THE END OF HISTORY MESSIAH CONSPIRACY

PHILIP N. MOORE

RAMSHEAD PRESS INTERNATIONAL CORPORATION
ATLANTA, GA
1996

The End of History—Messiah Conspiracy

Published by Ramshead Press International
P. O. Box 12-227, Atlanta, GA, USA 30355
1-800-726-7432 (1-800-RAMSHEAD)
404-233-8023 Fax (404) 816-9994
E-Mail: theconinc@aol.com (for questions or comments to our authors directly)
Web Page: http.//members.aol.com/theconinc/publish.htm and www.ramsheadpress.com

First Printing
Printed in the United States of America

Library of Congress Cataloging-in-Publication Data

Author:	Moore, Philip N., 1957-
Title:	The end of history—Messiah conspiracy / Philip N. Moore.
Published:	Atlanta, GA: RamsHead Press International, 1996.
Description:	xxiv, 1207 p. : ill. ; 23 cm.
LC Call No.:	BT230.M66 1996
Dewey No.:	236/.9 21
ISBN:	0964862301 and 1-57915-993-1
Notes:	Includes bibliographical references (p. [1180]-1196).
Subjects:	Jesus Christ - Messiahship.
	Messiah - Prophecies.
	Messiah - Judaism.
	Eschatology.
	Second Advent.
	Bible - Prophecies.

Library of Congress Catalog Card Number: 95-92646
Control No.: 95092646

In memory of my loving father, Nicholas George Moore, without whose support the research and writing of this book would not have been possible. Also, to my mother Marie and my brother Paul, who have been so understanding over the course of my writing. And finally, to the Messiah Jesus, who is my best friend, for comfort and guidance.

ACKNOWLEDGMENTS

Spring Mason, Melanie Lennox, Kim Mason and Debra Cole, for typesetting • Roy Ioannides and Constantine Terss, for assistance in Greek • Tal Moran, for double-checking Hebrew • Yakale Saar, of the State of Israel Government Press Office, photography department, for assistance in locating many unique photos • Polly Barr, of *Strictly Black and White*, Atlanta, GA, for such fine processing of my personal photos • George Chafin at Typo-Repro Service, Inc., for excellent pre-press work • Attorneys Jeff Young and Bill Gignilliat for outstanding legal assistance • Reverend Perrin Cook, Jeff Williams and Moshe Rosen, for encouragement • Reverend George Lauderdale, for the use of his Ben-Gurion letters and his personal letter helping to confirm Prime Minister Ben-Gurion's immense interest in the New Testament • Mike Bentley, for his Nostradamus photos • Artist Cathy Taibbi, for her incredible illustrations • Reverend William R. Meyers, for the use of some very extraordinary quotes from *Halley's Bible Handbook* • Dr. Arnold G. Fruchtenbaum, for encouragement and permission to quote from his lectures and books • Joseph Shulam, for helping to locate two interesting Talmudic references • Archaeologist Dr. Zvi Greenhut and Areah Rochman Haperin, for the use of photos from the Israel Antiquities Authority regarding the recent discovery of Caiphas' ossuary • Sophie Durocher, for helping me to obtain a photo of "Crucified Man" • Professor Michael Wise and Dr. Norman Golb, for permission to quote their works on the Dead Sea Scrolls • Dr. Ruth Fleischer, for warm encouragement and permission to quote her • Rabbi Dr. Arieh Bauminger, director of the Yad VaShem Holocaust museum in Jerusalem, for being so generous with his time • David Newman, Abraham Eliezer, Paul Blicksilver, Alfred Barnhart, Jerome Fleischer, Paul Liben, Donna Greenberg, Jacob Damkani, Sid Roth, Dan Segal, Patty Moore, George Moore, Jr., George Moore III, David Yood, John Akerman, Marie Nitschke, Nurit Benyahuda and Dean Lampman, for encouragement • Ruth Van Martin, for prayer • Professor Richard Popkin, of UCLA, for his time and advice regarding the Newton papers • Dr. Raphael Patai, for permission to use extensive quotes from his book, *The Messiah Texts* • Dr. Stefan C. Reif, of the Cambridge Taylor-Schechter Genizah Research Unit, for helping me to obtain what I consider to be the most interesting document in history, the Birkat ha-Minim • Dr. Arthur Kac, for his kindness and permission to quote his material • Dr. Ray A. Pritz, for his expert advice regarding why the word *minim*, from the Birkat ha-Minim, was removed from the Ashkenazic *Amidah* synagogue prayer • Prophecy experts Hal Lindsey, Grant Jeffrey, Jack Van Impe, Zola Levitt, Robert Morey and scholar Risto Santala, for permission to quote large portions of their works in support of my theses • Carol Lanning and Charlton Heston, for permission to quote from the video, *Charlton Heston Presents The Bible* • Grant Livingston, for his letter concerning Golda Meir and her newly found faith • Dr. Ron Bartour, for encouragement, assisting with research and his invaluble aid in obtaining permission to publish certain material from the Hebrew University Manuscript Department • Ari Sorko-Ram, and James Adair for advice and support • Elliot Klayman, for encouragment • Dr. Ofira Seliktar Heitov,[1] for proofreading both volumes in April and May of 1995, and suggested rephrasing of certain portions of text, some of which I used. My friends, Haim and Amy Haviv; my family and I were flattered by her comments on most of the research that went into this work. Again, we thank her for these compliments, yet we emphasize that anyone could have located this material if time permitted. I thank the Lord for allotting me the time—time which is priceless and so very precious.

Pooka (left), Philip and Daisy Moore.

---

[1]Ofira (who presently teaches at Gratz College in Melrose Park, Pennsylvania) authored *New Zionism and the Foreign Policy System of Israel* in 1986, under her previous married name Seliktar. I want to clarify that her political and idealogical opinions and views do not necessarily agree with mine and the ones in this work.

Philip Moore has done a tremendous work with His study, *The End of History—Messiah Conspiracy*. It is useful for all who love Israel. There is an old Hebrew saying מגלה טפח, מסתיר טפחיים "by opening one palm, you reveal two more"—every discovery challenges us to a new and more thorough study! One might raise some critical questions, but as a whole the book reveals many hidden treasures of importance to the reader!

Risto Santala, Hebrew Bible Scholar and Author[2]

---

[2] Risto Santala is the author of *The Messiah in the Old Testament, in the Light of Rabbinical Writings*, *The Messiah in the New Testament* and *Paul, the Man and the Teacher, in the Light of Jewish Sources*, widely read in Hebrew, French, Spanish, Finnish, German, Hungarian, Estonian, Russian and English. Regarding Santala's books, a prominent Aramaic scholar, Jacob J. Barclay, has noted: "No such material concerning the identity of our Lord has hitherto been condensed into such a succinct presentation as this" (Back cover *Messiah in the Old Testament*). It has been said that Santala is "stepping into the lion's den of the Rabbis and into the fiery furnace of the liberal theologians. But he hopes that others will follow him and promote a similar dialogue in the spirit of tolerance and spiritual democracy" (Ibid). And Moore is more than glad to do this. Santala's books may be obtained through Bible & Gospel Service, Kaivokatu 18100 Heinola, Finland, telephone 011-358-3-714-4215 and Karen Ahvah Meshihit, P.O. Box 10382, Jerusalem, Israel.

TABLE OF CONTENTS

TO THE READER

This work will prove to be of interest and reward to the layperson and the scholar. If you are a casual reader, just avoid the footnotes and comparison pages. Reading only the body of the text, you will encounter some very interesting material—an adventure that will literally take you out of this world and into the new one to come.

If, on the other hand, you are a professor, keep your eyes on the footnotes and references. You will find that you, too, are swept off your feet. The footnotes and comparisons will certainly not allow you to become bored, as my many professor friends have told me. I sincerely hope you find this work interesting enough to live up to their enthusiasm.[1]

Philip Moore

---

[1] Keep your eyes open for *The End of History—Messiah Conspiracy, Volume II, Essays*, which will be available in late 1996. Our *Volume II* takes a closer look at particular topics of interest from *Volume I*! An abridged version of our *Volume I* will also be available in late 1996. In addition, we offer two video cassettes: one featuring a tour of the Garden Tomb in Israel; and another featuring a tour of a kibbutz and the testimony of an Israeli believer in Jesus who tells how she came to believe. For further information, please contact us directly. Fax: (404) 816-9994, Tel: (800) RAMS-HEAD (800-726-7432), or E-Mail: pmoore000@aol.com. You may also order *The End of History—Messiah Conspiracy* through your local bookstore and amazon.com. "Then Abraham raised his eyes and looked, and behold, behind *him* a ram caught in the thicket by his horns; and Abraham went and took the ram, and offered him up for a burnt offering in the place of his son. And Abraham called the name of that place The LORD Will Provide, as it is said to this day, 'In the mount of the LORD it will be provided' " (Genesis 22:13-14 NASB).

The Hebrew prophet Zechariah further enlightened us: "Behold, I will make Jerusalem a cup of trembling unto all the people round about, when they shall be in the siege both against Judah *and* against Jerusalem. And in that day will I make Jerusalem a burdensome stone for all people: all that burden themselves with it shall be cut in pieces, though all the people of the earth be gathered together against it....And this shall be the plague wherewith the LORD will smite all the people that have fought against Jerusalem; Their flesh shall consume away while they stand upon their feet, and their eyes shall consume away in their holes, and their tongue shall consume away in their mouth" (Zech. 12:2-3; 14:12 KJV). Only nuclear heat can accomplish what Zechariah described.

A major point of our work, *The End of History—Messiah Conspiracy*, will be to present a response to several attempts, though ultimately unsuccessful, to rewrite some of the most crucial events in history in order to create a deception. These attempts include different subjects and time periods. To name only a few: 1. The claim that very few Jews in the first century believed in Jesus as Messiah, when in reality, nearly a million Jewish believers in Jesus existed;[2] 2. The denial by liberals of a plot at Yavne to cover up the Messiahship of Jesus by purging the Messianic Jews (Jews for Jesus) from the synagogue using economic sanctions, retranslations and the creation of the Birkat ha-Minim (BHM), a malediction to identify and expose Jewish believers in Jesus. In fact, the entire Yavne production of the BHM was an attempt to alter the course of history (see our chapters 7-9 on the Messiah Conspiracy); 3. The false notion that true Christians dislike Jews and are responsible for anti-Semitism, while in reality, the opposite is true.[3] We will document that more than a few true

---

[2]David Chernoff, *7 Steps to Knowing the God of Abraham, Isaac & Jacob*. Havertown, PA: MMI Publishing Co., © 1984, p. step 6. Available through POB 1024, Havertown, PA, USA 19083.

[3]At the MJAA Messiah Conference in 1994, Messianic Rabbi Barry Rubin pointed out in his class, "You Bring the Bagels, I'll Bring the Gospel—Sharing the Messiah With Your Jewish Neighbor": "If you're a Messianic Gentile [non-Jewish born-again Jewish believer in Jesus], a Gentile believer in Jesus, I need to tell you a few things about yourself. When it comes to witnessing to Jews, the first point you might want to write down is, uh, to some degree or another...you are seen as partially responsible for the crusades during which...Jews were killed, the Spanish Inquisition, during which you either converted to Catholicism or you were killed if you were Jewish, and the Holocaust....All non-Jewish believers are seen as part of all that. You weren't even born, but there's this generalized blame on the church towards the atrocities that have happened to the Jewish people. You've got to understand that's part of your background as seen by the Jewish community. But it's not true. What are Gentile believers, if not grafted—in believers...among the natural, the natural olive branches. That's the Jewish believer. Read Romans 11. This is Paul's expression of Gentile believers. A wild olive branch grafted in among the natural. That's the true position of a non-Jewish believer." 1994

An atomic blast occurred in the Middle East today. It was much worse than Hiroshima. We do not know where this is going to end. Stay in your homes, do not turn off your radios or television sets. Stay tuned to the Emergency Broadcast System for further information....

PREFACE

We choose to use this picture[1] to open our work on the Bible, Messiah Conspiracy and Apocalypse because we believe it represents Arab aspirations, since their recent acquisition of the bomb. However, we know from prophecy that they will not realize their hopes to the extent portrayed above, thank God!

Certainly the Scriptures predict our final conflict between the Arab and Israeli spheres of power through their ancient dispute, as described by King David: "O God, do not remain quiet; Do not be silent and, O God, do not be still. For, behold, Thine enemies make an uproar; And those who hate Thee have exalted themselves. They make shrewd plans against Thy people, And conspire together against Thy treasured ones. They have said, 'Come, and let us wipe them out as a nation, That the name of Israel be remembered no more.' For they have conspired together with one mind; Against Thee do they make a covenant...." (Psalm 83:1-5 NASB).

---

[1]This picture was created by Carl Chaplin, © used by permission. Available through ART NUKO, 1695 W. 7th, Vancouver, British Colombia, Canada V6J 1S4. Tel. (604) 736-1399.

believers laid the groundwork within Christian Zionism[4] for a Jewish return to Israel. Others saved many Jews from the Holocaust, at the risk of their own lives (see our chapter 12, "Christian Zionists Past and Present" and chapter 14, "Zionists—Evangelical Christians—the Most Loyal to Israel"); 4. The false idea that key Bible prophecies, such as Isaiah 53, Psalms 22 and Daniel 9, do not refer to the sufferings of the Jewish Messiah, and worse, that they are latter-day Christian interpretations. This train of thought is reflected in a number of books which attempt to repudiate Christian Messianic claims. These publications include: *The Real Messiah*; *You Take Jesus, I'll Take God; The Jew and the Christian Missionary;*[5] *Jews and "Jewish Christianity"; Faith Strengthened; The Passover Plot; A Guide to the Misled,* and; *Judaism Looks at Christianity.* However, the ancient Jewish commentaries (Midrashim and Targums),[6] and even segments of the Talmud all maintain that these prophecies did refer to Messiah. Of course, the prophecies never stopped being Messianic, as some may wish they had after the Jesus movement became popular and especially now, when so many Jews are espousing Jesus as their personal Messiah; 5. The attempted cover-up of coming events which will bring the Messiah back to usher in peace (see our chapters 26-29). Liberal ministers and rabbis around the world deny this greatest hope of mankind, while conservatives prove the coming of this great event by pointing out current political events which were predicted in the

---

MJAA Messiah Conference, Tape 37 CF 307. Available through Conference Taping, Inc., 1704 Valencia NE, Albuquerque, NM, USA 87110.

[4]Mount Zion is the hill in Jerusalem on which the Temple was built. Zionism is a worldwide movement to establish and maintain a national homeland for the Jews—*Israel*—the area formerly known as "Palestine." Many Christians support this movement and call themselves Christian Zionists. Mount Zion is also mentioned in the New Testament (Rev. 14:1).

[5]Rober Vasholz, Th.D., professor of the Old Testament, presented a very enlightening review of this book written by Gerald Sigal in Dr. Kac's newsletter, which revealed many of the author's inconsistencies, efforts to mislead and blatant dishonesty in his criticism of our New Testament faith. Rober Vasholz, Th.D., "The Interpreter," Fall 1994, pp. 221-224, Dr. Arthur W. Kac, editor. Ruth Fleischer, a precious friend of ours, referred to these books and the nature of their anti-Messianic intent, as a threat to Lubavitch Judaism. She said we (Messianic Jews) "have the truth and the truth is always going to reach people." Ruth Fleischer, Ph.D., 1993 MJAA Conference.

[6]The Targums are portions of Scriptures that were translated from Hebrew to Aramaic with certain portions interpreted or paraphrased. Some of these Scriptures in question predicted the Messiah. These validated Jesus' claim that these Scriptures were Messianic. One example is the Targum to Isaiah 52, where it mentions the word Messiah, while the biblical text does not. This shows that the interpretation of that time was Messianic. Today, most rabbis deny that Isaiah 52:13-53:12 is about the suffering of the Messiah, though the Targum, when brought to light, destroys their claim. Their claim is that Israel is the sufferer, in an attempt to discredit Jesus, since He proved Himself conclusively to be the suffering Messiah anticipated by ancient Judaism.

Bible thousands of years ago; 6. The false claim that evolution took place over creation, and that science and the Bible are incompatible (see our chapter 1, "How It All Began," and our Appendix 3, "Apes, Fakes and Mistakes," on evolution, which show that if you know Hebrew and the true meaning of Hebrew words you will see no contradiction between the claims of the Bible and science concerning creation, and that there is no true scientific evidence that evolution took place over creation).

THE GREATEST OF HISTORY'S SCIENTISTS BELIEVED IN THE BIBLE AND CREATION

The facts are that the greatest of scientists believed in the Bible. Dr. Norman Geisler, in his book, *Is Man the Measure?*, lists the scientists who accepted the Bible in total. Geisler writes: "Most of the famous people in the early years of modern science were creationists. They believed in the supernatural origin of the universe and of life. Included among them are: Johannes Kepler (1571-1630) Celestial mechanics, physical astronomy; Blaise Pascal (1623-1662) Hydrostatics; Robert Boyle (1627-1691) Chemistry, gas dynamics; Nicolaus Steno (1638-1687) Stratigraphy; Isaac Newton (1642-1727) Calculus, dynamics; Michael Faraday (1791-1867) Magnetic theory; Charles Babbage (1792-1871) Computer science; Louis Agassiz (1807-1873) Glacial geology, ichthyology; James Young Simpson (1811-1870) Gynecology; Gregor Mendel (1822-1884) Genetics; Louis Pasteur (1822-1895) Bacteriology; Lord Kelvin (1824-1907) Energetics, thermodynamics; Joseph Lister (1827-1912) Antiseptic surgery; James Clerk Maxwell (1831-1879) Electrodynamics, statistical thermo-dynamics; William Ramsay (1852-1916) Isotopic chemistry. In general, scientists before 1860 tended to be creationists. Sir Isaac Newton's statement about the origin of the universe is typical: 'This most beautiful system of the sun, planets, and comets, could only proceed from the counsel and dominion of an intelligent and powerful Being. And if the fixed stars are the centres of other like systems, these, being formed by the like wise counsel, must be all subject to the dominion of One.' After Charles Darwin published *The Origin of Species* (1859), there was a radical change."[7]

***

[7]Norman Geisler, *Is Man the Measure? An Evaluation of Contemporary Humanism.* Grand Rapids, MI: Baker Book House Company, © 1983, pp. 132-133, used by permission.

A LONDON PROFESSOR RECOMMENDED NEWTON'S BIBLICAL PAPERS BE BURNED

The greatest of all scientists, Sir Isaac Newton, also believed and wrote about Jesus as the Messiah and espoused creation by His pre-incarnate diety,[8] as is told in the first chapter of the Gospel of John. Of course, modern revisionists wish that no evidence of these writings existed.

We note that Harvard University, once a conservative Christian school, refused to accept Sir Isaac Newton's *religious* writings, which are now housed at the National Jewish Library at the Hebrew University in Jerusalem. Professor Richard Popkin, who revealed this fact,[9] was also quoted in an Israeli newspaper[10] as saying that a London professor told him: "Newton's writings on the Bible should be 'burnt,' because they are harmful to science." Isaac Newton said that he regarded his theological writings on the Bible as much more important than his scientific works and discoveries.

TRUE CHRISTIANS AND JEWS EXONERATED OF THE CHARGES

This book also exonerates Jews of the false, non-Christian, but rather Gentile/ecumenical accusation that they were "Christ killers,"[11]

---

[8]See our chapter 24, "Truth or Consequences—Will the Real Faith Please Stand?" for some very interesting quotes from Sir Isaac Newton. Also see our chapter 11, "Newton's Forbidden Works Rescued."

[9]This is documented by Professor Richard Popkin. He states: "In 1940, Yahuda became a refugee in the United States. He transported his vast manuscript collection with him to America where he tried, with the assistance of his close friend, Albert Einstein, to get **Harvard, Yale**, or **Princeton** to take over his very large collection of Newton's papers. **All three institutions** refused, even though Einstein tried to make them realize the importance of the papers for understanding how Newton's creative intelligence worked. Yahuda, on his deathbed in 1951, decided to leave his entire manuscript collection, which contains much Near Eastern material in addition to the Newton manuscripts, to what became the Jewish National & University Library...." James E. Force and Richard H. Popkin, editors, *The Books of Nature and Scripture*: *Recent Essays on Natural Philosophy, Theology, and Biblical Criticism in the Netherlands of Spinoza's Time and the British Isles of Newton's Time*. Boston: Kluwer Academic Publishers, © 1994, p. x, used by permission.

[10]*Al Hamishmar*, July 26, 1985.

[11]A recent example of this was brought up at the 1994 MJAA Messiah Conference by the evangelical believer and reporter, Dave Dolan, in his class, "Arab-Israeli Update." He said that a little Jewish girl once told him: " 'I've got a question for you. I go to Catholic school (her father's Catholic)...the kids come up to me and say, 'You killed Jesus.' " Dolan's reply was: "Well, of course my heart sank hearing that. 1994 and she's hearing that sort of thing. She said, 'What's that all about?' Well, God used it to open up an

made by those who are ignorant of New and Old Testament teachings. "I [Jesus] have power to lay it [His (Jesus') life] down, and I have power to take it again" (John 10:18 KJV; [ ] mine). "...he [Messiah] *was* wounded for our transgressions, *he was* bruised for our iniquities: the chastisement of our peace *was* upon him; and with his stripes we are healed. All we like sheep have gone astray; we have turned every one to his own way; and the LORD hath laid on him the iniquity of us all [the Jew and all the rest of mankind]" (Isa. 53:5-6 KJV; [ ] mine).

So said the Jewish prophet Isaiah in the fifty-third chapter of his book written 2700 years ago—seven hundred years prior to the writing of the New Testament (for a full report, see our chapter 5, "Which Prophecies Did Jesus Fulfill?").

opportunity to speak about *Yeshua* [Jesus in Hebrew] and I explained to her that *Yeshua* Himself rebuked Peter for saying, 'Don't go to Jerusalem and die.' That it was His intention to come and die for the sins of mankind and that it was Roman soldiers anyway that crucified Him. And yes, some Jewish leaders at the time did want to see Him crucified but many others didn't, and many turned to Him. And we went on and talked about *Yeshua*...." 1994 MJAA Messiah Conference, Tape 60, CF 307.

"...the rabbis proved afterward to be the greatest stumbling block for the Christian mission to the Jews."[1] Jacob Neusner, an unbelieving Jewish scholar

INTRODUCTION

The main theme of our title, *The End of History—Messiah Conspiracy*, is intended to illustrate that the rabbis, from the first century to the present day, have been engaged in a plot—a plot against the Jewish Messiah. You may ask, "How dare you make an allegation like that?" My answer is that for a group of religious leaders who are supposed to know the prophecies of their sacred writings, passed down from the Old Testament, to deny that Jesus is the Messiah, is not just a fib that can be taken lightly. Neither can we say that the rabbis are searching for another Messiah or an alternate faith!

The crystal-clear Jewish prophecies pointed to one Messiah who would come twice: once as a suffering Joseph figure and, after His rejection, as a David kingly personage to bring world freedom and peace. Yet the rabbis deny that Jesus is the Messiah, despite the hundreds of prophecies—a clear sign of an ongoing conspiracy.[2]

The Messiahship of Jesus has been proven by hundreds of Messianic prophecies throughout the Old Testament and even the ancient rabbinical commentaries on those prophecies. I have reproduced many of those commentaries in this work to show how the modern rabbinical leadership changed the established interpretation of

---

[1]Jacob Neusner, *First-Century Judaism in Crisis, Yohanan Ben Zakkai and the Renaissance of Torah.* New York: Abingdon Press, © 1975, p. 40, used by permission. We use the word unbelieving because he does not believe in Jesus as his Messiah, as we do in the Messianic and evangelical communities.

[2]Conspiracy has an evil element to its meaning. *The Oxford English Dictionary* says: "...conspire...*cónspíráre* lit. 'to breath together', whence, 'to accord, harmonize, agree, combine or unite in a purpose, plot mischief together secretly'.] 1. *intr.* To combine privily for an evil or unlawful purpose; to agree together to do something criminal, illegal, or reprehensible...." *The Oxford English Dictionary*, Vol. III. Oxford: Clarendon Press, © 1989, p. 783, used by permission. *The Barnhart Dictionary of Etymology* further notes: "...Before 1376 *conspiren,* in *Piers Plowman*; borrowed from Old French *conspirer*, learned borrowing from Latin *cónspíráre* accord, agree, combine for a purpose, plot together....**conspiracy** n. 1357, borrowed from Anglo-French *conspiracie,* Old French *conspiratie,* replacing earlier conspiration...borrowed from Old French *conspiration*, from Latin *cónspírátiónem* (nominative *cónspírátió*) act of plotting, conspiracy...." *The Barnhart Dictionary of Etymology.* Bronx, NY: The H.W. Wilson Company, © 1988, p. 210, used by permission. If Jesus is the Messiah of the Jews, and the rabbis from their Yavne hideaway attempted to cover it up from the first century until the twentieth century, what could be more evil or sinister? Nothing, since He (Messiah Jesus) is the answer to our eternal salvation, well-being and security.

these predictions in order to deliberately mislead young Jewish people who are searching for the Messiah.

What motive would this leadership have for taking their own people away from the only one in their history who could save them? We have a good explanation based on what occurred in the first century—fear of assimilation!

Many non-Jews were accepting Jesus as Messiah. These believers were not brought up to understand and practice Jewish traditions and holy days. When the first century rabbis realized that Gentiles were flocking into the faith in large numbers, they feared that the Jews who believed in Jesus would give up their heritage and tradition, melt into the Gentile world and disappear as a special race of people.[3]

God intended to eventually bring peace to the earth through their great leader, Messiah (in the Second Advent), but the rabbis tried, at all costs, to separate first century Jewish believers in Jesus from those Jews who did not believe. They taught that no trade relations or religious discussions were permitted. They introduced new prayers against Jewish believers who were still attending the synagogues, so as to isolate and ostracize them from other Jews. The first century Jewish leader Bar Kochba, who was proclaimed Messiah by Rabbi Akiva, even required that they be killed if they would not renounce their faith in Jesus as Messiah.[4]

This was just as inexcusable then as it is today, and this book is intended to expose and rectify the account of the most controversial person Judaism ever knew—Jesus. He is controversial because there has been such a tremendous amount of propaganda and prejudice against Him and His claim that He was **the Jewish Messiah**.

---

[3]David Berger and Michael Wyschogrod ask this of Jewish Christians: "...do they believe that it is the will of God that the seed of Abraham remain in the world as an identifiable people chosen by God? There is very little reason to think that they do....if it can be expected that Jews in this group will gradually be absorbed into the larger, gentile Christian community, then such a Jew is opting for the dissolution of the people God wants to remain his eternal people." David Berger and Michael Wyschogrod, *Jews and "Jewish Christianity."* New York: KTAV Publishing House, Inc., © 1978, pp. 65-66, used by permission.

[4]Johannes Weiss documents this from the ancient sources of Eusebius and Orosius, which reveal: " 'And indeed in the recent Jewish war, Bar-Kokhba, the leader of the uprising of the Jews, condemned the Christians alone to be led away to dreadful torture if they would not deny Jesus was Christ and blaspheme him;' Eusebius, *Chron*.....'Kokhba, who was leader of the rebellion of the Jews, inflicted various penalties on many of the Christians, since they would not go out to battle with him against the Romans;' Orosius 7:13." Johannes Weiss, *Earliest Christianity, A History of the Period A.D. 30-150*, Vol. II, p. 723.

Some may say this book or its title offends them. If it takes an offense to cause people to see the truth, as Jesus said, "I am the truth" (John 14:6), then may the offense be ever greater, as millions see who the truth is!

MODERN CHRISTIAN INTERPRETATION OF PROPHECY IS NOTHING LESS THAN YESTERDAY'S ANCIENT JEWISH INTERPRETATION

When Messianic prophecy is mentioned to contemporary rabbis, there is the common and familiar outcry, "You are reading into it your Christian interpretation."[5] This book disproves that statement, once and for all!

We will show that the modern "Christian interpretation" is nothing less than the ancient **Jewish interpretation**, unchanged and unbiased. We will prove this by quoting and reproducing the actual ancient rabbinical text of the interpretive passages which comment on the particular Messianic Scriptures in question. We will also reproduce the Hebrew text of the Scriptures along with the rabbinic interpretation, to remove any suspicion of fraud to the non-Hebrew speaking reader. Using these two mediums, we will illustrate that the New Testament agrees with the ancient Jewish beliefs on the Scriptures in question.

---

[5]In a June 1983 seminar entitled, "Jewish Answers to Christian Questions," conducted by Rabbi Shalom Lewis of the Atlanta Rabbinic Association, when this topic was being discussed, he told me adamantly: "At any rate, let me just again put to rest some of these things and, that is, that obviously, we are speaking different languages here. I will make a statement that I will stand by and I don't care what kind of statements are directed at me. The fact of the matter is that the Bible, the Tora, Nevim Ketuvim....the fact of the matter is that there is nothing there that refers to Jesus, that refers to Christianity whatsoever....The Bible is strictly, purely and absolutely a Jewish text. There is no statement there....what Judaism says...." Who says Rabbi Lewis can speak for or has a monopoly on all of Judaism? I know many Jews who are interested in and some who are believers in Jesus as Messiah! The rabbi continues: "...what Judaism says...is a very simple fact....Christianity came along and created a new religion. Not the continuation of Judaism, not a New Testament because I don't call it the New Testament....There's one Bible, the Jewish Bible, the Tanack [T.N.K. is an acronym for *Tora* "law," *Nevim* "the prophets," and *Ketuvim* "the writings," which are the three divisions into which Jews divide the Old Testament]. The New Testament is a s-document [we believe he meant to say document, while thinking of the word statement] put together by the early Christian fathers and the purpose was very simple...it was propaganda, propaganda. It was to make the Jews look bad and it was to make the Romans look good....When somebody starts to interpret my faith for me, my Bible for me, and starts to tell me what Judaism really means and what the Jewish attitude towards the Messiah really is, then I tell them they don't know what they're talking about. If you say that Christianity is the completion of Jud-

Modern rabbis, in an effort to protect the Jewish people from evangelical truth, which they fear might lead to the greatest Holocaust yet—assimilation, have forsaken these once cherished beliefs. Thus we believe our work will make evident the greatest fraud in the history of mankind—the claim that Jesus was not the Jewish Messiah and that He did not walk on Earth or fulfill many ancient Hebrew prophecies. (Such prophecies include Deut. 18:15; Lev. 17:11; Isa. 53; Dan. 9:26, and; Hos. 3:3-4).

We charge modern rabbis and many of those of the past 2000 years with a Messiah Conspiracy—an attempt to isolate the Jewish soul from its only opportunity for salvation through the acceptance of the Messiah and His blood atonement for sin. The Scriptures we will quote are from the authoritative Jewish document known to the world as the Old Testament, which avows to be the Word of God. Any Bible believing individual who reads these Old Testament proofs and facts about the Messiah and denies his fellow Jewish friend the knowledge of these incredible truths of life and death, commits anti-Semitism,[6] in its most subtle, yet heinous form.

***

---

aism, then I say to you that is utter garbage, that is not true. I respect Christianity, when Christianity stays in the church and when Christianity does what they do, but the moment Christianity tries to invade the synagogue and tries to say to Judaism, 'This is what you really mean, this is what you really mean by the Messiah,' quoting our books—that's when I have to say, 'You guys don't know...what you're talking about. You're not talking about Judaism. You are talking about the bastardization of Judaism through Christian eyes'....I will gladly send you pages, documents of a different analysis, the correct analysis of Isaiah 53, sections in the book of Daniel, sections in Deuteronomy where there's all sorts of Christian misinterpretations and fundamentalists' misinterpretations of what the text truly means." Rabbi Shalom Lewis, "Jewish Answers to Christian Questions," author's personal tape from lecture at the Atlanta Jewish Community Center, Zaban Park branch in Dunwoody, GA, June 1983. The book the rabbi mentioned was *You Take Jesus, I'll Take God.* We will be quoting this book to illustrate that his claims concerning the Tanack (Old Testament) cannot possibly stand, in light of true scholarship and honesty. We believe that after you read this text and hear the facts, you will discover there is plenty of evidence to support Jesus as the Messiah in the Old Testament portion of the Bible, as the New Testament and history claims, contrary to what this rabbi and many others presently assert!

[6]Anti-Semitism is a set of beliefs that are negative and often hostile prejudices toward Jews. However, the term is inaccurate, as the word Semite indicates any person who is of Semitic origin—this includes Arabs. The word Semitic is derived from the name of Noah's son Shem, from whom the Jewish people are descended. All three races on earth—caucasoid, negroid and Oriental/Asiatic—are directly descended from Noah's three sons, "Shem and Ham and Japheth" mentioned in Genesis 7:13 (see Gen. 9:18-19). Anti-Semitism developed from fear based on religious differences. The Nazi Holocaust—the extermination of millions of Jews during World War II—was a direct result of Adolf Hitler's anti-Semitism.

IF YOU TRULY LOVE YOUR JEWISH FRIENDS, YOU WILL TELL THEM!

All believers in Messiah, both Jew and Gentile/evangelical, should be aware of the consequences to all Jews and Gentiles of slipping through this life without a saving knowledge of Messiah, who Himself said: "I am the way, the truth and the life: no man cometh unto the Father, but by me" (John 14:6 KJV).

If you read these words and truly believe this statement, you should, at all costs, seek to share the knowledge you possess with your Jewish friends. "Thou shalt love thy neighbour as thyself" (Matt. 19:19 KJV). If you truly love them, as the New Testament commands, you are duty-bound to overcome your shyness and let them in on the facts regarding their Messiah, so they will share eternal life with you. To deny them the truth, out of fear of offending them or to avoid rabbinical opposition, is to condemn them.

If you do not know where to begin, we suggest you show your love for them by giving them this book or a similar one. If you do not tell them, they may never hear. They certainly deserve to hear. They have endured enough persecution over the past 2000 years to last throughout eternity.

THE JEWS' TIME TO HEAR IS UPON US, AS NEVER BEFORE

It is time we see to it that the Jews hear and witness the life we share in their Messiah, and the peace, security and fulfillment, we as believers, have found in their Bible. So that they, themselves, can have a fair chance to learn the facts and make a free choice for their Messiah, based on the ancient teaching of Judaism. To make the choice easier, we have printed all the sources in sequence.

The Old and New Testament verses are printed alongside the ancient rabbinical texts and their negation by contemporary rabbis. Never before have these texts been arranged in this way, which shows that the rabbis distorted the previously held Messianic interpretations after the death of Jesus. Apparently, His death prejudiced them against their former beliefs about the Messiah.

HOW, WHEN AND WHERE DID THE RABBIS CHANGE THE ANCIENT MESSIANIC BELIEFS? YAVNE! THIS WILL MAKE JEWS VULNERABLE TO THE FUTURE ANTICHRIST

In the years 70-110 AD, in Yavne, on the coast of Israel, the rabbis reconstructed Judaism with the central goal of isolating the Jew from Messiah. The consequences of this action were great, not only for the Jews in the Diaspora of the past 2000 years, but the quality of life in the world to come; the greater, more applicable consequence for our time (the last days) is the coming of the Antichrist.

The Jews, because they have been deprived of their true Messiah through this reconstruction, will be ever more vulnerable to the soon-coming false Messiah. Bible scholars and teachers know this anti-Messiah by his New Testament name, "Antichrist."

The ancient rabbis knew of the coming of Antichrist and wrote much about him. They attempted to warn the Jewish people about him. However, much of the apocalyptic Jewish material about the Antichrist was apparently destroyed by later rabbis after the time of Jesus.[7]

In this book, we have recovered some of their writings regarding the Antichrist (see our chapter 23, "The False Messiah Armilus Equals Antichrist"). If we do not tell the Jewish people about the true Messiah, they will accept the Antichrist as their Messiah. He will make the claim that he is the Messiah (II Thes. 2:4; Dan. 8:24). This time we must tell them what the Scriptures predict. When we tell them, they may not believe right away, but of those who are still around when the Antichrist arrives in a few years—after the Rapture[8]—many will be able to recognize him. Thus you will receive the blessing promised in Genesis 12:3: "And I will bless them that bless thee, and curse him that curseth thee [the Jews]...." (KJV).

After the seven-year reign of Antichrist, when Messiah returns with you and all other believers to put a halt to Armageddon (Rev. 19:20-21; Dan. 7:13; Matt. 24:29-30; Mark 14:62) and begin the 1000-year Messianic Kingdom of peace on Earth (Rev. 20:4-6; Isa. 2), you will be able to look forward to living in that kingdom with your friends with whom you took the time to share God's word. Shalom!

---

[7]D.S. Russell informs us: "L. Ginzberg has pointed out that in the entire rabbinic literature of the first six centuries there is not a single quotation from the extant apocalyptic literature; because of this it has sometimes been too readily assumed that rabbinic Judaism would have nothing whatever to do with the teaching and ideals contained in these books. C. C. Torrey, for example, affirms that from AD 70 onwards, so great was the devotion of the Jewish leaders to the Law and the sacred Scriptures, the decision was taken to destroy as undesirable all the Semitic originals of the 'outside books', including the apocalyptic writings, and so effect 'the sudden and complete abandonment by the Jews of their popular literature'. Thus, this once-popular literature was discontinued and the ideas which it perpetuated were rejected as dangerous and heretical." D.S. Russell, *The Method & Message of Jewish Apocalyptic, 200 BC - AD 100.* Philadelphia: The Westminster Press, © 1964, p. 30, used by permission.

[8]This will probably occur before the last half of the twenty-first century, as time parameters indicate, in conjunction with certain Bible verses we will discuss later.

A HISTORICAL PHENOMENON OF WHICH VERY FEW LAYMEN ARE AWARE—A SHORT, SECRET SPAN OF HISTORY WHEN JESUS WAS LOCKED OUT OF JUDAISM

Few are currently aware that Judaism underwent profound changes when it was reconstructed at Yavne by a select group of intellectual rabbis, headed by Yohanan ben Zakkai and Rabbi Gamaliel. The changes that were made—to create a new religion which would be called by the same name, Judaism, commonly known as Rabbinic Judaism—were sharp and abrupt. The rabbis felt it absolutely necessary to make these alterations so that Judaism could survive after its anticipated worldwide dispersion.[9] However, the changes at Yavne obliterated the Messianic interpretation of the Old Testament that existed for almost 1500 years.

As you read the latter pages of this book, you will be able to see just how this has reshaped Jewish beliefs and precious Hebrew hopes that the Messiah will redeem both the Jewish race and millions of Gentiles. This cover-up is nothing short of an intellectual crime against the Jewish people.

Some Jewish scholars are aware of these ancient sacred Jewish understandings of the Messianic prophecies. However, the majority of Jewish teachers and students are unfamiliar with the interpretative commentaries which we will reproduce for you. One of our purposes in writing this book is to inform the layperson of these long "lost"[10] secret commentaries, which demonstrate that the beliefs of Messianic Jews and born-again Christians, as pertaining to a Messiah, were wholeheartedly accepted by Jews over 2000 years ago. Today, however, in many cases, these Scriptures and commentaries are categorically denied by many rabbis and "scholars" as ever having been Messianically interpreted by the rabbis of Jesus' day. We believe the purpose of this denial is to stifle Jewish curiosity about the Messianic credentials of Jesus and this is horrible!

---

[9]This dispersion began in 70 AD under Roman General Titus, and became complete in 135 AD, when Rome defeated the Bar Kochba Rebellion. From that time until 1948, there was no Jewish state with any sizable Jewish population. The biblically predicted rebirth of Israel in 1948 marks the official end of the forced Roman dispersion between 70 and 135 AD, and the beginning of a new Messianic Age, which will culminate in the return of Jesus to save us and preserve Israel forever! Hallelujah!

[10]We say "lost" because these are not emphasized, studied or made reference to in the Jewish lay community. Indeed, most of the commentaries have not even been translated from their original Hebrew. Some of the rarer commentaries which we have quoted were only recently translated in 1979 by Dr. Raphael Patai. We thank Dr. Patai for this often unrecognized yet great service to humanity. We are eternally grateful to him.

A MODERN JEWISH SCHOLAR ADMITS ISAIAH 53 HAS BEEN DELIBERATELY OMITTED FROM HAFTAROT BECAUSE OF JESUS

All of the subsequent reinterpretations of the Scriptures are a frantic effort to seclude the Jew from understanding the true nature of the Messianic prophecies. To prove our point, we note that the famed literary work, *A Rabbinic Anthology*, written by two Jewish scholars, C. G. Montefiore and H. Loewe, admits: "Quotations from the famous 53rd chapter of Isaiah are rare in the Rabbinic literature. [Because of the christological interpretation given to the chapter by Christians, it is omitted from the series of prophetical lessons (*Haftarot*) for the Deuteronomy Sabbaths....the *omission* is *deliberate* and *striking*. (H.L.)]"[11]

We agree with the comments of F. F. Bruce, author of the scholarly book *The Spreading Flame,* on this publication. Bruce writes: "It is a distinguished orthodox Jewish scholar who tells us that the reason why the prophecy of the suffering Servant (Isaiah 52:13-53:12) is not included in the synagogue lectionary, although the passages immediately preceding and following it are found there, is the Christian application of that prophecy to Jesus."[12]

THOUGH THE PROPHETS PERSIST, THE RABBIS DENY JEWS A FREE CHOICE BY USING ASSIMILATION AS A SCARE TACTIC

It is clear that many rabbis want to isolate the Jewish people from Messianic expectations, especially those of His Second Advent to Earth to redeem Israel from an all-out Russian/Arab invasion. If you examine Zechariah 12-14 and Ezekiel 38-39 of the Old Testament, you will see that the Messiah that returns to save Israel has pierced hands, thus identifying Him as the Messiah of which the prophecies speak. This is the Messiah long rejected by the rabbis.

Why then have the rabbis kept these formerly held Messianic truths hidden? The *answer* is they want to guard against any possible vehicle that might induce assimilation. From the first century, they have not felt that Jews could be entrusted with a faith which has been embraced by millions of non-Jews (born-again believers). They fear that if the Jews are allowed the liberty to make a free choice for Messiah, based on ancient rabbinic interpretations and the New

---

[11]C.G. Montefiore and H. Loewe, *A Rabbinic Anthology*. New York: Schocken Books Inc., © 1974, p. 554, used by permission. Italics outside ( ) mine.

[12]F.F. Bruce, *The Spreading Flame*. Grand Rapids, MI:William B. Eerdmans Publishing Company, © 1958, pp. 267, used by permission.

Testament, the obvious would take place—a faith in Jesus.[13] In turn, they feel that this would cause the Jews to give up their Jewish culture. After all, most Gentiles who have professed a faith in Jesus have not adhered to Jewish customs. Thus the rabbis fear an extinction (so to speak) of the Jewish race by virtue of the Messiah.

Since the major task entrusted to the rabbis is to preserve the Jewish race through the perpetuation of Jewish culture and the observance of Jewish traditions, the rabbis feel that they must anticipate[14] any possible assimilation and, in turn, fight anything which could precipitate any threat of a Jewish "melt-down" into the ways of the non-Jewish nations. However, we state here that these rabbinical fears are unfounded in a historical and contemporary context.

Messianic congregations and even the worldwide *Jews for Jesus* movement are faithful to Jewish tradition in many ways and maintain a distinct Jewish identity. In fact, many Jewish Christians (*Christ* means "Messiah" and *ian* means "one that follows") state that they became more zealous in their Jewishness, and more committed to Israel and their Zionist causes, than before they embraced Jesus as the Jewish Messiah.[15]

IF ALL ELSE SHOULD FAIL, THE RABBIS WILL EMPLOY THEIR FINAL SCARE TACTIC—IDOLATRY

It is our firm conviction that all who desire to accept or reject faith in the Messiah should have a right to do so without being coerced

---

[13]Currently, many rabbis imply that if you are a Jew and you accept Jesus, you have left Judaism. Thus, as a Jew you do not have the choice of faith in Jesus—that is, if you want to remain a Jew. That, my friends, is a lie right out of the pit of Hell! We will address this later in further detail.

[14]An example of this fear, which we believe is without foundation, along with the use of the assimilation scare tactic and guilt trip of not being loyal to your race trick, is found in the book, *Jews and "Jewish Christianity,"* where Berger and Wyschogrod state: "In recent years various groups have come into being that consider themselves 'Jewish Christians.' They preach Jesus as their savior, yet seem intent on maintaining a form of Jewish identity. What is the Jewish reaction to such groups?....Some of them practice various Jewish customs, such as wearing *tsitsit* (fringes) and lighting candles on Friday nights....In fact, their primary identification seems to be with gentile, evangelical Christianity. As such, it is to be expected that the traditional pattern will be repeated. The descendants of Jews who come to believe in Jesus as the Messiah will disappear as Jews within two or three generations....every form of 'Jewish Christianity' in existence today teaches Jesus as God and not only as the Messiah. Any Jew who embraces this belief **commits idolatry**....he commits one of the gravest sins of which a Jew is capable." David Berger and Michael Wyschogrod, *Jews and "Jewish Christianity,"* pp. 65-66. Bold mine.

[15]See our chapter 16, "Was Christopher Columbus a Messianic Jew?", where we show he was both Jewish and a believer in Jesus. Though he was fearful of Catholic persecution, in secret he still used the B.H. Hebrew greeting in letters to his family. He also treasured a book that proved Jesus the Messiah from a Jewish viewpoint!

in either direction! In America and most non-communist countries, we are afforded freedom of religion. We would appreciate it if all were permitted to check out the facts and accept what they feel is in their best interest. We feel the right to believe as one wishes, free of harrassment, is presently being obstructed by many rabbis in their battle against Messianic Judaism and the *Jews for Jesus* movement.

The rabbis say it is fine for Gentiles to accept Jesus as Messiah, but it is idolatry[16] for Jews to accept Him. This is a double standard according to the Old Testament portion of the Bible, which both Jews and Christians use as their standard for what constitutes idolatry. What would be idolatrous for one should also be idolatrous for the other. This double standard can be seen in the book by David Berger and Michael Wyschogrod, *Jews and "Jewish Christianity,"* where they say: "In Jewish literature, the term that came to be used for the trinitarian concept of God was *shittuf* (partnership). The accepted Jewish view is that belief in *shittuf* does not constitute idolatry for gentiles but does so for Jews. The reason for this is that the definition of what constitutes idolatry is different for Jews and gentiles. Belief in *shittuf*, the belief that God shares his being in equal partnership with Jesus and the Holy Spirit, is not idolatry by the standard of idolatry demanded of gentiles. But the very same belief held by a Jew constitutes idolatry by the standard applicable to Jews. It is for this reason that Judaism does not condemn Christian trinitarianism as idolatry unless those holding the belief are Jews....for a Jew to believe that Jesus was God constitutes idolatry, while the same trinitarian belief is not idolatry when held by a gentile."[17]

---

[16]Idolatry is defined as the worship of a false god or statue of stone or gold. The film *Raiders of the Lost Ark* clearly illustrates the ridiculousness of idolatry. In the movie, we see natives bowing to a "golden head," which Belak took from Indiana Jones. Comparing believers' behavior to the natives' behavior is the sort of ridicule we must contend with when the rabbis accuse Jewish Christians of being idolaters. This is serious, insipid, a lie and disgusting—will they apologize?

[17]David Berger and Michael Wyschogrod, *Jews and "Jewish Christianity,"* pp. 30, 60. We wish to emphasize that it was never Israel's place to mislead the rest of mankind into thinking that it is permissable to commit idolatry while they worshipped the one true God, as many modern rabbis state in their polemical books against Messianic Jews! Abraham is clearly said to be a father of many nations (Gen.17:4), a fact which was borne out when many individuals in these nations accepted the God of Abraham, Isaac and Jacob through the sacrifice and atonement of Jesus the Messiah. Genesis 12:3 teaches of Israel's importance through Him: "...in thee shall **all** families of the earth be blessed" (KJV; bold mine). The purpose of Israel was to teach the whole world how to know the one true God through the Messiah, who is God Incarnate. Today, rabbis who cannot bring themselves to accept Jesus as their Messiah are, in a very real sense, attempting to spiritually denigrate the non-Jewish world by telling them that there are two different standards for idolatry. They maintain that if you are not Jewish you automatically fall into the lower one. This never was, nor is it today, Israel's purpose. In fact, it is a categorical denial of the truth of and purpose for the creation of the Jewish people. When

IF WE ALLOW THE SCARE TACTICS OF THE RABBIS TO GO UNCHALLENGED, ANTICHRIST WILL DECEIVE *MORE* OF OUR BELOVED JEWISH FRIENDS

Many of the quotes we list under the heading "Modern Rabbinic Comment/Refutation" are from a half-dozen books, written by rabbis and others, for the sole purpose of interfering with the beliefs of Messianic Jews.

One of the other changes accomplished by the rabbis at Yavne was to downplay the reading of apocalyptic literature,[18] as we will see later in our chapter 8, "The Messiah Conspiracy Continues in the *New* Old Testament." Apocalyptic literature in the Bible foretells the future events concerning final redemption and the Messiah's ruling kingdom at the end of time. The rabbis also successfully scrapped the ancient teaching about the coming of the Antichrist (a false Messiah), known to them in rabbinic lingo as the Armilus.[19]

Judaism once[20] taught that a suffering Messiah would appear, then disappear for a long period of time. This redeemer was known as the Messiah ben Joseph, because he suffered just as Joseph did when he was sold into slavery in Egypt by his brothers.

The teaching was that the suffering son (*ben*) of Joseph Messiah would die and be resurrected. Thereafter, he would disappear, and return as Messiah ben David, to defeat Gog and Magog along with their Arab counterparts. Seven years before the Messiah ben David appears to save Israel,[21] the Antichrist (Armilus) will appear on Earth and deceive the Israelis into believing he is the promised Messiah. However, the Israelis will later discover that he is not. They will begin to study the Bible to see exactly what it teaches concerning Messiah.

I read statements like these, I cringe. These ridiculous statements are pitiful examples of what most rabbis try to sell non-Jews who believe in Jesus, in their feeble attempt to discourage non-Jews from sharing Jesus' Messianic claims with interested Jews who would like to have God's purpose fulfilled within their lives.

[18]D.S. Russell wrote, "the Jews abandoned this once popular literature." D.S. Russell, *Method & Message of Jewish Apocalyptic*, p. 30.

[19]Along with a few Midrashic commentaries quoted in encyclopedias, nearly all that remains of the Jewish teachings of the end time Antichrist/Armilus, are found in Saadia Gaon's work of over 1000 years ago (see our chapter 23, "The False Messiah, Armilus Equals Antichrist").

[20]Raphael Patai, an Orthodox Jewish scholar and author of *The Messiah Texts*, a detailed account of 3000 years of Jewish legend, tells us: "...Messiah ben Joseph...would fall victim....The other, Messiah ben David, will come after him (in some legends will bring him back to life, which psychologically hints at the identity of the two), and will lead Israel to the ultimate victory, the triumph, and the Messianic era of bliss....According to an old tradition, the Messiah was perfectly prefigured in Moses. But Moses died before he could lead the Children of Israel into the land of promise. Consequently, for the parallel to be complete, the Messiah, too, had to die before accomplishing his great task of ultimate redemption." Raphael Patai, *The Messiah Texts*. Detroit: Wayne State University Press, © 1979, pp. 166-167, used by permission.

[21]To more fully understand the teaching of the two Messianic visits—one to suffer and a subsequent return to save the world from the apocalypse—see our chapters 23, 25-30 on the Second Coming, and our chapter 3, "Two Messiahs."

The Messiah ben David will come, defeat these invading powers and set up his kingdom, which will last 1000 years. This *true* Messiah will be Jesus in His Second Advent.[22]

CAN WE BE SURE THAT JESUS IS THE JEWISH MESSIAH DESPITE MOST RABBIS RAILING AGAINST HIM? YES!

How can we be sure that Jesus is the long awaited Jewish Messiah promised to Israel and ultimately the world? By studying His identity, which the Hebrew prophets earmarked so clearly in their hundreds of predictions throughout the Old Testament. This is sufficient proof that no other event in history can match!

The entire life of the Messiah was foretold hundreds of years prior to His birth in Bethlehem, Israel, 2000 years ago. That is proof enough for most individuals. However, those of you who are Jewish may sometimes wonder how we can know that these prophecies are being interpreted correctly in the Messianic sense. After all, modern rabbis apply many of these prophecies to the nation of Israel and her people.

Most Bible students would have difficulty answering this. However, there were many Jewish scholars and rabbis who wrote commentaries on these verses, some prior to the Coming of Jesus. These commentaries show conclusively that all prophecies in question were understood to apply to Messiah.

We have unearthed these commentaries from the Talmud, Targumim and Midrashim and aligned them beside their Old and New Testament parallels to illustrate to the average (layman) reader these proofs, which have for so long been limited to a handful of scholars. We have also placed a ready-made rabbinical refutation of the Messianic prophecies at the end of each one to highlight what most *current* Judaic authorities have done with these prophecies. We are sure you will see our point in showing these ancient rabbinical commentaries, which clearly legitimize the claim of Christians and Jews for Jesus that Jesus is indeed the Messiah, as recorded in the New Testament.

***

[22]See our chapter 28, "The Second Coming Event—Will He Yet Be Sent?"

SINCE JESUS IS THE MESSIAH, MESSIANIC JEWS ARE, IN FACT, THE TRUEST AND BEST JEWS, NO MATTER WHAT THE RABBIS SAY!

Most rabbis have tried to tell the Jewish people they cannot believe in Jesus and remain Jewish.[23] This notion was born from prejudice and intolerance, because the rabbis thought that if they could convince the Jewish people of this, most would forsake Jesus, even if He is the Messiah, rather than give up their rich national heritage.

The fact is that when Jews become believers in the Jewish Messiah, their Judaism, their holy days and their customs become all the more real and enjoyable to them. They become Jews in the truest sense of the word.

The Hebrew word for Jew means "a praiser of God." That is why Abraham, nearly 4000 years ago, was named the first Jew by God.

---

[23]Ruth Fleischer, Ph.D., noted of the Jewish community and the Messianic movement: "The real issue is over who is a Jew, isn't it? Isn't that the real issue? Can you be a Jew and believe *Yeshua* [Jesus] is the Messiah? Yes, you can and you should...the traditional answer has been no. The amazing thing about that is the fact that there are other people who have believed in Messiahs who weren't accepted by the establishment and yet they're not anathematizing [a curse] to Judaism. I'll name you one—Rabbi Akiba. He believed that Bar Kochba was the Messiah. Now we know that Bar Kochba was not the Messiah. It's pretty obvious from history, and yet Akiba is acclaimed as one of the greatest rabbis of Judaism. So why is it that he can believe in a false Messiah, but our believing that *Yeshua* is the Messiah puts us in a different category? *Yeshua* is the issue. The Talmud says that even if you are a bad Jew, you are still a Jew. You cannot stop being a Jew....It's from Sanhedrin 44." This passage reads: "R. Abba b. Zabda said: 'Even though [the people] have sinned, they are still [called] Israel.' R. Abba said: 'Thus people say, A myrtle, though it stands among reeds, is still a myrtle, and it is so called.' " Ruth also correctly observes: "We've seen a very interesting Jewish response in the last few years, and that's visible by the truck that's down over the hill over there. *Jews for Judaism*, yeah, you know why they're here? [parked just off of the campus of Messiah College at the '93 Messiah Conference.] Cause we're a threat to them. We are antagonists. The Lubavitch and the Messianic movement are antagonists....They know it, do you know it? What we are talking about is Lubavitch Judaism. They recognize us as an intrinsic threat to them and they know that, with us, they face their greatest challenge. Why? Well, we have the truth and the truth is always going to reach people. What they have is a system but not a personal relationship with the Lord. We need to pray for them....The greatest positive statement about the Messianic movement today is being made by the fact that they are seriously confronting us....Today, they see very clearly that we are a threat. We are a threat to the [religious Jewish] establishment because we offer our people something they don't have. And we are a growing movement and God has blessed us, and He is moving among us in a powerful way. And because of that, there are books being written that attack us. There are books being written that challenge what we believe because they know that God is working. He's moving among us. They may not see it that way, but that is what's happening and they can see clearly that something, something is there challenging them." Ruth Fleischer, Ph.D., Tape 30 cf179, *The Reemergence of Messianic Judaism*. Grantham, PA: 1993 Messiah Conference at Messiah College, © 1993, used by permission. [ ] mine.

He was the first man to leave the pagan and idolatrous customs, which had crept into man's history a few hundred years after the creation of Adam, and follow the true God of mankind. Thus, when a Jew by heritage begins to follow this Messiah predicted in his Bible, he has accepted the promises made by his forefathers, the prophets of the Bible, which the God of the Hebrews swore to provide from the beginning of creation. This does not make a Jew less Jewish; rather, according to the New Testament, it makes a non-Jew or Gentile an adopted Jew, giving those who were not born Jewish the promise of the Jewish people concerning atonement and forgiveness (Gal. 3:6-9, 16).[24]

We read in the first book of the Hebrew Bible that God originally intended to bless all nations of the earth through the Hebrew race (Gen. 12:1-3)! This began with the promise of the Messiah and will realize its full potential at Jesus' Second Advent to set up the Messianic Kingdom.

The *Jews for Judaism* truck, which Ruth Fleischer mentioned. *Jews for Judaism* is an organization dedicated to convincing Jews who believe in Jesus that they are wrong.

---

[24] "Even as Abraham believed God, and it was accounted to him for righteousness. Know ye therefore that they which are of faith, the same are the children of Abraham. And the scripture, foreseeing that God would justify the heathen through faith, preached before the gospel unto Abraham, *saying*, In thee shall all nations be blessed. So then they which be of faith are blessed with faithful Abraham....Now to Abraham and his seed were the promises made. He saith not, And to seeds, as of many; but as of one, And to thy seed, which is Christ" (Gal. 3:6-9, 16 KJV).

DO PRESENT DAY POLITICAL EVENTS THAT WERE PREDICTED IN THE BIBLE, INDICATE JESUS' RETURN AS MESSIAH WITHIN OUR GENERATION?

What is even more exciting about examining the prophecies and their ancient commentaries, is that they indicate that Jesus the Messiah is about to return to Earth to set up His kingdom of peace. Many recent political events, such as the rebirth of Israel in 1948, the establishment of the European Economic Community (EEC) in 1958, the existence of China's two hundred million-man army since the 1970's, the Russian/Arab abhorrence of the new State of Israel, the advent of nuclear power and its present proliferation, and so on, were all foretold by these very same Hebrew prophets. These prophets give us a hope of life, liberty and paradise that has not been known to man since the Garden of Eden.

Many scoff at us and our claim that the Bible is true and modern political events verify and fulfill what these prophets claim would occur just prior to the coming of the Antichrist,[25] and subsequently, the Messiah, who will destroy the evil plot of the Antichrist to wipe out world Jewry and renew Israel as the capital of the world (Deut. 28:13).[26] However, the account of how the Messiah will recreate this former state of paradise promised to the Jewish race in the Bible, and ultimately to all who accept Him, is also a major subject of this book. Need we mention that we do not mind giving such a scoffer a hard

---

[25]While on a trip to the Holy Land with the popular Christian author, Hal Lindsey, I gave him some of my research on the Antichrist. He lectured to our group, as even he was amazed at what the rabbis are publishing in their lack of Messianic knowledge. He said: "...And he will show no regard for the God of his fathers [Daniel 11:37]—now this is a Hebrew prophet speaking from a Hebrew point of view, so when he says he will show no regard for the God of his fathers, what kind of a person must he be speaking about—A Jew, *Elohim*? He will show no regard for the God of his fathers, this king of the end times...You know who this is? In the New Testament he's called the false prophet, he will be a pseudo-Messiah. My hair stood on end as I read some things that Philip—you know Philip's been doing some research for me and uh, he's done a good job. He found some very interesting things, but one of the things he found is a recent piece of literature written by several rabbinical writers. And what I read made my hair stand on end as we were driving on the bus because it was describing, from their point of view, the minimal requirements for a Messiah to be identified, and they said anyone who can come back and negotiate a peace between the Arabs and Israelis, can somehow bring about a settlement so that they can rebuild their temple and see that it's built, and will be able to deal in a wise way with the rest of the world, will be certainly the Messiah. Well, that's exactly what the false Messiah will do. I tell ya, they are primed to receive him because they really are not looking at their own prophets and seeing what kind of a person he was supposed to be." [ ] mine, transcribed from this author's personal tape made on location in Israel.

[26]"And the LORD shall make thee the **head** and not the tail; and thou shalt be above only, and thou shalt not be beneath; if that thou hearken unto the commandments of the LORD thy God, which I command thee this day, to observe and to do *them*...." (Deut. 28:13 KJV).

time! Maybe some of them will believe after they have seen our evidence.

DESPITE ALL THE PAST RABBINIC AND ECUMENICAL FORCES BLINDING JEWS TO THE MESSIAH, JEWS MUST HEAR, BECAUSE JESUS IS AT THE PROPHETIC DOORSTEP[27]

We do not believe that the rabbinical writings were inspired by God, as is the Bible. The Talmud and other rabbinical writings do not make this claim as the Bible does. In the Bible, God, personally speaking through the prophet Isaiah, reverberates into our century: "...I am God....Declaring the end from the beginning, and from ancient times *the things* that are not *yet* done, saying, My counsel shall stand, and I will do all my pleasure...." (Isa. 46:9-10 KJV).

The New Testament portion of the Bible also makes this claim in II Timothy 3:16: "All scripture *is* given by **inspiration of God**, and *is* profitable for doctrine, for reproof, for correction, for instruction in righteousness...." (KJV). However, the rabbinical writings do illustrate that the ancient rabbis reached the same interpretations of their Holy Scriptures, as have modern Evangelical Christians![28] This, of course, puts them in sharp contrast with later rabbis whose works we will also quote.

This work will prove conclusively that there has been a **cover-up** of the true Jewish view of Scripture, to isolate the Jew from the truth about Jesus. As we already stated, at the core of this deliberate conspiracy was the fear that Jews would be lost to the Gentile culture, as they accepted Jesus with so many more non-Jews. This certainly was not a serious possibility, since Gentiles who accepted Messiah also adopted Jewish custom, such as Passover (I Cor. 5:7-8), because they understood that the Messiah represents the Passover lamb and that He fulfilled this role (Isa. 53:7).

It was not until the age of Constantine in the fourth century that the Messianic and non-Jewish believers were forced out of the visible body of believers[29] known as the church. Even then they remained loyal to the Scriptures. The great majority of pagan Gentiles who were

---

[27]Jesus asked us to realize, "So likewise ye, when ye shall see all these things, know that it is near, *even* at the doors" (Matt. 24:33 KJV). The *things* Jesus is speaking of are prophecies of the end times, many of which are occurring today.

[28]In relation to prophecies said to be predictive of the Messiah, His birthplace, suffering and sacrifice, all of which, by no coincidence, actually realized fulfillment in Jesus' life!

[29]By this time, there were not very many believers in what had become the Christian body—the true church was already retreating underground. See chapter 10, "Early Christian History Versus Catholicism."

forced to convert to Catholicism by the Catholic Church, which began to develop around the time of Constantinople. They were not interested in the Bible and those few who might have been interested, were not permitted to study the Bible. They continued their pagan practices, which Roman Catholicism adopted.

Today, Messianic Jewish believers and Gentile born-again Christians stand with the first true believers regarding the fact that the visible "churches" of the Middle Ages were not Christian then, any more than most of the ecumenical and liberal theological organizations[30] are today!

This book will also present, in layman's terms, the ancient biblical hope of the return of the Messiah, which has been a Christian hope since the first century. All of the predicted signs of the Coming of Messiah are currently in place. Chief among them is the rebirth of Israel. The ancient rabbis held the same belief about these signs as we do, and their opinions on them (usually only known to unbelieving scholars) will be quoted in the context of the Bible. The only difference between them and us is that we have waited 2000 years longer and the signs of the times are now before us. We stand on the brink of this great promise while they stood thousands of years away from it.

While we study the words of Jesus and the prophets with excitement in relation to our near future and His promises, many so-called Christian churches remain in the dark regarding prophecy. If you truly love your Jewish friends, you owe them the opportunity to

---

[30]One telltale sign of a true believing Christian is a zealous desire to tell his friends about Jesus, so that they become fellow believers. This was commanded by Jesus (Acts 1:8) and emphasized by Paul, the apostle who wrote more than half of the New Testament. In his letter to the Roman congregations, he emphasized that the message of Jesus should be to the Jew first! Thus, those of us who are true believers, who are often scornfully called "fundamentalists" or "evangelicals" by liberal theologians and others who claim some sort of faith in Jesus, follow this New Testament teaching because we love our Jewish brothers and sisters. However, there are those who apparently do not believe that this biblical message applies. For example, in a publication entitled "Backgrounder," the question was asked, "Do all Christians support the efforts of 'Jews For Jesus' and other groups like them?" Part of the answer read: "Professor Tommaso Federici, a consultant to the Vatican, has called for an outright end to proselytism of the Jews, as has Dr. Krister Stendahl, dean of the Harvard Divinity School." "Backgrounder," June 1980, p. 3. From the Jewish Community Relations Council of Greater Philadelphia, a constituent of the Federation of Jewish Agencies. Proselytism is a word used to describe the kindness of evangelism in sharing the good news of Jesus' love. Obviously, these two individuals fall short of the standards set by Jesus and Paul. To separate the Jewish person from Jesus is a slap in the face to God, and if He is the Messiah for Israel as He claims, it is unusually cruel to call "for an outright end to the proselytism [sharing of Jesus—conversion to true Messianic Judaism] of the Jews." Ibid. [ ] mine. Isn't it? Yes!

see what their prophets wrote about their future. It is our prayer that you might loan them this book to read.

Thank you and bless you!
Sincerely and lovingly, Philip Moore

Orthodox Jews pray fervently at the Western Wall in Jerusalem.

PROLOGUE

"...he who hears a Midrash from the mouth of the Messiah **never forgets it**, because the Holy One, blessed be He, reveals Himself in the House of **Study** of the Messiah and pours out His Holy Spirit upon all those who walk in the world...."[1]

Yemenite Midrash

"The Law which man learns in this world is nothing in comparison with the Law of the Messiah."[2]

Midrash Qohel. on II

"**Study** to shew thyself approved unto God, a workman that needeth not to be ashamed, rightly dividing the word of truth." II Timothy 2:15 KJV.

"He that without better grounds then his private opinion or the opinion of any human authority whatsoever shall turn scripture from the plain meaning to an Allegory or to any other less naturall sense declares thereby that he reposes more trust in his own imaginations or in that human authority then in the Scripture ⟨and by consequence that he is no true beleever⟩. And therefore the opinion of such men how numerous soever they be, is not to be regarded. Hence is it and not from any reall uncertainty in the Scripture that Commentators have so distorted it; And this hath been the door through which all Heresies have crept in and turned out the ancient faith."[3]

Sir Isaac Newton, the greatest scientist that ever lived

Maimonides forbade the reading of certain rabbinical texts to prevent Jews from realizing the Bible's literal fulfillment[4] and the Messiahship of Jesus. Maimonides once wrote of Jesus: "...may his bones be ground to dust...."[5] These false ideas are still present within Judaism to varying degrees! We cannot allow them to go unchecked and unchallenged—not in light of the biblical and prophetic historical facts!

Philip Moore

***

---

[1]Raphael Patai, *The Messiah Texts*, p. 141. Bold mine. The famed rabbi of the twelfth century known as Rambam/Maimonides, once said: "...one should...not expatiate about the *midrashim*...." Ibid, p. 326. Midrashim are the Jewish commentaries on the Bible, which in many cases, as you will see in this book, authenticate our belief that Jesus is the Messiah. Is it any wonder Rambam said such a thing? We do not believe that they are inspired, but there is some truth to be found in them. More importantly, *if* they help the Jewish people see that the Messiah predicted in their Bible (our Old Testament) is, in fact, the Jesus spoken about in the New Testament, then we find them of particular and rare value, because Paul has instructed in the new covenant concerning the Gospel message: "...to the **Jew first,** and also to the Greek [Gentile/non-Jew]" (Rom. 1:16 KJV; [ ] mine). Maimonides' authority is definitely undercut by the Midrash and certainly by Timothy!

[2]W.O.E. Oesterley, D.D. and G.H. Box, M.A., *The Religion and Worship of the Synagogue*. London: Sir Isaac Pitman & Sons, 1911, p. 250.

[3]Frank E. Manuel, *The Religion of Isaac Newton*. London: Oxford University Press, © 1974, pp. 118-119, used by permission of the Oxford University Press. Manuel's source was *Yahuda Manuscript 1*. The spelling of believer, natural and real, is Newton's.

[4]In direct contradiction to the literal position stated in the rabbinic work Yalkut ha Makhiri, Rambam disrespectfully wrote: "...*The lion shall eat straw like the ox* (Isa. 11:7). And likewise, all the similar things said about the Messiah are but allegories." Raphael Patai, *The Messiah Texts*, p. 325. For details, see our comparison page in chapter 29, "After the Messiah Arrives and Ends the War—Paradise!"

[5]Abraham Halkin, *Crisis and Leadership: Epistles of Maimonides*. Philadelphia: The Jewish Publication Society of America, © 1985, p. 126, used by permission.

FOREWORD

Although I make no claim to every minute detail written herein, nevertheless, this work is filled with precious holy memories of faith, taken from the inherent power of the written word, holding true predictions inscribed by the Hebrew prophets of the Older Testament.

This book interestingly interprets the Bible, which is the cornerstone of Western civilization. It touches the heart through the living personalities in the Gospels. The scholarly research enhances a deeper and more genuine understanding of human history. This adds a spiritually significant dimension to the era in which we reside.

The second advent of the Redeemer is wonderfully illuminated through a unique insight of first century Jewish customs found in the New Testament. This gives humanity hope as we head into an exciting future with the promised Messiah in His coming kingdom reign.

Charlton Heston

An Israeli teacher, with Hebrew on her blackboard, the language in which the prophetic Holy scriptures were penned thousands of years ago.

"This most beautiful system of the sun, planets, and comets, could only proceed from the counsel and dominion of an intelligent and powerful Being. And if the fixed stars are the centres of other like systems, these, being formed by the like wise counsel, must be all subject to the dominion of One...."[1] Sir Isaac Newton, famed seventeenth century scientist

"Nature does exhibit remarkable coincidences and these do warrant some explanation." "One would have to conclude either that the features of the universe invoked in support of the anthropic principle are only coincidences, or that the universe was indeed tailor-made for life. I will leave it to the theologians to ascertain the identity of the tailor."[2] Bernard Carr and Martin Rees, astronomers

"When confronted with the order and beauty of the universe and the strange coincidences of nature, it's very tempting to take the leap of faith from science into religion. I am sure many physicists want to—I only wish they would admit it."

Tony Rothman, theoretical physicist

"The exquisite order displayed by our scientific understanding of the physical world calls for the divine." Vera Kistiakowsky, Association of Women in Science

"Astronomy leads us to a universe which has an underlying (one might say 'supernatural') plan." Arno Penzias, Nobel Prize-winner who discovered cosmic background radiation

"One cannot be exposed to the law and order of the universe without concluding that there must be design and purpose behind it all....They (evolutionists) challenge science to prove the existence of God. But must we really light a candle to see the sun?"[3] Dr. Wernher von Braun, the leading scientist who put us on the moon

"Thousands of fortune tellers, astrologers, demon possessed mediums, who ask the dead, make a fine living throughout Christendom and profit greatly by the desire of thousands to know a little about the future. And here in the Bible God has uncovered the future, but few of His people pay any attention to it."

Arno Gaebelein (see p. 19 to see what he means)

1

HOW IT ALL BEGAN

You may be asking, "In a book which is mainly about the future, why do we begin with the ancient past?" We need to know how we reached the present and where we will be going in the future, as one great Bible teacher has beautifully said: "...the account that we are investigating here is found in the record of the ancient Hebrew Scriptures. I believe that this account has proved to be the most

---

[1]Isaac Newton, *Mathematical Principles of Natural Philosophy*, published in the compilation *Great Books of the Western World*, Vol. 34. Chicago: William Benton for Encyclopedia Brittanica, Inc. in cooperation with the University of Chicago, © 1952, p. 369, used by permission.

[2]First quote Carr and Rees; Second quote Carr; from Hugh Ross, *Reasons to Believe*, Feb. 1994 broadcast. Ross' sources were *Discover* magazine and an article on the anthropic principle for *Nature* magazine. The following three quotes are from the same broadcast. For data on recent scientific discoveries in astrophysics, proving creation over evolution, write Dr. Ross at POB 5978, Pasadena, CA, USA 91117.

[3]*Bible Science Newsletter*, May 1974, p. 8.

consistent explanation....To understand what is happening today and in the near future, we must reach back into these ancient documents and look into events that occurred before man came into existence. The account of how an exalted supernatural being of incredible beauty, power, and intelligence named Lucifer came to be Satan is stranger than fiction....The key to understanding man's purpose and destiny is related to the pre-history conflict that began with Lucifer's revolt against God."[4]

OUR CREATION 6000 YEARS AGO IN JUST SIX DAYS? AFTER THE CHAOS OF *TOHU-VA-VOHU*

Many scoff at the biblical account of how the world began; however, the Bible does not really make such a simple claim—not to those of us who know[5] the original Hebrew.[6] In fact, there are two words in Hebrew for creation: *bara* (בָּרָא); and *asah* (עָשָׂה).[7] The first means to create something out of nothing—the true meaning of creation! However, the second means to create something from something else, in fact, to reconstruct something already in existence. There is also a third Hebrew word, which is located between creation and reconstruction; *tohu-va-vohu* (תֹהוּ וָבֹהוּ).

"Tohu-va-what?" you ask. This word means "chaos"; something beautiful and perfect that became obliterated into unorganized chaos. An Israeli friend told me the best way to express this word in modern language is "tossed salad."

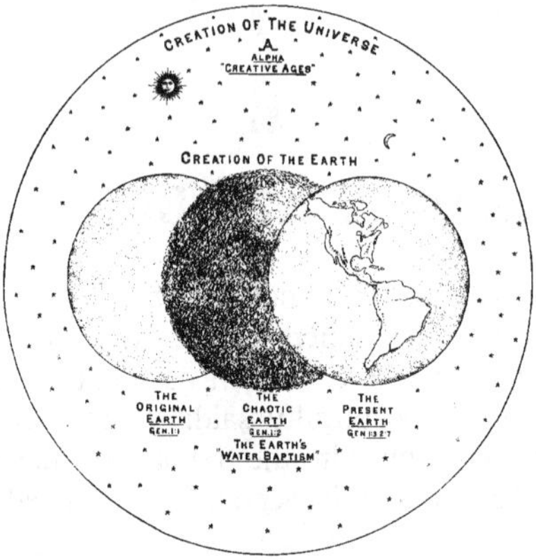

[4]Hal Lindsey with C.C. Carlson, *Satan is Alive and Well on Planet Earth*. Grand Rapids, MI: The Zondervan Corporation, © 1972, pp. 44-45, used by permission.

[5]I cannot give enough thanks to God for giving me the great privilege to live in Israel for eight years and learn His wonderful language—Hebrew! May all of my readers one day have a similar opportunity, if it be their desire, for if I had not been granted such an opportunity, this book would not be what it is today.

[6]See our *Vol. II*, chapter 40, "Two Creations—An Israeli Professor Comments on Our Findings."

[7]*Bara* is found in Genesis 1:1 and *asah* is found in Genesis 2:2 in the Hebrew Bible.

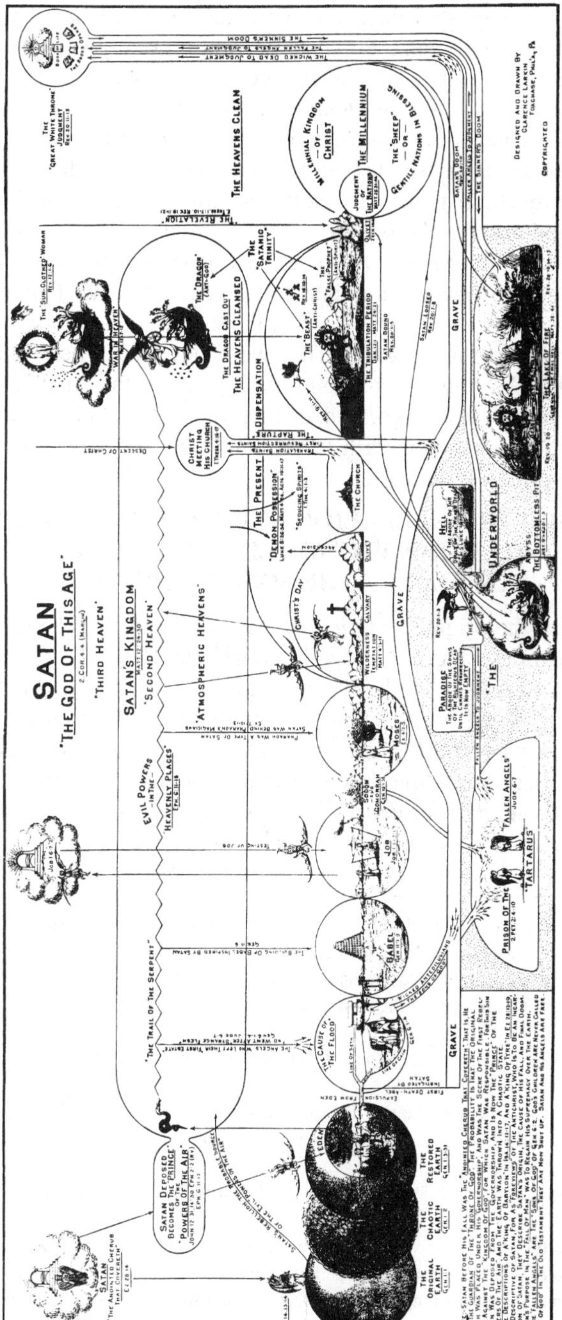

Diagram courtesy of Clarence Larkin Estate.

In our English Bibles the word *tohu-va-vohu* is translated as "without form and void." So what the Bible is really telling us is that: "God created the earth and it was good...." in Genesis 1:1,[8] and in Genesis 1:2, that it became *tohu-va-vohu*, which is the Hebrew word for shapeless and void in form, in other words, chaotic.

We can clearly see that in the interval between the two biblical verses, a rebellion took place and that this first creation, *bara*, was original and occurred before the *asah* (a second creation described later in the book of Genesis). *Asah*[9] means to construct something from material already made, or rather, to *re*construct. The famous Rabbi Nachman remarked of *bara*: "...that there is no other word to express production out of nothing."[10] Thus we believe that when Genesis 1:1 tells us that the original creation[11] took place in the hands of God, it was millions of years ago, and in fact, did not include man[12] or the modern life we have on earth today, but rather dinosaurs, mammoths, and other primitive animals.

LUCIFER'S REBELLION AND TRANSFORMATION TO SATAN WAS AFTER THE ORIGINAL BUT BEFORE THE SIX-DAY CREATION

After the original creation, there was a satanic rebellion led by God's mightiest angelic being, Lucifer[13] (in Hebrew, בֶּן־שַׁחַר or *ben Shahar*, means "son of the dawn"). Lucifer decided to rebel and be "like God." The Lord, speaking to Job, revealed that prior to Lucifer's rebellion, which transformed[14] him into the evil creature known to us as Satan, there was a time when all angelic beings were in a state of joy after the creation of the earth. These beings were known in Hebrew as *Bené Elohim* or "sons of God," and also as "morning stars."

---

[8]Genesis is the first book of the Old Testament portion of the Judeo-Christian Bible.

[9]G.H. Pember documents: "...*asah* signifies to make, fashion, or prepare out of existing material; as, for instance...to prepare a meal." G.H. Pember, *Earth's Earliest Ages*. Grand Rapids, MI: Kregel Publications, 1979, p. 29.

[10]Ibid.

[11]See our *Vol. II*, chapter 28, "The Gap Theory, as Expounded Upon by M.R. DeHaan, M.D."

[12]The Hebrew Bible uses the word *yatzar* (יָצַר) in reference to the origin of man. This word "means to shape, or mould, as a potter does the clay (Gen. ii. 7)." G.H. Pember, *Earth's Earliest Ages*, p. 30.

[13]The word *Lucifer* is derived from the Latin words for "light bringing" or "morning star."

[14]Lucifer's transformation was to *sitra acara*, which is Hebrew for "the other side" or "the evil side." We could not help being reminded of the transformation of something good and cute into something hateful and ugly when we saw Steven Spielberg's movie, *Gremlins*. It portrays this concept in a down-to-earth, understandable and comical way, though it does not directly relate. It sounds like Spielberg may have read Genesis, Ezekiel and Isaiah.

The Scriptures record God's question to Job: "Where were you when I laid the foundation of the earth? Tell *Me*, if you have understanding....When the morning stars sang together, And all the sons of God shouted for joy?" (Job 38:4, 7 NASB).

The Hebrew prophets Ezekiel and Isaiah describe Satan's nature in eons past. Ezekiel 28 tells us of his original unfallen state: "...'Thus says the Lord GOD, 'You had the seal of perfection, Full of wisdom and perfect in beauty. You were in Eden, the garden of God; Every precious stone was your covering: The ruby, the topaz, and the diamond; The beryl, the onyx, and the jasper; The lapis lazuli, the turquoise, and the emerald; And the gold, the workmanship of your settings and sockets, Was in you. On the day that you were created They were prepared. You were the anointed cherub who covers, And I placed you *there*. You were on the holy mountain of God; You walked in the midst of the stones of fire. You were blameless in your ways From the day you were created, Until unrighteousness was found in you' " (Ezek. 28:12-15 NASB).

Isaiah 14 reveals Satan's five *I wills*—his lofty boasts of triumph over God, his creator: "How art thou fallen from heaven, O Lucifer, son of the morning! *how* art thou cut down to the ground, which didst weaken the nations! For thou hast said in thine heart, **I will** ascend into heaven, **I will** exalt my throne above the stars of God: **I will** sit also upon the mount of the congregation, in the sides of the north: **I will** ascend above the heights of the clouds; **I will** be like the most High" (Isa. 14:12-14, KJV; bold mine).

We believe that once Lucifer, who was perfect in his ways from the day of his creation,[15] exercised his free will to attempt a conquest of God, the "Big Bang" (excuse the expression) took place. Lucifer led one-third of the angelic realm into rebellion against God. This rebellion resulted in *tohu-va-vohu*—chaos. Once this occurred, God exiled these fallen creatures from Himself. Jesus, speaking of this event which He witnessed prior to His physical birth into humanity, testified: "...'I beheld Satan as lightning fall from heaven' " (Luke 10:18 KJV).

TRULY, MODERN MAN WAS CREATED 6000 YEARS AGO IN THE SIX DAYS OF THE *ASAH* RECONSTRUCTION, IN ACCORDANCE WITH THE HEBREW SCRIPTURES

Revelation 12:3-4 maintains that Satan led a rebellion in which one-third of God's angelic realm were drawn over to his side. Once the rebellion was defeated and they were banned from His presence,

[15]Ezekiel 28:15.

God decided to create man (a creature out of the soil of the earth),[16] to whom He would give all that Satan had tried to steal.

The Bible says one day we will have bodies "like unto his glorious body"[17] (Phil. 3:21; Ps. 17:15).[18] These verses speak of the time when the Messiah returns and gives us our new bodies (see our chapter 29, "After the Messiah Arrives and Ends the War—Paradise!" and chapter 30, "New Heavens and a New Earth").

The popular Christian writer, Hal Lindsey, using the New Testament books of Hebrews and Corinthians, has eloquently remarked concerning our future that: "...God wanted to elevate man above the angelic realm and to fellowship with Him.

In the Book of Hebrews God shows that man will rule the world to come; angels will actually be under man's rule: 'For He did not subject to angels the world to come, concerning which we are speaking. But one has testified somewhere, saying, 'What is man that Thou rememberest him? Or the son of man, that Thou art concerned about him? Thou hast made him for a little while lower than the angels; Thou hast crowned him with glory and honor, and hast appointed him over the works of Thy hands; Thou hast put all things in subjection under his feet' ' (Hebrews 2:5-8).

The Apostle Paul says the same thing in 1 Corinthians 6:3: 'Do you not know that we shall judge angels? How much more, matters of this life?' "[19]

Thus, *after* the original creation, *after* the chaos, there was an *asah*. This word in Hebrew, as we have noted, means to "reconstruct." We believe God reconstructed the earth after the original creation of dinosaurs and other ancient creatures, some of which may have resembled the shape of man as chimpanzees and gorillas do today. Most, if not all fossils attributed to man prior to this date, have been proven either to be fakes, such as England's Piltdown Man, or mistakes.[20] For example, one Prosthennops find was believed to be an ape-man until 1922, when "he" was discovered to be the tooth of a pig.

---

[16]Modern science states that every element in the human body can be found in the soil.

[17]Jesus' glorified body, which He received at His resurrection—a body which can move through solid objects (John 20:26).

[18]Psalm 17:15 reads: "As for me, I will behold thy face in righteousness: I shall be satisfied, when I awake, with thy likeness" (KJV).

[19]Hal Lindsey with C.C. Carlson, *Satan is Alive and Well on Planet Earth*, p. 54.

[20]There have been entire "prehistoric" human skulls (i.e., Nebraska Man) built from a single tooth; however, scientists later discovered that the tooth belonged to an extinct pig. See our appendix 3, "Apes, Fakes and Mistakes," where we systematically expose all of these prehistoric men for the frauds they are, with proven evidence which has often been suppressed!

MODERN CREATION AND MAN IN JUST SIX DAYS APPROXIMATELY 6000 YEARS AGO! GOD ANTICIPATED OUR FALL

The chief creature in the creative reconstruction of earthbound life was unlike anything hitherto created by God. It was man, the only one to be made in the image of his creator, with mind, free will, emotion, and intellect.[21] Thus man was made to have a relationship with his Creator and he did. However, our great, great, great...grandparents were deceived at one point by, you guessed it, Satan himself.

Satan, knowing man was made to replace him, will always hate mankind, no matter how loyal a man may be to him (as in witchcraft, etc.), and in the end, **will destroy all who serve him**. Satan succeeded in causing man to rebel (Gen. 3), which resulted in man also becoming estranged from God, as Satan had been. He thought, "Now I've got him! If God forgives him, then God will also have to forgive me!" However, God knew man would fall temporarily because of the gift of free will. Thus He launched His ultimate plan, "Operation Redemption," through the Messiah. Redemption means to buy back.[22] **Ransom** is the greater part of its meaning. Jesus once said: "For even the Son of man came not to be ministered unto, but to minister, and to give his life a **ransom** for many" (Mark 10:45 KJV). Also, the Hebrew prophet Isaiah predicted (circa 700 BC) of the Messiah: "...he

---

[21]Man alone was created for fellowship and worship of God, possessing above any other creature the ability to write and pass down knowledge from one generation to another—a must for receiving and transmitting the Bible, God's written revelation of Himself and prophecy needed to guide us in worship. Animals may have limited intellect, but animals are set apart from us in relation to our worship of the Creator and the ability to receive and record revelation from generation to generation, which is a necessity for this worship.

[22] What is God interested in buying back? The Hebrew Bible said: "From any tree of the garden you may eat freely; but from the tree of the knowledge of good and evil you shall not eat, for in that **day**...you shall surely **die**" (Gen. 2:17; bold mine). In Hebrew, the word for life is plural. God said in Genesis 2:7 that He breathed life (וַיִּפַּח בְּאַפָּיו נִשְׁמַת חַיִּים) into man. In Hebrew, He said He breathed *heim* ("lives") into man. Thus man, from the beginning, was created with a dual life—two kinds of life, physical and spiritual. Man lost his spiritual life in the garden when he failed God's test. He disobeyed God for the first time by listening to the Satan-incarnated serpent (Gen. 2:17), which resulted in his spiritual death that very day! This death, which resulted in his expulsion from the garden (Gen. 3:23), later resulted in physical death: "...from it you were taken; For you are dust, And to dust you shall return" (Gen. 3:19 NASB). Likewise, once his spiritual life is restored through the acceptance of the ransom of the Messiah later (the Second Coming), his physical eternal life will be restored through resurrection, as Jesus and Daniel prophesied: "Marvel not at this: for the hour is coming, in the which all that are in the graves shall hear his voice, And shall come forth; they that have done good, unto the resurrection of life; and they that have done evil, unto the resurrection of damnation" (John 5:28-29 KJV). "And many of them that sleep in the dust of the earth shall awake, some to everlasting life, and some to shame *and* everlasting contempt" (Dan. 12:2 KJV).

was cut off out of the land of the living: for the transgression of my people was he stricken....Yet it pleased the LORD to bruise him....by his knowledge shall my righteous servant justify many....” (Isa. 53:8-11 KJV).

SOLUTION—GOD’S KINSMAN REDEEMER, THROUGH OPERATION MESSIAH!

The Messiah was to be God’s avenue for this redemption. In order for redemption to take place, it would have to be accomplished through a party who was not guilty, as man had become, and who was not invulnerable to death, as God is. It had to be someone who was between us. Hal Lindsey, my favorite Bible teacher, put it in these words: “...the redeemer had to be ‘next of kin’ to the human race. Hebrews 2:14, 15 explains why this was so: ‘Since then the children [mankind] share in flesh and blood, He Himself likewise also partook of the same [flesh and blood], that through death He might render powerless him who had the power of death, that is, the devil; and might deliver those who through fear of death were subject to slavery all their lives.’

You see, the price of redemption for man has always been the shed blood of an innocent substitute. Moses taught in the Law, ‘Without the shedding of blood, there is no remission of sin’ (Hebrews 9:22). However, the blood of animals could never take the sin away; it only atoned for, or covered it, temporarily until God provided a complete remission of sins through His ultimate sacrifice of Jesus (Hebrews 10:11-14).

But, since the redemption price had to be the shed *blood* of an *innocent* sacrifice, the redeemer had to be someone with blood in his veins who could actually experience death. In other words, a man, but one who was completely innocent of any sins.

That’s why we read about Christ’s death in 1 Peter 1:19, that it accomplished redemption ‘with precious blood, as of a lamb *unblemished* and *spotless*, the blood of Christ.’ ”[23]

Thus Genesis 3:15 was known within ancient Judaism and is still recognized among Evangelical Christians as the first Messianic prophecy: “...I will put enmity between thee and the woman, and between thy seed and her seed; it shall bruise thy head, and thou shalt bruise his heel” (KJV).[24]

***

[23]Hal Lindsey, *The Liberation of Planet Earth*. Grand Rapids, MI: The Zondervan Corporation, © 1974, pp. 106-107, used by permission of Western Front, Ltd./Hal Lindsey.

[24]This Scripture is the main theme in the design of our book cover. It is inlaid in the serpent’s tail.

ORIGINAL HEBREW TEXT WRITTEN 1450 BC

וַיֹּאמֶר יְהוָה אֱלֹהִים ׀ אֶל־הַנָּחָשׁ כִּי עָשִׂיתָ זֹּאת אָרוּר אַתָּה מִכָּל־הַבְּהֵמָה וּמִכֹּל חַיַּת
הַשָּׂדֶה עַל־גְּחֹנְךָ תֵלֵךְ וְעָפָר תֹּאכַל כָּל־יְמֵי חַיֶּיךָ׃ וְאֵיבָה ׀ אָשִׁית בֵּינְךָ וּבֵין הָאִשָּׁה
וּבֵין זַרְעֲךָ וּבֵין זַרְעָהּ הוּא יְשׁוּפְךָ רֹאשׁ וְאַתָּה תְּשׁוּפֶנּוּ עָקֵב׃

בראשית ג:טו-יז

OLD TESTAMENT SCRIPTURE TRANSLATION

"And the LORD God said unto the serpent, Because thou hast done this, thou *art* cursed above all cattle, and above every beast of the field; upon thy belly shalt thou go, and dust shalt thou eat all thy days of thy life: And I will put enmity between thee and the woman, and between thy seed and her seed; it shall bruise thy head, and thou shalt bruise his heel."

Genesis 3:14-15, KJV[25]

ANCIENT RABBINICAL COMMENTARY

"R. Tanhuma said in the name of Samuel Kozith: [She hinted at] that seed which would arise from another source, viz. the king Messiah."

Midrash Rabbah XXIII 5-6

NEW TESTAMENT RECORDED 65 AD

"...Adam was first formed, then Eve. And Adam was not deceived, but the woman, being deceived, was in the transgression. Notwithstanding, she shall be saved in childbearing...."[26] **I Timothy 2:13-15 KJV**[27]

MODERN RABBINIC COMMENT/REFUTATION

"From this verse Christian missionary theologians argue that the Messiah is to be born of the seed of a woman without a man's intervention. Yet there is absolutely no proof to assume that this verse is messianic or that the Messiah is to be born in a supernatural way. The Christian missionary claim of a direct and exclusive reference to Jesus is exegetically untenable. The phrase 'her seed' has nothing to do with the determination of the Messiah's lineage....'Her seed' simply means her descendants....the Christian missionary interpretation of Genesis 3:15 is yet another Christological dream...."

***The Jew and the Christian Missionary*, by Gerald Sigal, pp. 3-5; © 1981**

AUTHOR'S COMMENT—EVANGELICAL CHRISTIAN POSITION

It is quite obvious from this ancient rabbinical commentary that there was a seed, expected and predicted (Gen. 3:15; 4:25),[28] which was to be the Messiah of triumph. Thus the view of the majority of modern rabbis, voiced by Mr. Sigal under the guidance of Rabbi Bronznick, claiming that the seed of Genesis 3:15 is not Messianic, is dishonest and untrue when set in the framework of what was once believed by the rabbis of ancient Judaism.

Philip Moore

---

[25] This event occurred circa 4000 BC.

[26] This verse indicates that one day a woman would bear a child (the Messiah), by which all of humanity, including Eve herself, would be saved (redeemed). The New Testament identifies this one as Jesus.

[27] *The New Scofield Reference Bible*.

[28] Many brilliant Bible scholars have commented that Eve, remembering God's promised seed of Genesis 3:15, mistakenly thought her son Seth was the Messiah.

The essence of the prophecy is that the Messiah's heel would be bruised.[29] Jesus' heels were bruised when the Romans drove nails into His feet during the crucifixion. But as a result of His death, His innocence paid the penalty of Adam's original sin in the Garden, which was the beginning and root[30] that made all mankind, through the centuries until now, sin. This is the evil inclination, *yetzer hara*, of which Judaism teaches.

Original sin, which is denounced by modern Judaism, was once a chief tenet of ancient Judaism in keeping with the Bible. It is only because some modernists do not want an evident reason to show our need for a suffering Messiah to die for the sins of the world, that the whole idea of "original sin" is denied. Here is the proof:

An Israeli soldier hugs her lamb.

---

[29]"The *Talmud Sota*, fol. 49, col. 2, speaks of 'the heels of the Messiah' (עקבות), i.e., of the time when the heel of the Messiah shall be bruised by the serpent, with reference to the troubles in the Messianic time." Reverend B. Pick, Ph.D., *Old Testament Passages Messianically Applied by the Ancient Synagogue*, published in the compilation *Hebraica, A Quarterly Journal in the Interests of Semitic Study*, Vol. IV. New York: Charles Scribner's Sons, 1888, p. 25.

[30]Rabbinically speaking, it has been said: "Adam....became negligent by eating from the Tree of Knowledge...who failed the test and ate of the aftergrowth, and thereby caused damage in all the worlds....almost this entire story occurs to every man individually...." Raphael Patai, *The Messiah Texts*, p. 106. Patai's source was R. Nathan's introduction to R. Nahman of Bratzlav's *Sippure Ma'asiyyot*, 1973 ed., pp. 7-8.

ORIGINAL HEBREW TEXT WRITTEN 1450 BC

וַיִּיצֶר יְהוָה אֱלֹהִים אֶת־הָאָדָם עָפָר מִן־הָאֲדָמָה וַיִּפַּח בְּאַפָּיו נִשְׁמַת חַיִּים וַיְהִי הָאָדָם
לְנֶפֶשׁ חַיָּה׃ וַיִּטַּע יְהוָה אֱלֹהִים גַּן־בְּעֵדֶן מִקֶּדֶם וַיָּשֶׂם שָׁם אֶת־הָאָדָם אֲשֶׁר יָצָר׃ וַיַּצְמַח
יְהוָה אֱלֹהִים מִן־הָאֲדָמָה כָּל־עֵץ נֶחְמָד לְמַרְאֶה וְטוֹב לְמַאֲכָל וְעֵץ הַחַיִּים בְּתוֹךְ הַגָּן וְעֵץ
הַדַּעַת טוֹב וָרָע׃ .... וּלְאָדָם אָמַר כִּי שָׁמַעְתָּ לְקוֹל אִשְׁתֶּךָ וַתֹּאכַל מִן־הָעֵץ אֲשֶׁר צִוִּיתִיךָ
לֵאמֹר לֹא תֹאכַל מִמֶּנּוּ אֲרוּרָה הָאֲדָמָה בַּעֲבוּרֶךָ בְּעִצָּבוֹן תֹּאכֲלֶנָּה כֹּל יְמֵי חַיֶּיךָ׃
וְקוֹץ וְדַרְדַּר תַּצְמִיחַ לָךְ וְאָכַלְתָּ אֶת־עֵשֶׂב הַשָּׂדֶה׃ בְּזֵעַת אַפֶּיךָ תֹּאכַל לֶחֶם עַד שׁוּבְךָ
אֶל־הָאֲדָמָה כִּי מִמֶּנָּה לֻקָּחְתָּ כִּי־עָפָר אַתָּה וְאֶל־עָפָר תָּשׁוּב׃ וַיִּקְרָא הָאָדָם שֵׁם אִשְׁתּוֹ
חַוָּה כִּי הִוא הָיְתָה אֵם כָּל־חָי׃ וַיַּעַשׂ יְהוָה אֱלֹהִים לְאָדָם וּלְאִשְׁתּוֹ יְהוָה אֱלֹהִים
לְאָדָם וּלְאִשְׁתּוֹ כָּתְנוֹת עוֹר וַיַּלְבִּשֵׁם׃ וַיֹּאמֶר ׀ יְהוָה אֱלֹהִים הֵן הָאָדָם הָיָה כְּאַחַד מִמֶּנּוּ
לָדַעַת טוֹב וָרָע וְעַתָּה ׀ פֶּן־יִשְׁלַח יָדוֹ וְלָקַח גַּם מֵעֵץ הַחַיִּים וְאָכַל וָחַי לְעֹלָם׃ וַיְשַׁלְּחֵהוּ
יְהוָה אֱלֹהִים מִגַּן־עֵדֶן לַעֲבֹד אֶת־הָאֲדָמָה אֲשֶׁר לֻקַּח מִשָּׁם׃ וַיְגָרֶשׁ אֶת־הָאָדָם וַיַּשְׁכֵּן
מִקֶּדֶם לְגַן־עֵדֶן אֶת־הַכְּרֻבִים וְאֵת לַהַט הַחֶרֶב הַמִּתְהַפֶּכֶת לִשְׁמֹר אֶת־דֶּרֶךְ עֵץ הַחַיִּים׃

בראשית ב:ז-ט; ג:יז-כד

OLD TESTAMENT SCRIPTURE TRANSLATION

"And the LORD God formed man *of* the dust of the ground, and breathed into his nostrils the breath of life; and man became a living soul. And the LORD God planted a garden eastward in Eden; and there he put the man whom he had formed. And out of the ground made the LORD God to grow every tree that is pleasant to the sight, and good for food; the tree of life also in the midst of the garden, and the tree of knowledge of good and evil....And unto Adam he said, Because thou hast hearkened unto the voice of thy wife, and hast eaten of the tree, of which I commanded thee, saying, Thou shalt not eat of it: cursed *is* the ground for thy sake; in sorrow shalt thou eat *of* it all the days of thy life; Thorns also and thistles shall it bring forth to thee; and thou shalt eat the herb of the field; In the sweat of thy face shalt thou eat bread, till thou return unto the ground; for out of it wast thou taken: for dust thou *art*, and unto dust shalt thou return. And Adam called his wife's name Eve; because she was the mother of all living. Unto Adam also and to his wife did the LORD God make coats of skins, and clothed them. And the LORD God said, Behold, the man is become as one of us, to know good and evil: and now, lest he put forth his hand, and take also of the tree of life, and eat, and live for ever: Therefore the LORD God sent him forth from the garden of Eden, to till the ground from whence he was taken. So he drove out the man; and he placed at the east of the garden of Eden Cherubims,[31] and a flaming sword which turned every way, to keep the way of the tree of life."

Genesis 2:7-9; 3:17-24 KJV

ANCIENT RABBINICAL COMMENTARY

"...Adam whom I charged with one commandment which he was to perform and live and endure for ever'; as it says, *Behold, the man was as one of us* (Gen. III, 22). Similarly, *And God created man in His own image* (*ib.* I, 27), that is to say, that he should live and endure like Himself. Yet [says God] he corrupted his deeds and nullified My decree. For he ate of the tree, and I said to him: *For dust thou art* (*ib.* III, 19)....you have ruined yourselves like Adam, and so, *'Indeed, ye shall die like* Adam.' "[32]

Midrash Rabbah XXIII 5-6

---

[31] See our *Vol. II*, chapter 31, "The Mystery of the Temple Doors," from a lecture by Jonathan Cahn.

[32] *Midrash Rabbah, Numbers*, Vol. II. New York: Soncino Press Ltd., © 1983, p. 692.

"...The Tora was before the Holy One, blessed be He, containing six hundred thousand letters, in disarray. And when Adam the first man sinned, [God] arranged the letters into words, such as, *When a man dieth in the tent* (Num. 19:14), or the section about inheritance, and the section about levirate, and many more the like. For had Adam not sinned, the letters would have arranged themselves into other words. Therefore, in the Future to Come, when the sin of Adam will have been forgiven, the words will return to their primordial state, and the very Tora of Moses will contain the full complement of letters, neither fewer nor more, arranged into other words, as it would have been had Adam not sinned."[33]

Midrash Talpiyot, 58a

"R. Pinhas said: 'In the future time to come, the Holy One, blessed be He, will render the bodies of the pious beautiful like the beauty of Adam the first man when he entered the Garden of Eden.' "[34]

Zohar 1:113b, Midrash haNe'elam

NEW TESTAMENT RECORDED 96 AD

"And he showed me a pure river of water of life, clear as crystal, proceeding out of the throne of God and of the Lamb. In the midst of the street of it, and on either side of the river, *was there* the tree of life, which bore twelve *kinds of* fruits, *and* yielded her fruit every month; and the leaves of the tree *were* for the healing of the nations. And there shall be no more curse, but the throne of God and of the Lamb shall be in it, and his servants shall serve him...."

Revelation 22:1-3 KJV[35]

MODERN RABBINIC COMMENT/REFUTATION

"Judaism rejects these doctrines. Man was mortal from the first, and death did not enter the world through the transgression of Eve....There is no loss of the Godlikeness of man, nor of man's ability to do right in the eyes of God; and no such loss has been transmitted to his latest descendants....Judaism preaches the Rise of man; and instead of Original Sin, it stresses Original Virtue...."[36]

Chief Rabbi J. H. Hertz

AUTHOR'S COMMENT—EVANGELICAL CHRISTIAN POSITION

The ancient rabbinical commentaries we quoted clearly support the New Testament remedy of a future need to heal the nations of the world in order to reverse the ruin Adam brought upon the race. Rabbi Hertz denied original sin and claimed that Judaism believes in "original virtue." This is deceptive! Obviously, this rabbi lived in a fantasy world because the Old Testament, historic records, ancient rabbinical commentaries and New Testament all agree that man got sick and will one day get well! Look around you, see how much theft, murder, and cruelty tyrants have caused throughout history. The murder of six million Jews by Hitler and the murder of over fifty million innocent Chinese by Mao, along with the tens of thousands of murders and thefts occurring every day on our streets, illustrates man is not presently what he was created to be! Adam, when he failed God's test of obedience in the Garden, marred the spirit that God breathed into him (Gen. 2:7). That which the Bible says was made in God's image (Gen. 1:27), was now changed (Gen. 3), although it would be a temporary change; that change we know as original sin. Fallen man transmitted this evil desire like any other genetically transmitted disease, in his desire to control and manipulate others for his own selfish purposes. The

---

[33]Raphael Patai, *The Messiah Texts*, p. 256.
[34]Ibid, p. 263.
[35]*The New Scofield Reference Bible*.
[36]Arthur W. Kac, *The Rebirth of the State of Israel: Is It of God or of Men?* Grand Rapids, MI: Baker Book House, © 1976, pp. 185-186, used by permission.

hundreds of wars we have had throughout history are evidence that something terrible has happened to our race. If later rabbis (after the Coming of Jesus) are going to be successful in diminishing the Hebrew Bible's concept of the Messiah suffering for the sins of the Jewish people and ultimately the nations, they must destroy the reason for the Coming of the Messiah, and that reason is sin—*original* sin. This is why original sin, which was openly believed within Judaism until Jesus, is so vigorously contested by modern rabbis. You see, if original sin, the sin nature the Jewish Bible says all people possess (Ps. 53; Ecc. 7:20) really exists, you must have a redemption remedy for it—Jesus. And to eliminate the Messianic claim of Jesus' power to redeem, you must first eliminate the requirement for such redemption and that is the doctrine of original sin.

Philip Moore

GOD CREATED A VESSEL, ENTERED IT, AND TOOK HIS OWN PENALTY FOR US THROUGH THAT VESSEL—MESSIAH FORESHADOWED IN THE PASSOVER LAMB

At this point, for all of us who believe that the Messiah[37] took the rap for us and bought us out of the trouble our great...grandmother and grandfather got us into, we can be sure of the *olam haba* (in Hebrew, "the world to come"). One day this paradise will be realized, and presently we will have peace of mind in the knowledge that things do not just happen by accident and that we all do, in fact, have a very real and eternal future (see our chapter 29, "After the Messiah Arrives and Ends the War—Paradise!" and chapter 30, "New Heavens and a New Earth").

However, the price God paid for us to receive this redemption (salvation from what befell Adam and was transferred to us genetically from generation to generation) is unfathomable. God, as perfect and

---

[37]Ancient rabbinical teachings and commentaries agree with our view of original sin in the sense that it was handed down to us against the modern rabbinical stance that it was not. W.O.E. Oesterley and G.H. Box say: "According to Jewish teaching the 'Fall' was the transgression of *one* commandment, aggravated, however, by the absence of all repentance on the part of Adam; it was brought about by the subtilty of Satan—or the serpent, for the two are of course identical—because he was jealous of Adam, who had usurped the position formerly held by Satan....The Targums teach that death is one of the consequences of sin; this is expressed in one passsage, in the Jerusalem Targum to Genesis 3[6], by saying that at the moment in which Eve succumbed to temptation she saw Sammael the angel of death; as Satan is identical with Sammael, we must suppose that this passage is intended to teach that Satan revealed himself to Eve as the angel of death at the moment in which he overcame her....Further on in the same passsage, in the comment on Genesis 3[7], we read: 'His (Adam's) skin was a light garment, shining like his nails; when he sinned this lightness vanished, and he appeared naked.' As illustrating a deeper realization of the essence of Sin we may refer to the *Targum of Jonathan* to Is. 62[10], where it says that the imagination of sin is sin. While the existence of sin is presupposed before Adam fell, his sin was the means of death entering into the world, so that all generations to the end of time are subject to death (*Tanchuma, Bereshith* 8)." W.O.E. Oesterley, D.D. and G.H. Box, M.A., *The Religion and Worship of the Synagogue*, pp. 266-267.

mighty as He is, actually incarnated Himself into one of the descendants of Adam, whom **He** had created, and then took the penalty due us, while He Himself was innocent. He did this so He could, in the end, justify us before His law and His perfect standards for all the times we have and will fall short!

Pointing to this future (from the standpoint of Genesis 3:15, written about 4000 years ago) sacrificial redemption on the Messiah's part, was the Passover, instituted 3500 years ago within Hebrew antiquity, in which an innocent lamb's blood was placed over the doorposts of the Jews while they were in Egypt. Those who did this would be spared the consequence of the death angel when he "passed over," which was the death of the first-born son. (Diagram courtesy of Clarence Larkin Estate.)

THE PASSOVER

THE PRINCE OF THE POWER OF THE AIR

Until the Messiah returns to redeem the world physically, the earth in the natural sense (apart from those who have received Jesus spiritually into their hearts) is under a title deed of ownership. This deed once belonged to Adam but was forfeit to Satan at the time of Adam's fall. This is why Satan said to Jesus in the Gospel of Luke concerning "all the kingdoms of the world": "...All this power will I give thee, and the glory of them: for that is delivered unto me; and to whomsoever I will I give it. If thou therefore wilt worship me, all shall be thine" (Luke 4:6-7 KJV).

The New Testament calls Satan "the prince of the power of the air"[38] (Eph. 2:2 KJV). This is why there has been so much evil throughout history and in the present natural world. The Hebrew prophet Jeremiah affirms this in the Old Testament portion of the Bible, to which most Orthodox Jews still lay claim. "The heart *is* **deceitful** above all *things*, **and desperately wicked**: who can know it?" (Jer. 17:9 KJV; bold mine). Thus, only when the Messiah returns will Satan be incapacitated and the earth's full beauty realized. This will be the time when Jesus' wounded heel truly crushes Satan's ugly head, as foretold so long ago in Genesis 3:15.

Judiskt bokmärke från 1909

In the Garden of Eden, Satan obtained the title deed to the earth through the fall of Adam. One day it will be given back to us, when Jesus returns.

---

[38]Many rabbis say that the Old Testament does not teach of the existence of Satan in the same sense as the New Testament. If you are a Jew, ask your rabbi! See what he tells you! However, after you ask about the official Jewish view of Satan, remind him of I Chronicles 21:1 which says, "And Satan stood up against Israel...." (KJV). Also, Job 1:7, where it is written in the Jewish Bible that Satan came also among them. "And the LORD said unto Satan, Whence comest thou? Then Satan answered the LORD, and said, From going to and fro in the earth, and from walking up and down in it" (KJV). And if he tries to explain this away, ask him to read the iron-clad proof written in the ancient rabbinical commentary called Midrash wa Yosha', chapter 1:55, which says: " 'In This World there are wars and sufferings and Evil Inclination and Satan and the Angel of Death, and they have permission to rule the World. But in the World to Come there will be no sufferings, no hatred, no Satan, no Angel of Death, no sighs, no enslavement, no Evil Inclination, as it is written, *He will swallow up death forever, and the Lord God will wipe away tears from off all* (Isa. 25:8)' (Midrash waYosha', BhM 1:55)." Raphael Patai, *The Messiah Texts*, p. 261.

ORIGINAL HEBREW TEXT WRITTEN 1450 BC

וַיִּקַּח יְהוָה אֱלֹהִים אֶת־הָאָדָם וַיַּנִּחֵהוּ בְגַן־עֵדֶן לְעָבְדָהּ וּלְשָׁמְרָהּ׃ וַיְצַו יְהוָה אֱלֹהִים
עַל־הָאָדָם לֵאמֹר מִכֹּל עֵץ־הַגָּן אָכֹל תֹּאכֵל׃ וּמֵעֵץ הַדַּעַת טוֹב וָרָע לֹא תֹאכַל מִמֶּנּוּ
כִּי בְּיוֹם אֲכָלְךָ מִמֶּנּוּ מוֹת תָּמוּת׃ .... הֵן־בְּעָווֹן חוֹלָלְתִּי וּבְחֵטְא יֶחֱמַתְנִי אִמִּי׃

בראשית ב:טו-יז; תהלים נא:ז

OLD TESTAMENT SCRIPTURE TRANSLATION

"And the LORD God took the man, and put him into the garden of Eden to dress it and to keep it. And the LORD God commanded the man, saying, Of every tree of the garden thou mayest freely eat: But of the tree of the knowledge of good and evil, thou shalt not eat of it: for in the day that thou eatest thereof thou shalt surely die....Behold, I was shapen in iniquity; and in sin did my mother conceive me."

Genesis 2:15-17; Psalms 51:5 KJV

ANCIENT RABBINICAL COMMENTARY

"...'*These are the generations of the heaven and the earth*' (Gen. II, 4) and *Now these are the generations of Perez* (Ruth IV, 18)—the word '*toledoth*' whenever it occurs in the Bible is spelt defectively, and for a very significant reason. Thus the word is spelt fully [with a *waw*] in the case of '*These are the generations of the heaven and the earth*', because when God created His world, there was no Angel of Death in the world, and on this account is it spelt fully; but as soon as Adam and Eve sinned, God made defective all the '*toledoth*' mentioned in the Bible. But when Perez arose, his '*generations*' were spelt fully again, because from him Messiah would arise, and in his days God would cause death to be swallowed up, as it says, *He will swallow up death for ever* (Isa. XXV, 8); on this account is the '*toledoth*' of '*The heaven and the earth*' and of Perez spelt fully."[39]

Midrash Rabbah XXX. 3

NEW TESTAMENT RECORDED 60 AD

"When Adam sinned, sin entered the entire human race. His sin spread death throughout all the world, so everything began to grow old and die, for all sinned. [We know that it was Adam's sin that caused this] because although, of course, people were sinning from the time of Adam until Moses, God did not in those days judge them guilty of death for breaking his laws—because he had not yet given his laws to them, nor told them what he wanted them to do. So when their bodies died it was not for their own sins since they themselves had never disobeyed God's special law against eating the forbidden fruit, as Adam had. What a contrast between Adam and Christ who was yet to come! And what a difference between man's sin and God's forgiveness! For this one man, Adam, brought death to many through his *sin*. But this one man, Jesus Christ, brought forgiveness to many through God's *mercy*. Adam's *one* sin brought the penalty of death to many, while Christ freely takes away *many* sins and gives glorious life instead. The sin of this one man, Adam, caused *death to be king over all*, but all who will take God's gift of forgiveness and acquittal *are kings of life....*"

Romans 5:12-17 *The Living Bible*

MODERN RABBINIC COMMENT/REFUTATION

"Christian missionaries maintain that because of the sin of Adam, humanity has a sinful nature. By his disobeying God and eating of the Tree of Knowledge, Adam brought hereditary sin into the world, tainting all his descendants with what is called Original Sin. Thus, man is a sinner from birth, separated spiritually from a holy

[39] *Midrash Rabbah, Exodus.* New York: The Soncino Press Ltd., © 1983. pp. 349-350, used by permission.

God. Consequently, man has to be saved from sin and reconciled to God....First and foremost, God, and no one else, provides the means of reconciliation and fellowship...The missionary's question, 'Are you saved?' is thus a question having no basis in the Hebrew Scriptures. Its origin lies in the New Testament and has no bearing on the spiritual life of the Jew."

***The Jew and the Christian Missionary*,**
by Gerald Sigal, pp. 275, 281; © 1981

AUTHOR'S COMMENT—EVANGELICAL CHRISTIAN POSITION

"Are you saved?" most certainly does have a place in the spiritual life of the Jew. Mr. Sigal should educate himself and realize that the origin of original sin is not the New Testament but is also clearly seen in the Jewish commentary, Midrash Rabbah, as we have quoted. Regarding his comment as to whether the question, "Are you saved?" has its basis in the New Testament and has no bearing on the Jews, we ask you to see our *Vol. II*, chapter 25, "Saved, Saved from What?" Here you will discover how judgments have befallen the Jewish people many times on one particular day, the ninth of Av, the odds of which amount to hundreds of billions to one! You will see that God's judgment, from which we need to be **saved**, is predicted to occur shortly for those who are not ready! In our *Vol. II*, chapter 25, we also cover Isaac Newton's comments on a Protestant nation aiding in Israel's formation and the little known fact that Hyam Salomon (a Jew) saved the U.S. from complete financial ruin. **Philip Moore**

ENLIGHTENED ORTHODOX JEWISH FINDING

Israeli professor Dr. Flusser, of Jerusalem, ties the Jewishness of the son of man, the spirit of God and original sin together in the Messiah. This brilliant individual flattens the claims of many contemporary rabbis who deny the Jewishness of a divine Messiah who paid for our original sin. He brings to light: "The image of this *Bar Enash* is fascinating and unique. It is the figure of an almost superhuman judge, who is to sit on the throne of God and to separate the righteous from the wicked. He is to deliver the righteous to everlasting life and the wicked to everlasting punishment. There are hints of *Bar Enash* even in the sayings of the Sages. When Rabbi Akiva hinted at this figure, the other Sages rejected his view and advised him to go and occupy himself with the study of the Law, since the Messiah will be human, not an angel. The expression 'Son of Man' (Hebrew: *Ben Adam*) connects this figure with Adam, the first man. In one of the Jewish Apocrypha (*The Testament of Abraham*), this expression is interpreted literally as the son of the Biblical Adam and is identified with Abel, the brother of Cain, who will be the judge at the end of days. This connection between the Messiah and the Biblical Adam can also be found in the literature of the Sages: according to Reish Lakish, the spirit of the Messiah is identical with the breath of life which God breathed into Adam's nostrils. It is identified, on the one hand, with the spirit of God which moved upon the face of the waters, and on the other hand, with the spirit of God mentioned in Isaiah 11:2, which God will instill within the Messiah. In the writings of Paul, it appears that the spirit upon the waters is the spirit of Adam and also the spirit of the Messiah. The connection between the Messiah and Adam was accepted by Christianity, and brought about the further connection between Original Sin, the First Man, and the Last Man, who is Jesus the Christ. The Last Man atones for the sin of the First Man...."[40]

David Flusser, Ph.D.

---

[40]David Flusser, Ph.D., *Jewish Sources in Early Christianity.* Tel Aviv: The Israel MOD Publishing House, © 1989, pp. 56, 58, used by permission.

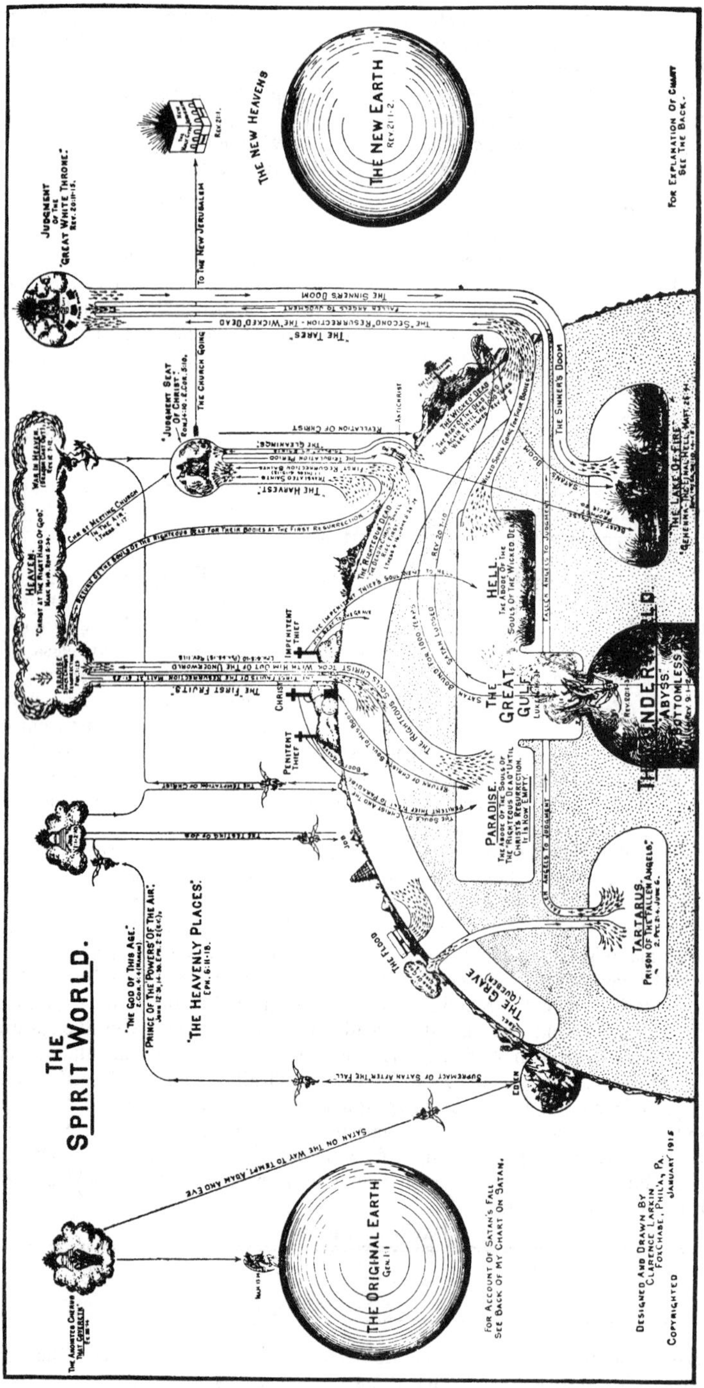
The Spirit World.
"The Heavenly Places." Eph. 6:11-18.
The Original Earth Gen. 1:1
The New Earth Rev 21:1-2
The New Heavens
Paradise.
Hell.
The Great Gulf
Tartarus.
The Lake Of Fire
The Underworld.
For Account Of Satan's Fall See Back Of My Chart On Satan.
For Explanation Of Chart See The Back.
Designed And Drawn By Clarence Larkin Fox Chase, Phila., Pa.
Copyrighted January 1915

"Thousands of fortune tellers, astrologers, demon possessed mediums, who ask the dead, make a fine living throughout Christendom and profit greatly by the desire of thousands to know a little about the future. And here in the Bible God has uncovered the future, but few of His people pay any attention to it."[41]

Arno Gaebelein

GOD'S SUPERNATURAL PROTECTION—OUR REFUGE

Meanwhile, our only true protection from the evil of Satan, who wishes to harm and destroy us, is in the refuge of Jesus' sacrifice. Daily, you can call on His protection silently to yourself—you will discover the hidden world of God's supernatural safety. This is the greatest power anyone can possess! Jesus tells those who believe in Him: "Behold, I give unto you **power** to tread on serpents and scorpions, and over all the power of the enemy: and nothing shall by any means hurt you. Notwithstanding in this rejoice not, that the spirits are subject unto you; but rather rejoice, because your names are written in heaven"[42] (Luke 10:19-20 KJV).

FALSE PROPHECY EQUALS RAW DEMONIC SATANIC SORCERY

When we speak of Satan's power and shielding ourselves from his attempts to destroy us, we want to emphasize that we are not speaking of an animated cartoon character with horns and a pointed tail, but rather a very real force who crushes all those who fall his way. This creature, who was once Lucifer and presently exists in the transformed composition of Satan, can be seen in the supernatural, occult and witchcraft of today. For example, while our Bible is the only book which contains prophecies that always come to true fulfillment, there are other books whose prophecies do not—other "prophets" like Jeane Dixon,[43] Nostradamus, and various astrologers and fortune tellers who are never one hundred percent accurate!

The Bible says *if a prophet is not one hundred percent correct in his prophecies, then he is not from God* (Deut. 18:22), and if he is not from God, the Scriptures state that he is to be killed (Deut. 18:20).

---

[41]A.C. Gaebelein, *The Prophet Daniel.* New York: Our Hope Press, 1911, p. 2.

[42]Bold mine.

[43]Zola Levitt, a precious Jewish Christian who is the author of over forty books on the Bible, noted of Mrs. D.: "A false prophet would be someone more like Jeane Dixon, the wizards and palm readers who haunt our avenues, or those who make up astrological forecasts for a fee. Again, we have always had false prophets, but the point may be fairly taken that our generation is seeing a great upsurge in this occult activity." Zola Levitt, *The Signs of the End.* Dallas: Zola Levitt, © 1978, p.5, used by permission. Available through Zola Levitt, POB 12268, Dallas, TX, USA 75225.

Quite a severe prescription for the ancient false prophet! Suffice it to say that these soothsayers have many modern counterparts who also claim to receive revelations, visions and prophecies from supernatural sources. Here, we must emphasize that they are not receiving their truths from the source of God's supernatural. We know this because the Bible states that if a prophet is not one hundred percent accurate in the law of Moses (Deut. 18:22), then he is not a prophet from God: "...How shall we know the word which the LORD hath not spoken?" (Deut. 18:21 KJV).

The penalty in ancient Israel for false prophecy was death by stoning (Deut. 13:1-10); seemingly harsh, but demanded as punishment and deterrent! Why? Obviously, their sources were supernatural—but not God's supernatural. That leaves only one other option, according to the Bible, and that is raw demonic satanic sorcery. Even though such "prophets" may claim God as their inspiration, we know that He is not!

THE ISSUE OF PROPHECY—HOLY SCRIPTURES VERSUS THE ASTROLOGER'S ASTROLOGY

Examples of "prophets" who have failed Moses' test of one hundred percent accuracy, thus placing themselves outside the Bible's criterion of a true prophet of God, are Jeane Dixon and Michel de Notredame. In her book, *The Call to Glory*, Dixon clearly claims: "...God has given me a gift of prophecy...."[44] She explains how she receives her prophecies from God: "I empty my mind in order that I may be filled with the Spirit of God. Finally, during my meditations, when my spirit is calm and He is ready, God talks to me. I know then, beyond all doubt, that the channel is coming directly to me from the Divine, the Lord our God, because I *feel it* and sense it. I know it is not the channel of Satan, because his channel I have felt and sensed too; and I definitely know the difference."[45]

DIXON'S SOURCE—DEMONIC[46] DIVINATION

God commanded through Moses in the Bible: "There shall not be found among you anyone who makes his son or his daughter pass through the fire, one who uses **divination**, one who practices witchcraft, or one who interprets omens, or a sorcerer...." (Deut. 18:10 NASB).

***

[44]Jeane Dixon, *The Call to Glory*. New York: Bantam Books, © 1971, p. 34.

[45]Ibid, p. 35.

[46]For additional facts from two Christian authors pointing out the source of Dixon's power, see our *Vol. II*, chapter 9, "Dixon's Prophecies Cannot Hold a Candle to the Bible."

Hal Lindsey, in his book, *Satan is Alive and Well on Planet Earth,* has noted regarding divination: "The most amazing display of divination is called 'inspirational divination' in which the medium is given direct communication from demons of events that could not have been known by normal means. In this form of divination, the medium is conscious of contact with real spirit beings, though erroneously thinking that it is the Spirit of God....If a person receives accurate secret knowledge which cannot be attributed to fakery, then there are only two possible sources. The person is either a prophet of God and receiving revelation from the Holy Spirit, or he is a divining medium receiving revelation from a demon, called in Acts 16:16 'a spirit of divination.' The Bible leaves us no other option."[47]

Dixon's powers to see into the future are documented by the fact that she accurately foretold that President Kennedy[48] would be assassinated in Dallas,[49] quite a while before the event became a reality, even attempting to warn[50] him before the trip was announced to the public. However, she flunked the Bible's test of a true prophet of God when she predicted on May 7, 1968, that the Vietnam War would "end in ninety days."[51] We all know it lasted well into the 1970's.

MICHEL DEE—WHAT DID HE SEE?

Nostradamus (1503-1566) is the Latin name of Michel de Notredame,[52] a French physician and astrologer who was a Jewish convert to Catholicism. This man is purported to have made many prophecies in his work, *Centuries,* completed in 1555. Was he a true prophet of God? Our question is answered by an inaccuracy in his predictions involving the Kennedy family. This puts him within the Bible's definition of a false prophet, whom we may dismiss (Deut. 18:22), in light of the fact that he missed the one hundred percent mark!

Nostradamus is said to have written about Kennedy: "The great man falls by lightning in the day. An evil foretold by the postulate

---

[47]Hal Lindsey with C.C. Carlson, *Satan is Alive and Well on Planet Earth*, p. 120.

[48]Dixon pinpointed the trip to Dallas a few months before it occurred and also stated in a 1956 *Parade* magazine interview (May 13) that a Democrat would be elected President in 1960 and thereafter assassinated.

[49]See Hal Lindsey with C.C. Carlson, *The Late Great Planet Earth*. Grand Rapids, MI: Zondervan Publishing House, © 1970, 1977, p. 15.

[50]J.H. Brennan, *Nostradamus, Visions of the Future*. London: The Aquarian Press, © 1992, p. 149.

[51]See Hal Lindsey with C.C. Carlson, *Satan is Alive and Well on Planet Earth*, p. 122.

[52]His original name was Gassonet before it was changed to Notredame. *Omni,* Dec. 1993, p. 44.

one...the ancient work will be accomplished from the roof, evil ruin shall fall on the great man, being dead they will accuse an innocent of the deed. The guilty one hidden in the misty woods...according to the forecast another falls in the hours of the night...the youngest son shall be slandered by a detractor when the enormous and martial deed shall be done the least part shall be doubtful to the eldest, soon after they shall be equal in government."[53]

SOME SAY MICHEL DEE SAW KENNEDY

In the Warner Brothers production, *The Man Who Saw Tomorrow*, a documentary on the prophecies of Nostradamus narrated by Orson Welles, the reportedly accepted interpretation runs something like this: The great man (JFK) is killed by lightning (rapid gunfire), foreseen by a postulator (Jeane Dixon), seemingly accomplished from the roof (sixth floor of the Texas School Book Depository building), while an innocent (Oswald) is falsely accused, when in fact, the real killer was "hidden in the misty woods" (the grassy knoll[54] with its trees and bushes still wet, as it had been raining one-half hour before Kennedy's motorcade passed).

***

---

[53]According to the documentary, *The Man Who Saw Tomorrow* (Warner Brothers), Nostradamus wrote this. I also read the equivalent in a recent English translation of Nostradamus' work, *Centuries*, by Erika Cheetham.

[54]While most press reports, the Warren Commission, and more recently, a 1993 book entitled *Case Closed*, insist that Oswald shot Kennedy from behind, C.A. Crenshaw, the doctor who attempted to save Kennedy in the emergency room, does not agree. In his book, Crenshaw, according to his expertise as a physician, admitted that the wounds were inflicted from the front. Thus Oswald's exoneration and the true sniper's nest, the misty woods (in the grassy knoll in front of JFK), predicted in this demonic prophecy over four centuries before, lines up with the doctor's eyewitness testimony. Kennedy was shot from the wooded area behind the grassy knoll just in front of his car. Crenshaw wrote: "I have wanted to shout to the world that the wounds to Kennedy's head and throat that I examined were caused by bullets that struck him from the **front**, not the back, as the public has been led to believe..." Charles A. Crenshaw, M.D., *JFK: Conspiracy of Silence*. New York: Signet, © 1992, p. 4. Bold mine. Spooky, huh? This verifies the Bible's claim of malevolence within the supernatural, outside of divinely inspired biblical prophecy. There is no way Nostradamus, nearly five centuries ago, could have just "guessed" at such an incident, is there? Clearly, there was an evil Satanic intelligence guiding and giving him this secret information containing such a high degree of accuracy concerning the future. As to why Kennedy was shot, see our *Vol. II*, chapter 20, "Motives for Kennedy's Demise and the Negative End of Politicians Who Mistreat Israel." This chapter also contains documentation on God's curse, as opposed to a blessing on past Presidents, based on the way they have treated Israel.

The other one who falls by night is said to be his brother (Senator Robert Kennedy), who was assassinated at night. Finally, the movie infers that the youngest of the three sons Nostradamus described, was Ted Kennedy. This man would be slandered by a detractor (the Chapaquidick incident) and be "equal in government" (President) soon after the "eldest" (JFK).

Our point is that Ted Kennedy did not become President "soon after," which confirms that this seemingly amazing prediction of Nostradamus' is in error! We emphasize that no matter how small that mistake may be, it shows Mr. N. was wrong! Since God does not make mistakes in His prophecies, as the Bible confirms (Deut. 18:22), we know that **Michel de Notredame's predictions were not**[55] **of divine origin**. The fact that his "prophecies" appear to be more accurate than sheer chance indicates that they lie most definitely within the **dangerous realm of the occult**. True believers need not fear Mr. N. because our Bible tells us so (Deut. 18:22).

THE HOPE OF THE SCRIPTURES FAR EXCEEDS THE GLOOM OF MR. N.

The Scriptures of the Old and New Testaments give us far greater hope than the famed Mr. N. ever could! The promises of the Messiah, who loves each one of us and who promises a new world soon to come (see our chapters 29-30), far outweigh a twentieth century presidency and assassination, wouldn't you say? In other words, all those future prophecies of doom Nostradamus is said to have made will not happen

---

[55]We recognize further falsehood in his "prophecy" and interpretation of Israel's demise, which will not be! The Bible clearly foretells that Israel will never again be dispersed, once regathered (Amos 9:15), though it predicts some hardship before Jesus' return (Zech. 14). However, the third century Quatrain 97, a prophecy said to be about Israel, predicts: "New law to occupy new land Around Syria, Judea and Palestine The great non-Christian empire will crumble Before the twentieth century is done." J.H. Brennan, *Nostradamus, Visions of the Future*, p. 192. We also note that V.J. Hewitt and Peter Lorie indicate: "The prophecy states that...Egypt, Syria and Iraq form a circle around the country...cutting off her Mediterranean access....when Israel begins to lose the war—for, as Nostradamus states, her enemies are too strong. Between 1996 and 1998 Israel is devastated...overrun by Arab armies....This rather doomy prediction seems to suggest the end of the modern nation of Israel almost 1,900 years after the devastation it suffered at the hands of Rome." V.J. Hewitt and Peter Lorie, *Nostradamus, The End of the Millennium, Prophecies to 2001*. New York: Simon and Schuster, © 1991, pp. 68, used by permission. The same book shows its anti-Christian colors when it infers concerning Rajneesh's death in 1990: "...that it is admitted that Rajneesh was deliberately given a slow-acting poison as a result of pressure on the authorities by the fundamentalist Christians who objected to his teachings." Ibid, p. 140. Rajneesh most probably died of AIDS, as symptoms indicated. Will persecution of Christians and Jews by the followers of Nostradamus ever stop? Only when Jesus returns.

the way he said, but the way our biblical Scriptures say—ending in our triumph with the Messiah Jesus' victory over the evils of Armageddon, which Satan and his "angels of light" will attempt to perpetrate upon us. "...for even Satan disguises himself as an angel of light. Therefore it is not surprising if his servants also disguise themselves as servants of righteousness...." (II Cor. 11:14-15 NASB).

AN INFAMOUS DELIRIOUS NOSTRADAMUS CANNOT SAVE US! YOU NEED NOT FEAR MR. N. OR MRS. D!

Mrs. D. and Mr. N. are looked upon as righteous prophets and do-gooders by millions today, as we can see from the popularity of their writings. We assure you that you need not fear Mrs. D.'s or Mr. N.'s prophecies of our end times because of their past mistakes. God, through Moses, wrote: "But the prophet, which shall presume to speak a word in my name, which I have not commanded him to speak, or that shall speak in the name of other gods, even that prophet shall die. And if thou say in thine heart, How shall we know the word which the LORD hath not spoken? When a prophet speaketh in the name of the LORD, if the thing follow not, nor come to pass, that *is* the thing which the LORD hath not spoken, *but* the prophet hath spoken it presumptuously: **thou shalt not be afraid of him**" (Deut. 18:20-22 KJV; bold mine).

We wish to point out that Nostradamus and his false demon-inspired prophecies have become a religion of sorts! Mr. N.'s prophecies are commonly compared or put on a par equal to the Bible's, while modern interpreters enjoy best-seller lists the world over. Should Nostradamus be exposed according to biblical standards? Should the public be informed of what the Bible has to say about prophecies which do not always realize fulfillment? This author says absolutely yes!

Confronting the problem of Nostradamus' immense popularity, Dava Sobel, in her *Omni* magazine article, "The Resurrection of Nostradamus, Tripping Through Time With the Man Who Saw Tomorrow," points out: "Now...as the millennium draws nigh, Nostradamus virtually springs from the grave in a tidal wave of public appreciation. Japanese author Ben Goto reached the top of his country's best-seller list in 1991 with *Predictions of Nostradamus: Middle East Chapter*....In France, England, and America, too, newly published books reexamine Nostradamus's centuries-old prognostications as foreshadows of recent history....followers of Nostradamus conjure Armageddon and apocalypse with the mere mention of his name....A book of remarkable popularity, the *Centuries* has remained continuously in print for more than 400 years. I had no trouble finding a copy at the bookstore in my neighborhood, where I frequently have to order the books I want to read. No other prophet since Biblical times has held as constant a place in the hearts and minds of the populace as Nostradamus....Indeed, although the works of Nostradamus lack the spiritual guidance of the Bible...Nostradamus finds followers everywhere: People worry about the future. Even those who scoff at the book and try to dismiss it seem to contribute to its endurance."[56]

SOME THINK NOSTRADAMUS' "POWER" IS DIVINE—HOWEVER, HIS USE OF OCCULT ARTIFACTS AND BOOKS PROVES OTHERWISE

Lee Roberts Amsterdam, the coeditor of *The Complete Prophecies of Nostradamus,* while speaking on *Secrets of the Unknown*, a worldwide television news production produced by Eric Nelson, said of Mr. N.'s prophetic abilities: "He would sit alone in his study at night....he had a brass tripod. He had a flame and he would concentrate and suddenly the **divine** power would enter him and he'd be able to make his predictions." Nostradamus, known by some as the doctor who was unable to save his own wife and two children from the plague,[57] referred to astrology as "celestial science."[58]

Some believed his interest in magic and the occult[59] began during the time he spent in Avignon because the library there was filled with books on the occult.[60] Mr. N. became something of a recluse as he began writing his "prophecies." In Salon, France he changed the attic[61] of his house into a study where he "worked...at night with his

---

[56]*Omni,* Vol. 16, No. 3, Dec. 1993, ©used by permission. Let's pray that the last sentence does not pertain to our publication. If you are a true believer, we ask that you pray (make a note in your Bible prayer list) that the Lord expose Nostradamus for who he really is—pray that the Bible increase and Nostradamus' books decrease, so that we will be blessed by moving away from astrology and false prophecy, as the Bible promises!

[57]See James Randi, *The Mask of Nostradamus, The Prophecies of the World's Most Famous Seer.* Buffalo, NY: Prometheus Books, © 1993, p. 232.

[58]Erika Cheetham, *The Prophecies of Nostradamus.* New York: Berkley Books, © 1973, p. 6.

[59]Ibid, p. 7.

[60]Ibid.

[61]See our *Vol. II*, chapter 44, "What Really Went On in Nostradamus' Attic? Was It Demonic?" To summarize a lengthy quote you will be reading in this chapter, we note that J.H. Brennan mentions: "...he was, in other words, attempting to make contact with the god and, in doing so, to prophesy. One wonders what would be the consequence of such an operation?....According to his own writings, as he completed the ritual a voice sounded which filled him with such terror that his arms trembled. Then, out of the darkness strode the splendid figure of a god, who took his seat upon the tripod stool....the

occult books,"[62] and, by his own admission, "burnt a lot of them once he had finished with them."[63]

Mr. N. quotes from *De Mysteriis Egyptorum* "line for line in his prophecies."[64] He drew up horoscopes on "the seven Valois children."[65] Their lives all ended tragically.[66] I myself have known people who, after having an astrological chart drawn on themselves, experienced unfathomable horror and tragedy[67] before they died.

Mr. N. told Catherine de' Medici "all of her children would be kings."[68] However, one died as a child; thus his inaccuracy and error is historically documented for all to see. This, according to the Bible (Deut. 18:22), removes any credibility of divine inspiration as the source of his prophecy.

A street named for Nostradamus in Salon de Provence, France.

---

weird little ceremony worked." J.H. Brennan, *Nostradamus: Visions of the Future*, pp. 17-18.

[62]Erika Cheetham, *The Prophecies of Nostradamus*, p. 9.

[63]Ibid. V.J. Hewitt and Peter Lorie also note: "...he gathered together all his papers, notes, books and documents—records of a lifetime of secret prophecy—and burned them to ashes. In the Preface to his prophecies, he writes that he offered them to Vulcan, the ancient Greek god who changed metals into weapons and tools. They burned with an extraordinary light, more brightly than might have been expected....Among the collection there were copies of centuries-old occult manuscripts and books...." V.J. Hewitt and Peter Lorie, *Nostradamus, The End of the Millennium, Prophecies to 2001*, p. 6.

[64]Erika Cheetham, *The Prophecies of Nostradamus*, p. 9.

[65]Ibid, p. 11.

[66]Ibid.

[67]If by chance you have had a chart drawn and are presently experiencing tremendous misfortune, having perhaps unknowingly tampered with the occult, we suggest you do the only thing possible to prevent a future of horrors and reverse the trend. That is to accept Jesus and plead His blood over the horoscope, trusting the power of His sacrifice over the evil of astrology. Simply say now, "Lord Jesus, thank you for dying for me and raising from the dead. Come into my life; save me and give me your power to live life in a new way. Start your plan of truth for my life now. Thank you." Once you say this, and mean it, you are forever free! You will be with us in the kingdom forever (Rom. 4:24).

[68]Ibid.

The view from the alleyway beside Nostradamus' house in Salon de Provence, where he lived from 1547 until his painful, self-predicted death in 1566.

The rear view of Nostradamus' home.

A mural of Nostradamus on an adjacent building.

A plaque marks the door of the house where Nostradamus lived from 1547 until his death in 1566.

Mr. N's desk in his home.

A print of Leonardo da Vinci's drawing of a Vitruvian man displayed in Nostradamus' home.

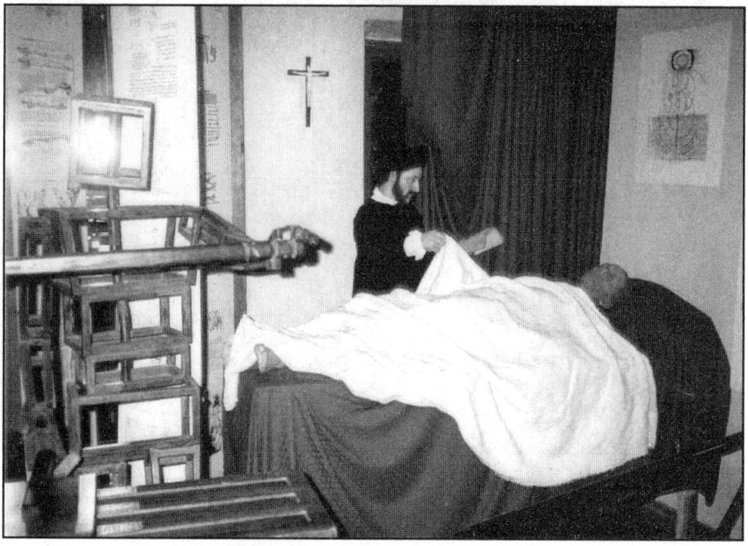

A wax exhibit of Nostradamus caring for a patient.

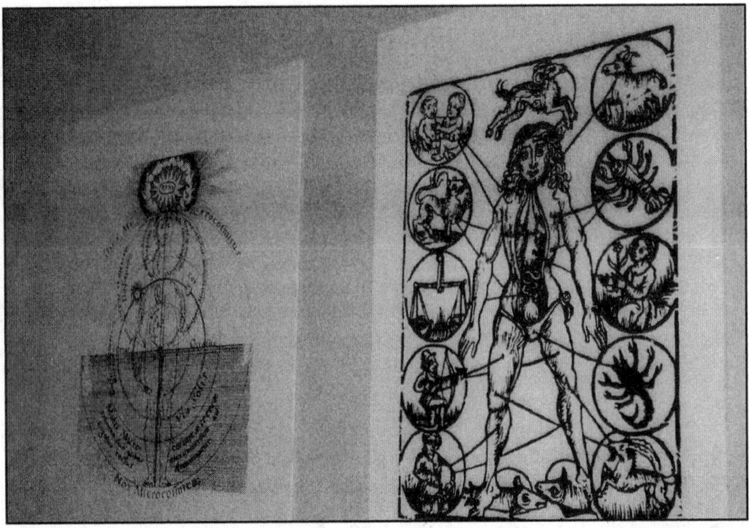

Nostradamus' mystical charts.

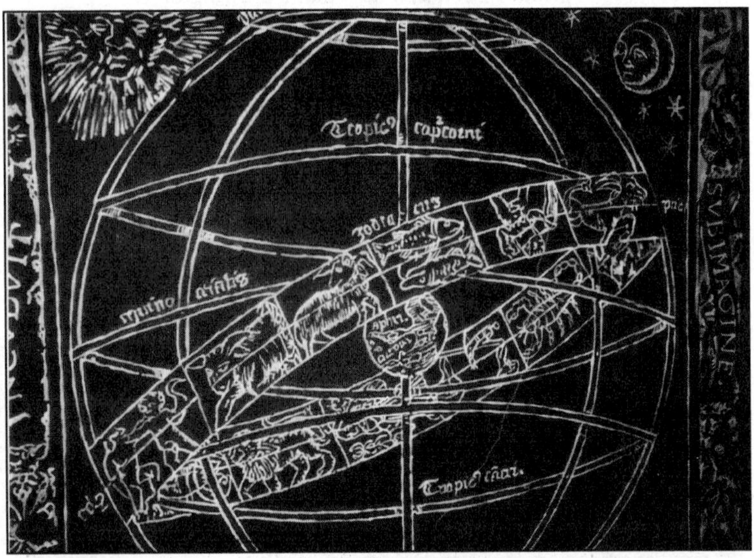

An occult astrological illustration in Nostradamus' home.

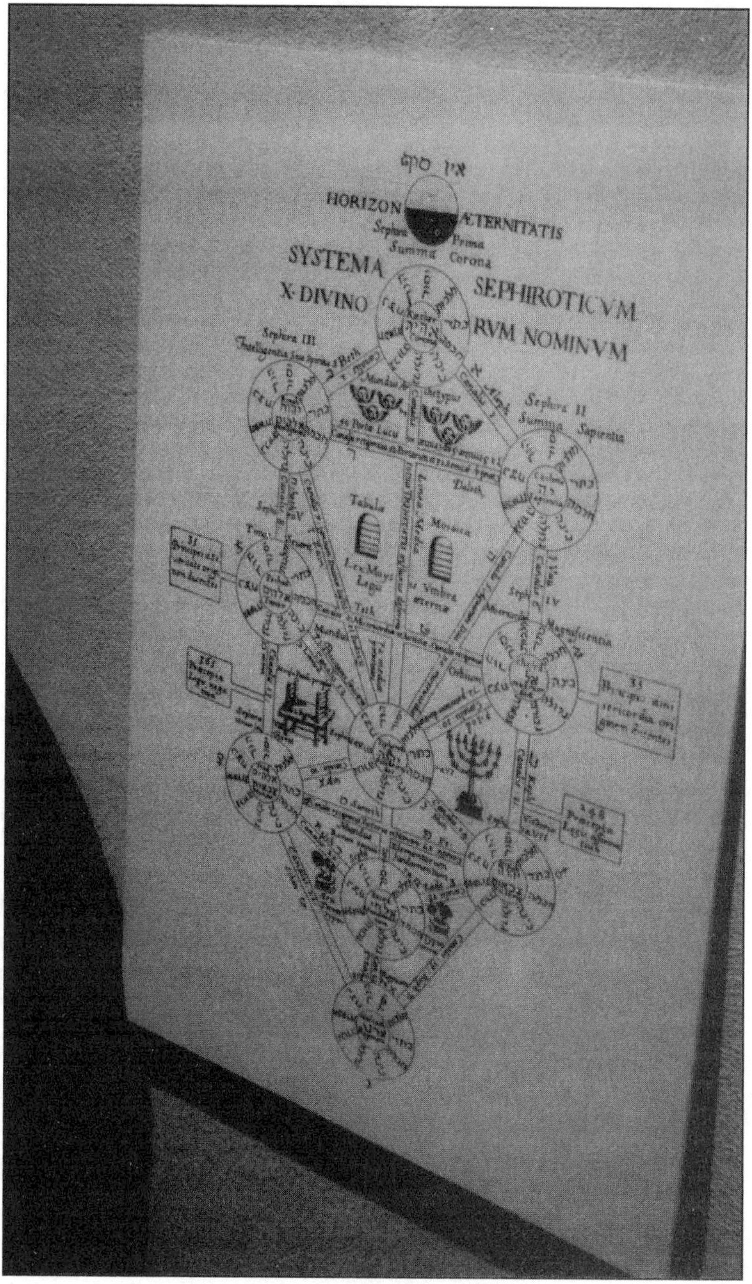

A Hebrew cabbalistic chart in Nostradamus' home.

The Catholic church where Nostradamus lies entombed.

Nostradamus' remains lie entombed behind this wall.

The interior of the Catholic church where Nostradamus' remains lie. His bones are just behind the left wall.

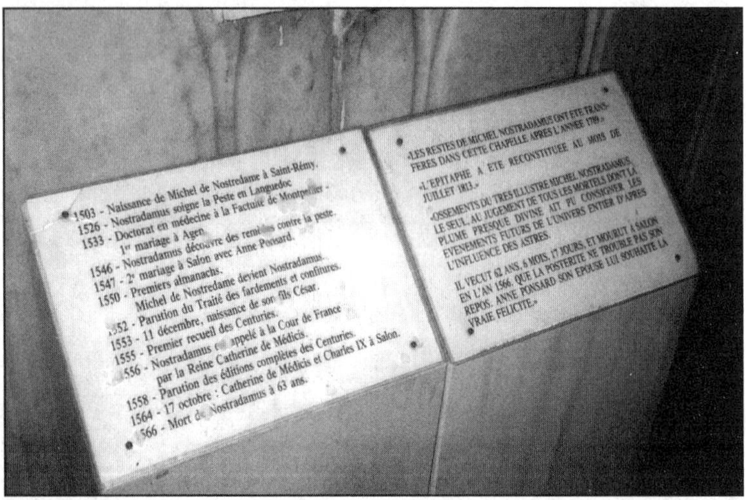

A chronology of Nostradamus' life exhibited outside his tomb.[69]

[69]All photographs relating to Nostradamus were taken by Michael Bentley, a missionary presently residing in France. He graciously made these photographs at our request. These are rare photos that you will most probably not find in other publications.

NOSTRADAMUS CLAIMED TO BE A DIVINE PROPHET, THOUGH THE EVIDENCE REVEALS THAT HE WAS AN OCCULT WITCH

I was having lunch with a friend of mine, Diana, who had some fascination with Nostradamus. I pointed out that Mr. N.'s prophecies are not from God, according to the Bible, because they contain mistakes. She was quick to mention that Nostradamus never claimed that his prophecies were from God, she thought they were "just his prophecies." Other people have told me this, as if the fact that he did not claim his predictions were from God somehow seemed to excuse his errors from the Bible's standards of false prophecy and mistakes.

We want to note that Professor Richard Popkin of UCLA confirms Nostradamus did claim his prophecies were of a divine nature: "In Nostradamus's explanations of what he was doing and how he did it, he first asserted that he was a prophet in the Biblical sense, namely that God had revealed future events to him and enabled him to make them known in a certain fashion....Nostradamus claimed to be a prophet in a more mundane and genetic sense—mundane in that he was simply indicating that a lot of human political and military disasters would occur before the end of the world (which he put soon after 1991, if anyone here is concerned)—and genetic in the sense that prophecy was in his biological make-up. He told King Henri II that he was a member of one of the Lost Tribes, the tribe of Issachar, which had been given the gift of prophecy.

Further, he told his son that God had revealed future events to him by means of astronomical revolutions, i.e. astrology. Everything is governed by God, and God can give power to his prophets to foresee and foretell future events. Nostradamus said he wrote out his quatrains for 'the common benefit of Mankind'....When the prophecies would be fulfilled, people could tell that he had predicted them, and would realise that God had fore-ordained these events. So, he saw himself as reinforcing people's awareness of Divine Providence."[70]

To what do we as believers in the Bible attribute Mr. N.'s prophetic power, since it is not from a divine source as some like to believe? Our answer lies in the supernatural—the supernatural of Satan. Satan's incentive can be seen in his writings. Even Hitler had

---

[70]Richard Popkin, *Predicting, Prophecying, Divining and Foretelling From Nostradamus to Hume*, published in the compilation *History of European Ideas,* Vol. 5, No. 2. London: Pergamon Press, © 1984, pp. 118-119, used by permission. Popkin's sources were: *Preface de M. Nostradamus a ses Propheties.* Ad Caesarem Nostradamum filium, in Leoni, *op. cit.*, pp. 120-131; *Nostradamus, Preface to Cesar Nostradamus*, in Leoni, *op. cit.*

Nostradamus' prophecies dropped over France; prophecies which predicted his victory there.[71]

No man can truly see the future without the help of God or demons. God is always right (Deut. 18:18-22; Isa. 46:5, 9-10). Demons, on the other hand, who have plans for the future of men, are not always correct because God can intervene. Thus, prophecies laden with errors, as Mr. N.'s have been, are the revelations of demons! Mr. N.'s life ended in tragedy and sickness. He was unable to cure his gout, which became dropsy.[72] Jesus cured dropsy (Luke 14:1-6). Wouldn't it have been something if Michel had known[73] Jesus?

NOSTRADAMUS' SATANIC "TO-DO LIST" WILL OFFER AN ALTERNATIVE TO THOSE LEFT BEHIND AFTER THE RAPTURE!

John Kinsella, the co-editor of Peter and Paul Lalonde's magazine, *This Week in Bible Prophecy*, in an article entitled "The Prophecies of Nostradamus," observed: "While Nostradamus wrote of the rise of Hitler, he did not see his fall. He wrote of the world wars, but he did not know how they came out. He anticipated people and major events, like wars and assassination, but not the outcome....Satan knew what he had planned for the future—he just didn't know how it would turn out. The writings of Nostradamus are little more than Satan's 'to do' list. The false prophecies of Nostradamus, Edgar Cayce, the so-called sleeping prophet, and many others are gaining tremendous influence[74] in this generation. Following the Rapture of the Church, those left behind will be lost, confused and looking for answers. Nostradamus writes of an alien spacecraft that many New Agers have claimed will come to evacuate some people off the planet in the last days. The Bible tells us those left behind will find answers they can live with. II Thessalonians 2:11-12...."[75]

---

[71]Erika Cheetham, *The Prophecies of Nostradamus*, p. 14.

[72]Ibid, p. 12.

[73]In this question, the author indicates his sorrow over the loss of Nostradamus' salvation, only obtainable when we ask Jesus into our hearts to know Him personally, as taught in the New Testament. Had Nostradamus truly believed in Jesus in the fundamental sense, he might have been a wonderful Bible teacher and writer and we would have seen him in the world to come.

[74]Hal Lindsey noted: "Although he [Cayce] has been dead for more than twenty years, when we called the local library to locate some of his books we were told that they were all checked out and we would have to be put on a waiting list." Hal Lindsey with C.C. Carlson, *The Late Great Planet Earth*, p.14. [ ] mine.

[75]John Kinsella, "The Prophecies of Nostradamus," *This Week in Bible Prophecy*, Vol.2, Issue 3, Mar. 1994, p. 21, © used by permission.

EDGAR CAYCE, THOUGH MEAGER IN COMPARISON TO MR. N., UNDERESTIMATED HITLER AND CALLED JESUS AN OCCULT DIVINER

Many have thought of Edgar Cayce as a well-meaning person and healer. However, Richard Lee and Ed Hindson, in their book *Angels of Deceipt,* document that: "Cayce claimed the world was a pantheistic manifestation of God, that reincarnation was the path to salvation, and that Jesus was the thirtieth reincarnation of Adam, Enoch, Melchizedek, and others. He claimed later 'psychic revelation' that indicated Jesus was an Essene, that He was initiated in the 'mystery societies' of Egypt and India, and that He used astrology and occult divination....despite his high percentage of accuracy, Cayce made numerous false 'prophecies' regarding Hitler, World War II, the submerging of New York City in the 1970s, the rise of Atlantis in the twentieth century, and even the prediction of his own miraculous healing on New Year's day, 1945. He died three days later!....In contrast to Cayce's revelations stands the warning of Scripture: 'In the latter times some shall depart from the faith, giving heed to seducing spirits, and doctrines of devils' (I Tim. 4:1). Edgar Cayce's apparent 'sincerity' does not excuse his making himself available to demonic spirits, nor does it legitimize the false doctrine he disseminated while in self-hypnotic trances."[76]

Bob Larson informs us: "He failed by underestimating Hitler's inclination for evil, and struck out again by declaring that New York would be dumped into the sea in the seventies....His claim to be a prophet is clearly without a Scriptural base. One hundred percent accuracy (Deut. 18:20-22) is the requirement for those who speak on behalf of God!"[77]

IT IS TIME WE SURPASS THE ERROR-LADEN PROPHECIES OF NOSTRADAMUS AND ADVANCE INTO THE TRUTH OF JESUS IN OUR END TIMES

Setting the psychics—Jeane Dixon, Edgar Cayce, Nostradamus—and their false prognostication of wars and the end aside, let's investigate what the Messiah has said! Jesus warned of the destruction of Israel by the Romans,[78] the times of the Gentiles,[79] wars

---

[76]Richard Lee and Ed Hindson, *Angels of Deceipt: The Masterminds Behind Religious Deceptions*. Eugene, OR: Harvest House Publishers, © 1993, pp. 163-164.
[77]Bob Larson, *Larson's Book of Cults*. Wheaton, IL: Tyndale House Publishers, © 1982, pp. 246-247, used by permission.
[78]Luke 19:41-44.
[79]Luke 21:24.

and rumors of wars,[80] outbreaks of horrendous incurable diseases,[81] earthquakes,[82] the rise of the Antichrist,[83] the Rapture,[84] a northern attack on Israel [85]and His return to save that nation and the world from ultimate destruction.[86] He foretold the truth of His predictions, giving a divine reason as to *why* these events will occur.

If you are interested in the reason for the existence of war, you will enjoy our next chapter. If you want to read and interpret predictions which include wars that could affect you, you may as well read the authentic ones foretold in the Bible.

[80]Matthew 24:6.
[81]Matthew 24:7.
[82]Ibid.
[83]Matthew 24:15; John 5:43.
[84]Luke 17:34-36.
[85]Matthew 24:16-27; Luke 21: 29-36; in light of Ezekiel 36-39.
[86]Mathew 24:22.

"What is the source of quarrels and conflicts among you? Is not the source your pleasures that wage war in your members? You lust and do not have; *so* you commit murder. And you are envious and cannot obtain; *so* you fight and quarrel. You do not have because you do not ask." James 4:1-2 New Testament, NASB

"The problem basically is theological and involves a spiritual recrudescence and improvement of human character that will synchronize with our almost matchless advances in science, art, literature, and all material and cultural developments of the past 2,000 years. It must be the spirit if we are to save the flesh."
General Douglas MacArthur

"...ye shall hear of wars and rumours of wars: see that ye be not troubled: for all *these things* must come to pass....except those days should be shortened, there should no flesh be saved...." Jesus the Messiah

"The unleashed power of the atom has changed everything, save our modes of thinking, and thus we drift toward unparalleled catastrophe."[1] Albert Einstein, 1946

2

WHY WAR ON PLANET EARTH?

Satan's favorite pastime is war and rebellion. His aim is to destroy as many of God's human creations as possible through bloody conflicts. He is doing it for the same reason[2] he fought so hard to cause man's fall.

The history of the world, as you are probably aware, is filled with wars, peace treaties and very little peace! As much as we would like to see all war end, we have yet to see this occur; and as terrible as wars are, we must remember Jesus foretold (in the New Testament Scriptures) that the end times will be accompanied by "wars and rumors of wars" (Matt. 24:6).

The Antichrist, known as the Armilus (the future false Messiah) in the ancient Jewish tradition,[3] will bring this world to a short period

---

[1]"The Fire Unleashed," *Close Up*, ABC News, © 1986.

[2]Against who or what is Satan at war? To find out what Satan is trying to destroy in relation to you, you only need to ask yourself who you are. The answer is that you came from your mother and father who were in turn, produced by your grandparents, and so on, all the way back to Adam, the first father. He was created by God, as you yourself are. Although Adam fell and you inherited that defect, God says you are not beyond the redemption for which the Messiah gave Himself to buy for you. God loves you and wants you back; Satan wants to destroy you by blinding you to what the Messiah sacrificed for all of us, in order to diminish what we are, forever. He desires to do this because your race (humanity), and you, were created by God to displace Lucifer himself (he is not very happy about this). Who do you let win? Do you receive redemption now or put it off another day, week, or year until your day of accounting?

[3] See our chapter 23, "The False Messiah Armilus Equals Antichrist."

of false peace. This false period of peace will precede the final war on our planet (see our chapter 26, "We Win Armageddon—Our Final Battle"). This will in turn, bring in the Second Coming of the true Messiah.

HATRED OF BELIEVERS BECAUSE OF THE NAMESAKE OF JESUS WILL BE A HALLMARK OF THE QUICKLY APPROACHING APOCALYPSE

The first book of the New Testament tells us Jesus' warning of these occurrences: "....as He was sitting on the Mount of Olives, the disciples came to Him privately, saying, 'Tell us, when will these things be, and what *will be* the sign of Your coming, and of the end of the age?' And Jesus answered and said to them, 'See to it that no one misleads you. For many will come in My name, saying, 'I am the Christ,' and will mislead many. And you will be hearing of **wars and rumors of wars;** see that you are not frightened, for *those things* must take place, but *that* is not yet the end. For nation will rise against nation, and kingdom against kingdom, and in various places there will be famines and earthquakes. But all these things are *merely* the beginning of birth pangs. Then they will deliver you up to tribulation, and will kill you, and you will be hated[4] by all nations on account of

---

4We can already see new key organizations, entertainers and wealthy personalities begining with their "Christian bashing," which is an obvious prelude to this hatred that will be perpetrated, particularly by the future Antichrist. An example of this can be seen in media magnate Ted Turner's remark, "Christianity is a religion for losers." Hal Lindsey, *Planet Earth—2000 A.D.* Palos Verde, CA: Western Front, Ltd., © 1994, p. 273. The underlying themes of the *Star Trek*® movies, especially *Star Trek V*, can certainly be interpreted as anti-Christian in the sense that certain similarities to biblical characters and verses are portrayed somewhat negatively and may influence our subconscious minds (see our *Vol. II*, chapter 26, "Star Trek Exposed—New Insights and Sad Memories"). Hal Lindsey lends interesting insight to the beginning of this hatred of Christians as he points out: "When Christians jammed the Capital switchboard with complaints about President Clinton's lifting of the ban on homosexuals in the military, for instance, the Washington Post published a story characterizing them as 'poor, uneducated and easy to command.' Can you think of another group of people who could be so carelessly insulted by a major newspaper? And consider this statement by ABC's Hugh Downs on the TV magazine show '20/20': 'During times of social stress, humanity usually regresses into the family....In the 1920s, the Ku Klux Klan urged the nation to adopt family values and return to old-time religion. Similarly, Adolf Hitler launched a family-values regimen. Hitler centered on his ideas of motherhood. Fanatics in the Ku Klux Klan, the Nazi Party, the Hezbollah, or any other intolerant organizations refer to themselves as religious warriors. As warriors, fanatics censor the thoughts of others and love to burn books. In the modern United States, new proponents of family values continue this tradition of fear and intolerance'....Greece is adopting laws that would forbid proselytism and impose restrictions on non-Orthodox religious minorities....In Vietnam, police routinely arrest Christians for holding unregistered meetings and worship services. Church property is often confiscated." Ibid, pp. 276-278.

My name. And at that time many will fall away and will betray one another and hate one another. And many false prophets will arise, and will mislead many. And because lawlessness is increased, most people's love will grow cold' " (Matt. 24:3-12 NASB).

THE WARS OF THE END TIMES—FORESEEN BY JESUS

This passage from the first book of the New Testament is quite startling. It details the tragedies of war foretold by the Messiah which will precede His Second Advent to Earth to bring peace. Are His words true? To answer that question, let's take a brief look at history's most brutal wars.

Jesus said that until His return there would be wars and rumors of wars. How true has Jesus' prophetic statement been? In the seventeenth century, ten nations fought for thirty years, killing nearly eight million people. The Manchu-Chinese War, beginning four years before the end of the Thirty Years' War, caused twenty-five million people to die. In the early 1700's, the War of Spanish Succession resulted in over one million dead. Six million people were lost in the French Napoleonic Wars between the years of 1792 and 1815. In the Taiping Rebellion, which was fought over a sixteen-year period (1850-1864), thirty million people died. In the six-year Lopez War (1864-1870), two million people fell. Gary DeMar notes that in "the wars that have been fought over the centuries" (over fourteen thousand) there have been "estimates of over 3.6 billion"[5] people killed.

COMMUNISTS MURDER OVER ONE HUNDRED MILLION, WHILE ABORTION SNUFFS OUT THREE-QUARTERS OF A BILLION

Dr. D. James Kennedy documented that "seven hundred and fifty million people worldwide"[6] have been destroyed in the abortionists' modern war[7] against the unborn. Abortion is the epitome of Jesus'

---

[5]Gary DeMar, *Last Days Madness*. Brentwood, TN: Wolgemuth & Hyatt Publishers, Inc., © 1991, p. 190, used by permission.

[6]He documented this in his Jan. 22, 1993 sermon on Channel 63, Atlanta, GA.

[7]*The Random House Dictionary* defines war as: "...to be in conflict or in a state of strong opposition...." p. 1482. Having seen the video *The Silent Scream*, by Dr. Bernard Nathanson, which is an ultrasound of an abortion performed at only twelve weeks, I noticed a most bizarre conflict. The child pitifully opposed and fought the suction equipment which ended his life. Many have changed their minds about abortion after viewing this film. This videotape is available through American Portrait Films, 1695 W. Crescent, Suite 500, Anaheim, CA, USA 92801. Tel. (216) 531-8600 or (800) 736-4567.

statement, "most people's *love* will grow *cold*."[8] More recently, we have experienced horrifying communist takeovers or revolutions, including: Russia–1917; Mongolia–1924; Bessarabia/ Bukovina–1940; Estonia–1940; Latvia–1940; Lithuania–1940; Albania–1944; Kurile Islands–1945; North Korea–1945; Carpatho Ukraine–1945; Yugoslavia–1945; Tannu Tuva–1945; Bulgaria–1946; Hungary–1947; Poland–1947; Romania–1947; Czechoslovakia–1948; East Germany–1948; China–1949; North Vietnam–1954; Cuba–1960; South Yemen–1969; Angola–1975; Madagascar–1975; Laos–1975; South Vietnam–1975; Ethiopia–1977; Mozambique–1977; Afghanistan–1978; Cambodia–1979.

THE RUSSIAN DISTRIBUTION OF NUCLEAR WEAPONS TO TERRORIST COMMUNIST-BASED NATIONS

Though most of these Communist countries have recently been liberated (perhaps temporarily?), we speculate that with the advent of the atom bomb and its rapid proliferation among unstable Communist and Moslem nations, we may be only a heartbeat away from the push of a button launching the third and most terrible world war. Because of the incredible destructiveness of nuclear weapons, only the Messiah will be able to save our planet. We grasp, as much as we can, from past fictional nuclear catastrophies in movies like *Fail Safe*[9] and *The Day After*,[10] some idea of just what Jesus really meant!

---

[8]Matthew 24:12 (NASB; italics mine). In the biblical language of Hebrew, the word for mercy is *raham*, while the word for womb is *reham*. The words share the same root base. A pro-life Israeli-Jewish minister, Barry Segal, mentioned in one of his sermons that the womb has now, in many cases, become a tomb, one of the most dangerous places a child can be. He noted the similarities between the Hebrew words for mercy and womb and pointed out that the one place God has allowed mercy is in the womb. God is merciful in allowing every succeeding human generation to come forth from this marvelous organ, yet today, many "doctors" wield the knife there without mercy. Some time after I heard this sermon, I mentioned it to an Israeli woman in response to her pro-abortion stance. When she heard the Hebrew (*raham* and *reham*) her relatively calm mood was transformed into one of uncontrollable anger. She was suddenly violently out of control, screaming, "You don't know what you are saying. You're playing with Hebrew, you are." BAM—she went into another room, slammed the door and started crying. Truly, there is nothing **colder** than placing a knife of steel, called a curette, into the womb of a woman for the purpose of sectioning her baby apart to be thrown away, is there? A baby like she once was, deserving love as her mother gave her. We can see there is not much love today as seven hundred million people have been eliminated by their own mothers—and this number continues to grow. The love of many has truly grown cold.

[9]This is a film which depicts Russia jamming our communications, which indirectly resulted in our mistakingly bombing them. After this, we bombed ourselves so that Russia would not bomb us. The author did not agree with this movie's latter action.

[10]*The Day After* was a made-for-television movie which we felt was intended as a propaganda tool of the left, designed to counter the American public's support of President Reagan's defense build-up. However, this backfired when he said, "This is

The day before Thanksgiving, 1992, the *McNeil/Lehrer News Hour* interviewed Senator Sam Nunn, Chairman of the Armed Services Committee, regarding the plutonium which had recently been smuggled[11] out of Russia. Nunn warned of the danger that "an unauthorized accident" could occur in the near future if proper measures were not taken.

This author is not saying that we might become vulnerable tomorrow, but rather that there are concerns for the future. Sometime before the mid-twenty-first century, materials bought or stolen today could easily result in a terrorist, communist, or Arab attack against America or Israel; an action that could escalate into a full-scale nuclear conflagration. It appears that the so-called "dead Soviet Union" is much more dangerous *dead* than it ever was when alive, because so much of its nuclear material has recently been stolen and sold off to enemy states!

BELIEVERS WILL BE SPARED THE HORRORS OF THE TRIBULATION AND ARMAGEDDON

If you have not put off your decision to accept Jesus until after the Tribulation begins, and are presently a true believer, you will not have to worry about most of these tragedies and wars affecting you directly (see our chapter 25, "The Rapture Factor"). In addition to the wars already listed, we have fought World War I, which we called "the war to end all wars" in which over thirty-seven million people perished.[12] Soon after, World War II was started by Hitler and his Nazi party.

Some have falsely perceived Hitler as right-wing. We must remember that in German, Nazi is short for *Nazional**sozialist***, or in English, National **Socialist**[13] German Workers Party. Hitler made

---

what we are trying to prevent." Our nation backed him with greater support after seeing the horrifying effects of nuclear war depicted in the movie.

[11]We are all probably familiar with what happened after the "plutonium" was stolen in the film, *Back to the Future*. Our beloved Dr. Brown was shot by an Arab terrorist with a machine gun. He had hoodwinked this Libyan by using the plutonium for his time machine instead of an Arab A-bomb. However, Marty was able to go back in time and warn him, so he would not be killed the second time. Of course, in reality, things don't always work out like they do in movie-land. We can only venture that in the future someone, or rather, some "many," other than Dr. Brown, will suffer death as a result of plutonium stolen from a country in disarray!

[12]This figure taken from the 1946 *World Almanac*.

[13]For insight into newly revealed secrets concerning Hitler and Stalin and their belief in world domination, which will probably startle you, see Philip Moore, *What If Hitler Won The War?*, Appendix 4, "What If Hitler Had Not Turned Against Stalin—What Would Russia Have Done?"

reference to individuals "meaning little" and emphasized that the state was the only thing of prime importance.

In a 1989 Israeli television documentary on Nazi Germany, it was said that in the 1928 elections the Nazis got nowhere, while only two years later they made major inroads. The documentary claimed that, due to an outbreak of foot-and-mouth disease, the demand for agricultural products was destroyed. This caused the ruin of the farmers, a factor which played into Nazi hands! Hitler stepped in and blamed the "farmer's difficulties on the *Jewish people* and the *democratic* system." The Nazis put up signs everywhere blaming the failed economy on "bank Jews." Concluding this point, the program said: "It worked in local elections. In 1929 some German villages supported the Nazis one hundred percent."

Six million Jews and many millions of others were murdered in Hitler's utterly cruel effort to bring his brand of socialism to our world.

ARMAGEDDON AND THE ACCOMPANYING PLAGUES—CAN WE HELP OURSELVES?

World War III will be a future conflict, the only one fought (if a smaller war does not occur prior to this) where we will have ready-made nuclear weapons. The Bible predicts this war and calls it Armageddon (Rev. 16:16). The Bible says only the Messiah will be able to save us from this war (Dan. 2:34-35; Matt. 24:6)!

In the 1980's, forty-five local conflicts[14] were ongoing. Presently, evidence is surfacing which seems to indicate that the AIDS

---

[14]In April of 1993, Paul Crouch, Sr. mentioned on his TBN broadcast *Praise the Lord* that there were sixty-eight wars being fought, many of which we do not even hear about on the news! These, of course, are not the cold wars of the 1980's but the beginning of the hot wars of the 1990's (massacres such as Bosnia). In Matthew 24, where the New Testament speaks of wars and nation rising against nation and kingdom against kingdom, the Greek word *ethnos* is used. This is where we get the English word, "ethnic"! The late President Richard Nixon noted: "Today, seventy-seven conflicts, based on tribal, national, ethnic, or religious hatreds, are being fought, and ruthless dictators such as Saddam Hussein, Kim II Sung, and Muammar Qaddafi are poised to attack their neighbors." Richard Nixon, *Beyond Peace*. New York: Random House, © 1994, p. 35, used by permission. With many smaller and less stable Moslem countries now obtaining the A-bomb, serious trouble is an imminent possibility. This is extremely dangerous—whether we are living in the late 1990's or just before the halfway mark of the twenty-first century, i.e. 2050 AD. Dangerous is not the word for it, is it? We pray that we are blessed so that we do not have a nuclear accident before President Clinton is relieved of office, lest we be put in a life-threatening situation. He cut our Star Wars defense program in May of 1993. Edward Teller, the father of the H-bomb, commented on *Close-Up*, a 1986 ABC news magazine entitled, "The Fire Unleashed": "I think shields are just very much less dangerous....I had wished for a defense for a long time...." Teller said this in reference to President Reagan's nuclear missile (Star Wars) defense shield program! If

virus might have been artificially produced to be used as germ warfare.[15] All these things illustrate that the human race, in its present unredeemed state caused by the Fall (Gen. 3), just can't help itself.

IF THERE IS A GOD—WHY WAR?

Many ask, "If there is a God, why is there so much war in the world?" In answer to this we affirm that war is indeed a tragedy, but what is more terrifying than war is the rejection of the only one capable of ending war for all time.

Man has adequately demonstrated his total inability to put an end to war, as we examine the record from ancient history right up to the present day. Who then holds the lock and key to war on planet Earth and why have they not yet put a stop to war?

The answer involves a people—in fact the *Jewish* people—whose most cherished religious and racial hope had been the Coming of their great deliverer king, called the **Messiah.** He, the Jewish Messiah, is the only one who possesses the awesome power to end war and grant everlasting resurrection bodies to those who accept and believe in Him. He would have done these and many other supernatural and wonderful things not only for the Jew but for the entire world, had His people, the Jews, accepted[16] Him (Luke 19:41-44; Dan. 9:26). We know this from

---

anyone should know, Teller should. Any future president who continues Clinton's policy of Star Wars cuts, plays Russian roulette with our children's lives.

[15]See our *Vol. II*, chapter 41, "Was AIDS Made?" This author does not take this position but is open enough to consider the possibility. This chapter quotes several qualified physicians who believe AIDS was created as germ warfare. Though this may seem out of the question to most, it is wise, if such technology exists today, to not put anything past anyone. We believe the spread of this disease is greatly perpetuated through promiscuity, however, its origin may have been deliberate. The theory involves cross-viral species jumps through growing sheep and cow viruses, which were genetically altered, in human tissue cultures in the lab. Why? Some speculate to control the population. Horrifying!

[16]There are many orthodox publications and writers, such as *The Real Messiah*, by Rabbi Aryeh Kaplan, *et al*, which state that Jesus could not have been the Messiah because: "...the missionaries never mention the most important prophecies concerning the Messiah that Jesus *did not* fulfill. The main task of the Messiah was to bring the world back to G-d, and to abolish all war, suffering and injustice from the world. Clearly, Jesus did not accomplish this. In order to get around this failure on the part of Jesus, Christians invented the doctrine of the 'Second Coming' (Hebrews 9:29, Peter 3). All the prophesies that Jesus did not fulfill the first time are supposed to be taken care of the second time around. However, the Jewish Bible offers absolutely no evidence to support the Christian doctrine of a 'Second Coming.' " Rabbi Aryeh Kaplan, *et al*, *The Real Messiah*. New York: National Conference of Synagogue Youth, 1976, p. 57. In answer to this, we say it certainly does. Hosea 5:15-6:2 illustrates this. Hosea says: "I will go *and* return to my place, till they acknowledge their offence, and seek my face: in their affliction they will seek me early. Come and let us return unto the LORD: for he hath torn, and he will heal us; he hath smitten, and he will bind us up. After two days will he

His words in the New Testament book of Matthew: "Oh Jerusalem, Jerusalem...how often would I have gathered thy children together, even as a hen gathereth her chickens under *her* wings, and ye would not!" (Matt. 23:37 KJV).

WOULD JESUS HAVE BROUGHT PEACE HAD HE BEEN ACCEPTED?

Jesus said these words, recorded by Matthew, with tears in His eyes (see Luke 19:41-44), as He predicted Israel's destruction. Moses predicted this event 2000 years before the Advent of Jesus (Deut. 28:64). These events, predicted to occur in Jesus' generation, were caused because they (the people of Jesus' day) would not know *the time of their visitation* by Messiah (Luke 19:44).

Both events—the Coming of the Messiah and Israel's destruction—were also forecast by Daniel, the Old Testament prophet, six hundred years before the birth of Jesus (Dan. 9:24-26). Thus, because He was not received and accepted at His First Coming, these great blessings of a promised permanent world full of peace and free of injustice have been postponed until the nation of Israel and world Jewry accept Him en masse (see the New Testament; Matt. 23:39; Rom. 11:26; and Old Testament; Isa. 2:4; Lam. 4:17-20; and Hos. 5:15-6:2). We patiently await this wonderful day with excitement and thanksgiving! You can help advance this process, in part, by telling your Jewish friends about Jesus today.

MOSES, DANIEL AND JESUS FORETELL THE CONSEQUENCES OF MESSIANIC REJECTION

As we have read, Jesus warned of the consequences of His rejection to the people of His day and future unbelieving generations when He said: "For the days shall come upon thee, that thine enemies shall cast a trench about thee, and compass thee round, and keep thee in on every side, And shall lay thee even with the ground, and thy children within thee; and they shall not leave in thee one stone upon another; because thou knewest not the time of thy visitation" (Luke 19:43-44 KJV).

According to Luke 21:24, written before the fact, and the historian, Josephus Flavius, writing after the fact, these events occurred within thirty-seven years of Jesus' prediction, in the year 33 AD, and culminated in the holocaust of 70 AD. History records the horrors of the Temple's destruction[17] and the forced, almost 2000-year dispersion

---

revive us: in the third day he will raise us up, and we shall live in his sight" (Hos. 5:15-6:2 KJV).

Hosea comes from the Old Testament portion of the Holy Scriptures, which Kaplan calls "the Jewish Bible"! Hosea indicates that the Messiah left for two days (according to Ps. 90:4, in this instance, 1000 years is likened to one day in rabbinical symbolism). The of the Jewish people by Rome. This was precisely detailed by Moses almost 3450 years ago when he predicted: "And the LORD shall scatter thee among all people, from the one end of the earth even unto the other...." (Deut. 28:64 KJV).

Additionally, the Jewish prophet Daniel, in circa 600 BC, clearly reaffirmed the Messiah's rejection as he pinpointed the divine discipline of the dispersion to Jesus' generation specifically.[18]

Jesus also made long-range predictions about wars throughout history, which He said would occur because of His people's refusal to let Him bring peace. Jesus said until He returns there would be wars and rumors of wars (Matt. 24:6). He also stated, as we have read: "O Jerusalem, Jerusalem...how often would I have gathered thy children together, even as a hen gathereth her chickens under *her* wings, and ye would not! Behold, your house is left unto you desolate. For I say unto you, Ye shall not see me henceforth, till ye shall say, Blessed *is* he that cometh in the name of the Lord" (Matt. 23:37-39 KJV).

***

Messiah then returns before the millenial kingdom. Hosea's words are: "After two days will he revive us: in the third day he will raise us up...." The Jewish Bible passage of Zechariah 12:10, written 2500 years ago, says that when the Messiah returns: "...they shall look upon me whom they have pierced, and they shall mourn for him...." When did the Messiah receive these marks all who look upon Him see (Rev. 1:7)? It is quite obvious that Jesus received them 2000 years ago. When He comes back we will see them and recognize Him. Furthermore, the ancient Jewish commentary Midrash Ruth Rabba clearly illustrates two Comings of the Messiah: "R. Berekhia in the name of R. Levi: 'The Last Redeemer [the Messiah] will be like the First Redeemer [Moses]. Just as the First Redeemer was revealed and then again was hidden from the Children of Israel....so the Last Redeemer will be revealed to them and then will be hidden from them....'(Ruth Rabba 5:6)." Raphael Patai, *The Messiah Texts*, p. 99. Also, the Jewish Talmud speaks of Him coming on "a donkey" (Zech. 9:9) and "coming on the clouds of heaven" (Dan. 7:13), in its Sanhedrin 98a section. The rabbinical legend and tradition of Messiah ben Joseph and Messiah ben David also illustrates the two roles in which the Messiah acts (see our "Messiah ben Joseph" section coming up in our next chapter). Rabbi Kaplan goes on to mock and attack the Christian faith and the Second Coming of the Messiah, as he says: "Jesus, therefore, was not the Messiah of the Jewish tradition. We still await the true Messiah who will accomplish all this in his first attempt." We believe, with good reason, based on the Jewish Bible and ancient Jewish commentaries, that Jesus was and is the Messiah of Jewish tradition. Furthermore, to blatantly ignore this and state that Jews still await the Messiah who will accomplish all this in His First Coming, is to disregard the fact that the Messiah was to suffer in His first attempt as Joseph and reign in His second as David. Thus, falsely saying that the Messiah will come and bring peace in His first attempt is to set a baited trap to deceive world Jewry into being fooled by the Antichrist, who will, according to Bible prophecy (see our chapter 23, "The False Messiah Armilus Equals Antichrist"), accomplish a short world peace on His first appearance, as Kaplan falsely claimed the "Messiah" was to do.

[17] See Josephus, *War of the Jews*.

[18] It is all there in black and white. All you have to do is open to the ninth chapter of the book of Daniel in the Bible.

THE TRAGEDY OF WAR CONTINUES UNTIL THE JEWS ACCEPT THEIR MESSIAH

We are still having wars today and will continue to do so until the world, with the Jews first in line, says: "Blessed *is* he that cometh in the name of the Lord"[19] to the Messiah, the Prince of Permanent Peace! It should be noted at this point that the Messiah is not punishing or "getting even" with His people through the existence and tragedy of wars; wars are the natural result of rejecting supreme protection. For example, if you have enemies who are bent on carrying out their brand of evil against you, yet you reject the army, police, security guards, or anyone else responsible for your protection—guess what? Consequences will follow, until you call your protector back.

CONSPIRACY AND HYPOCRISY OF THE HIGH PRIESTS—THE CORE REASON FOR REJECTION

The high priests in the days of Jesus could not bring themselves to believe that Jesus was the Messiah, primarily because it would have meant too much compromise on their part. Later on, in the section dealing with Jesus' trial, we will discuss the little-known historical fact that the Jewish priesthood had become corrupt and were unduly influenced by their political relations with the Roman government. This corruption was the chief reason for the Messiah leaving the earth until this day. As a result of the priests falsely swaying their nation into rejecting Him and consequently, the glorious benefits of peace and blessings Jesus would have brought, not only to Israel, but to us also, and we all suffer until now (Rom. 8:22-23; 11:15).[20]

Due to the rejection of the Jewish Messiah by the Jewish people, many great blessings, which were always central, cherished, and hopefully anticipated by Judaism, were postponed until Israel as a nation would accept Him. This will happen in our generation, as we will see later in our chapter 18, "Israel—is Real," and chapters 27-30 on the Second Coming.

***

---

[19]Matthew 23:39 KJV.

[20]In the New Testament book of Romans we read: "For we know that even the things of nature, like animals and plants, suffer in sickness and death as they await this great event. And even we Christians, although we have the Holy Spirit within us as a foretaste of future glory, also groan to be released from pain and suffering. We, too, wait anxiously for that day when God will give us our full rights as his children, including the new bodies he has promised us—bodies that will never be sick again and will never die....when the Jews come to Christ. It will be like dead people coming back to life" (Rom. 8:22-23; 11:15 *The Living Bible*).

MESSIAH—A TIME TO REJECT AND A TIME TO ACCEPT

God knew that Israel would, for a period, reject her Messiah. That is why we have two different pictures of the Messiah painted by the Bible's prophets thousands of years ago, long before the birth of Jesus. One picture of Him being scorned, mocked and rejected by His nation's high priests, and subsequently by His people, was painted by prophets such as Isaiah (see Isa. 53 in the Old Testament). Another picture, of a powerful conquering Messiah who returns to save Israel and the entire world from nuclear annihilation, was predicted by Zechariah in 487 BC (14:12-14). Look it up now, no doubt it will be interesting to see![21]

THE GREAT INTERLUDE BETWEEN THE TWO COMINGS—WHAT TAKES PLACE THEN?

The length of time between the two Comings is entirely dependent on the Jewish people. In other words, the King will not return until the King's people call upon Him in acceptance. Jesus clearly told the Jews: "For I say unto you, Ye shall not see me henceforth, till ye shall say, Blessed *is* he that cometh in the name of the Lord" (Matt. 23:39 KJV).

In the Old Testament, David exhorted God (referring to the modern Israelis) to: "...let the king [Messiah] hear us when we [Jews] call" (Ps. 20:9 KJV; [ ] mine). In chapter 5, "Which Prophecies Did Jesus Fulfill?", we will cover many of the prophecies of His First Advent nearly 2000 years ago. In chapters 6-10, we will review many of the designs which were undertaken to deceive[22] the world about Jesus during the period between His First and Second Comings. And finally, in chapters 18-22 and 26, we will investigate how current political events, which were foretold thousands of years ago as biblical prophecies, are changing the world, and how these prophecies will relate to His Second Coming in power and glory to save the earth and His people.

---

[21]For those of you who have never looked up a Bible verse, it will take all of five minutes to pull the book from the shelf, flip through to the prophet Isaiah and a few books past that to Zechariah and the other chapters listed in those predictions. Believe me, once you get started, it's fun exploring the future from your bookshelf—it is incredible!

[22]Deceptions such as: 1. a new translation of the Old Testament with the Messianic prophesies purposely removed; 2. the addition of new notes reinterpreting Messianic prophecies as "not being Messianic" in some Hebrew Bibles; 3. the insertion of the Birkat ha-Minim into the Jewish *Amidah* prayer. The BHM was a curse against the Jewish Christians of the early centuries which, was purposely devised to drive Jewish believers in Jesus out of the synagogues.

These events began to occur in the last forty-eight years, starting with the founding of the modern State of Israel in 1948, the creation of the EEC in 1958 and Arab terrorism and the proliferation of nuclear weapons, which have been smuggled, sold and stolen following the collapse of the former Soviet Union. The events are still unfolding. Finally, in chapters 29-30, you will take a crack at what God has in store for you in a recreated Earth, where He has planned a special eternal agenda for you in a completely new galaxy.

In our forthcoming chapter, we will examine the teaching that there would be two Messiahs. Wars have continued because the Messiah was not accepted. We await the Second Coming, not a second Messiah! However, it is extremely interesting to unravel what the rabbis did about the so-called "paradox of the Messiah." Did they invent a second Messiah to answer key questions about their inability to see the two Comings? Read on and see how this will affect you, as your journey of excitement nears its new beginning, as promised by Jesus.

The Israeli flag is raised over the newly founded State of Israel.

"Having searched & by the grace of God obteined after knowledg in ye [the] prophetique scriptures, I have thought my self bound to communicate it for the benefit of others....Let me therefore beg of thee not to trust to ye opinion of any man concerning these things....search the scriptures thy self...if thou desirest to find the truth. Which if thou shalt at length attain thou wilt value above all other treasures....understanding the sacred Prophesies & the danger by neglecting them is very great & that ye obligation to study them is as great may appear by considering ye like case of ye Jews at ye coming of Christ. For the rules whereby they were to know their Messiah were the prophesies of the Old Testament....Thus also ye Apostles & those who in ye first ages propagated ye gospel urged chiefly these Prophesies & exhorted their hearers to search & see whether all things concerning our Saviour ought not to have been as they fell out. And in a word it was ye ignorance of ye Jews in these Prophesies wch [which] caused them to reject their Messiah & by consequence to be...captivated by the Romans....Luke 19.42, 44....For they had some regard to these prophesies insomuch as to be in generall expectation of our Saviour about that time when he came, onely they were not aware of the manner of his two comings...they understood ye description of his second coming, & onely were mistaken in applying that to ye time of his first coming. Consider therefore, if ye description of his second coming was so much more plain and perspicuous then that of ye first, yt [yet] ye Jews who could not so much as perceive any thing of ye first could yet understand ye second...."[1]

Sir Isaac Newton, the greatest scientist to ever live,[2] 1642-1727

3

TWO MESSIAHS?

There were two completely different pictures of the Messiah painted by the prophets of the Jews, and the Old Testament is filled with them! One of a king and one of a sufferer. Most of the Jews in the days of Jesus expected these two strains of Messianic prophecy to either occur consecutively or simultaneously. Many only anticipated the prophecies about the king to be fulfilled. Furthermore, some believed then, as many do today, that two Messiahs might appear—one to separately fulfill each role. In all earnestness, we may say that they failed to comprehend the truth due to extenuating circumstances;

---

[1] *Yahuda Manuscript 1.* Used by permission of the Hebrew University Manuscript Department, Jerusalem. Spellings are Newton's from three hundred years ago. [ ] my clarification of Newton's shorthand/sixteenth century English. You should read "ye" as "the."

[2] John Herman Randall, Jr. (professor of philosophy at Columbia University), in his introduction to *Newton's Philosophy of Nature*, reminds us: "Isaac Newton is not only by general acclaim the greatest scientific genius the English-speaking peoples have produced, and one of the half-dozen towering giants of the intellectual movement that has distinguished the modern world from all other societies. He also gave his name to an entire age...he came to stand as the symbol of a broadly conceived new 'natural philosophy,' or physical science...." H.S. Thayer, *Newton's Philosophy of Nature,* Third Edition. New York: Hafner Publishing Company, © 1953, p. ix.

namely, that the Messiah would come twice, fulfilling each role in its era, separated by a valley of time spanning approximately two millennia!

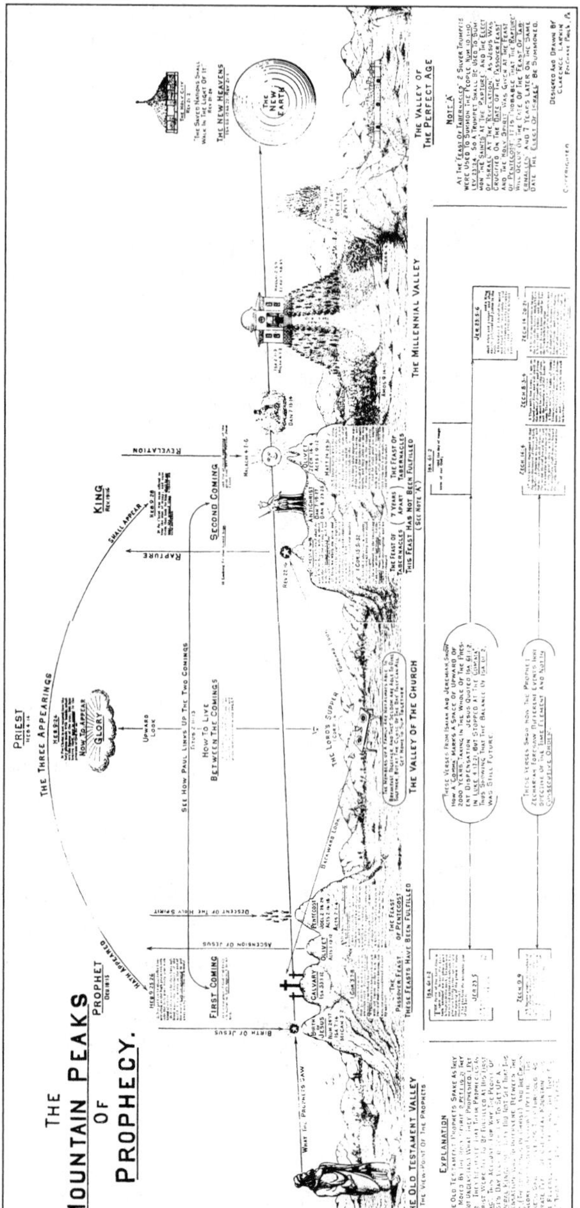

A chart by Rev. Clarence Larkin illustrating the mountain peaks of prophecy regarding the Messiah's two Comings.

AN ISRAELI RABBI'S INTEREST IN THE MESSIAH COMING TWICE, SPARKED BY ANCIENT COMMENTARIES

Hal Lindsey, in his book *The Late Great Planet Earth*, points out that the "rabbis at least a century before Jesus of Nazareth was born theorized that there would be two messiahs."[3] The idea of the Messiah coming twice or the Coming of two Messiahs is denied by many modern rabbis. I gave a rabbi a copy of the Hebrew edition of Hal's book while I was at a youth hostel in Israel. As he read the aforementioned passage, he jumped and exclaimed, "Ah, I've never heard such a thing!" However, when I showed him the following ancient rabbinical commentaries he began to stroke his long grey beard, mumbling, "Perhaps so. Perhaps you are right." The commentaries we looked at read as follows:

"R. Berekhia in the name of R. Levi: 'The Last Redeemer [the Messiah] will be like the First Redeemer [Moses]. Just as the First Redeemer was revealed and then again was hidden from the Children of Israel...so the Last Redeemer will be revealed to them and then will be hidden from them....' "[4] Ruth Rabba 5:6

"R. Alexandri said: 'R. Y'hoshu'a ben Levi explained:....'If they will be righteous, [the Messiah will come] *on the clouds of heaven* (Daniel 7:13); if they will not be righteous, [he will come] as *a poor man riding upon an ass* (Zech. 9:9).' ' "[5] Talmud B. Sanhedrin 98a

"R. Yishma'el said: Metatron said to me: 'Come and I shall show you the Curtain of the Place which is spread out before the Holy One, blessed be He, on which are engraved all the generations of the world and their deeds, whether they did them or will do them until the end of all generations.' And I went and he showed me with the fingers of his hand like a father who teaches his son the letters of the Tora....And I saw *Messiah ben Joseph* and his generation, and all the deeds which the nations of the world will do there. And I saw *Messiah ben David* and his generation, and all the battles and wars of their deeds, and their acts which they will perform with Israel, whether for good or for bad. And I saw all the battles and wars which Gog and Magog will do in the days of the Messiah, and all that the Holy One, blessed be He, will do with them in the Future to Come. And there were the chiefs of the generation, whether among Israel or among the nations of the world, whether they did or will do in the Future to Come, until all generations,

---

[3]Hal Lindsey with C.C. Carlson, *The Late Great Planet Earth*, p. 29.

[4]Raphael Patai, *The Messiah Texts*, p. 99. Patai is an unbiased Jewish Bible scholar who does not believe in the Christian interpretation.

[5]Ibid, p. 83.

all was engraved there on the Curtain of the Place. And I saw them all with my own eyes, and at the end when I had seen I opened my mouth and spoke in praise of the Place...."[6] Sefer Hekhalot, BhM 5:187-88

ONE DOWN AND ONE TO GO

As we will see, Jesus fulfilled the Messiah ben Joseph role and promised to fulfill the ben David role in our end time generation when Armageddon (Gog/Magog) converge upon us (for a clearer picture, see our chapter 26, "We Win Armageddon—Our Final Battle").

MESSIAH BEN JOSEPH

Messiah ben[7] Joseph, referred to in some legends as Messiah ben Ephrim after Joseph's son Ephrim, is in fact, the suffering servant who is often mentioned in the ancient rabbinical literature. The reason he is called Messiah ben Joseph is not hard to grasp. Joseph's life was one of an innocent sufferer who was first betrayed by his own people (his brothers), only later to gain acceptance by them on their second visit to Egypt to see Pharaoh (Gen. 43:15).

On this second appearance, Joseph saved the entire nation of Israel when he was recognized for who he was, Pharaoh's Vice-King of Egypt, and *unbelievably*, their brother. His kin were quite shocked to see that the brother they had sold into slavery (Gen. 45:3), and by then supposed dead and gone, was God's agent for their salvation. Joseph himself told his brothers: " 'And as for you, you meant evil against me, *but* God meant it for good in order to bring about this present result, to preserve many people alive. So therefore, do not be afraid; I will provide for you and your little ones.' So he comforted them and spoke kindly to them" (Gen. 50:20-21 NASB).

THE LIFE OF JESUS PARALLELS THE LIFE OF JOSEPH

The whole pattern of Jesus' life perfectly matches in every detail Joseph's prophetic foreshadowing of the Messiah. Jesus was betrayed for the price of a slave[8] (Zech. 11:12-13; Matt. 27:3-10), as was Joseph (Gen. 37:28). Joseph, for twenty shekels—Jesus, for thirty. The difference of ten shekels was due to inflation, which took place during

---

[6]Ibid, p. 168. Italics mine.

[7]In Hebrew, *ben* means "son of " or "descendant of."

[8]The Leviticus 27:5 price later changed to thirty shekels (Exo. 21:32).

the 1967 years that elapsed between the two events. Jesus was handed over to the Romans (non-Jewish Gentiles), just as Joseph was handed to the Ishmaelites (non-Jews), who were the ancient Arabs.

Jesus has been perceived by many as an insignificant person who met with misfortune, resulting in His death because His own people conspired against Him (John 19:15).[9] Jesus was betrayed to the Romans by a few corrupt priests representing the Jewish people, while many Gentiles since that time have enjoyed the knowledge of His kingship.

Joseph was considered unimportant and dead by his brothers (Gen. 42:36; 44:20). The coat of many colors, dipped in goat's blood, symbolized his death Jesus' clothes were also stripped from Him and, as a result of His whippings prior to His trial, were soaked with blood. Later, Joseph's brothers really believed him to be dead when they said, "his [Benjamin's] brother is dead" (Gen. 44:20 NASB; [ ] mine).[10]

Meanwhile, the Gentiles (Egyptians) enjoyed Joseph's rule in Egypt as Vice-Pharaoh (Gen. 41:39-43). Jesus was a stumbling stone to His people at His First Coming. At His Second Advent, the Hebrew prophets predict He will save Israel from the greatest war of all time—Armageddon (Matt. 24;[11] Rev. 16; Ezek. 38-39), which is yet to occur.[12]

MESSIAH BEN JOSEPH—JESUS, WILL HAVE HIS FAMILY REUNION WITH ISRAEL

Jesus told Israel that they would not see Him again until they said, "Blessed is He who comes in the name of the Lord" (Matt. 23:39). This will occur soon in a graphically portrayed family reunion, predicted in the writings of Zechariah, recorded in the Jewish Bible five centuries before the birth of Jesus. The prophet's words reveal: "And it will come about in that day that I will set about to destroy all the nations that come against Jerusalem. And I will pour out on the house of David and on the inhabitants of Jerusalem, the Spirit of grace and of supplication, so that they will look on Me whom they have pierced; and they will mourn for Him, as one mourns for an only son, and they will weep bitterly over Him, like the bitter weeping over a

---

[9]John 19:15 reads: "But they cried out, Away with *him*, away with *him*, crucify him. Pilate saith unto them, Shall I crucify your King? The chief priests answered, We have no king but Cæsar" (KJV).

[10]Rachel was the mother of Benjamin and Joseph, her two children from Jacob.

[11]In Matthew 24:22, Jesus says: "...except those days should be shortened, there should no flesh be saved; but for the **elect's** sake those days shall be shortened" (KJV).

[12]These passages regarding Armageddon will be covered in detail in the latter chapters of this book.

first-born. In that day there will be great mourning in Jerusalem, like the mourning of Hadadrimmon in the plain of Megiddo. And the land will mourn, every family by itself; the family of the house of David by itself, and their wives by themselves; the family of the house of Nathan by itself, and their wives by themselves...." (Zech. 12:9-12 NASB).

Joseph's brothers did not realize who he was until they visited him a *second time* in Egypt. Then they knew who he really was—their brother, savior and king of the Gentiles. They were terrified as Joseph cried, and then they accepted him (Gen. 45).

TWO FOR THE PRICE OF ONE— MESSIAH BEN JOSEPH AND MESSIAH BEN DAVID

When Jesus returns to save Israel from destruction by the Russian/Arab armies, as foretold by the prophet Ezekiel—just as Joseph saved Israel from destruction through famine—He will become known as the Messiah ben David. He will have fulfilled His future global role of saving the world (probably from a nuclear disaster)[13] as a mighty and powerful king, just as David was.

The ancient rabbinical legend concerning the Messiah, which we have investigated as Messiah ben David, will have been fulfilled and made evident in the only person who could possibly bring two seemingly contradictory roles into harmony; namely Jesus. Jesus suffered rejection by His brothers (the Jewish priests and rabbis), while being recognized by Gentiles (non-Jews), just as Joseph was neglected by his own, only to be received in Egypt as king. Pharaoh made him Vice-King and gave him a new name, *Zaphnath-paaneah* (Gen. 41:43-45 KJV), meaning "Saviour of the world"[14] in Egyptian (Gentile) language, and "revealer of secrets" in Joseph's Hebrew (Jewish) language.

Interestingly, until recent times and the advent of *Jews for Jesus* and the Jewish Messianic movements, Messianic salvation was kept secret from most Jews by the rabbis, while more and more Gentiles said, "What else is new?" We know that Jesus was not "a secret," but our Messiah-Savior.

---

[13]When we say disaster, we mean a global devastation. This author believes, along with many other evangelicals and some Jews who believe in Jesus as Messiah, that there may be a few nuclear "accidents" which will drive the world into the Antichrist's dictatorship, marking a seven-year period of his rule before a full-scale confrontation necessitates Jesus' return to stop it.

[14]J.N. Darby, in his study Bible, points out that *Zaphnath-paaneah* means, in "Egyptian, 'Saviour of the world,' " and in "Hebrew, 'Revealer of secrets.' " J.N. Darby, *The 'Holy Scriptures,' A New Translation from the Original Languages*, p. 55.

WHAT'S IN A NAME?
JESUS BECOMES MESSIAH BEN DAVID

Pharaoh called Joseph *Zaphnath-paaneah*, which had a double meaning (one meaning in Hebrew, another in Egyptian), because of Joseph's God-given ability to interpret his dream. This convinced Pharaoh to allow Joseph to grow and store enormous amounts of food, which saved Egypt and others, including Joseph's brothers, who came their way during the worldwide famine (Gen. 42). It is also interesting that, in a sense, the rabbis created a spiritual famine about Jesus as the Messiah, so that for many years Jews had to go to Gentiles to ask about the Messiah. The words of Amos the prophet, written in the eighth century BC, sound strangely familiar: " 'Behold, days are coming,' declares the Lord GOD, 'When I will send a famine on the land, Not a famine for bread or a thirst for water, But rather for hearing the words of the LORD' " (Amos 8:11 NASB).

Jesus, having already suffered rejection by the rabbis and crucifixion by the Romans—approximately 2000 years ago to date—fulfilled this suffering role, but He is still believed to be dead by many in the Jewish faith. In the same way, Joseph's bloody coat convinced his father that he was dead, while in Egypt—the land of the Gentiles (non-Jews)—he was being enjoyed as king.

Today, many rabbis refer to Jesus as "the God of the Gentiles," who "is not for the Jews." Soon, when Jesus returns, He will fulfill the role of a mighty king saving Israel and anyone else who looks to Him in that day. He will save the world from physical destruction by a future Russian/Arab invasion, known to us as Gog and Magog (see our chapters 19 and 20, "Russia is Crushed in Gog" and "Mohammed is Mad," for the details of these yet to be fulfilled Messianic prophecies). Just as Joseph saved Egypt from famine, the tailor-made role for a mighty warrior king like David will begin. Jesus will fulfill His role as Messiah ben David, as He decimates the enemies of Israel and consummates His predicted 1000-year rule over Israel and all nations (Zech. 14:16; Rev. 20; also see our chapters 25-30 on the Rapture, Second Coming and the millennium).

THE CONNECTION—PERSONAL
EXPERIENCES OF ISRAELI CONFORMATION

The rabbis and laymen alike do not really link this famous Messiah ben Joseph/David legend, as taught in the ancient rabbinical literature, with Jesus. However, I have had various opportunities to go into detail with dozens of individuals, especially in Israel, showing how Jesus and Joseph match so exactly. I saw many a smile arise on

Jewish faces; a look which seemed to say, "I cannot believe it, but I know you are right."

The legends of Messiah ben Joseph/David are taught today in Israel, apparently as school curriculum. If you were to mention the subject of the Messiah ben Joseph/David to any Israeli on the street, most would be captivated, as they awaited your comment. This Messiah legend is not very evident in the Diaspora[15] countries. With the possible exception of a handful of Orthodox yeshiva[16] students, most do not realize that there was ever such a famous legend about the Messiah. However, American Jews are acquainted with the history of Joseph and can easily grasp the parallels between Jesus and Joseph when someone takes the time to inform them of the historic details of the life of Jesus.[17]

DR. PATAI, A *JEWISH BIBLE SCHOLAR*, EXPOUNDS UPON THE MESSIAH BEN JOSEPH/DAVID LEGENDS

Raphael Patai, a Jewish Bible scholar who does not believe in Jesus, sheds considerable light on the history of this rabbinical legend about the Messiah, in his book, *The Messiah Texts*. Patai writes: "Scholars have repeatedly speculated about the origin of the Messiah ben Joseph legend and the curious fact that the Messiah figure has thus been split in two. It would seem that in the early legend, the death of the Messiah was envisaged, perhaps as a development of the Suffering Servant motif. A prophecy of Daniel, written about 164 B.C.E.,[18] is the earliest source speaking of the death of a *Mashiah* ('Anointed') sixty-two (prophetic) weeks...after the return and the rebuilding of Jerusalem (Dan. 9:24-26...)....When the death of the Messiah became an established tenet in Talmudic times, this was felt to be irreconcilable with the belief in the Messiah as the Redeemer who would usher in the blissful millennium of the Messianic age. The dilemma was solved by splitting the person of the Messiah in two: one of them, called Messiah ben Joseph...would fall victim....The other, Messiah ben David, will

---

15 The Diaspora refers to Jews outside of Israel, in all the countries of the world, after being exiled and dispersed there 2000 years ago, until 1948.

16 Yeshiva comes from two Hebrew words meaning "you sit." It is the Hebrew term used to describe a school where Jews sit and study the Jewish religion intensively.

17 To get a good idea of past and present rabbis' opinions on Jesus fulfilling the Messianic roles, read our *Vol. II*, chapter 7, "Discover Jesus is the Messiah—Some Rabbis Have and Are." This chapter names twenty-two rabbis who have!

18 This is the date given by many liberal scholars. The actual true date is mentioned in *The Scofield Reference Bible*. It was 553 BCE. Dates of different chapters of Daniel differ slightly because he wrote this book in Babylon over a period of about seventy years. He was taken there as a child and lived well into his nineties.

come after him...and will lead Israel to the ultimate victory, the triumph, and the Messianic era of bliss.

This splitting of the Messiah in two persons, which took place in the Talmudic period, achieved another purpose besides resolving the dilemma of the slain Messiah. According to an old tradition, the Messiah was perfectly prefigured in Moses. But Moses died before he could lead the Children of Israel into the Land of Promise. Consequently, for the parallel to be complete, the Messiah, too, had to die before accomplishing his great task of ultimate Redemption. Since, however, the Messiah would not be the True Redeemer of God if he did not fulfill that ultimate task, the only solution was to let one Messiah, like Moses, die, and then assign the completion of the work of Redemption to a second Messiah...."[19]

WHEN THE ESSENES PUT THE TWO AND TWO FROM THE SCRIPTURES TOGETHER, THEY GOT ONE AND ONE—ONE MESSIAH COMING TWO TIMES

In an article titled, "The Two Zadokite Messiahs," in *The Journal of Theological Studies*, the statement was made that: "Prof. Strack (following Prof. Schechter) thinks that the two are in reality only one...."[20] Jay Junior Smith, in his dissertation for a Ph.D. in religion, notes: "During the Pompeian era (63-31 B.C.) the two messiahs become one."[21]

Rev. Chuck Smith and Mark Eastman, M.D., in their book, *The Search for Messiah*, comment on a 1992 article in *The Biblical Archaeology Review*, which illustrates the historic truth of one Messiah Coming twice within the ancient Jewish theology of Jesus' day. They tell us: "In the Biblical Archaeology Review, December 1992, in an article by Hebrew scholars Michael Wise and James Tabor, we find a fascinating analysis of this text. ***'Our Qumran text, 4Q521, is, astonishingly, quite close to this Christian concept of the Messiah. Our text speaks not only of a single messianic figure...but it also describes him in extremely exalted terms, quite like the Christian view of Jesus as a cosmic agent.*** *That there was, in fact, an expectation of a* ***single messianic figure*** *at Qumran is really not so surprising....'*

*Wise and Tabor go on to state: '...**The Messiah of our text is thus much closer to the Christian Messiah, in this regard, than in***

---

[19]Raphael Patai, *The Messiah Texts*, pp. 166-167.

[20]G. Margoliouth, "The Two Zadokite Messiahs," *The Journal of Theological Studies*, Vol. XII, 1911, p. 447.

[21]Jay Junior Smith, Faculty of the Graduate School of Vanderbilt University, "A Study of the Alleged 'Two Messiah' Expectation of the Dead Sea Scrolls Against the Background of Developing Eschatology," May 1970, p. 29. Produced on microfilm-xerography in 1971 by University Microfilms, A Xerox Company, Ann Arbor, MI, USA.

***any previously published text** and requires us to reexamine the previously, rather restricted, views of messianic expectations at Qumran.'*

These recent discoveries from the Dead Sea Scrolls, have dramatically changed the belief that the Qumran community was expecting two Messiahs. For the past forty-five years, scholars have felt that the Essenes of Qumran, which was a devout sect of Judaism, were expecting and believed in two Messiahs. However, these new discoveries reveal strong evidence that the Qumran community was expecting only one Messiah!

The article goes on to state that there is abundant evidence from the Dead Sea Scrolls that the Messiah would in fact be both a ruling, reigning, and triumphant and yet a suffering rejected figure as well. On page 58 they state: '***there is no doubt that the Qumran community had faith in the ultimate victory of such a Messiah over all evil.** However, a closer reading of these texts reveals an additional theme, equally dominant—**that of an initial, though temporary, triumph of the wicked over righteousness. That is, there was the belief among the Qumran community that the Messiah would suffer initial defeat, but that he would ultimately triumph in the end of days**.*'

According to Wise and Tabor, the Qumran community believed that the Messiah would come once, 'suffer initial defeat' but at a later time he would 'ultimately triumph in the end of days.' Although not stated explicitly, this sounds like two appearances of a single Messiah! One appearance in humility and one in glory!

Wise and Tabor go on to show that because of Daniel's '70 weeks' prophecy, the Qumran community believed that the Messiah was going to come in the era in which they lived (First Century B.C.E.-First Century C.E.) '*We know the Qumran group was intensely interested in this seventy weeks prophecy of Daniel. They tried to place themselves within this chronological scheme as they calculated the eschaton. They must have made something out of this Messiah figure who was cut off.*'

Wise and Tabor admit that the person spoken of in Daniel's 70 weeks prophecy was believed by the Essenes of Qumran to be a Messiah of Davidic descent called the teacher of righteousness. The article goes on to state that: '*The teacher of righteousness, frequently referred to in the Qumran documents, appears to be a Messiah figure of Davidic descent, who is connected by the writers at Qumran specifically with the figure written about in Daniel 9:25.*' "[22]

---

[22]Mark Eastman, M.D. and Rev. Chuck Smith, *The Search for Messiah.* Costa Mesa, CA: The Word For Today, © 1993, pp. 91-92, used by permission. Eastman and Smith's source was Michael O. Wise and James D. Tabor, "The Messiah at Qumran," *Biblical Archaeology Review*, Dec. 1992. *The Search for Messiah* is available through The Word For Today, POB 8000, Costa Mesa, CA, USA 92628. Tel. (714) 979-0706.

ORIGINAL HEBREW TEXT WRITTEN 780 BC

אֵלֵךְ אָשׁוּבָה֙ אֶל־מְקוֹמִ֔י עַ֥ד אֲשֶׁר־יֶאְשְׁמ֖וּ וּבִקְשׁ֣וּ פָנָ֑י בַּצַּ֥ר לָהֶ֖ם יְשַׁחֲרֻֽנְנִי׃ לְכוּ֙ וְנָשׁ֣וּבָה
אֶל־יְהוָ֔ה כִּ֥י ה֛וּא טָרָ֖ף וְיִרְפָּאֵ֑נוּ יַ֖ךְ וְיַחְבְּשֵֽׁנוּ׃ יְחַיֵּ֖נוּ מִיֹּמָ֑יִם בַּיּוֹם֙ הַשְּׁלִישִׁ֔י יְקִמֵ֖נוּ וְנִחְיֶ֥ה
לְפָנָֽיו׃ **הושע ה:טו-ו:ב**

OLD TESTAMENT SCRIPTURE TRANSLATION

"I will go away *and* return to My place Until they acknowledge their guilt and seek My face; In their affliction they will earnestly seek Me. Come, let us return to the Lord. For He has torn *us*, but He will heal us; He has wounded *us*, but He will bandage us. He will revive us after two days; He will raise us up on the third day That we may live before Him."

Hosea 5:15-6:2 NASB

ANCIENT RABBINICAL COMMENTARY

"When King Solomon speaks of his 'beloved,' he usually means Israel the nation. In one instance he compares his beloved to a roe, and therein he refers to a feature which marks alike Moses and the Messiah, the two redeemers of Israel. Just as a roe comes within the range of man's vision only to disappear from sight and then appear again, so it is with these redeemers. Moses appeared to the Israelites, then disappeared, and eventually appeared once more, and the same peculiarity we have in connexion with Messiah; He will appear, disappear, and appear again—Numb. Rabba II. The fourteenth verse in the second chapter of Ruth is thus explained. 'Come thou hither' is the prediction of Messiah's kingdom. 'Dip the morsel in the vinegar,' foretells the agony through which Messiah will pass, as it is written in Isaiah (cap. 53.), 'He was wounded for our sins, He was bruised for our transgressions.' 'And she set herself beside the reapers' predicts the temporary departure of Messiah's kingdom. 'And he reached her parched corn' means the restoration of His kingdom."* **Midrash Ruth Rabba 5.**

***A Treasury Midrash*, by Samuel Rapaport, pp. 43-44**

NEW TESTAMENT RECORDED 63 AD

"And He said to the disciples, 'The days shall come when you will long to see one of the days of the Son of Man, and you will not see it. And they will say to you, 'Look there! Look here!' Do not go away, and do not run after *them.* For just as the lightning, when it flashes out of one part of the sky, shines to the other part of the sky, so will the Son of Man be in His day. But first He must suffer many things and be rejected by this generation.' "

Jesus, quoted from Luke 17:22-25 NASB

MODERN RABBINIC COMMENT/REFUTATION

"...commentators say that it [Isaiah 53] is speaking of the Prophet Isaiah himself. In any case it cannot be proven that this passage is speaking of the Messiah at all....The main thing is that a clear reading of the Jewish Bible offers absolutely no support to the 'proofs' of Christianity. In most cases, all you need is a good translation (or better still, the Hebrew original), and all those 'proofs' fall away. Many contemporary Christian scholars admit as much. However, the missionaries never mention the most important prophecies concerning the Messiah that Jesus *did not* fulfill. The main task of the Messiah was to bring the world back to G-d, and to abolish all war, suffering and injustice from the world. Clearly, Jesus did not accomplish this. In order to get around this failure on the part of Jesus, Christians invented the doctrine of the 'Second Coming' (Hebrews 9:29, Peter 3). All the

---

* Samuel Rapaport, *A Treasury of the Midrash.* New York: KTAV Publishing House, Inc., © 1968, pp. 43-44.

prophecies that Jesus did not fulfill the first time are supposed to be taken care of the second time around. However, the Jewish Bible offers absolutely no evidence to support the Christian doctrine of a 'Second Coming'....All the embarrassing prophecies that he did not fulfill are swept under the rug of a 'Second Coming.' "[23]

***The Real Messiah*, by Rabbi Aryeh Kaplan, *et al*, pp. 54-57; 1976**

AUTHOR'S COMMENT—EVANGELICAL CHRISTIAN POSITION

We can assure you that the prophecies of the Second Advent are not "swept under the rug," but are clearly dealt with throughout the New Testament, as we will detail in many chapters of this book. The authors[24] of *The Real Messiah* are representative of most of the modern rabbinical attitude toward the Messiahship of Jesus and are guilty of sweeping all of the many prophecies of the Messiah's First Coming, such as Isaiah 53 and Daniel 9:26, under the rabbinical carpet of intolerance and narrow-mindedness. In this book, we document these prophecies as being considered Messianic not only by Christians and Messianic Jews today but also by the most ancient rabbinical commentaries. Hosea, in his explanation of Messiah coming and returning to His place while reviving Israel after two days (2000 years) and living in their literal sight for the third day (1000 years), is speaking of the Messiah. There can be no doubt of this in light of the fact that the Targum Onkelos (ancient rabbinical commentary) identifies this passage with Messiah. This is documented in Alfred Edersheim's book, *The Life and Times of Jesus the Messiah*,[25] where it says Hosea 6:2 is Messianically applied in the Targum. **Philip Moore**

TOO FEW TRULY UNDERSTAND WHAT IS REALLY AT STAKE WHEN IT COMES TO THE MESSIAH

All too few in our modern age are aware that the commentaries of ancient Judaism are virtually identical to the teachings of those who propagate the modern Christian (Messianic) fundamentals of Jesus, as were prescribed by the New Testament 2000 years ago. The only answer to the human conditions of suffering, guilt and the question, "Where is world peace?", is the redeemer, the only true hope. The only individual who fits this bill is the carpenter from Nazareth, known to ancient Judaism[26] and modern Christians, both Gentile and Jewish alike, as Jesus the Messiah!

---

[23][ ] mine. Rabbi Kaplan's spelling of God as "G-d" is not a typo but the way Orthodox Jews sometimes refer to His name, considering it too holy to write or pronounce outside of a synagogue. In Israel, they say *Elohim* (God) in the synagogue, but *Elokim* outside the synagogue, leaving out the letter *hay*. This is where the written English form, G-d, originated.

[24]This publication is authored by several rabbis writing on various anti-missionary topics.

[25]See Alfred Edersheim, *The Life and Times of Jesus the Messiah*. Grand Rapids, MI: Wm B. Eerdmans Publishing Co., © 1971, p. 734.

[26]Here we refer to those many Jewish believers in Jesus who followed Him for the first three centuries of the Christian era, in accordance with the ancient interpretation held by some rabbis of the Messianic fulfillment of Jewish biblical prophecies. See our chapters 7, 15 and 27, "The Messiah Conspiracy," "Messianic Jewish Faith in Jesus," and "Speculating on Messiah's *Second* Coming—Whether They Know It or Not."

The ancient school of rabbinical interpretation of Messianic prophecy, in existence primarily before the birth, death and resurrection of Jesus, was unbiased by the events which took place in His life. These events were later recorded as fulfillments of prophecy by the New Testament because they matched exactly the specific predictions relating to the Jewish Messiah. Even secular sources outside the New Testament, such as *Josephus*, mention that many Jews and others received Him as Messiah as a result of these fulfillments. A case in point was His resurrection, predicted by King David.

YOU CAN TAKE THE OLD TESTAMENT OUT OF JESUS, BUT YOU CANNOT TAKE JESUS OUT OF THE OLD TESTAMENT

These predictions (in the Old Testament prophets and law) were viewed by many ancient schools of rabbis as sacred and breathed by the spirit of God. Today, and even in the early years after the crucifixion of Jesus, rabbis began to de-emphasize the importance of various Messianic prophecies in scope and magnitude. They even began to imply that such prophecies are not and never have been Messianic in their importance and meaning![27] They virtually reinterpreted the prophecies to be non-Messianic because Jesus fulfilled those designated for the Messiah's First Advent to Earth by assuming His role as the suffering Passover lamb. He removed guilt and prepared man for God's Messianic Kingdom, yet to be realized at the Messiah's Second Coming.

MESSIANIC INTERPRETATIONS—BEFORE AND AFTER

I have not, to this date, seen a list which illustrates the contrast between the rabbinic interpretations of the Messianic prophecies before and after the birth of Jesus. The absence of such a comparison is due

---

[27]F.F. Bruce tells us: "There was a good deal of contact between orthodox Jews and Jewish Christians in Palestine in the first and second centuries, and there are frequent echoes in the rabbinical literature of controversies between the two parties, on the interpretation of messianic prophecy, for example. In a number of instances interpretations which had formerly been regarded as quite proper and respectable by orthodox Jews were ruled out as inadmissible when Christians began to use them to prove that Jesus was the Messiah. There is one notable occasion recorded when the great Rabbi Akiba got into trouble because he favoured such an unacceptable interpretation. He and his colleagues were discussing the vision of the judgment day in Daniel 7·9-14, where 'one like a son of man' appears before the Ancient of Days to receive universal and eternal sovereignty from him. 'As I looked', says Daniel (verse 9), 'thrones were placed, and one that was ancient of days took his seat.' The question was raised: Why thrones in the plural? Akiba gave the traditional answer: 'One for God and one for David' (i.e. for Messiah, the son of David) But Rabbi José expostulated with him: 'Akiba, how long will you profane the Shekhinah? It is one for justice and one for righteousness.' " F.F. Bruce, D.D., F.B.A., *Jesus and Christian Origins Outside the New Testament.* Hodder and Stoughton, © 1984, pp. 64-65, used by permission.

to the false fear that accepting Jesus will promote assimilation. Therefore, we are devoting special pages of this work to illustrate how the ancient rabbinical commentaries diverge from the opinions of modern rabbis, and how they both relate to the Old and New Testaments. The Old Testament is still considered sacred by many Jews, though most orthodox authorities do not honestly interpret the Messianic prophecies as Messianic. The New Testament is neither believed nor studied because of the aforementioned fear above.

It is our goal to show that certain schools of ancient Judaism taught what Evangelical Christians and Jews for Jesus—both ancient (first century) and modern (twentieth century)—teach and embrace in connection with the roles of the Messiah.

ALL JEWS SHOULD BELIEVE IN JESUS, IF THEY ARE LOYAL TO THEIR HERITAGE

Our conclusion will show that contemporary Jews of all denominations and persuasions—orthodox, conservative and reformed—should believe in Jesus if they are going to be honest and loyal to their Jewish heritage and the biblical Jewish hope of "**the Messiah**." The Messiah will be positively shown to be Jesus throughout this writing. Contrary to what many Jewish leaders are presently teaching, a denial of Jesus is a denial of what being Jewish is all about. True Jewishness is based on the Jewish Bible, and not on external modern rabbinical criteria, which we believe have been designed to perpetuate the false teaching, which maintains that Jesus is not the Messiah, thus negating the truth of the Jewish Scriptures and their true Messianic meanings!

Incidentally, the Jewish Bible is the very document which was always used by the ancients to identify what was Jewish and what was not. It is "the document" which will show us the answer, because its purpose was to divinely designate the Jewish people as the ones to bring a pagan world back[28] to God from the depths of demon worship (which arose between the Fall of Adam until the call of Abraham), and lead it into a redemptive reconciliation with the one true God, through the acceptance of His Messiah.

---

[28]In the Jewish Bible (our Old Testament), it is said in Genesis: "And I will make you a great nation, And I will bless you, And make your name great; And so you shall be a blessing; And I will bless those who bless you, And the one who curses you I will curse. And in you all the families of the earth shall be blessed" (Gen. 12:2-3 NASB). The prophet Isaiah likewise proclaimed God's very words: "...'It is too small a thing that You should be My servant To raise up the tribes of Jacob, and to restore the preserved ones of Israel; I will also make You a light of the nations So that My salvation may reach to the end of the earth' " (Isa. 49:6 NASB).

PREVIOUSLY UNSEEN MANUSCRIPTS REVEALED WILL DESTROY RELIGION AND UNCOVER THE TRUTH

This book may arouse much hatred against me by those who continue to teach and perpetuate these modern misconceptions of the prophecies in question. However, what the Bible and history teach about the past and future is of paramount importance!

Regardless of how some may feel about my work to bring forth the unpopular truth from ancient manuscripts (until now, mostly unexamined by the common man), they must be shown! No doubt, most religious figures of many persuasions would rather you not check into these matters! Of course, the Orthodox Jewish rabbi would not want you to discover any hidden evidences that Jesus is the Messiah. The Moslem would not want you to be convinced that the Jews are the chosen people and that the true Christian faith is based on the Old Testament's Jewish prophecies. They want you to think Israel is fair game for all, including the Palestinians, and not the land of promise for the Jewish people, as true Evangelical Christians believe![29]

Without question, the ecumenical, Eastern Orthodox and Catholic "priests" would be uncomfortable with both Jews, Evangelical Christians and those without a faith discovering the Jewishness of Jesus and the teachings in the New Testament, since this conflicts with the man-made "holy traditions" found in many of their catechisms and early church council rulings.

There have been more wars fought over religion than most people will ever realize. As we have seen, the reason for all war was the rejection of the Messiah at His First Advent. Of course, as His Second Coming draws ever nearer, we will be confronted with that final war called Armageddon and Gog and Magog (discussed in full in the latter chapters of this work). Since the rejection of the Messiah the first time around has placed us in such a position of peril, we think it of prime importance to investigate why He was rejected, so that we may get to the truth of the matter! This is the subject of our next chapter.

***

[29]For the history and biblical reason for Christian Zionism, see our chapter 12, "Christian Zionists Past and Present," and chapter 14, "Zionists—Evangelical Christians—the Most Loyal to Israel."

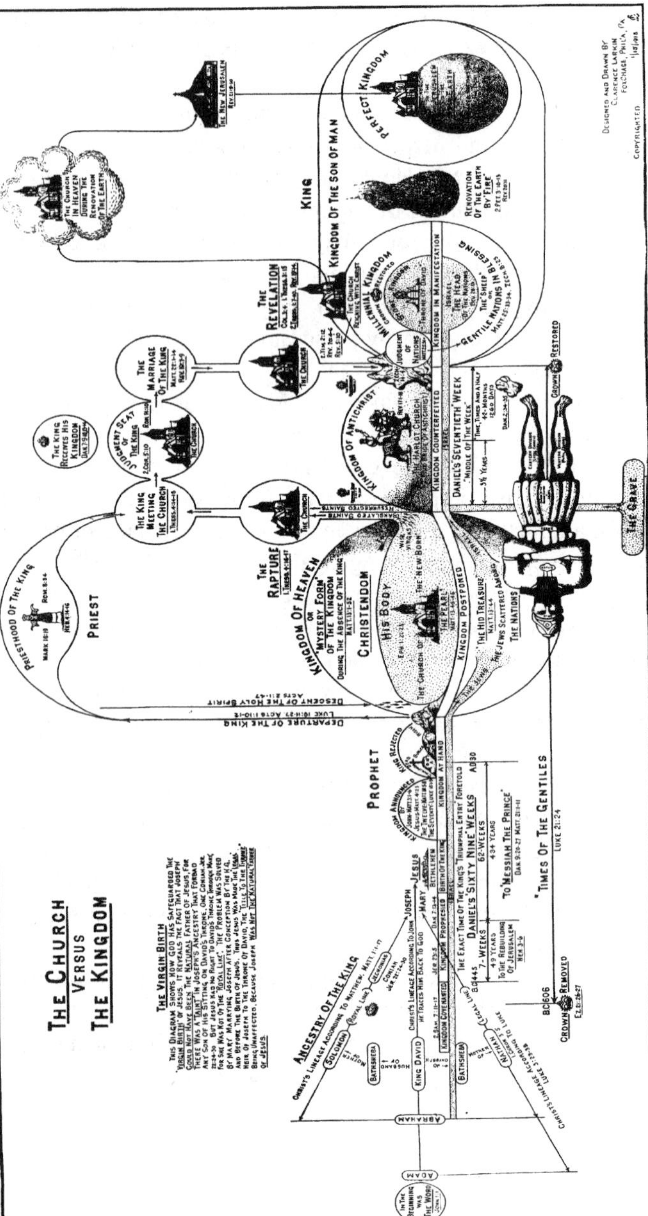

In this chart, Clarence Larkin illustrates that Scripture differentiates between the Church and the Jewish Messianic Kingdom. The Church was initiated because the kingdom was rejected.

"For if you believed Moses, you would believe Me; for he wrote of Me."[1]

Jesus' comment to the Jewish religious leaders, 2000 years ago

"...'What are we doing? For this man is performing many signs. If we let Him *go on* like this, all men will believe in Him, and the Romans will come and take away both our place and our nation.' "[2] The chief priests (Caiaphas and Annas) and Pharisees in a convened council, 2000 years ago

"Woe is me for the house of Boethus! Woe is me for their club! Woe is me for the house of Hanin [Annas]! Woe is me for their whisperings! Woe is me for the house of Kantheras! Woe is me for their pen! Woe is me for the house of Ishmael [ben Phiabi]! Woe is me for their fist! For they are the high priests; Their sons are the treasurers; Their sons-in-law are temple-officers; And their servants beat the people with cudgels!"[3] The Talmud, Pesahim 57a

"If the house of Kantheras is identical with the house of Caiaphas (cf. Schwartz 1990), then the last 'woe' is intended against Joseph Caiaphas and his family. The 'house of Hanin,' which means the mighty family of Annas, is accused of calumnies, and one could easily include among these calumnies the persecution of Jesus....The New Testament indicates that those who were active in delivering Jesus to Pilate were members of the high-priestly aristocracy....the leading figures in this fateful action were Annas and his clan together with Joseph Caiaphas, probably his son-in-law."[4] Israeli Professor David Flusser, Ph.D., of Jerusalem, 1992

"For centuries, professional and amateur archaeologists have been obsessed with **digging up** Israel, and with good reason. No place on earth has more alluring ancient treasures waiting to be discovered than does little Israel. For believers, virtually every turn of the spade provides further documentation of the inerrancy of Scripture."[5] Editor Elwood McQuaid, 1994

In 1990, Caiaphas, the high priest mentioned above, was "**dug up**" in Israel. This archaelogically validated his existence to the dismay of liberal "higher" critics throughout the world. It was Caiaphas who initiated, pioneered and led the way to a solidified Jewish rejection of Jesus, chiefly for political gain. Read on...!

Philip Moore, 1996

4

WHY WAS JESUS REJECTED BY THE JEWISH PEOPLE?

Why was the picture of the suffering Messiah swept aside in light of the many prophecies which came true in the life of Jesus? Jesus often reminded the religious leaders that these prophecies were indeed

---

[1]John 5:46 NASB.
[2]John 11:47-48 NASB.
[3]F.F. Bruce, *New Testament History*. New York: Doubleday & Co., © 1969, pp. 67-68.
[4]*'Atiqot,* Vol. XXI. Jerusalem: Israel Antiquities Authority, © 1992, p. 83.
[5]*Israel My Glory*, Vol. 51, No. 5, Oct./Nov., 1994, p. 21. Bold mine.

being fulfilled in His life! He said: " 'You search the Scriptures, because you think that in them you have eternal life; and it is these that bear witness of Me; and you are unwilling to come to Me, that you may have life....Do not think that I will accuse you before the Father; the one who accuses you is Moses, in whom you have set your hope. For if you believed Moses, you would believe Me; for he wrote of Me. But if you do not believe his writings, how will you believe My words?' " (John 5:39-40, 45-47 NASB).

After His resurrection, Jesus said to them: " '...These are My words which I spoke to you while I was still with you, that all things which are written about Me in the Law of Moses and the Prophets and the Psalms must be fulfilled'....'Thus it is written, that the Christ should suffer and rise again from the dead the third day; and that repentance for forgiveness of sins should be proclaimed in His name to all the nations, beginning from Jerusalem. You are witnesses of these things' " (Luke 24:44-48 NASB).

A COUPLE OF CORRUPT PRIESTS MISLEAD MANY COMMON PEOPLE INTO *REJECTING* THE MESSIAH

Our explanation of why He was rejected in the first century lies with the Jewish priests, on whom the common people relied for religious understanding. There is overwhelming evidence that the high priests at the time of Jesus had become so completely corrupt and involved in the political intrigues of the Roman rulers, that no matter how many Messianic proofs were laid out on the table, no honesty would be forthcoming, as far as they were concerned!

To illustrate our assertion, we quote from an extremely interesting book entitled, *The Trial of Jesus, From a Lawyers Standpoint*, by New York attorney Walter M. Chandler. Chandler, being as modest as possible, says: "We trust that these expressions will not offend our dear Israelitish readers, for they are based on the statements of eminent and zealous Jewish writers....Josephus the historian. Although endeavoring to conceal as much as possible the shameful acts committed by the priests composing this council, yet he was unable, in a moment of disgust, to refrain from stigmatizing them. 'About this time,' he says, 'there arose a sedition between the high priests and the principal men of the multitude of Jerusalem, each of which assembled a company of the boldest sort of men, and of those that loved innovations, and became leaders to them. And when they struggled together they did it by casting reproachful words against one another, and by throwing stones also. And there was nobody to reprove them; but these disorders were done after a licentious manner in the city, as if it had no government over it....Here is the explanation, to the shame of the Jewish assembly:

"For nearly a century a **detestable abuse** prevailed, which consisted in the arbitrary **nomination** and **deposition** of the **high priest**. The high priesthood, which for fifteen centuries had been preserved in the same family, being hereditary according to the divine command,[3] had at the time of Christ's advent become an object of commercial speculation. Herod commenced these arbitrary changes,[4] and after Judea became one of the Roman conquests the election of the high priest took place almost every year at Jerusalem, the procurators appointing and deposing them in the same manner as the praetorians later on made and unmade emperors.[5] The Talmud speaks sorrowfully of this venality and the yearly changes of the high priest.

"This sacred office was given to the one that offered the most money for it, and mothers were particularly anxious that their sons should be nominated to this dignity[6]....M. Derembourg, a modern Jewish savant, has remarked: '*A few priestly, aristocratic, powerful, and vain families, who cared for neither the dignity nor the interests of the altar, quarreled with each other respecting appointments, influence, and wealth.*'[7]"[6]

MESSIANIC REJECTION RESULTED FROM PHARISAIC PRIDE IN A LAW WHICH COULD NOT BE KEPT

We also note, in our explanation of why Jesus was rejected, that the Pharisees of Jesus' day were descended from a group of righteous men who returned from the Jewish captivity in Babylon several hundred years before. However, they had degenerated[7] into

---

[6]Walter M. Chandler, *The Trial of Jesus, From a Lawyer's Standpoint,* Illustrated Edition, Vol. II. Norcross, Georgia: The Harrison Company Publishers, © 1976, pp. 145, 142, used by permission. Bold mine. Mr. Chandler's documentary footnotes 3-7, preserved above, include the following sources: "3 Josephus, 'Ant.,' Book XX. Chap. X. 1; XV. III. 1."; "4 Josephus, 'Ant.,' Book XV. Chap. III. 1."; "5 Josephus, 'Ant.,' Book XVIII. Chap. II. 3; Book XX. Chap. IX. 1, 4."; "6 See 'Talmud,' 'Yoma,' or 'the Day of Atonement,' fol. 35, recto; also Derembourg, work above quoted, p. 230, note 2."; "7 'Essai sur l'histoire et la geographie de la Palestine,' p. 232." Ibid.

[7]*The New Scofield Reference Bible* informs us: "...'Pharisees' [comes] from a Hebrew word meaning *separate.* After the ministry of the postexilic prophets ceased, godly men called *Chasidim* (saints) arose who sought to keep alive reverence for the law among the descendants of the Jews who returned from the Babylonian captivity. This movement degenerated into the Pharisaism of our Lord's day—a letter-strictness which overlaid the law with traditional interpretations held to have been communicated by the LORD to Moses as oral explanations of equal authority with the law itself (cp. Mt.15:2-3; Mk.7:8-13; Gal.1:14). The Pharisees were strictly a sect. A member was a *chaber* (i.e. 'knit together,' Jud.20:11) and was obligated to remain true to the principles of Pharisaism.

interpreting God's law by the letter strictness of their self righteous traditions to such an extent that they had obscured its true meaning; the true intention of the law was to show people that they were sinful and needed atonement. Many Pharisees felt that they were not out of character with God's law because they labored under the false perception that they were keeping it.

Jesus emphasized the law's true heart meaning (Matt. 5:21-22). He maintained that if anyone claims to keep the law with perfection they must also do it in their hearts[8]—something impossible for a human being to do perfectly throughout their life! Jesus claimed this was a test to show us that we cannot be perfect, and that one man—the Messiah—would come and keep the law faultlessly. Thereafter, anyone who believed in Him would be considered worthy of keeping it and assured forgiveness, even in their areas of weakness. "If we believe not, *yet* he abideth faithful: he cannot deny himself " (II Tim. 2:13 KJV).

THE SUFFERING MESSIAH, WHO JUSTIFIED MAN THROUGH THE LAW, IS DITCHED

The New Testament book of Romans says: "...by the works of the Law no flesh [man] will be justified in His [God's] sight" (Rom. 3:20 NASB; [ ] mine). In the Old Testament, King David exhorts: "Hear my prayer, O LORD, give ear to my supplications: in thy faithfulness answer me, *and* in thy righteousness....enter not into judgment with thy servant: for in thy sight shall no man living be justified" (Ps. 143:1-2 KJV).

Hal Lindsey, a famous prophetic theologian, correctly notes: "The law was given to show mankind why it needed a 'suffering Messiah' who alone could make man acceptable[9] to God. Any person who hasn't come to see that his most basic problem is an inner spiritual one prefers a political deliverer to a spiritual one. It is not difficult,

---

They were moral, zealous, and self-denying, but self-righteous (Lk.18:9) and destitute of the sense of sin and need (Lk.7:39). They were the foremost persecutors of Jesus Christ and the objects of His unsparing denunciation, e.g. Mt.23:1-36; Lk.11:42-44." *The New Scofield Reference Bible*, p. 995.

[8]This was the whole reason He gave the Sermon on the Mount (for insight into the true meaning of the Sermon on the Mount, see our chapter 5 "Which Prophecies Did Jesus Fulfill?").

[9]So, believe it or not, it may sound too good to be true. If you want to keep the law, all you have to do is rest in Jesus. Read Romans 3-4 and Galatians 3-4 in your New Testament. He kept it for you!

therefore, to understand the basic attitude which rationalized away the prophetic portrait of the suffering Messiah."[10]

BORN AHEAD OF YOUR TIME—THE REJECTION OF THE SUFFERING POSTPONED THE KING

Jesus demonstrated the fact that He had fulfilled the prophecies of the suffering servant (such as Isa. 53; 49:5-7; and Ps. 22), and claimed He would also fulfill the kingly prophecies (Dan. 7:13-14) at a later date (Mark 14:62). The pro-Roman Sanhedrin[11] (Jewish Supreme Court), made up of a large number of Pharisees, chose to reject their Messiah. They were looking for the kingly fulfillments in their time; pride and misinterpretation prevented them from accepting the suffering one first. Jesus would have indeed become the king and national deliverer to them and the world, had His message been heeded (see Matt. 23:39; and the parables of Jesus in Matt. 21-22; and Luke 19:41-44).[12]

WHY DECEIVE THE COMMON MAN? FOR THE PRIESTS TO HAVE RECEIVED JESUS SPIRITUALLY WOULD HAVE MEANT THEIR DEMISE POLITICALLY

The common people (the general Jewish populace) rejected Him because most did not read or take the prophecies of the Messiah

---

[10]Hal Lindsey with C.C. Carlson, *The Late Great Planet Earth*, p. 31.

[11]F.F. Bruce tells us: "An attempt has been made to distinguish between two Sanhedrins at this time–a political body, dominated by the pro-Roman high-priestly party, and a religious body, controlled by leading rabbis. Now it is plain that the Mishnah regards a religious Sanhedrin as existing before A.D. 70, under the presidency of one of the great rabbis of the day. If there were in fact two separate Sanhedrins, then there is no doubt that the political Sanhedrin was the one which sentenced Jesus to death." Mr. Bruce's documentation of footnote 7 reads: "E.g. by the Jewish scholar Adolf Büchler in *Das Synhedrion in Jerusalem* (Vienna, 1902), and more recently by Solomon Zeitlin in *Who Crucified Jesus?* (Philadelphia, 1942), where it is argued that the pro-Roman political Sanhedrin was the only section of the Jewish nation responsible for the execution of Jesus. A thorough examination of Zeitlin's thesis by N.B. Stonehouse appears in *Paul before the Areopagus and Other NT Studies* (1957), pp. 41 ff." F.F. Bruce, *The Spreading Flame*. London: The Paternoster Press, © 1958, pp. 53-54. We note that the men of the "minor" Sanhedrin and the "great" Sanhedrin are mentioned in the Jewish commentary, *Midrash Rabbah, Lamentations*, published by The Soncino Press, p. 227.

[12]Arnold Fruchtenbaum, a Jewish believer in Jesus who holds a Th.M and Ph.D, reminds us in our dispensational faith: "Christ would have died even if Israel had accepted Him. The nation would have proclaimed Jesus as their King, which would have been viewed by Rome as a rebellion against Caesar. Jesus would then have been arrested, tried, and crucified for treason against Rome, as was the case anyway. Three days later, following His resurrection, He would have dispensed with Rome and set up the Messianic Kingdom. His death would have occurred regardless of what Israel did." Dr. Arnold G. Fruchtenbaum, *Israelology: The Missing Link in Systematic Theology*. Tustin, CA: Ariel Ministries Press, © 1993, pp. 624-625, used by permission.

literally.[13] Rather, they relied on the opinion of the religious leadership within the majority of the Sanhedrin, which at that time, had become pro-Roman.

According to the Talmud and other commentaries, both ancient and modern, the reason for this pro-Roman stand of the court was that the priests and many elders of that time thought in strictly secular terms. They reasoned that the best way to secure the welfare of the nation and their own wealth and position, would be to collaborate closely with the Roman authorities![14]

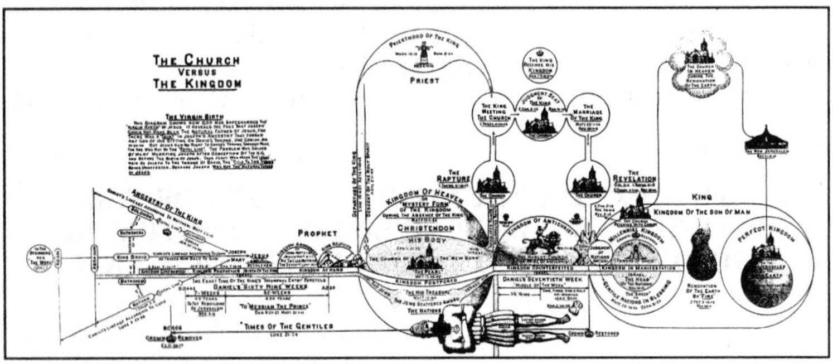

[13]See Hal Lindsey with C.C. Carlson, *The Late Great Planet Earth*, p. 31.

[14]F.F. Bruce proves this by using the Talmud's own admission outside of the New Testament. The Talmud is a Jewish book written for Jews. Using this volume, Bruce clearly exposes this issue when he writes: "This meant an unhealthy concentration of power in the hands of a few rich and influential families....'chief priests' exercised power out of all proportion to their numbers. The common people's attitude toward them and the families to which they belonged finds expression in a satirical chant preserved in the Talmud: Woe is me for the house of Boethus! Woe is me for their club! Woe is me for the house of Hanin [Annas]! Woe is me for their whisperings! Woe is me for the house of Kantheras! Woe is me for their pen! Woe is me for the house of Ishmael [ben Phiabi]! Woe is me for their fist! For they are the high priests; Their sons are the treasurers; Their sons-in-law are temple-officers; And their servants beat the people with cudgels![52]" Bruce's footnote 52 is *The Babylonian Talmud*, Pesahim 57a. F.F. Bruce, *New Testament History*, pp. 67-68. Dr. David Flusser of Jerusalem informs us of the fact: "If the house of Kantheras is identical with the house of Caiaphas (cf. Schwartz 1990), then the last 'woe' is intended against Joseph Caiaphas and his family. The 'house of Hanin,' which means the mighty family of Annas, is accused of calumnies, and one could easily include among these calumnies the persecution of Jesus....The New Testament indicates that those who were active in delivering Jesus to Pilate were members of the high-priestly aristocracy....the leading figures in this fateful action were Annas and his clan together with Joseph Caiaphas, probably his son-in-law." *'Atiqot*, Vol. XXI, © 1992, p. 83.

History Begins *Adam to Abraham*	**Call of Abraham, the first Jew** *Abraham to Jesus*	**Institution of Church replaces rejected king** *Jesus to present*	**Future after Second Coming** *1000 years of peace*
2000 years of general knowledge of God, the Fall and institution of sacrifice (Genesis).	2000 years of law. In this Dispensation, Jewish law is enforced.	Approximately 2000 years of Church, joined by many Jews and Gentiles through faith in the Jewish Messiah, Jesus.	Scriptures predict the 1000-year Jewish Messianic Kingdom of Jesus reigning on Earth, to be instituted by Jesus when He returns and is accepted by the Jewish people (Revelation 20).

God's timeline for the 7000 years known as the Millenial Dispensational Week.
Very probably in the 2030's, when we are 2000 years from the time Jesus left (33 AD), the millenial kingdom will begin—peace on Earth!

After all, the priests and several Pharisees commented on the miracles of Jesus: "If we let Him *go on* like this, all men will believe in Him, and the Romans will come and take away both our place and our nation" (John 11:48 NASB).

At this point, we should remind ourselves that if Israel as a nation had accepted Jesus then, there would have been no need for the institution of the Church, and the Jewish kingdom would have begun. Jesus said the kingdom was at hand (Matt. 3:2; 4:23) and if He had been accepted, He would have instituted this kingdom.

All the parallel prophecies concerning His Second Advent began **after** His rejection. What would have happened had He been received? He would have reached the pagan Gentile world by giving them the opportunity to accept the God of Israel through the Messianic Jewish Kingdom, instead of using the Church. He will do this at His Second Coming (Dan. 7:13-14; Rev. 20). However, His rejection has put approximately 2000 years between His First and Second Advents to Earth, as predicted in Hosea 5:15 and Matthew 23:39. These two pictures painted by the Jewish Bible could easily have occurred at the same time, had those to whom He came (present at His First Advent), received Him.

A PRIESTLY PARADOX LENGTHENS THE TIME BETWEEN THE TWO COMINGS OF THE MESSIAH!

In recent years there are some in "Christian circles" (liberals) who reject the idea that Jesus was offering the Messianic Kingdom to Israel, and that He would have set it up if received by His people. New Testament verses like Matthew 3:2 and 4:23 could not be more clear on this subject. However, many of the greatest evangelical scholars of our time, who truly believe the Bible, point out that *if* Jesus had been received at His First Coming, the two predicted Old Testament pictures of Messiah, one of a "suffering servant" and the other of a "reigning king," would have merged. Indeed, Jesus would have set up His kingdom of peace at that First Coming.

Hal Lindsey, foremost fundamentalist Christian author of a dozen best-selling books, pointed out this truth in his book, *There's A New World Coming*, when he said: "For anyone who cared to investigate, there was no lack of evidence to show that Jesus was indeed the long-awaited Messiah. Had the people received Him, He would have fulfilled the kingly prophecies in their day in addition to the ones regarding the suffering Messiah. But when the Jewish nation as a whole rejected Christ, the fulfillment of His kingship was postponed until the final culmination of world history. This is the subject of the Book of Revelation."[15]

HOW WOULD THE PROPHESIED CRUCIFIXION OF JESUS HAVE TAKEN PLACE HAD HE BEEN ACCEPTED?

Many Jews became believers as they witnessed the fulfillment of the prophecies in the holy writings of the Old Testament. We will look at a few of the incredible prophetic evidences of the resurrection later when we cover Psalms 16, 21 and 22 (in our chapter 5, "Which Prophecies Did Jesus Fulfill?").

Many wonder how these prophecies of the Messiah's death and resurrection would have been fulfilled had He been accepted. The answer is simple; the Romans would have executed Him, on their own, as a usurper[16] of Roman authority. The only reason they were lenient toward Jesus' claims of Messiahship was because, for selfish reasons, the corrupt priests denied His Messianic credentials. As a result, the Romans overlooked His Messianic credibility to the very end.

THE HIGH PRIESTS AND THEIR MOB BLACKMAIL PILATE INTO CRUCIFIXION

When the Jewish religious leaders told Pilate, "We have no king but Caesar," Pilate's entire political career was put in jeopardy. He knew they would leak word to Caesar in Rome, which in turn would

---

[15]Hal Lindsey, *There's A New World Coming*. Santa Ana, CA: Vision House Publishers, © 1973, p. 19, used by permission.

[16]Reverend Clarence Larkin also shed some light on this ancient view when he said: "But some one may ask, 'What would have happened if the Jews, as a nation, had **repented**, and accepted Jesus as King, would the earthly Messianic Kingdom have been set up?' Certainly, but not necessarily immediately, for certain Old Testament prophecies as to Jesus' death and ressurection had to be fulfilled, for He had to die for the redemption of the race, before He could assume His office as King. But this could and would have been fulfilled by the Roman Government seizing Jesus and crucifying Him as a usurper, and with Jesus' Ressurection and Ascension, Daniel's 69th week would have terminated, and the 70th week begun without a break, and at its close Jesus would have descended and set up His earthly Kingdom." Clarence Larkin, *Dispensational Truth or God's Plan and Purpose in The Ages.* Glenside, PA: Rev. Clarence Larkin Est., © 1918, p. 87. Available through Rev. Clarence Larkin Est., POB 334, Glenside, PA, USA 19038. The religious leaders, because of their corruption by Rome, deceived the people regarding the Messiah's Coming, and this created an approximate 2000-year interlude between the Messianic arrivals. We have discussed this with many rabbis who ridicule the assertion that their Bible spoke of two Comings of the Messiah. However, the ancient rabbinical expositors of centuries past confirm this. They expounded on the words of Hosea in their Bible, written nearly seven hundred years before the birth of Jesus, as refer-

destroy his "presidential" future.[17] Evidence of this is clearly revealed by the apostle John in the New Testament. "As a result of this Pilate made efforts to release Him, but the Jews [mobs that the priests had previously arranged to be at the scene] cried out, saying, 'If you release this Man, you are no friend of Caesar; everyone who makes himself out *to be* a king opposes Caesar'....Now it was the day of preparation for the Passover; it was about the sixth hour. And he said to the Jews, 'Behold, your King!' They therefore cried out, 'Away with *Him*, away with *Him*, crucify Him!' Pilate said to them, 'Shall I crucify your King?' The chief priests answered, 'We have no king but Caesar.' So he then delivered Him to them to be crucified" (John 19:12, 14-16 NASB).

PILATE'S *WOULD HAVE BEEN CONSEQUENCE*, DUE TO THE HIGH PRIESTS, CONVENIENTLY AND SKILLFULLY AVOIDED BY CRUCIFIXION

As you can imagine, if word had traveled back to Rome that the Roman governor, Pilate of Judea, allowed a Jew to openly proclaim himself king—a treasonable offense by Roman law—Pilate would have been finished. Thus when the priests and their hand-picked mob told Pilate they "had no king but Caesar," they were in a sense, blackmailing him into executing Jesus. A better understanding of this can be obtained from the eleventh chapter of the Gospel of John, which we will quote shortly.

A nineteen hundred and fifty-three-year-old inscription reading "Joseph, son of Caiaphas", with a clear first-century pattern of rosettes carved on the side of an ossuary excavated in 1990, in Jerusalem.

ring to the Messiah. They said His two days were symbolic of 2000 years, while His third day was to be the 1000-year kingdom of the Messiah, which will be set up after His 2000 years of patience with Israel, at their final acceptance of Him. Hosea 5:15-6:2 reads: "I will go *and* return to my place, till they acknowledge their offence, and seek my face: in their affliction they will seek me early. Come, and let us return unto the LORD: for he hath torn, and he will heal us; he hath smitten, and he will bind us up. After two days will he revive us: in the third day he will raise us up, and we shall live in his sight" (KJV). An authentically accepted ancient viewpoint on these words reads: "...as it is said, *After two days he will revive us* (Hos 6:2). These are the days of the Messiah, which [will last] for two thousand years. *On the third day*[192] *he will raise us, [and we shall live before him]* (Hos 6:2).[193]" Footnote 192 to this ancient rabbinical commentary reads: "The third millennium, considering a day as a thousand years." Footnote 193 reads: " 'Living' in convenantal terms meant living on the promised land with the Messiah." George Buchanan, *Revelation and Redemption*, pp. 405-406.

[17]In other words, any promotions in store for him would not be forthcoming.

1992 ARCHAEOLOGICAL EVIDENCE OF THE EXISTENCE OF CAIAPHAS VALIDATES THE HISTORICITY OF THE NEW TESTAMENT!

A recent *New York Times* article entitled, "Tomb in Jerusalem May Be That of Priest Who Doomed Jesus," displayed pictures of a stone ossuary (repository box for bones) which contained bones of a sixty-year-old man from the first century. The ossuary bore an inscription, in Semitic language, which read "Joseph, son of Caiaphas." Flavius Josephus, the first century Jewish historian, wrote: " 'Joseph...was called Caiaphas of the high priesthood.' "[18]

The article confirmed that a first century (43 AD) bronze coin was found in one of the ossuaries. The site was accidentally opened in 1990 by workers who were widening a road at the Peace Forest in Jerusalem. Ronny Reich, of the Israel Antiquities Authority, referred to the writing on the box as that of working class people/cemetery workers. There were several boxes located in the tomb, yet one "stood out in splendor....decorated with a rare, intricate pattern of rosettes." This was the ossuary bearing the high priest's name. Zvi Greenhut, Jerusalem's chief archaeologist, began excavating the tomb only hours after it was discovered. We note this recent archaelogical discovery to illustrate just how real the people in the New Testament were. They existed and still exist, though they may be only bones (that is, until the resurrection).[19] Consequently, this disproves the claims of those liberal scholars who in the past, denied that Pilate was real because he was only mentioned in the New Testament, until the stone bearing his name was found in Tiberius in 1961!

The photo of Caiaphas' ossuary above, with his sixty-year-old bones entombed, and those on page 78 are shown courtesy of the Israel Antiquities Authority.

[18]"Tomb in Jerusalem May Be That of Priest Who Doomed Jesus," *New York Times*, Aug. 14, 1992, p. 10A, © 1992 by the New York Times Co. Reprinted by permission.

[19]Throughout the centuries, Jews have buried many thousands of their loved ones on the Mount of Olives, as they do today, because they believe those buried there will be the first to see the Messiah at the resurrection when He comes to the Mount of Olives mentioned in the Bible's book of Zechariah. In this situation, we remember Jesus' statement to Caiaphus at His trial referring to His Second Coming. Caiaphus asked: "...Art thou the Christ, the Son of the Blessed? And Jesus said, I am: and ye shall see the Son of man sitting on the right hand of power, and coming in the clouds of heaven" (Mark 14:61-62 KJV). Isn't it interesting that after Caiaphus' 2000-year-old bones were studied, analyzed and dated, they were "reburied on the Mount of Olives" by Israel's Ministry of Religious Affairs, as was "customary"? *Biblical Archaeology Review*, Vol. 18, Sept./Oct., © 1992, p. 35. Thus Caiaphus is in position to get a bird's-eye view of Jesus in the resurrection of Messianic judgment, just as he was promised at Jesus' trial by Jesus Himself. Interesting, to say the least!

A10 L THE NEW YORK TIMES INTERNATIONAL FRIDAY, AUGUST 14, 1992

Israeli Antiquities Authority

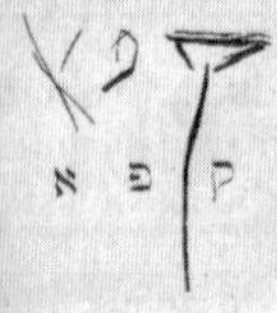

Two boxes of bones probably belonging to Caiaphas, the Jewish High Priest who tried Jesus, have been found. A translation of the Aramaic inscriptions, center, contains letters of Caiaphas's name.

Garo Nalbandian

Tomb in Jerusalem May Be That of Priest Who Doomed Jesus

Continued From Page A1

tion about the era in which Jesus lived. Such a pristine site is incredibly rare. We are so lucky."

The burial cave was in excellent condition, according to Zvi Greenhut, Jerusalem's chief archeologist, who began excavating the ruin within hours of its discovery. His article describing the contents of the cave, along with one by Ronny Reich of the Israeli Antiquities Authority discussing the significance of the Aramaic writing, will appear next week in the September-October issue of The Biblical Archeology Review.

12 Boxes in Cave

Twelve such ossuaries, limestone boxes in which the bones of the dead were often stored, were discovered in the cave, which had a pit in the floor making it just tall enough for mourners to stand in. As was the custom of the time, the bodies were almost certainly first laid out in a niche of a burial cave. After the flesh had decomposed, the bones were gathered and placed in the ossuary, possibly to await resurrection, Mr. Greenhut and others say.

Many boxes had been broken and their contents ransacked, ancient evidence, it appears, of grave robbers. But others seemed untouched and one in particular stood out in splendor. It was decorated with a rare, intricate pattern of rosettes and carried the inscription "Joseph, son of Caiaphas." Joseph was the nickname of the Jewish High Priest now known as Caiaphas, who ruled in Jerusalem from A.D. 18 to 36. Inside this uniquely elaborate ossuary were the bones of a 60-year-old man.

"The writing on the side is the equivalent of his nickname," Mr.

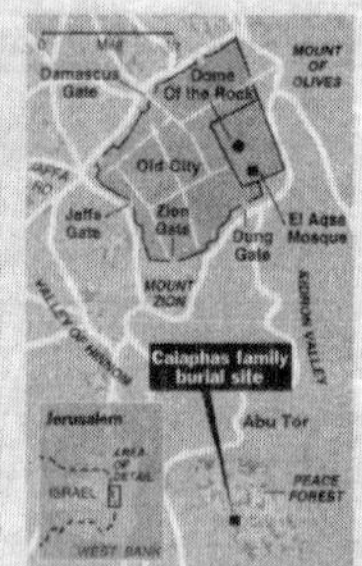

The New York Times

Workers accidentally opened burial cave in Jerusalem in 1990.

Reich said in an interview. He noted that the Aramaic writing on the wall and the ossuaries was the language used by working-class people of the time, cemetery workers, for example.

The New Testament provides the name Caiaphas only in Greek, but Flavius Josephus gives his full name as "Joseph who was called Caiaphas of the high priesthood." Josephus, the first-century Jewish historian, provides the only contemporary mention of Caiaphas outside the Talmud and the New Testament.

The writing on the ossuary is also the first contemporary evidence of the name in a Semitic language.

There is further evidence to place the burial site as first century: A bronze coin minted in A.D. 43, during the reign of Herod Agrippa I, was found in one of the ossuaries. It is the first known example of that pagan custom practiced at a Jewish burial site.

Caiaphas was one of the most important High Priests of Israel, largely, historians argue, because of his unusually close relationship with Pontius Pilate. It was during Caiaphas's reign, the Talmud says, that the Jewish high court, the Sanhedrin, was removed from the Temple Mount, thus weakening its power. And it was Caiaphas, according to the Gospels, who encouraged money changers and the sellers of animals to enter the main court of the Temple, strengthening his control of trade.

2,000 Years of Debate

Academic debates about Caiaphas's purpose or role in condemning Jesus and his desire to please the Romans have raged for nearly 2,000 years. Some historians contend that he played only a minor historical role; others, supported largely by the Gospels, suggest that without the decision by Caiaphas, Jesus would surely have lived.

In the Gospels, Jesus' expulsion of the vendors and money lenders from the temple is a central event: "It is written, My house shall be the house of prayer," Jesus is quoted as saying in Matthew 21:13. "But ye have made it a den of thieves."

This may have provided the crucial conflict between him and Caiaphas.

The denunciation of Jesus by Caiaphas may have been enough by itself to seal Jesus' fate, according to Mr. Chilton and others.

Although it was Pilate who put Jesus to death — and crucifixion was a uniquely Roman punishment — many historians have directed the blame toward Caiaphas, arguing in effect that the High Priest was well enough liked in Jerusalem to successfully protect Jesus from death.

"Caiaphas surely disliked Jesus," said David Flusser, a professor of religion at Hebrew University who specializes in the study of early Christianity. "He saw in Jesus a danger for the Romans, for the Jews and for his rule. I don't think it's hard to see why he did what he did. Perhaps it was not one of the noblest acts of history, but certainly it was understandable.

"Like many others, he was a man who by violence and condemnation retained his power."

Reproduction of *New York Times*[20] article on the archaeological discovery of Caiaphas' bones.

ANOTHER NEW TESTAMENT INDIVIDUAL'S OSSUARY IS FOUND—SIMON OF CYRENE

In the British newspaper *The Sunday Times* (March 31, 1996), in a news review article "The Tomb That Dare Not Speak Its Name", it was remarked by Tal Ham (who is Israel's foremost expert on early Christian and Jewish history) in relation to a recent tomb excavation, "The chance that this is the ossuary of the son of Simon of Cyrene, who carried Jesus's cross, is very likely." A following paragraph read "Clearly archaeology is making discoveries that show the New Testament to be accurate ... about certain individuals."

[20]*New York Times.* Article and map © used by permission. Photographs above of Caiaphas family member ossuary are courtesy of Chief Archaeologist Zvi Greenhut, of the Israel Antiquities Authority, Jerusalem, © used by permission.

This recently discovered stone bearing Pilate's name and title of governor was an embarrassment to those who denied his existence because he was "only mentioned in the New Testament."

THE PROPHECY OF A PRIEST DESPITE HIS BELIEF

The New Testament records a conversation between two chief priests about Jesus: "Therefore the chief priests and Pharisees convened a council, and were saying, 'What are we doing? For this man is performing many signs. If we let Him *go on* like this, all men will believe in Him, and **the Romans will come and take away both our place and our nation**.' But a certain one of them, Caiaphas, who was high priest that year, said to them, 'You know nothing at all, nor do you take into account that it is expedient for you that one man should die for the people, and that the whole nation should not perish.' Now this he did not say on his own initiative; but being high priest that year, he prophesied that Jesus was going to die for the nation, and not for the nation only, but that He might also gather together into one the children of God who are scattered abroad. So from that day on they planned together to kill Him" (John 11:47-53 NASB; bold mine).

TO THE SORROW OF MANY, JESUS WAS REJECTED—THE SECOND TIME AROUND HE WILL RULE WHEN HE TOPPLES THE ANTICHRIST AND HIS ESTABLISHMENT

From this we understand that the priests thought they were saving their nation, and their own selfish and wrongful rulership of it, by deciding that Jesus *must die.* In reality, Jesus was the only one who could have saved the nation! Had He been accepted, He would have risen up and overthrown the Roman Empire and its emperor, as predicted (Dan. 2:34-35, 45; Isa. 11:4).[21]

As a result of the way things actually happened, Jesus will accomplish this task at His Second Coming, when the empire is revived in its ten-nation form with the Antichrist as its new and future emperor. There is a difference between Daniel 7:23, which describes ancient Rome, and Daniel 7:24-25, which tells of a yet-to-be-built future ten-nation revived Rome (for details, see our chapter 22, "Rome Resurrected").

***

[21]The stone in Daniel's second chapter is the Messiah, who smashes the last rule of the future Gentile kingdom, represented head to toe by this statue. The rabbinical writings and Paul's letter to the Thessalonians in the New Testament identify this wicked individual, who is to be slain by the mouth of the Messiah, as the Armilus and Antichrist. The analogy concerning the stone "cut out without hands" indicates the divinity of the Messiah, in that He was not created but always existed.

HIS PEOPLE WOULD NOT ALLOW THE MESSIAH TO SAVE ISRAEL, THUS JESUS CRIES

Jesus was crying as He rode the donkey through the gates of Jerusalem, as predicted in Zechariah 9:9. His eyes were filled with tears (Luke 19:41) because He realized, as predicted by Daniel some six hundred years before, that His people, the Jews, would not allow Him to save them from the terrible onslaughts predicted in the Scripture. Read what Luke recorded in the New Testament concerning Israel and Rome: "...and when he [Jesus] approached, He saw the city and wept for it, saying, 'If you had known in this day, even you, the things which make for peace! But now they have been hidden from your eyes. For the days shall come upon you when your enemies will throw up a bank before you, and surround you, and hem you in on every side, and will level you to the ground and your children within you, and they will not leave in you one stone upon another, because you did not recognize the time of your visitation' " (Luke 19:41-44 NASB; [ ] mine).

RELIGIOUS HYPOCRISY FURTHER DELAYS THE PEACE—NO ACCEPTANCE, NO KING, THUS NO KINGDOM

Many have asked,[22] "If Jesus was the Messiah, why did He not overthrow the Romans and bring peace?" We think it is important to respect and appreciate the fact that the Messiah did not push His Messianic government on His people at a time when they were not ready to receive it! He was waiting for a national, royal and religious acceptance. This is why He did not set up the kingdom. The religious hierarchy that the people relied upon for spiritual guidance told them not to accept Him. Remember the words of Jesus to the Pharisees: "...woe unto you, scribes and Pharisees, hypocrites! for ye shut up the kingdom of heaven against men: for ye neither go in *yourselves,* neither suffer ye them that are entering to go in" (Matt. 23:13 KJV).

JESUS, LIKE JOSEPH, WAS BETRAYED FOR A PRICE AND MARKED FOR SACRIFICE

If you read the previously quoted Scripture again (John 11:47-53) you will discover its double meaning. Note the word "prophesied"

---

[22]For example, David Berger and Michael Wyschogrod, in their anti-missionary book directed at dissuading Jews who believe in Jesus from their faith, asked: "If Jesus was the Messiah, why have suffering and evil continued and even increased in the many centuries since His death?" David Berger and Michael Wyschogrod, *Jews and "Jewish Christianity,"* p. 19. Our answer is, because He was rejected. Jesus pointed this out in Matthew 23:39. We will discuss this later in further detail.

is used in verse 51, even though these men were plotting evil for personal gain. Similarly, Joseph made light of his brothers' plot against him when he said: "Fear not: for *am* I in the place of God? But as for you, ye thought evil against me; *but* God meant it unto good, to bring to pass, as *it is* this day, to save much people alive" (Gen. 50:19-20 KJV).

When the high priests handed Jesus over to the Gentiles, God, whose will was at work in spite of their plot, had His way. They reasoned that it would be better for one man to die than for the entire nation to perish.

While the priests thought they were relying on their own human "wisdom," in reality they were doing God's bidding. With the sacrificial death of one person, Jesus, not only would the Jewish nation be saved, but the entire world would be offered salvation as well. And guess who offered the sacrifice without knowing it? That's right, the same people God had appointed to offer all of the other blood-atoning precious sacrifices—the priests. Therefore, it was only because of disbelief that the priests went through with the sacrifice of Jesus. Yet, without realizing what they were doing, they played out the predicted scenario down to the last detail, including the price of betrayal. They paid Judas thirty shekels of silver for divulging the whereabouts of Jesus; the exact price Zechariah predicted five hundred years earlier.[23]

Hal Lindsey, in his book *The Promise*, points this out: "It's very unlikely that the priests who set the sum of 30 pieces of silver even faintly connected Zechariah's words with what they were doing. To them, no doubt, the figure of thirty shekels was meant to show their derision of Jesus since that was the official value of a slave (Exodus 21:32).

But to me, the greatest significance of what they did was that the money they gave to Judas for Jesus' betrayal was taken out of the Temple treasury which was where the money was kept to buy the sacrifices used in the Temple services. It was with these sacrifices that the priests made the blood offerings for the sins of the people. Little did they realize the implications of *this* 'sacrifice' which they were purchasing."[24]

***

---

[23]Zechariah 11:12-13 reads: "And I said unto them, if ye think good, give *me* my price; and if not, forbear. So they weighed for my price thirty *pieces* of silver. And the LORD said unto me, Cast it unto the potter: a goodly price that I was prised at of them. And I took the thirty *pieces* of silver, and cast them to the potter in the house of the LORD" (KJV).

[24]Hal Lindsey, *The Promise*. New York: Bantam Books, Inc., © 1984, p. 107, used by permission.

WHAT COULD HAVE BEEN BUT WAS NOT

As a result of this act, the physical redemption of Israel that was scheduled to occur during the First Advent has been postponed until Jesus is accepted by Israel as a nation. Then the physical nation will be delivered from a newly formed ten-nation Roman Empire, which will be headed by the false Messiah (Rev. 19; Isa. 11:4). This will be covered in our chapters 22, 23 and 26. Truly, had Jesus been received the first time around, a different scenario would have been realized. The priests, being sincere in their hearts and wanting the best for their nation, would have given Jesus their endorsement. As a result, the common people would have accepted Him as their Messiah King. This would have forced Rome to execute Him as a political usurper. Upon the resurrection of Jesus, Satan would have entered the Roman Caesar, of that day, and energized him as the Antichrist, only to be overthrown by Jesus.[25]

DESPITE THE PRIESTS' MISGIVINGS, MANY JEWS BEGIN TO BELIEVE, THUS THE MESSIAH CONSPIRACY IS CONTRIVED

Many Jewish people realized after the resurrection that Jesus was the Messiah. However, the religious leaders who rejected Him before, maintained their disbelief (Acts 5:17-19, 23, 27-32).[26] In fact, Jewish acceptance became so rampant that the rabbis became alarmed—so alarmed that they decided on a "Messiah Conspiracy"—a drastic step that began in the year 80 AD in a city called Yavne, where many of the rabbis who escaped death from the Romans gathered to reformulate Judaism for the Diaspora. In this city, they had to find a way to

---

[25]For a better understanding, see our chapter 22, "Rome Resurrected."

[26]"But the high priest rose up, along with all his associates (that is the sect of the Sadducees), and they were filled with jealousy; and they laid hands on the apostles, and put them in a public jail. But an angel of the Lord during the night opened the gates of the prison, and taking them out he said....'We found the prison house locked quite securely and the guards standing at the doors; but when we had opened up, we found no one inside'....And when they had brought them, they stood them before the Council. And the high priest questioned them, saying, 'We gave you strict orders not to continue teaching in this name, and behold, you have filled Jerusalem with your teaching, and intend to bring this man's blood upon us.' But Peter and the apostles answered and said, 'We must obey God rather than men. The God of our fathers raised up Jesus, whom you had put to death by hanging Him on a cross. He is the one whom God exalted to His right hand as a Prince and a Savior, to grant repentance to Israel, and forgiveness of sins. And we are witnesses of these things; and *so is* the Holy Spirit, whom God has given to those who obey Him' " (NASB).

separate the Messianic Jewish community from the non-traditional,[27] non-Messianic Jews (this will be discussed further in our chapter 6-7).

THOUGH JESUS WAS REJECTED AND CRUCIFIED, THESE VERY OCCURRENCES *FULFILLED MESSIANIC PROPHECIES,* WHICH ARE STILL DENIED BY THE RABBIS IN VAIN

In our forthcoming chapter, we will review some examples of the fulfilled prophecies which clearly acclaim Jesus as the suffering Messiah. I might add, I have met many who have said, "In the New Testament, Jesus never claimed to be the Messiah." Suffice it to say, these same people were dumbstruck after I showed them John 4:26, where Jesus emphatically makes the claim: "I who speak to you am *He* [Messiah]" (NASB; [ ] mine). For example, one questionable publication commented: "The missionaries claim that Jesus fulfilled all the prophecies pertaining to the Messiah. The truth, however, is that he did not fulfill even one of the important prophecies. All the things that he fulfilled were in reality quite trivial."[28]

This quote, from an anti-Christian missionary book entitled, *The Real Messiah*, represents the general Jewish view of most modern rabbis. We believe our chapter 5, "Which Prophecies Did Jesus Fulfill?" will show, once and for all, that this is not the case, thus proving such statements dishonest. In fact, we have devoted our chapter 5 to the many First Coming prophecies fulfilled by Jesus, such as: His birth at Bethlehem during a rare astronomical planetary conjunction (Micah 5:1-2; Num. 24:17); His miracles of healing (Isa. 35:5); His Messianic sufferings (Isa. 53); death by crucifixion (Ps. 22); and resurrection (Ps. 16; 21).[29]

Get ready for a roller coaster ride, as the next chapter will take you through the true meanings of prophecies about the Messiah stated by the ancients, as opposed to the modern rabbis' reinterpretation of these prophecies!

---

[27]Traditional Jews from this point on (once the Pharisees were eliminated as a sect), would honestly investigate prophecies concerning Messiah. The rabbis at Yavne created a non-traditional, radically new form of Judaism, which they used to separate Jews into two groups; those who believed and those who did not believe in Messiah. The ones who believed were thoroughly ostracized and accused of no longer being Jews! What insanity!

[28]Rabbi Aryeh Kaplan, *et al*, *The Real Messiah*. New York: National Conference of Synagogue Youth, 1976, p. 44. From Pinchas Stolper's chapter entitled, "Was Jesus the Messiah? Let's Examine the Facts."

[29]In our *Vol. II*, chapter 24, "Satanic Messianic Abortion—Jesus' Messianic Geneology," we cover Jesus' genealogy, as was prophesied in the Old Testament.

"As you know, the Jews were in Israel for around 1000 years before Jesus appeared. They had a definite concept of what the Messiah would be like—*there was a status quo regarding the nature of the Messiah.* The Christians appeared and introduced an entirely different[1] picture of what the Messiah would be like (son of God, God incarnate, born of virgin, two comings, etc.). Thus, *the Christians changed the status quo concept of the Messiah, and so the full burden of proof rests upon them.*"[2]

Samuel Levine, *You Take Jesus, I'll Take God*

"The ancient rabbinical views are nearly 180 degrees in opposition to those of modern rabbis. However, the vast majority of modern Jews have never been taught the ancient views. An examination of those ancient writings reveals that *the messianic 'status quo' spoken of by Samuel Levine never existed*...The messianic beliefs found in the Talmud and the Midrashim represent the majority opinions of the various rabbinical academies. As we examine these views we will see that the Christian beliefs regarding the birth, character, mission and destiny of the Messiah are in most cases identical to those of the ancient rabbinical ones. Therefore, the ancient rabbinical beliefs were not changed but embraced by the Christians. *The burden of proof, therefore, rests on modern rabbinical scholarship to explain their radically different view of the Messiah!*"[3]

Mark Eastman, M.D., *The Search for Messiah*

"This know also, that in the last days perilous times shall come. For men shall be lovers of their own selves, covetous, boasters...Ever learning, and never able to come to the knowledge of the truth."[4]

The New Testament, Paul's second letter to Timothy

5

WHICH PROPHECIES DID JESUS FULFILL?

In our review of prophecy concerning Messiah's First Advent to Earth, we ask, "Are the rabbis presently lying to their people by claiming that Jesus is not the Messiah?" We see them studying and learning, day in and day out, in their yeshivas,[5] deciphering cabbalistic

---

[1]The renowned Finnish scholar, Risto Santala, eloquently illustrates that Levine's accusation is untrue when he says: "...in connection with these 'twin' psalms [80, 110], we have had to speak about the Messiah as the Son of God, and even about the Zohar's 'mystery of the number three' which is associated with these psalms, it is worth pointing out that such ideas, usually associated with Christian theology, are also a natural part of **older Judaism**. They are **not,** in other words, **mere creations** of the Church." Risto Santala, *The Messiah in the Old Testament in the Light of Rabbinical Writings*, p. 21. [ ] and bold mine.

[2]Samuel Levine, *You Take Jesus, I'll Take God.* Los Angeles: Hamoroh Press, © 1980, p. 12, used by permission. Italics and underline mine.

[3]Mark Eastman, M.D., *The Search for the Messiah*, pp. 2-3. Italics and underline mine.

[4]II Timothy 3:1-2, 7 KJV.

[5]A *yeshiva* is a Jewish religious study school. In Hebrew, the word literally means "you sit," as a student does in class.

codes and obscure hypotheses on what the Scriptures may mean here or may teach there. However, it seems that concerning *the Messiah*, they are for the most part, ever "learning but not able to come to the knowledge of the truth" concerning the prophecies Jesus fulfilled, as we will discover in this chapter.

TO BE OR NOT TO BE? THAT IS THE *MESSIANIC* QUESTION

One of the most startling aspects of the Bible is that it predicts hundreds of events which **later** in history became facts, as they actually occurred before our very eyes. Many are forthcoming and will occur in our lifetime. These events are the most exciting and will be reviewed in the latter chapters of this book.

Here, in this section, we are going to read about some very interesting events which, against all odds, were predicted to take place in the life of the Messiah. These events, foretold hundred of years before the fact, took place 2000 years ago in the life of a man known throughout history as Jesus of Nazareth who, by no small coincidence, made the monumental claim of being the Jewish Messiah.

THE MESSIAH'S CONCEPTION WAS PREDICTED TO BE SUPERNATURAL DESPITE THE RABBIS' MISUNDERSTANDINGS

The first prediction,[6] of course, concerns His conception. Amazingly, it was foreseen by the prophet Isaiah nearly seven centuries beforehand. This Messianic personality was to be brought forth from the womb of a virgin, as foretold in the biblical writings. The prophet penned these words: "Therefore the Lord Himself will give you a sign: Behold, a virgin will be with child and bear a son, and she will call His name Immanuel" (Isa. 7:14 NASB).

Two chapters later, he elaborates: "For a child will be born to us, a son will be given to us; And the government will rest on His shoulders; And His name will be called Wonderful Counselor, Mighty God, Eternal Father, Prince of Peace. There will be no end to the increase of *His* government or of peace, On the throne of David and over his kingdom, To establish it and to uphold it with justice and

---

[6]For predictions prior to the birth of Jesus, such as His genealogies or Satan's attempts to destroy the Messianic line (the attempted corruption of pure human lineage by creating a half-demon race through the Nephalim in Genesis 6 at the time of Noah), see our *Vol. II*, chapter 24, "Sạtanic Messianic Abortion—Jesus' Messianic Genealogy." This chapter also documents the rabbis' attacks on His genealogy to be frivolous, even illustrating a passage from the Talmud which authenticates His required royal Davidic lineage.

righteousness From then on and forevermore. The zeal of the LORD of hosts will accomplish this" (Isa. 9:6-7 NASB).

Though these prophecies seem clear enough in both Hebrew and English, Rabbi Pinchas Stolper, in the book *The Real Messiah,* has the nerve to say: "Nowhere does the Bible predict that the Messiah will be born to a virgin. In fact, virgins never give birth anywhere in the Bible. The idea is to be found only in pagan mythology. To the Jewish mind, the very idea that G-d would plant a seed in a woman is unnecessary and unnatural. After all,—what is accomplished by this claim? What positive purpose does it serve?"[7]

OUR RABBI FRIEND'S QUESTION, SATISFACTORILY ANSWERED

In reply to the rabbi's question, which is a legitimate one, we have an answer. Remember, earlier we demonstrated that man was once in a state of innocence in the garden, in perfect harmony with God. At one point in time, he was tested and he failed. This failure marred the perfect image of God in which he was made (Gen. 1-3), because he exercised his free will, given by God, to rebel against God. This was his right within the realm of freedom of choice given by our creator. However, it resulted in our fall from His grace.

Once in the fallen state, he could only reproduce descendants who also inherited this newly acquired sin nature, which is imperfect and the seed of all violence and death on our planet. Human nature is guilty, and of course, in no way can a person redeem or pay for another's guilt—only their own—and that penalty is death and eternal judgment, according to the Bible. Thus, if the Messiah was to come into the world to be innocent and a guilt offering for all, He would have to bypass this *original sin nature* which has been passed down from generation to generation to all men since Adam, while still being a man. Thus, Genesis 3:15 said that the Messiah would be the "seed of woman," not man. So if God created the miracle of allowing His Spirit to genetically replicate an ovum within the womb of a virgin, Jesus bypasses inherited sin as required! There is your reason.

***

[7]Rabbi Aryeh Kaplan, *et al*, *The Real Messiah*, p. 45. From the chapter by Rabbi Pinchas Stolper entitled "Was Jesus the Messiah? Let's Examine the Facts."

THE DEEPER MEANING LIES IN THE QUESTION, "CAN GOD ACCOMPLISH THIS TO SERVE HIS PURPOSE?"

Now we have a true sinless redeemer without inherited original sin, not an impostor. Many have questioned how God can do such a thing. "No woman can have a child without a man, that story is a pagan fairytale for kids." Nope, sorry—God can do anything He wants. If He has told us in advance that He will, certainly we can expect He will follow through.

The same Jewish rabbinic challengers, with whom I have debated in the past, had no qualms about greater miracles. One example is the miraculous birth of Isaac. His mother was over ninety years old. Israel came from the miracle child Isaac, who was born of a mother the Bible said had already long lost the "manner of women" in relation to child-bearing (Gen. 18:11). As a matter of fact, the very name that God requested Sarah give the boy, Isaac, means "laughter" in Hebrew. Sarah laughed when she was told she was going to have a son. She did not believe God until her belly began to show and it became obvious!

The Orthodox Jews have no objection to God making Adam from dirt. The very Hebrew word *Adama* means "red mud." Where did man come from? Adam came from *Adama*, molded and breathed into by God. If Eve was made from the rib God removed from **Adam**, isn't that a little harder than creating a baby from a full-grown woman? Of course! So we remind those critics that the miracle of Jesus' supernatural birth is not out of the question and had a very specific important Messianic redemptive purpose and meaning! Any more questions, rabbi? We didn't think so!

THE ARGUMENT OF INTERPRETATION VERSUS MISINTERPRETATION

In Gerald Sigal's book, *The Jew and The Christian Missionary*, he argues that "Christians misinterpret and mistranslate" the Hebrew word for virgin. He says: "...but the Jews never believed, nor did their Holy Scriptures teach, that the Messiah would be born of a virgin....Seeking to substantiate the Christian-pagan concoction, the early Christians searched the Jewish Scriptures for justification of their claim of a virgin birth. They seized upon the word *almah*, which they mistranslated in an attempt to give credence to their spurious claim that the birth of Jesus was foretold by the Bible. This contention has made Judaism and Christianity forever incompatible...."[8]

However, nothing could be further from the truth. Moishe Rosen, founder and president of *Jews for Jesus*, answers the classical rabbinical objection in his book, *Y'shua, the Jewish Way to Say Jesus*. He tells us: "Matthew ties the virgin birth of Jesus to Isaiah 7:14, a passage that says, 'Therefore the LORD Himself shall give you a sign: behold, the young woman shall conceive and bear a son, and shall call his name Immanuel [God is with us].' The discussion focuses around whether the Hebrew term *almah*, employed here, should be properly translated 'young woman' or 'virgin'. Notice that the sign was to be not only the virgin birth, but the fact that God would be with us. You will not have to be a linguistics expert to understand the following points.

Usually, it is said that if Isaiah meant a virgin, he could have chosen another word, *bethulah*. But *bethulah*[9] could be used of a married woman who was not a virgin, as in Joel 1:8. *Almah,* however, can be shown to mean a virgin in its six other uses in the Hebrew Bible [Genesis 24:43; Exodus 2:8; Psalm 68:26; Proverbs 30:19; Song of Songs 1:3; 6:8.] and when Jewish scholars rendered the Scriptures into Greek during the third and second centuries B.C.E., they translated *almah* in Isaiah 7:14 by the Greek term *parthenos*, which could be understood only as meaning 'virgin.' That translation represented the best understanding of that day."[10]

"THE VIRGIN BIRTH IS JEWISH," SAYS PROFESSOR DAVID FLUSSER, PH.D.

In dealing with Isaiah's prophecy which predicted that the Messiah would be born of a virgin, many have said, as you have read, "This is a false Christian concept!" However, there is sufficient

---

[8]Gerald Sigal, *The Jew and the Christian Missionary: A Jewish Response to Missionary Christianity*. New York: KTAV Publishing House, Inc., © 1981, p. 20, used by permission.

[9]Gerald Sigal, in an attempt to evade the true meaning of this Hebrew word, writes: "According to some missionaries, proof that *betulah* does not necessarily always mean 'virgin' can also be derived from the fact that Genesis 24:16 uses the qualifying words 'neither had any man known her' in its description of Rebekah: 'And the maiden was very fair to look upon, a virgin [*betulah*], neither had any man known her.' Those who hold this view should read Rashi's commentary on this verse. Quoting from Bereshit Rabbah, Rashi states: 'A virgin': [This refers to] the place of virginity. 'Neither had any man known her.' [This refers to] an unnatural sexual act...." Ibid, p. 23. It goes without saying that Sigal's quotation of Rashi's commentary, "an unnatural act," proves nothing but desperation. In this passage, the Bible clearly pointed to a natural virginity.

[10]Moishe Rosen, *Y'shua, The Jewish Way to Say Jesus*. Chicago: Moody Bible Institute, © 1982, pp. 16-17, used by permission.

evidence to indicate that the Hebraically predicted manner in which the Messiah would enter the world, preceeding His thirty-three-year career, is genuinely Jewish.

Risto Santala documents a spectacular phenomenon found in the order of Hebrew letters in the original text of Isaiah 9:6 which relates to the Messiah. Let's investigate in Hebrew. The closed *mem* (*mem* is the Hebrew letter for "m") is always used in the Bible at the end of a word. The only exception, where it is placed in the middle of a word, is in a prophecy in Isaiah which indicates the increase of the Messiah's government. That word לְםַרְבֵּה (*lemarbe*) meaning "to increase" should read לְמַרְבֵּה with the double underlined second letter (reading from right to left) of the word open, not closed, as you see in the first example which appears in the Hebrew Bible.

In order to understand the spectacular meaning of the closed *mem*, Santala consults one of the ancient rabbinical commentaries, he points out that: "*The zohar*[11] *on the other hand decides that the closed 'm' refers to the fact that the Messiah will be born from a 'closed womb'*. Perhaps such things were in Professor David Flusser's mind when, on a visit to Finland in the summer of 1984, he was asked for his views on the New Testament's most difficult questions. Of the resurrection of Jesus he stated categorically: 'It is a historical fact... I was not there at the tomb myself, of course, but the resurrected Jesus did manifest himself to his disciples'....And the Virgin Birth? 'Nor does that go against Jewish thinking.' "[12]

---

[11]Israeli professor Yehudah Liebes mentions this closed *mem* in connection with the ancient rabbinical literature and Christological combined speculation. Delving a good bit deeper than Santala, he writes: "...the idea of the Messiah who splits open the closed womb of the Shekhina signified by the closed letter *Mem* developed in later Kabbalistic thinking—an idea which had its beginnings in the Zohar, in which Midrashic, Kabbalistic and Christological speculations were combined....This connection could easily have been made by interpreting the word *bara* in Genesis 1:1 according to its Aramaic rendering—son—especially if they utilized the statement of the rabbis discussed previously: 'In the beginning' (i.e., the word *bereshith*) is also a statement (by which God created the world).' This interpretation would have carried even more weight had Christians added to it the Talmudic passage which designated the closed final *mem* as a 'closed statement' along with their own understanding of this letter as representing the womb of the virgin, as mentioned above....parallel to the Sifra *di-Tseniutha's* 'half a statement'—born of a closed womb, albeit the Christological connection between the closed *mem* as the womb and closed statement....After a lengthy discourse on these ideas, Neckam substantiates them by interpreting the various combinations of the Hebrew letters found in the word *bereshith* (in the beginning): *Ab* (father), *bar* (son), *esh* (fire = Holy Spirit) and *yesh* (existence). He even interprets the final letter *Tav* as signifying the cross, among other things." Yehudah Liebes, "Jewish Thought and Spirituality, Christian Influences in the Zohar," *Immanuel*, Winter 1983/84, © 1983, pp. 55-57, used by permission.

[12]Risto Santala, *The Messiah in the Old Testament in the Light of Rabbinical Writings*, p. 194.

THE HEBREW SIGN, WHICH PROVES THE MESSIAH IS DIVINE, DAZZLES MOST RABBIS

Richard Wurmbrand, an eighty-five-year-old Jew I had the great pleasure of meeting at the 1994 Messiah Conference in Pennsylvania, is a Holocaust survivor who was persecuted for being both a Jew and a believer in Jesus. Wurmbrand explained the significance of the *mem* in his book, *Christ on the Jewish Road*: "I must add that, generally speaking, I have found many rabbis very ill-prepared to answer our arguments. I once talked to one of the Berlin rabbis, who had fled to Rumania. I showed him the text in the ninth chapter of Isaiah, which foretells the coming into the world of the Messiah, declaring: 'For unto us a child is born, unto us a son is given: and the government shall be upon his shoulder: and his name shall be called Wonderful, Counsellor, 'The mighty God, The everlasting Father, The Prince of Peace. Of the increase of his government and peace there shall be no end...' (Isa. 9:6-7). This passage contains an orthographical curiosity. In Hebrew, the letter M is written at the beginning and in the middle of a word with the sign, מ, and only at the end of a word as a closed square. This orthography is rigidly adhered to throughout the Old Testament, except in one particular case. In this verse, in the word *lemarbe* (increase), a final M, ם, appears in the middle of the word. This orthographical mistake has never been corrected. A final M, ם, which should occur only at the end of the word is written in the middle of one.

"I asked the rabbi if he could explain this, but he could give me no answer. I then told him of the Kabalistic tradition, that Isaiah put a ם in the middle of the word, in order to show the reader who was destined to understand it that the Divine Child of whom this prophecy speaks would be born of the closed womb of a virgin."[13]

OUR PERSONAL EXPERIENCE WITH THE MESSIAH'S FINAL *MEM* AND A RABBI IN JERUSALEM

This closed *mem* has undoubtedly caused trouble for more than a few. Since this is the only place in the Bible where a closed *mem* appears in the middle of a word, ancient rabbis have seen it as a secret divine symbol concerning the Messiah being born of a woman with a closed womb (a virgin).

A *mem sofi* or "final" *mem*, by Hebrew linguistic rule must always appear in words ending in "m." Only an **open** *mem* is allowed to be used in the middle or beginning of words. Most modern rabbis are unaware of the existence and meaning of this with regard to the ancient Hebrew mystical belief in the prophecy of the Messiah, until it is pointed out to them.

---

[13] Richard Wurmbrand, *Christ on the Jewish Road*, pp. 105-106.

When I was visiting in Jerusalem in 1988, I attended one of Samuel Golding's[14] so-called anti-missionary meetings in order to punch a few holes in his arguments against believers. I brought up the fact that the closed *mem* was considered of Messianic significance in connection with the supernatural conception of the Messiah within ancient rabbinical folklore. Golding laughingly denied this and even tried to say that this *mem*, the Hebrew letter in question, was a *samech* (one of the Hebrew letters for "s").

A *samech*, ס, resembles a *mem* in its closed form but, of course, is not exactly the same. As you can see, the corners are rounded. In trying to disprove me, he asked "his rabbi" in the back of the room, who, to the immense embarrassment of Golding, confirmed that it was a *mem.*

Golding has criticized Christians in his book, *A Guide to the Misled,* for not knowing or taking time to study Hebrew. However, in this case, it turns out that he should take time to study Hebrew, doesn't it?[15]

Johann Kepler explains his model of planetary orbit to Rudolf II, as we will see the Messiah's birth was not only foreshadowed in Hebrew letters but also within the science of astronomy.

---

[14]Samuel Golding's true name, before it was changed, was Frank Waddington. His lifelong story of having been an evangelical preacher who found out he was a Jew in the 1960's, is false. He was converted in Turkey. In the 1980's, he had the title *Rabbi* Shmuel Golding on his books. He was forced to remove it when the authorities found out he never was, nor is he now, a rabbi. We have copies in our file of both editions of this book entitled, *A Guide to the Misled.*

[15]I have this conversation in Golding's classroom recorded on videotape. If anyone is interested, they may write this author. Abba Hillel Silver says: "Already in Talmudic times this word with its closed *Mem* was regarded as holding Messianic meaning." Abba Hillel Silver, D.D., *A History of Messianic Speculation in Israel.* New York: The MacMillan Company, © 1927, p. 97. Talmudic times can be as early as 200 BC.

ORIGINAL HEBREW TEXT WRITTEN 740 BC

כִּי־יֶלֶד יֻלַּד־לָנוּ בֵּן נִתַּן־לָנוּ וַתְּהִי הַמִּשְׂרָה עַל־שִׁכְמוֹ וַיִּקְרָא שְׁמוֹ פֶּלֶא יוֹעֵץ אֵל גִּבּוֹר
אֲבִיעַד שַׂר־שָׁלוֹם׃ לְםַרְבֵּה הַמִּשְׂרָה וּלְשָׁלוֹם אֵין־קֵץ עַל־כִּסֵּא דָוִד וְעַל־מַמְלַכְתּוֹ
לְהָכִין אֹתָהּ וּלְסַעֲדָהּ בְּמִשְׁפָּט וּבִצְדָקָה מֵעַתָּה וְעַד־עוֹלָם קִנְאַת יְהוָה צְבָאוֹת תַּעֲשֶׂה־זֹּאת׃

ישעיה ט:ה-ו

OLD TESTAMENT SCRIPTURE TRANSLATION

"For a child will be born to us, a son will be given to us; And the government will rest on His shoulders; And His name will be called Wonderful Counselor, Mighty God, Eternal Father, Prince of Peace. There will be no end to the increase of *His* government or of peace, On the throne of David and over his kingdom, To establish it and to uphold it with justice and righteousness From then on and forevermore. The zeal of the LORD of hosts will accomplish this."

Isaiah 9:6-7 NASB

ANCIENT RABBINICAL COMMENTARY

"The prophet said to the house of David, For unto us a child is born, to us a son is given, and he shall receive the law upon him to keep it, and his name is called from eternity, Wonderful, Counsellor, Mighty God, Continuing for ever, the Messiah; for peace shall be multiplied upon us in his days."[16]

Targum to Isaiah 9:6

NEW TESTAMENT RECORDED 63 AND 37 AD

"And behold, you will conceive in your womb, and bear a son, and you shall name Him Jesus. He will be great, and will be called the Son of the Most High; and the Lord God will give Him the throne of His father David; and He will reign over the house of Jacob forever; and His kingdom will have no end." Jesus himself also said: " 'Verily I say unto you, That ye which have followed me, in the regeneration when the Son of man shall sit in the throne of his glory, ye also shall sit upon twelve thrones, judging the twelve tribes of Israel'....'For I say unto you, Ye shall not see me henceforth, till ye shall say, Blessed *is* he that cometh in the name of the Lord.' "

Luke 1:31-33 NASB; Matthew 19:28; 23:39 KJV

MODERN RABBINIC COMMENT/REFUTATION

"Jesus was *never called these names*; i.e., Wonderful, Prince of Peace, etc., even in the New Testament, and yet the verse says explicitly that the person referred to will be *called* those names. Furthermore, in desperation, the Christians say that Isaiah 9:6 refers to Isaiah 7:14. The absurdity of 7:14 referring to Jesus has been discussed before....How can this refer to Jesus—his government never began, let alone had any peace! If someone tells you that it refers to the second coming—well, by now, I think that you should be able to seek the weakness of that. Thus, this verse refers to someone, but surely not to Jesus...." In footnote 18, regarding names, Levine says: "...many Jewish commentaries translate the verse like this: 'And the Wonderful Counseler, the Mighty God, the Everlasting Father will call him (the boy that is born) the Prince of Peace.' Thus, the verse does not say that the Prince of Peace will be another name for God."

***You Take Jesus, I'll Take God,* by Samuel Levine, p. 54; © 1980. [ ] mine**

[16]Rev. B. Pick, Ph.D., *Old Testament Passages Messianically Applied by the Ancient Synagogue*, published in the compilation *Hebraica, A Quarterly Journal in the Interests of Semitic Study*, Vol. III, p. 35.

AUTHOR'S COMMENT—EVANGELICAL CHRISTIAN POSITION

With all due respect to Mr. Levine, we believe that if he is going to criticize Isaiah's Messianic prophecy using the New Testament, he should take the time to fully inform himself. Though Jesus may not have been called all these Messianic titles in the First Coming in His day, He is projected to be just who Isaiah proclaims in our near future, as the angel Gabriel in the New Testament book of Luke affirms to His mother, Miriam.[17] Revelation 22:6 assures us that the Messianic Kingdom of Jesus will soon take place. Apparently, Levine knows this prophecy in question is about the Second Coming; otherwise, why would he have mentioned it? I assure you there is no "weakness" in that. For details, see our chapters 26-30 on the Second Coming. Jesus points out that His Messianic Kingdom was postponed because He was rejected. It will only begin when He is accepted by the Jews. Lastly, Levine mentions that Jewish commentaries retranslate this passage. We have not seen them and he does not go to the trouble to name them, if they exist. Even if they do, that would prove our point that certain rabbis covered up the Messianic prophecies. The Jewish Targum to Isaiah of ages past quoted above clearly refers this passage to the Messiah whom Jesus claimed to be (Luke 24:42; John 4:26, 14:10).

Philip Moore

A STAR IS BORN, IN MESSIAH, TO HERALD THE COMING OF THE PROMISED ONE

The prophecy of Numbers 24:17, which speaks of a star in connection with the Messiah, has a two-fold meaning. Throughout the ages, the rabbinical sages have written about a star (tri-planetary conjunction) appearing in the sky in the zone of the Pisces constellation near the time of the Messiah's birth. Dr. Alfred Edersheim, a renowned nineteenth century Bible scholar,[18] confirms this point when he refers to a famous rabbi, Abarbanel, and his commentary. In his book, *The Life and Times of Jesus the Messiah,* Edersheim comments: "In his Commentary on Daniel that Rabbi [Abarbanel] laid it down, that the conjunction of Jupiter and Saturn in the constellation Pisces betokened not only the most important events, but referred especially to Israel....He further argues that, as that conjunction had taken place three years before the birth of Moses, which heralded the first deliverance of Israel, so it would also precede the birth of the Messiah, and the final deliverance of Israel."[19]

***

[17]This is the original Hebrew name of Jesus' mother, whom we know as Mary in English.

[18]Dr. Alfred Edersheim was a brilliant Jew who realized that Jesus is the Jewish Messiah.

[19]Alfred Edersheim, *The Life and Times of Jesus the Messiah,* p. 211. [ ] mine.

A PERSONAL TRANSLATION OF ABARBANEL'S INSIGHT, HERETOFORE UNTRANSLATED, JUST FOR YOU

While studying Isaac Newton's handwritten theological manuscripts at the Hebrew University in Jerusalem, this author made the aquaintance of "Dr. X," a high-ranking Hebrew University official who translated the passage. He later became apprehensive when he discovered my intent to publish this text and requested that I not mention his name under any circumstances.

"Dr. X" was the only person able to properly translate this due to his unique knowledge of astronomy and the technical terms involved therein. His interesting English translation reads as follows: "...because since the beginning of Creation until now, there have been only two conjunctions of Jupiter and Saturn in Pisces.[20] The first occurred in the year 2365 [A.M.][21] when Israel was in Egypt, 3 years before the birth of Moses, that is, 83 years before his prophecy and miracles, the Exodus of Israel from Egypt and the giving of the Torah....Since both of them are conjunctions of the same type, namely grand conjunctions in the sign of Pisces, the second one will be like the first—the one that accompanied the Exodus from Egypt—in every way. Therefore, since the first conjunction indicated Israel's Exodus[22] from exile to freedom, from slavery to redemption, and from lowliness to greatness and kingdom, and also wonders and miracles, the birth of Moses, and revenge from enemies—so also the second Israelite conjunction indicates for Israel prophecy, relief, salvation, and redemption, and there can be no doubt, the time of the birth of the man of God, our

---

20"Jupiter, Saturn and the Sun are all lined up in the sign of Pisces." This footnote is "Dr. X's" explanation to the layperson of the astronomical conjunction of which Abarbanel is speaking.

21A.M. stands for *anno mundi*— "from creation" (Latin: "in the year of the world").

22We note that Franklyn M. Branley, in his 1990 book *The Christmas Sky*, has commented concerning Pisces, Moses, the Exodus, conjunctions and the Jewish scholars: "Records of the planets tell us that there were three planets in the evening skies of the fall...and that these planets moved closer together as the months went by. The three planets were Mars, Jupiter, and Saturn. Saturn, in the constellation of Pisces, the fish....The Magi knew about the planets. They were astrologers, the astronomers of that time and place. They studied the planets, and they knew of their positions and their motions. They also knew that these three planets were in a constellation where centuries earlier, according to Jewish scholars, planets had appeared around the time of the birth of Moses. Moses was the prophet who was to lead the Israelites out of Egypt to the eastern borders of the Promised Land. Pisces was therefore considered the constellation of the Jews. The appearance of the planets in Pisces may have been a sign to the Magi that an event of great importance was occurring in the land of the Jews. The Star of Bethlehem might have been these three planets that had moved close together. They may have been the guide that the Wise Men followed to find the manger where Jesus was born." Franklyn M. Branley and Stephen Foster, *The Christmas Sky*. New York: Harper Collins, © 1966, 1990, pp. 43-44.

righteous Messiah, exalted from Abraham and higher than Moses and all according to its ways requires the conjunction to renew...."[23]

RABBI LIEVA OF PRAGUE AND THE BOOK OF REVELATION IN THE NEW TESTAMENT AGREE—THE MESSIAH IS ALSO THE STAR

Other rabbis have said, not only would there be a star in the sky at the time of the Messiah's Coming, but, in fact, the star *is* the Messiah. Rabbi Lieva of Prague has said: "A STAR shall proceed out of Jacob, and there shall come a SCEPTRE in Israel. The KING MESSIAH is here spoken of as a STAR."[24]

The Targum Onkelos, a recognized ancient rabbinical commentary, makes this claim: "I see him, but not now; I behold him, but he is not near; when a king shall arise out of Jacob and be anointed the Messiah out of Israel. He shall slay the princes of Moab and reign over all mankind."[25]

Revelation, the last book of the New Testament, says that Jesus is in fact the star. Jesus says: "I, Jesus...am the root and the offspring of David, the bright morning star" (Rev. 22:16 NASB).

Johann Kepler, founder of Exact Modern Science, established Jesus' birth through astronomical calculation.

---

[23]Quoted from "Dr. X's" handwritten translation for this author during his 1989 study at the Hebrew University.

[24]F. Kenton Beshore, D.D., LL.D., Ph.D., *"The Messiah" of the Targums, Talmuds, and Rabbinical Writers.* Los Angeles, CA: World Bible Society, © 1971, chart 4, used by permission. Available through World Bible Society, Box 1, Los Angeles, CA, USA 90053.

[25]Samson H. Levey, *The Messiah: An Aramaic Interpretation, The Messianic Exegesis of the Targum.* Jerusalem: Hebrew Union College/Jewish Institute of Religion, © 1974, p. 21, used by permission.

ORIGINAL HEBREW TEXT WRITTEN 1452 BC

אֶרְאֶ֙נּוּ֙ וְלֹ֣א עַתָּ֔ה אֲשׁוּרֶ֖נּוּ וְלֹ֣א קָר֑וֹב דָּרַ֨ךְ כּוֹכָ֜ב מִֽיַּעֲקֹ֗ב וְקָ֥ם שֵׁ֙בֶט֙ מִיִּשְׂרָאֵ֔ל וּמָחַץ֙ פַּאֲתֵ֣י

מוֹאָ֔ב וְקַרְקַ֖ר כָּל־בְּנֵי־שֵֽׁת׃   במדבר כד:יז

OLD TESTAMENT SCRIPTURE TRANSLATION

"I see him, but not now; I behold him, but not near; A star shall come forth from Jacob, And a scepter shall rise from Israel, And shall crush through the forehead of Moab, And tear down all the sons of Sheth."

Numbers 24:17 NASB

ANCIENT RABBINICAL COMMENTARY

"...a star will shoot out from the East, and at his head will be a staff of fire like a spear, and the Gentiles will say, 'This star is ours.' But it will not be so, but rather of Israel, as it is said, A *star has stepped out from Jacob* (Num. 24:17)."[26]

The Week of the Messiah Prayer

"Our rabbis have a tradition that in the week in which Messiah will be born, there will be a bright star in the east, which is the star of the Messiah."[27]

Pesikta Sotarta, Fol. 58, col. 1

NEW TESTAMENT RECORDED 37 AD

"Now after Jesus was born in Bethlehem of Judea in the days of Herod the king, behold, magi from the east arrived in Jerusalem, saying, 'Where is He who has been born King of the Jews? For we saw His star in the east, and have come to worship Him.' "   **Matthew 2:1-2 NASB**

MODERN RABBINIC COMMENT/REFUTATION

"...a whole mythology—mythology—was created around the persona of Jesus...and what you read about in the New Testament...from the three wise men[28] and all that kind of stuff—all **bubbameis**—all mythology. Beautiful, powerful stuff that obviously affects a billion souls in this world, but it's mythology."[29]

Rabbi Shalom Lewis, 1994

AUTHOR'S COMMENT—EVANGELICAL CHRISTIAN POSITION

Rabbi Lewis' statement is careless, inflammatory and without foundation. Marco Polo recorded an interview with the descendants of those who remembered the wise men setting forth from Saveh, Persia! Modern scientific fact documents that astronomy confirms the appearance of this star (constellation and tri-planetary conjunction) at the time of Jesus' birth, as the scientist Johanas Kepler discovered. Dr. Edersheim notes: "Kepler, who was led to the discovery by observing a similar

---

[26]George Wesley Buchanan, *Revelation and Redemption.* Dillsboro, NC: Western North Carolina Press, © 1978, p. 409, used by permission. Buchanan's source was *The Prayer, Secrets, and Mysteries of Rabbi Shimon ben Yohai.*

[27]Rev. B. Pick, Ph.D., *Old Testament Passages Messianically Applied by the Ancient Synagogue,* published in the compilation *Hebraica, A Quarterly Journal in the Interests of Semitic Study,* Vol. II, p. 129.

[28]The "wise men" are the magi mentioned in the book of Matthew. A *bubbameis* is known in Yiddish as a "grandmother's tale." Though Rabbi Lewis referred to the wise men/magi as mythology in 1994, in December 1968, *Sky & Telescope* magazine noted: "Marco Polo reported passing through a small Persian village called Saveh, whose people told him that it was the town from which the Magi set forth...." Roger W. Sinnott, "Thoughts on the Star of Bethlehem," *Sky & Telescope,* Dec. 1968, p. 386. The New Testament mentions magi but not three. In our opinion, the rabbi should check out the text before he criticizes it.

[29]Quoted from a personal tape of the 1994 seminar entitled, "Jesus: The Jewish Perspective," conducted at the Atlanta Jewish Community Center by Rabbi Shalom Lewis.

conjunction in 1603-4, also noticed, that when the three planets came into conjunction, a new, extraordinary, brilliant, and peculiarly colored evanescent star was visible between Jupiter and Saturn, and he suggested that a similar star had appeared under the same circumstances in the conjunction preceding the Nativity [birth of Jesus]."[30] **Philip Moore**

THE SCIENTIST, KEPLER, TRACKS MARS, JUPITER AND SATURN OVER BETHLEHEM AT THE MESSIANIC BIRTH DATE

Alfred Edersheim has collected some startling facts surrounding the birth of Jesus and the Star of Bethlehem (star in the original biblical language refers to constellations, planets and celestial phenomena),[31] which we read about in the New Testament and ancient rabbinical writings. Dr. Edersheim asks, "Did such a Star, then, really appear in the East...." His answer was: "Astronomically speaking...there can be no doubt that the most remarkable conjunction of the planets—that of Jupiter and Saturn in the constellation of Pisces, which occurs only once in 800 years—*did* take place no less than three times in the year 747 A.U.C.....(in May, October and December). This conjunction is admitted by all astronomers. It was not only extraordinary, but presented the most brilliant spectacle in the night-sky, such as could not but attract the attention of all who watched the sidereal heavens, but especially of those who busied themselves with astrology. In the year following, that is, in 748 A.U.C., another planet, Mars, joined this conjunction. The merit of first discovering these facts...belongs to the great *Kepler*, who, accordingly, placed the Nativity of Christ....Kepler, who was led to the discovery by observing a similar conjunction in 1603-4, also noticed, that when the three planets came into conjunction, a new, extraordinary, brilliant, and peculiarly colored evanescent star was visible between Jupiter and Saturn, and he suggested that a similar star had appeared under the same circumstances in the conjunction preceding the Nativity [birth of Messiah]."[32]

THE ANCIENT CHINESE AND THE ASTRONOMER GOLDSCHMIDT AGREE

Edersheim also points out: "In the astronomical tables of the Chinese...the appearance of an evanescent star was noted.....Moreover,

---

[30]Alfred Edersheim, *The Life and Times of Jesus the Messiah*, p. 213. [ ] mine.

[31]Dr. Edersheim documents: "*Schleusner* has abundantly proved that the word αστηρ, though primarily meaning a *star*, is also used for constellations, meteors, and comets—in short, has the widest application: 'omne designare, quod aliquem splendorem habet et emittit' (Lex. in N.T., t. i. pp. 390, 391)." Ibid, p. 204, footnote 2.

[32]Ibid, pp. 212-213. [ ] mine.

it has been astronomically ascertained [by the astronomer, Dr. Goldschmidt....],[33] that such a sidereal apparition would be visible to those who left Jerusalem, and that it would point—almost seem to go before—in the direction of, and stand over, Bethlehem."[34]

THE INTEREST OF THE ZOROASTRIAN PERSIAN MAGI IN THE MESSIAH'S STAR WAS INSPIRED BY THEIR LEADER, A STUDENT OF DANIEL

Why would magi,[35] who were, without a doubt, astrologers (Dan. 5:15),[36] be interested in the King of the Jews and the appearance of God's prophetic constellation at the designated time? We all know that astrology is strictly forbidden by the Bible (Deut. 18:10-12; Isa. 47:13). Interestingly, Matthew neither condones nor condemns this activity, but merely records the astrologers' inquiries, questions and answers, just as the book of Job in the Old Testament records Satan's conversation with God (Job 1:6-9, 12; 2:1-7).

Matthew, in recording the historic visit of these men, reaffirms both the existence of the star (constellation and tri-planetary conjunction) and the notion that it was a rabbinical tradition that such a

---

[33]Ibid, p. 213. Edersheim's footnote 1 inserted into text with [ ].

[34]Ibid.

[35]The dictionary defines magi as: "**1.** the three wise men who paid homage to the infant Jesus. Matt. 2:1-12. **2.** the class of Zoroastrian priests in ancient Media and Persia, reputed to possess supernatural powers." *The Random House College Dictionary*, 1975 Edition, p. 804.

[36]Joseph Good enlightens us regarding magi: "The Greek 'magi' is taken from the Babylonian word 'mag,' which has a number of meanings. It is true that the word does mean 'astrologer;' however, this is not its only usage. The same word is used for scientist, counselor, or scholar." Joseph Good, *Rosh HaShanah and the Messianic Kingdom to Come, A Messianic Jewish Interpretation of the Feast of Trumpets*. Port Arthur, TX: Hatikva Ministries, © 1989, p. 168. Available through Hatikva Ministries, POB 3125, Port Arthur, TX, USA 77643-3125. Rabbi Good is available at: Tel. (409) 724-7601. *The New Scofield Reference Bible* footnotes Matthew 2:1: "...there came **wise men** from the east to Jerusalem" with the following note: "(2:1) 'Wise men' is from the Greek *magoi*, a Persian word for men expert in the study of the stars. There is no evidence that these magi were only three in number or that they were kings. Their interest aroused by the star that signalized Christ's birth, they journeyed to Judæa to seek the newborn King of the Jews. They arrived some months after His birth. When Herod sent them to Bethlehem, the star reappeared and led them to the Christ child." *The New Scofield Reference Bible*, p. 993. Daniel identified the meaning of "wise men" in the Bible as he recorded his audience with King Belté-shaz'zar: "Then was Daniel brought in before the king. *And* the king spake and said unto Daniel, *Art* thou that Daniel, which *art* of the children of the captivity of Judah, whom the king my father brought out of Jewry? I have even heard of thee, that the spirit of the gods *is* in thee, and *that* light and understanding and excellent wisdom is found in thee. And now the wise *men*, the astrologers, have been brought in before me, that they should read this writing, and make known unto me the interpretation thereof" (Dan. 5:13-15 KJV).

phenomenon would signify the Coming of the Messiah. The fact that the constellation existed at that time was subsequently confirmed by the famous sixteenth century astronomer Kepler. Dr. Edersheim sheds light on why astrologers would have been interested in Jesus, when he states: "...from about 120 B.C. to the sixth century of our era, the kings of *Yemen* professed the Jewish faith. For if, on the one hand, it seems unlikely, that Eastern magi would spontaneously connect a celestial phenomenon with the birth of a Jewish king, evidence will, on the other hand, be presented to connect the meaning attached to the appearance of 'the star' at that particular time with Jewish expectancy of the Messiah."[37]

Thus, we can see why the magi were concerned about Jesus! They were apparently "half-converted" to Judaism, enough to realize the expected Messiah's arrival but not enough to have foregone the forbidden practice of astrology. Reverend Dr. D. James Kennedy has noted: "Tradition tells us that Zoroaster, the Persian religious leader, was a student of Daniel when he was in Babylon. He learned from him that a star would appear in the constellation Coma when that **One** whom it foretold was to be born."[38]

The wise men might have, in a sense, professed Judaism, but were not necessarily accepted as orthodox practitioners of the pure faith. We have apostates or phonies today, which the New Testament predicted (Matt. 24:11; Mark 13:22; I John 4:1). They say they believe in Jesus, while they deny both His deity and His ultimate power to save.[39] We know these are not wise men, don't we?

KEPLER AND SANTALA EMPHASIZE THAT GOD USED THE STARS TO TELL EVERYONE, EVEN THE BABYLONIANS, THAT THE MESSIAH HAD COME

Interestingly enough, the astronomer Kepler has commented on why the magi were intrigued with the Star of Bethlehem: "I do not doubt but that God would have condescended to cater to the credulity of the Chaldeans."[40]

My friend, Risto Santala, a Finnish Bible scholar, has recently pointed out: "The astral phenomemon which took place at that time

---

[37]Alfred Edersheim, *The Life and Times of Jesus the Messiah*, pp. 203-204.

[38]Dr. D. James Kennedy, "The Gospel in the Stars," p. 7. See our *Vol. II*, chapter 30, "The Gospel in the Stars," where we reproduce Dr. Kennedy's interesting sermon nearly in its entirety. Bold mine.

[39]See our *Vol. II*, chapter 4, "Cults, the Occult and the New Age."

[40]John Mosley, *The Christmas Star*. Los Angeles: Griffith Observatory, © 1987, p. 39, used by permission. Available through Griffith Observatory, 2800 East Observatory Road, Los Angeles, CA, USA 90027.

was, however, with great probability, interpreted Messianically....*The symbolic relevance of the portent was clear to the people of that time.* The constellations of the zodiac were generally identified with different nations, Pisces, for example, being considered the patron constellation of...Palestine, and the revealer of the End Times. Saturn was associated with Palestine in Babylonian astrology, whereas Jupiter was the royal planet, foreshadowing a political Golden Age. Thus, when Jupiter conjoined with Saturn in Pisces it was obvious that the Ruler of the End Times had been born in Palestine....This *coniunctio magna* [Grand Conjunction] lasted for nine months. In the first phase, from the 12th of April to the beginning of June, the planets drew gradually nearer to each other. A new conjunction began in the middle of July, fusing into a great brilliant star for ten days in the first weeks of October, perhaps at its brightest on the 3rd, the Great Day of Atonement. The third phase, in which the two planets receded from each other, began in the middle of November and lasted until the beginning of December. After this, in the beginning of January, Mars, the enemy of the Jews, drew near to both. The devout mind may well have seen this too as a portent of the persecution of the baby Jesus."[41]

Again, we emphasize that we are not endorsing astrology in any way, we are simply illustrating ancient Jewish Messianic beliefs and expectations as related by Matthew's account of the Star of Bethlehem. Further information on the stars and the Gospel of Jesus is included in our *Vol. II*, chapter 30, "The Gospel in the Stars," a sermon from Reverend D. James Kennedy. In this sermon, Kennedy expounds upon the true reason for the position of the stars in the night sky of that era; as they reveal God's plan and the Coming of His Messiah to redeem us. Astrologers have grossly perverted the sky's signs and the symbols God gave us (Gen. 1:14-16).

SKY & TELESCOPE CORROBORATES BABYLONIAN/JEWISH INTERCHANGE OF IDEAS, THE CONJUNCTIONS, AND THE VERY TOWN MARCO POLO FOUND

Is there any evidence or mention of the wise men of Persia and their quest for the Messiah, outside of the New Testament and the Hebrew Scriptures? Do historians note a Babylonian search for the Jewish king using His star? We are glad you asked! The reputable *Sky & Telescope* magazine reveals: "Marco Polo reported passing through a small Persian village called Saveh, whose people told him that it was the town from which the Magi set forth....If the Magi sighted a 'star,' why would they conclude that it marked the birth of a new king of the Jews? Babylonian and Jewish populations had been intermingled for

[41]Risto Santala, *The Messiah in the New Testament in the Light of Rabbinical Writings*, pp. 83-84. [ ] mine.

years, so some interchange of ideas was inevitable....Babylonians conversant with Old Testament prophecies might have been greatly impressed by planetary conjunctions....Observing the long-awaited sign, the Wise Men would, perhaps, know to go to Bethlehem by the prophecy in *Micah* 5:2 (referred to in *Matthew* 2:5)....These two conjunctions of the brightest planets could thus fit the story of the Star of Bethlehem....a highly unusual astronomical event in its own right."[42]

This illustation represents the constellation Pisces and the planets Mars, Saturn and Jupiter. The famed Rabbi Abarbanel said this planetary conjunction, which occurred at the birth of Moses, "must renew" at the Coming of the Messiah. This astral phenomenon is the "Star of Bethlehem," which occurred at the Nativity of Jesus, as confirmed by the astronomer Johann Kepler. Illustration by Cathy Taibbi.

---

[42]Roger W. Sinnott, "Thoughts on the Star of Bethlehem," *Sky & Telescope*, Dec. 1968, p. 386.

If you desire to see the fascinating beauty of this constellation/conjunction recorded in Matthew 2:16, it is now possible to do so. Thanks to modern science, you can go back in time, so to speak, by visiting the planetarium. Above is a photograph of an astral reproduction of the 2000-year-old constellation of Pisces with the three planets, Mars, Saturn and Jupiter. This photograph was taken at the Fernbank Science Center planetarium in Atlanta, Georgia.

THE ONE WHOSE BIRTH WAS SIGNALED BY THE STAR WAS TO BE BORN THE *SON OF GOD!*

More than once, I have been told by the rabbis that the Christian idea of a son of God is neither Jewish nor orthodox. One Jewish man even told me that he felt Islam was a closer kin to Judaism than Christianity. This is hard to understand, as an Arab in Israel once told me, "There is no 'son of God,' " with a look of intense hate on his face.

I showed another Jewish person and a rabbi the Jewish Midrash Tehelim which says: "When the time of the advent of Messiah will be near, then the blessed God will say to him: With him I will make a new covenant. And this is the time when he will acknowledge him as his son, saying 'This day have I begotten thee.' "

One of them hung his head in embarassment and shame and the other evaded the topic by pleading another appointment. Before I showed them the Midrash, I asked what they thought of Psalm 2:7, which says: "I will surely tell of the decree of the LORD: He said to Me, 'Thou art My Son....' " (NASB).

One said, "I'll need to see the original Hebrew"; the other said, "I'll check it out, but more likely, it's a Christian interpretation of a mistranslation." I then pulled out the ancient Jewish commentary Midrash Tehelim, which is highly respected among Orthodox Jews. From our encounter, it became quite clear to me that the rabbis are not happy about the Messiah being the Son of God, especially when they see it illustrated in their own commentaries.

THE MESSIAH IS THE SON OF GOD, MUCH TO THE RABBIS' DISMAY

Grant Jeffrey has also written and commented on his personal experience with the rabbis over this explosive issue. He relates: "In my discussions with orthodox rabbis and rabbinical students in Jerusalem, the conversation would often focus on Old Testament prophecies....The problem is that they have rejected Jesus partly because of their belief that the Messiah is not the Son of God but rather an anointed Messiah-King. In their understanding of the monotheism of the Old Testament, they believe that God could not have a 'son.' Despite the many verses in the Old Testament that refer to the concept of the Trinity, they see this as a contradiction....However, when I asked what would happen to Israel and the world to come when their Messiah-King became an old man and died, their reaction was pure astonishment. I explained, if they believed that the Messiah will not be the Son of God as Christians believe, but only an anointed human like King David, then He must die after seventy or so years. None of them had ever considered the fact of the death of their coming Messiah-

King. The tremendous expectations placed upon the Messianic Age could never be realized in just one lifetime of a normal, human king in Israel. Both the biblical prophecies and the Jewish teaching about the coming Messiah demand that the Messiah be more than just a man and that he must live forever to complete the transformation of all things in the Age of Redemption....Their understanding of Messiah's role is closer to Christians' understanding than they know."[43]

"The Presentation of Jesus in the Temple,"
as depicted by Rembrandt in 1631.

---

[43]Grant R. Jeffrey, *Heaven...The Last Frontier*. New York: Bantam Books, © 1990, pp. 93-94, used by permission.

ORIGINAL HEBREW TEXT WRITTEN 1000 BC

אֲסַפְּרָה אֶל חֹק יְהוָה אָמַר אֵלַי בְּנִי אַתָּה אֲנִי הַיּוֹם יְלִדְתִּיךָ׃

תהלים ב:ז

OLD TESTAMENT SCRIPTURE TRANSLATION

"I will surely tell of the decree of the LORD: He said to Me, 'Thou art My Son, Today I have begotten Thee.' " **Psalms 2:7 NASB**

ANCIENT RABBINICAL COMMENTARY

"When the time of the advent of Messiah will be near, then the blessed God will say to him: With him I will make a new covenant. And this is the time when he will acknowledge him as his son, saying 'This day have I begotten thee.' "[44]

Midrash Tehelim, fol. 3, col. 4

NEW TESTAMENT RECORDED 63 AD

"And the angel said to her, 'Do not be afraid, Mary; for you have found favor with God. And behold, you will conceive in your womb, and bear a son, and you shall name Him Jesus. He will be great, and will be called the Son of the Most High; and the Lord God will give Him the throne of His father David; and He will reign over the house of Jacob forever; and His kingdom will have no end.' And Mary said to the angel, 'How can this be, since I am a virgin?' And the angel answered and said to her, 'The Holy Spirit will come upon you, and the power of the Most High will overshadow you; and for that reason the holy offspring shall be called the Son of God.' " **Luke 1:30-35 NASB**

MODERN RABBINIC COMMENT/REFUTATION

"In the Christian missionary search for biblical proof of the belief in Jesus as the Son of God, proof has often been found where none exists by violating the integrity of the plain meaning of many scriptural passages. Prominent among these is Psalm 2:7, wherein it is stated: 'The Lord said to me: 'You are My son, this day I have begotten you'....Christian missionaries may argue that the references to sonship are typologies pointing to the existence of an actual divine sonship embodied in Jesus. But this argument is obviously based on purely subjective reasoning, with no facts from the Hebrew Scriptures to give it support. Psalm 2:7 could not at all refer to Jesus." ***The Jew and the Christian Missionary*,**

by Gerald Sigal, p. 87; © 1981

"...any talk of the Messiah as being the 'son of G-d' is totally unacceptable. In no place do the Prophets say that he will be anything more than a remarkable leader and teacher." ***The Real Messiah*,**

by Rabbi Aryeh Kaplan, *et al*, p. 14; 1976

AUTHOR'S COMMENT—EVANGELICAL CHRISTIAN POSITION

Obviously, Mr. Sigal, with the guidance of Rabbi Bronznick, is wrong in his claim about Christian subjective reasoning and his statement that "Psalms 2:7 could not refer to Jesus." The Jewish commentary called the Midrash on Psalms clearly refers to this passage as Messianic! We suggest that Mr. Sigal and his rabbi brush up on their Midrashim. With all due respect, I must comment that Psalms 2:7 does refer to Jesus and that the statement by Mr. Sigal—representative of modern rabbinic indifference and reluctance to admit Jesus' Messiahship—that the Christian

---

[44]Rev. B. Pick, Ph.D., *Old Testament Passages Messianically Applied by the Ancient Synagogue*, published in the compilation *Hebraica, A Quarterly Journal in the Interests of Semitic Study*, Vol. II, p. 129.

interpretation violates the integrity of the plain meaning of Psalms 2:7, is false. We know that this statement is false because, contrary to his claim, the ancient Hebrew tradition, as documented in the Midrash Tehelim, affirms that Psalms 2:7 was counted among the prophecies the Messiah was to fulfill in the Hebrew Scriptures. Rabbi Aryeh Kaplan maintains (in his chapter, "Why Aren't We Christians?" from *The Real Messiah*) that the Messiah will not be God's son and that any talk of such things is out of the question and out of line with the Jewish prophets. However, as you have read, the prophet King David expressly wrote in the volume of Psalms (which is part of the Christian Old Testament) that He would be just that, *God's son*. While some may try to claim that this is a Christian interpretation, we refer them to the Jewish commentary on this verse, which says God will acknowledge Him as His son, while quoting, "This day I have begotten thee," from Psalms itself.

Philip Moore

ARCHAEOLOGICAL DISCOVERY

Mark Eastman, M.D., and Reverend Chuck Smith, in their book, *The Search for Messiah*, comment on the newly released Dead Sea Scroll fragment 4Q246, and give indisputable proof that the idea of the Son of God is an authentic ancient Jewish belief! They tell us: "The discovery and translation of the Dead Sea Scrolls has been a tremendous boost to our understanding of the beliefs and culture of the Jewish people during the First Century C.E. In the Fall of 1991 the remaining unpublished portions of the Dead Sea Scrolls were released to libraries around the world. A number of new fragments have come forth which have provided remarkable new insights regarding the messianic beliefs of the Qumran Jews during that period. The people of the Qumran community, the apparent writers of the scrolls, have been described as 'religious end time zealots' by some scholars, and as mainstream Jews by others. One thing is certain, they wrote extensively about the Messiah. Therefore, if the Messiah was believed to be the Son of God by ancient Jews, then it should not be surprising to find that belief expressed in the writings of the Dead Sea Scrolls. In fact, that is exactly what we find....[In] A portion of the Dead Sea Scrolls, called the 'Son of God' fragment 4Q246, we see an astonishing reference to a supernatural Messiah who is called the Son of God: *'he shall be called the Son of the God; they will call him the Son of the Most High...He will judge the earth in righteousness...and every nation will bow down to him...with (God's) help he will make war, and...[God] will give all the peoples into his power.'* [45] The passage is filled with undeniable messianic images. The writer of this text believed that the Messiah would 'judge the earth in righteousness' and that the nations 'will bow down to him.' The text speaks not of multiple Messiah figures but of a *single* individual. This Messiah figure is triumphant and exalted and specially referred to as the 'Son of God...Son of the Most High!' His strength, accomplishments and character clearly reveal that he is not an ordinary man, but he was believed by these people to be a supernatural being. To find a messianic figure being called 'the Son of God', the 'Son of the Most High', by the Jewish believers in Qumran, is astonishing and conclusive! To them, the Messiah would be the Son of God!"[46]

---

[45]The italicized information is from an article by Michael Wise and James Tabor, *Biblical Archaeology Review*, Nov/Dec 1992.

[46]Mark Eastman, M.D., and Chuck Smith, *The Search For Messiah*, pp. 67-68. First [ ] mine.

MICAH'S PREDICTED BIRTHPLACE FOR GOD'S SON, WHO WOULD BE THE *MESSIAH*

Concerning the birthplace of Jesus, there is a beautiful and specific prediction, perhaps one of the most precise prophecies in the Bible, pinpointing the birth as occurring in the little town of Bethlehem. The prophecy states: "Now gather thyself in troops, O daughter of troops: he hath laid siege against us: they shall smite the judge of Israel with a rod upon the cheek. But thou, Beth-lehem Ephra-tah, *though* thou be little among the thousands of Judah, *yet* out of thee shall he come forth unto me *that is* to be ruler in Israel; whose goings forth *have been* from of old, from everlasting" (Micah 5:1-2 KJV).

One thing we should remember is that the Bible foretells very little about the birth of Jesus in comparison to the amount of details it reveals about His death for us, which was the reason for His birth!

The Scriptures foretell His humble birth in this small town, and the New Testament, over seven hundred years later, records the Star and shepherds appearing there at, and shortly after, His birth.

We learn from history that all Roman citizens and others were required to return to the town of their birth for the newly enacted tax census. Jesus' parents, Joseph and Mary, were both born in Bethlehem, and therefore, returned for the census. During their time there, Jesus was born!

MISCONCEPTIONS IN LATER TRADITION CONTRASTED WITH BIBLICAL FACT ABOUT THE BIRTH DATE

Christmas is not mentioned anywhere in the Old or New Testament of the Bible. It originated several hundred years after the birth of Jesus and is, in reality, of pagan origin.[47]

The date of December twenty-fifth was set in the fourth century[48] and, according to Sir Isaac Newton's calculations, is

[47]The Reverend Hislop reminds us: "That Christmas was originally a Pagan festival, is beyond all doubt. The time of the year, and the ceremonies with which it is still celebrated, prove its origin. In Egypt, the son of Isis, the Egyptian title for the queen of heaven, was born at this very time, 'about the time of the winter solstice.' The very name by which Christmas is popularly known among ourselves—Yule day—proves at once its Pagan and Babylonian origin. 'Yule' is the Chaldee name for an 'infant' or 'little child;' and as the 25th of December was called by our Pagan Anglo-Saxon ancestors, 'Yule-day,' or the 'Child's day,' and the night that preceded it, 'Mother-Night,' long before they came in contact with Christianity, that sufficiently proves its real character." Rev. Alexander Hislop, *The Two Babylons*. England: A&C Black, Ltd., © 1916, pp.

inaccurate for the time of Jesus' birth! The greatest scientist ever to live, according to all the authorities we have studied,[49] reveals: "...Luke tells us that when in circumcising Christ & purifying the virgin, they had performed all things according to the law (which was within forty days), they returned into Galilee to their own city Nazareth...Matthew acquaints us that they went first into Egypt & upon the death of Herod went from Egypt into Galilee to the city Nazareth whence...the time between the birth of Christ & death of Herod was very short....The Magi came to worship Christ while his parents stayed at Bethlehem in an inn & by consequence soon after his birth & Herod slew the children as soon as he found himself mocked of the wise men....And since Luke saith that when Christ was twelve years old he disputed in the temple at the Passover and only that he was about 30 years old when he was baptised...the death of Herod & a year and three-quarters before the vulgar era, will answer perfectly well to the Scriptures & to Josephus. Then might shepherds be able to watch their flocks all night in the fields, & then might the Jews go conveniently out of all Judea to Jerusalem....if any man had rather suppose that Christ was born at Christmas preceding; I might reply that Christmas was instituted in the room of a heathen festival & so is of no authority for determining the time: but I had rather say that the difference of three months in time is a nicety not worth disputing about."[50]

Frank Manuel, commenting on Newton's calculation, says that Newton wrote and calculated "through a meticulous historical reconstruction of the times,"[51] that Christ was not born on Christmas Day, which was a "pagan festival."[52] By the way, Newton would have had nothing to lose by accepting the idea of Christmas, if it were true, for Newton himself was born on December 25, 1642.

"CHRISTMAS" IS A NICE IDEA, BUT IS IT JEWISH OR BIBLICAL?

The Bible details the true Hebraic traditions and circumstances surrounding the birth of Jesus, which further identify Him as the Messiah. Although we may enjoy the Christmas tree with which many

---

[48]*The World Book Encyclopedia* says: "In A.D. 354, Bishop Liberius of Rome ordered the people to celebrate on December 25. He probably chose this date because the people of Rome already observed it as the Feast of Saturn, celebrating the birthday of the sun." *The World Book Encyclopedia*, 1970 Edition, p. 416.

[49]In regard to Sir Isaac Newton's unsurpassed scientific credentials and reputation, see our footnote 2 in chapter 3, "Two Messiahs?"

[50]*Yahuda Manuscript 25:20-21.*

[51]Frank Manuel, *The Religion of Isaac Newton*, p. 62.

[52]Ibid.

of us were raised, the biblical prophet Jeremiah says: "For the customs of the people *are* vain: for *one* cutteth a tree out of the forest, the work of the hands of the workman, with the axe. They deck it with silver and with gold; they fasten it with nails and with hammers, that it move not" (Jer. 10:3-4 KJV).

We born-again seekers of truth, including Messianic Jewish believers, may enjoy these traditions but we should not get too attached to them. The important thing is not celebrating His birth, giving gifts[53] or hanging balls and lights on a dead tree, or celebrating the twenty-fifth day of a Roman Julian calendar,[54] but rather realizing that He was born for us, to give His life for us[55] and to one day return as King to give us His Kingdom, where we will live forever in happiness with each other.

Neither Jesus nor the Old Testament ever told us to celebrate His birth. Rather Jesus told Pilate: "... I am a King [i.e., the Messiah]. To this end was I **born**...." (John 18:37 KJV; [ ] mine).

Jesus Himself asks that we celebrate the Last Supper or Passover in the form of communion (Luke 22:19-20) to signify His death until He returns, in remembrance of Him as our Passover lamb. Remember the New Testament words of Jesus: "...this do in remembrance of me" (Luke 22:19 KJV). Paul wrote: "...Christ our passover is sacrificed for us: Therefore let **us keep** the feast...." (I Cor. 5:7-8 KJV).

THE TRUE SEQUENCE OF EVENTS SURROUNDING THE BIRTH OF JESUS ACCORDING TO JEWISH TRADITION, THE NEW TESTAMENT, JOSEPHUS AND AN ECLIPSE!

Jesus was born during a shortage of hotel rooms in Jerusalem (Luke 2:7). He was taken to Egypt for protection during the time when King Herod was murdering male children (Matt. 2:13-15). He was brought back to Jerusalem after Herod died but in time to be dedicated in the Temple. According to Jewish law, this time of dedication had to be within forty days of birth (Lev. 12:2-4). In the New Testament, Luke speaks specifically of this: "And when eight days were completed before His circumcision, His name was *then* called Jesus,

---

[53]The wise men gave gifts to Jesus, not to each other.

[54]Jesus celebrated Hanukkah, "the feast of the dedication" (John 10:22 KJV), also known as the Festival of Lights, at about this time of year. Could this day also have a Messianic meaning, since Jesus is the "light of the world" as John recorded? Isaiah wrote: "The people who walk in darkness Will see a great light; Those who live in a dark land, The light will shine on them....I will also make You a light of the nations...." (Isa. 9:2; 49:6 NASB). As you will see in our next paragraph, December twenty-fifth is an absolute impossibility for the birth of the Messiah according to the historian, Josephus, and critical date computations found in the New Testament.

[55]"For even the Son of man came not to be ministered unto, but to minister, and to give his life a ransom for many" (Mark 10:45 KJV).

the name given by the angel before He was conceived in the womb. And when the days for their purification according to the law of Moses were completed, they brought Him up to Jerusalem to present Him to the Lord (as it is **written** in the **Law of the Lord**, 'EVERY *first-born* MALE THAT OPENS THE WOMB SHALL BE CALLED HOLY TO THE LORD'), and to offer a sacrifice according to what was said in the Law of the Lord...." (Luke 2:21-24 NASB). Thus, if we can establish the time of Herod's death (alive at Jesus' birth [Matt. 2] and dead before His dedication), we will discover the season of the birth of the Messiah. The Jewish historian, Josephus, based on an eclipse, put Herod's death in September.[56] Thus, Jesus had to have been born before mid-October in order to be taken to Egypt and brought back in time to be dedicated at the Temple. This would place the birth of Jesus during the Jewish feasts of Yom Kippur and Sukkot, which occur within five days of each other.

During these holy days, Jerusalem would overflow, creating a situation in which there would not be enough room for Mary and Joseph in the inn (Luke 2). What an appropriate time for His birth; Yom Kippur in Hebrew means "the day of atonement," which He said He was born to be (Mark 10:45).

The very word manger, in which He was born, in Hebrew means "booth" or *Sukkah* (Gen. 33:17; Luke 2:7). The feast of Sukkot ("booths") symbolizes that we leave our comfortable places and dwell in humble abodes. Today, when the Jews celebrate Sukkot in Israel, untold numbers of booths are constructed in their yards. Many Orthodox Israeli Jews not only eat in them but also sleep in them all week.

Jesus left Heaven to **tabernacle** among men (Heb. 9:11; Rev. 21:3). According to the prophet Zechariah (14:16-21), all nations will observe this feast during the millenium. This pre-mid-October date confirms Kepler's calculation of three planets coming together in a grand conjunction over Bethlehem to form the Star of Bethlehem.

In our opinion, if the world wants to celebrate "Christmas," which is not mentioned anywhere in the New Testament, they should celebrate these feasts with Israel and remember that the Jewish Messiah Jesus was born in Bethlehem during these feasts.[57] In Hebrew, *bait-lehem* means "house of bread." Jesus once said, "I am the bread of life" (John 6:48 NASB).

The Reverend Alexander Hislop notes: "Gill, in his *Commentary* on Luke ii. 8, has the following....'....From whence it appears that

---

[56]Joseph Good, *Rosh HaShanah and the Messianic Kingdom to Come, A Messianic Jewish Interpretation of the Feast of Trumpets*, pp. 172-173.

[57]For a fuller, more in-depth study of the true time of the birth of Jesus, using the Jewish priestly courses in force during first century Judaism as documented in the New Testament, see Luke 1:5, 8. Also see appendix 1, Ibid.

Christ must be born before the middle of October, since the first rain was not yet come'.....there is no doubt that it could not be later than there stated, according to the testimony of Maimonides, whose aquaintance with all that concerns Jewish customs is well known.' "[58]

The view from a tower in the town of Bethlehem where the most famous king in history was born. Upon Jesus' return, we will experience an ultimate kingdom over all the nations ruled from Israel by the only one who loves us all (Micah 5:2). In the Bible, Zechariah and David teach us of this time: "And I will cut off the chariot from Ephraim, and the horse from Jerusalem, and the battle bow shall be cut off: and he shall speak peace unto the heathen: and his dominion *shall be* from sea *even* to sea, and from the river *even* to the ends of the earth" (Zech. 9:10 KJV). And: "He shall have dominion also from sea to sea, and from the river unto the ends of the earth. They that dwell in the wilderness shall bow before him; and his enemies shall lick the dust. The kings of Tarshish and of the isles shall bring presents: the kings of Sheba and Seba shall offer gifts....His name shall endure for ever: his name shall be continued as long as the sun: and *men* shall be blessed in him: all nations shall call him blessed" (King David/Ps. 72:8-10, 17 KJV).

---

[58]Rev. Alexander Hislop, *The Two Babylons*, pp. 91-92.

STARTLING REVELATIONS ABOUT CHRISTMAS AND THE BIRTH OF JESUS

Ralph Woodrow sheds light on facts everyone should know about the birth of Jesus and its relation to Christmas. "The early Christians commemorated the *death* of Christ (1 Cor. 11:26), not his birth. *The Catholic Encyclopedia* says, 'Christmas was not among the earliest festivals of the Church. Irenaeus and Tertullian omit it from their lists of feasts.' Later, when churches at various places did begin celebrating the birthday of Christ, there was much difference of opinion as to the correct date. It was not until the latter part of the fourth century before the Roman church began observing December 25th. Yet, by the fifth century, it was ordering that the birth of Christ be forever observed on this date, even though this was the day of the old Roman feast of the birth of Sol, one of the names of the sun-god!

Says Frazer, 'The largest pagan religious cult which fostered the celebration of December 25 as a holiday throughout the Roman and Greek worlds was the pagan sun worship—Mithraism...This winter festival was called 'the Nativity'—the 'Nativity of the SUN'.' Was this pagan festival responsible for the December 25 day being chosen by the Roman Church? We will let *The Catholic Encyclopedia* answer. 'The well-known *solar* feast of Natalis Invicti'—the Nativity of the Unconquered Sun—'celebrated on 25 December, *has a strong claim on the responsibility for our December date*'!"[59]

The Bible tells us not to add to God's commandments, which, of course, include holy days and celebrations: "What thing soever I command you, observe to do it: thou shalt not add thereto, nor diminish from it" (Deut. 12:32 KJV).

JESUS WAS BORN *BEFORE* CHRISTMAS, BECAUSE THE SHEPHERDS BRING IN THEIR SHEEP BEFORE DECEMBER

Apparently, early American Christians realized the gravity of this statement in the fifth book of the Bible, because they enacted laws forbidding the observance of Christmas. "In Massachusetts, the following became law in 1659. *Whosoever shall be found observing Christmas, either by forbearing of labor, feasting, or any other way, every such person shall pay as a fine five shillings to the county.*"[60]

---

[59]Ralph Woodrow, *Babylon Mystery Religion*. Riverside, CA: Ralph Woodrow Evangelistic Association, Inc., © 1966, p. 151, used by permission.
[60]John Mosley, *The Christmas Star*, p. 69.

Regarding the birth of Jesus in Bethlehem, the New Testament reads: "...there were in the same country shepherds abiding in the field...." (Luke 2:8 KJV).

Shepherds, who still pasture their sheep in Bethlehem (as I have personally observed, having lived in Israel during eight Christmas seasons), have never been seen herding sheep in December, the middle of winter. A somewhat popular Christian commentator, Adam Clark, has written: "...our Lord was not born on the 25th of December, when no flocks were out in the fields...On this very ground the nativity in December should be given up."[61]

The only part of *The Real Messiah*, an anti-missionary book we have quoted, that we do not differ with, are the lines by Pinchas Stolper which point out: "What reason can Christians give for not celebrating Rosh Hashana and Yom Kippur which are clearly spelled out in the Torah?....Christmas and Easter are not mentioned in either the Jewish Bible or the Christian 'New Testament,'—these festivals are pagan in origin, adapted for Christian use. But Pesach, Sukkos and Shavuos are clearly spoken of in the Bible. On top of which, Jesus nowhere requests that the Biblical festivals no longer be observed."[62]

Finally, Stolper got something right. As the apostle Paul noted earlier: "...let us keep the Feast...." (I Cor. 5:8 KJV). What feast? The Jewish feasts, emphasizing their Messianic fulfillments and meanings. It is my prayer that believers who read these lines will get Zola Levitt's books on the feasts and start keeping them in their churches. What a testimony to our Jewish friends this would be. No doubt, many would find the Lord through this! And that's what it's all **about**, isn't it?

BETHLEHEM WAS THE PLACE WHERE THE HEBREW PROPHET, MICAH, PREDICTED DEITY WOULD TAKE UP HUMAN RESIDENCE

Back to the future Bethlehem of Micah's prophecy. One of the interesting points about this prophecy of Bethlehem, which is often overlooked, is the fact that it points to the pre-existence of the Messiah: "...whose goings forth *have been* from of old, from **everlasting**" (Micah 5:2 KJV; bold mine).

---

[61]Ralph Woodrow, *Babylon Mystery Religion*, p. 149. Woodrow's source was *Clark's Commentary*, Vol. 5, p. 370, "Luke.".

[62]Rabbi Aryeh Kaplan, *et al*, *The Real Messiah*, pp. 47-48. Quoted from Rabbi Pinchas Stolper's chapter entitled "Was Jesus the Messiah? Let's Examine the Facts." *Pesach*, *Sukkos* and *Shavuos* are Hebraic English renderings of Passover and the other Jewish feasts.

Since only God is everlasting, this prophecy indirectly affirms the deity of Jesus. Thus, the Messiah is foretold as being God—something no modern day rabbi wants to admit!

In connection with this prophecy made by Micah some seven hundred years prior to the birth of Jesus and its fulfillment in the New Testament, we find in the Gospel of Matthew, the first of the twenty-seven books of the New Testament (covenant), the prophet Micah quoted verbatim! The quote is made in reference to Herod's inquisition of the Hebrew scribes concerning the birthplace of the promised Jewish Messiah. The scribes' answer, as quoted by the apostle Matthew, was recorded as follows: "And they [the scribes] said unto him [Herod], In Bethlehem of Judæa: for thus it is written by the prophet, And thou Bethlehem, *in* the land of Juda, art not the least among the princes of Juda: for out of thee shall come a Governor, that shall rule my people Israel" (Matt. 2:5-6 KJV; [ ] mine).

HEROD'S PREDICTED HOLOCAUST AND JESUS' ESCAPE—*VERIFIED* BY ANCIENT EGYPTIAN RECORDS

As a result of their answer, King Herod murdered all male children—two years old and younger—to prevent the arrival of the Jewish king and preclude a challenge to his own rule (Matt. 2:16; predicted in Jer. 31:15).[63]

---

[63]Gerald Sigal, in his anti-missionary treatise, *The Jew and the Christian Missionary*, comments on Matthew's quotation of Jeremiah's words. We believe the words of Jeremiah had both a prophetic and historic meaning. Sigal states: "Eager to show fulfillment of prophecy in the life of Jesus, Matthew refers to Jeremiah 31:15 as a proof-text that Rachel wept for the allegedly slain children of Bethlehem....However, an examination of this quotation within its biblical context plainly shows us that it does not refer to slain, but rather to captive children....This is the substance of which New Testament fulfillment of prophecy is made. Let the believer beware." Gerald Sigal, *The Jew and the Christian Missionary*, pp. 189-190. However, Norman Golb, an unsurpassed scholar holding the Rosenberger Chair in Jewish History and Civilization at the University of Chicago, demonstrates the ignorance of statements like Sigal's in his book published fourteen years after Sigal's. This method of relating past events to present events was not unique to the writers of the New Testament. It was a literary communication device used by Jews who wrote the Dead Sea Scrolls *before* the New Testament was penned. Golb points out: "While nothing like the scriptural commentaries, i.e., the *pesharim*, appears in the New Testament, the same general understanding of the nature of the Jewish scriptures and use of its prophecies is found both there and in the scrolls. The way that New Testament texts—especially the Gospels—use those scriptures had for a long time been a puzzle to scholars....A famous example is Matthew 2.18, where, in connection with the birth of Jesus and the flight to Egypt, Herod's 'slaughter of the innocents' is said to fulfill Jeremiah 31.15, 'A voice was heard in Ramah...Rachel weeping for her children; she refused to be comforted, because they are no more.' In the context of Jeremiah, the prophecy refers uniquely to the

It was only after God warned Joseph in a dream that he took his stepson to Egypt, thus avoiding Jesus' death in the massacre. Egyptian records,[64] even today, reveal "the holy family of Jesus" spent a short time there during the Bethlehem peril.

My friend Rachel (left) weeps at Rachel's tomb in Bethlehem. The New Testament quotes Rachel's lament for her children, as a foresight to Herod's holocaust.

Babylonian Exile. This practice has led more than one reader of the Gospels to accuse the evangelists of misappropriation or even deliberate deception. In the scrolls, however, we find that the same procedure was followed by the biblical interpreters who authored the *pesharim*. The authors of these texts drew passages from the prophets out of their contexts and applied them to events in the immediate past or future—events that they believed had eschatological significance. Thus, the New Testament authors were using a method of argumentation and interpretation that would have been quite familiar to at least a portion of their Jewish audience. The early midrashists of rabbinic Judaism would themselves build upon this method, which must have been popular not only among members of the *Yahad* movement but also among many Jewish authors in intertestamental times...." Norman Golb, *Who Wrote the Dead Sea Scrolls? The Search for the Secret of Qumran*. New York: reprinted with the permission of Scribner, a Division of Simon & Schuster, © 1995, pp. 374-375.

[64]During my 1987 tour of Israel, Petra and Sinai, Egypt, the Egyptian tour guide on the bus quoted several historical Egyptian records and writings which referred to what she called "the holy family of Jesus" being in Egypt at this designated period. I was rather impressed that she volunteered such detailed information with such empathy, since she was a Moslem. However, someone told me that in keeping with historical accuracy, a tour guide is more or less bound by professional honor to tell the truth concerning documented historical events.

ORIGINAL HEBREW TEXT WRITTEN 710 BC

וְאַתָּ֞ה בֵּֽית־לֶ֣חֶם אֶפְרָ֗תָה צָעִיר֙ לִֽהְיוֹת֙ בְּאַלְפֵ֣י יְהוּדָ֔ה מִמְּךָ֙ לִ֣י יֵצֵ֔א לִֽהְי֥וֹת מוֹשֵׁ֖ל בְּיִשְׂרָאֵ֑ל
וּמוֹצָאֹתָ֥יו מִקֶּ֖דֶם מִימֵ֥י עוֹלָֽם׃ מיכה ה:א

OLD TESTAMENT SCRIPTURE TRANSLATION

"But as for you, Bethlehem Ephrathah, *Too* little to be among the clans of Judah, From you One will go forth for Me to be ruler in Israel. His goings forth are from long ago, From the days of eternity."

Micah 5:2 NASB

ANCIENT RABBINICAL COMMENTARY

"And you, O Bethlehem Ephrath, you who were too small to be numbered among the thousands of the house of Judah, from you shall come forth before Me the Messiah, to exercise dominion over Israel, he whose name was mentioned from before, from the days of creation."[65]

Targum Jonathan

" 'Son of Judah, Judaean! Tie your ox and tie your plow, for the King Messiah has been born!' ....He asked him: 'From where is he?' He answered: 'From the royal fort of Bethlehem in Judah.' "[66]

***The Jerusalem Talmud,* Berachoth, fol. 5a**

NEW TESTAMENT RECORDED 63 AD

"Now it came about in those days that a decree went out from Caesar Augustus, that a census be taken of all the inhabited earth. This was the first census taken while Quirinius was governor of Syria. And all were proceeding to register for the census, everyone to his own city. And Joseph also went up from Galilee, from the city of Nazareth, to Judea, to the city of David, which is called Bethlehem, because he was of the house and family of David, in order to register, along with Mary, who was engaged to him, and was with child. And it came about that while they were there, the days were completed for her to give birth. And she gave birth to her first-born son; and she wrapped Him in cloths, and laid Him in a manger, because there was no room for them in the inn."

Luke 2:1-7 NASB

MODERN RABBINIC COMMENT/REFUTATION

"...there is one more verse on the divinity of the Messiah which serves double duty by demonstrating his birth in Bethlehem as well. (Micah 5:1 = 5:2 in some translations). The Christological translation of the last phrase (*miqedem mimei 'olam)* is 'of old, from everlasting,' which demonstrates that this ruler is eternal and hence divine. But aside from the almost immediate reference to 'the Lord his God,' we are once again dealing with a mistranslation...according to the most probable reading of this verse, it not only fails to say that the Messiah is everlasting, it doesn't even say that he will be born in Bethlehem."

***Jews and "Jewish Christianity,"* by David Berger and Michael Wyschograd, pp. 44-45; © 1978**

---

[65] Samson H. Levey, *The Messiah: An Aramaic Interpretation, The Messianic Exegesis of the Targum*, p. 93.

[66] Raphael Patai, *The Messiah Texts*, p. 123.

AUTHOR'S COMMENT—EVANGELICAL CHRISTIAN POSITION

With all due respect, this verse certainly does indicate that the Messiah would be born in Bethlehem and be eternal. Many times this author has shown the Hebrew of Micah 5 to Jews in Israel. They would smile and say, "What an interesting verse. It is so specific about His birthplace, and yet, it shows that He is from forever, as you say." Also, the Jerusalem Talmud and Targum Jonathan, two major Jewish commentaries, say this verse refers to Bethlehem as the birthplace of the Messiah. Hoping not to offend, we suggest David Berger, and the other authors and rabbis of the anti-missionary writings we have quoted in this book, brush up on their Hebrew and ancient rabbinical commentary.

Philip Moore

THE VAIN ATTEMPT OF THE RABBIS TO REINTERPRET MICAH'S MESSIANIC PROPHECY

Today, there are numerous rabbis who deny that their prophet Micah was writing about the birth of the Messiah. Many others believe they deny this in order to counter the Christian/Messianic claim that Jesus fulfilled this specific prophecy. Mr. Berger wrote: "...there is one more verse on the divinity of the Messiah which serves double duty by demonstrating his birth in Bethlehem as well....(Micah 5:1 = 5:2 in some translations). The christological translation of the last phrase (*miqedem mimei 'olam*) is 'of old, from everlasting,' which demonstrates that this ruler is eternal and hence divine. But aside from the almost immediate reference to 'the Lord his God,' we are once again dealing with a mistranslation....according to the most probable reading of this verse, it not only fails to say that the Messiah is everlasting, it doesn't even say that he will be born in Bethlehem."[67]

There is another problem regarding the honesty and accuracy of this claim, apart from its lack of common sense; for anyone reading the prophecy in English or Hebrew understands that it refers to the Messiah. Moreover, the rabbis who wrote the ancient commentaries about the Old Testament would have been thoroughly embarrassed by their modern colleagues who emphatically deny its Messianic meaning. The Targum Jonathan says: "And you, O Bethlehem Ephrath, you who were too small to be numbered among the thousands of the house of Judah, from you shall come forth before Me the Messiah, to exercise dominion over Israel, he whose name was mentioned from before, from the days of creation."[68]

The Jerusalem Talmud tells us: " 'Son of Judah, Judaean! Tie your ox and tie your plow, for the King Messiah has been born!'....He

---

67 David Berger and Michael Wyschograd, *Jews and "Jewish Christianity,"* pp. 44-45.

68 Samson H. Levey, *The Messiah: An Aramaic Interpretation, The Messianic Exegesis of the Targum*, p. 93.

asked him: 'From where is he?' He answered: 'From the royal fort of Bethlehem in Judah.' "[69]

These commentaries quite clearly show that, once again, the modern rabbis have been caught trying to deny the Messiah His prophecies.

THE TRUE MESSAGE OF JESUS' PROMISED NEW COVENANT—AS THE BIBLE (OLD T.) TRULY TAUGHT

The Messiah brought in the new covenant promised in Jeremiah 31:31. This *new covenant* is characterized by God's grace. Grace means "undeserved love." God loves us even when we break His perfect law because of what His Messiah has done for us, by giving His life for our shortcomings.

This law was given to the ancient Hebrews in the first five books of the Bible, commonly referred to as the "Books of Moses" or simply "Torah." Throughout the many centuries between the giving of the law and the Coming of the Messiah many sincere people began to build tradition around the law in order to make it easier to keep, so that they would not have to feel as if they were breaking it constantly. When someone did break the law, they offered a sacrifice[70] in the Temple and the Jewish priest made intercession for them before God. In this practice we see the reason God gave the law to the nation of Israel. It showed that an innocent substitute—Temple sacrifice—had to die for whatever sin was committed against God's perfect standard, a standard that is impossible to keep. By the way, the Bible says that if you stumble in one point it is the same as breaking the entire law (James 2:10).

Now we are getting somewhere. We see that the law was given to show man's true nature of sin, a basic rebellion instilled in our innermost being by the fall of Adam.

***

---

[69]Raphael Patai, *The Messiah Texts*, p. 123. Patai's source was the Jerusalem Talmud, Berachoth, fol. 5a.

[70]Oesterley and Box inform us of the ancient Jewish sacrifice, which pointed to Jesus: "It is said several times in *Bemidbar rabbah* that no man in Jerusalem was burdened, or passed the night with a consciousness of sin; for the morning sacrifice atoned for the sins of the night, and the evening sacrifice for the sins of the day." W.O.E. Oesterley, D.D., *The Religion and Worship of the Synagogue*, p. 270.

SOME TEACH WHAT THE BIBLE DOES NOT, TO THE DETRIMENT OF US ALL

Many "Christian teachers" urge people to keep the Sermon on the Mount,[71] even though Jesus pointed out that breaking the law in your thoughts is just as bad as breaking it in deed (Matt. 5:8).

It is because these teachers take this wrong approach to God, that we realize they are certainly not Christian in any New Testament sense of the word. The true Christian or Messianic doctrine is revealed by Paul, the former Rabbi Saul, in Romans 3:20-25.

Accordingly, Jesus was trying to explain the difference between heart and behavior to the religious Jews of His day, the Pharisees, who, incidentally, believed they were keeping God's law. He showed them that God not only looked upon the outside performance but the heart as well; when their heart and motives were wrong, it was just as bad as when their actions were wrong. This, of course, stung these self-righteous Jewish religious leaders who attempted to please God through their actions and deeds.

The heart of Jesus' teaching and message was that it does not matter how many sins you commit: "Then came Peter to him, and said, Lord, how oft shall my brother sin against me, and I forgive him? till seven times? Jesus saith unto him, I say not unto thee, Until seven times: but, Until seventy times seven" (Matt. 18:21-22 KJV).

---

[71]We would like to comment at this point that contrary to the claims of some, Jesus' Sermon on the Mount teachings are authentically Jewish, and were so well liked that rabbis one hundred years *after* Him have been caught borrowing them. Risto Santala tells us: "...in the Talmud. Rabbi Terphon, who received his instruction from contemporaries of Jesus, the elder Gamaliel and Johanan Ben Zakkai, says that *'If someone urges you to remove the speck from your eye, he must be given the answer, 'Take the plank out of your own!''* [Arachin 16b] One hundred years later, a certain Johanan commenting on the first verse of Ruth—'In the days when the judges judged...' —says that, 'this generation judges its judges; *but if someone should say to you, 'Remove the speck from your eye,' say to him, 'Remove the plank from your own eye.'* " Risto Santala, *The Messiah in the New Testament in the Light of Rabbinical Writings*, p. 185. This passage from the Talmud is from the section Baba Bathra 15b. Though it does not credit Jesus (Matt. 7:3-5), for obvious reasons, we are not going to sue for plagiarism. We wouldn't even if we could! We are actually very flattered. On the back cover of Risto Santala's companion book it is stated: "This book about the Messianic Old Testament prophecies in the Light of Rabbinical Writings has already seen five Hebrew editions in Israel....The item is somewhat delicate. The writer is stepping into the lion's den of the Rabbis and into the fiery furnace of the liberal theologians. But he hopes that others will follow him and promote a similar dialogue in the spirit of tolerance...." Risto Santala, *The Messiah in the Old Testament in the Light of Rabbinical Writings*, p. back cover. Thus, you can see that the precious truths he brings to light, which may be embarrassing to some rabbis, may indeed provoke interest among the open-minded as well as anger among the stubborn! No matter what, we are determined to get the word out!

The Bible teaches that you really cannot help[72] your action of sin. The Scripture tells us to be honest with ourselves and God each and every time and remember that we are paid for by the death of an innocent substitute, justified by faith.

Take a look in Genesis; God said that He counted Abraham's faith to him for righteousness (Gen. 15:6).[73] Before the law was even given, God made a covenant[74] with Abraham. King David, whom God called "a man after his own heart," expressed God's truth when he said that none could hope to be sinless under the law: "For I acknowledge my transgressions: and my sin *is* ever before me" (Ps. 51:3 KJV).

The Jewish King Solomon, known throughout history as the wisest man on Earth, states God's inspired biblical words: "For *there* is not a just man upon earth, that doeth good, and sinneth not" (Ecc. 7:20 KJV).

These words are true and honest. They illustrate God's love and mercy toward all of us. However, the Pharisees of Jesus' day, 2000 years removed from Abraham, had built such a wall of hypocrisy and legalism around the law that few felt they could come to God for their needs. This was the real sin of that day!

SOME MINISTERS SAY YOU CAN KEEP *THE LAW* WHEN JESUS SAID YOU CANNOT—IF YOU COULD, HIS DEATH WOULD HAVE BEEN MEANINGLESS

The Pharisaic law estranged the common people from God and kept the Pharisees in power. This is why Jesus later said: "...The scribes and the Pharisees sit in Moses' seat....For they bind heavy burdens and grievous to be borne, and lay *them* on men's shoulders; but they *themselves* will not move them with one of their fingers....But woe unto you, scribes and Pharisees, hypocrites! for ye shut up the kingdom of heaven against men: for ye neither go in *yourselves*, neither suffer ye them that are entering to go in" (Matt. 23:2, 4, 13 KJV).

This is what is happening today in many so-called churches: Roman Catholic, Greek Orthodox, various legalistic Protestant denominations, etc. The teachers within these institutions insist on *keeping* the very things Jesus said you *cannot* keep. They teach these things to the masses, and the people who feel themselves to be

---

[72] Apart from drawing on the power of the Holy Spirit's strength, which can empower us to resist and live a Christian life of victory as we maintain our fellowship with the Father as we trust Jesus, something some Christians do not always do.

[73] "And he believed in the LORD; and he counted it to him for righteousness" (KJV).

[74] "In the same day the LORD made a covenant with Abram, saying, Unto thy seed have I given this land, from the river of Egypt unto the great river, the river Euphrates...." (Gen. 15:18 KJV).

Christians take this as an example of how Christian life should be lived when, in reality, the sermon was God's condemnation to men indicating that they, in *their own power*, cannot please Him.

The divine interpretation of what Jesus expounds historically in the Sermon on the Mount (Matt. 5:8), is found later on in the New Testament in Romans 3:20-4:25 and Galatians, chapters 3-4. There, the true New Testament teachings are made clear beyond the shadow of a doubt.

Free and eternal salvation[75] is not based on what you do for God but rather what God has done for you through the death of His innocent son, the Messiah. All we are required to do is accept it and believe it. The Messiah gets all the credit for it.

Any Jew who looks at the Sermon on the Mount as a way of keeping the law, can reach one of two conclusions. Either it is impossible to keep the law and thus, the Messianic or Christian faith is a hypocrisy, or he realizes that the Messiah, in His sermon, was pointing out that the true requirement is to seek God honestly and unselfishly, in an attempt to keep the law.

This is clearly stated in Galatians 3-4 and Romans 3:20-4:25. If you read these two portions of the New Testament now, you will sleep better tonight and for the rest of your life. I might add that the churches which I mentioned generally do not teach these passages of Scripture, and those people who are in their ecumenical grip usually live very uncomfortable lives because of the way they are taught. It is one thing to be instructed about another's interpretation of the New Testament; it is clearly another to truly read it for yourself! Read Romans 3 and 4—you will never be the same!

WHEN DID THE NEW TESTAMENT BEGIN? HOW TO GET IN AND TELL A FRIEND

In reality, the new covenant did not begin until the sacrifice and resurrection of the Messiah. That event, and the whole body of Paul's epistles,[76] are in actuality, the new covenant as predicted by Jeremiah.

---

[75]See our *Vol. II,* chapter 11, "Eternal Security for True Believers."

[76]Epistle is a fancy word for letter. Paul wrote half of the New Testament and that half is made up of various letters he wrote to Christian congregations. He wrote Romans to the Church at Rome, which resembled more of a Baptist Church than a Roman Catholic Church. He wrote Corinthians, Thessalonians, Colossians and Ephesians to the Greek congregations in Corinth, Thessalonica, Colosse and Ephesus, Greece. Of course, you can see from these letters which doctrine these churches followed. They, too, were very similar to contemporary evangelical born-again churches rather than the Greek Orthodox Church, which was part of the Roman Catholic that developed after the era of Constantine only to later break off into Eastern Orthodoxy because of council disagreements, etc. When I was in Greece, I sat in on Greek Orthodox services out of curiosity. Though my Greek is not perfect, I never once heard Paul's epistles taught. At

It is written on our hearts with love and we enjoy sharing our faith with others, bringing them into an eternal kingdom which one day will be physically realized when the Messiah returns. It is not written on our hands as a legalism to be followed under the whip[77] of a master, but on our hearts as joy.

We see our loved ones' admiration of our example as they ask, "What do you have that I don't?" Then we share with them, and if they accept, they are going to live with us and God throughout all eternity in God's forever love kingdom. This is the motivation and message of the New Testament. Accept Messiah; He in turn eternally saves you on the basis of His personal sacrifice. Thus, you become so grateful that you desire to tell all your friends so that you may spend eternity with them.

This was the teaching of the early believers for the first two hundred years, before Constantine took over the church and turned it into a politically subjective institution, which he used in an attempted rescue of the Roman Empire. At this time, the true believers in Messiah, Jew and Gentile alike, were persecuted. They retreated underground and became a secret community until after the Reformation in the late 1500's, when biblical truth began to be recovered.

IN PAST AGES, READING THE NEW TESTAMENT COST MANY THEIR LIVES—WHAT WAS SO VALUABLE THAT IT WAS WORTH DYING FOR? ETERNAL LIFE!

The Catholic Church of the medieval age would not allow the reading of the Bible. They burned those who attempted to translate it because any reading of this document would disprove the doctrines, traditions and dogmas which the church began to attach to the Scriptures in much the same way as the Pharisees.

The religious hypocrisy of the Catholic leaders would have been exposed if this book of God found its way into the hands of the common people. The few underground believers who knew the Scriptures, were tortured and executed for their beliefs, along with Orthodox Jews.

During the years in which this Roman institution held sway over the politics of the world, the Jews, along with the Jewish and Gentile

---

the most, a verse from Matthew's Sermon on the Mount was quoted and, of course, as we have mentioned, until Jesus went to the cross and rose from the dead long after that teaching was given, the Old Testament was still in force. It was the resurrection of Jesus which marked the start of the new covenant which God has revealed to us in Paul's letters. Try them, you'll like them!

[77] Jesus taught, "For My yoke is easy, and My load is light" (Matt. 11:30 NASB).

true Christians, when discovered, were put to the rack, burned at the stake, and enclosed in iron maidens.[78]

Don't forget, if you were a true believer and read the Bible, you might have realized that the sale of indulgences (paid forgiveness for sin) was unbiblical. If you told too many people about this, the "church" (Catholicism) would run short of money. Thus, you were a risk they could not afford.

If you are interested in finding out historical details of actual cases describing the treatment biblical Christians endured at the hands of this institution, we suggest you read the bestsellers *Foxes, Book of Martyrs* and *Halley's Bible Handbook.*

"St. Serapion," a persecuted Christian,
as illustrated by Francisco de Zurbaran in 1628.

---

[78]An iron maiden, as you will see pictured later, was a hollowed-out iron casement which on the outside looked like a woman, but on the inside was lined with iron spikes or knives. The "heretic" who did not believe the way the Roman Catholic authorities wanted him or her to believe, was placed in this structure, which was slowly closed, murdering them.

ORIGINAL HEBREW TEXT 997 BC

לְדָוִ֗ד מִ֫זְמ֥וֹר נְאֻ֤ם יְהוָ֨ה ׀ לַֽאדֹנִ֗י שֵׁ֥ב לִֽימִינִ֑י עַד־אָשִׁ֥ית אֹ֝יְבֶ֗יךָ הֲדֹ֣ם לְרַגְלֶֽיךָ׃

תהלים קי:א

OLD TESTAMENT SCRIPTURE TRANSLATION

"The LORD says to my Lord: 'Sit at My right hand, Until I make Thine enemies a footstool for Thy feet.' " **Psalms 110:1 NASB**

ANCIENT RABBINICAL COMMENTARY

"In the future God will seat the King Messiah at his right, for it is said: 'The Lord said unto my Lord, Sit thou at my right hand,' "[79]

Midrash on Psalm XVIII, 35 (36 in Hebrew)

NEW TESTAMENT RECORDED 63 AD

"And He [Jesus] said to them, 'How *is it that* they [religious leaders] say the Christ is David's son? For David himself says in the book of Psalms, 'THE LORD SAID TO MY LORD, 'SIT AT MY RIGHT HAND, UNTIL I MAKE THINE ENEMIES A FOOTSTOOL FOR THY FEET.' ' David therefore calls Him 'Lord,' and how is He his son?' "

Luke 20:41-44 NASB. [ ] mine

MODERN RABBINIC COMMENT/REFUTATION

"The Christians believe that this passage proves that Jesus sits at God's right side, that Jesus should be called Lord, and that he is...God ("*The Lord said unto my Lord*"). Once again, this interpretation rests on a mistranslation....the Psalm refers to the anxious time before Abraham had to fight the four kings, in Genesis 14. God is telling Abraham not to worry, sit, so to speak, at my side, until I take care of your enemies...."

***You Take Jesus, I'll Take God*, by Samuel Levine, pp. 37-38; © 1980**

AUTHOR'S COMMENT—EVANGELICAL CHRISTIAN POSITION

Now I know that by bringing the original ancient understanding of this prophecy to light, I may help to burst the bubbles of both liberal, so-called "Christians" and modern rabbis, who deny the deity and Messiahship of Jesus. However, I am obligated by the Bible to illuminate these truths to all who sincerely want to understand and accept this Scripture in its authenticity. It is not my purpose to offend, only to proclaim the absolute truth, even though it may cause discomfort to some. In proving our point beyond doubt, I would like to quote the learned Henry Frowde of Oxford University, who notes in his article, "The Christian Messiah in the Light of Judaism" that: "The New Testament in its citations from the Old Testament Scriptures preserves much of the old exegesis of the ancient synagogue, **which has often been refined away or modified by the later Rabbis** and teachers. An interesting example of this meets us in the case of Ps. cx (*The Lord said unto my Lord*). In the New Testament (St. Matt. xxii 44 and parallels) it is implied that the Messianic interpretation of this Psalm was the one generally accepted and current at the time among the Jews. Later, however, this view was largely displaced in favour of others, more especially of one which referred the words *my lord* to Abraham (so Rashi). But the older view is sometimes attested. Thus it reappears in the Midrash to Ps. xviii 36 in a comment on the words: 'Thy right hand hath upholden me.' 'R. Judan in the name of R. Chama says, 'that in the

[79]Rev. B. Pick, Ph.D., *Old Testament Passages Messianically Applied by the Ancient Synagogue*, published in the compilation *Hebraica, A Quarterly Journal in the Interests of Semitic Study*, Vol. II, p. 137.

time to come the Holy One—blessed be He—will make King Messiah sit at His right hand, as it is said (Ps. cx 1): *The Lord said unto my lord, Sit thou on my right hand'*...."[80] Frowde's scholarship certainly exposes Levine's error.

Philip Moore

The tomb of Lazarus (in Hebrew, *Eleazer*, אלעזר). After four days in this tomb, Jesus raised Lazarus from the dead (John 11).

[80]Henry Frowde, M.A., "The Christian Messiah in Light of Judaism," *Journal of Theological Studies*, Vol. XIII. London: Oxford University Press, 1912, pp. 327-328. Bold mine.

"The LORD said unto my Lord, Sit thou at my right hand, until I make thine enemies thy footstool." **Psalms 110:1 KJV, penned 997 BC**

"While the Pharisees were gathered together, Jesus asked them, Saying, 'What think ye of Christ? whose son is he?' They say unto him, *The son* of David. He saith unto them, 'How then doth David in spirit call him Lord, saying, The LORD said unto my Lord, Sit thou on my right hand, till I make thine enemies thy footstool? If David then call him Lord, how is he his son?' And no man was able to answer him a word, neither durst any *man* from that day forth ask him any more *questions*."
Matthew 22:41-46 KJV, spoken 33 AD

JESUS WILL SIT ON THE RIGHT UNTIL HIS ENEMIES CHALLENGE HIS MIGHT

The main reason we quoted Psalms 110:1, its ancient commentary and its New Testament references, was to illustrate that the Jewish Messiah, contrary to modern rabbinical thought and teaching, was almost always understood by ancient rabbis to be one and the same with God: "The *LORD* said unto my *Lord*."[81]

In other words, God would one day become incarnate within a prepared human body of flesh; something I will document later in this work by using many other references and rabbinical commentaries.[82]

---

[81]Italics mine.

[82]Hal Lindsey, in his book, *The Promise*, makes a very good case for deity in reference to Psalm 40 and its rabbinical commentary and the Targum. We share his intriguing words with you: "In this chapter you're going to have to put on your thinking-cap because the arguments and logic these Old and New Testament scholars use to present Messiah as a *divine* person who clothed himself with a human body at a point in history, is so close and so intriguing that you won't want to miss a single nuance of their meaning. To many devout worshippers of Jehovah God, it's the quintessance of blasphemy to say that there was a time when He took on a human body and lived on earth in that manner for any length of time. And yet, there are specific predictions in the Old Testament which indicate that very thing would happen when Messiah came to earth. Psalm 40 is one of the prophetic passages which alludes to this....The Psalmist predicted that there would come a time when God would no longer require sacrifice. It would be at a time when God prepared a body for the Promised One who was going to come and do God's will on earth....A very ancient Jewish interpretation in the Midrash concerning Messiah's geneology makes reference to Psalm 40 and says that this is definitely Messiah speaking through the Psalmist. The New Testament writer of the epistle to the Hebrews quotes Psalm 40:6-8 from the Greek Septuagint version and uses it as the basis for his climactic argument to convince the Hebrew followers of Jesus that his sacrificial death *fulfilled* and thus *annuled* the Mosaic animal sacrifice system....As might be expected, there's quite a present day dispute about the phrase in Psalm 40 '...a body you prepared for me.' In the official Hebrew Massoretic text it reads instead, 'My ears you have opened.' However, the Septuagint version of the Old Testament (250 B.C.E.) translates this phrase as 'but a body you prepared for me'....The best explanation is that the Septuagint translaters of the Hebrew Old Testament, writing sometime before 200 B.C.E. paraphrased the meaning of this portion of Psalm 40. This paraphrasing is known as *targumming* and it was a standard practice in the translating of the Biblical writings.

However, in this episode of Jesus' teachings to the Pharisees (Jewish religious leaders of His day), He mentions this particular predictive Messianic Psalm of David: "Sit at My right hand, Until I make Thine enemies a footstool for Thy feet" (Ps. 110:1 NASB).

This phrase contains interesting and specific prophetic events which have to do with our near future. The first segment of this phrase, "Sit at My right hand," is recorded in the New Testament as occurring when Jesus left the earth from the Mount of Olives in Jerusalem (see Acts I). After He was crucified, rejected and resurrected, He told His people, the Jews who received Him as Messiah, that the promised Messianic Kingdom of the Old Testament, a fervent hope of Judaism, would only be set up when He was accepted by all Israel, including their leaders. "For I say unto you, Ye shall not see me henceforth, till ye shall say, Blessed *is* he that cometh in the name of the Lord" (Matt. 23:39 KJV).

We know from other sections of the New Testament, chiefly Revelation, chapters 16-19, that this will not occur until the battle of Armageddon (see our chapter 26, "We Win Armageddon—Our Final Battle"). Until then, He will sit at God's right hand until the "restitution of all things, which God hath spoken by the mouth of all his holy prophets since the world began" (Acts 3:21 KJV).

The New Testament book of Hebrews clarifies: "But this man, after he had offered one sacrifice for sins for ever, sat down on the right hand of God; From henceforth expecting till his enemies be made his footstool" (Heb. 10:12-13 KJV).

***

Paraphrasing didn't deny the meaning of the original words, it usually put it into an idiom or concept which was more familiar to the people of their day. This is the case with the phrase 'to open or pierce a person's ears.' It was related to completely and voluntarily submitting one's self to another. The idea is beautifully expressed in Exodus 21:2-6 where the case of a slave who loves his master and volunteers to be a lifetime slave to him is discussed. Moses instructs the master to pierce the slave's ear with an awl and that will be a sign that he's volunteered to serve him for his lifetime.... This idea was interpreted and paraphrased in the Septuagint by the Hebrew scholars as 'a body you have prepared for me,' because this was a corresponding Greek idea of total submission which the Greek speaking readers of the Septuagint translation would be more familiar with. If the Messiah was to come and dwell in a special body which God had prepared for him, what would be the purpose of it? There are many facets to the answer of that question, but primarily it was so that, as a sinless man, God could place on him the sins of all mankind and then the body of this special man, which God counted as a fulfillment of the sacrificial lamb, could suffer sin's penalty which is death and God could accept this death as substitutionary for every man who would ever place faith in its efficacy for him." Hal Lindsey, *The Promise*. New York: Bantam Books, Inc., © 1984, pp. 152-155, used by permission.

BUT WHO ARE THE ENEMIES SPECIFICALLY AND PROPHETICALLY MENTIONED? GOG AND MAGOG!

Armageddon is known and described in the Old Testament as Gog and Magog (Ezek. 38-39). Jesus will be called upon, according to the prophet Hosea[83] (Zech. 12:10), to save Israel from this future war. We should remember that the parchment of Zechariah 12:10 is part of the *Old Testament*, and was written five hundred years before the birth of Jesus in anticipation of the Messiah's Second Coming.

Considering this fact, the passage is one of the most remarkable prophecies in the Bible because it speaks of the Messiah appearing to us for the second time, with pierced hands, five hundred years before His first appearance in Bethlehem. He is seen in the sky and mourned by Jewish on-lookers who are shocked by the fact that He is their Messiah, and has been all along for the past 2000 years, and He is saving them from the biblically predicted invasion (Gog and Magog) which we will prove to be Russia in our chapter 19, "Russia is Crushed in Gog."

Russia has been proven, through ancient rabbinical documents, including reliable geographical, historical, and even genealogical records, to be Israel's last great enemy. Also, it is important to note that Israel did not exist when the prophecy regarding Russia coming against Israel was written, 2600 years ago. Jews were captive in Babylon.

Today, as predicted, Israel is back in her land after 2000 years in exile. She has been reconstructed as a nation in our era. Ezekiel 36-39 speaks of this and, in the New Testament, the students of Jesus anticipated the rebirth of Israel (Acts 1:6). More will be said about this event in our chapter 18, "Israel—Is Real."

THE END TIME ENEMY, THOUGH THEY PRESENTLY LIE LOW, AWAIT THEIR FATAL ROLE, A FACT UNKNOWN TO MANY!

The reason we mentioned this is that in order for there to be an invasion of Israel, there obviously must be a State of Israel. During the past 2000 years, there was not a state; that is, until 1948. Thus, we know that we are in the general time-frame of this invasion. In an age of nuclear weapons, false peace treaties and terror, we are a heartbeat away! Though time will tell, we know that the Bible already has.

***

---

[83]Hosea 5:15.

While Russia is seemingly benevolent in 1996, do not count on it to last. This will change in the next twenty to thirty years, if not sooner. The Bible demands it!

IS THERE A MIDRASHIC HINT AS TO THE IDENTITY OF THE ENEMY IN PSALM 110?

The last segment of this Psalm, "until I make Thine enemies a footstool for Thy feet," is extremely interesting! What enemies are we talking about? Many have come to the superficial conclusion that it must be anyone who does not believe in the Messiah. We are not saying they are wrong, but there may be a deeper meaning to this prophecy. Could it be that they are the Gog and Magog (future Russian/Arab armies) of the Armageddon prophecy? Is there any evidence from the ancient rabbis that this passage might have been, in fact, referring to this future Russian invasion of Israel called Gog and Magog?

As we pored over the volumes of rabbinical literature written over a millennia ago concerning the Messiah and this anciently predicted invasion, which according to New Testament claims will herald the return of Jesus to save His people (Rom. 11:26; Rev. 19:11-18), we retrieved a Midrashic treasure! We found a rather breathtaking rabbinical commentary on this Psalm, which confirmed our suspicion that Gog and Magog will yet become the enemies which Jesus, in Matthew 22:44, claimed as His very own.

Why does He proclaim them His enemies? I suppose because they attempt to wipe out His people, the Jews. This rabbinical commentary was written many hundreds of years ago and is now accepted as a part of the rabbinical literature, even by the liberal rabbis, though it may not be studied or believed by all of the Orthodox. It reads: "[God says:] 'Ephraim, My firstborn, you sit on My right until I subdue the army of the hosts of Gog and Magog, your enemies, under your footstool....' " (Mid. Alpha Betot, 2:438-42).[84]

This commentary continues and explains the aftermath of the destruction of Gog and Magog accompanied by the Messiah's Coming. "The Messiah will arise over Israel, will gather the exiles of Israel in Jerusalem, and will rebuild Jerusalem....And all the kings of the nations of the world will come to the door of the Messiah and will serve before him and bring him presents...."[85]

***

---

[84]Raphael Patai, *The Messiah Texts*, p. 153.
[85]Ibid.

"The one like a man who sits upon the throne of God's glory [Luke 22:69, cf. Ps. 110; Dan. 7:13], the sublime eschatological judge, is the highest conception of the Redeemer ever developed by ancient Judaism. Only one artist has captured it. Jan Van Eyck. He depicted the Son of man, above the altar at Ghent, as a human being who is divine. Could Jesus of Nazareth have understood himself thus? Let us not forget that he felt he was God's chosen one, his servant, the only Son to whom the secrets of the heavenly Father were open. This very sense of sublime dignity could have led him in the end publicly to dare to identify himself with the Son of man; and in Judaism the Son of man was frequently understood as the Messiah."[86]

Israeli Professor David Flusser, Ph.D., world-renowned Jewish biblical scholar over the age of 70, residing in Jerusalem

The Son of Man over the alter at Ghent, as envisioned by the famous artist Jan Van Eyck in the fifteenth century.

---

[86]Donald Hagner, *The Jewish Reclamation of Jesus*, p. 266. Hagner's source was David Flusser, Ph.D., *Jesus*, pp. 103-104.

WE REST EASIER BECAUSE WE KNOW THAT GOD WILL SURELY DEFEAT ISRAEL'S LAST ENEMY!

It is comforting to know that Israel, who has known very little peace, will finally have peace forever when she recognizes the Messiah. We know that this peace will be permanent from a prophecy found in the book of Amos: "...I will plant them upon their land, and they shall no more be pulled up out of their land...." (Amos 9:15 KJV).

All past calamities which have come against the Jews were successful only because they failed to call upon the Messiah Jesus. This time they will call on Him and they will never know destruction or devastation again!

DEITY AND RELIGIOUS MISCONCEPTIONS

Some rabbis have attempted to undermine the Christian/Messianic Jewish belief that Messiah is God. They use arguments that sound very plausible on the surface and concepts very much in line with Judaism to promote their arguments. However, they amputate entire portions of prophecy concerning the Messiah and completely disregard the once-respected ancient rabbinical commentaries on those Old Testament biblical texts which show that, though the Messiah is a man, He is also, most importantly, God in the flesh—God Incarnate.

There are some religions that attempt to deify the flesh of Christ in wafers and who venerate Mary as the "Mother of God." The Catholic religion presents these claims almost as if they were biblical. These ideas fostered by the Catholic, and to some extent by the Eastern Orthodox Church, are diametrically opposed to the teachings of the Scriptures. Fundamental Christians and Messianic Jews are repulsed and offended by these heretical claims. Beliefs such as these are not Scriptural but are the result of traditions which have been taking shape for nearly 1600 years, beginning with the philosophy of Constantine in 312 AD.

True believers in Messiah, born-again Messianic Jews and Gentiles alike, believe in the Messiah's pre-existence and His incarnate deity. They base these beliefs on many claims in the Bible, starting with Genesis and running through the other sixty-five books, culminating in Revelation. They also treasure a number of ancient rabbinical writings that verify these beliefs.

***

HOW CAN GOD BE BOTH DEITY AND HUMAN AT THE SAME TIME IF HE IS ONE BEING?

Many rabbis have disclaimed the deity of the Messiah, inferring that this concept is pagan, not Jewish, and that the Trinitarian claim of the New Testament is somehow foreign to the Jewish Bible. We take exception to this because the ancient rabbinical writing known to us as the Zohar clearly affirms God in three persons. The Zohar tells us: "Come and see the mystery of the word YHVH: there are three steps, each existing by itself: nevertheless they are One, and so united that one cannot be separated from the other. The Ancient Holy One is revealed with three heads, which are united into one, and that head is three exalted. The Ancient One is described as being three: because the other lights emanating from him are included in the three. But how can three names be one? Are they really one because we call them one? How three can be one can only be known through the revelation of the Holy Spirit."[87]

A painting of a contemplating scholar, 1633, Louvre, Paris.

[87] Arnold Fruchtenbaum, "Jewishness and the Trinity." San Francisco, CA: Jews for Jesus, © 1987, p. 3, used by permission. Fruchtenbaum's source was *The Babylonian Talmud,* Zohar, Vol. III, p. 288; Vol. II, p. 43, Hebrew edition (see also The Soncino Press edition, Vol. III, p. 134). This pamphlet is available through *Jews for Jesus*, 60 Haight Street, San Francisco, CA, USA 94102-5895. Tel. (415) 864-2600.

ORIGINAL HEBREW TEXT WRITTEN 999 BC

כִּסְאֲךָ אֱלֹהִים עוֹלָם וָעֶד שֵׁבֶט מִישֹׁר שֵׁבֶט מַלְכוּתֶךָ: אָהַבְתָּ צֶּדֶק וַתִּשְׂנָא רֶשַׁע עַל־כֵּן ׀ מְשָׁחֲךָ אֱלֹהִים אֱלֹהֶיךָ שֶׁמֶן שָׂשׂוֹן מֵחֲבֵרֶיךָ:

תהלים מה:ז-ט

OLD TESTAMENT SCRIPTURE TRANSLATION

"Thy throne, O God, is forever and ever; A scepter of uprightness is the scepter of Thy Kingdom. Thou hast loved righteousness, and hated wickedness; Therefore God, Thy God, has anointed Thee With the oil of joy above Thy fellows."

Psalms 45:6-7 NASB

ANCIENT RABBINICAL COMMENTARY

" 'Thy Throne from God in heaven,...is for ever and ever' (for 'world without end,' עלמי עלמין) 'a rule of righteousness is the rule of Thy kingdom, O Thou King Messiah!' "[88] **Rabbi Levy in his Targum. Wörterb. vol. i. p. 390a**

NEW TESTAMENT RECORDED 64 AD

"But of the Son *He says*, 'THY THRONE, O GOD, IS FOREVER AND EVER, AND THE RIGHTEOUS SCEPTER IS THE SCEPTER OF HIS KINGDOM. THOU HAST LOVED RIGHTEOUSNESS AND HATED LAWLESSNESS; THEREFORE GOD, THY GOD, HATH ANOINTED THEE WITH THE OIL OF GLADNESS ABOVE THY COMPANIONS.' "

Hebrews 1:8-9 NASB

MODERN RABBINIC COMMENT/REFUTATION

"The errors of the author of this epistle [Hebrews] are as many as the quotations with which he strives to confirm his views....The words, 'Thy throne, O God, is for ever and ever,' are wrongly quoted from Psalm xlv. 6. We read there *Kis-au-hau Elohim*, which means, 'Thy throne (is) *of* God,' and not 'Thy throne, *O God*.' Thus we find, in 1 Chron. xxix. 23, 'And Solomon sat on the *throne of the Lord*.' "

***Faith Strengthened*, by Isaac Troki, pp. 291; 1850.[89] [ ] mine**

AUTHOR'S COMMENT—EVANGELICAL CHRISTIAN POSITION

The author (apolus) of this New Testament epistle (letter) of Hebrews, agrees with the ancient rabbinical commentary from Rabbi Levy's Targum. He is not "mistaken." Secondly, any Hebrew scholar can verify without question that Troki's comment that the Hebrew is "wrongly quoted," is in itself an error. Thirdly, I Chronicles xxix has no connection with Psalms 45:6-7, which was confirmed by ancient Jewish sources as being Messianic. Fourthly, the author of *Faith Strengthened* goes on to say that, based on the text, Jesus cannot be God, which we did not bother to quote here. In reading his book, you will see that he attempts to reinterpret almost all of the Messianic prophecies, distancing them from their natural and ancient meanings, in an attempt to scare Jews away from Jesus in today's world, through purposely perpetrated deception. In our opinion, this is not only wrong, but malicious! **Philip Moore**

---

[88] Alfred Edersheim, *The Life and Times of Jesus the Messiah*, p. 151, footnote 1.

[89] Isaac Troki, *Faith Strengthened.* New York: Hermon Press, 1850, p. 155.

PAGAN NOTIONS VERSUS SCRIPTURAL PREDICTIONS —WHAT IS THE DIFFERENCE IN BELIEF? A LOT!

It may be true that Eastern Orthodox and Roman Catholics engage in practices we believe to be nothing more than a type of candy-coated paganism. We, as true believers in Messiah, hold ourselves to be equal with the first believers in Jesus, whom others venerate. We believe Mary, whose true Hebrew name is Miriam (a common Hebrew name, even today), is not the "Mother of God" but rather a well-favored[90] woman, a virgin of God's choosing, selected to be the agency through which the Redeemer would be brought into the world. This was foretold in Isaiah 7:14, Jeremiah 23:5-6 and Isaiah 9:6.

We believe that God, being all-powerful, incarnated Himself in human form over 1900 years ago, just as He appeared to Jacob when He changed his name from Jacob to Israel. Listen to the nearly 4000-year-old words spoken by Jacob (Yacov) in the thirty-second chapter of the book of Genesis, the first book in the Bible: "Then Jacob was left alone, and a man wrestled with him until daybreak. And when he saw that he had not prevailed against him, he touched the socket of his thigh; so the socket of Jacob's thigh was dislocated while he wrestled with him. Then he said, 'Let me go, for the dawn is breaking.' But he said, 'I will not let you go unless you bless me.' So he said to him, 'What is your name?' And he said, 'Jacob.' And he said, 'Your name shall no longer be Jacob, but Israel; for you have striven with God and with men and have prevailed.' Then Jacob asked him and said, 'Please tell me your name.' But he said, 'Why is it that you ask my name?' And he blessed him there. So Jacob named the place Peniel, for *he said*, 'I have **seen God** face to face, yet my life has been preserved.' Now the sun rose upon him just as he crossed over Penuel,[91] and he was limping on his thigh. Therefore, to this day the sons of Israel do not eat the sinew of the hip which is on the socket of the thigh, because he touched the socket of Jacob's thigh in the sinew of the hip" (Gen. 32:24-32 NASB).

Obviously, this man was no ordinary man because Jacob said after his encounter with him, "I have seen **God**, face to face." This man was the hidden divine Messiah Jesus who changed Jacob's name from Jacob to Israel, which means a "Prince who has striven with God."

---

[90]The New Testament clearly tells us: "And the angel said to her, 'Do not be afraid, Mary; for you have found favor with God...you will conceive in your womb, and bear a son, and you shall name Him Jesus' " (Luke 1:30-31 NASB).

[91]In Hebrew, the word *pen* refers to "face," plural *penim*, and *el* of course, is "God."

THE QUESTION OF THE DEITY OF MESSIAH

ORIGINAL HEBREW TEXT WRITTEN 599 BC

בְּיָמָיו תִּוָּשַׁע יְהוּדָה וְיִשְׂרָאֵל יִשְׁכֹּן לָבֶטַח וְזֶה־שְּׁמוֹ אֲשֶׁר־יִקְרְאוֹ יְהוָה ׀ צִדְקֵנוּ׃

ירמיה כג:ו

OLD TESTAMENT SCRIPTURE TRANSLATION

"In His days Judah will be saved, And Israel will dwell securely; And this is His name by which He will be called, 'The LORD our righteousness.' "

Jeremiah 23:6 NASB

ANCIENT RABBINICAL COMMENTARY

"What is the name of the King Messiah? Rabbi Abba, son of Kahana, said: Jehovah; for it is written, 'This is his name whereby he shall be called, the Lord our Righteousness.' "[92] **Midrash on Lamentations I, 16**

NEW TESTAMENT RECORDED 64 AD

"But of the Son *He says*, 'THY THRONE, O GOD, IS FOREVER AND EVER, AND THE RIGHTEOUS SCEPTER IS THE SCEPTER OF HIS KINGDOM.' "

Hebrews 1:8 NASB

MODERN RABBINIC COMMENT/REFUTATION

"If the king is called 'The Lord our righteousness,' it would seem that he must be divine. The trouble is that this is a mistranslation."

***Jews and "Jewish Christianity,"* by David Berger and Michael Wyschogrod, p. 42; © 1978**

AUTHOR'S COMMENT—EVANGELICAL CHRISTIAN POSITION

This claim of mistranslation is a dishonest one. For anybody who knows Hebrew, this is evident. **Philip Moore**

ABRAHAM ALSO MEETS GOD FACE-TO-FACE, AS IF HE WERE A MAN

In Genesis 18, Abraham met God at his tent door. However, this time God appeared in the form of three men. In verse 3, Abraham clearly calls all three men, "My Lord." The passage reads: "And the LORD appeared unto him in the plains of Mamre: and he sat in the tent door in the heat of the day; And he lift up his eyes and looked, and, lo, three men stood by him: and when he saw *them*, he ran to meet them from the tent door, and bowed himself toward the ground, And said, My **Lord**, if now I have found favour in thy sight, pass not away, I pray thee, from thy servant...." (Gen. 18:1-3 KJV).

***

[92] Rev. B. Pick, Ph.D., *Old Testament Passages Messianically Applied by the Ancient Synagogue*, published in the compilation *Hebraica, A Quarterly Journal in the Interests of Semitic Study*, Vol. III, p. 176.

WHAT IS THE TRUE BUT CRYPTIC MEANING OF THE ANCIENT NAME OF DAVID FROM WHICH WE GET THE STAR OF DAVID

The Star of David is an illustration of God and man interwoven into one. In Israel, it is called the Shield of David for a very specific reason.

In Hebrew, *Magen* means "shield." In English we substitute star, because the Shield of David forms a star of six points. Actually, the six-pointed star is composed of two ancient *daleds* (a daled is a "d" in the Hebrew alphabet). One points up and one points down and they are interlaced and woven through each other.

The middle letter of David's name, *vav*, is not included in the modern Star of David. However, if it were, you would have a Jewish Star of David with a cross in the middle.

There is evidence that the ancient shape of the *vav* was similar to a Roman cross. All of the religious scholars in Israel know that the ancient shape for the Hebrew letter, *daled* (ד) was Δ. So David's name is spelled in Hebrew with two *daleds* and a *vav*. Its modern spelling would look like דוד. Its ancient spelling (the way David would have written it 3000 years ago before Hebrew was altered in the first dispersion), would look like this—ΔTΔ.

DAVID'S CONSOLIDATION OF HIS ANCIENT NAME CONTAINED MESSIANIC DEITY IN ITS MEANING!

As a famous king of Israel, David would have consolidated these letters to spell his name in a logo style, a trademark, so to speak, to separate him from all other Davids in Israel. The signature of the king would have been written in this way: one ancient *daled* inverted over the other, with the middle letter of his name, *vav*, inscribed in the middle of the symbol.

The modern Messianic Jews may not even be aware that when they wear this Jewish star with the cross inside of it, they are wearing the personal signature of David, called the Shield of David.

If you think about it, who was David's shield? Of course, it was the Messiah, who is God and man, and died on an ancient wooden *vav*. The triangle pointing skyward represents man created in the image of God, with three integral parts interlaced into one—mind, body and spirit;[93] while the triangle facing downward represents God's image of

93 "For there are three that bear record in heaven, the Father, the Word, and the Holy Ghost: and these three are one" (I John 5:7 KJV). "Now may the God of peace Himself

Father, Son and Holy Spirit. When they are woven into one another, as is the true Star of David, they represent the God Incarnate Messiah, who showed Himself to us in the body of a Jewish man, Jesus, whose name means "salvation" in Hebrew. Remember, God said let us make *man* in *our* image (Gen. 1:26).

YOUR PERCEPTION CHANGED FOREVER FOR THE BETTER—THE STAR OF DAVID, THE SYMBOL ON THE ISRAELI NATIONAL FLAG, PROCLAIMS JESUS' DEITY

You will never be able to view another Star of David or Israeli flag without knowing who it truly represents, Jesus, commonly called in the New Testament the Son of David (Matt. 1:1, 20; 9:27; 12:23; 15:22; 20:30-31; 21:9, 15; 22:42; Mark 2:25; 10:47-48; 12:35; Luke 3:31; 18:38-39).

DECKED BY MELCHIZEDEK

While I was in Jerusalem, I debated for two hours with a Hasidic rabbi about whether the Messiah was God. He said, "I see," in complete surprise, as we both read the passages about Melchizedek. As is well known, Melchizedek was the highest of high priests—even higher than the priesthood of Aaron—through whom Abraham paid his tithes to God.

The rabbi told me, "It all makes more sense to me. What you are saying is Jewish and very wise. Though at this moment I do not fully understand it, I'll take your New Testament and read it from cover-to-cover. Only, please do not tell anyone we have spoken about such things, for my life, family and reputation are at stake. It will be between myself and God...."

The passages we read were from Genesis, Psalms and the New Testament book of Hebrews. I explained to him, "Rabbi, in the Jewish Bible, we read of a unique person, a priest Melchizedek, whose priesthood reaches far above that of the Jewish high priests in the Temple. This individual, to whom Abraham paid his tithes (ten percent of his earnings), met Abraham when he was returning from Salem: '...Melchizedek king of Salem brought out bread and wine; now he was a priest of God Most High. And he blessed him and said, 'Blessed be Abram of God Most High, Possessor of heaven and earth....' ' " (Gen. 14:18-19 NASB).

***

---

sanctify you entirely; and may your spirit and soul and body be preserved complete, without blame at the coming of our Lord Jesus Christ" (I Thes. 5:23 NASB).

Over 1000 years later, King David penned the verses regarding the promised Messiah to come: "The LORD has sworn and will not change His mind, 'Thou art a priest forever According to the order of Melchizedek.' The Lord is at Thy right hand; He will shatter kings in the day of His wrath" (Ps. 110:4-5 NASB).

OUR NEW TESTAMENT DOCUMENTS THAT JESUS FULFILLED THE PRIESTHOOD OF MELCHIZEDEK

One thousand years after God predicted these words through David, Jesus came along. The writer of the New Testament book of Hebrews enlightens us regarding this high priest: "...no one takes the honor to himself, but *receives it* when he is called by God, even as Aaron was. So also Christ did not glorify Himself so as to become a high priest, but He who said to Him, 'THOU ART MY SON, TODAY I HAVE BEGOTTEN THEE'; just as He says also in another *passage*, 'THOU ART A PRIEST FOREVER ACCORDING TO THE ORDER OF MELCHIZEDEK'....being designated by God as a high priest according to the order of Melchizedek....For when God made the promise to Abraham, since He could swear by no one greater, He swore by Himself, saying, 'I WILL SURELY BLESS YOU, AND I WILL SURELY MULTIPLY YOU.' And thus, having patiently waited, he obtained the promise....This hope we have as an anchor[94] of the soul, a *hope* both sure and steadfast and one which enters within the veil,[95] where Jesus has entered as a forerunner for us, having become a high priest forever according to the order of Melchizedek. For this Melchizedek, king of Salem, priest of the Most High God, who met Abraham as he was returning from the slaughter of the kings and blessed him, to whom also Abraham apportioned a tenth part of all *the spoils*, was first of all, by the translation *of his name*, king of righteousness, and then also king of Salem, which is king of peace. Without father, without mother, without genealogy, having neither beginning of days nor end of life, but made like the Son of God, he abides a priest perpetually. Now observe how great this man was to whom Abraham, the patriarch, gave a tenth of the choicest spoils. And those indeed of the sons of Levi who receive the priest's office have commandment in the Law to collect a tenth from the people, that is, from their brethren, although

---

94The symbol of an anchor was carved into the rock on the face of Jesus' tomb in Jerusalem by the early Christians, and is still visible today (see photo in our Garden Tomb section coming up). The anchor, a first-century Christian symbol for eternal security, was also found carved on Jewish Christian tombstones in the Golan of Israel in 1994. We document this in our chapter 8, "The Messiah Conspiracy Continues in the *New* Old Testament," and our *Vol. II*, chapter 11, "Eternal Security for True Believers."

95For a fuller explanation of this veil, see our *Vol. II*, chapter 31, "The Mystery of the Temple Doors," from a lecture by Jonathan Cahn.

these are descended from Abraham. But the one whose genealogy is not traced from them collected a tenth from Abraham, and blessed the one who had the promises. But without any dispute the lesser is blessed by the greater. And in this case mortal men receive tithes, but in that case one *receives them*, of whom it is witnessed that he lives on. And, so to speak, through Abraham even Levi, who received tithes, paid tithes, for he was still in the loins of his father when Melchizedek met him. Now if perfection was through the Levitical priesthood (for on the basis of it the people received the Law), what further need *was there* for another priest to arise according to the order of Melchizedek, and not be designated according to the order of Aaron? For when the priesthood is changed, of necessity there takes place a change of law also....For it is witnessed *of Him*, 'THOU ART A PRIEST FOREVER ACCORDING TO THE ORDER OF MELCHIZEDEK.' For, on the one hand, there is a setting aside of a former commandment because of its weakness and uselessness (for the Law made nothing perfect), and on the other hand there is a bringing in of a better hope, through which we draw near to God. And inasmuch as *it was* not without an oath (for they indeed became priests without an oath, but He with an oath through the One who said to Him, 'THE LORD HAS SWORN AND WILL NOT CHANGE HIS MIND, 'THOU ART A PRIEST FOREVER' '); so much the more also Jesus has become the guarantee of a better covenant. And the *former* priests, on the one hand, existed in greater numbers, because they were prevented by death from continuing, but He, on the other hand, because He abides forever, holds His priesthood permanently. Hence, also, He is able to save forever those who draw near to God through Him, since He always lives to make intercession for them. For it was fitting that we should have such a high priest, holy, innocent, undefiled, separated from sinners and exalted above the heavens; who does not need daily, like those high priests, to offer up sacrifices, first for His own sins, and then for the *sins* of the people, because this He did once for all when He offered up Himself. For the Law appoints men as high priests who are weak, but the word of the oath, which came after the Law, *appoints* a Son, made perfect forever" (Heb. 5:4-7:28 NASB).

A RABBI'S ASTONISHMENT

After reading this, the rabbi was astonished. He said (I am paraphrasing), "I must be blind. Melchizedek was in our Bible all along and in the yeshiva [rabbinical study school], though I have a vague recollection of him in Genesis, I never once heard him mentioned in relation to this passage in Psalms. And of course, the New Testament passages I never read because I was always told the New Testament was a forbidden book for us. However, now that I have dared to read it with you, I see, at least concerning this passage on Melchizedek, it is quite an amazing book—one I must read from cover to cover. However, I have just one question. If all this is true about Melchizedek, why have our rabbis not expounded upon him in their writings?"

I answered, "In past times, they did, though they do not today. Of course, the Melchizedek passage from Psalms 110 was considered a dangerous passage to those who rejected Jesus because it made His claim to the Melchizedek priesthood even more solid. Though this passage was acceptable, being interpreted as Messianic even before Jesus' day, thereafter its Messianic interpretation was banned by many a rabbi as blasphemy."

The scholar, F. F. Bruce, sheds light on this when he says: "There was a good deal of contact between orthodox Jews and Jewish Christians in Palestine in the first and second centuries, and there are frequent echoes in the rabbinical literature of controversies between the two parties, on the interpretation of messianic prophecy, for example. In a number of instances interpretations which had formerly been regarded as quite proper and respectable by orthodox Jews were ruled out as inadmissible when Christians began to use them to prove that Jesus was the Messiah. There is one notable occasion recorded when the great Rabbi Akiba got into trouble because he favoured such an unacceptable interpretation. He and his colleagues were discussing the vision of the judgment day in Daniel 7.9-14, where 'one like a son of man' appears before the Ancient of Days to receive universal and eternal sovereignty from him. 'As I looked.' says Daniel (verse 9), 'thrones were placed, and one that was ancient of days took his seat.' The question was raised: Why thrones in the plural? Akiba gave the traditional answer: 'One for God and one for David' (i.e. for Messiah, the son of David). But Rabbi Jose expostulated with him: 'Akiba, how long will you profane the Shekhinah? It is one for justice and one for righteousness' [Bruce, in his footnote to righteousness, tells us that: "Akiba may have had in mind the divine invitation to the Messiah in Psalm 110. I: 'Sit at my right hand, till I make your enemies your footstool'—but the fact that Jesus in his reply to the high priest at his trial had conjoined this text with Daniel 7. 13 meant that its former messianic interpretation also was no longer favoured."]....Ever since Jesus had claimed, at his trial before the Sanhedrin, to be that Son of Man whom Daniel saw 'coming with the clouds of heaven' the messianic interpretation of the passage had become taboo for many Jewish teachers. The rabbis of this period, then, were not unacquainted with the story of Jesus and the activity of his followers, vigorously as they voiced their dissent from all that he and they stood for."[96]

---

[96]F.F. Bruce, *Jesus and Christian Origins Outside the New Testament*, pp. 64-65.

This exposition greatly impressed my friend! While Psalm 110:1 is a passage avoided even today by the rabbis (because it shows two persons in the Godhead), Psalm 110:4, three verses down, is feared even more because it indicates that the Messiah of Psalm 110:1 will indeed be *the* Messiah-priest Melchizedek, whom the redeemer of Israel would have to be! Jesus verifies all of this!

MESSIANIC MIRACLES OF HEALING

The Messiah, in the thirty-fifth chapter of Isaiah in the Jewish Bible, is understood to perform healings of the magnitude of miracles. Jesus also fulfilled this area of prediction when He opened the eyes of the blind (Matt. 15:31), raised the dead (Luke 8:54), opened the ears of the deaf and enabled the mute to speak, (Matt. 11:5) and healed the lame (Luke 7:22). However, when He was rejected and His earthly ministry came to an end, the full extent of His universal worldwide healing of all disease for all people was relegated to the future. When the Messiah returns, the Bible tells us that Jesus will heal everyone for all time in the millenial and eternal kingdom to come (Ezek. 47:12; Rev. 21:4; 22:1-5).

The interesting Messianic rabbinical commentary in the Yalkut on Joshua reflects these dual times of the Messiah's healings, as it speculates " 'then' may refer to the past and to the future."[97]

Concerning the past, it seems that if Jesus would have continued, nearly all of Israel would have been drawn to Him. As you may recall, the high priests were nervously worrying: "...'What are we doing? For this man is performing many signs. If we let Him *go on* like this, all men will believe in Him, and the Romans will come and take away both our place and our nation' " (John 11:47-48 NASB).

Interestingly enough, the first century Jewish historian, Flavius Josephus, though he mentions little of Jesus, speaks of His miracles as "wonderful works." In his *Antiquities* he wrote: "Now, there was about this time Jesus, a wise man [if it be lawful to call him a man], for he was a doer of **wonderful works**, a teacher of such men as receive the truth with pleasure. He drew over to him both many of the Jews, and many of the Gentiles. [He was the Messiah.] And when Pilate, at the suggestion of the principal men amongst us, had condemned him to the cross, those that loved him at the first did not forsake him [for he appeared to them alive again at the third day; as the divine prophets had foretold these and ten thousand other wonderful things concerning him]. And the tribe of Christians, so named from him, are not extinct at this day."[98]

---

[97]Rev. B. Pick, Ph.D., *Old Testament Passages Messianically Applied by the Ancient Synagogue*, published in the compilation *Hebraica, A Quarterly Journal in the Interests of Semitic Study*, Vol. I, p. 266.

[98]Moishe Rosen, *Y'shua: The Jewish Way to Say Jesus*, p. 102. Bold mine. Rosen's source was F.F. Bruce, *Jesus and Christian Origins Outside the New Testament*, p. 37.

"The Raising of the Cross," a Peter Paul Rubens masterpiece painted in 1609-1610.

The segment of Josephus is from *Antiquities* xviii 33, from the early second century. Dr. David Flusser, an unsurpassed expert in the field of Jewish and New Testament study, defends Josephus' *Jesus passage* with new and rock-solid evidence against the liberal critics, who have been crying "forgery" at the top of their lungs for as long as we can remember. Flusser notes: "Josephus (*Antiquities*, XVIII, 63-64)...tells us that Jesus was more than merely human...there are those who believe that the whole passage is a forgery interpolated into the text of Josephus. The late Professor Victor A. Tcherikover, an expert on Second Temple history, pointed to the end of that passage, which reads: 'And unto this day there are still people who are called Christians.' It is unlikely, he argued, that such a sentence would be a forgery, and it appears that these are the words of Josephus himself. The question remained undecided until Professor Shlomo Pines found a different version of Josephus' testimony in an Arabic version of the tenth century: 'At this time there was a wise man who was called Jesus, and his conduct was good, and he was known to be virtuous. And many people from among the Jews and the other nations became his disciples. Pilate condemned him to be crucified and to die. And those who had become his disciples did not abandon their loyalty to him. They reported that he had appeared to them three days after his crucifixion, and that he was alive. Accordingly they believed that he was the Messiah, concerning whom the Prophets have recounted wonders.' " David Flusser, Ph.D., *Jewish Sources in Early Christianity*, p. 14.

ORIGINAL HEBREW TEXT WRITTEN 713 BC

אִמְרוּ לְנִמְהֲרֵי־לֵב חִזְקוּ אַל־תִּירָאוּ הִנֵּה אֱלֹהֵיכֶם נָקָם יָבוֹא גְּמוּל אֱלֹהִים הוּא יָבוֹא
וְיֹשַׁעֲכֶם׃ אָז תִּפָּקַחְנָה עֵינֵי עִוְרִים וְאָזְנֵי חֵרְשִׁים תִּפָּתַחְנָה׃ אָז יְדַלֵּג כָּאַיָּל פִּסֵּחַ וְתָרֹן לְשׁוֹן
אִלֵּם כִּי־נִבְקְעוּ בַמִּדְבָּר מַיִם וּנְחָלִים בָּעֲרָבָה׃

ישעיה לה:ד-ז

OLD TESTAMENT SCRIPTURE TRANSLATION

"Say to those with anxious heart, 'Take courage, fear not. Behold, your God will come *with* vengeance; The recompense of God will come, But He will save you.' Then the eyes of the blind will be opened, And the ears of the deaf will be unstopped. Then the lame will leap like a deer, And the tongue of the dumb will shout for joy. For waters will break forth in the wilderness And streams in the Arabah." **Isaiah 35:4-6 NASB**

ANCIENT RABBINICAL COMMENTARY

"Come and see; all that the Holy One has wounded in this world he will heal in the future. The blind shall be healed; for it is said, 'The eyes of the blind shall be opened.' The lame shall be healed; for it is said, 'Then shall the lame man leap as an hart.' The dumb shall be healed; as it is said, 'And the tongue of the dumb sing'....The word 'then' (אז) may refer to the past and to the future. To the latter refers 'then thou shalt see and flow together' (Isa. LX.5); 'then shall thy light break forth as the morning' (*ibid* LVIII. 8); 'then the eyes of the blind,' etc.; 'then shall the lame man leap,' etc."[99]

Midrash on Genesis XLVI.28, section 85; Yalkut on I Samuel XXVIII.24 and Yalkut on Joshua X.12

NEW TESTAMENT RECORDED 63 AD

"...as He [Jesus] approached the gate of the city, behold, a dead man was being carried out, the only son of his mother, and she was a widow; and a sizeable crowd from the city was with her. And when the Lord saw her, He felt compassion for her, and said to her, 'Do not weep.' And He came up and touched the coffin; and the bearers came to a halt. And He said, 'Young man, I say to you, arise!' And the dead man sat up, and began to speak. And *Jesus* gave him back to his mother. And fear gripped them all, and they *began* glorifying God, saying, 'A great prophet has arisen among us!' and, 'God has visited His people!' And this report concerning Him went out all over Judea, and in all the surrounding district. And the disciples of John reported to him about all these things. And summoning two of his disciples, John sent them to the Lord, saying, 'Are You the Expected One, or do we look for someone else?' And when the men had come to Him, they said, 'John the Baptist has sent us to You, saying, 'Are You the Expected One, or do we look for someone else?' ' At that very time He cured many *people* of diseases and afflictions and evil spirits; and He granted sight to many *who were* blind. And He answered and said to them, 'Go and report to John what you have seen and heard: *the* BLIND RECEIVE SIGHT, *the* lame walk, *the* lepers are cleansed, and *the* deaf hear, *the* dead are raised up, *the* POOR HAVE THE GOSPEL PREACHED TO THEM. And blessed is he who keeps from stumbling over Me.' "

Luke 7:12-23 NASB. [ ] mine

---

[99]Rev. B. Pick, Ph.D., *Old Testament Passages Messianically Applied by the Ancient Synagogue*, published in the compilation *Hebraica, A Quarterly Journal in the Interests of Semitic Study*, Vol. I, p. 266.

MODERN RABBINIC COMMENT/REFUTATION

"The true Messiah is to reign as King of the Jews. Jesus' career as described in the New Testament lasted all of three years, at the end of which he was crucified by the Romans as a common criminal. He never functioned as anything but a wandering preacher and 'faith healer'....Only the gullible and superstitious are taken in by miracles...."

***The Real Messiah*, by Aryeh Kaplan, *et al*, pp. 46, 55; 1976**

ARCHAEOLOGICAL DISCOVERY

"...the scrolls do speak of the coming Jewish Messiah....Two of the fragments made newly available in the *Review's*[100] photo books are especially striking....the most important phrases are clear. Apparently referring to the coming Messiah, the text declares that he will 'heal the wounded, resurrect the dead [and] preach glad tidings to the poor.' The passage closely resembles the words of Jesus in the Nazareth synagogue (*Luke 4*)...."[101]

"Is Jesus In The Dead Sea Scrolls?", by Richard Ostling,
***Time*, September 21, 1992**

AUTHOR'S COMMENT—EVANGELICAL CHRISTIAN POSITION

Judging from the rabbinical commentary and especially the newly released Dead Sea Scroll[102] manuscripts on what the Jewish Messiah was supposed to accomplish

---

[100]*Biblical Archaeological Review.*

[101]Richard N. Ostling, contributor, "Is Jesus In The Dead Sea Scrolls?", *Time*, Sept. 21, 1992. Quebecor Printing Book Group, © 1992, Time, Inc., reprinted by permission. This article commented on the Dead Sea Scroll Text 4Q521. In Luke 4, Jesus reads Isaiah 61:1-2 to the congregation in His synagogue: " 'The Spirit of the Lord *is* upon me, because he hath anointed me to preach the gospel to the poor; he hath sent me to heal the broken-hearted, to preach deliverance to the captives, and recovering of sight to the blind, to set at liberty them that are bruised, To preach the acceptable year of the Lord' " (Luke 4:18-19 KJV). He then tells the people: "...'Today this Scripture has been fulfilled in your hearing' " (Luke 4:21 NASB). Thus, He was telling them, "I am the Messiah," because only the Messiah was to fulfill these prophecies (Isa. 35:5-6). Notice Jesus stopped short of completing the Isaiah passage which went on to read: "...and the day of vengeance of our God; to comfort all that mourn...." (Isa. 61:2 KJV). This was because He knew that this portion of the prophecy was not to be fulfilled until His Second Coming, when He will rescue Israel in victory from the war of Armageddon (II Thes. 1:7-8; Rev. 16:16; Ezek. 38-39)! The passage from Thessalonians in the New Testament reads: "And to you who are troubled rest with us, when the Lord Jesus shall be revealed from heaven with his mighty angels, In flaming fire taking vengeance on them that know not God...." (KJV).

[102]Although the rabbis were quoted from a 1976 publication and the newly released Dead Sea Scroll evidence shown here is from a 1992 secular news magazine, there is no indication that Stolper or present rabbis representing this train of thought have changed their minds. Based on our new evidence, if you are ever involved in a conversation on this issue, it might prove interesting to bring up this topic! You can try it, but I don't think you'll like it. The 1992 article notes that Britain's *Journal of Jewish Studies* is already attempting to dispute at least one supporting text. The *Journal of Jewish Studies* featured an article titled, "Qumran Corner—the Oxford Forum for Qumran Research Seminar on the Rule of War from Cave 4 (4Q825)," written by Geza Vermes from the Oxford Center for Post-Graduate Studies. Vermes admits in his criticizing footnote: "Of course the same consonants can be vocalized *wehemîtû*, 'and they will kill the Prince of the Congregation', proposed by Eisenman and Wise...." Geza Vermes, "Qumran Corner:

according to ancient Jewish expectation, it seems quite shocking and uncalled for that Rabbis Kaplan and Stolper would mock this credential of Jesus' Messiahship, doesn't it? *Time* magazine's major article, "Is Jesus in the Dead Sea Scrolls?" commented on the similarity between the Jewish Dead Sea Scrolls and Luke's New Testament report. These similarities regarding the activities of Jesus in the area of healing are a landmark of evidence for Evangelical Christians' faith in Jesus as the Jewish Messiah! This is illustrated in another part of the article, where Michael Wise of the University of Chicago mentions that these similarities are important in "underscoring the Jewishness of Jesus."

Philip Moore

THE DONKEY PROPHECY

For centuries, the rabbis have rejoiced in their tradition that the Messiah would enter Jerusalem on a donkey! One such rabbinic writing reads as follows: "...(Zech. 9:9) describes the Messiah, for when they laughed at him while he sat in prison, he submitted for the sake of Israel to the judgment imposed on him, and is therefore properly called submissive. Why is he spoken of as *yet he promises salvation?* Because after submitting to the judgment for their sake, he said: All of you deserve extermination; nevertheless, you will be saved, every one of you, by the mercy of the Holy One, blessed be He.

"*Afflicted, and he is riding upon an ass...*describes the Messiah. And why is he called *afflicted?* Because he was afflicted during all his years in prison while transgressors in Israel laughed at him.

"Why does Scripture say *riding upon an ass?* The ass represents the wicked who have no merit of their own and can manage to get along only by resorting to the merit of their fathers. But through the merit of the Messiah, the Holy One, blessed be He, shields them <and

---

The Oxford Forum for Qumran Research Seminar on the Rule of War from Cave 4 (4Q285)," *Journal of Jewish Studies,*Vol. 43, No. 1. Oxford Centre for Hebrew and Jewish Studies: Oxford, England, © 1992, p. 88. At the same time, Vermes harshly and falsely criticizes the world news media for emphasizing: "...their [Eisenman and Wise] claims without arguments to support them...." Ibid, p. 86. A bit schizophrenic, wouldn't you say? Mr. Vermes bases part of his argument against the pre-New Testament suffering Messiah of the Dead Sea Scrolls on the fact that, elsewhere in the scrolls, mention is made of the warring victorious Messiah who destroys the evil one, etc. We (Christians) believe this, too. This is going to be Jesus' Messianic Second Coming (see our chapter 23, "The False Messiah Armilus Equals Antichrist," and chapter 27, "Speculating on Messiah's *Second* Coming—Whether They Know It or Not"). Jesus will indeed end the war of Gog and Magog/Armageddon, destroying the evil Antichrist by the breath of his mouth (II Thes. 2:8; Isa. 11:4), carrying out judgment (Matt. 25) and finally bringing in peace (Rev. 21). It would benefit liberal Jewish scholars to study, realize and investigate the fact that the true evangelical dispensational Christian faith teaches two Comings of the Messiah. One in the past—suffering—as well as a victorious kingly role yet to occur, we believe before the mid-twenty-first century. Mr. Vermes may live to greet his returning Messiah Jesus. Let's hope he is ready! We invite our readers to send him a copy of this book. Maybe after he has received enough of them, he will read one.

guides them> in a straight way, and redeems them, as is said *They shall come with weeping, and with supplications will I lead them; I will cause them to walk by rivers of waters, in a straight way wherein they shall not stumble; for I am become a father to Israel, and Ephraim is My first-born* (Jer. 31:9)."[103]

ORIGINAL BIBLICAL WORD CONSTRUCTIONS IDENTIFY TWO COMINGS—ONE ON A *DONKEY* AND ONE ON THE CLOUDS

The Talmud Sanhedrin points out that there would be two Comings as prophesized in Zechariah 9:9 and Daniel 7:13.[104] What seems to reinforce this Talmudic interpretation is the interesting fact about the construction of the two Hebrew words which describe the Comings. The key word "humble" in Zechariah 9 denotes the First Coming, while the word "clouds" in Daniel 7 denotes the Second Coming.[105]

It should be pointed out that in the original Hebrew version, the term for humble or poor is *ani*, and clouds, in Aramaic,[106] is *anani*. In Zechariah the text says: עָנִי וְרֹכֵב עַל־חֲמוֹר ("**humble**, and mounted on a donkey") and in Daniel: וארו עִם־עֲנָנֵי שְׁמַיָּא ("and behold, with the **clouds** of heaven").

These two words are almost identical except that the first has one *noon* (which is the Hebrew "n"), while the second has two *noons*. This illustrates God's inspired use of the biblical language, which can in itself symbolize the two Comings, the First by one *noon*[107] and the Second by two.[108]

---

[103] William G. Braude, *Pesikta Rabbati* Piska 34, from *Pesikta Rabbati: Discourses for Feasts, Fasts, and Special Sabbaths*. New Haven, CT: Judaica Research at Yale University, © 1968, pp. 667-668, used by permission.

[104] Sanhedrin fol. 98, col 1: "R. Alexandri said: 'R. Y'hoshu'a ben Levi explained:....'If they will be righteous, [the Messiah will come] *on the clouds of heaven* (Daniel 7:13); if they will not be righteous, [he will come] as *a poor man riding upon an ass* (Zech. 9:9).''" Raphael Patai, *The Messiah Texts*, p. 83. Patai's source was the *Babylonian Talmud*.

[105] Santala also tells us: "It is possible to determine in any case that the Messiah should have come during the time of the Second Temple when it was still possible to determine His lineage according to the genealogical tables." Risto Santala, *The Messiah in the Old Testament in the Light of Rabbinical Writings* (Hebrew edition), p. 66.

[106] In the Hebrew Bible, this portion of Daniel was written in Aramaic because Daniel was in Babylon at the time. Aramaic uses Hebrew letters.

[107] The letter *noon* has a very special Messianic significance in Hebrew culture. Rabbi Michael Munk writes in the book *The Wisdom in the Hebrew Alphabet*: "No turmoil (bent נ) will last forever, because in the end it leads to the erect ן. This is demonstrated in the very term נון denoting perpetuation; in נון (fish) it represents propagation; in נין, descendant, it stands for the future of our people; and in ינון, Mashiach, it names the final Redeemer." Rabbi Michael L. Munk, *The Wisdom in the Hebrew Alphabet*. Brooklyn, NY: Mesorah Publications, ©1983, p. 158. The last Hebrew word Rabbi Monk mentions is a mystical name for the Messiah found in Psalm 72, ינון (*yinnon*). *Yinnon* has two

JESUS' DONKEY

Our New Testament records the event of Jesus riding the donkey into Jerusalem: "And after He had said these things, He was going on ahead, ascending to Jerusalem. And it came about that when He approached Bethphage and Bethany, near the mount that is called Olivet, He sent two of the disciples, saying, 'Go into the village opposite *you*, in which as you enter you will find a colt tied, on which no one yet has ever sat; untie it, and bring it *here*. And if anyone asks you, 'Why are you untying it?' thus shall you speak, 'The Lord has need of it.' And those who were sent went away and found it just as He had told them. And as they were untying the colt, its owners said to them, 'Why are you untying the colt?' And they said, 'The Lord has need of it.' And they brought it to Jesus, and they threw their garments on the colt, and put Jesus *on it.* And as He was going, they were spreading their garments in the road. And as He was now approaching, near the descent of the Mount of Olives, the whole multitude of the disciples began to praise God joyfully with a loud voice for all the miracles which they had seen, saying, 'BLESSED IS THE KING WHO COMES IN THE NAME OF THE LORD; Peace in heaven and glory in the highest!' And some of the Pharisees in the multitude said to Him, 'Teacher, rebuke Your disciples.' And He answered and said, 'I tell you, if these become silent, the stones will cry out!' " (Luke 19:28-40 NASB).

THE DAY THE STONES ALMOST CRIED

As you have just read, the response of the people was that of Messianic expectation. Notice Jesus' reply when the religious leaders denounced His followers for saying: "...'Hosanna to the Son of David; BLESSED IS HE WHO COMES IN THE NAME OF THE LORD; Hosanna in the highest!' " (Matt. 21:9 NASB).

Once Jesus had received this Messianic declaration offered by the few who really knew *and believed* the Scriptures, some of the

---

noons as does the Hebrew word *noon*, נ׳ן (a final *noon* is longer than the normal letter). Risto Santala comments on the name *Yinnon*: "Again it is worth recognizing that when looking at, for example, psalm 118 we saw that RASHI identifies this ruler with the 'cornerstone' which will be rejected, and with the *Yinnon* or 'flourish' idea in psalm 72:17. The *Yinnon* Messiah was before the sun, moon and course of the stars. This special name also describes how he will *'awake the children of the dust from the dead'* It is quite impossible to understand what the New Testament has to say without some familiarity with these roots of our faith which arise from the Jewish literature." Risto Santala, *The Messiah in the Old Testament in the Light of Rabbinical Writings*, p. 163.

[108] I would like to take time here to credit Itzchak Klugler for pointing this out to me in 1984. Itzchak is an Israeli Messianic Jew who immigrated to Israel in the early 1980's. This is the first time the interesting aspect of the two *noons* in relation to the Messiah's two Comings has ever been published!

Pharisees condemned this, saying, "Teacher, rebuke Your disciples." Clearly, they were angry at Jesus for receiving Messianic honors in the fulfillment of this "donkey prophecy." Jesus' answer to them was monumental. "I tell you, if these become silent, the stones will cry out!" (Luke 19:40 NASB).

By claiming "the stones will cry out" Jesus was alluding to the date of the Messiah's Coming. It had been said by the prophet Daniel, nearly six hundred years earlier, that the Messiah would enter Jerusalem four hundred and eighty-three years after the rebuilding of the second Temple (which was built out of *stone*, by the way). It was not a coincidence that the entrance of Jesus on the donkey occurred to the day of Daniel's predicted date!

Israeli children prepare for a donkey ride.

ORIGINAL HEBREW TEXT WRITTEN 487 AD

גִּילִי מְאֹד בַּת־צִיּוֹן הָרִיעִי בַּת יְרוּשָׁלִַם הִנֵּה מַלְכֵּךְ יָבוֹא לָךְ צַדִּיק וְנוֹשָׁע הוּא עָנִי וְרֹכֵב
עַל־חֲמוֹר וְעַל־עַיִר בֶּן־אֲתֹנוֹת׃ **זכריה ט:ט**

OLD TESTAMENT SCRIPTURE TRANSLATION

"Rejoice greatly, O daughter of Zion! Shout *in triumph*, O daughter of Jerusalem! Behold, your king is coming to you; He is just and endowed with salvation, Humble, and mounted on a donkey, Even on a colt, the foal of a donkey."
Zechariah 9:9 NASB

ANCIENT RABBINICAL COMMENTARY

"Rabbi Berachya said in the name of Rabbi Isaac: The last Redeemer will be like the first (Moses), as the first put his wife and his sons upon an ass (Exod. IV.20), the last one will also ride upon an ass; as the first fed his people with manna (Exod. XVI. 4), so will the last one also bring manna down from heaven (Ps. LXXII. 16); as the first made rise the well, so will the last one also bring forth water (Joel III.18). Thus, here is something of which it is said, Behold this is something new; but it has already been."[109] **Midrash on Ecclesiastes or Coheleth in loco**

NEW TESTAMENT RECORDED 90 AD

"On the next day the great multitude who had come to the feast, when they heard that Jesus was coming to Jerusalem, took the branches of the palm trees, and went out to meet Him, and *began* to cry out, 'Hosanna! BLESSED IS HE WHO COMES IN THE NAME OF THE LORD, even the King of Israel.' And Jesus, finding a young donkey, sat on it...." **John 12:12-14 NASB**

MODERN RABBINIC COMMENT/REFUTATION

"Zechariah 9:9—This is the verse dealing with the Messiah coming on a donkey....keep in mind that in the time of Jesus, riding on a donkey was not unusual at all. It is totally absurd to say that since Jesus rode into Jerusalem on a donkey, that proves conclusively that he is the Messiah, considering the fact that there were probably thousands of other Jews on donkeys going to Jerusalem at the same time. It makes more sense to say that the verse refers to the 20th[110] Century—while everyone else will fly to Jerusalem on a 747 jet, or drive a car, or ride in a bus or train, the Messiah will instead choose a donkey, which would be quite unusual."
***You Take Jesus, I'll Take God*, by Samuel Levine, p. 53; © 1980**

AUTHOR'S COMMENT—EVANGELICAL CHRISTIAN POSITION

Our point is that Jesus came on a specific day, on a donkey, which lined up with Daniel's prophecy of the Messiah, which could only be fulfilled on that day, excluding all days past and future. He was the only one being hailed as the Messiah as He came in on His donkey. Most importantly, the Messiah was predicted to come twice, once on a donkey (humbly), and again in glory on the predicted clouds of Heaven (Dan. 7:13). The author of *You Take Jesus, I'll Take God* should realize that Jesus' donkey and the time He appeared on it is one of the most unique correlations in history and that the Messiah's return cannot be on an animal—only

---

109 Rev. B. Pick, Ph.D., *Old Testament Passages Messianically Applied by the Ancient Synagogue*, published in the compilation *Hebraica, A Quarterly Journal in the Interests of Semitic Study*, Vol. III, p. 30.

110 We know that He will not be coming in the twentieth century, but rather in the twenty-first century. Isaac Newton has also testified to this. If you are reading this book in the year 2000, you will see old Newton was right! Now, if you give yourself between twenty to forty years, you will see things really start to happen!

on the clouds, as many rabbis admit! If Samuel Levine studies up, I'll bet he will hush up! **Philip Moore**

WHY THE MESSIAH CANNOT COME ON A DONKEY *TODAY* AS SOME HAVE ALLEGED—TIMING!

Because of a specifically predicted timetable given us by another Hebrew prophet, Daniel, there is in fact a certain absurdity to Levine's statement about "a twentieth century donkey" and his attempt to convince us that it would be more timely for the Messiah to come on a donkey in **our** generation. It is important to realize that He will come, and His Coming will be soon, but it will not be on a donkey! Not this time.

In our present generation, the prophecies of Daniel 7 and accompanying ancient rabbinical commentaries prove otherwise. For example, Daniel tells us: "I kept looking in the night visions, And behold, with the clouds of heaven One like a Son of Man was coming, And He came up to the Ancient of Days And was presented before Him. And to Him was given dominion, Glory and a kingdom...." (Dan. 7:13-14 NASB).

When this prophesied event occurs (commonly known as the Second Coming), Jewish people throughout the world will realize that their leaders (who have rejected the Messiahship of Jesus) were wrong. The Jews who see Jesus coming, will at that time be "**all righteous.**" As the prophet Isaiah wrote regarding that period: "...and the days of thy mourning shall be ended. Thy people also *shall be* **all righteous:** they shall inherit the land for ever, the branch of my planting, the work of my hands, that I may be glorified" (Isa. 60:20-21 KJV).

When they see the Messiah Jesus they will believe in Him, and that alone, **believing** in Him, will make them completely righteous. The New Testament says: "For even the Son of Man did not come to be served, but to serve, and to give His life a ransom for many" (Mark 10:45 NASB). "BEHOLD, HE IS COMING WITH THE CLOUDS, and every eye will see Him, even those who pierced Him; and all the tribes of the earth will mourn over Him. Even so. Amen" (Rev. 1:7 NASB).

Isaiah also said: "As a result of the anguish of His soul, He will see *it* and be satisfied; By His **knowledge** the Righteous One, My Servant, will justify the many, As He will bear their iniquities" (Isa. 53:11 NASB).

EVEN IN THE TALMUD, THE RABBIS CORROBORATE TWO COMINGS AND THE MANNER OF THE SECOND IS ON THE CLOUDS

In a discussion in the Talmud, the ancient rabbis clearly saw the two Comings of the Messiah. Once on a donkey, if Israel was unworthy, and again to a worthy Israel on the clouds of Heaven. In fact, these ancient rabbis cite the same two Scriptures in Zechariah and

Daniel that we have: "Rabbi Joshua ben Levi asked: In one place it is written, 'Behold, one like the Son of Man,' etc., and in another, 'Lowly and riding upon an ass' (Zech. IX. 9)! (He answered), If they be worthy, He (the Messiah) will come with the clouds of heaven; if not, He will come lowly and riding upon an ass.—*Talmud Sanhedrin*, fol. 98, col. 1."[111] For details of the Messiah's return on *"the clouds of Heaven"*, see our chapters 27-30 which deal with His Second Coming.

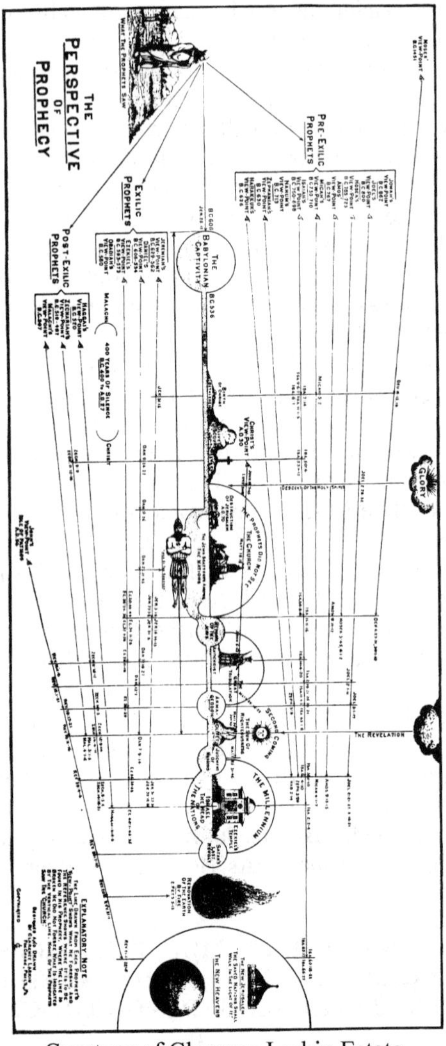

Courtesy of Clarence Larkin Estate.

[111]Rev. B. Pick, Ph.D., *Old Testament Passages Messianically Applied by the Ancient Synagogue*, published in the compilation *Hebraica, A Quarterly Journal in the Interests of Semitic Study*, Vol. III, p. 179.

ORIGINAL ARAMAIC TEXT WRITTEN 555 BC

חָזֵה הֲוֵית בְּחֶזְוֵי לֵילְיָא וַאֲרוּ עִם־עֲנָנֵי שְׁמַיָּא כְּבַר אֱנָשׁ אָתֵה הֲוָה וְעַד־עַתִּיק יוֹמַיָּא
מְטָה וּקְדָמוֹהִי הַקְרְבוּהִי׃ וְלֵהּ יְהִיב שָׁלְטָן וִיקָר וּמַלְכוּ וְכֹל עַמְמַיָּא אֻמַּיָּא וְלִשָּׁנַיָּא
לֵהּ יִפְלְחוּן שָׁלְטָנֵהּ שָׁלְטָן עָלַם דִּי־לָא יֶעְדֵּה וּמַלְכוּתֵהּ דִּי־לָא תִתְחַבַּל׃

דניאל ז:יג-יד

OLD TESTAMENT SCRIPTURE TRANSLATION

"I kept looking in the night visions, And behold, with the clouds of heaven One like a Son of Man was coming, And He came up to the Ancient of Days And was presented before Him. And to Him was given dominion, Glory and a kingdom, That all the peoples, nations, and *men of every* language Might serve Him. His dominion is an everlasting dominion Which will not pass away; And His kingdom is one Which will not be destroyed."

Daniel 7:13-14 NASB

ANCIENT RABBINICAL COMMENTARY

"Rabbi Joshua ben Levi asked: In one place it is written, 'Behold, one like the Son of Man,' etc., and in another, 'Lowly and riding upon an ass!' (Zech. IX. 9). (He answered), If they be worthy, He (the Messiah) will come with the clouds of heaven; if not, He will come lowly and riding upon an ass."[112]

Talmud Sanhedrin, fol. 98, col. 1

NEW TESTAMENT RECORDED 57 AD

"...Again the high priest was questioning Him, and saying to Him, 'Are You the Christ, the Son of the Blessed *One?*' And Jesus said, 'I am; and you shall see THE SON OF MAN SITTING AT THE RIGHT HAND OF POWER, AND COMING WITH THE CLOUDS OF HEAVEN.' And tearing his clothes, the high priest said, 'What further need do we have of witnesses? You have heard the blasphemy....' "

Mark 14:61-64 NASB

MODERN RABBINIC COMMENT/REFUTATION

"Daniel vii.13, 'I saw in the night visions, and, behold, one like the Son of Man came with the clouds of heaven, and came to the Ancient of days, and they brought him near before him.' The Christian expositors of Scripture ascribe the object of this prophecy to the advent of their Messiah, who, according to their view of this prophecy, was to be a superhuman being; otherwise how could he come with the clouds of heaven? Refutation.—The prophet speaks here of a dream....The clouds of heaven mentioned in the quotation at the head of this chapter, bring to mind the heavenly rule which ordains changes on high, in the region which lies beyond the reach and influence of man....The last-mentioned prediction is most decidedly not realised in the person of Jesus...."

***Faith Strengthened*, by Isaac Troki, pp. 195-197; 1850**

AUTHOR'S COMMENT—EVANGELICAL CHRISTIAN POSITION

It is quite obvious that Isaac Troki, in his "refutation," is grasping at straws. He not only rebuts the claim of the Christian New Testament, but also the Talmud, as you have read above, though he may be doing so unwittingly. The Talmud in this instance correctly reflects the true Christian realization that the Bible teaches the Messiah will come twice. Once "lowly" (Zech. 9:9) and once (yet to come) "kingly" (Dan. 7:13-14), just as Jesus promised in the New Testament Gospel of Mark. **Philip Moore**

---

[112] Ibid, p. 179.

DANIEL NINE—THE TIME

Daniel 9:24-26, outlines specific details as to how the Messiah would come the first time at an exact time.[113] Hal Lindsey, in his book, *The Promise*, beautifully illustrates the evidence: "...Daniel.... was himself in dispersion in Babylon with the rest of his nation when he wrote his remarkable prophecy of Daniel 9:24-27....this amazing prediction of the future events of Israel's career sets forth a divinely ordained time period of 'seventy weeks' of years (490 years) in which God would, in specific ways, *deal with the sin of the nation, bring in everlasting righteousness,* and *send the Messiah to the world.* This allotted time period was like a great divine 'time-clock' with 490 years of time marked off on it.

A specific event was to mark the beginning of this 490 years of God's unique dealing with his people. Daniel said that when the permission was officially given for the Jews to leave their Babylonian captivity and return to their land and restore and rebuild Jerusalem, that would mark the start of this 490 year period. Like a great stop-watch, God's finger pushed down on the button and the 490 year allotted countdown began clicking off April, 444 B.C.E. Archaeologists have confirmed to us that this was the year that Artaxerxes Longimanus, the Persian King, gave the Jews permission to leave their exile in Babylon.

Then Daniel predicted a strange thing. He said that after sixty-nine weeks of years (483 years) had clicked off on this allotment of time, the Messiah of Israel would be revealed to the Jews and then *killed*, and the city of Jerusalem and their Temple would be destroyed and their 490 year special time allotment would be temporarily cut short by 7 years.

There's no possible way that it could be coincidence that on the *very day* that Jesus rode into Jerusalem on a donkey and presented himself to Israel as their Messiah, exactly 483 years had transpired

---

[113] Although some contemporary rabbis attempt every mental gymnastic feat imaginable in order to get around this exact and powerful prophecy, this documentation is an infallible proof which has convinced many sincere rabbis of the Messiahship of Jesus. See the book *Rabbi's Edition* (Available through Good News Society, POB 7848, Johannesburg, South Africa, 2000) Tel. 1-610-449-1396, for testimonies of over twenty rabbis who have received Jesus as the Messiah. The prophecy is speaking of an exact time period of four hundred and eighty-three years counting from the command which allowed the rebuilding of the Temple, as we have quoted from Hal Lindsey's brilliant exposition. Rashi dishonestly attempts to apply this prophecy to Agrippa, liberal theologians attempt to link it to the murder of a former high priest, and all of the anti-Messianic Jewish polemical books we have quoted, such as: *You Take Jesus, I'll Take God*; *The Jew and The Christian Missionary*; *Faith Strengthened*; and *The Real Messiah*; deny this prophecy's Messianic application to Jesus, without foundation.

since the proclamation given by Artaxerxes. Daniel said that the city and Temple would be destroyed following the death of their Messiah, and within forty years the Roman Holocaust had taken place.

There's one critical fact that must be pointed out in this prophecy. *Whoever* the Messiah was to be, he had to have come to Israel *before* the city and Temple were destroyed in 70 C.E. Only one candidate fits that role—Jesus of Nazareth!"[114]

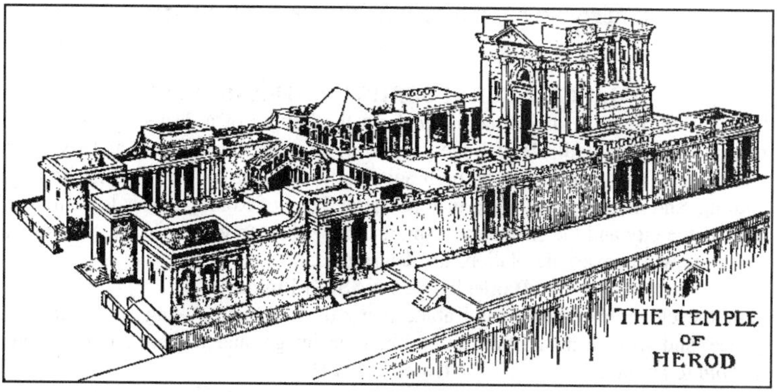

The Temple of Herod was burned to the ground in 70 AD, as Jesus foretold (Luke 12:5-6).

A fifty-to-one model of the Second Temple in Jerusalem, located at The Holyland Hotel.

[114]Hal Lindsey, *The Promise*, pp. 187-189.

ORIGINAL HEBREW TEXT WRITTEN 538 AND 785 BC

וְתֵדַע וְתַשְׂכֵּל מִן־מֹצָא דָבָר לְהָשִׁיב וְלִבְנוֹת יְרוּשָׁלִַם עַד־מָשִׁיחַ נָגִיד שָׁבֻעִים שִׁבְעָה
וְשָׁבֻעִים שִׁשִּׁים וּשְׁנַיִם תָּשׁוּב וְנִבְנְתָה רְחוֹב וְחָרוּץ וּבְצוֹק הָעִתִּים׃ וְאַחֲרֵי הַשָּׁבֻעִים
שִׁשִּׁים וּשְׁנַיִם יִכָּרֵת מָשִׁיחַ וְאֵין לוֹ וְהָעִיר וְהַקֹּדֶשׁ יַשְׁחִית עַם נָגִיד הַבָּא וְקִצּוֹ
בַשֶּׁטֶף וְעַד קֵץ מִלְחָמָה נֶחֱרֶצֶת שֹׁמֵמוֹת׃

דניאל ט:כה-כו

כִּי ׀ יָמִים רַבִּים יֵשְׁבוּ בְּנֵי יִשְׂרָאֵל אֵין מֶלֶךְ וְאֵין שָׂר וְאֵין זֶבַח וְאֵין מַצֵּבָה וְאֵין אֵפוֹד
וּתְרָפִים׃ **הושע ג:ד**

OLD TESTAMENT SCRIPTURE TRANSLATION

"So you are to know and discern *that* from the issuing of a decree to restore and rebuild Jerusalem until Messiah the Prince *there will be* seven weeks and sixty-two weeks; it [The Temple] will be built again....the Messiah will be cut off and have nothing, and the people of the prince [General Titus of Rome] who is to come will destroy the city and the sanctuary. And its end *will come* with a flood; even to the end there will be war; desolations are determined."

Daniel 9:25-26 NASB. [ ] mine

"For the children of Israel shall abide many days without a king, and without a prince, and without a sacrifice, and without an image, and without an ephod, and *without* teraphim...." **Hosea 3:4 KJV**

NEW TESTAMENT RECORDED 63 AD

"And while some were talking about the temple, that it was adorned with beautiful stones and votive gifts, He said, '*As for* these things which you are looking at, the days will come in which there will not be left one stone upon another which will not be torn down.' " **Luke 21:5-6 NASB**

HISTORICAL EYEWITNESS

"These Romans put the Jews to flight...and proceeded as far as the holy house itself. At which time one of the soldiers, without staying for any orders, and without any concern or dread upon him at so great an undertaking, and being hurried on by a certain divine fury, snatched somewhat out of the materials that were on fire, and being lifted up by another soldier, he set fire to a golden window, through which there was a passage to the rooms that were round about the holy house [second Temple]...on the north side of it."[115] **Josephus**

AUTHOR'S COMMENT—EVANGELICAL CHRISTIAN POSITION

As you can see from Jesus's prediction in Luke's New Testament gospel, and the eyewitness account of Josephus, the Romans tore the Temple down stone by stone. When it was accidentally burned, the gold melted and ran down between the stones. Thus, the Romans had to remove the stones of the Temple one by one until the ground level was reached to retrieve the gold, thereby fulfilling the six hundred-year-old prophecy of Daniel 9, which Jesus said would occur in His generation.

Philip Moore

---

[115]Thomas S. McCall and Zola Levitt, *Satan in the Sanctuary*. Dallas, TX: Zola Levitt, © 1983, p. 120, used by permission. [ ] mine.

THE TALMUD TELLS ON ITSELF, HUSHING UP THE MESSIAH'S DATE

The Talmud unwittingly refers to events that verify many New Testament claims. The Talmud records the secrecy of the specific date for the Coming of the Messiah as predicted in Daniel 9, where it tells us: "...a *Bath Kol* came forth and exclaimed, Who is this that has revealed My secrets to mankind? Jonathan b. Uzziel thereupon arose and said, It is I who have revealed Thy secrets to mankind. It is fully known to Thee that I have not done this for my own honour or for the honour of my father's house, but for Thy honour I have done it, that dissension may not increase in Israel. He further sought to reveal [by] a *targum* [the inner meaning] of the Hagiographa, but a *Bath Kol* went forth and said, Enough! What was the reason?—Because the **date** of the **Messiah** is **foretold** in it."[116] The Soncino English Talmud's footnote to the words, "the Messiah is foretold in it," reads: "The reference is probably to the Book of Daniel."[117]

THE ISRAELI BIBLE—ARMY STYLE—RESOLVES THE TIME CALCULATION CRISIS

The Israeli Army Bible, in its commentary footnotes on this segment of Daniel, identifies this time-period as weeks of years. Many liberals and even Christian allegorists argue that the weeks *of years* mentioned here is a modern Christian/Dispensational interpretation.

Since there are few Evangelical Christians in Israel, and thus no need to play down the Messiah, the Israeli Bible is honest and truthful about the time calculations! We would love to get these rabbis and "Christians" all together on an El-Al[118] flight to Israel, then upon arrival at Ben-Gurion Airport, take them over to one of the soldiers at passport control and have him pull out his Bible and translate the footnote to Daniel 9 where it says *weeks of years*! If such rabbis and liberals would be open-minded on this issue, then they might become Messianic and evangelical.

***

---

[116] *The Babylonian Talmud*, Megillah 3a, pp. 9-10. Bold mine.

[117] Ibid.

[118] El-Al is Israel's national airline. In Hebrew, *El* means "God" and *Al* means "flies." In support of Israel, we never fail to use it on our trips to the Holy Land.

ATTORNEY WALTER CHANDLER SAYS JONATHAN'S OMISSION COULD NOT BE COINCIDENCE—IT WAS BECAUSE OF THE TIME FACTOR!

Walter M. Chandler, the famous New York lawyer, in his book, *The Trial of Jesus: From a Lawyer's Standpoint*, sheds light on what seems to be an early rabbinic conspiracy centered around the time factor in Daniel's prophecy. Chandler wrote: "JONATHAN ben UZIEL, author of a very remarkable paraphrase of the Pentateuch and the Prophets....has purposely omitted Daniel, which omission the Talmud explains as due to the special intervention of an angel who informed him that the manner in which the prophet speaks of the death of the Messiah coincided too exactly with that of Jesus of Nazareth. Now, since Jonathan has intentionally left out the prophecies of Daniel on account of their coincidence with the death of Christ, it proves that....The Talmudists, in order to reward this person for having, through his hatred of Christ, erased the name of Daniel from the roll of the prophets, eulogize him in the most absurd manner. They relate that while engaged in the study of the law of God, the atmosphere which surrounded him, and came in contact with the light of his understanding, so caught fire from his fervor that the birds, silly enough to be attracted toward it, were consumed immediately."[119]

SIR ROBERT ANDERSON OF SCOTLAND YARD PUTS THE LAST NAIL IN THE COFFINS OF THOSE WHO DISPUTE DANIEL

Sir Robert Anderson, Chief of the Criminal Investigation Department of Scotland Yard and author of seven textbooks, spent his life investigating this prophecy. He even wrote a book, *The Coming Prince*, to illustrate the historical reliability which he uncovered during his investigation of Daniel 9:24-26. Anderson said: "Now it is an undisputed fact that Jerusalem was rebuilt by Nehemiah, under an edict issued by Artaxerxes (Longimanus), in the twentieth year of his reign. Therefore, notwithstanding the doubts which controversy throws upon everything, the conclusion is obvious and irresistible that this was the epoch of the prophetic period. But the month date was Nisan, and the sacred year of the Jews began with the phasis of the Paschal moon. I appealed, therefore, to the Astronomer Royal, the late Sir George Airy, to calculate for me the moon's place for March in the year in question,

---

[119]Walter M. Chandler, *The Trial of Jesus: From a Lawyer's Standpoint*, illustrated edition, p. 148. Chandler's sources were: The Talmud, "Succa" or "The Festival of Tabernacles," fol. 28, verso; David Ganz, "Chronol," 4728; Gesenius, "Comm. on Isaiah," Part I, p. 65; Zunz, "Culte divin des Juifs," Berlin, 1832, p. 61; Derembourg, work quoted above, p. 276; Hanneburg, "Revelat Bibliq.," ii, 163, 432.

and I thus ascertained the date required—March 14th, B.C. 445....Its *terminus ad quem* can thus with certainty be ascertained. Now 483 years (69 x 7) of 360 days contain 173,880 days. And a period of 173,880 days, beginning March 14th, B.C. 445, ended upon that Sunday in the week of the crucifixion, when, for the first and only time in His ministry, the Lord Jesus Christ, in fulfilment of Zechariah's prophecy, made a public entry into Jerusalem, and caused His Messiahship to be openly proclaimed by 'the whole multitude of the disciples'....Now the great characteristic of the Jewish sacred year has remained unchanged ever since the memorable night when the equinoctial moon beamed down upon the huts of Israel in Egypt, bloodstained by the Paschal sacrifice; and there is neither doubt nor difficulty in fixing within narrow limits the Julian date of the 1st of Nisan in any year whatever. In B.C. 445 the new moon by which the Passover was regulated was the 13th of March at 7h. 9m. A.M. And accordingly the 1st Nisan may be assigned to the 14th March....the language of the prophecy is clear: 'From the going forth of the commandment to restore and to build Jerusalem *unto Messiah the Prince* shall be seven weeks and threescore and two weeks.' An era therefore of sixty-nine 'weeks,' or 483 prophetic years reckoned from the 14th March, B.C. 445, should close with some event to satisfy the words, 'unto the Messiah the Prince'....What then was the length of the period intervening between the issuing of the decree to rebuild Jerusalem and the public advent of 'Messiah the Prince,'—between the 14th March, B.C. 445, and the 6th April....THE INTERVAL CONTAINED EXACTLY AND TO THE VERY DAY 173,880 DAYS, OR SEVEN TIMES SIXTY-NINE PROPHETIC YEARS OF 360 DAYS, the first sixty-nine weeks of Gabriel's prophecy....

But 476 x 365 = ...	173,740 days
Add (14 March to 6th April, *both* inclusive)	24 "
Add for leap years	116 "
	173,880 "

And 69 weeks of prophetic years of 360 days (or 69 x 7 x 360) = 173,880 days.

It may be well to offer here two explanatory remarks. First: in reckoning years from B.C. to A.D., *one* year must always be omitted; for it is obvious, *ex. gr.*, that from B.C. I to A.D. I was not *two* years, but one year. B.C. I ought to be described as B.C. O, and it is so reckoned by astronomers, who would describe the historical date B.C. 445, as 444 (see note, p. 124, *ante*). And secondly, the Julian year is Ilm. 10'46s., or about the 129th part of a day, longer than the mean solar year."[120]

[120] Sir Robert Anderson, *The Coming Prince*. Grand Rapids, MI: Kregel Publications, © 1984, pp. xlv-xlvi, xlvii, 123-124, 127-128, used by permission.

This is why biblical three hundred and sixty-day lunar years differ in length from our three hundred and sixty-five and one-quarter-day solar year. Anderson's calculations are indisputable.

MARK EASTMAN AND REVEREND CHUCK SMITH CORROBORATE ANDERSON

In their book, *The Search for Messiah*, authors Eastman and Smith clarify: "Is there any other way to check the accuracy of this date? Yes....The 1990 Encyclopedia Britannica states that the reign of Caesar Tiberius started on August 19th in the year 14 C.E.....scholars believe Jesus was baptized in the Fall season. Consequently, according to Luke chapter Three, the ministry of Jesus started with his baptism in the Fall of the 15th year of the reign of Caesar Tiberius and...lasted four Passovers or 3 1/2 years. The first Passover of Jesus' ministry would have been in the Spring of 29 C.E.....The Passover in that year fell on April 10th. Remarkably, according to Robert Anderson and the British Royal Observatory, the Sunday before that Passover was April 6th!!!

That day, April 6th, 32 C.E., was exactly 173,880 days after Artaxerxes gave the decree to restore and rebuild Jerusalem on March 14, 445 B.C.E! That day was the first day that Jesus of Nazareth allowed his disciples to proclaim him as Messiah!

This prophecy is one of the many proofs that God transcends time and is able to see the beginning of time from the end with incredible precision....Furthermore, it is well established that the Jews of the Qumran community (the writers of the Dead Sea Scrolls) believed that Daniel's seventy weeks prophecy pinpointed the time of the coming of the Messiah. In fact, many in the Qumran community based their messianic hope on similar chronological calculations.[121] They believed that they were living in the generation to which this

---

[121]Mark Eastman has strong ground for revealing this newly discovered Messianic evidence concerning this prophecy, its commentary on the Messiah, its date, the Coming of Jesus and the Essenes at Qumran, because James Tabor, in the *Biblical Archaeological Review*, reported: "...the question is: Given their triumphant view of the Davidic messiah figure, is it likely that the Qumran group conceived of such a one being crushed? Such a connection is implied in the fascinating text 11QMelch[izedek], which deals with the end of days. There Daniel 9:25 is quoted, which mentions the coming of a messiah who is subsequently (in Daniel 9:26) *cut off.* This verse is followed immediately in 11QMelch[izedek] by a quotation from Isaiah 61:2-3, a messianic text of hope and comfort (see 4Q521, which interprets Isaiah 61 as the messiah's triumph). We know the Qumran group was intensely interested in this 'Seventy Weeks' prophecy of Daniel. They tried to place themselves within this chronological scheme as they calculated the eschaton." James Tabor, "A Pierced or Piercing Messiah?—The Verdict is Still Out," *Biblical Archaeological Review*, Nov.-Dec. 1992, p. 58.

prophecy pointed!....However, according to the popular view (not the Biblical one) he was not what they expected or wanted in a Messiah. The truth had been hidden from their eyes."[122]

ANDERSON'S INSPIRATION

Anderson was, in part, inspired by a rabbi who denied and challenged our interpretation of Daniel's prophecy. "Very many years ago my attention was directed to a volume of sermons by a devout Jewish rabbi of the London Synagogue, in which he sought to discredit the Christian interpretation of certain Messianic prophecies. And in dealing with Daniel ix., he accused Christian expositors of tampering, not only with chronology, but with Scripture, in their efforts to apply the prophecy of the Seventy Weeks to the Nazarene. My indignation at such a charge gave place to distress....I decided to take up the study of the subject with a fixed determination to accept without reserve not only the language of Scripture, but the standard dates of history as settled by our best modern chronologists."[123]

WHAT EVENTS DID DANIEL PREDICT EXACTLY?

Daniel's prophecy reads as follows: "Seventy weeks are determined upon thy people and upon thy holy city, to finish the transgression, and to make an end of sins, and to make reconciliation for iniquity, and to bring in everlasting righteousness, and to seal up the vision and prophecy, and to anoint the most Holy. Know therefore and understand, *that* from the going forth of the commandment to restore and to build Jerusalem unto the Messiah the Prince *shall be* seven weeks, and threescore and two weeks: the street shall be built again, and the wall, even in troublous times. And after threescore and two weeks shall Messiah be cut off, but not for himself: and the people of the prince that shall come shall destroy the city and the sanctuary; and the end thereof *shall be* with a flood, and unto the end of the war desolations are determined" (Dan. 9:24-26 KJV).

Daniel clearly outlines that the Messiah would come four hundred and eighty-three years (sixty-nine weeks of years) after the command given for the Jews' release from Babylon, so that they could return to Israel and begin rebuilding the Temple. The date of this command, given by the Persian King Artaxerxes, was discovered in Persian archives during archaeological excavations.

---

[122]Mark Eastman, M.D., and Chuck Smith, *The Search for Messiah*, pp. 81-83.

[123]Sir Robert Anderson, *The Coming Prince*, p. ix.

The Old Testament prophet Nehemiah also verifies this in the second chapter of his biblical book.[124] Daniel predicted that once the Messiah came, He would be "cut off" (a Hebrew idiom for being killed, verse 26), then he says that the city of Jerusalem and the sanctuary (of the Temple) would be destroyed.

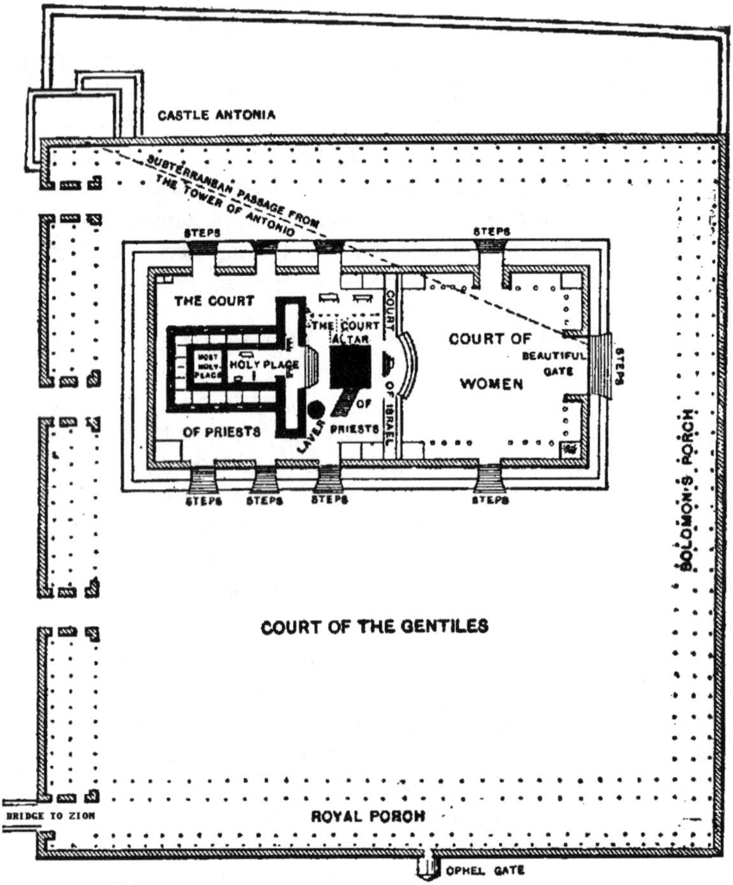

PLAN OF TEMPLE

---

[124]Nehemiah 2:1-10.

ORIGINAL HEBREW TEXT WRITTEN 538 BC

שָׁבֻעִים שִׁבְעִים נֶחְתַּךְ עַל־עַמְּךָ ׀ וְעַל־עִיר קָדְשֶׁךָ לְכַלֵּא הַפֶּשַׁע וּלְחָתֵם חַטָּאות וּלְכַפֵּר
עָוֺן וּלְהָבִיא צֶדֶק עֹלָמִים וְלַחְתֹּם חָזוֹן וְנָבִיא וְלִמְשֹׁחַ קֹדֶשׁ קָדָשִׁים׃ וְתֵדַע וְתַשְׂכֵּל
מִן־מֹצָא דָבָר לְהָשִׁיב וְלִבְנוֹת יְרוּשָׁלִַם עַד־מָשִׁיחַ נָגִיד שָׁבֻעִים שִׁבְעָה וְשָׁבֻעִים שִׁשִּׁים
וּשְׁנַיִם תָּשׁוּב וְנִבְנְתָה רְחוֹב וְחָרוּץ וּבְצוֹק הָעִתִּים׃ וְאַחֲרֵי הַשָּׁבֻעִים שִׁשִּׁים וּשְׁנַיִם יִכָּרֵת
מָשִׁיחַ וְאֵין לוֹ וְהָעִיר וְהַקֹּדֶשׁ יַשְׁחִית עַם נָגִיד הַבָּא וְקִצּוֹ בַשֶּׁטֶף וְעַד קֵץ מִלְחָמָה נֶחֱרֶצֶת
שֹׁמֵמוֹת׃ **דניאל ט:כד-כו**

OLD TESTAMENT SCRIPTURE TRANSLATION

"Seventy weeks have been decreed for your people and your holy city, to finish the transgression, to make an end of sin, to make atonement for iniquity, to bring in everlasting righteousness, to seal up vision and prophecy, and to anoint the most holy *place*. So you are to know and discern *that* from the issuing of a decree to restore and rebuild Jerusalem until Messiah the Prince *there will be* seven weeks and sixty-two weeks....Messiah will be cut off [killed] and have nothing, and the people of the prince [Titus of Rome] who is to come will destroy the city and the sanctuary. And its end *will come* with a flood; even to the end there will be war; desolations are determined."

Daniel 9:24-26 NASB. [ ] mine[125]

ANCIENT RABBINICAL COMMENTARY

"I have examined and searched all the Holy Scriptures, and have not found the time for the coming of MESSIAH, clearly fixed, except in the words of Gabriel to the prophet Daniel, which are written in the ninth chapter of the prophecy of Daniel."[126] **Rabbi Moses Abraham Levi**

NEW TESTAMENT RECORDED 63 AD

"And when He approached, He saw the city and **wept** over it, saying, 'If you had known in this day, even you, the things which make for peace! But now they have been hidden from your eyes. For the days shall come upon you when your enemies will throw up a bank before you, and surround you, and hem you in on every side, and will level you to the ground and your children within you, and they will not leave in you one stone upon another, because you did not recognize the **time** of your **visitation**.' " **Luke 19:41-44 NASB**

MODERN RABBINIC COMMENT/REFUTATION

"…It is most reasonable and probable to affirm that the annointed one that he referred to in Daniel 9:25 is Cyrus, and not Jesus. The reason why a Christian would have difficulty understanding this is because the compiler of the King James Bible was a shrewd person. In the original Hebrew, both Daniel 9:25 and Isaiah 45:1 use the exact same word—'moshiach.' However, in the Christian version of the Old Testament, the word, 'moshiach,' is translated in Isaiah 45:1 as 'anointed' whereas in Daniel 9:25, the same Hebrew word is translated as 'the Messiah.' ('Messiah' is the Anglicized version of 'Moshiach'; the pure translation of 'Moshiach' is 'an anointed one.') This deceptive translating makes it virtually impossible for the innocent reader who does not know Hebrew to discern the truth."

***You Take Jesus, I'll Take God,* by Samuel Levine, p. 31-32: © 1980.**

---

125 See Chapter 22, "Rome Resurrected," regarding details on Daniel's end-time prophecies as they relate to Rome's revival in our present-day Europe.

126 F. Kenton Beshore, D.D., LL.D., Ph.D., *"The Messiah" of the Targums, Talmuds and Rabbinical Writers*, pp. chart 13.

AUTHOR'S COMMENT—EVANGELICAL CHRISTIAN POSITION

Being a Christian who happens to know Hebrew, I can reassure my readers that contrary to what Levine claims, מָשִׁיחַ נָגִיד (Meshiack Nagid) translates "Messiah cut off." Those "dumb Christians who only read King James and don't know Hebrew" need not worry. Jesus cried because He saw His people were rejecting Him (not knowing the time of their Messianic visitation). He knew the consequences of this act for Israel from the ancient prophecies written in the law (Deut. 28:57). This prophecy of Moses indicated cannibalism. Luke 23:27-31 added details to this. The Jewish historian of the first century, Josephus, records that these events actually occurred just as Moses and Jesus predicted. These events happened thirty-seven years after Jesus said they would. Josephus verified: " 'This famine also will destroy us, even before that slavery comes upon us; yet are these seditious rogues more terrible than both the other. Come on; be thou my food, and be thou a fury to these seditious varlets and a bye-word to the world, which is all that is now wanting to complete the calamities of us Jews.' As soon as she had said this, she slew her son; and then roasted him and ate the one half of him, and kept the other half by her concealed."[127]

Philip Moore

WHAT DANIEL PREDICTED OF JERUSALEM, THE TEMPLE AND JESUS, HAS OCCURRED TO THE LETTER

Did it happen? Jesus rode into Jerusalem exactly to the day of the end of the four hundred and eighty-three years.[128] Soon thereafter, Jesus was crucified and within a generation the Temple and its sanctuary were destroyed. Who could dare to make such an accurate prophecy? Only God through his prophet Daniel.

Verse 27 of Daniel's ninth chapter deals with the time of the Antichrist and his false prophet. They will appear in the mid-21st century as the ruler of a newly formed revived Roman Empire and as Israel's Messiah. Much more will be said about this in our chapters 22, "Rome Resurrected," and 23, "The False Messiah Armilus Equals Antichrist."

A review of world history, and future, illustrated from biblical symbols.

[127] *Wars of the Jews*, published in the compilation *Josephus: Complete Works*. Grand Rapids, MI: Kregel Publications, © 1981, book 4, chapter 3, verse 3, used by permission.

[128] According to the three hundred and sixty-day biblical years, as foretold by Daniel.

THE MAIN POINT OF DANIEL'S PREDICTION, FULFILLED IN PAST AGES BUT STILL IN OUR FUTURE, POINTS TO JESUS REGARDLESS

Our point regarding these monumental prophecies of Daniel is that there is no way anyone can study them, including modern rabbinical "scholars," and being intellectually honest about them, infer that Jesus was not the Messiah or that the Messiah will come on a donkey in the twentieth century. He will come, but with pierced hands (Zech. 12:10) "on the clouds of heaven" (Dan. 7:13) to a weeping Jewish Jerusalem, which He saves from invading Russian-Arab armies known to Israel as Gog and Magog. Read the 2600-year-old writings of the Hebrew prophet Ezekiel, chapters 38-39 in your family Bible and you will see what we are talking about! This subject is covered in our chapter 19, "Russia is Crushed in Gog," and chapter 20, "Mohammed is Mad," where we show how these future political predicaments will result in biblically predicted fulfillments.

IN THE END, JESUS WILL BRING IN PEACE, AS PREDICTED BY ZECHARIAH AND DAVID

After the third world war (Rev. 16:16)[129] Jesus will fulfill the remainder of Zechariah's prophecy by inaugurating the long awaited Messianic Kingdom of peace. Jesus promised to fulfill this prophecy when Israel and the world's Jewry would receive Him (Matt. 23:39), when He would return "in the clouds of heaven" (Mark 16:42) from God's right hand, as predicted by King David (Ps. 110:1).

As you remember, Zechariah 9:9 dealt with the entrance of Jesus into Jerusalem on a donkey. The remainder of Zechariah's prophecy says: "And I will cut off the chariot from Ephraim, and the horse from Jerusalem, and the battle bow shall be cut off: and he shall speak peace unto the heathen: and his dominion *shall be* from sea *even* to sea, and from the river *even* to the ends of the earth" (Zech. 9:10 KJV).

It will be at this time (probably no more than one-half century away) that many great and unbelievable events will take place. Jesus will resurrect the dead (you and me, that is, if we have a chance to die before He returns). If you have partaken of Jesus' free gift of salvation you will live forever in a refurbished, regenerated New Earth.

These promises tingle my toes with vitality. Just think, happy-go-lucky, never to feel pain or suffering or to die, but to righteously enjoy, as God has always intended for us (see our chapters 29 and 30, which deal with new world Messianic conditions)!

---

[129] John the apostle calls this war Armageddon in the sixteenth chapter of his Apocalypse.

ORIGINAL HEBREW TEXT WRITTEN 712 BC

הֵן עַבְדִּי֙ אֶתְמָךְ־בּ֔וֹ בְּחִירִ֖י רָצְתָ֣ה נַפְשִׁ֑י נָתַ֤תִּי רוּחִי֙ עָלָ֔יו מִשְׁפָּ֖ט לַגּוֹיִ֥ם יוֹצִֽיא׃

ישעיה מב:א

OLD TESTAMENT SCRIPTURE TRANSLATION

" 'Behold, My Servant, whom I uphold; My chosen one *in whom* My soul delights. I have put My Spirit upon Him; He will bring forth justice to the nations.' "[130]

Isaiah 42:1 NASB

ANCIENT RABBINICAL COMMENTARY

"Behold, My Servant, the Messiah, whom I bring near, My chosen one, in whom My Memra takes delight; I will place My holy spirit upon him, and he shall reveal My law to the nations."[131] **Targum Jonathan**

NEW TESTAMENT PREDICTION 96 AD

"...He [Jesus] who sat upon it *is* called Faithful and True; and in righteousness He judges and wages war. And His eyes *are* a flame of fire, and upon His head *are* many diadems; and He has a name written *upon Him* which no one knows except Himself. And *He is* clothed with a robe dipped in blood; and His name is called The Word of God. And the armies which are in heaven, clothed in fine linen, white *and* clean, were following Him on white horses. And from His mouth comes a sharp sword, so that with it He may smite the nations; and He will rule them with a rod of iron; and He treads the wine press of the fierce wrath of God, the Almighty. And on His robe and on His thigh He has a name written, 'KING OF KINGS, AND LORD OF LORDS.' " **Revelation 19:11-16 NASB. [ ] mine**

MODERN RABBINIC COMMENT/REFUTATION

All anti-Christian rabbis believe that the Messiah will fulfill the above prophecies and bring peace, but that it is not Jesus coming back to do it. We could not find an anti-Christian refutation of Jesus in our selection of books. They finally missed one, didn't they? **Philip Moore**

AUTHOR'S COMMENT—EVANGELICAL CHRISTIAN POSITION

Psalms 2:8-9 says that through God's spirit the Messiah will bring justice to the nations. All true believers look to Jesus to carry out these promises when He returns, as the last book of the New Testament, Revelation, asserts.

Philip Moore

MEANWHILE, BACK AT THE TEMPLE, JESUS THROWS A FIT! WHY?

At that time, Judaism was still geared to accept any Gentile who wanted to be saved by accepting the Hebrew God of Israel. This is why there was a Court of the Gentiles at the Temple.

The Gentiles were placed in the outermost court, which was built at the instruction of God, so that any of the world's heathens who were

---

130 *The New Scofield Reference Bible* documents: "There is a twofold account of the Coming Servant: He is represented 1. as weak, despised, rejected, slain; and also 2. as a mighty conqueror, taking vengeance on the nations and restoring Israel (e.g. 40:10; 63:1-4. The former class of passages relate to the first advent, and are fulfilled; the latter to the second advent, and are unfulfilled." *The New Scofield Reference Bible*, p. 748.

131 Samson H. Levey, *The Messiah: An Aramaic Interpretation, The Messianic Exegesis of the Targum*, p. 59.

interested might have the opportunity to see and accept the true faith of Israel before the Messiah came.

Even though the Bible and Temple opened the door for Gentiles to enter into the biblical faith, the religious leaders at the time of Messiah Jesus had grown intolerant of these allotments which God had commanded. This is why, in John 2:15, we read that Jesus whipped the moneychangers in the Temple: "...He made a scourge of cords, and drove *them* all out of the temple, with the sheep and the oxen; and He poured out the coins of the moneychangers, and overturned their tables...." (NASB).

You see, they were changing the money of heathen governments to shekels, the only acceptable currency for the purchase of sacrificial animals. They were charging exorbitant rates of exchange but the real and terrible thing which upset Jesus was the fact that these animals, sold for sacrifice, were taking up the entire Court of the Gentiles! In other words, if Gentiles were interested and wanted to observe Jewish rites and consider accepting the biblical faith and the God of Israel, they could not make their way into the Temple area which God had instructed the nation of Israel to allow for them. These corrupt priests and leaders were using their space to store sacrificial animals. Thus, after He drives the moneychangers from the Temple (house) area, Jesus says: "...'Is it not written, My house shall be called of all nations the house of prayer? but ye have made it a den of thieves' " (Mark 11:17 KJV).

STRANGE PHRASES OF JESUS BECOME ALL TOO FAMILIAR WHEN WE LOOK BACK INTO THE OLD TESTAMENT

These two phrases: "a house of prayer for all nations," and; "a den of thieves" (indicating the Court of the Gentiles[132] and astronomical rates of exchange), were prophecies foretold hundreds of years earlier in the Bible of Israel! These were to be fulfilled in Jesus' day.

Jesus was quoting from Isaiah and Jeremiah, who explicitly predicted and instructed: "...the sons of the |foreigner| that join themselves to the LORD, to serve him, and to love the name of the LORD, to be his servants, every one that keepeth the sabbath from polluting it, and taketh hold of my covenant; Even them will I bring to my holy mountain, and make them joyful in my house of prayer; their burnt offerings and their sacrifices *shall be* accepted upon mine altar [including non-Jews (nations/Gentiles) who accepted the God of Israel]...." (Isa. 56:6-7 KJV; [ ] mine).[133]

---

[132]Gentile means "nation" or "non-Jew," from a nation other than Israel.

[133]*The New Scofield Reference Bible.*

Jeremiah's 2600-year-old prophecy included the words: "**Is this house**, which is called by my name, **become a den of robbers** in your eyes? Behold, even I have seen *it*, saith the LORD" (Jer. 7:11 KJV; bold mine).

THE PROPHECY OF PRICE WAS THIRTY SHEKELS!

It has been said that everyone has their price. Judas' price was thirty Israeli shekels of silver and his motives were complex.

The Messianic expectations among the Jews of that day were geared toward a mighty warrior king rather than a suffering servant. Judas thought that he could push Jesus into a situation where He would have to use military might or fall helplessly to Rome. Judas felt he would force Jesus to legitimize Himself and make some easy money at the same time. However, Jesus played right along with what was really prophesied to happen; that is the appearance of the suffering Messiah. He willingly allowed Himself to be arrested, tried and put to death.

When Judas witnessed the first two parts of this triple design, he felt guilty. He had been paid the money which Zechariah had foretold to the penny five hundred years beforehand (Matt. 26:14-15).

Once he saw that Jesus was going to allow Himself to be executed, he felt tremendous remorse, so he tried to give the money back to the priests. They would not take it, saying: "What is that to us? See to *that* yourself...It is not lawful[134] to put them into the temple treasury, since it is the price of blood" (Matt. 27:6 NASB).

---

134 Alfred Edersheim, a Jewish believer in Jesus and scholar of the last century, enlightens us: "...in the Temple the priests knew not what to do with these thirty pieces of money. Their unscrupulous scrupulosity came again upon them. It was not lawful to take into the Temple-treasury, for the purchase of sacred things, money that had been unlawfully gained. In such cases the Jewish Law provided that the money was to be restored to the donor, and, if he insisted on giving it, that he should be induced to spend it for something for the public weal. This explains the apparent discrepancy between the accounts in the Book of Acts and by St. Matthew. By a fiction of law the money was still considered to be Judas', and to have been applied by him in the purchase of the well-known 'potter's field,' for the charitable purpose of burying in it strangers. But from henceforth the old name of 'potter's field,' became popularly changed into that of 'field of blood' (Haqal Dema). And yet it was the act of Israel through its leaders: 'they took the thirty pieces of silver—the price of him that was valued, whom they of the children of Israel did value, and gave them for the potter's field!' It was all theirs, though they would have fain made it all Judas': the valuing, the selling, and the purchasing. And 'the potter's field'—the very spot on which Jeremiah had been Divinely directed to prophesy against Jerusalem and against Israel: how was it now all fulfilled in the light of the completed sin and apostasy of the people, as prophetically described by Zechariah! This Tophet of Jeremiah, now that they had valued and sold at thirty shekel Israel's Messiah-Shepherd—truly a Tophet, and become a field of blood! Surely, not an accidental coincidence this, that it should be the place of Jeremy's announcement of judgment: not accidental, but veritably a fulfillment of his prophecy! And so St. Matthew, targuming this prophecy...in true Jewish manner stringing to it the prophetic description furnished

Judas threw the silver into the Temple in a fit of rage and disillusionment (by the way, Zechariah's "house of the Lord," in which the prophecy indicates the payment was to be cast down, was the Temple!). Finally, once he had flung those infamous shekels onto the *hekel*[135] floor, the priest picked up the coins and decided, with mock concern, to use them to buy the "potter's field," where poor people would be buried. As we read in the New Testament: "...they counseled together and with the money bought the Potter's Field as a burial place for strangers. For this reason that field has been called the Field of Blood to this day" (Matt. 27:7-8 NASB).

Since the money had been taken from the Temple treasury it had to be used for the public good (and actually, it was, since Jesus truly was the sacrifice and the Temple treasury was used to purchase sacrificial offerings). So Zechariah gets three predictions in a row right about the Messiah's betrayal.

Zechariah predicted: "So it was broken on that day, and thus the afflicted of the flock who were watching me realized that it was the word of the LORD. And I said to them, 'If it is good in your sight, give *me* my wages; but if not, never mind!' So they weighed out thirty *shekels* of silver as my wages. Then the LORD said to me, 'Throw it to the potter, *that* magnificent price at which I was valued by them.' So I took the thirty *shekels* of silver and threw them to the potter in the house of the LORD" (Zech. 11:11-13 NASB).

The Potter's Field in Israel where Judas committed suicide.

---

by Zechariah, sets the event before us as the fulfillment of Jeremy's prophecy." Dr. Alfred Edersheim, *The Life and Times of Jesus the Messiah*, pp. 575-576.

[135] Another word for Temple.

ORIGINAL HEBREW TEXT WRITTEN 487 BC

וָאֹמַר אֲלֵיהֶם אִם־טוֹב בְּעֵינֵיכֶם הָבוּ שְׂכָרִי וְאִם־לֹא ׀ חֲדָלוּ וַיִּשְׁקְלוּ אֶת־שְׂכָרִי שְׁלֹשִׁים
כָּסֶף׃ וַיֹּאמֶר יְהוָה אֵלַי הַשְׁלִיכֵהוּ אֶל־הַיּוֹצֵר אֶדֶר הַיְקָר אֲשֶׁר יָקַרְתִּי מֵעֲלֵיהֶם וָאֶקְחָה
שְׁלֹשִׁים הַכֶּסֶף וָאַשְׁלִךְ אֹתוֹ בֵּית יְהוָה אֶל־הַיּוֹצֵר׃

זכריה יא:יב-יג

OLD TESTAMENT SCRIPTURE TRANSLATION

"And I said to them, 'If it is good in your sight, give *me* my wages; but if not, never mind!' So they weighed out thirty *shekels* of silver as my wages. Then the LORD said to me, 'Throw it to the potter, *that* magnificent price at which I was valued by them.' So I took the thirty *shekels* of silver and threw them to the potter in the house of the LORD." **Zechariah 11:12-13 NASB**

ANCIENT RABBINICAL COMMENTARY

"R. Hanin said, 'Israel will not require the teaching of the royal Messiah in the future, for it says, '*Unto him shall the nations seek*' (Isa. 11:10), but not Israel. If so, for what purpose will the royal Messiah come, and what will he do? He will come to...give...thirty precepts, as it says, '*And I said unto them: If ye think good, give me my hire; and if not, forbear. So they weighed for my hire thirty pieces of silver.*' (Zech. 11:12)" **Genesis Rabbah 98.9**

NEW TESTAMENT RECORDED 37 AD

"Then one of the twelve, named Judas Iscariot, went to the chief priests, and said, 'What are you willing to give me to deliver Him up to you?' And they weighed out to him thirty pieces of silver. And from then on he *began* looking for a good opportunity to betray Him....And while He was still speaking, behold, Judas, one of the twelve, came up, accompanied by a great multitude with swords and clubs, from the chief priests and elders of the people. Now he who was betraying Him gave them a sign, saying, 'Whomever I shall kiss, He is the one; seize Him.' And immediately he went to Jesus and said, 'Hail Rabbi!' and kissed Him....At that time Jesus said to the multitudes, 'Have you come out with swords and clubs to arrest Me as against a robber? Every day I used to sit in the temple teaching and you did not seize Me'....Then when Judas, who had betrayed Him, saw that He had been condemned, he felt remorse and returned the thirty pieces of silver to the chief priests and elders, saying, 'I have sinned by betraying innocent blood.' But they said, 'What is that to us? See *to that* yourself!' And he threw the pieces of silver into the sanctuary and departed; and he went away and hanged himself. And the chief priests took the pieces of silver and said, 'It is not lawful to put them into the temple treasury, since it is the price of blood.' And they counseled together and with the money bought the Potter's Field[136] as a burial place for strangers."

Matthew 26:14-16, 47-49, 55; 27:3-7 NASB

---

136 Matthew 27:9 mentions fulfillment of Jeremiah's prediction. Jeremiah 32:6-9 mentions a field. However, the fuller meaning is found in Zechariah 11:12-13, which is Matthew's exact quotation. *The New Scofield Reference Bible* quite accurately explains: "There may be an allusion to Jer. 18:1-4 and 19:1-3, but the reference is distinctly to Zech. 11:12-13. A Talmudic tradition states that the prophetic writings were placed in the canon in this order: Jeremiah, Ezekiel, Isaiah, etc. Many Hebrew manuscripts follow this order. Thus Matthew cited the passage as from the roll of the prophets and by the name of the first book." *The New Scofield Reference Bible*, p. 1041.

MODERN RABBINIC COMMENT/REFUTATION

"Here, again, we meet with the usual misapplication of Scriptural passages. The quotation, taken from Zechariah xi. 12, 13, runs as follows: 'So they weighed for my price thirty pieces of silver. And the Lord said unto me, Cast it unto the potter,' etc....The thirty pieces of silver are a figurative representation of the righteous men of the time, who were cast to their potter...."

***Faith Strengthened*, by Isaac Troki, pp. 246-247; 1850**

AUTHOR'S COMMENT—EVANGELICAL CHRISTIAN POSITION

I realize that the rabbinical commentary concerning the number thirty does not indicate the sale of Messiah for thirty shekels. Such a commentary is yet to be found, if in fact it exists. However, my point in using the quote from the Midrash is to illustrate to you, in the twentieth century, that the ancient rabbis saw Zechariah 11:12-13 as applying in some way to the Messiah; something modern Jewish scholars and rabbis categorically deny.

Philip Moore

Some of these olive trees in the Garden of Gethsemane in Israel are actually the same trees which were alive when Jesus was arrested after praying in this garden over 1960 years ago. It is a botanical fact that their life span averages well over 2000 years.

WHAT REALLY HAPPENED IN THE GARDEN OF GETHSEMANE?

The Garden of Gethsemane is a beautiful garden in Jerusalem, located at the foot of the Mount of Olives. This was the place where Jesus and His disciples were praying the night Judas led the Roman chiliarch[137] (a chiliarch was a commander of 1000 men, equal in rank to a modern general[138]) and his men, accompanied by the high priests and their henchmen, to Jesus. That same night, He was arrested by the Roman government for His claim of Messiahship.

As I stood in this beautiful garden I could feel the spirit of love and self-sacrifice. Even today, it seems to linger, to those who are sensitive to the things of God!

---

[137]This word is correctly translated by J.N. Darby in his study Bible in the passage John 18:12: "The band therefore, and the *chiliarch*, and the officers of the Jews, took Jesus and bound him...." J.N. Darby, *The 'Holy Scriptures,' A New Translation from the Original Languages*. Addison, IL: Bible Truth Publishers, 1976, p. 1295. Italics mine. Available through Bible Truth Publishers, POB 649, 59 Industrial Road, Addison, IL, USA 60101.

[138]Hal Lindsey, *A Prophetical Walk Through the Holy Land*. Eugene, OR: Harvest House Publishers, © 1983, p. 108.

ON YOUR BACK LOOKING UP AT GOD

Let's take a closer look at the events surrounding the visit of the Romans and Pharisees to the Garden. The New Testament text reads: "...He went forth with His disciples over the ravine of the Kidron, where there was a garden....Judas then, having received the *Roman* cohort, and officers from the chief priests and the Pharisees, came there with lanterns and torches and weapons. Jesus therefore...went forth, and said to them, 'Whom do you seek?' They answered Him, 'Jesus the Nazarene.' He said to them, 'I am *He*'....When therefore He said to them, 'I am *He*,' they drew back, and fell to the ground....'...if therefore you seek Me, let these go their way'...." (John 18:1, 3-6, 8 NASB).

JESUS CLAIMED HIS MEMORIAL NAME OF ALL GENERATIONS—"I AM," OR YAHWEH, FROM THE BOOK OF EXODUS, BEFORE THE PRIESTS, ROMAN SOLDIERS AND CHILIARCH

The "He" in verse 6 is not contained in the original language. If you have a New American Standard translation of the New Testament before you, notice that *He* is in italics, indicating that the word is not in the original language but was inserted afterward to make the English read more smoothly.

Jesus is claiming His ancient title of deity **I AM**, or in Hebrew, ***YAHWEH.*** This incredible Hebrew title comes from the Old Testament book of Exodus, the second book of the Jewish Bible. The conversation runs as follows: "Then Moses said to God, 'Behold, I am going to the sons of Israel, and I shall say to them, 'The God of your fathers has sent me to you.' Now they may say to me, 'What is His name?' What shall I say to them?' And God said to Moses, 'I AM WHO I AM'; and He said, 'Thus you shall say to the sons of Israel, 'I AM has sent me to you.' ' And God, furthermore, said to Moses, 'Thus you shall say to the sons of Israel, 'The LORD, the God of your fathers, the God of Abraham, the God of Isaac, and the God of Jacob, has sent me to you.' This is My name forever, and this is My memorial-name to all generations' " (Exo. 3:13-15 NASB).

God told Moses to address Him as such before the Pharaoh of Egypt. Of course, Pharaoh at that time had not become acquainted with the God of Israel, the one true God!

***

JESUS' MESSIANIC CLAIM OF DEITY REFERRED TO HIS ETERNAL PRE-EXISTENT SELF BEFORE ABRAHAM WAS BORN—"I AM"

Jesus was claiming this title not of His flesh, which was born at Bethlehem some thirty-three years before, of which God is the literal father, but rather His claim is based on His eternal pre-existence before His birth. This is beautifully illustrated in His conversation with some religious leaders in the Gospel of John. John records this revealing encounter as the authorities asked Jesus: " '...whom do You make Yourself out *to be*?' Jesus answered....'Your father Abraham rejoiced to see My day, and he saw *it* and was glad.' The Jews [religious minority leaders] therefore said to Him, 'You are not yet fifty years old, and have You seen Abraham?' Jesus said to them, 'Truly, truly, I say to you, before Abraham was born, **I am**' " (John 8:53-54, 56-58 NASB; [ ] and bold mine).

It is incredible that a century before, the Jewish leaders in charge would have fallen on their faces and worshipped Him for who He was (Messianic deity), but by the time Jesus arrived on the scene the religious leadership of Israel had been corrupted by Rome, as we have documented.

JESUS KNOCKED THE ROMANS AND PRIESTS (TOGETHER, OVER 1000 OF THEM) DOWN FLAT WITH THE UTTERANCE OF HIS ANCIENT NAME, "I AM"!

To get back to the subject, which is the event we were observing in the Garden of Gethsemane, verse 6 of John 18 says: "When therefore He said to them, 'I am *He,*' they drew back, and fell to the ground" (NASB).

Most do not realize the significance of the words, "they drew back." This phrase indicates that they were knocked flat on their backs, suddenly, as God's name released this power with the utterance of His true identity.

***

I have never seen this miracle of vast might, which was released when Jesus uttered His true divine name, ever portrayed in any of the movies about Him! Have you? In essence, Jesus told this group of Roman soldiers, including their leader, the chiliarch (John 18:12 Darby), that they could not arrest God on their own conditions. They had no choice but to let the disciples go, who otherwise would also have been arrested. After these events occurred, Jesus allowed the Romans and "religious leaders" to arrest Him so He could fulfill the Bible's predicted role for Him as a willing Passover lamb, sacrificed for you and me, so anyone believing in Him could receive atonement for all evils. What a relief!

IS ISAIAH 53 MESSIANIC OR NOT? OUR GREATEST SUFFERER

Isaiah eloquently predicted: "Behold, my servant shall deal prudently, he shall be exalted and extolled, and be very high. As many were astonied at thee; his visage was so marred more than any man, and his form more than the sons of men: So shall he sprinkle many nations; the kings shall shut their mouths at him: for *that* which had not been told them shall they see; and *that* which they had not heard shall they consider. Who hath believed our report? and to whom is the arm of the LORD revealed? For he shall grow up before him as a tender plant, and as a root out of a dry ground: he hath no form nor comeliness; and when we shall see him, *there is* no beauty that we should desire him" (Isa. 52:13-53:2 KJV).

The Jewish prophet Isaiah, seven hundred years before Christ, claimed that this one, God's servant, the Messiah, would be beaten beyond recognition and suffer so as to gain the interest of heathen kings and nations the world over. In essence, he said that the non-Jew would be given the grace of the God of Israel through the horrible sufferings and tortures of this man who would go almost unrecognized by the whole[139] of His own people, the Jews, to whom He was sent! Did this come true? Jesus, in His rejection by His fellow countrymen, was truly likened to "a tender plant," and "a root out of dry ground," due to the spiritual callousness and misunderstanding of the religious leaders of Israel!

History as well as the New Testament testifies to His brutal beatings (John 19:1-3)[140] and crucifixion by Roman soldiers, which

---

[139]Although there were nearly one million Jews who did accept Jesus in the first and second centuries, many other millions were convinced falsely by the rabbinical authorities of their day that He was not the Messiah. For a full understanding of this, see our chapters 7-9 on the Messiah Conspiracy.

[140]The apostle John records this mistreatment: "Then Pilate therefore took Jesus, and scourged *him*. And the soldiers platted a crown of thorns, and put *it* on his head, and they put on him a purple robe, And said, Hail, King of the Jews! and they smote him with their hands" (KJV). Hal Lindsey, in his book, *The Promise*, beautifully elaborates: "It's predicted that this Servant of the Lord would be treated in such a manner that he would be disfigured to the point that he would hardly look human (Isaiah 52:14). As unthinkable as it is, the Servant would be struck on both the back and face. He would be humiliated by being spit upon the face (Isaiah 50:4-11). It's well known that this is the kind of treatment that Jesus received during the six illegal trials he was subjected to. The officers of Herod's temple guard spat in Jesus' face after the Sanhedrin had condemned him. Then they blindfolded him and struck him in the face. A jagged crown of thorns was jammed down on his head and he was cruelly whipped with a Roman scourge. It was a sadistic whip made of many strips of leather to which pieces of bone or jagged metal were attached to make the effect more painful. None of this abuse of Jesus was either legal or warranted. There had been no criminal charges proven against him. Yet all

rendered Him so **marred,** He was unrecognizable. This is one of the reasons people from all nations and walks of life consider Him, saying, "Did He endure all of this terrible suffering so I could be set free? For me?" We can easily imagine that even a mighty king with unlimited political power and wealth would find this question intriguing.

"The Apostle Paul in Prison," as envisioned by Rembrandt in 1627.

---

of this happened to the Servant of the Lord just as Isaiah had prophesied that it would (Isaiah 52:13-53:12)." Hal Lindsey, *The Promise*, pp. 120-121.

ORIGINAL HEBREW TEXT WRITTEN 712 BC

הִנֵּה יַשְׂכִּיל עַבְדִּי יָרוּם וְנִשָּׂא וְגָבַהּ מְאֹד׃

ישעיה נב:יג

OLD TESTAMENT SCRIPTURE TRANSLATION

"Behold, My servant will prosper, He will be high and lifted up, and greatly exalted." **Isaiah 52:13 NASB**

ANCIENT RABBINICAL COMMENTARY

"Behold, my servant, the Messiah, shall prosper; he shall be exalted, etc. 'Behold, my servant shall deal prudently.' This is the King Messiah. 'He shall be exalted and extolled, and be very high.' He shall be exalted more than Abraham; for of Him it is written, 'I have exalted my hand to the Lord' (Gen. XIV.22). He shall be extolled more than Moses....(Num. XI.12)."[141]

Targum

NEW TESTAMENT RECORDED 90 AD

"...as Moses lifted up the serpent in the wilderness, even so must the Son of Man be lifted up; that whoever believes may in Him have eternal life....'When you lift up the Son of Man, then you will know that I am *He*, and I do nothing on My own initiative, but I speak these things as the Father taught Me.' "

John 3:14-15; 8:28 NASB

MODERN RABBINIC COMMENT/REFUTATION

"...the Christians assert, that the prophecy of Isaiah constitutes a prediction of Jesus, the Nazarene, concerning whom Isaiah has said, 'He shall be exalted and extolled, and be very high,' because to him alone it is asserted these words can be attributed....The word ישׂכיל 'he shall prosper,' is found again in the 1st Samuel xviii. 14, 'And David *was prosperous* in all ways.' 'My servant shall prosper,' relates to that period when Israel shall leave the countries of its captivity, and be elevated to the highest degree of happiness."

***Faith Strengthened,* by Isaac Troki, pp. 108-118; 1850**

AUTHOR'S COMMENT—EVANGELICAL CHRISTIAN POSITION

Isaac Troki's refutation of the Messianic interpretation and application of Isaiah 52:13 clearly flies in the face of the ancient rabbinical understanding. As you see, the Jewish Targum of many centuries past definitely explains this biblical passage to be about the Messiah. On the other hand, our Christian polemic friend would have us believe that it is about Israel's happiness. That's a new one on us. When Mr. Troki said, "The Christians assert," he was apparently ignorant of the fact that the Targum also "asserted"—Messiah! Right? Yes!

Philip Moore

[141]Rev. B. Pick, Ph.D., *Old Testament Passages Messianically Applied by the Ancient Synagogue*, published in the compilation *Hebraica, A Quarterly Journal in the Interests of Semitic Study*, Vol. I, p. 268.

RABBIS SAY SUFFERING AND REJECTION INDICATES HE IS NOT MESSIAH, HOWEVER, THE TREATMENT INFLICTED BY THEIR PREDECESSORS AUTHENTICATES JESUS' MESSIANIC CREDENTIALS

Isaiah went on to predict: "He is despised and rejected of men; a man of sorrows, and acquainted with grief: and we hid as it were *our* faces from him; he was despised, and we esteemed him not. Surely he hath borne our griefs, and carried our sorrows: yet we did esteem him stricken, smitten of God, and afflicted. But he *was* wounded for our transgressions, *he was* bruised for our iniquities: the chastisement of our peace *was* upon him; and with his stripes we are healed. All we like sheep have gone astray; we have turned every one to his own way; and the LORD hath laid on him the iniquity of us all" (Isa. 53:3-6 KJV).

Here, we see that the prophet Isaiah speaks of the Messiah's rejection by Jewish religious leaders and rabbis. He says that the peoples' leaders would cause the rejection of the exact one they were seeking! Was and is this true? Many contemporary, perhaps well-meaning rabbis have said, "Jesus could not possibly have been the Messiah, for if He was He would have been accepted by the Jewish leaders of the time." However, when we read the Jewish prophecies of Isaiah we find that one of the qualifications for Messiahship is in fact the Messiah's rejection by His own people! Does this settle the question in the rabbis' minds? Hardly.

When this quote regarding rejection is firmly stated to rabbis, they inevitably respond with the words, "Isaiah is not speaking about the Messiah in this particular passage, but rather Israel."

This line of thought has been contrived by modern "scholarship" to attack and counter the Messianic/Christian claims that Jesus is the suffering Messiah. However, if you quote the ancient rabbinical commentaries, the Talmud, Targums and Midrashim, in their references to these specific passages of Isaiah, you might find yourself on hostile ground in the rabbis office.

The older commentaries claim that this passage in Isaiah is indeed referring to the Messiah; something for which the rabbi has no answer in this case, if he is honest about his misunderstood interpretation that Isaiah 53 is referring to Israel.

***

ORIGINAL HEBREW TEXT WRITTEN 712 BC

נִבְזֶה֙ וַחֲדַ֣ל אִישִׁ֔ים אִ֥ישׁ מַכְאֹב֖וֹת וִיד֣וּעַ חֹ֑לִי וּכְמַסְתֵּ֤ר פָּנִים֙ מִמֶּ֔נּוּ נִבְזֶ֖ה וְלֹ֥א חֲשַׁבְנֻֽהוּ׃

ישעיה נג:ג

OLD TESTAMENT SCRIPTURE TRANSLATION

"He was despised and forsaken of men, A man of sorrows, and acquainted with grief; And like one from whom men hide their face, He was despised, and we did not esteem Him." **Isaiah 53:3 NASB**

ANCIENT RABBINICAL COMMENTARY

"...the Holy One will reveal to them Messiah, the son of David, whom Israel will desire to stone, saying, Thou speakest falsely; already is the Messiah slain, and there is none other Messiah to stand up (after him): and so they will despise him, as it is written, 'Despised and forlorn of men;' but he will turn and hide himself from them, according to the words, 'Like one hiding his face from us.' "[142]

Mysteries of Rabbi Shim'on Ben Yohai
Jellinek, Beth ham-Midrash (1855), part iii, p. 80

NEW TESTAMENT RECORDED 90 AD

" '...and I give eternal life to them, and they shall never perish; and no one shall snatch them out of My hand. My Father, who has given *them* to Me, is greater than all; and no one is able to snatch *them* out of the Father's hand. I and the Father are one.' The Jews took up stones again to stone Him. Jesus answered them, 'I showed you many good works from the Father; for which of them are you stoning Me?' The Jews answered Him, 'For a good work we do not stone You, but for blasphemy; and because You, being a man, make Yourself out *to be* God.' "

John 10:28-33 NASB

MODERN RABBINIC COMMENT/REFUTATION

"*He was despised, and rejected of men* [אישים*: 'men of high status'*]*, a man of pains, and acquainted with disease, and as one from whom men hide their face: he was despised, and we esteemed him not.* This verse, continuing the theme of the previous one, speaks of the servant as being generally despised. He is described as suffering from pains and diseases with which he is well acquainted. Terms having to do with wounds, sickness, pain, and disease are often used in the Scriptures to describe the humiliations and adversities suffered by the nation of Israel (Isaiah 1:5-6; Jeremiah 10:19, 30:12). The prophet quotes the Gentiles as saying that the suffering servant of the Lord 'was despised and rejected' by their leaders, the 'men of high status.' "

***The Jew and the Christian Missionary*, by Gerald Sigal, p. 39; © 1981**

AUTHOR'S COMMENT—EVANGELICAL CHRISTIAN POSITION

Mr. Sigal and Rabbi Bronznick just do not understand the ancient rabbinical commentaries about the servant of Isaiah 53 being the Messiah who is despised and expected to die for Israel. They employ an argument which began in the Middle Ages with Rashi, which was a fatalistic attempt to transfer the sufferings of the Messiah to Israel. Thus, their claim was and is that this passage refers to non-Jews against Jews. This is ironic because clearly Isaiah speaks of an individual dying for the sins of Israel and everyone else. When Isaiah said *we*, he was referring to himself as well as the rest of Israel. The rabbinical commentaries of ancient Israel

---

[142] *The Fifty-Third Chapter of Isaiah, According to the Jewish Interpreters,* published in the compilation by The Library of Biblical Studies. New York: KTAV Publishing House, Inc., © 1969, p. 32, used by permission.

said this person was the Messiah. Mr. Sigal and his advocates should get their facts right before they write! Wouldn't you say?

Philip Moore

A young Israeli shears a sheep on a kibbutz. This reminds us of Isaiah's prophecy that the Messiah was "as a sheep before her shearers is dumb, so he openeth not his mouth" (Isa. 53:7 KJV).

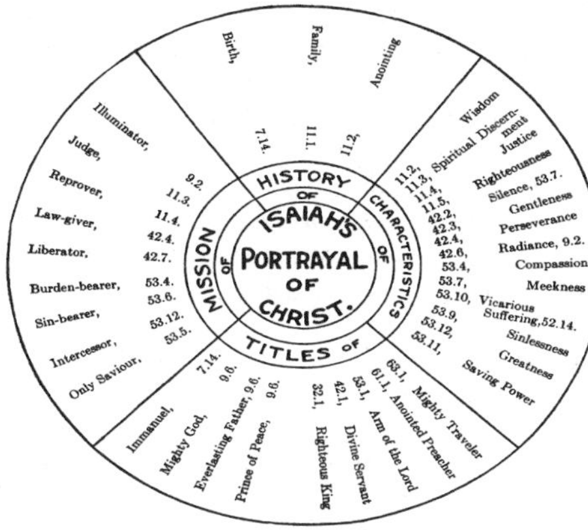

Isaiah, the Hebrew prophet, looking down through the centuries, predicted nearly every aspect of the Messiah's first coming to suffer.

ORIGINAL HEBREW TEXT WRITTEN 712 B.C.

לָכֵ֞ן אֲחַלֶּק־ל֣וֹ בָרַבִּ֗ים וְאֶת־עֲצוּמִים֮ יְחַלֵּ֣ק שָׁלָל֒ תַּ֗חַת אֲשֶׁ֨ר הֶעֱרָ֤ה לַמָּ֙וֶת֙ נַפְשׁ֔וֹ
וְאֶת־פֹּשְׁעִ֖ים נִמְנָ֑ה וְהוּא֙ חֵטְא־רַבִּ֣ים נָשָׂ֔א וְלַפֹּשְׁעִ֖ים יַפְגִּֽיעַ׃

ישעיה נג:יב

OLD TESTAMENT SCRIPTURE TRANSLATION

"Therefore, I will allot Him a portion with the great, And He will divide the booty with the strong; Because He poured out Himself to death, And was numbered with the transgressors; Yet He Himself bore the sin of many, And interceded for the transgressors." **Isaiah 53:12 NASB**

ANCIENT RABBINICAL COMMENTARY

"And when Israel is sinful, the MESSIAH seeks for mercy upon them, as it is written, 'By His Stripes we were healed, and HE carried the sins of many; and MADE INTERCESSION FOR THE TRANSGRESSORS.' "[143]

B'reshith Rabban, pp. 430, 671

NEW TESTAMENT RECORDED 57 AND 63 AD

"For even the Son of Man did not come to be served, but to serve, and to give His life a ransom for many....For I tell you, that this which is written must be fulfilled in Me, 'AND HE WAS NUMBERED WITH TRANSGRESSORS'; for that which refers to Me has *its* fulfillment." **Mark 10:45; Luke 22:37 NASB**

MODERN RABBINIC COMMENT/REFUTATION

"Isaiah 53:1-8 finds the prophet quoting the astonished exclamations of the Gentile spokesmen....In the latter part of verse 10 through verse 12, the prophet records the blessings with which God will reward His faithful servant for all the abuse and injury he endured for the sanctification of the Name of God....the servant, Israel, formerly despised by the nations, will now attain a place of honor and recognition among 'the great,' the sovereign nations of the world...."

***The Jew and the Christian Missionary*, by Gerald Sigal, pp. 37, 64; 1981**

AUTHOR'S COMMENT—EVANGELICAL CHRISTIAN POSITION

Where Gerald Sigal, under the direction of Rabbi Bronznick, gets the idea that Isaiah 53 concerns a "Gentile spokesman," eludes us. It would also have eluded the most brilliant ancient Jewish rabbinical commentators. This Messianic passage in Isaiah begins with: "Who hath believed **our** [Hebrew prophetic Jewish] report? and to **whom** is the arm of the LORD revealed?" (Isa. 53:1 KJV; [ ] mine). We all, even most rabbis and nominal "Christians," agree that it was the Jews who wrote the Old Testament in the midst of a pagan world as God's revelation to man. Further, Isaiah, who said *He bore **our** sorrows*, is Jewish! We believe Gerald Sigal and Rabbi Bronznick should read the ancient Jewish commentaries we have quoted, in their original Hebrew, if they know enough Hebrew. This passage cannot refer to Israel as implied by our friendly Jewish *Christian polemicist*. Though Israel will be sovereign when Jesus returns and establishes the millennium, this passage, as indicated by the ancient rabbinical commentary, refers to the Messiah, one who would be punished and beaten while praying for His enemies. This was never true of Israel but was true of Jesus! Furthermore, the Jewish Targum Jonathan to Isaiah 43:10-12, emphatically states that this servant is the *Messiah*. It says: " 'You are witnesses before Me,' says the Lord, 'and My servant is the Messiah, whom I have

[143] F. Kenton Beshore, D.D., LL.D., Ph.D., *"The Messiah" of the Targums, Talmuds and Rabbinical Writers*, pp. chart 26.

chosen; that you may know and believe Me, and that you may understand that I am He who was from the beginning, and also that all eternities belong to Me, and besides Me there is no God.' "[144] **Philip Moore**

THE ZOHAR'S ANSWER TO ATONEMENT AFTER THE TEMPLE FALLS IS THE SUFFERING OF THE MESSIAH

A clear example of a rabbinical cover-up of the true Messianic interpretation of Isaiah 53 can be seen in an obscure deletion in the Zohar. The Zohar is an ancient Jewish commentarial work which uses quotations from the Bible and other sources to answer many legitimate Jewish questions.

In response to questions regarding the atonement, the Bible and the Messiah, the Zohar says: "The souls which are in the Garden of Eden of Below roam about on every New Moon and Sabbath, and go to that place which is called Walls of Jerusalem, where there are my officers and detachments which watch over those walls....And they go to that place, but do not enter it until they are purified. And there they prostrate themselves, and enjoy the radiance, and then return to the Garden. [And again] they go forth from there and roam about in the world, and they see the bodies of the sinful suffering their punishment....And then they [continue to] roam and view those afflicted with sufferings and disease, and those who suffer for the Oneness of their Master, and then they return and tell [all this] to the Messiah.

"In the hour in which they tell the Messiah about the sufferings of Israel in exile, and [about] the sinful among them who seek not the knowledge of their Master, the Messiah lifts up his voice and weeps over those sinful among them. This is what is written: ***He was wounded because of our transgressions, he was crushed because of our iniquities (Isa. 53:5)***. Those souls then return to their places. In the Garden of Eden there is a hall which is called the Hall of the Sons of Illness. The **Messiah** enters that hall and summons all the diseases and all the pains and all the sufferings of Israel that they should come upon him, and all of them come upon him. And would he not thus bring ease to Israel and take their sufferings upon himself, no man could endure the sufferings Israel has to undergo because they neglected the Tora....As long as Israel dwelt in the Holy Land, the rituals and the sacrifices they performed [in the temple] removed all those diseases from the world; now the **Messiah removes** them from the children of the world...."[145]

---

[144] Samson H. Levey, *The Messiah: An Aramaic Interpretation, The Messianic Exegesis of the Targum*, p. 62.

[145] Raphael Patai, *The Messiah Texts*, pp. 115-116. Bold mine. These portions of the Zohar are quoted for you free of censorship. In modern versions of the Zohar this section

THE MODERN SONCINO ZOHAR HAS BEEN EDITED, APPARENTLY FOR MESSIANIC COVER-UP BECAUSE OF JESUS

We have just clarified that from time immemorial, rabbinical literature has admitted that the Messiah was to take up the slack when the Temple, the sacrifices, and the priests were no more. Incidentally, these were the claims made by Jesus in the New Testament.

This beautiful passage, which fits hand-in-hand with our New Testament Christian doctrinal happenings, is no doubt remarkable. However, there is a modern cover-up of this! What you just read was the original ancient version quoted from *The Messiah Texts*, by Raphael Patai. This version reaches back many, many hundreds of years.[146] However, in the modern English version of the same passage published by The Soncino Press, those precious words concerning the suffering Messiah are omitted, with a footnote explaining: "The first four and a half pages of this section (211b-216a) are declared by all the commentators to be an interpolation, containing much erroneous doctrine."[147] Obviously, the commentator who wrote these pages did not believe they were erroneous! Did he?

In Israel, an Orthodox Jew attempts the blood atonement by swinging a chicken over his head as part of the sacrificial ritual on Yom Kippur.

---

has been censored because of its ancient endorsement of Isaiah 53's Messianic significance.

146Some believe it reaches back to the time of Rabbi Shimon ben Yohai, nearly 2000 years ago.

147*The Zohar,* Vol. II. New York: The Soncino Press, © 1984, p. 301, footnote 1.

ORIGINAL HEBREW TEXT WRITTEN 712 BC

וְהוּא מְחֹלָל מִפְּשָׁעֵנוּ מְדֻכָּא מֵעֲוֹנֹתֵינוּ מוּסַר שְׁלוֹמֵנוּ עָלָיו וּבַחֲבֻרָתוֹ נִרְפָּא־לָנוּ׃

ישעיה נג:ה

OLD TESTAMENT SCRIPTURE TRANSLATION

"But He was pierced through for our transgressions, He was crushed for our iniquities; The chastening for our well-being *fell* upon Him, And by His scourging we are healed." **Isaiah 53:5 NASB**

ANCIENT RABBINICAL COMMENTARY

"The Patriarchs will one day rise again in the month of Nisan and will say to the Messiah: 'Ephraim, our righteous Messiah, although we are your ancestors, you are nevertheless greater than we, for you have borne the sins of our children, as it is written: 'Surely he has borne our diseases and carried our sorrows; yet we regarded him stricken, smitten of God, and afflicted. But he was wounded for our sins, bruised for our iniquities, upon him was the chastisement that makes us well, and through his wounds we are healed' (Isaiah 53:4-5). Heavy oppressions have been imposed upon you, as it is written: 'As a result of oppression and judgment he was taken away; but in his day, who considered that he was torn from the land of the living because of the transgressions of my people?' (Isaiah 53:8)."[148]

Pesiqta Rabbati, Friedmann's edition, chapter 37

NEW TESTAMENT RECORDED 60 AD

"...He Himself [Jesus] bore our sins in His body on the cross...for by His wounds you were healed. For you were continually straying like sheep, but now you have returned to the Shepherd and Guardian of your souls."

I Peter 2:24-25 NASB. [ ] mine

MODERN RABBINIC COMMENT/REFUTATION

"In verse 4 [of Isa. 53], the Gentile spokesmen depict the servant as bearing the 'diseases' and carrying the 'pains' which they themselves should have suffered. At the time of the servant's suffering, the Gentiles believed that the servant was undergoing divine retribution for *his* sins....we must conclude that this statement, made by the enemies of the suffering servant of the Lord, does not refer to Jesus, who, it is alleged, suffered as an atonement for mankind's sins. There is no indication in this verse that the servant of God suffered to atone for the sins of others....This is the confession of the Gentile spokesmen, who now realize that it was they and their people who deserved to suffer the humiliations inflicted on the servant of the Lord, as they stated in verses 4-6."

***The Jew and the Christian Missionary*,**
by Gerald Sigal, pp. 42-43, 52; © 1981. [ ] mine

AUTHOR'S COMMENT—EVANGELICAL CHRISTIAN POSITION

See our comments on previous Isaiah 53 comparison on page 184.

Philip Moore

---

[148]Arthur W. Kac, *The Messianic Hope.* Grand Rapids, MI: Baker Book House, © 1975, p. 80, used by permission.

CENSORING ISAIAH 53 FROM THE SYNAGOGUE LECTIONARY WAS DELIBERATE BECAUSE OF *JESUS,* AS THE SCHOLARS AFFIRM

Hal Lindsey, in his well-known book, *The Late Great Planet Earth,* comments on this passage in Isaiah: "Rabbis since the birth and death of Jesus of Nazareth have reinterpreted this passage....[because] the passage speaks of this person as bearing the consequences of the transgressions of Israel."[149]

Frederick Bruce, author of the scholarly book, *The Spreading Flame,* notes: "It is a distinguished orthodox Jewish scholar who tells us that the reason why the prophecy of the Suffering Servant (Isaiah 52:13-53:12) is not included in the synagogue lectionary, although the passages immediately preceding and following it are found there, is the Christian application of that prophecy to Jesus."[150]

This orthodox scholar mentioned by Professor Bruce is none other than the famous Herbert Martin James Loewe of Cambridge, who wrote the over eight hundred-page *Rabbinic Anthology* with C.G. Montefiore. His exact words are: "Quotations from the famous 53rd chapter of Isaiah are rare in the Rabbinic literature. [Because of the christological interpretation given to the chapter by Christians, it is omitted from the series of prophetical lessons (*Haftarot*) for the Deuteronomy Sabbaths....the omission is deliberate and striking. (H.L.)]"[151]

THE REINTERPRETATION OF ISAIAH'S MESSIANIC PROPHECY ORIGINATED AT YAVNE AND STILL DECEIVES TODAY

The groundwork for these new reinterpretations[152] was laid at Yavne a generation after Jesus, and they reached their zenith in Rashi's

---

[149]Hal Lindsey with C.C. Carlson, *The Late Great Planet Earth*, p. 37. [ ] mine.

[150]F.F. Bruce, *The Spreading Flame*, p. 267.

[151]C.G. Montefiore and H. Loewe, *A Rabbinic Anthology*, p. 544.

[152]Popular Christian author, Hal Lindsey, exposes the real veil over Israel's Messianic misunderstanding as clearly originating in this forsaken remnant of a town, when he mentions: "ORTHODOX JUDAISM....primarily the heir of the first century Pharisees. Until modern times this was the predominant form of Judaism practiced by Jews in the dispersion. Their doctrines were first formulated by the Pharisee scribes and priests who survived the A.D. 70 holocaust. They fled to a place called Yavneh (which is just southeast of modern Tel Aviv), where they reinterpreted Judaism so that it could be practiced without a Temple and animal sacrifices. In theory, this group fanatically holds to the Torah. But in reality they hold the rabbinical interpretations of the Torah as more authoritative. In my opinion, this tradition is the veil over the Israelite's heart that blinds

writings in the eleventh century. It would seem that the last couple of generations have seen these interpretations become standardized within mainstream Judaism. Not so long ago, many rabbis still agreed that Isaiah 53 was Messianic.

Isaiah 53 also predicted that the person in question would not be given justice[153] according to Jewish law. This came true during the trials of Jesus. All were amazed that Jesus did not defend Himself. "And when he was accused of the chief priests and elders, he answered nothing. Then said Pilate unto him, Hearest thou not how many things they witness against thee? And he answered him to never a word; insomuch that the governor marvelled greatly" (Matt. 27:12-14 KJV).

Isaiah's words, seven hundred years before, were: "He was oppressed, and he was afflicted, yet he opened not his mouth: he is brought as a lamb to the slaughter, and as a sheep before her shearers is dumb, so he openeth not his mouth" (Isa. 53:7 KJV).

THE MESSIAH WAS SLATED FOR JUDGMENT AND PRISON IN PROPHECY—WAS JESUS PUT IN JAIL JUST AS PROPHESIED?

Another unmistakable prediction says that the Messiah would die for Isaiah's people (Israel). This, of course, includes anybody who puts their trust in the God of Israel, even if they are not Jewish.[154] Isaiah miraculously predicts: "He was taken from prison and from judgment: and who shall declare his generation? for he was cut off out of the land of the living: for the transgression of my people was he stricken" (Isa. 53:8 KJV).

Seven hundred years *later*, we observe the obvious fulfillment of this prophecy in the New Testament's record, which reports: "Then the band and the captain and officers...took Jesus....and bound him, And led him away to Annas first; for he was father in law to Caiaphas, which was the high priest that same year....Now Annus had sent him

---

him to the truth. At Yavneh, every prophecy concerning the Suffering Messiah was explained away." Hal Lindsey, *The Road to Holocaust*, pp. 133-134.

[153] Walter M. Chandler, in his book, *The Trial of Jesus, From a Lawyer's Standpoint*, details the many Jewish laws that were broken during the illegal trials of Jesus.

[154] "And now, saith the LORD that formed me from the womb *to be* his servant, to bring Jacob again to him, Though Israel be not gathered, yet shall I be glorious in the eyes of the LORD , and my God shall be my strength. And he said, It is a light thing that thou shouldest be my servant to raise up the tribes of Jacob, and to restore the preserved of Israel: I will also give thee for a light to the Gentiles, that thou mayest be my salvation unto the end of the earth. Thus saith the LORD, the Redeemer of Israel, *and* his Holy One, to him whom man despiseth, to him whom the nation [Israel] abhorreth, to a servant of rulers, Kings shall see and arise, princes also shall worship, because of the LORD that is faithful, *and* the Holy One of Israel, and he shall choose thee" (Isa. 49:5-7 KJV), [ ] mine.

bound unto Caiaphas the high priest [here He spent time in the prophecied cell]....Then led they Jesus from Caiaphas unto the hall of judgment...." (John 18:12-14, 24, 28 KJV; [ ] mine).[155]

Between Jesus' many trials and His crucifixion, He was held in the pit[156] of a dungeon prison cell. The hole in the top of this jail (pictured on page 192) was the means by which prisoners were lowered into an *inescapable, hopeless stone dungeon.* To this day, Psalm 88 is on display in this room where Jesus was held. Many believe this Psalm, written 3000 years ago, to be the prophetic utterings of the Messiah, twenty centuries past, as He awaited His fate.

THE ANCIENT JEWISH SANHEDRIN'S TRIAL OF JESUS WAS SUCH A FARCE THAT EVEN A MODERN ISRAELI ATTORNEY IS ATTEMPTING TO GET IT THROWN OUT!

In his October 1993 sermon, "Christ in the Hands of the Police," Reverend D. James Kennedy noted that forty-eight different Roman and Jewish laws were violated during the trials of Jesus (these are carefully expounded upon in the book *The Trial of Jesus, From a Lawyer's Standpoint*, by the New York attorney Walter M. Chandler).

Kennedy interestingly pointed out that one Israeli attorney, Itzhak David, recently brought up the question of Jesus' guilt before the Supreme Court in Israel. He requested that the Court exonerate Jesus of the charges made by the Sanhedrin. In his sermon, Kennedy said: "I think as an aside, it is interesting that the UPI reported that an Israeli lawyer by the name of **Itzhak David, an Orthodox Jew, appealed** to the high court of Israel **to have Jesus Christ exonerated** and all charges against Him dropped and have it declared that this was, indeed, a mistrial and filled with violations of its own law. The Supreme Court heard this request for a *writ of certiorari* and they denied it. But David says he will try again. The court before which Christ was brought was, indeed, a farce and not really a trial."[157] Reverend Kennedy anticipated Jesus' Jewish exoneration at a future date, as do we![158]

---

[155]The prison cell in Caiaphas' basement where Jesus was held exists in Jerusalem to this day. I have seen it for myself! Israeli tour guides often lead tours there and explain the events in detail. I will never forget Helen Bar Yacov's lecture there during my May 1980 TBN tour to Israel.

[156]This brings to mind our beloved Joseph, who was also placed in a pit and put in Pharaoh's prison before he rose to prominence, saving all of Egypt from famine.

[157]Rev. D. James Kennedy, "Christ in the Hands of the Police," pp. 9-10. Bold mine. Reverend Kennedy's sermon is available in pamphlet form from Coral Ridge Ministries, POB 40, Fort Lauderdale, FL, USA 33302.

[158]We ask you to write the court and send them a copy of this book at their address in Israel. Write to Chief Justice Aaron Barak and Head Secretary (*Maskera Rashi*) Smayaho Cohen at Rehov Sharie Mishpat Kiayat Ben Gurion, Jerusalem, Israel 91950.

THE PSALMIST'S POETRY OF SORROW WAS JESUS' MESSIANIC REALITY OF SUFFERING FOR OUR INIQUITY

Were the words of the eighty-eighth Psalm the same words spoken by Jesus 1000 years later in a prayer to His Father? Many believe so. The Psalm reads: "O LORD God of my salvation, I have cried day *and* night before thee: Let my prayer come before thee: incline thine ear unto my cry; for my soul is full of troubles: and my life draweth nigh unto the grave. I am counted with them that go down into the pit: I am as a man *that hath* no strength: Free among the dead, like the slain that lie in the grave, whom thou rememberest no more: and they are cut off from thy hand. Thou hast laid me in the lowest **pit, in darkness**, in the deeps. Thy wrath lieth hard upon me, and thou hast afflicted *me* with all thy waves. Selah. Thou hast put away mine acquaintance far from me; thou hast made me an abomination unto them: ***I am* shut up**, and I cannot come forth. Mine eye mourneth by reason of affliction: LORD, I have called daily upon thee, I have stretched out my hands unto thee. Wilt thou shew wonders to the dead? shall the dead arise *and* praise thee? Selah. **Shall thy lovingkindness be declared in the grave**?[159] *or* thy faithfulness in destruction? Shall thy wonders be known in the dark? and thy righteousness in the land of forgetfulness? But unto thee have I cried, O LORD; and in the morning shall my prayer prevent thee. LORD, why castest thou off my soul? *why* hidest thou thy face from me? I *am* afflicted and ready to die from *my* youth up: *while* I suffer thy terrors I am distracted. Thy fierce wrath goeth over me; thy terrors have cut me off. They came round about me daily like water; they compassed me about together. Lover and friend hast thou put far from me, *and* mine acquaintance into darkness" (Ps. 88 KJV).

***

Tel. 011-972-2-759666. For if Israel were to do this, some Israelis who have been taught that the New Testament is a forbidden book because Jesus broke the law would then realize He did not, and that He was innocent before His accusers. This might open the way to their investigation of Jesus and His claims of being Messiah, free of prejudice. What a blessing this would be!

159 Bold emphasis illustrates what Jesus experienced and why. He was "shut up" in a dark, lifeless, stone dungeon and thereafter, crucified and died for us because of God's loving kindness, to provide a way to spare us!

This stone holding chamber where Jesus was imprisoned is located in Jerusalem, under the house of the high priest Caiaphas (Matt. 26:57). In Jesus' day, the left window and right stairwell had not yet been constructed; there was only the hole in the ceiling through which Jesus was lowered! Today, it is a tourist site visited by millions of pilgrims every year.

A little girl reads Psalm 88 on display in the corner of Jesus' jail cell.

THE ONE THEY INTENDED TO BURY UNDER THE CROSS WAS LAID TO REST MOST LUXURIOUSLY

Isaiah further details that this man would be buried in a pauper's grave as were the wicked. However, he emphatically states that when He finally dies He would receive burial with the *rich.* Isaiah predicted: "And he made his grave with the wicked, and with the rich in his death; because he had done no violence, neither *was any* deceit in his mouth" (Isa. 53:9 KJV).

We all should know that the Romans intended to bury Jesus as they buried all crucifixion victims, at the foot of the cross in a cheap grave befitting the wicked who were executed in this cruel Phoenician manner. However, because Jesus was the Messiah and had no deceit in His mouth and had done no wickedness, Isaiah's words, "with the rich in his death" literally came true, because of a Sanhedrin member who loved Jesus.

Rabbi Joseph of Arimathæa requested and obtained permission from the Roman governor, Pontius Pilate, to give Jesus a proper burial in his personal tomb. Joseph was a rich Pharisee whose elaborate stone-cut tomb can be visited in Jerusalem[160] to this day.

DESPITE THE NEW TESTAMENT, HISTORICAL AND ARCHAEOLOGICAL EVIDENCE, THERE ARE STILL SOME WHO IGNORANTLY MAINTAIN A DESPICABLE BURIAL

Bishop John Spong, a critic of Jesus' predicted proper burial and resurrection, arrogantly writes in his book, *Resurrection, Myth or Reality?*: "The tomb of Jesus was unknown because, in all probability, there was no tomb. There was no tomb because he was buried as a common criminal in a common grave...."[161]

Of course, nothing could be further from the truth. The tomb of Jesus is now known to us. I get an unfathomable spiritual high every time I visit it in Jerusalem. The description given of the tomb in the New Testament matches exactly this nineteenth and twentieth century excavation known as the Garden Tomb or, in Hebrew, *Gan Ha kever*, presently run by the British in Jerusalem.

---

[160]This tomb is known as the Garden Tomb and is located in Jerusalem, on Nablus Road, a few steps away from the main Arab bus station. Evangelical tours provide safe visits to the tomb yearly for hundreds of thousands of pilgrims. Lectures are given free of charge—expositions, in our opinion—which biblically authenticate this tomb as the true tomb of Jesus. The Garden Tomb is not to be confused with the Tomb of the Holy Sepulchre, which is held by Catholics, Coptics and Greek Orthodox to be His tomb, and is located a half-mile away within the city walls.

[161]John Shelby Spong, *Resurrection, Myth or Reality?* San Francisco: HarperSanFrancisco, © 1994, p. 228, used by permission.

Spong also claims that the burial and Nicodemus' portion of the Gospel's accounts of Jesus are legends which have evolved over time: "By the time the fourth Gospel was written, a brand-new element had entered the burial legend. There the Joseph of Arimathea story is joined by the tradition involving Nicodemus. John introduced this story by reminding his readers of Nicodemus's earlier visit to Jesus 'by night' (John 3:1-15). Then John said that Nicodemus 'came bringing a mixture of myrrh and aloes....' "[162] However, Nicodemus is not part of a New Testament legend, story or tradition. He was a real person written about in the Jewish Talmud under his Jewish name, Nakdimon ben Gurion.[163] Spong shows his ignorance again, doesn't he?

The Garden Tomb.

[162]Ibid, p. 223.
[163]See our footnote on this unique and precious biblical individual on page 250-251.

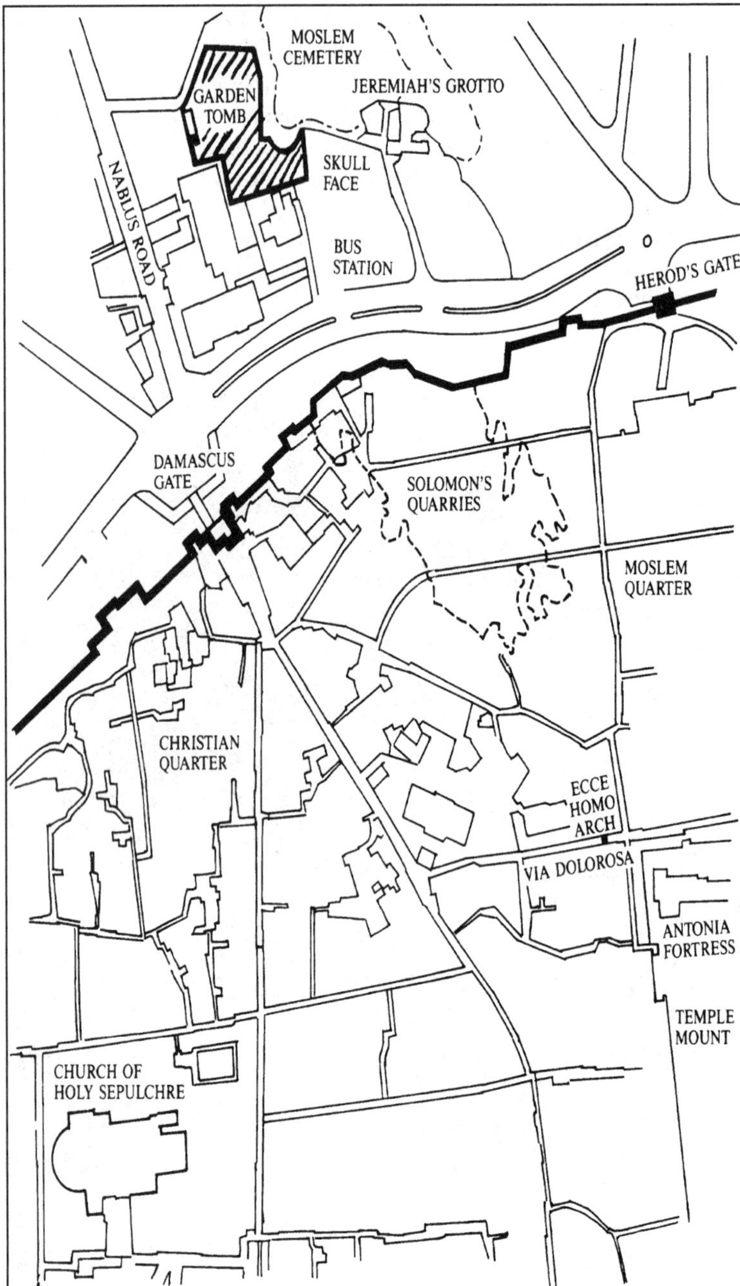

If you are in Jerusalem, show your taxi driver this map and you should be sure to arrive at the right place.

ISAIAH PREDICTED THAT BY BELIEF IN THIS ONE'S DEATH WE CAN ALL LIVE FREE OF GUILT AND TERROR

Isaiah goes on to emphasize that by the knowledge of this righteous servant, many would be *justified*, as he predicted: "Yet it pleased the LORD to bruise him; he hath put *him* to grief: when thou shalt make his soul an offering for sin, he shall see *his* seed, he shall prolong *his* days, and the pleasure of the LORD shall prosper in his hand. He shall see of the travail of his soul, *and* shall be satisfied: by his knowledge shall my righteous servant justify many; for he shall bear their iniquities" (Isa. 53:10-11 KJV).

This, of course, is the paramount claim of the New Testament regarding Jesus. That is, as a believer in Him, we are forgiven: "...if thou shalt confess with thy mouth the Lord Jesus, and shalt believe in thine heart that God hath raised him from the dead, thou shalt be saved" (Rom. 10:9 KJV).

"Saved" from what, some have asked. Saved from God's judgment now and for God's future world, in which eternity, Heaven on Earth, will one day be a reality (see our chapter 29, "After the Messiah Arrives and Ends the War—Paradise!" on the New Jerusalem, and our *Vol. II*, chapter 25, "Saved, Saved from What?").

To continue, Isaiah foretells: "...because he hath poured out his soul unto death; and he was numbered with the transgressors; and he bore the sin of many, and made intercession for the transgressors" (Isa. 53:12 KJV).[164]

The prophet predicted that because this man would be willing to die while being numbered with "transgressors" (thieves), the sins of many (all who would believe) would be borne (paid for) by Him. It is a well-known fact that Jesus claimed His death on the cross would be for all the sin of those who would accept it as just payment (Mark 10:45). It is also common knowledge that Jesus was numbered with two thieves, one crucified on each side of Him (Luke 23:39-43). One believed in Him and was promised Paradise, the other did not and was promised nothing.[165]

Interior of the Garden Tomb in Jerusalem.

[164] *The New Scofield Reference Bible.*

[165] This brings to mind the butler and the baker who were in jail with Joseph in Egypt. In the same way that Jesus told one of the thieves He would be in Paradise with Him, Joseph told the baker that he would be killed in three days, while the other was, of course, freed.

ORIGINAL HEBREW TEXT WRITTEN 712 BC

וַיהוָ֞ה חָפֵ֤ץ דַּכְּאוֹ֙ הֶֽחֱלִ֔י אִם־תָּשִׂ֤ים אָשָׁם֙ נַפְשׁ֔וֹ יִרְאֶ֥ה זֶ֖רַע יַאֲרִ֣יךְ יָמִ֑ים וְחֵ֥פֶץ יְהוָ֖ה וְחֵ֥פֶץ
יְהוָ֖ה בְּיָד֥וֹ יִצְלָֽח׃ ישעיה נג:י

OLD TESTAMENT SCRIPTURE TRANSLATION

"But the LORD was pleased To crush Him, putting *Him* to grief; If He would render Himself *as* a guilt offering, He will see *His* offspring, He will prolong *His* days, And the good pleasure of the LORD will prosper in His hand."

Isaiah 53:10 NASB

ANCIENT RABBINICAL COMMENTARY

"...my servant, the Messiah, in whom I am well pleased."[166]

Targum to Isaiah XLIII:10

NEW TESTAMENT RECORDED 37 AND 60 AD

"...Jesus went up immediately from the water; and behold, the heavens were opened, and he saw the Spirit of God descending as a dove, *and* coming upon Him, and behold, a voice out of the heavens, saying, 'This is My beloved Son, in whom I am well-pleased'.... while being reviled, He did not revile in return; while suffering, He uttered no threats, but kept entrusting *Himself* to Him who judges righteously; and He Himself bore our sins in His body on the cross, that we might die to sin and live to righteousness; for by His wounds you were healed. For you were continually straying like sheep, but now you have returned to the Shepherd and Guardian of your souls."

Matthew 3:16-17; I Peter 2:23-25 NASB

MODERN RABBINIC COMMENT/REFUTATION

"In this verse [Isaiah 53:10], the prophet reiterates, in bold terms, a basic biblical concept. In suffering there is purification. Thus, there are times that God presents crushing personal challenges to His most loyal followers in order to strengthen their spirit....No person is born pious or righteous....The words of Isaiah, 'If he would offer himself as a guilt-offering,' do not mean that the servant offers himself vicariously as a guilt-offering for others....Thus, Isaiah 53:10 cannot and should not be applied to Jesus." ***The Jew and the Christian Missionary*,**

by Gerald Sigal, pp. 59, 63; © 1981. [ ] mine

AUTHOR'S COMMENT—EVANGELICAL CHRISTIAN POSITION

In Gerald Sigal's modern interpretative comment, he argues without foundation that no one is born pious and that the suffering which Isaiah mentions is not a vicarious guilt-offering for others. However, the ancient rabbis did believe the Messiah would be pious from the womb (see Isa. 9:6-7 [5-6 in Jewish editions], and our quotes of rabbinical comments on this). The rabbinical Targums of ages past even insert the word, Messiah, into their interpretive translations in Aramaic because the Messiah was so clearly understood to be this sufferer at that early date, as we have demonstrated. Mr. Sigal and his rabbi are so anxious to say that it cannot be Jesus who claimed it as a Messianic prophecy referring to Himself (Luke 24:44), that we believe they have again either forgotten or neglected to do their homework.

Philip Moore

---

[166] Rev. B. Pick, Ph.D., *Old Testament Passages Messianically Applied by the Ancient Synagogue*, published in the compilation *Hebraica, A Quarterly Journal in the Interests of Semitic Study*, Vol I, p. 267.

A CASE OF MISTAKEN IDENTITY BY THOSE WHO SHOULD HAVE KNOWN BETTER

Jesus also made intercession for the transgressors who were crucifying Him. He said: "...Father, forgive them; for they know not what they do" (Luke 23:34 KJV).

This was because they thought they were crucifying an impostor or false Messiah. Remember Isaiah's prediction: "...we did esteem him...smitten of God...." (Isa. 53:4 KJV). However, in truth, the Passover lamb of God was offering Himself before God for all of their and our shortcomings. That many of them did not know who He was or what they were saying is clear from the priest's statement: "...If he be the King of Israel, let him now come down from the cross, and we will believe him. He trusted in God; let him deliver him now, if he will have him...." (Matt. 27:42-43 KJV).

This occurrence, which was also predicted by King David over 3000 years ago, reads: "He trusted on the LORD *that* he would deliver him: let him deliver him, seeing he delighted in him" (Ps. 22:8 KJV).

We can see that all of this was not by accident but was foretold. Only Jewish priests could offer sacrifice. However, these Jewish leaders[167] did not know they were offering the most important sacrifice of all time for all of us. They felt they were aiding Rome in ridding themselves of political friction.

Rembrandt, 1653.

---

[167]Caiaphas and Annas held the office of high priest, perhaps falsely, as we documented earlier. However, the fact that they were filling the shoes of the Aaronic line and there was no one else to do this, made them responsible to God in issues concerning the high priesthood.

ORIGINAL HEBREW TEXT WRITTEN 712 BC

אָכֵן חֳלָיֵנוּ הוּא נָשָׂא וּמַכְאֹבֵינוּ סְבָלָם וַאֲנַחְנוּ חֲשַׁבְנֻהוּ נָגוּעַ מֻכֵּה אֱלֹהִים וּמְעֻנֶּה׃

ישעיה נג:ד

OLD TESTAMENT SCRIPTURE TRANSLATION

"Surely our griefs He Himself bore, And our sorrows He carried; Yet we ourselves esteemed Him stricken, Smitten of God, and afflicted."

Isaiah 53:4 NASB

ANCIENT RABBINICAL COMMENTARY

"The rabbis say, His name is the leper of the house of Rabbi, as it is said, 'Surely he hath borne our sickness, and endured the burden of our pains, yet we did esteem him stricken, smitten of God, and afflicted' (Isa. LIII., 4)."[168]

Sanhedrin, fol. 98, col 2

NEW TESTAMENT RECORDED 60 AD

"...He Himself [Jesus] bore our sins in His body on the cross...for by His wounds you were healed. For you were continually straying like sheep, but now you have returned to the Shepherd and Guardian of your souls."

I Peter 2:24 NASB. [ ] mine

MODERN RABBINIC COMMENT/REFUTATION

"In verse 4 [of Isa. 53], the Gentile spokesmen depict the servant as bearing the 'diseases' and carrying the 'pains' which they themselves should have suffered. At the time of the servant's suffering, the Gentiles believed that the servant was undergoing divine retribution for *his* sins....we must conclude that this statement, made by the enemies of the suffering servant of the Lord, does not refer to Jesus, who, it is alleged, suffered as an atonement for mankind's sins. There is no indication in this verse that the servant of God suffered to atone for the sins of others....This is the confession of the Gentile spokesmen, who now realize that it was they and their people who deserved to suffer the humiliations inflicted on the servant of the Lord, as they stated in verses 4-6."

***The Jew and the Christian Missionary*,**
by Gerald Sigal, pp. 42-43, 52; © 1981. [ ] mine

AUTHOR'S COMMENT—EVANGELICAL CHRISTIAN POSITION

See our comments on previous Isaiah 53 comparison on page 184.

Philip Moore

ARCHAEOLOGICAL EVIDENCE OF THE DETAILS OF CRUCIFIXION FOUND IN ISRAEL!

In his recent book, *The Messiah in the New Testament in the Light of Rabbinical Writings*, my Finnish friend, Risto Santala, has archaeologically illustrated what happened to Jesus as He fulfilled David's prophecy. Risto reminds us: "In 1968 on the Givat Ha-mivtar

[168]Rev. B. Pick, Ph.D., *Old Testament Passages Messianically Applied by the Ancient Synagogue*, published in the compilation *Hebraica, A Quarterly Journal in the Interests of Semitic Study*, Vol. II, p. 27.

hill on the outskirts of Jerusalem, Israeli archaeologists found the remains of ancient ankle bones in which there was the remnant of a well-preserved nail. The cross in question had been made of olive wood and the bar to hold the feet of acacia.

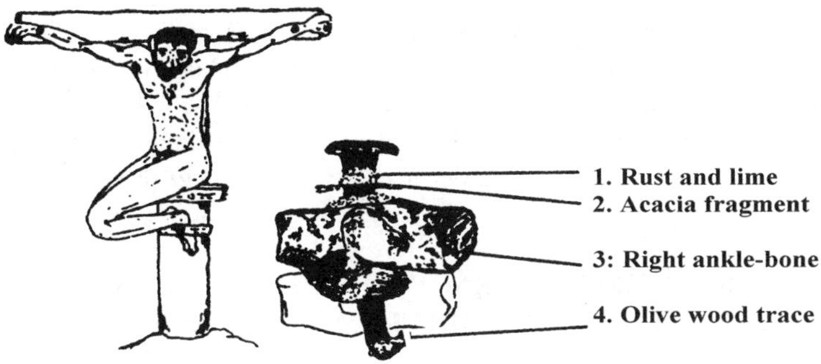

...It [Roman crucifixion] was referred to as the '*death of slaves*'. *Cicero speaks of it as 'the most terrifying' manner of death.* The Roman philosopher Seneca writes that, 'The life of the accused drained from him drop by drop.' The oldest extant illustrations of the cross depict it as a T (*crux commissa*), without the upper protrusion."[169]

"Crucified Man," the only crucified remnant ever discovered.
Courtesy Israel Antiquities Authority.

[169]Risto Santala, *The Messiah in the New Testament in the Light of Rabbinical Writings*, pp. 226-227. [ ] mine.

While we can be sure that this crucified heel is not that of Jesus[170] (He was resurrected), we are archaeologically assured that these are the remains of a wooden cross and the nail and heelbone of a man who was crucified in the same way the Scriptures confirm of Jesus.

The New Testament report of Jesus' sufferings takes on a uniquely intense, realistic light as we gaze at this photo, doesn't it? A cold but factual reminder of what He allowed Himself to go through for us. In His God Incarnate, sinless perfection, He did not permit pain to stand in the way of paying our penalty; He took *our* place and died in this cruelly and inhumanely devised manner—what mercy!

HOW DID ISAIAH KNOW ALL OF THIS? WAS HE IN THE CROWD AT THE CROSS? OBVIOUSLY NOT!

While reading these prophecies inspired by God (no man can foresee the future), you might have thought Isaiah himself, God's Jewish prophet in the Bible, was there among the crowd at the cross. The fact is that he lived and wrote all of these things seven hundred years before Jesus lived. What more supernatural proof could we ask for to confirm Jesus' Messiahship according to Jewish standards?[171]

THE PROPHECY OF CRUCIFIXION

Was Jesus' death on the Roman cross a random accident in antiquity or was His sacrifice for us a carefully predicted plan by God,

---

[170]We can be sure that this does not belong to Jesus because the ossuary bone box (ancient casket) bears the inscription of Yehohanan as documented in an article by Joseph Zias and Eliezer Sekele. The article also mentioned: "The nail in the right remains because the bend at the pointed end (which was probably caused by the nail's hitting a knot in the wood as it was driven in) likely resulted in its not being removed in order to avoid doing further injury to the body. When the feet were nailed to the cross, an olive wood plaque was put between the head of each nail and the foot, probably to prevent the condemned from pulling free of the nail. Evidence for this consists of wood fragments found below the head of the nail, which were identified as olive wood by the Department of Botany of the Hebrew University after analysis with a scanning electron microscope. Fragments of wood near the point of the nail could not be identified; thus, the type of wood the upright of the cross was made from could not be identified." Joseph Zias and Eliezer Sekele, "The Crucified Man from Giv^c^at ha-Mivtar—A Reappraisal," *Biblical Archaeologist*, Sept. 1985, © used by permission. Our thanks to Joe Zias who told me how to order this picture from the Israel Museum. We also thank Sophie Durocher and Areah Rochman Haperin of the Israel Antiquities Authority for sending this photo and giving us permission to use it.

[171]If you find all of this too hard to believe, as many do, go over to your bookshelf, pick up your Bible, blow the dust off of it and open those unread pages to the prophet Isaiah. In chapter 53 (a 2700-year-old piece of Hebrew literature) you will read the exact events of Jesus' life, which did not take place until 2000 years ago!

foreseen in the biblical Psalms of King David 1000 years prior to the event? We will positively prove the latter in this section, though it may astonish many.

THE ENTIRE EARTH ENVELOPED IN TOTAL DARKNESS

During the time of Jesus' crucifixion, the New Testament says darkness fell while Jesus was on the cross. Records show that an orator as far away as Athens, Greece, was awed as he witnessed the same darkness, which was of a global[172] nature. As God poured out all judgment for sin which was due us, He darkened the Earth so that no one could see what was going on between Him and His Son. God judged an innocent Jesus in our place so He could justify us and one day set us free. The orator, commenting on the blackness, said it must be "the death of a god."[173]

The prophet Amos, over seven hundred years prior to the event, predicted this darkness when he said: " '...it will come about in that day,' declares the Lord GOD, 'That I shall make the sun go down at noon And make the earth dark in broad daylight' " (Amos 8:9 NASB).

Matthew documented this when he said: "Now from the sixth hour[174] **darkness fell upon all the land** until the ninth hour" (Matt. 27:45 NASB; bold mine).

THOSE OPPOSING JESUS MISUSE HEBREW WORDS—THEIR IGNORANCE IS EXPOSED IN OUR PROPHETIC INSIGHT (DAN. 12:10)

Jesus uttered seven cries from the cross, one of them noted in the English Bible is a transliteration of the Hebrew, " 'Eli, Eli, LAMA sabachthani' " (Matt. 27:46 KJV), which in English means "My God, My God, why have you forsaken Me?"

This phrase has often been exploited by liberal "Christian" theologians and some rabbis, who attempt to dupe the public into believing that Jesus had given up and was admitting He was not the Messiah. For example, Gerald Sigal, under the "guiding light" of

---

[172]There was also a local eclipse, not to be confused with the global darkness. The eclipse, interestingly enough, adds to our evidence in that it gives us the exact date of the crucifixion, which we will later document.

[173]Hal Lindsey, "The Resurrection In the Old Testament," Tape 089. Available through Hal Lindsey Ministries, POB 4000, Palos Verdes, CA, USA 90274.

[174]Josh McDowell notes: "Because the Jews reckoned twelve hours from sunrise to sunset, it would make the sixth hour near noon and the ninth hour about three o'clock." Josh McDowell, *Evidence That Demands a Verdict*, San Bernardino, CA: Campus Crusade for Christ International, © 1972, p. 174.

Rabbi Bronznick, has written: "We must conclude that in those last agonizing minutes he truly felt personally abandoned, his mission coming to grief....Jesus could not be the Messiah that Christian missionaries believe him to be."[175] However, the words, "Eli, Eli, lama sabachthani," are the exact opening words of Psalm 22 of the Old Testament.

This Psalm, written by King David, was an admitted prophecy of the Messiah's sufferings (even in ancient rabbinical commentary)[176] foretold over 1000 years before the birth of Jesus. Jesus was, in essence, sending a secret message to all who knew this Scripture, to turn back to this Psalm in the Old Testament and read a very detailed account of Messianic suffering through crucifixion. Interestingly enough, at the time when David wrote "they pierced my hands and my feet" (Ps. 22:16 KJV), crucifixion had not yet been invented!

It is important to note that Jesus cried out, "My God" twice, speaking to the Father and to the Spirit,[177] which shows that the first and the third member of the Godhead were there, in darkness, judging the sin of all which was placed on the second member,[178] Jesus, to pay for us as our substitute. Having been made guilty and then judged, Jesus would allow all who believed that He took and paid for our guilt to be free through the law of double jeopardy. God will not punish us for sin for which Jesus already paid![179]

---

[175]Gerald Sigal, *The Jew and The Christian Missionary*, p. 97.

[176]*Midrash Pesiqta Rabbati*, chapters 36-37.

[177]Modern Judaism denies the legitimacy of the Trinity, claiming that it was pagan, only later to be adopted by the Christians. Apparently, the rabbis have not done their homework; for the Jewish commentary, Zohar, is in agreement with God's tri-unity when it says: "Come and see the mystery of the word YHVH: there are three steps, each existing by itself: nevertheless they are One, and so united that one cannot be separated from the other. The Ancient Holy One is revealed with three heads, which are united into one, and that head is three exalted. The Ancient One is described as being three: because the other lights emanating from him are included in the three. But how can three names be one? Are they really one because we call them one? How three can be one can only be known through the revelation of the Holy Spirit." *Zohar*, Vol. III, p. 288; Vol. II, p. 43, Hebrew editions. See also Soncino Press edition, Vol. III, p. 134.

[178]See our *Vol. II*, chapter 16, "Jesus' Cry from the Cross to His Father Indicates Trinity," which also verifies the darkness over Jerusalem caused by an an eclipse during the crucifixion, as related by Dr. Edersheim.

[179]There is a true story told of a court case. Once, after a judge had heard a particular case, the defendant, proven guilty, was to be sentenced to either pay a fine or serve time in jail. The merciful judge said, "I love you and want to set you free but, being just, if law is to abide, I cannot. This crime must be paid for." Having no money but wishing to pay his fine, the defendant hung his head as he began to walk toward his cell. Just then, the judge's son who was in the courtroom jumped up and said, "Dad, I will pay his fine, if he will accept my money for it!" Everyone smiled as the guilty man accepted the money and gave it to the judge. "Paid for in full," said the Judge, "You are free to go.

WHY WAS THERE DARKNESS? FOR JESUS' PRIVACY DURING A SUFFERING SO AWFUL WE WILL NEVER UNDERSTAND

Jesus took God's judgment on Himself at its worst, in darkness, as recorded in Matthew 27:45. This was because God did not want to disgrace this part of His tri-unity Godhead before humanity. What was taking place was a very personal suffering between Jesus and His Father, God.

Psalm 22 tells of this darkness when it says: "O my God, I cry by day, but Thou dost not answer; And by **night**, but I have no rest. Yet Thou art holy, O Thou who art enthroned upon the praises of Israel. In Thee our fathers trusted...." (Ps. 22:2-4 NASB).

In Hebrew, the phrase "and by night" means a night season; "but there is not rest," indicates a special darkness. Thus, the reason Jesus asked why He was *forsaken* was because though His Divine nature understood, His human nature did not realize the enormity of being abandoned and forsaken.[180] God (the Father and Spirit) must separate fellowship entirely from God (the Son) before judging Him for us. As a result, for the first and last time in all eternity, all the sins of the world were poured upon Jesus and He and God were separated. Jesus was forsaken by God for us. This is why Jesus cried out.

Through David, the pre-incarnate Messiah said, "Thou art holy." Jesus knew His Father would have to separate Himself from Him, once He was made sin for all of us, because God cannot have any direct fellowship with sin. Thus, if He is truly holy, the God of Israel would have to cease fellowship at the time the Messiah was made sin and judged guilty for it! Jesus had thus done exactly what He had promised in the Gospel of Mark: "For even the Son of man came...to give his life a ransom for many" (Mark 10:45 KJV).

This was accomplished in full when He said, "It is finished" (John 19:30 KJV), which in the original language of the Gospel means "paid in full." If we accept Jesus' death payment, all of our sins from birth to death are paid for in full. We are redeemed as a result of Jesus' horrendous suffering for us, having accepted this wonderful though horribly obtained gift.

***

My son paid for you! And you accepted it." The biblical analogy here is easy to see. God, the Father = Judge; Jesus = Son; Hell = jail; blood atonement = money; sacrificial substitutionary death = acceptance/payment.

[180]This reflects Jesus' dual nature. His human nature is subject to the Father because God the Father is greater than His humanity (John 14:28). His Divine nature is of one essence with God because they are equal (John 10:30).

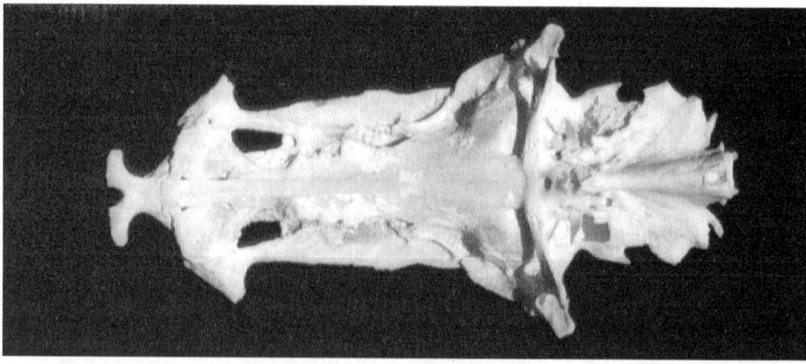

A portion of the Arius catfish skeleton, commonly known as the "crucifix fish," has an outline design resembling a man being crucified.

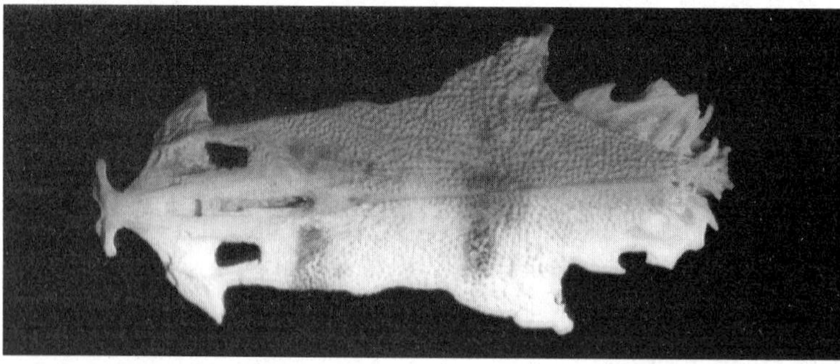

The reverse side of the skeleton resembles a Roman shield from Jesus' day. Some feel there are divine hints about Jesus in nature. Another example is the dogwood tree, which blossoms during the season in which Jesus was crucified. Each of the four white flower petals has a red tinge on the outer edge, resembling blood stains. The flowers' center resembles a crown of thorns.

ORIGINAL HEBREW TEXT WRITTEN 1000 BC

אֵלִי אֵלִי לָמָה עֲזַבְתָּנִי רָחוֹק מִישׁוּעָתִי דִּבְרֵי שַׁאֲגָתִי׃ אֱלֹהַי אֶקְרָא יוֹמָם וְלֹא תַעֲנֶה וְלַיְלָה
וְלֹא־דוּמִיָּה לִי׃ .... בִּרְכַּי כָּשְׁלוּ מִצּוֹם וּבְשָׂרִי כָּחַשׁ מִשָּׁמֶן׃ וַאֲנִי ׀ הָיִיתִי חֶרְפָּה לָהֶם
יִרְאוּנִי יְנִיעוּן רֹאשָׁם׃ תהלים כב:ב-ג; קט:כד-כה

OLD TESTAMENT SCRIPTURE TRANSLATION

"My God, my God, why hast Thou forsaken me? Far from my deliverance are the words of my groaning. O my God, I cry by day, but Thou dost not answer; And by night, but I have no rest....My knees are weak from fasting; And my flesh has grown lean, without fatness. I also have become a reproach to them; When they see me, they wag their head."

Psalms 22:1-2; 109:24-25 NASB

ANCIENT RABBINICAL COMMENTARY

"In the week when the Son of David comes, they will bring beams of iron and put them like a yoke on his neck until His stature is bent down. He cries and weeps, and his voice ascends to heaven, and in God's presence He will say: 'Sovereign of the world, how long will my strength last, how long my breath, my soul, and my limbs? Am I not flesh and blood?'....Then the Holy One—blessed be He!—says to Him: 'Ephraim, my righteous Messiah, you took all this upon yourself from the six days of creation....' "[181]

Pesiqta Rabbati, Friedmann's edition, chapter 36

NEW TESTAMENT RECORDED 90 AD

"...Pilate said to them, 'Shall I crucify your King?' The chief priests answered, 'We have no king but Caesar.' So he then delivered Him to them to be crucified. They took Jesus therefore, and He went out, bearing His own cross, to the place called the Place of a Skull, which is called in Hebrew, Golgotha. There they crucified Him, and with Him two other men, one on either side, and Jesus in between. And Pilate wrote an inscription also, and put it on the cross. And it was written, 'JESUS THE NAZARENE, THE KING OF THE JEWS.' Therefore this inscription many of the Jews read, for the place where Jesus was crucified was near the city; and it was written in Hebrew...." **John 19:15-20 NASB**

"Now from the sixth hour darkness fell upon all the land until the ninth hour. And about the ninth hour Jesus cried out with a loud voice, saying, 'ELI, ELI, LAMA SABACHTHANI?' that is, 'MY GOD, MY GOD, WHY HAST THOU FORSAKEN ME?' "

Matthew 27:45-46 NASB

MODERN RABBINIC COMMENT/REFUTATION

" 'My God, my God, why have you forsaken me?' is the opening sentence of Psalm 22. But why should Jesus have expressed this sentiment? Why should he have thought of himself as separated from God at the very moment when, according to Christian missionary theology, he was fulfilling God's plan?....Furthermore, it makes little sense to see in Psalm 22, prophecies depicting the agony felt by Jesus at his crucifixion....what sense does it make for Jesus to complain: 'My God, my God, why have you forsaken me?' "

***The Jew and the Christian Missionary*, by Gerald Sigal, pp. 96-97; © 1981**

AUTHOR'S COMMENT—EVANGELICAL CHRISTIAN POSITION

It makes every bit of sense that the agony of the Messiah, which had befallen Jesus, is detailed in Psalm 22 because the rabbis of old clearly interpreted this passage

---

[181] Arthur W. Kac, *The Messianic Hope*, p. 80.

from Pesiqta Rabbati, quoted above, as referring to the Messiah! Secondly, it was precisely God's plan to separate Himself (the Father and the Spirit) from God the Son, so that He might judge Him for the sin of all, thus legitimizing Him as redeemer for not only the Jew, but all mankind, as the Jewish Bible had always taught (Isa. 49:5-7). It seems a pity that Mr. Sigal and his rabbi apparently have not studied their Pesiqta Rabbati. **Philip Moore**

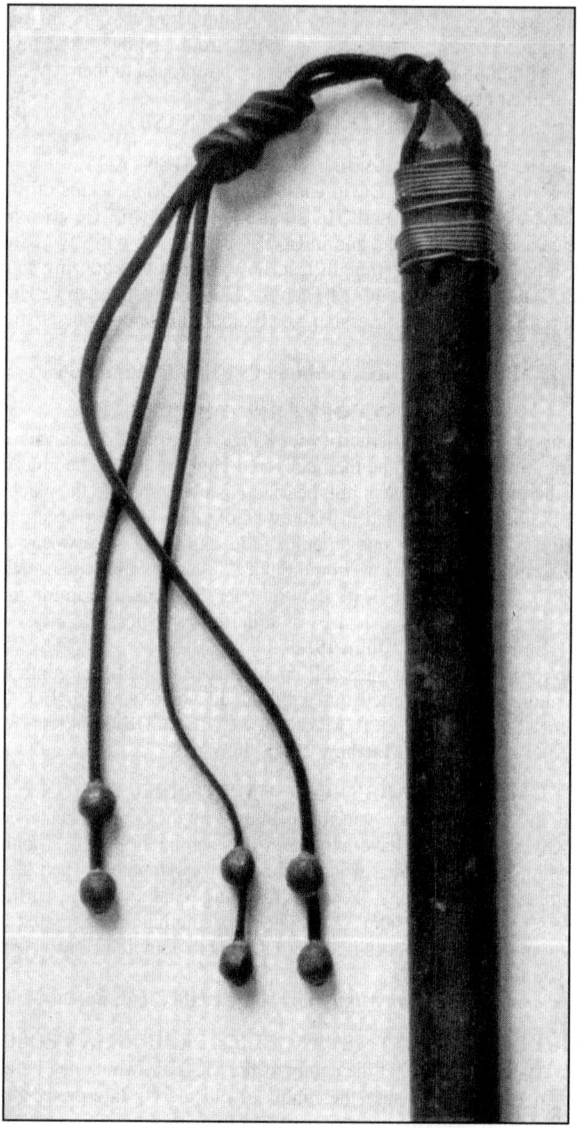

Jesus was whipped by Roman soldiers with an ancient weapon similar to this one. Notice the lead bits at the ends of the leather strips.

ORIGINAL HEBREW TEXT WRITTEN 1000 BC

וְאָנֹכִי תוֹלַעַת וְלֹא־אִישׁ חֶרְפַּת אָדָם וּבְזוּי עָם׃ כָּל־רֹאַי יַלְעִגוּ לִי יַפְטִירוּ בְשָׂפָה יָנִיעוּ
רֹאשׁ׃ גֹּל אֶל־יְהוָה יְפַלְּטֵהוּ יַצִּילֵהוּ כִּי חָפֵץ בּוֹ׃ .... כַּמַּיִם נִשְׁפַּכְתִּי וְהִתְפָּרְדוּ כָּל־עַצְמוֹתָי
הָיָה לִבִּי כַּדּוֹנָג נָמֵס בְּתוֹךְ מֵעָי׃ יָבֵשׁ כַּחֶרֶשׂ ׀ כֹּחִי וּלְשׁוֹנִי מֻדְבָּק מַלְקוֹחָי וְלַעֲפַר־מָוֶת
תִּשְׁפְּתֵנִי׃ כִּי סְבָבוּנִי כְּלָבִים עֲדַת מְרֵעִים הִקִּיפוּנִי כָּאֲרִי יָדַי וְרַגְלָי׃ אֲסַפֵּר כָּל־עַצְמוֹתָי
הֵמָּה יַבִּיטוּ יִרְאוּ־בִי׃ יְחַלְּקוּ בְגָדַי לָהֶם וְעַל־לְבוּשִׁי יַפִּילוּ גוֹרָל׃

תהלים כב:ז-ט; טו-יט

OLD TESTAMENT SCRIPTURE TRANSLATION

"But I am a worm, and not a man, A reproach of men, and despised by the people. All who see me sneer at me; They separate with the lip, they wag the head, *saying*, 'Commit *yourself* to the LORD; let Him deliver him; Let Him rescue him, because He delights in him'....I am poured out like water, And all my bones are out of joint; My heart is like wax; It is melted within me. My strength is dried up like a potsherd, And my tongue cleaves to my jaws; And Thou dost lay me in the dust of death. For dogs have surrounded me; A band of evildoers has encompassed me; They pierced my hands and my feet. I can count all my bones. They look, they stare at me; They divide my garments among them, And for my clothing they cast lots." **Psalms 22:6-8, 14-18 NASB**

ANCIENT RABBINICAL COMMENTARY

"The Patriarchs will one day rise again in the month of Nisan and will say to the Messiah....You have been a laughing-stock and a derision among the peoples of the world, and because of you they jeered at Israel, as it is written (Psalm 22:6). You have dwelt in darkness and in gloominess, and your eyes have not seen light, your skin was cleaving to your bones, and your body withered like wood. Your eyes became hollow from fasting, and your strength was dried up like a potsherd, as it is written (Psalm 22:15; 22:16 Heb.). All this happened because of the sins of our children, as it is written: 'And Jehovah laid on him the iniquity of us all' (Isaiah 53:6)."[182] **Pesiqta Rabbati, Friedmann's edition, chapter 37**

NEW TESTAMENT RECORDED 90 AD

"The soldiers therefore, when they had crucified Jesus, took His outer garments and made four parts, a part to every soldier and *also* the tunic; now the tunic was seamless, woven in one piece. They said therefore to one another, 'Let us not tear it, but cast lots for it, *to decide* whose it shall be'...."

John 19:23-24 NASB

MODERN RABBINIC COMMENT/REFUTATION

"Missionaries claim that Jesus fulfilled the prophecy that the Messiah would be killed by crucifixion...there is absolutely no evidence that this Psalm is speaking of the Messiah. From the opening verse, it would seem that King David, the author of this Psalm [22], was actually speaking of himself."

***The Real Messiah*, by Aryeh Kaplan, *et al*, p. 55; 1976. [ ] mine**

"This Psalm [22] voices the concerns of the Jewish people."[183]

***Their Hollow Inheritance*, by Rabbi Michoel Drazin, p. 143; © 1990. [ ] mine.**

---

[182] Ibid, pp. 80-81.

[183] Michoel Drazin, *Their Hollow Inheritance, A Comprehensive Refutation of Christian Missionaries*. Safed, Israel: G.M. Publications, © 1990, p. 143. The foreword to Drazin's book was written by Rabbi Gabriel Marzel.

AUTHOR'S COMMENT—EVANGELICAL CHRISTIAN POSITION

There is every evidence that this Psalm is indeed speaking of the Messiah since the rabbinical commentaries interpret it so. Even the thought that King David wrote of himself is preposterous, since the sufferer of Psalm 22 dies in immense agony before his enemies, while David was victorious and died a death quite different than the one predicted in the Messianic Psalm. Rabbi Kaplan would have done well to have studied the commentary on Psalm 22 before commenting so arrogantly.

Philip Moore

FOUR INTRICATE, DELICATELY BALANCED DETAILS OF THE PROPHECY OF CRUCIFIXION

We are dealing with three issues here: 1. The heavy wooden cross Jesus was forced to carry part of the way to the site of His crucifixion, which we believe the ancient rabbinical commentary described, in the ancient idiom, as "iron beams"; 2. Why did Jesus sound His fourth of seven cries, "My God, My God, why hast Thou forsaken me?" and; 3. Most importantly, the significance of His sixth cry, "It is finished," or *tetelestai*, more correctly translated as "paid for in full."

LINDSEY'S EXPOSITION OF JESUS' FULFILLMENT OF THE CRUCIFIXION PROPHECY DESTROYS SIGAL'S POTENTIAL TO INFLICT DOUBT

In answer to the author of *The Jew and the Christian Missionary*, we quote the popular and learned Christian writer, Hal Lindsey, who remarks: "Perhaps no other statement that Jesus made has provoked more curiosity and controversy than his cry from the cross, 'My God, my God, why have you forsaken me?' (Matthew 27:46)

I don't believe Jesus asked the question because he didn't know the answer. It's that he wanted us to find out what it was and sending us back to David's prophetic Psalm from where it is quoted was a good place to begin.

The Psalms make many predictions concerning the Messiah but the clearest and most graphic of these is Psalm 22. King David wrote this around 1000 B.C.E. yet the circumstances described in this Psalm do not fit anything that ever happened in the life of David himself as so many of his other Psalms do. David ruled the most powerful kingdom of his day and yet never fell into his enemies' hands even during his darkest times, as this Psalm describes of its central figure. David died a peaceful death in old age too, while this personage in Psalm 22 dies in great suffering and humiliation....What we have before us in Psalm 22 is a very personal prophecy of how Messiah *felt* in his sufferings and how he viewed the things going on around Him. David, in the power of the Spirit, speaks as if he were the Messiah, feeling his emotions and discouragement as if they were his own.

In one of the most amazing usages of prophecy anywhere in literature, David describes in unbelievably realistic terms the plight of one going through the tortures of crucifixion. Yet, crucifixion was a Phoenecian and Roman custom, unknown to the Jews until approximately 400 years *after* David wrote this Psalm.

It's fairly common knowledge that Jesus was executed on a Roman cross because he claimed to be the Son of God and Israel's Messiah."[184]

THIS WE BELIEVE AND THIS WE DO NOT BECAUSE ONE KNOWS HIS "STUFF" BETTER THAN THE OTHER

Question: Why should we hold what the author of *The Jew and the Christian Missionary* has said to be essentially a lie, while agreeing with the comments of Hal Lindsey? Answer: Hal Lindsey agrees with the ancient rabbinical writings, whereas Sigal and the rabbi advising him are either ignoring, shunning, or even worse, are oblivious to the ancient writings of their own forefathers such as the Pesiqta Rabbati and the Yalkut, which clearly show the Davidic literature in question to be Messianic.

WHAT REALLY HAPPENED TO JESUS? DID PSALM 22 IN JEWISH SCRIPTURE TRULY FORETELL SUCH DETAILS?

The Psalm foretells, "I am poured out like water...." (verse 14 KJV). This was true of Jesus as He sweat profusely after being lifted up on the cross into the Middle Eastern sun of Israel. The Psalm goes on: "...all my bones are out of joint...." (verse 14). Once a person was affixed to a cross, it was hoisted by a rope and knocked into a prepared hole in the ground. It was common knowledge that the sudden jerk would literally throw every bone in the body out of joint. Later, the ligaments would stretch, dislocating the bones even more.

Jesus experienced this horrifying agony of crucifixion predicted by David in verse 17:[185] "I may tell all my bones...." (KJV). Psalm 22 continues: "...my heart is like wax; it is melted in the midst of my bowels" (verse 14 KJV). John 19:34 records that Jesus' heart was pierced by a Roman spear. This would cause the poetic quote, "like wax it is melted in the midst of my bowels," to literally come true.

---

[184]Hal Lindsey, *The Promise*, pp. 134-136.

[185]Verse 18 in the Hebrew edition.

David's prophecy continues: "My strength is dried up like a potsherd; and my tongue cleaveth to my jaws; and thou hast brought me into the dust of death" (verse 15 KJV). This verse clearly describes the weakened condition of Jesus as He hung upon the cross. The mention, "dried up like a potsherd" (a potsherd is a broken piece of dried-up pottery which once contained water when whole), graphically illustrates what Jesus meant when He said, "I thirst" (John 19:28 KJV), after hanging so many hours in the merciless Mediterranean sun.

IS THE INTERPRETATION OF THIS PSALM CHRISTIAN INNUENDO OR WAS IT JEWISHLY CONSIDERED OF THE MESSIAH?

Chapter 36 of the ancient rabbinical commentary Pesiqta Rabbati speaks of these Davidic passages and clearly illustrates that these sufferings were to come upon Israel's Messiah: "The Fathers of the World [Abraham, Isaac, and Jacob] will in the future rise up in the month of Nissan and speak to him: 'Ephraim, our True Messiah! Even though we are your fathers, you are greater than we, for you suffered because of the sins of our children, and cruel punishments have come upon you the like of which have not come upon the early and the later generations, and you were put to ridicule and held in contempt by the nations of the world because of Israel, and you sat in darkness and blackness and your eyes saw no light, and your skin cleft to your bones, and your body dried out and was like wood, and your eyes grew dim from fasting, and your strength became like a **potsherd**. All this because of the sins of our children. Do you want that our children should enjoy the happiness that the Holy One, blessed be He, allotted to Israel, or perhaps, because of the great sufferings that have come upon you on their account, and because they imprisoned you in the jailhouse, your mind is not reconciled with them?' "[186]

Additional portions of this incredible Jewish rabbinical writing from the Pesiqta Rabbati read as follows: "During the seven-year period preceding the coming of the son of David, iron beams will be brought and loaded upon his neck until the Messiah's body is bent low. Then he will cry and weep, and his voice will rise up to the very height of heaven, and he will say to God: Master of the universe, how much can my strength endure? How much can my spirit endure? How much my breath before it ceases? How much can my limbs suffer? Am I not flesh-and-blood?....He will be told: Ephraim, our true Messiah, be thou judge of these and do with them what thy soul desires, for the nations

[186]Raphael Patai, *The Messiah Texts*, p. 113. Bold and [ ] mine. Decide for yourself if Psalm 22 is a Christian interpretation or a Jewish one!

would long since have destroyed thee in an instant had not God's mercies been exceedingly mighty in thy behalf, as is said *Ephraim is a darling son unto Me*....They will growl over him like lions who lust to swallow him, as is said *All our enemies have opened their mouth wide against us. Terror and the pit are come upon us, desolation and destruction* (Lam. 3:46-47)."[187]

WHEN KING DAVID RECORDED GOD'S PROPHECY OF CRUCIFIXION BY PIERCING, HE MEANT IT, ALONG WITH THE GORY DETAILS

David's Psalm continues: "For dogs have compassed me: the assembly of the wicked have inclosed me: they pierced my hands and my feet. I may tell all my bones: they look *and* stare upon me. They part my garments among them, and cast lots upon my vesture" (verses 16-18 KJV).

When the Psalm says "**dogs** have compassed [surrounded] me,"[188] and "the **assembly** of the wicked have inclosed me," two groups are indicated. Dog was common slang for Gentiles or non-Jews,[189] thus the many Roman soldiers are foreseen. Secondly, this wicked assembly refers to the priests and some unbelieving Sanhedrin members,[190] who said: "He saved others; himself he cannot save. If he be the King of Israel, let him now come down from the cross, and we will believe him. He trusted in God; let him deliver him now, if he will have him: for he said, I am the Son of God" (Matt. 27:42-43 KJV).

These phrases uttered by this *assembly of the wicked* almost match those foretelling this event in verse 8 of Psalm 22: "He trusted on the LORD *that* he would deliver him: let him deliver him, seeing he delighted in him" (KJV).

Perhaps the greatest and most disputed line of the entire Old Testament portion of the Bible is "they pierced[191] my hands and my

---

[187] *Pesikta Rabbati*, Yale Judaica Series, Vol. XVIII. New Haven, CT: Yale University Press, © 1968, pp. 680, 686-687, used by permission.

[188] [ ] mine.

[189] Hal Lindsey with C.C. Carlson, *The Late Great Planet Earth*, p. 40.

[190] See Matthew 27:41.

[191] What did they do, *Kaari* or *Kaaru*? That is the question. Moishe Rosen mentions: "Yalkut Shimoni (687):....'*Kaari' my hands and my feet*—Rabbi Nehemiah says, 'They pierced my hands and my feet in the presence of Ahasuerus.' [This shows that the reading 'pierced' was accepted by certain rabbis.]" Moishe Rosen, *Y'shua*, p. 74. Rosen has quoted from Rachmiel Frydland's unpublished manuscript, *Messianic Prophecy*, to show that the quoted passage illustrates that the ancient rabbis interpreted Psalm 22 as *Kaaru* כארו for "pierced," which here means *Kaari* "like a lion," which by no coincidence also pierces with its claws. The only differences between the two Hebrew words "like a lion" and "pierced," כארי (*Kaari*) and כארו (*Kaaru*), is that one contains a *ude* י (pronounced

feet," because it clearly indicates crucifixion, which is universally known to have been perpetrated upon Jesus.

The phrase, "I may count all my bones," describes a crucified man's efforts to pull himself up to breathe. The Romans bent the legs slightly before nailing the spikes into the feet. They placed a small seat in the middle of the cross in order to cause a person, while hanging, to push up off the seat to gasp for air. While doing this, every bone in the body could be felt along with a lot of other things. That is why, if a person lasted too long on a cross, the Romans would break his legs so he would soon suffocate. If a victim lost consciousness at any time, he would expire within moments!

---

yude) and the other a *vav* ו. A long *ude* is often mistaken for a short *vav* and a short *vav* mistaken for a long *ude*. There seems to be a disagreement between our ancient and modern rabbinical friends. History, for no mysterious reason, has seen the letter ו *vav* become a *ude*! Albert Barnes comments: "Gesenius candidly observes that 'all the ancient interpreters have taken כארי as a verb; and this is certainly possible if we regard כארו as the participle in Kal formed in the Chaldee manner, and in the plural number for כארים.' And he refers to two MSS. to prove that *'it was commonly held to be a verb.'* And in confirmation of this Vatablus declares that the ancient reading was twofold כארי and כרו; while according to the testimony of Genebrard, the Jews continued to write כארי in the margin and כארו in the text until the six hundredth year of the Christian era, and then began to insert the marginal reading into the text itself; and finally to omit כארו altogether." Albert Barnes, *Notes on the Old Testament*, Psalms Vol. I. Grand Rapids, MI: Baker Book House, p. 395. Hebrew is a precise language and, we believe inspired by God. That is why, in all the efforts to foil this Messianic prophecy, all that could be changed was the act of "piercing," to an animal which has four claws that also pierce! Hal Lindsey has elegantly commented on the motive for the rabbis' alteration of Psalm 22:16 (22:17 in Hebrew): "...the identity of the one whose sufferings are described in Psalm 22 is of utmost importance. Because of the remarkable features....because it does seem so specifically to allude to Jesus, later Rabbis and liberal Christian theologians have either avoided comment on it or sought to ascribe the central personage as someone other than Messiah. However, in the ancient Rabbinic collection of traditions called the Yalkut....the Rabbis said that God makes an agreement with the Messiah to the effect that the Messiah would suffer for the sins of all Jews who have lived before or after him, and to illustrate these sufferings, they quote from Psalm 22....here is the Messiah [in Ps. 22], saying through David's pen, that one day his hands and feet would be pierced. Obviously, the meaning of this phase is vigorously contested by the Rabbis since to admit that it means exactly what it says is tantamount to admitting that Jesus...was their Messiah. The main objection to this phrase revolves around one word, 'to pierce.' In the Hebrew Massoretic text, the Hebrew word is 'caari' which translates into 'like a lion.' thus the Jewish Bible reads, 'Like a lion they are at my hands and my feet.' However, the 3rd century B.C.E. translation of the Hebrew Old Testament into Greek (the Septuagint), designated this disputed word as 'caaru' which means 'to pierce.' Thus, 250 years before Jesus' crucifixion would have made anyone prejudiced about this reading, the Rabbis were translating the word as 'pierced.' The only minute difference in these two words is the length of the stem of the last letter of the Hebrew word, and it could easily have been altered by one tiny slip on one stroke of a scribe's pen." Hal Lindsey, *The Promise*, pp. 134-135, 138. [ ] mine.

The Romans were about to break Jesus' legs (John 19:33) because the priests wanted all of this finished before the Sabbath (John 19:31).

After they broke the legs of the two thieves on both sides, they noticed that Jesus looked dead. Since they were not sure, a soldier thrust a spear into Jesus' side and blood and water were released separately. This showed that His corpuscles had separated from the blood serum and indicated that He had been dead an hour or more. Thus, they forewent this "leg breaking," fulfilling Psalm 34:20, written 1000 years before: "He keeps all his bones; Not one of them is broken" (NASB). It is also interesting that God told the Israelis never to break a bone of the Passover lamb (Exo. 12). Jesus, as our Passover sacrifice, again fits the bill!

DAVID'S PREDICTION THAT THE MESSIAH WOULD BE STRIPPED, HIS GARMENTS TORN AND VESTURE (COAT) GAMBLED FOR, REALLY CAME TRUE

Did the Psalmist's prediction: "...they look *and* stare upon me. They part my garments among them, and cast lots upon my vesture" (Ps. 22:17-18) also come true? Before Jesus was nailed to the cross, He was stripped of both His garments and vesture, thus, He was without clothing.[192] This is what is meant by looking and staring.

Once Jesus was lifted up, the Romans at the foot of the cross divided His garments and gambled for His expensive seamless coat. This was a common practice for obtaining the clothes of victims. The eyewitness John, who wrote the book of Revelation of things yet to come, tells us in his Gospel: "Then the soldiers, when they had crucified Jesus, took his garments, and made four parts, to every soldier a part; and also *his* coat. Now the coat was without seam, woven from the top throughout. They said, therefore, among themselves, Let us not |tear| it, but cast lots for it, whose it shall be...." (John 19:23-24 KJV).[193]

WAS THIS MESSIANIC SUFFERING PROPHESIED AND ACCOMPLISHED FOR NOTHING? NO! IT WAS FOR *TETELESTAI*

When Jesus said, *tetelestai* or "paid in full," He was proclaiming His task completed. The human race was now spiritually redeemed

---

[192]The Romans crucified their victims naked. Hal Lindsey with C.C. Carlson, *The Late Great Planet Earth*, p. 40.
[193]*The New Scofield Reference Bible.*

from all guilt. Jesus was placed back into harmony with His Father and He gave up His life in aquiescence to His Father. This was also foreseen by David when he mentioned in the last two verses of Psalm 22: "...It will be told of the Lord to the *coming* generation. They will come and will declare his righteousness To a people who will be born, that He has performed *it*" (Ps. 22:30-31 NASB).

Performed it, in Hebrew, means the same as *tetelestai* in Greek. Since the death of Jesus, all true believers in Him have approached the world of unbelievers with the good news concerning redemption with the words, "he hath done this,"[194] or יָבֹאוּ וְיַגִּידוּ צִדְקָתוֹ לְעַם נוֹלָד כִּי עָשָׂה .

Jesus fulfilled all of the intricate details prophesied in King David's book of Psalms 1000 years after they were written, which is in itself amazing. However, when we talk about redemption, what do we really indicate when we say, "He, Jesus, performed it." What did Jesus finish when He said, "It is finished," or rather, *tetelestai*? What does this word really mean and what did Jesus precisely do when He redeemed the human race?

THE CRY OF JESUS PAYS THE DEBT OF SIN

Here again, we feel that Hal Lindsey has so beautifully illustrated the point of Jesus' sixth cry, that we quote him extensively. In his book, *The Liberation of Planet Earth*, Hal wrote: "To understand the nature of this DEBT OF SIN, we have to reach back into the practices of the criminal courts of the Roman Empire.

In the days of the great dominion of Rome, it was assumed by Caesar that every Roman citizen owed him perfect allegiance and obedience to his laws. Justice was swift to enforce this assumption, and if any citizen broke any law of the land, he soon found himself standing before the courts or Caesar himself.

NAILED TO THE PRISON DOOR

If the man were found guilty of breaking the law and sentenced to prison, an itemized list was made of each infraction and its corresponding penalty. This list was, in essence, a record of how the man had failed to live up to the laws of Caesar. It was called a 'Certificate of Debt.'

When the man was taken to his prison cell, this Certificate of Debt was nailed to his cell door so that anyone passing by could tell that the man had been justly condemned and could also see the limitations of his punishment....When the man had served his time and was released, he would be handed the yellowed, tattered Certificate of

---

[194]Psalms 22:31 KJV.

Debt with the worlds 'Paid in Full' written across it. He could never again be imprisoned for those crimes as long as he could produce his canceled Certificate of Debt.

But until the sentence was paid, that Certificate of Debt stood between him and freedom. It continued to witness to the fact that the imprisoned man had failed to live according to the laws of Rome and was, in essence, an offense to Caesar....man owes God perfect obedience to His holy laws as summarized in the Ten Commandments and the Sermon on the Mount. By his failure to live up to this standard of perfection, man has become an offense to the very character of God, and the eternal court of justice has pronounced the death sentence upon man.

A Certificate of Debt was prepared against every person who would ever live, listing his failure to live in thought, word, and deed in accordance with the law of God. This death sentence has become a DEBT OF SIN which has to be paid, either by man or, if possible, someone qualified to take his place (Colossians 2:14)....All we have to do is look inside ourselves and we'll see all kinds of emotions, lusts, drives, and temptations that overpower us from time to time and cause us to do things we know are wrong.

Those actions are what God calls 'sins,' and they *aren't* caused by our environment. They are caused by our 'reaction' to our environment, and that's an *internal* problem which man has.

Listen to how Jesus described man and his sinning: 'That which comes *out* of the man is what defiles him. For from *inside*, out of the heart of men comes the evil thoughts and fornications, thefts, murders, adulteries, deeds of coveting, and wickedness, as well as deceit, lust, envy, slander, pride and foolishness. All these evil things proceed from *within...'*....Misbehavior is not primarily the result of our environment; it's a problem of the heart....In using the word 'heart,' Jesus is talking about that inner part of man's being which has in it the 'sin nature,' or a disposition toward rebellion against God.

Have you ever done something which was totally stupid and senseless and you said to yourself afterwards, 'What on earth made me do that?' Your better judgment *knew* it was wrong, but you went ahead anyway. Well, it was your 'sin nature' which prompted you to do it.

The Bible uses the terms 'flesh' and 'sin' (in the singular) to describe that force within us that is in total rebellion against God. This 'nature' was not in man when God created him. It entered Adam and Eve the moment they disobeyed God and He withdrew His spiritual life from them....The Bible teaches that when Adam and Eve disobeyed God in the Garden of Eden, they didn't just lose their sense of fellowship with God and become unlike Him in their character; they actually had something *added* to them—a sin nature. And that made them sinners. Since that awful day of infamy, all men have been born with that same sinful nature, and that is the source of our sins....the day Jesus died....At noonday God drew a veil of darkness over the whole earth. It was pitch black. I believe God did this so that no one would be able to witness visually the horror of what was happening to Jesus as He hung there—because in that moment, the entire wrath of God was engulfing Him as He allowed the sins of all mankind to be put on Him. Until then Jesus hadn't uttered even a whimper.

But then, all of a sudden, the silence was broken and Jesus cried out in His humanity, '*Eloi, Eloi, lama sabachthani,'* which means, 'My God, My God, why have You forsaken Me?'

In that instant God had taken the Certificates of Debt of every human being from the beginning of mankind until the close of history, and nailed them to the cross, making Jesus responsible and guilty for each one!

And God had to turn His back on His own Son in His greatest hour of need, because Christ had voluntarily allowed Himself to be made a sinner on our behalf and God could have no fellowship with sinners of *any* kind until redemption was completed.

When I get to heaven I want to ask Jesus, 'Lord, what really happened in that awful hour of blackness?'

Even after He explains it to me, I know I won't be able to comprehend what it must have been like for the poured-out fury of a holy God to fall like an atomic blast on Jesus.

His scream was out of deep agony of soul because, for the first and last time for all eternity, the Second Person of the Godhead, Jesus, was separated from the other two members of the Godhead, the Father and the Spirit.

No one will ever be as alone as Jesus was there on the cross. He was separated from every person He'd ever loved and trusted. Forsaken by His closest friends, forsaken by God the Father and God the Holy Spirit, forsaken by all, He hung there in an aloneness that nobody will ever be able to fathom.

Do you know why He did it?

So that you and I would never have to be alone again. So He could tell those who believed in Him, 'I will never desert you, nor will I ever forsake you' (Hebrews 13:5)....But that's not the end of the story.

Just before Jesus gave up His earthly life and commended His Spirit to the Father, He shouted a word which is the Magna Carta of all true believers.

That victorious cry was '*Tetelestai*!'

Let that word burn like a firebrand into your mind, because that's the *exact same word* that a Roman judge would write across a released criminal's Certificate of Debt to show that all his penalty had been paid and he was free at last. The word used in this way means 'paid in full' and is translated in many Bibles as 'It is finished.' In the mind of God, 'Paid in Full' has been written across the Certificate of Debt of every man who will ever live because His debt to God has been fully paid by Jesus [provided the person accepts this!][195]....

JESUS DIED TWICE

When Jesus was hanging on the cross as our substitute, the writer of Hebrews tell us, it was that 'He might taste death for every one' (Hebrews 2:9). Since man's penalty for being a sinner is both spiritual and physical death, Jesus had to taste both kinds of death.

When He shouted out, 'My God, My God, why hast Thou forsaken me?' at that moment, there on the cross, He was actually made sin for us, and in His human spirit He died spiritually. The apostle Paul referred to this when he said, 'He made Him [Jesus] who knew no sin *to be sin on our behalf*, that we might become the righteousness of God in Him' (2 Corinthians 5:21).

This doesn't mean Jesus was actually sinful in Himself. It means He was treated by the Father as if He were actually sinful. Since Jesus was bearing our sins, God had to judge Him just as He would have had to judge us because of our sins.

In dying spiritually and physically as our substitute, God looked at Jesus' death and credited it to the account of fallen humanity. His spiritual death means God can give spiritual life to all men who will receive it; and His physical death, and defeat of it in the resurrection, means God can ultimately raise our physical bodies and give them immortality.

GOD'S ULTIMATE LAMB

There's little more that can be said to amplify this vivid picture of Jesus' substitutionary death on our behalf. The only thing to add is that in becoming a Lamb for the world's sins, Jesus *fulfilled the need* for one lamb for a man, one lamb for a family, and one lamb for a nation.

It was no mere coincidence that His crucifixion took place on the day of Passover. He was destined by God to be the world's Passover Lamb whose blood, when applied to the doorposts of our hearts, would cause God to 'pass over' us in judgment.

He was also the fulfillment of the lamb on the Day of Atonement upon whom the sins of the people were laid and who was slain in their behalf.

---

195 [ ] mine.

WHY?

The only question that might come to mind is, 'Why did He do it?' Jesus gave us the answer to that question when He told His disciples, 'Greater love has no one than this, that one lay down his life for his friends' (John 15:13).

Jesus died for us because He loved us!"[196]

PIERCING DECEPTIONS BETWEEN TRANSLATIONS

The writers of *The Real Messiah*, an anti-missionary publication which is distributed by the National Conference of Synagogue Youth, vainly attempt to explain away the Messianic prophecy of Psalm 22. In this joke of scholarship, it is commented that: "Missionaries claim that Jesus fulfilled the prophecy that the Messiah would be killed by crucifixion. They quote a Biblical verse, which, correctly translated, reads (Psalm 22:17), 'For dogs have encompassed me, a company of evil-doers have enclosed me, *like a lion*, they are at my hands and feet.' 'Like a lion' in Hebrew is *KeAri.* The fundamentalist Christian interpreters actually changed the spelling of the word from *KeAri* to *Kari.*

"If one then totally ignores Hebrew grammar, one can twist this to mean 'He gouged me.' Then, as in the King James' Version, they make this verse read 'they pierced my hands and feet.' However, this bears no relation to the original meaning of the verse. Even with the change in spelling, it is a forced translation. This is but one more example of the lengths missionaries go to to prove that they are right."[197]

We emphasize that there is no alteration of the Hebrew word *KeAri* כארי (also transliterated and pronounced *Kaari*) in verse 17 of Psalm 22 in Hebrew. *Kaari* means *KeAri.*[198] Rather, this word *Kaari* ("like a lion," a Hebrew idiom for being pierced) was originally *Kaaru* כארו, which can *only* mean "to pierce." Even in its present altered form, *Kaari* (changed from *Kaaru*) is not exclusively translated as "pierced" in the King James Version as *The Real Messiah* infers! In fact, it was translated as "pierced" in an English *Jewish* version from the 1930's, which reads: "...they pierced my hands and my feet."[199]

---

[196] Hal Lindsey, *The Liberation of Planet Earth*, pp. 45-49, 100-102, 118-119.

[197] Aryeh Kaplan, *et al*, *The Real Messiah*, p. 55.

[198] This explanation using the words *KeAri* and *Kari* is puzzling to us. *Kaari* in Hebrew means "like a lion." *Kaaru* means "to pierce"! We asked Tal Moran, a friend from Israel who grew up speaking Hebrew, where the authors of *The Real Messiah* might have come up with the idea that there were two versions of *KeAri*, one meaning "they gouged me." Tal did not have the slightest idea. We believe the author of *The Real Messiah* apparently invented the word *"Kari"*; along with his "explanation" of translation, it is neither a word nor an issue.

[199] *The Holy Scriptures.* New York: Hebrew Publishing Company, © 1930, p. 898.

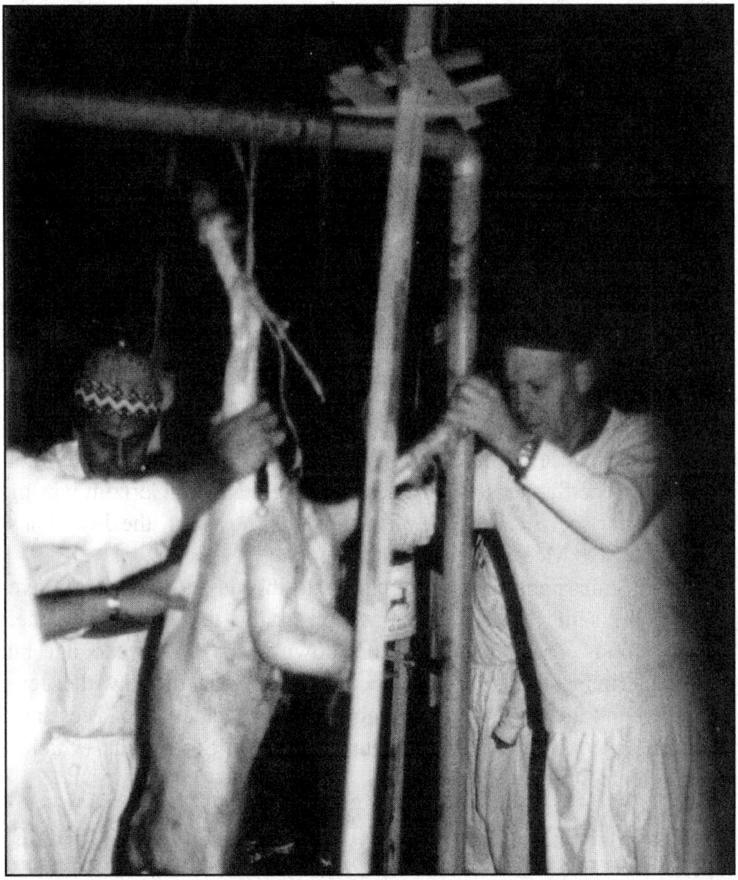

On Mount Gerizim in Israel, Samaritans place the Passover sacrifice on a wooden roasting rod with a crossbar, forming the shape of a cross, in order to prepare the sacrifice to be cooked over an open fire. This is in line with their understanding of Moses' instructions in Exodus 12 concerning the command to perform the original Passover. Moses wrote: "Your lamb shall be without blemish, a male of the first year: ye shall take *it* out from the sheep, or from the goats: And ye shall keep it up until the fourteenth day of the same month: and the whole assembly of the congregation of Israel shall kill it in the evening. And they shall take of the blood, and strike *it* on the two side posts and on the upper door post of the houses, wherein they shall eat it. And they shall eat the flesh in that night, roast with fire, and unleavened bread; *and* with bitter *herbs* they shall eat it. Eat not of it raw, nor sodden at all with water, but roast *with* fire; his head with his legs, and with the purtenance thereof. And ye shall let nothing of it remain until the morning; and that which remaineth of it until the morning ye shall burn with fire" (Exo. 12:5-10 KJV).

Samaritans are also mentioned in the New Testament (Matt. 10:5; Luke 9:52; John 4:9, 39-40; Acts 8:25). Jesus once made reference to a Samaritan who performed a good deed by saving the life of a man who had been robbed, beaten and left to die. Thus, we have the parable of the "Good Samaritan," which you have probably heard.

THE MODERN SAMARITANS PRESERVED THE ANCIENT EXODUS PASSOVER LAMB SACRIFICE

Here, we are dealing with modern Samaritans living in Israel (there are only about five hundred left on Earth), and the relationship between their ancient Passover custom and the manner in which the Messiah died on the cross.

The custom of sacrificing a lamb on Passover began during the bondage of the Jews in Egypt and continued as a symbol of their liberation. The Samaritans mistakenly thought Mount Gerizim was the place to offer sacrifice instead of the Temple; however, the Jews knew the Temple was Moses' designated area.

The Samaritans have continued, until this day, to offer a Passover lamb in the same fashion and tradition as did the Jews while their Temple stood. The Temple was torn down nearly 2000 years ago but Mount Gerizim still exists. We can get an idea of how the Jews sacrificed and ate the Passover lamb in their anticipation of Messianic redemption by observing the ancient feast of the Samaritans, which is still celebrated today.

JESUS' SUFFERING MESSIANIC CREDENTIAL IS VISIBLE STILL IN THE SAMARITANS' *PREPARATION* OF THE LAMB

We see the strong connection between the crossbar on which the Passover lamb was placed and the cross on which the Romans hung Jesus. They, of course, did not know that He was designated to be the sacrifice for all mankind. God knew, and we can see that this crossbar was also God's prophetic symbol pointing to the future Messiah's First Coming and atonement for us.

LEARNED JEWS ARE STARTLED BY A JEWISH COMMENTARY THAT MENTIONS A "CROSS ON HIS SHOULDERS" IN ISAAC'S ANCIENT ORDEAL

It is related in Genesis 22:6, concerning Isaac's near-sacrifice by Abraham, that: "...Abraham took the wood of the burnt-offering, and laid *it* upon Isaac his son; and he took the fire in his hand, and a knife; and they went both of them together" (Gen. 22:6 KJV).

Though many rabbis deny this verse foreshadows Jesus and His cross, we have surprised them when we pointed out the Midrash Shimoni's commentary on this verse; for we have read in Hebrew on page 58 of the Saloniki edition: "...and Abraham took the wood and he put it on his son as a person who carries a cross on his shoulders."

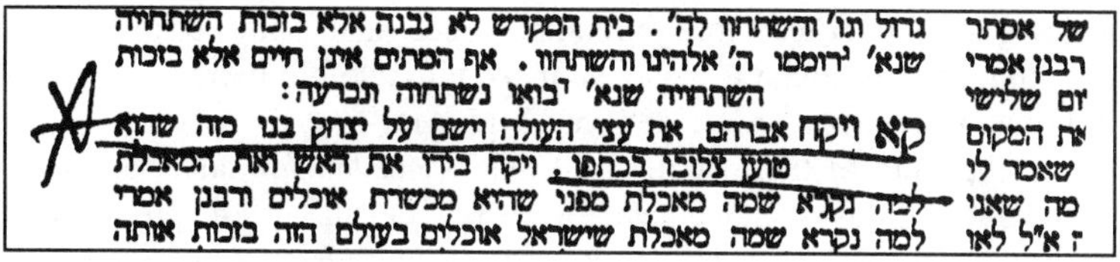

גדול וגו' והשתחוו לה'. בית המקדש לא נבנה אלא בזכות השתחויה
שנא' רוממו ה' אלהינו והשתחוו. אף המתים אינן חיים אלא בזכות
השתחויה שנא' בואו נשתחוה ונכרעה:
קא ויקח אברהם את עצי העולה וישם על יצחק בנו כזה שהוא
טוען צלובו בכתפו. ויקח בידו את האש ואת המאכלת
למה נקרא שמה מאכלת מפני שהיא מכשרת אוכלים ורבנן אמרי
למה נקרא שמה מאכלת שישראל אוכלים בעולם הזה בזכות אותה

של אסתר
רבנן אמרי
יום שלישי
את המקום
שאמר לי
מה שאני
ז א"ל לאו

Photo copy reproduction of Hebrew quote in *Midrash Shimoni*.

This verse of the Yalkut startles many learned Jewish scholars because it shows that the cross (*Tzlav* in Hebrew) is mentioned in Hebrew literature, even outside of the Old Testament (Ps. 22) in connection to sacrifice for God. Remember, God asked Abraham to give his only son but then allowed a ram to be sacrificed in his place!

THE PROPHECY OF THE NEW TESTAMENT, WHICH JESUS MADE POSSIBLE IN HIS DEATH

As Jesus gave the cup of Passover wine to His disciples,[200] He said: "...This cup *is* the new testament in my blood, which is shed for you" (Luke 22:20 KJV).

Today, many preachers seem to make salvation more difficult than the religious leaders of Jesus' day. Jesus rebuked these Pharisees. In Matthew, He said: "...they bind heavy burdens and grievous to be borne, and lay *them* on men's shoulders; but they *themselves* will not move them with one of their fingers. But all their works they do for to be seen of men: they make broad their phylacteries, and enlarge the borders of their garments....But woe unto you, scribes and Pharisees,

[200]Israeli Professor David Flusser interestingly points out that some early Jewish customs which were not given to us by other Jewish (Talmudic) literature, *are* revealed to us in the New Testament. The devout and orthodox Flusser enlightens us: "Early Christian literature thus reflects the world of the Sages at an earlier stage than its reflection in the Jewish sources. It reflects Jewish life in the Hellenistic diaspora, details of which we otherwise know chiefly from the writings of Philo of Alexandria. We can also learn from it about other Jewish diasporas and about Jewish customs which have not been recorded in early Jewish sources. Take an example: the Jewish custom of giving a boy his name during his circumcision ceremony is not known in our Talmudic literature, but in one of the Gospels (Luke 1:59-64) we are told that John the Baptist's father gave him his name during this ceremony. Or another example: the custom of passing around the glass of wine during the Kiddush (the blessing on the wine ushering in Sabbath and Holy Day meals) is unknown in the Talmudic sources, but the New Testament tells us that during the Last Supper Jesus asked that his cup should be passed among his Apostles (Luke 22:17 and parallel passages)." David Flusser, Ph.D., *Jewish Sources in Early Christianity*, p. 10.

hypocrites! for ye shut up the kingdom of heaven against men: for ye neither go in *yourselves*, neither suffer ye them that are entering to go in. Woe unto you, scribes and Pharisees, hypocrites! for ye devour widows' houses, and for a pretence make long prayer: therefore ye shall receive the greater damnation. Woe unto you, scribes and Pharisees, hypocrites! for ye compass sea and land to make one proselyte, and when he is made, ye make him twofold more the child of hell than yourselves" (Matt. 23:4-5, 13-15 KJV).

The truth of the matter is, all that is needed for salvation is the acceptance of Jesus' atonement for all of our sins—past, present and future. To accept this, all we need to do is invite Him to come into our hearts and give us His free gift of salvation.[201]

If you find this hard to believe, just take a moment to read the New Testament passages of Revelation 3:20, Ephesians 2:8-9, Romans 3:20-41, and Galatians chapters 3-4.

It is important for us to remember that Jesus' Sermon on the Mount (Matt. 5-8) was a lecture which condemned the people for attempting to gain favor and salvation from God by works, deeds and appeasement. This address was designed to show the religious people in the crowd that, by God's standards, they were sinners and that if they really wanted to be forgiven and partake in God's abundant plan for their salvation, they would have to accept the then future atonement of the Messiah by faith (faith comes by hearing, and hearing by the word of God [the Bible] Rom. 10:17). Mark 10:45 teaches that this is the meaning of the new covenant, of which Jesus reminded His disciples at the last Passover supper in Luke 22.

THE PHYSICAL AND SPIRITUAL

This new covenant, predicted six hundred years before Christ by the Jewish prophet Jeremiah, has two aspects to it: a spiritual and a physical. The spiritual occurred when Jesus offered Himself as the lamb of God at that fateful Passover in Jerusalem. As I Corinthians teaches, "Christ our Passover sacrificed for us." The physical aspect of this promise made by the Old Testament prophet Jeremiah, will occur at the Second Coming of Jesus when Israel sees and believes in Him as a nation. At that time, the words "new covenant with the **House** of **Israel**" will have been completely fulfilled.

Today, the new covenant is with a select but growing number of Jews for Jesus (born-again Messianic Jews) and born-again Gentiles (known commonly as Evangelical or Fundamentalist Christians), who accept the Jewish Messiah. By "accept the Jewish Messiah," we mean accepting that Jesus died for us as was Jewishly predicted in Isaiah 53:4.

---

[201] See Philip Moore, *Eternal Security for True Believers.*

THERE WERE SEVEN COVENANTS BEFORE THE NEW COVENANT

God had dealt with man using seven other covenants before the new covenant was instituted by the Messiah. *The New Scofield Reference Bible* lists these, with an abbreviated explanation and verse for each, as follows: "...(1) The Edenic Covenant (Gen. 2:16, *note*) conditions the life of man in innocence. (2) The Adamic Covenant (Gen. 3:15, *note*) conditions the life of fallen man and gives promise of a Redeemer. (3) The Noahic Covenant (Gen. 9:16, *note*) establishes the principle of human government. (4) The Abrahamic Covenant (Gen. 12:2, *note*) founds the nation of Israel and confirms, with specific additions, the Adamic promise of redemption. (5) The Mosaic Covenant (Ex. 19:5, *note*) condemns all men, 'for all have sinned' (Rom. 3:23; 5:12). (6) The Palestinian Covenant (Dt. 30:3, *note*) secures the final restoration and conversion of Israel. (7) The Davidic Covenant (2 Sam. 7:16, *note*) establishes the perpetuity of the Davidic family (fulfilled in Christ, Mt. 1:1; Lk. 1:31-33; Rom. 1:3), and of the Davidic kingdom over Israel and over the whole earth, to be fulfilled in and by Christ (2 Sam. 7:8-17; Zech. 12:8; Lk. 1:31-33; Acts 15:14-17; I Cor. 15:24). And (8) the New Covenant (Heb. 8:8, *note* 1) rests upon the sacrifice of Christ and secures the eternal blessedness, under the Abrahamic Covenant (Gal. 3:13-29), of all who believe. It is absolutely unconditional and, since no responsibility is by it committed to man, it is final and irreversible."[202]

IN THE SEVEN COVENANTS BEFORE MESSIAH'S FIRST COMING, THERE WERE SOME FAITHFUL, WHO JESUS SAYS WILL BE IN THE KINGDOM

With the exception of the new covenant in the New Testament, these covenants or testaments are all known as "the old covenant" or rather "Old Testament." They are meshed together in a simplified form today because they are all found in the old covenant section of the Bible, comprised of thirty-nine books from Genesis through Malachi.

The new covenant begins with the sacrifice of Jesus at the end of Matthew and ends with the epistles of Paul, formerly known as Rabbi Saul, who was a famous student of the well-known Rabbi Gamaliel.

The beginning of Matthew consists of Jesus' lectures under the last segment of the seven segments of the old covenant law. He makes known that the eighth segment of God's covenant will be brought in by

---

[202] *The New Scofield Reference Bible*, pp. 1317-1318.

His own sacrifice (predicted 700 BC in the old covenant by Isaiah, chapters 53 and 49:5-7). He also teaches that the prior covenant was designed to look forward to the time when Messiah would come and pay for all past and future peoples' shortcomings, so that they may have a joyous, eternal relationship with God. This would be fully realized after the Second Coming, when all are resurrected to everlasting life in the kingdom of God in and around Jerusalem (Isa. 60:21; Rev. 21:11-21).

Concerning past individuals, Jesus spoke of Abraham, Isaac and Jacob, who lived 4000 years ago, as being alive (meaning through their spirits; Matt. 8:11). Jesus declared that one day they would be resurrected and live in His kingdom with all who accept this covenant in their time (Luke 13:28-30). This covers all individuals who accept the God of the Hebrews under all eight covenants through all sixty-six books of the complete Bible—Genesis through Revelation—from the time of Adam until sometime in the near future.

What is most important for us is now. If you have read this, you now have sufficient proof that we are living under a new covenant and you owe it to yourself to check it out! If you are interested, send me a fax and I will send you a free New Testament.[203]

GOD HAD PLANS TO REACH THE NON-JEWS (GENTILES) EVEN IF HIS NEW COVENANT WAS REJECTED BY HIS JEWISH PEOPLE

Portions of the New Testament point out that God would, in addition to reaching out to the Jewish people, one day call those Gentiles who wanted to know Him. He knew that many Jews would not at first be receptive to His new covenant. Paul, in the New Testament, comments on these issues: "But I say, Did not Israel know? First Moses saith, I [Deut. 32:21][204] will provoke you to jealousy by *them that are* no people, *and* by a foolish nation I will anger you. But Esaias is very bold, and saith, I [Isa. 65:1][205] was found of them that sought me not; I was made manifest unto them [Isa. 65:1, 19-20; Isa. 42:6-7][206] that asked not after me. But to Israel he

---

[203] Fax (404) 816-9994.

[204] "They have moved me to jealousy with *that which is* not God; they have provoked me to anger with their vanities: and I will move them to jealousy with *those which are* not a people; I will provoke them to anger with a foolish nation" (KJV).

[205] "I am sought of *them that* asked not *for me*; I am found of *them that* sought me not: I said, Behold me, behold me, unto a nation *that* was not called by my name" (KJV).

[206] "I the LORD have called thee in righteousness, and will hold thine hand, and will keep thee, and give thee for a covenant of the people, for a light of the Gentiles; To open the

saith, All [Isa. 65:2][207] day long I have stretched forth my hands unto a disobedient and gainsaying people" (Rom. 10:19-21 KJV; [ ] mine).

"Simeon hath declared how God at the first did visit the Gentiles, to take out of them a people for his name. And to this agree the words of the prophets; as it is written, After this I will return, and will build again the tabernacle of David, which is fallen down; and I will build again the ruins thereof, and I will set it up: That the residue of men might seek after the Lord, and all the Gentiles, upon whom my name is called, saith the Lord, who doeth all these things" (Acts 15:14-17 KJV).

In a parable, Jesus alludes to temporarily[208] handing over the duties of God's word to the Gentiles, as He was addressing the belligerence and arrogance of the Pharisees. He said: "...A certain landowner planted a vineyard with a hedge around it, and built a platform for the watchman, then leased the vineyard to some farmers on a sharecrop basis, and went away to live in another country. At the time of the grape harvest he sent his agents to the farmers to collect his share. But the farmers attacked his men, beat one, killed one and stoned another. Then he sent a larger group of his men to collect for him, but the results were the same. Finally the owner sent his son, thinking they would surely respect him. But when these farmers saw the son coming they said among themselves, 'Here comes the heir to this estate; come on, let's kill him and get it for ourselves!' So they dragged him out of the vineyard and killed him. When the owner returns, what do you think he will do to those farmers? The Jewish leaders replied, 'He will put the wicked men to a horrible death, and lease the vineyard to others who will pay him promptly.' Then Jesus asked them, 'Didn't you ever read in the Scriptures: 'The stone rejected by the builders has been made the honored cornerstone; how remarkable! what an amazing thing the Lord has done'? What I mean

---

blind eyes, to bring out the prisoners from the prison, *and* them that sit in darkness out of the prison house" (KJV).

[207]"I have spread out my hands all the day unto a rebellious people, which walketh in a way *that was* not good, after their own thoughts; A people that provoketh me to anger continually to my face; that sacrificeth in gardens, and burneth incense upon altars of brick...." (KJV).

[208]We say "temporary" because after the Rapture and during the seven-year Tribulation, *until* the end of Daniel's seventieth week, God will again use the Jews to evangelize the world. Presently, this task has been carried out by the Fundamental Evangelical Church. Their members are of a majority Gentile, but once the Church (all who presently believe in Jesus, in a personal sense) is removed in the Rapture (see our chapter 25, "The Rapture Factor"), then God will again use the Jews as a whole people to tell the world about His work of atonement. Revelation, the last book of the New Testament, says that there will be 144,000 Jews sealed for this!

is that the Kingdom of God shall be taken away from you, and given to a nation that will give God his share of the crop. All who stumble on this rock of truth shall be broken, but those it falls on will be scattered as dust" (Matt. 21:33-43 *The Living Bible*).

Risto Santala notes an amazing parallel between Jesus' warning and an interesting point made by an ancient rabbi. "There is a discussion in the Talmud concerning Jeremiah 13:17, where the prophet 'weeps in secret' because of the pride which will not 'give glory to the LORD', and so 'the LORD's flock will be taken captive'. R. Shmuel Bar Yitshak says that, 'this is the result of Israel's sinfulness, and is the reason why the Torah will be taken from them and given to the Gentile nations'.[209] The Talmud itself understands this in the sense that God himself will allow the Temple to be destroyed and that even the 'angels of peace' will weep for it. There was something of the same sorrow in Jesus'[210] lament."[211] Here, we see that at least one rabbi shared the same sentiment as Jesus.

[209]Haggiga 5b.

[210]The lament is found in Luke 19:41-44. It dealt with Him crying over the city of Jerusalem because He realized the disasters that would follow in the Jewish expulsion by the Romans as a result of their rejection of His Messiahship.

[211]Risto Santala, *The Messiah in the New Testament in the Light of Rabbinical Writings*, p. 43.

ORIGINAL HEBREW TEXT WRITTEN 606 BC

הִנֵּה יָמִים בָּאִים נְאֻם־יְהוָה וְכָרַתִּי אֶת־בֵּית יִשְׂרָאֵל וְאֶת־בֵּית יְהוּדָה בְּרִית חֲדָשָׁה׃

ירמיה לא:ל

OLD TESTAMENT SCRIPTURE TRANSLATION

" 'Behold, days are coming,' declares the LORD, 'when I will make a new covenant with the house of Israel and with the house of Judah....' "

Jeremiah 31:31 NASB

ANCIENT RABBINICAL COMMENTARY

"When the time of the advent of Messiah will be near, then the blessed God will say to him: With him I will make a new covenant. And this is the time when he will acknowledge him as his son, saying 'This day have I begotten thee.' "[212]

Midrash Tehelim, fol. 3, col. 4

"...He will sit and expound the new Tora which He will give through the Messiah."[213] **Midrash Talpiyot, 58a**

NEW TESTAMENT RECORDED 37 AND 64 AD

"...for this is My blood of the covenant, which is poured out for many for forgiveness of sins. But I say to you, I will not drink of this fruit of the vine from now on until that day when I drink it new with you in My Father's kingdom."

Matthew 26:28-29 NASB

"For finding fault with them, He says, 'BEHOLD, DAYS ARE COMING, SAYS THE LORD, WHEN I WILL EFFECT A NEW COVENANT WITH THE HOUSE OF ISRAEL AND WITH THE HOUSE OF JUDAH...."

Hebrews 8:8 NASB

MODERN RABBINIC COMMENT/REFUTATION

"The Christians assert that the prophet Jeremiah here foretold the giving of a new law for the people of Israel—viz., the Gospel of Jesus of Nazareth....Scripture does not allude here to the substitution of a new law for the old one...."

***Faith Strengthened*, by Isaac Troki, p. 155; 1850**

AUTHOR'S COMMENT—EVANGELICAL CHRISTIAN POSITION

In spite of what Mr. Troki said, the Midrash Tehelim, which represents much of ancient rabbinical belief, specifically quotes the Scripture of Jeremiah and relates that when the Messiah's Coming nears, a new covenant will begin. Midrash Talpiyot says that the Messiah Himself would give this new Torah, and, needless to say, it would have benefited Troki to have reviewed these Midrashim before writing such untruth! There is no denying the New Testament within Judaism in light of the ancient writings of the rabbis! So much for Troki's argument!

Philip Moore

---

[212] Rev. B. Pick, Ph.D., *Old Testament Passages Messianically Applied by the Ancient Synagogue*, published in the compilation *Hebraica, A Quarterly Journal in the Interests of Semitic Study*, Vol. II, p. 129.

[213] Raphael Patai, *The Messiah Texts*, p. 256.

THE PROPHECY AND EVENT OF THE MESSIANIC RESURRECTION OF JESUS

No other faith in history can lay claim to a risen redeemer by demonstrating a body of proof such as that which Jesus left for us. The Jewish Bible predicted that the Messiah would die, and shortly thereafter, miraculously return to life to seal our own future resurrections and assure us that He was the true Messiah amongst many imposters (Matt. 24:5).

The greatest prophecy Jesus fulfilled from the Old Testament, recorded in the New, was His resurrection from death unto life: "...I am the resurrection, and the life: he that believeth in me, though he were dead, yet shall he live...." (John 11:25 KJV). Truly, if we believe in His salvation and resurrection we will one day at the end of time, be raised from death to life as He promised!

SOME HAVE SET OUT TO DISPROVE THE RESURRECTION ONLY TO END UP CONVERTING TO IT

Frank Morrison, a brilliant lawyer, believed that the resurrection was a "cruel hoax," and avowed to destroy the Christian faith by proving that Jesus never resurrected from the dead. Mr. Morrison used the best historical, legal and theological libraries of our day to gather research to be used to write a book which he would name, *Disproving the Resurrection of Jesus.* However, once all the research was in, he fell on his knees and asked forgiveness in the *name* of Jesus, the risen Lord. He did write a book, but not the one he had intended.

His book, entitled *Who Moved the Stone*, is filled with evidence *legally proving* the resurrection. The evidence he discovered turned a bitter enemy of Jesus into a believer in Him as the Messiah. Mr. Morrison's legal training forced him to be objective in his examination of the evidence he found!

Lew Wallace, author of the famous novel *Ben Hur*, planned to write a book disproving Jesus' deity and resurrection. However, if you have seen the movie or read his book, his theme is based on evidence which *defends* the resurrection.

A LAW PROFESSOR CONCLUDES THE EVIDENCE OF THE RESURRECTION INDISPUTABLE

Simon Greenleaf, professor of law at Harvard University (1833-48), "has been called the greatest authority on legal evidences in the history of the world."[214] Greenleaf wrote *A Treatise on the Law of Evidence.* This classic law work used in courtrooms throughout the world to determine good evidence from bad "is still considered the greatest single authority on evidence in the entire literature of legal procedure".[215]

Greenleaf was challenged by his students to take his laws of evidence and apply them to the resurrection of Jesus. Once he had done this, Greenleaf wrote *An Examination of the Testimony of the Four Evangelists by the Rules of Evidence Administered in the Courts of Justice,*[216] in which he concluded that the resurrection of Jesus was the most established fact in history. He clearly proved that there was more conclusive verifiable evidence of every type to substantiate the resurrection than any other event which has occurred in the history of the world!

We find it interesting that there have been booklets and treatises written over the centuries mocking the resurrection, and yet, there is clearly more evidence supporting the resurrection than there is testimony to the fact that Julius Caesar ever lived! Do you know anyone who has ever questioned Caesar's existence? Neither do we!

TWO OF THE MOST COMMON MOCKERIES USED TO DISPUTE THE RESURRECTION, RESOLVED

The two "contradictions" most often raised by liberal critics of Jesus' resurrection are: "How could He have eaten on the Passover and died on it, also?" and; "How could He have remained in the tomb three days and nights if He was buried on the Sabbath?" The answers to these two questions, still used to mock Christians today, would be

---

[214]D. James Kennedy, *Why I Believe*. Waco, TX: Word Books, © 1980, p. 106, used by permission. New York attorney Walter M. Chandler notes of Greenleaf: "The author can conceive of no more satisfactory way of establishing the principle of the admissibility of the Gospels in evidence under modern law than by quoting at length from the celebrated treatise on the 'Testimony of Evangelists,' by Mr. Simon Greenleaf, the greatest of all writers on the Law of Evidence. The opinion of Greenleaf on a subject of this kind is somewhat in the nature of a decision of a court of last resort, and his authority in matters of this import is unquestioned in every land where English law is practiced. *London Law Magazine*, a few years ago, paid him the following splendid tribute: 'It is no mean honor to America that her schools of jurisprudence have produced two of the first writers and best esteemed legal authorities of this century—the great and good man, Judge Story, and his worthy and eminent associate, Professor Greenleaf. Upon the existing Law of Evidence (by Greenleaf) more light has shone from the New World than from all the lawyers who adorn the courts of Europe.' " Walter M. Chandler, *The Trial of Jesus, From a Lawyer's Standpoint*, illustrated edition, p. 4.

[215]Josh McDowell, *Evidence that Demands a Verdict, Historical Evidences for the Christian Faith*, p. 199.

[216]In 1965, Baker Book House reprinted this book from its 1847 edition.

simple if those posing them would take the time to investigate the culture of Jesus and His land, along with the intricate meanings of Hebrew words.

The answer to the first question is that Jesus ate His last supper on the ancient Essene calendar Passover. The Essene holy day fell one day earlier in that year than the Pharisaic Passover observed by most of Israel. Risto Santala noted in his book, *The Messiah in the New Testament in the Light of Rabbinical Writings*, that Bargil Pixner, using Josephus and Philo as sources, deduced that there were about 6000 Pharisees and 4000 Essenes at that period in history. He also mentioned that some believed: "...that Jesus partook of the Paschal meal with his disciples in an Essene guest room and following their festive calendar, which would place the event...on Tuesday."[217]

Santala also mentioned that Jesus told Peter and John they would see a man carrying a pitcher of water, which was "a rare sight,"[218] who would show them the location of His Passover.

I will never forget my friend Meron Ten-Brink, an Israeli tour guide who asked me about Jesus eating and dying on Passover. He mentioned the water in connection with the Essene custom and the difference of a day in calendar dates. Jesus ate a Tuesday night Essene Passover and was crucified on a Wednesday Pharisaic Passover. We know this from the key sign given to us in the Gospel of Mark: "And he sendeth forth two of his disciples, and saith unto them, 'Go ye into the city, and there shall meet you a **man** bearing a pitcher of water: follow him. And wheresoever he shall go in, say ye to the goodman of the house, The Master saith, Where is the guest-chamber, where I shall eat the passover with my disciples? And he will shew you a large upper room furnished *and* prepared: there make ready for us' " (Mark 14:13-15 KJV; bold mine).

In the Essene tradition, a man would carry the water, not a woman, and since there were few Essenes in comparison to the Pharisees and a larger portion of the rest of Diaspora Jewry who would come to celebrate the Passover in Israel, this was indeed a *rare* sight.

In a 1994 facsimile from Israel, Tsvi Sadan explained to me why, in the Essene culture, only a man would carry the water for Passover. He noted: "The man thus is a celibate (Essene practice) who is forced to carry the water by himself."

Sadan also mentioned that Josephus wrote about an "Essene gate," which some believe indicated the existence of "a whole Essene

---

[217]Risto Santala, *The Messiah in the New Testament in the Light of Rabbinical Writings*, p. 205.
[218]Ibid, p. 204.

quarter in Jerusalem."[219] A person educated in the times and traditions of Jesus would know this.

It goes without saying that if you knew you were scheduled to die on Passover, you would observe it the day before, if you could, while at the same time honoring the other predominantly religious Jews (Essenes) along with the Pharisees. Jesus was fair, wasn't He?

Second, the word Sabbath means "rest" as well as "Saturday." It is still used in Israel to designate a major Jewish holy day or season. Any Israeli will admit it is *Shabbat* ("Sabbath") during the entire seven days of any given Passover celebration.

A Jewish day runs from one sundown to another, thus, Jesus was buried Wednesday night (of the Sabbath Passover week) and resurrected sometime Saturday night. This allows for three days and nights, as He predicted, using Jonah's example (Matt. 12:40). The tomb was found empty the next morning, on Sunday, by His disciples. Any questions?

DESPITE THE EVIDENCE FOR RESURRECTION HUXLEY LECTURED AGAINST IT

Thomas Huxley, Charles Darwin's strongest supporter, known as "his bulldog," made no secret of at least one of the primary goals[220] of "the theory of evolution," which he hoped his friend Darwin was justifying and legitimizing. One of the attractions in Huxley's speech-making tours was "lecturing against the resurrection of Christ."[221] In his writings, he proclaimed that "the promise of the Second Coming" was "allegorical."[222] The word "allegorical" is a fancy word which means that it will never literally happen.

---

[219]The facsimile was sent from the Messianic congregation named *Nativyah* ("the path of God" in Hebrew), headed by Joe Shulam in Jerusalem.

[220]See our *Vol. II*, chapter 5, "Darwinian Evolution: Fact, Fraud or Fiction?", where we reveal the evidence behind the real political motives of evolution. We show that Huxley, in reality, did not believe in evolution. This section documents Darwin's ulterior motive, the theft of theories from others and taking false credit for himself. We show that in his own autobiography, he admitted to his lifelong desire to "take a place by the other famous scientific men."

[221]Henry M. Morris, Ph.D., *The Troubled Waters of Evolution.* San Diego, CA: Creation-Life Publishers, © 1974, p. 58, used by permission. We also note that on the same page, Dr. Morris documents that Huxley "invented" the term "agnostic" and applied it to "himself." Agnostic means, "I do not know about God because I cannot see him, but if I find evidence, I will accept that. First show me this concrete evidence." This term was much more palatable to the public than atheist, which means "I do not believe God exists." Huxley was a master propagandist and activist.

[222]Thomas Henry Huxley, *Agnosticism and Christianity and Other Essays*. Buffalo, NY: Prometheus Books, 1992, p. 203.

These are the two most important truths of our Bible. They secure: 1. our resurrection, and; 2. our hope in the coming redemption. If Satan can destroy or discredit these two promises of God through a godless false philosopher, he has won. Huxley[223] was a tool, a weapon against Christians, and he should be exposed!

A RABBI TRIES TO QUASH THE RESURRECTION OF JESUS IN THE PSALMS

Rabbi Sh'lomo ben Yitzhak, the famous interpreter commonly referred to by his Hebrew acronym Rashi, does not live up to the high esteem which he has enjoyed in the Jewish community since his death in 1105. When you take the time to carefully study exactly what he taught, as I did, you discover his use of double standards to cover up what he knew to be prophetic references pertaining to the Messiah. These examples are Isaiah 53, Zechariah 12:10 and the case of the Messiah's resurrection, Psalm 21.

The Jewish scholar, David Baron, has documented this in his book, *Rays of Messiah's Glory*. Baron, catching the rabbi red-handed, notes: "Rashi....in his comments on Psalm xxi...says, 'Our Rabbis have expounded it of the King Messiah, but it is better to expound it further of David himself in order to answer heretics' [Jewish Christians]."[224]

Here the dishonesty of the double standard, used in order to escape any possible reference to the resurrection of Jesus, is clearly identified and exposed to all of us.

***

---

[223]H.G. Wells, the famous novelist known for his work, *The Time Machine*, was a student of Huxley. No doubt, his false evolutionary ideas connected with the Morlocks were influenced by this false teacher. *Benets Readers Encyclopedia*, third edition, tells us that Wells died in despair in 1946, worrying about how man's inventions were progressing faster than his intellectual and social development, while also mentioning that he was an advocate of Fabian socialism, feminism, evolutionarianism, naturalism, and studied under Thomas Huxley at the University of London. We believe Dr. A.E. Wilder-Smith was right when he said the " 'dead hand of Darwinism' has 'weighed heavily on [scientific] progress for over one hundred years.' " John Ankerberg and John Weldon, *The Facts on Creation vs. Evolution*. Eugene, OR: Harvest House Publishers, © 1993, p. 25, used by permission. Ankerberg and Weldon's source was A.E. Wilder-Smith, *The Creation of Life: A Cybernetic Approach to Evolution*, pp. 244-245. Though we may enjoy the adventure of *The Time Machine* in the book and movie, we should always bring ourselves back to the reality that the "Morlocks" at its end are as fictitous as evolution, not allowing ourselves to be subconsciously influenced toward the philosophy of Darwinism by Wells' casual expression.

[224]These "heretics" are Christian Jews. David Baron, *Rays of Messiah's Glory, Christ in the Old Testament*. Grand Rapids, MI: Zondervan Publishing House, p. 240. [ ] mine.

CONTEMPORARY ATTEMPTS TO CRUSH THE RESURRECTION EXPOSE FEAR WITHIN THE OPPOSITION

Jews for Judaism is an organization that distributes literature[225] which attempts to deny the resurrection. As we read a copy which was given to us, we were amused at their claim that since different Gospel writers list different resurrection events, this is somehow contradictory.

In reality, this method of investigation complements and corroborates the story. Say, for instance, that you and three of your friends are interrogated regarding a murder you all witnessed and you tell four different stories. However, in the end, all the stories come together beautifully. This is a firmer evidence of authenticity. When the story is fully reconstructed, there is actually no contradiction because each of you saw different aspects at different times, depending on when and where you were during this episode.

Yes, the women went to the tomb to embalm Jesus, only because they were not aware of the fact that Joseph and Nicodemus had already done so. The word "unaware" is not spelled out in the New Testament; it is something we see for ourselves. It does not take a detective as skilled as Colombo or Sherlock Holmes to discover the obvious, does it?

The New Testament states that Nicodemus embalmed Jesus, and, in another passage, says the women sought Him out to perform this ritual only to find that the body of Jesus was not there. *Jews for Judaism*[226] claim that this somehow presents a contradiction. In reality, this is merely a testimony to the fact that the women were not aware it had already been performed. How ignorant of this organization to say otherwise.

TWO JEWISH CONTEMPORARIES TAKE POT SHOTS AT THE RESURRECTION OF JESUS

Gerald Sigal, in *The Jew and the Christian Missionary*, says: "Belief in the resurrection of Jesus, so crucial to the theology of missionary Christianity, is based on unsubstantiated evidence. The Gospel accounts of the resurrection are not the result of objective observations by trustworthy eyewitnesses. As a result, the veracity of the resurrection accounts is highly questionable."[227]

---

[225]The piece was entitled *The Resurrection: What Is the Evidence?*, by Rabbi Tovia Singer. NJ: Jews for Judaism.

[226]This view is also held by liberal "Christian" theologians.

[227]Gerald Sigal, *The Jew and the Christian Missionary*, p. 238.

Sam Levine, in his book, *You Take Jesus, I'll Take God*, arrogantly wrote: "The resurrection story is a fabricated hoax; it never happened. However, those early followers just could not believe that their savior simply died and was no more....They therefore made up a story (perhaps it was a hallucination which they thought was true) and the story that they made up was one that could not be disproven."[228]

As you read on, these statements will be conclusively disproven! Don't worry, be happy...about the resurrection of Jesus and the evidence we will present, which proves it.

DR. KENNEDY EXPOSES THE "SWOON SURVIVAL THEORY" AS A NON-EXCLUSIVE AND RELATIVELY MODERN WORKING IMPOSSIBILITY

Dr. D. James Kennedy notes: "Only a handful of theories have been propounded by skeptics, atheists, and unbelievers who have turned their greatest guns upon the resurrection....there is the 'swoon' theory.[229] This has been set forth by Venturini; it is found in the writings of Mary Baker Eddy; it is found in the writings of Hugh Schonfield in *The Passover Plot*. It is interesting, however, that for over eighteen hundred years there was never a whisper from the friends or the most implacable enemies of Christianity that Jesus Christ had not died. Some of these recent writers have now conceived the idea that Jesus had simply swooned....Medical authorities state that if Jesus had swooned, open air was needed, not a closed tomb. Certainly what was not needed were grave clothes wrapped around his head and spices covering nose and mouth. Furthermore, to place a person in such a swoon in a cold grave would bring about a syncope or cessation of his heartbeat, if he had been alive."[230]

***

---

[228]Samuel Levine, *You Take Jesus, I'll Take God*, p. 71.

[229]The Jewish believer in Jesus, Dr. Arthur Kac, M.D., quotes the scholar Strauss, on this ridiculous swoon theory. He says: "Hear what Strauss has to say about this theory: - 'It is impossible that a being who had been stolen half dead out of a sepulchre, who crept about weak and ill, wanting medical treatment, who required bandaging, strengthening, and indulgence, and who still at last yielded to His sufferings, could have given to His disciples the impression that He was a Conqueror over death and the grave, the Prince of Life, an impression which lay at the bottom of their future ministry.' " Arthur W. Kac, *The Messiahship of Jesus*, p. 232. We suggest you read *The Proof of the Resurrection*, by our friend, Elliot Klayman, a precious Jewish believer in Jesus, available through The Messianic Literature Outreach, POB 37062, Cincinnati, OH, USA 45222.

[230]D. James Kennedy, Ph.D., *Why I Believe*, pp. 109, 114-115.

SCHONFIELD ATTEMPTS TO DEBAUCH THE RESURRECTION—A PERSONAL ENCOUNTER

Hugh Schonfield,[231] a Jewish writer, tried to discredit the resurrection in his 1965 book, *The Passover Plot.* Schonfield claimed that Jesus had a Messiah complex, and faked His death on the cross by having Himself drugged. "Jesus lapsed quickly into complete unconsciousness. His body sagged. His head lolled on his breast, and to all intents and purposes he was a dead man.

Directly it was seen that the drug had worked the man hastened to Joseph who was anxiously waiting for the news....It is the moment before sundown in Jerusalem. On the hill of Golgotha three bodies are suspended on crosses. Two—the thieves—are dead. The third appears so. This is the drugged body of Jesus of Nazareth, the man who planned his own crucifixion, who contrived to be given a soporific potion to put him into a deathlike trance. Now Joseph of Arimathea, bearing clean linen and spices, approaches and recovers the still form of Jesus. All seems to be proceeding according to plan....As arranged, Jesus was conveyed carefully to the nearby tomb. The women of his following, who had been observing everything at a distance, saw where he was taken....Jesus lay in the tomb over the Sabbath. He would not regain consciousness for many hours, and in the meantime the spices and linen bandages provided the best dressing for his injuries....Jesus was taken from the tomb at the first possible opportunity for the entirely legitimate purpose of reviving him....a plan was being followed which was worked out in advance by Jesus himself and which he had not divulged to his close disciples. What seems probable is that in the darkness of Saturday night when Jesus was brought out of the tomb by those concerned in the plan he regained consciousness...."[232]

SCHONFIELD'S LIE DISPROVED BY CRUCIFIXION PHYSICS

In order for Schonfield's theory to be true, a number of highly improbable things would have had to occur, including the total incompetence of the superbly trained Roman soldiers. Most important, the "drugged" Jesus would have suffocated within minutes,[233] once

---

[231]In 1983, before he died, I received two letters from Schonfield. I had attempted to share the Gospel with the very hurt and hardened man. He had once professed faith in Jesus in his earlier years, and had been a member of the Hebrew Christian Alliance.

[232]Hugh J. Schonfield, *The Passover Plot: New Light on the History of Jesus.* New York: Bantam Books, © 1971, pp. 160, preface, 161, 163, 165, used by permission of Element Books, Inc., POB 830/21 Broadway, Rockport, MA, USA 01966.

[233]The period of time between the moment His body sagged until permission was secured to take Him down would have been considerable—more than only a few minutes.

His body sagged, as was already discussed in our section dealing with the physics of crucifixion. He would have been long since dead.

This gaping hole in Schonfield's "theory" is an obvious one, but to our knowledge, has never been addressed. This same theme of survival after crucifixion was portrayed in a mini-series, *The Word*, starring David Jensen, airing on American television in the 1970's.

ATTEMPTS TO MAKE FICTION OUT OF THE RESURRECTION—NON-JEWS ARE GUILTY, TOO

Bishop Spong attempted to discredit the literal and bodily resurrection of Jesus in his 1994 book, *Resurrection, Myth or Reality?* He claimed: "The story of Jesus' burial and the account of the empty tomb are in fact late-developing[234] Christian legends....the tomb itself with its massive stone[235] and its female visitors, to say nothing of the

---

[234]Despite Spong's erroneous assertions, former professor of Semitic languages at Yale, Charles Cutler Torrey, reminds us in chapter 3 of his book: "Evidence was also given to show that these scriptures of the Nazarene sect were put forth at an early date; as soon as such works could well be prepared, and in the time when they were especially needed. The current guesses at the dates of Mark and Matthew, published in the standard textbooks and treatises, are based primarily on the mistaken belief that the Gospels were composed in Greek....'At the annual meeting of the Society of Biblical Literature and Exegesis, in New York City in December, 1934, I challenged my New Testament colleagues to designate even *one* passage from any of the Four Gospels giving clear evidence of a date later than 50 A.D., or of origin outside Palestine. The challenge was not met, nor will it be, for there is no such passage'....The datings generally proposed at present, for all four Gospels, are quite indefensible in the face of facts which are coming to light....Every feature of these Gospels indicates that they were composed while the Nazarenes were regarded as loyal Jews, even if mistaken. There is in them no indication, of any sort, clearly pointing to a later date....Unexpected confirmation of both conclusions, as to language and date, appears to be given by the Jewish tradition preserved in the Talmud....the Jews of Palestine in the first century had in their hands certain Semitic writings which they called 'the gospels' (plural number) and regarded as the authoritative Christian scriptures....There are in the Talmud numerous allusions to the Gospels, always brief and sometimes sharply polemical. These heretical scriptures are either called 'the *Gilyonim'* or else are spoken of as 'the books (or, writings) of the *Minim*'....The conclusion reached and stated by Professor Moore, in the course of the investigation which he published in 1911, that the allusion to the Christian Gospels in Tosephta Yadaim II, 13 comes from Johanan ben Zakkai, is certainly correct, and is extremely important....writings which had been put forth with the claim to prophetic inspiration, Messianic scriptures designed to show a new era of divine revelation and to supplement the older sacred books of Israel....There was a brief period of at least partial toleration under Johanan before he gave his mild but momentous ruling, that the Nazarene scriptures were of merely human origin....The tone of the decision, as has been shown, plainly implies an early date, before the time of the bitter hostility induced by the mission to the Gentiles and the disaster of the year 70. 'The Gospels' of the Nazarenes...addressed to the Jews, were already in circulation in or very soon after the middle of the first century, and cannot possibly have made their appearance as late as the war under Titus." Professor Charles Cutler Torrey, *Documents of the Primitive Church*. New York: Harper & Brothers Publishers, © 1941, pp. 91-93, 111, used by permission.

[235]See our photo, "Mike's Site," of a first-century Jewish tomb in Israel, including its *massive stone*, an archaeological find of preeminence—believe me, it is factual. I not

entire burial tradition, must all be dismissed as not factual....manifestations of the dead body that somehow was enabled to be revivified and to walk out of a tomb are also legends and myths that cannot be literalized. The risen Jesus did not literally eat fish....Resurrection may mean many things, but these details are not literally a part of that reality."[236] Bishop Spong has also made several ignorant and unfounded accusations, one of which is: "...we had to experience our literal understanding of the Bible as no longer trustworthy. In the reverberations of the knowledge explosion that began with Copernicus and continued through Galileo, Newton...and Einstein, among others, the literal Bible disintegrated."[237]

There is no doubt, from this statement, that Mr. Spong knows little about Galileo, Newton and Einstein, who not only believed in the Bible but held to quite literal fundamental positions (for Newton and Einstein's views, see our chapters 11 and 15, "Newton's Forbidden Works Rescued," and "Messianic Jewish Faith in Jesus").

Apparently, Bishop Spong imagines that these great scientists did not believe or helped to provide knowledge which has discouraged evidence to prove the literal prophetical claims of the Bible. Nothing could be further from the truth.

As you will see in this work, in our opinion, Spong arrogantly attempts to dress the neo-orthodoxy of the reformed nineteenth century German higher criticism of the Bible in new clothes. As is well known, the school of higher criticism says, in essence, that the Bible is not true or literal—a theory that has been disproved by modern archaelogical discoveries, including the Dead Sea Scrolls. Spong claims his findings are derived from *a new understanding from the ancient Jewish*[238] *traditions and Midrash.*[239] How absurd!

---

only photographed it, but touched it with my very own hands! The large stone, which the New Testament claims was over Jesus' tomb, was a traditional first-century Jewish burial custom among the wealthy; a group to which Joseph of Arimathea and Nakdimon ben Gorion (Nicodemus) definitely belonged.

[236]John Shelby Spong, *Resurrection, Myth or Reality?*, pp. back cover, 235-236.

[237]Ibid, p.11. Crossan and Ludemann also impotently attacked the resurrection in 1995-6.

[238]In our observation, Spong knows very little of Jewish culture and tradition. One example lies in his comment: "Jesus is quoted as saying to some of the scribes and Pharisees: 'For as Jonah was three days and three nights in the belly of the whale, so will the Son of man be three days and three nights in the heart of the earth' (12:40). If these words are to be taken literally, then the resurrection of Jesus would have to be located at sundown on Monday." Spong thinks that Sabbath means Saturday so he mistakenly calculates to Monday, but in actuality, the entire seven-day Passover feast is considered Sabbath. Spong continues: "Even then, the stated order would have to be reversed so that it would read three nights and three days....[and] the sun went down *ending* that day near the moment of Jesus' death." We note that Jewish days run from sundown to sunup as the Jews recognize correctly the phrase "the evening and the morning were the first day," as Zola Levitt reminds us: "In Hebrew reckoning, the day begins at sundown, or moonrise. This seemed to be God's intention at the very beginning ('And the evening and the morning were the first day,' Gen 1:5)." Zola Levitt, *The Seven Feasts of Israel.*

In our work, we have published numerous Midrashim supporting overall our fundamental position of biblical truth from creation, the birth and resurrection of Jesus, to the Apocalypse and the New Heavens and Earth promised us. How dare someone use the words *Jewish tradition* and *Midrash* to slander the resurrection of Jesus and fundamental truth, especially when archaeology has already disproved their view!

CAN SPONG ESCAPE MESSIANIC JUDGMENT? PERHAPS, *IF* HE TURNS TO JESUS

Bishop Spong and others who believe as he does should perhaps be reminded of Judgment Day, when they will cry out: "...Lord, Lord, have we not prophesied in thy name? and in thy name have cast out devils? and in thy name done many wonderful works?" Only to be answered: "...I never knew you: depart from me, ye that work iniquity" (Matt. 7:22-23 KJV).[240]

Regarding his chapter entitled, "Life After Death—This I do Believe," we ask why, if he really believes it, does he not do what the apostle Paul claims that all must do in order to get in on the Heaven side of life after death? Paul instructs in the New Testament: "That if thou shalt confess with thy mouth the Lord Jesus, and shalt believe in thine heart that God hath **raised** him from the dead, thou shalt be saved" (Rom. 10:9 KJV).

If Spong is truly a Christian, as he claims on page 107 of his spurious book,[241] *Resurrection, Myth or Reality?*, he should retract his books, which mock fundamental Christian truths, and open his heart truly and faithfully to Jesus. We definitely believe that if he dared to do such a thing he would hear these words in the future, when the believers are judged: "...Well done, good and faithful servant; thou hast been faithful over a few things, I will make thee ruler over many things: enter thou into the joy of thy lord" (Matt. 25:23 KJV).

Dallas, TX: Zola Levitt, © 1979, p. 3, used by permission. Spong's ignorance of Jewish customs is particularly glaring in the two statements he uses in an attempt to discredit the three day and three night time sequence for the resurrection in the New Testament, as stated by Jesus. On pp. 210-213 of his ridiculous book, *Resurrection, Myth or Reality?*, he attempts to create a contradiction between "After three days" and "on the third day." It would appear that his math training is also insufficient because it is possible to rise after three days at the end of the third day, still on the third day, moments before the fourth starts, isn't it? Yes! [ ] mine.

239 John Shelby Spong, *Resurrection, Myth or Reality?*, pp. 8-12.

240 This verse strictly applies to those who do not believe in Jesus and His exclusive saving power and resurrection. See our *Vol. II*, chapter 11, "Eternal Security for True Believers."

241 As far as his assertion that there has never been a literal and physical resurrection of Jesus.

If Spong is a Christian, as he claims, how could he forget the words of Jesus to the Pharisees? "...if ye believe not that I am *he*, ye shall die in your sins" (John 8:24 KJV).

Obviously, he is not a Christian in the New Testament sense of the word, is he? He makes claims such as: "I will not make any further attempt to convert the Buddhist, the Jew, the Hindu or the Moslem. I am content to learn from them and to walk with them side by side toward the God who lives, I believe, beyond the images that bind and blind us."[242]

From this, we know that he is not. We know this because Jesus instructed us to tell all nations of His Messiahship (Acts 1:8). Jesus has also said: "...'I am the way, the truth, and the life: no man cometh unto the Father, but by me' " (John 14:6 KJV). How can Spong be a follower of Jesus and be content to take lessons from the Moslems?

Pray that Bishop Spong may possibly change his heart and mind, and truly believe in Jesus' blood atonement and resurrection to life eternal. This will assure Spong a place with the Lord and us, instead of eternal separation from Him after the Judgment Day of the Messiah.

The Garden Tomb of Jesus in Jerusalem, Israel.

[242]Dave Hunt, *Global Peace and the Rise of Antichrist.* Grand Rapids, MI: Harvest House Publishers, © 1990, p. 130, used by permission. Hunt's source was *The Voice*, Diocese of Newark, Jan. 1989.

ORIGINAL HEBREW TEXT WRITTEN 1000 BC

לָכֵן ׀ שָׂמַח לִבִּי וַיָּגֶל כְּבוֹדִי אַף־בְּשָׂרִי יִשְׁכֹּן לָבֶטַח׃ כִּי ׀ לֹא־תַעֲזֹב נַפְשִׁי לִשְׁאוֹל לֹא־תִתֵּן
חֲסִידְךָ לִרְאוֹת שָׁחַת׃ תּוֹדִיעֵנִי אֹרַח חַיִּים שֹׂבַע שְׂמָחוֹת אֶת־פָּנֶיךָ נְעִמוֹת בִּימִינְךָ נֶצַח׃
.... כִּי־תְקַדְּמֶנּוּ בִּרְכוֹת טוֹב תָּשִׁית לְרֹאשׁוֹ עֲטֶרֶת פָּז׃ חַיִּים ׀ שָׁאַל מִמְּךָ נָתַתָּה לּוֹ אֹרֶךְ
יָמִים עוֹלָם וָעֶד׃ גָּדוֹל כְּבוֹדוֹ בִּישׁוּעָתֶךָ הוֹד וְהָדָר תְּשַׁוֶּה עָלָיו׃ כִּי־תְשִׁיתֵהוּ בְרָכוֹת
לָעַד תְּחַדֵּהוּ בְשִׂמְחָה אֶת־פָּנֶיךָ׃ **תהלים טז:ט-יא; כא:ד-ז**

OLD TESTAMENT SCRIPTURE TRANSLATION

"Therefore my heart is glad, and my glory rejoices; My flesh also will dwell securely. For Thou wilt not abandon my soul to Sheol; Neither wilt Thou allow Thy Holy One to undergo decay. Thou wilt make known to me the path of life; In Thy presence is fulness of joy; In Thy right hand there are pleasures forever....Thou dost set a crown of fine gold on his head. He asked life of Thee, Thou didst give it to him, Length of days forever and ever. His glory is great through Thy salvation, Splendor and majesty Thou dost place upon him. For Thou dost make him most blessed forever; Thou dost make him joyful with gladness in Thy presence."

Psalms 16:9-11; 21:3-6 NASB

ANCIENT RABBINICAL COMMENTARY

"Our Rabbis taught, The Holy One, blessed be He, will say to the Messiah, the son of David (May he reveal himself speedily in our days!), 'Ask of me anything, and I will give it to thee', as it is said, *I will tell of the decree* etc. *this day have I begotten thee, ask of me and I will give the nations for thy inheritance.* (Ps. II, 7 and 8). But when he will see that the Messiah the son of Joseph is slain, he will say to Him, 'Lord of the Universe, I ask of Thee only the gift of life'. 'As to life', He would answer him, 'Your father David has already prophesied this concerning you', as it is said, *He asked life of thee, thou gavest it him* [*even length of days for ever and ever*]. (Ps. XXI, 5.)"[243] **Talmud Sukkah 52a**

NEW TESTAMENT RECORDED 65 AND 96 AD

"And when they had carried out all that was written concerning Him, they took Him down from the cross and laid Him in a tomb. But God raised Him from the dead; and for many days He appeared to those who came up with Him from Galilee to Jerusalem, the very ones who are now His witnesses to the people. And we preach to you the good news of the promise made to the fathers, that God has fulfilled this *promise* to our children in that He raised up Jesus, as it is also written in the second Psalm, 'THOU ART MY SON; TODAY I HAVE BEGOTTEN THEE.' *And as for the fact* that He raised Him up from the dead, no more to return to decay, He has spoken in this way: 'I WILL GIVE YOU THE HOLY *and* SURE *blessings* OF DAVID. Therefore He also says in another *Psalm*, 'THOU WILT NOT ALLOW THY HOLY ONE TO UNDERGO DECAY.' For David, after he had served the purpose of God in his own generation, fell asleep, and was laid among his fathers, and underwent decay; but He whom God raised did not undergo decay. Therefore let it be known to you, brethren, that through Him forgiveness of sins is proclaimed to you, and through Him everyone who believes is freed from all things, from which you could not be freed through the Law of Moses. Take heed therefore, so that the thing spoken of in the Prophets may not come upon *you*: 'BEHOLD, YOU SCOFFERS, AND MARVEL, AND PERISH; FOR I AM ACCOMPLISHING A WORK IN YOUR DAYS, A WORK WHICH YOU WILL NEVER BELIEVE,THOUGH SOMEONE SHOULD DESCRIBE IT TO YOU.' [i.e.,

---

[243] *The Babylonian Talmud*, Sukkah 52a, p. 247. Last two ( ) are *The Babylonian Talmud*'s Scriptural documentary footnotes 5 and 6.

Hab. 1:5] And as Paul and Barnabas were going out, the people kept begging that these things might be spoken to them the next Sabbath. Now when *the meeting of* the synagogue had broken up, many of the Jews and of the God-fearing proselytes followed Paul and Barnabas, who, speaking to them, were urging them to continue in the grace of God. And the next Sabbath nearly the whole city assembled to hear the word of God." **Acts 13:29-44 NASB. [ ] mine**

"And when I saw Him, I fell at His feet as a dead man. And He laid His right hand upon me, saying, 'Do not be afraid; I am the first and the last, and the living One; and I was dead, and behold, I am alive forevermore, and I have the keys of death and of Hades." **Revelation 1:17-18 NASB**

MODERN RABBINIC COMMENT/REFUTATION

"The author of Acts claims that this is a foreshadowing of the resurrection of Jesus....Therefore He also says in another Psalm: 'You will not allow Your loyal one to see corruption.' For David, after he had served the purpose of God in his own generation, fell asleep, and was laid among his fathers, and did see corruption; but he whom God raised did not see corruption. (Acts 13:34-37) The application of David's words to explain the disappearance of Jesus' body is without foundation. These verses were seized upon as proof-texts by desperate men attempting to explain the disappearance of Jesus' body to his followers....Nothing definite can be said concerning its final disposition at the time of the alleged resurrection. All the information concerning this alleged event is derived from the New Testament. The New Testament, while not a contemporary document, is the earliest and only source of information on the subject of the resurrection of Jesus. However, it lacks the necessary factual information to allow one to learn about the final disposition of the physical remains of Jesus."

***The Jew and the Christian Missionary*, by Gerald Sigal, pp. 90-91; © 1981**

AUTHOR'S COMMENT—EVANGELICAL CHRISTIAN POSITION

The author of *The Jew and the Christian Missionary* and his colleagues would be wiser in their "scholarship" if they would heed the words of the prophet Habakkuk quoted in the forty-first verse of Acts 13. Furthermore, Mr. Sigal's "exposé" that the New Testament is the only source of information on the resurrection of Jesus is entirely inaccurate. The first-century Jewish historian, Josephus, speaks to us as an eyewitness concerning Christians who were still alive at Jesus' resurrection, in his book, *Jewish Antiquities* (93 C.E.). He has written to us: "Now, there was about this time Jesus, a wise man [if it be lawful to call him a man], for he was a doer of wonderful works, a teacher of such men as receive the truth with pleasure. He drew over to him both many of the Jews, and many of the Gentiles. [He was the Messiah.] And when Pilate, at the suggestion of the principal men amongst us, had condemned him to the cross, those that loved him at the first did not forsake him **[for he appeared to them alive again at the third day**; as the divine prophets had foretold these and ten thousand other wonderful things concerning him]. And the tribe of Christians, so named from him, are not extinct at this day."[244] What evidence! **Philip Moore**

---

[244] F.F. Bruce, *Jesus and Christian Origins Outside the New Testament*, p. 37. This passage was proclaimed a forgery by some until the recent discovery of a much older Arabic edition containing the Jesus passage. We thank Professor Shlomo Pines for this recent discovery and for his validation of Joseph's authenticity! Professor David Flusser made mention of Dr. Pine's find in his recent book, *Jewish Sources in Early Christianity*.

LET'S LOOK AT SOME OF THE CIRCUMSTANTIAL EVIDENCE REGARDING THE *EMPTY* TOMB

The chief priests approached Pilate after Jesus' death due to their fear that a resurrection would further confirm Jesus' Messiahship. They knew, based on similar incidents in the past, that the Romans were likely to react severely to such Messiah-like figures, and thus tried to pre-empt any punitive measures which would have threatened both the national interest and their position. A clear motive is revealed here!

The eyewitness account of Jesus' student, Matthew,[245] bears testimony to this: "Now on the next day, which is *the one* after the preparation, the chief priests and the Pharisees gathered together with Pilate, and said, 'Sir, we remember that when He was still alive that deceiver [Jesus] said, 'After three days, I *am to* rise again.'[246] Therefore, give orders for the grave to be made secure until the third day, lest the disciples come and steal Him away and say to the people, 'He has risen from the dead,' and the last deception will be worse than the first.' Pilate said to them, 'You have[247] a guard; go, make it *as* secure as you know how.' And they went and made the grave secure, and along with the guard they set a seal on the stone" (Matt. 27:62-66 NASB).

Very clearly, these priests did not want Jesus to come to fulfill **the prophecy of the Messianic resurrection**, thereby sealing His identity as Messiah, did they?

THE CIRCUMSTANTIAL *EVIDENCE OF THE OPPOSITION* AGAINST THE RESURRECTION, AS REVEALED BY DR. GREENLEAF

According to Professor Greenleaf, this conversation is very important evidence! It is what is called "the witness of the opposition." The witness of the opposition is considered among the most important

---

245 Critics who try to discredit the facts surrounding the resurrection of Jesus have often argued that the event did not happen, but rather that a legend or myth grew up around it over the centuries. Dr. D. James Kennedy answers this accusation for us: "Some have said that the resurrection was a legend that just gradually grew up. This was a popular theory in the last century when the higher critics said that the Gospels were written a hundred or two hundred years after the events, but the advance of archaeology has silenced this criticism. Now we know that the Gospels go right back to the authors whose names they bear, and that the testimony of the resurrection goes back to the very decade in which it took place. Therefore, there was no possible time for legend to develop." D. James Kennedy, *Why I Believe*, p. 113.

246 Luke 18:33; Matthew 16:1-4.

247 This phrase means "to take a guard" in the original language.

evidence in any courtroom. If Jesus had not existed, or had not been raised from the dead, as some claim, this conversation would not have occurred, nor would there be derogatory references to Him in the Talmud.[248] More importantly, Jesus risked all of His teachings on the claim that they would only be true if He came out of His tomb! This risk was unnecessary, since He was already considered by many to be the Messiah or at least a teacher unlike all others "come from God."[249]

Jesus put all at stake concerning His bodily resurrection. He knew with certainty that His resurrection would occur. He affirmed to the Pharisees: "Destroy this temple [body], and in three days I will raise it up" (John 2:19 NASB).[250]

THE ADDITIONAL EVIDENCE OF THE ROMAN MAXIMUM SECURITY OF THE TOMB OF JESUS

There were many precautionary steps taken by Rome, at the urging of the chief priests, that were designed to prevent any rumors of a resurrection which they feared would be faked. They feared that a fake resurrection would make Jesus all the more popular. These steps included: 1. Making sure that Jesus was in the tomb; 2. Closing the tomb with a seven-ton stone; 3. Sealing the tomb with the seal of Caesar, and; 4. Stationing sixteen Roman legionnaires outside the tomb, who were checked by a centurion at every watch! These soldiers knew that to fail or to fall asleep on duty meant capital punishment—*execution*—by Rome.

The New Testament reports the pathetic plot hatched by the religious leaders in an attempt to discredit the resurrection: "Now while they were on their way, behold, some of the guard came into the city and reported to the chief priests all that had happened. And when they had assembled with the elders and counseled together, they gave a large sum of money to the soldiers, and said, 'You are to say, 'His disciples came by night and stole[251] Him away while we were

---

[248]See our *Vol. II*, chapter 8, "Distasteful References to Jesus in the Talmud as Documented by R.T. Herford."

[249]See John 3, where Nakdimon ben Gorion, known to us as Nicodemus, one of the wealthiest and most powerful rabbis of Jesus' time, spoke of Jesus as "a teacher come from God."

[250]John 2:2 mentions that Jesus "spoke of the temple of his body."

[251]This accusation that the body was stolen is not isolated to the New Testament, as some liberals would have us believe. An unbelieving but inquiring Jew of the first century, Trypho, also asserts this in a dialogue with Justin Martyr. Dr. D. James Kennedy documents: "Trypho, one of the earliest and greatest Jewish apologists, in a dialogue with Justin Martyr speaks of 'one Jesus, a Galilean deceiver, whom we crucified; but his disciples stole him by night from the tomb, where he was laid when unfastened from the

asleep.'[252] And if this should come to the governor's ears, we will win him over[253] and keep you out of trouble.' And they took the money and did as they had been instructed; and this story was widely spread among the Jews, *and is* to this day" (Matt. 28:11-15 NASB).

It is also recorded, *outside the New Testament,* in the dialogue between Justin Martyr and the Jew, Trypho, that the rabbis and sages of the elitist rabbinical establishment of that day propagated the lie that Jesus was: "...a Galilean deceiver, whom we crucified, but his disciples stole him by night from the tomb where he was laid when unfastened from the cross, and now deceive men by asserting that he has risen from the dead and ascended to heaven.' "[254]

ADDITIONAL EVIDENCE—THE MAXIMUM SECURITY OF THE SEAL OF CAESAR IS APPLIED TO JESUS' TOMB

The seal of Caesar (Matt. 27:66) consisted of a piece of wax placed on both the *tomb closing stone* and the *wall* of the tomb. A leather thong was then pressed into both pieces of wax, and both were stamped with the insignia of Tiberius Caesar. Anyone breaking the band of leather out of either piece of wax would be guilty of breaking the **seal of Caesar**, which carried a mandatory **death sentence**.

In reference to this Roman seal and the "sleeping-on-duty" hoax, the lawyer Albert Roper, author of *Did Jesus Rise from the Dead?,* points out: "...upon the request of the high priests, the tomb in which the body of Jesus was laid was sealed by order of Pontius Pilate, the Roman governor, and a guard of Roman soldiers stationed about it (Matthew 27:65). Commanding the guard was a centurion designated by Pilate, presumably one in whom he had full confidence, whose name according to tradition was Petronius....The Roman seal affixed to

---

cross, and now deceive men by asserting that he has arisen from the dead and ascended into heaven.' " D. James Kennedy, *Why I Believe*, p. 117.

252Kennedy further points out: "In the entire history of jurisprudence there has never under any circumstances been a witness who has been allowed to testify to what transpired while he was asleep. 'While we were asleep, the apostles came.' For a Roman soldier to fall asleep on guard duty meant inevitably the death penalty. And this was rigorously applied." Ibid, p. 111.

253It should be emphasized that it was quite easy for the priests to convince the soldiers to lie. Since under Roman law the soldiers would have been executed for "loosing the body," the priests assured the soldiers that, if they would admit to sleeping on duty, they would use their connections with Pontius Pilate to get them off the hook. Of course, this fabrication served the priests well because they could claim that the body was stolen and the resurrection was a hoax.

254James Parkes, *The Foundations of Judaism and Christianity*. London: Vallentine, Mitchell & Co., Ltd., © 1960, p. 226, used by permission. Parkes' source was *The Ante-Nicene Fathers*, p. 235. Cf. Ch. 17.

the stone before Joseph's tomb was far more sacred to them than all the philosophy of Israel or the sanctity of her ancient creed. Soldiers cold-blooded enough to gamble over a dying victim's cloak are not the kind of men to be hoodwinked by timid Galileans or to jeopardize their Roman necks by sleeping on their post."[255]

THE *"DISCIPLE CONSPIRACY THEORY"* DISCREDITED AS A RABBINIC TRICK THAT *DID NOT* WORK

In response to the rabbinic allegations that Jesus was "a Galilean deceiver" who was stolen from the tomb, we ask you to consider these questions: Do you think it even remotely probable that the disciples, who had just witnessed the execution of their beloved leader and already terrified, could even have considered sneaking past sixteen Roman soldiers? Or that these same soldiers would all forget that it meant the death penalty to sleep on duty; or even more improbable, would not wake up when the seven-ton stone was moved during the theft of Jesus' body?

Rather, it is documented that when the stone was moved to show He was not there, the guards "became like dead men" (Matt. 28:4). Why? Because they knew they were going to be executed for their failure. Caesar was not going to buy the resurrection or any other explanation.

The maximum security precautions of the Romans are documented in *The Institutes of the Roman Legions*, by Vegetius (second-century Roman general). This book is in the U.S. Military Classic Library.

"The Resurrection of Christ," Rembrandt, 1637.

---

[255]Albert Roper, *Did Jesus Rise from the Dead?* Grand Rapids, MI: Zondervan Publishing House, Inc., © 1965, pp. 32-33, used by permission.

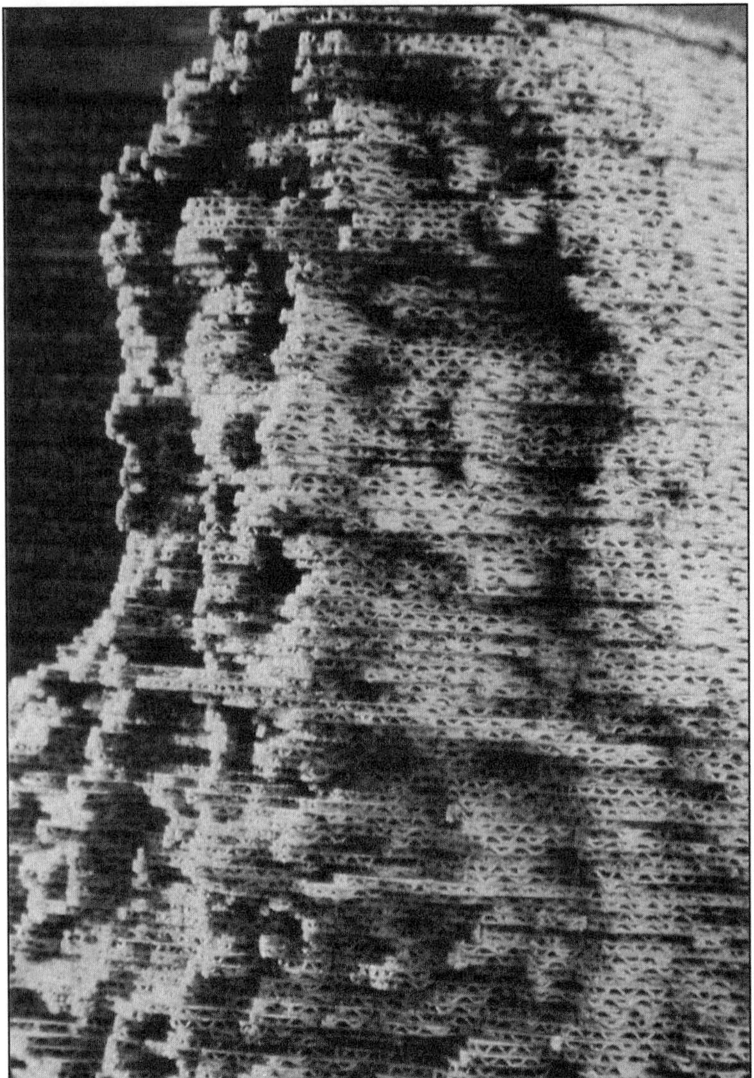

This three-dimensional computer-cut model of the image of a man from the Shroud of Turin may possibly be the image of Jesus, provided the carbon dating is in error, as it sometimes is. If this is the case, it is not entirely incomprehensible that this cloth may have been used to carry Jesus from the cross to the place of preparation where He was ceremoniously wrapped in linen, myrrh and aloes before being removed from the cloth and placed in the tomb. Photo used by permission of photographer Vernon D. Miller (see our *Vol. II*, chapter 36, "The Shroud of Turin—Did It Actually Envelop the Body of Jesus? Possibly!").

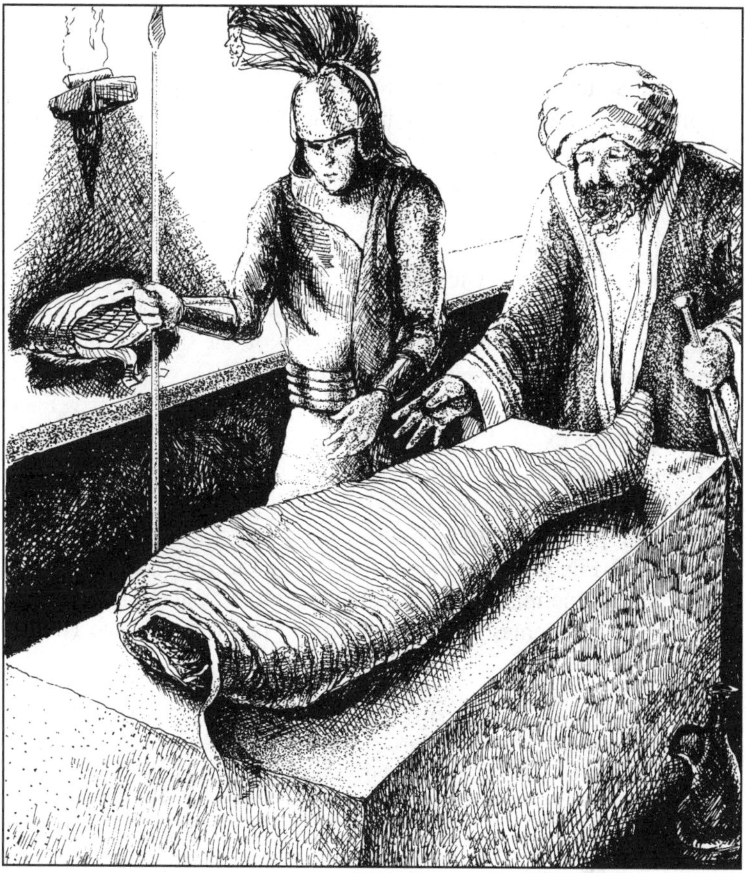

A Roman soldier and a priest are astonished at the sight of the empty graveclothes of Jesus, realizing His resurrection.

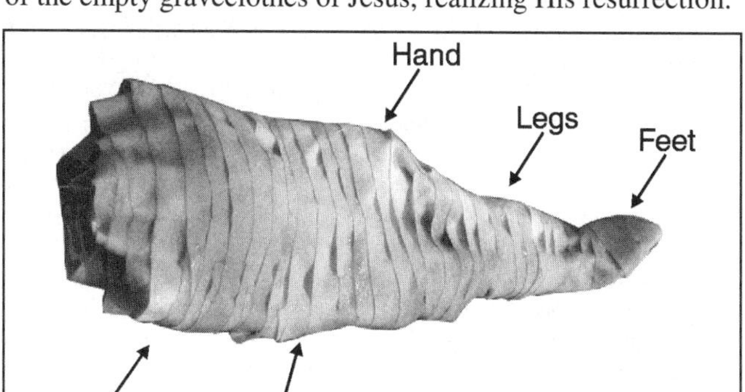

A model of the headless empty linen graveclothes, as they would have appeared after the resurrection of Jesus' body.

THE EVIDENCE OF THE UNDISTURBED GRAVECLOTHES

The Scriptures tell us that Nicodemus and Joseph of Arimathæa bought one hundred pounds of myrrh and aloes. The myrrh was a shellac-like tree sap, while the aloes were a powdered sachet. During the preparation of Jesus' body for burial, the myrrh and aloes were mixed and then coated onto one-foot strips of the finest linen, which were wrapped around the dead body of Jesus until the entire corpse resembled a mummy! Only the head was left unwrapped. A death mask of linen, which was easily removable, was placed on the victim's head. This was the ancient burial custom of the Jews, which they brought out of Egypt at the time of the Exodus.

At Yavne, a few decades after Jesus' time, a decision was made to forego this expensive burial custom[256] to help Judaism better survive outside of Israel. The New Testament Scriptures vividly attest to the ancient Jewish burial of Jesus: "And after these things Joseph of Arimathea, being a disciple of Jesus, but a secret *one*, for fear of the Jews, asked Pilate that he might take away the body of Jesus; and Pilate granted permission. He came therefore, and took away His body. And Nicodemus[257] came also, who had first come to Him by

---

256 Archdeacon Dowling tells us: "This Rabbi (Rabban Gamaliel) was the son of Simon and grandson of Gamaliel I, leader of the Sanhedrin at Jerusalem, referred to in Acts v, 34. He is called Gamaliel II, or Gamaliel, Prince of Jamnia, from his position as Patriarch of the first Rabbinic School re-opened in that city. He ranks as one of the seven great Rabbins of the Talmudists....It was an ancient custom among the Jews to bury their dead with great pomp. The heavy expenses which this entailed upon the poor sadly crippled their resources. Gamaliel forbade this extravagance, and ordered his family to bury him in simple white linen, and so did away with the extreme expensiveness of Jewish funerals." Archdeacon Dowling, "Jamnia During the Presidency of Gamaliel II, C. A.D. 80-117," *Palestine Exploration Fund*. London: Palestine Exploration Fund, 1914. p. 85. Rabbins is another word for rabbis.

257 Nicodemus was a rabbinic master of Israel (John 3:10). A rabbi of rabbis, highly respected and spoken of in the Talmud as Nakdimon ben Gorion. He put his entire reputation on the line when he stepped out and identified himself as a believer by helping Joseph to bury Jesus. The Talmud says of Nicodemus, who bought the very expensive burial preparations for Jesus: "There were in it [Jerusalem] three men of great wealth, Nakdimon b. Gorion, Ben Kalba Shabua and Ben Zizith Hakeseth. Nakdimon b. Gorion was so called because the sun continued shining for his sake...." Gittin 56a, *Talmud*. The Talmud continues: "It has been taught: His name was not Nakdimon but Boni and he was called Nakdimon because the sun had broken through [*nikdera*] on his behalf. The Rabbis have taught: For the sake of three the sun broke through, Moses, Joshua and Nakdimon b. Gurion." Taanith 20a, *Talmud*. [ ] mine. It is not hard to authenticate his New Testament title of Master of Israel when the Talmud records such honors in his prayer life as: "Nakdimon entered the Temple depressed. He wrapped himself in his cloak and stood up to pray. He said, 'Master of the Universe! It is revealed and known before Thee that I have not done this for my honour nor for the honour of my father's

night; bringing a mixture of myrrh and aloes, about a hundred pounds *weight*. And so they took the body of Jesus, and bound it in linen wrappings with the spices, as is **the burial custom of the Jews**.[258] Now in the place where He was crucified there was a garden; and in the garden a new tomb, in which no one had yet been laid. Therefore on account of the Jewish day of preparation, because the tomb was nearby, they laid Jesus there" (John 19:38-42 NASB; bold mine).

Thus, we know that once all but Jesus' head was securely wrapped, the myrrh would have hardened within twenty-four hours, creating a cocoon-like structure from which it would be impossible to escape without it being torn.

WHEN THE DISCIPLES SAW AN UNDISTURBED AND UNBROKEN COCOON OF WRAPPINGS, THEY REALIZED THE REALITY OF THE RESURRECTION PROPHECY IN THE JEWISH SCRIPTURES

The New Testament reports the surprised reaction of two of the disciples when they saw these graveclothes: "...and stooping and looking in, he [John] saw the linen wrappings lying *there*; but he did not go in. Simon Peter therefore also came, following him, and entered the tomb; and he beheld the wrappings lying *there*, and the face-cloth, which had been on His head, not lying with the linen wrappings, but rolled up in a place by itself. So the other disciple who had first come to the tomb entered then also, and he saw and believed. For as yet they

---

house, but for Thine honour have I done this in order that water be available for the Pilgrims'. Immediately the sky became covered with clouds and rain fell until the twelve wells were filled with water and there was much over." Taanith 19b-20a, *Babylonian Talmud*. The same Talmud's footnote 6 to Kethuboth 65a (another book within the Talmud) confirms that Nakdimon ben Gorion was Nicodemus. This note reads: "...'Nicodemus', one of the three wealthiest men in Jerusalem in the days of the siege by Vespasian and Titus v. Git. 58a, *Talmud*." Ibid. Jesus said to Nicodemus: "...Except a man be born-again, he cannot see the kingdom of God." He visited Jesus by night and said: "...we know that thou art a teacher come from God" (John 3:2-3 KJV). Thus we know that this man was not a man of fiction, but, according to a famous rabbinical source, was in fact a very real and godly individual. Imagine, the one the Talmud praises alongside Moses and Joshua was fascinated with Jesus! Interesting, to say the least.

258 Merrill C. Tenney, dean of the graduate school of Wheaton College, tells us: "In preparing a body for burial according to Jewish custom, it was usually washed and straightened, and then bandaged tightly from the armpits to the ankles in strips of linen about a foot wide. Aromatic spices, often of a gummy consistency, were placed between the wrappings or folds. They served partially as a preservative and partially as a cement to glue the cloth wrappings into a solid covering. When the body was thus encased, a square piece of cloth was wrapped around the head and tied under the chin to keep the lower jaw from sagging." Merrill C. Tenney, *The Reality of the Resurrection*. New York: Harper & Row, © 1963, p. 117, used by permission.

did not understand the Scripture,[259] that He must rise again from the dead" (John 20:5-9 NASB).

In Greek, the word for "saw"[260] means "to see and understand." What occurred when Peter saw, but was unable to understand, was that Jesus' body had risen through the graveclothes. This was *important* evidence, because you could look in the place where the head had been and perceive a hollow, unbroken cocoon. Jesus' new physical resurrected body passed through these clothes, just as it passed through the wall of a room later (see John 20:26). One day, we will have this kind of body in our resurrection when He returns (I John 3:2; Phil. 3:21).[261]

The molecular structure of such resurrection bodies enables them to pass through solid substance. This cocoon-like mummy and Jesus' physical appearance later, alive, was the reason hundreds of thousands of Jews came to believe within the early Jewish Christian/Messianic movement, as recorded in the New Testament, historical[262] and even rabbinical sources![263]

---

[259]This Scripture refers to the Old Testament prophecy of the resurrection, which was relatively obscure, primarily because it mentioned the idea of the Messiah's death, which was unpopular. Thus, the necessity of His resurrection was unthinkable among many of the greatest sages who instead, placed their emphasis on the Messianic predictions relating to a mighty reigning *King* Messiah!

[260]In John 20:5-9, there are three words used for "saw." The first, *blepei*, meant that John physically bent down, looked in, and physically saw the grave clothes; nothing more. The second word, *orei*, is used when Peter arrives after John and enters the tomb. This word means a very careful observation, a puzzlement with the purpose of apprehending the **importance** or the truth of what really happened. Finally, the third key word is *eidon*, and means "seeing with perception," which is connected with solving the puzzle. Once John entered he saw the clothes in the exact shape of Jesus' body and then realized that the Scriptures, in question by many, had indeed predicted the resurrection. Merrill C. Tenney notes: "The account says that 'he saw and believed' (20:8). The word 'saw' (Gr. *eidon*) implies mental perception or realization as well as physical sight. In modern language, he 'clicked.' The answer to the enigma was that Jesus had risen, passing through the graveclothes, which He left undisturbed as a silent proof that death could not hold Him, nor material bonds restrain Him." Merrill C. Tenney, *The Reality of the Resurrection*, p. 119.

[261]These New Testament verses promise: "Beloved, now are we the sons of God, and it doth not yet appear what we shall be; but we know that, when he shall appear, we shall be like him; for we shall see him as he is" (I John 3:2 KJV). "...Who shall change our vile body, that it may be fashioned like unto his glorious body, according to the working whereby he is able even to subdue all things unto himself" (Phil. 3:21 KJV).

[262]Such as Josephus, a secular Jewish historian.

[263]The Talmud of the rabbis, for one, continually speaks of the *minim* and how they must be combated. G. Alon notes in his unsurpassed work: "It is possible that the memory of a connection between *Birkat ha-Minim* and the Nazarenes lasted into Gaonic times....The editor notes that his ms. contains a marginal note: '*Birkat ha-Minim* was introduced after Yeshua ben Pandera, when heretics became **numerous**.' " G. Alon, *The*

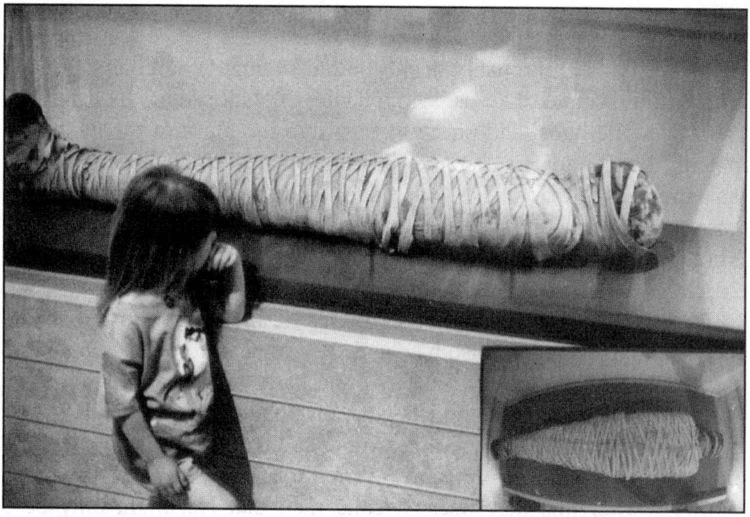

Katie Mason is captivated as she views an authentic Egyptian mummy at the Michael C. Carlos Museum in Atlanta, Georgia.

JESUS' GRAVE CLOTHES—WHAT DID THEY LOOK LIKE?

The Jewish outer wrapping for burial was borrowed from the time when Joseph the Patriarch received such a wrapping in Egypt (Gen. 50:26). Because the first-century Jewish practice of anointment and embalming was so similar (with the exception of removal of the body parts, soaking and drying of the skin and covering the head), this Egyptian mummy, which I photographed at the Michael C. Carlos Museum at Emory University in Atlanta, Georgia, gives you some idea of what the New Testament meant by "graveclothes."

You can see that for these to be **undisturbed** (John 20:5-9),[264] Jesus' escape from them had to be supernatural and miraculous. His resurrected body would have had to pass directly through them, as there was no other way to escape the tightly wrapped linen cocoon.

Unlike the mummies, who were wrapped completely from head to toe, Jesus' head and body were wrapped in separate pieces of cloth.

***

Jews in Their Land in the Talmudic Age, p. 290. Bold mine. *Yeshua ben Pandera* refers to Jesus, and of course *heretics*, coming from Rashi and the Jewish mind-set of a thousand years ago, to Jesus' followers (Christians). These Jewish Christians were the only sect of that era which became numerous after Jesus was presented as the Messiah!

[264]See our footnote 255 where we quoted Merrill C. Tenney on this fascinating subject.

THE EVIDENCE OF EYEWITNESSES

We have all probably heard the old saying, "doubting Thomas." Thomas, a disciple of Jesus, said: "Unless I shall see in His hands the imprint of the nails, and put my finger into the place of the nails, and put my hand into His side, I will not believe" (John 20:25 NASB). Jesus replied, "Reach here your finger, and see My hands; and reach here your hand, and put it into My side...." (John 20:27 NASB). Thomas, after touching Jesus, replied, "My Lord and my God" (John 20:28 NASB).

After the resurrection, some of Jesus' first words to those who knew Him were: "O foolish men and slow of heart to believe in all that the prophets have spoken! Was it not necessary for the Christ to suffer these things and to enter into His glory?" (Luke 24:25-26 NASB).

Jesus then, point-by-point, expounded upon all of the Messianic prophecies of the Jewish Bible, from Moses to the prophets (Luke 24:27). After this they became concerned that He might only be a spirit, as so many cults presently teach. Because they doubted His bodily resurrection, He replied: "Why are you troubled, and why do doubts arise in your hearts? See My hands and My feet, that it is I Myself; touch Me and see, for a spirit does not have flesh and bones as you see that I have....These are My words which I spoke to you while I was still with you, that all things which are written about Me in the Law of Moses and the Prophets and the Psalms must be fulfilled....Thus it is written, that the Christ should suffer and rise again from the dead the third day; and that repentance for forgiveness of sins should be proclaimed in His name to all the nations, beginning from Jerusalem. You are witnesses of these things" (Luke 24:38-39, 44, 46-48 NASB).

THE EVIDENCE OF CHANGED BEHAVIOR

The apostles, who were afraid and in hiding during Jesus' crucifixion,[265] became bold and daring after His resurrection. Most died martyrs' deaths while proclaiming the resurrection of Jesus rather than live and recant their testimony. Quite a change, wouldn't you say?

Peter, who denied Jesus three times while He was being beaten in the courtyard, was so transformed by the resurrection that when he was martyred he refused to recant his testimony and asked to be crucified upside down, proclaiming himself not worthy to die the death of his

[265]John was the only one at the site of the crucifixion. Peter was one of the most fearful, denying Jesus three times before the cock crowed, in a courtyard, as Jesus was nearly beaten to death by Roman soldiers (Luke 22:34).

Master! The secular **Jewish historian, Josephus Flavius, attests** to the resurrection of Jesus: "Now, there was about this time Jesus, a wise man [if it be lawful to call him a man], for he was a doer of wonderful works, a teacher of such men as receive the truth with pleasure. He drew over to him both many of the Jews, and many of the Gentiles. [He was the Messiah.] And when Pilate, at the suggestion of the principal men amongst us, had condemned him to the cross, *those that loved him at the first did not forsake him* [for he appeared to them **alive again** at the third day; as the divine prophets had foretold these and ten thousand other wonderful things concerning him]. And the.... tribe of Christians, so named from him, are not extinct at this day."[266]

We know we have quoted Josephus before, but here we wanted to emphasize his words, "those [Christians] that loved him [Jesus] at the first did not forsake him."[267] They did not **recant**, their behavior *changed* because "he appeared to them *alive* again"! This is **strong** evidence coming from a secular historian!

The entrance to the Garden Tomb in Jerusalem, Israel.

[266]Moishe Rosen, *Y'shua: The Jewish Way to Say Jesus*, p. 102. Bold mine. Rosen's source was F.F. Bruce, *Jesus and Christian Origins Outside the New Testament*, p. 37. The segment of Josephus is from *Antiquities* xviii 33, from the early second century.
[267]Ibid. [ ] mine.

The tomb of Jesus in Jerusalem, Israel. This tomb, unlike those of other rabbis which you will see in this book, is empty, and has been for nearly 2000 years! Why? This rabbi was the Messiah. As we read earlier, the central biblical condition which the Messiah must meet, as confirmed by the ancient rabbinical literature, was that of resurrection! Both our New Testament and the first century Jewish historian Josephus, confirm that Rabbi Jesus[268] fulfilled this prediction, as prophesied in the book of Psalms (16:10; 21:5), written nearly 3000 years ago.

---

[268]Jesus was called rabbi in the New Testament (John 1:38; 6:25). Nathanael said to Him: "...'Rabbi, You are the Son of God; You are the King of Israel' " (John 1:49 NASB). Nicodemus said to Him: "...'Rabbi, we know that You have come from God *as* a teacher; for no one can do these signs that You do unless God is with him' " (John 3:2 NASB). Rabbi was originally a Hebrew term meaning a teacher associated with Scripture and guidance. In our day, different Jewish groups ordain rabbis after they have met their required study.

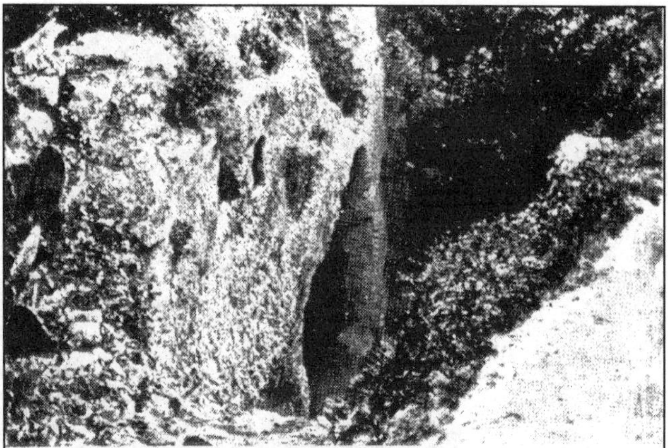

The Tomb when first unearthed 1867 ▲ ▼ The Tomb 1898

Jesus promised to overcome death, as Luke tells us: "...He [Jesus] took the twelve aside and said to them, 'Behold, we are going up to Jerusalem, and all things which are written through the prophets about the Son of Man will be accomplished. For He will be delivered to the Gentiles, and will be mocked and mistreated and spit upon, and after they have scourged Him, they will kill Him; and the third day He will rise again' " (Luke 18:31-33 NASB). Because Jesus kept this promise, something no other teacher of religion or philosophy has done to date, we can trust Him in His promise to resurrect all of us who believe in Him when He returns to establish the Messianic Kingdom for eternity. Jesus pledged in the New Testament: "And this is the will of Him who sent Me, that of all that He has given Me I lose nothing, but raise it up on the last day. For this is the will of My Father, that everyone who beholds the Son and believes in Him, may have eternal life; and I Myself will raise him up on the last day" (John 6:39-40 NASB).

MIKE'S SITE

Since the circular rolling stone of Jesus' tomb is missing (it was chipped up and collected as relics by early believers), we display a picture of a similar first-century tomb with its stone intact, so that you may better understand what the Gospel meant in its description of a *great stone*! I call this Mike's Site because Mike Bentley, a missionary of twenty years in Israel, made a special trip to the spot to allow me to photograph this almost unknown attraction, which lies hidden in the Israeli wilderness. The location of this tomb is described in Deuteronomy 1:7 as "hill-country." J. N. Darby, in his study Bible of exceptional translation, describes the area correctly as Shephelah in his footnote to the verse. It is just south of the valley of Elah, not far from Moresheth-Gath, mentioned in Micah 1:14-15, the birthplace of the prophet Micah, between the mountains of Judah and the Philistine plain.

A closer look at this first century tomb reveals
its interior and the massive size of its rolling stone.

To illustrate the prophetic fulfillment of Messiah Jesus and the resurrection, the New Testament qoutes the Resurrection Psalm uttered by King David nearly 3000 years ago. "Therefore my heart is glad, and my glory rejoices; My flesh also will dwell securely. For Thou wilt not abandon my soul to Sheol; Neither wilt Thou allow Thy Holy One to undergo decay. Thou wilt make known to me the path of life; In Thy presence is fulness of joy; In Thy right hand there are pleasures forever" (Ps. 16:9-11 NASB).

Traditional site, believed by many to be King David's tomb,
near the Western Wall in Jerusalem, open to tourists today.

RESURRECTION—KING DAVID'S PREDICTION

Simon Peter, a student of Jesus, gave a detailed exposition of the predicted words of David, recorded in Luke's New Testament book of Acts. "For David says of Him, 'I WAS ALWAYS BEHOLDING THE LORD IN MY PRESENCE; FOR HE IS AT MY RIGHT HAND, THAT I MAY NOT BE SHAKEN. THEREFORE MY HEART WAS GLAD AND MY TONGUE EXULTED; MOREOVER MY FLESH ALSO WILL ABIDE IN HOPE; BECAUSE THOU WILT NOT ABANDON MY SOUL TO HADES, NOR ALLOW THY HOLY ONE TO UNDERGO DECAY. THOU HAST MADE KNOWN TO ME THE WAYS OF LIFE; THOU WILT MAKE ME FULL OF GLADNESS WITH THY PRESENCE.' Brethren, I may confidently say to you regarding the patriarch David that he both died and was buried, and his tomb is with us to this day. And so, because he was a prophet, and knew that GOD HAD SWORN TO HIM WITH AN OATH TO SEAT *one* OF HIS DECENDANTS UPON HIS THRONE, he looked ahead and spoke of the resurrection of the Christ, that HE WAS NEITHER ABANDONED TO HADES, NOR DID His flesh SUFFER DECAY. This Jesus God raised up again, to which we are all witnesses. Therefore having been exalted to the right hand of God, and having received from the Father the promise of the Holy Spirit, He has poured forth this which you both see and hear. For it was not David who ascended into heaven, but he himself says: 'THE LORD SAID TO MY LORD, 'SIT AT MY RIGHT HAND, UNTIL I MAKE THINE ENEMIES A FOOTSTOOL FOR THY FEET' ' " (Acts 2:25-35 NASB).

THE *JERUSALEM TIMES/JEWISH PRESS* ALLOWS CRITIQUE OF A JEWISH SCHOLAR WHO ACCEPTS THE RESURRECTION OF JESUS

In recent years, Jewish scholars have begun to examine this type of evidence. One such scholar, Pinchas Lapide, highly respected in the Jewish religious community, wrote a book supporting the resurrection of Jesus. Although he does not accept Jesus as Messiah and does not follow other Christian claims, he does validate this aspect of the New Testament. In his book, *The Resurrection of Jesus, A Jewish Perspective*, he states: "...according to my opinion, the resurrection belongs to the category of the truly real and effective occurrences...a fact of history...."[269]

Quite an amazing statement from a traditional scholarly Jewish point of view, isn't it? Although Lapide is held in high esteem by the Jewish community in spite of his study and honesty regarding the

---

[269]Pinchas Lapide, *The Resurrection of Jesus, A Jewish Perspective.* Minneapolis, MN: Augsburg Publishing House, © 1983, p. 92.

resurrection issue, some Jewish opinions have been negative in regard to his findings.

The radical orthodox Jewish paper, *The Jerusalem Times/Jewish Press*, printed the following comment by Steve Jacobs: "I read with interest the article (P-O, April 25) which is headlined a 'Jewish Scholar (named Pinchas Lapide) Says Resurrection (of Jesus) was an Historical Event.' Nothing could be farther from the truth because his conclusion is based on the erroneous assumption the biographical stories about Jesus are historically reliable."[270]

This paper periodically runs anti-missionary comments, quotes and articles. We believe they printed Steve Jacobs' comments against the validity of Lapide's statement because they fear any evidence that might lend credibility to Jesus' Messianic movement from a Jewish point of view. Since Lapide is respected and is likely to be listened to by the Jewish community, he is given a bit of special attention in *The Jerusalem Times/Jewish Press*. We must remember, when considering his statement, that Lapide risked his professional reputation by publicizing his findings.

Earlier in a May 7, 1979 *Time* article entitled, "Resurrection? A Jew Looks at Jesus," it was reported that West German Jews considered Lapide's view outrageous and Rabbi Peter Levinson felt he had "overstepped the bounds of Jewish theology." Lapide countered that Jews were raised from the dead in the Old Testament (I Kings 17:22; II Kings 4:35; 13:21), noting that resurrection is "a Jewish affair" (in this case since it was witnessed in Israel by Jews), to be judged by Jewish standards! He maintained the evidence that if the disciples were so upset by the *real* crucifixion that it would take a real resurrection to transform them into such a zealous and "self-confident missionary society."

ORTHODOX JEWISH LUBAVITCHERS INDIRECTLY VERIFY THE JEWISH BELIEF OF A RESURRECTED MESSIAH

The fact that Orthodox Lubavitcher Jews have been sitting around the grave of Rabbi Menachem Schneerson, who died in 1994, claiming they expect his resurrection, has some Orthodox Jews worried. It is quite obvious to us that Menachem Schneerson will not rise from the dead as the Messiah, but these Jews rightly realize the Messianic implications of the Jewish belief in a resurrected Messiah. If

---

[270]*The Jerusalem Times/Jewish Press,* Vol. xxxv, No. 52, Week of Dec. 27, 1985 to Jan. 2, 1986, p. 12.

it once again became popular among modern Jewry, it would validate Jesus' resurrection as a Messianic expectation within Hebrew beliefs, as was customary in ancient Judaism! As a result, David Berger, in a July 1, 1994 letter to the editor of *The Jerusalem Times/Jewish Press*, calls on the leadership of Chabad to "denounce this position in the strongest possible terms."

Berger, the author of the book, *Jews and Jewish Christianity*, written at the request of the Jewish Community Relations Council of New York, has fought Messianic beliefs before, especially as they are embraced by Jews, purportedly "instigated" by missionaries. The deeper meaning of David Berger's worries can be understood in this context. It seems to us that Berger is so worried that the resurrection of the Messiah belief will give some credence to Jesus that he closes his letter with the frantic words: "If it is allowed to survive within Chabad even as a minority view, the movement will destroy its legitimacy as a form of Orthodox Judaism....The belief in a dead Messiah cannot be allowed a shred of legitimacy within Judaism. It must be extirpated in its infancy."[271]

As you may remember, Rashi worried about the Messianic interpretation of Psalm 21 nearly 1000 years ago, and was aware of the reference to the resurrection meaning in the Psalm and the implication of it regarding the acceptance of Jesus. As we have previously documented in our paragraph, "A Rabbi Tries to Quash the Resurrection of Jesus in the Psalms," he warned that the Psalm should be expounded upon differently; in other words, reinterpreted when dealing with "heretics" (Jewish Christians).

THE LUBAVITCHER JEWS BRIEFLY RETURNED TO THE ANCIENT MESSIANIC INTERPRETATION OF ISAIAH 53 IN 1994

The possibility of a Messianic interpretation of the circumstances surrounding the death of the Lubavitcher rabbi can be found in the *Lederer Messianic Ministries Newsletter*. Barry Rubin, the executive director of *Lederer*, interestingly notes of the Lubavitchers: "Surely, his loyal followers had believed, Rabbi Schneerson would declare his Messiahship, establish his Messianic reign, deliver all the faithful to the promised land, and even bring peace. But as the frail white-haired man lay helpless for months in a silent coma, scholars among the Lubavitch frantically searched for an explanation.

---

[271] *The Jerusalem Times/Jewish Press*, Fri., July 1, 1994, p. editor's page, © used by permission. David Berger is professor of history at Brooklyn College and Graduate School.

Then, on June 12 of this year, the rabbi slipped away, leaving in his wake a din of unanswered questions. At first the Lubavitch community held its collective breath, hoping for the resurrection of their leader. One follower declared, 'What happened Sunday (June 12) was only a test. The Messiah is coming, and the rebbe is the Messiah. We don't know how it happens, but he is going to get up'....Although most were shocked, some of Schneerson's flock argued that he *had* to die, according to the words in Isaiah 53, often referred to as the prophecy of the 'suffering servant.' After so many years of denying that this chapter spoke of Messiah, the rabbi's adherents are now relying on the passage's original historical interpretation in an effort to understand what had become of their leader. It is this very prophecy that had convinced me and so many other Jewish people that Jesus was the Messiah. With the rabbi gone and no successor named, the Orthodox community, worldwide, finds itself in the midst of turmoil."[272]

Rabbi Schneerson's followers saw to it that a replica of his New York home was built for him in Israel in which to stay when he visited. Believe it or not, this ninety-two-year-old rabbi never made it to Israel. Photograph courtesy of the State of Israel Government Press Office, photography department.

---

[272] *Lederer Messianic Ministries Newsletter*, Sept. 1994. Available through Lederer Messianic Ministries, 6204 Park Heights Avenue, Baltimore, MD, USA 21215. Tel. (410) 358-6471.

CHARLTON HESTON TELLS THE STORY OF THE GARDEN TOMB

Charlton Heston, in his video series, *Charlton Heston Presents the Bible*, says: " 'In the beginning was The Word....' John, chapter 1, verse 1—wonderful lines. Several centuries before Jesus was born, the Hebrew prophet Isaiah foretold the Coming of the Messiah in the Older Testament with these words: 'Unto us will a child be born. He shall be called The Prince of Peace and of His kingdom there shall be no end. Righteousness shall gird His loins....He will bear our grief yet we will esteem Him not, like sheep we have gone astray, so like a lamb will He be brought to slaughter.' Is Jesus this promised Messiah? Well, not many would even ask at the time, though maybe some of those who were in the stable that first night and saw the Star, thought of Isaiah's prophecy....The resurrection has been endlessly debated.... It's said by some to have happened here [the Garden tomb]....In 1883, General Gordon, of Khartoum, spotted a hill with a strange skull-like look to it. Beneath the hill was a garden, which research showed may have belonged to Joseph of Aramethea, as a small tomb carved from the living rock. There's a track where a stone could be moved to seal the entrance or rolled away....The resurrection is the crux of the New Testament, the focal point of the Gospels. Christ, having delivered His message to mankind and accepted the burden of their sins, comes back from the grave....significantly, to provide reliable living witnesses to His resurrection, and inspire them to spread the word He'd given them....to accept this witness requires an act of faith."[1]

Japanese Christian supporters of Israel and Israeli soldiers tour the tomb of Jesus.

[1]"Jesus of Nazareth," and "The Passion," *Charlton Heston Presents the Bible*, Vol. III and IV, © 1993, used by permission. Available through TTV Educational Media Company, Studios at Las Colinas, 6301 North O'Connor, Bldg. One, Irving, TX, USA 75039. Tel. (214) 869-3333.

The site of Jesus' crucifixion at Golgotha. A shape of a skull is clearly visible in the rock above the sign.

ABRAHAM'S NEAR SACRIFICE OF ISAAC (ON THE SAME HILL) FORESHADOWED THE FUTURE SACRIFICE OF OUR MESSIAH FOR US!

The word *Golgotha*, mentioned in the New Testament (John 19:17), means "skull" in Hebrew. The Romans crucified Jesus for proclaiming Himself "King of the Jews," i.e., Messiah, at the instigation of key religious leaders who saw Him as a challenge to their authority and a danger to the delicately balanced Israeli-Roman political relations of that day. They felt that an appearance by a "King" would have given Rome an excuse to destroy the occupied province.

To call yourself a King in the way Jesus did, was tantamount to treason in the eyes of the government represented by Pilate. That is why the words, "We have no king but Caesar" were repeated by a handful of religious leaders and their followers (John 19:15), to Pilate, the Roman governor of Jerusalem.

As you gaze at this hill, which is indeed shaped like a skull, it is important to realize that Abraham was asked by God to sacrifice Isaac, his son, on this same hill (Gen. 22:2). The angel of the Lord told Abraham he could lay down the knife, once God saw what he was willing to do for Him. The Lord, in effect, told Abraham and his people, the Jews, through scores of Old Testament prophecies, that He would one day give His very own Son, the Messiah, for not only Abraham and his people, but even for the non-Jews of the world if they would believe.

It is interesting to investigate key phrases from the story of Abraham in Hebrew. When Isaac asked Abraham where the sacrifice was, Abraham told Isaac: "God will provide for himself the lamb...." (Gen. 22:8. Also, see the New Testament John 1:29, 36).

Abraham later named this hill *Jehovah-ji reh*,[274] which in Hebrew means "the Lord will (future) Provide," in apparent anticipation of the Messiah's sacrifice for us; for Moses recorded: "And Abraham called the name of that place The Lord Will Provide, as it is said to this day, In the mount of the Lord it will be provided' " (Gen. 22:14 NASB).

***

[274]Genesis 22:14 KJV, *The New Scofield Reference Bible*.

"THEY TOOK JESUS THEREFORE, AND HE WENT OUT, BEARING HIS OWN CROSS, TO THE PLACE CALLED THE PLACE OF A SKULL, WHICH IS CALLED IN HEBREW, GOLGOTHA."[275]

The Gospel of John, from the New Testament, first century AD

Many believe this archaelogical discovery to be not a mere coincidence, but a modern miracle. This 2000-year-old verse from the New Testament matches this skull-shaped cliff located next to a first-century Jewish tomb.

Skull Hill in 1856; the top photo was taken in 1883.

[275]John 19:17 (NASB).

TANGIBLE EVIDENCE OF TODAY—THE GARDEN TOMB

In Jerusalem, near a skull-shaped hill, an ancient garden has been excavated containing a vineyard in which a first-century Jewish tomb was discovered only recently! One morning in 1883, the British General Gordon noticed the skull-shaped structure of a hill while gazing over the old city wall. This hill was an execution site in biblical times. It is located by Jeremiah's grotto, where Jeremiah wrote about the Messiah's sorrow in his lament, nearly six hundred years before the fact: "*Is it* nothing to you, all ye that pass by? behold, and see if there be any sorrow like unto my sorrow...." (Lam. 1:12 KJV).

His sorrow would be that of the whole world, as He would take all of its evils on His back for us.

General Gordon, who was also a Bible student, recognized the skull-shaped rock formation. He recalled that it was written in the first two books of the New Testament, Matthew and Mark, recorded nearly 2000 years ago, that Jesus was crucified near "the place of a skull," as it was called in Hebrew! "They took Jesus therefore, and He went out, bearing His own cross, to the place called the Place of a Skull, which is called in Hebrew, Golgotha" (John 19:17 NASB).

The area formerly considered to be used for Jesus' crucifixion, burial and resurrection, was chosen by Emperor Constantine in the fourth century following a dream had by his mother, Helen, and was located within the old city wall and gate. The New Testament says Jesus was taken "outside the city" [276] (Heb. 13:12).

NINETEENTH & TWENTIETH CENTURY ARCHAEOLOGY MOVES US TO THE SITE OF THE TRUE TOMB

In the nineteenth century, several archaeologists began to question the authenticity of this fabricated site, which still exists inside the wall. It is visited mostly by Coptic Greek Orthodox and Catholic pilgrims, few of which are informed of the more recent discovery which is presently visited by millions from Protestant Evangelical and Messianic Jewish congregations each year.

In 1842, the scholar Otto Thenius[277] of Dresden, was one of the first to suggest that the crucifixion occurred outside the city wall near the rocky knoll of Jeremiah's grotto. When excavations were begun adjacent to the skull formation, the tomb was discovered.

---

[276]It has been argued that the ancient wall and gate were at a different location, however, a recent archaeological dig uncovered the ancient gate directly under the modern one.

[277]"Jerusalem Garden Tomb" booklet, 5th edition, p. 4. Available through The Garden Tomb, Nablus Road, POB 19462, Jerusalem, Israel 91-193. Tel. 972-2 283402.

Also discovered within the garden area near this tomb were two cisterns and a wine-press. One cistern was stained with wine, the other held two hundred thousand gallons of water. The Jerusalem Fire Brigade took three full days to drain it, before this picture was taken.

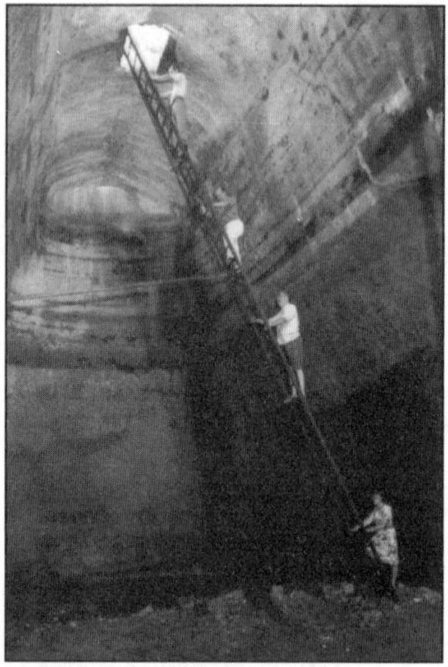

Empty two hundred thousand-gallon water cistern located under the garden surrounding the Garden Tomb in Jerusalem.

This wine-press was recently excavated within the garden—need we any more proof? Photos used by permission of The Garden Tomb Association.

THE CISTERN AUTHENTICATES THE GARDEN WHERE THE TOMB OF JESUS WAS FOUND, AS DOCUMENTED IN THE NEW TESTAMENT!

A cistern is a huge underground water storage area cut from the rock. All of these things indicate that this was truly an ancient first century garden, since a cistern would be needed for growing grapes, which require large amounts of water. Jesus' burial tomb is described in the New Testament as a place where: "...there was a **garden**; and in the garden a new sepulchre, wherein was never man yet laid" (John 19:41 KJV).

ARCHAEOLOGISTS AND ANCIENT CARVINGS CONFIRM FACTS THAT INDICATE THIS TOMB TO BE JESUS' VERY OWN

The archaeologist Dr. Conrad Schick found two crosses in the wall of this cistern in 1886,[278] which indicates that early Christians held this area in high esteem. Dr. Schick also reported that this tomb was Jewish,[279] and noted signs that it had been associated with early Christian interests.[280] Later in 1937, Sir Flinders Petrie agreed that the tomb was of first century Jewish Herodian origin. This was confirmed by Charles Marston.

In 1970, the famous British archaeologist, Dame Kathleen Kenyon, said: "It is a typical tomb of about first century A.D."[281] She also noted that it contained "several important features of special interest for Christians."[282]

One of these symbols, an anchor carved outside the door of the tomb, was an early Christian sign symbolizing eternal security in Jesus as Savior (Heb. 6:19).[283] This symbol of an anchor was discovered in 1994 on the tombs of Jewish Christians in the Golan Heights by a French archaeologist (for the documentation, see our chapter 8, "The Messiah Conspiracy Continues in the *New* Old Testament").

***

[278]Ibid.

[279]*The Palestinian Exploration Fund*, April 1892.

[280]"Jerusalem Garden Tomb" booklet, 5th Edition, p. 4.

[281]Ibid.

[282]*Jerusalem Garden Tomb* videotape.

[283]Hebrews 6:19 reads: "Which *hope* we have as an anchor of the soul, both sure and stedfast, and which entereth into that within the veil...." (KJV). See our *Vol. II*, chapter 11, "Eternal Security for True Believers."

The others were later symbols, crosses of the Byzantine era, indicating this tomb was recognized even at that late date. The New Testament states: "Now...there was a garden; and in the garden a new sepulchre, wherein was never man yet laid. There laid they Jesus therefore because of the Jews' preparation *day*; for the sepulchre was nigh at hand" (John 19:41-42 KJV).

Notice the mention of a new tomb where no one had ever been laid. An extremely interesting feature, which still exists to date, and shows the tomb to be still new in a sense, is that there are two places inside for bodies. One is finished (completely cut out), but the one on the right is still, as of our time, unfinished (not completely cut out). Apparently, Christians never allowed the tomb to be finished, because it was the tomb of Jesus.

This is where the body of Jesus lay in the left-hand loculus.
The loculus on the right remains unfinished.

In addition to these facts, the New Testament also stated that the tomb was: 1. owned by a wealthy Jew; 2. hewn out of rock; 3. near the place of crucifixion in a garden, and; 4. that it was possible for several people to view the loculi (body chamber) from outside. These, of course, are all true[284] of this particular tomb, which I hope you will one day visit, as I have, in Jerusalem, Israel!

[284]For evidence of these criteria, read the following New Testament passages: Matthew 27:57, 60; John 19:41; 20:5 and Luke 24:1-4.

THE CONVICTION OF THE TOMB

Many Jews who came to view this tomb and the empty linen cocoon which had encased Jesus, became believers in Him as the Messiah. They maintained their Jewish identity and served Jesus with ardent fervor. Many even became martyrs for their faith by both the Romans and their fellow countrymen. Hal Lindsey said it well: "A fact often overlooked and seldom emphasized is that the first 100,000 or more of the most ardent disciples of Jesus were all Jews who had been trained in Judaism, were familiar with the Rabbinic teachings about the Messianic prophecies, and for the most part were on the scenes of the public life and death of Jesus. In their minds, they hadn't 'converted' to another religion in order to believe in Jesus and his teachings. They saw in him the One that all of Judaism had been looking for for centuries and it was the most natural thing in the world to embrace." [285]

WERE THESE THE PROPHECIES OF FRAUDS OR TRUTH-BEARERS? LET'S CHECK THE RECORD OF HISTORY

If anything proves the historicity and truth of the words of the authors of the New Testament, it is the animosity of the Jewish leaders toward the early believers. They persecuted the followers instead of embracing Him; a belief that would have meant the loss of their dishonest position, as documented in John 11, *Josephus,* and the Talmud (mentioned in our chapter 4, "Why Was Jesus Rejected by the Jewish People?").

WERE THOSE WHO WROTE THE NEW TESTAMENT LIARS? NO! WHY? BECAUSE FULFILLED MESSIANIC PROPHECY HAS PUT THE WORD OUT

Beginning only fifty days after the death and resurrection of the Messiah, the exciting message of fulfilled prophecy was carried throughout the land of Israel by the disciples. If the fanatical Jewish "leaders" could have disproved these prophecies and their New Testament fulfillments as frauds, **they would have**, and thus dismantled the entire Messianic/Christian movement of Jesus from its beginnings. However, no refutation of the facts of prophetic fulfillment was offered; rather these non-believing "religious leaders" killed* many of Jesus' early followers, who were proclaiming these prophecies fulfilled throughout the land!

---

[285] Hal Lindsey, *The Promise,* pp. 167-8.

* The stoning of Steven is a prime case in point.

NO ACCEPTANCE, NO KINGDOM AND NO TEMPLE

Jesus also told these very same people that because He was rejected, there would not be a kingdom set up; rather the Temple would be destroyed: "...There shall not be left here one stone upon another...." (Matt. 24:2 KJV). Jesus also said that the Romans would "compass thee round, and keep thee in on every side" (Luke 19:43).

They were going to be scattered into every nation (Luke 21:24) until His Second Advent to save Israel, sometime in the distant future (our time; Matt. 23:39), when Israel, by necessity, would have become a nation once more. Remember He instructed Israelis to "flee into the mountains of Judea" for safety in this future apocalyptic era (Matt. 24:16, 21). For a full explanation, see our *Vol. II*, chapter 38, "They Escaped to Petra."

THE WARNINGS OF JESUS, FOUND IN THE NEW TESTAMENT, ARE ENLIGHTENING

As Jesus rode His donkey down the Mount of Olives toward the city, He wept and warned: "If thou hadst known, even thou, at least in this thy day, the things *which belong* unto thy peace! but now they are hid from thine eyes. For the days shall come upon thee, that thine enemies shall cast a trench about thee, and compass thee round, and keep thee in on every side, And shall lay thee even with the ground, and thy children within thee; and they shall not leave in thee one stone upon another; because thou knewest not the time of thy visitation" (Luke 19:42-44 KJV). Later, His disciples asked: "...wilt thou at this time restore again the kingdom to Israel?" (Acts 1:6 KJV).

From these New Testament verses, set to papyrus nearly 2000 years ago, we can look back as inhabitants of the twentieth and twenty-first centuries and see that Jesus Himself foretold the dispersion, persecution and regathering of Israel. The Romans truly destroyed Jerusalem in 70 AD. Israel was dispersed, persecuted in all the nations of the world where she sought refuge, and returned in 1948 as a nation.

Truly, nearly every newspaper which was printed after 1948 has been dominated by stories about the Middle East Crisis and **Israel**. We await the Second Coming, since three out of four of Jesus' predictions have already come true. What odds!

Truly, He is no fake, but ready to return in the clouds of Heaven, as predicted by Daniel and Mark so long ago! "I saw in the night visions, and, behold, *one* like the Son of man came with the clouds of heaven, and came to the Ancient of days, and they brought him near before him. And there was given him dominion, and glory, and a kingdom, that all people, nations, and languages, should serve him: his dominion *is* an everlasting dominion, which shall not pass away, and his kingdom *that* which shall not be destroyed" (Dan. 7:13-14 KJV).

"And Jesus said, 'I am: [the Son of the Blessed, mentioned in Daniel, to the high priest. See Mark 14:61] and ye shall see the Son of man sitting on the right hand of power, and coming in the clouds of heaven' " (Mark 14:62 KJV; [ ] mine).

AFTER JESUS ASCENDS, PREDICTED JEWISH PERSECUTIONS ARE PERPETRATED, PERSECUTIONS HE *WEPT* OVER!

After Jesus left the scene, ascending into the heavens, the Jews went through nineteen centuries of persecution! Why? One competent biblical answer is because they rejected their Messiah in the person of Jesus.

The Jewish Bible clearly stated that the Messiah would be the one who would bring in universal peace (Isa. 2:4) and protection for Israel and everyone else (Zech. 9:10). His protection of Israel as a nation is mentioned in the New Testament when He says: "O Jerusalem, Jerusalem....How often I wanted to gather your children together, the way a hen gathers her chicks under her wings, and you were unwilling. Behold, your house [Temple] is being left to you desolate! For I say to you, from now on you shall not see Me until you say, 'BLESSED IS HE WHO COMES IN THE NAME OF THE LORD!" (Matt. 23:37-39 NASB; [ ] mine).

He realized the price of His rejection and **cried for the Jewish nation**, as we read in the New Testament words of Luke: "And when He approached, He saw the city and **wept over it**, saying, 'If you had known in this day, even you, the things which make for peace! But now they have been hidden from your eyes. For the days shall come upon you when your enemies will throw up a bank....and will level you to the ground and your children within you, and they will not leave in you one stone upon another, because you did not recognize the time of your visitation' " (Luke 19:41-43 NASB).

IS JESUS' MESSIAHSHIP INDIRECTLY INDICATED IN THE ANCIENT JEWISH YOM KIPPUR PRAYER, IN THEIR BECKONING FOR MESSIAH'S *RETURN?*

There is a prayer which has been recited for centuries on Yom Kippur, the Day of Atonement, the most sacred Jewish holy day of the year. The portion of this prayer which deals with the Messiah reads: "...We are ever threatened by destruction because of our evil deeds, And God does not draw nigh us—He, our only refuge. Our righteous **Messiah has departed** from us, We are horror-stricken, and have none to justify us. Our iniquities and the yoke of our transgressions He carries, and He is wounded because of our transgressions. He bears on His shoulder the burden of our sins, To find pardon for all our iniquities. By his stripes we shall be healed—O, Eternal One, it is time that thou shouldst create **Him anew**!"[286]

Even though this prayer is read annually in synagogues throughout the world, it never seems to suggest "Jesus" to the Jewish mind. This is because the Jewish laymen of today are not familiar with the early rabbinical writings and the New Testament.

BAR KOCHBA, FALSE MESSIAHS AND *THE* FALSE MESSIAH (ANTICHRIST)

Bar Kochba was one of the first of a long line of men claiming to be Messiah, which launched a 2000-year-long plague of false Messiahs upon the Jewish people. Virtually every era has witnessed a false Jewish Messiah. To mention a few: Moses of Crete–fifth century; Abu Isa–eighth century; David Alroy–twelfth century; Abraham Abulafia–1240-1291; Abraham ben Samuel–circa 1300; David Reuveni–sixteenth century; Hayyim Vital–1574; Solomon Molko–sixteenth century; Sabbatai Zevi–1626-1676; and Jacob Frank–eighteenth century.

In the twentieth century, the Orthodox Lubavitcher Jewish community, numbering, according to some estimates, just short of three quarters of a million people, have acclaimed the recently deceased Rabbi Menachem Schneerson[287] as the Messiah. In fact, the

---

[286]Arthur W. Kac, *The Messianic Hope*, p. 84. Bold mine. This prayer was written by Eleazar ben Qualir over 1000 years ago.

[287]This rabbi never proclaimed himself the Messiah, nor did he have a worldwide following of larger portions of the Jewish community, as the previous men we have mentioned came closer to doing. We have mentioned him because his followers, being misled, really believed him to be Messiah. Actually, we think he was a great guy. We do not believe that he thought of himself as the Messiah, because he wrote a book anticipating the true Messiah's Coming entitled, *I Await His Coming Every Day*, published by the "Kehot" Publication Society, Brooklyn, NY. In fact, Barry Rubin, executive director of Lederer Messianic Ministries, noted in his September 1994 newsletter: "...a person I know who lead a Lubavitch-Hasid to the Lord, spent an hour with the rabbi—as the rabbi tried to 'de-program them.' Only God in heaven knows whether this new believer, in his defense of the faith, was able to prick the heart of this rabbi. Perhaps his simple testimony persuaded the venerated rabbi that the Messiah had already come and his name was 'Yeshua.' Only God knows!....Perhaps the death of this false messiah, will lead our Jewish people to the true Messiah, who both died *and* rose

ABC news magazine, *Nightline*, found Schneerson of such interest that they featured a segment on him entitled, "Waiting for the Messiah."

The last false Messiah will sadly be realized in the Antichrist in the twenty-first century! Martin Gilbert, in his book, *Jerusalem History Atlas*, provides an impressive chart[288] which gives the dates and places of false Messiahs from the fifth century to the eighteenth.

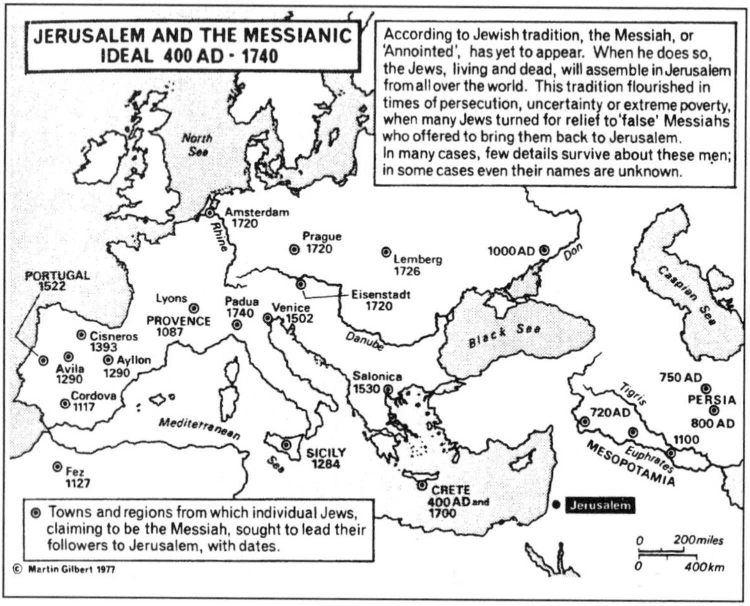
JERUSALEM AND THE MESSIANIC IDEAL 400 AD - 1740
According to Jewish tradition, the Messiah, or 'Annointed', has yet to appear. When he does so, the Jews, living and dead, will assemble in Jerusalem from all over the world. This tradition flourished in times of persecution, uncertainty or extreme poverty, when many Jews turned for relief to 'false' Messiahs who offered to bring them back to Jerusalem.
In many cases, few details survive about these men; in some cases even their names are unknown.
North Sea
Amsterdam 1720
Rhine
Prague 1720
Lemberg 1726
1000 AD
Don
Caspian Sea
PORTUGAL 1522
Lyons
PROVENCE 1087
Padua 1740
Venice 1502
Eisenstadt 1720
Danube
Black Sea
Cisneros 1393
Avila 1290
Ayllon 1290
Cordova 1117
Mediterranean Sea
Salonica 1530
Tigris
750 AD
PERSIA
720 AD
800 AD
1100
MESOPOTAMIA
Euphrates
SICILY 1284
Fez 1127
CRETE 400 AD and 1700
Jerusalem
Towns and regions from which individual Jews, claiming to be the Messiah, sought to lead their followers to Jerusalem, with dates.
0 200 miles
0 400 km
© Martin Gilbert 1977

JESUS WARNS ABOUT THE KING OF FALSE MESSIAHS—THE ANTICHRIST OF THE TWENTY-FIRST CENTURY

Jesus clearly told His people that He would return and save them upon their acceptance of Him as their Messiah (Matt. 23:39). However, He also foretold that a fake Messiah would come in His own name and be temporarily received by the masses of world Jewry, just prior to the time when His people would finally accept Him at the height of global Armageddon. Jesus proclaimed to the Jewish religious leaders of His time: "...ye will not come to me, that ye might have life. I receive not honour from men. But I know you, that ye have not the love of God in you. I am come in my Father's name, and ye receive me not: if another shall come in his own name, him ye will receive....And this gospel of the kingdom shall be preached in all the world for a wit-

again-according to the Scriptures." *Lederer Messianic Ministries Newsletter*, Sept. 1994, Rosh HaShanah, 5755, p. 2.

[288]Martin Gilbert, *Jerusalem History Atlas*. New York: Macmillan Publishing Co., ©1977, p. 37, used by permission.

ness unto all nations; and then shall the end come....For then shall be great tribulation, such as was not since the beginning of the world to this time, no, nor ever shall be. And except those days should be shortened, there should no flesh be saved: but for the elect's sake those days shall be shortened....For there shall arise **false Christs** [Messiahs]...." (John 5:40-43; Matt. 24:14, 21-22, 24 KJV; [ ] mine).[289]

This false Messiah mentioned in John 5:43 is most probably alive today, awaiting his fatal role in the lives of the Jewish people and the world. Nearly every generation has witnessed a false Jewish Messiah. As we approach the second quarter of the twenty-first century, watch out![290]

THE FUTURE ANTICHRIST/FALSE MESSIAH, UNLIKE HIS PREDECESSORS, WILL *APPEAR* TO BRING IN MESSIANIC PEACE

The Bible teaches that the crowning king of false Messianism will bloom and realize itself in the person of the Antichrist mentioned throughout the Old and New Testaments. The Antichrist is mentioned in Daniel 8:25, II Thessalonians, III John and Revelation 13 and 17.

It cannot be overstressed that he is to appear in our generation. More will be said regarding this evil individual in chapter 23, "The False Messiah Armilus Equals Antichrist."

It should be emphasized that not one of the false Messiahs previously mentioned fulfilled even a few of the hundreds of Messianic prophecies outlined in the Jewish Bible as Jesus did! However, it is important to know that the Bible also foretells that the Antichrist will appear to fulfill some of the Scriptures concerning the Kingly Messianic prophecies, which Jesus is yet to fulfill at His Second Coming, such as bringing in world peace and prosperity. However, his "prosperity and peace" will be false, short-lived and will soon crumble into global Armageddon as he tries to destroy the Jewish people (Dan. 8:25; Ezek. 38-39). Jesus will then save His Jewish people, destroy the Antichrist, save Israel and bring in everlasting world peace (Isa. 11:4; II Thes. 2:7-8; Matt. 24; Rev. 20-21).

***

[289]"Christ" is anglicized Greek for the Hebrew word (מָשִׁיחַ) for Messiah.

[290]See Isaac Newton's quote regarding the Antichrist in our chapter 23, "The False Messiah Armilus Equals Antichrist." Newton believed Jesus would return in the twenty-first century. See our chapter 11, "Newton's Forbidden Works Rescued."

THE CHANGES WITHIN JUDAISM THAT OCCURRED IN THE FIRST AND SECOND CENTURIES AUTHENTICATED THE MESSIANIC CLAIM OF JESUS

Getting back to the subject at hand, just after Jesus fulfilled the prophecies regarding the First Coming of the Messiah, certain things began to occur within Judaism and Israel. If Jesus was truly the Jewish Messiah, we would expect unusual occurrences to take place within the world of Judaism, as He said they would! The Temple in Jerusalem fell as He foretold (Matt. 24:1-2).

The Jews were dispersed worldwide, as He foretold. Nearly a million Jews discovered His Messiahship and, despite persecution, most followed Him to their deaths.

The rabbis became so alarmed at this large Jewish following of Jesus that they devised a plan; a conspiracy to sabotage it. This conspiracy had its roots in a hidden school established by Yohanan ben Zakkai at Yavne, with the permission of Rome.

The school, an academy, was run primarily by Rabbi Gamaliel II. The Messiah Conspiracy and the changes that took place within Judaism after Jesus left the scene in the dawn of the second century, are the subjects of our next four chapters.

My friend, Eddy Sussman, took this photograph in Sanhedria in Jerusalem. During our trip, we saw some of the most ornate tombs ever designed. The tomb in this photo is an example of the elaborate manner in which the Sanhedrin judges buried their dead.

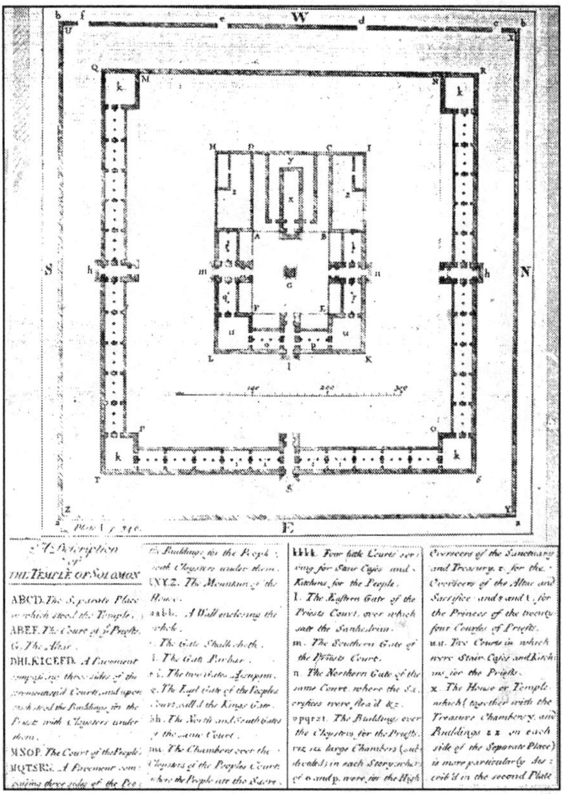

Sir Isaac Newton's plan of Solomon's Temple, from Newton's book, *The Chronology of Ancient Kingdoms Amended.*

Sir Isaac Newton studies light rays.

Rembrandt, circa 1635.

"...the LORD shall scatter thee among all people, from the one end of the earth even unto the other...." Moses, the law-giver, Deuteronomy 28:64 KJV; 1451 BC

"Yet our eyes failed; *Looking* for help was useless. In our watching we have watched For a nation that could not save. They hunted our steps So that we could not walk in our streets; Our end drew near, Our days were finished For our end had come. Our pursuers were swifter Than the eagles of the sky. They chased us on the mountains; They waited in ambush for us in the wilderness. The breath of our nostrils, the LORD'S anointed, Was captured in their pits, Of whom we had said, 'Under his shadow We shall live among the nations.' "

Prophet Jeremiah, Lamentations 4:17-20 NASB; 588 BC

"...there shall be great distress in the land, and wrath upon this people. And they shall fall by the edge of the sword, and shall be led away captive into all nations: and Jerusalem shall be trodden down of the Gentiles, until the times of the Gentiles be fulfilled." Messiah Jesus' prediction of Israel's Dispersion, Luke 21:23-24 KJV; 33 AD

"...Ye men of Israel, take heed to yourselves what ye intend to do as touching these men....And now I say unto you, Refrain from these men, and let them alone: for if this counsel or this work be of men, it will come to nought: But if it be of God, ye cannot overthrow it; lest haply ye be found even to fight against God."[1]

Gamaliel I, a well-respected Sanhedrin judge of Jesus' day, The Acts 5:35, 38-39 KJV; 33 AD,

6

THE HANDWRITING ON THE WALL SPELLED "THE TEMPLE FALLS"

It is not our purpose to bore you or bog you down with scholarly references and quotations. However, this chapter and the next three: "The Messiah Conspiracy," "The Messiah Conspiracy Continues in the *New* Old Testament," and "The Messiah Conspiracy Concludes in Preventing Healings," are highly controversial. As a matter of fact, the main purpose of this book is to establish that such a conspiracy took

---

[1]This quote is what Gamaliel forcefully told the chief priests after the apostles were supernaturally released from jail. The priests said to the apostles: "...Did not we straitly command you that ye should not teach in this name? and, behold, ye have filled Jerusalem with your doctrine, and intend to bring this man's blood upon us" (Acts 5:28 KJV). Peter replied: "...We ought to obey God rather than men. The God of our fathers raised up Jesus, whom ye slew and hanged on a tree. Him hath God exalted with his right hand *to be* a Prince and a Saviour, for to give repentance to Israel, and forgiveness of sins" (Acts 5:29-31 KJV). Needless to say, the priests should have heeded the wise counsel of Gamaliel. Need we wonder what we should do if our civil government asked us to go against the Bible? No! This Gamaliel is not to be confused with his grandson, Gamaliel II, who instituted the Messiah Conspiracy at Yavne, which is the subject of our next three chapters.

place. We believe this is a new thesis yet to be proven in the way we will attempt. Much of the evidence involving this conspiracy is relatively new. We are exposing this evidence for the first time, in layman's terms.

The aim of this conspiracy was to cover up the true identity of the Messiah, preventing millions of Jews throughout the ages from receiving the benefits of Messianic redemption. This conspiracy has literally changed the course of history for both the Jew and the Christian. We intend to expose this deception to the world and, in particular, to the Jew, from a literal, biblical, evangelical perspective. We intend to reveal the truth.

We also want to enlighten Evangelical Christians and believing Jews and afford them the opportunity to help the unbelieving Jewish world realize what happened and see the reality which has been so carefully covered up. Once the truth is revealed, we believe the benefits of salvation and, especially Jewish salvation, which the world has yet to see,[2] will then be realized, revolutionizing our planet. In order to accomplish our task, much scholarly quotation is necessary. However, keep in mind that your reading will be much easier and more casual, after these sections are completed.

THE TEMPLE COMES TUMBLING DOWN, JUST AS JESUS PREDICTED!

Circumstantial evidence proved the Jewish Christians correct. Thus, when the rabbis read the "handwriting on the wall" (Jesus had warned the Temple would fall thirty-seven years beforehand; Matt. 26:6; Luke), they reacted! This provided further evidence that Jesus was who He said He was—"the atoning Jewish Messiah"!

The scholar George Foot Moore comments eloquently on this issue when he tells us: "...the generation following the disastrous end of the Jewish war the 'disciples of Jesus the Nazarene,' finding an effective argument[3] in the calamity of the people and the destruction of the temple, which they interpreted as a judgment on the nation for its rejection of the Messiah and the precursor of the direr judgments to

---

[2]On a large scale, more in proportion to Gentile numbers.

[3]C.C. Torrey, professor of Semitic languages at Yale University, pointed out: "The fact that there is no trace of this 'effective argument' in any one of our four Gospels, though they are all addressed to the Jewish people, is one of the many items of evidence tending to show that these writings saw the light before the war under Titus." Charles Cutler Torrey, *Documents of the Primitive Church*, p. 101. This shows that all four Gospels were on the scene before 70 AD. This observation has embarrassed the liberals who place very late dates on the Gospels to discredit the supernatural element of prophecy, in an attempt to undermine our faith.

follow, had had such success as to rouse the apprehension of the rabbis and prompt them to take measures to check the growth of the sect....The vehemence with which the leading rabbis of the first generation of the second century express their hostility to the gospel and other books of the heretics, and to their conventicles, is the best evidence that they were growing in numbers and influence; some even among the teachers of the Law were suspected of leanings toward the new doctrine. The war under Hadrian brought about a complete separation of the Nazarenes from the body of Judaism, and after the war the animosity diminished with the danger of the spread of infection within the synagogue."[4]

A NEW MAINSTREAM JUDAISM PLANNED

As we will see, after the destruction of the Temple in 70 AD, the rabbis retreated to Yavne where they established a rabbinical school. It was at Yavne that they decided to end all sectarianism within Judaism. This meant no more Pharisees, Sadducees, Essenes and, especially **no more** Messianic Jews.

They worked exceptionally hard on the Messianic Jews. They felt they were particularly dangerous to their plan; to mold Judaism, as they saw fit, into a mainstream traditional religion! Their work was aimed at unifying Judaism, as they felt this would be its best hope for survival in the second Diaspora, which would become complete at the defeat of Bar Kochba in 135 AD, just over one-quarter century after their Yavnean activity! They made it their duty to see that Judaism as a nation did not become extinct. They had their own ideas and plans about how to rid Judaism of its Messiah worshippers. These plans were not very pleasant.

WHY DID THE RABBIS "ASSASSINATE" THE JEWS FOR JESUS MOVEMENT?—GENTILES!

The rabbis decided to "assassinate" the Jewish Messianic movement because it brought the threat of assimilation. In view of the fact that so many Gentiles were coming into the faith, they felt it would not be long before the rich tradition of the Messianic Jews merged with the pagan culture of the Gentile newcomers, to whom the New Testament gave the same blessings as the children of Abraham (Gal. 3:29).[5] This seems to be supported by the scholar Kenneth L. Carroll,

---

[4]George Foot Moore, *Judaism In The First Centuries Of the Christian Era, The Age of The Tannaim*, Vol. I. London: Humphrey Milford Oxford University Press, © 1927, pp. 243-244, used by permission.

[5]Galatians 3:29 reads: "And if ye *be* Christ's [Messiah's], then are ye Abraham's seed, and heirs according to the promise" (KJV; [ ] mine).

Ph.D., who says: "Had the Jewish Christians been the only members of the new faith it is quite possible that the breach between the two groups might have been healed...."[6]

James Parkes is even clearer as he reminds us: "When the armies of Titus approached Jerusalem, the Judeo-Christians retired to Pella. At the same time the rabbinical leaders retired to Jabne....The fall of the city [of Jerusalem], however, reacted differently upon the two different groups [Jews who believed in Jesus as Messiah and non-Messianic Jews]....Had the Judeo-Christians been the only members of the new faith, the breach between them and the Jews might have been healed....But the rabbis at Jabne were not unaware of their contact with Gentile Christians who did not observe the Law at all....It was only a step from this condemnation to the refusal to accept as orthodox the conformity of the Judeo-Christians."[7]

TWO REASONS THE RABBIS ABHORRED JEWISH CHRISTIANS—FEAR OF ASSIMILATION AND RABBINIC PRIDE

The "sages" felt that the identifiable Jewish race might be threatened by assimilation into a world populated mainly by pagan peoples. After all, every non-Jew was pagan by definition of the Scripture.[8] In addition to this fear, these famous and dedicated rabbis of Yavne, who were restructuring Judaism for its survival in the Diaspora, were personally and professionally insulted by the Scriptural attitude of Messianic Jews. The attitude of the Jews who followed Messiah Jesus was that they considered themselves the new spiritual Israel of God (Gal. 6:16), thus excluding all Jews who did not acknowledge the Messiah from God's promise of atonement.

SUPERNATURAL EVENTS IN THE TEMPLE REGARDING ATONEMENT CEASE AFTER JESUS!

God's rejection of the blood atonement available in the Temple through the Levite priest (Cohen), became evident in that the red cord of wool, ceased to render its supernatural transformation on Yom Kippur[9] after the crucifixion of Jesus. The Jewish traditional oral law

---

[6]Ken Carroll, Ph.D., *The Fourth Gospel and the Exclusion of Christians*, p. 22.

[7]James Parkes, *The Conflict of the Church and the Synagogue*. New York: Jewish Publication Society of America, © 1981, p. 77, used by permission. [ ] mine.

[8]There were some Gentiles attending synagogue, even before the time of Jesus, who were known as "God Fearers." However, the Scriptures teach that in order to be right with God you have to be a believer under the Old Testament covenant, and once Jesus came as the fulfillment of that covenant, a believer in Him.

[9]Yom Kippur is the Jewish "Day of Atonement," the holiest holiday in the Jewish calendar. Today, without a Temple, it is celebrated with fasting instead of Temple sacrifice.

known as the Talmud, revered by Jews in the past and still respected by Jews today, records these events most vividly. Colin Deal comments on this: "Even the Talmud (canonical and civil law of the Jews) bears witness to Christ's fulfillment of Passover though the Jewish Nation as a whole never accepted Jesus as the Messiah. The Talmud records an astonishing event that occurred approximately forty years before the destruction of the Temple by Titus' army in 70 A.D. This is the approximate time Jesus died on the cross....It reads, 'Forty years before the Holy Temple was destroyed the following things happened: The lot for the Yom Kippur goat ceased to be supernatural; the red cord of wool that used to change to white (as a symbol of God's forgiveness) now remained red and did not change and the western candle in the candlestick in the sanctuary refused to burn continually while the doors of the Holy temple would open of themselves. (Tractate yoma 39:b).' "[10]

The English *Soncino Babylonian Talmud's* exact words are: "Our Rabbis taught: During the last forty years before the destruction of the Temple the lot ['For the Lord'] did not come up in the right hand; nor did the crimson-coloured strap become white; nor did the westernmost light shine; and the doors of the *Hekal* would open by themselves...."[11]

NOT ONE STONE WAS LEFT UPON ANOTHER!

The Talmud comprises dozens of volumes. This passage is not likely to sound familiar to many Jews. It is not publicized because it shows, indirectly, that God had transferred His acceptance of the Temple sacrifice and ritual to the sacrifice of Messiah. Thus, within forty years of the time God ushered in His new covenant through the Messiah's atonement, He allowed the destruction of the Temple, which was expected by all of the Messianic Jews.

Jesus predicted it would be His generation which would not see one stone left upon another in the Temple (Matt. 24:1-2). This occurred when Rome attacked Jerusalem in 70 AD, fulfilling the prophecy of Jesus and the expectations of the Messianic Jews. Presently, all that remains of the Temple site is the outer retaining wall, known as the Wailing Wall; named for the many Jews who have come there to weep over the destruction of the Temple. The Wall is the holiest national shrine in Israel today.

---

[10]Colin Deal, *The Day and Hour Jesus Will Return*. North Carolina: Rutherford College Press, © 1981, p. 128, used by permission. For a full exposition on how the redemption of Jesus ties into the Garden of Eden and the second Temple, see our *Vol. II*, chapter 31, "The Mystery of the Temple Doors," from a lecture by Jonathan Cahn.

[11]*The Babylonian Talmud*, Yoma 39b, p. 186.

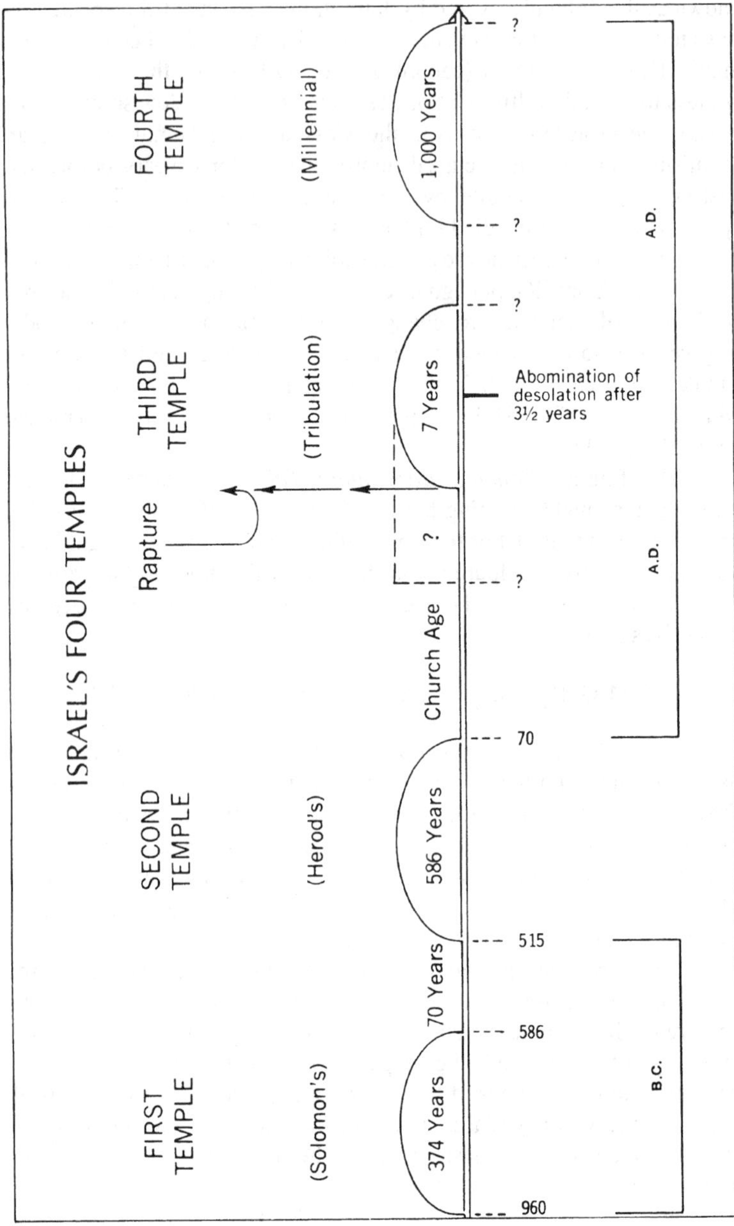
ISRAEL'S FOUR TEMPLES
FIRST TEMPLE
(Solomon's)
374 Years
70 Years
SECOND TEMPLE
(Herod's)
586 Years
Church Age
Rapture
?
THIRD TEMPLE
(Tribulation)
7 Years
Abomination of desolation after 3½ years
FOURTH TEMPLE
(Millennial)
1,000 Years
960
586
515
70
?
?
?
?
B.C.
A.D.
A.D.

TEMPLES—HOW MANY AND WHAT FOR?

There are two more Temples planned for Israel in the prophecies of the Bible. This chart from Zola Levitt's book, *Satan in the Sanctuary*,[12] shows the two previously existing Temples, and the two yet to come. The Bible identifies these Temples as follows: First–II Chronicles 3 (over 1000 BC); Second–Ezra 5 (445 BC); Third–Daniel 9; II Thessalonians; Revelation 11, and; Fourth–Ezekiel 40-48.

The next Temple to be built will be constructed at the urging of the Antichrist. Many Jews of the twenty-first century will believe in him as Messiah until, after three and one-half years of Jewish favor, he desecrates the Temple.

The Bible speaks of this horrifying event in various places. In Matthew, Jesus warns the believers of the future: "When ye therefore shall see the abomination of desolation, spoken of by Daniel the Prophet, stand in the holy place, (whoso readeth, let him understand:) Then let them which be in Judæa flee into the mountains: Let him which is on the housetop not come down to take anything out of his house: Neither let him which is in the field return back to take his clothes. And **woe** unto them that are with child, and to them that give suck in those days! But pray ye that your flight be not in the winter, neither on the sabbath day:[13] For then shall be great tribulation, such as was not since the beginning of the world to this time, no, nor ever shall be" (Matt. 24:15-21 KJV).

ANTICHRIST ATTEMPTS SECOND HOLOCAUST AFTER TEMPLE DESECRATION BUT JESUS STOPS IT!

In II Thessalonians, a letter in the New Testament, Paul writes of this future man we know as "anti-Christ": "Who opposeth and exalteth himself above all that is called God, or that is worshipped; so that he as God sitteth in the temple of God, shewing himself that he is God. Remember ye not, that, when I was yet with you, I told you these things? And now ye know what withholdeth that he might be revealed in his time. For the mystery of iniquity doth already work: only he who now letteth *will let*, until he be taken out of the way. And then shall that Wicked be revealed, whom the Lord shall

---

12This material is used by permission of Zola Levitt Ministries.

13Woe is mentioned in connection with pregnancy, small children, winter and the Sabbath, because all four will make a rapid escape/evacuation from that area to safety; more difficult at that future time. In Israel, the religious will have control and will enforce a ban on travel during the Saturday Sabbath. For those of you who may not know, modern Jewish observance of the Sabbath precludes the use of machinery and any form of labor, which includes driving cars and other means of lengthy travel.

consume with the spirit of his mouth, and shall destroy with the brightness of his coming: *Even him*, whose coming is after the working of Satan with all power and signs and lying wonders...." (II Thes. 2:4-9 KJV).

DANIEL'S DATED DETAILS CONFIRM THESE EVENTS!

Daniel predicted in the Old Testament: "And he shall speak *great* words against the Most High, and shall wear out the saints of the Most High, and think to change times and laws: and they shall be given into his hand until a time and times and the dividing of time....And his power shall be mighty, but not by his own power: and he shall destroy wonderfully, and shall prosper, and practise, and shall destroy the mighty and the holy people. And through his policy also he shall cause craft to prosper in his hand; and he shall magnify *himself* in his heart, and by peace shall destroy many: he shall also stand up against the Prince of princes; but he shall be broken without hand....And he shall confirm the covenant with many for one week: and in the midst of the week he shall cause the sacrifice and the oblation to cease, and for the overspreading of abominations he shall make *it* desolate...." (Dan. 7:25; 8:24-25; 9:27 KJV).[14]

As a result of Jewish disapproval in this yet to occur desecration, the Antichrist will attempt another Holocaust upon the Jewish people (as indicated in Dan. 8:24) which will be impossible to stop, aside from the return of Jesus, the true Messiah, who will slay him and bring peace to Israel, as foreseen by Isaiah: "...he shall smite the earth with the rod of his mouth, and with the breath of his lips shall he slay the wicked [one]" (Isa. 11:4 KJV).[15]

In chapter 19 of Revelation, this is mentioned as a prime event during Jesus' Second Advent. The Jewish interpretative Targum Jonathan to Isaiah 11:4 also says: "But he shall judge the poor in truth, and shall reprove in faithfulness for the needy of the people. He shall smite the guilty of the land with the words of his mouth, and with the speech of his lips he shall slay Armilus the wicked."[16]

---

[14]In these 2600-year-old verses of Daniel, the Antichrist is described as speaking against the most high (blaspheming the Rapture; see our chapter 25, "The Rapture Factor"); as persecuting the saints (those who missed the Rapture because they were unbelievers before it occurred); as having power from Satan "not his own"; as destroying the holy people, the Jews, through a false peace; as being destroyed by the "Prince of princes" (Jesus, the real Messiah), without human hand (through God's power in Jesus), at the end of the Tribulation when he desecrates the Temple. Interesting, isn't it?

[15][ ] mine, to emphasize literal Hebrew. An individual wicked one is indicated in the original Hebrew text, though in English, wicked may sound as if it is plural.

[16]Samson H. Levey, *The Messiah: An Aramaic Interpretation, The Messianic Exegesis of the Targum*, p. 49. Levey's footnote to Armilus admits: "Armilus...is found in the late

THE PROPHETS HOSEA, DAVID AND PETER CORRELATE AN APPROXIMATE TIME-CLOCK FOR THE RETURN OF JESUS

The fourth Temple will be constructed under the supervision of Jesus (Zech. 6:12-13) after His return, probably sometime just before the mid twenty-first century. (That just falls into your lifetime, kid! But, if something happens to you, don't worry, Jesus promised to raise all believers into a body of glory. Read all about it in John 5-6). We know this from a prophecy in the Old Testament book of Hosea, which states: "I will go *and* return to my place, till they acknowledge their offence, and seek my face: in their affliction they will seek me early. Come, and let us return unto the LORD: for he hath torn, and he will heal us; he hath smitten, and he will bind us up. After two days will he revive us: in the third day he will raise us up, and we shall live in his sight" (Hos. 5:15-6:2 KJV).

In verse 15, Hosea is prophetically speaking of the Messiah Jesus returning to His place in Heaven after rejection. This occurred 2000 years ago. The offense he speaks of is the rejection of Jesus by the Jewish people. The affliction spoken of is the Antichrist's persecution of the Jews, which will cause many Hebrews to investigate the prophecies concerning the Messiahship of Jesus. Jesus spoke of this in Matthew 23:39.

Chapter 6, verse 1 of Hosea's prophecy makes reference to the Jews being dispersed (torn) and regathered to Israel (healed).

Verse 2 is the time-clock key. The two days represent 2000 years, as Jesus returned to His Father approximately 1962 years ago, in approximately 33 AD (Ps. 90:4; II Peter 3:2-9[17] mention a day being represented as 1000 years). Peter lends special emphasis to this

---

apocalypses and is a Messianic legend mentioned by Saadia Gaon, representing the anti-Messiah." Ibid, p. 154.

[17]For those of you who were too lazy to get that dusty old Bible off the shelf, II Peter 3:2-9 reads: "...be mindful of the words which were spoken before by the holy prophets, [including Hosea] and of the commandment of us the apostles of the Lord and Saviour: Knowing this first, that there shall come in the last days scoffers, walking after their own lusts, And saying, Where is the promise of his coming? for since the fathers fell asleep, all things continue as *they were* from the beginning of the creation. For this they willingly are ignorant of, that by the word of God the heavens were of old, and the earth standing out of the water and in the water: Whereby the world that then was, being overflowed with water, perished: But the heavens and the earth which are now, by the same word are kept in store, reserved unto fire against the day of judgment and perdition of ungodly men. But, beloved, be not ignorant of this one thing, that one day *is* with the Lord as a thousand years, and a thousand years as one day. The Lord is not slack concerning his promise, as some men count slackness; but is longsuffering to us-ward...." (KJV; [ ] mine).

analogy, applying it to the Second Coming of the Lord and pleading that we **not** be ignorant about it. Look it up in your Bible and read it.

In verse 2, the third day represents the 1000-year (millennial) kingdom spoken of in Revelation 20. This prophecy[18] of Hosea is covered in more detail in our chapter 28, "The Second Coming Event—Will He Yet Be Sent?"

WHAT IS THE PURPOSE OF THE FOURTH TEMPLE AND WHAT HAPPENED AFTER THE SECOND WAS DESTROYED—FAITH SPREAD LIKE WILDFIRE

The Scriptures which speak of this new Temple are Ezekiel 40-48 and Revelation 21:22. This Temple will remain on Earth during the 1000-year reign of Messiah, when Jesus will rule and judge in peace from the throne of King David (Luke 1:33; Isa. 9) and Israel will be head of all nations (Deut. 28:13).[19]

Once the first century Temple was destroyed, the Messianic Jews began to multiply rapidly, as we have shown. Many Jews in synagogues throughout the East were seeing evidence proving the claims of those who believed in Jesus as prophet, priest and king. In many instances, they began to heed the teachings of the attending Messianic Jews in the regular synagogues. Thus, Messianic Judaism, known to many as Hebrew Christianity, spread like wildfire through tens of thousands of synagogues in the Diaspora. The renowned Israeli politician and scholar, Abba Eban, documented the existence of these synagogues in the PBS television special, *Heritage, Civilization and The Jews.*

THE RABBIS' WORST FEARS REALIZED—THE MESSIANIC JEWISH MOVEMENT GROWS BY LEAPS AND BOUNDS

Even before the destruction of the Temple, the good news was spreading rapidly among the Jews. For the most part, it reached the poor and lowly. James, the brother of the Lord and the head of the Messianic community, was known as the Father of the People, an indication of the high esteem in which he was held. As one observer put it: "James was the Father of the People because the Messianic movement was essentially a movement of the *People*."[20]

---

[18]*The New Scofield Reference Bible*'s footnote to Hosea's prediction reads: "(5:15) Taken with Matthew 23:37-39, this passage gives in broad outline the course of Israel's future restoration to God." *The New Scofield Reference Bible*, p. 922.

[19]Today, most of the world, aside from born-again believers, feels that Israel is the tail.

[20] Jacob Jocz, *The Jewish People and Jesus Christ*, p. 165.

Of course, the destruction of the Temple only added to the spread of the movement. Believers could point out fulfillments of Jesus' predictions and convince their fellow Jews that He was not an imposter, as the rabbis maintained. One testimony to the accelerated growth of the movement was the large number of Jewish elders mentioned by Eusebius, an early historian of the Church.[21]

HOW DID THE RABBIS AT YAVNE REACT TO THE SPREAD OF THE MESSIANIC FAITH?—NEGATIVE!

The personal integrity of the rabbis at Yavne and their belief regarding what constituted Judaism was at stake. They had to find a way to stop the spread of Messianic Judaism from reaching world Jewry. They felt that Judaism should be remolded into a cultural cement designed to keep Jewish and Gentile identities separate for all time. They felt that Jesus was a common personality whose message might threaten Jewish racial purity because so many Gentiles were accepting Him along with their Jewish friends. They were becoming interested in Jewish feasts and traditions, because their (the Gentiles') Messiah was Jewish.

Incidentally, this phenomenon has currently been revived among true Evangelical Christians. Representatives of *Jews for Jesus*[22] have been invited to thousands of churches to demonstrate Passover and reveal its secret Messianic meaning.[23]

YAVNEAN MAGIC—THIS WE CHANGE, THIS WE DON'T—OR DO WE?

In desperation, the rabbis at Yavne came up with a benediction which could identify any secret Messianic Jew in any orthodox congregation at that time. It was called the Birkat ha-Minim, which we will discuss in more detail in our next chapter.

---

[21] Ibid, p. 169.

[22] *Jews for Jesus* is the name of a large organization of Jews throughout the world who accept Jesus as their Messiah. They maintain their Jewish identity, as did the first century Jewish Christians who frequented the Temple and synagogues. They have a great deal of teaching material and are eager to help other Jews and Christians understand that Jesus is the Messiah from the Old Testament prophecies of the Bible. The can be reached through Jews for Jesus, 60 Haight Street, San Francisco, CA, USA 94102-5895. Tel. (415) 864-2600. In Canada: POB 487, Station Z, Toronto, Ontario, Canada M5N 2Z6. Tel (416) 787-7816.

[23] If you are interested in learning the secret symbols of Jesus hidden within the Passover, see our *Vol. II*, chapter 35, "The Secrets of Jesus in Passover Versus the Errors of Easter."

Rabbi Gamaliel instructed Rabbi Samuel the Lesser to concoct and compose this malediction, as the Talmud reveals: "Said Rabban Gamaliel to the Sages: Can any one among you frame a benediction relating to the *Minim?* Samuel the Lesser arose and composed it."[24]

They then wrote letters which were circulated throughout the Diaspora with a copy of this malediction and instructions to add it to the Amidah Prayer, which was recited daily in all synagogues of that time.

Through their emissaries, they propagated the idea that Messianic Jews were not legitimate members of the community, were not to be acknowledged, and in some cases, were even worthy of death. The first century patristic Father Justin Martyr noted: "But these Jews, though they read the books, fail to grasp their meaning, and they consider us as their enemies and adversaries, killing and punishing us, just as you do, whenever they are able to do so, as you can readily imagine. In the recent Jewish war, Bar Kocheba, the leader of the Jewish uprising, ordered that only the Christians should be subjected to dreadful torments, unless they renounced and blasphemed Jesus Christ."[25]

JESUS FORETELLS MARTYRDOM OF JEWISH CHRISTIANS—HISTORIAN CONFIRMS THEIR DEATH

Indeed, Jesus warned of this when He said: "These things have I spoken unto you, that ye should not be offended. They shall put you out of the synagogues: yea, the time cometh, that whosoever killeth you will think that he doeth God service. And these things will they do unto you, because they have not known the Father, nor me. But these things have I told you, that when the time shall come, ye may remember that I told you of them. And these things I said not unto you at the beginning, because I was with you. But now I go my way to him that sent me...." (John 16:1-5 KJV).

When the rabbis' propaganda machine began to work, it resulted in Jewish persecution of Messianic Jews for a time. However, when the Jewish believers in Jesus refused to fight under Bar Kochba because Rabbi Akiva demanded that he be recognized as the Messiah, this tool devised by the rabbis went into full operation. Initially, the Messianic Jews were willing and did fight against the Romans for Israel's national security. They fought the Roman soldiers and died for their country, until Bar Kochba, supported by Rabbi Akiva, demanded

---

[24]*The Babylonian Talmud*, Berakoth 28b, p. 175.

[25]Thomas B. Falls, D.D., Ph.D., *Saint Justin Martyr*. Washington: Catholic University Press, © 1948, p. 67, used by permission.

that he be recognized as the Messiah. The Messianic Jews were faced with giving up God and their Messianic faith in favor of this secular rebel at war with the Romans. Of course, as loyal Jews they said, "Okay, we will keep our faith, and if we are not welcome to fight alongside other Jews because it is against our faith to accept a false Messiah, we won't."[26]

At this time, Bar Kochba began to persecute Messianic Jews because of their refusal to render him Messianic recognition. Johannes Weiss documents this fact when he tells us: "The fate of the Jerusalem church underwent a decided change under Hadrian (117-138). In the great uprising of the Jews under the Messiah-prophet Bar-Kokhba (132-135), Jerusalem fell into the hands of the rebels; and even during the Bar-Kokhba revolt, the Christians had much to suffer at their hands...."[27]

---

[26]Paul Liberman, a twentieth century Messianic Jew, notes: "Because Messianic Jews used the destruction of the Temple as proof that the Messiah had made the final sacrifice, there was an upsurge in the movement, with many Jews beginning to join it. Finally, the Rabbis decided to end these discussions and forbade any contact with the Messianic Jewish community. Messianic Jews were expelled from the synagogue. It wasn't until later that they were expelled from the community. The Bar-Cochba Revolt occurred between 132 and 135 A.D. It was the second Jewish uprising against Roman rule It eventually changed the nature of the dispute between Jewish believers and the Rabbinical Jewish community. Then, there was a radical change. So many non-Jews accepted Messianic claims, the movement became more and more of a Gentile religion. This marked the rejection of the Messianic movement as a force in the Jewish community. During the first year of the revolt, Messianic Jews fought alongside their other Jewish brethren. But a year later, Rabbi Akiba declared Bar-Cochba to be the Jewish Messiah. As the result, Jewish believers pulled out of the revolt. They could not accept that concept, and it created the final split between the two Jewish communities." Paul Liberman, *The Fig Tree Blossoms: Messianic Judaism Emerges*. Indianola, IA: Fountain Press, © 1976, pp. 36-37, used by permission. F.F. Bruce affirms the often denied fact that the Messianic Jews refused to fight because they could not allow Rabbi Akiva to belittle their faith through the recognition of a false Messiah. He says: "When Hadrian issued his ban on circumcision in A.D. 132, which precipitated Ben-Kosebah's revolt, Jewish Christians who maintained this covenant-sign must have been affected by it as much as other Jews; yet they were unable to take part wholeheartedly in the revolt because they could not acknowledge Ben-Kosebah's messianic claim. Perhaps they joined with others who rejected this claim in calling him Bar-koziba, 'the son of falsehood', as a counterblast to the designation Bar-kokhba, 'the son of the star', given him by Aqiba who hailed him as the messianic 'star out of Jacob' predicted by Balaam (Num. 24:17). At any rate their refusal to acknowledge Ben-Kosebah as the Messiah stamped them in the eyes of many of their fellow-Jews as traitors to the national cause, and brought severe reprisals on them." F.F. Bruce, *New Testament History*, p. 390. In footnote 86, Bruce notes: "The name Ben-Kosebah is now attested from contemporary Hebrew documents; cf. the Murabba'at texts 24 B $_3$, C $_3$, 20, E $_2$, G $_3$: 43. 1, 8." Ibid.

[27]Johannes Weiss, *Earliest Christianity: A History of the Period A.D. 30-150,* Vol. II., p. 722.

SECOND CENTURY JEWS FOR JESUS FALSELY ACCUSED OF BEING TRAITORS, TORTURED AND MURDERED

Though this may sound hard to believe, Weiss footnotes his comment with such credible sources as Eusebius and Orosius, who tell us: " 'And indeed in the recent Jewish war, Bar-Kokhba, the leader of the uprising of the Jews, condemned the Christians alone to be led away to dreadful torture if they would not deny Jesus was Christ and blaspheme him;' Eusebius, *Chron.* (ed. Schoene, ii, 168 ff)....'Kokhba, who was leader of the rebellion of the Jews, inflicted various penalties on many of the Christians, since they would not go out to the battle with him against the Romans;' Orosius, 7:13."[28]

In the article, "Outside Books," Joshua Bloch said: "The Jews fought their enemy by themselves. The Nazarenes were thus disloyal to the Jewish national cause. Regarding them as blasphemous and as spies and therefore guilty of treason, Bar Kokba made them pay dearly. Because they refused to take part in the national war—they were only idle onlookers at the fearful spectacle—he displayed considerable hostility against them. Gradually his hatred for them increased and many of them were put to death. Those who survived were, for one reason or another, forced to withdraw gradually from the Jewish community."[29]

At this time, the propaganda concocted in Yavne by Rabbi Gamaliel and Rabbi Samuel the Small, began to take an alarming toll on Messianic Jewish life. They used the refusal of the Messianic Jews to fight against Rome as proof that they were not really Jews (a false accusation) and that they were, in fact, traitors to the Jewish nation. This is where the current view originated.

Some Orthodox Jews call Jews for Jesus "traitors"[30] and really do not know why. Well, now you know why it has been a tradition, even though it was a lie from the beginning, to call Jews who believed in the Messiah "traitors" to Israel's national cause.

---

[28]Ibid, p. 723.

[29]Joshua Bloch, "Outside Books," *Mordecai M. Kaplan, Jubilee Volume*. New York: The Jewish Theological Seminary of America, © 1953, pp. 96-97, used by permission. The reason the Messianic Jews refused to fight was because Rabbi Akiva claimed Bar Kochba was the Messiah. The Christian Jews knew better and were forced to stop fighting or go against the faith they realized to be true. Could this have been a ploy on the part of Akiva to alienate Jewish believers from the Jewish community? We may never know.

[30]The Hebrew word *meshumud* can be heard in the whisperings of rabbis when they discuss Jews who believe in Jesus. Read Zola Levitt's book, *Meshumud*, available through Zola Levitt, POB 12268, Dallas, TX, USA 75225.

GAMALIEL, YOHANAN BEN ZAKKAI, MEIR, AKIVA AND AQUILA

These rabbis, their descendants and other leaders closely associated due to their anti-Christian zeal, incited riots throughout the Roman world, causing the Roman authorities to view the Messianic Jewish movement as a threat. They also convinced Rome that the Messianic Jews, who were the first Christians, were not a sect of Judaism, and therefore not entitled to the same rights as the Jews, including absolution from taking an oath to the pagan gods of Rome and Greece. Maurice Goguel tells us in his scholarly book, *The Birth of Christianity*: "...right up to Paul's trial, the Roman authorities in Palestine do not seem to have made any distinction between Jews and Christians. At first the same was true in the diaspora: for a long time Christians were confused with the Jews. But the latter went to work to clear up this confusion with such perseverance that we cannot help but think that they were working according to a set plan. So far as they succeeded they rendered the situation of the Christians in the empire very precarious. As soon as they ceased to enjoy the favoured treatment which had been awarded to Judaism, they found themselves without legal status, on the fringe of society and subject to the penalty of death, because they practised an illicit religion.

Judaism enjoyed an exceptional position in the empire. It had received considerable privileges through a series of public decrees which had been renewed and confirmed by Caesar and Augustus....Jewish communities possessed wide powers of self-government; they had rights of association and could exercise discipline over their members. Jews were exempt from all participation in public worship; they could take oaths without calling upon the gods....All this was possible because Judaism was considered to be the national religion of a people who had been the friend and ally of the Roman people before they became vassals....the means used by the Jews [rabbinical leaders] to hinder the Christian mission were indirect. They made every effort to persuade the Roman authorities that Christians were not Jews or had ceased to be so and consequently had no right to the privileges of Judaism. They seem also sometimes to have created riots for the purpose of giving the impression that the existence of Christian communities was a perpetual cause of agitation and disorder. According to the early church, the Jews [certain elite rabbis at Yavne] organised a proper campaign to fight the preaching of the gospel. Justin Martyr, who mentions several times the way in which Christ and the Christians were cursed in the synagogue, when addressing the Jew Tryphon says as follows, 'When you knew that he (Jesus) was risen from the dead and had ascended into heaven, as the prophets foretold, you not only refused to repent but chose delegates whom you sent into the whole world to say that an impious heresy, that of the Christians, had appeared and to publish calumnies against us which people who do not know us repeat.' "[31]

Hugh Schonfield, in his book, *Saints Against Caesar*, sheds some light on Goguel's statements: "But already in the first century it was Rabbinical Judaism which had taken the initiative in trying to force the Nazarenes out of the Synagogue. The Romans no doubt did not in Palestine distinguish between one brand of Judaism and another until they came to appreciate that there was a body of Christians still inside the Jewish Community....when the emperor decreed a search for members of the house of David, and started a persecution of the Christians. According to Hegesippus there were some Jewish heretics who denounced certain of the Nazarenes to the authorities."[32]

Since such stigma and fear were laid at the feet of the believers by these intolerant rabbis, it made it easier for the Romans to justify feeding Christians to the lions for entertainment in their coliseums!

THE REAL McCOY

Incredibly, at least three of these rabbinical personalities[33] who persecuted the Jewish believers were Gentile converts to rabbinicism.

---

[31]Maurice Goguel, *The Birth of Christianity*. London: George Allen & Unwin Ltd., © 1953, pp. 468-470, used by permission. [ ] mine.

[32]Hugh Schonfield, *Saints Against Caesar, The Rise and Reactions of the First Christian Community*. London: Macdonald & Co. Ltd., © 1948, p. 181.

[33]Concerning Aquila and Akiva, Philip Carrington tells us: "In the new generation, which flourished from about 90 to the war of 131, the greatest name was that of Akiba. He was a proselyte of Arabian origin, a convert to the faith....Akiba was the tutor of Aquila, another proselyte, who was a native of Sinope in Pontus, like Marcion....Aquila made a new Greek translation of the Hebrew scriptures....It was intended for use in connexion with the theological methods of Aquila...." Philip Carrington, *The Early Christian Church,* Vol. 1, *The First Christian Century*. London: The Syndics of The Cambridge University Press, © 1957, pp. 426-427, used by permission. Aquila made a fraudulent Greek translation of the Old Testament, which removed Messianic prophecies, in a deliberate attempt to mislead millions of unsuspecting Greek-speaking Jews for hundreds of years to come. We will cover this in detail in our chapter 8 "The Messiah Conspiracy Continues in the *New* Old Testament." Carrington notes of Akiva's rebellion, which caused the death of well over one-half million Jews: "He [Akiva] was destined to ruin Israel by his military and political adventures; and yet, by his genius, he laid the foundations of the New Judaism which would survive the disaster for which he was largely responsible." Ibid. This disaster was one of the main causes of Jews being separated, alienated and isolated from Jesus to this day, and may have been a deliberate attempt to cause just such an alienation. Arnold Fruchtenbaum, one of the foremost leaders of Messianic Judaism, noted: "In 132 A.D. another Jewish revolt occurred against the Roman Empire, led by Bar Cochba. At the beginning of this revolt the Hebrew Christians joined the battle with their Jewish brethren, identifying with them as this was a national cause. As the revolt progressed, Rabbi Akiba declared Bar Cochba to be the Messiah. Hebrew Christians pulled out of the revolt inasmuch as they refused to acknowledge Bar Cochba as the Jewish Messiah. A complete break took place between

Ironically, they have become known as the sages of the Jewish religion, partially due to their persecution of those who were truly Jews and believed in Jesus as their Messiah. Their deeds have not been recognized by history, but I am sure will not go unnoticed by those who read this book!!

Too few Jewish laymen are aware of the fact that these men were not Jews,[34] and all too few Jewish believers in Jesus and Gentile fundamentalist Christians are aware of the fact that these men were the architects of a Messianic cover-up and campaign of persecution against the first Jews for Jesus.

The early believers in Jesus suffered much from these men. This scandal must be exposed in our generation, so we can all make a fair decision about who, where, and what Jesus was, is and will be, in eternity and in our present lives.

WHAT HAPPENED TO MESSIANIC JEWISH IDENTITY?

From the time of Bar Kochba, growing numbers of rabbis began to successfully strip away the Jewish identity of Messianic Jews, thus exposing them to ostracism by the Jewish community. The later development of the Gentile institution of Catholicism finished their dirty work for them by declaring the original Jews who believed in

---

the Jewish people and the Jewish Christians. From this time on, Jewish believers in the Messiahship of Jesus have been ostracized. If anyone can be blamed for turning Christianity into a 'Gentile religion,' that one is Bar Cochba. The complete break between church and synagogue was a result of the Bar Cochba revolt. Even after Bar Cochba Jews were turning to Jesus as the Messiah. Throughout the past nineteen centuries there have always been Jewish believers in the Messiahship of Jesus Christ. Sometimes the number has been small, but there has always been a number." Arnold Fruchtenbaum, "Jewishness and Hebrew Christianity." Englewood Cliffs, NJ: Sar Shalom Publications, p. 13, © used by permission. It is quite obvious, for those of you who are able to read between the lines, that Akiva and Bar Kochba knew they could not win a Jewish war against Rome, which controlled virtually the entire world at that time! It is also obvious that they both knew that the Jews who believed in Jesus would not fight under another "Messiah," aside from Jesus. Voilà! What better way to turn the world's Jews against Jesus-believing Jews, than to: 1. start a Jewish war; 2. proclaim its leader "Messiah"; 3. watch the Christian Jews pull out, and; 4. announce to Jews everywhere what traitors they were to Israel's national cause, thus resulting in their rejection for all time. Have you ever thought of it that way? Dr. Daniel Smith Christopher, the associate professor of theological studies at Loyola Mary Mount University, made an interesting statement regarding another reason why certain elements secretly wanted Jerusalem to be leveled. "Had Jerusalem been able to carry on, had it survived the Roman destruction...of the common era, I think that Christianity would have had a quite different character. There would have been a much stronger Judeo-Christian tradition based in Jerusalem, a much stronger and more heavily Jewish version of Christianity...." Daniel Smith Christopher, *Mysteries of the Bible*. Arts & Entertainment Network, Nov. 18, 1994.

[34]One ancient rabbinical writing says: "The rabbis taught: 'The proselytes and those who play with children hold back the Messiah.' This is understandable as far as the

Jesus to be "Christian heretics."[35] Paul Liberman notes: "Traditional Jews considered all believers Gentiles. On the other hand, Gentiles were uneasy with them as Jews. The Messianic Jew had no place to backslide to.

Meanwhile, with Gentile Christianity becoming established in its own right, the struggle began with Gentile and Jewish believers. The dispute essentially was over whether Jewish believers should be allowed to continue certain Jewish practices. A key conflict developed over the question of Resurrection Day and when it should be celebrated. It was not called Easter then. Gentile Christianity began to push for a strictly Sunday celebration; Messianic Jews disagreed. They thought it should be celebrated on the 14th day of Nisan, as the Bible states.

In 196 A.D., a council was held in Caesarea, but no Jewish representatives attended. This council decreed that Resurrection Day was to be celebrated on Sunday. Messianic Jews did not object to Sunday worship since they were worshipping on Sundays anyway. They went to the synagogue on Saturday and they worshipped among themselves on Sunday. The issue was whether the resurrection of the Messiah was to be celebrated on what we now call Easter Sunday, calculated from the 14th day of the month of Nisan which was the date of the Passover according to the Bible.

When Messianic Jews learned of the decision, they bolted. They considered Resurrection Day impossible to change because it was fixed by the Lord Himself. In fact, Jewish believers considered Passover to be even more important than the observance of the Sabbath.

In the third century, Gentile and Jewish believers began to split over the observance of Passover. The gulf widened....As the Gentiles gained dominance over the movement and the Jewish believers' position became less threatening, rabbinical restrictions softened....Meanwhile, the Gentile Christians were penetrating into Judea from the coast. Ever since the Greek invasion about 300 B.C., the entire coastal plain of Israel primarily had been Gentile. Most of the Gentile churches in the land were along the coastal strip.

---

proselytes are concerned, for R. Helbo said: 'The proselytes are as bad for Israel as a sore on the skin'....(B. Nid 13b)" Raphael Patai, *The Messiah Texts*, p. 59. Certainly this is pertinent here since these rabbis, who were mostly proselytes (converts to Judaism), set up barriers to prevent Jewish people from realizing Jesus is the Messiah. This has prevented a large Jewish acceptance which has delayed the return of Jesus until this day (see the book of Romans in the New Testament, verses 8:22-23; 11:15). No doubt, the writer of this wise but little known Jewish Talmudic commentary probably did not have Jesus in mind, yet we agree on the fact that "proselytes" hold back the Messiah, whom we, with good reason, believe to be Jesus.

[35]For greater detail, see our chapter 7, "The Messiah Conspiracy."

The fourth century marked the end of Messianic Jewish movement as such. Gentile Christian writers of this period included Apathames, Heggissipus and Jerome, all of whom were heavily influenced by Jewish believers. Among the Gentile leaders, there was a desire to consult with educated Jewish believers to discuss the theological issues. Jewish believers by this time, however, were less well-equipped theologically. They were considered less of a threat because of their diminished ability to defend their beliefs. A century earlier, when they had knowledge of the text, they were able to convince many people to believe in Yeshua.

But in the fourth century this did not occur as frequently as before. After that time the Messianic Jewish community practically stopped trying to evangelize other Jewish people. The believing Jewish community began to dwindle in numbers. In Gentile Christian writings, reference was made to Jews as 'them.' During the fourth century, St. Apathames even refused to acknowledge Jewish believers were Christians. He called them heretical because they celebrated Jewish festivals.

Obviously Messianic Judaism was flourishing within the established synagogues where these festivals were celebrated. It is difficult to visualize this occurring in a Gentile environment. As far as Gentile Christians were concerned....They considered the Nazarenes stupid for believing that biblical prophecies were to be literally fulfilled in the Jewish nation....The concerns of the Jewish believers were virtually unknown to a large part of the Gentile church. They were only known among the Gentile churches in the area that was by then called Palestine. In 325 A.D., the Council of Nicea re-emphasized the importance of keeping Easter on a Sunday. None of the bishops involved in the decision were Jewish. Several years later in the Council of Antioch, they went even further. It was determined that anyone who celebrated the 14th day of Nisan as the Passover was to be excommunicated. One of the church fathers criticized Jewish believers who attended synagogues during feasts, observances of the Sabbath....By the end of the fourth century, Messianic Judaism disappeared as a movement. From that point on, the history of the movement is a tableau of individual Jewish believers. The Messianic movement disappeared because of its inability to defend itself against majority forces—Rabbinical Judaism on the one hand; Gentile Christianity on the other."[36]

Scholar F. F. Bruce notes of the Messianic Jewish population: "As for the remnant of Jewish Christians, their subsequent history is

---

[36]Paul Liberman, *The Fig Tree Blossoms: Messianic Judaism Emerges*, pp. 40-43.

but scantily documented....alienated alike from orthodox Jews and catholic...."[37]

MEANWHILE, BACK AT THE TEMPLE IN AD 70, ONE MILLION WERE TRAPPED WITHIN THE WALLS AND CANNIBALISM OCCURRED

The terrible events which occurred at the fall of the second Temple as a result of the Messiah's rejection, were prophesied thousands of years earlier. Deuteronomy, the fifth book of the Bible, predicted cannibalism: "The tender and delicate woman among you, which would not adventure to set the sole of her foot upon the ground for delicateness and tenderness, her eye shall be evil toward the husband of her bosom, and toward her son, and toward her daughter, And toward her young one that cometh out from between her feet, and toward her children which she shall bear: for she shall eat them for want of all *things* secretly in the siege and straitness, wherewith thine enemy shall distress thee in thy gates" (Deut. 28:56-57 KJV).

The prophet Jeremiah later clarified: "The hands of compassionate women Boiled their own children; They became food for them Because of the destruction of the daughter of my people" (Lam. 4:10 NASB).

Jesus indicated that such things would occur soon after His Ascension. In His instructions to the daughters of Jerusalem on the way to His crucifixion, He said: " '...Daughters of Jerusalem, weep not for me, but weep for yourselves, and for your children. For, behold, the days are coming, in the which they shall say, Blessed *are* the barren, and the wombs that never bare, and the paps which never gave suck. Then shall they begin to say to the mountains, Fall on us; and to the hills, Cover us. For if they [Rome] do these things in a green tree [while relations are good with the Jewish nation], what shall be done in the dry?' " (Luke 23:28-31 KJV; [ ] mine).

The Jewish historian, Josephus, recorded these terrifying occurrences forewarned by Moses and Jesus. " 'This famine also will destroy us, even before that slavery comes upon us; yet are these seditious rogues more terrible than both the other. Come on; be thou my food, and be thou a fury to these seditious varlets and a bye-word to the world, which is all that is now wanting to complete the calamities of us Jews.' As soon as she had said this, she slew her son;

---

[37]F.F. Bruce, *New Testament History*, p. 391.

and then roasted him, and ate the one half of him, and kept the other half by her concealed."[38]

INSIGHT FROM A LEVITE

Zola Levitt, a contemporary Jewish believer in Jesus, comments on Jesus' warning to His people at that time: "They [the Jews who had rejected Messiah][39] should have listened to Jesus. The catastrophe of the destruction of the second Temple is almost beyond imagination.

At least 1.1 million Jews died in the five-month siege of Jerusalem by the Roman legions.

Approximately 600,000 starved to death in the streets. Their bodies were thrown over the city walls at the rate of 4,000 per day.

Josephus records cannibalism among the panicky and starving 3 million people crammed within the city walls.

***

[38]Josephus, *Wars of the Jews,* published in the compilation *Josephus: Complete Works*, book 4, chapter 3, verse 3, p. 579.

[39][ ] mine. The true Jewish believer in Jesus realized the prophecy of destruction given by Jesus in Luke 21:21 and heeded His warning to escape the impending doom. They were criticized for their wise evasion of danger, even though the alternative was to neglect Jesus' warning and die for nothing! Arnold Fruchtenbaum details this when he says: "In 68 A.D. the great Jewish revolt against the power of Rome broke out. Soon the Roman army came to Jerusalem and surrounded the city. The Zealots among the Jews took up arms against the Romans, but the Hebrew Christians did not. They were caught in a dilemma. They remembered a prophecy spoken by Jesus: *But when ye see Jerusalem compassed with armies, then know that her desolation is at hand. Then let them that are in Judea flee unto the mountains; and let them that are in the midst of her depart out; and let not them that are in the country enter therein* (Luke 21:21 NASB). According to this prophecy, the Temple and Jerusalem were both to be destroyed. The Hebrew Christians were told that when they saw the armies surrounding Jerusalem they were to flee. For this reason these Jewish believers refused to take up arms against the Romans. Not because they wished to betray the Jewish cause but because they felt bound to obey the words of Jesus of Nazareth. When the Roman legions temporarily lifted the siege of the city for a few days, the Hebrew Christians fled to the mountains in Trans-Jordan. Later the Romans returned and in 70 A.D. destroyed the city and the Temple. Because the Hebrew Christians fled the city earlier in the siege, they have since been called *Meshumod*, or *Meshumodim*, a Hebrew word meaning destroyers, or in modern terminology, traitors. The destruction of Jerusalem and the Temple was taken by the Hebrew Christians as a fulfillment of the words of Jesus and accepted by them as a further evidence of His Messiahship. This led many Jewish people to accept Jesus as their Messiah. Josephus, the ancient Jewish historian, described the Jewish followers of Jesus as numbering 'myriads,' a Greek word meaning a very great number." Arnold Fruchtenbaum, "Jewishness and Hebrew Christianity," pp. 11-12.

And the Temple was razed so thoroughly that our Lord's prophecy was completely fulfilled—not one stone was left upon another."[40]

GOLD-GLAZED STONES—PROPHECY FULFILLED

The prophecy Zola refers to is an exact one in which Jesus foretold that every stone of the Temple would be dismantled: "...as some spake of the temple, how it was adorned with goodly stones and gifts, he [Jesus] said, *As for* these things which ye behold, the days will come, in the which there shall not be left **one stone upon another,** that shall not be thrown down....And when ye shall see Jerusalem compassed with armies, then know that the desolation thereof is nigh....For these be the days of vengeance, that all things which are written may be fulfilled. But woe unto them that are with child, and to them that give suck, in those days! for there shall be great distress in the land, and wrath upon this people. And they shall fall by the edge of the sword, and shall be led away captive into all nations: and Jerusalem shall be trodden down of the Gentiles until the times of the Gentiles be fulfilled" (Luke 21:5-6, 20-24 KJV).

This was carried out to the letter because the gold which melted when the fire was accidentally[41] started in the Temple, ran down between the stones, necessitating the removal of all the stones to retrieve the gold.

PREDICTIONS OF THE DISPERSION—THE REASON FOR IT—AN AMAZEMENT TO ALL THE WORLD

Jesus pinpointed these prophetical events to occur in His generation as a result of His rejection as Messiah by Israel's leaders. He spoke of this time in which the Messiah was to come as the time of visitation (Dan. 9:26; Luke 19:41-44).

The prophet Ezekiel, hundreds of years earlier, also revealed God's foreknowledge of this dispersal and the understanding of the non-Jew. "And the heathen shall know that the house of Israel went into captivity for their iniquity: because they trespassed against me, therefore hid I my face from them, and gave them into the hand of their

---

[40]Zola Levitt and Thomas S. McCall, *Satan in the Sanctuary*, p. 171. This book deals with the Antichrist (Satan in the flesh) coming into a yet to be built sanctuary in the New Temple in Jerusalem—reading is a must for the ardent student of prophecy.

[41]See our *Vol. II*, chapter 25, "Saved, Saved from What?" The Temple was ordered to be saved by the Roman army because it was a crown jewel of the Middle East. A crazed Roman soldier threw a torch into the area containing the flammable olive oil used for the lamps, which ultimately fulfilled the prophecy of Jesus as recorded in Matthew 24.

enemies: so fell they all by the sword. According to their uncleanness and according to their transgressions have I done unto them, and hid my face from them" (Ezekiel 39:23-24 KJV).

The Old Testament writings of Jeremiah the prophet describe the details of where and why the first century dispersion of Israel began, in the person of the transgressors. "As for us [Jewish priests and leaders], our eyes as yet failed for our vain help: in our watching we have watched for a nation [Rome] *that* could not save *us*. They hunt our steps, that we cannot go in our streets: our end is near, our days are fulfilled; for our end is come. Our persecutors are swifter than the eagles of the heaven: they pursued us upon the mountains, they laid wait for us in the wilderness. The breath of our nostrils, the anointed [Messiah] of the LORD was taken in their pits, of whom **we** said, Under **his shadow** we shall live among the **heathen** [in the dispersion]" (Lamentations 4:17-20 KJV; [ ] and bold mine).

Ezekiel 39:27 and Lamantations 22 deal with Israel re-gathering in her land *after her punishment is accomplished.* This is, in itself, a miracle, which began in 1948 with the rebirth of Israel. This will be detailed in our chapter 18, "Israel—is Real."

THERE IS PLENTY IN VERSE 20

In Lamentations 4:20, Jeremiah mentions that religious Jews turned up their noses in the Messiah's shadow. This occurred while He was on the cross. By rejecting Him, they assured their fate of dispersion among the heathen nations, which occurred only thirty-seven years after the crucifixion. Interesting, to say the least. So many prophetical facts detailed in such a short line of Hebrew poetry—so many hundreds of years before they actually took place. Truly, there is no literature on Earth which can even attempt to surpass the Hebrew Scriptures and the New Testament.

THE RABBIS' CONSPIRACY ENDANGERED THE JEWS AND THE WORLD

Most of the priests and rabbis ignored these prophecies. They were not even impressed by the terrible judgment brought down by the destruction of the Temple. For 2000 years, the Jews and the world's people, by and large, had to pay the penalty of hunger, misery and war. What's more, even worse things lie in store (see our chapters 23 and 26). They hindered the salvation of the Jewish people and delayed the mission of redemption and peace that Jesus had in store for us when He came for the first time. They have perpetuated this delay through their Messiah

Conspiracy, which began at Yavne. This terrible act is the subject of our forthcoming chapter.

"They shall put you out of the synagogues: yea, the time cometh, that whosoever killeth you will think that he doeth God service."

Jesus, speaking to the Jews who would believe in Him
in the generation to come (John 16:2 KJV), predicted 33 AD

"Give me Jabneh and its wisemen, and the family chain of Rabban Gamaliel."

The Talmud Gittin, 56. Y. b. Zakkai's request of Gen. Vespasian, 69 AD;
Jabneh (Yavne) was the location of the Messiah Conspiracy's contrivance

"How shall we maintain ourselves against the Minim [Messianic Jewish Christians]?"[1] The students of Rabbi Joshua at his deathbed, circa 135 AD

"...you appointed chosen men and sent them into all the civilized world, proclaiming that 'a certain godless and lawless sect has been raised by one Jesus of Galilee....the priests and teachers of your people have caused His name to be profaned and blasphemed throughout the whole earth."[2]

Justin Martyr, Christian philosopher, 135 AD

"The Jewish practice of excommunication during the period under consideration is **shrouded in mystery** despite all that has been written on the subject."

Douglas Hare, assistant professor of the New Testament,
Pittsburgh Theological Seminary, 1967

"I have been accumulating research for a number of years for a book...thanks to Philip, I have some incredible material to write this....He...has done research...and contributed incredible documentation for it. The book will be called *The Messiah Conspiracy*. And I really am thankful to Philip...he's got a simple-hearted purpose, that's to love the Lord and serve Him."[3]

Hal Lindsey, best-selling Christian author, 1986

The discovery of the Messiah Conspiracy to the unique new depth you will see in this and the next two chapters, is the product of over twelve years of relentless research on our part—enjoy! Author Philip Moore, 1996

7

THE MESSIAH CONSPIRACY

Vapors have been rising from this terrible conspiracy for two millennia. Various historians have gotten a whiff here and a taste there of how the rabbis sought to cover up the early evidence of Jewish

[1]Hugo Mantel, *Studies in the History of the Sanhedrin.* Cambridge, MA: Harvard University Press, © 1961, p. 191, used by permission. [ ] mine.

[2]A. Lukyn Williams, D.D., *Justin Martyr, The Dialogue With Trypho.* India: Diocesan Press, © 1930, pp. 224, 242.

[3]Quoted from a personal tape made while on tour in Israel with Hal Lindsey, during a dinner tribute. This included a word of thanks to the author for doing research for Dr. Lindsey (referenced on our front cover). We hope that Hal's next book will be the one mentioned.

belief in Jesus' claimed Messiahship of Israel. However, we have never seen these bits and pieces put together in a comprehensive chronological order. Moreover, in studying this subject, one would practically have to become a biblical scholar.

One of the aims of this chapter is to present a comprehensive overview of how and why this rabbinical plot to deny the Messiahship of Jesus began and just what the purpose was. It is our hope that we will inform the layman and casual reader of one of history's greatest secrets, which has been a blinding force for the Jew thus far, as to who Jesus said He was, and what He came to do for all mankind.

TWENTY CENTURIES OF DECEPTION

For nearly twenty centuries, rabbis of all branches of contemporary Judaism, which was reconstructed at Yavne, have been successful in convincing nine-tenths of world Jewry that Jesus is not for the Jews and that He is not worthy of Messianic consideration because such a consideration would be at the expense of "Jewish heritage and identity." Of course, nothing could be further from the truth!

It is our hope that all of our readers will recognize the magnitude of this problem through the evidence we are about to present! Remember, a deception can be best corrected only after it is fully understood.

We believe, after you have read all of our documentation in relation to the Birkat ha-Minim (BHM) and other devices used by the first century rabbis to excommunicate the Jewish Christians, that we will be able to dispel the status quo.[4] As Douglas Hare has well said: "The Jewish practice of excommunication during the period under consideration is *shrouded in mystery*. Despite all that has been written on the subject."[5]

YAVNE'S MESSIAH CONSPIRACY—UNTIL NOW, NO ONE HAS DARED TO CALL IT A *CONSPIRACY*

Conspiracy? Was there a conspiracy concerning the Messiah nearly 2000 years ago? Are the rabbis of Yavne responsible? If **there**

---

[4]By this statement the author is not implying that he is uncovering all, but is rather partially removing the present veil of the secret conspiratorial activities of certain rabbis against the Jewish Christians of this period, through heavily and intensely researched documentation involving some relatively recent archaeological discoveries.

[5]Douglas Hare, *The Theme of Jewish Persecution of Christians in the Gospel According to St. Matthew*. London: Cambridge University Press, © 1967, p. 48. Italics mine.

was and if **they** are, what can you do to expose and remedy the consequences of their actions?

All through history there have been blatant lies about the Jewish people plotting to take over the world,[6] but in truth, the Jewish people have not been the conspirators, rather they have been the victims of a conspiracy perpetrated upon them by a small group of elitist rabbis who gathered at Yavne nearly 2000 years ago. These individuals set out to isolate the Jew from any possible opportunity to hear of or make a decision about Jesus' Messianic claims, free of guilt and prejudice.

Hal Lindsey, foremost prophetic author and television personality, whose books have sold millions, commented on this event at Yavne: "In 70 AD when Titus conquered the city...a million and a half Jews were killed....The surviving rabbis who managed to escape went to a place called Yavne on the coast of Israel, and there they hammered out a basic rabbinic way of teaching that would...be the basic way of teaching in the synagogues for the next nineteen some hundred years on how the Jews would live without the Temple and without sacrifice. In Yavne, they hammered out the basis of rabbinic Judaism....the curse was this—that at the heart of this rabbinic teaching was a systematic teaching with a vengeance to isolate and insulate the Jewish person completely from Jesus—**completely**. And to explain away the Messianic prophecies—to explain away the significance of Jesus' claims—to pervert, to distort, and down through the centuries this has been done....there was a tradition that helped the race survive. On the other hand, it helped blind them to the very thing [an acceptance of Jesus as Messiah][7] that could have meant a secession of the suffering—that could have meant a secession of the dispersion."[8]

---

[6]A classic example is *The Protocols of the Elders of Zion*, a lie which presumes to detail, step by step, the idea that the Jews have been, and are now contriving plans to take over the world by inter-marriage with ultra-rich families, economics, or other means. Even today this book is heavily circulated among Arab countries. Jewish Messianic scholar, Michael Brown has noted: "Saudi leaders have followed in Abdul Aziz' foosteps; King Faisal highly praised the notoriously anti-Jewish book called *The Protocols of the Eders of Zion*, (conclusively proved to be a forged work of lying propaganda) and gave it to all his international guests to read. In 1972, he stated that 'all countries should wage war against the Zionists.' " Michael L. Brown, *Our Hands are Stained with Blood: The Tragic Story of the "Church" and the Jewish People*. Shippensburg, PA: Destiny Image Publishers, © 1992, p. 54, used by permission. Available through Messiah Biblical Institute, POB 7163, Gaithersburg, MD, USA 20898-7163. Tel. (301) 977-0156. For an in-depth understanding of the evil lies and purpose behind such satanic literature as the *Protocols*, we also suggest you read *The History of a Lie, "The Protocols of the Wise Men of Zion,"* by Herman Bernstein, and; *The Truth about the Forged Protocols of the Elders of Zion*, by Lucien Wolf.

[7]We believe that once there is a national Jewish acceptance of Jesus as Messiah, He will completely restore the world's Jews to Israel and set up a worldwide Messianic Kingdom

TIME IN REVERSE—2000 YEARS—LET'S GO BACK TO THE FUTURE FORWARD OF THE FIRST CENTURY

Outside, there is a man in a coffin waiting to be carried out of the city of Jerusalem. This man is not dead, nor is he Dracula. He is none other than *Rabbi Yohanan ben Zakkai* carefully being smuggled out to see Vespasian, who will secure Yavne for him, a small coastal town in Israel. It will be in this city that the most devious conspiracy of all time will be devised by Yohanan and his colleagues, Samuel the Small, Gamaliel, Aquila, and Joshua, to name only a few.

This **conspiracy** concerned the Jewish people and the purposeful intention to isolate them from exposure to and knowledge of the identity of the Messiah. The prime instrument in this effort was the Birkat ha-Minim, which was a benediction cursing the believers! An obscure passage of the Talmud reveals: "Our Rabbis taught: Simeon ha-Pakuli arranged the eighteen benedictions in order before Rabban Gamaliel in Jabneh. Said Rabban Gamaliel to the Sages: Can any one among you frame a benediction relating to the *Minim?* Samuel the Lesser arose and composed it."[9]

A few lines above this record in the Berakoth section of the Talmud are the words: "These eighteen are really nineteen?—R. Levi said: The benediction relating to the *Minim* was instituted in Jabneh." The Talmud's footnote to Jabneh clearly says, "After the rest." Thus, we see that this ancient sacred prayer reported to have been arranged by Ezra,[10] was doctored to include a curse against the defenseless

---

of peace. See our chapters 29 and 30, entitled, "After Messiah Arrives and Ends the War—Paradise" and "New Heavens and a New Earth." Jesus said, "until" in Matthew 23:39. Therefore it is theoretically possible for Israel to accept Jesus at any time and thereby initiate His Second Coming. However, according to prophecy, it is impossible, for they will only call on Him when the great Arab/Russian invasion occurs at the end of the seven-year Tribulation yet to begin at some point in our near future. The Bible's offer of the Advent of Messiah at Israel's anytime acceptance is indeed a bona fide offer. However, we know from prophecy its actual time is at Israel's last possible moment of distress, God's appointed time (Hos. 5:15). Even the rabbinical writings show this. The ancient rabbinic work known as Midrash Rabba maintains: "A time has been appointed by God for the coming of Messiah. Yet if Israel but repent [of] his sins, the glorious redemption will be hastened, and Messiah will make His appearance before the appointed time. (Exod. Rabba 25)." [ ] mine. Interesting, isn't it?

[8]Hal Lindsey, *From Abraham to the Middle East Crisis*, © used by permission. [ ] mine. This audio tape series is available through Hal Lindsey Ministries, POB 4000, Palos Verdes, CA, USA 90274.

[9]*The Babylonian Talmud*, Berakoth 28b-29a, p. 175.

[10]Attorney Walter Chandler documents the mutilation of this wonderful 2500-year-old piece of Jewish literature: "As soon as Samuel Hakaton had composed this malediction, it was inserted as an additional blessing in the celebrated prayer of the synagogue, the 'Shemonah-Essaria' (the eighteen blessings). These blessings belonged to the time of Ezra—that is to say, five centuries before the Christian era; and every Jew has to recite it

Minim/Nazarenes by Gamaliel in Yavne, the town secured by Yohanan.

Y.B.Z. —HOW DID HE GET FROM JERUSALEM TO YAVNE[11] AND WHAT DID HE DO WHEN HE ARRIVED?

Solomon Grayzel elaborated on the details of how Y.B.Z. obtained Yavne and the academy. He mentions: "When he saw the end of Jerusalem approaching, Johanan decided that the time had come for him to act. A famous story[12] tells what happened after this. Some of Johanan's pupils announced that their master had died and asked permission to carry his body for burial outside of Jerusalem. Theirs was a dangerous mission, doubly dangerous, since the suspicious Zealots were on one side of the walls and the cruel Romans on the other. But they managed to carry the living Johanan beyond the lines of danger, where he rose out of his coffin and made his way to Vespasian, the Roman general....Vespasian knew that the man before him was a very influential man, whose good will would have restraining effect upon the moderates among the Jews in and outside of Palestine....One can imagine Vespasian's astonishment when all that Johanan requested was permission to open a school in a little town by the seacoast which the Jews called Jabne and the Romans Jamnia. Vespasian...must have thought the request ridiculous and Johanan a foolish old man. He certainly would not have believed that the school would save the Jewish people...and prove, more than any other single event in history, that Spirit is mightier than Sword."[13]

Because Vespasian granted Yohanan's request for Yavne, Vespasian also arranged safe passage for Yohanan and these rabbis to this coastal town where they formulated their work leading to the excommunication of Jewish Christians from Judaism. The results of their misguided and irresponsible actions are still echoing in our twentieth century, in that many Jews think it is taboo to even consider Jesus' Messianic claims. In the minds of these rabbis (including many of their modern contemporaries), part of saving the Jewish people involved separating them from their faith in Jesus. This was not and is

---

daily. St. Jerome...says: '*The Jews anathematize three times daily in their synagogue the name of the Christian....*' " Walter M. Chandler, *The Trial of Jesus, From a Lawyer's Standpoint*, Illustrated Edition, Vol. II, p. 149.

[11]This author uses the spelling Yavne, because it appears on a highway sign in Israel directing the way to its ruins. Other spellings include Jabne, Jabneh, Jamnia, Yavneh and Yavnah.

[12]The story he mentioned is in the Gittin 56 section of the Babylonian Talmud.

[13]Solomon Grayzel, *A History of the Jews.* Philadelphia: The Jewish Publication Society of America, © 1970, pp. 194-195, used by permission.

not true. What it is, is extremely misleading, wrong and evil (as we will document later in this and the next two chapters)!

HOW YOHANAN'S CALCULATED *GUESS*, WHICH HE CLAIMED WAS A "PROPHECY," PAID OFF, RESULTING IN THE GENERAL AWARDING HIM YAVNE—TEDIOUS

Max Dimont, in his book, *Jews, God and History*, lends incredible insight into how an old bearded rabbi (Y.B.Z.) was able to dupe a fearless Roman general into giving him Yavne, the town used for Judaism's reformulation, where the Messiah Conspiracy took place! Of course, Yohanan was not a prophet or a writer of part of the Bible, but a shrewd and realistic rabbi obsessed with preserving the people of Judaism under one unassimilated roof.

The keys to his plan were playing dead and making a fantastic guess cleverly disguised as a prophecy. As Dimont documents of the time: "[In] Besieged Jerusalem....People were dying by the thousands of starvation and pestilence. Leaving the city was forbidden on pain of death. Suspected Peace Party members were thrown over the wall by the Zealots, who held as tight a grip inside the city as the Romans did outside. To outwit the Zealots, Jochanan ben Zakkai resorted to a ruse. He took a few of his disciples into his confidence and outlined his plan to them. The disciples then went out into the street, tore their clothes according to the plan, and in mournful voices announced that their great rabbi, Jochanan ben Zakkai, had died of the plague. They asked and received permission from the Zealot authorities to bury the revered rabbi outside the gates of Jerusalem to check the spread of pestilence in the city. With a show of great grief, clad in sackcloth and ashes, the disciples carried a sealed coffin with the live Jochanan ben Zakkai in it out of Jerusalem and to the tent of Vespasian, where they opened the coffin and the rabbi stepped out....The general waited, and the rabbi spoke. He had a prophecy and a request to make, said the rabbi. The general indicated he would listen. Boldly Jochanan ben Zakkai prophesied that Vespasian would soon be emperor, and in such an eventuality, would Emperor Vespasian grant him, Jochanan ben Zakkai, and a few of his disciples, permission to establish a small school of Jewish learning....Stunned by the prophecy and surprised by the modesty of the request—which to a soldier like Vespasian made no sense—he promised the favor would be granted provided the prophecy came true.

It was not superstition on which Rabbi ben Zakkai had based his prediction. He had made a shrewd and calculated guess. That same year Nero had committed suicide. As the Romans had no laws of succession, it stood to reason that eventually the throne would go to the strongest man, who, in ben Zakkai's mind, was Vespasian. In that same year, three political and military hacks held the throne of Rome in succession, each assassinated after a few months in office. Jochanan ben Zakkai had guessed right. In the year 69 the Roman Senate offered the throne to Vespasian. Unlettered and superstitious as Vespasian was, he could not help but be awed by the bearded rabbi's prophecy. He kept his promise to Zakkai, who now founded the first yeshiva—Jewish academy of learning—in the town of Jabneh, north of Jerusalem. It was destined to play a central role in Jewish survival."[14]

THE RABBIS, FROM THEIR YAVNE HIDE-AWAY, HAVE DECEIVED THE JEWISH PEOPLE AND DELAYED REDEMPTION TO THIS VERY DAY

Now that you have been briefed on Yavne and Y.B.Z., back to the doctored curse of the conspiracy. We believe this conspiracy is the most heinous of all time, because in a sense, it has delayed world redemption until this very date. It has kept us from realizing the fruits of the world to come and the New Jerusalem,[15] which will only be brought in by the Messiah Jesus at His Second Coming, as we find in the New Testament book of Romans: "For all creation is waiting patiently and hopefully for that future day when God will resurrect his children....For we know that even the things of nature, like animals and plants, suffer in sickness and death as they await this great event. And even we Christians, although we have the Holy Spirit within us as a foretaste of future glory, also groan to be released from pain and suffering. We, too, wait anxiously for that day when God will give us our full rights as his children, including the new bodies he has promised us—bodies that will never be sick again and will never die" (Rom. 8:19, 22-23 *The Living Bible*).[16]

---

[14]Max I. Dimont, *Jews, God and History*. New York: The New American Library of World Literature, Inc., Signet Books, © 1962, pp. 103-104, used by permission. [ ] mine.

[15]In Hebrew, *olam haba* (world to come) and *Yerushalim hadash* (New Jerusalem).

[16]The rest of this passage in Romans ends on quite a positive note for Israel and the world. It reads: "...think how much greater a blessing the world will share in later on when the Jews, too, come to Christ....And how wonderful it will be when they become Christians [Messianic believers in their Messiah]!" (Rom. 11:12, 15 *The Living Bible*). *The Living Bible* simplifies the more difficult verses of certain English translations of the New Testament. However, when it says Christians, it may be confusing to some Jews who do not realize that the word Christians does not designate a religion foreign to Judaism. This word is actually derived from the Greek *Christos*, which means "Messiah" (in Hebrew *Meshiak*), predicted by the Old Testament in our true faith. *Ian* simply means "one who follows Christ," i.e. Messiah! "...When God turned away from them it meant that he turned to the rest of the world to offer his salvation; and now it is even more wonderful when the Jews come to Christ. It will be like dead people coming back to life. And since Abraham and the prophets are God's people, their children will be too. For if

These elitist rabbis have instilled identity crises and guilt trips by using the formula of the Birkat ha-Minim to detect,[17] ostracize and alienate believers. They have succeeded, even into our modern time, in making Jesus a stranger to the Jewish heart. The Bible teaches that only after[18] the Jews have believed in Him as Messiah, as foretold by the holy prophetic writings of the Hebrews known to us as the Old Testament (Zechariah 12:10; Romans 8:19-23; 11:11-12, 25-26), can world redemption and the prophesied Second Coming of Jesus to initiate this begin[19] (Isaiah 11:6-8).

What these rabbis did from their little hide-out at Yavne, in their attempt to destroy the Christian (Messianic) faith among the Jews, drastically affected the lives of everyone on planet Earth during the last 2000 years. When you finish reading this book and clearly see exactly what they did, you will begin to see how to remedy and reverse this conspiracy which has affected us all! That remedy will involve using cautious knowledge and loving sensitivity to inform your Jewish friends about the misinformation given them, and to show them, using the prophecies of the Bible, that Jesus, *Yeshua*,[20] is the Messiah who loves them and alone can bring redemption!

***

---

the roots of the tree are holy, the branches will be too....I want you to know about this truth from God, dear brothers, so that you will not feel proud and start bragging. Yes, it is true that some of the Jews have set themselves against the Gospel now, but this will last only until all of you Gentiles have come to Christ—those of you who will. And then all Israel will be saved. Do you remember what the prophets said about this? 'There shall come out of Zion a Deliverer....' " (Rom. 11:15-16, 25-26 *The Living Bible*; [ ] mine). Though this conspiracy and consequent Jewish rejection is wrong, God is presently allowing it to continue to a lesser degree, as long as non-Jews are converting to Jesus!

[17]Ken Carroll, Ph.D. of religion at Southern Methodist University in Dallas, quite accurately pointed this out regarding first century Jewish believers in Jesus: "Since they did not withdraw from the community of Israel, they had to be cast out. This end was to be obtained by the various devices for the detection of the *Minim*—the Formula against the *Minim*." Ken Carroll, Ph.D., *The Fourth Gospel and the Exclusion of Christians*, p. 20.

[18]See our *Vol. II*, chapter 22, "Only the Family of David Can Welcome the Son of David Back to the City of David," which illustrates the Messianic parallel of David in II Samuel, as it relates to the return of Jesus, only *after* His brothers receive Him. This interesting material is from Michael Brown's book, *Our Hands are Stained with Blood: The Tragic Story of the "Church" and the Jewish People*.

[19]We are not talking about the first part of the Second Coming known as the Rapture, which could happen at any time, when Jesus will save Israel. This occurs seven years before His kingdom begins (see our chapter 25, "The Rapture Factor"). It will be between the Rapture and the second phase of the Second Coming, seven years afterward, that the majority of Jews (including the 144,000) will begin to realize that Jesus is the Messiah.

[20]*Yeshua* ישוע is Jesus' Hebrew name.

Tomb of Rabbi Yohanan ben Zakkai in Tiberias, Israel.

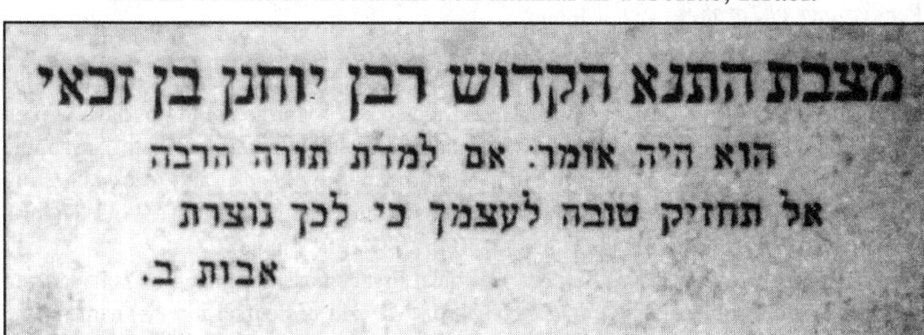

מצבת התנא הקדוש רבן יוחנן בן זכאי
הוא היה אומר: אם למדת תורה הרבה
אל תחזיק טובה לעצמך כי לכך נוצרת
אבות ב.

JUST WHO WAS YOHANAN BEN ZAKKAI? WHO WAS HE TO PUT IN HIS TWO CENTS?

Let's look at Yohanan ben Zakki's true outlook as he lay on his deathbed: "In his last hours, Rabban Yohanan ben Zakkai kept weeping out loud [to his disciples]....'Do I then go to appear before a king of flesh and blood, whose anger if he should be angry with me, is but of this world?....I go rather to appear before the King of Kings of Kings, the Holy One, blessed be he, whose anger, if he should be angry with me, is of this world, and the world to come....Moreover I have before me two roads, one to Paradise and one to Gehenna, and I know not whether he will sentence me to Gehenna or admit me into Paradise.' "[21]

Yohanan ben Zakkai's statements about his fear of *Gehenna* (Hebrew for Hell), are a far cry from those of Yohanan ben Zebedee[22] (better known as the apostle John) who emphatically stated to us for all time: "And the witness is this, that God has given us eternal life, and this life is in His Son. He who has the Son has the life; he who does not have the Son of God does not have the life. These things I have written to you who believe in the name of the Son of God, in order that you may **know** [not hope or think or doubt] that you have eternal life" (I John 5:11-13 NASB; [ ] mine).

The apostle John knows that the words he uttered in the New Testament are true because he witnessed firsthand[23] both the resurrection of Yeshua ben Joseph[24] (Jesus), who gave the promise of eternal life, and the empty tomb from which He rose.[25] Yohanan ben Zakkai, though he was a scholar and chief reformer of what became modern Judaism, is still in the tomb which bears his name in Hebrew, as you see pictured.

***

---

[21]Jacob Neusner, *First-Century Judaism in Crisis, Yohanan Ben Zakkai and the Renaissance of Torah*, p. 199. [ ] mine.

[22]The apostle John was also called rabbi (John 3:26).

[23]The apostle John, who wrote the fourth book of the New Testament, attests to his witness of Thomas actually touching the resurrected Jesus, for he could not have written about it in the present tense if he had not actually seen it. John tells us that: "...saith he [Jesus] to Thomas, 'Reach hither thy finger, and behold my hands; and reach hither thy hand, and thrust *it* into my side: and be not faithless, but believing.' And Thomas answered...'My Lord and my God' " (John 20:27-28 KJV; [ ] mine).

[24]Yeshua ben Joseph is Jesus' Hebrew rabbinical first century designation. Yohanan ben Zebedee is John's. In Hebrew, *ben* means "son of" and of course, the last name is the father's first name.

[25]As we saw in our chapter 5, "Which Prophecies Did Jesus Fulfill?"

A RISEN RABBI'S WORDS ARE SUPERIOR TO A DEAD ONE'S

These words, "I know not whether he will sentence me to Gehenna [Hell],"[26] expressed by the one who is considered the greatest reformer of modern Orthodox Judaism, are very shaky! They bring to mind the words of Jesus: "A disciple is not above his teacher...." (Matt. 10:24 NASB).

Can we really follow a man who has no real security, who is himself groping in the dark? Jesus also said: "...if the blind lead the blind, both shall fall into the ditch" (Matt. 15:14 KJV).

The truth is that the Bible gives us absolutes whereby we may know if we are headed for eternal Paradise or eternal Hell. Both are formative tenets of ancient Judaism.[27] This is something about which Yohanan ben Zakkai had no peace. We know this because in his last hours he was crying out on his deathbed in fear of where he might end up—Hell!

A RABBI WHO SURVIVED HITLER'S HOLOCAUST THROWS OFF THE SHACKLES OF Y. B. Z. TO EMBRACE THE BIBLE'S TRUTH OF MESSIAH

A rabbinical student and survivor of Hitler's Holocaust, Rachmiel Frydland, read these words of Y.B.Z.: "...I know not whether he will sentence me to Gehenna [Hell] or admit me into Paradise." Mr. Frydland had been taught that this prominent rabbi: "...saved Judaism from extinction after the destruction of the temple in Jerusalem in the year A.D. 70."[28] His reaction to the rabbi's expression of insecurity and doubt regarding something as important as your eternal destiny, was: "If this Rabbi Yohanan was not certain, what hope was there for me?"[29]

Rachmiel Frydland left his rabbinical school, Yeshivat Emek Halacha, in Warsaw, Poland, to investigate who the Messiah might be, using the Bible as his guide. He became one of the leaders of modern Messianic Judaism; Judaism which accepts Jesus for who He said He was, namely the Jewish Messiah. He wrote a comprehensive biography[30] regarding his life of survival and discovery, which we

---

[26] [ ] mine.

[27] See our *Vol. II*, chapter 33, "The Reality of the Ancient Jewish Acknowledgment of Hell, Covered Up Until Now."

[28] Rachmiel Frydland, *When Being Jewish Was a Crime*. Nashville: Thomas Nelson Publishers, © 1978, p. 66, used by permission.

[29] Ibid, p. 67.

[30] Frydland's biography is available through Messianic Literature Outreach, POB 37062, Cincinnati, OH, USA 45222.

believe is a must for all who inquire into the true history of the Nazi Holocaust. His book, *When Being Jewish Was a Crime*, details the many times he was almost killed in Poland during the Nazi persecutions and how, as a result of his religious search, he realized Jesus was the Messiah. He details that many who died in German ovens were Messianic Jews who believed in Jesus. There is an untold story of the many Jews who secretly believed in Jesus[31] in the camps, which history has yet to record!

The sign reads: "Rabbi Gamaliel, the president, the son of Rabbi Shimon, the son of Old Hillel from the line of the presidents, from the seed of King David from the great sages (*tannim*), the wisest people in Yavne."

---

[31]See our *Vol. II*, chapter 21, "Nazis Murdered Over One-Quarter Million Messianic Jews for Jesus—Unknown to Most." This chapter contains the testimony of Rachmiel Frydland and Arnold Fruchtenbaum, Ph.D.

OUR VISIT TO THE GAMALIEL TOMB IN YAVNE

Behind the plaque on this wall, in the building you see pictured on the opposite page, lies the late Rabbi Gamaliel who has long since passed into eternity. Rabbi Gamaliel, according to the Talmud, contrived and began a consorted effort to drive hundreds of thousands of Jews who believed in Jesus from the synagogue.

In the early centuries shortly after Jesus left the earth, Rabbi Gamaliel helped to reconstruct Judaism into a new form of cultural cement which denied many biblical doctrines previously taught and accepted as truly Jewish and Scriptural within the former biblically based Jewish faith. He initiated this effort with the Birkat ha-Minim in a coordinated plan to destroy the acceptance of those who were Jewish and who had believed in the Messiah. His new mainstream Judaism, which continues today, is a tragedy for the many who are kept from the wonderful world of Messiah's assurance, joy and hope! I will never forget the spirit of gloom which overwhelmed me when I visited Gamaliel's tomb.

THE BAKER PAPER—UNFORESEEN REVELATIONS CONCERNING RABBI GAMALIEL AND HIS BIRKAT HA-MINIM

Julie Baker, whom I had the pleasure of meeting through Mike Bentley in Israel a few years ago in 1987, provides interesting insight into the Birkat ha-Minim. She notes in her paper, "Yavneh: Achievements and Significance," concerning Judaism's first century reconstruction: "It was Gamaliel who 'introduced the policy of exclusion and brought about the permanent fissure in Judaism between Rabbinic Judaism and Christianity.' The primary way Gamaliel II accomplished this was by instituting the Birkat ha-Minim which was added to the 18 Benedictions. These were recited in the synagogues and so the purpose of the 19th Benediction was to keep the Minim out of the synagogue by making them very uncomfortable. Ultimately, it did just that. The word minim is a general term for heretics but a number of 'tannaitic restrictions directed against minim clearly refer to Jewish Christians, as can be shown by their context and date.' Jerome, as well as a Genizah fragment found in 1925 also support this contention. This shows that 'the Sages at Jamnia regarded the Jewish Christians as a menace sufficiently serious to warrant a liturgical innovation.'[32]

---

[32] Julie Baker's source was Phillip Sigal, *The Emergence of Contemporary Judaism.*

The Sages at Yavneh also took other actions to thwart the influence of these Messianic Jews. The Septuagint was set aside because it had been taken over by the Greek converts to Christianity as well as the Jewish believers. So a new translation was begun by Aquila of Pontus....Social ostracism was also practiced and Jewish people were told not to sell to Jewish believers or take anything from them or teach them or obtain healing from them.

There are a number of factors that account for these drastic measures taken against Jewish believers....The fact that in the decades since 30 CE the Jewish believers had been having a fair amount of success in spreading their beliefs was a reason to worry. When approximately 20% of the people of Israel become adherents to a new way, this was something to cause consternation especially later with the presence of the spiritual void brought about by the Destruction of the Temple. It is not surprising to see that the leaders at Yavneh reacted in a hostile fashion to people they believed were inhibiting their ability to put the nation back together again."[33]

JULIE BAKER'S CORRECT CONCLUSION SHOULD LEAD US TO PRAY THAT THE JEW RETURNS TO THE BIBLICALLY BASED TRUTH!

Julie points out that Y.B.Z. deposed the priesthood and sacrifice. She quotes a statement made by Rabbi Phillip Sigal,[34] which is: "Yohannan ben Zakkai did nothing less than restate Judaic theology." She correctly concludes that in the rabbis' attempt at Yavne to lock out Jewish Christians and substitute their brand of "replacement Judaism," the Jewish faith from that time on was removed from its true biblical base.

Julie notes: "Yavneh did allow Judaism to survive only in a drastically different form. The Sages passed measures to hold onto the land and to build up the economy so that the people could get back on their feet monetarily. But more than anything the Sages changed the theology and structure of Judaism and moved it further from its Biblical basis. Rabbinical Judaism had been born and this is the shape Judaism would keep, with slight modifications, to the present day."[35]

We pray that this book, along with its newly uncovered documentation concerning the ancient truth of Judaism and its prophetic fulfillments found in the New Testament, and the Jews who

---

[33]Julie Baker, "Yavneh: Achievements and Significance," submitted to Dr. Goldberg at The Moody Bible Institute of Chicago, April 16, 1986, used by permission.

[34]Baker's source was Phillip Sigal, *The Emergence of Contemporary Judaism*, p. 23.

[35]Julie Baker, "Yavneh: Achievements and Significance," April 16, 1986.

believed in Jesus as the Messiah, will help to restore the Jewish faith in its true and biblical[36] form before the Antichrist makes his entrance into humanity and deceives Jews wholesale with his predicted false claims of Messianic identity (see our chapter 23, "The False Messiah Armilus Equals Antichrist")!

MIN AND *MINIM*

Before we go into greater detail about the Birkat ha-Minim, let's see who the *minim* were. What are *min* and *minim*? Most of you who just read these words are probably scratching your heads and saying, "Does this writer have all of his marbles, or not?" I admit these words sound very strange to twentieth century ears. However, they have had great significance in the past, especially the first century. In reality, they are Hebrew acronyms coined by the early rabbis to identify Jews who accepted Jesus as Messiah. This was the so-called blessing for the believers in Jesus from Nazareth which was inserted into the eighteen benediction Amidah synagogue prayer for the purpose of driving a schism between early Jews for Jesus and the other non-believing sects of Judaism.

MIN AND *MINIM*—WHAT DO THEY *REALLY* MEAN?

The acronyms *min* and *minim* mean just this in plain English: "m" (*mem* מ) stands for the Hebrew word *Maamine*, which means "to believe"; the "i" (*ude* י) stands for the Hebrew word *Yeshua,* which means "Jesus"; the "n" (*noon* נ) stands for the Hebrew word *Nazaret* (נצרת), in English, Nazareth. This is the town in northern Israel, a despised town, by the way, where Jesus grew up; a fact predicted by the prophet Isaiah.[37] The "im" (*ude mem* ים) simply makes the Hebrew word *min* plural. It was used to refer to a group of believers.

You now know one of the hidden secrets of history. We know who the *minim* were and still are today: *Mem* = believers; *ude* = in

---

[36] In an article entitled "Sparks Fly Over 'Messianic' Congregation," a rabbi by the name of Cohen commented: " 'They [Messianic Jews] are basing their approach on what they perceive as a biblical approach and bypassing rabbinic Judaism, which is not the Jewish thing to do. We are a rabbinic religion....' " Rick Hellman, "Sparks Fly Over 'Messianic' Congregation," *The Kansas City Jewish Chronicle*, Apr. 16, 1993, p. 18A. [ ] mine. These words still reflect the standard of most rabbis. Let us work hard to get our Bibles out and enlighten them, as the Scriptures command—in love!

[37] Matthew 2:23 says: "And he came and dwelt in a city called Nazareth: that it might be fulfilled which was spoken by the prophets. He shall be called a Nazarene" (KJV). This verse refers to Isaiah 11:1, where Christ is spoken of as a *netzer* (or "rod") out of the stem of Jesse. Few realize that in the time of Jesus, Nazareth was despised. This verse also refers to Jesus being despised, as was predicted of the Messiah in Isaiah 53.

Jesus; *noon* = from the despised town of Nazareth; *ude mem* = plural, a group of them.

JOCZ AND DERENBOURGH CONFIRM *MINIM* IS A RABBINIC "PUN" FOR BELIEVERS!

Though there are some who deny that *minim* is an acronym for believers, Professor Jakob Jocz of Wycliffe College in Toronto correctly identifies the word and meaning of the Hebrew word *minim* with what we believe to be the truth.

Minim were Jewish believers in Jesus; the name is the initials in the form of an acronym for "believers in Jesus from Nazareth." Jocz quotes the authority Derenbourgh as evidence. In the words of Professor Jocz: "... Derenbourgh's theory, which explains *minim* as a contraction of the initials *maamine Yeshua nozri* or *min* for *maamin Jeshua nozri* is by no means too far-fetched, especially when we remember how fond the Rabbis were of making puns and juggling with words....the *minim* called themselves *maaminim.* Herein lay their distinction from the rest of the people: they were *the believers* [*maaminim* is Hebrew for believers]."[38]

THE TALMUD ADMITS TO THE COMPOSITION OF THE BIRKAT HA-MINIM AT YAVNE AT THE REQUEST OF GAMALIEL

With the knowledge we have just obtained, we can now move on to better understand who these individuals were and how history has treated[39] them. First, we will investigate the benediction which was inserted into the famous 2500-year-old Amidah synagogue prayer, which contained eighteen separate benedictions. As the Talmud admits: "Our Rabbis taught: Simeon ha-Pakuli arranged the eighteen benedictions in order before Rabban Gamaliel in Jabneh. Said Rabban Gamaliel to the Sages: Can any one among you frame a benediction

---

[38]Jakob Jocz, *The Jewish People and Jesus Christ.* London: Baker Book House, © 1949, p. 177, used by permission. [ ] mine.

[39]Was there a rabbinic lynching of believers? Did first century rabbis agree that it was all right for the Jewish Christians' (*minim*) lives to be placed in jeopardy? Douglas Hare documents: "The most extreme treatment that the rabbis will countenance is that the lives of Minim may be endangered and not saved, Tos. B. Mezia 2:33: 'The Minim and the apostates and the betrayers are cast in [to a pit] and not helped out' (translation by R. Travers Herford, *Christianity in Talmud and Midrash* ([1903], p. 94)." Douglas Hare, *The Theme of Jewish Persecution of Christians in the Gospel According to St Matthew*, p. 39. Hare's source was the Talmud, Jewish rabbinic law and history of that time, which can be found in any good library.

relating to the *Minim*? Samuel the Lesser arose and composed it" (Berakoth 28b, Babylonian Talmud).

WHY BHM THE MESSIANIC JEWS? ASSIMILATION MIGHT HAVE OCCURRED BECAUSE THEY WERE IN EVERY SYNAGOGUE OF THE EAST

Rabbi Gamaliel II, the grandson of the famous Sanhedrin judge mentioned in the New Testament book of Acts, feared the fact that so many Jews were accepting Jesus as the Messiah along with millions of pagans in the Roman world. He falsely reasoned that because so many pagan Gentiles (non-Jews) were accepting Jesus, they would have a strong bond in common with the Jews who also believed in Jesus. Thus, since the pagans were not brought up celebrating the Jewish traditions and holy days, he reasoned that the intermingling of Jews with these millions of non-Jews would bring about assimilation (a situation in which Jews forsake Jewish heritage, religion and identity), something greatly feared by the rabbis. Thus he felt Jews might be absorbed into the Gentile world and would be lost to Jewish heritage and culture, which would result in the extinction of the race! This neither happened in the first century, nor has it happened today in the modern *Jews for Jesus* movement.

Messianic Jews maintain that their acceptance of Jesus has shown them what Judaism is all about. They even claim that they are more proud than ever to be Jews.[40] Due to the fear of assimilation, Rabbi Gamaliel and Samuel the Small devised this prayer to detect and isolate Jews who believed in Jesus, which amounted to nearly twenty percent of the first and second century synagogues. The rabbis felt that these Jews should be expelled from the Jewish community in order to prevent them from sharing Jesus with unbelieving Jews who were attending the same synagogues. We read in Aldolf Harnack's book, *The Mission and Expansion of Christianity in the First Three Centuries*: "Jerome (Ep. ad Aug. 112, c. 13) does assert that Nazarenes were to be found in every Jewish synagogue throughout the East. 'What am I to say about the Ebionites who allege themselves to be Christians? To this day the sect exists in all the synagogues of the Jews, under the title of 'the Minim'; the Pharisees still curse it, and the people dub its adherents 'Nazarenes,' etc. ('Quid dicaru de Hebionitis,

---

[40]We suggest you read *The Fig Tree Blossoms*, by Paul Liberman; *Everything You Need to Build a Messianic Synagogue*, by Phillip Goble; Zola Levitt's many books; MMI's many publications; and *Jews for Jesus*' extensive materials, all of which confirm that there is a greater and more complete Jewish meaning to the faith once a Jew accepts Messiah Jesus.

qui Christianos esse se simulant? usque hodie per totas orientis synagogas inter Judaeos heresis est, quae dicitur Minaeorum et a Pharisaeis nune usque damnatur, quos vulgo Nazaraeos nuncupant').' "[41]

THE RABBIS HAD A UNIVERSAL PROBLEM ON THEIR HANDS—HUNDREDS OF THOUSANDS OF JEWS WERE BELIEVING IN JESUS

Messianic Jews were attending "every synagogue of the east." It is clear from this interesting evidence that the Messianic Jews were not merely a local problem for the rabbis.

The apostles spread the good news of His Messiahship throughout the world as Jesus had requested (Acts 1:8). They used the fulfilled prophecies to back up His claim. The bottom temporarily fell out of rabbinicism. Hundreds of thousands of Jews throughout the Diaspora were becoming Messianic Jews. They were experiencing new life, hope and happiness as they saw the evidence and received it with open hearts. This was proof that He had become the Passover lamb—Messiah ben Joseph—securing the final blood atonement and assuring eternal salvation, as promised throughout the Old Testament. They realized He would be returning to fulfill the kingly prophecies at the height of a future global war (Gog and Magog/Armageddon), resulting in all of world Jewry accepting Him. These were His conditions of return in the role of Messiah ben David (the kingly portrait of Messiah promised in the Old Testament; Matthew 23:39; Romans 11:26).

PARKES RECONSTRUCTS THE ANTI-CHRISTIAN LETTER, *USED TO EXCOMMUNICATE THE JEWISH FOLLOWERS OF JESUS*, SENT OUT BY YAVNE, FROM JUSTIN EUSEBIUS AND JEROME

Because this **problem** of Jews for Jesus persisted in strength throughout the Diaspora (see James 1:1),[42] the rabbis devised a plan to sabotage the movement. They sent emissaries and letters with copies of the famed Birkat ha-Minim to virtually every synagogue in the

[41]Adolf Harnack, *The Mission and Expansion of Christianity in the First Three Centuries.* New York: G.P. Putnam's Sons, © 1908, p. 100.

[42]James 1:1 of the New Testament says: "James, a servant of God and of the Lord Jesus Christ, to the twelve tribes [of Jews] which are *scattered abroad*, greeting" (KJV; [ ] and italics mine). For an overview of the twelve tribes, see Genesis 49. "Scattered abroad" refers to the Diaspora, where Jews were scattered throughout the other countries.

world, in an attempt to drive out those Jews who believed in the Messiah.

We read in the scholarly work of James Parkes: "...the rabbis at Jabne, had decided that the presence of these people could not be tolerated, the Judeo-Christians, however much they disagreed from other Jews on the question as to whether the Messiah had or had not come, still considered themselves to be Jews; and it is not too much to suppose from this that there were also Jews who considered that a disagreement on this point did not make fellowship with them impossible. They must have been generally accepted, or it is incredible that they should have continued to frequent the synagogue. They were evidently there as ordinary members, since it needed the introduction of this formula to detect them....It is reasonable also to date the letters and 'Apostles' sent out to the Jews of the diaspora to the end of the first century. Through his emissaries the Jewish Patriarch of Palestine was able to keep in fairly close touch with the Jews in the rest of the world because of the annual collection which was made by all the synagogues to the central organisation. The decision which is marked by the inclusion of the test malediction on the heretics into the Eighteen Benedictions was an important one. The matter touched the diaspora even more closely than Palestine itself. We may therefore presume that before the end of the century all the synagogues of the diaspora had been informed of the new malediction and warned to have no dealings with the Christians[43]....It is difficult, but necessary, to try to distinguish what was sent out officially from Palestine....If we take the substance of what is told us by Justin, Eusebius and Jerome, we can make a fair reconstruction of the letter. It contained a formal denial of the truth of the Christian account of the teaching and resurrection of Jesus. Christianity [Messianism] was a denial of God and of the Law. It was based on the teaching of Jesus, who was a deceiver, and who had been put to death....His disciples had stolen His body, and then pretended that He had risen again from the dead and was the Son of God. It was therefore impossible for Jews to have anything to do with such teaching, and His followers should be formally excommunicated. (Justin, *ibid.,* and Jerome, *On Isaiah,* xviii, 2; P.L., XXIV, p. 184.) Jews were to avoid all discussions of any kind with the Christians. [Messianic Jews] (Justin, XXXVIII, and Oregon, *Celsus,* VI, 27; P.G., XI, p. 1333.)....letters also contained a copy of the Birkath-ha-Minim, with instructions to include it into the Eighteen Benedictions. For the daily cursing of Christ in the synagogue is very closely associated with

---

[43]Messianic Jews, or if you please, ancient Jews for Jesus who had accepted the Jewish Messiah in accordance with the biblical promises.

the letters. (Justin, xvi, xlvii, xcv, cxxxiii.)....All three writers insist on the official character of these letters, and on their wide dispersion."[44]

"I, BELIEVING THEM, CRUCIFIED HIM"—*PILATE*

Additional evidence of this conspiratorial schism can be found in an ancient document known as *The Acts of Pilate.* The information revealed in this piece of literature exposes an admitted plot to cover up Messianic truths simply because they would cause a split in the synagogue of that day.

Pilate, the Roman governor, made these statements in a letter to Tiberius Caesar in an attempt to explain why he killed Jesus. Again, we have more evidence of how the priests and rabbis sold out the Jewish population at large for their own gains and purposes.

James Parkes, in *The Conflict of the Church and the Synagogue,* summarizes *The Acts of Pilate*, as he notes: "The next development is that the High Priest, also impressed by the events of the Crucifixion, calls a meeting to examine carefully whether the prophecies really prove that Jesus was the Messiah. The meeting finds that He was; and their decision comes to the ears of Pilate, who sends to them to adjure them to tell him the truth. They admit that He was the Messiah, but say that they have decided to conceal the fact, 'lest there should be a schism in our synagogues'. They implore Pilate to keep silence. Pilate, however, writes to the emperor Tiberius that 'the Jews through envy have punished themselves and their posterity with fearful judgments of their own fault; for their fathers had promises that God would send them His Holy One, and when He came, and performed marvelous works, the priests through envy delivered Him to me, and I, believing them, crucified Him."[45]

THE JEWISH CHRISTIAN SCHOLAR, JACOB JOCZ, REVEALS TO US THE MOTIVE, MEANS AND OPPORTUNITY FOR THE MESSIAH CONSPIRACY

Jacob Jocz, the famous Jewish professor and scholar, while agreeing with Jesus' claims, is most honest with the facts of this period. He tells us in his book, *The Jewish People and Jesus Christ*: "The *Shemoneh Esreh,* which is the *Tephillah* par excellence and 'the central feature of the three daily prayers', contains a strange 'blessing', the much discussed *Birkat ha-minim.* It is associated with the names of

---

[44]James Parkes, *The Conflict of the Church and the Synagogue*, pp. 78-80. Parkes' footnotes were inserted into his text for clarification using ( ). [ ] mine.
[45]Ibid, p. 103.

Gamaliel (*circa* A.D. 100) and Samuel the Small (died *circa* A.D. 125). The classical Talmudic passage recording the introduction of the 'benediction' reads: Our Rabbis have taught: Simeon the cotton-dealer (Dalman transl. *Flachsschäler*) arranged the eighteen benedictions in order in the presence of Rabban Gamaliel at Jabneh. Rabban Gamaliel asked the sages: 'Is there anyone who knows how to word the benediction relating to the *minim*?' Samuel The Small stood up and worded it. The *Shemoneh Esreh*, which according to tradition, was drawn up by the Men of the Great Synagogue, has thus acquired an *extra* 'benediction', though it still retained the former name of 'Eighteen' (benedictions). Immediately preceding the passage quoted above the question is being asked: 'As to those eighteen benedictions;—there are nineteen! R. Levi said: The benediction relating to the *minim* was subsequently instituted at Jabneh....It is obvious from this passage that the Rabbis have tried to find some justification for the introduction of a curse into the otherwise lofty prayers of the *Shemoneh Esreh*. Jewish scholars[46] have for a long time maintained that the *Birkat ha-minim* was mainly directed against heresy as such, and only indirectly against Hebrew Christianity. Even Israel Abrahams in his notes to *Singer's Prayer Book* says that the benediction 'was directed against...sectarians (*minim*) within the Synagogue....'...The Jewish believers in Jesus of Nazareth were the real and immediate danger to the Synagogue. There can be little doubt who

---

46Why did the scholar Akiva abhor Christians and their books? We verify from scholar Joshua Bloch, in his article "Outside Books" that: "The Nazarenes and their books became objectionable not so much because of their belief about the role of Jesus but because of their persistent attempt to exalt him to a position almost equal with that of God....they evidently became quite dangerous in the days of Rabbi Akiba....Rabbi Akiba and his circle regarded the teachings of the christian books current in their day about the 'divinity' of Jesus of Nazareth, as a serious infringement of the belief in the Divine Unity...." Hence, the deity of Jesus was taught in the first century—a concept that is denied by many rabbis and liberal "Christian scholars." Bloch also notes: "...the Nazarenes are specifically named. The text from the Genizah which Schechter published (*Jewish Quarterly Review*, London, 1898, v. 10, pp. 654-659) is directed against 'the Notzerim and the Minim,' which Marcel Simon (*Verus Israel*, Paris, 1948, p. 236) translated by 'the Nazarenes and the other Minim.' In the wording of the prayer as it is now familiar ולמלשינים is substituted for מינים. The text of the prayer in current prayer books has the appearance of having been modified more than once in the course of centuries and adapted to new conditions and surroundings (see S. Baer, *Abodat Yisrael*, p. 93 f.; Singer, *Authorized Daily Prayer Book*, p. 48 with I. Abrahams' note, p. LXIV f. Cf. G.F. Moore, *op. cit.*, v. 1, p. 292 and v. 3, p. 97, note 68 and S. Krauss, 'Imprecations against the *Minim* in the Synagogue,' in *Jewish Quarterly Review*, April, 1897, v. 9, pp. 515-518.)." Joshua Bloch, "Outside Books," *Mordecai M. Kaplan, Jubilee Volume*, pp. 95, 99-100.

are meant by the *minim*. There was no other sect or heresy which could compare in importance with Hebrew Christianity.

The Hebrew Christians were steeped in the traditions of Judaism, many of them were loyal to the 'traditions of the elders'. They were spiritually alive, abounding in religious zeal. They were aggressive, and, above all, they were the enthusiastic bearers of the greatest Jewish heritage—the Messianic hope. They were dangerous because they had the advantage of attacking [the new false rabbinical] Judaism from *within*."[47]

They were exposing what real Judaism was all about—the Messiah, Jesus. The religious leaders of the new cultural Judaism could not swallow this! It was a slap in the face to the false Judaism of cultural cement they were attempting to construct to guard against assimilation during the coming 1900-year Diaspora. Jocz continues: "It therefore became imperative for the Synagogue to isolate them. For that purpose the *Birkat ha-minim* was composed. Loewe [the scholar who helped write *A Rabbinic Anthology* with C. G. Montefiore] rightly calls it a 'test passage'; its intention being to 'separate the sheep from goats, and compel the *minim* to declare themselves'. It naturally had the effect of widening the breach between the Jesus-believing and the non-believing Jews in that it made it impossible for the believers to worship in the synagogues."[48]

Jocz makes the following observations based on the most up-to-date scholarly sources: "(1) The *Birkat ha-minim* had no precedent in the Synagogue; it was a new creation, entirely dictated by internal necessity. (2) It was composed at an early date, not many years after the destruction of Jerusalem....the introduction of the *Birkat ha-minim* resulted, not only in widening the breach between Hebrew Christians and orthodox Jews, but also in further prejudicing the Jews against Jesus of Nazareth....Israel Abrahams has shown that the Synagogue's dealings with *minut* [Messianic Jewish believers in Jesus] must be viewed as an internal affair. Its main purpose was self-defence. For that purpose, it introduced the *Birkat ha-minim*; it altered its liturgy; it changed its emphasis, especially with regard to Messianic teaching; it created barriers."[49] One such barrier would be to de-emphasize Jesus' deity. Was it done? A.J.B Higgins said: "...the tendency in post-

---

[47]Jakob Jocz, *The Jewish People and Jesus Christ*, pp. 51-53. [ ] mine.
[48]Ibid, p. 53. [ ] mine.
[49]Ibid, pp. 57, 190. [ ] mine.

Christian Judaism was to tone down messianic dogma and to emphasize the human nature of the Messiah."[50]

RABBI SAFRAI VERIFIES BRUCE'S CLAIM IN OUR ARCHAEOLOGICAL ARCHIVES OF THE ORIGINAL BHM, DURING A CHAT AT HIS FLAT

I thought it important to obtain a modern scholarly Jewish opinion on this subject from a rabbi who would not be biased—one who would only be interested in the true facts, even those facts which have remained hidden from the eyes of history, such as Rabbi Safrai. I say this because the text of the BHM was changed from *minim* and *Nazarenes* to **slanderers** soon after its true purpose was considered successful.

The scholar F. F. Bruce, author of *New Testament History,* speaks of the powers of the Sanhedrin and its strong hold on the Jewish synagogues of that era: "...it was indeed through the synagogue that the Sanhedrin exercised its authority. An outstanding example of this is provided by the effective exclusion of Nazarenes and other 'heretics' from participation in Jewish worship when, about A.D. 90, a member of the Sanhedrin named Samuel the Less reworded one of the blessings recited daily in the synagogue so as to make it include a curse on such persons. In the present Jewish prayer book this blessing appears as the twelfth of the Eighteen Benedictions; it runs thus: 'And for slanderers let there be no hope, and let all wickedness perish as in a moment; may all Thy enemies be speedily cut off, and the kingdom of arrogance do Thou speedily uproot and break in pieces, cast it down and humble it speedily, in our days. Blessed art Thou, O Lord, who breakest enemies in pieces and humblest the arrogant.' But towards the end of the first century it was given this form: 'For apostates let there be no hope, and the kingdom of arrogance do Thou speedily uproot in our days; and let Nazarenes and heretics (*minim*) perish as in a moment; let them be blotted out of the book of life and not be enrolled with the righteous. Blessed art Thou, O Lord, who humblest the arrogant.' This revised edition of **the prayer was authorized by the Sanhedrin and adopted in synagogues, so that Jewish Christians, by keeping silence at this point, might give themselves away and be excommunicated**. The 'heretics' or *minim* were members of other sects of which the Sanhedrin disapproved. It is only after A.D. 70 that

---

[50]A.J.B. Higgins, *Jewish Messianic Belief in Justin Martyr's Dialogue with Trypho*, published in the compilation by Leo Landman, *Messianism in the Talmudic Era.* New York: KTAV Publishing House, Inc., © 1979, pp. 183.

we can begin to talk about normative Judaism and of deviations from the norm; in the days of the Second Temple there was a much greater variety of Jewish religious life and practice, and no one form could claim to represent the standard by which others were to be judged.

When the rabbis of Jamnia discussed the recognition of canonical books and the rejection of others, one group to which they paid attention was 'the books of the *minim*'. These contained the name of God, and yet their contents were unacceptable....they certainly included Jewish Christian writings."[51]

Recent discoveries in an ancient Egyptian synagogue proved the near original words were *minim* and **Nazarene**. Many modern rabbis, interested in maintaining this secret, deny that the BHM was ever used for the purpose of excommunicating Messianic or Christian Jews from the synagogue in the first to the fourth centuries. As we will see shortly in greater detail, many even deny that there was a sizable Jewish Messianic community in existence.[52] Ask any rabbi and compare what he says to the historical facts you are reading here and see if it all lines up. Most likely it will not![53]

In 1984, while in Israel doing research on this subject for a popular Christian writer, I interviewed world-renowned Hebrew scholar and professor, Rabbi Shmuel Safrai, of the Hebrew University in Jerusalem. We had a cozy little chat in his apartment. He agreed with me that F. F. Bruce was accurate! He told me about his book, *A History of the Jewish People,* as he pulled it from his bookshelf and handed it to me.

THE ISRAELI RABBI SAFRAI ADMITS THE TRUTH ABOUT THE TRUE INTENTION OF THE BHM—IT WAS TO *CUT OFF CHRISTIANITY*, ESPECIALLY THE JUDEO-CHRISTIANS!

In Rabbi Safrai's unique book, we found the following: "Throughout the Jabneh era, from immediately after the destruction of the Temple until the Revolt of Bar Kokhba (70-132), many steps were taken that were to have a decisive influence on the coherence of the nation under the contemporary conditions. The sages were able to gain control over the different groups and trends that were competing within

[51]F.F. Bruce, *New Testament History*. New York: Doubleday & Company, Inc., © 1971, pp. 385-386, used by permission. Bold mine.

[52]One example lies in several statements by Rabbi Shalom Lewis, which have recently been factually contradicted by archaeology. See this interesting contrast documented in our forthcoming chapter 8, "The Messiah Conspiracy Continues in the *New* Old Testament."

[53]If it does not, don't you think that is interesting? Something is wrong somewhere and it is not here!

the nation....Decisive steps were also taken to **cut off Christianity** [Messianism]....One such measure was the insertion into the *Amidah* prayer of an additional, nineteenth benediction, *Birkat Haminim* ('benediction against the heretics'), which, in its earliest Palestinian formula, was directed primarily against the Judeo-Christians, who 'shall have no hope' in their belief that the Messiah has already appeared on earth. Of the men who established and shaped the institutions of national and community leadership in Jabneh, none belonged to those circles that had formed the social *élite* in the days of the Temple. Those elements had completely vanished from public life....These sages were known by the designation 'rabbi', and from them the president of the Sanhedrin chose his executives and emissaries....R. Joshua was one of their emissaries whose travels resulted in wide-ranging contacts with the outside world....We find him in the role of spokesman for [Yavne's newly formed rabbinical] Judaism in disputations with Christians...."[54]

ALON'S TRUER RESULT—THE BHM HAD THE FAR-REACHING CONSEQUENCE OF REMOVING THE JEWISH BELIEVER FROM HIS PEOPLE, AS NEWER SOURCES INDICATE

It is not our point to bore you with scholarly references. This book is for the layman as well as professors. However, in the interest of answering any rabbis who may try to take exception to our facts, we think it necessary to carefully document these new and exciting discoveries, which have helped to uncover the *Messiah Conspiracy* of the first century!

G. Alon is an expert on the subject of first century Jewish Christian activities. Concerning Rabbi Gamaliel and his fear of Jewish Christians (Messianic Jews) and assimilation, he says: "...these were sectarians who had *not* given up their Jewish identity.

In any case, it is likely that the process of intermingling between these various sects created a situation in which the Jewish Sages could no longer tell them apart; and lumping them all together, read them out of the Jewish fold. The fact remains, however, that the 'loyal' sects were never put on a par with the others.

What then was the purpose of *Birkat ha-Minim*? Most scholars believe that it was designed to keep the *Minim* away from worship in the synagogue, and they may well be right. But it is probably truer to

---

[54] H.H. Ben-Sasson and Shmuel Safrai, *A History of the Jewish People*, Part IV. Tel Aviv: Dvir Publishing House, © 1969, 1976, p. 325, used by permission. [ ] and bold mine.

say that that was the end result, rather than the original purpose. It is likely that the main intention was to make all Jews aware of the fact that the *Minim* were to be regarded as *apostates*, and could *no longer be called Jews.*

Whichever way we look at it, it will be seen that the Beth Din [rabbinical school which reformulated Judaism] of Rabban Gamaliel at Yavneh took a fateful step, one that was to have far-reaching historical consequences. They declared [wrongfully, with a vengeance unparalleled in religious bigotry] in unequivocal terms that the Jewish Christians could no longer be considered part of the Jewish community nor of the Jewish people."[55]

Professor Alon mentions some of his sources in his footnote 53, which reads: "[The study of the Jewish Christians has naturally been affected by the discovery of new source-materials bearing on the subject. For examples, see 'The Dead Sea Sect and Pre-Pauline Christianity,' by David Flusser, in *Scripta Hierosolymitana*, vol. IV (1958), pp. 215 ff.; and 'The Jewish Christians in the Early Centuries of Christianity According to a New Source,' by Shlomo Pines, in Proceedings of *The Israel Academy of Sciences and Humanities,* vol. II, no. 13]."[56]

NEW DISCOVERIES IN OUR CENTURY OF THE ORIGINAL FORMULATION OF THE BHM OBLITERATE TALL TALES AND INDICATE CHRISTIANS

Chief among this recently discovered evidence of the Messiah Conspiracy was the discovery of the Genizah fragments, which contain the earliest copies to date of the **original** BHM document. This came to light in 1925. G. Alon, in his work, *The Jews in Their Land in the Talmudic Age,* documents this monumental find: "The twelfth paragraph of the 'Eighteen' Benedictions *(ve-lamal-shinim)* is referred to in Talmudic literature as '*Birkat ha-Minim*'—the prayer concerning the sectarians. The same sources inform us that this part of the liturgy dates from the Academy of Yavneh: Simeon Hapakuli arranged the Eighteen Benedictions in their proper order in the presence of Rabban Gamaliel at Yavneh. Said Rabban Gamaliel to the Sages: Is there anyone that can formulate the *Birkat ha-Minim*? Up rose Samuel the Lesser and recited it. What was the nature of this 'benediction'? As it appears in most Ashkenazic versions of the liturgy today, it says not a

---

[55]G. Alon, *The Jews in Their Land in the Talmudic Age*, Vol. I. Jerusalem: EJ Brill, © 1980, p. 307. [ ] is our opinion reached after years of research on this subject.
[56]Ibid.

word about sectarians or *Minim*. But there was a time when the *Minim* were explicitly mentioned. Just who were they?

The Talmud uses the word frequently, and always in the sense of 'sectarians'—Jews whose religious beliefs and practices set them apart from the rest of the people. Some scholars hold that the term invariably refers to one or another kind of Jewish Christian....when the field is narrowed down to the *Minim* of Eighteen Benedictions, the definition becomes more plausible. For one thing, there is the evidence provided by several Church Fathers. The earliest to mention the subject is Justin Martyr, born a pagan at what is now Nablus at the end of the first century. In his 'Dialogue With Trypho', written around the year 150, he says: 'You Jews pronounce maledictions on the Christians in your synagogues'....more direct testimony comes from Epiphanius, who writes that the Jews denounce the *Nazarenes* in their prayers three times a day. Note that he speaks only of *Jewish* Christians (Nazarenes). And Jerome, in his Commentary on Isaiah, chapter 52, verse 4, says practically the same thing.

That was about all we knew **until 1925**, when the question was settled by the discovery of Genizah fragments containing portions of the liturgy according to the ancient Palestinian rite. In these versions, *Birkat ha-Minim* reads like this: May the apostates have no hope, unless they return to Thy Torah, and may the **Nazarenes** and the Minim disappear in a moment. May they be erased from the book of life, and not be inscribed with the righteous. The provenance of this text, which calls down wrath on...Nazarenes and *Minim*—leaves little room for doubt that **we are looking at something very close to the original formulation as laid down in the days of Rabban Gamaliel.** The wording might give the impression that Nazarenes are one thing and *Minim* another; or that *Minim* is a generic term for schismatics. But that can scarcely be true; for why would Rabban Gamaliel have reacted to any heresy except one that posed a special threat in his own time? There was nothing new about non-Pharisaic sects like the Sadducees. They and others had been numerous in Temple days.

We must therefore assume that in this liturgical fragment, *Minim* and *Notzrim* are synonymous, and that both refer to the Jewish Christians. The assumption is borne out by Jerome, who writes that in his lifetime (4th to 5th centuries) there was a sect of Jews called *Minim—also known* as Nazarenes. He says they wanted to be both Jews and Christians...."[57]

***

[57]Ibid, pp. 288-290. Bold mine.

ONCE THE DECEPTION WAS ACCOMPLISHED, THE NAMES WERE CHANGED TO PROTECT THE *GUILTY*

It is important to realize that after the rabbis achieved their desired goal of splitting the Jews who believed in Jesus from those who did not, they changed the Birkat ha-Minim by removing the words Nazarene and *minim*, in an apparent attempt to cover up their plot to excommunicate the masses of Jews who believed in Jesus!

Today, many rabbis claim there were very few Jews who accepted Jesus, even though there were many. To admit it would cause the modern Jewish community to ponder the question of whether Jesus might qualify to be the Jewish Messiah! It is interesting to note that the modern Amidah prayer, which contains the Birkat ha-Minim benediction, contains the word "slanderers" instead of *minim* (an acronym for "believers in Jesus from Nazareth") or Nazarene (the largest denomination of ancient Jews for Jesus).

Archaeology, like it or not, tells it like it is and shows that all is not the way many rabbis have led us to believe, no matter what the cost. Will you read on and further investigate these findings? Will you give yourself an opportunity to make a decision about your eternal destiny, based on who Jesus really is? You owe it to yourself to check it out!

Solomon Schechter at work, sorting out tens of thousands of Geniza fragments at Cambrige in 1898

A LEAP IN THE DARK

The Cairo Geniza constitutes a fabulous listening device, a 'bug' planted in the heart of time and recording for our elucidation the loftiest visions and most intimate secrets of the Dark Ages. But how is the scholarly puzzle being solved?

Abraham Rabinovich

THE *JERUSALEM POST* REVEALS THE SIGNIFICANCE OF THE GENIZA AND SOME OF ITS SECRETS

As you have read, prior to the 1925 discovery of the Cairo Geniza Birkat ha-Minim fragment, the word *Notzrim* and the true meaning of this "prayer" rabbinically contrived at Yavne, was one of the best-kept secrets of our age. However, after the archaeological find, as a result of the "bug" in the hidden synagogue chamber that lay silent and unknown to scholars for centuries, the exact words and the true reason for the creation of the Birkat ha-Minim became all too evident.

The fragment that was found, because of its early origin, shows that *minim* were really ancient Jewish Christians, contrary to some "scholarly" claims that *minim* referred merely to apostates.[58] I believe the word *notzrim* was discovered beside *minim* as a clarifying noun because the *notzrim* were the largest sect of believers in Jesus, Messianic Jews, or put more simply, Messiah followers (in English, Christ (Messiah); ians (followers).

CAIRO'S GENIZA WAS DIFFERENT—IT WAS NEVER EMPTIED! IT CONSTITUTED A "BUG"

We have reprinted portions of an article from the *Jerusalem Post* magazine entitled "A Leap in the Dark," so you will be able to grasp the immense importance of this chamber found in the Ben Ezra Cairo Synagogue, called the Geniza, where the authentic Birkat ha-Minim was discovered. The subtitle of this article reads: "The Cairo Geniza constitutes a fabulous listening device, a 'bug' planted in the heart of time and recording for our elucidation the loftiest visions and **most intimate secrets** of the Dark Ages. But how is the scholarly puzzle being solved?"[59]

***

[58]We remind you of our quote from Alon, the Jewish scholar who informed us otherwise, according to the latest findings. "That was about all we knew until 1925, when the question was settled by the discovery of Genizah fragments containing portions of the liturgy according to ancient Palestinean rite. In these versions, *Birkhat ha-Minim* reads like this: May the apostates have no hope, unless they return to Thy Torah, and may the Nazarenes and the *Minim* disappear in a moment. May they be erased from the book of life, and not be inscribed with the righteous. The provenance of this text, which calls down wrath on...Nazarenes and *Minim*—leaves little room for doubt that we are looking at something very close to the original formulation....We must therefore assume that in this liturgical fragment, *Minim* and *Notzrim* are synonymous, and that both refer to the Jewish Christians." Ibid, pp. 289-290.

[59]"A Leap in the Dark," *Jerusalem Post* magazine, Mar. 10, 1989, © used by permission. Bold mine.

This article shows that even a casual, unscientific observer would be amazed to realize that this synagogue compartment has yielded secrets unknown to history for over 1000 years. The magazine devoted several pages to this feature story and even printed a full page photo of Solomon Schechter sorting out thousands of Geniza fragments. The article went into detail describing the conditions and reasons for the find; it documented the major importance of this discovery and emphasized that most of the general public is still unaware of the "knowledge of the documents." We believe the following words from the article are ironic, since many of us are still **unaware** and **unenlightened** with regard to the Birkat ha-Minim, which we will bet you just learned about by reading this book. The article reads: "The Geniza collection stems from the Jewish practice of not destroying old prayerbooks or any other Hebrew writing on which the name of God might appear, including private letters. These are usually stored in a cupboard or other space in a synagogue until they are ceremonially buried in a cemetery.

For reasons that scholars do not understand, the *geniza* (repository) in the Ben Ezra Synagogue in old Cairo was operated differently. It became a catch-all for every kind of written document, including those in non-Hebrew languages that clearly did not bear God's name in the holy tongue.

In addition, the Cairo Geniza was apparently never emptied in the course of centuries....Because of the relatively dry climate, the parchment, paper, papyrus and cloth on which these documents were written survived the centuries in remarkably good condition.

The Cairo Geniza constitutes a fabulous listening device, a scholarly 'bug' planted in the heart of time and recording for our titillation and elucidation the loftiest visions and most intimate secrets of an age.

These secrets began to leak last century....For the general public, the world of the Geniza is still a dark age unlit by knowledge of the documents' revelations. In time, presumably, the knowledge of this rich world will seep into the general consciousness."[60]

THEY DID NOT *COUNT* ON OUR DISCOVERY— IT WAS SUPPOSED TO HAVE BEEN *BURIED*

Those, whoever they may be, who concealed and perhaps destroyed previous copies of this document containing the word *notzrim*, in their attempt to cover up the evidence of its true target, did not count on this conspicuous find at the Cairo Geniza revealing their conspiracy in our time! Also, "those" in charge of the synagogue in

---

[60]Ibid. Bold mine.

Cairo, who stored this BHM document, did not count on and had no intention of having the twentieth century lay eyes upon this writing. Paul E. Kahle, in his book *The Cairo Geniza*, states: "...the room which is of interest to us [held]....A great number of fragments of MSS [manuscripts] and of printed books, documents and letters had been stored there for many hundreds of years. The Jews used to deposit all sorts of written and printed material in such rooms which were provided in or near their synagogues; they were **not** intended to be **kept** as in archives, but were to remain there undisturbed for a certain time. The Jews were afraid lest such writings which might contain the name of God should be profaned by misuse. So such written—and in later times also printed—matter was taken from time to time to consecrated ground and buried; thus it perished.

It was by mere chance that the Cairo Geniza was forgotten and its contents so escaped the fate of other Genizas. **These old writings** have been **saved quite contrary to the intention of those who stored them** there."[61] As you read this "prayer" in modern Jewish prayer books,[62] you will see the word slanderers remains in the place of our discovery.

[61]Paul E. Kahle, *The Cairo Geniza.* Oxford: Basil Blackwell, © 1959, p. 4, used by permission. Bold and [ ] mine.

[62]The words Nazarenes/*minim* have been replaced by the word slanderers in modern Jewish prayer books. The authorized daily prayer book by S. Singer reads as follows: "And for slanderers let there be no hope, and let all wickedness perish as in a moment; let all thine enemies be speedily cut off, and the dominion of arrogance do thou uproot and crush, cast down and humble speedily in our days. Blessed art thou, O Lord, who breakest the enemies and humblest the arrogant." F.F. Bruce, *The Spreading Flame*, p. 267.

The discovery of the century. The word *notzrim* ("Christians" in Hebrew) is circled in this reproduction of the Birkat ha-Minim discovered in the Cairo Geniza, at the Ben Ezra Synagogue in Cairo, Egypt.

BARRIER, WHAT BARRIER? THERE ARE SOME WHO DENY THAT THE SAGES OF YAVNE BUILT A BARRIER BETWEEN JESUS AND THE JEWS!

Although some scholars may attempt to disprove[63] what we are about to quote, it is recorded history for those who accept the Talmud. This includes Orthodox Jews, who accept it totally, and nearly all the rest of the Jews, in addition to quite a few non-Jewish Bible students. Some teach that Yavne was not a breeding ground for building a barrier around Judaism, forcing the Jew who believed in the Messiah away from the mainstream Jewish community. However, we will present evidence quite to the contrary.

Many have asked, "Why would the rabbis want to keep the people from the Messiah, if it can be genuinely and Jewishly proven that Jesus is the Messiah?" Well, *answering* this question is one of the main purposes of our work. The answer is two-fold. The priests in the time of Jesus refused to accept Him because of their self-interest and corruption. A half-century later, the rabbis at Yavne decided that they had to save the Jews as a cultural group. This "cultural salvation" was, of course, considered more important than allowing the Messiah[64] to save the individual souls of the people. So, in essence, the rabbis made the decision to save the body of cultural Jewish heritage, which they incorrectly assumed was in danger, even at the expense of the Jewish soul. This was nothing short of spiritual suicide performed in the name of preserving Jewish culture, which was not, and never will be lost, even to the Jew who accepts Jesus as their Messiah, based on the fulfillments of Jewish prophecies.

BARRIER, WHAT BARRIER? TO GET STRAIGHT TO THE POINT, CUTTING OFF JESUS FROM THE JEW!

The point of this segment is to illustrate how some Jewish historical writings were purposely created to build a barrier against Jesus as Messiah. Here is a quote from the Talmud to prove this point, though its reproduction here may be much to the dislike of Gentile liberal scholars and orthodox rabbis, as it clearly exposes the truth.

The Talmud tells us: "Once it happened that Rabbi Eleazar ben Dama was bitten by a snake, and Jacob of Kefar [James of the New Testament] Sama came to heal him in the name of Yeshua ben Pantera

---

[63]Men like Rabbi Asher Finkel and Steven Katz, whom we will soon review.

[64]Truly, the Jewish people had the door slammed on them by the Jewish leaders concerning knowledge of the Messiah.

[rabbinical slang of that time for Jesus' name]. Rabbi Ishmael would not permit it, saying: 'Ben Dama, you are not allowed!' He answered: 'But I can prove to you that it is permissible for him to heal me.' However, before he could manage to cite his proof, he died. Rabbi Ishmael exclaimed: 'Happy are you, ben Dama, because you have departed in peace without having broken down **the barrier erected by the Sages**...' "[65]

Rabbi Ishmael believed that "the most fundamental prohibitions...may be violated to save a life."[66] Thus, when he states "without having broken down the **barrier** erected by the sages,"[67] we know with certainty that he is talking about the barrier erected between the Jewish believers and the newly forged rabbinic Judaism, in order to separate Jews from Jesus, forever.

WHY DO THEY ANSWER, "BARRIER, WHAT BARRIER?" BECAUSE THEY ARE AFRAID!

If you were to inquire about the rabbinical barrier built to keep the Messianic Jews away from the new mainstream Judaism created at Yavne by the rabbinical sages of the first century, most modern rabbis would say, "Barrier, what barrier? None of our people ever believed in Jesus. He was accepted by non-Jews."[68]

These rabbis are either unaware of the more than a million Jews for Jesus who existed in the first century, or they are not willing to, or at least find it hard to admit, that such a movement existed! Why? Because they are either lacking in study or are afraid that Jews will begin to investigate the Jewishness of the Messianic movement, thus breaking down the barrier that was erected by the rabbinical sages, designed to sabotage the Jewish Messianic faith, which later led to a mainly non-Jewish church.

***

---

[65]G. Alon, *The Jews in Their Land in the Talmudic Age*, p. 292. [ ] and bold mine.

[66]Ibid. [ ] mine.

[67]So we see in this passage that this poor rabbi lost his life because Rabbi Ishmael was afraid that if Jacob were to miraculously heal him in Jesus' name, he might become a believer in Him and "break down the barrier of the sages." These "sages" were none other than a small group of desperate rabbis at Yavne attempting to reformulate Judaism, even if it meant deceiving the Jewish people out of the Jewish Messiah. Some sages, wouldn't you say?

[68]Read Rabbi Kaplan's comments in *The Real Messiah* later in this chapter to see our point, that despite the fact that many Jews believed, it is still arrogantly denied by many modern rabbis.

RABBINIC WATERGATE—YAVNE AND TODAY! WHY DID THEY *COVER UP* THE COVER-UP?

We cannot overemphasize that there has been a concerted effort to disguise the cover-up, though it has been concealed and kept quiet among popular readers throughout the centuries until today. In the Ashkenazic (European and American) Jewish prayer books, the words *minim* and Nazarenes (believers in Jesus from Nazareth) have been removed and in their place the word slanderers is found, as we read in a previous footnote.

In the Sephardic prayer books (used by Jews from Arab countries), the word *minim* is intact. However, the very obvious word, Nazarenes, is no longer there. In the Western world, a sizable Christian community has flourished since that era. In the Arab countries since Mohammed's time, where Christians were massacred wholesale, there were virtually none. In the non-Arab/Sephardic countries, the Jewish leaders of that time were challenged, with respect to the BHM and its reference to Christians by the word *minim*, in order to escape the issue of the early Jewish believers and the BHM's direct reference to Jesus' followers, the prayer book was edited.

Ray Pritz, a trusted friend and author of the scholarly book, *Nazarene Jewish Christianity*, affirms: "It has long been recognized that rabbinic self-censorship of anti-Christian material was more extensive in those countries where the church controlled civil life. This was clearly the case also with the excision of the words *minim* and *notzrim* in those areas where they had been added to the Twelfth Benediction"[69]

In countries like the United States, where there are so many who believe in Jesus as the Jewish Messiah, there is a fear among rabbis that their Jewish flock could be affected; therefore, they do not want there to be any possibility of their congregations becoming curious about Jesus as Messiah.[70] If evangelicals could point to the fact that the BHM was a device used by the rabbis of the first three centuries to chase the ancient Jews for Jesus from the synagogue, many Jews today might become curious and investigate why so many Jews of Jesus' day

---

[69]Ray A. Pritz, quoted from this author's personal facsimile received from Jerusalem on Aug. 20, 1995.

[70]In our opinion, this is illustrated in the recent statement of Rabbi Aron Lieberman of Synagogue Inverrary-Chabad. "Any dialogue that relates to interfaith is destructive to the Jewish community as a whole." John Levitt: "Messianic Jews in shul? The rabbi invited them." *Broward Jewish Journal,* Dec. 31, 1992. We can certainly see why he has something to fear. If Jesus fulfilled Jewish prophecies in the Scriptures, folks might be led to the truth of Judaism—the Messiah Jesus—the discovery of the ages. This is not destructive, it is constructive.

accepted Him as Messiah, in order to find out why this formula (BHM) was needed. Thus, long ago they removed this word *minim*, and have not replaced it to this day,[71] hoping to conceal their cover-up of Jesus as Messiah in the early centuries.

INDIRECT EVIDENCE OF THE ASHKENAZIC COVER-UP, BY WHAT THE SEPHARDIC JEWS *DID NOT DO*

In Arab countries, where there were virtually no believers in Jesus sharing their faith in Him as Messiah, there was no need to disguise their *cover-up*. Therefore, to this day, you can pick up a Sephardic prayer book and read ***minim*** in bold black letters in this benediction against those ancient Jews for Jesus who—let me say it clearly, so my opposition can hear, even if they don't like it—**existed in large, large numbers**.

There is still a reason to investigate. Could it be that Jesus was really the Messiah for the Jewish people? Oh, how true were the words of Douglas Hare when he said: "The Jewish practice of excommunication during the period under consideration is **shrouded in mystery**. Despite all that has been written on the subject...."[72]

In our opinion, the rabbis took great care to conceal what they were doing and hoped that their Messiah Conspiracy would not be detected by future generations. Of course, as you read this book, you will find that at the end of the twentieth century, their scandal has been brought to light!

We challenge you to read on and discover for yourself if Jesus is Messiah or not! We must ask ourselves, where is our end time leading? Will He return and save the approaching troubled twenty-first century from nuclear annihilation, as predicted by the prophets of the Old Testament and as He promised in the New Testament? Or are we headed blindly for destruction from a God who couldn't care less? I challenge you to read on concerning your very own future, covered extensively in the latter chapters of this work. You will not be disappointed.

***

---

[71]If you are reading this book at a later date in the twenty-first century, it probably will not be worth your time to recheck the prayer books because we do not believe there will be any change, which would be the honest thing to do. Slanderers should be changed back to the word *minim* with a footnote as to who the *minim* were. For several hundred years, Jewish leaders have been free to replace this word with *minim*, explaining that they were Nazarenes, and have not.

[72]Douglas Hare, *The Theme of Jewish Persecution of Christians in the Gospel According to St. Matthew*, p. 48.

THE HEBREW WORD, *NAZARENE, IS THE KEY* TO UNRAVELING ATTEMPTS TO OBSCURE THE CONSPIRACY

We know now that the term **Nazarene** was used in the BHM! However, there are those who would deny its widespread use, thus carrying the 2000-year-old conspiracy of Yavne into the present day!

Rabbi Asher Finkel, in his article, "Yavneh's Liturgy and Early Christianity," pathetically attempts to refute the fact that the BHM of the Cairo Geniza Amidah fragment (recently discovered and published by Solomon Schecter) had anything to do with an anti-Christian plot, on the basis that the word Nazarene was more or less only mentioned in *that* fragment and not in other copies of the Amidah prayer.

Our response to Mr. Finkel's highly questionable hypothesis is that this is why we have documented this plot against the early Jewish believers—precisely because it is mentioned in only a few obscure and *recently* discovered copies! It was played down, altered, and covered up in later copies. As you have read, the modern Ashkenazic Jewish prayer books have been edited. They delete the words *minim* and Nazarene ("Christians") and use "slanderers" in their place.

The mention of the word *notzrim*/Christians at least once is all the more proof of a documented conspiracy. After all, how many times does it take to document an event? Once! Once is enough—too much really![73] Do you remember what Simon Greenleaf said about the witness of the opposition in our Resurrection section? Well, here it is again, in a twentieth century article on the BHM. This oppositional article attests to our conviction of just such a plot against the Jewish believers in Jesus. A plot which has lasted to this day and which must be overthrown! It is our hope and prayer that this book will be instrumental in helping to accomplish this. We ask all believers to pray that the Messiah Conspiracy be toppled in our decade!

WHAT FINKEL ATTEMPTS TO ASSERT DOES NOT LINE UP WITH CONTEMPORARY SCHOLARSHIP

Portions of Finkel's article read: "Contemporary scholarly consensus maintains that, while these Pharisaic leaders were putting their own house in order, they also set up fences against the burgeoning influence of early Christianity. Specifically, Rabban Gamaliel II introduced, through the standardization and emendation of the public synagogal prayer, a malediction against Jewish Christians. The twelfth edited liturgical piece of Yavneh reads, in the Palestinian recension of

---

[73] Actually, we wish it had never happened, but it did.

Genizah material: 'Let the Nazarenes [Jewish Christians] and *minim* [a catch-all word for heretics] perish swiftly. Let them be blotted out of the Book of Life and let them not be inscribed with the righteous.' Judaism, in its quest for survival, apparently was threatened by Christianity. In its response, Yavneh not only formulated a negative view of Christianity but purposely aimed at the exclusion of Christians from Jewish services. An act of excommunication was enforced by Yavneh's missionary activities....The consensus still favors the view that 'Nazarenes' were included in the original[74] liturgical text and that Yavneh meant to designate Jewish Christians in the malediction. This central argument of Davies' thesis will be demonstrated as historically untenable.

At the outset, it should be said one cannot present a historical case from sources argued retrojectively unless there is ample evidence for such a development. Secondly, one cannot simply collect various rabbinic statements on a particular question as evidence without examining them organically....One cannot assume that a reading of a late manuscript first published by S. Schechter as a Palestinian recension was the exact reading at the time of its inception....Yavneh amended the petition on the elimination of evildoers and the 'insolent kingdom' by the inclusion of '*minim*' only....During the Yavneh period, a test for a '*min*' in time of worship was not one's faith in the Messiah...*minim* are like the idolators, barbarians, and Zoroastrians who reject monotheistic providence....**At Yavneh, no act of excommunication was employed against these Jewish Christians**....it was simply an intra-synagogal matter. The reference to epistulary action by the rabbis (Justin, *Dialogue* 108) does not indicate that Diaspora communities should introduce anti-Christian prayer or issue a ban against Christians, as scholars wish us to infer. It simply appeals to Jews to refrain from heated discussion with Christian missionaries....The original intent and meaning of the emended 'so called' malediction can be studied in the context of the other eleven benedictions, which comprise the middle section of the daily Jewish

---

[74]Despite Rabbi Finkel's assertion, we have not only ample, but conclusive manuscript evidence! My friend, Dr. Ray A. Pritz, who presently works at the Bible Society as its director, documents the fact that: "In subsequent years further manuscripts came to light from widely scattered provenances which would seem to prove conclusively that a very early version of the *birkat ha-mînîm* (if not the original of Shmuel *ha-qatan)* contained the words *nôẓrîm* and *mînîm.* In 1907 Marx published a text of the Siddur of R. Amram Gaon. The manuscript dates from 1426 and reads והנוצרים והמינים יכלו כרגע ('may the *nôẓrîm* and *mînîm* be destroyed in a moment.') In 1925 another Geniza fragment was published with exactly the same words at the point in question of Schechter's fragment." Ray A. Pritz, *Nazarene Jewish Christianity.* The Magness Press, Hebrew University, 1988, p. 104, used by permission.

Prayer....The existential petitions appear as penultimate to the last six eschatological petitions....In light of the above discussion, Yavneh did not formulate an anti-Jewish Christian prayer. Rather, it defined an eschatological hope...."[75]

DAVIS' ARGUMENT THAT JEWISH CHRISTIANS *WERE* DESIGNATED IN THE MALEDICTION IS VALIDATED BY RABBI SIGAL, DESPITE FINKEL'S FANTASIZED ASSERTION

The Jewish scholar Rabbi Phillip Sigal, in his book, *The Emergence of Contemporary Judaism,* in his appendix entitled, "The Impact of Christianity at Yavne," tells us: "During the last three decades of the first century CE the rabbinic academy at Jabneh issued a significant number of decisions, whose intention was to bring unity to Jewish worship and practice. If the assumption is correct that Jewish Christians were actively seeking converts to their messianic faith within the synagogue communities of Palestine and the Diaspora, it appears probable that some of the actions taken at Jabneh were directed against the Christians, whose sectarian activity threatened the unity of the Jewish community.

W. D. Davies is one of the few contemporary scholars who has made a serious attempt to assess the Christian influence at Jabneh. His section entitled 'Jamnia' in *The Setting of the Sermon on the Mount* (1964) remains unsurpassed....If a good case could be made for the view that *nosrim* did not occur in the original form of the benediction prepared by Samuel the Small but was added later and/or elsewhere than at Jabneh, *or* that *nosrim* refers not to Jewish Christians but to some other Jewish sect, then it could be argued that the central element in Davies' argument has been demolished. The consensus, however, still favors the view that *nosrim* was part of the original text, and that it did designate Jewish Christians."[76]

DR. PRITZ AND RASHI HELP US TO QUESTION RABBI FINKEL'S MODERN ATTEMPT TO COVER UP YAVNE'S BHM CONSPIRACY

What Rabbi Finkel infers, or rather states, is that because the original copy of the BHM (formulated at Yavne) has yet to be found, we may assume that the word Nazarene may not have been there.

---

[75]Rabbi Asher Finkel, "Yavneh's Liturgy and Early Christianity," *The Journal of Ecumenical Studies*, Spring 1981, pp. 232-233, 235, 237, 239, 241, 243-246. Bold mine.
[76]Phillip Sigal, *The Emergence of Contemporary Judaism.* Pittsburgh: The Pickwick Press, © 1980, pp. 297-298, used by permission.

Thus, there was no plot against the early Jewish believers in Jesus. His defense is that the fragment found was a late one. However, the fragment is one of the earliest to be discovered,[77] and the fact that it was first published by Solomon Schechter in 1925 is meaningless within the context of our thesis! The fact that Solomon Schechter was actually an unbiased Jewish scholar is a point in our favor, as evidence that there was a carefully devised Jewish rabbinical conspiracy against the Jewish believers in Messiah.

All things aside, even Rashi, the highly revered rabbi of the eleventh century, admitted the reason for the BHM when he said: "They revised it at Yavne after a long time in the vicinity of the teaching of the nôẕrî...."[78]

I owe this piece of knowledge to a dear friend of mine, Dr. Ray A. Pritz, who is presently the director of the Bible Society in Jerusalem. In his book, *Nazarene Jewish Christianity*, Ray documented what is clearly an irrefutable proof in a comment by Rashi, in a section of the Talmud which, itself, was later covered up and censored. Ray documents: "In the first Venice printing of the Talmud we find this comment by Rashi (missing in later, censored editions) at Brachot 30a (=28b in today's pagination): 'They revised it' [The ancient Jewish eighteen benediction Amidah synagogue prayer by adding a curse (No. 12) against the Jewish believers in Jesus]....at Yavne after a long time in the vicinity of the teaching of the *nôẕrî* [Jesus], who taught to overturn [in Rashi's warped opinion] the ways of the living God."[79]

RASHI EXPOSES RABBI FINKEL'S DOUBLE STANDARD WITHIN THIS CONSPIRACY

It is also interesting that Rabbi Finkel mentions nearly a dozen Christian scholars in reference to what he calls "his widely accepted thesis." At the same time he conveniently fails to mention some of the unbiased Jewish scholars who agree with us, many of whom are quoted in this chapter—this includes our friend, Rashi.

---

[77]Dr. Pritz, whose field of study lies squarely within this area, informed me in a letter from Jerusalem in 1993, that: "The oldest dated document found in the geniza was from the mid-eighth century." This is an extremely early copy by archaeological standards.

[78]Ray A. Pritz, *Nazarene Jewish Christianity*, p. 104.

[79]Ibid. [ ] mine. "See *Halakhot Gedolot*, ed. Hildesheimer, Berlin 5652, p. 27. The editor notes that his ms. contains a marginal note: '*Birkat ha-Minim* was introduced after Yeshua ben Pandera, when heretics became numerous.' " G. Alon, *The Jews in Their Land in the Talmudic Age*, p. 290. In his book *Christianity in Talmud & Midrash*, (1903), Herford documents that Yeshua ben Pandera was a derogatory and sarcastic Hebrew name for Jesus.

Now we can say without a guilty conscience, "Rabbi Finkel, you can hang it up!" Even the famed Rashi (Rabbi Shlomo Hisaki) of the eleventh century testified against you nearly, 1000 years ago.

DOES RABBI FINKEL ATTEMPT TO DENY THE CONSPIRACY SO JESUS WILL REMAIN CLOAKED IN "CHRISTIAN CLOTHES," TO CIRCUMVENT JEWISH INTEREST?

We ask why Rabbi Finkel has continued to deny something that even Rashi admitted nearly 1000 years ago. Well, we have seen how even that admission was concealed and censored. Why? We believe that such knowledge will arouse interest in the person of Jesus in light of His true historical Messianic Jewish acceptance. An honest investigation into this forbidden subject might prove dangerous to the rabbis' desires to stonewall the Messianic credentials of Jesus and perpetuate the continued rejection of Him among the Jewish youth of today.

Oh, what tragedy, what shame, and what judgment lies ahead for these who would, in many cases, deliberately try to hide the truth from their own people. For what? A doctrine of ego—assimilation. Is that worth eternal life? God will certainly judge these men seriously. He warns in Proverbs: "An ungodly witness scorneth judgment: and the mouth of the wicked devoureth iniquity" (Prov. 19:28 KJV).

Jesus once said of those who would cause little children to be misled: "...'It is inevitable that stumbling blocks should come, but woe to him through whom they come! It would be better for him if a millstone were hung around his neck and he were thrown into the sea, than that he should cause one of these little ones to stumble' " (Luke 17:1-2 NASB).

IS THERE ANOTHER "FINK" HIDING IN THE THEOLOGICAL JOURNALS?

In 1984, Steven Katz wrote an article on Yavne entitled "Issues in the Separation of Judaism and Christianity After 70 C.E.: A Reconsideration." In our opinion, this article is very similar to Rabbi Finkel's in that it attempts to blatantly deny the obvious! At one point, Katz remarks: "One would expect to find a better indication of Jewish propaganda, to the extent that it existed, in the Jewish sources, namely, Mishna, Tosefta, and the Tannaitic Midrashim. However, these sources contain almost no references at all to Jesus or to early Jewish Christianity."[80]

We remind our readers that almost is not all; it either does contain a mention of Jesus or it does not! If it does not, you do have a point. If it does contain even one mention, you **do not** have a point. So what is the use in saying "almost no mention of Jesus"? It is like saying, "I am almost a virgin." Katz's arguments, upon close examination, are obviously absurd; especially when you stand them up against the documentation in this book. They fall down.

When I looked up this article at the Pitts Theological Library at Emory University in Atlanta, Georgia, the ATLA Religion database printed out a descriptive comment under the article listing, which read: "Note: The article re-examines the main arguments that have been put forward regarding claims of official Jewish persecution of early Christians. Based on the rabbinic sources, these claims are examined and, in general, **shown to be without foundation** *despite the long tradition in Christian apologetic and scholarly circles to the contrary.*"[81] Suffice it to say that the latter comment is appreciated for its honesty in making a truthful point of scholarship for us.

THEY SAY A CAT HAS NINE LIVES—WE URGE KATZ TO FIND TRUTH IN HIS ONE, BEFORE IT IS TOO LATE!

Katz, like his predecessor Finkel, suggestively denies that the BHM mentioned *notzrim* ("Jewish Christians"), as the recently discovered Schechter fragment has clearly indicated! Without foundation, Katz arrogantly writes: "...the rabbinic evidence suggests a concern with heretical groups and manifestations that is broader in scope than Jewish (or Gentile) Christianity. As a consequence, the tendency to see Jewish Christianity as a major or even primary concern of the sages must be tempered, even rejected....with regard to method....we should not overestimate the importance of Christianity to the sages at Yavneh and, reading backwards, impute into their age, work, and consciousness the later significance of Christianity....Our investigation justifies the conclusion that the Yavnean sages were not overly preoccupied with Jewish Christianity[82]....one can suggest with

---

[80]Steven T. Katz, "Issues in the Separation of Judaism and Christianity After 70 C.E.: A Reconsideration," *Journal of Biblical Literature*. Mar. 1984, Dartmouth College, © used by permission.

[81]Bold and Italics mine.

[82]In response to Katz's off-the-wall statement insinuating a nonchalant attitude of the Yavnean rabbis in their concern about Jewish believers in Jesus, we ask, "Were the Jewish Christians so numerous, with biblical Jewish proof of the truth of their faith, that

confidence that the Yavneans....text did not include an explicit reference to *Notzrim*. Instead, in all probability, it addressed itself to 'outsiders' (*perushim*)...and the 'arrogant of the nations' (*zedim*)....and as such the entire role of the *Birkat ha-Minim* in the history of Jewish-Christian relations must be rethought....there was no official anti-Christian policy at Yavneh or elsewhere before the Bar Kochba revolt and no total separation between Jews and Christians before (if immediately after?) the Bar Kochba revolt....despite strong claims to the contrary, the *Birkat ha-Minim* did *not* signal any decisive break between Jews and Jewish Christians."[83]

KATZ TRIES TO ADOPT A DIFFERENT SOLUTION TO THE ANTI-JEWISH CHRISTIAN BHM, BUT PROFESSOR ALON BRINGS HIM BACK DOWN TO EARTH

Katz further writes: "Had Justin, writing within two decades of the Bar Kochba revolt, cited the form of the *Birkat ha-Minim* that includes the term 'Nazarenes,' it would have provided strong grounds for a direct link of this prayer with Jewish Christianity. The lack of such a mention suggests the need for a different solution regarding the *Birkat ha-Minim*."[84] We remind our readers what the scholar, G. Alon, has documented of Justin and Jerome: "...Justin Martyr, born a pagan at what is now Nablus at the end of the first century. In his 'Dialogue With Trypho', written around the year 150, he says: 'You Jews pronounce maledictions on the Christians in your synagogues'....more direct testimony comes from Epiphanius, who writes that the Jews denounce the *Nazarenes* in their prayers three times a day.' Note that he speaks only of *Jewish* Christians (Nazarenes). And Jerome, in his

---

they became a large enough threat to warrant that rabbis send out letters worldwide (containing copies of the BHM) to all synagogues in an effort to convince universal Jewry that the believer's faith was an untrue heresy?" Douglas Hare comments: "The insertion of the *Birkath ha-Minim* into the Eighteen Benedictions is clear proof that the rabbinic authorities regarded Christianity as a threat to a beleaguered Jewry. Even without further evidence it should be assumed that notice of this liturgical innovation was transmitted to synagogues throughout the Diaspora. We are not limited to assumptions, however. We have the testimony of Justin that selected men were sent out from Jerusalem 'into all the world' ε*l*ς πᾶσαν τηὺ λῆν to report the outbreak of the Christian heresy. In addition we have the evidence of Tos. Sanh. 2:6 that letters were on at least one other occasion sent out to all the Diaspora communities on the subject of liturgical matters." Douglas Hare, *The Theme of Jewish Persecution of Christians in the Gospel According to St. Matthew*, p. 65.

[83]Steven T. Katz, "Issues in the Separation of Judaism and Christianity After 70 C.E.: A Reconsideration," *Journal of Biblical Literature*, pp. 61-62, 66, 62, 68-69, 72.

[84]Ibid, p. 71.

Commentary on Isaiah, chapter 52, verse 4, says practically the same thing.

That was about all we knew until 1925, when the question was settled by the discovery of Genizah fragments containing portions of the liturgy according to the ancient Palestinian rite. In these versions, *Birkat ha-Minim* reads like this: May the apostates have no hope, unless they return to Thy Torah, and may the Nazarenes and the Minim disappear in a moment. May they be erased from the book of life, and not be inscribed with the righteous.

The provenance of this text, which calls down wrath on...Nazarenes and *Minim*—leaves little room for doubt that we are looking at something very close to the original formulation as laid down in the days of Rabban Gamaliel. The wording might give the impression that Nazarenes are one thing and *Minim* another; or that *Minim* is a generic term for schismatics. But that can scarcely be true; for why would Rabban Gamaliel have reacted to any heresy except one that posed a special threat in his own time? There was nothing new about non-Pharisaic sects like the Sadducees. They and others had been numerous in Temple days.

We must therefore assume that in this liturgical fragment, *Minim* and *Notzrim* are synonymous, and that both refer to the Jewish Christians. The assumption is borne out by Jerome, who writes that in his lifetime (4th to 5th centuries) there was a sect of Jews called *Minim—also known* as Nazarenes."[85]

IS KATZ A CO-CONSPIRACTOR? WE MAY NEVER KNOW, UNTIL . . . .

These men (Justin and Jerome), specifically alluded to the BHM in reference to Christians being cursed. The Amidah prayer containing the eighteen benedictions (the twelfth being the BHM) was recited three times a day! The blindness of Katz eludes us! And I bet it eludes you, too!

We believe he should reconsider his reconsideration! Unless, of course, he knows better, and is himself a co-conspirator in the present attempt at a Messiah Conspiracy cover-up. Could it be? You may never know! Until the return of the Messiah, of course.

***

[85]G. Alon, *The Jews in Their Land in the Talmudic Age*, pp. 289-290.

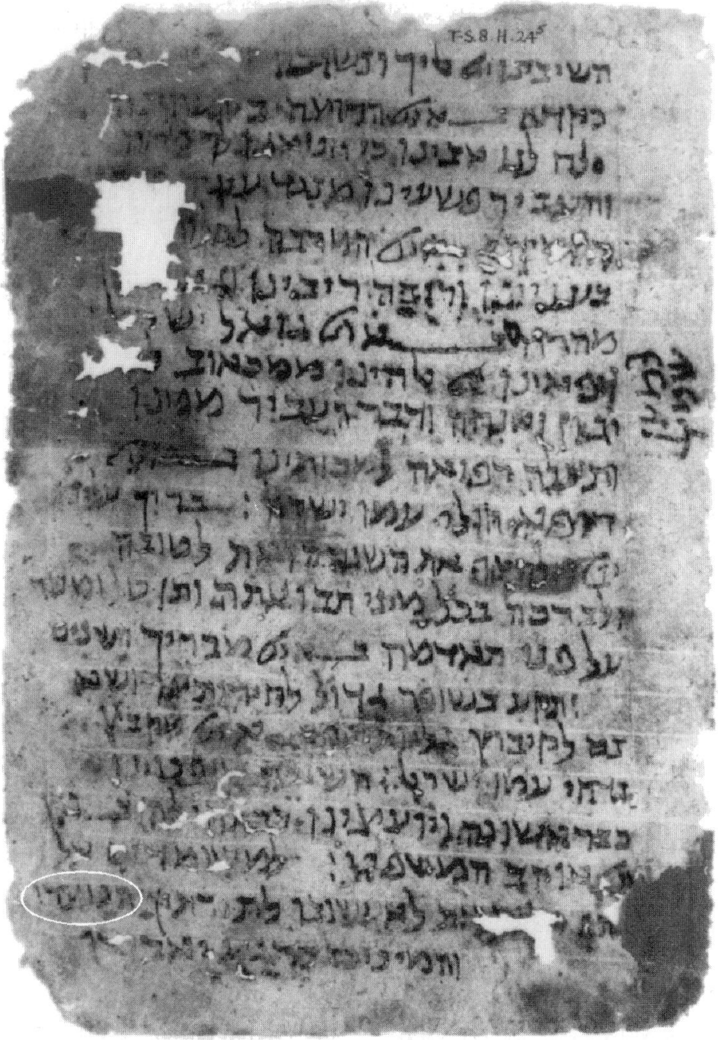

In fragment T-S.8.H.24^{5} of the Birkat ha-Minim, the word *notzrim*, which targets Christians, is almost unreadable, as previously illustrated. However, with the use of ultraviolet photography, this word can be clearly identified, as you see in this photograph.[86] This document, one of the most interesting in history, now stares its readers in the face, as we have exposed its creator's intent. The "prayer's" author is guilty before all. His true purpose is revealed; an attempt to systematically neutralize Jewish believers in Jesus as Messiah.

---

[86]Previous three photographs, courtesy of the Syndics of Cambridge University Library.

Prior to its discovery in 1925, many snickered[87] at the reports of Justin Martyr and other witnesses who, writing a generation after Jesus left the earth, recorded that the rabbis *sent special men out from Jerusalem into all the world*[88] for the attempted elimination of "Jews for Jesus," if you please, from the synagogue.

AN INTERESTING PARTY AROUND THE MICROFILM PROJECTOR AT THE HEBREW UNIVERSITY LIBRARY

When I asked several individuals at the Hebrew University of Jerusalem, in the Givat Ram library to translate Schechter's fourth century BHM for me from the microfilm projector,[89] they were shocked. When they read the word *notzrim* (Jewish Christians), one professor asked me, "What are you studying?" Another library attendant asked, with a dumbfounded look on his face, "What are you going to do with this?" As they encircled me and the microfilm screen displaying the Cambridge Schechter fragment,[90] I answered, "I am going to publish it." Then Benjamin, from the archives department, gave me an order form for the Cambridge Geniza Research Unit in England. I filled it out, and shortly thereafter received the prints of the fragment you saw.

That is how I came to retrieve this treasure for you! It was interesting and unforgettable! I might add that in all of the journals, articles, books and literature I have searched through over the past twelve years, I never once saw a photo of the Schechter fragment. You have a true rarity before you; a treat few have ever laid eyes on.

The word, "Christian" (*Notzri*), was removed from the prayer after Jewish Christians were no longer considered a threat. Today, most modern Hebrew Jewish readers have not seen this word, and most are not aware it existed in earlier copies of the synagogue prayer, just

---

[87]Ray A. Pritz, *Nazarene Jewish Christianity*, p. 102.

[88]Justin Martyr, of the late first and early second centuries, attested: "...you appointed chosen men and sent them into all the civilized world, proclaiming that 'a certain godless and lawless sect has been raised by one Jesus of Galilee, a deceiver, whom we crucified, but His disciples stole Him by night from the tomb, where He had been laid after being unnailed from the cross, and they deceive men, saying that He is risen from the dead and has ascended into heaven'....the priests and teachers of your people have caused His name to be profaned and blasphemed throughout the whole earth." A. Lukyn Williams, *Justin Martyr, The Dialogue With Trypho*, pp. 224, 242.

[89]At that time in the late 1980's, my Hebrew was not what it is today, so I asked for assistance.

[90]I wish to thank my friend Shosh Basson, the librarian for the Institute of Microfilmed Hebrew Manuscripts, for retrieving this important BHM document we were viewing earlier that day.

as many are not aware of the fact that there was an incredibly large number of Jewish believers in Jesus' Messiahship frequenting the synagogues in the first and second centuries.[91] If the rabbis would openly admit this, they would have to contend with Jews who are becoming increasingly more curious about the question of Jesus.[92]

A JEWISH PROFESSOR COMES CLEAN WITH THE BIRKAT HA-MINIM

Lawrence H. Schiffman, professor of Hebrew and Judaic studies at New York University, wrote the book, *Who Was A Jew? Rabbinic and Halakhic Perspectives on the Jewish-Christian Schism*, in 1985. In his book, he attempts to tell it the way it was, with honesty, in relation to the BHM controversy. On the back cover of his work, it is written: "In recent years the issue of 'Who is a Jew?' has become predominant in the Jewish community both in America and Israel. This book masterfully explains the relationship between *halakhah* and the issue of 'Who Was a Jew,' showing that the Jewish-Christian schism was a result of the halakhic definition of Jewish identity. Using Talmudic sources, Professor Schiffman examines the *halakhot* governing the Jew by birth...and the Rabbinic reaction to the early Christians, and discusses the narratives illustrating Rabbinic contact with Jewish Christians. He concludes that the Christians were regarded initially by the Rabbis as *minim*, Jews who had heretical beliefs....This book is required reading for both historians of Judaism and Christianity and those who would seek to formulate educated views about the issue of Jewish status in contemporary times."[93]

***

---

[91]David Chernoff, in his publication, *7 Steps to Knowing the God of Abraham, Isaac & Jacob*, noted that estimates of the number of Jewish believers in Jesus in the first century run as high as "one million Messianic Jews." His pamphlet is available through MMI Publishing Co., POB 1024, Havertown, PA, USA 19083.

[92]Dr. Kac notes of Professor Pinchas Lapide: "According to Lapide a 'Jesus wave' is now passing through Judaism. In proof of this he states that in the first twenty-seven years following the reconstitution of the present State of Israel 187 Hebrew books, research articles, poems, dissertations and essays have been written about Jesus. More has been written in Hebrew about Jesus in the last twenty-five years than in all the eighteen previous centuries." Arthur W. Kac, *The Messiahship of Jesus*. Grand Rapids, MI: Baker Book House, © 1980, p. 76, used by permission.

[93]Lawrence Schiffman, *Who Was a Jew? Rabbinic and Halakhic Perspectives on the Jewish-Christian Schism*. New York: KTAV Publishing House, Inc., © 1985, p. back cover, used by permission.

UNLIKE SOME, PROFESSOR SCHIFFMAN ADMITS THAT THE CAIRO GENIZA DISCOVERY ELUCIDATES THE IDENTIFICATION OF THE *MINIM* AS JEWISH CHRISTIANS

Professor Schiffman tells us: "A number of tannaitic restrictions directed against *minim* clearly refer to the early Jewish Christians, as can be shown from their content and date. These regulations show how the Rabbis attempted to combat those beliefs which they regarded as outside the Jewish pale while never rejecting the Jewishness of those who held them....Indeed, this benediction probably went a long way toward making the Jewish Christians feel unwelcome in the synagogue and causing them to worship separately.

A *baraita'* in B. Berakhot 28bf. states: Our Rabbis taught: Simeon Ha-Paqoli ordered the Eighteen Benedictions before Rabban Gamliel at Yavneh. Rabban Gamliel said to the Sages: Is there no one who knows how to compose a benediction against the *minim?* Samuel Ha-Qatan stood up and composed it. Another year (while serving as precentor), he (Samuel Ha-Qatan) forgot it and tried to recall it for two or three hours, yet they did not remove him.

Despite some ingenious claims to the contrary, the Gamliel of our *baraita'* is Rabban Gamliel II of Yavneh in the post-destruction period. Simeon Ha-Paqoli set the Eighteen Benedictions in order before Rabban Gamliel as part of the general effort at Yavneh to fix and standardize *halakhah.* Rabban Gamliel (II) asked for a volunteer to compose the benediction against the *minim*....In a later year, he was called upon to serve as precentor. In the course of the service, he was unable to recite the benediction against the *minim.* Nonetheless, even after several hours of trying to recall it, the Rabbis did not remove him as precentor.

B. Berakhot 29a asks why he was not removed. After all, it was the purpose of this blessing to ensure that the precentor was not one of those heretics cursed in the benediction. The Talmud answers that since Samuel Ha-Qatan had himself composed it, it could be assumed that he was not a *min.*

Since the term *min* can refer at different times to various forms of heresy that threatened Rabbinic Judaism in Talmudic times, it is essential to clarify who the *minim* of this benediction are. Palestinian texts of the Eighteen Benedictions from the Cairo Genizah present us with a text of the benediction which elucidates the identification of the *minim*: For the apostates may there be no hope unless they return to Your Torah. As for the *noserim* and the *minim*, may they perish immediately. Speedily may they be erased from the Book of Life and may they not be registered among the righteous. Blessed are You, O Lord, Who subdues the wicked.

While other specimens of the Palestinian liturgy show slight variation, the *noserim*, (usually translated 'Christians') and *minim* are included in the best texts of this benediction. Some may wish to debate whether the *noserim* and *minim* here mentioned are to be taken as one group or two. Yet the fact remains that the *noserim* were included with apostates and heretics in the Genizah documents.

May we assume that this version of the benediction represents the text as it was recited by Samuel Ha-Qatan before the sages of Yavneh? On the one hand, the Palestinian liturgical material found in the Cairo Genizah generally preserves the traditions of Palestinian Jewry in the amoraic period. On the other hand, there may be external evidence that this benediction was recited during the tannaitic period and that it included explicit reference to *noserim*."[94]

PROFESSOR SCHIFFMAN ADMITS THAT *YOU CANNOT ESCAPE* THE PRESENT EVIDENCE THAT THE PASSAGE OF THE BHM WAS ALREADY BEING RECITED IN THE SECOND CENTURY IN REFERENCE TO BELIEVERS

Schiffman also mentions: "Three passages in the Gospel of John (9:22, 12:42, 16:2) mention the expulsion of Christians from the synagogue. The Gospel of John was most probably not composed until at least the last decade of the first century. The actual setting of the Gospel is not known, although some would place it in a Syrian or Palestinian milieu. The most we can conclude from John is that the community to which it was directed *may* have already been subject to the benediction against the *minim* when this book was composed.

Justin Martyr, writing in the middle of the second century C.E., in his Dialogue with Tryphon referred several times to the cursing of Christians in the synagogue. Justin castigates his interlocutor Trypho as follows (XVI): For you slew the just one (Jesus) and his prophets before him, and now you...dishonour those that set their hope on him, and God Almighty and Maker of the Universe that sent him, cursing in your synagogues them that believe in Christ....he appeals to the Jews in CXXXVII not to revile Jesus: As the rulers of your synagogues teach you, after the prayer.

It is difficult to escape the conclusion that these passages are a polemical and confused reflection of the recitation of the *birkat ha-minim* in the synagogues of Palestine (Justin grew up in Samaria).

---

[94]Ibid, pp. 54-56.

These passages present evidence that some version of the benediction was already recited in the mid-second century C.E. and that it included explicit reference to the Christians.

Similar testimony comes from Origen (c. 185-c. 254 C.E.), who accuses Jews of blaspheming and cursing Jesus and in another passage says: Enter the synagogue of the Jews and see Jesus flagellated by those with the language of blasphemy....Explicit reference, however, comes from Epiphanius and Jerome. Epiphanius (c. 315-403 C.E.), speaking of the Nazoraeans, a Judaizing Christian sect, says: ...the people also stand up in the morning, at noon, and in the evening, three times a day and they pronounce curses and maledictions over them when they say their prayers in the synagogues. Three times a day they say: 'May God curse the Nazoraeans.' "[95]

A RABBI WHO KNOWS HIS HISTORY AND HIS NEW TESTAMENT, PULLS BACK THE CURTAIN ON YAVNE

In 1985, Rabbi Phillip Sigal, of Grand Rapids, Michigan, known for his great wisdom regarding Judaism and the New Testament, wrote *Judaism, The Evolution of a Faith.* This work was published three years later. In it, Sigal helps us peel away the sheath covering up the true events at Yavne in connection with the Hebrew Christian. This contradicts Rabbi Finkel and others who would have us believe that it is all "make-believe." Sigal tells us: "Yohanan's segment of the proto-rabbinic movement remained aloof from the rebellion of 66 C.E., as did Christian Jews. It attempted to still the stormy waters of a new rising tide of militancy after 73 C.E. but failed. As it failed, the position of apolitical Christian Jews became precarious. When Yohanan was deposed as leader of the academy at Yabneh, the fate of Christian Judaism as a variant form of Judaism was sealed. The irony of this particular development is that the person behind the expulsion of Christians from the synagogue was Rabbi Gamaliel II, grandson of Gamaliel I, who saved Peter from potential disaster before the Sanhedrin (Acts 5:34-35)....Yohanan ben Zakkai and his Yabnean associates did nothing less than restate the theology of Judaism....Yabneh was the center of great liturgical development. Prayers of old were brought together, recast, and joined with newly composed prayers, and a fixed form of worship was arranged....It is clear that Yohanan set in motion the mechanism of consolidation and the restatement of Judaic theology. But Yohanan was ousted from leadership sometime between 80 and 90 C.E., when the Romans saw fit

---

[95]Ibid, pp. 56-57.

to bestow government-backed authority upon Gamaliel II, naming him Nasi (president or prince) at Yabneh. This erstwhile supporter of anti-Roman policies in the late 60s thus became presiding rabbi at Yabneh....As soon as **Gamaliel II** assumed authority he **moved against Christians**, and sometime between 90 and 100 C.E. he had the *amidah* redacted to include a paragraph that invoked God's curse upon all sectarians including *notzrim*, Christians. **This change made it impossible for a Christian to pray in a synagogue**. In addition, Gamaliel sent out letters for the expulsion of Christians from synagogues that led to the permanent fissure in Judaism between Rabbinic Judaism and Christianity....This anti-Christian clause has long been removed from the *amidah*....The major source of irritation to Gamaliel II was the Christian Jewish movement, and as noted, he saw to their exclusion."[96]

RABBI SIGAL'S CREDENTIALS—IMPRESSIVE

Rabbi Sigal has admitted to a fact that many rabbis dare not! We praise him for his unbiased honesty in our quest to uncover the Messiah Conspiracy! Marilyn Schaub of Duquesne University makes an impressive comment on the back cover of Rabbi Sigal's book: "His rare qualification as both rabbinic and Christian Testament scholar makes his discussion of the relationship between Judaism and Christianity **particularly valuable**. The book should have wide appeal...."[97]

One comment from the cover flap of this wonderful rabbi's book states: "As both rabbi and New Testament scholar, Sigal pays particular attention to the relationship between Judaism and Christianity. His unique perspective illuminates the Jewish matrix which gave birth to Christianity, and his analysis, including some original interpretations, explores both the tensions and the ongoing interaction between the two faiths....Phillip Sigal was Rabbi of Congregation Ahavas Israel in Grand Rapids, Michigan, until his death in 1985."[98]

***

[96]Phillip Sigal, *Judaism, The Evolution of a Faith.* Grand Rapids, MI: William B. Eerdmans Publishing Co., © 1988, pp. 67, 93-95, used by permission. Bold mine.
[97]Ibid, p. back cover. Bold mine.
[98]Ibid, p. cover flap.

A BRILLIANT ISRAELI PROFESSOR TAKES THE LID OFF THE BARREL OF THE CONSPIRACY AT YAVNE

In the summer of 1987, *Immanuel*, an Israeli journal of religious thought and research, published a fascinating and revealing, albeit technical article on the subject of changes which took place at Yavne; changes which deliberately targeted Jewish Christians. This article is extremely important and most revealing because, in addition to its comments on the BHM, it mentions that the *et zemah* Davidic Messianic blessing was removed in order to stifle the Christian movement among Jews. Again, this is something only coming to light in this century, as presented by Dr. Liebes!

The article is also amazing in that it mentions hidden Christian influence in Jewish blessings as they are presently recited; a fact revealed only recently in an honest manner by its author, Yehudah Liebes, who is a Jewish Israeli professor at the Hebrew University in Jerusalem. Since Liebes is not a believer, these credentials provide us with an unbiased viewpoint. We found it of such interest that we will quote Liebes at length. Though it may be four pages, it will prove extremely enlightening to the uninformed Jewish readers who desire to put the last nails in the coffins of the arguments used by Rabbis Finkel and Katz. Their teachings are clearly outdated by the brilliant and enlightened Professor Liebes, who helped us remove the lid from the barrel of the Messiah Conspiracy!

EARLY ON, JEWS FOR JESUS AND THE REST OF THE JEWS WORSHIPPED IN THE SAME SYNOGOGUE UNTIL THE *ET ZEMAH* BLESSING CAME INTO QUESTION

Dr. Liebes tells us: "...the earliest Christians did not separate themselves from the community of Israel, but worshipped in the same synagogues, and even served as prayer leaders. One may therefore conclude that, during the first generation following Jesus, these Jews were not yet rejected nor perceived as a danger (the above mishnah was written at a later period). Essentially, there was no disagreement between them and other Jews save that concerning the identity of the Messiah, which was the kind of question over which internal Jewish disagreement was acceptable—much as there was disagreement on this score between R. Akiba and R. Johanan ben Torta concerning the messianic claims of Bar Kokhba. True, the Christians believed that their messiah had already left this world, but this did not affect their basic hope for the coming of the Messiah and the national redemption. As we know from many documents, the essential belief of the Jewish

Christians crystallized around their hope for the Second Coming of Jesus, and through him the redemption of Israel....It was natural enough that the Jewish Christians should wish to introduce a change into that prayer dealing with the coming of the Messiah son of David namely, the blessing *Et Zemah*. What could be more natural than a Christian attempt to mention the name of Jesus within the framework of this blessing? Thus, the formula *mazmiah qeren le-David* was replaced by *mazmiah qeren yeshuàh*. In so doing, the Jewish Christians did not intend to alter the original intention of this blessing, but merely to reinterpret it in light of their own views, utilizing the then-accepted option to vary the formulae of blessings. Neither did they remove David's name from the blessing entirely, but they retained the opening formula, 'the shoot of David your servant speedily cause to blossom...'; they saw no reason to eliminate this, as they considered Jesus as the Davidic messiah. Nevertheless, the name of Jesus, which they alluded to in the word *yeshuàh* ('salvation') in the concluding formula, and possible also in the body of the blessing, was stressed more than that of David...."[99]

PROFESSOR LIEBES TELLS US THE SECRET REASON THE RABBIS REACTED AGAINST THE JEWISH BELIEVERS AT YAVNE, BY *REMOVING* A CRITICAL HEBREW BLESSING

"There was also a ritual expression to this break. The Sanhedrin, convened under the leadership of Rabban Gamaliel II in Yavneh at the beginning of the second century, introduced a number of changes directed against the Christians within the text of the prayers. The most striking and best-known of these changes was the introduction of *Birkat ha-Minim* as a separate, independent blessing, which was reformulated in an anti-Christian manner. According to the text of the Palestinian liturgy discovered in the Cairo genizah, this blessing speaks explicitly against the 'apostates' and **'Christians'**....But this was not the only change introduced in the prayer book at that time. At that time the blessing *et zemah* was removed from the prayer book, and from then on this blessing was no longer recited in the Palestinian ritual. This omission was not performed, as thought by some, to preserve the total number of eighteen blessings following the introduction of *Birkat*

---

[99]Yehudah Liebes, "Who Makes the Horn of Jesus to Flourish," *Immanuel*, No. 21, Summer 1987. Israel: The Ecumenical Theological Research Fraternity in Israel and The Anti-Defamation League of B'nai B'rithin, pp. 56-58, © used by permission. Liebes' original and unabridged Hebrew article was originally published in *Jerusalem Studies in Jewish Thought*, iii, © 1984, pp. 313-348. Professor Liebes presently teaches in the Department of Jewish Thought at the Hebrew University in Jerusalem, Israel.

ha-Minim; such a reason would be inadequate justification for eliminating from the prayer text an important blessing, dealing with such a central principle as the coming of the Messiah....The main motivation for the elimination of *et zemah* was the same as that which led to the introduction of *Birkat ha-Minim*—namely, the distancing of Christianity. The sages knew that the Jewish Christians expressed their belief in Jesus in this blessing, and that one of its most widespread concluding formulae was even introduced by the Christians as an allusion to the name of their Messiah—as were also, possibly, the references to *yeshu'ah* in the body of the blessing. Therefore, they decided at Yavneh to eliminate this blessing entirely, with all the associations involved in it. This is not merely a theoretical conjecture, but is based upon the evidence of a midrash preserved in Numbers Rabba. This midrash states that two blessings of the Amidah—*Birkat ha-Minim* and *et zemah*—are excluded from the rubric of 'Forgive all iniquity and accept that which is good (tov)' (Hosea 14:3—*Tov* in gematria equals 17, which is the number of blessings left in the Amidah after one removes the above two), as it was introduced 'after' Jesus Christ—that is, because of him or on his account. While Jesus' name is not explicitly mentioned in this midrash, it may clearly be inferred there, not only because the subject and matter and the context require it, but also because of certain exact linguistic parallels in which his name is mentioned as such, albeit not in connection with *et zemah* but only in relation to *Birkat ha-Minim.*

Another anti-Christian ritual change was made at Yavneh. Following the elimination of *et zemah David*, no reference to King David remained in the Amidah. This was the opposite of the intention of the rabbis of Yavneh, whose main complaint against the Christians was precisely that they had removed David's name from the conclusion of the blessing *et zemah*, substituting for it the name of their messiah. Thus, those making these changes felt the need to restore David to his rightful place. But this could no longer be done in the separate blessing of *et zemah*, because of its association with heresy; instead, the name of David was added to the previous blessing, concluding the blessing for Jerusalem with the formula, *Elohei David u-voney Yerushalayim* ('God of David, who rebuilds Jerusalem'). The Jerusalem Talmud, following the directive to behave thus in prayer, alludes to the political situation which brought about the institution of this version, emphasizing that the Messiah would be none other than David himself, to counter the view of those who had erased David's name from the blessing and placed that of Jesus in its stead."[100]

---

[100]Ibid, pp. 63-64. Bold mine.

PROFESSOR LIEBES INFORMS US THAT JEWS HAVE UNKNOWINGLY BEEN RECITING A "CHRISTIAN" PRAYER FOR CENTURIES, WHICH IS EVIDENCE OF THE JEWISHNESS OF THE TRUE CHRISTIAN FAITH

"The destiny of the concluding formula, *mazmiah qeren yeshu'ah,* was far more fortunate than that of its Jewish Christian authors. While the blessing *et zemah David*, including its ending, was abolished in the Palestinean rite, it was retained in Babylonia, where there were no Jewish Christians. Indeed, the Babylonians did not even know of them, and therefore had no reason to cast suspicions upon this formula, particularly as it was already widely accepted; they ruled in their Talmud that one should recite it. Thus, once the rulings of the Babylonian Talmud had become accepted among all Jewish communities, the entire Jewish people throughout the centuries recited the formula *mazmiah qeren yeshu'ah* three times a day, without knowing who introduced this formula or why. Indeed, they would have been unable to imagine a Christian origin for it....It should be noted that *mazmiah qeren yeshu'ah* is far more indicative of the Jewishness of Christianity in its earliest years than of Christian influence upon the text of the prayer book. There is no more impressive testimony to this than the presence of the name of the Christian Messiah in the Amidah prayer, but this is not the only evidence of such. One who examines it attentively is liable to discover many other remnants of the Jewish Christian spirit surviving in Jewish literature."[101]

A portion of Professor Liebes' footnote 28 reads: "There may be other such survivals in Jewish ritual, such as the angelic names recited between the Shofar blasts on Rosh Hashanah in some rituals, which refer to *Yeshu'a Sar ha-Panim* together with Elijah and Metatron, a combination found in other sources as well. See now my article, 'The Angels of the Shofar and Yeshu'a Sar ha-Panim' (Heb.) in *ha-Mistiqah ha-Yehudit ha-Qedumah* [=*Mehqerey Yerushalayim be-Mahshevet Yisra'el* vi: 1-2] (1987), pp. 171-195."[102]

THERE ARE SOME WHO DENY THE TRUTH AND SOME WHO TELL THE TRUTH AS *IT IS* DOCUMENTED

Despite the fact that Finkel, Katz and others deny that the true purpose of the BHM was to eliminate Jewish Christians from the

---

[101] Ibid, pp. 66-67.
[102] Ibid.

synagogues, we provide the truth, as documented by many an authority, including some very unusual ones!

IT IS DOCUMENTED BY DOCTOR KAC

The real purpose and result of the BHM has been well documented by several foremost scholars. Examples include the Jewish Christian, Arthur W. Kac, M.D., who stated: "Jewish hostility to the Hebrew Christian dates back to the first century when the Messianic movement of Jesus was still strongly Jewish. The so-called Birkat Ha-minim prayer of hate was composed before the end of the first century and was designed to separate the Hebrew Christian from his Jewish brethren."[103]

BY PFEIFFER

Robert H. Pfeiffer tells us in his book, *History of New Testament Times*: "The revolt of Bar Cocheba marks the last flaming outburst of militant Messianic hope. Normative Judaism relinquished the utopian dreams of apocalyptic writings to the Christians, and retrenched itself increasingly within the citadel of the written and the oral law, thus separating itself more and more from the Gentiles. The final break between the Christian Church and the synagogue took place at this time when the Nazarenes—a Jewish-Christian group worshiping in the synagogues but teaching that Jesus was the Messiah—were forced to become a sect, equally repudiated by the Rabbis and by the Bishops. Henceforth the teachers of the Law—scribes and Pharisees, Tannaim, Amoraim, Geonim, rabbis—became the leaders of Israel."[104]

BY FORKMAN

The scholar, Goran Forkman, in his article "The Limits of the Religious Community," informs us: "The effect of this point in the prayer was very ingenious. It was from now on impossible for someone who knew himself to be a Christian or who in any other way deviated from the normative Judaism, to read the Eighteen Benedictions aloud or to respond with an 'amen'....the prayer had to be read every morning, and just this must have resulted in the deviator leaving the Jewish community. Birkat ha-minim therefore acted as a

---

[103] Arthur W. Kac, *The Messiahship of Jesus*, p. 139

[104] Robert Pfeiffer, *History of New Testament Times*. New York: Harper & Brothers Publishers, © 1949, p. 45, used by permission.

total, definite expulsion. The level of formality was low. Without any formal decisions, without any trials and expulsion sentences, the deviator was in this way thrust out of the community. Judaism was no longer pluralistic."[105]

BY PRESIDENT ROSEN

Moishe Rosen, president of *Jews for Jesus*, comments on the purpose of the Birkat ha-Minim; to throw the believers out of the synagogues in the first and second centuries. He notes: "A Jewish Christian could hardly be expected to recite a prayer against himself; the *Birkat Haminim*, therefore, was an effective tool to dissociate the Jewish believers from the synagogue. It was not that they decided to leave—they were forced out by the leadership."[106]

BY DOCTOR FRUCHTENBAUM

In 1985, Dr. Arnold Fruchtenbaum, director of Ariel Ministries, informed us in the article entitled, "A Quest for a Messianic Theology": "Theology has often developed as a result of conflict and controversy. The same is true for Messianic theology. With Jewish Christianity of the first four centuries, this conflict came from....the Jewish community which, at a time when rabbinical Judaism was being developed, tended increasingly to ostracize the Jewish believers. Some time after the first Jewish revolt of 66-70 A.D., around A.D. 90, a curse formula against Jewish Christians...was introduced into the daily prayers of the synagogue (the Birkat-Ha-Minim of the Shmoneh-Esreh)...effectively separated the Jewish Christians from the synagogue."[107]

BY M. AVI YONAH

M. Avi Yonah enlightens us: "The leaders of the Jewish nation were in the end obliged to combat the Judaeo-Christian activities. In

---

[105] Göran Forkman, *The Limits of the Religious Community, Expulsion from the Religious Community Within the Qumran Sect, Within Rabbinic Judaism, and Within Primitive Christianity*. Sweden: Studentlitteratur Lund, © 1972, pp. 91-92, used by permission.

[106] Moishe Rosen, *Y'shua, The Jewish Way to say Jesus*, p. 110.

[107] *Mishkan*, Winter 1985, No. 2. Jerusalem: Arnold Fruchtenbaum, © 1985, p. 3. Arnold Fruchtenbaum has produced many tapes and books worthy of study, which may be ordered through his ministry. Ariel, POB 3723, Tustin, CA, USA 92681. His book, *The Footsteps of the Messiah*, features a foreword by Charles Ryrie.

the first and second generations after the destruction of the Temple disputes with them were fairly common. Their influence was regarded as doubly dangerous because they were still living within the Jewish people, and took part in the synagogue services....The 'Blessing concerning the Minim' was therefore composed and included with the 'Eighteen Benedictions' of daily prayer. This text was composed by Rabbi Samuel ha-Katan and approved by Rabban Gamliel II and the Sanhedrin in the last quarter of the first century....An old version, which was found in the Cairo Genizah, contains the version 'the *Minim* and the *Notserim*' (Christians). Some scholars consider this the original version...."[108]

BY JOHN KOENIG

Koenig admits: "Sometime around the year 85 C.E. the rabbinic sages at Jamnia made a critical decision. They felt compelled to draw a sharp line between themselves and that element within the Christian church which wished to consider itself Jewish. This decision to institutionalize the separation of synagogue and church took a form that was consistent with the pacifism of the rabbis. No persecutions were ordered. No edict prohibited Christians from attending synagogue services. Rather, a change was introduced into one of the chief synagogue prayers, the so-called Eighteen Benedictions. The twelfth bendiction was altered so as to include Christians and other groups deemed heretical in a curse. Apparently, the theory was that wherever this new version of the Benedictions was prayed, Jewish Chrisians could not in good conscience participate. If a local synagogue ruler had some doubt about whether a man taking part in the service was actually praying the curse, he could have the person called up before the Torah niche to *lead* the prayer as a 'delegate of the congregation.' "[109]

BY ATTORNEY W. M. CHANDLER

The famed legal authority, Walter M. Chandler, author of *The Trial of Jesus, From a Lawyer's Standpoint*, writes: "Samuel Hakaton, or *the Less*. Surnamed to distinguish him from Samuel the prophet....some time after the resurrection of Christ, composed the famous imprecation against the Christians, called 'Birchath

---

[108]M. Avi Yonah, *The Jews of Palestine*, 1976, pp. 141-142.

[109]John Koenig, *Jews and Christians in Dialogue*. Pennsylvania: Westminster Press, © 1979, p. 122, used by permission.

Hamminim' (Benedictions of Infidels). The 'Birchath Hamminim,' says the Talmud, and the commentary of R. Jarchi, 'was composed by R. Samuel Hakaton at Jabneh, where the Sanhedrin had removed after the misconduct of the Nazarene, who taught a doctrine contrary to the words of the living God.' The following is the singular benediction: '*Let there be no hope for the apostates of religion, and let all heretics, whosoever they may be, perish suddenly. May the kingdom of pride be rooted out; let it be annihilated quickly, even in our days! Be blessed, O Lord, who destroyest the impious, and humblest the proud!*' As soon as Samuel Hakaton had composed this malediction, it was inserted as an additional blessing in the celebrated prayer of the synagogue, the 'Shemonah-Essara' (the eighteen blessings). These blessings belonged to the time of Ezra—that is to say, five centuries before the Christian era; and every Jew has to recite it daily. St. Jerome was not ignorant of this strange prayer. He says: '*The Jews anathematize three times daily in their synagogue the name of the Christian, disguising it under the name of the Nazarene.*' "[110]

BY KEN CARROLL, PH.D.

Kenneth L. Carroll, professor of religion at Southern Methodist University in Dallas, Texas, tells us in his article, "The Fourth Gospel and the Exclusion of Christians from the Synagogues": "...the bitterest assault upon these Jewish Christians took place from the turn of the first century to the middle of the second century....They were judged to be more dangerous because they were more secret. Since they did not withdraw from the community of Israel, they had to be cast out. This end was to be obtained by the various devices for the detection of the *Minim*—the Formula against the *Minim*.

The *Birchath ha-Minim*, composed about A.D. 90 by Shemuel ha-Qaton, 'represents the official condemnation by the Rabbis of the spurious Judaism which was growing in their midst, and at the same time furnished a means of detection'. This declaration about heretics, which was inserted into the Blessings recited daily, was so worded that Jewish Christians could not repeat it. We can not be certain of the actual wording of the original malediction; later forms only contain the word *Minim* (heretics). According to Jerome, however, it contained the express condemnation of 'Nazarenes'.

The purpose of this malediction was to make possible the detection of the *Minim* who would inevitably omit this particular

---

110 Walter M. Chandler, *The Trial of Jesus, From a Lawyer's Standpoint*, Illustrated Edition, Vol. II, pp. 148-149.

paragraph when invited to pronounce the *Eighteen Benedictions* 'The very fact that this addition was made to the synagogue service shows that the Jewish Christians were still frequenting the synagogue service, since it needed the introduction of the formula to detect them.' In other words, the Jewish Christians still regarded themselves as Jews at this time—no matter how much they disagreed with other Jews on the subject of whether or not the Messiah had already come.

By the end of the first century all of the synagogues of the diaspora had probably been informed of the new malediction and warned not to have any dealing with the Christians—through letters, and emissaries sent out by the Jewish Patriarch of Palestine. Christians were to be excommunicated, and Jews were to avoid discussions of all kinds with the Christians. Undoubtedly these letters contained a copy of the *Birchath ha-Minim* with instructions that it was to be included in the *Eighteen Benedictions*, for the daily cursing of Christians in the synagogues is very closely associated with these letters. Jerome, Origen, and Justin all three 'insist on the official character of these letters, and on their wide dispersion'.

At the time that Christianity and Judaism were parting company, faithful Jews were warned not to read the gospels. This shows that the Christian writings were sufficiently popular among Jewish readers to necessitate such a warning against perusing them. This in turn illustrates how very Jewish the movement of Jesus was at this time."[111]

NO MORE IDENTITY CRISES

The rabbinic formula against the *minim* has almost worked for the past 2000 years. However, present Messianic synagogue movements are making the rabbis very uneasy because the objective of the "Birkat ha-Minim," which is to convince Jews that "you cannot be Jewish and believe in Jesus," is being destroyed.

Jewish Christians now maintain that they are more Jewish (in understanding the meanings[112] of their traditions and faith) because they believe in the Jewish Messiah. You can cast the Messianic Jews

---

[111]Kenneth L.Carroll, Ph.D., "The Fourth Gospel and the Exclusion of Christians from the Synagogues," *Bulletin of the John Rylands University Library of Manchester*, 40, 1957-58, pp. 19-32.

[112]I heard this explained by Eric Wittmayer in a Messianic Passover demonstration on a PTL broadcast hosted by Messianic Rabbi Robert Solomon. When the rabbi asked Eric if, after having been raised in an orthodox home, the Passover Seder had taken on more meaning since he came to know the Messiah Jesus, he replied, "Oh, so much more richness and life. The spirit of God, the *Rauch ha Kodesh*, the Holy Spirit is with us as we celebrate together...."

out of the synagogue but you cannot prevent them from founding Messianic synagogues, which arouse interest among the Jewish community. The modern Messianic Jewish synagogue removes the identity crisis the rabbis of the first two centuries sought to create so that Jews would not accept Jesus in the Diaspora.

TODAY'S CHURCH, SYNAGOGUE, AND MESSIANIC SYNAGOGUE VERSUS THE WAY THE MESSIAH WAS WORSHIPPED IN ANCIENT TIMES

Rabbis are becoming overly alarmed at the seemingly new (though not new at all) Messianic synagogue. They are also becoming fearful of the *Jews for Jesus*' Passover demonstrations.

A Passover demonstration is an explanation of how Jesus fulfilled this Jewish holy day in all of its ritual and sacred meaning. As we have explained before, it illustrates how the first century believers in Jesus celebrated Passover as a Messianic holy day rather than Easter, which, in its name and origin, was and is pagan. Easter, which is actually the name of a pagan fertility goddess,[113] was added as a holiday in later years by the Roman Catholic Church and was totally unknown to the early Jewish believers in Jesus. Even Paul says in the New Testament, "Christ [Messiah] our passover [not Easter] is sacrificed for us...." (I Cor. 5:7 KJV; [ ] mine).

---

[113]The late Reverend Alexander Hislop, author of *The Two Babylons,* shows a unique and intelligent insight into how Easter replaced Passover: "It was called Pasch, or the Passover, and though not of Apostolic institution, was very early observed by many professing Christians, in commemoration of the death and resurrection of Christ....That festival was not idolatrous, and it was preceded by no Lent....The forty days' abstinence of Lent was directly borrowed from the worshippers of the Babylonian goddess....Such a Lent of forty days was held in spring by the Pagan Mexicans....in honour of the sun.' Such a Lent of forty days was observed in Egypt....in commemoration of Adonis or Osiris, the great mediatorial god....'An egg of wondrous size is said to have fallen from heaven into the river Euphrates....out came Venus, who afterwards was called the Syrian Goddess'—that is, Astarte. Hence the egg became one of the symbols of Astarte or Easter...." Reverend Alexander Hislop, *The Two Babylons*, pp. 104-105, 109. Reverend Woodrow further informs us: "The word translated 'Easter' here is *pascha* which is—as ALL scholars know—the Greek word for *passover* and has no connection with the English 'Easter.' It is well-known that 'Easter' is not a Christian expression—not in its *original* meaning. The word comes from the name of a pagan goddess—the goddess of the rising light of day and spring. 'Easter' is but a more modern form of Eostre, Ostera, Astarte, or Ishtar, the latter, according to Hislop, being pronounced as we pronounce 'Easter' today....How, then, did this custom come to be associated with Christianity? Apparently some sought to Christianize the egg by suggesting that as the chick comes out of the egg, so Christ came out of the tomb." Ralph Woodrow, *Babylon Mystery Religion*, pp. 143, 145.

The rabbis are perfectly content that these false Christian holy days are still being observed by many so-called Christian organizations, since this continues to obscure the Jewish identity of the Messiah. For example, a Jew will look at these so-called Christian holidays and say, "What's Jewish about Christmas and Easter?" One who believes in Jesus might conversely look at Hanukkah and Passover and say, "What's Christian about these holy days?"[114] Of course, all we need to do is look at the New Testament, for we see Jesus and His followers both celebrating the two Jewish holidays (Matt. 26:2; John 10:22).

Why then are the rabbis so worried about *Jews for Jesus* explaining how Jesus celebrated His Passover with His disciples, and how all early believers in Jesus continued these practices until overthrown by the vicious half-pagan Roman Catholics centuries later? We will tell you why. They are worried that Jews might see the truth of Jesus' New Testament Jewish Messianism. Then these Jews might become interested in it and even accept it for the truth that is contained therein.

In the *Jerusalem Times/Jewish Press* there was an article explaining the rabbis' concern about Jews returning to the original authentic Messianic faith in Jesus. In an article entitled "Beware of Missionary Forge S'Dorim [Passover Meal],"[115] author Aryeh Julius referred to their Passover as a "trap," and "the queerest 'Seder.' " He listed many locations to avoid in Israel, reminding Jews of their "beautifully decorated Haggadahs" and "set tables."

Rabbi Eckstein, in his book, *What Christians Should Know About Jews and Judaism*, stated his concern regarding the recent large-scale emergence of the Messianic synagogue. We know from history that the first church (group of believers, not a building or organization) met in their own synagogue buildings. In Hebrew, synagogue means "house of gathering;" literally *bait conesset*.

THE ANCIENT SYNAGOGUE OF THE NAZARENES THAT SOME SAY NEVER EXISTED—ARE THEY LYING?

Jakob Jocz, author of *The Jewish People and Jesus Christ*, notes: "The formation of separate Synagogues seems to have been a feature of Jewish life in Jerusalem. Soon there was added a new Synagogue,

---

[114]Jesus celebrated the Passover in Matthew 26:2. John 10:22-23 records His attendance at the feast of Hanukkah, which is also called the Festival of Lights and the Festival of the Dedication.

[115]Aryeh Julius, "Beware of Missionary Forge S'Dorim," *Jerusalem Times/Jewish Press*, Apr. 10-16, 1987. [ ] mine.

that of the Nazarenes."[116] Grant Jeffrey documents: "Archaeologists in Jerusalem have discovered, in the basement of the site of the Upper Room, the remains of a first-century Judeo-Christian congregation that met in a synagogue."[117]

The famous Jewish authority, Abba Eban, also admits the previous existence of the Messianic Jewish synagogues! More about these synagogues will be documented in our next chapter.

AN ABSURD OBJECTION TO THE TRUTH, IRONICALLY, BY A RABBI WHO CLAIMS TO BE A BRIDGE BETWEEN THE JEWISH AND EVANGELICAL COMMUNITIES

Denial of the existence of early Messianic Jews is only one aspect of the cover-up. Misinterpreting their faith is another part of the same problem. Rabbi Eckstein objects to the return of Jews to the original Jewish-Christian style of synagogue worship. He states the following in his book: " 'Messianic Jews,' or 'Hebrew Christians' as they are sometimes known (the terms are used here interchangeably)....believe in Jesus as the Christ, while maintaining selective portions of Jewish law and tradition....the movement is bitterly resented by the Jewish community. It is a major source of potential discord between evangelical Christians, who constitute their best supporters, and Jews.

Hebrew Christians link themselves theologically with the first-century Jerusalem church, which likewise affirmed its Jewish identity while, nevertheless, believing in Jesus as the Messiah. However, the Jewish and Christian communities separated and developed beyond any sort of theological compatibility that may have existed at the time of the early Jerusalem church. Two thousand years of history have intervened....the sociological composition of the church changed and in a short time became almost entirely Gentile. The fact that Christianity severed virtually all of its links with its Jewish origins also had important, irreversible theological implications....The church, in short, made certain decisions that effectively brought about its severance with the Jewish people and faith. It must now live by those decisions."[118]

Oh, must it really? "Hebrew Christians also insist that they constitute the only truly fulfilled Jews and that far from abandoning

---

116 Jakob Jocz, *The Jewish People and Jesus Christ,* p. 164.

117 Grant R. Jeffrey, *War in the Middle East & The Road to Armageddon.* Toronto: Frontier Research Publications, © 1991, p. 264, used by permission. Available through Frontier Research, POB 129, Station "U", Toronto, Ontario, Canada M8Z 5M4.

118 Rabbi Yechiel Eckstein, *What Christians Should Know About Jews and Judaism.* Waco, TX: Word Books Publisher, © 1984, pp. 294-296, used by permission.

their Judaism, they are really completing it. In fact, by sprinkling their Christian lives of faith with Jewish customs and rituals taken out of their proper, historic context, they pervert Jewish symbols and make a mockery of the Jewish faith....Messianic Judaism is an anathema[119]....The very term 'messianic Jews' is also seen as an anomaly....What is so disturbing to Jews about the Hebrew Christian movement is....that these groups are telling the Jewish community that only through Jesus can Jews become fulfilled as Jews....these groups profess that Jews become authentically Jewish through their act of acceptance of Jesus....messianic Jewish groups appear to engage in outright deception, justifying a little duplicity for the sake of the greater good. Others are pushy, overly aggressive, conniving....There are a number of proselytizing groups using Jewish-sounding names in an attempt to lull Jews into believing that they are really legitimate Jewish groups....The fact that many of the Hebrew Christian groups give themselves Jewish-sounding names and advertise in the newspapers under the category of Jewish 'synagogues' rather than Christian 'churches' leads Jews to mistakenly believe they are Jewish houses of worship....Is it any wonder that Jews[120] are so deeply offended by such groups and tend to regard them as essentially no different from cults?[121]....So as not to alienate Jews from coming to Jesus they refer to him as 'Yeshua' and do not place crucifixes in their 'synagogues' but instead use only Jewish symbols. In presenting themselves to Christian audiences, on the other hand, they generally claim to be an evangelical Christian group seeking to bring Jews to Christ and meriting their funding and support....The costs Evangelicals have to bear in fostering better relations with Jews, on the other hand, are exceptionally high....they ought to abandon and denounce the overly zealous and deceptive means usually employed by various Hebrew Christian groups."[122]

---

[119]Anathema means curse. This word is used by the apostle Paul in the New Testament book of I Corinthians 16:22.

[120]Rabbi Eckstein should speak for himself, for there are tens of thousands of Jews who are devoutly interested in Messianic Judaism.

[121]The evangelical community is highly incensed and offended at this statement! The rabbi should apologize and retract such double-talk. While it is fine for a Gentile to believe, if a Jew believes, while retaining his Jewish identity, he calls them a cult. Enough with this double standard; *it* is deceptive, not the believer!

[122]Ibid, pp. 295-299. The writer of these words should know that the first century Messianic Jewish community never used crucifixes in their synagogues. Crucifixes were added over three hundred years later when Constantine started his new religion known as Roman Catholicism, which deviated from the original New Testament teachings. *Yeshua* was Jesus' authentic Hebrew name used by Jews of the first century. Why does the fact that Jews desire to return to the original form and terminology of the true first century Messianic faith in Jesus disturb Rabbi Eckstein? Why does he falsely claim that Jews

THE RABBI'S WORDS SOUND STRANGELY FAMILIAR

These sound like the words of the rabbis at Yavne, which we discussed earlier, don't they? They are desperate words spoken by someone who we believe represents the desperation of many rabbis who are against the observance of Christian (Messianic) rituals in their original form, for fear that the Jewish people will see the truth. We believe the words of Israel Abrahams accurately illustrate the point we are trying to make. Mr. Abrahams, in his article "Studies in Pharisaism and the Gospels" says: "The very development of Christianity from a dependent Jewish sect (*minuth*) to an independent world-religion made the new faith less obnoxious to the Synagogue. As Inge well writes: 'Paul, he [Tyrrell] says, 'did not feel that he had broken with Judaism.' "[123]

In other words, the rabbis at that time were happy when Roman Catholicism, later Greek Orthodoxy and other organizations under the name of "Christian," usurped and overthrew the true believers in Jesus and disposed of their original feasts and practices. It pleased them because it helped blind the Jews further in their vision of who and what the real Jesus was and had come to do in His original Jewish context, for all humanity, both Jew and Gentile. I believe the rabbis' encouragement of misinformation concerning what is truly Christian is absolutely criminal.

Paul Liberman, a Messianic Jew and author of *The Fig Tree Blossoms*, illustrates how early Messianic believers were more or less forced to abandon their forms of worship by the Roman Catholic leaders. He says: "...with Gentile Christianity becoming established in its own right, the struggle began between Gentile and Jewish believers. The dispute essentially was over whether Jewish believers should be allowed to continue certain Jewish practices. A key conflict developed

---

who accept Messianic Judaism are "thought assimilated," when in fact, they are more proud of their Jewish Messianic faith than ever? I believe he and other modern rabbis feel that Bible believing Jews are a threat and a challenge to their authority as rabbis. After all, Messianic Jews and their rabbis, and the "traditional" anti-Messianic Jesus rabbis cannot both be right. If one is wrong, he would have to admit it and open his mind to the Bible, accept the truth and teach otherwise, or else go home and give up being a rabbi. In other words, he would become a full-fledged hypocrite. Other reasons for not accepting the truth may stem from jealousy, envy and spiritual bigotry. The last reason, I believe, is first century Gamaliel's fear of assimilation, which I can partly understand. However, the very fact that Messianic Jews love their Jewish identity and follow the Bible shows that their fears are unfounded.

[123] Israel Abrahams, "Studies in Pharisaism and the Gospels" for Cambridge University. New York: KTAV Publishing House, Inc., © 1917, 1967, p. 57, used by permission.

over the question of Resurrection Day and when it should be celebrated. It was not called Easter then. Gentile Christianity began to push for a strictly Sunday celebration; Messianic Jews disagreed. They thought it should be celebrated on the 14th day of Nisan, as the Bible states."[124]

TRY IT, YOU'LL LIKE IT

Since we have spent some time explaining Messianic synagogues, both ancient and modern, we think it is only fair to provide you with a list of some of these fabulous meeting places, which are more authentically Christian and Jewish than anything called Christian or Jewish.

Jewish means those who are born Jews from the lineage of Abraham, Isaac and Jacob, and who truly understand all Hebrew practices and ritual holiday worship in their predicted Messianic meanings, as well as their traditional ones.

If you visit a Messianic synagogue,[125] you will see what the liberal "Christian" and "orthodox" rabbinical fuss is all about. These synagogues are the embodiment of what both of the others claim to be. They expose both error and hypocrisy, while at the same time providing the believer with the spiritual fulfillment only the Jewish Messiah can give.

We have heard it said that every human has a Messiah-shaped void in their heart, at the core of their being. If this is true, no one can be spiritually satisfied until that void is filled, and of course, only the Messiah Jesus can fill it, when invited to do so. When you visit one of these places of worship, with so many other people who have the Messiah in their lives, you are overwhelmed with a spiritual sensation, unknown in power, intensity, and scope of understanding. Thus, we hope you can see why we recommend that you visit one of these wonderful places of worship!

THE ALTERNATIVE WITHIN MODERN JUDAISM OBSTRUCTS SPIRITUAL FULFILLMENT

The rabbis of the first century surgically removed the Messiah from Judaism in a frantic attempt to prevent what they perceived as a gateway toward assimilation. Their fear of assimilation, however, was

---

[124] Paul Liberman, *The Fig Tree Blossoms: Messianic Judaism Emerges*, pp. 40-41.

[125] For a list of some of the Messianic congregations, including their addresses so you can visit—remember Jesus welcomes all—see our *Vol. II*, chapter 19, "Messianic Synagogues—How to Get There." You may find the services very interesting.

unfounded, as we presently see so many Jews who believe in Jesus and maintain their pride in being Jewish. You cannot remove the Messiah from Judaism and still have Judaism. You might create a cultural Judaism built around some Jewish tradition, but essentially that is all you have left. You do not have religious Judaism without the Messiah, the core of all true biblically based Judaism.

Today, we have true Judaism in the Messianic synagogue. The Messianic synagogue is Judaism based on Scripture. I visited many of them throughout the United States and Israel; Jesus is praised as the Messiah and Jewish traditions and prayers are enjoyed. In a beautiful way, all of the Jewish holy days have a Messianic significance and truly, if you take time to learn about the Jewish holy days you will begin to understand why the apostle Paul, also known as Rabbi Saul, wrote in I Corinthians: "...Christ [Messiah] our passover is sacrificed for us...." (I Cor. 5:7 KJV; [ ] mine).

There is historical proof that the first believers gathered in a building in Jerusalem called the Synagogue (house of gathering) of the Nazarenes (Jewish believers in Jesus). Sometimes we forget that those who believed in Jesus as Messiah (Christ) for several decades after He left for the heavens were almost all Jewish.

Modern rabbinical Judaism is, of course, a cultural institution made up of four sects (Reformed, Conservative, Orthodox and Hasidic[126]). It serves to hold Jews together as a race and cultural religion. When compared to Messianic Judaism, it is seriously lacking because it is a religion with a spiritual void at its core. We say this because the Messiah, the chief cornerstone of the faith (Ps. 118:22),[127] was cut out and tossed aside centuries ago.

A MESSIANIC JEW EXPOSES THE FALSEHOODS OF "JUDAISM" VERSUS THE TRUTHS OF MESSIANIC JUDAISM

Phillip Goble, a Messianic Jew, drives the truth of our point home when, as a Jew, he tells us: "...God's gracious provision through his divine Word Yeshua has forced the whole world into a crisis of decision. When we look into the Jewish face of Yeshua, we are confronted eyeball to eyeball by the divine Word of God himself. We cannot obey the God of Israel nor can we receive his Holy Spirit unless we obey God's Word become Man, Yeshua Ha Mashiach.

---

[126]Hasidic Jews are those you see dressed in black, usually concentrated in New York City and Jerusalem. They call themselves Hasidic, which is Hebrew for "the righteous." They consider themselves orthodox, and some Christians refer to them as ultra-orthodox.
[127]"The stone which the builders rejected Has become the chief corner *stone*" (NASB).

Therefore, the task of Messianic Judaism is to lead people to follow the Jewish Messiah Yeshua in order that they may receive the Holy Spirit. Those who really do follow Yeshua, and are not hypocrites as some of his so-called followers have been, become true spiritual Jews and love our Jewish people just as they love our Jewish Messiah.

The theology of Messianic Judaism preserves the essentials of the faith of Israel that other brands of Judaism have largely lost. For example, Messianic Judaism maintains in the death of Yeshua the Torah's demand for blood sacrifice: 'It is the blood that maketh an atonement for the soul' (Leviticus 17:11). Messianic Judaism also preserves the true significance of such Jewish institutions as the high priesthood, the sage, and the prophet, and such Jewish doctrines as those concerning the Messiah king, the Holy Spirit, and salvation. Through the resurrection from the dead of the great high priest, sage, prophet, and Messianic King Yeshua and through the coming of the Holy Spirit at Pentecost...all these Jewish essentials are imperishably maintained."[128]

OBSCURE SOURCES REVEAL THE CONSEQUENCES TO THE JEWISH BELIEVERS AS A RESULT OF YAVNE

To continue our story regarding the extermination of the Jewish-Christians from the synagogue through letters, emissaries and the BHM, we will quote a few more examples. This should leave no doubt in the minds of the learned as to what was really done to the Jews who believed in Jesus 1500 to 2000 years ago. Since we have substantiated their existence against obnoxious claims that they "never were," where did they really go?

Professor Yehudah Liebes asks: "What became of the Jewish Christians? They continued to exist throughout most of the first millennium, but they did not have an easy existence. They frequently suffered from persecutions, and were at times even forced to live an underground existence. They were considered as aliens both by the Jews, following the period of Yavneh, as well as in the eyes of the Christian Church....[Ecumenical Catholicism, much of which is still indifferent to the Messianic Jewish movement]."[129]

---

[128]Phillip E. Goble, *Everything You Need to Grow a Messianic Synagogue*. S. Pasadena, CA: William Carey Library, © 1974, p. 5, used by permission. Available from William Carey Library, 533 Hermosa Street, South Pasadena, CA, USA 91030. Tel. (213) 799-4559.

[129]Yehudah Liebes, "Who Makes the Horn of Jesus to Flourish," *Immanuel*, p. 65. [ ] mine.

The scholar James Parkes was a man with tremendous empathy for the Jewish people. Some of his writings are even published by the Jewish Publication Society. He has said: "...the Judeo-Christians, where they formed separate Churches of their own, as in Palestine, lived a more or less peaceful life. It cannot be said that they were looked upon with favour, but they were rarely disturbed. Apart from the murder—or execution—of James in 62 no judicial action is known to have been taken against them, until their fellowship with the nascent churches of the Diaspora brought the whole matter within the scope of Jochanan ben Zakkai and the Jabne group's policy towards all dissidents. This was in the last decades of the first century, and until then it seems that they continued to share in common worship in the synagogue with other Jews. In any case the first step towards their exclusion from this fellowship was the inclusion in synagogue worship of a new Benediction, or rather Malediction, on the 'Nazarenes.' As we know that the author of this Malediction was Samuel the Small, a contemporary of Gamaliel II, we can date it to the period between 80 and 100. At about the same time, or a little later, a formal condemnation of the Nazarenes was drawn up by the Sanhedrin, and circulated officially to the synagogues of the Diaspora. We have many references to this document in Christian literature from the middle of the second century onwards, and its most likely date is some time before the revolt of Bar Cochba. We have not its text, but it denounced Jesus of Nazareth as a deceiver and excommunicated his followers from membership of the synagogues."[130]

JEWISH SCHOLARLY UNBIASED TRUTH UNCOVERED, CONCERNING THE "LETTERS," BY A JEWISH PROFESSOR FROM OVER A GENERATION AGO

Professor H. Graetz, who published his little-known book, *History of the Jews*, in 1893, has written on this subject. He maintains: "The Synhedrion of Jamnia must have occupied itself with the question what position the Jewish Christians should occupy in the Jewish community, and whether they should in fact be considered as Jews at all...."[131] The Jewish professor admits: "The Christian writings were condemned, and were put on a par with books of magic. Even to enter into business relations, or to receive menial services, was strictly forbidden, especially the use of magical cures which the Christians

[130] James Parkes, *Judaism and Christianity*. Chicago: The University of Chicago Press, © 1948, pp. 109-110, used by permission.

[131] Professor H. Graetz, *History of the Jews,* Vol. II. Philadelphia: The Jewish Publication Society of America, © 1893, p. 379, used by permission.

performed on animals or men in the name of Jesus was prohibited. A form of curse (which bore the name of Birchath ha Minim) was likewise employed against the Minæans in the daily prayers, as also against the informers. The Patriarch, Gamaliel, confided the composition of this prayer to Samuel the Younger. This circumstance confirmed the idea that the various ordinances against the Jewish Christians, even if not proceeding direct from the Patriarch, yet had his consent. The form of curse appears to have been a sort of trial of faith in order to recognize those who secretly adhered to Christianity. For, in connection with it, it was decreed that whosoever refrained at the public prayers from pronouncing the curse, or from praying for the restoration of the Jewish State, was to be dismissed from his office of precentor. The Synhedrion published all the enactments against the Jewish Christian sects by **circular letters** to the communities....Following the natural instinct of self-preservation, they, on the one hand, shut out the Jewish Christian sects from the Jewish community...."[132]

LETTERS, WHAT LETTERS? WERE THESE TRULY THE ONES DISPATCHED BY A SECRET PORTABLE SANHEDRIN? YES!

These letters can be a touchy subject. Once, over ten years ago, while I was doing research at the Pitts Theological Library at Emory University, I ran into Rabbi Shapiro and asked him about these letters of excommunication. He said, "Letters, there were no letters sent out. What are you talking about?" I then showed him a couple of my sources and suddenly I noticed a puzzled look on his face.

We know conclusively that these letters are not the ones referred to in the New Testament which Paul received from the Sanhedrin in Jerusalem. Rather, they came from an exiled Sanhedrin hidden in Yavne sinking ever deeper into the masterful anti-Christian plot of two millennia to come! We know that the Sanhedrin of Jerusalem moved ten times and on its third move landed in Yavne.

Although some Christian historians (Justin, for example) have referred to it as Jerusalem because the Sanhedrin was there for such a long time, the Jewish Talmud itself records: " '...the Sanhedrin wandered to ten places of banishment, as we know from tradition', namely, from the Chamber of Hewn Stone to Hanuth, and from Hanuth to Jerusalem, and from Jerusalem to Jabneh...and from Jabneh to Usha, and from Usha [back] to Jabneh, and from Jabne [back] to Usha, and

[132]Ibid, pp. 379-380, 382. Bold mine.

from Usha to Shefar'am, and from Shefar'am to Beth She'arim, and from Beth She'arim to Sepphoris, and from Sepphoris to Tiberias...."[133]

DID MOST OF DIASPORA JEWRY BLINDLY FOLLOW THESE ABSURD YAVNEAN DECISIONS ABOUT THE MESSIANIC JEWS, TO THEIR DETRIMENT?

The book, *History of the Jewish People,* elaborates on the attitude of the Jewish people worldwide toward decisions and instructions given from Yavne, pointing out: "The two leading Torah personalities at the end of the Second Temple period were Rabban Yochanan ben Zakkai, dean of the Sanhedrin, and Rabban Shimon ben Gamliel, of the family of Hillel....Rabban Shimon ben Gamliel, in his capacity as president or *Nasi* of the Sanhedrin, participated in the central government....Rabban Yochanan ben Zakkai assumed the crown of leadership over the mightiest spiritual empire on earth in its capital city—henceforth Yavneh....Rabban Yochanan ben Zakkai reorganized the Sanhedrin....From Yavneh he sent instructions to the scattered Jewish communities in matters of law and observance, and Jews from all over the Diaspora turned to Yavneh for answers and advice. Without any formal declaration, Yavneh became the new center of the Jewish people."[134]

Obviously, if this is true, it clearly shows that a great many Jewish people relied more on their rabbis than on their Bible. Since the rabbis have been shown to have intentionally altered known Messianic prophecy into false alternative interpretations (see our chapter 5, "Which Prophecies Did Jesus Fulfill?"), this was an unwise decision on their part! David has advised us in God's words, "*It is* better to trust in the LORD than to put confidence in man" (Ps. 118:8 KJV).

These Jewish communities would have done well to have taken David's advice! If most of the Jewish community had done this, these disastrous instructions from Yavne, including the secret letters against the Jewish-Christians that were carried to the outer limits of the world through emissaries, might have been widely disregarded and discarded. To follow Yavnean decisions on the matter of believers in Messiah would be a spiritual and ethical mistake. If the rabbis have

---

[133] *The Babylonian Talmud*, Rosh Hashanah 31a-31b, p. 149.

[134] Rabbi Hersh Goldwurm, *History of the Jewish People, The Second Temple Era*, adapted from Dr. Eliezer Ebner's translations of Yekutiel Friedner's "*Divrei Y'mei HaBayit HaSheini*." Brooklyn, NY: Mesorah Publications, Ltd., © 1982, pp. 183, 185, 201, used by permission.

intentionally changed the interpretation of prophecy relating to Messiah, how can we possibly trust them? Why did they do this?

The rabbis felt, no doubt, that the end justifies the means. "So what if we lie—we save our people from assimilation." It is not too late for Christians and Messianic Jews to inform their Jewish friends about the Messiah Conspiracy orchestrated by the rabbis. They should tell their friends to use the Bible and follow David's command to put their trust in God instead of men (Ps. 118:8).

THE SECRET EMISSARIES

These emissaries were documented as having been sent out to "all the world" to abolish the Gospel of Jesus and His apostles. Justin Martyr, the famous second century Christian historian, recorded: "Yet not only did you not repent, when you learned that He had risen from the dead, but, as I said before, you appointed **chosen men and sent them into all the civilized world,** proclaiming that 'a certain godless and lawless sect has been raised by one Jesus of Galilee, a deceiver, whom we crucified, but His disciples stole Him by night from the tomb, where He had been laid after being unnailed from the cross, and they deceive men, saying that He is risen from the dead and has ascended into heaven'....In addition to all this, although your city has been taken, and your land laid waste, you do not repent, but dare even to curse Him and all them that believe on Him. And, as for us, we do not hate you, nor them that because of you accept such suspicions of us, but we pray that even now you may repent and find mercy from God the Father of the universe, who is tender-hearted and full of compassion."[135]

ANTI-CHRISTIAN APOSTLE AGENTS TO EFFECT ASSASSINATION

Hugo Mantel, in his work, *Studies in the History of the Sanhedrin,* documents the existence, mission and work of these counter-apostle agents mentioned by Justin, who were sent out to the ends of the earth to effect the assassination of Jewish Christianity. In his section entitled, "The Dispatch of Apostles (Shelihim)," he notes: "The Nesi'im dispatched apostles...." He tells us that in Hebrew they were called *shelihim*. He says: "Justin alleges that the apostles advised ordinary people against holding religious discussions with Christians (*Dialogues of Justin*, 38, I, pp. 74-750; 112, 4, p. 231)." Mantel

[135] A. Lukyn Williams, D.D., *Justin Martyr, The Dialogue With Trypho*, p. 224.

mentions a very interesting passage from the Talmud concerning Rabbi Joshua's fear of these Christian-Jewish *minim*: "Thus the disciples of R. Joshua, at the deathbed of their master, were dismayed: 'How shall we maintain ourselves against the Minim?' "[136] He further informs us of the great distance the apostles penetrated, reaching Jewish communities throughout the world. "The apostles reached the Jewish communities throughout and beyond the Roman Empire, including Media and southern Arabia. Jewish communities considered it a privilege to act as hosts to the apostles."[137] Mr. Mantel proves his claim that the apostles got as far as Media, when he notes in footnote 138: "The inscription on a girl's grave in Venose states that at her funeral two apostles delivered eulogies...." (referencing Krauss, p. 381, *Die jüdischen Apostel*).

THE EMISSARIES' DIRTY TASK—JAMES SOCKS IT TO US

The chief task of these emissaries was to deliver a letter written by Rabbi Gamaliel of Yavne, containing the Birkat ha-Minim and instructions on how it was to be used to expel Jewish Christians from the synagogue. James Parkes gives us the evidence: "...Paul was converted while on an inquisitorial mission from the high priest to the Jewish community of Damascus; we are told that, fifty years later, the rabbinic authorities of Palestine sent out letters to the synagogues of the Diaspora formally rejecting the messianic claims made on behalf of Jesus of Nazareth and providing for the exclusion from the community of Jews who accepted them....It was a long process and included many incidents of which the adherents of neither religion can be proud, incidents where to a hostile Roman authority Jews denounced Christians....That the sect of the Nazarenes was attracting a number of Gentile converts was well known to the Jewish authorities....they set out to procure a new uniformity in religion as the necessary basis for a new unity....the very thought of consciously creating and **securing national unity by means of religious uniformity was without precedent in human history**....So far as the Judeo-Christians were concerned, they introduced into the synagogal service a formula which Judeo-Christians could not pronounce. This was an **additional** clause, the ***Birkath ha-Minim***....The clause stated 'and for the Nazarenes may there be no hope'. That such was its original form has recently been discovered from an Egyptian papyrus, for the present form...conceals

---

[136]Hugo Mantel, *Studies in the History of the Sanhedrin*, p. 191.
[137]Ibid, p. 195.

the word *Nozrim* behind the more neutral *minim* or *meshummadim*....then **a spy could observe whether it was included** or not, for synagogal services were open to all....action taken **by the synagogal authorities was to send out 'apostles' carrying a letter to all Jewish congregations in the Diaspora**. The existence of this letter is known to us only from the constant references to it in Christian literature....Even apart from its contents or occasion it is, however, of particular interest as almost the sole example of communications passing officially by 'apostles' and in writing from the central Jewish authorities in the Land of Israel to the diaspora Jewries. If we are to take the text of Justin, then the rabbis sent out chosen and ordained men throughout all the world to proclaim that 'a godless and lawless heresy had sprung from one Jesus, a Galilean deceiver, whom we crucified, but his disciples stole him by night from the tomb where he was laid when unfastened from the cross, and now deceive men by asserting that he has risen from the dead and ascended to heaven.' Moreover, you accuse him of having taught those godless, lawless, and unholy doctrines which you mention to the condemnation of those who confess him to be Christ and a Teacher from and Son of God."[138]

YAVNE AND ITS CONSPIRATORS UNVEILED, IN LIGHT OF PRESENT DISHONESTY

Further evidence as to why this small coastal town in Israel was a hotbed for breeding a Messiah Conspiracy against Jewish Christians, is seen in a plot to systematically drive down the number and destroy the credibility of believers within the Jewish community. As Raymon Hanson writes, to create a "death blow to any favorable if not quasi-official relationship that might have existed between the Judeo-Christians and the Jewish community."[139]

Today, one of the points a rabbi will most frequently use to verify his assertion that Jesus was not the Jewish Messiah is, "Jesus was never accepted by the Jewish people of his own day and thereafter. Thus, this is sufficient proof for us to dismiss the whole idea of his

---

[138]James Parkes, *The Foundations of Judaism and Christianity*, pp. 106, 223, 225-226. Bold mine.

[139]Raymon Hanson, "The Schism Between the Judeo-Christians and Mainstream Judaism," Hebrew University, May 24, 1984. Raymon, a friend with whom I still keep in touch, became a trusted buddy when I met him in Israel in 1984. His paper on the Jewish background of Christianity was submitted to Dr. Daniel Schwartz of the Hebrew University on May 24, 1984. For additional contents of this paper, see our *Vol. II*, chapter 14, "Interesting Excerpts from 'The Schism Between the Judeo-Christians and Mainstream Judaism,' by Raymon Hanson."

even remotely, possibly being our Messiah!" This consensus is echoed in Rabbi Aryeh Kaplan's writings, in a book entitled *The Real Messiah*, containing statements designed to dissuade Jews from considering Jesus' Messiahship. In the chapter entitled, "Why Aren't We Christians?", Kaplan writes: "Although all of Jesus' disciples were Jews, they could not convince their fellow Jews of their teachings.... Christianity was rejected by the Jews....the Jew stood firm....and walked his own way....If Christianity made any contribution at all, it was to the non-Jewish world."[140]

At the beginning of this same chapter, Kaplan explained the reason for his comment: "We hear quite a bit today about a movement called 'Jews for Jesus.' A small number[141] of Jews seem to be finding the teachings of Christianity very attractive."[142]

Many modern rabbis are saying, in so many words, "There really weren't very many[143] Jews of Jesus' day who believed in His Messiahship." We must answer, if this is so: 1. Why was there formulated a special benediction against them, which was inserted into the eighteen benediction Jewish synagogue prayer called the Amidah? 2. Why was this curse, called the BHM, then systematically circulated by emissaries in the form of a letter to virtually every synagogue in the entire world? 3. Why has the Talmud asked that there be no Orthodox Jewish contact with the *minim* and Nazarenes (believers)? 4. Why did Rabbi Akiva of the second century claim that Christians should be tortured if they did not recant and turn from Jesus?[144] Finally, why does *The Jewish Encyclopedia* overtly admit: "The cessation of sacrifice, in consequence of the destruction of the Temple, came,

---

[140]Rabbi Aryeh Kaplan, *et al*, *The Real Messiah*, pp. 16-17.

[141]On April 14, 1989, the *Jewish Echo* newspaper of Glasgow, Scotland, quoted this "small number" to be 350,000. The same newspaper predicted the number would swell to 500,000 by the year 2000. The *Jewish Echo*'s source was the Jewish Community Relations Council of New York.

[142]Ibid.

[143]Messianic Rabbi David Chernoff, in his book, *7 Steps to Knowing the God of Abraham, Isaac and Jacob*, documents that the estimates of first century Jews who believed in Jesus as Messiah ran as high as one million. We have also read these estimates stated by scholars, which shows us Rabbi Kaplan did not have his facts straight, or at least did not want anyone else in his day to realize such a large number of Jews believed in Jesus.

[144]Johannes Weiss quotes Eusebius and Orosius as follows: "And indeed in the recent Jewish war, Bar-Kokhba, the leader of the uprising of the Jews, condemned the Christians alone to be led away to dreadful torture if they would not deny Jesus was Christ and blaspheme him....Kokhba, who was leader of the rebellion of the Jews, inflicted various penalties on many of the Christians, since they would not go out to battle with him against the Romans." Johannes Weiss, *Earliest Christianity: A History of the Period A.D. 30-150*, Vol. II, p. 723.

therefore, as a shock to the people. It seemed to deprive them of the divine Atonement....Joshua ben Hananiah, who cried out in despair, 'Wo unto us! What shall atone for us?' only expressed the sentiment of all his contemporaries (IV Esd. ix. 36: 'We are lost on account of our sins'). It was then that Johanan b. Zakkai...declared works of benevolence to have atoning powers as great as those of sacrifice.

"This view, however, did not solve satisfactorily for all the problem of sin—the evil rooted in man from the very beginning, from the fall of Adam (IV Esd. iii. 20, viii. 118). **Hence a large number of Jews** accepted the Christian faith in the Atonement by the blood 'shed for many for the remission of sins' (Matt. xxvi 28; Heb. x. 12; Col. i. 20) or in Jesus as 'the Lamb of God' (John i. 29; Apoc. of John vii. 14, and elsewhere)."[145]

Triumphal Arch of Titus, erected by Rome in commemoration of the defeat of the Jews in 70 AD. Notice the laurel-crowned Romans as they make away with the ruined temple's gold menorah and other treasures.

---

[145] Isidore Singer, Ph.D, *et al*, *The Jewish Encyclopedia, A Descriptive Record of the History, Religion, Literature, and Customs of the Jewish People, from the Earliest Times to the Present Day*, Vol. II. New York: Funk and Wagnalls Company, © 1902, p. 278. Bold mine to emphasize Rabbi Kaplan's misinformation, which is commonly echoed within the Jewish community as accurate.

SYNAGOGUE EXCOMMUNICATION—WAS IT FORESEEN AND IS IT WIDELY ADMITTED TODAY?

ORIGINAL HEBREW OF ISAIAH 66:5

שִׁמְעוּ֙ דְּבַר־יְהוָ֔ה הַחֲרֵדִ֖ים אֶל־דְּבָר֑וֹ אָמְרוּ֩ אֲחֵיכֶ֨ם שֹׂנְאֵיכֶ֜ם מְנַדֵּיכֶ֗ם לְמַ֤עַן שְׁמִי֙ יִכְבַּ֣ד
יְהוָ֔ה וְנִרְאֶ֥ה בְשִׂמְחַתְכֶ֖ם וְהֵ֥ם יֵבֹֽשׁוּ׃ **ישעיה** סו:ה

OLD TESTAMENT SCRIPTURE TRANSLATION

"Hear the word of the LORD, ye [Jewish-Christians] that tremble at his word; Your brethren [rabbinical sages of Yavne] that hated you, that cast you out [of the synagogue] for my name's sake, said, Let the LORD be glorified: but he [Messiah Jesus] shall appear [at His Second Coming] to your joy, and they [the sages] shall be ashamed [of themselves]."

Predicted by the prophet Isaiah in the Jewish Bible, seven hundred years before the fact. Isaiah 66:5 KJV. [ ] mine.

DANIEL, 2600 YEARS AGO, PREDICTED THE MESSIAH'S SECOND COMING TO THE EARTH

"I saw in the night visions, and, behold, *one* like the Son of man came with the clouds of heaven, and came to the Ancient of days, and they brought him near before him. And there was given him dominion, and glory, and a kingdom, that all people, nations, and languages, should serve him: his dominion *is* an everlasting dominion, which shall not pass away, and his kingdom *that* which shall not be destroyed." **Daniel 7:13-14, 555 BC KJV**

"...the high priest asked him, and said unto him, Art thou the Christ, the Son of the Blessed? And Jesus said, 'I am: and ye shall see the Son of man sitting on the right hand of power, and coming in the clouds of heaven....These things have I spoken unto you, that ye should not be offended. They shall put you out of the synagogues: yea, the time cometh, that whosoever killeth you will think that he doeth God service. And these things will they do unto you, because they have not known the Father, nor me. But these things have I told you, that when the time shall come, ye may remember that I told you of them. And these things I said not unto you at the beginning, because I was with you. But now I go my way to him that sent me....' "

The words of Jesus, spoken in 33 AD, recorded by Mark 14:61-62 and John 16:1-5 KJV

JUSTIN MARTYR, ONE HUNDRED YEARS AFTER JESUS

"...you curse in your synagogues all who have become Christians through Him. And the other nations, who make the curse effective, are slaying them who only acknowledge that they are Christians....you appointed chosen men and sent them into all the civilized world, proclaiming that 'a certain godless and lawless sect has been raised by one Jesus of Galilee, a deceiver, whom we crucified, but His disciples stole Him by night from the tomb, where He had been laid after being unnailed from the cross, and they deceive men, saying that He is risen from the dead and has ascended into heaven'....the priests and teachers of your people have caused His name to be profaned and blasphemed throughout the whole earth."[146]

AN OBJECTIVE, HONEST, MODERN SCHOLAR, DOUGLAS HARE, COMMENTS ON JUSTIN'S STATEMENT

"...Jewish Christians, were indeed excluded from the synagogue...all personal and business contact with them was forbidden, and they were formally cursed in the *Shemoneh Esreh*....The insertion of the *Birkath ha-Minim* into the Eighteen

[146] A. Lukyn Williams, *Justin Martyr, The Dialogue With Trypho*, pp. 202, 224, 242.

Benedictions is clear proof that the rabbinic authorities regarded Christianity as a threat to a beleaguered Jewry....this liturgical innovation [BHM] was transmitted to synagogues throughout the Diaspora....We have the testimony of Justin that selected men were sent out from Jerusalem 'into all the world' ε*l*ς πᾶσαν τὴν λῆν to report the outbreak of the Christian heresy."[147]

***The Theme of Jewish Persecution of Christians*, by Douglas Hare. [ ] mine**

A MODERN RABBINIC COVER-UP COMMENT ON THE ABOVE

While Mr. Hare and Justin Martyr perceive and document the facts of history correctly, most of today's rabbinical leaders ignore the record and make irresponsible statements such as: "Although all of Jesus' disciples were Jews, they could not convince their fellow Jews of their teachings....Christianity was rejected by the Jews....the Jew stood firm....and walked his own way....If Christianity made any contribution at all, it was to the non-Jewish world."

***The Real Messiah*, by Rabbi Aryeh Kaplan, *et al*, p. 16; 1976**

AUTHOR'S COMMENT—EVANGELICAL CHRISTIAN POSITION

Rabbi Kaplan's statement, which represents common contemporary Jewish misconception, is proven untrue when we examine the above evidence. Many Jews did believe in Jesus and were treated brutally.[148]

Philip Moore

USUAL MESSIANIC INTERPRETATIVE STANDARDS WERE DECEPTIVELY *ALTERED* SHORTLY AFTER THE APPEARANCE OF JESUS!

How did the rabbis get away with calling the Messianic Jewish movement (Christian faith) a "heresy," as Justin documents, when in fact, according to their very own rabbinic interpretation of the Bible, Jesus fit the bill? Answer: They banned and changed their interpretations! These rabbis also made a new Greek translation of the Old Testament, which removed many of the Messianic prophecies fulfilled by Jesus. This fact is illustrated by the scholar, F. F. Bruce.

---

[147]Douglas Hare, *The Theme of Jewish Persecution of Christians in the Gospel According to St Matthew*, p. 65. [ ] mine.

[148]We need not wonder if believers were lynched in the name of religion in the first century. Many rabbis of that time felt there was nothing wrong with putting the believers' (*minim*/Jewish Christians') lives in jeopardy. Douglas Hare documents: "The most extreme treatment that the rabbis will countenance is that the lives of Minim may be endangered and not saved, Tos. B. Mezia 2:33: 'The Minim and the apostates and the betrayers are cast in [to a pit] and not helped out' (translation by R. Travers Herford, *Christianity in Talmud and Midrash* [1903], p. 94)...." Ibid, p. 39. The Jewish-Christians were persecuted to no end, while today, many who know this unbelievably try to deny they ever existed! This, to me, is as horrible as trying to say the Holocaust never happened! It is inexcusable and incomprehensible. We ask here that those who have written these things apologize and retract this false statement that Christianity was rejected by the Jews, which is a general denial of there ever having been a sizable community of Jewish-Christians in the first century. This only serves to facilitate ignorance of the existence of many thousands of Jewish Christians who suffered exclusion, persecution and even execution.

This further proves our point that the rabbis' actions were based on personal bias and prejudice against Jesus and His unique[149] claim to be the Jewish Messiah as He fulfilled the Messianic prophecies.

The new modern Judaism formed at this time at Yavne, would alter the interpretation of a formerly accepted prophetic understanding to show that the verses in question had nothing to do with the Messiah. Thus, He was not the Messiah! Dr. Bruce comments on two of the most famous prophecies concerning the Messiah (Dan. 7:13; Ps. 110:1), and documents the following interesting points: "There was a good deal of contact between orthodox Jews and Jewish Christians in Palestine in the first and second centuries, and there are frequent echoes in the rabbinical literature of controversies between the two parties, on the interpretation of messianic prophecy, for example. In a number of instances interpretations which had formerly been regarded as quite proper and respectable by orthodox Jews were ruled out as inadmissible when Christians began to use them to prove that Jesus was the Messiah.

There is one notable occasion recorded when the great Rabbi Akiba got into trouble because he favoured such an unacceptable interpretation. He and his colleagues were discussing the vision of the judgment day in Daniel 7. 9-14, where 'one like a son of man' appears before the Ancient of Days to receive universal and eternal sovereignty from him. 'As I looked', says Daniel (verse 9), 'thrones were placed, and one that was ancient of days took his seat.' The question was raised: Why thrones in the plural? Akiba gave the traditional answer: 'One for God and one for David' (i.e. for Messiah, the son of David). But Rabbi José expostulated with him: 'Akiba, how long will you profane the Shekhinah? It is one for justice and one for righteousness.' "[150] Bruce notes in his footnote: "Akiba may have had in mind the divine invitation to the Messiah in Psalm 110.I: 'Sit at my right hand, till I make your enemies your footstool'—but the fact that Jesus in his reply to the high priest at his trial had conjoined this text with Daniel

---

[149]We designate *unique* because Jesus pointed to dozens of prophecies that had been and were being fulfilled in His life, which proved from a biblical prophetic and *ancient* rabbinic standpoint, that He was the Jewish Messiah (Luke 24; John 5). None of the pseudo or false Messiahs of the past were able to do this. For example, Bar Kochba was one of the first of a long line of men claiming to be Messiah, who avalanched a twenty century-long plague of false Messianism and "Messiahs" on the Jewish people. Virtually every era has witnessed a false Jewish Messiah. Just to mention a few: Moses of Crete—fifth century; Abu Isa—eighth century; David Alroy—twelfth century; Abraham Abulafia—1240-1291; Abraham ben Samuel—circa 1300; David Reuveni—sixteenth century; Solomon Molko—sixteenth century; Hayyim Vital—1574 C.E.; Sabbatai Zevi—1626-1676; and Jacob Frank—eighteenth century.

[150]F.F. Bruce, *Jesus and Christian Origins Outside the New Testament*, pp. 64-65.

7·13 meant that its former messianic interpretation also was no longer favoured."[151]

Bruce continues: "Ever since Jesus had claimed, at his trial before the Sanhedrin, to be that Son of Man whom Daniel saw 'coming with the clouds of heaven' the messianic interpretation of the passage had become taboo for many Jewish teachers.

The rabbis of this period, then, were not unacquainted with the story of Jesus and the activity of his followers, vigorously as they voiced their dissent from all that he and they stood for."[152]

LINDSEY CONFIRMS BRUCE'S POINT THAT JESUS DARED TO FULFILL THE TWO MOST IMPORTANT PROPHECIES OF THE MESSIAH'S COMING

Hal Lindsey, in his book *The Late Great Planet Earth,* points out just how important these two prophecies were to the Jewish religious "leaders" and Jesus Himself during the first century. "Jesus promised under oath before the high priest at His trial [concerning His future Second Coming to Earth to judge]: '...nevertheless I tell you, hereafter you shall see the Son of Man sitting at the right hand of Power [God], and coming on the clouds of heaven' (Matthew 26:64 NASB).

This statement was the official ground of His condemnation for blasphemy and the death sentence. Jesus dared to be the One who would fulfill two of the best-known prophecies concerning the Messiah's coming in glory to rule the earth. The first is from Psalms, predicted before 1000 B.C.: 'The LORD [God, the Father] said unto my Lord [God, the Son], Sit thou at my right hand, until I make thine enemies thy footstool' (Psalm 110:1).

The second is from Daniel, predicted about 550 B.C.: 'I saw in the night visions, and behold, one like the Son of man came with clouds of heaven, and came to the Ancient of days, and they brought him near before him. And there was given him dominion, and glory, and a kingdom, that all people, nations, and languages should serve him: his dominion is an everlasting dominion, which shall not pass away, and his kingdom that which shall not be destroyed' (Daniel 7:13, 14 KJV).

No wonder the Jewish supreme court (the Sanhedrin) went into orbit. When Jesus made such a fantastic claim as that in one terse sentence, they either had to fall down and worship Him or kill Him. They chose the latter."[153]

---

[151]Ibid, p. 65.
[152]Ibid.
[153]Hal Lindsey with C.C. Carlson, *The Late Great Planet Earth*, p. 161. First [ ] mine.

A SMALL AMOUNT OF BACKLASH OCCURS, AS A RESULT OF RABBINIC REINTERPRETATION

After the rabbis began to reinterpret Isaiah 53, due to the huge number of Jews freely accepting Jesus, and claim that it was no longer to be understood as referring to Messiah, opposition to this mutilation of rabbinic understanding, which had prevailed for centuries rose up. For example, Dr. Kac, quoting David Baron, notes: "Rabbi Moshe Cohen Iben Crispin (fourteenth century) states that those who for controversial reasons apply the prophecy of the Suffering Servant to Israel find it impossible to understand the true meaning of this prophecy, 'having forsaken the knowledge of our teachers, and inclined after the stubborness of their own opinions.' Their misinterpretation, he declares, 'distorts the passage from its natural meaning,' for 'it was given of God as a description of the Messiah, whereby, when any should claim to be the Messiah, to judge by the resemblance or non-resemblance to it whether he were the Messiah or no.'

Rabbi Elijah de Vidas...affirms that 'the meaning of 'He was wounded for our transgressions,...bruised for our iniquities,' is, that since the Messiah bears our iniquities....whoso will not admit that the Messiah thus suffers for our iniquities must endure and suffer for them himself'....Rabbi Moshe el Sheikh...who was chief Rabbi of Safed, makes this statement....'Our Rabbis with one voice accept and affirm the opinion that the prophet is speaking of the King Messiah, and we shall ourselves also adhere to the same view.' "[154]

THE NEW FIXED INTERPRETIVE NOTES FURTHER ISOLATE THE JEWS OF ALL AGES FROM THEIR MESSIAH

Dr. Bruce lends deep insight into how the rabbis altered the interpretation of the prophecies through interpretive notes. Today, many Jewish copies of the Bible in Israel have commentary footnotes explaining how certain Scriptures are to be understood! When and where did these ideas originate?

Bruce informs us: "The assiduity with which the Nazarenes appealed to the Old Testament writings, in both their Hebrew and Greek forms, led to a consideration of the various forms in which the text of the Old Testament was current at the time. Under Rabbi Akiba, about the beginning of the second century, a standard form of the consonantal Hebrew text of the Old Testament was fixed...."[155]

---

[154] Arthur W. Kac, *The Messianic Hope*, pp.75-76. Kac's source was David Baron, *Rays of Messiah's Glory*, Zondervan Publishing House.

[155] F.F. Bruce, *The Spreading Flame*, p. 265. Bruce explains in his footnote: "The Hebrew script originally expressed consonant-sounds only; the later system of vowel signs belongs to the eighth and ninth centuries A.D." Ibid.

Bruce continues: "...not only the text, but its interpretation also, had to be fixed, in order especially that an authoritative explanation might be provided of those scriptures which Christians were continually invoking to support their claim that Jesus was the Messiah and Son of God. In some cases interpretations which had previously been perfectly admissible were now banned because they lent themselves too readily to Christian propaganda."[156]

Bruce further notes in his book, *New Testament History*: "A good example of the Christian use of the Septuagint and Jewish refusal to admit the validity of the Christian premises and arguments is provided in Justin's *Dialogue with Trypho the Jew*, a work whose dramatic date is A.D. 135, soon after the suppression of the second Jewish revolt....Lines of interpretation, too, were laid down by the rabbis of this period which carefully excluded the messianic exegesis favoured by Christians. Hence, for centuries to come, although the Hebrew scriptures in text or in translation were venerated as holy writ by Jews and Christians alike, they were read in accordance with two divergent and contradictory interpretative traditions, to a point where what should have served as a bond of union might almost have been two different bodies of literature."[157]

A sign points the way to Rabbi Akiva's tomb.

---

[156]Ibid.

[157]F.F. Bruce, *New Testament History*, pp. 388-389.

Rabbi Akiva's tomb in Tiberias, Israel.

A Samaritan High Priest displays a 2000-year-old Torah scroll in a Samaritan synagogue in Schem, Israel.[158]

[158]Photograph courtesy of the State of Israel Government Press Office photography department.

"Among the Greek-speaking Jews the Septuagint, as we call the older Greek version of the Old Testament, fell into disfavour....Many of the expressions in the Greek of the Septuagint might almost have been providentially framed with a view to Christian propaganda....As a result, the Septuagint, which had originally been produced by Jews for Jews, was entirely abandoned to the Christians. For Greek-speaking Jews a new Greek translation was commissioned, which should represent as closely as possible the text and interpretation of the Hebrew scriptures established by Akiba and his colleagues."[1] F.F. Bruce, Ph.D., professor emeritus, University of Manchester

"One of the great works undertaken at Jabneh was a new Greek translation of the Scriptures by Aquilas of Pontus, a Roman aristocrat who converted first to Christianity and then to Judaism and became a pupil of Rabban Gamaliel, whom he accompanied on his travels. His translation was made under the supervision of the leading scholars of Jabneh, who greatly admired his work. It reflects the system of interpretation of the *tannaim* (and particularly of R. Akiva)....The earlier Greek translation of the Old Testament, the Septuagint....had been accepted as sacred by the Christian church...."[2] Rabbi Samuel Safrai, Hebrew University

8

THE MESSIAH CONSPIRACY CONTINUES IN THE *NEW* OLD TESTAMENT

The conspiracy rolls on with ingenious new innovations: the retranslation of the Greek version of the Old Testament; cleverly devised instructions which permitted copies of the New Testament to be burnt, and; the change of the name of Jesus. His Hebrew name was changed from *Yeshua* "salvation" to *Yeshu* "a curse," demanding that His name and memory be wiped out; literally, *ymah shemo vezihro*, in Hebrew. This wrongful acronymous name is still uttered by the unlearned and misinformed in modern Israel.

Additionally, a stern but false contemporary denial of the existence of Jewish believers in Jesus in the early Christian era is propounded by Rabbis Kaplan and Lewis. We "disclaim" this claim through an archaeological discovery made in 1994 by the French archaeologist, Claudine Dauphine, in the mountains of the Golan Heights, presently still within the borders of Israel. We hope these beautiful, green, majestic mountains will not be handed back to the Arabs, Syrians and Palestinians by the radical liberals, especially since so much precious Israeli blood[3] was shed to gain them! In essence,

---

[1]F.F. Bruce, *The Spreading Flame*, p. 266.
[2]H.H. Ben-Sasson and Shmuel Safrai, *A History of the Jewish People*, Part IV, p. 326.
[3]Originally Israel wanted to live in peace, but the Arabs just kept attacking them.

"Palestinians" are nomads from the surrounding Arab countries, who briefly roamed in, over and out of this area before Israel's refounding in 1948.

GREEK-SPEAKING JEWS SHORT-CHANGED FOR CENTURIES BY THE NEW FRAUDULENT TRANSLATION

Many people are totally unaware that in the second century a man named Aquila produced a deliberately fraudulent translation of the Old Testament in an effort to aid the rabbis in their attempt to split Jews and Messianic Jews.

Before we discuss this new translation, perhaps we should examine the character of the man who produced this new book. Aquila, who is mentioned in the Talmud,[4] was born a pagan, yet wanted to be accepted by the Messianic Jewish community of his day. However, he was unable to forfeit the practice of astrology, which was strictly forbidden by the Old and New Testaments of the Bible (Deut. 18:10-12; Isa. 47:13; Acts 16:16-18).

Because Aquila was unable to wean himself from this demonic counterfeit prophetic craft, the believers in Jesus refused to fellowship with him. Philip Carrington, in his book, *The Early Christian Church*, notes: "This is all introductory to the story of Aquila....He was still a Gentile, but he was deeply impressed by the Christian teachers whom he found in Jerusalem and asked for baptism, which was granted. Unfortunately he failed to renounce his interest in astrology and calculated horoscopes every day. He was warned by the Christian teachers, but persisted in his error. Finally, he was excommunicated. Mortified by this treatment, he had himself enrolled as a Jewish proselyte and was circumcised. He devoted himself to the study of the Hebrew language, and produced his new translation of the Old Testament with the objective of giving a new rendering of those passages on which the Christians principally relied...."[5]

AQUILA THE ASTROLOGER—THE DEFECTOR TAKES HIS PLANS OF REVENGE AGAINST THE CHRISTIANS TO THE RABBIS

It is quite clear what Aquila's motives were; he was contemplating revenge on the Christian community for not accepting him, along with his deceptive and forbidden craft. Thus, he took his

---

[4]Jerusalem Talmud, Megillah i 71-c.

[5]Philip Carrington, *The Early Christian Church,* Vol. 1, *The First Christian Century*, p. 439.

proposition to the rabbis, who were anxious to hear his plan to further widen the gap between Messianic Jew and Jew.

He wanted to produce a new translation of the Scriptures, primarily differing only in the Messianic prophecies. In effect, Aquila said, "I'll show you how to get rid of the problem of these repulsive Christians, right at the source of their proofs." His plan was to retranslate the Messianic prophecies which were fulfilled by Jesus. These prophecies were originally predicted thousands of years ago by the Hebrew prophets, in Hebrew, and were translated to Greek more than two hundred and fifty years before Christ.

The original translation of the Bible into Greek, known as the Septuagint, was carried out by seventy rabbis trying to reach out to those portions of Israeli Jewry and Jews in the Diaspora who could not read Hebrew. This Greek Bible was held in high esteem[6] until the time of Aquila (120 AD), and in fact, was used to spread the Messianic message.

The Messianic Jews would show traditional Jews the Messianic prophecies in the Old Testament, such as Isaiah 7:14, and explain the events which had transpired in Israel proving Jesus' fulfillment of prophecy. Many were becoming believers. Realizing this, Aquila considered these Scriptures dangerous. Thus, he set out to make his own translation, intending to create a barrier[7] to Messianic understanding of the Scriptures. He deliberately changed the wording of the Messianic prophecies.

---

[6]Reverend M. Abrahams tells us: "...there is no doubt that a feeling of theological antagonism to the Septuagint had long prevailed among the Jews. This was certainly the case already in the second century when Aquila flourished. The Septuagint, it is true, was originally made by Jews for Jews, but it was adopted as the inspired Bible of the Church. It is freely quoted in the New Testament, and it contained certain renderings which became objectionable to Jewish sentiment because of the use made of them in sectarian [Messianic Jewish] controversies....In Philo's age, the Jews of Egypt regarded the Septuagint with a reverence, as Dr. Swete puts it, 'scarcely less than that which belonged to the original Hebrew.' We can hardly wonder that within a century of Philo's death the Jewish attitude towards the Septuagint had entirely changed. For that century was the one which saw the birth and early growth of the Christian Church which adopted the Septuagint as its very own, as its one and only Bible." Reverend M. Abrahams, B.A., *Aquila's Greek Version of the Hebrew Bible*. London: Spottiswoode, Ballantyne & Co. Ltd., 1919, pp. 2-3. [ ] mine.

[7]Scholar F.F. Bruce illustrates this when he says: "His [Aquila's] version...proved a barrier to Christian interpretations. Christians, for example, might quote the Septuagint form of Isaiah 7:14, 'See, a virgin (Gk. *parthenos*) will conceive and give birth to a son and call his name Immanuel' (as is done in Matthew 1:23), and press it upon their Jewish acquaintances as a clear prediction of the virginal conception of Jesus; but now the Greek-speaking Jew could retort that the Greek version which *he* recognized as authoritative made no mention of a virgin (Gk. *parthenos*) but simply of a young woman (Gk. *neanis*)." F.F. Bruce, *The Spreading Flame*, pp. 266-267.

575 ISAIAS 7 9—25

μορων, καὶ ἡ κεφαλὴ Σομορων υἱὸς τοῦ Ρομελιου· καὶ ἐὰν μὴ
πιστεύσητε, οὐδὲ μὴ συνῆτε.
[10]Καὶ προσέθετο κύριος λαλῆσαι τῷ Αχαζ λέγων [11]Αἴτησαι σε- 10 11
αυτῷ σημεῖον παρὰ κυρίου θεοῦ σου εἰς βάθος ἢ εἰς ὕψος. [12]καὶ 12
εἶπεν Αχαζ Οὐ μὴ αἰτήσω οὐδ᾽ οὐ μὴ πειράσω κύριον. [13]καὶ εἶπεν 13
Ἀκούσατε δή, οἶκος Δαυιδ· μὴ μικρὸν ὑμῖν ἀγῶνα παρέχειν ἀν-
θρώποις; καὶ πῶς κυρίῳ παρέχετε ἀγῶνα; [14]διὰ τοῦτο δώσει κύ- 14
ριος αὐτὸς ὑμῖν σημεῖον· ἰδοὺ ἡ παρθένος ἐν γαστρὶ ἕξει καὶ τέ-
ξεται υἱόν, καὶ καλέσεις τὸ ὄνομα αὐτοῦ Εμμανουηλ· [15]βούτυρον 15
καὶ μέλι φάγεται· πρὶν ἢ γνῶναι αὐτὸν ἢ προελέσθαι πονηρὰ ἐκ-
λέξεται τὸ ἀγαθόν· [16]διότι πρὶν ἢ γνῶναι τὸ παιδίον ἀγαθὸν ἢ 16
κακὸν ἀπειθεῖ πονηρίᾳ τοῦ ἐκλέξασθαι τὸ ἀγαθόν, καὶ καταλειφθή-
σεται ἡ γῆ, ἣν σὺ φοβῇ ἀπὸ προσώπου τῶν δύο βασιλέων. [17]ἀλλὰ 17
ἐπάξει ὁ θεὸς ἐπὶ σὲ καὶ ἐπὶ τὸν λαόν σου καὶ ἐπὶ τὸν οἶκον τοῦ
πατρός σου ἡμέρας, αἳ οὔπω ἥκασιν ἀφ᾽ ἧς ἡμέρας ἀφεῖλεν Εφραιμ
ἀπὸ Ιουδα, τὸν βασιλέα τῶν Ἀσσυρίων. [18]καὶ ἔσται ἐν τῇ ἡμέρᾳ 18
ἐκείνῃ συριεῖ κύριος μυίαις, ὃ κυριεύει μέρους ποταμοῦ Αἰγύπτου,
καὶ τῇ μελίσσῃ, ἥ ἐστιν ἐν χώρᾳ Ἀσσυρίων, [19]καὶ ἐλεύσονται πάν- 19

9 24—27 ΔΑΝΙΗΛ 924

πόλιν Σιων συντελεσθῆναι τὴν ἁμαρτίαν καὶ τὰς ἀδικίας σπανίσαι
καὶ ἀπαλεῖψαι τὰς ἀδικίας καὶ διανοηθῆναι τὸ ὅραμα καὶ δοθῆναι
δικαιοσύνην αἰώνιον καὶ συντελεσθῆναι τὸ ὅραμα καὶ εὐφρᾶναι
25 ἅγιον ἁγίων. [25]καὶ γνώσῃ καὶ διανοηθήσῃ καὶ εὐφρανθήσῃ καὶ
εὑρήσεις προστάγματα ἀποκριθῆναι καὶ οἰκοδομήσεις Ιερουσαλημ
26 πόλιν κυρίῳ. [26]καὶ μετὰ ἑπτὰ καὶ ἑβδομήκοντα καὶ ἑξήκοντα δύο
ἀποσταθήσεται χρῖσμα καὶ οὐκ ἔσται, καὶ βασιλεία ἐθνῶν φθερεῖ
τὴν πόλιν καὶ τὸ ἅγιον μετὰ τοῦ χριστοῦ, καὶ ἥξει ἡ συντέλεια
αὐτοῦ μετ᾽ ὀργῆς καὶ ἕως καιροῦ συντελείας· ἀπὸ πολέμου πολε-
27 μηθήσεται. [27]καὶ δυναστεύσει ἡ διαθήκη εἰς πολλούς, καὶ πάλιν
ἐπιστρέψει καὶ ἀνοικοδομηθήσεται εἰς πλάτος καὶ μῆκος· καὶ κατὰ
συντέλειαν καιρῶν καὶ μετὰ ἑπτὰ καὶ ἑβδομήκοντα καιροὺς καὶ ἑξήκοντα δύο ἔτη ἕως καιροῦ συντελείας πολέμου καὶ ἀφαιρεθήσεται
ἡ ἐρήμωσις ἐν τῷ κατισχῦσαι τὴν διαθήκην ἐπὶ πολλὰς ἑβδομά-
δας· καὶ ἐν τῷ τέλει τῆς ἑβδομάδος ἀρθήσεται ἡ θυσία καὶ ἡ
σπονδή, καὶ ἐπὶ τὸ ἱερὸν βδέλυγμα τῶν ἐρημώσεων ἔσται ἕως
συντελείας, καὶ συντέλεια δοθήσεται ἐπὶ τὴν ἐρήμωσιν.

24 το οραμα ult.] τα -ματα 88; + ※και προφητην 88 Sy || 27 ετη] ετων 88

Aquila altered the words "virgin" and "Christ" (Messiah), as illustrated in the Septuagint[8] text.

---

[8]*Septuaginta*. Stuttgart: Deutsche Bibelgesellschaft, © 1935, pp. 575, 924, used by permission.

AQUILA CONVENIENTLY REMOVES THE WORDS MESSIAH AND VIRGIN FROM THE JEWISH SEPTUAGINT BIBLE BECAUSE OF JESUS' FULFILLMENTS!

The Greek words χριστὸς "Christ/Messiah" and παρθένος "virgin" were removed by Aquila in a new fraudulent translation of the Greek Old Testament. He did this under the direction of Rabbi Akiva, one of, if not the most anti-Christian rabbi of his day![9]

There can be no doubt why Aquila and Akiva chose to change these two key words with regard to Messiah. They did not want people to be reminded that Jesus fulfilled the prophecy according to a fixed timetable given by Daniel. Aquila removed the word Messiah. When the New Testament recorded the virgin birth of Jesus, Aquila and Akiva thought it convenient to change Isaiah's word, which the Septuagint had previously translated quite a while before the birth of Jesus as *parthenos* "virgin," to *neanis,* which only means "young woman."

REVEREND ABRAHAMS POINTED OUT THAT AQUILA'S FAULTY TRANSLATION INFECTED THE JEWISH BIBLES IN AMERICA

Reverend M. Abrahams, in his book, *Aquila's Greek Version of the Hebrew Bible*, elaborates on this when he tells us: "...we know from Justin Martyr that the Jews [Jewish leaders of Yavne] of the first half of the second century strongly objected to the Septuagint rendering of the passage. The Jews [certain rabbis of Yavne] maintained that the correct translation of '*almah* was not 'parthenos' but 'neanis,' not virgin but young woman....my point is that the very word 'neanis' is the one chosen by Aquila, and this fact explains why, on the one hand, the Emperor Justinian—Christian as he was—preferred the Septuagint, while the Jews of his day were fonder of Aquila. It is interesting to note that Aquila's rendering of Isaiah vii.14...has been adopted in the new Jewish Version recently published in America....Epiphanius, in fact, asserts that the sole purpose of Aquila was precisely to introduce these variations. So, too, with Irenaeus. In his 'Treatise against Heresies,' written about the year 200, he devotes the whole of the

[9]Johannes Weiss documents: "The fate of the Jerusalem church underwent a decided change under Hadrian (117-138). In the great uprising of the Jews under the Messiah-prophet Bar-Kokhba (132-135), Jerusalem fell into the hands of the rebels; and even during the Bar-Kokhba revolt the Christians had much to suffer at their hands...." Weiss' footnote states: "And indeed in the recent Jewish war, Bar-Kokhba, the leader of the uprising of the Jews, condemned the Christians alone to be led away to dreadful torture if they would not deny Jesus was Christ and blaspheme him....'Kokhba, who was leader of the rebellion of the Jews, inflicted various penalties on many of the Christians, since they would not go out to battle with him against the Romans;' Orosius, 7:13." Johannes Weiss, *Earliest Christianity: A History of the Period A.D. 30-150,* Vol. II, pp. 722-723.

twenty-first chapter of Book III. to...what he calls the misinterpretation of Isaiah vii.14, by Theodotion of Ephesus and Aquila of Pontus, both, as Irenaeus says, proselytes to Judaism. Against Aquila, Irenaeus quotes the Septuagint, and makes great play with the argument that the Septuagint, made in pre-Christian times by Jews, confirmed the Christian interpretation of the text in question."[10]

After Aquila's dirty deed was done, within a few centuries his translations became rather scarce. Mysteriously, there are only a few fragments of his deceptively fraudulent translations existing in the twentieth century. The fragment we have reproduced[11] is commonly known as fragment TS 20.50. As you can see, the Greek is written over the Hebrew.

EVEN *THE JEWISH ENCYCLOPEDIA* CONFIRMS THAT AQUILA HAD AN ANTI-CHRISTIAN BIAS

The Jewish Encyclopedia tells us: "...the need of a Greek version for Jews disappeared when Greek ceased to be the *lingua franca* of Egypt and the Levant....fragmentary manuscripts of the translation....were discovered in 1897, partly by F. C. Burkitt, among the mass of loose documents brought to Cambridge from the *geniza* of

[10]Reverend M. Abrahams, B.A., *Aquila's Greek Version of the Hebrew Bible*, p. 5. [ ] mine.

[11]Courtesy of the Syndics of Cambridge University Library.

the Old Synagogue at Cairo through the enterprise of Dr. S. Schechter and Dr. C. Taylor, master of St. John's College, Cambridge."[12]

F. C. Conybeard published *The Dialogue of Timothy and Aquila* in 1898. This work mentions Aquila's anti-Christian bias.[13]

Aquila altered Daniel's word χριστὸς (*Christos*, i.e. "Messiah"), found in the Bible in Daniel 9:26, to ἠλειμμὲνος, which only means "a responsible person." Daniel's Hebrew original was exactly and correctly translated in the Septuagint (from משיח "Messiah"), but in order to mislead as many Greek-speaking Jews as possible, the rabbis mistranslated Messiah to ἠλειμμὲνος (*elemenous*), a fraudulent translation.[14]

ABRAHAMS DOCUMENTS THAT AQUILA CUT THE WORDS *MESSIAH* AND *JESUS* OUT OF HIS GREEK TRANSLATION

Reverend M. Abrahams further notes: "There were phrases in the Septuagint which Jews came to dislike. Two instances of this must suffice. The first instance is general, the second particular. The general instance concerns the word *Christos*, which merely comes from a Greek verb meaning to anoint, and thus corresponds to the Hebrew verb משח which has the same sense. The Greek word Christos, like the Hebrew equivalent משיח (Messiah), literally denotes 'anointed.' In the Septuagint the Hebrew משיח is quite correctly rendered Christos. Thus, in Daniel ix. 26, the word משיח is rendered Christos, where the Authorized English Version has 'the anointed one'....But, in the New Testament, Christos, or Christ, was used as a personal name for the Messiah. We can realise that Jews would dislike a translation in which

---

[12]*The Jewish Encyclopedia*, p. 34.

[13]Ibid.

[14]Joseph Reider, Ph.D., tells us in his thesis: "Special emphasis is laid on his rendering of משיח [Messiah] by ἠλειμμὲνος [responsible person] instead of χριστὸς [*Christos*] in passages like Dan. 9.26 and of עַלְמָה Isa. 7.14 by νεανις [young woman] as against παρθένος [*parthenos*, "virgin"] of the Septuagint." In Reider's footnotes 83 and 84, he says: "Comp. Schürer, *Geschichte des jüdischen Volkes im Zeitalter Jesu Christi*, II, 613, n.12. This is another of á's translations which Field characterizes by the word ἐτυμολογικῶς (*Prolegomena,* xxii), for he likewise renders מָשַׁח by ἀλείφειν Lev. 8.10 *et al.*, and מִשְׁחָה by ἄλειμμα Lev. 21.12. On this crucial point in the controversy between Jews and Christians comp. Swete's *Introduction to the O.T. in Greek*, p. 30.—Aquila's rendering here must have been particularly distasteful to the Christian Church, since elsewhere (Gen. 24.43) the same word is translated by ἀπόκρυφος [to uncover], while νεανις [young woman] is also used for בתולה [virgin] Deut. 22.28." Joseph Reider, Ph.D, *Prolegomena to a Greek-Hebrew & Hebrew-Greek Index to Aquila.* Philadelphia: College of Hebrew and Cognate Learning, 1916, pp. 59-60. [ ] mine. We thank our friend Roy Ioannides, an expert in Greek, for clarifying the meaning of ἠλειμμένος and ἀπόκρυφος; two very difficult and ancient Greek words.

the word Christos occurred at all. In Aquila's Version the word is altogether avoided. It is also significant that whereas the Septuagint mostly renders the Hebrew name Joshua by Jesus, Aquila carefully abstains from so doing; although, among Greek Jews, Jesus must have been a fairly common personal name."[15]

AQUILA'S LETHAL RESULT IS REALIZED—A DEATH BLOW TO THE SPREAD OF MESSIANIC BIBLICAL (GOSPEL) TRUTH ENSUES

Thus, after a considerable amount of time elapsed and Aquila's translation was in large circulation, the desired result began to take effect. Messianic Jews would attempt to tell Jews who were interested, about the Messiah's birth and other prophecies. The traditional Jews would look it up, and bang! It was not in their Bible—Aquila's "version" of the Bible that is!

This dealt a terrible blow to the understanding of Messianic biblical truths during that age and ages to come. It is clear Aquila wanted, out of spite and revenge,[16] to make sure no one else became interested in the Messianic Christian faith, as he once had. So he did everything in his power to hinder the biblical movement of Messianic Jews by making a new biased translation of the Holy Scriptures. He maintained his "version" was more literal[17] and accurate. He wrote his Greek directly over the original Hebrew, which few Diaspora Jews could even read with understanding. However, even today *The Jewish Encyclopedia* admits: "Aquila's renderings of the Hebrew tenses are

---

[15]Reverend M. Abrahams, B.A., *Aquila's Greek Version of the Hebrew Bible*, p. 4.

[16]Rabbi Abrahams informs us: "...Epiphanius further records that Aquila was a relative of the Emperor Hadrian, and that having witnessed various miraculous healings by Christians, he joined that faith. Owing, however, to his determined resolve to practise magic, he was excommunicated by the Church, and, in **revenge**, attached himself to the Synagogue, devoting himself to the task of removing Christian evidences from the Bible." Ibid, p. 6.

[17]Regarding this new Greek translation of Aquila's, Jakob Jocz informs us: "...the main reason for the prohibition to use the LXX [Septuagint] is closely connected with the Jewish-Christian controversy. To provide a more reliable translation which would eliminate the LXX from general use was attempted by the Greek proselyte, Aquila (middle second century), a convert from Christianity to Judaism. His aim was to give a literal translation closely related to the masoretic text. But though upheld by the Synagogue, it was not a success. Joseph Reider describes it as something of a monstrosity, 'its Greek vocabulary and grammatical forms being often uncouth and barbaric'. Its significance lies in that it provided a separate Greek version authorized by the Synagogue, while 'the Septuagint became the official Bible of the Christian.' " Jakob Jocz, *The Jewish People and Jesus Christ*, p. 50. [ ] mine.

often most inadequate."[18] Whose word will you take regarding the true translation of the Bible? A disgruntled pagan rejected by the Christians or seventy[19] blood-born Jewish rabbis who were scholars?

THEY SPREAD THIS FAKE TRANSLATION THROUGHOUT THE GREEK-SPEAKING WORLD TO PRECLUDE CHRISTOLOGICAL REFERENCES, SO ADMIT SCHOLARLY JEWISH SOURCES

In an article entitled "Aquila's Translation of the Bible," in the series *Jerusalem to Jabneh: The Period of the Mishnah and its Literature—Units 11,12,* it is documented that the rabbis of Yavne succeeded in spreading this faulty translation of the Old Testament, which Aquila had produced, throughout the entire Diaspora (to Jews everywhere in the Greek-speaking world of that time). You can see our point in the following documentation, which includes an impressive quote from G. Alon's book, *A History of the Jews*: "We can find evidence of the Sages' concern for the Hellenistic Diaspora in yet another area. They saw to it that the Torah was translated into Greek once again, the much earlier Septuagint version being considered inaccurate. This translation was made in the beginning of the reign of Hadrian (c. 120 C.E.), by the famous convert Aquila from Pontus, under the direction of R. Eliezer, R. Joshua ben Hanania and R. Akiva. What was the reason for this new translation? According to G. Allon, this translation was aimed at the Hellenistic-Roman Diaspora. 'The Sages wanted to give them a Greek version that would accord with the Massoretic Bible as decided upon by the Sages at Jabneh. The Septuagint, by contrast, was quite far from the Palestinian Hebrew Bible. (It is also possible that **the Sages wanted to word the new Greek version in such a way as to preclude Christological references** which were based on the LXX.) The fragments and quotes from the Aquila version in our possession show that faithfulness to the Massoretic Bible outweighed considerations of Greek style and syntax. Sometimes the translation is based on 'midrash exegesis' which resulted in strange Greek forms. At any rate, **we have much evidence**

---

[18]*The Jewish Encyclopedia*, p. 35.

[19]The word Septuagint comes from seventy. Rabbi Abrahams also noted that Jews began to regain a limited interest in the Septuagint when he said: "It was not till the age of De Rossi, in the sixteenth century, that Jewish scholars again interested themselves in the Septuagint, and even then their motive was literary rather than religious." Reverend M. Abrahams, B.A., *Aquila's Greek Version of the Hebrew Bible*. As you can see, it was too late. This did not help the Greek-speaking Jews of the first six centuries to see the Messianic evidence that was kept from them. Most modern Jews do not know Greek except for scholars and those who live in Greece.

that the sages of Jabneh succeeded in making the Aquila version available to the entire Diaspora, though it did not supplant the LXX entirely.' "[20]

The article mentioned that Aquila "had" a close relationship with the Rabban Gamaliel of Jabneh, and we all know how much Gamaliel hated Jewish-Christians. He found the perfect henchman in the person of Aquila.

THE ONLY POSSIBLE CONCLUSION! A TRAITOR BETRAYS THE JEWS OUT OF THEIR PROPHESIED MESSIAH

It is surprising to us that a person who created a fraudulent translation with the express purpose of deceiving the Greek-speaking populace could be "a favorite personage" of Jewish tradition and legend. As *The Jewish Encyclopedia* says of Aquila: "In Rabbinical Literature: 'Aquila the Proselyte' (עקילם הגר) and his work are familiar to the Talmudic-Midrashic literature. While 'the Seventy' and their production are almost completely ignored by rabbinical sources, Aquila is a **favorite personage** in Jewish tradition and legend. As historical, the following may be considered. 'Aquila the Proselyte translated the Torah (that is, the whole of Scripture...) in the presence of R. Eliezer and R. Joshua, who praised him and said, in the words of Ps. xlv. 3 [A.V. 2], 'Thou art fairer than the children of men: grace is poured into thy lips; therefore God hath blessed thee forever.' This contains a play upon the Hebrew word 'Yafyafita' (Thou art fairer) and the common designation of Greek as 'the language of Japhet' (Yer. Meg. i. 71*c)*."[21]

Hopefully, now that we have exposed what this man has done to the Jewish people, the world, including the rabbinical community, will reconsider and think of Aquila as not "fairer than the children of men," as past rabbis have claimed, but rather as a spiteful charlatan[22] who deliberately deceived Jews with respect to their Messiah and the prophecies He fulfilled.

---

[20]*Jerusalem to Jabneh: The Period of the Mishnah and its Literature—Units 11,12*. Tel Aviv: Everyman's University Publishing House, Open University of Israel, © 1981, p. 48, used by permission. Bold mine.

[21]*The Jewish Encyclopedia*, Vol. II, p. 36. Bold mine.

[22]Remember what one rabbinical source says of proselytes (converts to Judaism) such as Aquila: "The rabbis taught: 'The proselytes and those who play with children hold back the Messiah.' This is understandable as far as the proselytes are concerned, for R. Helbo said: 'The proselytes are as bad for Israel as a sore on the skin....' " (B. Nid. 13b). Raphael Patai, *The Messiah Texts*, p. 59. The book of Romans 8:21-23 and 11:15, 26 of the New Testament indicates that when enough Jews believe in Jesus, the world will go from "death to life" and Jesus the Messiah will return. Until then, He is still being "held back." Though we do not believe the writer of the commentary had Jesus in mind. His words are certainly an interesting parallel.

THE POWER OF THE NEW TESTAMENT CAUSED FEAR AMONG THE RABBIS

Was the New Testament so powerful a tool in the first century that it evoked immense fear among the rabbis? Were the rabbis alarmed at its wide distribution among the common Jews? The answer is an unequivocal yes! The rabbinical literature of this period indicates deliberate attempts to censor and cover up certain passages by blaming them on "scribal corruption," or writing errors made by early scribes.

Louis Ginzberg, in his article, "Some Observations on the Attitude of the Synagogue Towards the Apocalyptic-Eschatological Writings," describes how the popular scholar, George Foot Moore, discovered a corruptive error in the Jerusalem Talmud of the Jews, which we believe he (Moore) properly translated. Ginzberg's interesting words on this are: "The result of the thorough examination by Prof. Moore of the Tannaitic sources [from Yavne] bearing upon this question may be briefly summed up as follows: The ספרים החיצונים [External Books] the reading of which is strongly condemned by Rabbi Akiba, Sanhedrin X, 1 refer to the heretical, in particular to the early Christian writings. The ספרי המירס spoken of by Rabban Johanan ben Zakkai, Yaddaim IV, 6 in connection with the defilement of the hands and the reading of which books is permitted in Yerushalmi, Sanhedrin X, 28a owe their existence to a scribal error; המירס is nothing but a corruption of המינים. Consequently the text of Yerushalmi is to be emended to read as follows:

הקורא בספרים החיצונים כגון ספרי בן לענה וספרי המינים אבל ספר (י) בן סירא וגו'"

The translation of this passage as given by Prof. Moore reads: 'He who reads in the arch-heretical books, such as the books of Ben-Laana (Gospels) and the books of the heretics (Christians)....'...The inference which Prof. Moore draws from these premises is that **the attempt** authoritatively **to define the Canon** of the Hagiographa **was dictated by** the danger that threatened the Synagogue from **the circulation among Jews of the Gospels** and other **Christian books**."[23]

***

[23]Louis Ginzberg, "Some Observations on the Attitude of the Synagogue Towards the Apocalyptic-Eschatological Writings," *Journal of Biblical Literature,* Vol. IV. New Haven: Yale University Press for The Society of Biblical Literature and Exegesis, © 1922, pp. 120-122. [ ] and bold mine.

THE GREATEST BEST-SELLER OF ALL TIME WRITTEN BY THE PERSECUTED JEW

Even though the New Testament has become the greatest best-seller of all time, written by a group of highly persecuted, yet inspired Jews, the Talmud records the feelings of the leading rabbis of Yavne toward the books of the New Testament: "...the Books [New Testament books] of the Minim [believers in Jesus] may not be saved from a fire, but they must be burnt in their place, they and the Divine Names occurring in them. Now surely it means the blank portions of a Scroll of the Law? No: the blank spaces in the Books of Minim. Seeing that we [rabbis] may not save the Books of Minim themselves, need their blank spaces be stated?—This is its meaning: And the Books of Minim are like blank spaces.

It was stated in the text: The blank spaces and the Books of the Minim, we may not save them from a fire. R. Jose said: On weekdays one must cut out the Divine Names which they contain, hide them, and burn the rest. R. Tarfon said: May I bury my son if I would not burn them together with their Divine Names if they came to my hand. For even if one pursued me to slay me, or a snake pursued me to bite me, I would enter a heathen Temple [for refuge], but not the houses of these [people]....And just as we may not rescue them from a fire, so may we not rescue them from a collapse [of debris] or from water or from anything that may destroy them."[24] In the Talmud's footnote to this passage, it is said: "R. Meir called it (the Gospel) '*Awen Gilyon*, the falsehood of blank paper; R. Johanan called it' *Awon Gilyon*, the sin of etc."[25]

DID RABBIS YOHANAN BEN ZAKKAI AND ME'IR DEGRADE THE NEW TESTAMENT?

Evangelion is Greek for "good news/Gospel" and was the main term used to describe the message of the New Testament. Modern English derives the words "evangelist" and "evangelical" from this term. However, the rabbis of Yavne said many ugly and distasteful things about the faith and its book, the New Testament itself, by changing the vowels in the word *evangelion*. F. F. Bruce confirms: "Some leading rabbis, like Yohanan ben Zakkai and Aqiba's pupil Me'ir, made derogatory puns on the word *evangelion,* altering the vowels to *'awen-gillayon or 'awon-gillayon* ('iniquity of the margin')."[26]

---

[24]*The Babylonian Talmud,* Shabbath, 116a-b, pp. 570-571. First and third [ ] mine. Rabbi Finkel denies that these words refer to the Christian Gospel. However, as you have read, the monumental Jewish work known as the Soncino Talmud admits that it refers to the Gospel.

[25]Ibid, p. 571.

[26]F. F. Bruce, *New Testament History*, p. 378.

Remember, *evangelion* is the Greek word for "Gospel." The words created by altering the vowels sound similar but are perversions, or in effect, Hebrew word curses which sound almost identical to the original term "Gospel," *evangelion*.

Why was such disrespect and intolerance mounted against the Messianic faith by these rabbis? Could it have been that they felt jealous or threatened in their leadership and ability to rule and hold the Jews together as one people? Might their authority have been challenged and their egos damaged? In their pride, they became too narrow-minded to hear any testimony or prophecy regarding the exciting faith of their Messianic brothers in Jesus.

RABBI TARPHON BURNS THE NEW TESTAMENT RATHER THAN CURSE HIMSELF

Foremost scholar, James Parkes, in his book, *The Conflict of the Church and the Synagogue,* comments on this issue with added details: "...the rabbis show a knowledge of the New Testament and of the details of the life of Jesus. The gospels are known as 'Aven-gillayon' by Rabbis Meir of Jabne and Jochanan. The word is an offensive pun [in Hebrew] meaning 'revelation of sin' or 'falsehood of blank paper'. There is a discussion reported as to what shall be done with 'external books'....Rabbi Meir says that they are not to be saved from the fire, but to be burned at once, even with the names of God in them. Rabbi Jose says that on a week-day the name of God ought to be cut out and hidden away. Rabbi Tarphon invoked a curse on himself if he did not burn the books, names of God and all."[27]

The tomb of Rabbi Meir, on the Sea of Galilee in Tiberias, Israel.

[27]James Parkes, *The Conflict of the Church and the Synagogue*, p. 109. [ ] mine.

THE "MAIN-STREAM" AGAINST THE JEWISH CHRISTIANS' "FALSEHOOD OF THE SCROLL"

Scholar F. F. Bruce also adds interesting comments in his book, *Jesus and Christian Origins Outside the New Testament*: "...the *minim* in question appear to be Jewish Christians....we are dealing with the controversies between Jewish Christians and the representatives of what was now main-stream Judaism in the period after A.D. 70, when Jewish Christians were excluded from the synagogue. Discussions sometimes arise about the status of 'the books of the *minim*'....Derogatory puns on *evangelion*, the Greek word for 'Gospel', are ascribed to rabbis of the Tannaitic period: They called it '*awen-gillayon* or '*awon-gillayon*, which means something like 'falsehood of the scroll' or 'perversion of the scroll'. Any claim that such works should be granted canonical recognition was decisively rejected. Some rabbis thought they might well be burnt; others suggested that the occurrences of the name of God which they contained should be cut out first."[28]

RABBIS' VEHEMENCE AGAINST NEW TESTAMENT GOSPEL—EVIDENCE THAT OTHER RABBIS WERE BECOMING BELIEVERS

Bruce further elaborates on this little-known subject of the rabbis' abuse and intolerance of the New Testament, in his book, *New Testament History*: "It is only after A.D. 70 that we can begin to talk about normative Judaism and of deviations from the norm; in the days of the Second Temple there was a much greater variety of Jewish religious life and practice, and no one form could claim to represent the standard by which others were to be judged.

When the rabbis of Jamnia discussed the recognition of canonical books and the rejection of others, one group to which they paid attention was 'the books of the minim'. These contained the name of God, and yet their contents were unacceptable....it is unlikely that the idea of extending canonical recognition to the Christian books was seriously entertained: they were mentioned only to be condemned. 'The *gilyonim* and the books of the *minim* are not sacred scripture' [Talmud, Tosefta, *Yadaim* 2:13].[29] Some leading rabbis, like Yohanan ben Zakkai and Aqiba's pupil Me'ir, made derogatory puns on the word *evangelion*, altering the vowels to '*awen-gillayon* or *awon- gillayon*' ('iniquity of the margin'). But 'the vehemence with which the leading rabbis of the first generation of the second century

---

[28]F.F. Bruce, *Jesus and Christian Origins Outside the New Testament*, p. 60.

[29][ ] contain Bruce's footnote reference to the Talmud where this is documented.

express their hostility to the gospel and other books of the heretics, and to their conventicles, is the best evidence that they were growing in numbers and influence; some even among the teachers of the Law were suspected of leanings towards the new doctrine.' "[30]

RABBIS TARPHON, AKIVA AND ISHMAEL ALL INSTRUCT—BURN THE NEW TESTAMENT

The widely respected Jewish scholar, G. Alon, quotes the Talmud and other sources as he tells us: "Blank writing surfaces (*gilyonim*) and books of the *Minim* are not to be rescued (on the Sabbath) but should be allowed to burn right where they are, along with their *azkarot* [the explicit names of God, יהוה]. Rabbi Jose of Galilee says: On a week-day, one should cut out the *azkarot* and bury them, then burn the rest. Said Rabbi Tarphon: May I lose my sons if I would not burn any such books that fell into my hands, *azkarot* and all! Indeed, if I were fleeing from a deadly pursuer, I had rather take refuge in a house of heathen worship than enter into the house [Messianic synagogue of the Nazarenes] of such as these. For the heathen do not know Him and (so) deny Him; but these do know Him, and (yet) deny Him....The same question is the subject of a disagreement between Rabbi Ishmael and Rabbi Akiba in Sifre on Numbers: Rabbi Ishmael says: The way to deal with books of the Minim is this: one cuts out the *azkarot* and burns the rest. Rabbi Akiba says: One burns the whole thing, because it was not written in holiness."[31]

WHY DID RABBI AKIVA ABHOR THE CHRISTIANS AND THEIR NEW TESTAMENT BOOKS?

In our quest to discover the reason for Rabbi Akiva's actions, we find a most plausible answer in an article by scholar Joshua Bloch, entitled, "Outside Books." Bloch notes: "Rabbi Akiba and his circle became apprehensive. Seeing that the teachings contained in them were rapidly gaining followers and that the ranks of the Nazarenes were being swelled by the influx of many of the common people, Rabbi Akiba denounced those who indulged in the reading and study of 'outside books'....The Nazarenes and their books became objectionable not so much because of their belief about the role of Jesus but because of their persistent attempt to exalt him to a position almost equal with that of God....they evidently became quite dangerous in the days of Rabbi Akiba....Rabbi Akiba and his circle regarded the

---

[30] F.F. Bruce, *New Testament History*, pp. 386-387.
[31] G. Alon, *The Jews in Their Land in the Talmudic Age*, p. 291. [ ] mine.

teachings of the Christian books current in their day about the 'divinity' of Jesus of Nazareth, as a serious infringement of the belief in the Divine Unity....The close of the first century found the Jews and the Nazarenes going further and further apart....In maintaining that those who indulge in the reading of 'outside books' have no portion in the World to Come Rabbi Akiba made a significant contribution to the various measures then taken by authoritative Jewish leaders to bring about 'the final separation of the Nazarenes from the rest of the Jews. Hitherto these 'disciples of Jesus the Nazarene' had been a conventicle within the synagogue, rather than a sect.' "[32]

SOME RABBIS CALL THE ANCIENT MESSIANIC SYNAGOGUES "HOUSES OF DESTRUCTION"

The Talmud describes this house in question as a Messianic synagogue, so to speak. The words in the Talmud used for Messianic congregation are *Be Nitzraphi*, which is described as: " בי נצרפי; a meeting place of the Nazarenes, Jewish Christians, where local matters were discussed and religious debates were held. (Levy)."[33]

R. Travers Herford, an authority on Christianity in the Talmud, also mentioned that the Talmud called these ancient meeting places *Be Abidan*. He explains: " 'Be Nitzraphi' is a synagogue or meeting-place of Christians, more particularly Jewish Christians or Nazarenes, Notzrim."[34] Herford goes on to describe these houses as: "The meeting place of early Christians where religious controversies were held."[35] He shows that the word, *Be*, in fact, is short for *Bait* (Hebrew for "house"), and *Abidan* is actually a word denoting destruction. Thus, the Yavnean rabbis who were protesting early Jewish faith in Jesus were calling their synagogues (Houses of Gathering) "Houses of Destruction." To quote Herford: "Now what are the 'Be Abidan' and 'Be Nitzraphi'? 'Be' is a shortened form of Beth, house....'Abin' is apparently connected with the root 'abad' (אבד), to destroy....Nitzraphi [the vocalization is uncertain] is almost certainly connected with the word Notzri, Nazarene, while the form suggests a niph'al from the root

---

[32]Joshua Bloch, "Outside Books," *Mordecai M. Kaplan, Jubilee Volume*, pp. 94-95, 97-99. This shows that the deity of Jesus was taught very early, not later as liberal scholars assert in an effort to discredit our fundamentals. This, however, was not a legitimate reason for the hatred vented by Rabbi Akiva against the Messianic Jews, if Jesus was deity as He claimed. Akiva was worried about the implications of belief in Jesus' Messiahship and how it would affect Jewish survival outside of Israel.

[33]*The Babylonian Talmud*, Shabbath, 116a, footnote 7, p. 570.

[34]R.Travers Herford, *Christianity in Talmud & Midrash*. New York: KTAV Publishing House, Inc., © 1903, p. 170.

[35]*The Babylonian Talmud*, Shabbath, 116a, footnote 5, p. 570.

tzaraph (צרף), to unite....'Be Nitzraphi' denotes a meeting place of Jewish Christians; and I would explain the name as a hybrid, combining a reference to Notzrim, Nazarenes, with the notion of assembly (root, tzaraph)."[36]

THE REAL MEANING OF SYNAGOGUE/CHURCH AND MESSIANIC SYNAGOGUE

The word church, meaning those "called out" to believe in Messiah Jesus, was only used to describe the people who believed, not the buildings in which they met. Synagogue (*bait conesset*) literally means "house of gathering."

By this time, the Messianic Jews had been forced out of their home synagogues[37] by the biased, narrow-minded, propagandistic rulings of these self-appointed "rabbis" of Yavne, who managed to become the formulators of a new mainstream Judaism.

As you have read, the Birkat ha-Minim was their principal tool. Thus, the Messianic Jews were pressured to form their own Messianic synagogues similar to the ones being initiated now.[38] Jakob Jocz, a Jewish believer in Jesus and survivor of the Holocaust, wrote a standard work about Jesus as the Messiah from a Jewish point of view. His book is widely read in seminaries throughout the world. Regarding these Messianic synagogues of the second century, Jocz commented: "The formation of separate Synagogues seems to have been a feature

---

[36]R.Travers Herford, *Christianity in Talmud & Midrash*, pp. 164, 170.

[37]Professor Yehudah Liebes noted of Jewish and Jewish Christian synagogues: "Prof. Shlomo Pines has recently discovered evidence for such correct relations between Jews and Jewish Christians during the early years. In the following source relating the history of their sect, which originated among the Jewish Christians themselves, the situation following the death of Jesus is described as follows: After him, his disciples were with the Jews and the Children of Israel in the latter's synagogues, and observed the prayers and the feasts of (the Jews) in the same place as the latter. (However) there was a disagreement between them and the Jews with regard to Christ.' " Yehudah Liebes, "Who Makes the Horn of Jesus to Flourish," *Immanuel*, pp. 56-58. Thus, we see that the Jews and Jewish Christians, in at least some cases, early on shared the same synagogues. This remarkable evidence uncovered by Professor Pines should silence those rabbis who are saying there were not many or any Jews who believed in Jesus at that time! Professor Liebes' source was S. Pines, "The Jewish Christians of the Early Centuries of Christianity According to a New Source," *Proceedings of the Israel Academy of Science and Humanities*.

[38]After a few hundred years, Messianic congregations were persecuted as heretical by the Catholic Church and forced underground. Today, Catholicism no longer dominates the world. Their persecution (stocks, burning, iron maidens) stopped after the Reformation, and Messianic synagogues and congregations have re-emerged in the twentieth century.

of Jewish life in Jerusalem. Soon there was added a new Synagogue, that of the Nazarenes."[39]

The famous Jewish authority, Abba Eban, made reference to these synagogues of Jewish believers in Jesus being challenged by other synagogues in the second century, on a PBS special entitled, "Heritage, Civilization and the Jews," which aired in 1984.[40]

ARCHAEOLOGISTS UNEARTH AN ANCIENT MESSIANIC SYNAGOGUE IN ISRAEL

Grant Jeffrey, in his book, *Messiah, War in the Middle East & The Road to Armageddon*, documents under his section "Jewish Christian Synagogues": "Archaeologists in Jerusalem have discovered, in the basement of the site of the Upper Room, the remains of a first-century Judeo-Christian congregation that met in a synagogue. A fascinating article by Dr. Bargil Pixner in the *Mishkan* Magazine reveals startling archaeological evidence of the Church of the Apostles on Mount Zion (Jerusalem: Fall, 1990). He reports that when a mortar shell hit this site in the 1948 War of Independence, damage was done to the tomb of David. The Israeli archaeologist, Jacob Pinkerfield, studied the damage in 1951 and found evidence of an extremely old synagogue, with a niche to hold the ark of the Torah oriented in such a manner as to suggest Christian ownership. Further, he found some plaster in the original wall on which were written, in ancient Greek letters, the words that translated, 'Conquer, Savior, mercy,' and 'O Jesus, that I may live, O lord of the autocrat [the all-powerful].' "[41]

We find it interesting that John Elson, in an article entitled, "The New Testament's Unsolved Mysteries," quoted "scholar," R. T. France, who said: "...'no 1st century inscription mentions him [Jesus] and no object or building has survived which has a specific link to him.' "[42] France should have some fun reviewing the finds of 1951.

DESPITE THE EVIDENCE, SOME RABBIS ARE ATTEMPTING TO REWRITE HISTORY BY TELLING US THAT JEWISH CHRISTIANS NEVER REALLY EXISTED!

There are many rabbis today who obnoxiously and deceptively (perhaps ignorantly, in some cases) attempt to claim that Jewish

---

[39]Jakob Jocz, *The Jewish People and Jesus Christ*, p. 164.

[40]This telecourse special was produced by WNET, New York.

[41]Grant R. Jeffrey, *Messiah, War in the Middle East & The Road to Armageddon*, p. 264.

[42]John Elson, "The New Testament's Unsolved Mysteries," *Time*, Dec. 18, 1995. [ ] mine.

Christians between the first and the fourth century **never** existed[43] in notable numbers. It is the rabbis' apparent hope that this will scale down the present Jewish interest in Jesus as Messiah. For example, Rabbi Kaplan, in *The Real Messiah*, wrote: "Although all of Jesus' disciples were Jews, they could not convince their fellow Jews of their teachings....Christianity was rejected by the Jews....the Jew stood irm...and walked his own way....If Christianity made any contribution at all, it was to the non-Jewish world."[44]

RABBI LEWIS TOLD ME TO MY FACE, 2000-YEAR-OLD JEWISH CHRISTIANS ARE A MISCONCEPTION—NEW TESTAMENT PROPAGANDA

More recently, in a 1983 question and answer session/meeting entitled, "Jewish Answers to Christian Questions," conducted by Rabbi Shalom Lewis of the Atlanta Rabbinic Association, he asked a question concerning the existence and practices of Jews who believed in Jesus 2000 years ago. Lewis said: "A statement is directed at, you know, at the Jewish community by a Christian and that is, that it worked 2000 years ago where you had Jews accepting Jesus, so why can't it work today? How do you answer that question?" Someone in the group answered, "They didn't accept Jesus 2000 years ago either." The rabbi replied falsely: "That is correct, that is a misconception. The apostle, who was the apostle who was most successful? Was it Peter or Paul?" I said, "Paul." He answered, "Paul. Who was Paul going after?" I said, "Gentiles." Again he asked, "Who was Peter going after?" I said, "Jews." The rabbi said: "Who was successful? Paul, by your own admission, because the Jews realized that you can't have Jesus and still be Jewish 2000 years ago and Judaism recognizes that today and the Jewish community instinctively recognizes that today as well....Peter

---

[43]This attempt to rewrite history reminds me of a personal experience. A member of *Jews for Judaism* approached me at a Messiah Conference in 1991. He proceeded to tell me that Rachmiel Frydland never really believed in Jesus and because he was now dead, how could I know what he had believed? I told him I met Rachmiel several years before he died and that he had personally shared his testimony with me. I also said that attacking a dead man who could not defend himself was disgusting. He turned red with anger. This also reminds me of the neo-Nazis, who are cruelly trying to spread the propaganda that the Holocaust never happened. One of my friends, a Holocaust survivor, told me in despair, "In a few years when we (all Holocaust survivors—even the children who survived the Holocaust are now approaching seventy years of age) are all dead, the neo-Nazis are going to have a party, the likes of which few have seen." Jewish believers in Jesus died for their beliefs. To say they never existed is incomprehensible, evil and wrong!

[44]Rabbi Aryeh Kaplan, *et al*, *The Real Messiah*, pp. 16-17.

eventually just threw his hands up in the air because he realized he wasn't getting any place."

My friend, Dan Levine, who introduced himself to Rabbi Lewis as "a Messianic Jew of the New Testament," then commented: "I was also noticing, reading in Acts 21:20, that there were myriads, ten thousands of Jewish people in Jerusalem who believed in *Yeshua* and observed Torah [law]." Lewis answered sharply: "It's propaganda. **Do you believe** everything that comes out of Russia? Of course not."

By the way, when the rabbi said "by your own admission," he never gave me a chance to answer. He cut me off [45] with his answer to my question, as he did my friend Dan. Though Peter had less success than Paul because the world contains many more non-Jews than Jews, Peter succeeded greatly, as Dan pointed out before he was rudely cut off by Rabbi Lewis' remark.[46]

THOUGH THE SCRIBES DECORATED[47] THE TOMBS OF THE PROPHETS, MODERN RABBIS HAVE IGNORED THOSE OF THE JEWISH BELIEVERS, BUT NOW (DUE TO A RECENT ARCHAEOLOGICAL DISCOVERY), THEY NO LONGER CAN

We now ask Rabbi Lewis, "**Do you believe** what's *coming out of the Golan Heights* in archaeological discoveries in Israel eleven years after the fact?!" In another seminar held in January and February of 1994, Lewis reiterated his point that Jews of 2000 years ago never believed, emphasizing that Jews "disappear" within one generation after accepting Jesus. As we will see, Jewish believers existed for over

---

[45]Eleven years later, in a similar seminar held in January and February of 1994, he calmly told the group (while I quietly sat in), "...I refuted step by step by step all the arguments that they had." This was definitely an untruth. He said, "Every time they were caught in a corner, they kind of jumped out of it, not by logic or not by being very clever, but by being evasive;" when in fact, he was the one "jumping out of corners" by cutting us off and sharply answering his own questions to us and then moving quickly on to the next issue. If I had been allowed to finish my statement concerning the evangelism of Peter and Paul, I would have reminded the rabbi that Paul also shared the Gospel of Jesus with many Jews in the synagogues of his time. Paul lectured in the synagogues at: Salamis Acts 13:5; Iconium 14:1; Lystra 8; Antioch 19; Thessalonica 17:1; Berea 10; Athens 17; Corinth 18:4; Ephesus 18-19; and Tyrannus 19:8-10. However, I doubt the rabbi would have cared.

[46]Our quotes are from this author's personal tape of these talks and meetings. Anyone wishing to verify authenticity may hear the tape upon request!

[47]Jesus' New Testament words to the Pharisees and religious leaders were: " 'Woe to you, scribes and Pharisees, hypocrites! For you build the tombs of the prophets and adorn the monuments of the righteous, and say, If we had been *living* in the days of our fathers, we would not have been partners with them in *shedding* the blood of the prophets, Consequently you bear witness against yourselves, that you are the sons of those who murdered the prophets' " (Matt. 23:29-31 NASB).

three hundred years in the fourth century until they were completely shut out by the rabbis. This is substantiated by a popular Israeli magazine!

The tombstones of Jewish believers in Jesus have been discovered at the base of the Mount of Olives. They were identifiable from the Jewish symbols and Christian inscriptions in Greek and Hebrew and are now located in the Basilica of Dominus Flevit (Franciscan).[48] Recently, *Biblical Archaeological Review* featured an interesting article about the tombs of such believers. They existed, whether today's rabbis want to admit it or not.

The ancient Israeli towns of Anea and Yettra were whole cities composed almost completely of Jewish believers in Jesus. The rabbis of that era called the town of Bainah "an engulfed town" because the majority of its population were Jewish Christians.[49]

More recently, an article entitled "Filling in the Blanks," by Abraham Rabinovich reported: "French archaeologist Claudine Dauphine discovered that in addition to Jews and Christians, there were Jewish Christians on the Golan. In villages like Farj and Er-Ramthaniyeh, she found stones that were carved with symbols belonging to both religions, such as a *lulav* (palm branch), fish, or ship, and symbols associated specifically with Christian Jews, such as a cross superimposed on a ship's mast.

In 66 C.E., after the death of James, Jesus' brother, the Jewish Christian followers of James left Jerusalem for Pella in Transjordan. They subsequently moved northward, to the Bashan and eastern Golan. Two major groups were the Ebionites and the Nazarenes. Both clung to Jewish practices such as circumcision and Sabbath observance, but regarded Jesus as the Messiah....Dauphine believes she has found Ebionite remains from **as late as the fourth century** on the Golan. It is the first time, she says, that ancient carvings were found with Jewish and Christian symbols overlaid, not just beside each other—negating

---

[48]The Jewish believer in Jesus, Arnold Fruchtenbaum, Ph.D., visits this site during his extensive five-week tours of Israel, usually taken only once every two years. For information, write Ariel Ministries, POB 3723, Tustin, CA, USA 92681-3723.

[49]Arnold Fruchtenbaum documented this information in his class, "Messianic Jewish History," at the July 1994 MJAA Messiah Conference. This tape #505 CF307 is available from CTI, Inc., 1704 Valencia NE, Albuquerque, NM, USA 87110. These towns are also mentioned in a rare but interesting book by Fr. Bellarmino Bagetti, O.F.M., *The Church from the Circumcision, History and Archaeology of the Judaeo-Christians*, a publication of the Studium Biblicum Franciscanum, Jerusalem: Franciscan Printing Press, 1971, pp. 16-17.

the possibility that they may have been carved at different times by different peoples."[50]

THE HEBREW COVER-UP OF THE APOCALYPTIC BOOKS

Humanity is posed with an interesting question. Why did the leaders of the very people who wrote the apocalyptic literature want to cover them up? We also ask why Jews have not had an apocalyptic end-time teaching within mainstream Judaism for the last nineteen centuries?

While there is ample teaching in the Bible for the Jews to look forward to the apocalyptic signs of the end (as witnessed by this book, the Baptist Church and Dallas Theological Seminary teachings on the Old Testament), there is no significant emphasis on these exciting hopes at all within Orthodox or Conservative Judaism throughout the world. The only small exception to this rule lies within a few hard to find works noted in some of the writings of obscure rabbis, which are mainly glossed over in the Diaspora.[51]

It is much easier to locate rabbis who are willing to discuss the subject of the soon-coming apocalypse, based on biblical writings, in Israel, as I have done! They even have a library which specializes in the subject called the Rav Cook Library of Jerusalem. However, every rabbi I questioned in the U.S. said, "We do not emphasize any such teaching," or "We live for today. If the Messiah comes, He comes! We don't dwell on it. The Lubavitchers[52] may be fanatical about it but that's outside of normative mainstream Judaism!" Thus we ask,

---

[50]Abraham Rabinovich, "Filling in the Blanks," *ERETZ*, © May/June 1994, pp. 54-55, used by permission. Bold mine. This also disproves the hysterical fear of many modern rabbis who maintain that a Jew who believes in Jesus is absorbed into the Gentile culture within one generation, losing all Jewish identity. Clearly, Jewish believers' graves have been found as late as the fourth century. They did not assimilate in "one generation." They became dispersed after that time because the Catholics on one side and the *rabbis* on the other *forced them out.* Rabinovich writes in the same article: "By the fifth century, Jewish Christian groups disappeared, as hardening lines within both religions made it impossible to dwell in both camps." Ibid. Let's not let the rabbis destroy today's Messianic Jewish identity, as they are attempting to do through groups like *Jews for Judaism* and polemical books, such as *The Real Messiah.* Rabinovich's text cited above and in this footnote is annotated by the words: "The archaeological teams that set out to explore the Golan after the Six Day War weren't expecting very much. They were in for a big surprise." Ibid, p. 5. Bold mine.

[51]Countries outside of Israel—this is another reason why you should give your Jewish friends a copy of this book.

[52]An orthodox group of Hasidic Jews, which was headed by Rabbi Menachem Schneerson, numbering over one-half million, differing from most Jews in their emphatic expectation of the Messiah.

"Could ignoring the Hebrew apocalyptic writings be an added component of the historical rabbinical conspiracy to keep the Jew from becoming interested in the Messiah, thus possibly discovering His true identity—Jesus?"

Robert H. Pfeiffer of Harvard and Boston Universities, in his book, *History of New Testament Times*, tells us: "Normative Judaism relinquished the utopian dreams of apocalyptic writings to the Christians, and retrenched itself increasingly within the citadel of the written and the oral law, thus separating itself more and more from the Gentiles. The final break between the Christian Church and the synagogue took place at this time when the Nazarenes—a Jewish-Christian group worshiping in the synagogues but teaching that Jesus was the Messiah—were forced to become a sect, equally repudiated by the Rabbis and by the Bishops. Henceforth the teachers of the Law—scribes and Pharisees, Tannaim, Amoraim, Geonim, rabbis—became the leaders of Israel."[53]

AFTER 70 AD, JEWISH LEADERS DECIDE TO DESTROY HEBREW APOCALYPTIC ORIGINALS

D. S. Russell, author of *The Method & Message of Jewish Apocalyptic*, informs us: "L. Ginzberg has pointed out that in the entire rabbinic literature of the first six centuries there is not a single quotation from the extant apocalyptic literature; because of this it has sometimes been too readily assumed that rabbinic Judaism would have nothing whatever to do with the teaching and ideals contained in these books. C. C. Torrey, for example, affirms that from AD 70 onwards, so great was the devotion of the Jewish leaders to the Law and the sacred Scriptures, the decision was taken to destroy as undesirable all the Semitic originals of the 'outside books', including the apocalyptic writings, and so effect 'the sudden and complete abandonment by the Jews of their popular literature'. Thus, this once-popular literature was discontinued and the ideas which it perpetuated were rejected as dangerous and heretical."[54]

Russell goes on to say: "...the very fanaticism of the apocalyptists would in itself be a warning to the rabbis of the dangers inherent in such teachings....Thus, they were a challenge both to rabbinic authority and to the safety of the State. Another, and perhaps decisive, factor in the decline of apocalyptic would be the rapid growth of Christianity and the adoption and adaptation by the Church of many Jewish apocalyptic writings whose messianic and eschatological

[53]Robert H. Pfeiffer, *History of New Testament Times*, p. 45.

[54]D.S. Russell, *The Method & Message of Jewish Apocalyptic: 200 B.C. - A.D. 100*, p.30.

teachings were eminently suitable for the purpose of Christian propaganda....With the return of more peaceful times the original Hebrew and Aramaic texts would be no longer in existence. Such books as survived would owe their survival to the fact that they had already been translated into other languages, and such apocalyptic ideas as persisted within rabbinic Judaism would be the result of oral transmission. This attempted solution is only a guess and cannot be proven; but it underlines the fact that, for whatever reason, the apocalyptic books were perpetuated not in the original Hebrew and Aramaic tongues but in Greek and in the many other languages of the Dispersion. By reason of the antipathy of many rabbis to them and because they were no longer available for study in their original texts, it was inevitable that they should at last fall out of use [among Jews]."[55]

Several of these apocalyptic writings included commentaries on the Bible by ancient rabbis whose originals were written in Hebrew. There is an extensive list in the back of Raphael Patai's book, *The Messiah Texts*, in his section, "Abbreviations and Annotated Biography." W. Bousset, in his book, *Antichrist Legend, A Chapter in Christian and Jewish Folklore*, quotes from many translated apocalyptic writings.

SEMITIC FRAGMENTS OF MATTHEW'S GOSPEL HAVE BEEN REVEALED, BUT WILL THE ENTIRE HEBREW GOSPEL BE EXCAVATED IN ISRAEL? PRAY!

To conclude our comments regarding all of the attempts to destroy and cover up certain original apocalyptic writings dealing with predicted future events,[56] we would like to ask you a question. Could all the talk about the burning of the New Testament by rabbis such as Me'ir, Akiva, Jose and Tarphon, have been connected with the destruction of these writings? If the New Testament was hunted down and destroyed in its original Hebrew editions, could this be the reason why we have been unable (as of yet) to discover the original[57] Hebrew New Testament, which is the question of the century?

---

[55]Ibid, p. 32. [ ] mine.

[56]D.S. Russell outlines most of what is included under the apocalyptic prophecies when he notes: "...The apocalyptic books....express belief in such things as the heavenly bliss of the righteous, the resurrection of the dead, the heavenly banquet, the coming judgment, the fires of Gehenna, the angelic destruction of Jerusalem and the coming of the New Jerusalem, the advent of the Messiah, the travails of the messianic age, wonders and portents heralding the last days and so forth." Ibid.

[57]Pinchas Lapide, an unbiased Jewish scholar, wrote as recently as 1976 that: "It is certain, however, that all four Greek Gospels display distinct traces of an **original** Hebrew text in their vocabulary, grammar, syntax, and semantic patterns. Hence we

Fragments of an original document have been found and many wait for the original Hebrew New Testament to reappear from archaeological excavations in Israel. Such a find would impress a new openness to Jesus upon many Israeli rabbis' eyes (see our appendix 1, "It's All *Hebrew* to Me")! We urge all true believers to pray that we soon discover the "Hebrew New"!

A CASE OF MISTAKEN IDENTITY—*YESHU* WHO?

You have probably heard many people ask, "What's in a name?" You may have shrugged your shoulders and agreed, "You are right, nothing." In reality, nothing could be further from the truth. A name can contain incredible blessings or horrendous incantations. In our case, we are dealing with the greatest name known in history, which was mutilated by the early rabbis through the removal of the last letter. In order to obscure its true meaning, they attempted to transform the greatest name into the worst curse.

As previously noted, Jesus' given name was *Yeshua* ("salvation"). The rabbis changed it to *Yeshu*, an anagram of שמו וזכרו ימח(ישו) (*ymah shemo vezihro—Yeshu*). The only difference in the two words in Hebrew is the soft au pronounced at the end. This may sound strange to those unfamiliar with the Hebrew language. All Hebrew words stem from roots usually containing three letters. Each consonant has eleven vowel sounds. The words built from the roots are changed by adding prefixes and suffixes and changing the vowel sounds. A minor change can completely alter the meaning of a word. The words *neshek* and *nesheka* are an example. The word *nesheka*, with the soft a sound, means "kiss" in Hebrew. The word *neshek* without the soft a sound, means "weapon."

By exploiting this linguistic device, the rabbis tried to change the blessing of our salvation into a curse, since the literal meaning of *ymah shemo vezihro* is "may his name and memory be blotted out." In the Hebrew culture, this is the worst curse that can befall any man. Changing Jesus' Hebrew name *Yeshua*/salvation to the curse *Yeshu*, is no doubt, one of the worst rabbinic crimes ever committed in human history! May they apologize.

---

cannot seriously question the existence of a 'Hebrew gospel'—no fewer than ten Fathers of the Church testify to it....Papias (Eusebius, *Hist. Eccl.* III, 39, 1); Irenaeus (*ibid.*, V, 8, 2); Hegesippus (*ibid.*, IV, 22, 4); Jerome (*Contra Rufinum* VII, 77; *De vir. ill.* II; *In Matt.* 6, 11; *In Ezech.* 18, 7; *Adv. Pel.* III, 2 et al.); Origen (*In Matt.* XV, 14); Epiphanius (*Panarion* I, 29, 7 and 9); Theodoret of Cyprus (*Haer,* Fab. II, 1); Nicephorus Callistus (*Eccl. Hist.* III, 13); Clement of Alexandria (*Strom.* II, IX, 45, 5); Pantaenus (Eusebius, *ibid.*, V, 10, 3)." Pinchas Lapide, *Israelis, Jews, and Jesus*. New York: Doubleday & Company, Inc., © 1979, p. 3, used by permission.

REDISCOVERING THE HEBREW NAME OF JESUS AFTER TWO MILLENNIA OF SCANDAL

So, what's in a name? Today, we are rediscovering Jesus' true Hebrew name after twenty centuries of rabbinic cover-up—a name which, surprisingly, is still a secret to many in Israel! Quite a few modern Israelis are unaware of the true meaning of *Yeshu*. They do not know that this acronym, formulated by the rabbis in the early centuries after Jesus, really means "let His name and memory be blotted out." They think it is the true name of Jesus. Thus the rabbis have deceived nearly all of Israel from the first century to the present day with this false acronym.

Some rabbis, ashamed of what earlier ones did with the first three letters of Jesus' name, try to deny the true meaning of these letters. For instance, the noted authority, Professor Joseph Klausner,[58] is one of those who denies this. However, the modern Hebrew dictionary used in Israel,[59] compiled by Abraham Even-Soshan, defines these three letters, *ude* י, *shin* שׁ, and *vav* ו, as standing for י (ימח) *ymah* ("it will be blotted out") שׁ (שׁמו) *shemo* ("his name") ו (וזכרו) *vezihro* ("and his memory").

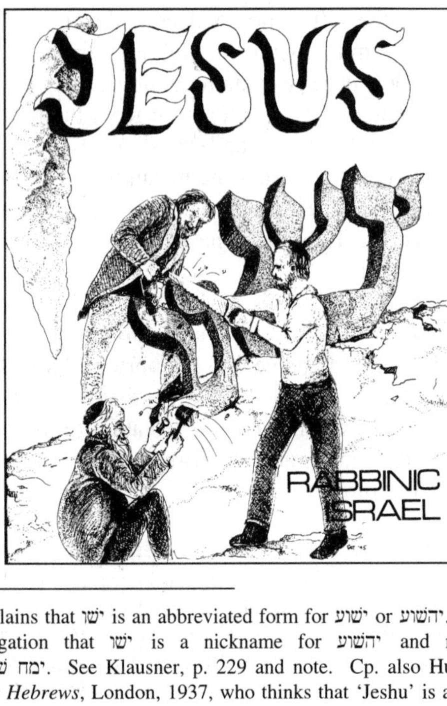

---

[58]"Klausner explains that ישו is an abbreviated form for ישוע or יהשוע. He categorically denies the allegation that ישו is a nickname for יהשוע and made up of the initials: ימח שמו וזכרו. See Klausner, p. 229 and note. Cp. also Hugh J. Schonfield, *According to the Hebrews*, London, 1937, who thinks that 'Jeshu' is a north-Palestinian contraction of Jeshua, where the letter *ayin* was not sounded (p. 221)." Jakob Jocz, *The Jewish People and Jesus Christ*, p. 337.

[59]*New Dictionary*. Jerusalem: Kiryat Sephen, © 1973, p. 512, used by permission.

Israel, like all other nations of the world, has the right to know the true name of Jesus, whether the religious like it or not! Especially since Jesus' name is the Hebrew name Joshua (*Yeshua* or *Yehoshua* in Hebrew). It is ironic that the nations of the earth generally know when and why Jesus came while it is forbidden for Israelis to look into it, according to the religious minority. Are we going to let the "Black Hats," two or three percent of the population, push Israel around? Many say no! Israel can make up its own mind after investigating these long hidden facts about the concealment of Jesus' Hebrew name.

DR. KAC'S CONFIRMATION OF THE ABBREVIATION

Additional evidence that this abbreviated name, *Yeshu*, was intended to be a curse has been documented by the Jewish scholar, Dr. Arthur Kac, who believes in Jesus. He tells us: "There was a time when the name of Jesus was never mentioned by Jews except in derision. One who wanted to refer to Him used circumlocution, such as *oto ish* ('this man') or *ish ploni* ('the unnamed one'). It became customary to alter His name by omitting one Hebrew letter. Thus the name *Yeshua* became Yeshu, which was meant to represent an anagram for a malediction.

According to a scurrilous parody of Jesus' life, a medieval tale fabricated to dishonor the mother of Jesus and to declare Him a bastard, His real name was Yehoshua, but when His origin became known it was altered to Yeshu...."[60] Dr. Kac's footnote to malediction reads: " 'Yeshu' was supposed to stand for 'his name and memory be blotted out.' "[61]

AN ISOLATED ISRAELI'S REDISCOVERY—PERSONAL TESTIMONY

I have had the opportunity to show many Israelis what this name really means. For quite a while, I carried a photocopy of the Hebrew dictionary documentation around in my briefcase. On many occasions when I would speak to them about *Yeshua* (Jesus) and point out the various prophecies, they would say, "Oh, you mean *Yeshu*." I would reply, "No, I mean *Yeshua*—His real name." This would confuse them, so I would pull the photocopy out of my briefcase for them to read. They would then say, "Oh no, that's a curse and a very wicked one at that" or something similar. Each time I used the documented proof of what the name *Yeshu* was intended to mean to inform my

---

[60] Arthur W. Kac, *The Messiahship of Jesus*, p. 148.

[61] Ibid, p. 153.

Israeli friends of what they had been falsely taught;[62] they never again ever referred to Jesus as *Yeshu*, but rather *Yeshua*, which as we now know, in Hebrew means "salvation," or more precisely "Jehova [God] saves."

RESTORATION OF THE *INE* ("EYE") LENDS INSIGHT TO BIBLE TEXT AND CONTEXT

Interestingly enough, the Hebrew letter *ine* ע, which the rabbis removed, is the symbol for "sight" in Hebrew. The Hebrew word for "eye" is *ine*. In Hebrew symbology, they are in a sense, deliberately blinding themselves to the true meaning of the word by removing the letter for sight. When we restore the last letter *ine* ע, the true meaning—*Yeshua*/Jesus, God's Messiah *Savior*—returns and the falseness of the curse falls away.

The fact that Jesus was named ישוע, *Yeshua* after Joshua (see Neh. 3:19 in the Hebrew Bible for the same spelling[63]) is even more symbolic here. Matthew, the author of the first book of the New Testament, clearly illustrates the intention and meaning in the context of his words: "...thou shalt call his name JESUS: for he *shall save* his people from their sins" (Matt. 1:21 KJV; italics mine). *The New Scofield Reference Bible* footnotes Jesus in this passage with the explanation, "Greek form of Hebrew, Johoshua meaning Jehovah is salvation."[64]

ISRAELIS REVERSE THE CURSE AND DENOUNCE RABBINIC DECEPTION

When Israelis are shown Messianic prophecies like Isaiah 53, Micah 5:2 and Zechariah 12:10, they realize that they cannot, in good conscience, refer to their Messiah in this way, suspecting that one day they may very well stand before Him. If Jesus is the Messiah, they do not want to continue using a curse to describe Him. After realizing what it means, they become more sympathetic with the life and person of Jesus and curiosity causes many to open their Bible and see who He really is. Once they see that He is the Messiah, as He claimed, they become disgusted with the rabbinical sages who deceived them into calling the Messiah by their curse of *Yeshu*.

***

---

[62]That *Yeshu* is Jesus' name instead of *Yeshua*.

[63]This name was also spelled with the extra letter, *hay*, earlier in the Torah.

[64]*The New Scofield Reference Bible*, p. 992.

ISRAEL *SEES THE LIGHT* (OF JESUS)
IN ITS OWN MENORAH

Jesus' real name, as it is spelled in the modern Hebrew translation of the New Testament, lights the menorah (Hebrew candlestick, see Exo. 25:31)[65] in Hebrew letters. This gives us another interesting insight into His true purpose, as found in His vibrant words recorded in the Gospel of John: "I am the light of the world; he that followeth me shall not walk in darkness but shall have the light of life" (John 8:12 KJV).

This was foretold seven hundred years before His birth within the Jewish prophetic writings of Isaiah: "And now says the LORD, who formed Me from the womb to be His Servant, To bring Jacob back to Him, in order that Israel might be gathered to Him (For I am honored in

[65]The menorah, or candlestick, Israel's national symbol, has seven branches. It should not be confused with the *hanukia* menorah, which is used on Hanukkah and has nine branches. Menorah means "lamp" in Hebrew.

the sight of the LORD, And My God is My strength), He says, 'It is too small a thing that You should be My Servant To raise up the tribes of Jacob, and to restore the preserved ones of Israel; I will also make You a **light** of the nations So that My salvation may reach to the end of the earth.' Thus says the LORD, the Redeemer of Israel, *and* its Holy One, To the despised One, To the One abhorred by the nation, To the Servant of rulers, 'Kings shall see and arise, Princes shall also bow down; Because of the LORD who is faithful, the Holy One of Israel who has chosen You.' Thus says the Lord, 'In a favorable time I have answered You, And in a day of salvation, I have helped You; And I will keep You and give You for a covenant of the people, To restore the land, to make *them* inherit the desolate heritages....' " (Isa. 49:5-8 NASB).

Thus, many Israelis, after realizing all that has been hidden from them (as we have documented in the last few pages), become indifferent to the rabbis and begin to study the Bible on their own, to find out what it really says about the truth and their Messiah.

A FEW ORTHODOX KNOW THE MEANING OF THE *NAME CURSE* BUT ARE UNMOVED

Anyone outside of Israel and rabbinical circles, who does not know Hebrew has probably never heard the word *Yeshu*. This name is virtually unknown, with the exception of a few English-speaking, American, Canadian and European Orthodox Jewish groups, which use this name in the Diaspora form of *Yesheka*.[66] It sounds worse than *Yeshu*, doesn't it? Most of them know its meaning. It is part of the anti-missionary and anti-Jews for Jesus campaign, which is drilled into the heads of orthodox students in yeshivas the world over. However, their numbers pale when compared to the whole of world Jewry. One rabbi told me that there are many more Jews for Jesus than there are Jews in all of the yeshivas[67] in the world.

---

[66]This word, using the spelling *Yoshkeh*, was used in the New Jerusalem Times edition of *The Jewish Press*, April 16, 1987, in a front page article entitled, "Beware of Missionary Forge S'Dorim," by Aryeh Julius. The article used this obscenity in the heading, "Jews for Yoshkeh Congregations." It described Jews for Jesus who would be celebrating Passover and elaborating on Jesus' fulfillment of this Jewish holiday. The article dealt with the announcement that spies of *Yad La Akim* ("the Hand to the Brothers," an anti-missionary organization) would be sent to watch over believers' Passover dinners at Baptist Village (Petah Tikva), Beit Hisda (Haifa), Assaf Congregation (Netanya), Beit Emmanuel Congregation (Yaffo), Hesed V'Emet Congregation (Eliat) and Netiv-ya (Jerusalem), as well as to the private homes of missionaries throughout Israel. They called their people "emissaries" and their mission "Operation Seder." If this sounds as silly to you as it did to me, you can look it up in the library archives. For more details on Passover and this instance, see our *Vol. II*, chapter 6, "Disapproval of the Believers' Passover in Israel."

[67]A yeshiva is an Orthodox Jewish study school where portions of the Old Testament and Jewish writings, such as the Talmud, are studied and chanted. In Hebrew, the word

JESUS' NAME IN HEBREW—WE ARE WINNING!

In the first century, the rabbis at Yavne changed Jesus' Hebrew name from *Yeshua* to *Yeshu* and nearly all rabbis today still use this despicable name, especially in Israel. It is worth noting that not only does the Hebrew edition of the New Testament call Jesus *Yeshua*, Rabbi Abarbanel, a famous Jewish sage who did not believe in Jesus, also called him *Yeshua* (ישוע). Rabbi Abarbanel wrote:

"והיתה אמונת ישוע אשר לקחו בני אדום מתחדשת בעולם בתחלת זאת המחברת."[68]

"...and there was the belief in *Yeshua* that the sons of Adom were renewing since the beginning of these Scriptures."[69]

The greatly respected sage, Rambam/Maimonides, of nearly 1000 years ago, referred to Jesus not by *Yeshu* but *Yeshua*. Risto Santala pointed this out in his latest book, *Paul: The Man and the Teacher, In the Light of Jewish Sources*, when he said: "It is worth remembering that the famous mediaeval scholar Maimonides wrote the name of Jesus in the form 'Yeshua' in his book Hilkhot Melakhim. So do Israeli Messianic Jews in order to avoid the secret abuse connected with the shorter form Yeshu: "May his name and memory be blotted out.' "[70]

The Orthodox Jews in Israel who call Jesus *Yeshu*, may not be aware that two of their most respected sages called Jesus by His true name, *Yeshua*. If the Orthodox Jews were made aware of this fact, then quite possibly most of them would cease to persist in calling Him by the name *Yeshu*? So tell them! However, in spite of the orthodox religious zeal to strike the true name of Jesus from Israel, there is apparently a slow but growing awareness within Israeli culture that His true name is really *Yeshua*, and not *Yeshu*. We gather this from Pinchas Lapide's book, *Israelis, Jews, and Jesus*, where he documents that recently at least three Israeli textbooks have begun to use the name *Yeshua*.[71]

***

yeshiva means "you sit," as they sit and study all day. I have an anti-missionary tape produced by a yeshiva in Israel. A rabbi teaching a course made the statement, "There are more Jews studying Christianity than there are Jews studying Judaism (Orthodox)." He called these people "Jews for Yesheka." Anyone wishing to verify this may contact me at the POB on the back of this book.

[68]דון יצחק אברבנאל, מעיני הישועה, © 1948, p. ת״ב. (Don Itzhak Abarbanel, *Matters of Salvation*, © 1948, p. 412; originally published in the sixteenth century.)

[69]English translation of previous Hebrew quote.

[70]Risto Santala, *Paul: The Man and the Teacher, In the Light of Jewish Sources*. Jerusalem: Keren Ahvah Meshihit, © 1995, p. 23, used by permission.

[71]Pinchas Lapide, *Israelis, Jews, and Jesus*, p. 39. Lapide is a Jewish scholar who, as far as we know, did not believe in Jesus as the Messiah.

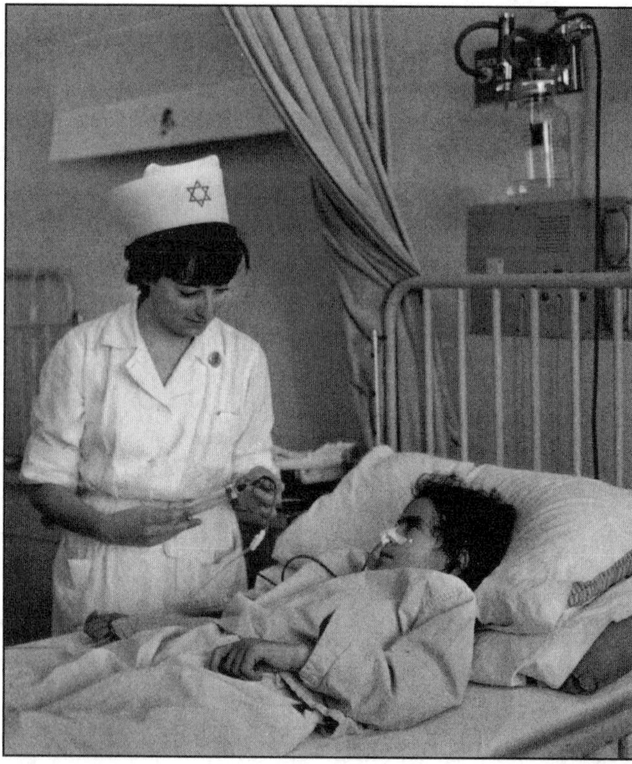

"A man shall have no dealings with the heretics, nor be cured by them, even for the sake of an hour of life. There was the case of Ben Dama nephew of R. Ishmael, whom a serpent bit. There came Jacob [The apostle James of the New Testament] the heretic of the village of Sechanya to cure him (in the name of Jeshu[1] ben Pandera *var. leg.*); [Jesus] but R. [Rabbi] Ishmael would not allow him. Ben Dama said to him, R. Ishmael, my brother, do allow him, that I may be cured, and I will produce a text from the Law to prove that this is permitted. But hardly had he finished his discourse when his soul departed, and he died."

The Talmud, Abodah Zarah 27b. [ ] mine

"The grandson of R. Joshua ben Levi had something stuck in his throat. There came a man and whispered to him in the name of Jesus, and he recovered. When the healer came out, R. Joshua said to him, What was it you whispered to him? He said to him, A certain word. He said to him, It had been better for him that he had died rather than that."

The Talmud, Shabbath 14b

"R. Akiba said, He who reads in external books, and he who whispers over a wound, and says, 'None of the diseases which I sent on Egypt will I lay on thee, I am the Lord thy healer' (*Exodus.* XV, 26), has any share in the world to come."

The Talmud, Sanhedrin X,1

9

THE MESSIAH CONSPIRACY CONCLUDES IN PREVENTING HEALINGS

Healings! Were there secret healings performed in the name of Jesus? Obviously, as you have just read in the quotes by the ancients of rabbinical literature, the answer is yes! Hugh Schonfield, though we do not agree with all of his ideas, rightly admits: "These quotations confirm the evidence that we have from other sources that the Jewish Christians practised healing in the name of Jesus....it is interesting to note in...Mark's Gospel that 'these signs shall follow them that believe;

[1]As you previously read, the name *Yeshu*, here anglicized to Jeshu, is the true name of Jesus. *Yeshua*, which means "salvation," was reduced to a curse by earlier rabbis through the removal of the last letter. The remaining three letters meant "may his name and memory be blotted out." This reproduction is just that, a reproduction, thus providing additional evidence of the antagonistic spirit of the rabbis against Jesus! It shows their stubborn resolve and arrogance in rejecting Him as the Messiah of salvation. We wish to appeal to rabbis to change the word *Yeshu* in the present Talmud, which is extremely offensive to knowledgeable Gentile Christians and Messianic Jews, back to Jesus' true Hebrew name, *Yeshua*; if not change it to *Yeshua*, at least change it to Jesus or "Jeshua" in English Talmuds. We make this appeal to return His true name to future editions, for the sake of good will, good relations and as an apology. We further

in my name...they shall lay hands on the sick, and they shall recover.' Epiphanius informs us that he was told by the Jewish Christian Joseph that before his conversion, when lying dangerously ill, one of the elders, a student of the Law, whispered in his ear, 'Believe that Jesus the son of God was crucified under Pontius Pilate, and that he will come again to judge the living and the dead.' This kind of thing was of frequent occurrence, writes the Bishop of Constantia, and mentions another Jew, who told him that once when on the point of death he heard a whisper in his ear from one of those who stood by, that 'Jesus Christ who was crucified, the son of God, will hereafter judge thee.' By means of their healing art, the Jewish Christians were thus able openly or secretly to reach and influence their brethren. McNeile has well explained R. Akiba's condemnation of those who whisper *Exodus* XV, 26, over wounds. The last words 'I am the Lord that healeth thee,' have the numerical value of the name Jesus, and would be used by crypto-Christians as a substitute, when they dared not pronounce the name of Jesus openly."[2]

THE EQUATION OF THE AGES

In order to understand the "healing connection," we have to present the "equation of the ages." The letters of the Hebrew alphabet all have a corresponding numerical value. The numerical value of the letters in *Yehoshua* יהושע is equal to the numerical value of the phrase "the Lord that healeth thee," אני יהוה רפאך in Hebrew. *Yehoshua* is an alternative and popular spelling of *Yeshua* (Jesus in Hebrew); it means

appeal to rabbis to make their peace with the present Jewish believers and evangelicals for the terrible mistreatment of the early Jewish-Christians by the rabbis of the early centuries of the Christian era. As Douglas Hare commented in his quotation of the Talmud: "The most extreme treatment that the Rabbis will countenance is that the lives of Minim may be endangered and not saved, Tos. B. Mezia 2:53: 'The Minim and the apostates and the betrayers are cast in [to a pit] and not helped out'...." Douglas Hare, *The Theme of Jewish Persecution of Christians in the Gospel According to St. Matthew*, p. 39. We ask for a public confession of wrongdoing for calling believers "apostates and betrayers." We ask for an apology and help in clearing up the question of Messianic prophecies fulfilled by Jesus in a worldwide rabbinic forum of public inquiry and confession. If you are a rabbi, and if you are interested in righting the wrongs of the past in order to improve relations between the rabbinical and Jewish-Christian communities, we invite you to contact Philip Moore, c/o RamsHead Press, POB 12-227, Atlanta, GA, USA 30355. Fax (404) 816-9994. Letters received will be published in a book and distributed. All three Talmud captions cited from Hugh J. Schonfield, *The History of Jewish Christianity, From the First to the Twentieth Century*. London: Duckworth, © 1936, pp. 78-80. The fact that Jacob is James is documented by Dr. David Flusser, *Jewish Sources in Early Christianity*, p. 13.

[2]Hugh J. Schonfield, *The History of Jewish Christianity, From the First to the Twentieth Century*, p. 80.

"Savior," as Joshua (*Yehoshua*) of the Old Testament was called. For a good example of interchangeability, see Nehemiah 3:19 in the Hebrew Bible, which uses the name *Yeshua* (ישוע). *Yehoshua* adds as follows: י 10 + ה 5 + ו 6 + שׁ 300 + ע 70 = 391. The Hebrew words for "the Lord that healeth thee" from Exodus 15:26, add as follows: א 1 + נ 50 + י10 + י 10 + ה 5 + ו 6 + ה 5 + ר 200 + פ 80 + א 1 + ך 20 = 388. Since there are three Hebrew words, when you add three to the equation—voilà—you get the same 391.

If you have any doubt about what I have just simplified, you don't have to take my word for it. The scholar Louis Ginzberg relates his opinion in the *Journal of Biblical Literature*: "I fully agree with the view which finds in the Mishna Sanhedrin a statement by R. Akiba directed against Christians. The severe condemnation by Rabbi Akiba of the use of Exodus 15 in connection with medication is certainly directed against certain Christian healers, as has been felt by many scholars, though they were unable to explain why just this biblical verse was so opprobrious to the Rabbis. The answer to this question is very simple. The last three words of this verse אני יהוה רפאך have the same numerical value (three hundred eighty-eight plus three for the three words = three hundred ninety one) as the name of Jesus (יהושע = three hundred ninety one). It is not unlikely that some crypto-Christians who were afraid to openly perform cures 'in the name of Jesus' would use this verse in which they found his name indicated....The very strong condemnation of the use of Exodus 15 cannot, however, be explained otherwise than on account of the favour this verse enjoyed among the Christian healers."[3]

HEALING IN THE NAME OF JESUS, HEBRAIC STYLE—A PROBLEM?

Did the rabbis in early times have difficulty preventing the witness of Jesus' Messiahship through the healings which were performed by believers in His name?[4] Could it have been that the healings were so real and persuasive in support of Jesus as Messiah that the rabbis really had something to worry about? Hugh Schonfield, a Jewish scholar who claimed in his early life to have believed in Jesus and later recanted, tells us in his book, *Saints Against Caesar*: "Another aspect of Nazarene activities which gave the rabbinists concern was their medical ministrations....they did employ the single

---

[3]Louis Ginzberg, "Some Observations on the Attitude of the Synagogue Towards the Apocalyptic-Eschatological Writings," *Journal of Biblical Literature*, Vol. XLI, 1922. New Haven: Yale University Press, © 1992, pp. 123-124, used by permission.

[4]The numerical equivalent of Jesus' name in the Hebrew Scripture.

name of Jesus. And when, as so often, their cures were successful, a conviction was created of the effective power of this name, thus inspiring the faith of the delighted household in the person of the Nazarene Messiah. At the end of *Mark's* Gospel it is said: 'These signs shall follow them that believe; in my name...they shall lay hands on the sick, and they shall recover.'

The rabbinists found the influence of the Nazarene physicians the hardest of all to stop, because those in need could not easily be prevented from privately sending for one of the heretical community. To the list of those declared by Rabbinical Judaism to have no share in the world to come, Rabbi Akiba, inveterate enemy of the Nazarenes early in the second century, added: 'Also he that reads the heretical books, or that utters charms over a wound, and says, 'I will put none of the diseases upon thee which I have put upon the Egyptians: for I am the Lord that healeth thee'...'I am the Lord that healeth thee' (*Exod.* XV. 26) have the numerical value of the name Jesus in Hebrew...."[5]

THE WITNESS OF THE OPPOSITION

It goes without saying that if there were no real healings performed in Jesus' Hebrew name, influencing further belief in Jesus as the Messiah, then of course, the Talmud would be silent on this issue. The very fact that the Talmud reveals several incidents of healing in connection with Jesus' name is evidence that it was occurring. The rabbis, however, opposed its use for their own relatives despite evidence of its effectiveness, as we saw in the second quote on the opening page of this chapter. This is clear evidence, the best evidence, the evidence of the opposition. This was established by the Harvard law professor Simon Greenleaf, in his book, *The Testimony of the Evangelists*.[6]

THE NAME OF JESUS IS MYSTERIOUSLY ENCODED IN ISAIAH'S PROPHECY ABOUT THE MESSIAH

In the latter portions of Isaiah 52 and all of chapter 53, we are introduced to the suffering servant of the Lord. Many rabbis of ancient times, along with the New Testament, rightly interpreted this prophecy to refer to the Messiah, as you previously read.

---

[5]Hugh Schonfield, *Saints Against Caesar, The Rise and Reactions of the First Christian Community*, pp. 78-79.

[6]We noted this in detail in our section on the Resurrection in chapter 5, "Which Prophecies Did Jesus Fulfill?"

When we take the fascinating phenomenon of the original Hebrew and count out every eighth word starting at the first *ude* in verse 13 of Isaiah 52, we discover that the Hebrew letters spell Jesus' name! In the Bible, the number eight symbolizes new beginnings. Jesus brought us the New Covenant/New Testament (new beginnings) predicted by Jeremiah. Interesting, wouldn't you say? Below, we enlarge the letters which spell the name of Jesus (Hebrew is read from right to left).

כִּי לֹא בְחִפָּזוֹן תֵּצֵאוּ וּבִמְנוּסָה לֹא תֵלֵכוּן כִּי־הֹלֵךְ לִפְנֵיכֶם יְהוָה וּמְאַסִּפְכֶם אֱלֹהֵי יִשְׂרָאֵל׃
יהֶם הִנֵּה **י**ַשְׂכִּיל עַבְדִּי יָרוּם וְנִשָּׂא וְגָבַהּ מְאֹד׃ כַּאֲשֶׁר **שָׁ**מְמוּ עָלֶיךָ רַבִּים כֵּן־מִשְׁחַת
מֵאִישׁ מַרְאֵהוּ **ו**ְתֹאֲרוֹ מִבְּנֵי אָדָם׃ כֵּן יַזֶּה גּוֹיִם רַבִּים **ע**ָלָיו יִקְפְּצוּ מְלָכִים פִּ
כִּי אֲשֶׁר לֹא־סֻפַּר לָהֶם רָאוּ וַאֲשֶׁר לֹא־שָׁמְעוּ הִתְבּוֹנָנוּ׃

Isaiah 52: 12-15

יֵשׁוּעַ = Jesus

The above words with their first letter in bold type are translated as: יַשְׂכִּיל "he will deal wisely"; שָׁמְמוּ "they shall be astonished"; וְתֹאֲרוֹ "and his appearance"; עָלָיו "concerning him." Here you have the key meaning, of salvation, and the Jews' response to Jesus' wisdom in giving Himself for their atonement. Today, as we tell Jews about Jesus and show them these prophecies, they are indeed astonished.

THE NAME OF GOD IS ENCODED IN HIS ACCOUNT OF CREATION IN GENESIS

Likewise, *Yahweh* (Yehovah) is spelled out in Hebrew at twenty-two letter intervals[7] (there are twenty-two letters in the Hebrew alphabet). This is the ancient and most holy name of God, encoded in the beginning verses of His account of creation.

בְּרֵאשִׁית בָּרָא אֱלֹהִים אֵת הַשָּׁמַיִם וְאֵת הָאָרֶץ׃ וְהָאָרֶץ הָיְתָה תֹהוּ וָבֹהוּ וְחֹשֶׁךְ עַל־פְּנֵי
תְהוֹם וְרוּחַ אֱלֹהִים מְרַחֶפֶת עַל־פְּנֵי הַמָּיִם׃ וַיֹּאמֶר אֱלֹהִים יְהִי אוֹר וַיְ**ה**ִי־אוֹר׃ וַיַּרְא
אֱלֹהִים אֶת־הָאוֹר כִּי־ט**וֹ**ב וַיַּבְדֵּל אֱלֹהִים בֵּין הָאוֹר וּבֵין **הַ**חֹשֶׁךְ׃ וַיִּקְרָא אֱלֹהִים ו
לָאוֹר יוֹם וְלַחֹשֶׁךְ קָרָא לָיְלָה וַיְהִי־עֶרֶב וַיְהִי־בֹקֶר יוֹם אֶחָד׃

Genesis 1:1-5

יהוָה = Yahweh/God

---

[7]There are exactly twenty-two letters between the letters in bold type.

DECODING THE MESSIANIC MYSTERY OF THE FIRST TEN NAMES IN HEBREW HISTORY

We would like to point out that the very meanings of the Jewish names of our original ancestors reveal God's plan to send His suffering Messiah, as a mortal, who would die for us.

Missler points out that: "In Hebrew: *Adam* (אָדָם) means 'man'; *Seth* (שֵׁת) means 'appointed'; *Enosh* (אֱנוֹשׁ) means 'mortal'; *Kenan* (קֵינָן) means 'sorrow'; *Mahalalel* (מַהֲלַלְאֵל) means 'the blessed God'; *Jared* (יֶרֶד) means 'shall come down'; *Enoch* (חֲנוֹךְ) means 'teaching'; *Methuselah* (מְתוּשָׁלַח) means 'his death shall bring'; *Lamech* (לֶמֶךְ) means 'the despairing'; and *Noah* (נֹחַ) means 'rest' or 'comfort.' "[8]

Reading this genealogy of names as a sentence, translating them from Hebrew to English, we get: "Man is appointed mortal sorrow. The blessed God shall come down, teaching that his death shall bring the despairing comfort." This, indirectly but clearly, shows that the God Incarnate Messiah would give His life for us, as Jesus did.

SOME RABBIS RECANT

Rabbi Eliezer ben Hyrcanus, one of the most famous and honored rabbis in Jewish history since the first century, held beliefs few Orthodox Jews may realize. As a matter of fact, he may have believed in Jesus, or at least had a profound interest and respect for the Jewish Messianic community, as revealed by a story in the rabbinic literature. This story runs as follows: Rabbi Eliezer was suspected of being a believer of "heretical" things and arrested. The Roman judge released him because he misunderstood Rabbi Eliezer's reply, "The judge is right." Later, in a conversation with Rabbi Akiva about this, Eliezer admits his conversation with and admiration for "Jacob of Kephar," who has been proven to be James[9] of the New Testament.

---

[8]Chuck Missler, "Mystery of the Messiah." Coeur d'Alene, ID: Koinonia House, © 1994, used by permission. ( ) mine. Audio tape available through Koinonia House, POB D, Coeur d'Alene, ID, USA 83816-0347. The following translation, ibid.

[9]In the Greek manuscripts of the New Testament and all foreign language translations from them, excepting English, the word *Yacov* for the apostle James is translated Jacob, which is the same name used in the first book of the Bible when it speaks of Abraham, Isaac and Jacob. Remember, the apostles were Jews and this is a Jewish name. The name James came to be in the English Bible because King James of England wanted his name in the Bible. When the honored and respected King James Version of the Bible was written, James asked that his name be used in place of Jacob. This is a documented fact for scholars of English literature. Don't get me wrong, I love and swear by the KJV—it is my favorite English translation.

For a more complete understanding of this summary, I will quote the actual ancient conversation between Akiva and Eliezer as recorded in the rabbinical text. This is from the book, *Israelis, Jews, and Jesus*, by the Jewish scholar, Pinchas Lapide. He tells us: "The oldest rabbinical passage which speaks of Jesus deals with one of the bright lights of the early tannaitic period, Rabbi Eliezer ben Hyrcanus, also named Eliezer the Great, whose magisterial opinions are quoted more than 320 times in the Mishnah. In two tannaitic texts [9. Tos. Hullin II, 24, and Aboda Sara 16b]...Rabbi Eliezer praises a decision on religious law which was passed on to him in the name of Jesus.

'When Rabbi Eliezer was arrested for heresy, they led him to the place of judgment to pass sentence on him. The Roman judge said to him, 'How can an old man like you bother with such trifling things?' Eliezer answered, 'The judge is right.' The Roman judge thought that Eliezer was talking about him, whereas Eliezer was actually speaking of his Father in heaven. Then the Roman judge said, 'Since you agree with me, you shall be set free.' When Eliezer got back home, his disciples came to him, to console him. But he refused all consolation. Then Rabbi Akiba said to him, 'Rabbi, ...perhaps you once heard something heretical, and it pleased you. Perhaps you were arrested on account of that.' Eliezer answered, 'Akiba, you have just reminded me! Once I was going about the upper marketplace of Sepphoris, and there I met a disciple of Jesus the Nazarene named Jacob, from the village of Shechania. He said to me, 'It is written in your Torah, 'You shall not bring the hire of a harlot into the house of the LORD' [Deut 23:18]. But may one use the harlot's wages to build a toilet for the high priest?' 'You have spoken well,' I said, since at the time I could not remember the Halakah. As soon as he saw that I agreed, he added, 'Jesus of Nazareth taught me that. Jesus was speaking in reference to the prophet Micah, where it says, 'For from the hire of a harlot she gathered them, and to the hire of a harlot they shall return' [Mic 1:7]. Jesus added, 'It came from filth, and it shall once again become filth.' ' This pleased me, and that is why I was arrested for heresy [or Christian sympathies]....' "[10] Rabbi Eliezer, "a believer in Jesus"? Decide for yourself.

ADDITIONAL EVIDENCE

The scholar, R. T. Herford, has interestingly noted: "...it is curious to observe the embarrassment of R. Eliezer when on his trial. One would have thought that he could have saved himself by declaring

[10]Pinchas Lapide, *Israelis, Jews, and Jesus*, pp. 78-79. Lapide's sources inserted with [ ] for clarity.

that he was not a Christian, whereas he only made a skillful evasion, and owed his escape to the vanity of his judge."[11]

Herford further comments on another scholar's opinion concerning the famous rabbi's activities. He notes: "Grätz...associates the incident much more closely with the subsequent arrest and trial. He says that by reason of his intercourse with Christians R. Eliezer was looked upon as a member of the Christian community, and therefore accused as a heretic."[12]

AHER IN THE QUAGMIRE

Our professor friend Jakob Jocz tells us: "R. Eliezer ben Hyrcanus is by no means an isolated case. An even more interesting person is the much discussed Elisha ben Abuyah, often referred to as *Aher* ('the other'). Elisha, who flourished at the end of the first and the beginning of the second century, was a famous *Tanna* and the teacher of R. Meir. The references concerning him are obscure....we do know that he was suspected of hiding in his clothes *sifre minim*[13] while he was still functioning as a teacher in the schoolhouse...."[14]

Professor Jocz' footnote documents this evidence from the Talmud: "202. *Hagigah*, 15b: 'It is told of Aher that when he used to rise (to go) from the schoolhouse, many *sifre minim* used to fall from his lap'. May there not be some significance in the fact that R. Meir, R. Akiba's greatest pupil and 'Aher's' devoted disciple, is credited with the pun on ευαγγελιον [evangelos/good news] = ' און גליון ' which Johanan further developed into ' עון גליון '? (See Bacher, *Agada der Tannaiten*, II, p. 36, note.)"[15]

Remember that these are those evil rabbinical puns for the New Testament, *awen-gillayon* and *awon-gillayon,* meaning "scroll of sin," which we read about earlier. We ask, "Could it have been that Rabbi Meir was angry that his famed teacher became a believer in the New Testament?" Sounds like it, doesn't it?

COMPOSER FORGETS HIS COMPOSITION?

Jakob Jocz, author of *The Jewish People and Jesus Christ,* exposes evidence from rabbinical writings which might well indicate

---

[11]R. Travers Herford, *Christianity in Talmud & Midrash*, p. 142.
[12]Ibid, p. 144.
[13]*Sifre* means "book" and *minim* means "sect" outside the mainstream—referring to Christian Gospels, no doubt. Aher kept losing the New Testament books and Gospels he was hiding and secretly reading as his students worked. He was absentminded, as many professors are, and when he would get up out of his chair they would fall before he realized what had happened.
[14]Jakob Jocz, *The Jewish People and Jesus Christ*, pp. 181-182.
[15]Ibid, p. 376. [ ] mine.

that the rabbi who formulated the Birkat ha-Minim curse against believers may have become a believer himself. He obviously used "forgetfulness" as a front to avoid suspicion due to his apparent refusal to use his own formulation. Jocz says: "Samuel the Small, the composer of the *Birkat ha-minim*, a year after he had composed the prayer, was leading the service at the synagogue. When he came to recite the *Birkat ha-minim*, he could not remember it. He tried to recall the prayer '*shetayim we-shalosh sha'ot*', but he was not dismissed. The question is asked, why did they not dismiss him? The rule laid down by Rab Jehudah (died 299) on the authority of Rab (i.e. Abba Arika, 167-247) was that if the precentor errs in any of the benedictions they do not dismiss him, but if he errs in the *Birkat ha-minim*, they dismiss him, because there is the possibility of his being a heretic. But in the case of Samuel the Small it is different, because he himself composed it. But could not he have changed his mind? To this, Abaje (died 338/9) replied that there is a traditional saying: A good person does not become bad."[16]

In our personal copy of the Talmud, which is the Soncino English version, we ran across a slightly different and more informative account of what happened to Samuel: "These eighteen are really nineteen?—R. Levi said: The benediction relating to the *Minim* was instituted in Jabneh....Our Rabbis taught: Simeon ha-Pakuli arranged the eighteen benedictions in order before Rabban Gamaliel in Jabneh. Said Rabban Gamaliel to the Sages: Can any one among you frame a benediction relating to the *Minim?* Samuel the Lesser arose and composed it. The next year he forgot it [29a] and he tried for two or three hours to recall it, and they did not remove him. Why did they not remove him seeing that Rab Judah has said in the name of Rab: If a reader made a mistake in any of the other benedictions, they do not remove him, but if in the benediction of the *Minim*, he is removed, because we suspect him of being a *Min?*—Samuel the Lesser is different, because he composed it. But is there not a fear that he may have recanted?"[17]

"DR. CALLOWAY" RABBIS MUST COME CLEAN BEFORE THE MESSIAH CONSPIRACY IS EXPOSED

The movie *Capricorn One* is about a conspiracy to convince the world that astronauts had actually reached Mars. Dr. Calloway is the character who creates the deception. The astronauts were made to appear as if they were on Mars due to a barrage of technical tricks.

---

[16]Ibid, p. 55.

[17]*The Babylonian Talmud,* Berakoth 28b-29a, p. 175.

Calloway even attempted to have the astronauts killed to seal the cover-up for all time. The movie concludes with the President speaking in honor of the astronauts at a funeral service, which of course was being covered by the media. The television cameras turn from him to the surviving astronaut as he approaches his own funeral.

In the same way, we hope to turn the world's attention away from the imaginary claims of the "Dr. Calloway" rabbis, who say there was no Messiah Conspiracy, to the true picture of Jesus as Messiah, returning to all of us, including the Jews.

The only way you will be able to appreciate what we have said is to watch the movie, *Capricorn One*, on video. It is not a very patriotic movie and I do not agree with its implications, though it certainly presents drama, suspense and conspiracy with the same seriousness as the greatest conspiracy—the Messiah Conspiracy.

Dr. Calloway conspiratorially sets out to deceive the world into believing that the astronauts went to Mars, when in fact they never left Earth. Likewise, the rabbis want everyone to believe that Jesus is not the Messiah, as you have reviewed in the anti-missionary publications we have quoted. They use a host of literary tricks to try to convince us to believe what they want us to believe. I cannot help but believe that many of them know otherwise, just as Calloway (played by Hal Holbrook) knew.

When the astronaut approaches his own funeral, as the President is giving a eulogy for him, the television cameras turn from the President to the astronaut. Calloway's expression is that of ultimate embarrassment. Watch the movie! I picture some rabbis looking like this when the Messiah returns and turns out to be Jesus! The expression on Calloway's face is that of a conspirator who has been caught red-handed—unforgettable! This is a strong analogy but a proper one to conclude this chapter.

Up until this point, we have covered the Jewish guns which have been pointed at the Messianic Jewish believers in Jesus. We will now examine the Gentile guns. Roman Catholicism arose about the time the rabbis considered their work against the believers a success. The leaders of Catholicism finished the job and were even more ruthless than the rabbinic community. The Catholic "Church" persecuted true believers in Jesus, both Jews and Gentiles, to no end. This is the subject of our chapter 10, which separates the false Christians from the true ones.

***

"Beware of false prophets, which come to you in sheep's clothing, but inwardly they are ravening wolves. Ye shall know them by their fruits. Do men gather grapes of thorns, or figs of thistles?" Jesus of Nazareth, Matthew 7:15-16, 33 AD

"[In] The Protestant Netherlands....During the 16th and the 17th Centuries, Amsterdam was known among Europe's Jews as the new Jerusalem....Pre-Reformation semi-sectarian minority movements expressing millenarian yearnings had to remain underground. They were persecuted and suppressed by the Church in Rome...."[1] Regina Sharif, an accurate comment on the 1500's

" '...For if it had not been for the Christians, our remnant would surely have been destroyed, and Israel's hope would have been extinguished amidst the Gentiles, who hate us because of our faith....But God, our Lord, has caused the Christian wise men to arise, who protect us in every generation.' "[2] Rabbi Emden, 1757

"...on the Continent of Europe small hidden Christian societies, who have held many of the opinions of the Anabaptists, have existed from the times of the apostles. In the sense of the direct transmission of Divine Truth, and the true nature of spiritual religion, it seems probable that these churches have a lineage or succession more ancient than that of the Roman Church."[3] Robert Barclay, 1876

"In 1208 a crusade was ordered by Pope Innocent III; a bloody war of extermination followed; scarcely paralleled in history....in 1229 the Inquisition was established and within a hundred years the Albigenses were utterly rooted out...."[4]
Henry Halley, 1965

The true Bible believing Christians mentioned above, along with the Huguenots and Anabaptists, the near equivalent of modern Evangelical Zionist Christians, aided and protected the Jews against Catholicism's medieval persecutions when they were able. Philip Moore, 1996

10

EARLY CHRISTIAN HISTORY VERSUS CATHOLICISM

The secret events of true Christian history have been hidden from our eyes for centuries! Today, many have been led to believe that church history is synonomous with the record of the Roman Catholic

---

1Regina Sharif, *Non-Jewish Zionism*. London: Zed Press, © 1983, pp. 15-17, used by permission. [ ] mine.
2Pinchas Lapide, *Israelis, Jews, and Jesus*, p. 105. Lapide's source was *Lechem Shamayim*, Hamburg, 1757, p. 30 ff.
3John T. Christian, A.M., D.D., LL.D., *A History of the Baptists: Together With Some Account of Their Principles and Practices*, Vol. II. Nashville, TN: Sunday School Board of the Southern Baptist Convention, © 1926, p. 85.
4Henry H. Halley, *Halley's Bible Handbook*. Grand Rapids, MI: Zondervan Publishing House, © 1965, p. 785, used by permission.

Church. However, this is not true. In this chapter, we will differentiate between the two, separating the sheep from the goats in an objective manner, so as to inform those who are truly interested, of the actual events.

Many are now taught that "Christianity" (Roman Catholicism, which is not really New Testament Christianity) has in the past, persecuted the Jews. While it is true that Roman Catholicism has ruthlessly murdered Jews and Protestants, it is also true that true New Testament Christians have rescued and even given their lives to save Jews from Catholic persecution and Hitler's Holocaust. These subjects will be covered in greater detail later in this book.

This chapter picks up where the last one left off and continues to illustrate the plight and persecution of true Christians throughout history, from the latter half of the first century until today.

THE BETRAYAL OF CHRISTIANS TO ROME—TRAITORS EXPOSING THOSE THEY FELT TO BE TRAITORS

The Jewish scholar, Hugh Schonfield, in his book, *Saints Against Caesar*, documents the persecution of Jewish Christians in the first century while Judaism was still a protected religion within Roman law. "But already in the first century it was Rabbinical Judaism which had taken the initiative in trying to force the Nazarenes out of the Synagogue. The Romans no doubt did not in Palestine distinguish between one brand of Judaism and another until they came to appreciate that there was a body of Christians still inside the Jewish Community....when the emperor decreed a search for members of the house of David, and started a persecution of the Christians. According to Hegesippus there were some Jewish heretics who denounced certain of the Nazarenes to the authorities."[5]

Maurice Goguel, in his unsurpassed work, *The Birth of Christianity*, sheds even more light on the subject when he notes: "...right up to Paul's trial, the Roman authorities in Palestine do not seem to have made any distinction between Jews and Christians. At first the same was true in the diaspora: for a long time Christians were confused with the Jews. But the latter went to work to clear up this confusion with such perseverance that we cannot help but think that they were working according to a set plan. So far as they succeeded they rendered the situation of the Christians in the empire very precarious. As soon as they ceased to enjoy the favoured treatment which had been awarded to Judaism, they found themselves without

---

[5]Hugh Schonfield, *Saints Against Caesar, The Rise and Reactions of the First Christian Community*, p. 181.

legal status, on the fringe of society and subject to the penalty of death....Jewish communities possessed wide powers of self-government; they had rights of association and could exercise discipline over their members. Jews were exempt from all participation in public worship; they could take oaths without calling upon the gods....All this was possible because Judaism was considered to be the national religion of a people who had been the friend and ally of the Roman people before they became vassals....the means used by the Jews [rabbinical leaders] to hinder the Christian mission were indirect. They made every effort to persuade the Roman authorities that Christians were not Jews or had ceased to be so and consequently had no right to the privileges of Judaism."[6]

WHAT ROME DID TO THE BELIEVERS IN PRE-CATHOLIC TIMES

Before Catholicism was decreed the state religion of Rome by Constantine in the fourth century AD, the empire was pagan. They worshipped many gods, including Greek and Roman deities. Though they permitted Jews to swear oaths without calling on the gods, they persecuted the believers in Jesus (both Jew and non-Jew) with a zeal unknown by most today.

THE MURDEROUS DEEDS AGAINST TRUE BELIEVERS BY PAGAN ROME'S ANTI-CHRISTIAN CAESARS

Emperor Nero put Christians to death while mocking them. He had their bodies covered with animal skins, and confined them to areas where wild dogs would devour them. He nailed them to crosses and covered them with flammable materials, setting them on fire to light his garden by night.[7]

Emperor Domitian (AD 95) instituted the persecution in which Flavius Clemens perished. Thousands of Christians were murdered in Rome and Italy under his orders.

Under Emperor Trajan (98-117 AD), many Christians were murdered, among them Simeon (Jesus' brother), who was crucified in 107. Ignatius of Antioch was thrown to wild beasts in 110 AD.

Concerning these horrible persecutions, Pliny, the governor of Bithynia, reported the progress of his extermination of Christians in a letter to Trajan, which we will partially reproduce for you here. Pliny

---

[6]Maurice Goguel, *The Birth of Christianity*, pp. 468-470. [ ] mine.

[7]See Will Durant, *Caesar and Christ: A History of Roman Civilization and of Christianity from Their Beginnings to A.D. 325*. New York: Simon and Schuster, © 1944, p. 281.

wrote to Trajan: "...the method I have observed towards those who have been denounced to me as Christians, is this; I interrogated them whether they were Christians; if they confessed I repeated the question twice again, adding a threat of capital punishment; if they still persevered, I ordered them to be executed....Those who denied that they were Christians, or had ever been so, who repeated after me an invocation to the gods, and offered religious rites with wine and frankincense to your statue (which I had ordered to be brought for the purpose, together with those of the gods), and finally cursed the name of Christ (none of which, it is said, those who are really Christians can be forced into performing), I thought proper to discharge....I therefore thought it proper to adjourn all further proceedings in this affair, in order to consult with you. For the matter is well worth referring to you, especially considering the numbers endangered: persons of all ranks and ages, and of both sexes, are and will be involved in the prosecution. For this contagious superstition is not confined to the cities only, but has spread through the villages and the countryside. Nevertheless it seems still possible to check and cure it. The [pagan] temples, at least, which were once almost deserted, begin now to be frequented, and the sacred solemnities, after a long intermission, are again revived; while there is a general demand for sacrificial animals which for some time past have met with but few purchasers. From hence it is easy to imagine what numbers might be reclaimed from this error [believers in Jesus] if the door is left open for repentance."[8]

THE EMPEROR'S EMPTY HEART

Under Emperor Hadrian (117-138), Telephorus and many other well-known Christians suffered martyrdom. Under Emperor Antonius Pius (138-161), Polycarp and many others were martyred. Emperor Marcus Aurelius (161-180) persecuted Christians with the enthusiasm of Nero. Under his rule, many thousands were beheaded and thrown to the lions, including our beloved Justin Martyr.

Emperor Septimius Severus (193-211) persecuted Christians in Egypt and North Africa. He burned, crucified and beheaded many martyrs in Alexandria. Origen's father, Leonidas, was one of his victims.

Under Emperor Maximin (235-238), many Christian leaders were executed. Emperor Decius (249-251) murdered untold numbers

---

[8]Hugh Schonfield, *Saints Against Caesar, The Rise and Reactions of the First Christian Community*, pp. 238, 188-189. [ ] mine.

of Christians throughout Rome, North Africa, Egypt and Asia Minor. The famed Cyprian proclaimed, "The whole world is devastated."[9]

Emperor Valerian (253-260) persecuted believers even more severely than his predecessor, Decius. Many Christian leaders were executed, including Cyprian, Bishop of Carthage. Emperor Diocletian (284-305) was known for the most severe persecution of Christians among the emperors.

Henry Halley notes that under Diocletian: "For ten years, Christians were hunted in cave and forest; they were burned, thrown to wild beasts, put to death by every torture cruelty could devise. It was a resolute, determined, systematic effort to abolish the Christian Name."[10]

ROME'S UNDERGROUND CATACOMBS—THE HIDDEN TOMBS OF A FORGOTTEN PEOPLE

Under the city of Rome lies the remains of a people so persecuted, so horribly tortured for their belief, it would almost seem as if none could begin to truly understand their plight.[11] These were the first and second century Christians of Rome, who existed underground in secret tunnels called catacombs.

The catacombs of Rome are vast subterranean chambers, roughly eight feet wide by five feet high. They extend for hundreds of miles under the city. They were used by Christians for secret worship, burial and sanctuary from Rome's persecution. There are an estimated seven million Christian graves and four miles of inscriptions to be found in these ancient galleries today.[12]

CHURCH FATHERS EXTERMINATED —THE UNPOPULAR HOLOCAUST

During these times of persecution, some of the greatest Christian philosophers were systematically murdered. These people are historically known as "the church fathers." Our list includes: **Polycarp** (AD 69-156), John the apostle's pupil who was arrested, brought before the governor, and offered his freedom if he would curse Jesus. Polycarp was burned alive when he refused; **Ignatius** (AD 67-110), also John's student, was sentenced to be thrown to wild beasts by

---

[9]Henry H. Halley, *Halley's Bible Handbook*, p. 762.

[10]Ibid.

[11]However, they are promised to inherit the earth, along with the believers from all other ages, in all its future beauty and with all its treasure, when Jesus returns!

[12]For a more complete history, see Ibid, p. 763.

the Emperor Trajan in Rome; **Papias** (AD 70-155) was martyred at Pergamum; **Justin Martyr** (AD 100-167) was martyred at Rome; **Iranaeus** (AD 130-200) died a martyr; **Origen** (AD 185-254) died in prison while being tortured under Emperor Decius.

WHO CONVERTED WHOM? IF YOU CAN'T BEAT THEM, JOIN THEM! DID IT HAPPEN?

Constantine erroneously reported that "he saw in the sky, just above the setting sun, a vision of the cross, and above it the words, 'In This sign Conquer.' "[13]

Obviously, no words or cross appeared in the sky telling him to fight. We believe Constantine used this as a ploy, which also illustrates that he never truly believed in Jesus.

Evangelist Ralph Woodrow defends this logic when he writes: "...if Constantine did have such a vision, are we to suppose its author was Jesus Christ? Would the Prince of Peace instruct a pagan emperor to make a military banner embodying the cross and to go forth conquering and killing in that sign?

The Roman Empire (of which Constantine became the head) has been described in the Scriptures as a 'beast.' Daniel saw four great beasts which represented four world empires—Babylon (a lion), Medo-Persia (a bear), Greece (a leopard), and Rome. The fourth beast, the Roman Empire, was so horrible that it was symbolized by a beast unlike any other (Daniel 7:1-8). We see no reason to suppose that Christ would tell Constantine to conquer with the sign of the cross to further the beast system of Rome!

But if the vision was not of God, how can we explain the *conversion* of Constantine? Actually, his conversion is to be seriously questioned. Even though he had much to do with the establishment of certain doctrines and customs within the church, the facts plainly show that he was not *truly* converted—not in the *Biblical* sense of the word. Historians admit that his conversion was 'nominal, even by contemporary standards.'

Probably the most obvious indication that he was not truly converted may be seen from the fact that *after* his conversion, he committed several *murders*—including the murder of his own wife and son!....These things are summed up in the following words from *The Catholic Encyclopedia*: 'Even after his conversion he caused the execution of his brother-in-law Licinius, and of the latter's son, as well as of Crispus his own son by his first marriage, and of his wife

---

[13]Henry H. Halley, *Halley's Bible Handbook*, p. 759.

Fausta....It has consequently been asserted that Constantine favored Christianity merely from *political* motives, and he has been regarded as an enlightened despot who made use of religion only to advance his policy.'

Such was the conclusion of the noted historian Durant regarding Constantine. 'Was his conversion sincere—was it an act of religious belief, or a consummate stroke of *political* wisdom? *Probably the latter*...He seldom conformed to the ceremonial requirements of Christian worship. His letters to Christian bishops make it clear that he cared little for the theological differences that agitated Christendom—though he was willing to suppress dissent in the interests of imperial unity. Throughout his reign he treated the bishops as his political aids; he summoned them, presided over their councils, and agreed to enforce whatever opinion their majority should formulate. A real believer would have been a Christian first and a statesman afterward; with Constantine it was the reverse. Christianity was to him a *means*, not an *end*.'

Persecutions had not destroyed the Christian faith. Constantine knew this. Instead of the empire constantly being divided—with pagans in conflict with Christians—why not take such steps as might be necessary to *mix* both paganism and Christianity together, he reasoned, and thus bring a *united* force to the empire?....Though he had his statue removed from pagan temples and renounced the offering of sacrifices to himself, yet people continued to speak of the divinity of the emperor. As pontifex maximus he continued to watch over the heathen worship and protect its rights. In dedicating Constantinople in 330 a ceremonial that was half pagan and half Christian was used....While professing to be a Christian, he continued to believe in pagan magic formulas for the protection of crops and the healing of disease. All of these things are pointed out in *The Catholic Encyclopedia*."[14]

Richard Booker, author of the book, *Jesus in the Feasts of Israel,* insightfully pointed out: "In A.D. 312, the Emperor Constantine decreed that Christianity was to be the official religion of Rome. But, of course, no one can decree that another person become a Christian. Christianity is a matter of the heart. But the people had to outwardly obey even though inwardly most never actually accepted Jesus personally and experienced the new birth. Rome embraced Christianity, but the Romans themselves did not become Christians. People joined a religious system, but they never had a change on the inside.

---

[14]Ralph Woodrow, *Babylon Mystery Religion*, pp. 55-58.

During the next 1,200 years, many unbiblical practices were taught by the institutional church. Church leaders did not clearly teach the biblical declaration that salvation is based on a personal relationship with Jesus Christ, and the necessity of the new birth. The significance of the Feast of Passover was unknown to the common man. People sought salvation through religious rituals rather than through personal faith in Jesus Christ as their human Passover Lamb."[15]

ERRONEOUS FORCED CHANGES IN CHRISTIAN ACTIVITIES AND CUSTOMS

Constantine changed the Sabbath from Saturday to Sunday. Halley documents: "He made the Christians' day of Assembly, Sunday, a Rest Day; forbidding ordinary work...."[16]

The original meaning of the word "church" was a group of people who believed in Jesus as Messiah (*ecclesia*), who gathered together, both Jews and non-Jews, and met anywhere, usually in a house. The New Testament testifies: "The churches of Asia |greet| you. Aquila and Priscilla |greet| you much in the Lord, with the church that is in their house" (I Cor. 16:19 KJV).[17]

Constantine issued an edict[18] for the construction of church buildings everywhere and set aside Sunday for Christians to rest. The New Testament never revoked Saturday as the biblical day of rest, something Christians and Jews should remember today. Sabbath (*shabbat*) is Hebrew for the "seventh day" and "rest." Sunday is the first day.

In Jewish-Christian debates, rabbis sometimes say, "You Christians have the wrong day." More correctly they should say, "Constantine has the wrong day." According to history, Constantine does not speak for true Christians. Many of us go to church on Sunday, to Messianic congregation service on Friday night/Saturday morning and trust the Lord every day of the week. *Every day* we trust that His will be done in our lives, that we meet the right people He has to bring our way so that we may tell them about Him. After all, what's

---

[15]Richard Booker, *Jesus in the Feasts of Israel*. Shippensburg, PA: Destiny Image Publishers, © 1987, p. 30, used by permission. Available through Destiny Image Publishers, POB 351, Shippensburg, PA, USA 17257. Tel. (717) 532-3040.

[16]Henry H. Halley, *Halley's Bible Handbook*, p. 760.

[17]*The New Scofield Reference Bible*. Also see Romans 16:6; Colossians 4:15; and Philemon 2.

[18]Henry H. Halley, *Halley's Bible Handbook*, p. 760.

in a day? He made all seven. If you are a believer, I guess you have two in which to rest instead of one, thanks to Constantine.

THE UNWELCOME CHANGES OF EMPEROR THEODOSIUS—PAGAN INJECTION

Halley not only documents the changes Constantine made, but the period of time under Emperor Theodosius just after him: "Emperor Theodosius (A.D. 378-398), made Christianity the State Religion of the Roman Empire, and made Church Membership Compulsory....This Forced Conversion filled the Churches with Unregenerate People.

Not only so, Theodosius undertook the Forcible Suppression of all other Religions, and Prohibited Idol Worship. Under his decrees, Heathen Temples were torn down....Up to this time Conversion was Voluntary, a Genuine Change in Heart and Life.

But now the Military Spirit of Imperial Rome had entered the Church. The Church had Conquered the Roman Empire. But in reality the Roman Empire had Conquered the Church, by Making the Church over into the Image of the Roman Empire....[It] had become a Political Organization in the Spirit and Pattern of Imperial Rome....The Imperial [Roman Catholic] Church of the 4th and 5th centuries had become an entirely different institution from the persecuted [true believers'] church of the first three centuries....Ministers became Priests. The term 'priest' was not applied to Christian ministers before A.D. 200. It was borrowed from the Jewish system, and from the example of heathen priesthood. Leo I (440-61) prohibited priests from marrying, and Celibacy of priests became a law of the Roman Church....The Goths, Vandals and Huns who overthrew the Roman Empire accepted Christianity; but to a large extent their conversion was nominal and this further filled the Church with Pagan practices."[19]

The devout and knowledgeable Henry Halley further notes: "The Church was founded, not as an institution of Authority to Force the Name and Teaching of Christ upon the world, but only as a Witness-Bearing institution to Christ, to hold Him before the people. Christ [Messiah] Himself, not the Church, is the Transforming Power in Human Life. But the Church [which] was founded in the Roman Empire, and gradually developed [for itself] a form of Government like the Political World in which it existed, become a vast Autocratic organization, ruled from the top."[20]

---

[19]Ibid, pp. 760-761. [ ] mine.
[20]Ibid, p. 767. [ ] mine.

THOUGH CATHOLICISM HAS PERSECUTED, TRUE CHRISTIANS HAVE ALWAYS LOVED THE JEW

Throughout the next few pages, it will not be our intention to bore you with historical facts regarding a long line of popes and their deeds. However, a review of these facts is necessary to make clear that what has been labeled "Christian history," was absolutely not!

While true Christians were underground[21] and unable to surface until the fierce battles of the Reformation in the sixteenth century, it is also interesting to see how Roman Catholicism, which attempted to call itself "the only true church of Christianity," developed through many of its leaders into a torture machine unsurpassed in human history. It was responsible for the murder of millions of Protestants and many tens of thousands of Jews.

I have found it an interesting pastime to read Regina Sharif's book, *Non-Jewish Zionism,* which records four hundred years of Christian Zionism and Protestant Christian love of Jews. This hit like an avalanche in the sixteenth century, when Christians began to be freed from the Catholic Church and permitted to openly study Bible prophecy! Even though Sharif's book attempts to discourage Christian support for Israel, it is a wealth of information on the little studied, little known subject of Christian colonial love and support (of hundreds of years past) for the Jews and their providential divine right to return to their state, the State of Israel, as prophesied in the Bible (Ezek.

---

[21]Regina Sharif indirectly referred to this little-known issue when she wrote: "...Millenarians regarded the future of the Jewish people as an important element in the events to precede the End of Time. In fact, the literal interpretation of the apocalyptic writings in the Bible led them to conclude that the Millennium was to be heralded by the physical Restoration of the Jews as a nation (Israel) to Palestine....After Christianity became the official religion of the Roman Empire in AD 380, the early Church Fathers, such as Origen and Augustine, were determined to wipe out millenarian ideas and expectations. Augustine, in his book, *City of God*, seemed to have settled this problem, at least until the 16th Century. Using the allegorical methodology, Augustine interpreted the Millennium as a spiritual state into which the Church collectively had already entered at the time of Pentecost, i.e. just after the death and resurrection of Christ. Pre-Reformation semi-sectarian minority movements expressing millenarian yearnings had to remain **underground**. They were persecuted and suppressed by the Church in Rome and their teachings were branded as heresies." Regina Shariff, *Non-Jewish Zionism*, pp. 16-17. In her footnote to heresies, Sharif points out: "Pre-Reformation movements with strong millenarian tendencies included the Waldensians in the 12th Century in southern France, the Passagii sect appearing at the same time in northern Italy and the Hussites of 15th Century Bohemia." Ibid, p. 30. So much for those who claim that true Christian love of the Jew in Israel is a phenomenon of the last half-century—believe me, they are many. We have had to show this quote to more than one arrogant soul, much to their dismay.

36:24; Isa. 11:12. See our chapter 12, "Christian Zionists Past and Present" and chapter 14, "Zionists—Evangelical Christians—the Most Loyal to Israel").

LET'S EXAMINE THE POPE AND PAPACY

At any rate, let's get through the Pope's Catholic history and investigate the objections which are always mentioned when a contemporary born-again Christian starts talking about Jesus. Author Henry Halley starts by explaining to us: "The word 'Pope' means 'Papa,' 'Father.' At first it was applied to all Western Bishops. About A.D. 500 it began to be restricted to the Bishop of Rome, and soon, in common use, came to mean Universal Bishop."

Halley notes that: "The Roman Catholic list of Popes includes the Bishops of Rome from the 1st century onward."[22] However, he documents: "...for 500 years Bishops of Rome were **NOT** Popes. The idea that the Bishop of Rome should have Authority over the Whole Church was a slow growth, bitterly contested at every step...."[23]

THE FICTION OF THE PAPAL INVENTION

We owe it to ourselves to briefly re-scan papal Roman Catholic history, from its early inception until now, and compare its councils, decrees and deeds to those individuals who claimed to be truly Christian, and illustrated this by their deeds of love and life-saving acts. These (born-again) Christians will be listed later in our chapter 12, "Christian Zionists Past and Present,"[24] which documents some of those who saved Jews from Hitler.

As we study, we will see a sharp contrast between the true believers and the evil events throughout history perpetrated by "traditionals" who claimed to be believers. Remember the words of Jesus: "Beware of false prophets, which come to you in sheep's clothing, but inwardly they are ravening wolves" (Matt. 7:15 KJV).

Jesus said that He would tell these people on Judgment Day: "...I never knew you...." (Matt. 7:23 KJV).

***

[22] Henry H. Halley, *Halley's Bible Handbook*, p. 767.

[23] Ibid, pp. 767-768.

[24] Some of these heroes are mentioned in our chapter 14, "Zionists—Evangelical Christians—the Most Loyal to Israel."

A BRIEF SURVEY OF POPES AND THEIR INSIPID CLAIMS

Pope Calixtus I (218-223) was actually just a bishop who tried to base his claim on the easily falsely interpreted authority of Matthew 16:18. Tertullian called him a "usurper in speaking as if Bishop of Bishops."

"Pope" Silvester I (314-335) was alive when Emperor Constantine made Catholicism the state religion of Rome; however, Constantine regarded himself as "head of the Church" and called the Council of Nicaea in 325, where many unorthodox, unchristian and unbiblical decisions were made for those who supposedly were part of the Church. A few years later we see Siricius (385-398), who claimed "Universal Jurisdiction" over Catholicism.

Innocent I (402-417) called himself "Ruler of the Church of God" (Roman Catholicism's conception of the Church of God).

During the years 440 through 461, a man named Leo I, who was called "the First Pope" by certain historians opportunistically used the tragedies of the empire.

Leo claimed to be "Primate of All Bishops" and Emperor Valentinian III recognized this claim in 452. After persuading Attila the Hun to spare Rome, Leo's reputation and popularity were enhanced. He then felt confident to erroneously proclaim himself "Lord of the Whole Church" (all Catholicism). This man was the first to advocate the "Exclusive Universal Papacy" (Pope-hood). He claimed that "Resistance to his authority was a Sure Way to Hell." While also supporting the death penalty for heretics (those who did not believe as he did), in spite of his struggle for power and his claim, the Ecumenical Council of Chalcedon (451) ordered that the Patriarch of Constantinople had equal prerogative with the Bishop of Rome.

POPES FREED FROM CIVIL GOVERNMENT WHEN THE EMPIRE FELL APART

Simplicius was the Catholic Pope in 476, during the dissolution of the Western empire between the years 468 and 483. Once this occurred, the Popes were freed from civil authority. The many new kingdoms of barbarians into which the West was now divided, gave future Popes the opportunity for alliances which benefited themselves personally. Slowly, the Popes became the most powerful figures in the Western world.

Between 590 and 604, Gregory I, who is generally regarded as the first Pope, "established for himself complete control over the churches [Catholicism][25] of Italy, Spain, Gaul and England." When the Patriarch of Constantinople called himself "Universal Bishop," Gregory was tremendously irritated, considering this title vicious and haughty.

CRIMES OF THE POPES

Pope Steven II (752-757) requested that Pepin lead an army into Italy, thus conquering the Lombards. He then gave their land—a good chunk of central Italy—to guess who? Pope Steven II. Thus began the "Papal States," known to us as the "Temporal Dominion of the Popes."

The civil control of Rome and central Italy established by Steven, which Pepin recognized in 1754, was later also confirmed by Charlemagne (742-814). Charlemagne, known to us as "one of the greatest rulers of all time," saved Europe from Mohammedism; however, he became the chief component who would bring the papacy to a reorganized position of world power.

Pope Leo III (795-816) gave Charlemagne the title of "Emperor over the Holy Roman Empire" in return for his papal support. This "Empire," which was really only a name, was brought to its deserved end by Napoleon in 1806.

FORGERIES—THE EPITOME OF LITERARY FRAUD

Pope Nicholas I was the first Pope to put a king's crown on his head. In promoting his claim to universal legitimacy and authority in Catholicism with the Pope as "head of all": "...he used with great effect the 'PSEUDO-ISIDORIAN DECRETALS,' a book that appeared about 857, containing documents that purported to be Letters and Decrees of Bishops and Councils of the 2nd and 3rd centuries, all tending to exalt the power of the Pope. They were Deliberate Forgeries and....Nicolas...Lied in stating that they had been kept in the archives of the Roman Church from ancient times....they served their purpose....'The Papacy, which was the Growth of Several Centuries, was made to appear as something Complete and Unchangeable from the very Beginning.' 'The object was to Ante-Date by Five Centuries the Pope's Temporal Power.' 'The Most Colossal Literary Fraud in History.' "[26]

***

[25] [ ] mine.

[26] All previous unreferenced quotes from Henry H. Halley, *Halley's Bible Handbook*, pp. 768-773.

CATHOLICISM'S CLEAVAGE

The schism of Catholicism into Western and Eastern (Greek Orthodox) organizational spheres occurred in the year 869, due to Nicolas meddling and interfering with the Eastern Catholics. Nicolas "excommunicated" the "Patriarch" of Constantinople. This "Patriarch," Photius, excommunicated Nicolas (laughable, isn't it?). This led to a complete split by the year 1054.

When the empire was divided in 395, there began a bitter struggle for supreme power between the "Popes" of Western Rome and the "Patriarchs" of Constantinople in the East. After 869, their "Ecumenical Councils" were held separately, while the Popes continued their claim to be "Lord of all Catholicism." The East avowed separation. From the point of separation, history witnesses the differences between these two massive organizational groups.

To this date, any difference in dogma or practice began with this series of schisms leading up to their complete separation. For example, Greek priests must be married to be ordained "Priests." A Catholic must be unmarried. This explains why there are Western and Eastern (Greek) Catholics in existence today.

A GREEK TRIES TO TAKE CREDIT FOR WHAT WE OWE THE JEW, THOUGH TODAY, MOST ARE QUITE BASHFUL ABOUT BEING RESPONSIBLE FOR THE MESSIAH

In the "Greek Orthodox Church," there is much ceremony similar to Catholicism, which has its roots not in Hebraic tradition, but rather in heathenism. While reading the book, *Understanding the Greek Orthodox Church*, by Demetrios J. Constantelos, we were dismayed by the incredibly arrogant statement which read: "...Christianity became an ecumenical religion. As T. R. Glover has put it: 'The chief contribution of the Greek was his demand for this very thing—that Christianity must be universal...the Greek really secured the triumph of Jesus....' "[27]

Jesus in no way owes His triumph to the Greeks. He was a Jew and still is. It is the Jew who is responsible for the triumph of Jesus, His parents and lineage, and the entire scheme of Jewish prophecy in the Old Testament, which proclaimed the many hundreds of prophecies of the Messiah centuries before His birth. These prophecies were fulfilled later in Jesus' life!

---

[27]Demetrios J. Constantelos, *Understanding the Greek Orthodox Church: Its Faith, History and Practice*. New York: The Seabury Press, © 1982, p. 80, used by permission.

Jesus is a Jew who claimed to be the Jewish Messiah (John 4:25-26). The very word "Messiah" is anglicized Hebrew from which Christ (anglicized Greek for *Christos*) emerged in our present English New Testament.

Constantelos, in his section entitled "The Ancient Church," goes on to claim: "The New Testament books themselves...were written in Greek....Christianity is Greek...."[28]

It is interesting to note that, in reality, at least the first three Gospels of the New Testament were clearly written in Hebrew and later translated into Greek. This is obvious from various Hebrew idioms found in the New Testament which do not make sense in Greek or any other language. For example, in Luke 9:51 it says He "set His face to go to Jerusalem" (NASB). This is not a Greek or English idiom, but in Hebrew, even today, this is how you say, "He turned to go to Jerusalem" in proper Hebrew.[29] See our appendix 1, "It's All

---

[28]Ibid, p. 81.

[29]David Bivin and Roy Blizzard, Jr., rightly expound: "The idiom used in Luke 9:51 is also a Hebrew 'face' idiom. To 'set one's face' simply means to 'turn in the direction of.' This idiom appears several times in the Old Testament (II Kings 12:17; Daniel 11:17; Genesis 31:21). Just like the verb 'turn' in English, 'set one's face' can be followed by 'to' in the sense of 'toward' or by 'to' plus an infinitive (i.e., 'to go,' 'to come,' to attack,' etc.) as in Luke 9:51. Apparently, none of our English translators recognized this Hebrew idiom in Luke 9:51. Most translations, even some of the most recent, have retained the word 'face,' and thus unwittingly transmitted a Hebraism. A few translators attempted to give a more English flavor: 'He resolutely set out' (New International Version); 'He resolutely took the road' (Jerusalem Bible); 'He proceeded with fixed purpose' (Weymouth); 'He moved steadily onward with an iron will' (Living Bible). This unnecessary emphasis on resoluteness eventually resulted in the translation, 'As the days drew near when Jesus would be taken up to heaven, *he made up his mind*...and set out on his way to Jerusalem' (Good News For Modern Man). From this last translation one might get the impression that Jesus, after much soul searching, at last decided to go through with his crucifixion—as if, until then, he had not been able to make up his mind. The way translators have translated Luke 9:51 illustrates what happens when a translator of the Gospels is solely dependent on the Greek text and makes no effort to recover the Hebrew behind the Greek: his translation gets clogged with literalisms such as 'face.' In the case of Luke 9:51, many translators were further misled by the verb of the idiom. Greek has several words for 'set.' Because the 'set' found in the Greek of Luke 9:51 carries 'fix' or 'establish' as its particular shade of meaning, translators began to insert the idea of *fixed* purpose. The Hebrew idiom, however, does not connote resoluteness or firmness of purpose. How then should Luke 9:51 be translated? Literally, the text reads: 'And when the days of his ascension were fulfilled, and he put his face to go to Jerusalem.' This is good Hebrew, but scarcely Greek or English. An accurate English translation would be: 'When the time came for him to be taken up to heaven, he headed for Jerusalem.' In other words, when the time came, Jesus went. This verse is simple narration, a description of events. It should not be made to imply that Jesus, after an inner struggle, finally found the courage to go to Jerusalem." David Bivin and Roy Blizzard, Jr., *Understanding the Difficult Words of Jesus: New Insights From a Hebraic*

Hebrew to Me." It will give you conclusive evidence that the original language of Jesus was Hebrew!

This modern Greek Orthodox writer also claims "Christianity is Greek." Don't we all wish we could give him the book, *Christianity is Jewish*, by Edith Schaeffer, or quote the words of Jesus to him, "salvation is of the Jews" (John 4:22 KJV)? He also asserts that "Greek missionaries carried the Christian message." However, we can be sure that they were not Greek "Orthodox"[30] but clearly evangelical.

It seems obvious that Roman Catholicism, Greek Orthodoxy (which split from Rome), the Mormons and many other cults and religions would like to lay claim to the original church in order to authenticate the traditions and dogmas of their particular group. This, above all, proves that those of us who follow the New Testament and its teachings *are* the true believers. Jesus said: "Ye shall know them by their fruits" (Matt. 7:16 KJV).

THE TRUE NEW TESTAMENT BELIEVER IS IDENTIFIED BECAUSE HE PUTS HIS MONEY WHERE HIS MOUTH IS! REMEMBER, JESUS SAID TALK IS CHEAP

Who saved the Jews from the Holocaust? Who is laboring to tell them Jesus is the Messiah out of love for their eternal future, as Jesus commanded? (Acts 1:8). Who has been supporting Israel? It is certainly not the Greek Orthodox, whom we have never seen evangelizing (telling the good news of Jesus to unbelievers). Is it any wonder? It is not part of their belief to evangelize, even though Jesus told us to do so in the New Testament.

The Baptists, the Church of God and various other evangelical New Testament believers are doing all of this, following the epistles of Paul and the words of Jesus. Thus, since they are using the Bible as their guide, we can see from their actions that they are authentic, as they follow the loving words of Jesus.

We want all of our friends to be in the Messianic Kingdom of Jesus when He returns. That is why we, as true believers, tell our friends and spread the message to invite Jesus into your heart (Rev. 3:20).[31] We have had Greek, Anglican, Catholic, and Episcopalian

---

Perspective. Austin, TX: Center for Judaic-Christian Studies, © 1983, 1984, pp. 165-167, used by permission.

[30]Robert A. Baker notes: "It was Cyprian, then, who corrupted the New Testament pattern of authority. Instead of the local church, the territorial bishop became the final word of authority. The universal (Catholic) church rested upon the sole sovereignty of the bishops as successors of the apostles. Local churches lost every vestige of authority. The fourth type of Christian literature—*systematic* development of doctrine—does not concern Episcopal development. In the New Testament the pattern of worship consisted

officials and priests alike criticize us for talking with Jews and others about believing in Jesus.

ESTABLISHED LITURGICAL OFFICIALS ARE NOT ANXIOUS TO GIVE JESUS BACK TO OUR JEWISH BRETHREN

An example of ecumenical indifference to following through and telling the Jews about Jesus can be seen in the recent article entitled, "Ads For Jesus Who's Right the Bishop of Oxford or the American Based Organisation Jews for Jesus? Asks Steve Parish." Steve Parish replies: "Now the brazen approach of *Jews for Jesus* is plainly not everybody's cup of tea. To everything a season: maybe St Peter could get away with telling the whole house of Israel that 'this Jesus you crucified has been made both Lord and Christ'....His [Bishop of Oxford] response to the advert is not to bemoan the lack of sensitivity, or its transatlantic hype, but to support Judaism in its own right and to discourage Jews from abandoning their historic faith to turn to Christianity. Christian organisations working amongst Jews should, he reckons, encourage Jews—especially those from 'agnostic or non-observant homes'—to explore with a Rabbi the depth of Judaism. This is, he says, 'surely basic to Christian integrity'....But it seems very strange for a Christian bishop to discourage anyone from becoming a Christian. Imagine the pearly gates, when Bishop Harries meets St. Peter, who persuaded 3000 Jews to turn to Christ in his first sermon.

---

principally of singing, Scriptures, prayer, and preaching. The service required no altar or ritual, for God was recognized as spirit and could be reached through spirit. But a change had occurred by 325. The idea that the sacraments were magical brought a change to the nature of worship. Instead of magnifying his prophetic or preaching ministry, the local presbyter began to function as a priest. In fact, after the fourth century the very name 'presbyter' began to drop out, and the title of this office became 'priest.' This development could be expected when the sacraments became magical; it required a priestly qualification to administer this sort of rite. Consequently, the center of worship became the observance of the Lord's Supper...." Robert A. Baker, *A Summary of Christian History*, Nashville: Broadman Press, © 1959, 1987, p. 48, used by permission. The true church was never a Greek Orthodox cathedral or Roman Catholic building, but according to the New Testament, always was and is, a group of believers who truly believe in Jesus and fellowship together. To this our New Testament testifies: "The churches of Asia |greet| you, Aquila and Priscilla |greet| you much in the Lord, with the church that is in their house" (I Cor. 16:19 KJV; *The New Scofield Reference Bible*. See also Rom. 16:6; Col. 4:15; Philemon 2). Paul's New Testament letter to the Ephesians (Greeks who lived in Ephesis, Greece) clearly said Jesus was the head of the church! This leaves out the Greek Orthodox Bishop or Patriarch and the Roman Pope.

[31] " 'Behold, I stand at the door, and knock: if any man hear my voice, and open the door, I will come in to him, and will sup with him, and he with me' " (Rev. 3:20 KJV).

'Well, Peter, I think you should have first sent them all off to have a chat with their Rabbi...' "[32]

A MAN WHO THINKS HE IS A CHRISTIAN VENTS HIS HATRED ON JEWS AND OTHER BELIEVERS WHO SHARE JESUS WITH THE HEBREWS

This same hypocrisy is echoed by the "Reverend" Dave Selzer, who, in a newspaper article entitled, "Jews for Jesus Perpetuate Myth," made this unbiblical claim: "I know each Jew is complete in and of her/himself, and does not need Christianity or another religion to be 'saved'. I know that to perpetuate this myth upon Jews is to continue the practice of persecution and to deny the realities of the Holocaust and of G-d working through the Chosen People of Israel even to this day....Jews for Jesus is another attempt to deny Jewish identity to Jews and another in a long series of persecutions by Christians of Jews. As a Christian I oppose the group and any other identifying themselves as 'completed' or 'Messianic' or 'Christian' Jew, and I urge others to do so as well."[33]

While the chaplain claims he is a Christian—"as a Christian I oppose"—we, as true believers in the Scriptures, note that if he holds this view, he cannot be a Christian. The heart of the New Testament teaches that the Gospel of Jesus as the Messiah is to be taken as good news to all the world, and especially to the Jews. As a matter of fact, it says, "to the Jew first." Jesus presented His message to the most religious Jews of His day. Only later did the Greeks begin to express interest.

To oppose the preaching of the Gospel to the Jews is to slap Jesus in the face, and is a lie right out of the pit of Hell. Nevertheless, we ask that you pray for the chaplain, that he may come to the light of the New Testament, so that one day he will truly be a New Testament chaplain. Remember, Jesus said to pray for your enemies. Anyone who denounces Jesus' message of love to His people, the Jews, is a definite enemy. Remember, Jesus said, "He that is not with me is against me...." (Matt. 12:30 KJV).

***

[32]Steve Parish, "Ads For Jesus Who's Right the Bishop of Oxford or the American Based Organisation Jews for Jesus? Asks Steve Parish." *CWN Series*, Jan. 30, 1989. [ ] mine.

[33]Dave Selzer, "Jews for Jesus Perpetuate Myth," *Minnesota Daily*, Tues., May 8, 1990, reprinted by permission.

A MISSIONARY FRIEND JAILED

My friend, Mike Bentley, an Evangelical Baptist, was once jailed in Greece for passing out pamphlets which detailed New Testament verses describing how to receive Jesus as Savior, in Greek. When his release was secured (it was not easy but Michael had a "friend," a Christian, who had a "friend"...), he told the Greek police, "It was only Christian literature." They told him, "Don't ever do that again." Apparently, the Orthodox fear[34] the real Jesus of the New Testament; otherwise, such anti-missionary laws would not exist.[35]

Michael's high-ranking friend told him, "If I had not insisted, they would have thrown the key away and no one would have ever known what had happened to you." So much for the Greek Orthodox "monopoly" on what is Christian. It speaks for itself. In our opinion, it is a head philosophy of investigation and ceremony, rather than a secure faith of the heart based on Jesus and the New Testament!

***

---

[34]The Greek fear of the real Jesus of the New Testament is deeply rooted. The New Testament affirms salvation in Jesus with no connection to a "church" or priesthood, etc. The Greek Orthodox, like the Catholic, maintains a priesthood. The Greek priest has a robe with bells along the bottom, complete with a Holy of Holies (which was the most sacred place of the Jewish Temple in Jerusalem, where the Jewish priests offered sacrifice on the Day of Atonement) built into his church building, wherever his "church" may be. Thus, what the Jews dare not do (because there is no Temple), the Greek "High Priest" does, by entering a "Holy of Holies." In the true church, according to the New Testament, there can be no place for a priest or a Holies of Holies sacred chamber in true Christian terms. Born-again believers realize this because the New Testament book of Hebrews (5:7-10) tells us so. Thus, according to the New Testament, the Greek "priest" is committing sacrilege by the very act of wearing such garments, because this was an office of sacred duty to God ordained for Israel to practice until the Messiah came. God appointed Jesus to fulfill this duty and office for all of us, once and for all (Heb 9:12). As the New Testament book of Hebrews teaches, to continue to carry out this function is to ignore God's honor, sacrifice and the priesthood of Jesus. It is completely contrary to New Testament instruction. No matter what kind of fanciful explanation the Orthodox may attempt to offer, Hebrews 5:7-10 testifies that the very acts of priesthood are fulfilled. A Greek priest is a sacrilege.

[35]It is our understanding that recently missionaries are being permitted to evangelize. The laws may have been reversed under the pressure of world opinion. However, in 1993, Greek officials were still trying to get Paul Crouch's evangelical Trinity Broadcasting Network banned from Greek television. Why? Something is wrong if the Greek Orthodox will not love and welcome Greek Christians. How can they claim to have Jesus' love?

"Constantine....In the course of his wars with competitors, to establish himself on the throne, on the eve of the battle of Milvain Bridge, just outside Rome (October 27, A.D. 312) [said], he saw in the sky, just above the setting sun, a vision of the Cross, and above it the words, 'In This Sign Conquer.' "[36]

Henry H. Halley

---

[36] Henry H. Halley, *Halley's Bible Handbook*, p. 759. [ ] mine.

"The 200 years between Nicolas I and Gregory VII is called by historians the midnight of the dark ages. Bribery, Corruption, Immorality and Bloodshed, make it just about the Blackest Chapter...."[37] Henry H. Halley

THE DARKEST OF THE DARK— THE CRIMES OF THE POPES PART II

All of these things happened while true Christians were **underground**, hiding, in fear for their lives. If you were not considered part of Catholicism, you were a "heretic" (someone against the "church"). Being a heretic, which true believers in Jesus were considered, practically guaranteed death, following brutal torture by the Catholic establishment.

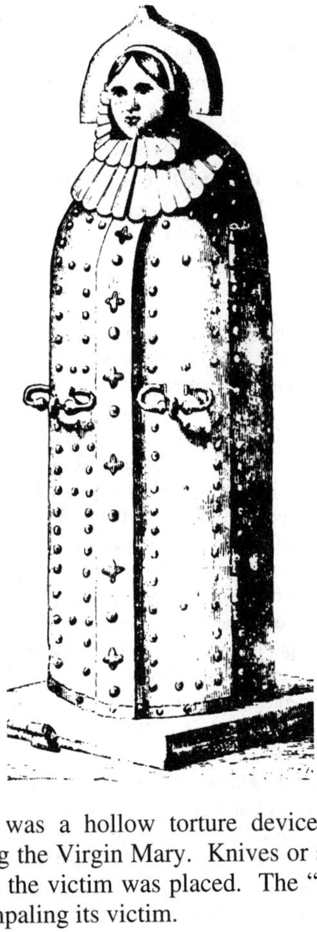

An "iron maiden" was a hollow torture device in the shape of a woman, representing the Virgin Mary. Knives or spikes were attached to the inside, where the victim was placed. The "maiden" would then be closed slowly, impaling its victim.

[37]Ibid, p. 774.

EVIDENCE OF THE ANCIENT UNDERGROUND PRO-ISRAEL CHURCH, FROM THE OPPOSITION

I know many may raise an eyebrow over our use of the word, **underground.**[38] Therefore, I will present some incredible documentation which may startle you, if not, it will certainly enrich your understanding of true history; events which many may not want you to know about.

Regina Sharif is no friend of Christians who support Israel,[39] and thus a witness of the opposition. She provides insight into the existence of the underground and its adherants' Zionist yearnings.

Incredibly, these true Christians were forced underground due to their millennial hope of the Second Coming of the Messiah. This was contrary to the doctrine of Augustine. This man, one of the official authorities of Catholicism, reinterpreted the Second Coming millennial promise as a "spiritual state," not a real event. He did this because he felt God was "finished with Israel!" True Christians, however, realizing the relevance of the Bible's prophecies of Jesus' return and the return of the Jew to Israel, believed otherwise and were persecuted for this belief!

---

[38]Once, while I was lecturing on this, an Orthodox Jew from Israel said to me, "What do you mean underground? What a myth. Name one underground Christian." We list several pro-Zionist Christians, their movements and books in our chapter 12, "Christian Zionists Past and Present."

[39]Sharif comments: "It will also be obvious that current Western attempts to find a solution to the Palestine problem will remain futile as long as the West does not come to grips with its own inherent Zionist prejudices embedded in its past and present....It is highly unlikely that any proposed 'solution' to the problem of Palestine coming from the West will ever do justice to the Palestinian or Arab cause until the West faces up to the intrinsic nature of Zionism and frees itself from its deeply entrenched Zionist prejudices. Nothing less than a major re-orientation is required....Biblical fundamentalism, as an outgrowth of the Protestant tradition, further developed the myth of Israel's Restoration. What was posited was a supra-rational relationship between the land of Palestine and the Jewish people as the direct descendants of the ancient Biblical Hebrew tribes of Israel. It was Protestant Christian theology which established the unbroken continuity between the two, the land and the people....Viewing American support for Israel from the vantage point of the long history and tradition of non-Jewish Zionism, it is evident....that American attitudes towards the Middle East reflect not only a strong emotional pro-Israel bias, but that this bias is accompanied by an equally pervasive dislike and distrust of the Arabs." Regina Sharif, *Non-Jewish Zionism*, pp. 4, 7, 133-138. This is our reply to Sharif's ridiculous accusations: True Christians will never abandon Israel and the accusations of Arab prejudice are ridiculous. There are many missionaries sharing the gospel with truly interested Arabs. However, we will always take a strong stand against terrorism and Moslem hatred of the Jew. Despite what Sharif and others have written in anger against Christian Zionism and the love of God's people, we will stand by Israel until Jesus returns, as our New Testament book of Romans commands.

In the section entitled, "Jewish Restoration and Christian Millenarianism," from Sharif's book, *Non-Jewish Zionism*, she wrote: "One of the most definite effects of the Protestant Reformation was the emerging interest in the fulfillment of Biblical prophecies concerning the End of Time. The core of millenarianism was the belief in the Second Coming of Christ whose return would establish God's Kingdom on earth, which was to last for 1,000 years (that is, a millennium). Millenarians regarded the future of the Jewish people as an important element in the events to precede the End of Time. In fact, the literal interpretation of the apocalyptic writings in the Bible led them to conclude that the Millennium was to be heralded by the physical Restoration of the Jews as a nation (Israel) to Palestine....After Christianity [Catholicism] became the official religion of the Roman empire in AD 380....Augustine in his *City of God* seemed to have settled this problem [of millennial teachings], at least until the 16th Century. Using the allegorical methodology, Augustine interpreted the Millennium as a spiritual state....Pre-Reformation semi-sectarian minority movements expressing millenarian yearnings had to remain **underground**. They were persecuted and suppressed by the Church in Rome....It [millenarianism] continued to find followers in every period of history after the Reformation and finally culminated in 20th Century American fundamentalism which insists that the state of Israel presents the literal fulfillment of prophecy in modern history."[40]

MORE EVIDENCE—ANABAPTIST CHURCHES FROM THE DAYS OF THE APOSTLES EVADE ROME BY HIDING UNDERGROUND

Quite a piece of evidence! Our second piece of evidence brings to mind the line used by Ronald Reagan to announce his second Presidential term. "You ain't seen nothing yet!" This evidence will show, to our twentieth century eyes, that still another unbiased historical figure provides critical information about the existence of these true Christian churches.

John T. Christian shows that these churches have existed during the entire Christian era and even before the Roman Catholic Church, which many people are taught was the first and only church until the Reformation. In Christian's book, *History of the Baptists*, we read: "Robert Barclay, a Quaker, who wrote largely upon this subject...says of the Baptists: We shall afterwards show the rise of the Anabaptists took place prior to the Reformation of the Church of England, and

---

[40]Regina Sharif, *Non-Jewish Zionism*, pp. 16-17. [ ] mine.

there are also reasons for believing that on the Continent of Europe small **hidden** Christian societies, who have held many of the opinions of the Anabaptists, have **existed** from the **times of the apostles**. In the sense of the direct transmission of Divine Truth, and the true nature of spiritual religion, it seems probable that these churches have a lineage or succession more ancient than that of the Roman Church (Barclay, The Inner Life of the Societies of the Commonwealth, 11, 12. London, 1876)....Cardinal Hosius, a member of the Council of Trent, A.D. 1560, in a statement often quoted, says: If the truth of religion were to be judged by the readiness and boldness of which a man of any sect shows in suffering, then the opinion and persuasion of no sect can be truer and surer than that of the Anabaptists since there have been none for these twelve hundred years past, that have been more generally punished or that have more cheerfully and steadfastly undergone, and even offered themselves to the most cruel sorts of punishment than these people (Hosius, Letters *Apud Opera*, 112-113. *Baptist Magazine* CVIII, 278. May, 1826).

That Cardinal Hosius dated the history of the Baptists back twelve hundred years[41]...for in yet another place the Cardinal says: The Anabaptists are a pernicious sect. Of which kind the Waldensian brethren seem to have been, although some of them lately, as they testify in their apology, declare that they will no longer re-baptize, as was their former custom; nevertheless, it is certain that many of them retain their custom, and have united with the Anabaptists (Hosius, Works of the Heresæics of our Times, Bk. I. 431. Ed. 1584).

From any standpoint that this Roman Catholic testimony is viewed it is of great importance. The Roman Catholics were in active opposition to the Baptists, through the Inquisition they had been dealing with them for some centuries, they had every avenue of information, they had spared no means to inform themselves, and, consequently, were accurately conversant with the facts. These powerful testimonies to the antiquity of the Baptists are peculiarly weighty. The Baptists were no novelty to the Roman Catholics of the Reformation period."[42]

***

[41]From the year 1560, which gives us the date 360 AD, the era in which the Catholic Church consolidated itself.

[42]John T. Christian, *A History of the Baptists: Together With Some Account of Their Principles and Practices,* Vol. I. Nashville, TN: Sunday School Board of the Southern Baptist Convention, 1926, pp. 85-86.

BACK TO THE CRIMES OF THE POPES

Pope Sergius III (904-911) is reported to have had a mistress, Marozia, who "filled the papal chair with her illegitimate children." Bible scholar Henry Halley documents the fact that this era of the papacy is "called in history The Rule of the Harlots (904-963)."

Halley also tells us Anastasius was made Pope by Theodora, Marozia's mother, for reasons of passion, only to be smothered to death by Marozia. After this, Marozia made both Leo IV (928-929) and Steven VII (929-931) Pope. Finally, John XI (931-936), her very own illegitimate son, was appointed "Pope," along with her other illegitimate sons. They were Leo VII (936-939), Steven VIII (939-942), Martin III (942-946), and Agapetus II (946-955).

Pope John XII (955-963), Marozia's grandson, raped virgins, lived with his father's mistress and was killed one day by the husband of the woman with whom he was sleeping!

Pope Boniface VII (984-985) murdered Pope John XIV and lived on stolen money. "The Bishop of Orleans, referring to John XII, Leo VIII and Boniface VII, called them 'monsters of guilt, reeking in blood and filth....' "

Hildebrand, Pope Gregory VII (1073-1085), attempted to straighten out Roman Catholicism's simony problem. Simony is the purchase of church offices, such as bishop or priest, with money. At the time, Roman Catholicism owned a large share of all properties. Gregory was very upset that anyone, regardless of qualification, could purchase such offices. This caused Gregory great bitterness toward Henry IV, Emperor of Germany, who deposed Gregory. After this, Gregory deposed Henry, which caused war to follow. In the end, Gregory was driven out of Rome, calling himself "Overlord of Kings and Princes."

Popes Victor III, Urban II and Pascal II (1086-1118) kept the war going with the German Emperor. Pope Alexander III (1159-1181) renewed the war, and terrible slaughters resulted between German and papal armies. In the end, Alexander III was also driven from Rome.

INNOCENT WAS NOT SO INNOCENT, WAS HE?

Innocent III (1198-1216) was the "most powerful of all the Popes." He claimed "to be 'Vicar of Christ,' " and to be "Supreme Sovereign over the Church and the World." Innocent "claimed the right to depose Kings and Princes," and said, "All things on earth and in heaven and in hell are subject to the Vicar of Christ," i.e., himself.

It was under Innocent that transubstantiation (the belief that the symbolic bread and wine became the body and blood of Jesus) was decreed. This man confirmed auricular confession and ordered two vicious crusades. He declared papal infallibility, condemned the Magna Carta ("great charter" of English liberties; the guide used to draft the U.S. Constitution) and forbade vernacular reading of the Bible. Innocent ordered that all "heretics" (those who did not agree with his guidelines of "faith") be exterminated. Innocent instituted the Inquisition, which he called the "Holy Office." This was Catholicism's means of detecting and murdering the "heretics," who were Jews and Protestant Christians. Scholar Henry Halley says of this monstrous creature: "More Blood was Shed under his direction, and that of his immediate successors, than in any other period...except in the Papacy's effort to Crush the Reformation [Protestant Christian Reformers and their flocks which numbered in the millions][43] in the 16th and 17th centuries."

Pope Innocent ordered the massacre of the Albigenses (Protestant Christians of Albi). Later, this "Inquisition Office" would be used to effect the death of over 900,000 additional Protestants in a war that lasted thirty years, between 1540 and 1570. This was "the Pope's war for the extermination of the Waldenses [biblical Christians of France]."[44]

Our wise and astute friend, Henry Halley, asks us to: "Think of Monks and Priests, in holy garments, directing, with Heartless Cruelty and Inhuman Brutality, the work of Torturing and Burning alive Innocent Men and Women, and doing it in the Name of Christ, by the direct order of the 'Vicar of Christ.'

The Inquisition was the Most Infamous and Devilish Thing in Human History. It was devised by Popes, and used by them for 500 years, to Maintain their Power. For its record none of the subsequent line of 'Holy' and 'Infallible' Popes have ever apologized."

As Evangelical Christians of the 1990's, we too ask Roman Catholicism and its present leaders, "Where is your apology?" Though it will not bring back the millions of our brothers and sisters who are presently with the Lord, it would be only decent to render an acknowledgment and apology for Catholicism's history of crimes.

THE CRIMES OF THE POPES, PART III

Boniface VIII (1294-1303), in his "Unam Sanctam," declared salvation was not possible if you were not subject to the "Roman

43[ ] mine.
44[ ] mine.

Pontiff." Dante, who visited the Vatican while Boniface was in office, took note of his horrible corruptions along with Nicolas II and Clement V, calling the Vatican a "Sewer of Corruption."

John XXIII (1410-1415) "lived in adultery with his brother's wife," and "sold Cardinalates to children of wealthy families; and openly denied the future life."

Nicolas V (1447-1455) "authorized the King of Portugal to war on African peoples, take their property and enslave people."

Sixtus IV (1471-1484) "decreed that money would deliver souls from Purgatory," a temporary Hell that does not exist, and "was implicated in a plot to murder Lorenzo de Medici, and others who opposed his policies." Sixtus sanctioned the Spanish Inquisition—the murder and torture of innocents, the likes few have known.

Innocent VIII (1484-1492) "multiplied church offices, and sold them for vast sums of money." He appointed Thomas of Torquemada the Inquisitor General of Spain, who then brutally murdered untold numbers of Christians. Innocent ordered that all rulers deliver "heretics" (believers) to him. He also "decreed the extermination of the Waldenses, and sent an army against them."

Alexander VI (1492-1503) has been called "the most corrupt of the Renaissance Popes." He bought the papacy, appointed various new Cardinals for monetary gain, openly had many illegitimate children, whom he later appointed to high church offices, and together, they murdered anyone who stood in the way.

Leo X (1513-1521) offered ecclesiastical offices and "church" honors for sale. Creating many new offices: "He appointed Cardinals as young as 7. He was in endless negotiations with kings and princes, jockeying for secular power...." Leo supported Unam Sanctam, whereby it is claimed that if you are not Roman Catholic, you are not saved. He also sold indulgences (certificates of forgiveness) and "declared burning of heretics a divine appointment."

Pope Paul III (1534-1549) produced numerous illegitimate children, considered himself an enemy of Protestants and "offered Charles V an army to exterminate them."[45]

***

[45]All previous unreferenced quotes from Henry H. Halley, *Halley's Bible Handbook*, pp. 774-780.

THE TRUE BELIEVING CHRISTIAN WHO SUPPORTED THE JEWS' RIGHT TO RETURN TO ISRAEL, IS PERSECUTED AND MURDERED

Under Pope Julius III (1550-55), Michael Servetus was burned as a Judaizer. Francis Kett, who wrote of the restoration of the Jews to Israel, was burned under Sixtus V (1585-90).

The views of Paul Felgenhauer, Holger Paulli and Anders Pederson Kempe, seemingly unknown to modern history, were concerned with support for the Jews and their right to return to Israel. Kempe, of Sweden, rightly called Rome: "...the Grandmother of all fornication...[for believing] that the Jews were forever disinherited and rejected by God...."[46]

Regina Sharif documents: "In 1655, Paul Felgenhauer (1593-1677) published his *Good News for Israel* in which he maintained that the Second Coming of Christ and the arrival of the Jewish Messiah were one and the same event. The sign that was to announce the advent of this Judaeo-Christian Messiah would be, in typical millenarian fashion, 'the permanent return of the Jews to their own country eternally bestowed upon them by God through his unqualified promise to Abraham, Isaac and Jacob'....In Denmark, Holger Paulli called upon Europe's monarchs to undertake a new crusade, this time to liberate Palestine and Jerusalem from the infidel in order to settle the original and rightful heirs, the Jews. In 1696 he submitted a most detailed plan to William III of England, appealing to the English king to re-conquer Palestine for the Jews so that they might re-establish a state of their own....In Sweden, Anders Pederson Kempe (1622-89), an ex-army officer turned theologian, was forced to leave Stockholm because of his role in the spreading of German messianism. He settled near Hamburg where in 1688 he published his own *Israel's Good News*, a violent attack[47] on traditional Christendom [Catholicism, which certainly needed straightening out at that time on its anti-Jewish stance]: 'You heathen Christians, you let yourselves be persuaded by false teachers, especially the Grandmother of all fornication, Rome, to believe that the Jews were forever disinherited and rejected by God and that you were now the rightful Christian Israel, to possess the Land of Canaan forever.' (Rengstorf and Kortzfleisch, op. cit., p. 63.)....A voluminous religious literature on the role and the destiny of the Jews spread rapidly during the 17th Century and, by its millenarian nature,

---

[46] Regina Sharif, *Non-Jewish Zionism*, p. 28. [ ] mine.

[47] We think this is not so violent as Sharif states but rather a justifiable condemnation of Catholic heretical teaching in contrast to the Bible's truth!

never fell out of vogue. Many millenarians were rebuked, persecuted and sometimes even executed for their heretical beliefs."[48]

TRUE BELIEVERS (AND THEIR DESCENDANTS)[49] WHO SAVED JEWS ARE NOT LIABLE FOR CATHOLICISM'S PERSECUTION—RABBIS SHOULD LEARN WHY!

The reason we mention all these true Christians is to show that Catholicism was not the monopoly of the time, though it tried to establish itself as one by executing "heretics." These so-called heretics were millennial Zionists who supported the Jews and their right to life, liberty and freedom, and especially their God-given sovereignty to return to their land, as the Christian Bible predicted.

So, it is important for us to realize that the Catholic "Church" not only persecuted Jews but also those who loved them and anyone who dared to differ from the doctrines of Catholicism. Thus, true Christians who love the Jewish people are not responsible in any way for their persecution in the name of Catholicism. Some gave their lives to save the Jewish people from these horrors. Today, when a rabbi tells you, "Don't talk about Jesus to the Jewish people, we've heard enough from the Crusades," you can confidently give him this book saying, "We have too, and we have saved some of you *from* the Crusades." Please, won't you hear our side, as documented by this rare list of Christian heroes of the Holocaust and Christian Zionists who saved Jews from the Spanish king and Catholic Church[50] in the Netherlands? Israel has recognized righteous Gentiles who saved Jews from the Holocaust; won't you read this documentation of the reason? If so, thank you!

THE CATHOLIC CHURCH PERSECUTES NOT ONLY THE JEWS BUT THEIR WRITINGS, TOO!

While persecuting Christians who loved Jews, the Catholic Church also persecuted Jews because they mentioned the name of Jesus in the Talmud. The following decree by Polish rabbis in 1631 illustrates this point: " 'We forbid under penalty of the great anathema the publishing of anything in new editions of the Mishnah or the

---

[48]Ibid, pp. 28-29. [ ] mine.

[49]I have heard some Christian leaders attempt to shame evangelicals for the Holocaust. We hold our heads high and now shame them for being ignorant and attempting to rewrite history. True believers were also persecuted. As we have documented, some lost their lives saving Jews. We stand beside the Jew and condemn the Catholicism of the Middle Ages, not true born-again supporters of Israel. For an in-depth history and list of true millennial Zionist Christians, see our forthcoming section on Christian Zionism!

[50]Ibid, p. 27.

Gemara which refers to Jesus of Nazareth. Should this order not be scrupulously obeyed...that will bring still greater suffering upon us than in the past.'"[51]

This shows that anyone who denies the existence of Jesus' name in the rabbinical literature is in error. This also exposes the Catholics for their lack of belief in Jesus' command to "love thy neighbor," and exposes their unwarranted persecutions. The Jewish scholar, Pinchas Lapide, documents: "In the period from the fourth to the sixteenth century no fewer than 106 popes and 92 Church councils issued anti-Jewish laws and regulations."[52]

ON THE BORN-AGAIN SIDE OF THINGS, WONDERFUL ANTICIPATIONS OF A NEW NATION, ISRAEL, WERE HELD

Just to be sure that God was not on the side of the "Church" of Rome, we note that all of their persecution did not stop the true followers of Jesus from expressing love and anticipation of a future reborn State of Israel. As the Protestant faith spread, many true believers began reviving the millennial hope that was considered heresy and punishable by death! Incredibly, in light of the rebirth of Israel in 1948, we read of the testimony of two seventeenth century scientists. Sharif notes: "Isaac Newton in his *Observations upon the Prophecies of Daniel and the Apocalypse of St. John*, first published five years after his death, concluded that the Jews will indeed return to their homeland: 'The manner I know not. Let time be the interpreter'....Another scientist who was a strong believer in the messianic mission of the Jewish people was the chemist and discoverer of oxygen, Joseph Priestley....[he] remained convinced that Judaism and Christianity were complementary and hence conversion to Christianity would be simple. His plea to the Jews to acknowledge Jesus as the Messiah was therefore coupled with his prayer that the God of Heaven, the God of Abraham, Isaac and Jacob whom we Christians as well as you worship, may be graciously pleased to put an end to your suffering, gathering you from all nations, resettle you in your own country, the land of Canaan and make you the most illustrious...of all nations on the earth."[53]

***

[51] Pinchas Lapide, *Israelis, Jews, and Jesus*, p. 74.

[52] Ibid, p. 81.

[53] Regina Sharif, *Non-Jewish Zionism*, pp. 36-37. [ ] mine.

BACK TO THE CRIMES OF THE POPES

Urban VIII (1623-44), aided by the Jesuits, "blotted out Protestants in Bohemia." Pope Clement XI (1700-21) "declared that kings reign only with his sanction [and][54] issued a bull against Bible reading."

Pope Pius VII (1800-20) "issued a bull against Bible societies." Pope Leo XII (1821-29) condemned religious freedom, translations of the Bible, and announced that: "Everyone separated from the Roman Catholic Church...has no part in eternal life." Pope Pius VIII (1829-30) also denounced Bible societies.

Gregory XVI (1831-46) also condemned Bible societies. Pope Pius IX (1846-78) decreed the deity of Mary and the Immaculate Conception, denounced Bible societies, and "declared that Protestantism is 'No Form of the Christian Religion.' "

Pope Leo XIII (1878-1903) announced that "he holds on this earth the Place of Almighty God." He declared Protestants "enemies of the Christian name."

Pope Pius X (1903-1914) "denounced leaders of the Reformation as 'enemies of the Cross of Christ.' "

In 1928, Pope Pius XI (1922-1939) "re-affirmed the Roman Catholic Church to be the only Church of Christ, and the re-union of Christendom impossible except by submission to Rome."

The last few Popes of this century have abstained from such harsh criticism of believers, perhaps because there are presently so many of them and they cannot do anything about it. Crusades, after all, are not legal today, are they? Having lost their political power, they are in dismay.

THE EXTERMINATION OF BIBLICALLY-MINDED CHRISTIANS BY ROMAN CATHOLICISM'S HOLOCAUST

These true Christians dared to be different and Catholicism's penalty was death. Henry Halley documents the terrible mass persecution and torture when he tells us that the: "Albigenses or Carthari. In Southern France, Northern Spain and Northern Italy. Preached against the...worship of saints and images...[they] made great use of the Scriptures....By 1167 they embraced possibly a majority of the population of South France....In 1208 a crusade was ordered by Pope Innocent III; a bloody war of extermination followed; scarcely

---

[54] [ ] mine.

paralleled in history...in 1229 the Inquisition was established and within a hundred years the Albigenses were utterly rooted out."[55]

The unchallenged historical volume, *Cyclopædia of Universal History*, by John Clark Ridpath, documents: "...the religio-civil war with the Albigenses broke out in the south of France. From the year 1209 to 1218, the best portions of the kingdom were ravaged with a ferocity that would have done credit to the Mamelukes. The harmless fathers of French protestantism were made to feel how cruel a thing the sword is when backed by religious intolerance....Louis VIII., who, acting under the instigation of the Pope, renewed the war against the Albigenses....to fill up the cup of bitterness which the papal party now mixed for the heretics to drink, the Inquisition, with its Chamber of Horror, was organized to complete their extermination. Notwithstanding the fierce persecutions to which these early protestants were subjected, the name of the Albigensian sect survived to the close of the thirteenth century, and even after the beginning of the fourteenth, adherents of the party were still found, not only in Southern France, but also in secluded parts of Italy and Spain."[56]

THE WALDENSES, BIBLE BELIEVING CHRISTIANS, WERE WIPED OUT—THEY DID NOT FOLLOW THE DOCTRINES OF CATHOLICISM

History has almost forgotten that the Waldenses in southern France and northern Italy were another Protestant group of Bible believers who were persecuted, tormented and murdered during the Inquisition. Waldo, its leader, rejected Catholic Mass and Purgatory. He taught that the Bible was the sole rule for our lives.

John Wycliff, who was a teacher in Oxford, England, exposed the priesthood and opposed Popes, Cardinals, and monks. He also showed that auricular confession was unbiblical. His followers were called Lollards, and today in England, some tours detail their horrible persecution. One stop on these tours is a place called Lollard's Pit, where Lollards were thrown to their death in untold numbers.

John Huss, rector of the University of Prague, Bohemia, also dismissed Purgatory and the worship of saints, which is, of course, condemned by the New Testament. For his true faith in Jesus, and rejection of the doctrines of Catholicism, he was burned at the stake, and those of his followers, who comprised the majority of Bohemia,

---

[55]All previous unreferenced quotes from Henry H. Halley, *Halley's Bible Handbook*, pp. 781-785.

[56]John Clark Ridpath, L.L.D., *Cyclopædia of Universal History*, Vol. II—Part II/*The Modern World*. Cincinnati: The Jones Brothers Publishing Company, © 1885, p. 419.

suffered near extermination at the hands of the Pope, who ordered a crusade.

Savonarola of Florence, Italy, who was said to have "Preached, like a Hebrew prophet,"[57] was murdered by hanging and burned in the square of Florence before the time of Luther.[58]

THE PROTESTANT REFORMATION—WHAT WAS SO BAD ABOUT IT?

The Protestant Reformation was brought about by "the direct contact of the mind with the Scriptures."[59] Harnack remarked: "The Greek Church is Primitive Christianity, plus Greek and Oriental Paganism. The Roman Catholic Church is Primitive Christianity plus Greek and Roman Paganism.[60] The Protestant Church is an effort to Restore Primitive Christianity Free from All Paganism."[61]

If you are asking yourself, "What is Protestant?" and "What are we protesting against?", it all goes back to 1529 at the Diet of Spires. There, Roman Catholics ruled that Catholicism could be taught in Lutheran states, while forbidding Lutheran teachings in Catholic states. To this, the Lutheran princes made formal protest, and thus they: "...henceforth were known as 'Protestants.' The name, originally applied to Lutherans, has now come to be applied in popular use, to those protesting against Papal Usurpation—including all Evangelical Christian Bodies."[62]

It is clear from this history lesson that the body of Catholicism did not want to tolerate freedom of religion among individuals. According to the papacy, it was wrong to fight for the right to read the Bible and believe in its fundamentals. Does this sound familiar?

Presently, in U.S. courts, the ACLU and other anti-Democratic and anti-biblical[63] organizations are fighting the rights of Christians to pray and read their Bibles in school. They are challenged by the Christian organization, The American Center for Law and Justice,[64]

---

[57]Henry H. Halley, *Halley's Bible Handbook*, p. 786.

[58]Ibid, pp. 785-786.

[59]Ibid, p. 786.

[60]To better understand the pagan practices in question, see Ralph Woodrow, *Babylon Mystery Religion*, pp. 15-17.

[61]Henry H. Halley, *Halley's Bible Handbook*, p. 758.

[62]Ibid, p. 788.

[63]In our opinion.

[64]This was stated in the *Journal of the American Center for Law and Justice*, Vol. II, No. 5, October 1993, article entitled, "The ACLU's Greatest Antagonistonist," and it is! This journal mentions many of the ongoing court cases between the leftist political organizations presently battling Christians' rights to life, liberty and dignity under the

which we believe we should all support to preserve our freedom, while we still have a chance. If we allow the Bible to be removed from our national life, history could repeat itself.

WHAT HAPPENED IN HISTORY THAT WE DARE NOT REPEAT?

What happened when the Bible was taken from us in the past? How was it taken? Who took it? Obviously those who did not like it, because it afforded freedom, dignity and self-rule.

The Anabaptists were a true Bible-reading group of believers. Henry Halley beautifully expounds on our point in connection with the Anabaptists when he documents: "In the Netherlands the Reformation was received early...Anabaptists were already numerous. Between 1513 and 1531 there were issued 25 different translations of the Bible in Dutch, Flemish and French. The Netherlands were a part of the dominion of Charles V. In 1522 he established the Inquisition, and ordered all Lutheran writings to be burned. In 1525 prohibited religious meetings in which the Bible would be read. 1546 prohibited the printing or possession of the Bible, either vulgate or translation. 1535 decreed 'death by fire' for Anabaptists. Philip II (1566-98), successor to Charles V, re-issued the edicts of his father, and with Jesuit help carried on the persecution with still greater fury. By one sentence of the Inquisition the whole population was condemned to death, and under Charles V and Philip II more than 100,000 were massacred with unbelievable brutality. Some were chained to a stake near the fire and slowly roasted to death; some were thrown into dungeons, scourged, tortured on the rack, before being burned. Women were buried alive, pressed into coffins too small, trampled down with the feet of the executioner. Protestants of Netherlands, after incredible suffering, in 1609, won their independence; Holland, on the North became Protestant; Belgium, on the South, Roman Catholic. Holland was the first country to adopt public schools supported by taxation, and to legalize principles of religious toleration and freedom of the press."[65]

***

guise of "civil liberties." They claim that our faith offends the minority. Their would-be remedy was to outlaw prayer and Bible reading in public places. This excellent journal can be obtained by writing The American Center for Law and Justice, POB 64429, Virginia Beach, VA, USA 23467. We want to commend Jay Sekulow, a Jewish lawyer, who fought and won many of the cases documented in this journal. He is chief counsel for The American Center for Law and Justice and a true believer in *Yeshua* (Jesus).

[65]Henry H. Halley, *Halley's Bible Handbook*, p. 789.

John Ridpath, in his unsurpassed *Cyclopædia of Universal History*, also documents: "...Charles V...spared no effort to check and repress the religious revolution which he saw going on in the Netherlands. Against the Protestant leaders he launched one edict after another, and finally, in hope of extirpating the heresy, established the Inquisition in Flanders. Before the death of Charles, the fangs of persecution had already been fixed in Holland, and several thousand of her people had been put to death on account of their religious belief....Prince WILLIAM OF ORANGE....was amazed and horrified, while residing at the French court, to hear coolly discussed the various measures which the princes of the Catholic world were then debating for the destruction of the Protestants....letters followed from Philip ordering the Inquisition, backed by the government, to proceed with all rigor against the heretics, and declaring that though a hundred thousand lives all his own should perish, he would not hesitate in the work of upholding and reëstablishing the ancient faith in all his dominions.

Now it was, however, that William of Orange, who at this time held the office of governor of Holland and Zealand, supported by a league of others, like-minded with himself, interposed to prevent the work of the Inquisition. He declared that his countrymen should not be put to death on account of their religious opinions. For the moment the situation was critical and full of peril. Many of the Flemings and Hollanders fled. Thirty thousand of them, the best artisans and merchants in Europe, left...."[66]

THE HUGUENOTS ARE NOT! ANY IDEA WHY?

The Huguenots were a compassionate Christian people of France. They loved to read the Bible and share their faith. Many of them were Zionist, recognizing the prophecies of the Bible. They realized the Jews would return to Israel before Jesus would return, thus, the reason for their leaders' encouraging the restoration of Palestine as the Jewish national homeland for Israel. This was advocated by Isaac de La Peyrere and Philippe Gentil de Langallerie.

In the 1550's, their numbers had swollen to nearly one-half million. Henry Halley tells us: "By 1559 there were about 400,000 Protestants. They were called 'Huguenots.' Their earnest piety and pure lives were in striking contrast to the scandalous lives of the Roman clergy. In 1557 Pope Pius urged their extermination. The king issued a decree for their massacre, and ordered all loyal subjects to help in hunting them out....on the night of August 24, 1572, 70,000

[66]John Clark Ridpath, *Cyclopædia of Universal History*, pp. 679-681.

Huguenots, including most of their leaders, were Massacred. There was great rejoicing in Rome. The Pope and his College of Cardinals went, in solemn procession, to the Church of San Marco, and ordered the Te Deum to be sung in thanksgiving. The Pope struck a medal[67] in commemoration of the Massacre; and sent a Cardinal to Paris to bear the King and Queen-Mother the Congratulations of Pope and Cardinals....Following St. Bartholomew's Massacre the Huguenots united and armed for resistance; till finally, in 1598, by the Edict of Nantes, they were granted freedom of conscience and worship. Pope Clement VIII called the Toleration Edict of Nantes a 'cursed thing'; and after years of underground work by the Jesuits, the Edict was Revoked, (1685)...."[68]

THE FORGOTTEN HUGUENOT HOLOCAUST—ONE-HALF MILLION TRUE CHRISTIAN MEN, WOMEN AND CHILDREN SLAUGHTERED BY FRENCH DRAGOONS

John Ridpath further documents that when it was: "...agreed that the whole scheme of toleration, which had been devised and proclaimed in April of 1598 by Henry of Navarre as the fundamental condition of the religious peace of France, should be reversed and abrogated, to the end that Catholic absolutism might be reëstablished throughout the kingdom.

"After certain prepatory steps, such as local persecutions of the Huguenots, the shutting up of their churches in various places, and their expulsion from public offices, an edict was finally prepared for the purpose of destroying French Protestantism at a single stroke. All Protestants were ordered to abjure their religion and return to the communion of Rome under penalty of having their property confiscated and themselves put beyond the protection of the law. Nor was the measure coupled with the poor provision for voluntary exile. Instead of permitting the Huguenots to go into self-banishment in foreign lands the most stringent orders were given to prevent their escape from France. It was decreed that any who should be caught in such an attempt should be sent to the galleys. Troops of dragoons were then sent into the districts where the Huguenots lived and a persecution was organized against them which has been made perpetually infamous in history under the name of the *Dragonade*. The minister Louvois

---

67"He [the Pope] ordered the papal mint to make coins commemorating this event. The coins showed an angel with sword in one hand and a cross in the other, before whom a band of Huguenots, with horror on their faces, were fleeing. The words *Ugonot-torum Stranges 1572,* which signify 'The slaughter of the Huguenots, 1572,' appeared on the coins." Ralph Woodrow, *Babylon Mystery Religion*, p. 108. [ ] mine.

68Henry H. Halley, *Halley's Bible Handbook*, pp. 789-790.

declared the will of the king to be that the greatest rigor should be visited on those who would not adopt his religion, and that such stupid vanity on the part of the Huguenots should be pursued to the last extremity.

"The king's dragoons were accordingly ordered to quarter at will in the houses of those who refused to give up the religion in which they had been nurtured. One cruelty succeeded another. Menace was followed by imprisonment, imprisonment by isolated murders, and these by general and brutal massacres. The Huguenot peasants were hunted into the woods like wild beasts and were shot down or tortured at the caprice of their persecutors. Neither the decrepitude of old age nor the pleading weakness of infancy stirred any remorse in the breasts of the bloody butchers who went about cutting down all ages, sexes, and conditions....The regions where the Huguenot population predominated were reduced to a desolation, and it is estimated that France by her frightful barbarity to her own people lost fully half a million of her most industrious inhabitants...."[69]

Artist Jorg Breu the Elder's sixteenth century woodcut of indulgence sales.

Inquisition Torture room, by seventeenth and eighteenth century artist, Picart.

[69]John Clark Ridpath, *Cyclopædia of Universal History*, pp. 822-823.

The persecution of the Huguenots during the Inquisition.

THE JEWISH CONSEQUENCE OF THE LOSS OF PROTESTANTS AND HUGUENOTS

Concerning what befell these precious Huguenots, is it any wonder why so few true Christians were able to help the Jews in times of persecution, as the Bible commands? Every time there arose a sizable number of true believers, the Roman Catholics seem to have come in and wiped them out. As for the Huguenots' pro-Jewish stance, Regina Sharif writes: "The Protestant Netherlands, under the ruling House of Nassau-Orange, was a case in point. During the 16th and the 17th Centuries, Amsterdam was known among Europe's Jews as the new Jerusalem....In the Calvinist Netherlands, Zionist ideas were especially entrenched in popular feeling. Spanish Jews fleeing from the Inquisition had found a secure haven in the Netherlands and were welcomed as allies against the common enemy of the Spanish King and the Catholic Church....France at the time also had its share of millenarian Zionists, most notably among the Huguenots in the southern regions. Their distinguished representative was Isaac de La Peyrere (1594-1676) who wrote *Rappel des Juifs*. De la Peyrere called for the Restoration of Israel as the Jewish nation in the Holy Land, despite its unconverted state. He sent his appeal to the French monarch, but his treatise was only allowed to appear in print nearly two centuries later after Napoleon had called for the assembling of a Jewish Sanhedrim in May 1806. The author, nevertheless, remained an influential scholar. He was even appointed French ambassador to Denmark in 1644. Another Frenchman, Philippe Gentil de Langallerie (1656-1717), did not fare so well. When he presented his plan for Jewish settlement in Palestine, offering Rome to the Ottoman emperor in exchange for a Jewish Palestine, he was arrested and tried for conspiracy and high treason."[70]

After realizing what occurred in the Netherlands and similar instances of the protection of Jews by true Protestant believers in Jesus, we can better understand Rabbi Emden's beautiful words: "For if it had not been for the Christians, our remnant would surely have been destroyed, and Israel's hope would have been extinguished amidst the Gentiles, who hate us because of our faith....But God, our Lord, has caused the Christian wise men to arise, who protect us in every generation."[71]

ROMAN CATHOLICISM'S WORLDWIDE ATTACK ON PROTESTANTS

Organizational Catholicism and its armies reduced large populations of innocent people to rubble in their attempts to maintain power throughout the world. In some cases, over three-quarters of the population was destroyed by some of the most horrifying torture

[70]Regina Sharif, *Non-Jewish Zionism*, pp. 15, 27.

[71]Pinchas Lapide, *Israelis, Jews, and Jesus*, p. 105. Lapide's source was *Lechem Shamayim* (Hamburg, 1757), p. 30 ff.

imaginable. This kind of onslaught cannot be called anything less than a holocaust. Henry Halley, addressing these events, informs us: "In Bohemia, by 1600, in a population of 4,000,000, 80 per cent were Protestant. When the Hapsburgs and Jesuits had done their work, 800,000 were left, all Catholics.

In Austria and Hungary half the population Protestant, but under the Hapsburgs and Jesuits they were slaughtered.

In Poland, by the end of the 16th century, it seemed as if Romanism was about to be entirely swept away, but here, too, the Jesuits, by persecution, killed Reform.

In Italy, the Pope's own country, the Reformation was getting a real hold; but the Inquisition got busy, and hardly a trace of Protestantism was left.

In Spain the Reformation never made much headway, because the Inquisition was already there. Every effort for freedom or independent thinking was crushed with a ruthless hand. Torquemada (1420-98), a Dominican monk, arch-inquisitor, in 18 years burned 10,200 and condemned to perpetual imprisonment 97,000. Victims were usually burned alive in the public square; made the occasion of religious festivities. From 1481 to 1808 there were at least 100,000 martyrs and 1,500,000 banished. 'In the 16th and 17th centuries the Inquisition extinguished the literary life of Spain, and put the nation almost outside the circle of European civilization'....In 50 years the Reformation had swept Europe, with most of Germany, Switzerland, Netherlands, Scandinavia, England, Scotland, Bohemia, Austria, Hungary, Poland in its grasp; and making headway in France. This was a terrific blow to the Roman Church, which, in turn, organized the Counter-Reformation; and by means of the Council of Trent (in session 18 years, 1545-63)....Rome was organized for an aggressive onslaught on Protestantism; and under the brilliant and brutal leadership of the Jesuits regained much of the lost territory; South Germany, Bohemia, Austria, Hungary, Poland, Belgium, and crushed the Reformation in France. Within a hundred years, by 1689, the Counter-Reformation had spent its force. The principal Rulers who fought the Pope's Wars were: Charles V (1519-56) of Spain, against German Protestants; Philip II (1556-98), of Spain, against Holland, England; Ferdinand II (1619-37), of Austria, against Bohemians; Catherine de Medici, mother of three kings of France, Francis II (1559-60), Charles IX (1560-74), Henry III (1574-89), in the wars for the extermination of French Huguenots.

The Reformation movement was followed by a hundred years of religious war: 1. War on the German Protestants (1546-55); 2. War on the Protestants of the Netherlands (1566-1609); 3. Huguenot Wars in France (1572-98); 4. Philip's attempt against England (1588); 5.

Thirty Years War (1618-48). In these wars political and national rivalries were involved, as well as questions of property, for the Church in most countries owned one-third to one-fifth of all lands. But every one of these wars was STARTED by Roman Catholic Kings, urged on by Pope and Jesuit, for the purpose of crushing Protestantism. They were the Aggressors. The Protestants were on the Defensive. Dutch, German nor French Protestants became Political Parties till after years of persecution....The number of Martyrs under Papal Persecutions far outnumbered the Early Christian Martyrs under Pagan Rome: hundreds of thousands among the Albigenses, Waldenses, and Protestants of Germany, Netherlands, Bohemia and other countries. It is common to excuse the Popes in this matter by saying that it was the 'spirit of the age.' Whose age was it? and who made it so? The Popes. It was their world. For 1000 years they had been training the world to be in subjection to them. If the Popes had not taken the Bible from the people, the people would have known better, and it would NOT have been...."[72]

Halley further documents that the Roman Catholics martyred "untold millions"[73] of innocent people because they chose to be Protestant and follow Jesus according to the New Testament.

Persecution of the Albigenses.

[72]Henry H. Halley, *Halley's Bible Handbook*, pp. 790, 792-793.
[73]Ibid, p. 793.

Victims of The Inquisition in The Netherlands.

HARD TO BELIEVE?

Many of you who have just read our sections, "The Crimes of the Popes" and all of the documentation in our review of the brutal history of Catholicism may be saying, "This is not true!" Some contemporary Catholics may also object to the accuracy of such documentation. However, the majority of these crimes are admitted to by respected Catholic historians, in the *Catholic Encyclopedia* and elsewhere.

Ralph Woodrow, in the book, *Babylon Mystery Religion*, gives many exact footnotes from the *Catholic Encyclopedia,* which admits to many of these events. Thus, if you are a Catholic or one who finds these things difficult to believe, we suggest that you read through the *Catholic Encyclopedia* and also the New Testament for a comparison of the truth.

We write off religion in the ecumenical sense and believe that all who consider the claims of Jesus and the truth of becoming born-again, should check out Jesus' Messianic ideals, teachings and claims for themselves. The New Testament itself is the only pure source (Rev. 22:18-19), changing the lives of millions for the better! Is it any wonder why so many modern liberals attack it and why many Popes of the past forbade the reading of it?

We live in a time when the Roman Catholic Church has lost the power to force its will by "condemning Bible readings and societies," which it has done in the past. However, we still live prior to the time when liberals will make laws which will remove our rights or ban us from our New Testament sharing of the Gospel (or proselytizing, as some would call it), which will become a reality during the time of the Antichrist. Thus, we feel that we should appreciate this present freedom and give out as many readable New Testaments as possible, before it is too late!

THE POPE AND ZIONISM—WHAT WAS THE SCORE IN 1904?

The Catholic "Church" has apparently never been happy about the return of Israel to her land, as are true Christians who believe in the fulfillment of biblical prophecy.[74] Instead, they have reacted with anger, illustrating their ignorance of the Scriptures and the promises of Jesus to His true followers. For example, Pope Pius X wrote to Theodor Herzl, the father of modern Zionism: "We [the Roman Catholic establishment] are unable to favor this movement [Zionism].

---

[74]Romans 11:26; Acts 1:6; and Luke 21:24.

We cannot prevent the Jews from going to Jerusalem—but we could never sanction it. As the head of the Church I cannot answer you otherwise....if you come to Palestine and settle your people there, we will be ready....(Pope Pius X to Theodor Herzl on January 26, 1904)"[75]

The historical record shows that the Pope was not able to prevent God's prophetic plan of a Jewish return to Israel, as was so hoped for and so anticipated by true born-again Bible believing Christians. The Reverend Hechler, a true Bible believer, greatly encouraged Theodor Herzl, who wrote the following in his *Diary*: "The Reverend William Hechler, Chaplain of the English Embassy here, came to see me. A sympathetic, gentle fellow, with the long grey beard of a prophet. He is enthusiastic about my solution of the Jewish Question. He also considers my movement a 'prophetic turning point'—which he had foretold two years before....From a prophecy...."[76]

Quite a contrast to the Pope's statement, which characterizes the majority of Catholic and liberal "Christian" opinion, which says, "Israel is not prophetic and modern Zionism is not biblical."

THE CATHOLIC CHURCH DENIES ISRAEL AGAIN—THE LEAVEN OF 1987

In October of 1987, *Nightline* aired a segment in which one of the announcers pointed out: "In 1948, still another affront, the Vatican was critical of the establishment of the State of Israel in Palestine. At that time *Observatori Romano* (the official Vatican newspaper) wrote, 'Zionism is not the embodiment of Israel as it is described in the Bible,' implying that Israel did not have justification. Today, 37 years later, the Vatican and Israel still do not have full diplomatic relations."[77] In this same broadcast, a clip from *Good Morning America* was aired, showing the Catholic theologian, Daniel Maguire, Ph.D., admitting: "We [Catholics], in fact, in the late eleventh century, conducted the first holocaust in Northern France, in Germany and so forth. We were the people that first said Jews had to live in ghettos and wear special things. Anything to do with Jews, we should recognize

---

[75]Marvin Lowenthal, *The Diaries of Theodor Herzl*. New York: Dial Press, © 1956, pp. 428-429, used by permission. [ ] mine. From Esther Yolles Feldblum, *The Introduction of The American Catholic Press and The Jewish State 1917-1959*. New York: KTAV Publishing House, Inc., © 1977. I wish to thank my friend, Ron Bartour, Ph.D., for retrieving this book from the Hebrew University for me.

[76]Regina Sharif, *Non-Jewish Zionism*, p. 71.

[77]*Nightline*, ABC News. © 1987. [ ] mine. This U.S. television program documented Jewish anger as a result of the Pope's visit to Waldheim. We were also angry.

that we come into this, heavy with guilt. And Christians [Catholics][78] are not able to just sit back and say, 'Gee, it's terrible what happened in the Holocaust.' A great deal of what happened, was us."[79]

We should remark that the majority of those killed in the Middle Ages were innocent Protestants! Their crimes were believing the New Testament, refusing to follow Roman Catholic doctrine and saving Jews from the armies of the Spanish king and the Pope. We think it is very decent that a Catholic theologian admitted to this crime of Catholicism, with apparent sorrow, on national television. Though it does not bring back those who were killed, it does break the long tradition of stonewalling silence.

THE DECEMBER DECEPTION

On December 30, 1993, the Roman Catholic Vatican signed an agreement with Israel intended to establish diplomatic relations. However, we believe that the Vatican's recognition of Israel was not sincere, but rather a device to secure Rome's interests, including a say in the Palestinian question and the fate of Jerusalem. As a result of this, Chief Rabbi Shlomo Goren,[80] who constantly praised Evangelical Christians for their support of Israel, characterized a visit to the Vatican by the Chief Ashkenazi Rabbi Meir Lau as a "blasphemy beyond expression."[81]

We believe that the well-known Christian author, Hal Lindsey, is correct when he says: "...it may be because of the pending talks about the future status of Jerusalem that the Vatican chose this moment in history to bridge new relations with Israel. According to the newly signed Israel-Palestine Liberation Organization agreement, negotiations on Jerusalem are scheduled to begin within the next two years. The Vatican, you see, has a long-term vested interest in the fate of Jerusalem. Rome has always desired a role in its future....The Bible

---

[78][ ] mine. Here, we stress that we are drawing a line of differentiation between "Christians" (the Catholic establishment) and true Bible believing Christians who, many times in history and even during the Holocaust of Hitler, risked their lives to save Jews from death. There is a special museum in Israel called Yad VaShem ("the hand and name" in Hebrew), which documents the atrocities of the German Holocaust. However, in order to enter this museum, you must walk down the pathway known as "The Way of the Righteous," where hundreds of carob trees are planted in memory of the righteous Gentiles who risked their own lives to save Jews. I have been there many times.

[79]Ibid.

[80]Rabbi Goran died in 1995; God rest his soul. He was so thankful to the Christians who supported Israel. We will always remember him.

[81]Hal Lindsey, "Israel's New Closer Links to Europe," *Countdown...*, Feb. 1994. Palos Verdes, CA: Hal Lindsey Ministries, p. 7, used by permission.

prophesies a time—in the very near future—when the seat of a one-world religion and government will be Jerusalem. This could only occur, of course, with at least compliance by the world's most important religious leader—the Roman Catholic pope. This does not mean, however, that this pope—or some future one—is or will be the antichrist. It merely suggests that after the Rapture, when all true believers are taken up to be with the Lord, the false church—Catholic or Protestant—that remains on earth will very much be a part of this one-world system.

Also, the Vatican has historically promoted the notion of world government. Pope John Paul II has, according to some insiders, recognized the dangers inherent in such an idea. He has even expressed fears, say some, about the future role of his church in such a globalist system.

Interestingly, when Rabbi Lau visited the pope in September, he also attended a large interfaith meeting in Milan. The headline speaker was Mikhail Gorbachev who addressed the ecumenical gathering on the topic: 'Religion, Peace and Justice in the New World Disorder.'

'The union of politics, science, religion and ethics holds the key to the solution for the future problems of modern man,' he said. 'Only a reasonable, responsible, ethical man can open the way to a peaceful future for humanity'....Israel and Jerusalem do indeed seem to be emerging as centers of political and religious activity on the world stage—just as the Bible predicted for the last days. Diplomatic ties between the Vatican and Jerusalem is just the latest profound development.

'This will strengthen Israel's international standing without a doubt,' explained Avi Pazner, Israel's ambassador to Italy. 'It is important that we have ties with representatives of such a great religion.' "[82]

Time will tell if the treaty is sincere. We doubt it! We believe this to be a political ploy rather than a spiritual reconciliation,[83] with Israel having the most to lose. The Vatican has no business having a say over the territory of the Jewish state, which God has given to modern Israelis, does it?

***

---

[82]Ibid.

[83]*New York Times* journalist Clyde Haberman pointed out: "Beilin's Vatican counterpart at the ceremony, Monsignor Claudio Celli, did not utter the word 'reconciliation' or say anything that could remotely be construed as contrition, as some Israelis had demanded." Clyde Haberman, "Israel, Vatican Begin Diplomatic Ties: But Animosities Aren't All Buried," *Atlanta Journal and Constitution*, © Dec 31, 1993, p. A8, reprinted by permission. Reproduction does not imply endorsement.

WHAT'S THE SCORE IN 1994 THAT'S DIFFERENT THAN BEFORE?

The editor of *Parade*, Tad Szulc, was recently granted an interview with the Pope. Portions of this interview were printed in the article, "An Interview with Pope John Paul II," in the *Atlanta Journal and Constitution.* A quote from the Pope that even startled us read: " 'It must be understood that Jews, who for 2000 years were dispersed among the nations of the world, had decided to return to the land of their ancestors. This is their right.' 'And this right...is recognized even by those who look upon the nation of Israel with an unsympathetic eye.' "[84]

This sounds very different than any previous thoughts to come out of Rome thus far. However, this Pope has recently met with evangelicals and has told young people "they must have a personal experience with Jesus." That is New Testament talk at the expense of Catholic dogma.

Jack Van Impe even mentioned on his video, *Startling Revelations*, that Catholics threw dung at the Pope-mobile recently. This Pope almost seems as if he may be a true believer. However, he is old and we can see from Scripture that in the very end days, no doubt past his time unfortunately, Israel will not be treated kindly by Roman Catholicism. Thus, we can only question how the Vatican will treat the Jews after he is gone, as the Tribulation period draws ever closer.

A later portion of the article feeds our fears as it reflects the attitude still rampant within this organization, when it says: "There are Vatican conservatives who think that John Paul II has gone much too far in being a 'protector of Jews,' as the charge is whispered among some in Rome and elsewhere, and who would prefer to see their Church remain immutable in its attitudes as in bygone centuries."[85]

CONTEMPORARY PERSECUTION OF EVANGELICALS BY CATHOLICS?

Even in Mexico, which has laws protecting freedom of religion, persecution sometimes occurs. And why? Because many are becoming believers, shedding their ecumenical skin like a snake sheds its skin. Apparently, Catholic leaders and Pope John Paul II[86] were not

---

[84]Tad Szulc, "An Interview with Pope John Paul II," *Atlanta Journal and Constitution*, Apr. 3, 1994, reprinted by permission. Reproduction does not imply endorsement.

[85]Ibid.

[86]There is no contradiction in this issue and the one we previously mentioned. Here, we are speaking of an event which occurred in 1990. The previous change in attitude with

very happy about this. The *Fort Worth Star-Telegram* reported in May of 1990: "Pope John Paul II left a warning for the country's overwhelming Catholic population toward the end of his whirlwind eight-day tour of Mexico: Beware of proselytizing inroads by evangelical Protestants.

The proselytizing—particularly by independent evangelicals and Pentecostals who emphasize door-to-door evangelism...is an increasingly vexing problem for Mexico's Catholic leaders.

On Friday, the pope pleaded with converts to return to the Roman Catholic faith....Rosa Maria Davila, a volunteer crowd-control monitor, joined Catholic leaders in criticizing the Protestant attempts to woo Catholics.

'We've been invaded by a lot of sects from other parts of the world.' she said. 'They come here to break all the unity of our religion in Mexico. One thing that unites us is our Catholic faith.'

'They are making a lot of propaganda,' she said. 'All I want is for them to leave us alone and not try to convert us'....Patricia Montelongo, a Mexico City journalist, said the evangelicals lure Catholics with gifts and special treatment.

'They take them to dinner, give them clothes and other things, and then try to win them away from the Catholic faith,' she said.

During a homily to 200,000 at Villahermosa in southern Mexico, where evangelicals have made the deepest inroads, John Paul directed his remarks to those who have left the Catholic Church.

'I would like to meet with each one of you to say: Come back to the breast of your church, your mother....a more solid training in the truths of our Catholic faith so as to form a front against the solicitations of the sects and groups that try to pull you away from the true fold of the Good Pastor [Christ].'

He said no Catholics in Mexico can consider themselves exempt from an obligation to persuade those who have left the Catholic Church to return.

The population of Mexican Protestants grew from 875,000 in 1970 to 2.4 million in 1980, according to census figures.

Mexican bishops have expressed concern about growing numbers of Protestants....Catholic bishops from northwestern Mexico and California issued a pastoral letter earlier this year alerting Catholics to proselytizing efforts by non-Catholic church groups, some of them disparagingly referred to as 'sects.'

But the so-called sects also have reason to worry.

---

regard to young people and Jews was documented in 1993-1994, after an obvious change of heart!

Although Mexico's constitution guarantees religious freedom, evangelicals have faced harsh treatment and even exile, especially in the southern state of Chiapas, where Protestants have recorded the most growth.

In the community of Mitontic in Chiapas state, officials evicted more then 600 evangelical Presbyterians....Pasqual Hernandez of San Juan Chamula told a reporter that he and his family had been roused from their sleep at midnight by police and locked in a school with four other Protestant families.

Later, Hernandez said, he and 60 other men, women and children, were jailed. Police released them after Domingo Perez, a Protestant pastor who previously had been expelled, contacted a civil-rights attorney, Hernandez said....Specialists at the Center for Religious Studies in Mexico, a non-denominational research center, told *The New York Times* that they believe the 1990 census will list about 6 million Protestants in Mexico and said that by the turn of the century Roman Catholics will be a minority in some Mexican states.

The Protestant growth has manifested itself especially among the Indian population near the Guatemalan border in southern Mexico. Protestants have translated the Bible into Indian tongues for the first time and found a receptive audience....Mexican church leaders, having seen the results of Protestant proselytizing in other Latin American countries, have mounted major missionary efforts recently that focus on the urban poor, peasants and Indian groups.

At least 25 million of Brazil's 150 million people have abandoned the Catholic Church, and in Peru evangelical Protestants represent a major force."[87]

THERE IS NO END TO ECUMENICAL INTOLERANCE OF TRUE EVANGELICAL CHRISTIANS

The Bible commands evangelism, but Roman Catholic and Eastern Orthodox "Christians" do not like competition. In direct defiance of the New Testament, they prefer to restrict, by law, the work of those who would spread the saving message of Jesus!

On July 25, 1993, the *Atlanta Journal and Constitution* printed two articles entitled: "Vying for the Soul of Russia: Some Sects Fear Persecution" and "New Wave of Missionaries Includes Many Americans: Are Some Americans Too Pushy About Their Beliefs?" The first article argues that the Russian Orthodox Church does not like

[87] Jim Jones, "Pope Urges Mexicans to Keep Faith," *Fort Worth Star-Telegram*, Mon., A.M., May 14, 1990, section 1, p. 6, © used by permission.

competition from evangelicals. To quote: "...fears that a new Russian law soon will fetter efforts by all foreign missionaries to spread their faith....The new flowering of diverse spirituality in Russia could be stunted under a law pushed by the Russian Orthodox Church, passed by the Russian Parliament and awaiting only the signature of President Boris Yeltsin to take effect....The deputy who sponsored the bill, the Rev. Vyacheslav Polosin,[88] said his amendments to a 1990 law stipulate 'that foreigners are denied the right to carry out missionary, publishing and advertising and propagandistic activities.' They would not be permitted to recruit new members, he said....maverick liberal Gleb Yakunin, said the restrictions constitute 'a new discriminatory law' aimed at benefiting the current administration of the Russian Orthodox Church, 'which is using...its lobby in the Supreme Soviet to muzzle all competing organizations'....The law's sponsors say it is merely aimed at calming....TV preaching by American evangelists—an expensive promotion against which the Russian Orthodox Church says it cannot compete....While Westerners and reformers want Mr. Yeltsin to oppose the restrictions, the Orthodox Church is promoting them....The Russian Orthodox Church, which claims 60 million members, is angling to reassert itself as a powerhouse of Russian society by aligning with conservative, anti-reform elements.

The Russian Orthodox Church....became the state religion through the reign of the czars.

But the church today—conservative, nationalistic and authoritarian—has been discredited in the eyes of some Russians....it weakly survived the ensuing Communist decades by often cooperating with Soviet authorities, who used the church as a cover for spying both at home and abroad, according to recently published archives." [89]

The existence of such a law in 1993 is an insult to modern freedom. It shows us who the real believers in Jesus are. As the first evangelicals were outlawed by Rome, so are their modern successors in Russia. In the article, "New Wave of Missionaries Includes Many Americans: Are Some Americans Too Pushy About Their Beliefs?", Elizabeth Kurylo informs us: "If residents of Russia and Eastern Europe feel deluged by polite people carrying Bibles, they've got a reason.

Thousands of U.S. missionaries—from Southern Baptists...to... Billy Graham...are flocking to what was once a land of official atheism,

---

[88]Russian Orthodox priest.

[89]Marcia Kunstel and Joseph Albright, "Vying for the Soul of Russia: Some Sects Fear Persecution," *Atlanta Journal and Constitution*, © July 25, 1993, pp. B1, B6, reprinted by permission. Reproduction does not imply endorsement.

spreading their gospel through good works, crusades and, of course, TV ministries.

But rather than being praised for filling a spiritual vacuum, American evangelists are being accused of 'sheep stealing' by resurgent Orthodox and Roman Catholic churches.

Since the collapse of the Berlin Wall, the number of American religious groups working in Russia and Eastern Europe has at least doubled....Among the most active are the Southern Baptists, who had nine missionaries in the region five years ago and now have close to 200.

American preachers such as...Robert Schuller...and Pat Robertson have appeared on Russian television....'I think it is unprecedented, but it may be short-lived,' said Mark Elliott, history professor and director of the Institute for East-West Christian Studies at Wheaton College in Illinois. 'Both the Catholic Church and the Orthodox Church are uncomfortable with competition.'

In Russia, Bulgaria and Albania, lawmakers are seeking to ban foreign missionaries....In Russia, the ban is strongly supported by the Russian Orthodox Church....Dr. Thangaraj [professor of religion at Emory University] supports Russian efforts to control U.S. missionary activity.

'I personally think somebody has to do something like that because people think the floodgates are open. Somebody has to kind of have a little bit of control over this influx of over-enthusiastic Christians'....One thing that American theologians [liberal false prophets, in our biblical belief] hope Eastern Europe can avoid is television evangelists and their simple solutions to complex problems."[90]

Jesus once said: "For my yoke *is* easy, and my burden is light" (Matt. 11:30 KJV). Peter has written unto us: "Casting all your care upon him; for he careth for you" (I Pet. 5:7 KJV).

Jesus has changed the lives of millions, myself included. It is interesting that these individuals who call themselves theologians find the truth so disturbing. This reminds us of the conversation between Jesus and Judas regarding the ointment: "Then took Mary a pound of ointment of spikenard, very costly, and anointed the feet of Jesus, and wiped his feet with her hair: and the house was filled with odour of the ointment. Then saith one of his disciples, Judas Iscariot, Simon's *son*, which should betray him, Why was not this ointment sold for three

---

[90]Elizabeth Kurylo, "New Wave of Missionaries Includes Many Americans: Are Americans Too Pushy About Their Beliefs?", *Atlanta Journal and Constitution*, © July 25, 1993, pp. B1, B6, reprinted by permission. Reproduction does not imply endorsement. [ ] mine.

hundred pence, and given to the poor? This he said, not that he cared for the poor; but because he was a thief, and had the bag, and bare what was put therein. Then said Jesus, 'Let her alone: against the day of my burying hath she kept this. For the poor always ye have with you; but me ye have not always' " (John 12:3-8 KJV).

We ask, "Will the liberal theologians ever leave the true Christian alone?" We doubt it! Why? Because, as Jesus forewarned: "Beware of false prophets, which come to you in sheep's clothing, but inwardly they are ravening wolves" (Matt. 7:15 KJV).

The stench of intolerance, censorship and outright Christian persecution is evident in these articles. However, this does not lessen our loving obligation to help the innocent Russian people, despite what their religious leaders are attempting to do to them.

Maybe you could send a copy of this book to some of the main Eastern Orthodox priests in Russia. It is not impossible that a few of them will find the true Jesus mentioned herein. Write a letter of love and personal testimony and send it with a copy of this book and the New Testament in Russian. We can still make a difference before the Antichrist comes.

A PRIEST BECOMES A BELIEVER

Even now, in an era in which Roman Catholicism has undergone a good deal of reform and become more benevolent, it still does not satisfy the inner spiritual needs of man. Only Jesus, as He promised, can do this! These two points can clearly be seen in the testimony of one of Catholicism's greater contemporary personalities, Carlo Fumagalli, former Roman Catholic priest and professor.

Fumagalli testifies of his life, before he was born-again: "I was born in Italy, north of Milano, in 1934. When nine years old, I entered the Seminary of Milano. After five years I joined a missionary society, the Consolata Fathers....The Consolata Society *motto* was taken from Isaiah 66:19: 'They will declare my glory among the nations', but rather than being spoken of the Lord, it was applied to Mary....A document that was heavily pounded in our minds was '*blind obedience to superiors*,' written by the Jesuits' founder, Ignatius of Loyola....in 1961, I took my final step, and I was ordained a Roman Catholic Priest.

My first assignment was to teach in a Consolata Seminary....After five years of teaching and hard work, to the surprise of all (mine too), I was appointed spiritual director of the whole seminary....I was assigned to begin a Theological College in London, England....I barely started classes when I had to fly back to Italy. My brother Vittorio, also a Consolata priest with a Ph.D. from a Roman

University, had died in a car accident. After the funeral, I had a chance to read through his personal diary. It was a very sad account, often in poetry, of an unhappy, frustrated and sour life, stemming mainly from lack of appreciation and warmth within the society. The wish that often surfaced in his diary was to be able to love a woman. This, however, was denied by the church law and by the vow of celibacy. My brother's diary touched the depth of my soul and opened my eyes to the tyranny of a system which was primarily using and manipulating people and their lives by *denying the divine right to marry*. (*See 1 Timothy 4:1-4*).

Coming back to Buffalo, I plunged into the study of cultures, societies, archaeology and evolution. In four years, I earned two degrees at the University of Buffalo, a B.A. and a M.A. in Anthropology, while still functioning as a priest. Although I had some questions about certain areas and tenets of evolution, I found no basic conflict between Catholic doctrine and evolution. Pius the XII (1939-1958), in his encyclical '*Humani Generis.*' August 1950, explicitly accepted the idea that the human body could have developed from previous living matter. I know now that such position is in open conflict with the teaching of the Bible (*Genesis 2:7*). I soon started to question a lot of things, doctrine and practice of the Catholic Church for which I had no answer....By September 1977, I had my Ph.D. in Anthropology, and by December of the same year I obtained full dispensation of priestly duties from Rome. All along, I kept searching mainly in the areas of the occult and oriental religions. But there was *much emptiness* in my soul, and *hunger and thirst* that nothing could satisfy.

In early March 1979, I bought a book in downtown Buffalo, *The Late Great Planet Earth*, by Hal Lindsey. I had no idea what the book was about. As usual, I started to read the book very critically and skeptically. But after a few chapters I stopped. I had never read anything like that in my life before. Here were *several prophecies* that, written some 2500-2600 years ago, were *coming to pass under my very eyes.* I knew from all the years of college that not even the best scientist with the most sophisticated equipment can predict with accuracy what may happen the following day. Therefore, I had to conclude that the *Bible has to be true*, and *it can only come from God.* At that very moment, still sitting at my desk, *I was convicted of my sins.* I strongly felt that I was a sinner, and I had no chances in making it on my own. But I clearly perceived that *Jesus Christ had died for me on Calgary, and the only way to be saved was to ask Him to forgive my sins and to come into my heart and be my Lord and Savior.* And so I did. At that very moment I started to weep, and I felt the sovereign and divine power of Jesus cleansing and purging me from all my sins, filth, heaviness and guilt. In that very moment, *I was born again of the incorruptible seed of the Word of God.* (1 Peter 1:23)

I found myself trying different churches, mostly Full Gospel, while fellowshipping in various *home prayer groups and Bible studies.* I *witnessed* about Jesus, salvation, and the Bible to *all my Catholic friends and relatives,* but most of them did not want to hear about it....Catholic traditions and doctrines are placed above the Word of God....The Church of Rome teaches that every mass is the repetition of the sacrifice of the cross and the renovation of Jesus' death for the sins of the world. If anybody was made to believe that the Second Vatican Council has dramatically changed things and done away with such blasphemy, a fresh quotation will clear away any doubt. *The Documents of the Vatican II*, by Walter M. Abbott, S.J., pg. 154, say: 'At the Last Supper, on the night He was betrayed, *our Savior instituted the Eucharistic Sacrifice of His Body and Blood.* He did this *in order to perpetuate the sacrifice of the Cross* throughout the centuries until He should come again.' The Bible, however, teaches a very different story. Jesus Himself, on the cross, before giving up His spirit, said: '*It is finished*' (*See John 19:30*). And again, in *Hebrews 9:12*, 'Through his own blood He (Jesus) entered the holy place *once and for all*, having obtained redemption.' *Hebrews 7:27*: 'Who (Jesus) does not need daily, like those high priests, to offer up sacrifices...because *this He did once for all* when He offered up Himself.' *Hebrews 10:12*: 'He (Jesus), having offered *one sacrifice for sins for all times,* sat down at the right hand of God.' *Hebrews 10:18*: 'Now.....there is *no longer any offering for sin.*' Scripture teaches explicitly that Jesus offered up Himself for sins of all times once for all, and that now He sits at the right hand of the Father in glory. He will come again in power and glory, this time, to rule as a King. (*Revelation 19:11-16*)

The *truly born again believer* can understand why the Church of Rome has opened the door to false idolatrous beliefs and practices such as: devotion to Mary, prayer to saints, cults to relics, purgatory, praying for the dead, indulgences, sacraments, rituals and liturgies, transubstantiation, and sacrifice of the mass, and why Jesus in Catholic churches is still kept nailed to the cross. The reason behind all this is that the Catholic Church, as a system of doctrines and practices, does not really believe in the Word of God which teaches that *Jesus paid it all on the cross of Calvary,* and that *He is the only Mediator between God and men.* (*See 1 Timothy 2:5*).

I know now that no religion, no church, no denomination, no priest, no minister or pastor, no good work, no clean and moral life, and neither a total commitment to any good cause can save any body. All men, good as they may be, *need to, and must be born again.* (*See John 3:3-7*). Salvation is a free gift of God that is made available to us because of Jesus' sacrifice on the cross, where He shed His blood for us, and He paid a debt we could not pay.

The Bible clearly states (*Ephesians 2:89*), '*For by grace you have been saved through faith;* and that not of yourselves, *it is the gift of God, not as a result of works,* that no one should boast.' "[91]

STARTLING CATHOLIC REVELATION

Jack Van Impe, while offering one of his latest videotapes during a 1993 broadcast, quoted Pope John Paul II telling young people at a recent meeting, "You must have a personal experience with Christ." Dr. Van Impe's tape concerns the Pope being upset about apostasy within Catholicism. It would seem from these indications that this Pope may have recently become a true believer. If this is true, we expect that he will not be Pope much longer. We shall see. As of early 1996, he still is.

We want to emphasize that in no way do we criticize or disapprove of our Catholic charismatic brothers who have truly received Jesus into their hearts and renounced the evils of the history of the Catholic Church, including all of the terrible persecutions their ancestors have perpetrated upon Jews and true believers.

There is a growing number of Catholics who are being born-again through personally receiving Jesus. Many disassociate themselves from the church altogether, while some remain, attempting to share the true Gospel of Jesus with their Catholic friends and family. We commend this.

NEWTON AND HIS RELIGIOUS OPINIONS—REVEALING!

Isaac Newton was a true believer in Jesus. He has been classified as a Christian Zionist by many. However, he differed with many Catholic doctrines. A great deal of Newton's religious writings remain unpublished. These writings and his mostly unknown religious opinions are the subject of our next chapter—enjoy!

***

[91]Quoted from the testimony pamphlet of Carlo Fumagalli, formerly a Roman Catholic priest. Available through Gospel Sunrise, Inc., #1 King St., Dayton, VA, USA 22821.

18 VII NEW YORK HERALD TRIBUNE BOOKS, SUNDAY, JULY 12, 1936

Notes for Bibliophiles

Edited by LEONARD L. MACKALL

Newton's Manuscripts

NOT until too late for mention last week did we receive the catalogue of a most unexpected and important sale—of the main body of Sir Isaac Newton's papers—to be sold at auction by Sotheby & Co., London, at 1 o'clock on Monday and Tuesday, July 13 and 14.

Some seven years ago, when a large and particularly important part (858 volumes in all, not included in the sale at Thame in 1920) of Newton's Library was discovered, and offered for sale by Messrs. Henry Sotheran, London, we gave a brief account of its history and scope (Books, September 8, October 6, 1919).

Newton's manuscripts, on his death in 1727 (he was born in 1642), passed (in accordance with an arrangement detailed in the documents in lot 178 in the present sale) into the keeping of John Conduitt, who had married Catherine Barton, Newton's niece. From him they descended to his daughter, the first Viscountess Lymington, mother of the second Earl of Portsmouth, and the collection remained intact in the Portsmouth family until 1872, when the then Earl presented a portion of the strictly scientific papers to the University of Cambridge, where Newton had been a student and then a Fellow of Trinity College. See the "Catalogue of the Portsmouth Collection of Books and Papers, written by or belonging to Sir Isaac Newton, the scientific portion presented by the Earl of Portsmouth to the University of Cambridge" (Cambridge University Press, 1888; our copy is one of those on hand-made paper).

The Earl retained, however, all those papers dealing with Alchemy, Chronology and Theology, all those connected with Newton's thirty years at the Mint, and everything of mainly personal interest. It is this portion in its entirety which is now offered for sale, and, except for a few scattered items of minor interest, it includes all the Newton Papers which can ever come into the market—among them some three million words (a conservative estimate) of unpublished autograph manuscripts! briefly but ably described in the "Catalogue of The Newton Papers, Sold by Order of The Viscount Lymington, to whom they have been descended from Catherine Conduitt, . Viscountess Lymington, Great-Niece of Sir Isaac Newton" (4 leaves, 144 pp.; the illustrated copies have 16 Plates), of which copies may doubtless be obtained from Sotheby's American representative, Lathrop C. Harper, 8 West 40th St., New York. Our account is necessarily based on that catalogue and its excellent Foreword:—

Newton is commonly thought of simply as a mathematical physicist. Actually his pre-eminence as such was but one of the manifestations of his genius. His greatest discoveries in this particular field (the Calculus, the Law of Gravitation, and the Composition of Light) were all made before he was twenty-four. In later years mathematics became tedious to him. Alchemy and theology were apparently his two abiding interests.

The MSS. on Alchemy, forming the first section (121 lots) of the present catalogue, contain over 650,000 words in his hand—including at least six long lists of writers and books on Alchemy and Chemistry. They show him to have assimilated the whole corpus of Alchemical Literature and to have been perhaps the most learned "adept" of all time. He was also a very skillful experimenter and a great part of his thirty-five years at Cambridge was spent among retorts and furnaces in the laboratory he had built for himself. From the letter (17 Jan., 1727-8; in lot 219) of his assistant (Humphrey Newton; apparently not a relative) at some of these experiments, we learn that for many weeks in the year the furnace burnt continuously, he and Newton sitting up alternate nights to attend it. . . . "What his aim might be I was not able to penetrate into, but his Pains, his Diligence . . . made me think he aimed at something beyond ye Reach of humane Art and Industry." . . . And so he did, for he had set himself to discover the Elixir of Life, and how to transmute base metals into gold. See for instance lot 72 on "The Philosopher's Stone," and lot 78 on "The Three Mysterious Fires."

Newton was more than usually secretive about these romantic pursuits. Although so much of his life was thus spent in the company of Diana's Doves, chasing the Red and Green Lyons through the Twelve Gates, or elevating Mercury with the full complement of Ten Eagles, he published only one chemical paper ("De natura acidorum") and this gave no inkling of the ultimate and grandiose object of his researches. After his appointment to the Mint, of course, any open association of his name with Alchemy would have been most indiscreet. The rumor that the Master of the Mint could transmute copper farthings into bright golden guineas would have spread panic throughout the nations. The Alchemy that Newton practiced had more than its vocabulary in common with Mysticism, and no doubt it was by way of Alchemy that Newton entered upon the Interpretation of the Prophecies (e. g. lot 228 on the Apocalypse) which form so large a part of his Theological writings, amounting to more than one-and-a-quarter million words, and mostly unpublished. It is difficult now to assess them at their proper value, but at least Newton himself regarded them as the most important of all his works, all of which he considered of value only in so far as they contributed to the knowledge of the Creator of the Universe. During his life there were rumors that his religious opinions were unorthodox. His MSS. show most definitely that they were, and for this reason they were deliberately suppressed by several orthodox divines who had the overlooking of them. Newton did not believe in the Doctrine of the Trinity as formulated by Athanasius, and this was a very serious matter in Newton's time, when Arians and Socinians were disbarred from all positions of trust, and men were frequently sent to prison for holding the very opinions held in secret by Newton himself.

Closely associated with the Theological MSS. are those on Chronology, amounting to nearly a quarter of a million words, and including some extremely interesting papers on Calendar Reform; the series covering the posthumous publication (late 1727, dated: 1728) by Conduitt of Newton's "The Chronology of Ancient Kingdoms Amended," includes (in lot 224A) a very remarkable autograph letter from Pope (10 Nov. 1927).

A most important series of nine autograph letters (1686/7; lot 137) from Halley give in detail the history of the publication in 1687 of Newton's "Principia," for which Halley alone was responsible. A whole section (lots 271-284) consists of papers relating to the Infinitesimal Calculus, and the extraordinary controversy that raged about it; many are in Newton's hand and are highly important, including the draft of his reply to Leibnitz's claim to the invention as printed on the famous "Charta Volans," 29 July, 1713, of which four copies are here, two of them printed on a single folio sheet being still unseparated. There are also notable autograph letters to Newton from Boyle (19 Aug., 1682, telling him of "Ye Apparition of a Comet . . . in ye North part of the sky at or a little after ten . . . at night"—which we suppose was "Halley's Comet"), from Locke (26 July, 1692, inclosing two Alchemical Recipes, and mentioning Boyle), and one from Pepys (21 Dec., 1693, asking for further explanations of Newton's calculations made for him of the chances involved in throwing dice).

The Mint Papers contain several hundred thousand words, and cover wider questions of Trade and Credit and Finances and Economics, besides incidentally supplying a complete documentation of the great Recoinage of 1696/9. Lot 337 is "Proposals for coyning half pence and farthings of copper for the English Plantations in America."

The Personal Papers are most important beyond any question, and include the collections formed by Conduitt for his unwritten biography of Newton, and intensely interesting original Note Books kept by Newton 1659-1661 and 1662-1669. Finally there is the famous portrait of Newton painted by Kneller in 1702; another by Kneller done in Newton's old age, and Newton's Death Mask.

Books of the Week

Continued from Page 16

Thomas Stock. Abingdon Press. Vocational and religious counsel. $1.

A PREFACE TO LIFE. By Father James. Bruce. Is life worth living? $1.50.

A DIARY OF PRIVATE PRAYER. By John Baillie. Scribners. Morning and evening prayers for the month. $1.50.

GOD TRANSCENDENT. By Karl Heim. Scribners. The quest of God. $3.50.

IT SHALL BE DONE UNTO YOU. By Lucius Humphrey. Richard R. Smith. A technique of thinking on "Creative Principle." $2.50.

THE DOCTRINE OF THE WORD OF GOD. By Karl Barth. Scribners. Prolegomena to Church Dogmatics, Vol. I, Part I. $7.50.

JUVENILE

TALES OF TROY AND GREECE. By Andrew Lang. Longmans, Green. Classical stories. $2.

A DAY AT SCHOOL. By Agnes McCready. Photographs by Ruth A. Nichols. Dutton. Authentic story of a real first grade. $1.

ELEPHANT TWINS. By Inez Hogan. Dutton. Sequel to the "Bear Twins." $1.

LITTLE ME: In Picture and Verse by Fanny Y. Cory. Dutton. The story of a three-year-old. $1.

THE DOLL HOUSE AT WORLD'S END. By Marjorie Knight. Illustrated by Clinton Knight. Dutton. An animated dollhouse in the attic. $1.50.

MISCELLANEOUS

FOUR HOURS A YEAR. Time, Inc. A picture-book story of "The March of Time."

STANFORD HORIZONS. By Ray Lyman Wilbur. Stanford. Academic addresses. $2.

REPORTING NEWS. By William E. Hall. Heath. Newspaper technique. $2.

A LAY VIEW OF THE PROBLEMS OF HIGHER EDUCATION. By Mark

" '...he [Newton] was much more sollicitous in his inquirys into Religion than into Natural Philosophy [science]....he had written a long explication of remarkable parts of the Old and New Testament, while his understanding was in its greatest perfection....That he would not publish these writings in his own time because they show'd that his thoughts were some times different from those which are commonly receiv'd, which would ingage him in disputes, and this was a thing which he avoided as much as possible. But now its hop'd that the worthy and ingenious Mr. Conduit will take care that they be **publish'd** that the world may see that Sr. Is: Newton was as good a Christian as he was a Mathematician and Philosopher.' "[1]

Letter from Newton's friend, John Craig, to John Conduit,
days after Newton's death, April 7, 1727

"...Newton entered upon the Interpretation of the Prophecies (e.g. lot 228 on the Apocalypse) which form so large a part of his Theological writings, amounting to more than one-and-a-quarter million words, and mostly **unpublished**....Newton himself regarded them as the most important of all his works...."[2]

"Newton's Manuscripts," Leonard L. Mackall, July 12, 1936

"When the various components of Newton's Bible scholarship are examined and evaluated, he can indeed be seen to be in the forefront of the critical scholarship...in the forefront in applying modern science to understanding the Bible, and in the forefront of those offering new historical data for interpreting prophecies....Perhaps, when his theological manuscripts have been **published**, we will be able to assess more accurately his entire theory and see his originality and his stature as a commentator on the scriptures."[3] "Newton was convinced that God had presented mankind in Scripture with certain most important clues about the future history of humanity. Newton's explorations of the problems involved in uncovering the text and discovering the true meaning of the text was carried on in private in the vast amount of unpublished manuscripts that he drafted for almost sixty years."[4]

Professor Richard H. Popkin, UCLA, 1990, 1994

11

NEWTON'S FORBIDDEN WORKS RESCUED

I will never forget that day. It was Thursday, May 23, 1991. I was at the Hebrew University in Jerusalem requesting the manuscripts of Sir Isaac Newton, the great English scientist. The librarian, for

[1]"Catalogue of The Newton Papers," p. 56. Compiled for the auction of Newton's papers by Sotheby & Co. on May 13, 1936. Spellings are John Craig's of three hundred years ago. [ ] mine.

[2]"Notes for Bibliophiles," *New York Herald Tribune Books*, July 12, 1936, p. 18.

[3]*Essays on the Context, Nature, and Influence of Isaac Newton's Theology*. Boston: Kluwer Academic Publishers, © 1990, p. 114, used by permission. James E. Force and Richard H. Popkin, editors.

[4]*The Books of Nature and Scripture*, p. viii.

some reason, could not find Newton's Yahuda manuscript 9.2 123-170 on microfilm, so they brought the original as I had ordered. The librarian, Moshe, told me, "I don't dare to change the order in this box. They are very old. Here are Newton's papers eight through fourteen—nine is here."

A LIBRARIAN'S MISPLACED EMPHASIS AND NONCHALANT SARCASM SOBERED ME!

Ephraim, the library attendant, removed number 9.2, looked at it curiously as he read and said to me, "The end of the world." He smirked, tossing the manuscript down before me and saying carelessly, "We all hope it will come soon."

The opening page of Newton's document 9.2 spoke of judgment and the end of the world. I thought to myself, he takes so lightly what the greatest of all scientists considered his most important writings. I thought, "He is missing out on a lot!" He, like others, has misplaced his values and doesn't know when or how to appreciate incredible truths—especially the treasure that lay before us.

THE REALIZATION OF NEWTON'S *SCRIPTURAL REALITY* BROUGHT ME TO TEARS AS I TOUCHED THE VERY PARCHMENT HE INSCRIBED

As I carefully picked up the forty-seven pages of ancient parchment written in Newton's own hand, with his quill, almost three hundred years ago, I walked over to the tables and cautiously sat down. As I turned first one page and then another, I was struck by the reality of what I was reading; the very commentaries and calculations on the end days, Revelations, the Hebrew prophets, the millennial kingdom and the new world to come, written by the most famous scientist ever to live in England, or anywhere else for that matter.

Tears welled up in my eyes as I realized how faithful to God and the Bible Newton was, as I read his incredible words and quotations of Scripture. I held in my hand what few have ever seen or will see and what had been unknown of the man for nearly three centuries.

I remembered my high school classmate, Clay Turner, who once quoted Newton in an attempt to disprove God—an empty attempt, without substance. If only he could see these writings I had before me. I have never felt more touched in all of my studies on Revelations and Newton as I was then. It is my hope that all those who read these words about Newton's description of the world to come (see our chapters 29 and 30), will take a piece of this unfathomable joy with them.

When the Messiah comes and sets up His kingdom on Earth, we shall see Newton[5] and all the other famous believers we read about in our history books and we will enjoy a beautiful bliss together, forever! Only then will we be able to appreciate the true happiness God has in store for all of us who trust in His wonderful promises.

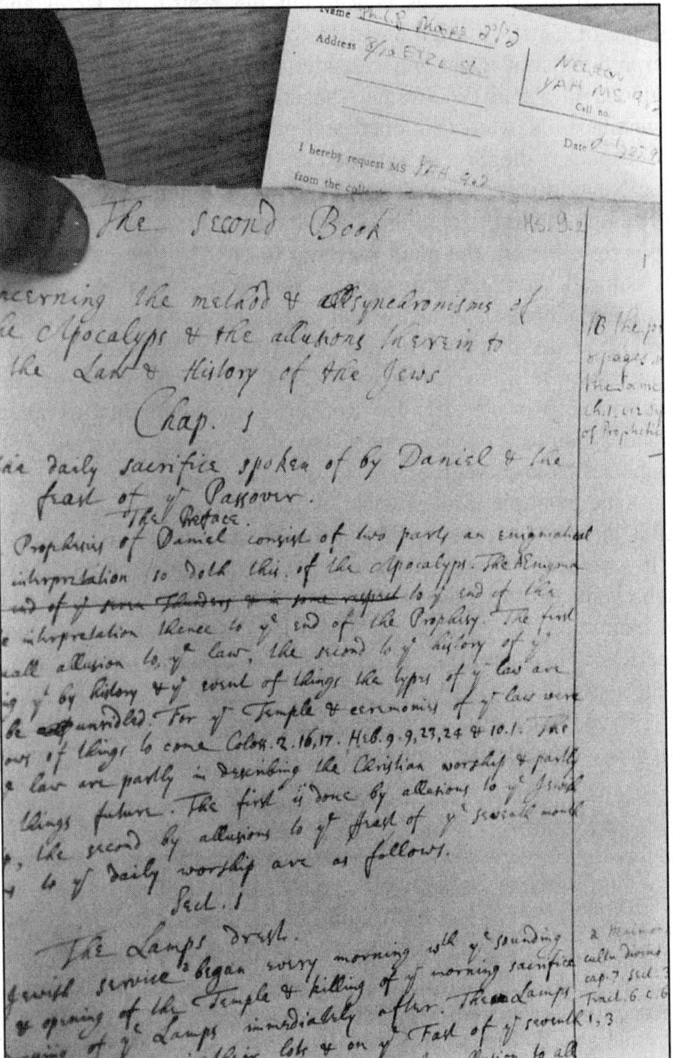

Yah. Ms. 9.2 Newton, courtesy of the Jewish National & University Library; photo by the author.

[5]He waits in his grave at Westminster Abbey cemetery in England, for the soon-coming resurrection, as his soul is with Jesus.

NEWTON ON THE CATHOLIC CHURCH VERSUS THE LITERAL *INTERPRETATION* OF PROPHECY CONCERNING ISRAEL

We are all aware that Roman Catholicism has spiritualized and allegorized the prophecies concerning the rebirth of Israel and the Coming of Christ to reign on Earth for 1000 years. These allegorical interpretations of what we consider to be a true historical event, grounded in a real time-frame,[6] began to appear around the time of Augustine.[7] Newton cautioned and gave careful guidelines to those who espouse allegory as opposed to literal biblical interpretations. Isaac Newton clearly says: "He that without better grounds then his private opinion or the opinion of any human authority whatsoever shall turn scripture from the plain meaning to an Allegory or to any other less naturall sense declares thereby that he reposes more trust in his own imaginations or in that human authority then in the Scripture and by consequence that he is no true beleever. And therefore the opinion of such men how numerous soever they be, is not to be regarded."[8] Thus we can write off the Roman Catholic claims of allegory, especially since, in past years, the literal interpretations of these prophecies have come true!

One example is the rebirth of Israel in 1948. Whether Newton said it[9] or not, it happened. Thus we don't have to take Newton's word for it—we just look at the fulfilled prophecy in modern political events. Such events disprove the past and present Catholic allegorical claims. For example, you yourself can go to Israel, walk on her ground and experience her people. Nothing could be more literal and less allegorical.

True believers were right in their interpretation of this prophecy,[10] while Catholicism and ecumenicism, which includes

---

[6]We believe within a generation, meaning one hundred years or slightly less in accordance with a timetable which puts four generations at four hundred years, as recorded in Genesis concerning Israel's previous Exodus. At most we probably have one-half century to wait. That is short when you consider past generations have already waited nearly twenty centuries, isn't it?

[7]Regina Sharif, *Non-Jewish Zionism*, p. 16.

[8]*Yahuda Manuscript 1*. Jerusalem: Hebrew University Manuscript Department, © used by permission. Spellings are Newton's.

[9]In a July 26, 1985 interview with Professor Popkin, the Hebrew newspaper, *Al Hamishmar*, quoted Newton saying that the Jews will return to Jerusalem in the twentieth century.

[10]Literally, in accordance with the apostles' question in Acts 1:6-7, where the New Testament records: "...when they had come together, they were asking Him, saying, 'Lord, is it at this time You are restoring the kingdom to **Israel**?' He said to them, 'It is not for you to know....' " (NASB). Jesus did not deny Israel or indicate any mistake, did He? Later, using the fig tree as an analogy for Israel, He spoke of our end times: " 'Now

Russian and Greek Orthodox Churches, are still wrong. For instance, they did not even anticipate[11] or hope for a new State of Israel, as the Old and New Testaments predicted in the true oracles of the Christian writings and events. Rather, the Catholic Church, through Pope Pius X, tried to halt Jewish immigration. The Pope informed Herzl in a letter: "We [Catholics] are unable to favor this movement [Zionism]. We cannot prevent the Jews from going to Jerusalem—but we could never sanction it. As the head of the Church I cannot answer you otherwise....if you come to Palestine and settle your people there, we will be ready...."[12]

NEWTON KNEW THE BIBLE BETTER THAN THE POPE—HE FORESAW ISRAEL'S RETURN CENTURIES BEFORE, WITH LOVING ANTICIPATION!

Two centuries before the Pope made this absurd statement, Newton, referring to the literal rebirth of Israel as predicted by the Bible, said: " '...since the commandment to return precedes the Messiah...it may perhaps come forth not from the Jews themselves, but from some other kingdom friendly to them, and precede their return from captivity and give occasion to it; and, lastly, that the rebuilding of Jerusalem and the waste places is predicted in Mich. vii. 11, Amos ix. 11, 14, Ezek. xxxvi. 33, 35, 36, 38, Isa. liv. 3, 11, 12, lv. 12, lxi. 4, lxv. 18, 21, 22...and thus the return from captivity and coming of the Messiah and his kingdom are described in Daniel vii, Rev. xix., Acts i., Mal. xxiv., Joel iii., Ezek., xxxvi., xxxvii., Isa., lx., lxii., lxiii., lxv., and lxvi., and many other places of Scripture. The manner I know not. Let time be the interpreter.' "[13]

Newton also noted that few Christians of his day realized the truth of the prophets' claims of Israel's return: "So then the mystery of this restitution of all things is to be found in all the Prophets: which makes me wonder with great admiration that so few Christians of our

---

learn the parable from the fig tree: when its branch has already become tender, and puts forth its leaves, you know that summer is near; even so you too, when you see all these things, recognize that He is near, *right* at the door. Truly I say to you, this generation will not pass away until all these things take place' " (Matt. 24:32-34 NASB). All of this is in accordance with the Old Testament prophecies of Ezekiel 36:24, and Isaiah 11:12: "For I will take you from the nations, gather you from all the lands, and bring you into your own land....And will assemble the banished ones of Israel, And will gather the dispersed of Judah From the four corners of the earth" (NASB).

[11]With the exception of a few individuals who were considered heretics and risked punishment for studying and interpreting the Bible.

[12]Marvin Lowenthal, *Diaries of Theodor Herzl*, pp. 428-429. First [ ] mine.

[13]Franz Kobler, "Newton on the Restoration of the Jews," *The Jewish Frontier*, © March 1943, pp. 22-23, used by permission. Kobler's source was *Yahuda Manuscript 9.2*.

age can find it there. For they understand not that the final return of the Jews captivity...."[14] Frank Manuel notes that Newton referred to the institution of the papacy as the "Whore of Babylon."[15]

NEWTON SAID, "ALL ISRAEL WILL BELIEVE IN JESUS"

Newton stated that there would be a great many unbelieving Jews who would become believers in Jesus during the same era that Israel would achieve national status, which would culminate in the entire nation of Israel (all Jews) believing in Jesus upon His Second Coming. He notes: "Hence I observe these things, first that the restauration of the Jewish nation so much spoken of by the old Prophets respects not the few Jews who were converted in the Apostles days, but the dispersed nation of the unbelieving Jews to be converted in the end when the fulness of the Gentiles shall enter, that is when the Gospel (upon the fall of Babylon) shall begin to be preached to all nations. Secondly that the prophecies of Isaiah described above by being here cited by the Apostle is limited to respect the time of the future conversion and restitution of the Jewish nation...."[16]

NEWTON HAD A PERSONAL RELATIONSHIP WITH GOD

Newton taught, as do the true born-again Evangelical Christians of today, that one can have a **personal** relationship with God through Jesus Christ. Frank Manuel comments on and quotes Newton regarding this issue: "...one of the constants of his [Newton's] religious and scientific outlook, was embodied in the argument that God is a Creator, a Master, that men have a personal relationship to...."[17]

Manuel goes on to quote Newton as follows: "...'I, Isaac Newton, the lad from Lincolnshire, have a plain religious faith based on my **personal** obedience to the Lord, and I will not be entrapped by the Leibnizian subtleties. Metaphysics wrought havoc in the early centuries of Christianity, as the history of the apostolic creed and of the church councils bear witness....' "[18]

***

---

[14]*Yahuda Manuscript 6.*

[15]Frank E. Manuel, *The Religion of Isaac Newton*, p. 95.

[16]*Yahuda Manuscript 9.2, fol. 158.*

[17]Frank E. Manuel, *The Religion of Isaac Newton*, p. 75. [ ] mine.

[18]Ibid. Manuel's source was *Yahuda Manuscript 11.3, fol. 5r.* Differences in spelling are Isaac Newton's.

Here, we can see that Isaac Newton, the "Greatest Scientist ever to live," outlines how the corruption of the true believers' church was precipitated by Roman Catholicism and metaphysics!

NEWTON DREW THE LINE BETWEEN THE FALSE AND THE TRUE CHURCHES

Newton gives further definition to the church: "...before the end of the second century corruption had slowly crept into the Latin churches, first by the addition of new articles couched in the language of Scripture, thus setting a precedent for a 'creed-making authority', and then by the introduction of metaphysical terminology nowhere to be found in Scripture. All was brought into confusion, and the drama of apostasy in the Church had begun."[19]

In Newton's writings, he clearly draws a line between the true church of believers and the false church of history. The false church, due to its corrupt leaders' wrongly contrived creeds and bizarre traditions, shows itself to be counterfeit in accordance with the words of Jesus: " 'Ye shall know them by their fruits....' " (Matt. 7:16 KJV).

Newton has also inscribed the following interesting and beautiful words concerning the prophetic Scriptures and the true church for us: "Having searched ⟨[and by the grace of God obteined⟩ after knowledg in the prophetique scriptures, I have thought my self bound to communicate it for the benefit of others....For it was revealed to Daniel that the prophecies concerning the last times should be closed up and sealed untill the time of the end: but then the wise should understand, and knowledg should be increased. Dan 12. 4, 9, 10....If they [the prophetic Scriptures] are never to be understood, to what end did God reveale them? Certainly he did it for the edification of the church; and if so, then it is as certain that the church shall at length attain to the understanding thereof. **I mean not all that call themselves Christians, but a remnant, a few** scattered persons which God hath chosen...."[20]

NEWTON SAID NOT TO DESERT THE TREASURE OF LITERAL SCRIPTURES, EVEN IF THEY CALL YOU "HOT-HEADED"

Today, many rabbis, Catholic ecumenical priests and liberal Protestant teachers attempt to disuade us from reading and interpreting

---

[19] *Yahuda Manuscript 15.5 fol. 92.*

[20] *Yahuda Manuscript 1* (as quoted from *The Religion of Isaac Newton*). < > are Manuel's indications of words that Newton crossed out as he wrote. [ ] and bold mine.

the Bible literally for ourselves! We should note that Isaac Newton encourages us, that is **you** and me, not to accept the opinion of others concerning the Bible, but to adventurously search these treasures (literal interpretation of the Scriptures) out for ourselves. In Newton's own words: "Let me therefore beg of thee not to trust to the opinion of any man concerning these things....search the scriptures thy self....if thou desirest to find the truth. Which if thou shalt at length attain thou wilt value above all other treasures....search into these Scriptures which God hath given to be a guide...and be not discouraged by the gainsaying which these things will meet with in the world.

[They will call thee it may be a ⟨hot-headed fellow⟩ a Bigot, a Fanatique, a Heretique etc: And tell thee of the uncertainty of these interpretations, and vanity of attending to them: Not considering that the prophesies concerning our Saviour's first coming were of more difficult interpretation, and yet God rejected the Jews for not attending better to them. And whither they will beleive it or not, there are greater judgments hang over the Christians for their remissness than ever the Jews yet felt. But the world loves to be deceived, they will not understand, they never consider equally, but are wholly led by prejudice, interest, the prais of men, and authority of the Church they live in: as is plain becaus all parties keep close to the Religion they have been brought up in, and yet in all parties there are wise and learned as well as fools and ignorant. There are but few that seek to understand the religion they profess, and those that study for understanding therein, do it rather for worldly ends, or that they may defend it, then...to examin whither it be true with a resolution to choose and profess that religion which in their judgment appears the truest. And as is their faith so is their practise....And when thou art convinced be not ashamed to profess the truth. For otherwise thou mayst become a stumbling block to others, and inherit the lot of those Rulers of the Jews who beleived in Christ but yet were afraid to confess him least they should be put out of the Synagogue. Wherefore when thou art convinced be not ashamed of the truth but profess it openly and indeavour to convince thy Brother also that thou mayst inherit at the resurrection the promis made in Daniel 12. 3, that they who turn many to righteousness shall shine as the starrs for ever and ever. And rejoyce if thou art counted worthy to suffer in thy reputation or any other way for the sake of the Gospel, for then great is thy reward."[21]

***

[21] Ibid. Spelling per original text.

SOME NETWORK NEWS SHOWS EQUATE FUNDAMENTALISTS WITH TERRORISTS— WHAT WOULD THEY HAVE SAID ABOUT NEWTON, HAD THEY BEEN THERE?

Newton finally gives us, as believers in Jesus, a beautiful scenario of truths about the great and loving personal God whom we serve. He wrote: "We must beleive that there is *one God*....We must beleive that he is the father of whom are all things, and that he loves his people as his children....We must beleive that he is παντοκρατωρ Lord of all things with an irresistible and boundless power and dominion....We must beleive that he is the God of the Jews who created the heaven and earth all things therein as is exprest in the ten commandments that we may thank him for our being and for all the blessings of this life....yet to us there is but one God...one Lord Jesus Christ...."[22]

THE DISCOVERY OF A FORBIDDEN LETTER OF CONCERN FOR PROTESTANTS AND JEWS

One of the major considerations pointed out by Albert Einstein and Abraham Shalom Yahuda, while urging that Newton's religious writings be released to the public, was that they were against the Catholic Church, and thus of interest to both Protestants and Jews. Newton's writings were donated at Yahuda's death to the Hebrew University in Jerusalem.

[22]*Yahuda Manuscript 15.5, fol. 46r.*

In a March 23, 1941 letter, Professor Yahuda and perhaps Einstein wrote:

> 12 Stockton Street
>
> Princeton, N.J.
>
> 23
> March 2~~1st~~.1941
>
> My dear Professor Isaacs,
>
> It is very kind of you to take so much interest in the Newton Collection. But I am afraid we shall not succeed in getting any library to but it from its own funds. It was Professor Sarton who suggested that I should approach Babson, because no other source would be avai-lable.
>
> My opinion is that some rich Jew should be interested in the collection, which is of great <u>Biblical and religious</u> interest for Protestants and Jews alike. All his treatises against the Catholic Church is still of actu-ality and they should be made public.
>
> The presentation of the collection to Harvard would be very a propos as Newton's tercentenary will soon be celebrated. Would it be difficult to get such a maecenas? Or would it be, perhaps, easier to find a group 2-3 donars ?
>
> I hardly need tell you how much I appre-ciate your cooperation in my attempt to find an adequate home for this unique collection. The owner would naturally prefer to have it disposed to Harvard than to disperse it.
>
> By the way, Sarton told me that he per-sonally is not interested in Newton's non-mathematical works, as he is a scientist and his special interest ins in Arabic medicine and mathematics. He is as little an expert in Newton's chronologie cal or religious writings as a medical man would be for Maimonides' rabbinical books.
>
> With my cordial regards,
>
> Yours very sincerely,

This unsigned letter (courtesy of Jewish National & University Library: Yah.Ms. Var.3) is obviously a combination of the writings of the two professors, Yahuda and Albert Einstein (the librarian wrote "Yah. Ms. Var. 1/42 Nathan," on the back of this document). They were living together at the time. The reference to the owner in the second person could only be a statement by Einstein in reference to Yahuda!

I make this clarification because upon my request to publish this letter, the Chairman of the Manuscript Department at the Hebrew University stated in his letter of permission that this was Yahuda's letter. However, Moshe Ron, of the Edelstein Scientific History Library, insisted and proved to my satisfaction that this was Einstein's letter after all, as I had always believed. I said, "What about Raffi?" He looked me straight in the eye and told me what he thought of him, which I will not repeat. Rafael Weiser is the Chairman of the Manuscript Department. Professor Richard Popkin of UCLA, who has done a great deal of research on these papers, also agreed with Moshe Ron's opinion after I read him this letter during a telephone call from Jerusalem to California in 1991. Here are Einstein's[23] letters from September and December 1940, expressing great interest in Newton's papers. He praises Newton and encourages that the manuscripts be made public.

Mein lieber Yahuda:

Newton's Schriften uber biblische Gegenstände scheinen mir deshalb besonders interessant, weil sie einen tiefen Einblick in die gesitige Eigenart und die Arbeitsweise dieses bedeutenden Menschen gewähren. Der göttliche Ursprung der Bibel steht für Newton unbedingt fest, welches Vertrauen in einem eigentümlichen Gegensatz steht zu der kritischen Skepsis, die seine Stellung gegenüber den Kirchen kennzeichnet. Aus diesem Vertrauen stammt die feste Ueberzeugung, dass die dunkel erscheinenden Teile der Bibel wichtige Offenbarungen enthalten mussen, zu deren Aufhellung es nur der Entziffe rung der in ihnen verwendeten symbolischen Sprache bedürfe. Diese Entzifferung, bezw. Deutung sucht Newton mittels seines scharfen systematischen Denkens unter sorgfältiger Verwendung aller ihm zur Verfügung stehenden Quellen.

Während die Entstehungsweise der die bleibende Bedeutung Newtons ausmachenden physikalischen Werke in Dunkel gehüllt bleiben muss, weil Newton seine vorbereitenden Arbeiten offenbar vernichtet hat, besitzen wir auf diesem Gebiete der Arbeiten über die Bibel Entwürfe und deren wiederholte Abänderung; diese zum grossen Teil unveröffentlichten Schriften gestatten daher einen höchst interessanten Einblick in die geistige Werkstatt dieses einzig - artigen Denkers.

gez. A. Einstein. September 1940, Lake Saranac

P.S. Ich halte es für sehr wunschbar. dass die erwähnten Schriften Newtons an einer Stelle vereinigt und dort der Forschung zuganglich gemacht werden.

Einstein's letter to Yahuda, published here for the first time.
Courtesy of The Jewish National & University Library
(Yah.Ms. Var. 3/Einstein).

[23] Einstein had more than a passing interest in Newton and his faith. One example of this, and his great reverence for Newton, is seen in the fact that he had a portrait of Newton in his bedroom, which was removed when he (Einstein) died. Roger Highfield and Paul Carter, *The Private Lives of Albert Einstein*, p. 273.

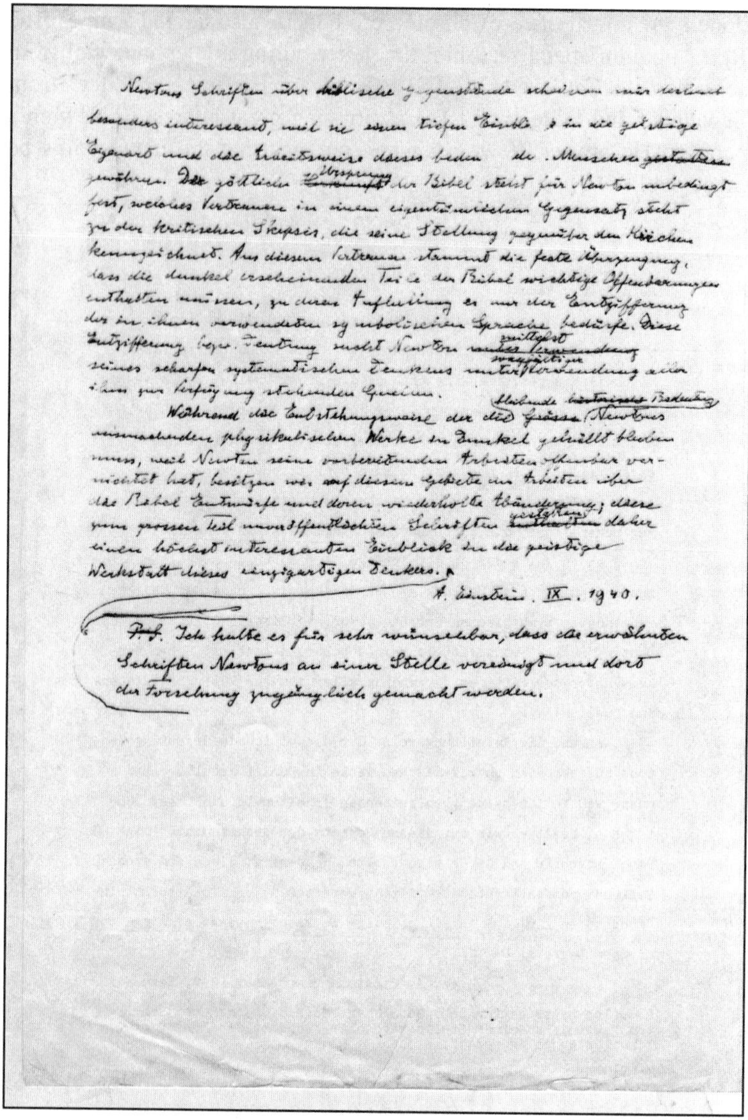

Newtons Schriften über biblische Gegenstände scheinen mir deshalb besonders interessant, weil sie einen tiefen Einblick in die geistige Eigenart und die Arbeitsweise dieses bedeutenden Menschen gewähren. Der göttliche Ursprung der Bibel steht für Newton unbedingt fest, welches Vertrauen in einem eigentümlichen Gegensatz steht zu der kritischen Skepsis, die seine Stellung gegenüber den Kirchen kennzeichnet. Aus diesem Vertrauen stammt die feste Überzeugung, dass die dunkel erscheinenden Teile der Bibel wichtige Offenbarungen enthalten müssen, zu deren Aufklärung es nur der Entzifferung der in ihnen verwendeten symbolischen Sprache bedürfe. Diese Entzifferung bezw. Deutung sucht Newton mittelst seines scharfen systematischen Denkens unter sorgfältiger Verwendung aller ihm zur Verfügung stehenden Quellen.

Während die Entstehungsweise der bleibende Bedeutung Newtons umschaffenden physikalischen Werke im Dunkel gehüllt bleiben muss, weil Newton seine vorbereitenden Arbeiten offenbar vernichtet hat, besitzen wir auf diesem Gebiete der Arbeiten über die Bibel Entwürfe und deren wiederholte Abänderung; diese zum grossen Teil unveröffentlichten Schriften gestatten daher einen höchst interessanten Einblick in die geistige Werkstatt dieses einzigartigen Denkers.

A. Einstein. IX. 1940.

P.S. Ich halte es für sehr wünschbar, dass die erwähnten Schriften Newtons an einer Stelle vereinigt und dort der Forschung zugänglich gemacht werden.

Courtesy of The Jewish National & University Library
(Yah.Ms. Var.3/Einstein).[24]

24On the back of the copy of this letter made for us, a librarian wrote: "Yah. Ms. Var. 1/42 Einstein." However, we credited the letter exactly the way Raphael Weiser asked in his letter dated December 27, 1990. Weiser's letter appears later in this chapter.

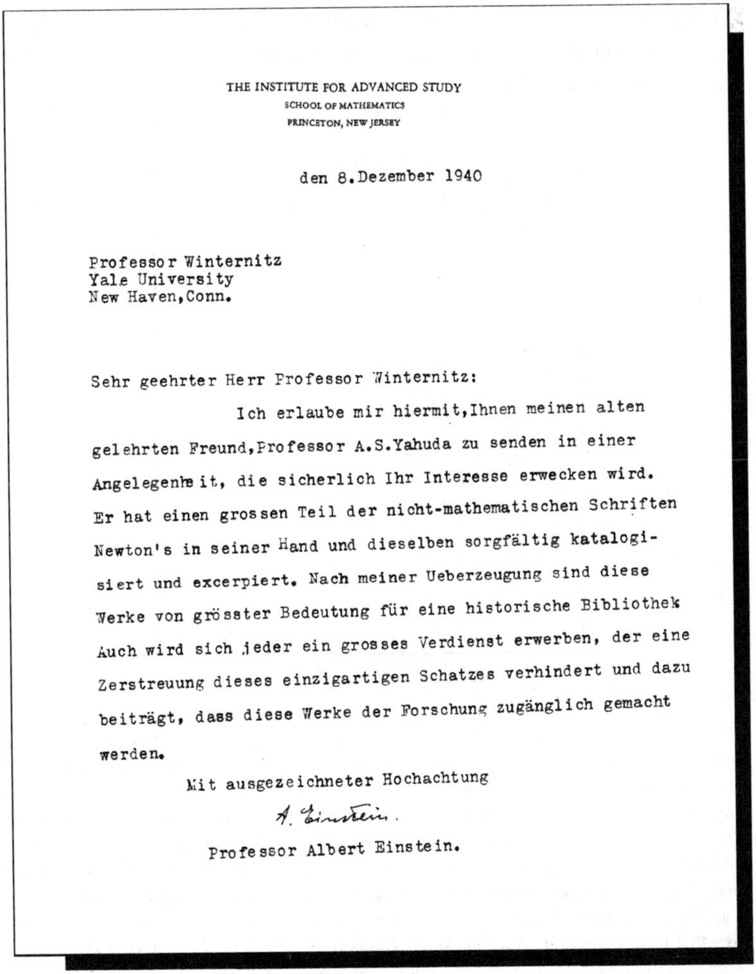

THE INSTITUTE FOR ADVANCED STUDY
SCHOOL OF MATHEMATICS
PRINCETON, NEW JERSEY

den 8.Dezember 1940

Professor Winternitz
Yale University
New Haven,Conn.

Sehr geehrter Herr Professor Winternitz:

Ich erlaube mir hiermit,Ihnen meinen alten gelehrten Freund,Professor A.S.Yahuda zu senden in einer Angelegenheit, die sicherlich Ihr Interesse erwecken wird. Er hat einen grossen Teil der nicht-mathematischen Schriften Newton's in seiner Hand und dieselben sorgfältig katalogisiert und excerpiert. Nach meiner Ueberzeugung sind diese Werke von grösster Bedeutung für eine historische Bibliothek Auch wird sich jeder ein grosses Verdienst erwerben, der eine Zerstreuung dieses einzigartigen Schatzes verhindert und dazu beiträgt, dass diese Werke der Forschung zugänglich gemacht werden.

Mit ausgezeichneter Hochachtung

A. Einstein.

Professor Albert Einstein.

A letter from Einstein to Professor Winternitz.
Courtesy of The Jewish National & University Library
(Yah.Ms. Var.3/Einstein).

Einstein's letters on Newton's religious works, urging Newton's religious writings be made public, are published here in full, for the first time in history, for your eyes to see the truth[25]. It took me three months[26] to get into this supposedly forbidden archive of the Yahuda Manuscript Var. at the Hebrew University! At the top of the catalog containing mention of these letters, the Hebrew word *ASUIE*, meaning "forbidden" and "off limits" was penned in with no signature.

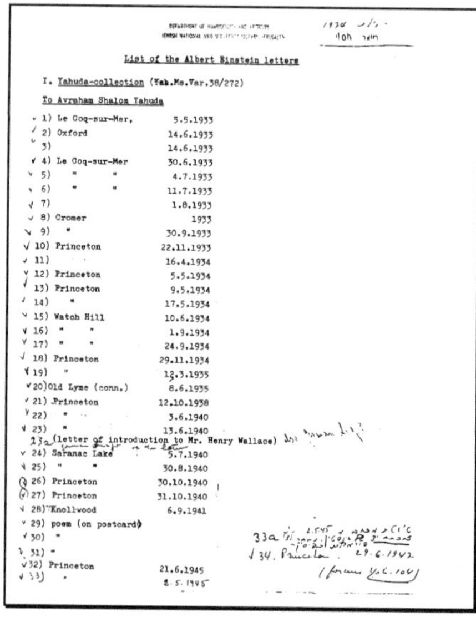

List of the Albert Einstein letters

I. Yahuda-collection (Yah.Ms.Var.38/272)

To Avraham Shalom Yahuda

1) Le Coq-sur-Mer,	5.5.1933
2) Oxford	14.6.1933
3)	14.6.1933
4) Le Coq-sur-Mer	30.6.1933
5) " "	4.7.1933
6) " "	11.7.1933
7)	1.8.1933
8) Cromer	1933
9) "	30.9.1933
10) Princeton	22.11.1933
11)	16.4.1934
12) Princeton	5.5.1934
13) Princeton	9.5.1934
14) "	17.5.1934
15) Watch Hill	10.6.1934
16) " "	1.9.1934
17) " "	24.9.1934
18) Princeton	29.11.1934
19) "	13.3.1935
20) Old Lyme (conn.)	8.6.1935
21) Princeton	12.10.1938
22) "	3.6.1940
23) "	13.6.1940
23a (letter of introduction to Mr. Henry Wallace)	
24) Saranac Lake	5.7.1940
25) " "	30.8.1940
26) Princeton	30.10.1940
27) Princeton	31.10.1940
28) Knollwood	6.9.1941
29) poem (on postcard)	
30) "	
31) "	
32) Princeton	21.6.1945
33) "	8.5.1945
33a	
34. Princeton	24.6.1942

---

[25]See pages 518-19 for translated portions of these Einstein letters.

[26]While it took us over a year of letter writing and help from friends to bring these treasures to you, don't feel too bad for this author. Richard Westfall (another research author on Newton) has told us that the Bodmer Library in Geneva never allowed him or any other scholar to see their Newton manuscripts (they possess some which no one else does). Westfall wrote: "I have examined all of the theological papers the location of which is known except the one in the Bodmer Library (Geneva), which apparently regards it as a perishable resource which reading would exhaust....only a chance to see it, a privilege which the Bodmer Library does not grant to mere scholars concerned to study Newton, can determine its content." Richard S. Westfall, "Newton's Theological Manuscripts," *Contemporary Newtonian Research*. Boston: D. Reidel Publishing Company, © 1982, p. 129. Some have said that Newton calculated the time of the Messiah's Coming. Perhaps it is in the Geneva Library, since they are so adamant about no one seeing it! It has been rumored that he had speculated the mid-twenty-first century. On page 135 of *Contemporary Newtonian Research*, it is said that Newton's final speculation post-dates the twentieth century. We will soon see, won't we? We should not dismiss the fact that all of the signs Jesus gave for His return have been upon us since the advent of the A-bomb in 1944, and the rebirth of Israel in 1948. We do not have another generation to wait! Have we? In 1995, as we were putting the finishing touches on our work of over twelve years, we noted that *The Books of Nature and Scripture*, edited by Force and Popkin, quotes from "Bodmer MS." Apparently some, if not all of these manuscripts, have recently been released.

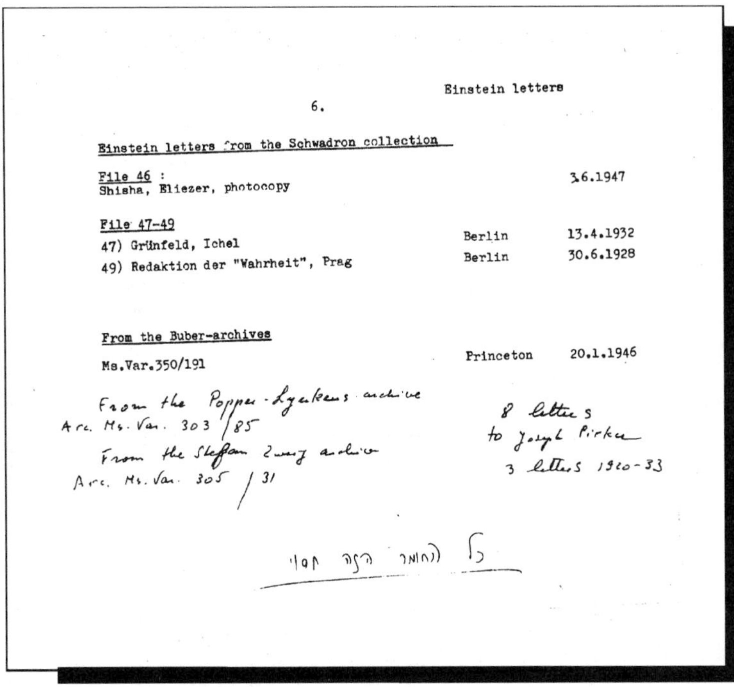

Einstein letters

6.

Einstein letters from the Schwadron collection

File 46 :
Shisha, Eliezer, photocopy — 3.6.1947

File 47-49
47) Grünfeld, Ichel — Berlin — 13.4.1932
49) Redaktion der "Wahrheit", Prag — Berlin — 30.6.1928

From the Buber-archives
Ms.Var.350/191 — Princeton — 20.1.1946

From the Popper-Lynkeus archive
Arc. Ms. Var. 303/85
From the Stefan Zweig archive
Arc. Ms. Var. 305/31

8 letters
to Joseph Pirker
3 letters 1920-33

כל החומר הזה אסור

Homer "material" and *asuie* "forbidden" are the first and the last handwritten Hebrew words on pages one and six of the Einstein letter catalog. As a Jerusalem newspaper reporter cautiously reminded me, "It is not signed." Dr. Jonathan Yoel is a high-ranking official of the Hebrew University library. After receiving letters from me and my lawyer, he apparently saw to it that my final permission letter was properly written by Mr. Weiser (pictured on page 507). This occurred just before our story about why these letters were so forbidden was to be published in an Israeli daily. The following correspondence illustrates part of this struggle.

SHIMON ORI ADVOCATE

שמעון אורי עו"ד דין

12c KORESH ST. P.O.B. 337, JERUSALEM 91002, TEL: 02-225386-225048

רח' כורש 12, כניסה ג', ת.ד. 337, ירושלים 91002, טל. 02-225386-225048

3/ ~~18~~ באוקטובר 1990

ירושלים .... Jerusalem

תיק מס' .... Ref

לכבוד

הספריה .הלאומית

האוניברסיטה העברית בירושלים, גבעת רם

ג.א.נ.,

הנדון: <u>אישור בכתב שהובטח למר פיליפ מור</u>

בשם מרשי, מר פיליפ מור, אני פונה אליכם ודורש שתתנו למרשי אישור בכתב כי הוא רשאי לצטט מכתבים באמור במכתב שהכין עבורכם ביום 2.9.90 שתצלומו מצ"ב, וכפי שדרש כבר במכתבו ב-5.9.89.

מרשי סיפר לי שמר רפי וייזה העובד בספריה הלאומית הבטיח לו יותר מ-30 פעם שיתן לו אישור בכתב לגבי ציטוט מכתבי ניוטון שבאוסף יהודה ויבדוק עד כמה יוכל לאשר לצטט ממכתבי איינשטיין לגבי פירוש ניוטון לתנ"ך ולברית החדשה.

אני מתפלא שלמרות ההבטחות החוזרות ונשנות לא טרח מר רפי וייזר להמציא למרשי את האישור.

הנכם נדרשים לתת למרשי את האישור תוך 14 ימים, שאם לא כן ייאלץ לנקוט בהליכים משפטיים.

אם אינכם מסכימים שמרשי יצטט ממכתבי איינשטיין, אבקש למסור לו, תוך 14 ימים, הסבר בכתב מדוע ולהראות למרשי את המסמכים שבהם נאמר שאסור לכם לאפשר לצטט את כל המכתבים, ובכל מקרה מרשי דורש את הסכמתכם בכתב לצטט חלקים קטנים, כפי שהוא רשאי, ע"פ החוק.

בכבוד רב,

ש. אורי, עו"ד

Letter from Shimon Ori to the Hebrew University.

Jerusalem, 31 October 1990

The National Library
The Hebrew University of Jerusalem
Giva'at Ram

Dear Mesdames/Messrs.,

Re: Permission in writing promised to Philip Moore

In the name of my client, Mr. Philip Moore, I am turning to you to request that you give my client permission in writing, authorizing him to quote the letters referred to in the letter he prepared for you on 2.9.90, the photocopy of which is attached to this letter, and as he requested in his letter of 5.9.89.

My client has told me that Mr. Raffi Weiser, who works in the National Library, promised more than 30 times to give him permission in writing regarding quotation from the Newton letters, which are in the Yahuda Collection, and that he would check how much quoting he would be able to authorize from the Einstein letters regarding Newton's commentary on the Bible and the New Testament.

I am surprised that despite the continual and recurring promises, Mr. Raffi Weiser has not taken the trouble to secure the authorization for my client.

We hereby request that you give my client permission within 14 days, or he will otherwise be forced to take legal action.

If you do not consent to my client quoting the Einstein letters, I request that you deliver an explanation as to why not, in writing, to him within 14 days and show my client the documents in which it appears that it is forbidden to permit quotation of all the letters.

In any event, my client requests your consent in writing to quote small parts, as he is entitled according to the law.

Respectfully yours,

S. Ori, Advocate

English translation of Shimon Ori letter to the Hebrew University.

ILAN WINKLER, ADVOCATE אילן וינקלר, עורך־דין

Jerusalem ירושלים

Ref. מספרנו

24, December 1990

Dear Mr. Weizer,

Thank you very much for the letter you sent to Attorney Ori. However you mentioned in the former letters the photocopies Philip Moore gave you on Newton and Einstein. Since in the future there is no guarantee that these photocopies will not be lost and since Mr. Moore's publishers must translate your letters and will have to contact your library on exactly which photocopies Philip handed in so that they will not have to have said photocopies mailed, in order to save all parties much red tape we feel a more proper permission letter naming the letters would be in order.

We have also noted that in Philips letter that it is nowhere specificly mentioned that he has permission, only "we're sorry about not answering untill now" and "remember to document the place of reference and to give us two copies of the book". Between these two statements there should be a clear clause of permission, in Philips letter. According to legal literary specifications, thus we suggest strongly, you sign the one I have prepared.

Thus we are sending you a letter ready to sign which I would like you to mail to Mr. Philip Moore within two weeks.

Attention: Philip Moore
8/10 Etzel
French Hill
Jerusalem

Thank you,
sincerely

Ilan Winkler, adv.

P.S. Please send me the call numbers to the material you require Mr. Moore to refer to for the mentioned letters of Einstein if you would like him to mention something other than YEHUDA MANUSCRIPT VAR.

Yahuda manuscript VAR. is the designation frank manuel uses in his book in refference to an Einstein letter located there. (See inclosed example).

13 M. Ben Hillel St., Jerusalem 94231 • Tel. 248833, 247733, 245475 טל' • 94231 רח' מרדכי בן הלל 13, ירושלים

Letter from Ilan Winkler to Rafael Weiser.[27]

[27]A copy of this letter was hand-delivered to Jonathan Yoel by this author.

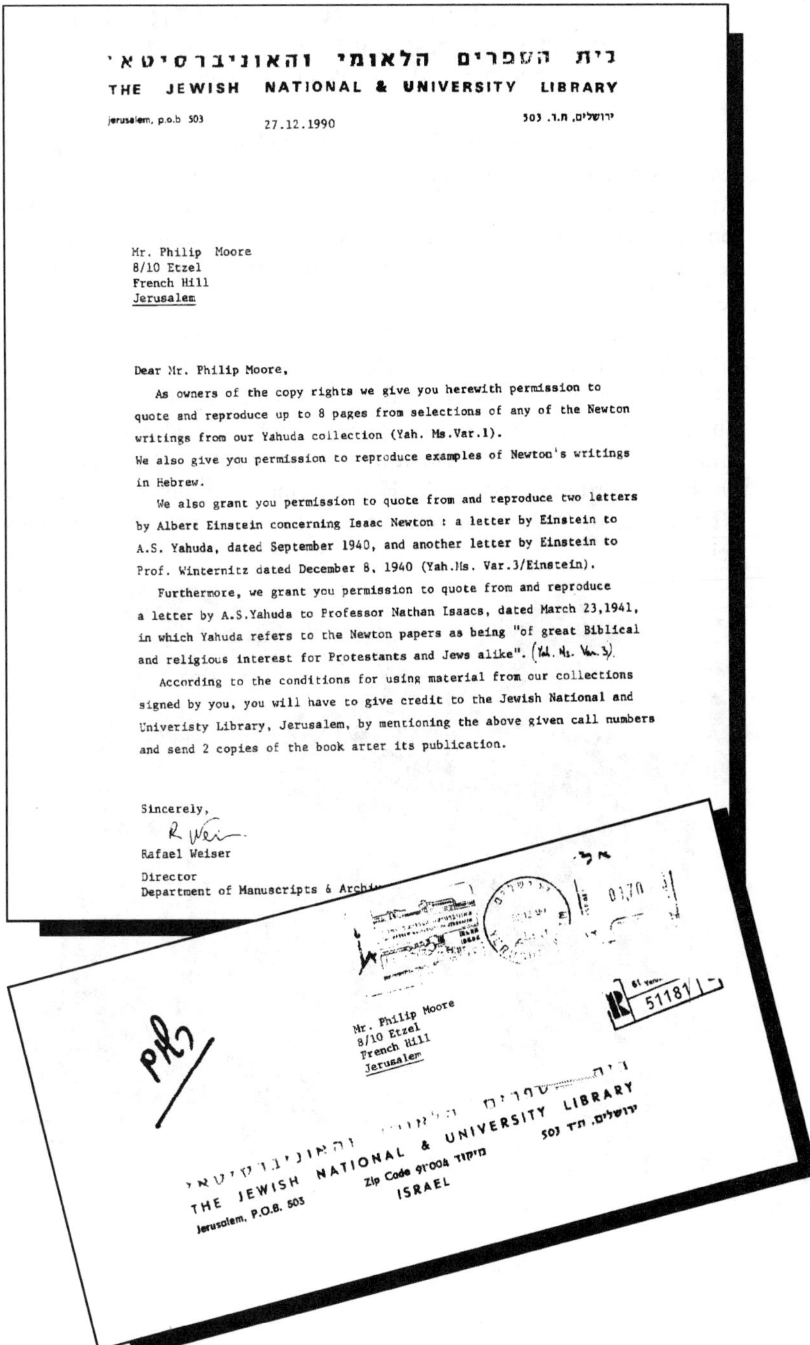

בית הספרים הלאומי והאוניברסיטאי
THE JEWISH NATIONAL & UNIVERSITY LIBRARY

jerusalem, p.o.b 503 27.12.1990 ירושלים, ת.ד. 503

Mr. Philip Moore
8/10 Etzel
French Hill
Jerusalem

Dear Mr. Philip Moore,

As owners of the copy rights we give you herewith permission to quote and reproduce up to 8 pages from selections of any of the Newton writings from our Yahuda collection (Yah. Ms.Var.1).
We also give you permission to reproduce examples of Newton's writings in Hebrew.

We also grant you permission to quote from and reproduce two letters by Albert Einstein concerning Isaac Newton : a letter by Einstein to A.S. Yahuda, dated September 1940, and another letter by Einstein to Prof. Winternitz dated December 8, 1940 (Yah.Ms. Var.3/Einstein).

Furthermore, we grant you permission to quote from and reproduce a letter by A.S.Yahuda to Professor Nathan Isaacs, dated March 23,1941, in which Yahuda refers to the Newton papers as being "of great Biblical and religious interest for Protestants and Jews alike". (Yah. Ms. Var. 3).

According to the conditions for using material from our collections signed by you, you will have to give credit to the Jewish National and Univeristy Library, Jerusalem, by mentioning the above given call numbers and send 2 copies of the book arter its publication.

Sincerely,

R Wei

Rafael Weiser

Director
Department of Manuscripts & Arch

Letter from Rafael Weiser to this author.

WHY DO SO MANY DENY NEWTON'S AUTHORITY? DO THEY CONSIDER IT A DANGER TO THEIR OWN CONVICTION?

This letter of authorization gives you and all the world the right to read this material! We believe that it is not an exaggeration to say, as Frank Manuel has: "Most of Newton's manuscripts on religion were long concealed from the world....suppressed...lest what were believed to be shady lucubrations tarnish the image of the perfect scientific genius."[28]

Another reason we believe the Hebrew University procrastinated in giving written permission authorizing publication of Newton's biblical commentary was that they suspected my book was of a Christian fundamentalist nature. They knew that I had worked on the evangelical film, *Jesus*, in Hebrew there in Israel in 1989 and 1990. Shosh, one of my friends at the Hebrew University library, tipped me off that one of Weiser's fellow workers had seen one of the articles below.

---

[28]Frank E. Manuel, *The Changing of the Gods*. Hanover: University Press of New England, © 1983, p. 17, used by permission.

If they did not want fundamental Christian beliefs encouraged and supported by Newton, they would naturally delay permission as long as possible, or try to deny it all together, without giving a clear reason as to why. My friend, Moshe Ron, the Director of the Edelstein Division of the Jewish National and University Library, advised me how to work around Mr. Weiser by appealing to his superiors. He told me in a taped interview: "*...if—if, you see, Newton's authority is behind those ideas, then they are far more dangerous than if it is your authority or mine. You see, that's why they are so anxious to cover them up. Because it was Newton who wrote these things. And Newton is a very believable important person—you see what I mean?*"[29]

Over thirty years before Newton's death, the philosopher and medical doctor, John Locke, wrote: "Mr. Newton is really a very valuable man, not only for his wonderful skill in mathematics, but in divinity also, and his great knowledge in the Scriptures, wherein I know few his equals."[30]

THE SECRET HISTORY OF HOW NEWTON'S PAPERS WERE KEPT FROM THE PUBLIC FOR OVER TWO HUNDRED AND FIFTY YEARS

It has been an uphill battle since Newton's death to see these papers made public. John Mills first spoke of it in 1727, in a letter to John Conduit: " 'According to your desire I here sent (sic) you a short account of the surprising discoverys and improvements, which the incomparable Sr. Is. Newton has made....And this I know that he was much more sollicitous in his inquirys into Religion than into Natural Philosophy [science]....he had written a long explication of remarkable parts of the Old and New Testament, while his understanding was in its greatest perfection....That he would not publish these writings in his own time because they show'd that his thoughts were some times different from those which are commonly receiv'd, which would ingage him in disputes, and this was a thing which he avoided as much as possible. But now its hop'd that the worthy and ingenious Mr. Conduit will take care that they be **publish'd** that the world may see

---

[29]Quoted from Moshe Ron, from a transcribed letter signed by Moshe Ron. Used by permission.

[30]Franz Kobler, "Newton on the Restoration of the Jews," *Jewish Frontier*, © Mar. 1943, p. 21. Dr. Locke was a believer in a government of, for and by the people. Jefferson adopted many of his ideas and incorporated them into the Declaration of Independence. Locke was a true believer. He has been called the "intellectual ruler of the eighteenth century." See his article in *The World Book Encyclopedia* Vol. 12, © 1970, by Field Enterprises Education Corporation.

that Sr. Is: Newton was as good a Christian as he was a Mathematician and Philosopher.'"[31]

Later, Mills' family was warned by Cambridge University officials not to show these papers to anyone.[32] As time passed, the Earl of Portsmouth[33] inherited them, and decided to have them sold. In 1936, they were auctioned in England at the Sotheby & Co. sale. After the sale, Professor Abraham Shalom Yahuda,[34] a collector fascinated by the Bible and science, bought most of the manuscripts back from the new owners, piece by piece, at bargain prices. Afterward, scientist Albert Einstein and Professor Yahuda urged that

---

[31] *Catalogue of The Newton Papers.* [ ] mine.

[32] Ruvic Rosenthal, "The Ostracized Newton," *Al Hamishmar*, July 26, 1985.

[33] "Newton's manuscripts, on his death in 1727...passed...into the keeping of John Conduitt, who had married Catherine Barton, Newton's niece. From him they descended to his daughter, the first Viscountess Lymington, mother of the second Earl of Portsmouth, and the collection remained intact in the Portsmouth family until 1872, when the then Earl presented a portion...to the University of Cambridge...." "Notes for Bibliofiles," *New York Herald Tribune Books*, p. 18.

[34] Professor Popkin enlightens us: "...A. S. Yahuda....a Palestinian Jew who was a very important Arabic scholar and a great collector of manuscripts, argued in the early 1930's that there was evidence of the historical accuracy of the Bible. He contended that the story of the Exodus was written by somebody who knew Egyptian and, hence, who was an actual participant or eyewitness to the events....Yahuda lectured and wrote on the accuracy of the Bible in pre-Hitler Germany and then in England. Yahuda, a product of sophisticated German scholarly training....acquired most of the [Newton] theological papers....the interests Yahuda had in Newton's religious writings was in understanding Newton's reasons for believing in the historical accuracy of the Bible....Against 17th— and 20th—century Bible critics, Yahuda contended that the authors were eyewitnesses and not merely recounting traditional stories at a much later time. Newton, to Yahuda's pleasure, went even further and argued that one could date events in the Old Testament from the astronomical descriptions and then show from this dating that Biblical events were the oldest known human events and that the Bible was the oldest known book....he saw Newton as pointing to something significant about the uniqueness of the Bible....attempting to provide further evidence of the accuracy of scripture against modern day skeptics....(I have been told by an eyewitness that Yahuda's close friend, **Albert Einstein, was present when Yahuda first advanced his theory and that Einstein wept with joy when he heard that one could establish the accuracy of the the Bible on the basis of historical and philological research**.) For Newton, once one accepted that the Bible was accurate in a significant sense, then one could use materials contained in it to explain the origins of mankind, of human institutions, and of human social and cultural abilities, for example, writing. Newton left a lot of manuscripts on these subjects. He was also convinced that one could find some basic understanding of the universe in the plans God laid down for building Solomon's Temple, a microcosm of the macrocosm. Newton's essay on the sacred cubit of the Hebrews and his analysis of the construction of the Temple show that he was sure that there was a mystical architecture in its dimensions that explained God's total dominion over all of creation." *Essays on the Context, Nature, and Influence of Isaac Newton's Theology*, pp. 174-175, 112. [ ] and bold mine.

they be made public.[35] A London professor insisted, "I hope they will be burned because they are harmful to Newton's scientific reputation."[36] Harvard, Yale and Princeton rejected[37] them. Finally, upon Yahuda's death in 1951, it was discovered that his collection was willed to the Hebrew University. However, his wife tried to prevent this donation by contesting the will, falsely claiming he was not of sound mind, because the will was made on his death bed. She ended up committing suicide over the matter.[38]

Only in 1969 was it decided that Yahuda's will would not be broken. The papers were then delivered to the library in Jerusalem after eighteen years of court battles. And of course, you have read of my difficulties, such as having to use a lawyer and the press to coerce Rafael Weiser, Department Head of Manuscripts, to finally give me written permission to quote the manuscripts, after thirty-three verbal promises to do so.

THE PROGRESS OF SCIENCE.

PROFESSOR EINSTEIN'S ENGLISH VISIT.

RELATIVITY AND REALITY.

(By Our Scientific Correspondent.)

Although Professor Einstein brought little to add to his theory of Relativity, it has been a pleasure to British men of science to meet personally the author of a great addition to human thought. ...

EINSTEIN AND NEWTON.

THE NEW MEANING OF SPACE.

LECTURE AT KING'S COLLEGE.

Professor Einstein lectured last evening at King's College on "The Development and Present Position of the Theory of Relativity." ...

---

[35]*Al Hamishmar*, July 26, 1985.

[36]Ibid.

[37]Professor Popkin documents: "In 1940, Yahuda became a refugee in the United States. He transported his vast manuscript collection with him to America where he tried, with the assistance of his close friend, Albert Einstein, to get **Harvard**, **Yale,** or **Princeton** to take over his very large collection of Newton's papers. **All three institutions** refused, even though Einstein tried to make them realize the importance of the papers for understanding how Newton's creative intelligence worked. Yahuda, on his deathbed in 1951, decided to leave his entire manuscript collection, which contains much Near Eastern material in addition to the Newton manuscripts, to what became the Jewish National & University Library...." *Books of Nature and Scripture*, p. x. I personally read the letters in the *Yahuda Manuscript Var.* by various professors illustrating how these most valuable papers were being politely turned down.

[38]This is according to Professor Popkin, an expert on the subject, who informed me of these details during a 1991 telephone conversation between California and Jerusalem.

Chairman Raffy Weiser
The Jewish National &
University Library
Manuscripts & Archives Dept
P. O. B. 503
Jerusalem, 91004

September 5, 1989

Dear Chairman Raffy Weiser,

I would like a short letter of permission to reproduce and quote short selected sections of your Yahuda manuscripts on Isaac Newton—I would also like your permission to reproduce Einstein's letter to Roosevelt and Einstein's letter praising the Newton papers.

Just write me a letter of two or three lines saying the above is OK. I know you told me I don't need anything other than your verbal permission for such short quotes but just in case the publisher might give me trouble I feel it is best. Here I have enclosed two examples of letters of permission which I received two weeks ago. Both companies told me on the phone it is OK. I asked for a letter just in case, so they mailed me what I have enclosed.

Even though I may not need it I would feel much safer with a short letter from you.

Thanks.

Sincerely your friend,

Philip Moore

It was nice to see you on Jaffa Road just before Passover! Tell our friend Ron Bartour Philip says Shalom next time you see him. Shalom Raffy Kol Tuv.

Letter from this author to Rafael Weiser.

April 18, 1990

Dear Beit Arye,

I have been to Raffy Weiser about 7 times asking for written permission. He gave me verbal permission when I told him I wanted it in writing as it is customary for publication of a book he said "just remember us, you have my verbal permission". Later I insisted with this letter dated September 5th 1989. He told me the first time "come in two weeks", I did, he told me when I came, "you remind me of my sins, come next week, it will be ready". I came three weeks later, he told me again "you remind me of my sins", the next time he told me the same thing. Two weeks after that, he told me it was being typed and I would receive it at the end of the week. Then, his letter of permission promised never arrived. It had been a month — last week before Passover, Moshe allowed me in the office to ask Raffy about the letter, Yaron Sakhish said "I'll ask him" when he (Mr. Sakhish) came out of Raffy's office, he had a mad look on his face and said "we are closed". I said, Moshe let me in to check with Raffy, did he send me my package as promised. Mr. Sakhish rudely said "he sent it". I told him, mail takes three days, I will wait ten days, then I'm going to the administration. He then rudely let me out.

Thank You,

Philip Moore

P.S. If possible, ask Mr. Weiser if I can receive permission for this material already promised within 30 days. I may be leaving Israel soon.

Thank you very much,
Bait Arye
Shalom

Letter from this author to Bait Arye.

October 22, 1990

To Whom it may concern at the Hebrew University,

Mr. Paz here at the acum copyright society in Tel-Aviv has told me no matter how restricted any material is said to be and (the material in question) may not be "restricted" I have the right to publish portions of it for academic reasons, under the fair use publishing laws giving credit to those who presently own the letters, thus I request the FORMALITY of your proper permission and approval to quote portions of the mentioned letters, if they are restricted, because I signed a paper saying that I wouldn't quote your material without your permission. This permission, as you can see from my Sept. 1989 letter, I have been requesting for over 1 year is absolutely necessary for the publication of my book which is of a Pro Israel Pro God Pro Bible nature and I have never understood why it is always next week that I will receive the permission as Mr. Weiser has kept telling me next week you'll receive it in the mail and it never arrives. I have asked him over 30 times for this permission in April 1990 Mr. Beitarie, the director of the university library, spoke to him about it.

The letter (here enclosed) which I have prepared for him to sign I have written, because one of his excuses in the beginning was "I didn't have time to write it for you yet."

The contents of this letter are within the legal limits of the university, concerning fair use of the mentioned letters on Einstein if they are restricted, and chairman Raffy Weiser has told me "I'll write that you can quote anything from Newton's own writings in the Yahuda manuscript because that is completely open"—thus if Mr. Weiser doesn't sign this letter or one similar to it, which is a normal service offered by the Hebrew University and has been provided for thousands of other researchers who have also come from over seas to study here, I am going to seek legal advice as you can see I already have a lawyer interested in this case and she's got a friend at the newspapers who is getting ready to cover this story.

It is my feeling that Raffy Weiser may be stalling in his letter, he's told me he is going to write and give me so many times, because of personal reasons.

I don't want to cause any trouble or any hard feelings, only I want the letter which is due me so I can do justice to my book and give proper praise and credit to the Hebrew University of whom I am so thankful to.

Sincerely,

Philip Moore
Author

Letter from this author to the Hebrew University.

The final letter of authorization from Mr. Weiser was the culmination of more than a year of struggle between us. Thus in 1996[39] you are able to see the material against which Satan fought for centuries, hoping you would never see.

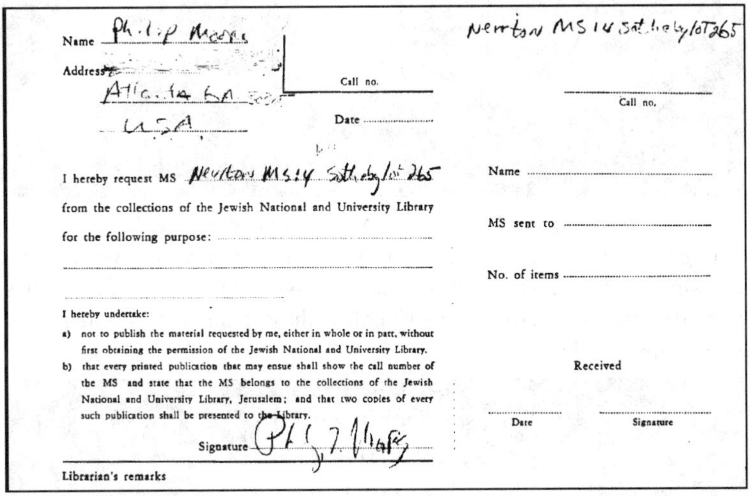

Name Philip Moore

Address

Atlanta GA

USA

Call no.

Date

I hereby request MS Newton MS 14 Sotheby lot 265

from the collections of the Jewish National and University Library

for the following purpose:

I hereby undertake:

a) not to publish the material requested by me, either in whole or in part, without first obtaining the permission of the Jewish National and University Library.

b) that every printed publication that may ensue shall show the call number of the MS and state that the MS belongs to the collections of the Jewish National and University Library, Jerusalem; and that two copies of every such publication shall be presented to the Library.

Signature

Librarian's remarks

Newton MS 14 Sotheby lot 265

Call no.

Name

MS sent to

No. of items

Received

Date Signature

Although today the public may view the Newton religious papers, anyone wishing to publish them must first obtain permission, as illustrated by the contractual restriction above, which I was asked to sign before being permitted to see the manuscripts. You may be asking why I went to such lengths. Read our quotes by Newton and the letters by Einstein, and see if you can guess!

---

39 A very small amount of Newton's religious writings were published in 1727 (see Frank Manuel, *Changing of the Gods*, p. 27), and in 1973, Manuel published additional material in his rare scholarly book, *The Religion of Isaac Newton*. In 1981, David Castillejo published a few passages in his book, *The Expanding Force in Newton's Cosmos*, and Professor Popkin, with whom we have personally conversed, published portions in 1990 and 1994. Aside from these brief quotes and the ones in our book, the vast majority of Newton's religious writings still lie in the Hebrew University's strong room, locked up and unpublished. However, to our great joy, we have recently learned that microfilms of Newton's writings were released to several other libraries—whether our difficulties with the library had anything to do with this is impossible to tell. It is a good first step! However, Professor Popkin told me in October 1994 that Robert Iliffe will publish four Newton manuscripts in a series on "Voltaire and the Enlightenment," and that James Force plans to publish the manuscripts on CD-ROM. However, as of early 1996, most remain unpublished.

Professor Richard Popkin of UCLA, pictured above with the author, may be the one to finally publish the remaining Newton manuscripts. Popkin, though over seventy years of age and lacking funds, has recently obtained permission to publish these manuscripts and is still very optimistic.[40]

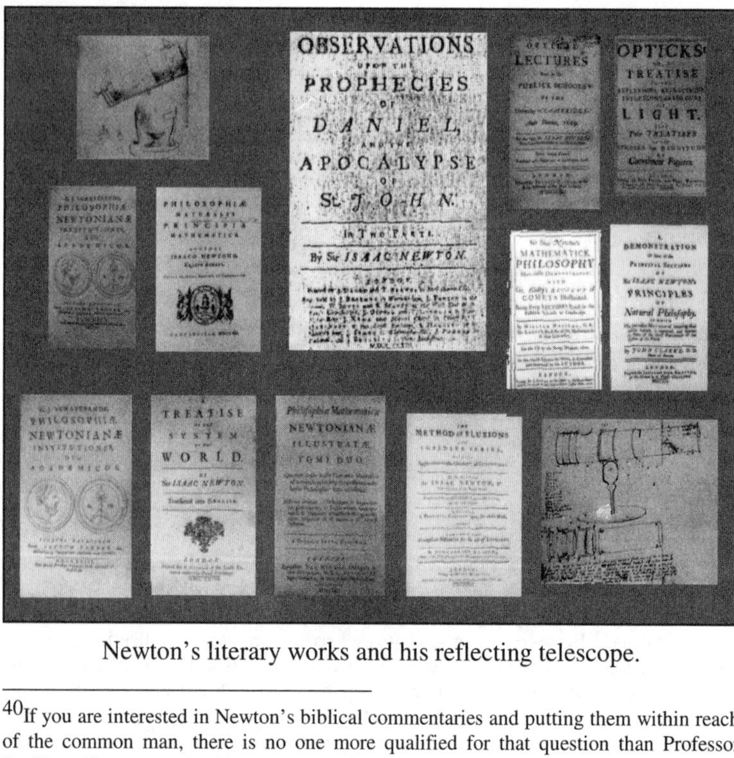

Newton's literary works and his reflecting telescope.

---

[40]If you are interested in Newton's biblical commentaries and putting them within reach of the common man, there is no one more qualified for that question than Professor Popkin. You can write him at: Attention Professor Popkin, Department of History, UCLA, Los Angeles, CA, USA 90024.

OURNAL—5—דער מארגען זשורנאל—5 MARCH 26, 1943

זוי די מלחמה האָט פאַרשאַרפט נעגער-פראַגע אין דער סאוטה

אמעריקאנער זשורנאלען דיסקוטירען איצט די נעגער פראגע. — די מענות פון א נעגער פיהרער. — וואס ניוטאן האט געזאגט וועגען אידען און ארץ ישראל. — א "פארטיידיגונג" פאר דעם יאפאנעזישען קעניג.

א שפאציר איבער זשורנאלען און צייטשריפטען
פון אהרן צייטלין

אידישע פליהער אין טלית און תפילין

דאס מערקווירדיג בילד ווי אידישע זעלנער וואס ווערען געלערענט אף פליהער דאווענען אין טליתים און תפילין איז גענומען געווארען אין די באקא ראטאן פילד, פלארידא. דער טשאפלעין איז הרב אליעזר ווערפעל א מוסמך פון דער ישיבה רבנו יצחק אלחנן. דאס בילד איז גענומען געווארען פון "ארמי עיר פארסעס טעכניקעל קאמאנד".

מען זאָגט מיר . . .

פון דר. יחזקאל לעוויט

מען זאגט מיר: "מענש, פארגעס דיין פאלק,
פארלאז די אלטע קברים!
גיב דיין נשמה אפ צו אונז —
וועסטו נים לעבען ארים".

מען זאגט מיר: "מענש, נים טראכט דערפון
צו בויען די רואינען
פון יענער שטאט, פון וועלכער נאר
איין וואנט קאן מען געפינען" . . .

מען זאגט מיר: "מענש, נים חלום מעהר
צו איפוועקען די אידען,
וואס זיינען מים דעם גלות-שלאף
אפנים גאנץ צופרידען" . . .

* * *

פארשטומט ווערט, איהר פאלשע נביאים!
איהר דארפט נאר פון הרפה אנטלויפען . . .
איך וועל מיין ירושה די אלטע
פאר גאלדענע בערג נים פארקויפען.

מיין גאט און מיין פאלק וועל איך שטענדיג
פון אלן אין דער וועלט מעהרער שאצען.
פאר מיר צווישען אידען א קבר
איז בעסער פון פרעמדע פאלאצען . . .

A Yiddish article on Newton detailing his views on the end times and redemption.

EINSTEIN'S EXCERPTS—NEWTON IS STILL GUIDING US

Professor Albert Einstein said: "...his own work would have been impossible without Newton's discoveries. [Newton's concepts]... are even today still guiding our thinking in physics."[41]

Einstein also made several impressive comments to Professor Yahuda and Professor Winternitz on this handwritten collection of Newton's biblical interpretations. For example, he wrote: "My Dear Yahuda, Newton's writings on biblical topics seem to me especially interesting, because they reveal a deep insight into the spiritual character and the working method of this significant man. For Newton, the divine origin of the Bible is unconditionally certain....From this belief arises the firm conviction that the parts of the Bible that appear obscure must contain important revelations, which

---

[41]*The World Book Encyclopedia*, 1970 Edition, p. 308. [ ] mine. *The World Book* also says that Newton was: "...an English scientist, astronomer, and mathematician, [he] invented a new kind of mathematics, discovered the secrets of light and color, and showed how the universe is held together. He is sometimes described as 'one of the greatest names in the history of human thought,' because of his great contributions to mathematics, physics, and astronomy. Newton discovered how the universe is held together through his theory of gravity. He discovered the secrets of light and color. He invented a branch of mathematics, *calculus*...He made these three discoveries within 18 months from 1665 to 1667....Newton said the concept of a universal force came to him while he was drinking tea in the garden and saw an apple fall. He suddenly realized that one and the same force pulls the apple to earth and keeps the moon in its orbit. He found that the force of universal gravitation makes every pair of bodies in the universe attract each other....Newton's discoveries on the laws of motion and theories of gravitation were published in 1687 in *Philosophiae Naturalis Principia Mathematica* (Mathematical Principles of Natural Philosophy). The book generally is considered one of the greatest single contributions in the history of science....Newton's discoveries in optics were equally spectacular. He published the results of his experiments and studies in *Opticks* (1704). Newton's discoveries explained why bodies appear to be colored. They laid the foundation for the science of spectrum analysis. This science allows us to determine the chemical composition, temperature, and even the speed of such hot, glowing bodies as a distant star or an object heated in a laboratory....He was considered a poor student. His youthful inventions included a small windmill that could grind wheat and corn, a water clock run by the force of dropping water, and a sundial. He left school when he was 14 to help his widowed mother manage her farm. But he spent so much time reading, he was sent back to school....Newton did not enjoy the scientific arguments that arose from his discoveries. Many new scientific theories are opposed violently when they are first announced, and Newton's did not escape criticism. He was so sensitive to such criticism that his friends had to plead with him to publish his most valuable discoveries. Newton was a bachelor who spent little of his time studying mathematics, physics, and astronomy....He also spent a great deal of his time on questions of theology and Biblical chronology. As a professor, he was very absent-minded. He showed great generosity to his nephews and nieces and to publishers and scientists who helped him in his work. He was modest in his character. He said of himself shortly before his death, 'I do not know what I may appear to the world, but to myself I seem to have been only like a boy playing on the seashore, and diverting myself in now and then finding a smoother pebble or a prettier shell than ordinary, whilst the great ocean of truth lay all undiscovered before me.' " Ibid. [ ] mine.

require only the decoding of the symbolic language used in them in order to be illuminated. Newton attempts this decoding or interpretation by means of his acute, systematic thinking, in which he carefully makes use of all the sources available to him....in this area of works on the Bible, we do possess his sketches and their repeated revisions. These writings, mostly unpublished, thus provide a highly interesting insight into the spiritual workshop of this unique thinker. Signed: A. Einstein, September 1940, Lake Saranac. P.S. I consider it very desirable that the writings of Newton mentioned here be collected in one place and there made available for research."[42]

In a second letter written in December of 1940, Einstein wrote: "Dear Professor Winternitz: Permit me to introduce to you herewith my learned old friend Professor A.S. Yahuda, in regard to a matter which will certainly awaken your interest. He has in his possession a great part of Newton's non-mathematical writings....I am convinced that these works are of the greatest significance for a historical library. Anyone who prevents the scattering of this unique treasure, and thus helps to make these works available for research, will be doing a great service. Most respectfully yours, Professor Albert Einstein."[43]

ניוטון המנודה
המשמר

An Israeli interview in Hebrew, on the subject of
Isaac Newton, with Jewish Professor Richard Popkin.[44]

[42]*Yahuda Manuscript*, "Einstein's Letter to Yahuda," Sept. 1940, from the collection at the Hebrew University, Jerusalem, © used by permission of the Hebrew University Manuscript Department.

[43]*Yahuda Manuscript Var. 3.* Both Einstein letters were translated by James B. McMahon, Ph.D., Associate Professor of German at Emory University in Atlanta. He is accredited for German to English translation by the American Translators Association.

[44]Newspaper cover and article illustration used by permission of the Israeli newspaper, *Al Hamishmar*.

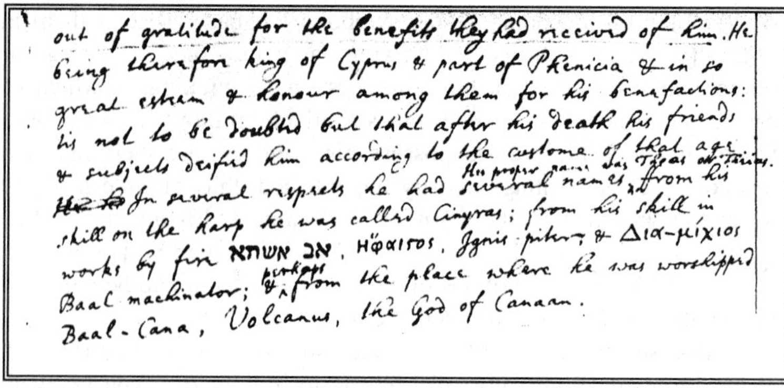
out of gratitude for the benefits they had received of him. He
being therefore king of Cyprus & part of Phenicia & in so
great esteem & honour among them for his benefactions:
tis not to be doubted but that after his death his friends
& subjects deified him according to the custome of that age.
His proper name was Thoas ... In several respects he had several names, from his
skill on the harp he was called Cinyras; from his skill in
works by fire אב אשתא, Ἥφαιστος, Ignis pater, & Δια-μίχιος
Baal machinator; & perhaps from the place where he was worshipped
Baal-Cana, Volcanus, the God of Canaan.

Yah. Ms. Var. 1. Courtesy of the Jewish National & University Library.

NEWTON KNEW HEBREW

Of particular interest to those Jews and Protestants who interpret the Bible literally, we should also note that Newton wrote in Hebrew, as we can see from this reproduction of one of his commentaries. We find it interesting that of the several recently published books on Newton, photos of his Hebrew writings have not been among the illustrations. You have a first before you!

Matt Goldish, an Israeli graduate student at the Hebrew University, confirms our claim in *The Books of Nature and Scripture*, where he noted: "Richard Westfall, Richard Popkin and Jose Faur have taken particular notice of Newton's intense study of Jewish history and ideas, especially through the medium of Maimonides' writings. The purpose of this study appears to have been directly related to Newton's interpretation of the prophecies—**he studied Hebrew so he could read the Old Testament in the original;** he studied the laws of the Temple in Jerusalem so he could better understand the vision of the Temple in the Apocalypse; he studied Jewish history because he saw it as the oldest and most reliable annal by which other nations' fabulous histories might be measured."[45]

NEWTON'S APOCALYPTIC OUTLOOK—HE PREDICTED AND BIBLICALLY SPECULATED (AS PERMITTED) BUT HE DID NOT "CABAL," AS SOME HAVE INFERRED

In Hebrew, every letter in the Bible has a special meaning and numerical value. Frank Manuel gives us insight into Newton's enthusiasm with Hebrew: "Into a few terse phrases from the

[45]*The Books of Nature and Scripture*, p. 90. Bold mine.

Apocalypse he compressed a wealth of scriptural evidence for his belief that the world was moving inexorably toward a cataclysm, a great conflagration, to be followed by a yet undefined form of renewal. His explication is in one of the normative exegetical traditions of the Talmudic rabbis and Puritan divines, whose underlying assumption was that Scriptures do not contain a single superfluous phrase, or even a letter[46] that does not have significant meaning—a sort of law of parsimony."[47]

Manuel also states: "In his interpretation of prophecy Newton made use of numerous 'mathematical' calculations which were among the standard techniques of the cabalists: one, known as 'gematria,' involved the translation of a name or a noun into its numerical equivalent (*A* being equal to *1*, *B* to *2*, and so forth) in order to prognosticate a future date, the coming of the Messiah, for example."[48]

While Newton made accurate mathematical calculations[49] based on his biblical studies, which may have seemed similar to those used by mystics who engaged in cabbala,[50] he clearly spoke against this and all other forms of mysticism in keeping with Moses and the Scripture. Manuel mentions of Newton: "The emotional outbursts against Catholicism that punctuated Newton's ecclesiastical history do not obscure...its basically rationalist framework. In the proemium of a Latin version of the history, Newton laid down the thesis that 'the true understanding of things Christian depends upon church history'. Only through a circumstantial account of the degradation of the Church in a series of stages and its doctrinal deviation from the primitive creed could Christianity be stripped of its spurious accretions. The original Christian religion was plain, but 'men skilled in the learning of heathens, Cabbalists, and Schoolmen corrupted it with metaphysicks, straining the scriptures from a moral to metaphysical sense and thereby making it unintelligible.'

As the historian of apostasy in the first centuries of the Church, Newton distinguished three principal agents in the propagation of the

---

[46]See our chapter 9, "The Messiah Conspiracy Concludes in Preventing Healings," where we illustrate that at precise numerical intervals in Hebrew, words are spelled out in the original biblical text. Somewhat of a mathematically improbable occurrence, which illustrates the Bible's divine inspiration.

[47]Frank E. Manuel, *The Religion of Isaac Newton*, p. 41.

[48]Frank E. Manuel, *A Portrait of Isaac Newton*. London: Frederick Muller Limited, © 1980, p. 370, used by permission. [ ] mine. We believe Newton's calculations, if they were ever recorded, were from the spirit of God!

[49]See caption in our chapter 18, "Israel is Real," on the rebirth of Israel, a quote from an Israeli newspaper on the exact century.

[50]Cabbala is Jewish mysticism forbidden by the Scripture, as is all mysticism (Deut. 18:10-12; Isa. 47:13-14).

metaphysical evil: the **Jewish Cabbalists**, the philosophers, among whom Plato and the Platonists were the worst offenders, and the Gnostics, of whom Simon Magus was the arch-culprit....the Cabbalists were not contemporary Jewish mystics but ancients who lived in the early ages of Christianity. His use of the term Cabbalists to identify those who propagated esoteric and theosophical doctrines among Jews in Egypt and Palestine about the time of the primitive Church and his stress on Hellenic influence in their inventions would enjoy favour among many present-day scholars who trace the roots of Cabbala back to that period."[51]

Manuel states that Newton, in his history of cabbalism, said: "...the Cabbalist Jews, through contact with Chaldean seers during the Babylonian captivity and with Egyptian priests and Greek philosophers in Alexandria, had exposed their pure Mosaic monotheism to contamination by this doctrine of emanation. It led them to conceive of the infinite, the *en-soph*, as emitting ten gradual subordinate emanations which they called *sephirot* and which were merely reifications of the attributes of God."[52]

YOUR PRIVILEGE OF READING NEWTON'S BIBLICAL COMMENTARIES IS MY PLEASURE

Because these papers of Isaac Newton's "spiritual workshop," as Professor Einstein put it, have been indeed made public in our time[53] (partly due to Einstein's urgings), you will have the unique privilege of reading, probably for your first time, some very interesting commentaries, most of which were not permitted to be seen until our era. These include foresights based on Scripture, some of which have and are also about to come true. The list includes such subjects as: the

---

[51]Frank E. Manuel, *The Religion of Isaac Newton*, pp. 68-69

[52]Ibid, p. 70. Bold mine. *En-soph* in Hebrew means "no end."

[53]As Frank Manuel said: "For the first time since the great dispersion, virtually everything that Newton wrote on religion is freely available." Ibid, p. 11. By dispersion, Manuel refers to the Sotheby & Co. sale of 1936, which scattered his manuscripts worldwide. Yahuda bought most of them back, but they did not become available until eighteen years after his death. We emphasize that available doesn't mean published . They are available to those who go to the library where the copies and originals are kept. However, you must first sign a form agreeing not to publish unless you first obtain permission. Professor Popkin mentions that the Jewish National Library houses most of Newton's religious papers "where they are now available for public examination by scholars." It would seem that if you are not a scholar, you may be out of luck, doesn't it? *Essays on the Context, Nature and Influence of Newton's Theology*, p. 15. Since we still possess nearly all of the manuscripts which were reproduced for our selections, you are more than welcome to see them, should you have any difficulty with the library! Write or fax me at the POB/facsimile number listed in the front of this book.

Messiah's First Coming; the return of the Jews to Israel in the twentieth century; the coming of the Antichrist; the war of Gog/Magog (Armageddon), and the Second Coming of Jesus to stop that war and bring peace in the twenty-first century!

NEWTON USED ADVANCED ASTRONOMICAL DATING TO VERIFY THE BIBLE'S ACCURACY

One of Newton's little-known revolutionary innovations was the use of astronomy to scientifically verify the time-frame of biblical events. Professor Richard Popkin of UCLA notes of Sir Isaac Newton: "Newton, using astronomical discoveries, constructed a chronology based upon the positions of the stars described in scripture and in other ancient writings....Using his astronomical method of dating, Newton came to the conclusion that the Bible was historically accurate and was the oldest historical record that we have. Scriptural history is more accurate than Greek, Phoenician, Babylonian....The procession of various stars in these constellations was measurable and followed a uniform law. From present observations, we could calculate backward to where these stars were historically described as being and date when the stars were in the positions described in early Greek history.

For Newton, the dramatic result of using this astronomical method to calculate the date of previous events was that it showed that the earliest events described in the Bible took place *before* the earliest events in Greek history. Newton calculated that Jason's voyage took place in 937 B.C. The earliest known events in Egyptian history also postdated the earliest Biblical events. Therefore, our earliest historical knowledge came from the Bible. The ancient Israelites were the first civilization and had the first monarchy. All other cultures and kingdoms, Newton declared, were derivative from the original Hebrew one.

Newton's elaborate astronomical argument and his debunking of pagan chronological and historical claims aimed to show that the Bible was accurate as history....And, assumed Newton, the message in the Bible was still of the greatest importance to mankind. The fact that the Bible was accurate historically meant that God had presented His message from the very beginning of the world through the history of the Hebrews and through the prophetic insights given to them."[54]

Popkin further notes: "Newton did a great deal of original historical research to discern the events in world history which constituted the fulfillment of the prophecies. Some of his

---

[54]Ibid, p. 111.

interpretations have been accepted by later Bible interpreters, especially among the fundamentalists. Newton studied the history of the Roman Empire, the European Middle Ages, and the rise of Islam in the Middle East in order to identify what actually happened in history with what was predicted in prophecy....Newton broke new interpretive ground both in the application of modern scientific techniques to the understanding of the Bible and in the historical interpretation of prophecies."[55]

NEWTON AND THE FUNDAMENTALIST—WHEN WILL THE MANUSCRIPT BE PUBLISHED?

In relation to the use of Newton's scientific proof of prophetic Scripture, as quoted in our work and also by evangelical ministers in the recent past, Popkin states: "Newton's historical research into the interpretation of historically fulfilled prophecies was taken over by many 19th-century fundamentalists who regarded him as one of the very best in this field. When the various components of Newton's Bible scholarship are examined and evaluated, he can indeed be seen to be in the forefront of the critical scholarship of his time, in the forefront in applying modern science to understanding the Bible, and in the forefront of those offering new historical data for interpreting philosophies....Perhaps, **when his theological manuscripts have been published**, we will be able to assess more accurately his entire theory and see his originality and his stature as a commentator on the scriptures. We will then be able to see if he was as great a thinker in this area as he was in the sciences."[56]

In 1994, I met Richard Popkin at Emory University in Atlanta. He spoke of hopefully getting the manuscripts published, despairing of the funds it would take. Later, toward the end of 1994, in his book, *The Books of Nature and Scripture*, he spoke of the study of the *unpublished* manuscripts with an air of futility, or so it seemed to me. His words were: "Further study of the unpublished manuscripts may deepen our understanding of Newton's contributions as a scholar of Scripture."[57]

In 1995, Popkin was optimistic about James Force publishing large portions of Newton's religious manuscripts on computer CD ROM; however, this is yet to be seen. If you think you have the resources to help Professor Popkin, write him in care of the History Department, UCLA, Los Angeles, CA, USA 90024.

---

[55]Ibid, pp. 113-114.
[56]Ibid, p. 114. Bold mine.
[57]*Books of Nature and Scripture*, p. xi.

HOW WE OBTAINED PERMISSION TO PUBLISH THE CONFRONTATIONAL CORRESPONDENCE OVER NEWTON'S PAPERS AND EINSTEIN'S LETTERS

You are probably wondering how we finally obtained permission to publish these letters of permission which allowed you to read the Newton/Einstein material. Let me tell you, it was not easy. After I requested permission from Mr. Ben Natan (from public relations), he forwarded it to our "friendly" Rafael Weiser, who wrote:

בית הספרים הלאומי והאוניברסיטאי

THE JEWISH NATIONAL & UNIVERSITY LIBRARY

P.O.B. 503 Jerusalem 91004
Tel. (02)660351 Telex 25367
Fax 972-2-511771
ת״ד 503 ירושלים 91004
טלפון 660351 טלקס 25367

8.12.1992

Mr. Philip Moore

Dear Mr. Moore,

Your Fax of 6.12.1992 to Mr. Ben-Nathan - forwarded to us - concerning your request to publish material from our collections and letters we wrote to you, is hardly legible.

Please, send us copies of the whole material (including the letters you received from us) you intend to publish, in normal size, to enable us to read it. Only then we can decide whether we can grant you permission to publish the material.

Sincerely,

Rafael Weiser
Director
Department of Manuscripts & Archives

One hundred years of the Library 1892 - 1992
מאה שנים לבית הספרים תרנ״ב - תשנ״ב

After receiving this letter, I sent all of the material and letters you have read to Rafael Weiser, in the sizes he requested. However, just as I expected, more than three months passed without an answer! When it became obvious to me that I would not get an answer and would be ignored, I phoned my good friend, Ron Bartour.[58] Ron worked with me on the dubbing of the film *Jesus* into Hebrew. More than once, he assisted me in my research at the Hebrew University by helping me locate hard-to-find books! Ron was involved in radio broadcast narration and is presently working on a very interesting book of his own.

AN INSIDE FRIEND HELPED OPEN THE DOOR FOR US

Ron has strong connections within the University and knew the right people. He asked me, "Philip, what do you want?" with that warm Israeli concern of his. I told him which letters I wanted to reproduce and sent them to him along with a draft letter. In his reply, he wrote: "I hope the attached letter which Raffi signed following my talk with head of the University Libraries...on my wife's library stationery is satisfied,[59] I hope you don't intend to print it but only to use it with your publisher."[60]

March 11,1993

Dear Phillip,

I hope the attached letter which Raffi signed following my talk with head of University Libraries) on my wife's library stationary is satisfied, I hope you don't intend to print it but only to use it with your publisher.

Yours,

Ron

---

[58]Ron's credentials are quite impressive. He was the director of the *Tarbut ha Dibor*, the Israeli Institute for Speech Culture. This institute was recognized by the Speech Communications Association, consisting of over 6000 professors, located in Avondale, VA. The institute instructs students, teachers and rabbis how to read the Bible rhetorically in Hebrew. Ron just finished his stay as visiting professor at Heidelberg University in Germany, where he taught Hebrew in the Jewish Studies department. Ron also holds a Ph.D. in the history of contemporary Jewry; was the narrator for the "Voice of Israel" (Kol Israel), Israel radio, was the emissary for the Jewish Agency in Albany, NY; was a graduate student in education in the American history department of the University of Wisconsin; was an officer of education in the Israeli Army's College of Education, and; was a volunteer (*Tzua Kavar*) in the Israeli Defense Force (IDF), where he obtained the rank of major. He is presently working on a book, *American Holy Land.*

[59]i.e., satisfactory.

[60]As you can see, we did not publish Raffi's letter, as Ron asked.

I realize that these letters, and especially the one which Ron asked that I not print, may prove to be embarrassing[61] to Rafael Weiser (Director of the Department of Manuscripts of the Hebrew University), but I felt it necessary to reveal the difficulty I had in fighting for the opportunity for my readers to have the privilege of reading Newton's material. I would like to thank my good friend, Ron Bartour, whom I greatly appreciate and will never forget.

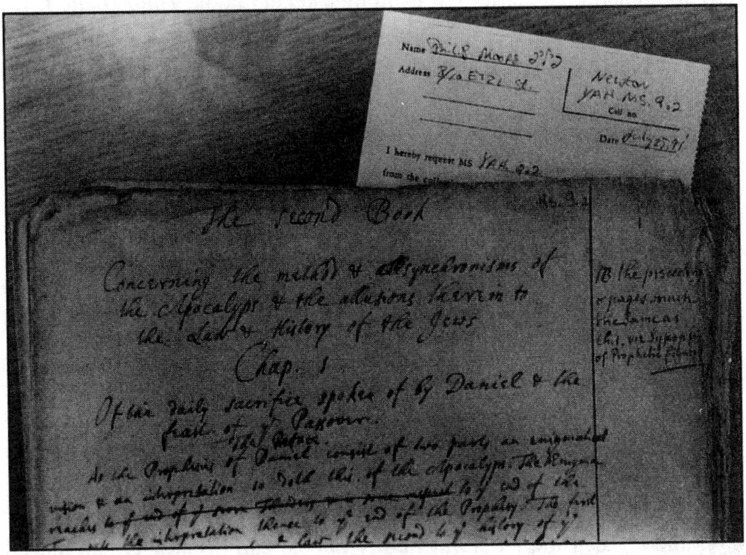

Hesitance to allow certain of Newton's Manuscripts to be made public in a Christian book may have been due to the beliefs he held. As David Castillejo said: "Newton believed that Christ dominates both the Old and the New Testament. All appearances of Jehova in the Bible are in fact appearances of Christ: it was Christ who walked in the Garden of Eden, who gave Moses the ten Commandments, who appeared to Abraham as an Angel, who fought with Jacob, who gave the prophecies to the prophets. He is the Prince Michael mentioned by Daniel, and he will come to judge the quick and the dead. The Jews are ruled by Christ in an absolute monarchy, and he is their lord."[62] This is no doubt something about which a Hebrew University official who does not believe in Jesus may have had reservations.

---

61 No doubt, Mr. Weiser would be embarrassed, as the letter was written on Ron's wife's stationery and stamped "Manuscript Department," thus indicating that Raffi had a little helpful push in the decision to grant me permission.

62 David Castillejo, *The Expanding Force in Newton's Cosmos.* Madrid: Ediciones De Arte Y Bibliofilia, © 1981, p. 60, used by permission.

DESPITE ALL, WE ARE STILL GRATEFUL TO THE HEBREW UNIVERSITY, SINCE OUR PERMISSION TO QUOTE HAS EXCEEDED OTHERS, WHO IN SOME CASES, COULD ONLY PARAPHRASE

We are grateful that the Einstein letters landed[63] at the Hebrew University! Had they not, you may have never seen them. Roger Highfield and Paul Carter tell us in their recent book, *The Private Lives of Albert Einstein*: "All the efforts of Dukas and Nathan were devoted to ensuring that Einstein retained his mystery, and that his reputation continued undimmed.

Biographers and researchers who attempted to investigate Einstein's life, or to make use of his writings, found their efforts constantly thwarted. Crucial sources of information were either suppressed or censored....scholars suspect that vital material was kept hidden or destroyed. Mark Darby, librarian and archivist at the Institute, says, 'The rumour is, and I don't know if it's true, that they threw stuff[64] out. Part of the problem, I guess, was with Helen Dukas and Otto Nathan, who did not—absolutely distinct, clear, did not—want anything to be made public that made Albert Einstein look anything less than perfect'....As a Jew, she [Elizabeth] sympathized with his suggestion that the letters be given to the Hebrew University in Jerusalem, which was subsequently to become the ultimate repository of the archive. But she may have felt under pressure closer to home to keep the letters in family hands, and eventually she placed them under a trust with Hans Albert's grandson, Thomas Einstein. Stachel did not know what the letters contained....Just before her death, Dukas and Nathan had handed control over Einstein's estate to the Hebrew University, in accordance with his will. The original documents of the archive were transferred to the Jewish National and University Library in Jerusalem. However, Nathan continued to harry the Einstein scholars in America until his own death on 27 January 1987, aged ninety-three. The biographer of Einstein's American years, Jamie Sayen, was close to both Dukas and Nathan....Their passing was not mourned by many Einstein scholars: Jagdish Mehra remarked that

---

[63]We are also truly grateful that the majority of Newton's religious papers have ended up there. We could not imagine him being more pleased that these are in the Jewish National Library in the new state which he so ardently forsaw and foretold!

[64]Some have speculated that Einstein may have been a true believer. Some of the "stuff" they threw out may have been evidence of his faith that Jesus was the Jewish Messiah. We have a provocative (for a Jew) quote stating his admiration for Jesus from a *Saturday Evening Post* article, in our chapter 15, "Messianic Jewish Faith in Jesus." However, it in itself, is by no means conclusive proof.

'everybody rejoiced' when Nathan died....In 1992, however, the Hebrew University gave permission for their [Einstein's letters to Elsa] contents to be published by Princeton University Press. It was a decision that marks a clean break with the censorship established by Dukas and Nathan, and the promise of a new era that will allow the systematic publication of all the papers. This, in turn, will allow an objective assessment of both Einstein the scientist and Einstein the man. All those interested in his life will be in the Hebrew University's debt."[65]

On the front cover of Highfield and Carter's book it is revealed: "In fact, so intensely guarded and obscured were the true details of Einstein's personal life that it took the authors six months to gain permission to quote from Einstein's correspondence, and even then many letters could only be paraphrased that have never before been published."[66] So now I can at least suspect that I was not personally singled out during my one-year quest because of my beliefs—nice to know!

NEWTON WAS ONLY ONE OF MANY CHRISTIAN ZIONISTS—THERE ARE SEVERAL MORE

My love for Isaac Newton is greatest when I remind myself of his Zionism and his predictions of Israel's rebirth. Still, there were quite a few Christian Zionists, though most have been lost to layman's history. Consequently, the subject of our forthcoming chapter, "Christian Zionists Past and Present," is one of my favorites. I hope it will be one of yours also!

***

[65]Roger Highfield and Paul Carter, *The Private Lives of Albert Einstein.* New York: St. Martin's Press, © 1993, pp. 273, 276, 279, 282. [ ] mine.
[66]Ibid, front cover.

Mary Ann Evans (George Eliot), John Locke, John Milton and Harry S. Truman—Christian Zionists? Yes!

"Say not a Christian e'er would persecute a Jew; A Gentile might, but not a Christian true. Pilate and Roman guard that folly tried. And with that great Jew's death an empire died!"[1] Will Houghton, past president of Moody Bible Institute

"...for the first time in more than 2000 years Jerusalem is now completely in the hands of the Jews [this] gives the student of the Bible a thrill and a renewed faith in the accuracy and validity of the Bible...."[2]

L. Nelson Bell, Billy Graham's father-in-law, speaking for the Evangelical Christians on July 21, 1967, hailing Israel's Six Day War victory

"The evangelical community is the largest and fastest growing block of pro-Israeli, pro-Jewish sentiment in this country."[3]

The late Rabbi Marc Tannenbaum, the American-Jewish Committee's national interreligious affairs director, 1981

"Your [Christian] sympathy, solidarity and belief in the future of Israel—this to us is tremendous. We consider you part of the fulfillment of the prophetic vision expressed by Zechariah in Chapter 14. Your presence here will always remain a golden page in the book of eternity in heaven. May the Lord bless you out of Zion."[4] Chief Rabbi Shlomo Goren, 1980

"Indeed, the manifestation of growing support from our Christian friends all over the world was a source of encouragement to me and my colleagues."[5]

Israeli Prime Minister, Menachem Begin, 1983

12

CHRISTIAN ZIONISTS PAST AND PRESENT

Do true born-again Christians really love Israel? Can we be sure Christian Zionism is not just a lot of talk? How? By putting our money where our mouth is. At the 1990 Christian Feast of Tabernacles held at the Benyenei Ha Uma Auditorium in Jerusalem, where 5000 Christians from many different nations came to express their support for the State of Israel, Prime Minister Yitzhak Shamir was presented with a check for one million dollars to help Soviet Jews come to Israel. Many Israelis were amazed to see that Christians could love Israel so much. Being born-again is just what it means.

---

[1]Elwood McQuaid, "The Biblical Injunction." *Israel My Glory,* Apr.-May 1993, p. 6, © used by permission.

[2]Dan O'Neill and Don Wagner, *Peace or Armageddon.* Grand Rapids, MI : Zondervan Publishing House, © 1993, p. 81, used by permission. [ ] mine. O'Neill and Wagner's source was *Christianity Today*, July 21, 1967.

[3]Ibid, p. 83. O'Neill and Wagner's source was the *Washington Post*, Mar. 23, 1981.

[4]"The Press of Israel on the International Christian Embassy Jerusalem," Jerusalem: International Christian Embassy.

[5]Ibid.

A representative of the International Christian Embassy presents Israeli Prime Minister Yitzhak Shamir with a check for one million dollars to help Russian Jews emigrate to Israel.

ALL PROTESTANTS ARE NOT TRUE-TO-THE-BIBLE SUPPORTERS OF PROPHECY AND ZIONISM

Before we list the true believers who have extended a helping hand to Jews throughout the ages, we would like to emphasize that many "Protestant" reformers who emerged from Catholicism, either mistreated the Jews,[6] or worse, killed Christian Zionists.[7] The true believers, the millennial Zionists or pre-millennialists, as they are sometimes called, have a virtually sterling record in their love and support of the Jew, as they adopt the New Testament commands in this respect. The command of love toward the Jew is one of the most important facets of their faith and loyalty to Jesus! These were and are Christians who believed the Jews would return to Israel before Jesus returns to set up a 1000-year (millennial) kingdom (Matt. 19:28).

Hal Lindsey, in his well-known book, *Road to Holocaust*, defines the Christian pre-millennial faith: "One of the fundamental elements of a Premillennialist's faith is that God has bound Himself by unconditional covenants to the Jews and that even though they are currently under His discipline He will punish anyone who mistreats them. As God swore to Abraham and reconfirmed to his successors, **'I**

---

[6]For an illustration of this, see Martin Luther's anti-Semitic publication, *Concerning the Jews and Their Lies*, written in 1544. For English excerpts of this see Regina Sharif, *Non-Jewish Zionism*, p. 21; and Hal Lindsey, *The Road to Holocaust*, p. 23.

[7]Regina Sharif documents the persecution of these Christian Messianic Zionists by Lutheran and Calvinist sects. She writes: "On the Continent messianic hopes were voiced by...the Anabaptists...but Lutheran and Calvinist official churches ruthlessly persecuted them as disruptive heretical forces....In Holland and Switzerland, a few messianic sects survived at the price of adopting a certain measure of conformity. In Germany, they were stamped out when Lutheranism had achieved a position of equality with Catholicism to form an alliance with the established order." Regina Sharif, *Non-Jewish Zionism*, p. 17. Several eyewitness accounts of this persecution of true believers are recorded in John T. Christian's book. He documents: "Henry VIII was already interested in the extermination of the Baptists, and his zeal extended to foreign lands. He extended his help in exterminating the Baptists in Germany....The Baptists died with the greatest fortitude. Of them Latimer says: 'The Anabaptists that were burnt here in divers towns in England...went to their death, even intrepid, as ye will say, without any fear in the world, cheerfully....'...In October, 1538, the king appointed a Commission composed of Thomas Cranmer, the Archbishop of Canterbury, as President...to prosecute the Anabaptists....the books of the Baptists were burnt wherever they were found....'...Anabaptists, and the like, who sell books of false doctrine, are to be detected to the king or Privy Council'....All strangers who 'lately rebaptized themselves' were ordered from the kingdom, and some Baptists were burnt at the stake....In the reign of Edward VI (1547-1553) the laws against the Baptists were enforced, and the two persons burned at the stake in this reign were Baptists....criminals were pardoned, but to be a Baptist was a grave crime." John T. Christian, A.M., D.D., LL.D., *A History of the Baptists: Together With Some Account of Their Principles and Practices*, Vol. I, pp. 191-193, 196.

will bless those who bless you, and whoever curses you I will curse....' "[8]

Lindsey goes on to show that the original church of Jesus' day taught and authorized these beliefs: "...the early Church...firmly believed that Israel was yet to be redeemed as a Nation and given her unconditionally promised Messianic Kingdom. They [the early Church until Augustine] believed that this theocratic kingdom would be set up on earth by Christ at His Second Coming, and that it would last for a thousand years. This teaching was called the doctrine of Chiliasm. (Chilias [χιλιας] is the Greek word for one thousand. The term chiliasm meant the belief in a literal one thousand year Messianic Kingdom on earth.)"[9]

Many of these individuals who espoused Chiliasm wrote books on the return of Jewry to Israel hundreds of years before it began to occur. Later, during the Holocaust, they saved Jews and Jewish children, at the risk of their own lives.[10] Indeed, some died in this service[11] when they were caught by the Nazis and murdered for helping Jews escape Hitler.

Lindsey further details: "Premillennialists believe that Christ will return to the earth with a cataclysmic judgment of the whole world. He will then separate the surviving unbelievers from the believers, casting the unbelievers off the earth directly into judgment (Matthew 25:31-46).

"Premillennialists believe that the Lord Jesus will at that time remove the curse from nature and restore the earth to its original pre-sin condition during the one-thousand-year Messianic Kingdom (Isaiah 65:17-25; Romans 8:18-25, etc.).

"The believers who survive the seven-year Tribulation period will be taken as mortals into a global Theocratic Kingdom over which Jesus the Messiah will reign for a thousand years. He will reign on the Davidic throne from Jerusalem.

---

[8]Hal Lindsey, *The Road To Holocaust*, p. 2.

[9]Ibid, pp. 10-11. First [ ] mine.

[10]Sholem Asch, Jewish scholar and writer, remarked concerning: "*...events associated with the Nazi period*....Christianity also distinguished itself, in the particular of rescuing Jewish children, by the highest degree of self-sacrifice. It may be stated without exaggeration that almost the entire remnant of Israel which was found in the liberated countries—no matter how small its number—has the Christians to thank for its preservation, Christians who, by performing this action, placed their own lives in danger." Arthur W. Kac, *The Messiahship of Jesus*, p. 18.

[11]Several of these cases were related to me by Arieh L. Bauminger, a rabbi, Holocaust survivor and former keeper of Yad VaShem (Israel's Holocaust Memorial Museum). I interviewed him in Israel regarding the number of righteous Gentiles who saved Jews, in connection with his famous work, *Hasdi Umot Ha Olam*, now translated as *The Righteous Among The Nations.*

At this time, the believing survivors from the physical descendants of Abraham, Isaac, and Jacob will receive all the things promised to them in the Abrahamic, Palestinian, Davidic, and New Covenants. (These will be defined in chapters four and five.)

Premillennialists also believe in a distinct, sudden snatching out of believers to meet the LORD in the air. In this event, believers will be instantaneously transformed from mortality to immortality without experiencing physical death (1 Corinthians 15:50-53; 1 Thessalonians 4:13-18, etc.). This is commonly called 'the Rapture.' The Church will return to the earth with Christ at His Second Advent in immortal form to reign with him as priests during the millennium."[12]

In this particular work, Hal's arguments were directed against the Christian Reform Movement and Dominion Theology, which deny the biblical truth about the millenium. We agree!

A CHECKLIST ON PREMILLENNIALISTS—THEIR HISTORY, BOOKS, AND DEEDS

Now that we have finished reading about the Church of Rome and their commission of some of the most atrocious acts ever recorded in history,[13] let's look at some of the good and loving deeds performed by those who claim to be true followers of Jesus.

Seemingly unknown to history, in the past several hundred years there were many true believers who, in the face of Catholic persecution, stood up for the rights of the Jews, as God's people, to return to their homeland! Many of these people risked and even lost their lives protecting and saving Jews from their Roman Catholic persecutors. Thus we as ardent searchers for history's hidden truths, should list these brave born-again heroes of the faith. And in so doing, not only honor these heroes, but uncover for ourselves the other side of the coin.

Few are aware of the "underground true believers" and their deeds, books, and love. While the Roman Catholic Church was murdering innocent Protestants and Jews, there was an effort of true Bible believing Christians to teach the precious truth of Bible prophecy, in order to save Jews, and organize movements, which would allow their desire to return to Israel to become a realistic possibility. It is also our strong assertion that just as Roman Catholicism has been historically noted and condemned for its vicious persecutions of Jews, space in this historical record should be taken to recognize and commend the true believing Christians for saving the Jews and advocating the literal fulfillment of the prophecies which

[12]Hal Lindsey, *The Road to Holocaust*, pp. 30-31.

[13]In our chapter 10, "Early Christian History Versus Catholicism."

predict the Jewish return to Israel. We believe this heritage of true believers has yet to be documented and credited in popular layman's terms.

WHO WERE THE CHRISTIAN ZIONISTS?

The great theologian, Thomas Brightman (1562-1607), stated in his *Apocalypsis Apocalypseos*: "...the Jews as a nation shall return again to Palestine, as the land of their early Fathers...."[14]

Joanna and Ebenezer Cartwright, Puritans who lived in Amsterdam, wrote a petition which was sent to the government of England in 1649. In it were these words: "That this Nation of England, with the inhabitants of the Netherlands, shall be the first and the readiest to transport Israel's sons and daughters on their ships to the land promised to their forefathers, Abraham, Isaac and Jacob for an everlasting inheritance."[15]

Michael Servetus and Francis Kett of England, who wrote about the restoration of Jews as God's chosen people, to their land, Israel, were burnt alive at the stake by "Church" authorities for their unwillingness to recant their faith. they were branded as Christian Judaizers and burnt 1553 and 1589.[16]

Isaac de La Peyrere (1594-1676), the French Ambassador to Denmark, was the leader of a large group of Christian Millennial Zionists in France. La Peyrere wrote a book entitled, *Rappel des Juifs*, calling for the "Restoration of Israel as the Jewish nation in the Holy Land."[17] He sent this treatise to the French government. This work was only allowed into publication two centuries after he wrote it, when Napoleon requested that the Jewish Sanhedrin be reestablished in 1806.

In 1655, Paul Felgenhauer (1593-1677) of Germany, published a book entitled *Good News for Israel*. In this book he: "...maintained that the Second Coming of Christ and the arrival of the Jewish Messiah were one and the same event. The sign that was to announce the advent of this Judaeo-Christian Messiah would be, in typical millenarian fashion, 'the permanent return of the Jews to their own country eternally bestowed upon them by God through his unqualified promise to Abraham, Isaac and Jacob.' "[18]

---

[14]Regina Sharif, *Non-Jewish Zionism*, p. 18.

[15]Ibid, p. 24. Sharif's source was Don Patinkin, "Mercantilism and the Readmission of the Jews to England," *Jewish Social Studies*, Vol. 8. © July 1946, pp. 161-178.

[16]Ibid, p. 17.

[17]Ibid, p. 27.

[18]Ibid, p. 28. Sharif's source was *Rengstorf and Kortzfleisch*, pp. 59-60.

In 1696, Denmark's Holger Paulli submitted a plan to William III of England asking the King to "re-conquer Palestine for the Jews so that they might re-establish a state of their own."[19] Paulli called on Europe's Monarchs "to liberate Palestine and Jerusalem from the infidel in order to settle the original and rightful heirs, the Jews."[20] In his plan to the King of England, he referred to the King as "Cyrus the Great and the Almighty's instrument."[21] Cyrus had allowed the Jews to return to Israel from their Babylonian captivity 2600 years ago (Isa. 44).

Germany's Anders Pederson Kempe (1622-89), who became a theologian after leaving the army, was forced out of Stockholm because of his outspokenness regarding German Messianism. In 1688, near Hamburg, he published his book, *Israel's Good News*, in which he wrote: "You heathen Christians, you let yourselves be persuaded by false teachers, especially the Grandmother of all fornication, Rome, to believe that the Jews were forever disinherited and rejected by God and that you were now the rightful Christian Israel, to possess the Land of Canaan forever."[22] These were statements clearly in defense of the Jews against Catholicism and in support of their right to return to Israel!

MEN OF THE CLOTH, PHILOSOPHY AND SCIENCE WERE ALSO AVID CHRISTIAN ZIONISTS

John Locke, the great English philosopher, wrote in his New Testament commentary on Paul's epistles: "God is able to collect the Jews into one body...and set them in flourishing condition in their own Land."[23]

Sir Isaac Newton, the greatest scientist who ever lived, quoted elsewhere in this work, wrote "in his *Observations upon the Prophecies of Daniel and the Apocalypse of St. John*, first published five years after his death...that the Jews will indeed return to their homeland: 'The manner I know not. Let time be the interpreter.' He even attempted to set up a timetable for the events leading to the Restoration and expected the intervention of an earthly power on behalf of the dispersed Jews to effect their return."[24]

---

[19]Ibid.
[20]Ibid.
[21]Ibid.
[22]Ibid. Sharif's source was *Rengstorf and Kortzfleisch*, p. 63.
[23]Ibid, p. 36.
[24]Ibid.

Joseph Priestly, the famous chemist who discovered oxygen, was a Zionist. Regina Sharif writes of him: "...Priestly remained convinced that Judaism and Christianity were complementary....His plea to the Jews to acknowledge Jesus as the Messiah was therefore coupled with his prayer that 'the God of Heaven, the God of Abraham, Isaac and Jacob whom we Christians as well as you worship, may be graciously pleased to put an end to your suffering, gathering you from all nations, resettle you in your own country, the land of Canaan and make you the most illustrious...of all nations on the earth.' "[25]

James Bicheno published his work, *The Restoration of the Jews, The Crisis of All Nations*, in 1800. In 1802, Jung-Stilling, the famous eye specialist, wrote in his book, *Das Heimweh von Heinrich Stilling*: "...'God has proclaimed through the prophets of old that the people of Israel would be scattered throughout the world. Who can deny that this has taken place? Yet the same prophets have prophesied that in the latter days God would gather his people again from the four corners of the earth, and bring them back to the land which he promised to their fathers long ago to be an everlasting possession....The land of Palestine will again become the possession of the Jewish people.' "[26]

In 1894, William Hechler, the chaplain of the British Embassy in Vienna, an Evangelical Christian and the closest friend of Theodore Herzl (the father of modern political Jewish Zionism), wrote in his book, *The Restoration of the Jews to Palestine*, of "...'restoring the Jews to Palestine according to Old Testament prophecies'. "[27] This book predates Herzl's great work *Der Judenstaat* by two years. Herzl spoke fondly of the chaplain in his diary. Hechler often expressed his "great love"[28] for the Jewish people.

MILTON, AUTHOR OF *PARADISE LOST*, A ZIONIST?

John Milton, in his celebrated *Paradise Regained*, wrote of Israel's restitution. However, few may recall his exact words, which were: "Yet He at length, time to himself best know Remembering Abraham, by some wondrous call May bring them back...."[29]

Sharif grudgingly documents Milton's deep fundamental prophetic faith: "Milton stated it clearly: Israel would be restored to

---

[25]Ibid, pp. 36-37.

[26]Kurt E. Koch, *The Coming One*. Grand Rapids, MI: Kregal Publishing, © 1972, p. 88, used by permission. This book was first published in German under the title *Der Kommende*, © 1971.

[27]Regina Sharif, *Non-Jewish Zionism*, p. 71.

[28]Ibid.

[29]Ibid, p. 34.

Palestine, not by conquest but rather by some supernatural event. His *De Doctrina Christiana* (not published until 1825) testifies to Milton's own millenarian convictions and belief in Israel's revival."[30]

BROWNING'S ZIONIST POETRY

The well-known English poet, Robert Browning, was also a true believer in Jesus! As a Millennial Zionist Christian, he made his points of view known in his poetry. He was an expert[31] in Jewish literature and often read the Bible (Old Testament) in the original Hebrew. In Browning's poem "The Holy Cross Day," written in 1855, he beautifully illustrates his enthusiastic faith in the return of Jews to Israel, according to Bible prophecy. A portion of this poem reads: "The Lord will have mercy on Jacob yet, And again in his border see Israel yet, When Judah beholds Jerusalem, The strangers shall be joined to them; To Jacob's House shall the Gentiles cleave, So the Prophet saith and the sons believe."[32]

OLIPHANT'S ZIONIST IDEAS RAISE HOPE IN THE GHETTOS

Laurence Oliphant of England (1829-1888), though he may be unknown to most of the world, is honored in Israel to this day. An Israeli reporter, Beth Uval, noted: "His parents were fanatically religious and raised him with...Evangelical strictness...."[33]

Oliphant was known for being "the only Christian member of the English Hovevei Zion branch [a Jewish Zionist charter]."[34] Later in his life he settled in Haifa, Israel. He lived there in 1882 with his wife, Alice.[35]

In an article which pictured a street named for him in Jerusalem, Uval, in the March 1989 *Jerusalem Post*, wrote: "Oliphant became interested in Zionism....His interest was based on...the belief, prevalent in the Evangelical circles in which Oliphant grew up, that the Jews' restoration to Jerusalem was a prerequisite for the Second Coming of the Messiah....Oliphant's efforts to obtain a Turkish concession for Jewish settlement in Palestine took him to Damascus and the Sultan's court in Constantinople (in 1879)....Oliphant's public support for the Zionist idea raised high hopes in the ghettos of Eastern Europe, and he

---

[30] Ibid.
[31] Ibid, p. 45.
[32] Ibid.
[33] Beth Uval, "An Oliphant Not Forgotten," *Jerusalem Post*, March 3, 1989, © used by permission.
[34] Ibid. [ ] mine.
[35] Ibid.

was inundated with letters calling him 'Redeemer' and 'the second Cyrus.'

Laurence and Alice Oliphant settled in Haifa toward the end of 1882. Their Hebrew-language secretary was Naphtali Herz Imber, who wrote 'Hatikva' [*The Hope*—Israel's national anthem]...."[36]

MARCH 3, 1989 **IN JERUSALEM**

(Zeev Ackerman)

Oliphant Street looking south toward Pinsker from D'Israeli. Inset shows Laurence Oliphant in 1854 at age 25.

An Oliphant not forgotten

Street scene/Beth Uval

Talbieh's Laurence Oliphant Street, notable for its gracious homes and lush gardens, probably would have appealed to Oliphant's romantic spirit.

The son of Scottish aristocrats who became the only Christian member of the English Hovevei Zion branch, Oliphant (1829-1888) was in some ways strikingly modern. After spending most of his life in an adventurous search for action and meaning – that included travel throughout Europe and the Far East and prolonged involvement with a dubious mystic sect in the U.S.– Oliphant embraced Zionism as his final cause and spent his latter years in Haifa.

His parents were fanatically religious and raised him with a curious mixture of indulgence and Evangelical strictness, a combination that left its mark on his character, according to his biographers. One writer described him as "brilliantly intelligent, perceptive, and intuitive, with a gift of wit and fluent expression, but also impulsive, emotional, moody, and given to precious brooding about religion and morality."

These qualities found expression in a remarkably chequered career that included writing popular travel books, satire, novels, and religious tracts; a stint as London's *The Times* correspondent in the Franco-Prussian War; and international diplomatic activity as a secret agent of the British government.

The same qualities apparently also made him susceptible to the ultimately disastrous influence of Thomas Lake Harris, one of the self-styled prophets who roamed the U.S. at the time. Unfortunately for Oliphant, Harris was preaching in England at a time when Oliphant, despite the promise of a brilliant political career and the success of his writing, was suffering a bout of depression and, some speculate, syphilis as well. Oliphant fell into the clutches of the unscrupulous and manipulative Harris, who had formerly been preaching in the backwoods of Georgia.

In the summer of 1867, Oliphant left his Parliamentary seat and invitations to dine with royalty for Harris's "Brotherhood of the New Life" commune on the shores of Lake Erie in upperstate New York. According to one biographer, "the end of [Oliphant's] long journey from Mayfair was an empty shed with a few wooden crates out of which he had to construct his bed, a table and [illegible] to sit on. His meals were sent over to him in a basket and he was not allowed to speak to more than one or two people."

[illegible] some 20th-century sect leaders, Harris somehow convinced people like Oliphant [illegible] spend their days carting manure, and maintain celibacy though married while he, Harris, lived in a 30-room mansion which he shared only with a few select women, his wife not among them.

Oliphant became interested in Zionism after a crisis precipitated by Harris's refusal to let him see his wife, Alice. His interest was based on both British strategic considerations in the Middle East and the belief, prevalent in the Evangelical circles in which Oliphant grew up, that the Jews' restoration to Jerusalem was a prerequisite for the Second Coming of the Messiah. He was probably also motivated by his taste for international intrigue and a genuine desire to be of service to humanity in a big way.

Oliphant's efforts to obtain a Turkish concession for Jewish settlement in Palestine took him to Damascus and the Sultan's court in Constantinople (in 1879). Like Herzl several years later, Oliphant left the Sultan empty-handed. According to an eyewitness account, Oliphant himself "put a stopper on it [the concession] by telling the Sultan's secretary that he was seeking to fulfil the Scripture that the end of the world was to come when the Jews were restored to their native land, and his Majesty had no desire to hurry that event."

Although his diplomatic efforts were ultimately fruitless, Oliphant's public support for the Zionist idea raised high hopes in the ghettos of Eastern Europe, and he was inundated with letters calling him "Redeemer" and "the second Cyrus."

Laurence and Alice Oliphant settled in Haifa toward the end of 1882. Their Hebrew-language secretary was Naphtali Herz Imber, who wrote "Hatikva" while working for them. In addition to befriending the local Druse and helping the Jewish settlers in the Galilee, the Oliphants (although finally free of Harris) became deeply involved in increasingly far-fetched mystic doctrines.

According to a contemporary observer, "the Turkish authorities themselves learned to reckon with the Oliphants for they were naturally credited with that measure of madness which is deemed throughout the East to derive from God."

Expressing what seem to have been the sentiments of many of his contemporaries, the same observer wrote that it was "difficult to understand Oliphant, but impossible not to love him."

A *Jerusalem Post* article by Beth Uval, featuring Laurence Oliphant, a nineteenth century Christian Zionist. The photo is of a street in Jerusalem named for Oliphant.

---

[36] Ibid. [ ] mine.

GEORGE ELIOT FORESEES AND ENCOURAGES THE EXISTENCE OF ISRAEL

The famous English novelist, George Eliot,[37] who may be familiar to you from your high school English literature classes, made a landmark contribution to what we are calling the "Christian Zionist Movement," as a millennial Zionist! She was a true believer who loved, supported and encouraged the Jews in their right to reestablish the State of Israel! In 1874, she began writing *Daniel Deronda.* Sharif describes the novel as follows: "Eliot's debt to...Evangelism, though unacknowledged, must be considered. The Gentile author created in *Daniel Deronda* a true Zionist hero who discovers for himself his Jewish nationality and heritage.

The novel represents the apex of non-Jewish Zionism in the literary field, the culmination of a long tradition that began with the Protestant idea of Restoration....George Eliot....was a deeply religious Christian...caught up in the full tide of the Evangelical movement....She regularly visited Jewish synagogue meetings and....met Moses Hess, the Jewish Zionist....[of her novel *Daniel Deronda*, Sharif comments] *Daniel Deronda* displays the possibility of having contemporary Jewish prophets and leaders as in ancient times. The heritage of the Jews is presented as most worthy of rediscovery and accepted as a way of national revival and final redemption. She strongly believed that 19th Century Jews in Europe were renouncing their own unique national heritage by striving for assimilation and amalgamation with other nations.

Daniel Deronda was the 'literary introduction' to the Balfour Declaration....[part of Eliot's *Daniel Deronda* reads] 'There is store of wisdom among us to found a new Jewish polity, grand, simple, just, like the old—a republic where there is equality of protection, an equality which shone like a star on the forehead of our ancient community, and gave it more than the brightness of Western freedom amid despotisms of the East. Then our race shall have an organic

---

[37]George Eliot was the pen name used by Mary Ann Evans to increase her readership. In her day, the literary works of men were more widely read and respected than than those of women. *The Jewish Encyclopedia* says that George Eliot was: "...a friend of the talmudic scholar Emanuel Deutsch, and began to study Hebrew and to show an interest in Jewish matters at an early age. *Daniel Deronda* (1874-76), her celebrated 'Zionist' novel....the hero of this novel, after discovering his Jewish identity only in his 20's, eventually leaves for Palestine to help 'revive the organic center' of his people's existence. *Daniel Deronda* influenced the early Zionist thinker Eliezer Ben-Yahuda, and such Hebrew writers as I.L. Peretz and P. Smolenskin....George Eliot discussed the Jewish question again in 'The Modern Hep-Hep' a strong attack on anti-Jewish prejudice published in a collection of essays entitled *Theophrastus Such* (1878)." *The Encyclopaedia Judaica Jerusalem*, Vol. 6. Jerusalem: Keter Publishing House Ltd., © 1971, pp. 663-664, used by permission.

centre, a heart and a brain to watch and guide and execute; the outraged Jew shall have a defence in the court of nations, as the outraged Englishman or American. And the world will gain as Israel gains'...."[38]

Eliot, in 1879, wrote in "The Modern Hep, Hep, Hep": "The hinge of possibility is simply the existence of an adequate community of feeling as well as widespread need in the Jewish race, and hope that among its finest specimens there may arise some men of instruction and ardent public spirit, some new Ezras, some modern Macabees, who will know how to use all favouring outward conditions, how to triumph by heroic example over the indifference of their fellows and foes, and will steadfastly set their faces toward making their people once more one among the nations."[39]

"ELIOT'S" (EVANS') SEVENTEENTH CENTURY FEAT—AN EXAMPLE FOR ALL EVANGELICALS TO FOLLOW IN THEIR ZIONIST SUPPORT OF ISRAEL

Quite a feat of inspirational support for a nation yet to exist, coming from this famed true believer in Jesus, isn't it? An example for today's Evangelical Millennial Zionists, found among the Baptists, Church of God,[40] Plymouth Brethren and several other denominations, who cheer Israel on in total agreement with the prophecies found in the Old and New Testaments of the Bible!

PROFESSOR POPKIN REMINDS US THAT CHRISTIAN SCHOLARS OF THAT TIME STUDIED HEBREW AND BUILT JEWISH TEMPLES

Richard Popkin tells us in his book, *Jewish Christians and Christian Jews*: "In the Netherlands, from the 1620's onward Christian scholars were learning Hebrew and were discussing religious points with Jews. Christians were also attending Jewish religious services. Two rabbis became quite involved with Christians in projects of joint concern. Rabbi Judah Leon and the leader of the Collegiants, Adam Boreel, joined forces to construct an exact accurate model of Solomon's Temple. Boreel financed the project to the point of having

---

[38]Regina Sharif, *Non-Jewish Zionism*, pp. 46-47. [ ] mine.
[39]Ibid, p. 47.
[40]The Church of God should not be confused with the Worldwide Church of God, which is a cult. We are referring to the Church of God, such as the one in Atlanta, Georgia with Pastor Paul Walker. This church sticks to the Scriptures and is pro-Zionist. We will recommend Pastor Walker any day.

rabbi Judah Leon living in his house for some years. The Temple model became one of the glories of Amsterdam, was on display in rabbi Judah Leon's garden for years until he took it to England to give to Charles II, after which it has still not been traced. They also joined forces in a project, which lasted at least thirty years, on editing the *Mishna* in Hebrew with vowel points, notes, and translations of the text into Spanish and Latin.

The other rabbi who became important, and much more important, in Christian circles, was Menasseh ben Israel, who was born in La Rochelle, France, was raised in Lisbon, and then turned up in Amsterdam in his teens, and became a teacher of Hebrew. It is not known where he received his education, but Menasseh by the 1620's exhibited a broad knowledge of Jewish and Christian literature."[41]

A RABBI OF THE 1620'S TEACHES CHRISTIANS HEBREW, AS HE SHARES THEIR EXPECTATION OF MESSIAH

Professor Popkin tells us: "We find in the late 1620's that Menasseh was teaching Christians Hebrew and that they were consulting him on various subjects. He became the first Hebrew printer in The Netherlands, and was an important bookseller, obtaining Hebrew books for Jewish and Christian scholars from Poland, Italy and the Levant....one finds Menasseh in contact with all sorts of learned Christians, people coming from various countries to hear him preach and to confer with him....He became friendly with John Dury, the Scottish Millenarian who was preacher for Princess Mary. He was in contact with the leading mystical Millenarians, and apparently shared their expectation....Boreel started the publication project with his work with rabbi Templo on the Hebrew text of the *Mishna*, (finally published in 1646 by Menasseh, and paid for by Dutch Millenarians). Menasseh's name was listed as editor instead of Boreel, because as Boreel explained the Jews would not buy the edition if a Christian was the editor. One of the reasons for the *Mishna* project is that the texts include the most exact descriptions of the Temple and the ceremonies held therein. This would be crucial information if Jerusalem was about to be restored....When Menasseh came to London in September 1655 he was wined and dined by leading English Millenarians. Robert Boyle's sister, Lady Ranlegh had dinner parties for him. Adam Boreel, the leader of the Dutch Collegiants, came to London and held a dinner for him with Boyle and Henry Oldenburg."[42]

---

[41]*Jewish Christians and Christian Jews*. Dordrecht, Holland: Kluwer Academic Publishers, © 1994, p. 59, used by permission. Richard H. Popkin and Gordon M. Weiner, editors.

[42]Ibid, pp. 60-61, 63.

A BELIEVER OF THE 1600'S FINANCIALLY BACKS A HEBREW PRESS, WHILE PUNISHING THOSE WHO ACCUSED THE JEWS

Allison Coubert reminds us of this little known fact: "...von Rosenroth spent his entire adult life in the service of Christian August of Sulzbach; for Christian August had equally wide interests and ecumenical sympathies. Not only was he intrigued by the Christian Hebraica to the point of subsidizing a Hebrew press, but his policy toward the Jews, whom he invited to settle in Sulzbah in 1666, was both liberal and protective. The charge of ritual murder was brought against the Sulzbach Jews twice during Christian August's regime, in 1682 and again in 1692. On both occasions he actively combatted the charges and ordered corporeal punishment for anyone bringing false accusations against Jews in the future....it is apparent that seventeenth-century Europe was criss-crossed by networks of millenarian Christians...."[43]

A MEMORIAL PRESENTED TO PRESIDENTS HARRISON AND WILSON—GIVE PALESTINE BACK TO THE JEW

Arthur Kac documented: "On March 5, 1891, William E. Blackstone, of Chicago, presented a memorial to President Harrison on behalf of Israel's restoration to the Holy Land. This was signed by over five hundred of America's leading Protestant clergymen, civil leaders, editors, and publishers. In 1917 Mr. Blackstone repeated his effort, reintroduced his memorial, and that time sent it to President Wilson. Part of the memorial reads as follows: 'Why not give Palestine back to them [the Jews] again? According to God's distribution of nations it is their home—an inalienable possession from which they were expelled by force. Under their cultivation it was a remarkably fruitful land, sustaining millions of Israelites, who industriously tilled its hillsides and valleys. They were agriculturists and producers as well as a nation of great commercial importance—the centre of civilization and religion.

'Why shall not the powers which under the treaty of Berlin, in 1878, gave Bulgaria to Bulgarians and Servia to Servians now give Palestine back to the Jews? These provinces, as well as Rumania, Montenegro, and Greece were wrested from the Turks and given to their natural owners. Does not Palestine as rightfully belong to the Jews?' "[44]

---

[43]Ibid, p. 75.

[44]Arthur W. Kac, *The Messiahship of Jesus*, pp. 296-297.

GO BACK TO THE LAND OF ABRAHAM

In 1897, John Stoddard wrote: "In a place so thronged with classic and religious memories as Palestine, even a man who has no Hebrew blood in his veins may indulge in a dream regarding the future of this extraordinary people....'Take again the land of your forefathers. We guarantee you its independence and integrity. It is the least that we can do for you after all these centuries of misery. All of you will not wish to go thither, but many will. At present Palestine supports only six hundred thousand people, but, with proper cultivation it can easily maintain two and a half million. You are a people without a country; there is a country without a people. Be united. Fulfill the dreams of your old poets and patriarchs. Go back,—go back to the land of Abraham.' "[45]

PROPHECY IN MODERN HISTORY

Concerning today's evangelical love and support of Israel among the millennial Protestants, in their lineage and in relation to their counterparts of centuries past, Regina Sharif says: "One of the most definite effects of the Protestant Reformation was the emerging interest in the fulfilment of Biblical prophecies concerning the End of Time. The core of millenarianism was the belief in the Second Coming of Christ whose return would establish God's kingdom on earth, which was to last for 1,000 years (that is, a millennium). Millenarians regarded the future of the Jewish people as an important element in the events to precede the End of Time. In fact, the literal interpretation of the apocalyptic writings in the Bible led them to conclude that the Millennium was to be heralded by the physical Restoration of the Jews as a nation (Israel) to Palestine....Pre-Reformation semi-sectarian minority movements expressing millenarian yearnings had to remain underground. They were persecuted and suppressed by the Church in Rome and their teachings were branded as heresies....it [millenarianism] did maintain a certain presence and its ideas percolated down to the masses. It continued to find followers in every period of history after the Reformation and finally culminated in 20th Century American fundamentalism which insists that the state of Israel presents the literal fulfilment of prophecy in modern history."[46]

---

[45]John L. Stoddard, *John L. Stoddard's Lectures*, Vol. II. Boston: Balch Brothers Co., 1897, pp. 220-221. There are ten volumes of his lectures: "Illustrated and embellished with views of the world's famous places and people, being the identical discourses delivered during the past eighteen years under the title of the Stoddard lectures." This author thanks Dan Levine for pointing out these long-forgotten lectures.

[46]Regina Sharif, *Non-Jewish Zionism*, pp. 16-17. Spelling of fulfillment per original. [ ] mine.

PRESIDENT HARRY S. TRUMAN
BAPTIST—ZIONIST

President Harry S. Truman was elected in 1948, the year of Israel's rebirth! Sharif said: "...Truman had shown a sympathetic understanding of Zionism. His own Southern Baptist background and training stressed the theme of the Jews' Restoration to Zion. The members of the Southern Baptist convention were the most enthusiastic pro-Zionist congregations, championing both the religious and historical claims of the Jews to the land of Palestine. Most Baptists were theologically conservative or even fundamentalist and tended to regard the creation of the Jewish state as the evident fulfilment of Biblical prophecies....Truman's religious background played a great part in his later life. By and large a self-taught man, like Abraham Lincoln, he had educated himself in part through the Bible itself. 'As a student of the Bible he believed in the historic justification for a Jewish homeland and it was a conviction with him that the Balfour Declaration of 1917 constituted a solemn promise that fulfilled the age-old hopes and dreams of the Jewish people.' Truman's autobiography, full of Biblical quotations and allusions, also indicates his marked tendency to dwell upon the Judaeo-Christian tradition.

As a Baptist, Truman sensed something profound and meaningful in the idea of Jewish Restoration. It was a known fact that his favourite Biblical passage was the Psalm 137, beginning 'By the rivers of Babylon, there we sat down, yea, we wept, when we remembered Zion'. Truman once confessed that he could never read the account of the giving of the Ten Commandments at Sinai without a tingle going down his spine. 'The fundamental basis of this nation's law,' he declared, 'was given to Moses on Mount Sinai.'

When Eddie Jacobson introduced Truman in 1953 to an audience at a Jewish theological seminary as 'the man who helped create the State of Israel', Truman's response invoked the enduring Zionist theme of exile and Restoration: 'What do you mean 'helped create'? I am Cyrus, I am Cyrus.' Who could forget that it was Cyrus who made possible the return of the Jews to Jerusalem from their exile in Babylon?"[47]

There is no doubt of the President's loyalty and great contribution to Israel and the Jewish people, is there? President Truman further stated in October of 1948: "...'What we need now is to help the people in Israel, and they've proved themselves in the best traditions of pioneers. They have created out of a barren desert a

---

[47]Ibid, pp. 106-107.

modern and efficient state with the highest standard of Western civilization....' "[48]

President Truman is honored in Israel with a forest named for him. I have visited this wonderful place on several occassions.

REAGAN AND REXELLA ARE ZIONIST

President Ronald Reagan once called Israel "a young, strong, brave nation," in the face of liberal criticism while she was defending herself against terrorism in the 1980's. Reagan, who allotted annual grants of three billion dollars to Israel, often listened to the evangelical ministers Mike Evans and Pat Robertson and was thoroughly convinced of the importance of supporting this biblically prophesized nation (Gen. 12:3).

In 1993, Rexella Van Impe, of Jack Van Impe Ministries, interestingly pointed out that several Christian scholars of the past four centuries, whom we have yet to mention, had very accurately foreseen the rebirth of Israel. In the May/June 1993 edition of *Perhaps Today* magazine, Rexella Van Impe said: "In 1669 a man by the name of Increase Mather, the president of Harvard College, wrote a book entitled *The Mystery of Israel's Salvation.* In it he stated: 'There is no doubt the Jews will return to the land of their fathers.'

Dr. Winchester wrote a book in 1800 explaining that the return of the Jews to their own land was certain.

In 1852 Reverend Bickersteth wrote a volume entitled *The Restoration of the Jews to Their Land*....Were these biblical scholars right? Did it happen? Let's see. In 1900 there were 50,000 Jews in Palestine. In 1922 there were 84,000. In 1931 there were 175,000. In 1948 there were 650,000, and in 1952 there were 1,421,000. Today, there are approximately three and one-half million Jews in Israel. Thus, the number of Jews has increased one hundred and twenty times in the last one hundred years. That's prophecy on the move."[49]

Jack Van Impe, Rexella's husband, an eminent Bible prophecy scholar and teacher, added: "Think of this—it had never happened in twenty-five centuries. Thus, what occurred was not just happenstance. It was the fulfillment of God's Word as predicted by these scholars. But where are these prophecies found? In Ezekiel 36:24, God says, *I will* [gather] *you from among the* [Gentiles—all nations], *and will* [put—place] *you into your own land.*"[50]

---

[48]Ibid, p. 135.

[49]Jack and Rexella Van Impe, "1999? Global March to Israel," *Perhaps Today*. Troy, MI: Jack Van Impe Ministries, May/June 1993, p. 5, used by permission.

[50]Ibid.

After reading these pages, no self-respecting rabbi[51] or liberal Protestant can say with a straight face that most Christians are anti-Semitic or against the Jews. True Christians truly love the Jews. Jesus said, "for salvation is of the Jews" (John 4:22 KJV), and no one who follows His teachings, thus becoming true Christians, can love Jesus, "THE KING OF THE JEWS" (Matt. 27:37 KJV), and still hate the Jews!

WHO SABOTAGED THE POTENTIAL NUMBERS OF CHRISTIAN ZIONISTS, WHICH MADE THE HOLOCAUST POSSIBLE?

As we documented, the eighteenth century was a time of great revival for true Bible believing Zionist Christians. However, in the nineteenth century, an attack was brought against our faith, which has extended into our own day. This attack was not one perpetrated with arms, but "philosophy." While we praise the value of true philosophers, such as John Locke and Isaac Newton, we absolutely condemn the anti-God indoctrinations which have been taught under the guise of "philosophy."

It is my belief that there would have been millions more Christian Zionists who love the Jews, had these malignant ideas not been introduced to the world under the concept of philosophy. Had this been the case, I do not believe Hitler could have mounted the Holocaust, which took so many Jewish lives. I also doubt that communism, which is responsible for over one hundred million murders, would have become a reality in the twentieth century.

The philosophical foundations which have plagued us all were chiefly introduced by a group of men who desired to reason away the absolutes the Bible teaches. These men, Kant, Hegel, Kierkegaard, Marx, Darwin and Freud, and the disastrous fruits of their writings, are the subjects of our next chapter.

"The Nightmare," by John Henry Fuseli, 1785-90.

---

[51] See Rabbi Stolper's comment on page 578. Many Christians lost their lives rescuing Jews during World War II. Christine Gorman wrote in a March 16, 1992 *Time* Magazine article entitled "A Conspiracy of Goodness" (which numbered the Jewish lives saved at nearly one-half million), "The rescuers have not escaped controversy. Their very existence has been denied by some Jews who feared the horror of the Holocaust might be white-washed by acknowledging their presence."

"See to it that no one takes you captive through **philosophy** and empty deception, according to the tradition of men, according to the elementary principles of the world, rather than according to Christ." The New Testament, from the apostle Paul's letter to the residents of Colosse, written for all Christians under the inspiration of God, Colossians 2:8 NASB

"Our dialectical **philosophy** abolishes all the notions of absolute and definitive truth."[1] Friedrich Engels' eulogy for Karl Marx

"We do not want any other God but Germany itself."[2]
Adolf Hitler, the German Führer

"God manifested himself not in Jesus Christ but in Adolf Hitler. Christ is a false prophet, for he was a Jew and Judaism is the source of all woes."[3]
Dr. Joseph Paul Goebbels, Hitler's propaganda director

13

PHILOSOPHICAL SABOTAGE OF OUR BIBLE RESULTED IN HOLOCAUST

In light of Engels' comment, we should keep in mind what Jesus said to certain Jews who had come to believe in Him: "...'If you abide in My word, *then* you are truly disciples of Mine; and you shall know the truth, and the truth shall make you **free**' " (John 8:31-32 NASB).

After the world was released from Roman Catholic domination by the Reformation, we ask who sabotaged the unconditional acceptance the Bible was beginning to enjoy and why? I believe these questions can be answered by studying a select group of men who have literally changed the course of modern history with their philosophic ideas. As we discuss these men, you will see how each one, building upon the foundations of his predecessor, developed concepts which have led to socialism, communism, secular humanism, and existentialism. All of these movements have mushroomed in our day and fuel the fires of atheism. I believe the men we are about to study subverted the message of the Old and New Testaments just as the dominance of Roman Catholicism, which kept the Bible out of the hands of the people for over 1000 years, began to wane.

---

[1]Hal Lindsey with C.C. Carlson, *Satan is Alive and Well on Planet Earth*, p. 84.
[2]*Führer, Rise of a Madman*. Videotape MP 1203: Matjack Productions, Inc.
[3]Ibid.

Why were so many people prevented from receiving the truths of the Bible after it was freed from the chains of Catholic rule? We think you will find a very good case as to why in the written philosophies of Kant, Hegel, Kierkegaard, Marx,[4] Darwin and Freud!

HAL DECKS ALL SIX, WHILE DUNPHY FANTASIZES AND WISHES FOR US TO BECOME A "ROTTING CORPSE"

Hal Lindsey, the famous author who writes prolifically on the subject of Bible prophecy, says of these six men: "Satan took their concepts and wired the underlying frame of reference for our present historical, educational, philosophical, sociological, psychological, religious, economic, and political outlook. You and I and our children have been ingeniously conditioned to think in terms that are contrary to biblical principles and truths in all of these areas—and without our even realizing it."[5]

In the post-Reformation era, once Catholicism's governmental rule dissolved and we were freed from the grip of the Catholic Church, true believers began to emerge and freely teach their biblical faith. However, these men of philosophy laid the groundwork for godless liberalism and secular humanism. They attempted, with some degree of success, to undermine the basic fundamental beliefs in absolute truth, freedom and redemption, so cherished by Bible believing, born-again Christians, and the silent majority of our society.

There is no doubt that the philosophies we are about to briefly wade through were constructed as a deliberate and well organized challenge to the biblical beliefs of Western society. Read what John Dunphy had to say: "I am convinced that the battle for humankind's future must be waged and won in the public school classroom by teachers who correctly perceive their role as the proselytizers of a *new faith*...these teachers must embody the same selfless dedication as the most rabid fundamentalist preachers, for they will be ministers of

---

[4]"Lenin had said '*Marxism is materialism. As such, it is ruthless toward religion.*' Marx had written '*Man is for man the supreme being.*' Now, men are different and think differently. Which type of man is for man the supreme being? Surely, the Marxian type. When Marx was still young he made a poem: 'My will is to build to myself a throne, Its peak should be cold and gigantic. Its bulwark should be superhuman fright. And dark pain should be its marshall.' FREDERICK ENGLES, the co-founder of modern Socialism, wrote about him after their first meeting '*He rages* unceasingly, with his evil fist clinched, *as if ten thousands of devils would have got him.*' (Quoted from 'Genius and richness' by ROLV HEUEL, Berthelman's Publishing House, in German)." Pastor Richard Wurmbrand, "The God of Marxism," *Jesus to the Communist World, Inc., "The Voice of the Martyrs," 1967-1977*, Oct. 1967. Glendale, CA: Jesus to the Communist World, Inc., used by permission.

[5]Hal Lindsey with C.C. Carlson, *Satan is Alive and Well on Planet Earth*, pp. 84-85.

another sort, utilizing a classroom instead of a pulpit to convey humanist values in whatever subject they teach....The classroom must and will become an arena of conflict between the old and the new, the rotting corpse of Christianity, together with all its adjacent evils and misery, and the new faith of humanism...."[6]

PHILOSOPHER I: KANT
BORN 1772, DIED 1804

Immanuel Kant was a German who never travelled farther than sixty-nine miles from his birthplace in Prussia. Prior to Kant, classical philosophy was based on absolute standards. In other words, if one and one are two, they cannot become three. Philosophical values were absolute. Kant questioned absolutes and consequently, drastically altered philosophy by proposing the idea that: "...no one can know anything except by experience. He believed that individual freedom lies in obedience to the 'moral law that speaks within us.' "[7]

The World Book Encyclopedia notes of Kant: "The central problem of his chief work, the *Critique of Pure Reason* (1781), is the nature and limits of human knowledge."[8] Kant was obsessed with the limits of human knowledge because of David Hume's erroneous idea that there are no absolutes. Our reference points out: "Hume asked how we can possibly know that *all* bodies gravitate...."[9]

Interestingly enough, the greatest of all scientists, Sir Isaac Newton, who went on to be with Jesus when Kant was only three years old, had already proven in several scientific formulas and calculations that *all bodies do indeed gravitate toward one another.* This is the basic law of gravity, and we believe it applies to all of creation, including the Bible's absolutes regarding God's diagnosis of man's dilemma—sin. Without Newton's formulas, we would never have landed a man on the moon. Fortunately, science did not take Kant as the last word. We agree with the encyclopedia's closing words, which point out: "...some philosophers regarded this refusal to claim absolute knowledge as too serious a limitation on a system of philosophy."[10] Kant's objection to absolute values led to a further modification of philosophy, which was introduced by a second philosopher.

---

[6]Johanna Michaelsen, *Like Lambs to the Slaughter*. Eugene, OR: Harvest House Publishers, © 1989, pp. 30-31. Michaelsen's source was John Dunphy's award-winning essay published in the January 1983 edition of *The Humanist*.

[7]Hal Lindsey with C.C. Carlson, *Satan is Alive and Well on Planet Earth*, p. 86.

[8]*The World Book Encyclopedia*. Chicago: Field Enterprises Educational Corporation, 1970 Edition, © 1957, p. 200, used by permission.

[9]Ibid.

[10]Ibid.

PHILOSOPHER II: HEGEL
BORN 1770, DIED 1831

Georg Wilhelm Hegel, another German who became known as the "philosophical dictator of Germany," pressed the ideas of Kant* forward.[11] Hegel taught that a thought (thesis) turned against another thought (antithesis) would in turn result in a new fact he called "synthesis." Hegel taught that the state need not keep moral laws and agreements and that all was relative—no absolutes. Absolutes are facts and truths which we use to reason and discover the logic of cause and effect. The biblical writer, Hal Lindsey, rightly commented: "When Hegel introduced the philosophical basis for relative thinking and rejected absolutes, he literally altered the future course of the world....As Hegel did away with cause-and-effect logic, there was no need for ultimate truth. With the elimination of an ultimate cause or truth, man could plunge headlong away from any necessity of believing in a Creator-God."[12]

Later, Hegel's "philosophy of relative thinking" found its way into the majority of American and European universities. The educational standard became *the smarter you get, the closer you come to realizing that there is no god or absolutes*, or, *everything is relative.* Hegel's philosophy was studied and followed by Adolf Hitler and Karl Marx.[13]

PHILOSOPHER III: KIERKEGAARD
BORN 1813, DIED 1855

Sorën Kierkegaard of Denmark is known as the "father of contemporary existentialism." Few laymen may know that Kierkegaard was a very despondent and depressed man; yet with books titled *Fear and Trembling* and *The Sickness Unto Death,* one does not have to

---

*Kant and Hume greatly contributed to the foundations of modern racism. In Kant's work, Observations on the Feeling of the Beautiful and Sublime, he wrote: "Mr. Hume challenges anyone to cite a simple example in which a Negro has shown talents, and asserts that among the hundreds of thousands of blacks who are transported elsewhere from their countries, although many of them have been set free, still not a single one was ever found who presented anything great in art or science or any other praiseworthy quality; even among the whites some continually rise aloft from the lowest rabble, and through superior gifts earn respect in the world. So fundamental is the difference between the two races of men, and it appears to be as great in regard to mental capacities as in color. Kant, at one point wrote: "this fellow was quite black from head to foot, a clear proof that what he said was stupid." Why are such "philosophers" still creditworthy and respected within academic circles? Good question. Few realize that the French Abbé of the time, Henri Grégoire, who wrote the essay, "How to Make the Jews Happy and Useful in France" fought for the rights of blacks and Jews—why? He was a jansenist millenarian Christian who believed all are created co-equal by God to enjoy the coming millennial kingdom. Racism would have been eliminated before our time if the academics had valued the Christian thought and view over secular anti-Bible philosophies.

[11]Hal Lindsey with C.C. Carlson, Satan is Alive and Well on Planet Earth, p. 86.

[12]Ibid, pp.86-87.

[13]Ibid, p. 87.

guess. In his book, *Fear and Trembling*, you will find that he resents the idea "that a light shines upon the Christian world whereas a darkness broods over paganism."[14] To remedy this, he advocated the rejuvenating effect of "the eternal youth of the Greek race"; clearly a call to pagan worship and an expression of contempt for the Christian faith.

Kierkegaard greatly influenced the theology of his time. You do not have to wonder where liberal theology got its boost. There are people such as Jesse Jackson[15] and Jimmy Carter calling themselves "Christians" and teaching Sunday school, without having the slightest idea of what it's all about! Liberal Protestant Christians deny the literal and fundamental understanding of the Scriptures. Fundamental writer Hal Lindsey says of Kierkegaard: "His writings are a denial of the basic tenets of the Christian faith and show a disdain for those who do not agree with his intellectual pursuits. He was the first man to launch a system of thought in which despair[16] was the underlying current....Kierkegaard was one of the foremost proponents of the philosophy which has swept the intellectual world right down to our time. He introduced the tenets of Kant and Hegel into the theology of the Christian faith....This was the beginning of 'existential thought.' "[17]

COMMUNIST PHILOSOPHER IV: MARX
BORN 1818, DIED 1883

Karl Marx, a German Jew who did not care much for Jews,[18] collaborated with his only lifelong friend, Friedrich Engels, and decided to pit the working class (proletariat) against the property-owning class he called the bourgeoisie. In the revolution he envisioned, he hoped to abolish private property and the Christian faith, which he maintained was the "opiate of the masses." Hal Lindsey notes: "Marx became involved at the University of Berlin

---

14 Ibid, p. 88.

15 See our *Vol. II*, chapter 27, "The Differences Between Pro-Israel Evangelicals and Indifferent Liberals," which contains information and documentation of the anti-Christian/anti-Jewish actions of Jesse Jackson and a liberal (in our opinion and observation) Kierkegaardian "Christian" Jimmy Carter telling a respectable Bible believing minister, Dr. Falwell, to "Go to Hell", [Atlanta Journal/Constitution, Sept. 12, 1986).

16 *The World Book Encyclopedia*, in its column on Kierkegaard, mentions: "When Kierkegaard was 22, he learned that his father, as a poor youth, had once cursed God and that his father had seduced his mother before marrying her. These revelations disturbed Kierkegaard...." *The World Book Encyclopedia*, 1970 Edition, p. 244. *The World Book* also informs us of Kierkegaard's narrow and intolerant view: "Kierkegaard regarded those who offered rational proofs for religion as having 'betrayed religion with a Judas kiss'....[He felt that] people who were officially Christian...did not possess the unconditional faith demanded by Christianity." Ibid. [ ] mine. Certainly, all who believe in Jesus fundamentally are Christian, whether K. likes it or not. The Scriptures teach that Jesus is sufficient to save us within Himself, if we believe in His atonement and resurrection (Rom. 10:9).

17 Hal Lindsey with C.C. Carlson, *Satan is Alive and Well on Planet Earth*, pp. 87-88.

18 See our section in chapter 19, "Russia is Crushed in Gog," which deals with the anti-Semitic writings of Marx.

with a left-wing group which followed the philosophy of Hegel. Their main thrust at that time was to throw out[19] Christianity."[20]

Marx used Hegel's philosophy of change—thesis, antithesis, synthesis—to legitimize his brand of revolutionary change. In the Marx version, the rich were the thesis, the working poor and middle class were the antithesis and their clash was expected to produce a new state, "communism," which was the synthesis. We can see this design quite clearly in Marx's whole philosophical plan of operation.

Marx thought that all evil could be traced to "**the evil**" of private property (you need not wonder if he had any—he did not). Almost everything he owned was pawned. He did not even take care of his own family, allowing his children to starve.[21] Marx and his friend Engels, influenced by Rabbi Moses Hess, argued that if the abolition of private property and the "oppressing force" of religion could be destroyed, the world would live in peace under a "classless society." In this society, property, or as Marx called it, "means of production," would be owned by the government. In reality, as we know, the communist elite owned the property and used it to control the people. This is a religion within itself. Our fundamental friend, Hal, accurately relates to us: "It is time for the world to realize that Communism is not just another political philosophy, but a religion—a religion which promises utopia to its devotees. The state is worshipped in place of God. Communism deals with such basic issues as: What is man? What is man's most basic problem? How can man be delivered from his problem? What is man's destiny? In all these points Communism gives answers which are diametrically opposed to God's truth."[22]

NATURALIST PHILOSOPHER V: DARWIN BORN 1809, DIED 1882

Charles Darwin is one of the most misunderstood philosophers of our time. He had no scientific degrees or credentials and never proved to any degree that evolution was responsible for our existence. What he did do was unscientifically steal[23] a philosophy, which he dubbed

---

[19]*The World Book Encyclopedia* pointed out that Marx predicted a revolution in England which never occurred. He was driven out of France (1854) and exiled from Germany in 1849. Isn't it something that this unwanted criminal's writings became the seed for the murder of millions when his theories were put into action by Lenin and those following him?

[20]Hal Lindsey with C.C. Carlson, *Satan is Alive and Well on Planet Earth*, p. 89.

[21]For details, see J. Edgar Hoover, *Masters of Deceit*.

[22]Hal Lindsey with C.C. Carlson, *Satan is Alive and Well on Planet Earth*, p. 91.

[23]See Henry M. Morris, Ph.D., *The Troubled Waters of Evolution*, San Diego, CA: Creation Life Publishers © 1974, pp. 54-57.

"natural selection." He then called it "my theory" and claimed that it explained the beginning of our existence (see our *Vol. II*, chapter 5, "Darwinian Evolution: Fact, Fraud or Fiction?", which details what really transpired in his hidden fiasco).

Is it any coincidence that the philosophies of Hegel and Marx were so beautifully justified by the philosophy of Darwin's theory? Darwin's entire unproved model of natural selection, which describes how one species struggles to survive over another, producing a "mutation" which is better able to survive, is based on Hegel's thesis/antithesis produces a synthesis formula.

Marx asked Darwin if he could dedicate his book, *Das Kapital*, to Darwin, himself![24] Lindsey says of this issue: "Conflict! Hegel and Marx would be happy—a scientist using their theories of thesis, antithesis, and synthesis....Hegel introduced the philosophical basis for man to see no necessity for a Creator-God. Darwin introduced what **seemed** to be a scientific basis for not believing in a Creator-God....The impact of this thought bomb is that since man had no special beginning, he has no special purpose or destiny."[25]

PSYCHOANALYTICAL PHILOSOPHER VI: FREUD BORN 1856, DIED 1939

Sigmund Freud is known as "the founder of psychoanalysis." Though few realize it, Freud was a man greatly influenced by Darwin's train of thought. It was clear that after Darwin introduced this "scientific proof" of evolution, it would only be a moment until all of our lives were changed permanently regarding our conception of God and human freedom, when the social application of all of these philosophic scratches were seemingly justified by Freud. Freud, an atheist, believed that: "The human race is motivated chiefly by pleasure...."[26]

Dr. A. A. Brill, in his book, *The Basic Writings of Sigmund Freud*, documents that Freud was: "...'very attracted to Darwin's theories because they offered the prospect of an extraordinary advance of human knowledge.' "[27] Hal Lindsey comments: "What did Freud believe?....Man is repressed by society in the fulfillment of his

---

[24]See page 781 for an illustration of this handwritten request by Darwin himself.

[25]Hal Lindsey with C.C. Carlson, *Satan is Alive and Well on Planet Earth* , p. 92. Bold mine.

[26]Ibid, p. 93.

[27]Ibid, p. 92. Lindsey's source was Dr. A.A. Brill, *The Basic Writings of Sigmund Freud.* New York: Random House Publishers, © 1938.

unconscious drive for gratification of his erotic desires; this repression makes him unhappy. The consequence of the conflict between our pleasure-seeking instincts and the repression exerted by our society is neurosis."[28]

In our friend's opinion, Boris Sokoloff rightly notes: " 'Freud's doctrines, and particularly his ethics, are the product of his concept of the human race. There is no purpose in man's existence. There is no goal in mankind's presence on earth. There is no God...and if this is so, all is permitted.' "[29] This includes the loss of human freedom of worship, freedom of life, and freedom to vote, accompanied by the government being permitted to impose communism, using terror, murder and even genocide.

It was Lenin who picked up on these philosophies and made the philosophical writings of Marx a reality. He also referred to religion as the "opiate of the masses." As an atheist, he used terror, murder and secret police to overpower the people and bring himself to rule in Russia. Lenin said: " '...we will destroy the entire bourgeoisie [property owner of middle-class or higher, even a farmer with a crop], grind it to a powder....I will be merciless with all counter-revolutionaries.' "[30]

As you read this, it may remind you of at least one communist country that resulted from the philosophies[31] which fed Lenin. China, with over one billion people held captive, unable to legally learn of God through the Bible,[32] is just one result of these philosophies.

THE CONSEQUENCE OF THE HOLOCAUST AND THE REAL MIND BEHIND THE EVIL OF HITLER

Adolf Hitler, the man responsible for attempting the greatest Jewish genocide in the history of humanity, was influenced by the

---

[28]Ibid, p. 93.

[29] Ibid.

[30]Ibid, p. 95. [ ] mine.

[31]The word philosophy originated from two anglicized Greek words; *philo*, meaning "love of" and *sophy*, meaning "wisdom." These "philosophies" mentioned above do not do justice to the name of philosophy. There has been more heartache, torture and brutal murder as a result of these philosophies and those who followed them than from any other single thing in this planet's history. Fifty-five million Chinese were exterminated because they did not agree with communism. This is just one case in point! If you tried to count to fifty-five million, you would probably die long before you had finished. Just think, these were innocent people just like you.

[32]In China, a strict new law was enacted in 1994 making it illegal to proselytize (convert to Christianity). *The 700 Club* documented this on their 1994 news update. However, this is really nothing new. Prior to 1994, from the foundation of the communist state, Chinese Christians were hunted down and brutally put to death.

same philosophers. Few people realize that most of Hitler's anti-Semitic ideas concerning the Hebrew race, which were adopted by the Nazi party, were taken from a book on race and history entitled *Foundations of the Nineteenth Century*, by Houston Steward Chamberlain. He was, by his own admission, demon-possessed. This little-known figure was an Englishman who became a German citizen. Chamberlain was well-versed in all the philosophies we have covered. He wrote about Kant and dabbled in the occult. It would be this book, translated into English in 1911, which would become championed by the Nazis and used to aggravate anti-Semitism worldwide.

R. L. Hymers, author of *Holocaust II*, says that this book dealt with: "...a fantastic race theory. He [Chamberlain] believed the Western nations were being weakened by oriental peoples breeding with the 'pure' Nordic races. He held that the Jews were the worst group of orientals."[33]

Hitler thoroughly adopted Chamberlain's ideas about the Jewish people. These evil, horrifyingly perverted views about the Jews were probably responsible for much, if not all, of his wicked hatred against the people who gave this world the Holy Bible, both Old and New Testaments, through their ancestors, the Hebrew prophets and apostles!

HITLER'S PHILOSOPHICAL PROPHET SWEATS WITH OCCULT FEVER

Hal Lindsey, quoting William Shirer's book, *The Rise and Fall of the Third Reich*, documents details about Chamberlain, his book and its influence on the one who murdered the people of God:[34] "Here is Shirer's description of Chamberlain, the man who inspired Hitler and his insane reign of terror and power: 'Hypersensitive and neurotic and subject to frequent nervous breakdowns, Chamberlain was given to seeing demons who, by his own account, drove him on relentlessly to seek new fields of study and to get on with his prodigious writings. One vision after another forced him to change from...philosophy, to biography, to history. Once, in 1898, when he was returning from Italy, the presence of a demon became so forceful that he got off the train at Gardone, shut himself up in a hotel room for eight days and, abandoning some work on music that he had contemplated, wrote

[33]Dr. R.L. Hymers, *Holocaust II*. Van Nuys, CA: Bible Voice, Inc., © 1978, p. 30, used by permission. [ ] mine. For extensive information on *The Protocols of The Elders of Zion* and Chamberlain, see Philip Moore *What If Hitler Won the War?*, Appendix 5, "The Philosophical Basis for German Anti-Semitism Uncovered and Examined".

[34]Since there are many liberal "Christian" theologians who would deny that the Jews are and were chosen by the Lord for His special dealings with mankind, while still claiming to believe the Bible, we list two biblical passages—one from the Old Testament and one from the New—which state that God chose the Jew: Deuteronomy 7:6-10 and Romans 11:1-26.

feverishly on a biological thesis until he had the germ of the theme that would dominate all of his later works: race and history.

'Since he felt himself goaded on by demons, his books...were written in the grip of a terrible fever, a veritable trance...he says in his autobiography, *Lebenswege*, he was often unable to recognize them as his own work....His racial theories and his burning sense of the destiny of the Germans and Germany were taken over by the Nazis, who acclaimed him as one of their prophets. During the Hitler regime books, pamphlets and articles poured from the presses extolling the 'spiritual founder' [Chamberlain] of National Socialist Germany.' "[35]

OCCULT BOOKS, HITLER'S FAVORITE— THE JEWS BECOME THE TARGET

Hitler, the greatest German racist who ever lived, believed the German people who produced him were the "master race." Thus anyone surpassing them in any way was to be destroyed. The Jews, of course, became a prime target, since their intellect just might be a little higher than that of the Germans. The Jews, with their rich heritage (which included the very oracles of God)[36] and brilliant intellect, had to be detected and destroyed. Hitler wanted no competition with his "master race."

Hitler idolized paganism and believed in using the occult to realize his ends. He created a Genealogical Research Society endowed with the task of finding "every Jew," no matter how diluted their origin. People who had only one great, great grandparent, who were one-sixteenth Jewish, who did not even know they had Jewish blood coursing through their veins, found themselves arrested and led off to the death camps. R. L. Hymers documents Hitler's fascination with the occult: "This emphasis on magic revealed Hitler's interest in the occult and black magic. He even directed the Nazis to create an occult research bureau, which was named the 'Bureau of Ancestral Heritage,' referring to the fact that its purpose was to research and publicize the ancient occult practices of Germany."[37]

Joseph Carr noted that Hitler idolized the "Bavarian mountain tribesmen," who were pagans.[38] Carr goes on to quote the authority

---

[35]Hal Lindsey with C.C. Carlson, *Satan is Alive and Well on Planet Earth*, pp. 96-97. [ ] mine.

[36]The New Testament tells us of the Jews: "...unto them were committed the oracles of God" (Rom. 3:2 KJV).

[37]Dr. R. L. Hymers, *Holocaust II*, p. 29.

[38]Joseph Carr, *The Twisted Cross*. Shreveport, LA: Huntington House, Inc., © 1985, p. 18, used by permission.

Kubizek on Hitler's obsession with the occult. Carr notes: "Included among Hitler's private books were numerous volumes on...*the occult and magic symbols.* Kubizek reports in his own book that he once found Adolf in a great state of excitement over a book on witchcraft....Hitler was also fascinated with tales of Germanic and nordic mythology, especially the mythical heroes of gigantic proportions and pagan gods from the era before Christian missionaries 'corrupted' the Germanic tribesmen....Kubizek also tells us that books on the occult were among Hitler's favorite reading matter. This interest was confirmed decades later when U.S. Army historians catalogued Hitler's personal library and found numerous occultic volumes heavily annotated in Hitler's fancy handwriting."[39]

HITLER FOLLOWED THE ADVICE OF HIS OCCULT ASTROLOGERS OVER THAT OF HIS GENERALS

Few know that astrology is a form of the occult and that Hitler used it extensively. In the video documentary, *The Rise and Fall of Adolf Hitler: Black Fox*, the narrator documents: "April, 1940, Hitler invades Denmark and Norway. Defenseless Denmark capitulates in four hours. Norway fights back hard, aided by a desperate expedition of British troops, but Norway is secured by the Nazis in twelve weeks. Hitler had ordered the North Sea action against the advice of his army staff. Now, flushed with victory, certain of weakness of the West, Hitler is, more than ever, convinced of his own military genius. May, 1940, again, against the advice of his cautious generals, but **with the advice of his astrologers,** Hitler orders attack. Through neutral Belgium and Holland, as in 1914, a German war machine slashes its way. The Maginot fortifications are bypassed. The Dutch, Belgium, French and British armies are smashed. At the Channel port of Dunkirk, the Allied survivors are driven into the sea. What the German armies of the first World War could not do in four years of battle, Hitler's legions accomplish in six weeks."[40]

WHERE DOES THE OCCULT LEAD? TO THE ATTEMPTED DESTRUCTION OF GOD'S PEOPLE!

There is no doubt that Hitler's great interest in the occult encouraged his belief that Jews and Christians were to be destroyed as

---

[39]Ibid, pp. 31, 93.

[40]Louis Clyde Stoumen, *The Rise and Fall of Adolf Hitler: Black Fox.* W. Long Beach, NJ: White Star, © 1962, used by permission. Videotape documentary available through White Star, 121 Hwy 36, West Long Beach, NJ, USA 07764. Tel. (201) 229-2343.

inferior races and faiths. Few realize that Hitler wanted to secretly kill all true Evangelical Christians, because he rightly understood that their faith was derived from biblical Judaism. R. L. Hymers, in his book *Holocaust II*, documents: "A cleavage developed in the German churches. Catholics and Protestants were divided into both camps; there were some of each on both sides. The first group accepted Hitler's ideas, rejecting historic Christianity. The second group led by Bonhoeffer and others, became known as the 'Confessing Church,' for they confessed Christ, rather than Hitler, as their Lord and Leader.

Dr. Barth observed: Since the autumn of the previous year (1936), the State Party and Secret Police of the Third Reich have embarked upon a new attack...on the Evangelical Church...."[41]

HITLER HATED TRUE CHRISTIANS, WHOSE FAITH IS DERIVED FROM BIBLICAL JUDAISM

In Hymers' little-known evidence, he goes on to cite a Nazi war song which clearly mentions the destruction of Jews, Christians, ministers and churches. He says: "A 'fighting song' of the young Nazi anti-church disciples of Hitler contained these words: The old Jewish shame at last swept away....German men, German women, beat the black band to a jelly. Hang them on the gallows...Ravens have been waiting. Plunge the knives into the minister's body. We'll be ready for any massacre. Hoist the Hohenzollerns high on the lamp-post! Hurl the hand grenades into the churches."[42]

We have always found it odd that some people have classified Hitler as a "Christian," when in fact he hated **true** Christians, perhaps as much as he hated Jews! Hymers, in his "Religion of the Nazis" section, excellently illustrated Hitler's hatred of Christianity because it is, in essence, part of the Jewish faith. Hymers, citing his quote from H. G. Baynes' book, *Germany Possessed*, says: "Adolf Hitler hated Christianity. He was bent on its destruction, saying, Christianity is a hoax, a gangrene to be cut out. Germans have for too long been held in the bondage of a Jewish derived faith."[43] The *World Book Encyclopedia* says: "...Hitler....hated Christianity, which he said was a religion for weaklings."[44]

We might well point out that those whom Hitler's twisted mind perceived as weaklings were, in fact, infinitely braver than all; for they,

---

[41]Dr. R. L. Hymers, *Holocaust II*, p. 90.

[42]Ibid, pp. 54-55. Hymers' source was Peter Viereck, *The Roots of the Nazi Mind.* New York: Capricorn Books, © 1965, p. 259.

[43]Ibid, p. 28.

[44]*The World Book Encyclopedia*, 1970 Edition, p. 236.

due to their faith, risked their lives and in some cases, lost them, in order to save Jews from the Holocaust. The Jewish scholar, Sholem Asch, speaking for an increasing number of Jews, said: "...Christianity also distinguished itself, in the particular of rescuing Jewish children, by the highest degree of self-sacrifice. It may be stated without exaggeration that almost the entire remnant of Israel which was found in the liberated countries—no matter how small its number—has the Christians to thank for its preservation, Christians who, by performing this action, placed their own lives in danger."[45]

THOUSANDS OF EVANGELICAL CHRISTIANS MURDERED BECAUSE THEIR FAITH LED THEM TO COURAGEOUSLY RESCUE THE JEWISH PEOPLE

It is a matter of public record that Hitler endorsed those who said that the Christian faith and National Socialism do not mix. Hence, Hitler was not a Christian, as opposed to what some misguided persons have thought and taught. He was a neo-paganist.

Thousands of Evangelical Christians were put to death by Hitler for helping the Jewish people escape his grasp. In a 1995 article, Elwood McQuaid told this story: "Considering the devastating attacks on the Bible and biblically orthodox Christianity brought by liberal theologians and their secular-humanist counterparts, it is little wonder that many nominally religious Germans were less than incensed at events taking place about them....the Nazis intended to destroy Christianity in Germany. Martin Bormann and Heinrich Himmler, encouraged by Hitler, promoted a return to the old paganism of the early tribal Germanic gods and a brand of neo-paganism created by Nazi fanatics. In 1941, Bormann stated publicly that 'National Socialism and Christianity are irreconcilable'....The Pastor's Emergency League, made up largely of younger men, responded forcefully to what they regarded as the heathen theology of the German Church. 'We refuse,' they affirmed, 'to earn the reproach of being dumb dogs. We owe it to our congregations and to the Church to resist the falsification of the Gospel. We emphatically recognize the Holy Scripture of the Old and New Testaments as the unique test of our faith and life.' Such commitment to biblical principles spawned acts of courageous opposition to the persecution of the Jewish people and other atrocities brought about by the Nazis, such as state approved euthanasia....By the end of 1935, 700 Confessional Church pastors were arrested by the Gestapo. Hundreds more were forced to join them in the concentration camps in 1936. In 1937, 807 more pastors and

---

[45] Arthur W. Kac, *The Messiahship of Jesus*, p. 18.

leading laymen were picked up as subversives. Before the reign was over, thousands of evangelicals attested to the quality of their faith by choosing death over capitulation or life behind the barbed wire of the Nazi concentration camps. These people—mostly unknown and unheralded—march in the ranks of Righteous Gentiles who could not endure forsaking their Savior of His Jewish brethren."[46]

LET'S HELP SAVE OUR JEWISH FRIENDS BY NOT LETTING HISTORY REPEAT ITSELF—KEEP THE ANTI-GOD LIBERALS OUT OF OFFICE

It is clear to us that a country full of prophecy-loving, born-again Christians anticipating the new State of Israel would have never been able to mount the Holocaust against God's people, the Jews! If there had been a fair number of people with the mind-set of Bonhoeffer, Hitler would have failed before he began.[47] It took a state stripped of

---

[46]Elwood McQuaid, "Holocaust: A Christian Atrocity?", *Israel My Glory*, © Apr./May 1995, pp. 6-7, used by permission. Available through Friends of Israel Gospel Ministry, Inc., POB 908 Bellmawr, NJ, USA 08031.

[47]Bonhoeffer was one of the true believers who, unfortunately, was in the greatest of minorities. *The 700 Club*, hosted by Pat Robertson, documented: "...though the Jewish people bore the brunt of hideous torture and systematic death, true Christians opposed to Hitler's demonically inspired genocide often met similar fates. Dietrich Bonhoeffer was one such man, a modern martyr whose crucible experience at the hands of the Nazis created a new understanding of the cost of discipleship....at an early age, Dietrich Bonhoeffer announced that he intended to study theology and enter the ministry....He felt an immediate enmity towards the Nazis....Bonhoeffer soon became involved in a network of underground seminaries, formed a guard theology study against the taint of Nazi ideology....the Gestapo closed in and terminated the secret schools as Hitler's forces whipped the German people into a war-thirsty frenzy. The hysteria and pageantry of Nazism supplanted the nation's spiritual life, with Hitler obtaining a near demonic glorification....Throughout the terrible first years of World War II, Bonhoeffer worked secretly against the Nazis....he was implicated in the conspiracy to assassinate Adolf Hitler and, in 1943, was arrested and held in a Berlin military prison. It was while incarcerated that Dietrich Bonhoeffer distilled the theological obstructions that had directed his personal Christian walk. During the next twelve months, he poured forth a lifetime of work, outlining a new concept of Christian service....On April the 9th, 1945, Dietrich Bonhoeffer was brought to a Nazi extermination camp at Flossenburg. There, he was condemned to die by hanging just one month before the final collapse of the Third Reich. A prison doctor who witnessed the execution later described the death scene: 'Through the half-open door in one room of the huts, I saw Professor Bonhoeffer before taking off his prison garb, kneeling on the floor praying fervently to his God. I was most deeply moved by the way this lovable man prayed, so devout and so certain that God heard his prayer. At the place of execution, he again said a short prayer and then climbed the steps to the gallows, brave and composed. His death ensued after a few seconds. In the almost fifty years that I have worked as a doctor, I have hardly ever seen a man die so entirely submissive to the will of God.' [Pat Robertson commented] 'What an incredible human being. Yeah....I was in Dachau. It was one of the most moving experiences when I went there, of course, way after—just recently. And...there was...a barracks or a couple of barracks dedicated to evangelical pastors who refused to submit to Nazism, and they went into the gas chambers along with the Jews. And...that's awful to overlook....

prayer, the Bible, and laden with Hitler's godless philosophy of secularism underpinned by evolution, to very nearly wipe the Jew from the face of the earth!

If efforts to secularize and demoralize America continue unchallenged, this author does not put another Holocaust out of the realm of possibility. Though I pray night and day that this never occurs, if the same breeding grounds are again laid down by our bleeding heart political liberals, as were previously laid down in Nazi Germany, we may again bear the same bitter fruit that was borne in Germany half a century ago.

We should learn from the past that the mistakes of pagan philosophies and liberal politics can destroy a nation practically overnight. We should learn this lesson so that we may prevent history from repeating itself! All believers in Jesus who love Israel owe it to themselves, God, and especially their Jewish friends, to fight anything that cheapens life for as long as possible. This includes godless liberalism, abortion, legal attempts to ban prayer from schools under the guise of "separation of church and state," and anything else that threatens religious freedom!

Most believe that the protest for our right to pray in the public schools is a twentieth century Christian issue. Let us not forget that the famed seventeenth century Dutch Jewish philosopher Baruch de Spinoza set down his epochal convictions regarding the right of free worship and free speech in his book *The Political Tractate*.[48]

---

that...these people were standing for freedom, as...well as others.' " Pat Robertson, *The 700 Club*, Sept. 12, 1994.

[48]Professor Popkin has noted that Spinoza "... made Christ the spirit that provided the basis for moral-religious life....Spinoza never joined any Christian group, though he spent the rest of his life with Christians, mainly Millenarian ones." Popkin *Jewish Christians*, p. 66

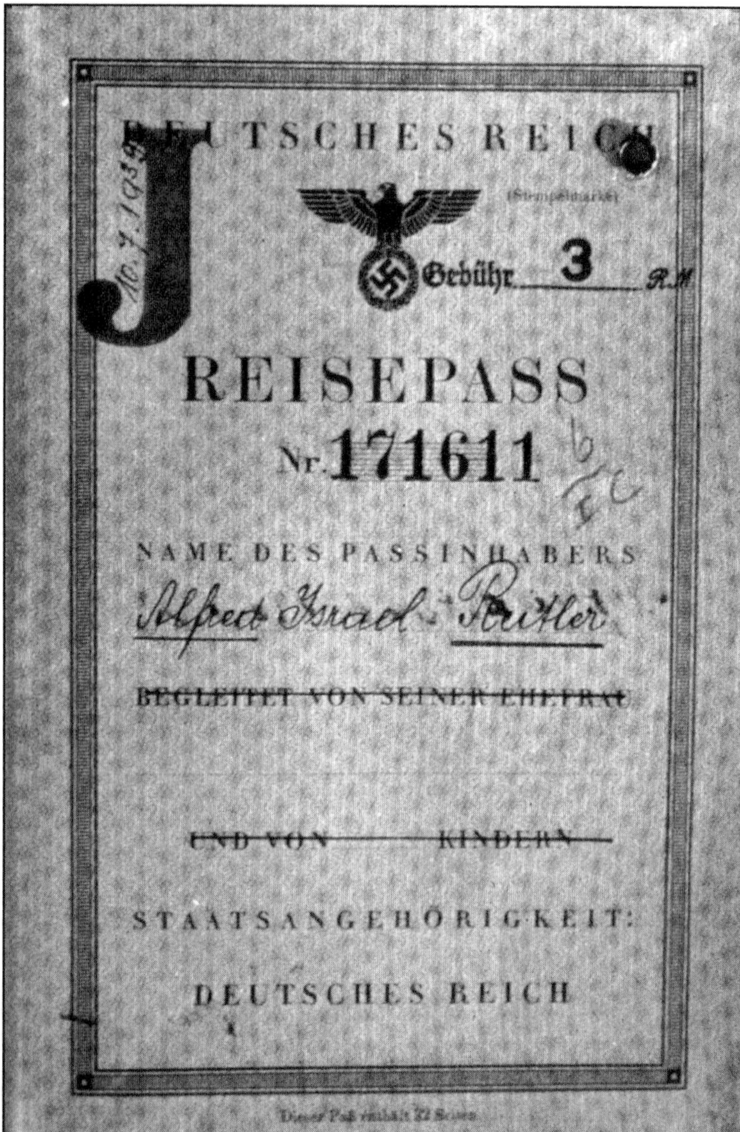

A German passport from Hitler's day, marked with a "J," indicating its owner was Jewish.[49] This is what happens when we let government become more powerful than the people. Christians are obligated to try to make sure that this never happens again—especially here in the U.S.!

49Photo courtesy of State of Israel Government Press Office, photography department.

"Beware of false prophets, which come to you in sheep's clothing, but inwardly they are ravening wolves. Ye shall know them by their fruits. Do men gather grapes of thorns, or figs of thistles? Even so every good tree bringeth forth good fruit; but a corrupt tree bringeth forth evil fruit." Jesus' words of precaution to us,
Matthew 7:15-17 KJV

" 'You worship that which you do not know; we worship that which we know, for salvation is from the Jews.' " Jesus' discourse with woman of Samaria,
John 4:22 NASB

"For I could wish that myself were accursed from Christ for my brethren, my kinsmen according to the flesh: Who are Israelites; to whom *pertaineth* the adoption, and the glory, and the covenants, and the giving of the law, and the service *of God*, and the promises; Whose *are* the fathers, and whom as concerning the flesh Christ *came*, who is over all, God blessed for ever. Amen....As concerning the gospel, *they are* enemies for your sakes: but as touching the election, *they* [the Jews] *are* beloved for the fathers' sakes." The apostle Paul's New Testament letter to the Romans 9:3-5; 11:28 KJV. [ ] mine

"It's not possible for a man to say, 'I'm a Christian,' and not love the Jewish people. You cannot be a Christian without being Jewish in spirit."[1] Rev. John Hagee

"One of the great questions in the world is 'Who is a Jew?' An equally great question is 'Who is a Christian?' Millions who profess Christianity could not possibly be true Christians in the biblical sense. For example, if a professing Christian is not dominated by love of neighbor, then he or she cannot possibly be called Christian. Thus many of the persecutions of history were caused by false Christians....I am an evangelical Christian who believes that God can be experienced in daily life and that we are known not only by the creeds we repeat but by the love we live out in our relations with our fellow men and women. Evangelical Christians especially have an affinity for the Jews because the Bible they love is essentially a Jewish book...."[2]
World-renowned evangelist, Dr. Billy Graham

14

ZIONISTS—EVANGELICAL CHRISTIANS—THE MOST LOYAL TO ISRAEL

In April 1988, the *Jerusalem Post* ran an interesting article which many Israelis talked about for some time. They were quite surprised to discover that the American evangelical community supported their struggle one hundred percent, while the American Jewish community

---

[1]Rev. John Hagee, *Why We Honor the Jews*. This audio tape is available through John Hagee Ministries, POB 1400, San Antonio, TX, USA 78295.

[2]Leonard C. Yaseen, *The Jesus Connection, To Triumph Over Anti-Semitism*. New York: The Crossroad Publishing Company, © 1985, p. ix, used by permission.

was split, many siding with the Arabs and the liberal left-wing.[3] The article said: "For many of the delegates to this week's Christian Zionist Congress, the battle in the West Bank is not between a modern-day Shlomo and Ahmed, but rather between biblical Isaac and Ishmael....'When we see on television a six-year-old Arab boy hurl a rock at an Israeli soldier, we are seeing the manifestations of this age-old struggle,' says Cal Hubbard, U.S. spokesman of the International Christian Embassy, which sponsored the five-day congress.

Hubbard sees the current riots in theological, not political, terms. 'It is the story of the covenant son coming back to regain his biblical promise and Ishmael not wanting to give it back. The Arabs can throw rocks from now until the millennium, but it won't make a difference,' he says. 'The Jews' return to their land is the greatest God-inspired event in the last 2,000 years.'

The return to the land, he emphasizes, is a return to the *whole* land, including the West Bank. 'You can no more separate the Jews from Judea and Samaria than power from the body of a horse'....Israel is enjoying the support of an estimated 30 million Evangelical Christian Zionists in the U.S.....Whereas America's Jewish community is deeply divided by recent events in the West Bank...the Christian Zionists are not wavering in their support....The Baltimore businessman who 'feels Jewish in my heart' says, 'The restoration of the Jews to Israel, including Judea and Samaria and especially Jerusalem, represents for us a stage in the redemptive process that will end in the millennium and the coming of the Messiah'....'If Israel left Judea and Samaria, there would be deep disappointment among many Christians worldwide,' Hubbard says. 'There would be a serious re-examining by some of what they see as a divinely inspired regathering of the Jews. Practically, this could mean that Christian Zionists would begin to find more fault with Israel if it abuses its authority.'

The prospect of Jews voluntarily relinquishing part of their biblical promise also sends shudders through Polly Grimes, a Los Angeles gospel concert promoter. But, she says, it would influence neither her faith nor her support for the Jewish state. 'Our faith is not based on what happens day to day,' Grimes says. 'And love is not based on performance.' "[4]

***

---

[3]In recent years, we have seen the birth of a conservative Jewish movement which supports Israel. We pray that this constituency continues to grow.

[4]Herb Keinon, "West Bank Uprising, Christian Zionists Have No Doubts Over the Outcome," *Jerusalem* magazine of the *Jerusalem Post*, © Apr. 15, 1988, p. 14, used by permission.

APRIL 15, 1988 **IN JERUSALEM**

West Bank uprising

Christian Zionists have no doubts over the outcome

By Herb Keinon

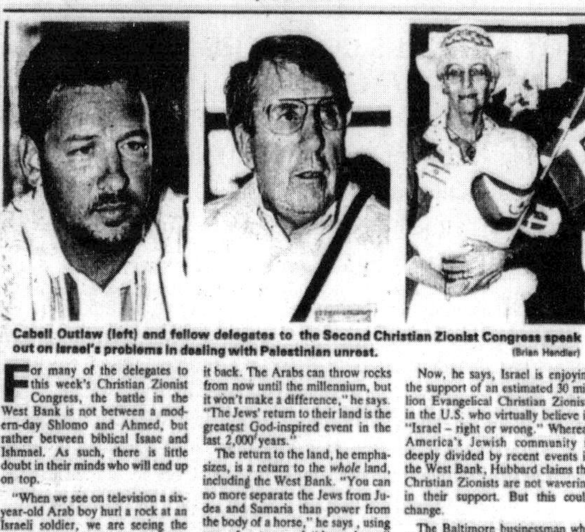

Cabell Outlaw (left) and fellow delegates to the Second Christian Zionist Congress speak out on Israel's problems in dealing with Palestinian unrest. (Brian Hendler)

For many of the delegates to this week's Christian Zionist Congress, the battle in the West Bank is not between a modern-day Shlomo and Ahmed, but rather between biblical Isaac and Ishmael. As such, there is little doubt in their minds who will end up on top.

"When we see on television a six-year-old Arab boy hurl a rock at an Israeli soldier, we are seeing the manifestations of this age-old struggle," says Cal Hubbard, U.S. spokesman of the International Christian Embassy, which sponsored the five-day congress.

Hubbard sees the current riots in theological, not political, terms. "It is the story of the covenant son coming back to regain his biblical promise, and Ishmael not wanting to give it back. The Arabs can throw rocks from now until the millennium, but it won't make a difference," he says. "The Jews' return to their land is the greatest God-inspired event in the last 2,000 years."

The return to the land, he emphasizes, is a return to the *whole* land, including the West Bank. "You can no more separate the Jews from Judea and Samaria than power from the body of a horse," he says , using one of a trove of "down home" expressions.

Hubbard recently received a death threat after calling Yasser Arafat a "rattlesnake" on a radio show beamed from Maine to California. He says that the riots have enabled him to speak in a number of forums and "try to present the whole loaf of bread, not just a single slice."

Now, he says, Israel is enjoying the support of an estimated 30 million Evangelical Christian Zionists in the U.S. who virtually believe in "Israel – right or wrong." Whereas America's Jewish community is deeply divided by recent events in the West Bank, Hubbard claims the Christian Zionists are not wavering in their support. But this could change.

The Baltimore businessman who "feels Jewish in my heart" says, "The restoration of the Jews to Israel, including Judea and Samaria and especially Jerusalem, represents for us a stage in the redemptive process that will end in the millennium and the coming of the Messiah."

So if Israel would ever decide to leave the West Bank, the theological base upon which this "Final Days" scenario rests could be undermined .for some Christian Zionists.

"If Israel left Judea and Samaria, there would be deep disappointment among many Christians worldwide," Hubbard says. "There would be a serious re-examining by some of what they see as a divinely inspired regathering of the Jews. Practically, this could mean that Christian Zionists would begin to find more fault with Israel if it abuses its authority."

The prospect of Jews voluntarily relinquishing part of their biblical promise also sends shudders through Polly Grimes, a Los Angeles gospel concert promoter. But, she says, it would influence neither her faith nor her support for the Jewish state. "Our faith is not based on what happens day to day," Grimes says. "And love is not based on performance."

Robert Eskridge, an ordained minister and a Los Angeles businessman, says that terriorial compromise would not shatter his End of Days scenario, "because we trust in God's timing. Giving up land wouldn't be the end of the line, it wouldn't spell defeat," he says. "But it would be a small detour."

Both Grimes and Eskridge see the divine hand behind the recent events in the territories, although neither would risk interpreting what it all means theologically. After hearing that some ultra-Orthodox Jews have said the riots are the result of Friday night movies in Jerusalem, Grimes says, "I can't say that, but I do know that God works in an 'if you do this, I'll do that' manner."

This "if, then" philosophy forms the cornerstone of Cabell Outlaw's support for Israel. Outlaw, a restaurateur from Orange Beach, Alabama, stresses that his love for Israel is based on the scriptural passage that those who bless Israel will be blessed, and those who curse it will be cursed.

"I want to be on the side of the blessing, not the curse," he says, explaining that he is not "pro-Israel, but pro-Scripture."

In Orange Beach, a town of 6,000 souls on the Gulf of Mexico, Outlaw says there are only limited opportunities to tangibly express one's feelings towards Israel. "There aren't demonstrations, and my pastor doesn't sermonize on the issue," the owner of the town's only Cajun restaraunt says. "So in Orange Beach all we have is prayer, and there is plenty of prayer for Israel."

A *Jerusalem Post* article on Christian Zionists by Herb Keinon.

While in the past, people who call themselves Christians may have persecuted Jews, true Christians (identified by the words born-again, taken from the New Testament books of John and I Peter),[5] love Israel and the Jewish people as Jesus commanded! They care for Israel, we venture to say, even more than a large portion of the Jews in America.

True Christians love and do not persecute Israel—past, present and future. The New Testament commands believers to love their brothers. Remember the definition of neighbor (less intimate than brother) from the New Testament (Luke 10:29-37 NASB),[6] where it is demonstrated that the hated Samaritan was called a neighbor to the dying Jew, whereas the Levi and Cohen were indifferent to his condition. The Samaritan saved the life of the Jew, though the Jews as a group had been in a state of war with the Samaritans for five hundred years. The Samaritan saved the Jew when no one else would, even his own.

GEORGE OTIS TRACKS DOWN THE REASON FOR THE *CHRISTIAN*—MISNOMER

George Otis, a major contemporary evangelical speaker, once said: " 'is Christian' semantically one of the most abused words. Satan has tried to pin that label on almost everything and everybody that isn't

---

[5]These passages from the New Testament read as follows: "Seeing ye have purified your souls in obeying the truth through the Spirit unto unfeigned love of the brethren, *see that ye* love one another with a pure heart fervently: Being born again, not of corruptible seed, but of incorruptible, by the word of God, which liveth and abideth for ever....There was a man of the Pharisees, named Nicodemus, a ruler of the Jews: The same came to Jesus by night, and said unto him, Rabbi, we know that thou art a teacher come from God: for no man can do these miracles that thou doest, except God be with him. Jesus answered and said unto him, Verily, verily, I say unto thee, Except a man be born again, he cannot see the kingdom of God" (I Pet. 1:22-23; John 3:1-3 KJV).

[6]Jesus details the Samaritan-Jewish situation in this passage where He speaks with a lawyer: "But wishing to justify himself, he [the lawyer] said to Jesus, 'And who is my neighbor?' Jesus replied and said, 'A certain man was going down from Jerusalem to Jericho; and he fell among robbers, and they stripped him and beat him, and went off leaving him half dead. And by chance a certain priest was going down on that road, and when he saw him, he passed by on the other side. And likewise a Levite also, when he came to the place and saw him, passed by on the other side. But a certain Samaritan, who was on a journey, came upon him; and when he saw him, he felt compassion, and came to him, and bandaged up his wounds, pouring oil and wine on *them*; and he put him on his own beast, and brought him to an inn, and took care of him. And on the next day he took out two denarii and gave them to the innkeeper and said, 'Take care of him; and what ever more you spend, when I return, I will repay you.' Which of these three do you think proved to be a neighbor to the man who fell into the robbers' *hands*?' And he said, 'The one who showed mercy toward him.' And Jesus said to him, 'Go and do the same' " (Luke 10:29-37 NASB).

a Jew. And, let's face it, he's enjoyed a measure of success in this terrible word-fogery. He has also taken advantage of some Jewish spiritual blindness in order to perpetuate this long, long distortion.

Oh, how Satan loves to breed enmity between the Christian and the Jew! My fury grew as I thought about his rotten tactic. I said to myself, 'You Serpent. You've gotten too much mileage out of this already.'

If there is any race loved and appreciated by true born-again Christians, it is the Jews. There are good reasons why the Lord told us to love and bless the Jews. We know they are beloved of Him in a very special way. Christians appreciate the Jews' faithfulness in carrying down through harsh millennia, both the Word and the worship of God.

And we're still awed by God choosing a Jewish frame and also a Jewish mother for His beloved Son! We owe much culturally, as well as spiritually to the indestructible Jew. And it's true that our hearts burn to share with them Messiah-Jesus. How, oh how could such love still be hidden to them?....My news article continued: 'Many Christian missionaries here are not only praying for and loving Israel, but are working for her as well....All real Bible-loving Christians are truly one with Israel."[7]

A JEWISH AUTHOR SAYS, "JEWS HAVE CHRISTIANS TO THANK FOR HOLOCAUST SURVIVAL"

Remember Jesus' words: "This is My commandment, that you love one another, just as I have loved you. Greater love has no one than this, that one lay down his life for his friends. You are My friends, if you do what I command you" (John 15:12-14 NASB).

These words have been fulfilled in history before! The Jewish author, Sholem Asch, wrote: "...Christianity also distinguished itself, in the particular of rescuing Jewish children, by the highest degree of self-sacrifice. It may be stated without exaggeration that almost the entire remnant of Israel which was found in the liberated countries—no matter how small its number—has the Christians to thank for its preservation. Christians who, by performing this action, placed their own lives in danger."[8]

***

[7]George Otis, *The Ghost of Hagar*. Van Nuys, CA: Time-Light Books, © 1974, pp. 44, 47, used by permission.

[8]Arthur W. Kac, *The Messiahship of Jesus*, p. 18.

DR. BAUMINGER SAYS 7000 RISKED THEIR LIVES TO SAVE JEWS

Dr. Arieh Bauminger, who was in charge of the Righteous Gentiles Archives at the Yad VaShem Holocaust and Memory Museum in Israel, told me in 1989 that they have discovered: "...six thousand righteous Christian Gentiles, who risked their lives to save Jews in Hitler's Holocaust. And in the next few years, we believe it will finally be discovered that in fact the total number was seven thousand."

Dr. Bauminger, a rabbi, told me these words when I interviewed him in Jerusalem for this book. A very delightful man whom I will never forget, he kindly gave me several hours of his time, for which I will always be grateful'!

RABBI EMDEN SAYS, "IF IT HAD NOT BEEN FOR THE CHRISTIANS, OUR REMNANT WOULD SURELY HAVE BEEN DESTROYED"

A famous Hasidic rabbi of Germany wrote: "For if it had not been for the Christians, our remnant would surely have been destroyed, and Israel's hope would have been extinguished amidst the Gentiles, who hate us because of our faith....But God, our Lord, has caused the Christian wise men to arise, who protect us in every generation."[9]

From Jesus' quotations in John 15, which represent the true Christian attitude toward humanity and especially the Jews, it would seem evident that most of what has been historically recorded as Christendom, is not! Richard Wurmbrand, a precious Jewish believer in Jesus, rightly notes of the World Council of Churches: "What communion can we have with the leaders of the World Council of Churches? They have never helped with one cent the families of Christian martyrs: on the contrary, they **give money to communist guerrillas in AFRICA.**"[10]

Concerning the Catholic Church, Sir Isaac Newton said: "Having searched, and by the grace of God obtained, after knowledg in the prophetique scriptures, I have thought my self bound to communicate it for the benefit of others....For it was revealed to Daniel that the prophecies concerning the last times should be closed up and sealed until the time of the end: but then the wise should understand, and knowledg should be increased. Dan 12, 4, 9, 10...and therefore the

---

[9]Pinchas Lapide, *Israelis, Jews, and Jesus*, p. 105. Lapide's source was *Lechem Shamayim* (Hamburg, 1757), p. 30 ff.

[10]Pastor Richard Wurmbrand, *Jesus to the Communist World, Inc., "The Voice of the Martyrs," 1967-1977*. Available through The Voice of the Martyrs, Inc., POB 11, Glendale, CA, USA 91209.

longer they have continued in obscurity, the more hopes there is that the time is at hand in which they are to be made manifest. If they [the prophetic Scriptures] are never to be understood, to what end did God reveal them? Certainly he did it for the edification of the church; and if so, then it is as certain that the church shall at length attain to the understanding thereof. I mean not all that call themselves Christians, but a remnant, a few **scattered persons** which God hath chosen, such as without being (blinded)."[11]

THOUGH FEW "CHRISTIANS" ARE CHRISTIAN, THIS DOES NOT MAKE THOSE FEW ANY LESS TRUE

Clearly the minority, as far as world Christendom is concerned, those who are referred to as born-again believers (I Pet. 4:12), are truly Christian and practice Jesus' words. Thus no one can truthfully say real Christians persecuted Jews in the past or present to indict Jesus or His true followers in order to cause doubt about His Messiahship. If they were true Christians in accordance with these passages, they would not have hurt anyone. In fact, they would have done the exact opposite; helped and pitied the Jewish people in troubled times.

We believe, along with others, that true Christian attitudes toward the Jewish people and Israel are represented in these words from several of today's well-known evangelical ministers, quoted from the television documentary *Israel—America's Key to Survival.* The quotes run as follows:

"The primary target of Soviet expansionism in the Middle East is Israel. World public opinion is turning against Israel. Once again, acts of anti-Semitism are on the increase throughout the world. As a supporter of law and justice, as a born-again Christian, as a God-fearing person, you have a responsibility to do something to stop these forces of destruction right now!" Hal Lindsey, author/film maker

"As Evangelicals, we're not ashamed to say that our God is the God of Israel. As Americans, we're not ashamed to say it...."

Mike Evans, evangelical minister/author

"We look to Israel to be a leader among the nations of the earth. A leader of peace, a leader of technology, a leader of the improvement of mankind. We feel that all of us here in America who call ourselves Evangelical Christians are prepared to stand behind you in your struggle for peace, in your struggle for dignity, in your struggle for liberty in these critical days. You can count on us. We are with you in every respect." Pat Robertson, evangelical broadcaster

"What a fulfillment of prophecy, what a testimony, what a future Israel has, and what a contribution Israel has made, is making and will make. All of us in the Christian faith here in America, salute you. We send you our warmest love and

---

[11] *Yahuda Manuscript 1.* Newton's spelling of three hundred years ago. [ ] mine.

greetings. You're constantly in our prayers and we too say, 'Oh Jerusalem, Oh Jerusalem' and we send our love and our prayers. God richly bless you."
Oral Roberts, evangelist

"We are also praying for the peace of Jerusalem, because the word of God commands, 'Pray for the peace of Jerusalem.' We see fulfilled the prophecies of the Old Testament daily in all of the things that have taken place in your great land [Israel]." Rex Humbard, television evangelist. [ ] mine

"Our heart is with you one hundred percent upon the biblical positions of the word with no compromises, no discussions. We are putting together 10,000 leaders and one million Evangelicals backing them up, that are going to be personally praying. More important than anything is prayers to God, but secondly after that, standing upon the biblical positions of the word of God [supporting Israel]."[12] Mike Evans, evangelical minister and author, to Prime Minister Begin. [ ] mine

"This is one of the great phenomena in our generation, the Christian friends of Israel—indeed an historic phenomenon."[13] Israeli Prime Minister Menachem Begin's reply

"Many of you who are watching this program may be having a hard time believing that Israel's survival is actually being threatened by such ominous forces as the PLO, the Soviet Union and more recently, by world public opinion. Now, if you are one of the skeptics, I urge you to do two important things. First, if you haven't already done it, undertake a serious thorough study of what the Bible says about the fate of modern Israel. Second, start being more analytical about what you see, what you hear, what you read in the media. Don't take everything at face value. Finally, I would encourage everyone of you to pick up your phones right now and call to add your name to the petition which is going to be given to our President [Reagan] urging him and other members of our government to stick by Israel at this most crucial time. Our leaders must understand that forcing Israel into some quick easy solution can only result in international catastrophe. Please, will you call and will you do it right now?" Pat Boone, Christian singer/entertainer. [ ] mine

"It was prophesied in the word of God and He has done it. And I thank God for it. I believe in the fact that God has raised up the nation of Israel again. Think about how fortunate we are as Christian people—we're watching God Almighty—the God of Abraham, Isaac and Jacob. We're watching Him move again just like in Bible days. Praise God." Kenneth Copeland, television evangelist

"We believe that God honors His word, God blesses His people and God honors those who honor His word and His people. For humanitarian reasons, we support the State of Israel. For historical reasons, believing that Palestine belongs to the Jewish people, we support the State of Israel. For legal reasons dating back to 1948, we believe the land of Palestine belongs to the Jewish people. And for theological reasons, first and foremost, we believe that God has given the land to the people."[14] Reverend Jerry Falwell, renowned television preacher

---

[12]From a meeting with Prime Minister Begin and key evangelical leaders in Jerusalem, led by Mike Evans.

[13]Ibid.

[14]Mike Evans, *Israel, America's Key to Survival*, broadcast aired June 1983. Menachem Begin, Prime Minister of Israel, presented the prestigious Jabotinsky Award from the government of Israel to Jerry Falwell in appreciation of his Christian support for Israel and the Jewish people. After Israel bombed Iraq's nuclear reactor, Begin first called Jerry Falwell, because of his great trust in Falwell's love of Israel, and asked him to "tell America why Israel needed to protect herself." Dan O'Neill and Don Wagner, *Peace or Armageddon*, pp. 83-84.

"It's not possible for a man to say, 'I'm a Christian,' and not love the Jewish people. You cannot be a Christian without being Jewish in spirit."[15] Rev. John Hagee

AS COMPARED TO EVANGELICAL CHRISTIANS AND JEWS FOR JESUS, JUST HOW LOYAL ARE LEFT-WING[16] AMERICAN JEWS TO ISRAEL?

In answer to this, we quote a segment from an article in the *Jerusalem Times/Jewish Press* entitled, "Rallies Tout Opposing Views on Uprisings." A portion of the article read: "...the so-called peaceniks carried the PLO flag next to that of Israel and noted that 'a good number of them were wearing 'Jackson for president' buttons...."[17]

The article also stated that this view was representative of a very small percentage of American Jews. Several speakers drew comparisons between Israel and Nazi Germany and the Israeli army and barbarians. Mordecai Levy, of the Jewish Defense Organization, was shocked by the outcome of what was supposed to have been a "peace" rally.

The sons of Israel have died in the heroic effort to salvage their land, which God promised to them (Gen. 17:7-8)! What is the response of a growing number of liberals living comfortably in the West? In 1989, *The Jewish Tribune*, a Miami-based Jewish newspaper, addressed this issue and pointed out that liberal American Jewry is potentially lethal to Israel. This newspaper published a letter to the editor by Lee Halpern entitled, "Reader Criticizes Liberals," which read: "Sadly, a number of wealthy American Jewish liberals have been using their financial might to force their ideology on Israel. The American Jewish Committee, for example, has been arranging meetings between young Israelis and Arabs—meetings which give the Arabs a golden opportunity to propagandize and undermine the morale and self confidence of the Israel teens. The organization known as the 'New Israel Fund' sends millions of dollars each year to Israeli groups like the left-wing Association for Civil Rights which defends the civil rights of...Arab terrorists—a classic case of liberalism gone haywire. This sort of liberal meddling will be Israel's undoing. Thank heavens there are those like Irving Moskowitz and 'Americans for a Safe Israel' to offer some straight thinking before it's too late."[18]

---

[15]Rev. John Hagee, *Why We Honor The Jews*.

[16]There is an appreciable Jewish community on the right side of the political spectrum, which is growing and is more or less solidly pro-Israel, as is the true born-again Christian.

[17]Julius Liebb, "Rallies Tout Opposing Views on Uprisings," *Jewish Press*, May 6, 1988, p. 60.

[18]Lee Halpern, "Reader Criticizes Liberals," *Jewish Tribune*. Miami, Mar. 10, 1989.

מעריב

11.1.1985

שגרירות בלי מדינה

ENGLISH SUMMARY

MA'ARIV, Israel's leading mass-circulation daily newspaper, published a major feature article about the International Christian Embassy Jerusalem in its popular weekend magazine. The article, entitled "Embassy Without a Country" was later reprinted in translation by the Israel Government Press Office for distribution to the overseas press stationed in Israel. It emphasizes the Embassy's across-the-spectrum appeal to all kinds of Christian supporters of Israel and unveils plans for a world-wide gathering of Christian Zionists to be convened in Basle, Switzerland in 1985.

במחנה

THE I.D.F. JOURNAL

„אשרת היכן שאלוה

ENGLISH SUMMARY

BAMAHANE is the official publication, in Hebrew, of the Israel Defense Forces. This monthly, especially popular amongst younger Israelis, looks at Jan Willem van der Hoeven, Jr.'s voluntary service in the Army and explains how the inspiration of the ICEJ and the teaching of his father, ICEJ Spokesman Jan Willem van der Hoeven, accounted for his uncommon decision to join up. It notes that Jan Jr.'s total faith and abiding ideology are a shining example to his fellow soldiers who have come to respect him. He, in turn, has endured the rigors of the army life with a handy book of Psalms secure in the knowledge that he is following a path shown him by the Lord.

הארץ

לאחר לבנון – יהודה ושומרון

ENGLISH SUMMARY

Israel's proximity to Lebanon has helped to focus ICEJ's attention on the pressing humanitarian needs of the Christian refugees of that war-torn nation. In the above article, appearing in 1984 in HA'ARETZ, Israel's intellectual daily newspaper, ICEJ Spokesman van der Hoeven, adds his analysis of developments in Lebanon to the marketplace of ideas. Below is one of numerous reports resulting – in this case in the *Jerusalem Post* – from an ICEJ fact-finding mission to southern Lebanon.

Christians warn of Lebanon carnage

THE JERUSALEM POST

MISSION OF FRIENDSHIP

By DAVID KRIVINE / Jerusalem Post Correspondent

ISRAEL SCENE

Diplomatic mission

Here are a few magazine and newspaper clippings illustrating the pro-Israel stance and born-again Christian concern for Israel. Courtesy of the International Christian Embassy, Jerusalem.

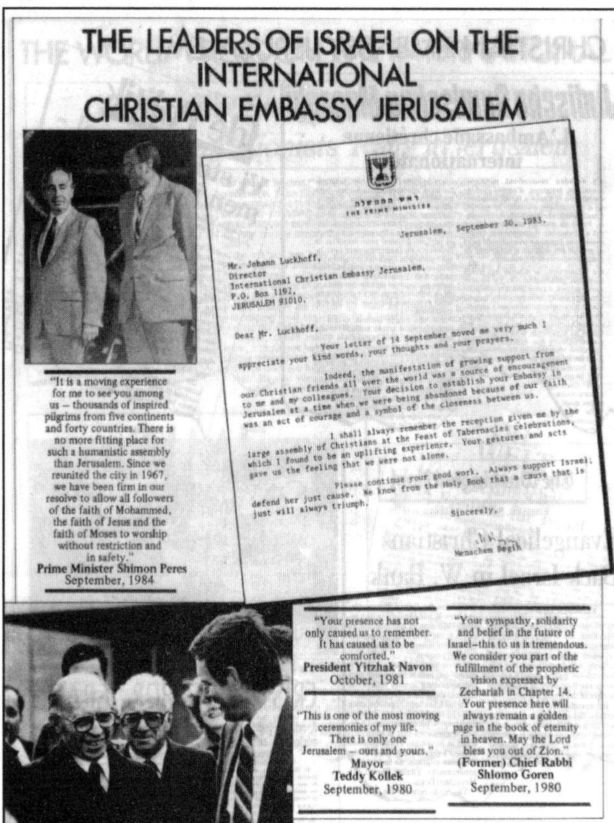

ראש הממשלה
THE PRIME MINISTER

Jerusalem, September 30, 1983.

Mr. Johann Luckhoff,
Director
International Christian Embassy Jerusalem,
P.O. Box 1192,
JERUSALEM 91010.

Dear Mr. Luckhoff,

Your letter of 14 September moved me very much I appreciate your kind words, your thoughts and your prayers.

Indeed, the manifestation of growing support from our Christian friends all over the world was a source of encouragement to me and my colleagues. Your decision to establish your Embassy in Jerusalem at a time when we were being abandoned because of our faith was an act of courage and a symbol of the closeness between us.

I shall always remember the reception given me by the large assembly of Christians at the Feast of Tabernacles celebrations, which I found to be an uplifting experience. Your gestures and acts gave us the feeling that we were not alone.

Please continue your good work. Always support Israel; defend her just cause. We know from the Holy Book that a cause that is just will always triumph.

Sincerely,

Menachem Begin

"It is a moving experience for me to see you among us – thousands of inspired pilgrims from five continents and forty countries. There is no more fitting place for such a humanistic assembly than Jerusalem. Since we reunited the city in 1967, we have been firm in our resolve to allow all followers of the faith of Mohammed, the faith of Jesus and the faith of Moses to worship without restriction and in safety."
Prime Minister Shimon Peres
September, 1984

"Your presence has not only caused us to remember. It has caused us to be comforted."
President Yitzhak Navon
October, 1981

"This is one of the most moving ceremonies of my life. There is only one Jerusalem – ours and yours."
Mayor Teddy Kollek
September, 1980

"Your sympathy, solidarity and belief in the future of Israel–this to us is tremendous. We consider you part of the fulfillment of the prophetic vision expressed by Zechariah in Chapter 14. Your presence here will always remain a golden page in the book of eternity in heaven. May the Lord bless you out of Zion."
(Former) Chief Rabbi Shlomo Goren
September, 1980

When the chips are down, virtually one hundred percent of the pro-Israel Zionist Christians and Jews for Jesus will support Israel! Can half of America's Jewish community make this claim? In light of the reports we quoted, it seems the answer is no. A very sad no; a no which is to be pitied because of the blood of those who have fought to ensure a safe Israel for their children and for the future of the Jewish people. Israelis are aware of this. This is a photo of an Israeli protest of an American left-wing government official in the late 1970's.

At present, the greater majority of Israelis are conservatives, or what many would call "right-wing." They are concerned for their nation and children and, my God, why shouldn't they be! It's time for conservatives who believe in a safe nation with freedom for all to draw the line! Wouldn't you ? Maybe this will happen in the next Israeli election.

DID TRUE BELIEVING CHRISTIANS SAVE THOUSANDS OF JEWS FROM HITLER?

In times of true need, as documented here, the only true and measurable help for the Jews can be found in the hearts and hands of Evangelical Christians. Israel has a memorial located near Mount Herzl called Yad VaShem, which is dedicated to displaying the horrifying acts perpetrated by the Nazis upon the Jewish people.

Outside of this memorial, Israel has planted a forest of trees called, "The Forest of the Righteous Gentiles." Each tree was planted in memory of someone who saved the Jewish people from Hitler. If you look carefully at the pictures, you will notice a name under each tree.

"...Yet I have left *me* seven thousand in Israel...." God, I Kings 19:18 KJV[19]

Just how many and who are the righteous Gentiles represented by the many trees planted outside the Yad VaShem Holocaust Museum in Israel? Rabbi Arieh L. Bauminger, director of the museum, member of the Committee for the Righteous Among the Nations, and himself a Holocaust survivor, told me there were: "...six thousand righteous Christian Gentiles, who risked their lives to save Jews in Hitler's Holocaust. And in the next few years, we believe it will finally be discovered that, in fact, the total number was seven thousand."

Dr. Bauminger was in charge of establishing the criteria by which these people were chosen. He told me it was decided that this title was not given to those who merely saved or helped Jews escape, but rather those who helped in spite of a danger to their own lives and the lives of their loved ones—this is why another 1000 are expected to be discovered through intense investigation. Many thousands were killed and can only be found through others who testify that they were helped by them.

[19]In this verse, God said to Elija that He still had 7000 Jews loyal to Him. Amazingly enough, there are approximately 7000 righteous Gentiles who saved the children of Israel from the Holocaust!

"Then come unto him the Sadducees, which say there is no resurrection; and they asked him, saying,...And Jesus answering said unto them, Do ye not therefore err, because ye know not the scriptures, neither the power of God?...and as touching the dead, that they rise: have ye not read in the book of Moses, how in the bush God spake unto him, saying, I *am* the God of Abraham, and the God of Isaac, and the God of Jacob? He is not the God of the dead, but the God of the living: ye, therefore do greatly err. And one of the scribes came, and having heard them reasoning together, and perceiving that he had answered them well, asked him, Which is the first commandment of all? And Jesus answered him, The first of all the commandments *is*, Hear, O Israel; The Lord our God is one Lord: And thou shalt love the Lord thy God with all thy heart, and with all thy soul, and with all thy mind, and with all thy strength: this *is* the first commandment. And the second *is* like, *namely* this, Thou shalt love thy neighbor as thyself. There is none other commandment greater than these."

Jesus' answer to a Jewish doctor of the law, as recorded in the New Testament, Mark 12:18, 24, 26-31 KJV

"In this book, writing from the depths of our hearts, we render infinite thanks and homage to the Righteous People who risked their lives to rescue Jews during one of the most tragic periods in the history of the Jewish nation."

Abba Eban, in his foreword to Arieh Bauminger's book, *The Righteous*

"If G-d is 'Love,' how can Christians explain the silence and indifference of the Church and most Christian nations while six million Jews were being gassed and burned by the Germans?"[20]

Rabbi Pinchas Stolper, quoted from the anti-missionary publication, *The Real Messiah*

Abba Eban, the famous Israeli statesman, comments on those Christians who saved so many Jews in his foreword to Dr. Bauminger's book, *The Righteous.* Eban, a Jew speaking for many Jews today, wrote: "In this book, writing from the depths of our hearts, we render infinite thanks and homage to the Righteous People who risked their lives to rescue Jews during one of the most tragic periods in the history of the Jewish nation....These saviours were men and women impelled by the Bible's behest, 'Love thy neighbour as thyself!'....they chose to hazard their own existence and to jeopardize the welfare of their nearest and dearest....In the name of that selfsame justice, we owe a debt of everlasting gratitude and of tribute to these Righteous People."[21]

***

[20]Rabbi Aryeh Kaplan, *et al*, *The Real Messiah*, pp. 57-58.

[21]Rabbi Arieh L. Bauminger, *The Righteous,* 3rd Edition. Jerusalem: Yad VaShem; Martyrs and Heroes Remembrance Authority, © 1983, p. foreword, used by permission.

The entrance to the Garden of the Righteous Gentiles, which leads to the Yad VaShem Holocaust Museum in Jerusalem.

"It is our duty to discover these knights of morality [righteous Gentiles], to establish contact with them, to pay them our debt of gratitude and to express to them our admiration for their courage...These few saved not only the Jews but the honour of Man."[22]
Kadish Luz, Speaker of Israel's Parliament

Dr. Bauminger also wrote: "There were not a few Gentiles who risked their own lives, and imperilled their families, in aiding Jewish fugutives, feeding and clothing them, sheltering them, furnishing them with forged 'Aryan' papers. Conscious of the hideous consequences if they were caught, they yet rendered salvation, and the deeds of these Righteous People are all the more to be marvelled at and be thankful for against the background of an overwhelming populace...even ready to betray hidden Jews to the Gestapo for a price."[23]

Just to name a few of these people, Bauminger writes: "It is impossible not to mention Vladas, a village schoolmaster in Lithuania...who for years hid nine Jews in his home, thwarting every Gestapo inquisition; even his young son was adamantly silent about the hidden Jews, though the Nazis thrashed him savagely. Eduardo Focherini, a newspaper editor in Bologna, was put to death by the Gestapo for smuggling Jews out of Italy....Oswald Bosko....(was arrested because of his pro-Jewish activities, charged by the Gestapo with treason, and executed on 18 September 1944.)"[24]

Corrie Ten Boom, the loving old woman whose book, *The Hiding Place*, later became a film,[25] saved many Jews in her own personal "hiding place" behind a double wall in her home. Corrie was a wonderful Evangelical Christian who said she was willing to save Jesus' people, the Jews, from the Holocaust even if it meant her death. Even though she was relentlessly beaten by the Gestapo, she never turned in any of the Jews she was hiding. Recently, Corrie died and her tree was placed in the Yad VaShem Memorial Park in Israel.

***

[22]Ibid, p. 11.
[23]Ibid, p. 10.
[24]Ibid, pp. 10-14.
[25]This film is now available on home video.

Corrie Ten Boom's name plaque and tree.

The famous Christian Swedish diplomat, Raul Wallenberg, who some feel is still alive and incarcerated in Russia, saved 100,000 Jews. Dr. Bauminger describes this "angel of mercy":[26] "...Wallenberg rented 32 houses that he proclaimed a Swedish extraterritorial zone. Into these houses Wallenberg brought his 'protected Jews,' after having duly provided them with forged papers in the name of the Swedish Embassy and the Red Cross."[27]

Bauminger went on to tell how Wallenberg hid the Jewish children in "churches or private Christian homes," and that: " 'All this was done by a courageous man who had the strength of his convictions to act according to his conscience and beliefs. As in the case of King Christian of Denmark, Wallenberg's deeds once more bring to mind the poignant thought: how much greater could have been the number of survivors in the lands of extermination, had there been others like him....' "[28]

---

[26]Ibid, p. 79.
[27]Ibid.
[28]Ibid, p. 81. Attorney General of Israel at the Eichmann trial.

The Wallenberg Memorial, built to honor the man who saved 100,000 Jews from the Holocaust.

The phrase from the Talmud, in the lower right-hand corner of the Wallenberg Memorial, says that if you save one person, you also save their children, grandchildren, great-grandchildren... (See Sanhedrin 37a).

PAST CHRISTIAN ZIONISTS (WHO SAVED JEWS FROM THE HOLOCAUST) ECHO THE FUTURE OF CHRISTIAN ZIONISM—PROTECT ISRAEL

In a recent edition of the *Jerusalem Courier*, David Allen Lewis pointed out: "It is encouraging to discover that many American Evangelicals did actually denounce Hitler. Pentecostal preachers were almost universally clear in their anti-Nazi declarations. Voss and Rausch state: 'During Hitler's 'final solution' to the Jewish problem, Fundamentalist-Evangelicals believed that the Jewish people were being exterminated by the millions, while more liberal Christians and periodicals, such as *The Christian Century*, were labeling the reports of atrocity propaganda. Gaebelein's *Our Hope* magazine gave factual reports of atrocities against the Jewish people during the 1930s and 1940s. The Fundamentalist-Evangelical world view lent itself very well to such convictions, even when they seemed beyond the realm of belief....'...The good news is that there are many Evangelicals and Pentecostals who are in tune with Biblical truth in relation to Israel and the Jewish people. How I thank God for those who refuse to be intimidated, who rise above the general apathy that attends this subject.

One might smugly take comfort in the fact that many American Evangelicals did resist Hitler from afar...."[29]

Malcolm Hedding, in his article entitled, "Christian Zionism," noted: "...famous Christian Zionists such as Orde Charles Wingate, John Hayes Holmes, Professor Reinhold Niebhur and Corrie Ten Boom who, at great personal risk during the Second World War, rescued Jews from the hands of Nazism. All these believed that Scripture promised the restoration of the Jewish State in Palestine. Most of them died in hope but some, like Corrie Ten Boom, lived to see the impossible come true.

Yes, Christian Zionism has a long history. Today the movement has swelled to embrace thousands. All of them see their task as being far from over, since the same forces that sought the destruction of Israel in decades past are still at work today. The survival and preservation of Israel is dependent upon the same kind of help and support that made her existence a reality. Christian Zionists believe that in seeking her peace they are in the long run working for the world's peace (Isaiah 2:1-4). The International Christian Embassy Jerusalem, Christians United For Israel and the National Christian Leadership Conference for Israel are in the forefront of this struggle for Israel's survival, peace and blessing."[30]

WHY DID TRUE CHRISTIANS SAVE THE JEWS? BECAUSE OF THE BIBLE'S AND JESUS' TEACHINGS OF LOVE

The reason has been truthfully and beautifully stated in the article entitled, "Gentiles Who Dared To Save Jews," by Peter Colón. He wrote: "The wonderful thing about the Avenue of the Righteous Gentiles is its acclamation to the testimony of ordinary people. Recent studies on the specific motives of the more religiously minded rescuers revealed that there were some basic spiritual considerations for their conduct. Foremost was the teaching of God's love and protection for the Jews as recorded in the Bible. Passages such as 'I [God] have loved thee [Israel] with an everlasting love' (Jer. 31:3) and 'he that toucheth you [Israel] toucheth the apple of his [God's] eye' (Zech. 2:8) were strong incentives. Other biblical passages—such as the golden rule of Matthew 7:12; the story of the good Samaritan in Luke 10:25-37; the love-for-God-and-neighbor commandment of Matthew 22:34-

---

[29]David Allen Lewis, "Was Hitler a Christian?", *Jerusalem Courier*, Vol. 7, No.. 2. Springfield, MO: David A. Lewis Ministries, Inc., © 1988, p. 2, used by permission.
[30]Malcolm Hedding, "Christian Zionism," *Jerusalem Courier*, Vol. 7, No.. 2, © 1988, p. 6, used by permission.

40; and the impending judgement to come of Matthew 25:33-46—were strong motivating factors that incited devout Christians to help the Jews. For them, the evils of anti-Semitism did not infiltrate their Christian theology."[31]

Colón listed a few of the righteous Christians and their deeds done out of love for the Jews, in the same article: "Their names are immortalized on a narrow walkway that leads to the Israeli Holocaust Memorial called Yad Vashem. This street is affectionately referred to as the 'Avenue of the Righteous Gentiles.'

On both sides of the path to the memorial thousands of evergreen carob trees are planted. At the base of each tree is a plaque inscribed with a name to commemorate an individual—exceptional individuals who believed that all people were created in the image and likeness of God and were therefore worth saving. The details of their heroic deeds are shining tributes to their humanity and sense of decency in helping the oppressed.

Along the path, one tree salutes a heroic man named Joop Westerweel, a Dutch Plymouth Brethren teacher. The father of four, he felt compassion for the plight of Jewish children and devised a plan to smuggle them from Nazi-occupied Holland into neutral Spain. The scheme worked and thousands of children were saved. Eventually he was caught, and Gestapo agents tortured him daily then condemned him to die in a horrid concentration camp. Today his carob tree is beautifully maintained by some of those same children, now adults, whom he sacrificed his life to save....In Vilna, Poland, a simple librarian named Anna Simaite hid Jewish children. She helped feed starving Jews using her own food rationing card. She also helped forge identity passes. At the same time the daring Jadzia Duniec supplied weapons to the Jewish underground. He was caught and murdered by the Gestapo. Another brave woman, Sophia Debicka, turned her humble home into a base for the Jewish resistance.

Abbe Alexander Glasberg of France rescued 2,000 French Jews and even managed to maintain a 'safe house' for 65 Jewish teens. A simple French pastor with the heart of a lion personally traveled to the various concentration camps and boldly requested the release of Jewish children. In many cases he was successful....In Belgium, Louis Celis rasied four young Jewish children as his own. When it was safe, he spirited them to their ancient homeland, Israel. Ingebjorg Fortyedt Sletten, a member of the Norwegian resistance, saved several Jewish families in Oslo, including the chief rabbi of the city."[32]

---

[31]Peter Colón, "Gentiles Who Dared To Save Jews," *Israel My Glory*, © Apr./May 1995, p. 12, used by permission.
[32]Ibid, pp. 11-12.

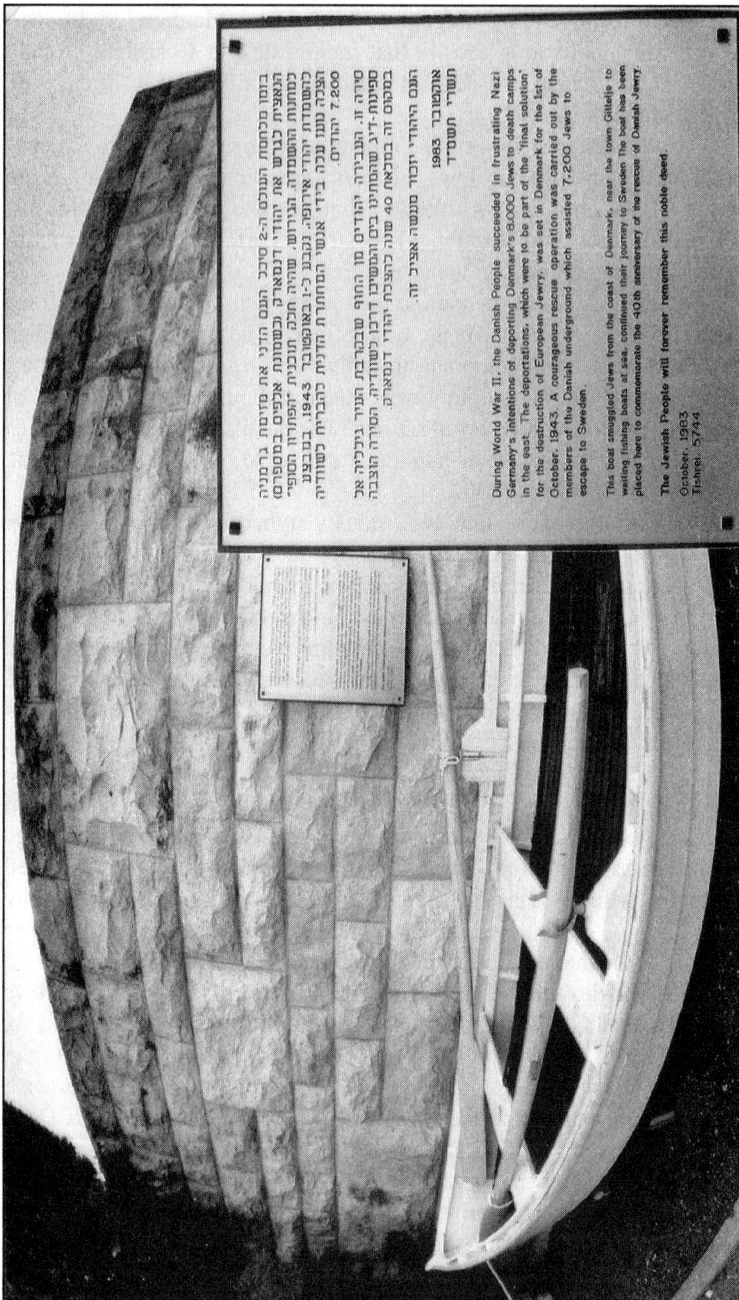

This small boat was used by the Danes to smuggle Jews from Gillelje, Denmark, to fishing boats at sea, on their way to the safety of Sweden.

Here are a few books written by Jewish survivors of the Holocaust. They say they owe their lives to those Christians who aided them in their fight for suvival and Jesus, the one they came to realize is the Jewish Messiah, through whom they were miraculously preserved.

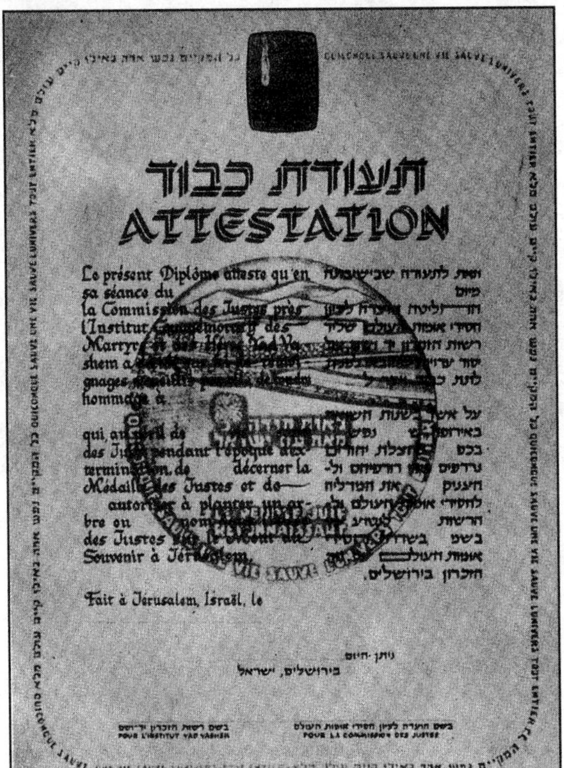

This citation is presented by Yad VaShem to righteous Gentiles in honor of their commitment to save Jews during the Nazi Holocaust.

I will never forget the feeling I had when I performed the Heimlich maneuver on my dear friend Eddie Sussman's son, Elad, dislodging the food he was choking on from his throat. His mother, Ruth, brought her little boy out of the kitchen, blue, saying, "I've tried and I can't get it!" When Elad began to breathe again, I realized what the Lord had done through me that night in Jerusalem and I thanked Him! This frightening close call gives me some small idea of what it must have felt like for those ancient believers when they saved people during the Holocaust.

The heavy coverage of the Christian Zionist Congress by the *Jerusalem Post* shows Israel's interest in Christian Zionism.

Arieh Bauminger, pictured here, author of *The Righteous* and *Roll of Honour*, documents an incredible number of righteous who saved countless Jews from Hitler's Holocaust.

"...For if it had not been for the Christians, our remnant would surely have been destroyed, and Israel's hope would have been extinguished amidst the Gentiles, who hate us because of our faith....But God, our Lord, has caused the Christian wise men to arise, who protect us in **every generation.**"[33] Rabbi Emden of Hamburg (concerning true believers), 1757

TWO RESPECTED JEWISH AUTHORITIES AFFIRM TRUE CHRISTIANS WERE HEROES AND THAT THEY RISKED THEIR LIVES TO SAVE JEWS

Have you ever heard that familiar statement, "The world stood by and watched while six million Jews were murdered"? Did the true followers of Jesus do this? While the "world" might have, those who truly believed in Jesus as Messiah did just the opposite! Jesus once said *you are in the world but not of the world*[34] (John 15:19).

Let's hear the testimonies of two eminent Jewish personalities on this issue, Dr. Arieh Bauminger and Sholem Asch. The famed Jewish author, Sholem Asch, who does not believe in Jesus as Messiah, wrote: "Christianity also distinguished itself, in the particular of rescuing Jewish children, by the highest degree of self-sacrifice. It may be stated without exaggeration that almost the entire remnant of Israel which was found in the liberated countries—no matter how small its number—has the Christians to thank for its preservation. Christians who, by performing this action, placed their own lives in danger."[35]

Israeli children are being taught the **novel truth** in Israel today, and that is that true Christians risked their lives to save Jews. On field trips to the museum, they not only see the Yad VaShem Holocaust Memorial Forest, in which each tree was planted in memory of one who saved Jews from Hitler, but they study a book called *Roll of Honour*, which describes heroes from twenty-three nations who risked their lives, and in some cases, were even murdered while rescuing Jews in World War II.[36] Dr. Bauminger told me in a personal interview that

---

[33]Pinchas Lapide, *Israelis, Jews, and Jesus*, p. 105. Bold mine. Lapide's source was *Lechem Shamayim* (Hamburg, 1757), p. 30 ff.

[34]The New Testament uses the word "world" as a generic term to describe all those who have not believed in Jesus. In contemporary terms we can say all those who are not born-again or who have not accepted Jesus as their personal Messiah, Savior and forgiver! This includes the majority of Catholic "churches" and a sizable portion of Protestantism!

[35]Arthur W. Kac, *The Messiahship of Jesus*, p. 18.

[36]They are taught from: "...a little booklet by school inspector Dr. Arie L. Bauminger which was introduced in 1967 in all classes beyond primary level and has been in continual use since then as a teaching aid. It is entitled *Honor Roll*, and it recounts in sixty pages the glorious deeds of some of the 'just men of the nations' who risked their lives—many in fact were killed—to rescue Jews during World War II....these roughtly eight hundred 'heroes of charity' came from twenty-three different countries...." Pinchas Lapide, *Israelis, Jews, and Jesus*, p. 63.

there are now 5000 Christian heroes and within a few years, we will discover perhaps 7000 who risked their lives to save Jews.

DESPITE THE WARNINGS OF FOREIGN RABBIS, ISRAEL'S NATIONAL TEXTBOOKS PORTRAY JESUS FOR THE HERO THAT HE IS!

This new knowledge about true Christians is arousing Israeli children's interest[37] in the New Testament and the person of Jesus. There is a new openness that was not there before to talk about Jesus! This is evidenced by the fear of a group of American and English rabbis who have warned against Jesus' heroism, as portrayed in Israel's schoolbooks. The Jewish scholar Pinchas Lapide documents: "...the present day schoolbooks of Israel contain what is undoubtedly the most sympathetic picture of Jesus ever offered to a generation of Jewish children by their teachers. This fact is confirmed by, among other things, the protests of a group of Rabbis (most are recent immigrants from America and England) who recently issued a public warning in Jerusalem that the 'heroic Jesus' presented in the schools today could pave the way for conversion efforts among the Jews by the ever-active missionary societies."[38]

Schoolchildren playing a Hanukkah game in their classroom.

---

[37]On March 26, 1987, the *Jerusalem Times/Jewish Press* ran an interesting article entitled "The Scandal of Avoda Zara in Kibbutzim." The author of the article was obviously very upset at the circulation of the Hebrew New Testament within Israel. He reported that the Hebrew New Testament, bound together with the Old Testament, was prevalent in the kibbutzim (social farms in Israel) and that a kibbutznik teacher said that they were **not** being thrown away. I know this is true because my friend Michael Bentley gave one hundred and fifty of the kibbutzim, several thousand Bibles containing New Testaments in the 1980's, before he was forced to leave Israel. There are about three hundred kibbutzim presently operating within the land of Israel.

[38]Ibid, pp. 67-68.

"We'll read what we want to read." Judy Derberg, an Israeli student, reads *Hasidi Oumout Olam* (*The Righteous of the World* in Hebrew), by Dr. Arieh Bauminger.

Can there be any wonder why so many Israelis feel that these foreign rabbis with an identity crisis should keep their opinions to themselves? In other words, let Israel be Israel, and let "us" decide what we want to know about Jesus for "ourselves"!

The following pictures[39] are of the International Christian Feast of Tabernacles. Christians from many nations, numbering in the thousands, come to Israel every year to celebrate this feast with the Jewish people. The prophet Zechariah predicts that when Jesus returns, all nations will come to Jerusalem and celebrate this feast.

The old city of Jerusalem and Golden Gate,
viewed from the Mount of Olives.

[39]The following photos in this chapter, with exception of the last three photos in the right-hand column, are courtesy of the International Christian Embassy Jerusalem.

True Christians will stand by Israel until the redemption arrives.

Until the end.

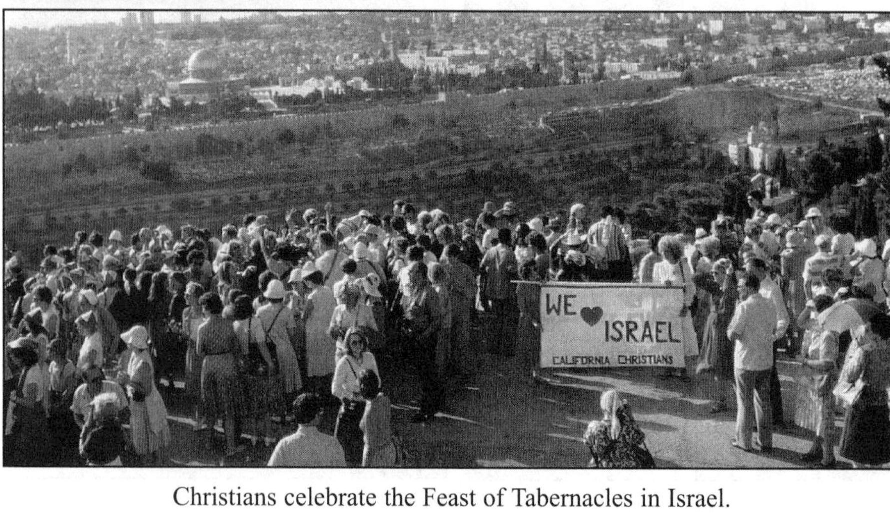

Christians celebrate the Feast of Tabernacles in Israel.

Christian Zionism continues until this day, and shall continue.

Jhan Moskowitz, of *Jews for Jesus*, offers Messianic literature at the Messiah Conference.

"I don't think there are many Jews—fanatics and ill-informed excepted—who are not fascinated by the Person and Teaching of Jesus. Perhaps much more so than many Gentiles and so-called 'Christians.' I might add that the approach of Jews to Christianity can only be made via the Message of Jesus....There is now a growing sense of inquiry here [in Israel], concerning the things of Jesus and Christianity. The reasons being that prejudices are dying down....there is a growing tendency within Christendom to make room for the rise of the Antichrist. He will be an imitator of Christ, of Jesus, whose teachings he will twist and pervert."[1]

Israeli professor of Jewish studies, David Flusser

"In the Diaspora Jesus looked alien to the Jew, an outsider, an interloper. But in Israel he is seen as the Jew from Nazareth, a native of this country, a Sabra, with claims to the land as strong as any. He cannot be brushed aside as a foreign influence....When the Jews left their land two thousand years ago, the land was holy for them alone; when they returned, the land was holy also to more than half of the world. The land had become sanctified in the meantime to millions and millions of non-Jews. The same applies to the Bible which had been a book holy to the Jews alone and which has become a holy book for millions of non-Jews. Both the Book and the Land have become sanctified to the world and this was not the work of the Diaspora Jews who, in spite of the injunction, did not become 'a light to the Gentiles,' but was the work rather of a single Jew and his band of Jewish followers, all of them Sabras. They were all born and bred in the Land, which is in this sense the most fruitful land on earth."[2]

English scholar and professor, Ferdynand Zweig

"If you're a Jew who believes that Yeshua is the Messiah, you've returned to Judaism, to the kind of Judaism the Bible teaches. You haven't converted to another religion. If you are a Gentile believer you have come to the faith of Abraham through the Messiah."[3]

Second generation Messianic Jewess, Ruth Fleischer, Ph.D.

15

MESSIANIC JEWISH FAITH IN JESUS

As we saw in chapters 5 and will see in chapter 27,[4] much ancient rabbinic commentary agrees with Christian interpretation involving the Messiah and end time prophecy! Why then have the religious leaders of Israel and their rabbinical successors, to this day, fought so hard to maintain a distance from Jesus as Messiah? Answer: The religious leaders of Jesus' day (Caiaphas and Annas, mentioned in

---

[1]Arthur W. Kac, *The Messiahship of Jesus*, p. 41. [ ] mine.

[2]Ibid, p. 63. Zweig is a well-known English scholar. He served several years as visiting professor in labor relations and sociology at the Tel Aviv and Hebrew Universities.

[3]Ruth Fleischer, Ph.D., *The Reemergence of Messianic Judaism.* Tape 30 CF179. Grantham, PA: The Messiah Conference at Messiah College, © 1993. This audio tape is available through Manna Conference Taping, Inc., 1704 Valencia N.E., Albuquerque, NM, USA 87110.

[4]The last two pages of this chapter illustrate a remarkable parallel of the projected events of the end times between the rabbinical writings and the New Testament words of Jesus.

John 11) were corrupt,[5] as we read in our earlier Messiah Conspiracy chapters. They wanted to control the power and wealth of Israel for themselves. Talmudic and modern rabbinic sources speak of the corruption of these first century religious leaders, as we documented earlier in our chapter 4.

RABBIS CONSPIRED TO COVER UP AN HONEST LOOK AT THE MESSIAHSHIP OF JESUS

As previously documented in our chapters dealing with the "Messiah Conspiracy," the rabbis at Yavne created a rigid, normative Judaism as distant as possible from its Messianic inspiration. As a result, for 2000 years, Jews who have expressed any interest in Jesus were branded as ignorant, deviant, heretics, or traitors. However, modern Messianic Jews, like their ancient counterparts, are neither misinformed nor deviant. They are the most courageous and bold sector of the Jewish community because they investigate the Bible for themselves and make their own decisions. They have the courage to believe and proclaim their views, even if it puts them at odds with their fellow Jews. These are the qualities of true heroes. *I will believe the truth and tell others even if my "leader" (the rabbi) disagrees and tells me otherwise. I will do what the Bible and God tells me, not what man says.* Psalms 118:8 states: "It is better to take refuge in the LORD Than to trust in man" (NASB).

IN OUR CENTURY, MORE JEWS ARE REALIZING THE MESSIAHSHIP OF JESUS THAN IN ANY OTHER PERIOD!

The Messianic Jewish movement lay virtually dormant until the middle of the twentieth century, when end time prophecy began to become reality. In 1948, Israel was born, and in 1967, against all odds, Israel was victorious in a war against five Arab nations.

The miracle of the Six Day War, and the return of Old Jerusalem to Jewish hands, enabled born-again Gentile Christians to show the Jews that the Messianic prophecies were being fulfilled. They were also able to show God's true love for the Jewish people through their caring in the Messiah.[6]

We began to see movements such as *Jews for Jesus* and Messianic synagogues popping up all over the world (for a short list of these, see our *Vol. II*, chapter 19, "Messianic Synagogues—How to Get There"). At last, Jews are returning to the pre-Yavnean Judaism which

---

[5]See our rabbinical references, both ancient and modern, which prove this, in chapter 4.

[6]Isn't it interesting that Einstein once wrote: " '...Only the church stood squarely across the path of Hitler's campaign....I am forced to confess that what I once despised I now praise unreservedly.' " Arthur W. Kac, *The Messiahship of Jesus*, pp. 36-37. Kac's source was *The Evening Sun*, Baltimore, April 13, 1979.

existed before the destruction of the Temple in the days of Jesus. They are returning to the only Judaism which can fill their hearts with God's forgiveness; they are beginning to appreciate the true Judaism of the Scriptures, which was penned by the ancient Hebrew prophets, from Moses to Malachi, under the direct inspiration of God. This is the Judaism in which Jesus believed and which He partially fulfilled in His First Coming;[7] the Judaism[8] that the Gentile followers of Jesus accept when they accept the Messiah Jesus.

While the present return of Jews to their Messiah is unprecedented, a steady stream of Jewish people have been coming to know Him since the turn of the century.

THE JEWISH RECLAMATION OF JESUS—A HISTORY OF THE *MODERN* MESSIANIC JEWISH MOVEMENT

Oppressed by the rabbis and the ecumenical "church," Jewish believers lost their autonomy in the Middle Ages when the last Messianic congregations disappeared. However, as previously mentioned, the *true* Christian carried the message of the Jewishness of the Messiah forward.

The ancient seed of Abraham would have to wait for a more fertile soil to take root. This time arrived at the end of the nineteenth century. After centuries of living in Europe, millions of Jews, seeking security and a better life, began emigrating to America. This "New World" became a new "promised land" for four million Jews who came to the United States at the turn of the century.

In the 1880's, Arno C. Gaebelian and Ernest Stoeter established The Hope of Israel, a Messianic missionary outreach. An article published in their quarterly, *Our Hope*, entitled, "Christian Judaism," proclaimed: "...Christian Judaism was 'not a nineteenth century invention,' but was 'as old as the days of the apostles, yea as old as the Psalms of David and the prophecies of Isaiah and Zechariah. Its roots lie in the oath-bound covenants of God with Abraham....' "[9]

---

[7]When Jesus returns, He will fulfill the kingly prophecies of the Messiah, which He promised to do in His Second Coming, as taught in the New Testament in Matthew 24, Luke 21, Revelation and portions of Paul's epistles.

[8]The word Judaism comes from Judah in the Old Testament, one of the twelve sons of Israel, and is connected with praising God. When Leah, Jacob's wife, gave birth to her son, Judah, she said: "...Now will I praise the LORD...." (Gen. 29:35 KJV). Thus, the word Judaism, in reality, is a very broad generic term that does not necessarily describe only today's Jewish culture, it describes a true biblical faith as well, which includes that of Christians who fundamentally believe the Old and New Testament in their praise to the God of Israel through His Messiah Jesus.

[9]David A. Rausch, *Messianic Judaism: Its History, Theology, and Polity*. New York: The Edwin Mellen Press, © 1982, p. 56.

In 1901, a group of Jewish believers met together in Boston to talk about forming an organization. The Hebrew Christian Alliance of America was created in 1915. By 1932, the Alliance had branches in a number of American cities and in Toronto, Ontario, Canada.

In 1954, the Hebrew Christian Alliance organized the "World Congress of Hebrew Christians." This was the largest gathering of Jews who believed in Jesus since the first and second centuries. Representatives came from Europe, Australia, South Africa and Canada.

In the 1960's and 1970's, Messianic Judaism became a household word. Many people were familiar with the movement. Throughout the 80's and into the 90's, this movement has grown to worldwide proportions, with thousands of congregations. Nearly every major U.S. city has its own congregation, advertised in the religious sections of major newspapers.[10]

Sherry Sussman (right), a Messianic Jew in Israel, celebrates Hanukkah with her friend in Jerusalem.

[10]For a more comprehensive history, see Robert I. Winer, *The Calling: The History of the Messianic Jewish Alliance of America 1915-1980.*

"The Reverend William Hechler, Chaplain of the English Embassy here, came to see me. A sympathetic, gentle fellow, with the long grey beard of a prophet. He is enthusiastic about my solution of the Jewish Question. He also considers my movement a 'prophetic turning-point'—which he had foretold two years before. From a prophecy...."[11]

Theodor Herzl, founder of modern political Zionism, quoted from his private diary

Theodore Herzl, founder of modern political Zionism.

[11]Regina Sharif, *Non-Jewish Zionism*, p. 71.

FAMOUS JEWS ASSOCIATED WITH ISRAEL AND HER FOUNDING—DID THEY HAVE AN INTEREST IN JESUS?

Theodor Herzl (1860-1904) grew up in Budapest, Hungary. He was the founder of political Zionism and the father of the State of Israel. Chaplain William H. Hechler (a true evangelical born-again Christian), author of *The Restoration of the Jews to Palestine*, was Theodor Herzl's best friend. In 1994, Professor Popkin told me that Herzl died in the arms of Hechler. Dr. Arthur Kac documents the following concerning Reverend Hechler and Theodor Herzl: "The remarkable story of William H. Hechler's Zionist activities is recounted in *The Prince and Prophet* by Claude Duvernoy, translated from the French by Jack Joffe, and published by Christian Action for Israel, Box 3367, Jerusalem. Hechler, a British clergyman, was born to missionary parents in India in 1845. The Grand Duke Frederick of Baden, Germany, appointed him as his private chaplain and tutor to his two sons. During his chaplaincy at the British Embassy in Vienna, Hechler met Herzl, the father of modern Zionism, whom he introduced to many leading political and ecclesiastical persons, including the Grand Duke, who subsequently became Kaiser Wilhelm II. For nine years Hechler played a most significant role in Herzl's preoccupation with Zionism. In times of despondency and disillusionment Herzl was spurred on by this dedicated evangelical Christian. 'God chose you,' he would say to Herzl. 'Your people will get its promised land. God is with you.' Based on his studies in the book of Daniel, Hechler predicted in 1895 that 1897 would be a fateful year in Jewish history. As we know, the First Zionist Congress was convened in 1897. To the German-Jewish philosopher Martin Buber, Hechler said in 1913: 'Your fatherland will soon be given back to you. For a serious crisis will occur, whose deep meaning is the liberation of your Messianic Jerusalem from the yoke of the nations...We are moving towards a world war...' Shortly before his death, he said this to the family of the Zionist leader Nathan Sokolov: 'Part of European Jewry is going to be sacrificed for the resurrection of your biblical fatherland.' "[12]

Some speculate that Herzl, influenced by his friend William Hechler, may have died a secret believer in Jesus as Messiah. Herzl once said, "But I think that he wants to convert me."[13]

Herzl certainly was interested in the Messiah. This we know from his dreams as he wrote: "One night I had a wonderful dream: King Messiah came, and he was old and glorious. He lifted me in his

---

[12]Arthur W. Kac, *The Messiahship of Jesus*, p. 299.

[13]Claude Duvernoy, *The Prince and the Prophet*. Jerusalem: Claude Duvernoy, 1979, p. 50.

arms, and he soared with me on the wings of the wind. On one of the clouds, full of splendor, we met the figure of Moses....and the Messiah called to Moses: 'For this child I have prayed!' Then he turned to me: 'Go and announce to the Jews that I will soon come and perform great miracles for my people and for the whole world!' I woke up, and it was a dream. I kept this dream a secret and did not dare to tell it to anybody."[14]

The twenty-sixth Zionist Congress in session at Binyanei Ha Oma, an auditorium in Jerusalem, January 1964.

The Christian Zionist Congress held in Jerusalem in 1988.

---

[14]Raphael Patai, *The Messiah Texts*, p. 273. Patai's sources were Reuben Brainin, *Hayye Herzl*, pp. 17-18; Joseph Patai, "Herzl's School Years," pp. 58-59.

International Christian Embassy Jerusalem

SUPPLEMENT – April 11, 1988

THE JERUSALEM POST

Second International Christian Zionist Congress

Massive support for Israel

Melanie Rosenberg

AN HISTORIC conference of Christian supporters of Israel from around the world, gathering in Israel for the first time, has opened at Jerusalem's Binyenei Ha'uma. The four-day Second International Christian Zionist Congress, spearheaded by the International Christian Embassy Jerusalem, coincides with Israel's 40th anniversary and gives voice to an international show of Christian support for Israel.

"Delegates to the Congress are involved spiritually, educationally and practically in demonstrating their commitment to Zion," declares Johan Lückhoff, director of the ICEJ. "We are looking to the participants to mobilize all the great Christian support for Israel in all parts of the globe. During the congress they will attend in-depth seminars examining issues ranging from the biblical basis for Christian Zionism to analyses of anti-Semitism and anti-Zionism."

The discussions at the congress embrace a view of history with contemporary reality. The delegates will gather today in Tel Aviv at the museum where independence was declared in 1948 and then proceed to an open-air concert in Malchei Yisrael Square.

A gala banquet in the Knesset on Tuesday will be preceded by a reception with prominent Israelis present.

Wednesday's activities will be devoted to a memorial to Holocaust victims, culminating in a session calling on Christians to aid the causes of Soviet Jewry and aliya. Ida Nudel will deliver a message to the congress.

At Mount Herzl the congress delegates will unveil a plaque commemorating Reverend William Hechler, an Anglican Church cleric from England who a century ago used his good offices to convince the Grand Duke of Baden to grant Theodor Herzl an audience. The Duke consequently opened the door for Herzl to be received by the Kaiser.

Director Johann Lückhoff points out the special significance of the Christian Zionist Congress being held on the occasion of Israel's 40th anniversary. "Biblically speaking, the number 40 holds a very great significance. It often marks the entry into a new phase. Just as the Children of Israel ended 40 years in the desert to inherit the land promised to them, so Israel today is on the threshold of entering a new dimension of its existence.

"The Christian world, too, must grasp this moment to understand the challenge facing us. What happens in Israel is reflected in the Church. The 40th years offers us a unique opportunity to consider our responsibility to the Jewish people in the light of our spiritual inheritance.

"The Christian Zionist Congress in Jerusalem is our tribute to the Jewish People and the State of Israel. Israel has many friends. We're convening here to deliver that message to the Israelis and to the nations of the world."

The spirit of Basel

THIS WEEK'S International Christian Zionist Congress in Jerusalem was conceived three years ago at the first congress of world-wide Christian supporters of Israel in Basel, Switzerland.

"In retrospect Basel was a turning point in Christianity's global mobilization to strengthen the State of Israel," attests ICEJ Director Johann Lückhoff. "The interest and excitement generated in that historic meeting – in the same hallowed hallways where Theodor Herzl convened the first Zionist Congress nearly a century before – set the tone for our ongoing work."

At Basel 600 delegates from 27 countries participated in the deliberations and decision-making. In addition to western countries, delegates from Gabon, India, Zaire, Sri Lanka, Ivory Coast and a number of other countries that do not even maintain diplomatic ties with Israel, played active roles.

The Congress adopted several resolutions urging world recognition of Jerusalem as Israel's capital, Jewish sovereignty over all of the Land of Israel, and aliya as a main principle of Diaspora Jewish life. Anti-Semitism and anti-Zionism were forcefully condemned.

"We are especially gratified that resolutions calling for Ethiopian Jewish aliya and Spain's closing the diplomatic vacuum with Israel preceded their actual occurrence," says ICEJ spokesman Jan Willem van der Hoeven. "And more recently our activists in Europe were able to nip the first signs of corporate boycotts of Israeli products in the bud through effective counter-pressures."

Even as all eyes turn towards Jerusalem, the vision expounded at Basel in 1985 will continue to grow today in the Binyenei Ha'uma.

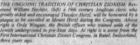

THE ONGOING TRADITION OF CHRISTIAN ZIONISM: Reverend William Hechler, (left) a 19th century Anglican cleric who greatly aided and encouraged Theodor Herzl, will be honoured by a plaque to be unveiled at Mount Herzl during the Congress. Above right is Orde Wingate, the British officer who trained units of the Jewish underground in pre-State days. At right is a scene from the First International Christian Zionist Congress, in Basel, Switzerland, three years ago.

Congress Highlights

SUNDAY	7:30 p.m.	Opening night at the Binyenei Ha'uma
MONDAY	3:00 p.m.	Short ceremony at the Museum Building in Tel Aviv, where Ben-Gurion proclaimed Israel's statehood in 1948, followed by march through downtown Tel Aviv to Malchei Israel Square.
TUESDAY		Reception at the Hilton Hotel Banquet in the Chagall Room at the Knesset
WEDNESDAY	3:30 p.m.	Visit to Mt. Herzl
	7:30 p.m.	Holocaust Memorial evening with focus also on the issue of Soviet Jews
THURSDAY	7:30 p.m.	Closing night, with brief speeches and special music

** Every morning from 8:30 a.m. to 12:30 p.m. there will be different seminars held at Binyenei Ha'uma.

Theodore Herzl, memorialized on
Israeli currency and postage stamp.

The great Albert Einstein,[15] father of the theory of relativity, revolutionized our understanding of the atom. He was invited by Israel to be their President and was also partly responsible, along with Professor Yahuda, for bringing Newton's prophetical biblical writings to the public eye, through certain letters he wrote in the 1940's.

---

[15]Einstein was an ardent Zionist, whom we appreciate. In his book, *Cosmic Religion with other Opinions and Aphorisms*, he said: "In view of the present situation of world Jewry, it is now more than ever necessary to preserve the Jewish community in a vital form. This end can best be attained by the colonization of Palestine, a work in which world Jewry is united, and by the fostering of the Jewish spiritual tradition. The publication of my book in the language of our fathers fills me with particular delight....The rebuilding of Palestine as the Jewish National Home differs fundamentally from all other Jewish activities of our time....In recent years large and valuable stretches of Palestinian land have become the property of the Jewish people. Jewish hands are reclaiming more and more neglected and waste lands and transforming them into fertile fields and orchards." Albert Einstein, *Cosmic Religion with other Opinions and Aphorisms*. New York: Covici, Friede Inc., © 1931, pp. 76-78.

"I am a Jew, but I am enthralled by the luminous figure of the Nazarene....No one can read the Gospels without feeling the actual presence of Jesus. His personality pulsates in every word. No myth is filled with such life." [16] Albert Einstein, October 26, 1929

---

[16]Arthur W. Kac, *The Messiahship of Jesus*, p. 36. Kac's source was *The Saturday Evening Post*, Oct. 26, 1929.

FAMOUS ISRAELIS—DID THEY HAVE AN INTEREST IN JESUS?

David Ben-Gurion, the legendary Zionist leader and the first Prime Minister of Israel, was said to have had a tremendous interest in Jesus. In 1971, Reverend George Lauderdale, a friend of mine, was personally invited to Israel by Ben-Gurion to discuss the subject of prophecy. The Reverend gave the Prime Minister a special edition of the Amplified Bible with fulfilled prophecy footnotes. George told me how happy Ben-Gurion was and how much he enjoyed receiving the Bible and reading the notes relating to Israel and Jesus' fulfilled prophecy!

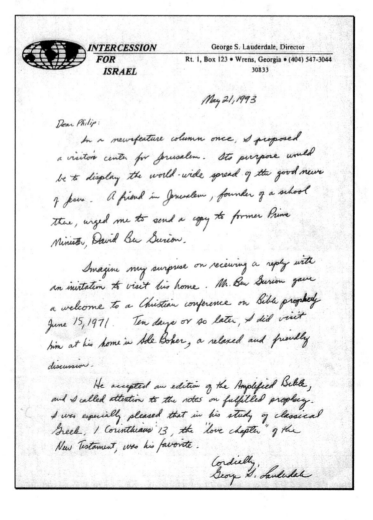

INTERCESSION FOR ISRAEL

George S. Lauderdale, Director
Rt. 1, Box 123 • Wrens, Georgia • (404) 547-3044
30833

May 21, 1993

Dear Philip:

In a newsfeature column once, I proposed a visitors center for Jerusalem. Its purpose would be to display the world-wide spread of the good news of Jesus. A friend in Jerusalem, founder of a school there, urged me to send a copy to former Prime Minister, David Ben Gurion.

Imagine my surprise on receiving a reply with an invitation to visit his home. Mr. Ben Gurion gave a welcome to a Christian conference on Bible prophecy June 15, 1971. Ten days or so later, I did visit him at his home in Sde Boker, a relaxed and friendly discussion.

He accepted an edition of the Amplified Bible, and I called attention to the notes on fulfilled prophecy. I was especially pleased that in his study of classical Greek, I Corinthians 13, the "love chapter" of the New Testament, was his favorite.

Cordially,
George S. Lauderdale

More recently, the Israeli newspaper, *Maariv*, mentioned Ben-Gurion's fascination with Jesus. It said, "The subject of Jesus was always interesting to him." The same article also had the famous Israeli author, Sholem Asch, quoting Ben-Gurion: "Anyone who hates the Jews, also hates Jesus Christ."[17]

While we can only venture a guess that Ben-Gurion was a secret believer, some people seem to think so. My Israeli friend, Yossi Oveda, told me that Ben-Gurion read the New Testament and Hal Lindsey's book, *The Late Great Planet Earth*, just before his death.

מעריב

8

ספרות סופרים ספרים

שלום אַש בעין הסערה

Maariv article, dated April 21, 1989, entitled "Sholem Asch in the Eye of the Storm," featuring a letter of sympathy from Ben-Gurion to Asch. In the photo, Asch is second from the left. Courtesy of *Maariv*.

[17]Nahaman Tamid, "Sholem Asch in the Eye of the Storm," *Maariv*, April 21, 1989.

Ben-Gurion's desk, exacly as it appeared at the time of his death. Notice, lying on the chair to the right of his desk, his copy of *The Late Great Planet Earth*, the best-selling Christian book on Bible prophecy.[18]

[18]Photo of *The Late Great Planet Earth*, by Hal Lindsey and C.C. Carlson, reproduced by permission of Zondervan Publishing House.

David Ben-Gurion's personal Bible, including the New Testament, sits atop his desk at his home in Israel.

A closer look reveals the words *Brit Ha Dasha* (ברית חדשה), the "New Testament" in Hebrew.

When I visited Ben-Gurion's home in Kibbutz Sdeh-Boker, I photographed these two books in his library, which we pictured previously. The Bible on his desk is one volume containing both the Old and New Testaments. The most worn book in his library, Hal Lindsey's *The Late Great Planet Earth*, is lying beside his desk.

I gave this picture to Hal a few years ago and he mentioned this fact in his 1989 book, *Road to Holocaust.* Hal wrote: "In writing *The Late Great Planet Earth*, I had the Jews constantly in mind. I prayerfully and deliberately sought to present my prophetic case in such a way that it would especially appeal to them. It has been published in more than fifty foreign editions and has been instrumental all around the world in bringing tens of thousands of Jews to faith in Jesus as their Messiah. I run into them everywhere. They continue to write me from virtually every part of the world. The first Prime Minister of Israel, David Ben Gurion, was reading it shortly before he died. Since everything in his room has been kept the way it was when he died, a copy of *The Late Great Planet Earth* remains on his desk. A friend of mine who is one of Israel's top military commanders passed out hundreds of copies of the Hebrew translation of *The Late Great Planet Earth* to the Israeli Defense Forces, even though he personally hasn't as yet believed in Jesus as the Messiah."[19]

David Ben-Gurion in his library, at his home in Sdeh-Boker, May 14, 1968.

[19]Hal Lindsey, *The Road To Holocaust*, p. 195.

Entrance to Ben-Gurion's home in Kibbutz Sdeh-Boker.

Prime Minister David Ben-Gurion, visiting an agricultural station near Eliat, Israel, June 13, 1957.

Israeli press photo of the prime minister's desk, 1968.

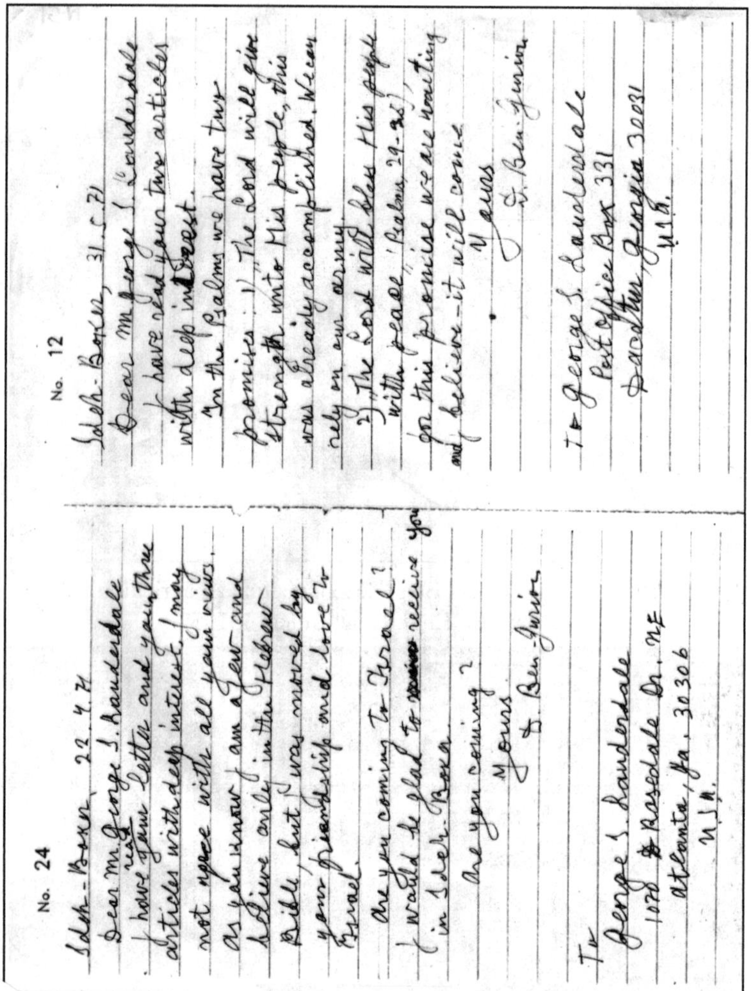

No. 24

Sdeh-Boker, 22.4.72

Dear Mr. George S. Lauderdale

I have read your letter and your three articles with deep interest. I may not agree with all your views.

As you know I am a Jew and believe only in the Hebrew Bible, but I was moved by your friendship and love to Israel.

Are you coming to Israel? I would be glad to receive you in Sdeh-Boker.

Are you coming?

Yours
D. Ben-Gurion

To George S. Lauderdale
1070 Rosedale Dr. NE
Atlanta, Ga. 30306
U.S.A.

No. 12

Sdeh-Boker, 31.5.71

Dear Mr. George S. Lauderdale

I have read your two articles with deep interest.

In the Psalms we have two promises: 1) "The Lord will give strength unto His people", this was already accomplished. We can rely on our army.

2) "The Lord will bless His people with peace" (Psalms 29-[illegible]), on this promise we are waiting and believe—it will come.

Yours
D. Ben-Gurion

To George S. Lauderdale
Post Office Box 331
Decatur, Georgia 30031
U.S.A.

Two letters from David Ben-Gurion to Reverend George Lauderdale of Atlanta, Georgia.

David Ben-Gurion and George Lauderdale at Ben-Gurion's home in Kibbutz Sdeh-Boker, Israel.

My friend, Grant Livingston, told me of the testimony of Golda Meir's radiologist, Dr. Larry Samuels.[20] He was treating her just before her death from cancer. Grant said: "...he was her doctor administering radiology to her at Hadassah Hospital in 1977. Dr. Samuels said Golda had prayed with him to receive Christ [Messiah Jesus]."[21]

We all think about what is really important and true when we know we are going to die. The Prime Minister of Israel, Golda Meir, knew she was dying of cancer! Her doctor was a believer in Jesus and, according to his testimony, she died a true believer in Jesus as Messiah, although it was never shouted from the rooftops or made public in the world press.

---

[20]"The Interpreter," a newsletter distributed by Dr. Arthur W. Kac, featured an article entitled, "Golda Meir and the Christian Professor from America." The article stated: "For twelve months Professor Larry Samuels maintained a warm personal relationship with Mrs. Meir, which went far beyond the provision of diagnosis and nuclear drugs to the 80 year old 'mother of Israel.' He became part of the family circle around Mrs. Meir who, in her final illness, found this completely dedicated, spiritual physician from America a tower of strength and hope and more than that, a friend and comforter. Often he would pray and read Scripture with Golda at her own request, or at the request of the family....Professor Samuels may be a Swedish-American, and may have all the gentle manner and informality of a Midwestern Yankee, but he is no less convinced that his roots, like those of every living Christian, are deeply embedded in the Holy Land. Golda Meir was for him, not merely a redoubtable public figure among the leaders of a spunky little Middle Eastern country. She was part of a people and land intimately linked to the personal faith and experience of folk for whom the Scriptures are the living Word of God. He declares without hesitation, 'It is in our unity with the Jewish people, in our oneness, that we are grafted on to the root of Jesse. If we reject the very roots upon which we grow, then we're cutting off our lifeblood, for our true roots are right here in this land, no matter where we may live.' As Golda Meir's body lay in state in the Knesset Plaza, and endless lines of Israelis filed past the bier throughout the day and night in a chilly Jerusalem December rain, Professor Samuels confided to a group of Christian friends: 'I really feel that if I should die this moment, my whole reason for going to medical school, my whole reason for studying nuclear medicine, my whole reason for following the Lord and coming to Jerusalem, would have been fulfilled. I am personally encouraging Christians to speak out, to organize their support, and not only by means of prayer, but also by applying political pressure. One Christian I spoke to recently is sending out a thousand letters to political figures, challenging them: 'Stand up for Israel's rights and freedom!' The reservoir of Christian backing for Israel is being tapped more and more as the Spirit of God moves over the people of America. It is part of a general spiritual revival, with a substantial number of those who are renewed spiritually coming to believe in the fulfillment of the Biblical promises for Israel. Meanwhile, here in Jerusalem we have organized a Christian prayer team to intercede daily with God for the patients and for the work of the Hospital. We have seen the Lord move in power through his Holy Spirit. As long as the Lord is my partner, giving me supernatural supervision, Jerusalem will be my home.' " Dr. Larry Samuels, "Golda Meir and the Christian Professor from America," *The Interpreter*, Vol. XXXVII, No. 1, Winter 1995. Available through The Interpreter, POB 110, Lutherville, MD, USA 21093-0110.

[21][ ] mine.

Golda Meir receives a bouquet of flowers from school children at Lod Airport, upon her return from the U.S., October 7, 1969.

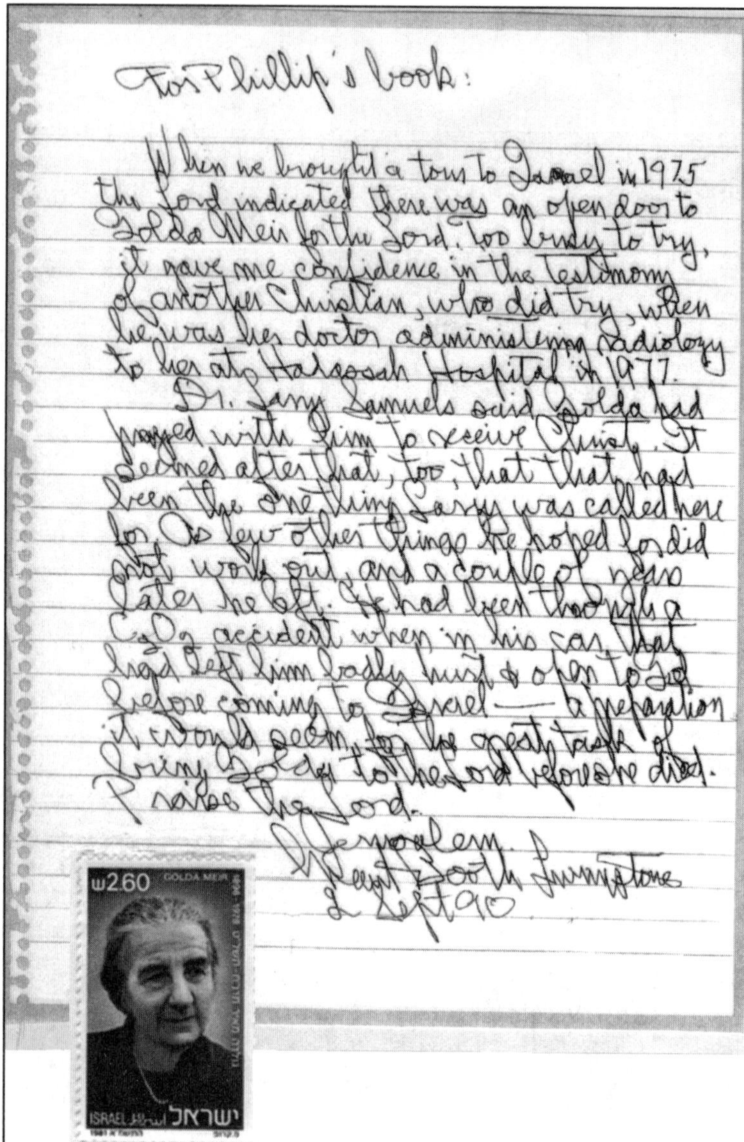

For Phillip's book:

When we brought a tour to Israel in 1975 the Lord indicated there was an open door to Golda Meir for the Lord. Too busy to try, it gave me confidence in the testimony of another Christian, who did try, when he was her doctor administering radiology to her at Hadassah Hospital in 1977.

Dr. Larry Samuels said Golda had prayed with him to receive Christ. It seemed after that, too, that that had been the one thing Larry was called here for, as few other things he hoped for did not work out, and a couple of years later he left. He had been through a car accident when in his car that had left him badly hurt & open to God before coming to Israel — a preparation it would seem, for the great task of bring Golda to the Lord before she died. Praise the Lord.

Jerusalem.
Grant Booth Livingstone
2 Sept 90

We have written confirmation from evangelist Grant Livingston that Golda Meir died a fulfilled Messianic Jewess. An Israeli postage stamp celebrates a beloved former Prime Minister, Golda Meir (1898-1978).

JEWISH ECHO
GLASGOW
SCOTLAND
14/04/89

The numbers of 'Messianic' Jews is said to be growing

HOW MANY MESSIANIC JEWS ARE THERE?

A 1989 article by Susan Birnbaum entitled, "The Numbers of 'Messianic' Jews is Said to be Growing," reports: "Some 350,000 Jews already believe in Jesus as their saviour, and the number may swell to half a million by the year 2000....The results were reported by the Jewish Community Relations Council of New York....Barret writes that of the 350,000 Jews...about 140,000 have continued to identify as Jews and have chosen to affiliate with 'Messianic synagogues....' "[22]

The article maintains that within ten years, another one hundred and fifty thousand Jews will accept Jesus as Messiah, and that approximately fifteen thousand Jews every year are coming to faith in Jesus. These Jews are not being duped or fooled, they are carefully studying and asking and observing end time Bible prophecies. They look at the current political situation and circumstances and compare them to the predictions of the Bible. Once they put two and two together, they make the wise and necessary decision—one which will determine their forgiveness and eternal future. Remember Daniel's words: "...the wise [studied] shall understand" (Dan. 12:10 KJV; [ ] mine).

---

[22]Susan Birnbaum, "The Numbers of 'Messianic' Jews is Said to be Growing," *Jewish Echo*, Glasgow, Scotland, Apr. 14, 1989, © used by permission.

An Orthodox Jew at the Wailing Wall in Jerusalem asked Hal Lindsey, the author of one of the most popular books on the end time events, *The Late Great Planet Earth*, "How long before the end and the Coming of the Messiah?" Of course, we as honest Christian Zionists, do not know the exact time, as Jesus said (Matt. 24:36). We only know that it is very close, as He indicated in Luke 21:28.

The thriving Messianic movement produces a large volume of literature. These Messianic materials vastly surpass the anti-Messianic and anti-Christian polemics in quality. The proof is in the reading! I have touched on some of this literature in my book.[23]

The Messianic materials present the truth about the Messiah, unencumbered by rabbinical camouflage. They also attempt to answer the onslaught of recent polemics from rabbis who fear the **truth** and are trying to invent new "interpretations" that would divert Jews away from an interest in Jesus. As in times of old, the contemporary Messianic movement provokes the hostility of the Orthodox Jews and their secular allies.

ISRAEL AND ITS RESPONSE TO CLAIMS THAT JESUS IS MESSIAH—WHAT DO THE PROS AND CONS SAY?

Jewish distrust—misunderstanding and anger against Jews and Evangelical Christians who love Jews and are intent on sharing the good news—is rampant. This is reflected in the large number of books, pamphlets, and posters being circulated, some of which are pictured here. To illustrate our point, I have used excerpts from these publications throughout this book under the heading, "Modern Rabbinic Comment/Refutation."

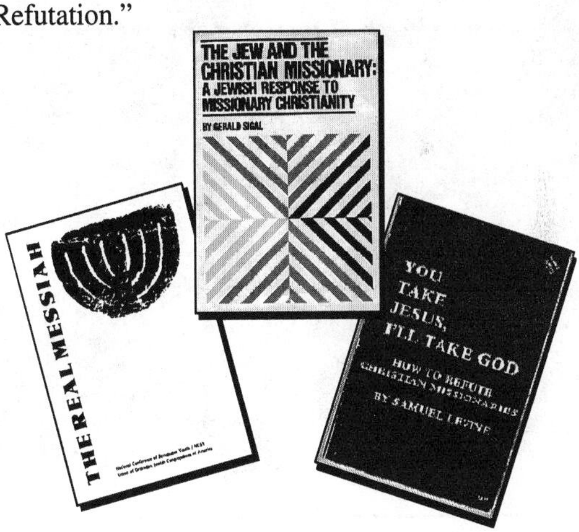

[23]Other books are available through specialized publishing houses and many can be found at the week-long Messiah Conference, at Messiah College in Grantham, Pennsylvania. This annual conference is held around the Fourth of July and is open to Jews and Christians who love the Jewish people. The conference draws participants from around the world, including Israel, England, South America, and of course, the U.S. For information on attending, write to the Messianic Jewish Alliance of America, POB 417, Wynwood, PA, USA 19046. Tel. (610) 896-5812 or (800) 225-MJAA.

For those interested in Messianic Judaism, there is a host of materials and books, whose scholarship regarding Messianic prophecy and future events promised in the Bible **far** exceeds the anti-missionary books we have pictured.

When you beat someone at their own game, it is not funny, it is annoying. Some Orthodox Jews go beyond writing and participate in demonstrations. A small group of the ultra-Orthodox Jews from *Mea Sha'arim* protested at the 1987 Feast of Tabernacles parade, where 5000 Christians from seventy nations marched in support of Israel. While the Israeli public cheered the marchers, the Orthodox Jews tried to surround the Messianic Jews in the procession with signs that read, "Messianic Jews = Christians" and "Beware Missionaries," framed with a skull and crossbones.

The police quickly dispersed this hindrance, but remember, you can always gauge the truth of a moment by the witness of the opposition. If something is not true, people will not blink an eye; if it is, anger and blood flows. Remember Cain and Abel.

The same opposition surfaced at a 1988 Messianic Conference of 1500 believers, half from the United States and half from Israel, in the Jerusalem Diplomat Hotel. *Yad la' Ahim*, a motley militant group that works against the "missionaries," showed up at the airport and tried to stop them. The Israeli police dragged the militants off to jail, fining them three hundred shekels apiece, while welcoming the Messianic Jews.

This picture was taken seconds before police destroyed the signs of ultra-Orthodox Jews who were trying to cause trouble and protesting against Messianic Jews during the Feast of Sukkot March in Jerusalem. This march is held annually on the Feast of Tabernacles (see Zech. 14), always with thousands of Evangelical Christians in support of Israel.

In Hebrew, the banner says, "Messianic Jews '*Yehudim Meshihim*' " and is carried through the streets of Jerusalem in the Sukkot March.

THE SUPREME COURT—THE SANHEDRIN OF OLD?

The pressure of the Orthodox Jews on contemporary Messianic Jews is unrelenting. One of the major battle in the war is the law. The Ministry of Interior, which is in charge of granting Israeli citizenship to new immigrants, has always been controlled by a religious party—a major coalition partner in all Israeli governments. Since citizenship is based on the Law of Return, which makes Jewish immigrants automatically eligible, the Orthodox have an exclusive say in defining who is a Jew. They occasionally use this power to block the immigration of Messianic Jews.

One such case involved Gary and Shirley Beresford. When this Messianic couple wanted to become Israeli citizens, they were told they were "not Jewish" because they believe in Jesus. The Beresfords sued the Ministry of Interior in the Supreme Court. However, they knew their chances were not good because the Supreme Court, under intense pressure from the Orthodox Jews, ruled against somewhat similar requests in the past. Even so, Gary and Shirley were brave enough to challenge the Orthodox status quo. When the court ruled against them in September 1992, they realized the rulings of Yavne could not be bent.

Even though it appears they lost, God used the Beresfords in a supernatural, miraculous way. The intense publicity surrounding the case reopened the debate (within the media and academia) concerning the Messianic identity of Jesus, which had been silenced at Yavne.[24] One day, Yavne will be but straw and hay as Jesus' fulfillment of Jewish prophecy becomes more widely known! Even now, many Jews are realizing Jesus is the Messiah, to the dismay of many rabbis who endorse Yavne and the controversial decision made there. The Beresfords plan to appeal—pray for them!

A LIBERAL FEMINIST, PNINA PELI, IS UPSET THAT ISRAELI COURTS STILL CONSIDER WHETHER BELIEVERS ARE PART OF TRUE JUDAISM

The very presence of Messianic Jews has tested the limits of tolerance in the liberal elements of Israeli society. Surprisingly, even some liberals seem to think that the message of Jesus should not be shared. An article by one Pnina Peli makes this point: "After years of

---

[24]See Gary Beresford and Shirley Beresford, *The Unpromised Land: The Struggle of Messianic Jews*. Baltimore, MD: Lederer Messianic Publications, ©1994, pp. 133, 160, 164.

surreptitious operations in various places throughout Israel, they have come out into the open to practice their missionary work, as announced in an article by Haim Shapiro in *The Jerusalem Post.* It is their claim that the followers of Jesus were mistaken in negating the relevance and spiritual importance of Tora. They contend that...a Jew who continues to follow the precepts of Judaism (Shabbat, kashrut, etc.) and accepts the Messiahship of Jesus...are the 'true believers.'

Hebrew-Christian groups lure new believers from among Israelis into their fold by bringing them the 'good news' that as Christians they will actually become better Jews.

This distorted version of 'Who is a Jew?' has at least twice been the subject of costly, highly publicized legal battles in Israeli courtrooms at the behest of those who feel it is fitting for the state to acknowledge that Christianity is, after all, also true Judaism.

According to the *Hebrew Christian* quarterly, there are such Messianic groups actively operating in Jerusalem, Rehovot and Haifa....'Hebrew Christians,' 'Messianic Jews,' and 'Jews for Jesus' are outstanding examples of groups intent on fudging the historical lines separating Christianity from Judaism. Such attempts have often aroused sharp opposition in Jewish, as well as in Christian circles.

'Faith in Jesus,' states the Rev. Ole Kvarme, of the Caspari Institute in Jerusalem, 'is not something that turns a Jew into a non-Jew.' "[25]

Peli's comments are nothing short of astonishing. They imply that sharing the Gospel somehow contaminates Judaism. She claims: "Such attitudes demonstrate little respect for the basic integrity of Judaism...."[26] That old Yavnean paranoia strikes again.

PELI IS UPSET AT THE RAPID GROWTH OF MESSIANIC JUDAISM WITHIN ISRAEL

Peli grudgingly describes the growth of the Messianic Jewish movement in Israel: "By their own admission, there has been a significant growth in the number of 'Hebrew Christians' operating in Israel in the past few years as hundreds of Israelis have been drawn into their ranks. Though some of their leaders, like Menahem Benhayim, now function openly...."[27]

***

---

[25]Pnina Peli, "Doubting the Blessings of Christian Zionism," *Jerusalem Post*, Sept. 20, 1985, © used by permission.
[26]Ibid.
[27]Ibid.

PELI SHAMES CHRISTIANS FOR BEING ZIONIST, TELLING THE TRUTH ABOUT THE MIDDLE AGES, AND HOLDING A ZIONIST CONFERENCE

Peli admits that many Israeli Messianic Jews are sharing the Gospel with fellow Israelis. However, she argues that they do it under cover and that Messianic Judaism is unpopular[28] among Israelis.

Peli wraps up her article by insinuating that Evangelical Christians should be ashamed to express their love for Jews, hold Christian Zionist meetings or wear Jewish artifacts. She lambasts the Reverend Van der Hoeven, head of the Christian Embassy in Jerusalem and one of Israel's best friends, for telling the truth that those who harmed Jews in the Middle Ages were not true Christians[29] (see chapters 10 and 12[30]).

Peli concludes with what appears to be extreme bitterness: "To claim, as did Van Der Hoeven in a radio interview with Avraham Ben-Melech, broadcast on Kol Israel prior to the Christian Zionist Congress, that those who have done harm to the Jewish people were not the 'real' Christians is not convincing enough. Such an argument rejects the accountability of Christians for acts committed in the name of Christianity and is a theological and historical cop-out of the first order.

Nor should Christians express their 'love' of Judaism and the Jewish people by taking over cherished and unique Jewish symbols, such as the menora or, for that matter, by holding a Christian Zionist Congress."[31]

[28]In our opinion, this is a false assumption on her part. We have met many Israelis who are very open and interested in Messianic Judaism.

[29]Many Jews are unaware of this fact and should be informed.

[30]In these chapters we show the difference between Christian Zionists of the past and certain "Christians" of the Middle Ages who persecuted Jews and Protestants.

[31]Ibid.

Market-place of ideas

1-10-1985 By DAVID KRIVINE

IT WOULD not be wrong to accuse the International Christian Embassy in Jerusalem of entertaining a vision of the future other than that which possesses the mind of the Lubavicher *rebbe*. That is quite right.

It follows according to Pnina Peli ("Doubting the blessings of Christian Zionism," *The Jerusalem Post*, September 20) that the Christian Zionists are acting in their own self-interest. That is correct, too, though one should insert a rider: "their own *spiritual* self-interest." The Christian hope is that one day the Jews will of their own accord recognize that Jesus was the Messiah.

That hope can be said to serve their spiritual self-interest, because they believe that only after the Jews make their act of contrition can the world be redeemed.

Continuing her argument, Peli concludes that "the people of Israel can no longer afford to underestimate the relentless determination of the other monotheistic religions to take over their rightful inheritance historical and geographical."

That is made to sound like a deduction from what was said before. It is nothing of the sort. That the Christians would like to sell an idea to the Jews does not mean that they want to take over the Jews' rightful inheritance.

What is our rightful inheritance? I imagine Peli means our identity as a separate religious community ("historical"); and our country Israel ("geographical"). Let us start with the geographical. Not only is the Christian Embassy free of any desire to dispossess us of our territory (for whose benefit – the Moslems?), but they also actively support in their information work the integral Land of Israel concept cherished by the nationalists of Herut.

Concerning our "historical" inheritance, the Christian Embassy expressly wishes the Jews to retain their separate identity, religion and nationhood. Their hope, and perhaps their conviction, is that the Jews will one day see sense (by the embassy's lights). The change can not be forced on us, because the change they have in mind is not one of affiliation or obedience, but of belief.

In the Middle Ages the Christians forced belief down the infidels' throats, and that memory dies hard among the Jews. The Christian Zionists reject these methods with revulsion. Mrs. Peli does not believe them? I will not argue the point, because that is not the main reason why conversion by force is no longer a possibility.

The real reason is that the sovereign state of Israel has been restored. We are no longer at the mercy of the gentiles. The ICEJ is situated inside our country and is subject to its laws. The foreigner does not have the power to make the Jew in Israel do anything he does not want to do.

CAN THE missionaries inveigle him to convert? This is the point at issue, and this is where the Christian Zionists take great care to tread very cautiously. Their forebears have been trying to turn all the Jews into Christians for two thousand years.

They have not done it. Their methods were cruel, and Christians now feel penitent about that. They know that the Jews have become hyper-sensitive over the issue. They therefore decided to renounce – while in Israel – the function of being missionaries.

The question is whether they mean it. At this juncture I am prepared to follow in Mrs. Peli's footsteps and to suspect with her that the good Mr. Van der Hoeven and his team are stuck in a very frustrating dilemma. They "know" that the Christ is the Messiah. They believe that the Jews' obstinate refusal to perceive that obvious and patent truth postpones endlessly the day of salvation for all humanity.

Like all people possessed of absolute belief, they are sure that if only the dissenter can be made to listen, he will be convinced. And yet they must remain silent. They have to wait patiently until the Jews come round of their own accord to recognize the truth of the revelation. It is going to be a long wait.

Meanwhile there are other Christian pastors carousing in and around Israel, who have not undertaken to refrain from preaching the gospel. How is the ICEJ to relate to them? It cannot cold-shoulder fellow-believers, hush them up, chase them away, send them to Coventry. The message of the Christians to the Jews gets through here and there – it cannot be bottled up completely; and this is what drives bigots of Jewish orthodoxy out of their wits.

WHY SHOULD the utterance by foreigners of heretical ideas be so repugnant? The problem here is not the Christian Zionists; it is the Jewish bigots. The great majority have never met a missionary in their lives. If they were told that one was passing by, they would flee in holy terror. They visualize these evangelists as satanic creatures who "lure" people into their fold, who harbour "ulterior motives," who "enhance themselves at our expense" – to quote Pnina Peli's article.

Missionaries are in fact ordinary human beings with a bee in their bonnets, like our own clerical dogmatists. The human race is argumentative. Everybody is selling ideologies – the communists, the liberals, the feminists, the Quakers, the spiritualists, the Zionists, the vegetarians, the Seventh Day Adventists, the ecologists, the Society for the Prevention of Cruelty to Animals, the Sandinistas, the Moonies and countless others.

The world is a market-place of ideas: that is what makes life interesting. Peli wants to slam the door on all that: an attitude that I did not believe could exist among Jews in this day and age (except among a small mindless fringe) until orthodox fundamentalism exploded recently into political activity.

A difference of opinion became visible that has widened into a yawning gulf between two sectors in our society: the ultra-Orthodox who have been saturated with talmudic studies all their lives to the exclusion of anything else; and liberal-minded people who are exposed to modern civilization in all its variety and amplitude, comprising everything that has been developed from Jewish, Hellenic and other sources over the centuries.

The difference between the two over the issue of missionaries is this: the liberals say that a man is a Jew by choice. He listens to what the missionaries and others say and makes up his own mind.

The Orthodox believe that people are Jews because they were told to be Jews. Freedom of choice is anathema. They must think the thoughts drilled into them by the rabbinate. They must close their eyes and ears to outside influences. Missionaries must not be allowed in the country.

The argument for that is self-defeating.

Once the Jew listens to the nonsensical heresies propounded by other faiths – our religious leaders say – he will cease to be Jewish, and will join the other faiths. The Orthodox have lost their age-old confidence in the superior logic of their own creed.

They are stuck in the past, fearful of the present, unable to compete in the market-place of ideas, cling to old rituals, systematically segregate their acolytes from all contact – even social – with the remaining 99.9 per cent of the human race.

The Jews of the Diaspora, who outnumber the Jews of Israel by two to one, are not locked up in this theocratic seclusion. They breathe the air of religious freedom. What has happened there is the development of Judaism in new directions. Vital Orthodox, Conservative and Reform congregations have sprung up in the West. The Orthodox in Israel say this is abominable, and proof of what happens when you let people do their own thinking. Ezra Austern put it bluntly in a letter to the editor (September 22). We must choose, he says "between (a) the democratic ideal with its train of 'blessings,' including the end of the state as a Jewish entity, and (b) a more intensely Jewish, albeit less democratic society."

Democracy means letting people talk, even missionaries, and letting people listen, even Jews. Out of this exchange of ideas comes progress. The International Christian Embassy is a participant in this exchange of ideas. It extends the hand of friendship to the Jews.

The anti-missionary society Yad le'Ahim rejects this friendship; it prefers the hostility with which it is familiar. It likes to be rejected by humanity at large; anti-Semitism serves the Orthodox purpose.

The Jew then remains cornered in his ghetto, frozen in his own past, isolated from the world – a puppet in the hands of his rabbinical masters. "The perpetuation of the Jewish [that is, the ultra-Orthodox Jewish] character of Israel is paramount and transcends all other considerations," stresses Mr. Austern. Which says it all.

1-10-1985

The writer is a member of The Jerusalem Post editorial staff

David Krivine, a writer for the *Jerusalem Post* editorial staff, countered what we believe is Peli's narrow-mindedness, in his article, "Market-place of Ideas."

JERUSALEM POST STAFF WRITER, KRIVINE, EXPOSES THAT THE MINDLESS FRINGE, INCLUDING PELI, WANTS TO SLAM THE DOOR ON DEMOCRACY

Krivine made eight important points: "It follows according to Pnina Peli ('Doubting the Blessings of Christian Zionism,' the *Jerusalem Post*, September 20) that the Christian Zionists are acting in their own self-interest. That is correct, too, though one should insert a rider: 'their own *spiritual* self-interest.' The Christian hope is that one day the Jews will of their own accord recognize that Jesus was the Messiah.

That hope can be said to serve their spiritual self-interest, because they believe that only after the Jews make their act of contrition can the world be redeemed....The message of the Christians to the Jews gets through here and there—it cannot be bottled up completely; and this is what drives bigots of Jewish orthodoxy out of their wits. WHY SHOULD the utterance by foreigners of heretical ideas be so repugnant? The problem here is not the Christian Zionists; it is the Jewish bigots. The great majority have never met a missionary in their lives....They visualize these evangelists as satanic creatures who 'lure' people into their fold, who harbour 'ulterior motives,' who 'enhance themselves at our expense'—to quote Pnina Peli's article.

Missionaries are in fact ordinary human beings....Everybody is selling ideologies—the communists, the liberals, the feminists, the Quakers, the spiritualists, the Zionists, the vegetarians, the Seventh Day Adventists, the ecologists, the Society for the Prevention of Cruelty to Animals....The world is a market-place of ideas: that is what makes life interesting. Peli wants to slam the door on all that; an attitude that I did not believe could exist among Jews in this day and age (except among a small mindless fringe) until orthodox fundamentalism exploded recently into political activity....Democracy means letting people talk, even missionaries, and letting people listen, even Jews. Out of the exchange of ideas comes progress. The International Christian Embassy is a participant in this exchange of ideas. It extends the hand of friendship to the Jews.

The anti-missionary society Yad la'Ahim rejects this friendship; it prefers the hostility with which it is familiar. It likes to be rejected by humanity at large; anti-Semitism serves the Orthodox purpose.

The Jew then remains cornered in his ghetto, frozen in his own past, isolated from the world—a puppet in the hands of his rabbinical masters."[32]

MENAHEM BENHAYIM PUTS PELI IN HER PLACE, AS ONE WHO WOULD LIKE TO TAKE OUR FREEDOM FROM US

Menahem Benhayim, a Jewish believer in Jesus, to whom Peli[33] referred in her article, responded in his article "Hebrew Christians." Among his wise words we read: "Sir,—Pnina Peli...expresses her viewpoint on Christian Zionism....Mrs. Peli expresses her abhorrence for the open sharing of their faith by Jewish believers in Jesus. Israel, however, is not a rabbinic theocracy....The fact that some of us are pursuing a return to the Jewish roots of a faith that was born among Jews in the Land of Israel is no doubt shocking to many Jews and Christians; but either the words of our national hymn about being 'a free people in our land' include even such offbeat and heretical Jews as we are reputed to be, or we are still strapped by Galut prejudices and stereotypes."[34]

***

[32]David Krivine, "Market-place of Ideas," *Jerusalem Post*, Oct. 1, 1985, © used by permission.

[33]Just who is this Pnina Peli? Barbara Livingston told me personally that Peli was a recent feminist immigrant to Israel seeking to annoy Jewish believers in Jesus there!

[34]Menahem Benhayim, "Hebrew Christians," *Jerusalem Post*, Fri., July 3, 1987, p. 22, © used by permission.

HEBREW CHRISTIANS

To Editor of The Jerusalem Post

Sir, – Pnina Peli ("Doubting the Blessings of Christian Zionism" – September 20) expresses her viewpoint on Christian Zionism with great skill, but has allowed certain inaccuracies to mar her presentation. Neither I nor anyone else in Jerusalem or elsewhere is "the movement's head" of the "Messianic Jews" or "Hebrew Christians" or "Jews for Jesus." 4 -10- 1985

Concerning my connection with the the International Christian Embassy, we do share a number of common views, but neither party is responsible for the other's policies or statements. The sale by the Embassy of a recently published book of mine about the New Testament and the problem of anti-Semitism is hardly threatening. Is it better that the New Testament be interpreted through the warped lenses of traditional Church anti-Semitism?

Mrs. Peli expresses her abhorrence for the open sharing of their faith by Jewish believers in Jesus. Israel, however, is not a rabbinic theocracy. We live in a period of Jewish national history when atheists and secularists openly organize to press for a Judaism without God or halacha, while others find spiritual attraction in a variety of Jewish and universal frameworks.

The fact that some of us are pursuing a return to the Jewish roots of a faith that was born among Jews in the Land of Israel is no doubt shocking to many Jews and Christians; but either the words of our national hymn about being "a free people in our land" include even such offbeat and heretical Jews as we are reputed to be, or we are still strapped by Galut prejudices and stereotypes.

MENAHEM BENHAYIM
4 -10- 1985 *Israel Secretary, IHCA*
Jerusalem.

BACK IN THE U.S., RABBI SPIVAK IS UPSET WITH *JEWS FOR JESUS*' USE OF THE FIRST AMENDMENT

There have been articles of discouragement and dishonesty about Messianic Jews in U.S. newspapers. The *Jerusalem Times/Jewish Press* article, "The Mask is Off," contained the following: "They stand there with a smile painted on their faces, offering you 'salvation' if you'll only take the little flyer they're handing out. What good people! Oh yes, what evil could possibly lurk in the heart of the missionary? What evil?"

We want to clarify that the rabbi infers that *Jews for Jesus* are "evil" without any foundation, excepting his possible prejudice. It is not the claim of *Jews for Jesus* that if someone will "only take the little flyer" that salvation is assured! Asking Jesus into the heart is the real issue, if He is Messiah, this rabbi, in his sarcasm, is obviously quite misinformed.

The article continued: "Jews for J..., champions of democracy! Lovers of the First Amendment....who demand from the Supreme Court their right to spread their poison in public places...."[35]

---

[35]Rabbi Yaakov Spivak, "The Mask is Off," *Jerusalem Times/Jewish Press*, Fri., July 3, 1987, p. 22. In this article, "J...," refers to Jesus. We surmise that Rabbi Spivak harbors such contempt for Jesus and Christians that he cannot even write His name.

The right was not demanded, as public evangelism has always been legal, it was merely defended against its opponents who desired we be stripped of it.

Rabbi Spivak threatened *Jews for Jesus* by saying that when they returned to Grand Central Station, he and EMES would be there as well. The same paper warned Jews to stay away from two Messianic conferences and one interdenominational national gathering.

RABBI ECKSTEIN CLAIMS TO BE A FRIEND OF EVANGELICAL CHRISTIANS, BUT CALLS MESSIANIC JEWS A "CURSE"—WHO IS REALLY BEING DECEPTIVE?

"Rabbi Eckstein....has worked for over a decade to break down the walls of fear and ignorance that separate Christians and Jews. In their place, he has built bridges of understanding between the communities....Yechiel Eckstein is an Orthodox rabbi, whose message of reconciliation and role as liaison have been heartily endorsed by Christian and Jewish leaders around the world."[36] So reads the biographical description on the J-card of one of his audio cassette tapes.

What troubles us is the claim of a bridge being built between two communities. A growing number of Christians are becoming aware of what Eckstein is really trying to do. He is not building bridges and breaking down walls, but rather is erecting walls and trying to break down bridges built between the Evangelicals and the Orthodox.

The main bridge of which I speak is Messianic Judaism and *Jews for Jesus*, which this rabbi opposes. He attempts to build the wall by saying, *We Jews have our own interpretation to these Messianic prophecies and we find Messianic Judaism deceptive.* What he fails to realize is that Messianic Jews and Evangelical Christians are the strongest bridge between the Jews and Christians. Would Rabbi Eckstein think so? We will let him answer in his own words. Read a few pages of his book, *What Christians Should Know About Jews and Judaism*. There he says: " 'Messianic Jews,' or 'Hebrew Christians' as they are sometimes known (the terms are used here interchangeably)....believe in Jesus as the Christ, while maintaining selective portions of Jewish law and tradition....Messianic Judaism is an anathema [curse] to the overwhelming number of Jews. Whether or not it comprises normative, genuine Christianity is, essentially, a matter for Christians to decide....they ought to abandon and denounce the

---

[36]*Selections from Ask the Rabbi*, by Yechiel Eckstein. Holyland Fellowship of Christians and Jews, © 1988, used by permission. This audio tape is available through HFCJ, 36 South Wabash Ave., Chicago, IL, USA 60603.

overly zealous and deceptive means usually employed by various Hebrew Christian groups."[37]

ECKSTEIN BRAGS ABOUT INCITING THE "CHRISTIAN COMMUNITY" TO ATTACK THE SLAVIC GOSPEL GROUP FOR SHARING JESUS WITH RUSSIAN JEWS

The *Jerusalem Post* provides further evidence of Rabbi Eckstein's deception: "Eckstein admitted that discussing Christian missionary work with evangelicals is a delicate issue. 'We can't start out by demanding that they stop proselytizing; that would mean asking evangelicals to stop being evangelicals....In Chicago, I got the Christian community to attack a deceptive attempt by the Slavic Gospel group to convert Russian Jewish immigrants....It took over 50 years of dialogue with liberal Protestants...before they reached the point where they have no active missionary work aimed at Jews.'

Eckstein has no contact with evangelicals who actively seek to convert Jews, or with the so-called Messianic Jews (those who profess to be Jews while accepting Jesus as the Messiah).

He says that a clash between the Jewish community and the evangelicals may be looming over the 'moral America' debate.

'They are trying to reverse the growing incidence of violence, drugs, abortion and the general breakdown of the family. And they are consistently opposed by certain Jewish defence organizations or Jews in leading roles in the American Civil Liberties Union.' "[38]

---

[37]Rabbi Yechiel Eckstein, *What Christians Should Know About Jews and Judaism*, pp. 294-295, 299. [ ] mine.

[38]Charles Hoffman, "Dialogue with Evangelicals," *Jerusalem Post*, Aug. 8, 1987, © used by permission. Rabbi Eckstein seems to us to generalize and include most Jews with the liberal political camp, in opposition to Christian Evangelicals. We would here like to emphasize that a growing number of Jews are becoming politically conservative. Eckstein does not speak for all Jews, especially after the era of the 80's with Jesse Jackson's anti-Semitic remarks and President Reagan's strong support of Israel. Many Jews are joining the conservative, moral viewpoints for which the true evangelical stands. To illustrate our point, we will quote from Jerry Falwell's article entitled, "Jewish Fear of Fundamentalist Activism Exaggerated." Rabbi Aryeh Spero of Agudas Achim Congregation of Canton, Ohio, stated in this article: "The Conservative agenda, finding both Jewish and Christian adherents, cannot be construed as an advancement of one religion over another....As euthanasia is viewed by many Secularists as a form of murder, so too is feticide, abortion. These issues and many others are not, as the committee would have us believe, inclusively religious, but more the traditional split between political Conservatives versus political Liberals. The committee is actually guilty of using religion. It is exploiting an age-old fear of religious ulterior motives, as a means to frighten Jews from Conservatism into their political party. As a Rabbi I am offended by their exploitation of religion for their secular political purpose." Jerry Falwell, "Jewish Fear of Fundamentalist Activism Exaggerated," *The Fundamentalist Journal*, Oct. 1986, © used by permission. We note that it is not Jews with whom evangelicals are upset concerning the ACLU, as implied by Rabbi Eckstein, but rather a hidden goal apparently

Geoffrey Wigoder, in an article entitled, "Evangelical Challenge," says of Eckstein: "...he feels that certain Israel-oriented Jewish groups have gone too far in giving legitimation to missionizing Hebrew-Christian groups on the basis of their pro-Israel activities...."[39]

EVANGELICAL CHALLENGE

By GEOFFREY WIGODER 14-10-1984

DURING THE Feast of Tabernacles (Succot), thousands of evangelical Christians will participate in what has become an annual celebration organized by the International Christian Embassy. Colourful groups from different parts of the world will converge on Jerusalem for a week of meeting, celebration and prayer.

Israelis welcome this expression of identification with the State of Israel although many are confused by these groups and their attitude towards Jews. A useful recently issued publication is *Understanding Evangelicals: A Guide for the Jewish Community* by Yechiel Eckstein, a Boston rabbi who has been active in inter-religious affairs on behalf of the Anti-Defamation League. The booklet has been issued in New York by the National Jewish Resource Centre.

Although there are very many variations of evangelicals, he writes, three ideological characteristics distinguish the evangelical from the "mainstream" Christians: the centrality of Scripture, the stress on the person of Jesus, and the experience of being "born again" which means that it is not enough to have been baptized while a baby but the individual on reaching maturity must make a personal decision to accept Jesus as his personal saviour.

Underlying all these principles is the belief in the Christian imperative to actively disseminate the gospel, or "good news" of Christianity. Eckstein is careful to differentiate the evangelist from the fundamentalist. Until a few decades ago the terms were used interchangeably – and still are in some circles. The fundamentalists originally implied a return to the fundamentals of the church (as opposed to liberal Christians who were seen as having overaccommodated themselves to modernity). Now the more generic term is "evangelical," with "fundamentalist" reserved for the more conservative right-wing of the evangelical community. Indeed, "fundamentalist" today often has the pejorative connotation of "backward."

THERE IS A wide spectrum of evangelicals, who are said to number 40-50 million in the U.S. alone (although all figures must be treated with caution). The major theological issue dividing the "liberal" from the "conservative" evangelical is whether Scripture is infalible. Major differences divide the various groups of evangelicals and it is wrong to lump them together. According to a recent Gallup poll, 20 per cent of evangelicals regard themselves as "left of centre," 31 per cent as "middle of the road" and 37 per cent as "right of centre" on the evangelical scale.

The left are concerned with issues of peace and justice, and oppose many of Israel's policies. On the other hand, they tend to be close to the American Jewish establishment on many domestic and social-justice issues. Those in the centre (he mentions the late Dr. Douglas Young as an outstanding example) are inclined to support Jews and Israel, though not uncritically.

Their solidarity stems more from their sense of justice for the Jewish people and for moral, strategic and geopolitical reasons than from eschatological considerations (i.e. the return of the Jews to their land as a necessary stage preceding the Second Coming of Jesus) – although the latter aspect is not absent. In the U.S. a number of dialogues have been conducted between Jews and this segment of evangelism. Although the members of this group will not – and could not – agree to end evangelism to Jews, its members rarely engage in aggressive, proselytizing efforts which single out the Jews for missionary activities.

The evangelical centre is generally supportive of Israel – but not unqualifiedly so. It is the evangelical right which is most sold on Israel – and on missionizing. They are aggressive in the U.S. on behalf of right-wing causes, hoping to bring America back to what they often call its "Judeo-Christian" moral foundations. They were particularly visible in the U.S. during election times, including the present.

The largest of the Christian far right groups calls itself the Moral Majority which claims a membership of four million. It has become so well-known that other evangelicals complain that the public tends to confuse them with the Moral Majority, towards which they themselves have mixed feelings.

MANY OF THESE right-wing evangelicals believe America has been blessed because it has treated Jews and Israel favourably and they express support for Jews. However, anti-Semitic remarks have been heard in their ranks. Some Jews such as Eckstein excuse these as inadvertent or naive; others take them as betraying a basic underlying anti-Semitism.

However, there is no gainsaying the genuineness of their Zionist enthusiasm, derived from biblical promises and expectations – drawn from both the Old and New Testaments. Events in the Middle East are interpreted as signs of the imminent return of Jesus, the battle of Armageddon and the ultimate conversion of the Jews. Evangelicals differ as to the order in which these events will take place and this can affect the priority given to missionizing. The evangelical right, which received enthusiastic endorsement from Menachem Begin, is the most politically active pro-Israel evangelical group, expressing its support through political lobbying, tourism, and positive media presentations of Israel and its policies (often supporting "Greater Israel" policies as fulfilment of biblical prophecy).

Eckstein points out, however, that on the Awacs issue, the most significant showdown over Israel between the Reagan Administration and the American Jewish establishment, all the evangelical representatives and senators supported the Democratic administration against the declared interests of Israel.

Jews in America are concerned with the declared objective of the evangelical right to "Christianize America." The Moral Majority has spoken of its desire to establish a "Christian republic," although it explains this as an attempt to arrest the moral decline in the country. Most official Jewish groups oppose its programme which supports prayers in schools, and opposes abortion, equal women's rights, and rights for homosexuals. One Jewish group, the right-wing Orthodox, Rabbinical Alliance, however, has affirmed its support for much of the Moral Majority's agenda.

In general, much confusion reigns among the Jewish community (as elsewhere) about evangelicals. Many Jews oppose cooperation with evangelicals, especially its right wing. These include Reform leaders and the American Jewish Congress, who are alarmed at the use of religion as an instrument of political coercion and the endorsement of reactionary causes.

ECKSTEIN DESCRIBES divergent Jewish views. Some warn against "selling their souls" to the Christian Right just because of its strong support for Israel. Others feel that the beleaguered State of Israel should ignore their underlying motivations and expectations and accept their support. Still others feel that Jews should seek out responsible evangelical circles and hold a dialogue with them on a variety of issues, which could prove potentially helpful.

Many Jews are uneasy about becoming involved in the evangelical world-view and suspect that inasmuch as the support for Israel may be related to the hope for the conversion of the Jews, when this does not happen, the relationship could misfire and Jews would be blamed as delaying the final redemption of the world – leading to strong resentment of the Jews for their "backsliding." Others fear that at a certain point the evangelicals will "call the chips in" and ask Jews to support various ultra-conservative causes as a *quid pro quo* for their support for Israel.

Eckstein himself optimistically feels that the development of dialogue will bring new understanding for Jewish concerns for pluralism and civil liberties and the dispelling of anxieties on either side. He recognizes that the relationship is based on a basic conflict – the determination to evangelize versus the Jewish determination to survive – but feels that a modus vivendi can be built up, involving give and take [illegible] sides.

Jews, he suggests, will be[illegible] recognize the centrality of mission for many Christians but in turn will demand the cessation of crude frontal activities in this direction and its restriction to frameworks of dialogue, model and example, without insistence on conversion. Jews, he feels, should develop the relationship but without compromising their own central Jewish commitments (although he feels that certain Israel-oriented Jewish groups have gone too far in giving legitimation to missionizing Hebrew-Christian groups on the basis of their pro-Israel activities).

Here in Israel, much can be learned from this document. We must be aware of the perception of a growth in missionary activity expressed in certain quarters but at the same time should keep the entire issue in proper perspective and not be drawn into panicky steps which play into the hands of anti-democratic tendencies in our midst.

The writer is editor-in-chief of the Encyclopedia Judaica *and a regular contributor to* The Jerusalem Post.

---

voiced by its founder, Roger Baldwin, who has stated from the beginning: "...'I am for Socialism, disarmament, and ultimately for abolishing the state itself as an instrument of violence and compulsion. I seek social ownership of property...Communism is the goal.' " Baldwin's quote is cited from Dr. D. James Kennedy's letter to me of July 13, 1993. Concerning the mention of abortion by Rabbi Eckstein, he should note that many Jewish defense organizations are presently working in Israel to curb abortion until their pro-life laws are enacted—laws that will have the potential to save up to 40,000 Israeli babies a year.

39 Geoffrey Wigoder, "Evangelical Challenge," *Jerusalem Post*, Oct. 14, 1984, © used by permission.

By CHARLES HOFFMAN
Jerusalem Post Reporter

Orthodox rabbi – man with a mission

Dialogue with evangelicals

Rabbi Yehiel Eckstein, an American rabbi ordained at Yeshiva University and with strong family ties to the Karliner hassidim, is a man with a mission. This is no ordinary mission, however, since it is something of a one-man effort to establish a dialogue on Jewish-Christian relations with one of the most powerful religious groups in America: the evangelical ("born-again") Christians.

To some people, the term evangelical conjures up images of fire-and-brimstone preachers, slick television ministries raking in millions of dollars from the faithful, uninhibited calls for making America into a "Christian nation," and lately, sex scandals and power struggles.

And there is also that curious combination of firm support for Israel, mixed with occasional old-fashioned anti-Semitism.

In a recent interview in Jerusalem, Eckstein noted that while these images are accurate to some extent, they are basically stereotypes that do an injustice to many evangelicals. "In my 10 years of working with evangelicals, I have found that many of them are reasonable people who we, as Jews, can and should be talking to.

"According to surveys, about 68 million Americans describe themselves as born-again Christians, or evangelicals. Over 40 per cent of Americans with TV sets watch an evangelical programme at least once a month – as many as tune in to *Dynasty*. Jews have had very little contact with this group, whose influence, wealth and political sophistication has grown tremendously in the past 15 years."

Eckstein is a former national co-director of inter-religious affairs for the Anti-Defamation League of B'nai Brith. Four years ago he founded the Holyland Fellowship of Christians and Jews. Jews provide about 65 per cent of the funds for his organization, while Christians supply the rest.

The 36-year-old rabbi was in Israel to advise on Christian participation in Israel's 40th anniversary celebrations.

Most Jews, he said, tend to lump all evangelicals together as fundamentalists. "There is an important mainstream or centrist approach among evangelicals, represented by Billy Graham, which is analogous to Yeshiva University among the American Orthodox.

"Then there are the fundamentalists, represented by Jerry Falwell and Bailey Smith; and what are called the charismatics, the preachers like Jimmy Swaggert, Pat Robertson and Jim Bakker, who tend to predominate on television."

As an example of how contact can have a positive influence, Eckstein cited the case of the infamous remark made some six years ago by Bailey Smith who declared that "God Almighty does not hear the prayers of a Jew."

"When this happened," Eckstein recalled, "I realized that Jews had no relations with this powerful group of fundamentalists. I made contact with Smith, brought him to Israel and tried to make him aware of certain Jewish sensitivities. You know, he did apologize for that remark. But I found out that he had never even met a Jew until he was 33."

Asked if Smith's apology pointed to a real change of heart, Eckstein said: "I don't care what he really thinks. This is a matter of faith for him. But unchecked statements like this can spill over into practical activity such as aggressive missionary work or efforts to make prayer in the schools compulsory.

"Later he asked me to preach at his church. It was a big thing for him to give up his pulpit to a rabbi."

Starting out mainly as an interpreter of Jewish life, Eckstein has found that he is being sought out by Jewish organizations as an expert on the evangelical community.

He noted that some people have criticized him for his efforts. "They say that I am beating my head agains a wall, and that there is no real possibility of Jewish-evangelical understanding. As evidence they cite repeated statements by leading preachers that their goal is to build a 'Christian America,' and the basic tenet of the evangelical faith that they must actively bring the world to accept Jesus as saviour."

Eckstein admitted that discussing Christian missionary work with evangelicals is a delicate issue. "We can't start out by demanding that they stop proselytizing; that would mean asking evangelicals to stop being evangelicals.

"What can we do? We can tell them: Go ahead and preach, but do it without the harassment and deception that one finds in some groups like Jews for Jesus. In Chicago, I got the Christian community to attack a deceptive attempt by the Slavic Gospel group to convert Russian Jewish immigrants.

"Now if you are talking about long-term changes, that is another matter. It took over 50 years of dialogue with liberal Protestants and the Catholic church before they reached the point where they have no active missionary work aimed at Jews."

Eckstein has no contact with evangelicals who actively seek to convert Jews, or with the so-called Messianic Jews (those who profess to be Jews while accepting Jesus as the messiah).

He says that a clash between the Jewish community and the evangelicals may be looming over the "moral America" debate.

"They are trying to reverse the growing incidence of violence, drugs, abortion and the general breakdown of the family. And they are consistently opposed by certain Jewish defence organizations or Jews in leading roles in the American Civil Liberties Union."

Eckstein wants to make evangelicals aware of Jewish sensitivity to the civil liberty aspects of these issues, but in a language that they can understand.

Eckstein's own mission has become so taxing that he has borrowed an effective evangelical technique: he is going electronic. In November, he will launch a daily radio show called *Ask the Rabbi*, a five-minute spot on stations belonging to the "electronic church" that will deal with many of the issues raised in his book, *What Christians Should Know About Jews and Judaism*. He also makes occasional TV appearances on the *700 Club* show, which is broadcast on Middle East TV.

"On one of these shows, an interviewer started out by asking me, as they would any Christian guest, 'When did you find the Lord?' So you see, they still have a long way to go in understanding the nature of Jewish faith."

ON THE ONE HAND, RABBI ECKSTEIN TELLS EVANGELICALS HE IS THEIR FRIEND, WHILE ON THE OTHER, HE TAKES THEIR MONEY AND TRIES TO SILENCE THEIR MESSAGE TO JEWS ABOUT JESUS

The 1987 article, "Dialogue with Evangelicals," also mentioned: "Eckstein is a former national co-director of inter-religious affairs for the Anti-Defamation League of B'nai Brith. Four years ago he founded the Holyland Fellowship of Christians and Jews. Jews provided about 65 per cent of the funds for his organization, while **Christians supply the rest**."[40]

We have a question. Should Christians support (give credence and respect to) one Rabbi Yechiel Eckstein? Should they supply thirty-five percent of the funds needed to fuel his organization? In our opinion, it is clear that Rabbi Eckstein is not a friend of the evangelical community, as he likes to portray and think of himself. He is clearly against their efforts to bring the message of salvation through Jesus (who we believe is the Jewish Messiah) to all people, which includes the Jews. He would like Jews exempted and left out of all this, and yet Jesus: "...told his disciples, 'I have been given all authority in heaven and earth. Therefore go and make disciples in **all**[41] the nations, baptizing them into the name of the Father and of the Son and of the Holy Spirit, and then teach these new disciples to obey all the commands I have given you; and be sure of this—that I am with you always, even to the end of the world' " (Matt. 28:18-19 *The Living Bible*).

---

[40]Charles Hoffman, "Dialogue with Evangelicals," *Jerusalem Post*, Aug. 8, 1987. Bold mine.

[41]"All" includes Israel. Bold mine.

Jesus also said: "...when the Holy Spirit has come upon you, you will receive power to testify about me with great effect, to the people in **Jerusalem**, throughout **Judea**, in **Samaria**, and to the **ends of the earth**, about my death and resurrection.' It was not long afterwards that he rose into the sky and disappeared into a cloud, leaving them staring after him" (Acts 1:8-9 *The Living Bible*).

Concerning the message of Jesus to the Jews, the apostle Paul said: "...for it is the power of God for salvation to everyone who believes, to the Jew first and also to the Greek" (Rom. 1:16 NASB).

FINALLY IN THE 90'S, THERE ARE SOME COURAGEOUS RABBIS READY FOR DIALOGUE AND TO REALISTICALLY ACCEPT THE MESSIANIC JEWS FOR WHO THEY ARE!

In answer to the question, "Do Christians see Rabbi Eckstein as a bridge builder and wall breaker?"—responsible Evangelical Christians say no. Rather, many evangelicals endorse Paul Liberman's book, *The Fig Tree Blossoms*, as a true reconciler and bridge builder. Read his book; it is a much more honest attempt at bridge building.

Lately, there has been some encouragement coming from courageous rabbis. Rabbi Edward Maline from Florida, invited local Messianic Jews to a debate. The *Fort Lauderdale Sun-Sentinel* reported: "What may be an unprecedented event in South Florida—a meeting in a synagogue between Jews and Jewish-born Christians—will take place at Broward County's oldest temple on Sunday morning.

Messianic Judaism...will be the topic at the 'Breakfast with the Rabbi' session at Temple Emanu-El. Doing a dialogue-style session with Rabbi Edward Maline, will be Neil Lash, host of a local TV show and founder of the messianic Temple Aron Kodesh. Both congregations are in Lauderdale Lakes....[Rabbi Maline said] 'The way I look at it, they exist, they're here in the community, so let's hear them'....'we'll understand each other only through dialogue.' "[42]

RABBI MALINE WANTED TO TALK *TO* THE MESSIANIC JEWS RATHER THAN *ABOUT* THEM—AGREEING THAT THEIR FAITH *WAS* A JEWISH SECT IN THE FIRST CENTURY

In a companion article written after the debate took place entitled, "Messianics Welcomed at Temple," the secular newspaper noted: "The rare event occurred over coffee and bagels on Sunday as

[42]James D. Davis, "Messianic Judaism, Topic of Discussion," *The Ft. Lauderdale Sun-Sentinel*, Dec. 4, 1992, © used by permission. [ ] mine.

Jewish-born Christians, who call themselves messianic Jews, took part in 'Breakfast with the Rabbi' at Temple Emanu-El, Lauderdale Lakes. They compared notes, argued and swapped business cards....' This is all to the good,' said Rabbi Edward Maline of Temple Emanu-El when it was all over. '[Messianics] are part of the real world. Instead of talking *about* each other, we should talk *to* each other.'

Local leader Neil Lash, Maline's messianic guest, even called it unprecedented....The event drew 150 people, most from Temple Emanu-El; about 25 were from Aron Kodesh; a dozen were from a class in Jewish history taught by Maline at Florida Atlantic University. There were also a few area church members....The rabbi agreed with messianics that Christianity was a Jewish sect in the first century....[the rabbi told one man] 'Religion is supposed to be a source of reconciliation and unity'....Temple Emanu-El members were positive about the exchange, and about their synagogue's part in it.

'We have a real neat temple,' said Fern Walker, who had come with her husband, Randall. 'Any kind of dialogue is beneficial. Jesus was a good man, a good rabbi, a social reformer.'

Ben Baena, a Jewish-born Christian on vacation from Bridgeport, Conn., was effusive. 'This was monumental. It brought a tear to my eye. This gives me credibility with other Jews, who say we wouldn't be allowed into a temple.'

Even the rabbi's wife, Marilyn Maline, was enthusiastic. 'A lot was accomplished here. It opened our ears, for the first time, to what the other side was saying. We learned to look at their faith in an intellectual light, rather than emotional. This is new meat for us.' "[43]

MOST AMERICAN RABBIS, FOLLOWING THE ATTITUDE OF ECKSTEIN, DO NOT GIVE MESSIANIC JEWS AN AUDIENCE, FOR FEAR OF JEWISH QUESTIONS OF LEGITIMACY!

We now see a stark contrast to Rabbi Eckstein's intolerable statement: "Messianic Judaism is an anathema [curse]...."[44]

Rabbi Edward Maline was truly kind, honest, open to dialogue and invited the Messianic Jews to his synagogue to speak with him. After the meeting, many Messianic Jews showed inquisitive members of the congregation Bible verses which support Messianic Judaism. The Messianic guests, Neil and Jaime Lash, reported in their newsletter

[43]James D. Davis, "Messianics Welcomed at Temple," *The Fort Lauderdale Sun-Sentinel*, Dec. 4, 1992, © used by permission.
[44][ ] mine.

"Love Song to the Messiah": "In the days that followed, we received calls from Jewish people asking questions and looking for information. One personal letter that Neil received led to an interesting phone conversation about the supernatural, the Jew, and God today."[45]

We now see one reason why so many rabbis, such as Eckstein, remain hostile in their attitudes and comments to true open-minded dialogue and acceptance of Messianic Jews. They are afraid the non-believing Jews will start to ask questions. Could Jesus really be the Messiah of the Jews?

We recovered one of the posters, which were plastered on a few of the bulletin boards at the Hebrew University, before it was removed by the university staff. It was hand drawn, apparently by another American studying there. This Lone Ranger attempt to damage the reputation of Jews for Jesus failed, like so many others. We reproduced this poster to illustrate the hate and frustration apparent in the will of the opposition to drive a wedge between Jews for Jesus and Evangelical Christians.

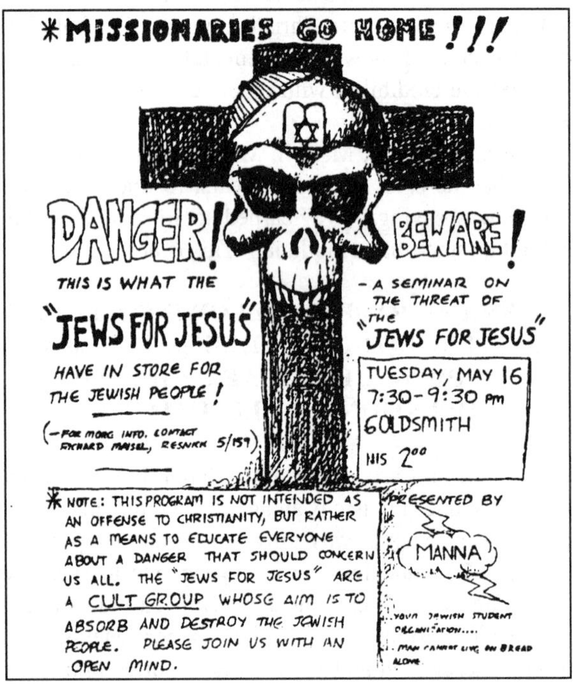

---

[45]Neil and Jaime Lash, "Love Song to the Messiah," Jan. 1993. Messianic newsletter available through LSM, POB 4386, Ft. Lauderdale, FL, USA 33338-4386. Tel. (305) 733-0656.

What do we as believers have to say about the hate directed at us (for sharing the Gospel with the Jews) and the misrepresentation of our faith? Before we answer that, let's look at the many secular articles in Israeli newspapers regarding the Israelis' appreciation of the believers' Zionism.

דולי רוזן

ברית עולם

היחיד שמובטח לו מקום בגן־עדן

מדירה סטנדרטית בירושלים, עם אשה,
שני ילדים וקסטות של טינה טרנר, יוצא
הקול הקורא לנו במודעות ענק לעבור
לנצרות החדשה

Israeli newspapers print favorable articles on Messianic Jews. In this article, our friend, Mino Kalesher, an Israeli born citizen, was interviewed regarding his faith. Mino's father, Zvi, a Holocaust survivor, is also a Messianic Jew. Illustration courtesy of Col Hyer, Jerusalem.

פי האתון

עיתון הסטודנטים בירושלים / אפריל תשמ"ח גליון מס' 7

מופץ חינם ללמעלה מ־25,000 סטודנטים ואנשי סגל.

משיח כבר בא

המנו"ף המרכזי

מרכז נופש ופנאי (מנר"ף) של האונ' מופעל כיחידה צבאית. העובדים מתלוננים על יחס רודני מצד המנהל. מי שמעז לנקוט יוזמה מוצא עצמו מפוטר בתואנות שונות. שמא כאן טמונה הסיבה מדוע חלה ירידה חדה במספר הסטודנטים הפעילים בספורט?
ראה עמ' 7.

עוד בגליון זה

כמו גדולים
ראה עמ' 4 — 5

המנוף המרכזי
ראה עמ' 7

יהודים משיחיים
ראה עמ' 9

שונא בינוניות יחייה
ראה עמ' 11

מרובינא עד ריטה
ראה עמ' 15

איסת"א לשרותך
ראה עמ' 20

Even the Hebrew University shows interest in Messianic Jews (*Yehudim Meshihim*) and especially Israeli Messianic Jews. They interviewed Yakov Damkani, one of the leading Israeli believers, for a full page article and published this photo I shot during the Feast of Tabernacles March in their monthly newspaper, *P-Haeton* (פ האתון). Illustration courtesy of P-Haeton.

IN JERUSALEM

Believers in Jesus

By Herb Keinon

David Stern of the Messianic Jewish community is also a veteran of Jews for Jesus campaigns in the U.S. (Brian Hendler)

David Stern says he keeps kosher. His Manahat home contains many Jewish ceremonial objects. What he calls his *ketuba* (marriage contract), written in Hebrew and English, hangs on the wall. The text includes numerous references to "Jesus, our Messiah."

Every Saturday night and Sunday afternoon, Stern prays at the Netivyah Congregation on Rehov Narkiss. The language of prayer is Hebrew. The congregation has a Tora scroll. At the end of the blessings, congregants intone the name of "Jesus, our Messiah."

Netivyah is one of the cornerstones, and Stern one of the members, of Jerusalem's so-called Messianic Jewish community. Members, about 100 souls organized into two Jerusalem congregations – Netivyah and the Israeli Messianic Assembly – were among the nearly 1,200 participants from around the world who recently attended a Messianic Jewish conference at the capital's Diplomat Hotel.

The Messianic Jews claim they are Jewish although they believe in Jesus. They have provided a rare point of agreement between Jerusalem Reform Rabbi Tuvia Ben-Horin and Yad Le'ahim, an ultra-Orthodox, anti-missionary organization.

Ben-Horin and the Yad Le'ahim representatives say that by believing in Jesus these individuals have placed themselves beyond the Jewish pale.

"Historically, any time Jews have pinned their Messianic hopes on any particular individual – the false Messiahs – they have found themselves outside the borders of Judaism. Halachically they may still be Jews, but they are surely not honourable Jews," Ben-Horin says.

A Yad Le'ahim representative, who would identify himself only as Ze'ev, was more blunt: "You can't stab your mother in the back and then claim to love her."

Joseph Shulam, a leader of Netivyah, rejects the notion that he is stabbing his mother. The Bulgarian-born Shulam, who was brought to this country when he was two and says he "became converted" in the early Sixties after reading the New Testament as part of a high school project, says his belief in Jesus, whom he refers to as Yeshua, doesn't place him outside the Jewish pale "any more than it places outside of Judaism those who believe that the Lubavitcher Rebbe is the Messiah."

Ben-Horin counters, saying that although there are those who may attribute messianic qualities to the rebbe, few actually pin their messianic dreams on him.

According to Halacha, a person born of a Jewish mother remains a Jew till his death, no matter what. However, a person who was born Jewish but converted to another religion is not entitled to receive Israeli citizenship under the Law of Return.

The High Court of Justice is considering a case involving a couple from Zimbabwe, Jerry and Shirley Beresford, who say they have Jewish mothers, who have not converted though they share beliefs similar to Shulam's, and who are trying to obtain Israeli citizenship under the Law of Return.

Ben-Horin says that although Messianic Jews already in the country have the right to congregate as they wish, the Jewish establishment should figure out what is lacking in today's Judaism that sends Jews into the open arms of Christianity.

"I'm afraid that what these people find in the Messianic Jewish community is a love and concern they haven't found in Judaism," he says.

At Netivyah's Sunday afternoon services, this "love and concern" seems to be abundant. People greet each other, and strangers are welcomed warmly, in a way rarely seen in Jerusalem's synagogues.

Although Shulam ordinarily delivers the Sunday afternoon sermon, it was recently given by Ernie Stewart, a tall, silver-haired, non-Jewish American – speaking English with a heavy Southern drawl – who preached on the virtues of patience.

The style of Stewart's delivery brought to mind small Baptist congregations in the American Midwest. His voice rose steadily to a crescendo, and in the middle of the sermon he called upon a congregant to stand. Stewart used this woman, who he said had undergone a great deal of physical pain in her life, to illustrate the virtues of a long-suffering nature.

During the sermon, after Stewart had cited a New Testament passage, one bearded man wearing *tzitziot* attached to his four-cornered shirt and a green yarmulke emblazoned with the Hebrew words "Jesus the Messiah," stopped him, and offered what he said was a more appropriate New Testament passage.

Instead of a traditional "amen corner" providing a steady din throughout the sermon, the noise at Netivyah came from a full-throated man in the back translating every word into Russian. Shulam was also translating the sermon into Hebrew, and earphones to pick up this translation were handed out to about 10 of the nearly 40 people present.

The reason Netivyah holds its services on Saturday night and Sunday afternoon, Shulam says, "is so people don't desecrate the Sabbath."

According to Yad Le'ahim, many of those who identify with the Messianic Jewish congregations are, in fact, not Jews according to the halachic definition. Even Stern admits that at the recent conference here, only about 500 of the 1,200 participants were born of Jewish mothers.

Stern, who made aliya from California, is a veteran of Jews for Jesus campaigns in the U.S. Both he and Shulam, however, stress that the Messianic Jewish congregations in Israel are not affiliated with the American "Jews for Jesus," which is made up primarily of Jews who have joined Christian churches.

"The Jews for Jesus have bought into Evangelical garbage," Shulam says, explaining this means speaking in tongues and faith healing.

Yad Le'ahim representatives say that theologically the differences between Jews for Jesus and the Messianic Jews here are slight. "In America they stay within the church and tend to stress the Jewishness of Jesus, while here they have their own congregations and try to stress their own Jewishness," a Jerusalem anti-missionary says.

In the U.S., she adds, Jews for Jesus have for years waged a very aggressive missionary campaign, while here it has been much more low-key, because they are watched here every step of the way.

Some may argue that divisions are the only thing the local Messianic Jewish community has in common with Judaism. In addition to the two formal congregations, a number of informal ones meet in people's homes. Off the record, some Netivyah congregants hint that the Israeli Messianic Assembly doesn't stress its Jewish links enough.

Victor Smadja, a congregant of the Israeli Messianic Assembly who came to Israel from Tunisia more than two decades ago, replies that his congregation is as "Jewish" as Netivyah is.

Like Netivyah, he says, his congregation celebrates the Jewish pilgrimage holidays – Succot, Pessah and Shavuot – rather than Christmas and Easter. But these holidays take on Messianic overtones. For instance, during Pessah the Israeli Messianic Assembly commemorates Jesus' resurrection.

According to Ze'ev of Yad Le'ahim, the intra-congregational argument is absurd. "One Jew who believes in Jesus," he says, "can't be more 'Jewish' than another Jew who believes in Jesus."

The *Jerusalem Post* interviews David Stern, an Israeli Messianic Jew.

Now we can reply to the question, "What do we as believers have to say about the hate directed at us and the misrepresentation of our faith?" We must not let those few minority groups intimidate us. Remember, Jesus said: "Blessed *are* they which are persecuted for righteousness' sake: for their's is the kingdom of heaven. Blessed are ye, when *men* shall revile you, and persecute *you*, and shall say all manner of evil against you falsely, for my sake. Rejoice, and be exceeding glad: for great *is* your reward in heaven: for so persecuted they the prophets which were before you" (Matt. 5:10-12 KJV).

We must push on to inform as many Jews as possible, so that they too will have a fair hearing of the Gospel, that Jesus is the Messiah and redeemer for all those who accept His gift of life into their heart. Remember, Paul taught all who truly believe in the New Testament: "...to the Jew first...." The Bible teaches that there are gifts for those that share. "For what *is* our hope, or joy, or crown of rejoicing? *Are* not even ye in the presence of our Lord Jesus Christ at his coming? For ye are our glory and joy" (I Thes. 2:19-20 KJV).

You might say, to call yourself a Christian or a believer in Jesus and not share the good news of Jesus, which He commanded of all who believe, is the epitome of hypocrisy! Listen to Daniel's words in his Old Testament book, chapter 12, verses 2 and 3. Read them now. He speaks of a resurrection of those who have turned many to righteousness (the only way to be righteous is to be forgiven through the Messiah). In this resurrection they will shine as the stars of Heaven forever (John 6).

What more incentive do we as believers need to encourage us to share the gift of living forever with our friends, with those in God's eternal kingdom on Earth (see our chapters 29-30), who otherwise may never know?! Those of our beloved Jewish friends, many of whom have not yet realized that Jesus is their Messiah and Savior, are at your mercy! Tell them. Don't forget the New Testament incidents between the Pharisees and the apostles in Acts 5.[46]

***

---

[46]The Pharisees said: "...Did not we straitly command you that ye should not teach in this name? and, behold, ye have filled Jerusalem with your doctrine....Then Peter and the *other* apostles answered and said, We ought to obey God rather than men" (Acts 5:28-29 KJV). Tell your orthodox friends that the New Testament Rabbi Gamaliel gave your predecessors advice which was well worth taking. "Then stood there up one in the council, a Pharisee, named Gamaliel, a doctor of the law, held in reputation among all the people, and commanded to put the apostles forth a little space; And said unto them, Ye men of Israel, take heed to yourselves what ye intend to do as touching these men....Refrain from these men, and let them alone: for if this counsel or this work be of men, it will come to nought: But if it be of God, ye cannot overthrow it; lest haply ye be found even to fight against God" (Acts 5:34-35, 38-39 KJV).

THE MESSIANIC JEWISH CONCLUSION

While many American immigrants and visiting rabbis come to Israel and try to quash and intimidate Evangelical Christians and Messianic Jews in their sharing of the Gospel of Messiah, the Israelis welcome them, as you saw in the closing photos of chapter 14.

They welcomed them with a love, rarely seen during the Messiah Conference at the Diplomat Hotel, where 1500 Messianic Jews gathered during Shavuot 88. I heard the cab drivers who drove them to their hotel say, "Make Alia [immigrate]. This country is for all of us, even those of you who think Jesus is the Messiah."

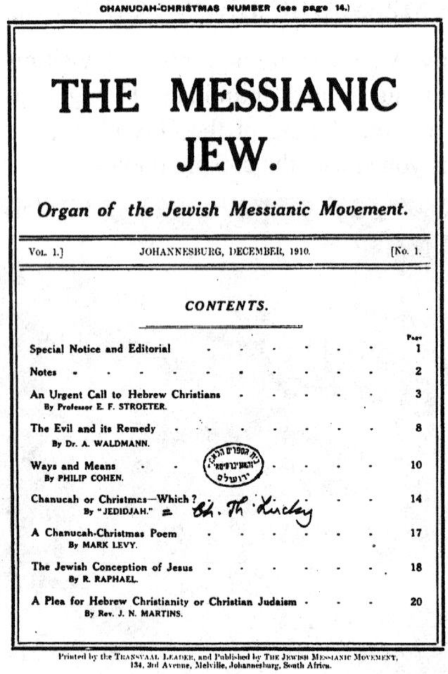

CHANUCAH-CHRISTMAS NUMBER (see page 14.)

THE MESSIANIC JEW.

Organ of the Jewish Messianic Movement.

VOL. 1.] JOHANNESBURG, DECEMBER, 1910. [No. 1.

CONTENTS.

Printed by the TRANSVAAL LEADER, and Published by THE JEWISH MESSIANIC MOVEMENT, 134, 3rd Avenue, Melville, Johannesburg, South Africa.

An article entitled, "High Court Asked: Is a Jew Who Believes in Jesus Still a Jew?",[47] featuring a picture of Gary and Shirley Beresford, stated that the "Dahaf Polls" show seventy-eight percent of the Israeli population welcomes Messianic Jews as new immigrants (*Olim*) to Israel. This worried Julius Berman, who is chairman of the Task Force on Missionaries and Cults of the Jewish Community Relations Council of New York. He warned: "The Jewish communities of the West recognize these Hebrew Christian groups for what they are and have not given them any credibility. Is the Israeli Jewish community willing to accept the responsibility of granting such legitimacy?"[48] Berman also said the Messianic Movement was "a little more than ten years old." The picture shown here of a Messianic publication from 1910, shows he needs to brush up on his facts. Hugh Schonfield wrote a book entitled, *Jewish Christianity, From the First to the Twentieth Century*, which traced the Messianic movement from the era of Jesus until today. We believe in letting Israel be Israel and New York be New York. If Israel realizes Messianic Jews are Jews, go back to New York. Israel is fully capable of deciding who is a Jew! Let Israel keep its deeper understanding of Messianic Judaism.

---

47 "High Court Asked: Is a Jew Who Believes in Jesus Still a Jew?", *Jerusalem Post*, Feb. 5, 1988.

48 Julius Berman, "Hebrew Christians," letter to the editor, *Jerusalem Post*, Mar. 2, 1988.

The religious Jew may one day take the place of the police and be in a position of civil authority. When the majority of American Jews come to Israel, those who are religious may successfully keep the Israelis from hearing the Gospel, which is the apparent wish of the Orthodox Jews and liberals such as Peli. We believe this because of Jesus' words, which indicate the Orthodox will have enormous political power just prior to His return.[49] Jesus' words of instruction and prediction read: "But pray that your flight may not be in the winter, or on a Sabbath...." (Matt. 24:20 NASB).

---

[49]After the Rapture (see our chapter 25, "The Rapture Factor") but before the Coming of Jesus to stop the war of Gog and Magog/Armageddon to save Israel, and therefore being fully and publicly recognized as Messiah. The Scriptures teach there will be religious persecution of those who believe in Jesus. This refers to those who believed after the Rapture, but before the Second Coming seven years preceding that. It refers especially to those Jewish believers in Jesus whose identity will be revealed to the Antichrist by their own zealous, self-righteous Orthodox brothers, who think the antichrist is the Messiah.

An Israeli, Jacob Damkani, and friends distribute Hebrew Messianic literature in Tel Aviv, Israel.

The Shelter (*Ha Meklat*), established by John and Judy Pex, is a Messianic congregation and youth hostel in Eliat, Israel. *Ha Meklat* is a welcome sight to travelers who are interested in the Gospel.

UMJC
FOSTERING & STRENGTHENING MESSIANIC CONGREGATIONS
SPIRITUAL LEADERS FELLOWSHIPS
LEADERSHIP ACCOUNTABILITY
LEADERSHIP TRAINING
EDUCATIONAL MATERIALS
The Union of Messianic Jewish Congregations
YESHIVAH PROGRAM

JEWS FOR JESUS
movement
Free Literature
CASSETTES RECORDS
KOSHER FOR PASSOVER
Y'SHUA
GOYIM

Sandra
Sheskin
Sings
Messianic Jewish
also Hosts Love Tours
to Israel
YESHUA
I AM the
ROOT and the
OFFSPRING
of DAVID, the
BRIGHT and
MORNING
STAR
sheskin

Over 2000 Messianic Jews enjoy an evening of singing and dancing at the annual Messiah Conference in Grantham, Pennsylvania.

"The fact is that much more has been written about Jesus in Hebrew in the last quarter century than in the eighteen previous centuries."[50]

Jewish scholar, Pinchas Lapide

These books are a small sample of Israel's Messianic publications presenting Jesus as the Jewish Messiah. Space does not permit us to include all of the books,[51] which number in the hundreds.

---

[50]Pinchas Lapide, *Israelis, Jews and Jesus*, p. 32.

[51]Many of these books are available through Yanetz Ltd., attention Victor Smadja, Industrial Park, POB 151, Talpiot, Jerusalem, Israel. Tel. 011-972-2-671-4536.

ARE ISRAELIS INTERESTED IN BOOKS ABOUT JESUS?

One of the greatest prophetic "signs of the times" concerning the imminent return of Jesus, is the tens of thousands of Jews who are becoming interested and even accepting Him as Messiah. The apostle Paul (Rabbi Saul) reminds us of the Old Testament predictions in Deuteronomy 32:21 when he writes: "And did they understand [that God would give His salvation to others if they refused to take it]? Yes, for even back in the time of Moses, God had said that he would make his people jealous and try to wake them up by giving his salvation to the foolish heathen nations" (Rom. 10:19 *The Living Bible*; [ ] mine).

In Romans 11:8, Paul says: "This is what our Scriptures refer to when they say that God has put them to sleep, shutting their eyes and ears so that they do not understand what we are talking about when we tell them of Christ. And so it is to this very day" (*The Living Bible*).

According to Paul and the Old Testament, one day **all** of Israel will believe! "I want you to know about this truth from God, dear brothers, so that you will not feel proud and start bragging. Yes, it is true that some of the Jews have set themselves against the Gospel now, but this will last only until all of you Gentiles have come to Christ—those of you who will. And then all Israel will be saved" (Rom. 11:25 *The Living Bible*).

This may not be true now, but we certainly are beginning to see the blindness fall from the eyes of hundreds of thousands of Jews! One indication of this ongoing process is the enormous volume of Hebrew Messianic books being written, printed, translated and read in Israel.

One of the foremost contemporary Jewish scholars, Pinchas Lapide, speaks of a "Jesus wave" moving through Judaism, while pointing to the large amount of literature in Hebrew recently published on the subject. Lapide writes: "The 187 Hebrew books, research articles, poems, plays, monographs, dissertations, and essays that have been written about Jesus in the last twenty-seven years since the foundation of the state of Israel, justify press reports of a 'Jesus wave' in the present-day literature of the Jewish state. The fact is that much more has been written about Jesus in Hebrew in the last quarter century than in the eighteen previous centuries."[52]

***

[52]Pinchas Lapide, *Israelis, Jews, and Jesus*, pp. 31-32.

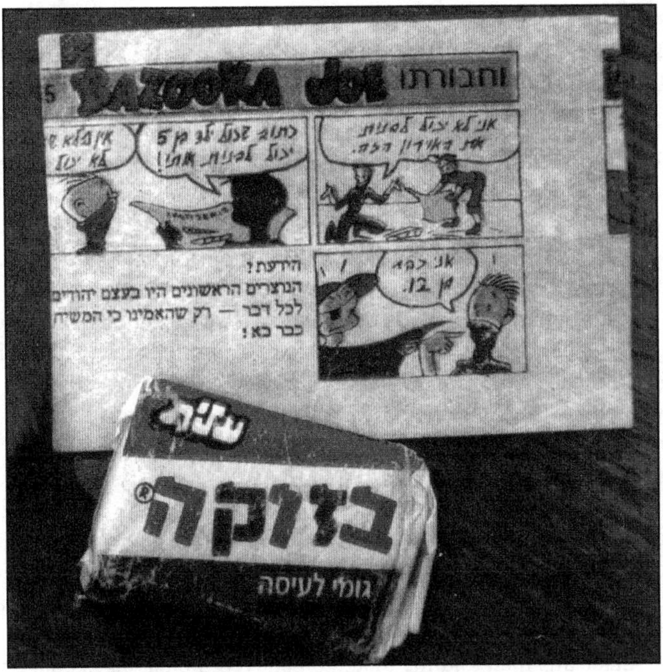

Bubble gum enlightens Israelis.

ISRAELI COMPANIES PRINT WHAT THEY LIKE, IF THEY BELIEVE IT IS TRUE

Israelis are becoming increasingly aware that the first century Christian movement *was* a Jewish one, organized and supervised by Jews! This recognition seems to be spreading to popular culture, as the picture of the bubble gum wrapper illustrates. This photo of a Bazooka bubble gum wrapper contains a "believe it or not" fact in the lower left-hand corner. Remember that the bubble gum distributers are, of course, secular, and thus unbiased. The Hebrew caption reads: "Did you know that the ancient Christians were in fact Jewish in every way, only they believed that the Messiah had already come?"

We believe there is absolutely no question that Israeli believers in Jesus and the Messianic Jews around the world are still Jews in every respect; only they now believe[53] that Jesus came as Messiah and will return soon to bring world redemption when He will be recognized by all. This is foretold in Zechariah 12:10, written in the Jewish Bible over 2500 years ago.[54]

---

[53]Because they are loyal to the Jewish prophecies of the Bible.

[54]I felt I had to include this paragraph because so many modern and reformed rabbis attempt to induce guilt in those Jews who presently believe in Jesus as Messiah, implying

ISRAELI MILITARY AND GOVERNMENT OFFICIALS DISCREETLY PONDER THE IMPORTANCE OF JESUS, IN RELATION TO THEIR APOCALYPTIC PROPHECIES

In Israel, there are government officials and others who believe in their hearts that Jesus is the Jewish Messiah. Why? One reason for so many secret believers in Jesus is the apparent popularity of Hal Lindsey's book, *The Late Great Planet Earth*. The book has been read by generals such as Ariel Sharon, and Prime Ministers such as David Ben-Gurion.

Lindsey himself documented the reaction of Israelis to his book, which outlines Israel's part in the final war predicted in the Bible, while biblically and prophetically revealing Jesus as the Messiah and only hope as its central theme. Hal wrote: "...I was introduced to one of the greatest fighter pilots alive today....at the Miramar Naval Air Station outside of San Diego.

In my book I had written a great deal about Israel, expressing my love for the Israeli people and my concern for their survival....we talked for quite some time. Later, he and I became close friends. Before we parted that night, I gave the young pilot a copy of *Late Great*, and he read it from cover to cover.

Later this man told me that...he believed the passages concerning the Middle East and its future to be absolutely true. He said that having fought for Israel nearly all his life, he had seen the very things the book dealt with taking place. He was amazed to discover that these events had been so precisely foretold thousands of years ago by his own people's prophets....On numerous occasions I have been asked how Israel has responded to *The Late Great Planet Earth*....In 1971, I accompanied a newspaper reporter on a fact-finding tour of Israel sponsored by the U.S. Department of State. Early in the tour I met a major assigned to Israeli army intelligence. This officer, an attractive woman, served as our interpreter and became a good friend.

After the major read my book she urged that it be translated into Hebrew. My publisher contacted an Israeli book firm, and a Hebrew edition was soon available. My major friend helped with the translation, using modern-day Israeli vernacular that made the book even more readable.

As a result of her work, the book caught on like wildfire. A great many copies circulated among military men and government officials as well."[55]

---

that they are not Jews or are disloyal to their race. We as believers, feel this is a lie. The bubble gum wrapper illustrates that even the unbiased secular Israeli authorities concur with us.

[55]Hal Lindsey, *The 1980's*: *Countdown To Armageddon*, pp. 4-5, 7.

IN CONCLUSION, ARE JEWISH BELIEVERS IN JESUS STILL JEWS? WE ANSWER TRUTHFULLY—YES!

Many rabbis say, "Stop converting Jews." They imply that we want to change Jews and somehow rob them of their Jewishness. However, nothing could be further from the truth! We as true believers in Jesus, feel that we have found hidden/forbidden[56] prophecies in the Jewish Bible (Old Testament), which prove Jesus to be the Jewish Messiah. We desire to share this knowledge with everyone, Jew and non-Jew alike, for the betterment of all. We want to let our Jewish friends in on the secret of the Messiah Club, which they can join while remaining Jews forever.

Paul (Rabbi Saul) realized this truth yet never denied his rich heritage as a Jew. To the contrary, he wrote over one-half of the New Testament, proclaiming he was: "...an Hebrew of the Hebrews...." (Phil. 3:5 KJV). He was proud to proclaim his Jewishness. Jesus, a Jew, said, "...for salvation is of the Jews" (John 4:22 KJV).

While many rabbis now attempt to frighten Jews by telling them they will no longer be Jews, there are many Messianic Jewish congregations which maintain Jewish services and praise Jesus as Messiah.

The emphasis on Jewishness is a real challenge to the Orthodox Jews because it exposes their double standard. They do not "excommunicate" atheist Jews, even though they follow no religious traditions, nor even believe in God. Yet they never tire of arguing that Messianic Jews, in spite of the many Jewish traditions they devoutly follow, are not Jewish.

Since when does any group of Jews have a monopoly on Judaism? The Karaite Jews did not accept the prophets or have rabbis, but their Jewishness was never challenged or denied. Messianic Jews believe in the prophets, have Messianic rabbis and realize the Messiahship of Jesus based on Jewish prophecies, and yet, are ridiculed as not being actual Jews. We are appalled; we protest; we will not be quiet until Jesus returns to set the Orthodox straight, as He promised He would (Matt. 23:37-39)!

***

---

[56]Forbidden in the sense that most rabbis would rather these not be considered to apply to the Jewish Messiah and Jesus as we consider their Messianic applications, comparing ancient Jewish writings with the New Testament and original Old Testament prophecy. Rather, many rabbis reinterpret these prophecies and consider their Messianic implications "forbidden" and off-limits to the modern Jewish explorer. This is evidenced by several polemical books against our faith. Examples are: *The Jew and the Christian Missionary*; *You Take Jesus, I'll Take God*, and; *The Real Messiah.*

A model of the Santa Maria, Columbus' flagship,
and a photo of Columbus' likely birthplace.

"...I will leave within you the meek and humble, who trust in the name of the LORD.» These are the remnant whom the apostle calls to mind when he quotes from an ancient prophesy: «Though the number of the Israelites be like the sand by the sea, only the remnant will be saved.» These are the remnant of that nation who have believed in Christ."[1] Christopher Columbus, discoverer of America

"Throughout the *Book of Prophecies* the Admiral makes frequent reference to Rabbi Samuel's expositions of the Biblical texts. Rabbi Samuel was Nicholas of Lyra, a Jewish convert to the Christian faith, who was the greatest Hebraist of the Middle Ages and the author of the first printed commentary on the Bible. In his *Glossa ordinaria*, commenting on Matthew 24:14, Rabbi Samuel says: «And the Gospel of the kingdom will be preached, that is the Gospel of Christ, which shows the way to the kingdom of heaven... It must be taken into account that one thing is the future preaching of the gospel among all the peoples, as regards its effectiveness, and another [thing] that all the peoples will receive that faith in Christ. This will take place at the consummation of the world.» (Fol. 21 of [Columbus'] *Book of Prophecies*)"[2] Kay Brigham's astute commentary on Columbus'quotation of an interesting Jewish opinion on the Messiah's return

16

WAS CHRISTOPHER COLUMBUS A MESSIANIC JEW?

First, let's examine the evidence which indicates Columbus was a Jew. Walter McEntire, author of *Was Christopher Columbus a Jew,* quotes a newspaper article which asked, "Was Columbus a Jew?" The article reads: "...'to the best of our knowledge the blood that flowed in Columbus' veins was three-quarters Jewish.' " McEntire then mentions that the editor adds: "...that 'it wasn't very safe in those days in Spain to call yourself a Jew, and Columbus knew that, and called himself 'a Genoese navigator,' without saying much about his origin'; that 'investigation shows that his mother came of a well known Jewish family, the Ponti Rossi, and that the name 'Colón,' which is the real name of Columbus, was that of Jews.' "[3] McEntire continues: "In two

---

[1]Kay Brigham, *Christopher Columbus's Book of Prophecies, Reproduction of the Original Manuscript with English Translation.* Barcelona: Clie, p. 267, © for the English translation, used by permission. Clie books may be ordered from TSELF, Inc., POB 8337, Fort Lauderdale, FL, USA 33310. Tel. (800) 327-7933. In Brigham's footnote, "LORD" is referenced with Zephaniah 3:9-12 and saved with Romans 9:27 (see Isa. 10:22).

[2]Kay Brigham, *Christopher Columbus: His Life and Discovery in the Light of His Prophecies.* Barcelona: Clie, © 1990, pp. 158-159, used by permission. [ ] mine. Clie books may be ordered from TSELF, Inc., POB 8337, Fort Lauderdale, FL, USA 33310. Tel. (800) 327-7933.

[3]Walter F. McEntire, *Was Christopher Columbus a Jew.* Boston: The Stratford Company, © 1925, pp. i-ii, used by permission.

other papers we found editors saying that 'as you honor Columbus, bear in mind the fact that in all probability three-quarters, if not all, of his blood was Jewish.' "[4]

McEntire points out that Don Garcia discovered: "...that the name of Columbus' mother was Susanna [Shoshana in Hebrew, שׁושׁנה], (a Jewish name)...."[5] He (Garcia) also found: "...in the archives of Pontevedra, a record setting forth that in the fifteenth century, there lived in that city, a family by the name of Colon, 'several members of which bore the same forenames as are to be found among the Colombos of Genoa, the kinsmen of Christopher Columbus. In 1434 and 1437, there was at Pontevedra a Domingo Colon; in 1438 a Bartolomé Colon; in 1496 a Cristobo Colon; in 1434 a Blanca Colon. As we shall see, Domenico was the name of Columbus' father; Bartolomeo that of his younger brother; and Bianchinetta was the name of Columbus' sister."[6] He also notes: "...the devoted friends of Columbus, Juan Cabrero, Luis de Santangel, Gabriel Sanchez, and Alfonso de la Caballeria, [were] all men of Jewish extraction."[7]

Columbus' portraits contain features common to people of Semitic origin, as can be seen here.

The portraits of Columbus look Jewish!

[4]Ibid, p. ii.
[5]Ibid, p. 8. [ ] mine.
[6]Ibid, pp. 7-8.
[7]Ibid, p. 63. [ ] mine.

MODERN SOURCES OF THE 1990'S, EVANGELICAL CHRISTIAN AND JEWISH ALIKE, ADMIT COLUMBUS WAS A JEW

The *Jerusalem Times/Jewish Press* article entitled, "Why Should Catholic Church Honor Queen Isabella?" acknowledges that Columbus was Jewish, while rightly criticizing the fact that the Catholic Church "wouldn't admit that Columbus was a Jew!" Arnold Fine notes: "...Colon, who changed his name to Columbus....was a *Cohen.* The name Colon, is the equivalent of Cohen....The fact remains that Columbus was a Jew."[8]

J. R. Church, minister of the Southwest Radio Church, mentioned in a 1991 radio broadcast: "Columbus used the Jewish calendar in his logs and the Hebrew alphabet for numbers in some cases."[9]

In a taped message, "Why We Honor the Jews," the famous pro-Zionist American television minister, John Hagee, said: "Consider America's debt to the Jewish people—would you be shocked to know that America was discovered by a Jewish sailor named Christopher Columbus? That's a historic fact."[10]

COLUMBUS HAD A SECRET AUTOGRAPH THAT HAS BEEN A MYSTERY TO MANY

William Curtis, in his book, *The Authentic Letters of Columbus,* describes the confusion of historians regarding the interpretation of Columbus' cryptic autograph: "The signature or rubric of Columbus which appears at the close of all his communications, as the sign of the cross appears at the beginning, has never been satisfactorily interpreted. It was the custom in his time for men of importance to adopt sign manuals of a peculiar sort, as they adopted mottoes for their escutcheons, which had some apparent or concealed significance."[11]

MORISON'S SPECULATION—"THE EXACT MEANING WAS A SECRET THAT COLUMBUS TOOK TO HIS GRAVE"

Samuel Morison, in his book, *Christopher Columbus, Admiral of the Ocean Sea*, was also mystified about the meaning of Columbus' autograph and relates that it "was a secret that Columbus took to his

---

[8]Arnold Fine, "Why Should Catholic Church Honor Queen Isabella?" *Jerusalem Times/Jewish Press,* Fri., Jan. 18, 1991, p. 36, © used by permission.

[9]Radio broadcast, Jan. 1991. J.R. Church's material is available through his ministry, Southwest Radio Church, POB 1144, Oklahoma City, OK, USA 73101. Tel. (800) 475-1111.

[10]John Hagee, *Why We Honor the Jews.*

[11]William Eleroy Curtis, *The Authentic Letters of Columbus*, Vol. 1, No. 2. Chicago: Field Columbian Museum Publication 2, 1895, p. 117.

grave." But was it really? In a moment, we will ask Maurice David! Morison tells us: "...these signatures of Columbus have been preserved, each with the pyramid of letters arranged in exactly the same way....Columbus attached great significance to it, and in his *mayorazgo* or entail instructed his heirs to continue to 'sign with my signature which I now employ....'...he never revealed the meaning, which has aroused endless speculation. The problem has particularly interested those endeavoring to prove that Columbus was a Jew....Speculate as we may, it is unlikely that any certain solution of the cipher will be found; the exact meaning was a secret that Columbus took to his grave."[12]

DAVID'S DISCOVERY—COLUMBUS' MYSTERY DECODED

I believe Maurice David, in his book, *Who Was "Columbus"?*, has unraveled the mystery of Columbus' autograph. He says: "...the mystic signature in the shape of a triangle, considered by Colón as his own family emblem, is nothing less than an abbreviation of the 'last confession' of the Jews and also a substitute for the Kaddish—in lieu of the real Kaddish, which was interdicted.

The abbreviation in this case should read:

. S .	**ש.**
. S . A . S .	**ש.א.ש.**
. X . M . Y .	**י. מ. ח.**
X . p . o . ferens	**נושא. ע. פ. ח.**

In Hebrew:

Shadai, Shadai	**ש ד י**
Adonoy Shadai	**שדי אדני שדי**
Yehova molai chesed	**יהוה מלא חסד**
Nauthai ovon, pesha, chatuo	**נשא עון פשע חטאה"[13]**

In a recent article entitled, "Was the Discoverer of America Jewish?", by Newton Frohlich, it was noted: "...the letters stand for a Latinized Hebrew prayer: *Sanctus. Sanctus, Adonai, Sanctus. Chesed Moleh Yehovah* (God. God, Lord, God. Lord grant mercy). The last

---

[12]Samuel Eliot Morison, *Christopher Columbus, Admiral of the Ocean Sea.* London: Oxford University Press, © 1939, pp. 356-357, used by permission.

[13]Maurice David, *Who Was "Columbus"?* New York: The Research Publishing Co., © 1933, p. 103, used by permission.

two lines are said to be Columbus' signature: *Xpo FERENS* has been translated as a Greco-Latin form of his name and *El Almirante* means 'the admiral.' "[14]

THE TELLTALE EMBLEM ON COLUMBUS' LETTERS "BH"—AN ANCIENT HEBREW INSCRIPTION OF GREETING

Maurice David and Mosco Galimir also reveal the comparatively unknown meaning of another insignia Columbus inscribed at the beginning of his letters to family members. David writes: "*On all of these thirteen intimate letters but one, the attentive reader can plainly see at the left top corner a little monogram which may seem cryptic to him, but which is, in fact, nothing more nor less than an old Hebrew greeting or benediction, frequently used among religious Jews all over the world even to this day.*

This monogram, consisting of two characters, 'beth,' and 'hai,' the second and fifth letter of the Hebrew alphabet—written from right to left, like all Semitic script—is an abbreviation of the Hebrew words, 'Boruch hashem' (Praised be the Lord)....I have stated that the Hebrew monogram appears on all, but one, of the thirteen letters from Columbus to his son. Its omission from that one is probably **more revealing** than its appearance on the others. Because this particular letter begins with the traditional; 'Muy caro fijo' (My dear son), but its contents show that it was intended to reach the eyes of Queen Isabelle. Colón therein advises his son that he is sending him by special messenger two bags of large gold nuggets, the first found in India by the Spanish explorers, and directs him to hand them over to the Queen together with the letter, adding: 'To you, I am writing another long letter, which will leave here tomorrow.' "[15]

Mosco Galimir also enlightens us: "The famous Admiral took special care to leave in obscurity and mystery his origin, ancestry and place of birth....In his thirteen letters to his son, he puts a small monogram at the upper left hand side of the paper, an old sephardic greeting, beginning with the Hebrew letters 'B H'...."[16]

***

---

[14]Newton Frohlich, "Was the Discoverer of America Jewish?", *Moment*, Dec. 1991, p. 43, used by permission.

[15]Ibid, p. 66. Bold mine.

[16]Mosco Galimir, *Cristobal Colón, The Discoverer of America.* New York: Galimir, 1950, pp. 21, 23.

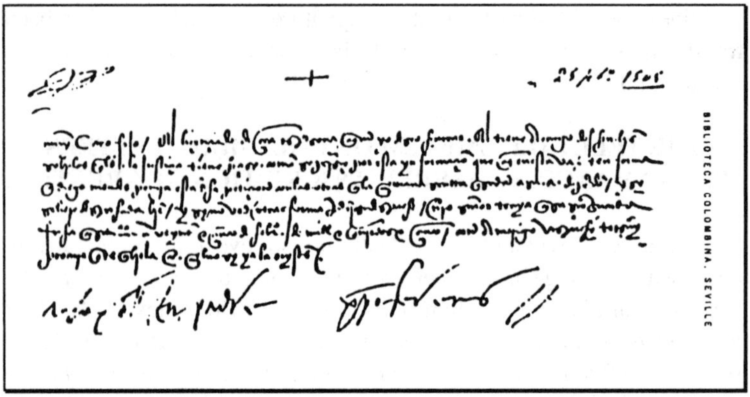

Notice the "bh" (ב״ה) in the upper-left corner, in Columbus' hand.

COLUMBUS CONCEALS THE "BH" FROM ISABELLA TO AVOID PERSECUTION BECAUSE OF HIS FAITH

I believe Columbus omitted this Hebrew monogram from the letter to be read by Queen Isabella because she was ruthlessly ordering Jews and Moors to be burned.[17] He also knew that Jews bearing the surnames Colón[18] and Colom, the two names he had used, were being condemned.[19] We believe Columbus kept his origin and identity a secret because **he was both a true believer in Jesus and a Jew!!**

Columbus obviously kept his (born-again) faith a secret from the Catholics, just as he kept his Jewish ancestry concealed, both of which remain a historical secret even today! But, for those of you who are brave and inquisitive enough to read between the lines, you will see for yourself the obvious fact—his words are unmistakenly those of one who has a personal relationship with and trust in God, as defined by modern evangelical standards.

---

[17]Dr. Meir Kayserling, *Christopher Columbus and The Participation of the Jews in the Spanish and Portugese Discoveries*. New York: Hermon Press, © 1968, p. 122. Available through Stephen Hermon Press, 1265 46th Street, Brooklyn, NY, USA 11219. Tel. (718) 972-9010.

[18]Mosco Galimir writes: "In Tortosa, Salonica and Amsterdam, the name of Colón is found; all bearers of this name are Sephardic Jews." Galimar continues: "Colombo is a Spanish name. The change of name was a custom amongst Jews. Palumbus, Palombo, Columbus, Colombo. Thus the evolution to Colombo, Colón. The Colombos were Jews from Catalonia. Colón is a common Jewish name found on the Mayorcas." Mosco Galimir, *Cristobal Colón, Discoverer of America*, pp. 29-30.

[19]He gives Columbus' answer to Antonio about his *final* name change: "I belong to the family of the Counts of Colombo....It is to distinguish myself from other members of my family, that I call myself Columbus." Ibid, p. 33.

COLUMBUS' FAITH ILLUSTRATED IN HIS USE OF THE BIBLE VS. REASON AND SCIENCE TO LOCATE THE INDIES

The well-documented volumes, *The Prophetic Faith of our Fathers,* record the following facts, events and words of Christopher Columbus: "CHOSEN TO PROCLAIM GOD'S NAME IN NEW WORLD—Columbus was a voluminous writer, and kept a minute diary of his voyages. These writings reflect a deep religious spirit. There is frequent citation of Scripture concerning Biblical characters and episodes. Columbus found land 'with the aid of the Lord.' He took possession of San Salvador, the first land of the Western Hemisphere that he sighted, in these words: 'O Lord, Eternal and Almighty God, by thy sacred word thou hast created the heavens, the earth and the sea; blessed and glorified be thy name, and praised be thy Majesty, who hath designed to use thy humble servant to make thy sacred name known and proclaimed in this other part of the world'....The story is told that even before his voyages, while he lay ill near Belem, Portugal, an unknown voice whispered to him in a dream, 'God will cause thy name to be wonderfully resounded through the earth, and will give thee the keys of the gates of the ocean, which are closed with strong chains!'....**Columbus expressly declares** that the discovery of the New World was not prompted by speculation, mathematics, or mere navigation, but by the compulsive conviction **that all the divinely inspired prophecies of Scripture must be fulfilled before the approaching end** of the world,[20] including the proclamation of the gospel to the ends of the earth. No trial or disappointment could turn him from his purpose....In September, 1501, Columbus began the preparation of his *Libro de las Profecías* (Book of the Prophecies)....He [in this work] continually invokes the Bible and the prophets, claiming to owe all he knew and all he had accomplished to the leading of God. He also quotes ecclesiastical writers, Christian and Jewish.

Columbus affirms the world must have an end, and a second advent of Christ, and that the Lord gave an account of the signs preceding it, which are mentioned in the Gospels....*Libro de las Profecías* contains a letter...a remarkable report, which reads like a theological treatise. 'At this time I both read and studied all kinds of literature: cosmography, histories, chronicles, and philosophy and other arts, to which our Lord opened my mind unmistakably to the fact that it was possible to navigate from here to the Indies, and He evoked

---

[20]For Columbus' exact words, see our caption at the opening of our chapter 28, "The Second Coming Event—Will He Yet Be Sent."

in me the will for the execution of it....All those who heard of my plan disregarded it mockingly and with laughter. All the sciences of which I spoke were of no profit to me nor the authorities in them....Who would doubt that this light did not come from the Holy Spirit, anyway as far as I am concerned, which comforted with rays of marvelous clarity and with its Holy and Sacred Scriptures....'...In this letter Columbus presses the providential guidance of his Western discoveries as a miracle intended to encourage the undertaking of the **restoration of Jerusalem**....'...I have already said that in order to execute the enterprise of the Indies neither reason, nor mathematics, nor maps profited me; what Isaiah said was fully realized, and this is that which I wish to write here in order to bring to the mind of Your Highnesses, and in order that you rejoice of the other, which I shall tell you about Jerusalem through the same authorities, about whose enterprise, if there is any faith, hold victory for more than certain.' "[21] Mosco Galimir raises the question: "Was not his heart beating for his lost fatherland, Palestine?"[22]

COLUMBUS' TRUE FAITH AND ANCESTRY REVEALED, FROM HIS HIDDEN NAME AND A BOOK HE TREASURED

We believe Columbus kept his true faith and Jewishness discreet, because in those days the Catholic Church used torture and inquisition to persecute people for their beliefs and heritage. Remember the newspaper articles quoted by McEntire which said: "...that it wasn't very safe in those days in Spain to call yourself a Jew, and Columbus knew that, and called himself 'a Genoese navigator'...."[23]

We believe the words recorded in his diary, book of prophecies and other writings are the utterances of a true New Testament Bible believer rather than the thoughts of a ceremonial Roman Catholic. We believe Columbus was both a Jew and true believer in Jesus. That is

---

[21]Leroy Edwin Froom, *The Prophetic Faith of our Fathers,* Vol. I. Washington, D.C.: Review and Herald, © 1948, pp. 167-171, 173, used by permission. [ ] mine.

[22]Mosco Galimir, *Cristobal Colón, Discoverer of America*, p. 53.

[23]Mosco Galimir asked: "Was Cristobal Colón secretive about his past and origin out of fear of being spied upon by the inglorious Inquisition?" Ibid, p. 37. And W. F. McEntire notes that Mier Kayserling asked: " '...What must have been the feelings of Christopher Columbus, or Colón, when he heard that members of the Jewish race bore his name, and had been condemned by the Inquisition?' [McEntire says that] The connection of Cristóbal Colón with the Jewish family of Colom is not apparent until in a footnote to the above paragraph we find that 'he was also called Colo*m*.' " Walter F. McEntire, *Was Christopher Columbus a Jew*, p. 77. [ ] mine. McEntire continues: "In Spain the Christoforo Colombo of Genoa chose to call himself Cristóval Colón, and the *Historie* tells us that he sought merely to make his descendants distinct of name from their remote kin." Ibid, pp. 77-78.

why he kept his origin and identity a secret, while he treasured to the end of his days a book which proved Jesus to be the Jewish Messiah of the Old Testament. Walter McEntire shares some interesting details regarding this highly prized and beloved book of Christopher Columbus: "What may be another bit of evidence aiding us in our effort, is the record that Columbus prized most highly a book written by a Marano—not a 'forced convert Jew,' but a freely baptized earnest 'convert Christian.' Of this book a Jewish historian writes: 'In Spain, he (Columbus) read with religious zeal the tract on the Messiah, which was written by the proselyte Samuel Ibn Abbas of Morocco, for the purpose of converting R. Isaac of Sujurmente; it had been translated into Spanish in 1339, and into Latin a hundred years later. This book interested Columbus so much that he excerpted three whole chapters.' (Kayserling.) Think of the zeal of a 'convert Jew' who would write an erudite and scholarly treatise on the Messiah, for the purpose, and only purpose, of 'converting' another Jew."[24]

This brings to light two important revelations about Columbus: 1. If he were not a Jew, why would he be so fascinated in seeing Jesus from the perspective of the proofs in the Old Testament prophecies? 2. If he were only a Marano (who may not have believed in Jesus), why would he care? The book would have been of little interest to him! The same reasoning follows if he were merely a ceremonial Roman Catholic. His love and prized value of this book shows he had a deep spiritual evangelical faith and interest in Jesus from a Jewish perspective. It was something only a Jew who truly believed in Jesus—a true believer—could sincerely appreciate.

CHRISTOPHER COLUMBUS, BELIEVE IT OR NOT, WAS A MESSIANIC JEW

If it were the case that Columbus was a true believer in Jesus and a Jew, modern Messianic Jews can claim one of the most famous discoveries of all time. This illustrates more than ever the legitimacy of the Jewish movement for Jesus! Columbus' dying words were: "Into Thy hands, Oh, Lord, I commit my spirit."[25] These were the same words uttered by Jesus while He was on the cross. Walter McEntire comments beautifully: "...**Columbus was deeply interested in the prophecies**. To him they had a special meaning; and he frequently meditated upon them....[He points out that] A Jewish

---

[24]Ibid, p. 66.

[25]*Commemoration of the Fourth Centenary of the Discovery of America.* From the Report of the Madrid Commission, 1892. Washington: Government Printing Office, 1895, p. 266.

historian writes: 'Some of his biographers have seen in his career not the triumph of science but that of religion; and a learned Spaniard[26] has in all seriousness asserted that without his strong religious faith Columbus would never have discovered America' (Kayserling).

Columbus' career *was* the triumph of religion; and without the faith he possessed he never could have accomplished the wonderful work he wrought: that millions of the suffering sons of man might be made peaceful and happy in the world he found and gave them."[27]

We will close this chapter with the dazzling words of Mosco Galimir. He writes: "And so should the life of Colón and his ancestors be pieced together, piece by piece, with patience and reverence, aided by the yet unseen documents kept probably in the archives of the Inquisition period, mostly in Madrid. One day, when all the data are assembled, the truth[28] will come to light."[29]

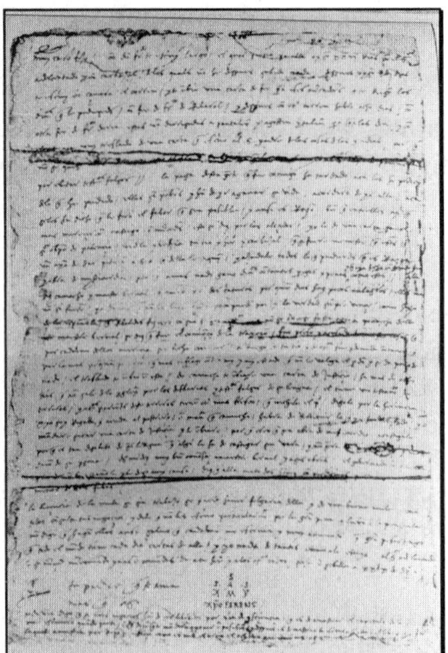

[26]This biographer was S. de la Rósa y López, *El Libros y Autografos de D. Chr. Colón*, Seville, 1891.

[27]Walter F. McEntire, *Was Christopher Columbus a Jew*, pp. 142-144. [ ] mine.

[28]As of the 1990's the truth is still kept tightly under wraps by the Vatican. In an article entitled, "Was the Discoverer of America Jewish?", by Newton Frohlich, it was noted: "In Simon Wiesenthal's study of Columbus, *Sails of Hope* (Macmillan, 1973)....He writes, 'When I inquired in Rome I was informed that the Vatican's documents on Columbus are not accessible.' He then adds, 'Can other reasons have decisively affected the Vatican's decisions, reasons based on documents being withheld from scholars....If some day the secret archives of the Vatican are opened...new facts may be brought to light.' It would be ironic, indeed, if Columbus were a Jew...." Newton Frohlich, "Was the Discoverer of America Jewish?", *Moment*, Dec. 1991, p. 42.

[29]Mosco Galimir, *Cristobal Colón, Discoverer of America*, p. 55.

"I felt very special when I looked down at my footprints on the moon. The scientists said that they would be there for a million years. Looking up I could see the earth the size of a marble. It was so beautiful and so far away, and yet, I felt strangely at home on the moon....The days I spent on the moon were very exciting. Not because I was there but because God was there. I could feel His presence....When I was on the moon, I was inspired to quote from Psalm 121, 'I will lift up mine eyes unto the hills, from whence cometh my help?' I knew my help was coming from the Lord who made the heavens and the earth. He made the moon and made it possible for Jim Irwin to place his footprints there....I believe Jesus Christ walking on the earth is more important than man walking on the moon. Just as surely as He walked 2000 years ago, He wants to walk today in your life. All you have to do is call upon Him....invite Him into your life by faith. Jesus said, 'I am the way, the truth and the life. No man cometh unto the Father but by me.' John 14:6....yield your life to the Master and let Him guide your footprints."[1]

James B. Irwin, Apollo 15 astronaut

17

A MOON-WALKING ASTRONAUT GIVES HIS TESTIMONY IN ISRAEL

James B. Irwin, the famous astronaut, was also a devout believer. The photograph shown here is a personal gift which Jim gave to me in Jerusalem in 1984.

---

[1]James B. Irwin, "Footprints on the Moon." This pamplet is available through High Flight Ministries, POB 1387, Colorado Springs, CO, USA 80901. This is Irwin's personal testimony from a tract which he gave to me in June of 1984 during a visit to Jerusalem. He also told us these very same words in his sermon at the Scottish Chapel near the railroad station in Jerusalem.

When I mentioned to Jim that his mother looked Jewish, he told me that he always felt he was part Jewish. If it is true that Jim's mother may have been of Jewish ancestry and that Jewish blood coursed in his veins, we can be doubly proud that, in a sense, a Messianic Jew for Jesus walked on the moon!

Those who speak against Messianic Jews should reconsider. Columbus was a Messianic Jew and discovered America, while Jim may have been, and helped us discover some of the moon's most closely guarded secrets.[2] Truly, the greatest discoverer is Jesus,[3] whom they both knew. We suggest you read Jim's personal account of his moon voyage in his book *To Rule The Night, The Discovery Voyage of Astronaut Jim Irwin*, available through High Flight Ministries. In his book, he tells of his ups and downs, his young life, and how he became a believer in Jesus through the Southern Baptist Church. In addition, he details every step of his 1971 trip to the moon.

In 1972, Jim presented Israeli Prime Minister Golda Meir with an Israeli flag which had been to the moon with him.

---

[2]Read about the white Genesis rock Jim found on the moon on p. 77 of his book, *To Rule the Night, The Discovery Voyage of Astronaut Jim Irwin.*.

[3]Jesus discovers our hearts when we invite Him in—He becomes a part of our lives and truly knows us!

Jim also wrote *Destination Moon*[4] (1989), a picture book. In another book, *More than an Ark on Ararat* (1985), he shared the adventures he had when climbing Mount Ararat in Turkey, which is where the Bible says Noah's Ark finally came to rest. Jim nearly died from a fall during his search for the Ark. His more recent planned expedition was postponed by Saddam Hussein's Gulf War. Jim went home to be with the Lord in August of 1991. His memory will be with us always until we see him again in God's soon-coming kingdom.

[4]Available through Multnomah School of the Bible, 8435 N.E. Glisan Street, Portland, OR, USA 97220, and; High Flight Ministries. He is also the author of *More than Earthlings*, Broadman Press, © 1983.

U.S. postage stamps commemorating the exploration of the moon.

INTERESTING INSIGHT FROM *TO RULE THE NIGHT*

Some of the more interesting comments Jim included in his book, *To Rule the Night*, were: "When you lean far back and look up, you can see the earth like a beautiful, fragile Christmas tree ornament hanging against the blackness of space, It's as if you could reach out and hold it in your hand. That's a feeling, a perception, I had never anticipated. And I don't think it's blasphemous for me to say I felt I was seeing the earth with the eyes of God. I believe, looking back on it now, the good Lord did have His hand in it. For me to travel such a roundabout way, and finally end up in the space program, and then go to the moon—it's amazing it ever happened....the beauty of the mountains of the moon had moved me, and that I had felt the presence of God....The moon has a powerful force; it seems to affect the feelings and the behavior of everybody. I cannot imagine a holier place.

I think of it as a very friendly place, too. When I am flying across the Rockies in a light plane and the moon rises in front of me, I look at it with fond attachment. There is the place I spent my vacation that summer of 1971: my favorite resort....It seems plain to me that the hand of God has been in my life as far back as I am able to remember. I think Providence has been a factor in every important thing that has ever happened to me. As strange as it sounds, my flight on Apollo 15 was the fulfillment of a dream I had all my life. I have talked of wanting to go to the moon since I was a young kid. My mother says that she remembers this, and some old neighbors of ours whom she talked to recently also remembered that when I was a little boy I used to point up to the moon and say, 'I'm going to go up there some day.' " This actually happened to Jim over thirty years later—the most relaxed moment of his voyage, just before he was to leave. Jim continues: "August the second, 1971....I started running around the Lunar Module in circles, and I did some broad jumping. Just having a ball—you know, like a little kid. Even in the space suit, I could broad jump about ten feet, about three or four feet in the air. No telling how far I could have jumped if I hadn't had that suit on. It was the most relaxed time I had on the surface.

Houston was urging us to get into the Lunar Module. It was time to come home. 'Move the baggage into the *Falcon* and climb in.' CapCom got a bit lyrical. 'As the space poet Rhysling would say, we're ready for you to come again to the homes of men on the cool green hills of Earth'....A combination of factors had led to my decision to become a Southern Baptist and join the Nassau Bay church. One, of course, was Bill Rittenhouse....In the spring of 1971, I had taken the family with me on a trip to Florida. We drove through the little town of New Port Richey, where I had lived years ago, and we saw the little church where, as a youngster, I had stepped forward to accept Christ....I appreciated their looking after me, and I knew they were Southern Baptists, actually members of the Nassau Bay Baptist Church....One Sunday morning I told the children that I was going to make a decision for Christ and asked if any of them wanted to go with me. Jill, my second daughter, was the only one. At the end of the morning service, when Brother Rittenhouse invited us to make a decision for Christ or to rededicate our lives, Jill and I stepped forward. Jill accepted Jesus Christ as her personal Lord and Savior, and I rededicated my life to Christ. We both decided that we wouldn't be baptized until I got back from the flight.

I feel now that the power of God was working in me the whole time I was on the flight. I felt His presence on the moon in the most immediate and overwhelming way. There I was, a test pilot, a nuts-and-bolts type who had gotten rather skeptical about God, and suddenly I was asking God to solve my problems on the moon. I was relying on God rather than on Houston."[5]

[5]James B. Irwin with William A. Emerson, Jr., *To Rule the Night, The Discovery Voyage of Astronaut Jim Irwin.* Nashville, TN: Holman Bible Publishers, © 1982, pp. 11, 21-23, 85-86, 122-124, used by permission. [ ] mine.

UNITED
STATES

Jim Irwin and moon photos, with exception to
the Golda Meir photo, courtesy of NASA.

In the following chapters 18-22, we address several spheres of power; those who will interact with one another in the scenario which the Bible predicted for the last days. These spheres include: Israel, Russia, the Arab nations, China and revived Rome.

"...And in a word it was the ignorance of the Jews in these Prophesies which caused them to reject their Messiah and by consequence to be...captivated by the Romans...."[1] "The Jews will return to Jerusalem in the 20th century."[2]

Sir Isaac Newton, 1600's

"Israel's regathering to its land is the trumpet of the Messiah that is blasting out over the earth. Already we hear the footsteps of the Messiah in the corridors."[3]

Israel's first Prime Minister, David Ben-Gurion, 1973

"Everywhere you turn in Israel today the Bible is coming to life. I'm not talking only about archeological discoveries, but about the international political scene as it affects us today. If you read the Biblical prophecies about Armageddon and the end days, and you look at the current realities in the world and especially the Middle East, things certainly begin to look familiar. 'The vast number of archaeological discoveries in Israel have all tended to vindicate the pictures that are presented in the Bible. If therefore the Bible has been proven true concerning the past, we cannot look lightly at any prognostication it makes about the future.' "[4]

Israeli Major General, Chaim Herzog, 1977

"I have the survivability of a super power."[5] Israeli General, Ariel Sharon, 1987

"We [Israel] will have a war with Russia because Ezekiel 38 and 39 predicts it."[6]

Israeli President, Yitzhak Navon, 1993

18

ISRAEL—IS REAL

God told Abraham, nearly 4000 years ago: "...I will make of thee a great nation, and I will bless thee, and make thy name great; and thou shalt be a blessing: And I will bless them that bless thee, and curse him that curseth thee: and in thee shall all families of the earth be blessed....in thy seed shall all the nations of the earth be blessed; because thou hast obeyed my voice" (Gen. 12:2-3; 22:18 KJV).

---

[1] *Yahuda Manuscript 1.*

[2] Ruvic Rosenthal, "The Ostracized Newton," *Al Hamishmar*, July 26, 1985, p. 10.

[3] Birgitta Yavari, *Min Messias*. Jerusalem: Rahm & Stenström Interpublishing, © 1979, p. 10, used by permission. Ben-Gurion quite accurately identifies this generation as the one which will see the Messiah come. Israel was established in 1948 and Genesis 15 indicates a maximum generation is approximately one hundred years.

[4] Hal Lindsey, *The 1980's: Countdown to Armageddon*. New York: Bantam Books, Inc., © 1980 The Aorist Corporation, Inc., p. 35, used by permission.

[5] Morris Cerillo, "Evangelical Newsletter," 1987.

[6] *Perhaps Today*, May/June 1993, p. 7. [ ] mine.

Few realize that Sir Isaac Newton, known today as the greatest scientist to ever live, was also a prophetical *Bible commentator*. In our opinion, he is unsurpassed in history. He foresaw Israel's return.[7]

[7]Our design consists of a portrait of Sir Isaac Newton and a modern satellite photo of Israel and the ancient Sinai.

The promise meant that one day all the world will return to the God of Israel from the pagan and atheistic culture that had developed in the 2000 years between Adam's creation and Abraham's time. This plan included the very redemption of man from the Fall, described in the Torah book of Genesis, and the creation of the "New World," commonly referred to in Hebrew tradition as the *olam haba*, which will even surpass that of the Garden of Eden before the Fall.

It was the Messiah who would come out of this nation, Israel, and be a blessing to all the world. The Messiah, as we read in a previous chapter, had two clearly predicted roles: one of suffering servant and one of kingly redemption. When He came at the exact time that Daniel said He would, He was rejected, as predicted in Isaiah 53, ushering in this suffering role. Because of the rejection, His earthly kingdom was postponed 2000 years (Hos. 5:15-6:2).

These Messianic events had profound implications for the dispersion and return of Israel. Moses had already outlined the two dispersions, and Jesus pinpointed the time of the second one.

THE FIRST JEWISH DISPERSION (AND RETURN), FORETOLD IN ITS SEVERITY AND LENGTH BY ISAIAH, JEREMIAH AND MOSES HIMSELF

Moses predicted in his fifth book, Deuteronomy: "The LORD shall bring a nation against thee from far, from the end of the earth, *as swift* as the eagle flieth; a nation whose tongue thou shalt not understand; A nation of fierce countenance, which shall not regard the person of the old, nor shew favour to the young...." (Deut. 28:49-50 KJV).

This occurred when the Babylonians overran Jerusalem and carried its inhabitants to Babylon in the year 606 BC. This was predicted by the prophet Isaiah: "Behold, the days come, that all that *is* in thine house, and *that* which thy fathers have laid up in store until this day, shall be carried to Babylon: nothing shall be left, saith the LORD" (Isa. 39:6 KJV).

Jeremiah the prophet indicated that the captivity would last for seventy years. "And this whole land shall be a desolation, *and* an astonishment; and these nations shall serve the king of Babylon seventy years" (Jer. 25:11 KJV).

Of course, every detail occurred precisely as predicted. The Jews were invaded by Babylon and there they remained captive exactly seventy years (II Chr. 36:15-21). At the end of the Babylonian captivity, the Jews were permitted to return to their land (II Chr. 36:23) by King Cyrus! If you check Isaiah 44:28-45:4, you may be amazed to see that this king was predicted by his very name two hundred years before his birth: "That saith of **Cyrus**, *He is* my shepherd, and shall perform all my pleasure: even saying to Jerusalem, Thou shalt be built; and to the temple, Thy foundation shall be laid....For Jacob my servant's sake, and Israel mine elect, I have even called thee by thy name: I have surnamed thee, though thou hast not known me" (KJV; bold mine).

MOSES FORETOLD THE SECOND DISPERSION (70 AD), GIVING ISRAEL'S DISOBEDIENCE AS THE REASON FOR GOD'S DISCIPLINE

Moses, nearly four thousand years ago, in his famous discourse in Deuteronomy, went on to warn the Jewish people that a second dispersion would occur. However, unlike Babylon's, which was local, it would be a worldwide event in which the sons and daughters of Israel would be *scattered into all nations* (Deut. 28:64). This of course, would occur because of Israel's disobedience. Moses wrote: "Moreover all these curses shall come upon thee, and shall pursue thee, and overtake thee...because thou hearkenedst not unto the voice of the LORD thy God, to keep his commandments and his statutes which he commanded thee...." (Deut. 28:45 KJV).

Chief among these statutes was the **acceptance** of the Messiah, mentioned in Deuteronomy 15:18; thus when Israel rejected her Messiah (Jesus), this predicted worldwide dispersion became a historical reality! Moses continued: "And the LORD shall scatter thee among all people, from the one end of the earth even unto the other....And among these nations shalt thou find no ease, neither shall the sole of thy foot have rest: but the LORD shall give thee there a trembling heart, and failing of eyes, and sorrow of mind: And thy life shall hang in doubt before thee; and thou shalt fear day and night, and shalt have none assurance of thy life: In the morning thou shalt say, Would God it were even! and at even thou shalt say, Would God it were morning!....And the LORD shall bring thee into Egypt...and there ye shall be sold unto your enemies for bondmen and bondwomen, and no man shall buy *you*" (Deut. 28:64-68 KJV).

***

Nazis hold Jews at gunpoint during the Holocaust.

This illustration, published before the rebirth of Israel in 1948, represents 2000 years of Jewish persecution.

JESUS, THE GREATEST PROPHET, PINPOINTED THE SECOND JEWISH DISPERSION TO HIS VERY OWN GENERATION, THIRTY-SEVEN YEARS BEFORE THE FACT

Jesus pinpointed the time of the second dispersion, of which Moses warned, in His discourse in the Gospel of Luke shortly before He was arrested and crucified. Jesus, the greatest of the Hebrew prophets (being the Messiah), foretold: " But woe unto them that are with child, and to them that give suck, in those days! for there shall be great distress in the land, and wrath upon this people. And they shall fall by the edge of the sword, and shall be led away captive into all nations: and Jerusalem shall be trodden down of the Gentiles, until the times of the Gentiles be fulfilled" (Luke 21:23-24 KJV).

Jesus also remarked that it would be His generation that would see this dispersion: "Verily I say unto you, All these things shall come upon **this** generation" (Matt. 23:36 KJV).

JESUS WANTED TO SAVE THE FIRST CENTURY JEWISH NATION—WITH TEARS IN HIS EYES HE PREDICTED HER FATE, EXPLAINING WHY

Jesus also implied that, had He been received, He would have remained and saved Israel under His wings. He said these words with tears in His eyes: "...'If thou hadst known, even thou, at least in this thy day, the things *which belong* unto thy peace! but now they are hid from thine eyes. For the days shall come upon thee, that thine enemies shall cast a trench about thee, and compass thee round, and keep thee in on every side, And shall lay thee even with the ground, and thy children within thee; and they shall not leave in thee one stone upon another; because thou knewest not the time of thy visitation....O Jerusalem, Jerusalem, *thou* that killest the prophets, and stonest them which are sent unto thee, how often would I have gathered thy children together, even as a hen gathereth her chickens under *her* wings, and ye would not!' " (Luke 19:42-44; Matt. 23:37 KJV).

JESUS WOULD HAVE SAVED ISRAEL HAD THE RELIGIOUS LEADERS NOT MISLED THE PEOPLE REGARDING HIS IDENTITY AND ABILITY TO BRING PEACE

Because the religious leaders and political factions succeeded in convincing the majority of the people to continue to reject the Jewish Messiah instead of setting up a royal kingdom, Jesus, the *rejected* king, left the scene forty days after the resurrection and ascended into the clouds with the promise to return upon **acceptance**. What righteous king would force His kingdom? Some of Jesus' last words to the religious leaders who rejected Him were: "...how often would I have gathered thy children together, even as a hen gathereth her chickens under *her* wings, and ye would not! Behold, your house is left unto you desolate. For I say unto you, Ye shall not see me henceforth, till ye shall say, Blessed *is* he that cometh in the name of the Lord" (Matt. 23:37-39 KJV).

AFTER JESUS LEFT, HIS AND MOSES' PREDICTIONS OF DEFEAT, DISPERSION, SLAVERY AND WORTHLESSNESS BECAME REALITY

Luke's eyewitness testimony of the departure of Jesus included: "And He led them out as far as Bethany, and He lifted up His hands and blessed them. And it came about that while He was blessing them, He parted from them. And they returned to Jerusalem with great joy, and were continually in the temple, praising God" (Luke 24:50-53 NASB).

As history has recorded, less than forty years after these events, Titus and the Roman armies destroyed Jerusalem and dispersed her inhabitants into "all the earth." The Romans slaughtered hundreds of thousands by "the sword." Some survived, and were shipped to the slave markets in Egypt. When the supply of slaves there exceeded the demand, they "became worthless, even as lowly slaves." Moses' prediction said, as you recall: "And the LORD shall bring thee into Egypt **again** with ships...and there ye shall be sold unto your enemies for bondmen and bondwomen, and no man shall buy *you*" (Deut. 28:68 KJV).

THE PROPHET MOSES PREDICTED THE GREATEST OF ALL PROPHETS (JESUS), BUT BECAUSE HIS PEOPLE REFUSED TO "HEARKEN" AS MOSES FORESAW, MUCH TRAGEDY EXISTS TO THIS DAY!

No prophets have been more precise regarding the dispersion than Moses and Jesus. Remember, the Bible of the Jews predicted through Moses: "The LORD thy God will raise up unto thee a Prophet from the midst of thee, of thy brethren, like unto me; unto him ye shall hearken....And the LORD said....I will raise them up a Prophet from among their brethren, like unto thee, and will put my words in his mouth; and he shall speak unto them all that I shall command him. And it shall come to pass, *that* whosoever will not hearken unto my words which he shall speak in my name, I will require *it* of him" (Deut. 18:15, 17-19 KJV).

This was the Messiah Jesus, for He, like Moses, dealt with the true interpretation of the Jewish law (Matt. 5-7)![8] Because Israel's religious leaders did not hearken to this prophet's words spoken in God's name, remember Jesus said, "I am come in my Father's name, and ye receive me not...." (John 5:43 KJV). It truly was and still is being **required** of Israel, for there was a terrible dispersion, and anti-Semitism[9] continues to the present day!

An illustration of the destruction of Jerusalem and dispersion of Jews by the Romans under Titus (70 AD).

[8]The lives of Jesus and Moses were beautifully paralleled in events and meanings. For example: "Both were preserved in childhood, Ex. 2.2-10; Mt. 2.14,15. — Contended with masters of evil, Ex. 7.11; Mt. 4.1. — Fasted forty days, Ex. 34.28; Mt. 4.2. — Controlled the sea, Ex. 14.21; Mt. 8.26. — Fed a multitude, Ex. 16.15; Mt. 14.20, 21. — Had radiant faces, Ex. 34.35; Mt. 17.2. — Endured murmurings, Ex. 15.24; Mk. 7.2. — Discredited in the home, Nu. 12.1; Jn. 7.5. — Made intercessory prayers, Ex. 32.32; Jn. 17.9. — Spoke as oracles, De. 18.18. — Had seventy helpers, Nu. 11.16, 17; Lu. 10.1. — Established memorials, Ex. 12.14; Lu. 22.19. — Re-appeared after death, Mt. 17.3; Ac. 1.3." Frank Charles Thompson, D.D., Ph.D., "Condensed Cyclopedia of Topics and Texts," *Thompson Chain Reference Bible*. Indianapolis, IN: B.B. Kirkbride Bible Co., Inc., © 1964, p. 95.

[9]Our point is that had Jesus been accepted, He would have set up the kingdom, defeated Rome and created a world free of disease, hunger and war. As we will see in our chapters 29 and 30, He will soon. Had His nation accepted Him, He would have accomplished this in the first century and there would be no opportunity for anti-Semitism today. Jesus would not have allowed this. His reign, which will be free of anti-Semitism is still in our future, but moving ever closer! I believe we are within approximately thirty years of this date.

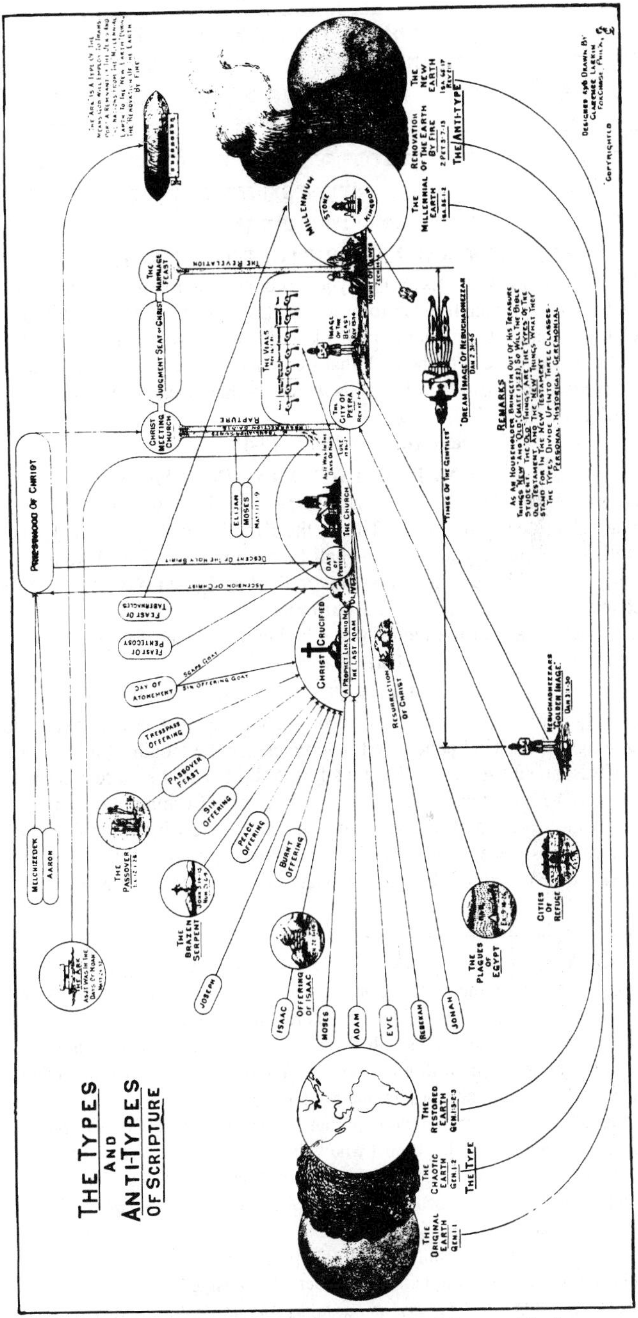

A chart by Reverend Clarence Larkin, entitled, "The Types and Anti-Types of Scripture."

ORIGINAL HEBREW TEXT WRITTEN 1451 BC

נָבִיא מִקִּרְבְּךָ מֵאַחֶיךָ כָּמֹנִי יָקִים לְךָ יְהוָה אֱלֹהֶיךָ אֵלָיו תִּשְׁמָעוּן: .... וַיֹּאמֶר יְהוָה אֵלָי
הֵיטִיבוּ אֲשֶׁר דִּבֵּרוּ: נָבִיא אָקִים לָהֶם מִקֶּרֶב אֲחֵיהֶם כָּמוֹךָ וְנָתַתִּי דְבָרַי בְּפִיו וְדִבֶּר
אֲלֵיהֶם אֵת כָּל־אֲשֶׁר אֲצַוֶּנּוּ: וְהָיָה הָאִישׁ אֲשֶׁר לֹא־יִשְׁמַע אֶל־דְּבָרַי אֲשֶׁר יְדַבֵּר בִּשְׁמִי
אָנֹכִי אֶדְרֹשׁ מֵעִמּוֹ: אַךְ הַנָּבִיא אֲשֶׁר יָזִיד לְדַבֵּר דָּבָר בִּשְׁמִי אֵת אֲשֶׁר לֹא־צִוִּיתִיו לְדַבֵּר
וַאֲשֶׁר יְדַבֵּר בְּשֵׁם אֱלֹהִים אֲחֵרִים וּמֵת הַנָּבִיא הַהוּא:

דברים יח:טו; יז-יט

OLD TESTAMENT SCRIPTURE TRANSLATION

"The LORD your God will raise up for you a prophet like me from among you, from your countrymen, you shall listen to him....the LORD said to me'....I will raise up a prophet from among their countrymen like you, and I will put My words in his mouth, and he shall speak to them all that I command him. And it shall come about that whoever will not listen to My words which he shall speak in My name, I Myself will **require** *it* of him.' "

Deuteronomy 18:15, 17-19 NASB

ANCIENT RABBINICAL COMMENTARY

"Behold, my servant, the Messiah, shall prosper; he shall be exalted, etc. 'Behold, my servant shall deal prudently.' This is the King Messiah. 'He shall be exalted and extolled, and be very high.' He shall be exalted more than Abraham; for of Him it is written, 'I have exalted my hand to the Lord' (Gen. XIV. 22). He shall be extolled more than **Moses**...."[10] **Yalkut in loco**

"Rabbi Berachia said in the name of Rabbi Levi: 'As the first redeemer, so the last....' "[11] **Ruth Rabba, sec. 5**

NEW TESTAMENT RECORDED 33 AD

"And now, brethren, I know that you acted in ignorance, just as your rulers did also. But the things which God announced beforehand by the mouth of all the prophets, that His Christ should suffer, He has thus fulfilled. Repent therefore and return, that your sins may be wiped away, in order that times of refreshing may come from the presence of the Lord; and that He may send Jesus, the Christ appointed for you, whom heaven must receive until *the* period of restoration of all things about which God spoke by the mouth of His holy prophets from ancient time. Moses said, 'THE

---

[10]Rev. B. Pick, Ph.D., *Old Testament Passages Messianically Applied by the Ancient Synagogue*, published in the compilation *Hebraica, A Quarterly Journal in the Interests of Semitic Study*, Vol. I, p. 268. Though this rabbinical commentary says the Messiah will be more extolled than Moses, which is a point in our favor, the learned scholar, Risto Santala, enlightens us with a Hebrew Targum on this very verse in Deuteronomy. He tells us: "The Targum attaches an interpretation to this verse which from the point of view of Christian theology is of great importance: 'The Lord your God will raise up from your midst a prophet by the Holy Spirit who will be like me', and, 'A prophet I will raise up from amongst your brethren, through the Holy Spirit.' " Santala's footnote to Holy Spirit reads: "In Hebrew, respectively, *be-Ruah qudsha* and *de-Ruah qudsha*." Risto Santala, *The Messiah in the Old Testament in the Light of Rabbinical Writings.* Jerusalem: Keren Ahvah Meshihit, © 1992, p. 58, used by permission. Available through Keren Ahvah Meshihit, POB 10382, Jerusalem, Israel.

[11]Rev. B. Pick, Ph.D., *Old Testament Passages Messianically Applied by the Ancient Synagogue*, published in the compilation *Hebraica, A Quarterly Journal in the Interests of Semitic Study*, Vol. II, p. 30. In this Midrash it is understood that the first redeemer is Moses and the second is the Messiah.

LORD GOD SHALL RAISE UP FOR YOU A PROPHET LIKE ME FROM YOUR BRETHREN; TO HIM YOU SHALL GIVE HEED in everything He says to you. And it shall be that every soul that does not heed that prophet shall be utterly destroyed from among the people.' And likewise, all the prophets who have spoken, from Samuel and *his* successors onward, also announced these days. It is you who are the sons of the prophets, and of the covenant which God made with your fathers, saying to Abraham, 'AND IN YOUR SEED ALL THE FAMILIES OF THE EARTH SHALL BE BLESSED.' "

Acts 3:17-25 NASB

"Now the Passover, the feast of the Jews, was at hand. Jesus therefore lifting up His eyes, and seeing that a great multitude was coming to Him, said to Philip, 'Where are we to buy bread, that these may eat?' And this He was saying to test him; for He Himself knew what He was intending to do. Philip answered Him, 'Two hundred denarii worth of bread is not sufficient for them, for everyone to receive a little.' One of His disciples, Andrew, Simon Peter's brother, said to Him, 'There is a lad here who has five barley loaves and two fish, but what are these for so many people?' Jesus said, 'Have the people sit down.' Now there was much grass in the place. So the men sat down, in number about five thousand. Jesus therefore took the loaves; and having given thanks, He distributed to those who were seated; likewise also of the fish as much as they wanted. And when they were filled, He said to His disciples, 'Gather up the leftover fragments that nothing may be lost.' And so they gathered them up, and filled twelve baskets with fragments from the five barley loaves, which were left over by those who had eaten. When therefore the people saw the sign which He had performed, they said, 'This is of a truth the **Prophet** who is to come into the world.' "

John 6:4-14 NASB

MODERN RABBINIC COMMENT/REFUTATION

"Furthermore there is no evidence that the original passage (Deuteronomy 18:18) speaks of the Messiah at all. The verse merely states that the future prophets of Israel in general would share Moses' saintly qualities."

***The Real Messiah*, by Rabbi Aryeh Kaplan, *et al*, p. 54; 1976**

AUTHOR'S COMMENT—EVANGELICAL CHRISTIAN POSITION

Rabbi Kaplan should have read his Midrashim and Targumim more carefully! It is an accepted fact within Judaism, and particularly in the rabbinic writings produced by the Jewish sages, that the Messiah would be extolled **more** than Moses!

Philip Moore

The land of the prophets is once again blooming,
as predicted by Ezekiel (chapter 37) nearly 3000 years ago.

"....the Apostles and those who in the first ages propagated the gospel urged chiefly these Prophesies and exhorted their hearers to search and see whether all things concerning our Saviour ought not to have been as they fell out. And in a word it was the ignorance of the Jews in these Prophesies which caused them to reject their Messiah and by consequence to be...captivated by the Romans....Luke 19. 42, 44."[12]
Sir Isaac Newton's comment on Jewish dispersion in 70 AD

For the next 1800 years, until 1948, the Jewish people wandered over the earth. They were people without a country, persecuted in every land through which they passed, just as Moses and Jesus had warned. Genuine Evangelical Christians were virtually the only ones who offered true love and shelter, as you previously read in our "Christian Zionist" and "Christian Heroes of the Holocaust" sections. Remember Moses' warning: "...thy life shall hang in doubt...." (Deut. 28:66); and Jesus' words: "...they shall fall by the edge of the sword, and shall be led away captive into all nations...." (Luke 21:24 KJV).

We see that Israel, her dispersions and judgments, have truly been a sign to all other nations, as Moses predicted. "And thou shalt become an astonishment, a proverb, and a byword, among all nations whither the LORD shall lead thee....And they shall be upon thee for a **sign** and for a wonder, and upon thy seed for ever" (Deut 28:37, 46).

Israel has indeed become a sign before the entire world because she was warned, did not heed that warning, and suffered the consequences, which fell exactly as foretold by the Bible. This shows all who read the Bible that God is not playing games. He is to be taken seriously and truly loves all of us who return. The same prophets who foretold the dispersion, including Jesus, also foretold the second ingathering of Israel to her land, which occurred in 1948, when Israel became a sovereign Jewish State.

12Frank E. Manuel, *The Religion of Isaac Newton*, pp. 108-109

This sign, which reads in Hebrew "Blessings to Those Coming to Jerusalem" (ברוכים הבאים לירושלים) lies at Jerusalem's entrance to welcome all who love her—we do!

ORIGINAL HEBREW TEXT WRITTEN 713, 587 BC

וְהָיָה ׀ בַּיּוֹם הַהוּא יוֹסִיף אֲדֹנָי ׀ שֵׁנִית יָדוֹ לִקְנוֹת אֶת־שְׁאָר עַמּוֹ אֲשֶׁר יִשָּׁאֵר מֵאַשּׁוּר
וּמִמִּצְרַיִם וּמִפַּתְרוֹס וּמִכּוּשׁ וּמֵעֵילָם וּמִשִּׁנְעָר וּמֵחֲמָת וּמֵאִיֵּי הַיָּם׃ וְנָשָׂא נֵס לַגּוֹיִם
וְאָסַף נִדְחֵי יִשְׂרָאֵל וּנְפֻצוֹת יְהוּדָה יְקַבֵּץ מֵאַרְבַּע כַּנְפוֹת הָאָרֶץ׃

ישעיה יא:יא-יב

וָאָפִיץ אֹתָם בַּגּוֹיִם וַיִּזָּרוּ בָּאֲרָצוֹת כְּדַרְכָּם וְכַעֲלִילוֹתָם שְׁפַטְתִּים׃ .... וְלָקַחְתִּי אֶתְכֶם
מִן־הַגּוֹיִם וְקִבַּצְתִּי אֶתְכֶם מִכָּל־הָאֲרָצוֹת וְהֵבֵאתִי אֶתְכֶם אֶל־אַדְמַתְכֶם׃

יחזקאל לו:יט-כד

OLD TESTAMENT SCRIPTURE TRANSLATION

"Then it will happen on that day that the Lord Will again recover the second time with His hand The remnant of His people, who will remain, From Assyria, Egypt, Pathros, Cush, Elam, Shinar, Hamath, And from the islands of the sea. And He will lift up a standard for the nations, And will assemble the banished ones of Israel, And will gather the dispersed of Judah From the four corners of the earth."

Isaiah 11:11-12 NASB

"Also I scattered them among the nations, and they were dispersed throughout the lands. According to their ways and their deeds I judged them....For I will take you from the nations, gather you from all the lands, and bring you into your own land."

Ezekiel 36:19, 24 NASB

ANCIENT RABBINICAL COMMENTARY

"When Moses our Master heard these words in the presence of Messiah ben David, he rejoiced with great joy, and turned back his face to the Holy One, blessed be He, and said to Him: 'Master of the World! When will this built-up Jerusalem descend?' The Holy One, blessed be He, said: 'I have not revealed the time to anybody, neither to the first ones nor to the last ones. How could I tell it to you?' Moses said to him: 'Master of the World! Give me a hint of the events!' The Holy One, blessed be He, said to him: 'I shall first scatter Israel with a winnowing fork in the gates of the earth, and they will be dispersed in the four corners of the world among all the nations....Then I shall stretch forth My hand a second time and shall gather....' "[13]

B'reshit Rabbati, pp. 136-37

"He who wrought miracles and portents in those days and at that time, may He work for us miracles and portents in these days and in this time, and gather us from the four winds of the world and lead us to Jerusalem, and make us rejoice in her, and let us say Amen, *Selah*!"[14]

Midrash waYosha', BhM 1:56-57

NEW TESTAMENT RECORDED 65, 37 AD

"...when they had come together, they were asking Him, saying, 'Lord, is it at this time You are restoring the kingdom to **Israel**?' He said to them, 'It is not for you to know....' "

Acts 1:6-7 NASB

"Now learn the parable from the fig tree: when its branch has already become tender, and puts forth its leaves, you know that summer is near; even so you too, when you see all these things, recognize that He is near, *right* at the door. Truly I say to you, this generation will not pass away until all these things take place."

Matthew 24:32-34 NASB

---

[13]Raphael Patai, *The Messiah Texts*, p. 228.

[14]Ibid, p. 218.

MODERN RABBINIC COMMENT/REFUTATION

"In 1862 Zevi Hirsch Kalischer, an Orthodox rabbi, wrote...redemption would come about through human initiative and natural causes rather than through God's intervention and miracles. He urged Jews to colonize Palestine...."

***What Christians Should Know About Jews and Judaism*, by Yechiel Eckstein, p. 218; © 1984**

"We consider ourselves no longer a nation, but a religious community, and therefore expect neither a return to Palestine, nor a sacrificial worship under the sons of Aaron, nor the restoration of any of the laws concerning the Jewish state."

"Pittsburgh Platform," *Encyclopaedia Judaica Jerusalem*, p. 1415; © 1885

ON THE SPOT EYEWITNESS REPORT, MAY 1948

"The first independent Jewish State in 19 centuries was born in Tel Aviv as the British Mandate over Palestine came to an end at midnight on Friday....As 'Medinat Yisrael' (State of Israel) was proclaimed, the battle for Jerusalem raged, with most of the city falling to the Jews."

***Palestine Post* (now the *Jerusalem Post*), Vol. XXIII, May 16, 1948**

MODERN FACTS HISTORICALLY RECORDED IN SECULAR NEWS

"With the war won, Israel soon became a sort of modern miracle....the nation sprang almost overnight from a picturesque wilderness to an enclave of clanging energy. Deepwater ports were dredged, power and irrigation plants built, modern cities and industries created. The desert bloomed, the orange trees blossomed, and Israel was suddenly the land of milk and honey. For 14 wondrous years, its gross national product soared by at least 10% a year, until by 1964 Israel had achieved a standard of living that rivaled Western Europe's."

"Israel: A Nation Under Siege," *Time*, p. 40, June 9, 1967

AUTHOR'S COMMENT—EVANGELICAL CHRISTIAN POSITION

There are many "Bible teachers" today who deny that the New Testament speaks of the rebirth of Israel, which occurred in 1948. The dominion theologists and liberals are a good example. Gary DeMar, in his book, *Last Days Madness*, claims that the New Testament is silent on the subject of Israel's rebirth, and that Ezekiel's prophecy refers to the first restoration from Babylon. Nothing could be further from the truth. This is expressed by Jesus' words when questioned on the subject of Israel by His apostles. Notice that He did not tell them, "You are wrong, Israel will not be restored." In answer to their question, He clearly told His disciples that they were not to know when it would occur. In retrospect, we see that though some rabbis of a hundred years ago denied Israel's miraculous rebirth, the secular news magazine, *Time,* described it as a "miracle." Interesting, isn't it? In addition, the prophetic Christian writer, Lance Lambert, noted in his book, *Israel: A Secret Documentary*: "An Israeli captain, again totally irreligious, said that at the height of the fighting on the Golan, he looked up into the sky and saw a great, gray hand pressing downwards, as if it were holding something back. In my opinion that was exactly what happened. Without the intervention of God, Israel would have been doomed. Shimon Peres, once a key adviser to Golda Meir and the present Minister of Defense, has said, 'The miracle is that we ever win. The Arab nations occupy eight percent of the surface of the world. They possess half the known oil resources and are immensely rich. They have more men in their armies than we have people in our state, and on top of the Arabs come the Russians, who have built for them a great war machine. On our side we have only America....[Lambert detailed of the

'73 war] Three days before the war began the Soviet Union launched two orbital Sputniks, which crossed Israel at the best time for aerial photography. Russia then relayed information to Syria and Egypt as to whether Israel was prepared....the war was originally planned for six o'clock in the evening of Yom Kippur, but was moved up to two o'clock. The Russians had passed on the information that preparations had begun on the Israeli side."[15] Hence, even though the enemy used the most modern, sophisticated, scientific technology of the time, Israel won as a result of her miracles. **Philip Moore**

THE BIBLE SAID THE WORLD WAS ROUND BEFORE SCIENCE FIGURED IT OUT MATHEMATICALLY

Remember the quote we used to illustrate Israel's rebirth, Isaiah 11:12, mentioned "four corners." Well, many philosophers have tried to use this to claim that the Bible said the world was flat instead of round. Hence, they maintain that the Bible is wrong and that there really is no God. I will never forget my high school English literature teacher, Mrs. Young, who always tried to pound this idea into my head.

The Scripture uses figurative language to describe the future of God's regathering of Jews from all areas of the earth. Thus, Isaiah says "corners." Since the voyage of Christopher Columbus,[16] Bible critics have used this verse from the Bible to try to convince the world that the Bible is in error (I Tim. 6:20-21)[17] because it states the world is flat. Thus, it is not a reliable document in which to place one's faith.

Let it be known, from now on, that the Bible taught the world was spherical and suspended in space long before Columbus took his first breath or the advent of modern science, which made it possible to photograph the earth from the moon. The oldest book of the Bible, Job, written over 3500 years ago, says: "He stretcheth out the north over the empty place, *and* hangeth the earth upon nothing" (Job 26:7 KJV). Isaiah, writing over 2600 years ago, added: "...have ye not understood from the foundations of the earth? *It is* he that sitteth upon the circle of the earth, and the inhabitants thereof *are* as grasshoppers; that stretcheth out the heavens as a curtain, and spreadeth them out as a tent to dwell in...." (Isa. 40:21-22 KJV).

---

[15]Lance Lambert, *Israel: A Secret Documentary.* Wheaton, IL: Tyndale House Publishers, Inc., © 1975, pp. 15-17, used by permission.

[16]Columbus was a Jewish-Christian, as you can see from the evidence in our chapter 16, "Was Christopher Columbus a Messianic Jew?"

[17]I Timothy 6:20-21 of the New Testament reads: "O Timothy, guard what has been entrusted to you, avoiding worldly *and* empty chatter *and* the opposing arguments of what is falsely called 'knowledge' — which some have professed and thus gone astray from the faith. Grace be with you" (NASB).

The ancient rabbinical writing, *Midrash Rabbah Numbers*, intended as a commentary on the Old Testament and written before the time of Columbus, reads: "He brought ONE SILVER BASIN (MIZRAK) as a symbol of the world which is shaped like a ball that can be thrown (*nizrak*) from hand to hand."[18]

AS WE CAREFULLY STUDY THE WORDS OF JESUS, WE SEE THAT HE KNEW THE WORLD WAS ROUND 2000 YEARS AGO

Only recently was it scientifically accepted that winds blow in cyclic currents. Yet the Bible foretold thousands of years ago: "The wind goeth toward the south, and turneth about unto the north; it whirleth about continually, and the wind returneth again according to his circuits" (Ecc. 1:6 KJV). This is illustrated in this photo of Earth taken on the way back from the moon—notice the white swirls.

There are cyclic wind patterns which illustrate that what the Bible says is true. Jesus illustrated His knowledge that the world was round and that it rotated on an axis. He said that when He came the second time, two would be working and sleeping at the same time, thus inferring day on one side of the earth and night on the other side.

We believe Columbus, being a believer and ardent Bible student, realized from these verses that the world was not flat. He was not afraid, as many were, of falling off the edge when navigating the globe, because Jesus, in the Gospel of Luke, had predicted: "I tell you, in that night there shall be two *men* in one bed; the one shall be taken, and the other left....Two *men* shall be in the field; the one shall be taken, and the other shall be left" (Luke 17:34, 36 KJV).

"Field" implies day because people did not work at night. Since this statement of Jesus' consists of one instant in time, when we will be Raptured (see our chapter 25, "The Rapture Factor"), it shows Jesus knew that the world was not flat, but round. In order to have day and night at the same moment, a spherical Earth would have to have one side facing toward the sun while the other would obviously have to be facing away. The Hebrew word translated as "circle" in Isaiah 40, means a three-dimensional sphere.

---

[18]*Midrash Rabbah Numbers*, Vol. II, Rabbah 13:14. New York: The Soncino Press Ltd., © 1983, p. 528.

"The Jews will return to Jerusalem in the 20th century."[19]

Scientist Sir Isaac Newton, 1642-1727

JESUS GAVE SPECIAL INSTRUCTIONS FOR JEWISH SAFETY, WHICH APPLIED TO THE ERA AFTER ISRAEL'S BIRTH BUT IMMEDIATELY BEFORE HIS SECOND ADVENT

Jesus foretold warnings to the Jews living in Israel during the general time of His return! Thus, we are able to observe from His words, He was aware that after dispersion, His people would be regathered into their own land. Jesus remarked, "But pray ye that your flight be not in the winter, neither on the sabbath day...." (Matt. 24:20).

From Jesus' special instructions for Jewish safety just prior to the terrible war which He will return to stop, we see that there would have to be a new Israel in existence and that Jesus, as a prophet and the Messiah, clearly saw this nearly 2000 years earlier. As a matter of fact, the Temple (not yet rebuilt), according to Jesus' words, will soon be erected. He said in Matthew 24:15: "When ye therefore shall see the abomination of desolation, spoken of by Daniel the prophet, stand in the holy place, (whoso readeth, let him understand:)...." (KJV).

The "abomination of desolation" refers to the taking of an unholy thing into the Holy of Holies chamber of the Temple. It occurred once before in 165 BC, when a pig was sacrificed in the second Temple.

Paul, in the New Testament book of Thessalonians, described Jesus' warning regarding Daniel's prophecy. The apostle wrote: "Let no one in any way deceive you, for *it will not come* unless the apostasy comes first, and the man of lawlessness is revealed, the son of destruction, who opposes and exalts himself above every so-called god or object of worship, so that he takes his seat in the **temple** of God, displaying himself as being God....that lawless one will be revealed whom the Lord will slay with the breath of His mouth and bring to an end by the appearance of His coming...." (II Thes. 2:3-4, 8 NASB).

THE FIG TREE (ISRAELI NATION) HAS PUT OUT LEAVES, INDICATING OUR ERA AS THE GENERATION TO SEE JESUS ARRIVE AT THE PROPHETIC DOOR

Jesus also used the parable of the fig tree. The fig tree is an Old Testament symbol of Israel, along with the olive tree, clearly foretelling Israel's rebirth as a key apocalyptic sign for His return. His presence at the door, ready to return to save His people, is imminent.

---

[19]Ruvic Rosenthal, "The Ostracized Newton," *Al Hamishmar*, July 26, 1985, p. 10.

In His very words: "Now learn a parable of the fig tree; When his branch is yet tender, and putteth forth leaves, ye know that summer *is* nigh: So likewise ye, when ye shall see all these things, know that it is near, *even* at the doors" (Matt. 24:32-33 KJV).

If you are asking, as many have in past times, "Who is the fig tree?", we will make use of a first century document, *The Apocalypse of Peter*, for our answer. This early writing, which only fully came to light in 1910, identifies the fig tree parable Jesus used as a reference to Israel. It also speaks of the future Antichrist's attempt to kill those who reject his (Antichrist's) claim that he is Messiah. Although we realize this is not a canonical part of the New Testament, and therefore not divinely inspired, it nevertheless sheds light on our understanding of the New Testament in reference to the age of Jesus and Israel today, in relation to the parable of the fig tree. It reads: " 'And ye, receive ye the parable of the fig tree thereon: as soon as its shoots have gone forth and its boughs have sprouted, the end of the world will come.' And I, Peter answered and said unto him 'Explain to me concerning the fig tree...' And he answered and said unto me: 'Dost thou not understand that **the fig tree is** the house of **Israel**?'....Verily I say unto you, when its boughs have sprouted at the end, then shall deceiving saviors come and awaken hope, saying: 'I am the Savior who am now come into the world.' And when they shall see the wickedness of their deeds (even of the false saviors) they shall turn away after them and deny him to whom our fathers gave praise, the first Messiah whom they crucified and thereby sinned exceedingly. And this deceiver is not the messiah. And when they reject him he will kill them with the sword, and there shall be many martyrs..."[20]

Jesus cursed[21] the fig tree for unbelief. This tree was a representation of Israel's unbelief at that time. This disfavor for unbelief peaked in Israel's dispersion in the first century. However, Jesus blessed it in a parable of the future, exclaiming it would one day again bring forth fruit!

This began in 1948 with the rebirth of Israel. Jesus said that the generation[22] which saw Israel reborn would not pass until all (which includes His Second Coming) would be fulfilled. In reference to the generation of the fig tree, Jesus said: "Verily I say unto you, **This generation** shall not pass, till all these things be fulfilled" (Matt. 24:34 KJV; bold mine).

---

[20]G. Alon, *The Jews in Their Land in the Talmudic Age*, p. 619. Bold mine.

[21]Matthew 21:19-21 KJV. The literal meaning is "disfavored."

[22]See our *Vol. II*, chapter 1, "A Liberal Interpretation on the Prophecy of Israel—Disproved," for the opinion of a writer who denies the prophecy of Israel as told by Jesus.

HOW LONG CAN A BIBLE GENERATION BE? APPROXIMATELY ONE HUNDRED YEARS—ISRAEL IS ALREADY FORTY-EIGHT YEARS OLD—CLOSE, MAYBE IN YOUR LIFETIME!

Genesis 15:13-16 says a generation can be as long as one hundred years, thus some Bible teachers believe that sometime within the next few decades, before 2048, we may see the Second Coming of Jesus, the resurrection of the dead and world redemption. However, this author refuses to set any exact dates because Jesus said, "But of that day and hour no one knows...." (Matt. 24:34 NASB).

Genesis 15:13-16 is God's prophecy to Abraham, given approximately one hundred and fifty years before the fact, predicting that the Israelis would be captive for four hundred years, which would be four generations before they would return to Canaan (Israel). The Amorite mentioned in verse 16 was given four hundred years to repent, but did not.

While Israel was in Egypt, the Amorites (a name used for the people who occupied Palestine in that day) sacrificed their children to demon gods, yet God gave them every opportunity to turn away from paganism and to Him. They had their last chance four hundred years later, and their iniquity (sin) became full. Only then did Moses lead the Hebrews to their land, Canaan, which today bears the name Israel.

Our main point is that God clearly identifies to Abraham that a generation is one hundred years; four hundred equals four generations! A "generation" is specifically named in Jesus' time clock for His Second Coming in connection with Israel, in Matthew 24 and Luke 21.

According to the prophecy of Genesis 15, a generation (one hundred years) may not pass after the rebirth of Israel *before* redemption will be realized. The fig tree of Israel, as Jesus called it, blossomed forty-eight years ago (as we look back from 1996). We are almost to the halfway mark. If you are in your twenties, thirties, or even your forties, it may very well occur in **your** lifetime. Keep in mind, a full generation is not required to pass. Jesus said, concerning these events leading up to and during His Second Advent: "...This generation shall not pass, till all these things be fulfilled" (Matt. 24:34 KJV). Thus, perhaps ninety-nine years, or eighty, or seventy may tick off out of this hundred before He returns. It could happen tomorrow, but no later than one hundred years. So, don't think that if you are old you have no hope. You do! It could happen tomorrow!

***

RECENT ISRAELI POLITICAL EVENTS AND WAR RESULTS/PREPARATIONS ARE INDICATIONS THAT THE SIGNS OF THE SECOND ADVENT OF JESUS ARE *ALMOST* AT THE DOOR

Though we realize we can not know exactly when, Jesus did give us indications of the approaching *nearness* of His return! These signs of His Second Coming include: 1. The Rapture of all true believers sometime after Israel's rebirth—obviously yet to occur, if you are a believer[23] still on Earth reading this book (see chapter 25, "The Rapture Factor"); 2. The coming of the Antichrist, whose rule will last seven years (see our chapter 23, "The False Messiah Armilus Equals Antichrist"), ending at Armageddon, at a point three and one-half years after he enters the rebuilt Temple in Jerusalem to proclaim himself God (II Thes. 2:3-4). This is called the abomination of desolation. Jesus spoke of it in Matthew 24:15 when He warned His future Jewish people to "flee to the mountains for safety" (see our *Vol. II*, chapter 38, "They Escaped to Petra").

The construction of this Temple would be impossible unless Israel owned the area of old Jerusalem. In the Six Day War of 1967, Israel's victory over five Arab armies put this piece of land, along with their most sacred holy shrine (the Wailing Wall), back into their hands for the first time in two millennia. Thus we are one step closer to the rebuilding of the Temple.

After the victory, the Israeli General Moshe Dayan marched to the Wailing Wall and proclaimed: "We have returned to our holiest of holy places, never to leave her again."[24] "No power on earth will remove us from this spot again."[25] Later, Israeli General Ariel Sharon said: "I have the survivability of a superpower!"[26]

The full thrust of this statement was later revealed in a *Time* magazine article written during the Yom Kippur War, which quoted Dayan and Prime Minister Golda Meir. " 'The Third Temple (a term for modern Israel) is falling,' Dayan reportedly told his prime minister. 'Arm the doomsday weapon.' One of the world's worst-kept military secrets is that Israel has strategic nuclear capabilities."[27]

***

---

[23]That is, if you were born-again before it occurs.

[24]Hal Lindsey with C.C. Carlson, *The Late Great Planet Earth*, p. 55.

[25]Grant R. Jeffrey, *Armageddon, Appointment with Destiny*. New York: Bantam Books, © 1988, p. 109, used by permission.

[26]Morris Cerillo, "Evangelical Newsletter," 1987.

[27]Hal Lindsey, *The 1980's: Countdown to Armageddon*, p. 39.

Recently, an Israeli nuclear technician publicly confirmed that as of 1982, Israel had at least two hundred nuclear weapons.[28] During the 1991 Gulf War, Prime Minister Shamier put Israel on full nuclear alert. Had Iraq dropped a chemical bomb on Israel, she would have gotten more than Saddam Hussein bargained for. Shamier said: *Our retaliation will be so terrible that it will be impossible to imagine. Iraq will never be able to forget it.*[29] Thus, Israel is not going to disappear.

THE FUTURE JEWISH TEMPLE, PRESENTLY FORESHADOWED BY THE PRODUCTION OF ITS ORNAMENTS

At present, ornaments are being manufactured for use in the new Temple by the Temple Institute (see our *Vol. II*, chapter 17, "Jewish Plans for Rebuilding the Temple"). Richard K. Ostling, in a *Time* magazine article entitled, "Time for a New Temple?", commented: "During six years of research, the institute has reconstructed 38 of the ritual implements that will be required when Temple sacrifices are restored; it will complete the other 65 items as funds permit. A museum of the completed pieces has drawn 10,000 visitors...."[30] The same article mentioned: "Temple restoration is also a fixation for literal-minded Protestants, who deem a new Temple the precondition for Christ's Second Coming. Two Talmudic schools located near the Western (Wailing) Wall are teaching nearly 200 students the elaborate details of Temple service."[31]

In a more recent article by the national news magazine, *U.S. News & World Report*, which had the words, "Waiting for the Messiah" blazing across the cover of its December 19, 1994 edition, the latest and most startling information was revealed. The article was entitled, "The Christmas Covenant." A profile of the article regarding the anticipated rebuilding of the Temple pointed out: "The first step, says Chaim Richman of the Temple Institute, is replication down to the precise detail of Temple objects, half of which have now been made. In addition, a Mississippi cattle farmer has agreed to provide special

---

[28]Grant R. Jeffrey, *Armageddon, Appointment with Destiny*, p. 203. This was also confirmed in the May 16, 1982 issue of the *Toronto Star*.

[29]This author heard Shamier's address on Israel TV in Jerusalem.

[30]Richard K. Ostling, "Time For a New Temple?", *Time*, Oct. 25, 1989, p. 63, used by permission.

[31]Ibid, p. 62.

unblemished red heifers,[32] the ashes of which are required for a purification ritual.

Others also prepare for the miracle. Rabbi Nahman Kahane of the Old City has created a data base of all Jews descended from Aaron, the priestly brother of Moses. They will be called into service if the Temple is rebuilt."[33]

Gershom Soloman, an Israeli member of the Temple Mount Faithful who is greatly interested in working for the Temple's rebuilding, said recently: "We must start immediately the rebuilding of the third Temple because this is a condition for the coming of the Messiah."[34]

I will not be surprised if Soloman's wish is accomplished within twenty-five to thirty years of our writing! However, it will be the Antichrist's negotiation of a temporary peace between Israel and the Arabs which will allow this Temple to be rebuilt.

THE *GLORY* OF THE MESSIAH'S RETURN, WHEN WILL IT BE? PSALM 102 GIVES US A CLUE—ZION

Because God is faithful, it will not be our fate that His Messiah will be late. He will be right on time. His scheduled time to arrive is to be found in Psalm 102:16.

When Jesus came 2000 years ago it was a Coming in humiliation, to suffer. However, He made reference to His Second Coming "when the Son of Man shall come in all of His **glory**" (Matt. 24:30). Psalm 102 references this glory as follows: "When the LORD shall build up Zion [Israel], he shall appear in his glory" (Ps. 102:16 KJV; [ ] mine). Thus according to David's inspired line, He will be right on time.

Jesus could not have returned to Earth until Israel became a nation in 1948, as this Psalm clearly says that when He shall build up Zion (Israel), the Lord (Messiah) shall appear (come) in His glory to save the earth and usher in the royal Messianic Kingdom. This kingdom was promised by hundreds of prophecies, inspired by God, throughout the Old Testament. So, since He promised to come in the generation of Israel's rebirth (Matt. 24:32-34), and a generation cannot

---

[32]Concerning the past search for the red heifer and presently the Ark (see our *Vol. II*, chapter 37, "The Vendyl Jones Adventure"), it was not what it was cracked up to be. Prospective Christian donors should know.

[33]Jeffrey L. Sheler, "The Christmas Covenant," *U.S News & World Report*, Dec. 19, 1994, p. 70, © used by permission. Quoted from the profiles by Gareth G. Cook and David Makovshy, "Jerusalem Temple, Preparing for the Messiah," *U.S. News & World Report*.

[34]*The 700 Club*, Christian Broadcasting Network, Dec. 8, 1994.

be more than one hundred years (Gen. 15:13-16), and since Israel was born in 1948,[35] we do not have long to wait!

CARL MARX

THE PALESTINE POST

STATE OF ISRAEL IS BORN

Most Crowded Hours in Palestine's History

JEWS TAKE OVER SECURITY ZONES

Egyptian Air Force Spitfires Bomb Tel Aviv; One Shot Down

U.S. RECOGNIZES JEWISH STATE

Proclamation by Head Of Government

2 Columns Cross Southern Border

Etzion Settlers Taken P.O.W.

Special Assembly Adjourns

A Good Thing

EMERGENCY

2 Villages Taken In Road Battle

The front page of the May 16, 1948 edition of what is now *The Jerusalem Post* reporting the rebirth of Israel. Courtesy of *The Jerusalem Post.*

---

[35]Risto Santala comments: "The Talmudic scholars picture the Messiah arriving in the middle of a crisis for humanity. These birth-pangs connected with the last generation relate to individual morals, the history of the nations and the whole of creation. Just a short example of this: '*If you see kingdoms arming themselves one against another, you can expect the coming of the Messiah.*' '*The Messiah, the Son of David, will not come until the whole world is filled with apostates* (Heb. *minût*, by which the Rabbis seem to understand the 'Christians'). '*The Son of David will not come until judges and authorities cease to be in Israel.*' '*The Messianic footsteps will appear when insolence increases....*' We could add here the so-called '*Messianic signs*' according to which *in that time there will be dreadful diseases, plagues and epidemics*', '*the whole world will be bathed in blood*' '*the sun will be darkened and the moon changed to blood*'. There are descriptions corresponding to these both in the words of Christ and the letters of Paul. It is worth keeping this symmetry in mind when studying Jewish scholars' expositions of psalm 102, which gives a description of the '*last generation*'." Risto Santala, *The Messiah in the Old Testament in the Light of Rabbinical Writings*, pp. 141-142. Santala's footnote to "blood" reads: "Jellinek, *Beit ha-Midrash,* vol. II pp58-63 'The Messianic signs' and vol. V1117-120 'The wars of the Messiah-King'." Ibid, p. 142.

This is the school presently preparing the ornaments for the Temple. It is located in Jerusalem's Old City, next to the Moriah Bookstore.

The author and Hal Lindsey examine the garments recently woven for the high priest at the Jerusalem school. These garments may one day be used by a future priest in the Temple.

"Yea, though I walk through the valley of the shadow of death, I will fear no evil: for thou *art* with me; thy rod and thy staff they comfort me." Psalms 23:4 KJV

HAVE NO FEAR—JESUS AND AMOS ASSURE US THAT ISRAEL WILL BE SAVED, NEVER AGAIN TO BE PLUCKED UP OUT OF HER LAND!

Before the final war is over, it is predicted that Jesus will return to save Israel by wiping out her enemies and thereby inaugurating the millennial kingdom. Jesus said those days would be cut short: "And except those days should be shortened, there should no flesh be saved: but for the elect's sake those days shall be shortened" (Matt. 24:22 KJV).

Amos, the Old Testament prophet, foretells that Israel, once regathered the second time from all the nations, will never be scattered again. "And I will bring again the captivity of my people of Israel, and they shall build the waste cities, and inhabit *them*; and they shall plant vineyards, and drink the wine thereof; they shall also make gardens, and eat the fruit of them. And I will plant them upon their land, and they shall no more be pulled up out of their land which I have given them, saith the LORD thy God" (Amos 9:14-15 KJV).

GOD SPEAKS TO THE JEW, THROUGH EZEKIEL, IN THE FIRST PERSON, "I....WILL BRING YOU INTO YOUR OWN LAND," AND HE IS STILL DOING IT!

The prophet Ezekiel had much to say about Israel's dispersion, regathering and last war, recognizing her Messiah and her permanent re-establishment on the land God gave to Abraham! Ezekiel tells us: "Therefore say unto the house of Israel, Thus saith the Lord GOD; I do not *this* for your sakes, O house of Israel, but for mine holy name's sake, which ye have profaned among the heathen, whither ye went. And I will sanctify my great name, which was profaned among the heathen, which ye have profaned in the midst of them; and the heathen shall know that I *am* the LORD, saith the Lord GOD, when I shall be sanctified in you before their eyes. For I will take you from among the heathen, and gather you out of all countries, and will bring you into your own land. Then will I sprinkle clean water upon you, and ye shall be clean: from all your filthiness, and from all your idols, will I cleanse you. A new heart also will I give you, and a new spirit will I put within you: and I will take away the stony heart out of your flesh, and I will give you an heart of flesh. And I will put my spirit within you, and cause you to walk in my statutes, and ye shall keep my judgments, and do *them*. And ye shall dwell in the land that I gave to your fathers; and ye shall be my people, and I will be your God. I will also save you from all your uncleannesses: and I will call for the corn, and will increase it, and lay no famine upon you. And I will multiply the fruit of the tree, and the increase of the field, that ye shall receive no more reproach of famine among the heathen. Then shall ye remember your own evil ways, and your doings that *were* not good, and shall lothe yourselves in your own sight for your iniquities and for your abominations. Not for your sakes do I *this*, saith the Lord GOD, be it known unto you: be ashamed and confounded for your own ways, O house of Israel. Thus saith the Lord GOD; In the day that I shall have cleansed you from all your iniquities I will also cause *you* to dwell in the cities, and the wastes shall be builded. And the desolate land shall be tilled, whereas it lay desolate in the sight of all that passed by. And they shall say, This land that was desolate is become like the garden of Eden; and the waste and desolate and ruined cities *are become* fenced, *and* are inhabited. Then the heathen that are left round about you shall know that I the LORD build the ruined *places*, *and* plant that that was desolate: I the LORD have spoken *it*, and I will do *it*" (Ezek. 36:22-36 KJV).

EZEKIEL'S 2600-YEAR-OLD EXPOSÉ ON ISRAEL IN THE LAST DAYS—FULFILLMENT IS IMMINENT

"After many days thou shalt be visited: in the latter years thou shalt come into the land *that is* brought back from the sword, *and is* gathered out of many people, against the mountains of Israel, which have been always waste: but it is brought forth out of the nations, and they shall dwell safely all of them. Thou shalt ascend and come like a storm, thou shalt be like a cloud to cover the land, thou, and all thy bands, and many people with thee. Thus saith the Lord GOD; It shall also come to pass, *that* at the same time shall things come into thy mind, and thou shalt think an evil thought: And thou shalt say, I will go up to the land of unwalled villages; I will go to them that are at rest, that dwell safely, all of them dwelling without walls, and having neither bars nor gates, To take a spoil, and to take a prey; to turn thine hand upon the desolate places *that are now* inhabited, and upon the people *that are* gathered out of the nations, which have gotten cattle and goods, that dwell in the midst of the land....And the heathen shall know that the house of Israel went into captivity for their iniquity: because they trespassed against me, therefore hid I my face from them, and gave them into the hand of their enemies: so fell they all by the sword. According to their uncleanness and according to their transgressions have I done unto them, and hid my face from them. Therefore thus saith the Lord GOD; Now will I bring again the captivity of Jacob, and have mercy upon the whole house of Israel, and will be jealous for my holy name; After that they have borne their shame, and all their trespasses whereby they have trespassed against me, when they dwelt safely in their land, and none made *them* afraid. When I have brought them again from the people, and gathered them out of their enemies' lands, and am sanctified in them in the sight of many nations; Then shall they know that I *am* the LORD their God, which caused them to be led into captivity among the heathen: but I have gathered them unto their own land, and have left none of them any more there. Neither will I hide my face any more from them: for I have poured out my spirit upon the house of Israel, saith the Lord GOD" (Ezek. 38:8-12; 39:23-29 KJV).

THE CRISIS OF THE LAST WAR IN ISRAEL, AS DESCRIBED IN ZECHARIAH AND EZEKIEL, BRINGS MANY ISRAELIS TO FAITH IN JESUS!

Hal Lindsey accurately said: "...these prophets forecast that Israel will be brought to the brink of annihilation just before the coming of the Messiah, who will save the Israelis (see Zachariah chapters 12-14 and especially chapter 13, verses eight and nine). According to Ezekiel, Israel's great crisis will cause many Jews to believe in their true Messiah.

Zachariah speaks of this holocaust and the repentence which follows: 'And I will pour out on the House of David and all the inhabitants of Jerusalem the spirit of grace and supplication, so that they will look on Me whom they have pierced; and they will mourn for Him as one mourns for an only son' (Zachariah 12:10)."[36]

WE WILL SOON BE CELEBRATING ISRAEL'S FUTURE VICTORY AND ENJOYING TABERNACLES WITH THE PEOPLE OF ISRAEL AND JESUS—EVERY YEAR!

For those of us who know the Bible's predictions, we have nothing to fear and have only to wait. If we are believers now, we will one day soon enjoy seven years in Heaven, while these terrible end-time events, which unbelieving men will perpetrate on themselves, occur (see our chapter 25, "The Rapture Factor").

---

[36]Hal Lindsey, *The 1980's: Countdown to Armageddon*, p. 46.

After this seven-year period, we will enjoy Israel's victory with Jesus, thereafter dining with all the world's peoples who receive Him, in Israel, as they are granted entrance. Zechariah tells us: "...it shall come to pass, *that* every one that is left of all the nations which came against Jerusalem shall even go up from year to year to worship the King, the LORD of hosts, and to keep the feast of tabernacles" (Zech. 14:16 KJV).

Jesus will sit with the twelve tribes of Israel. Remember what He promised at the last Passover supper: "That ye may eat and drink at my table in my kingdom, and sit on thrones judging the twelve tribes of Israel" (Luke 22:30 KJV). But now, let's see what the Russians have to do with all of this end-time trouble, which is the subject of our next chapter.

We conclude our chapter on Israel with a collection of photographs representing all walks of life within the land of Israel.[37]

The Mount of Olives is one of the highest places in Jerusalem. Many believe the Messiah will return to the vicinity of the church here, located at the top of this mountain.

[37]The following photos, courtesy of the State of Israel Government Press Office, photography department, with the exception of above, El Al Office, Pisgat Ziev, The Jerusalem Great Synagogue, McDavid's, and Talithakumi, which were taken by this author.

David Ben-Gurion, during a 1956 address in Tel Aviv.

דשיון כניסה לארץ־ישראל
מספר 07452
השם ושם המשפחה בורשטין ברוך
שם האב אברהם שם האם אלקה
מקום הלידה פולניה תאריך הלידה 1921
לאומיות סלידה עברית
נמצא עי נציגי מוסדות הישוב מתאים לעליה לארץ־ישראל.
1 MAR. 1946
מחלקת הבריאות
HEALTH DEPARTMENT
REPATRIATION DEPARTMENT

PERMIT TO ENTER EREZ-ISRAEL (PALESTINE)
07452
SURNAME BORSTEYN Name BARUH
Father's Name Abraham Mother's Name Elka
Place of Birth POLAND Date of Birth 1921
Nationality by Birth Jewish
HAS BEEN FOUND QUALIFIED BY THE REPRESENTATIVES OF THE YISHUV FOR RE-PATRIATION TO PALESTINE.
Authority: a) "And they shall abide in the land that I have given unto Jacob my servant, wherein your fathers abode, and they shall abide therein even they, and their children, and their children's children for ever". (Ezekiel, XXXVII)
b) "With great mercies will I gather thee." (Isaiah, LIV)
c) Lord Balfour's Declaration of 2nd November, 1917.
d) The Mandate for Palestine.
FOR OFFICIAL USE ONLY
REPATRIATION DEPARTMENT
מחלקת הבריאות
1 MAR. 1946
HEALTH DEPARTMENT

Dr. Chaim Weizman, the first President of Israel.

David Ben-Gurion, first Prime Minister of Israel,
and 1948 and 1967 Israeli war victories.

Yemenite Jews, who resemble
Arabs in their dress, immigrate to Israel.

Israeli Prime Minister, Golda Meir.

Israeli school children and scenic views of Israel.

Sabras (natives of Israel) and the flag of Israel.

Israeli settlements and an Israeli Army air show. The planes fly in the formation of the Hebrew initials meaning the "Army of Israel's Defense" ("TSA-HAL" or צהל), and the Star of David.

Israel is built and trees are planted as the desert is pushed back.

Downtown Israel, the suburbs, and a new sabra in his baby carriage.

Pisgat Ziev condominiums,
settlements, and a farm owner.

McDavid's fast food restaurant, and Israel's replica of the U.S. Statue of Liberty, in front of the Kol Bo Shalom department store.

Israel's statue of Abraham Lincoln, and
a replica of the U.S. Liberty Bell.

The Israeli Army, the Temple Mount as viewed from the summit of the Mount of Olives, and the Western Wall on Yom Ha Zicharon ("Day of Rememberance," for those lost in the Holocaust).

Eshcol Lake, and Israel's army and weaponry.

The Jerusalem Theater, a morning service under a prayer shawl prior to a Barmitzva on the top of Masada, and a bonfire during Lag b'Omer (a Jewish festival commemorating an unsuccessful revolt against the Romans in the second century AD).

An Israeli hospital, kibbutzniks at work, a drill team forming the Star of David, an amphitheater, religious holiday, and a field of flowers.

Religious ceremonies and sights in Jerusalem.

An Israeli child builds a menorah in the sand,
and an aerial view of a circular moshav (private farm) called Nahalal .

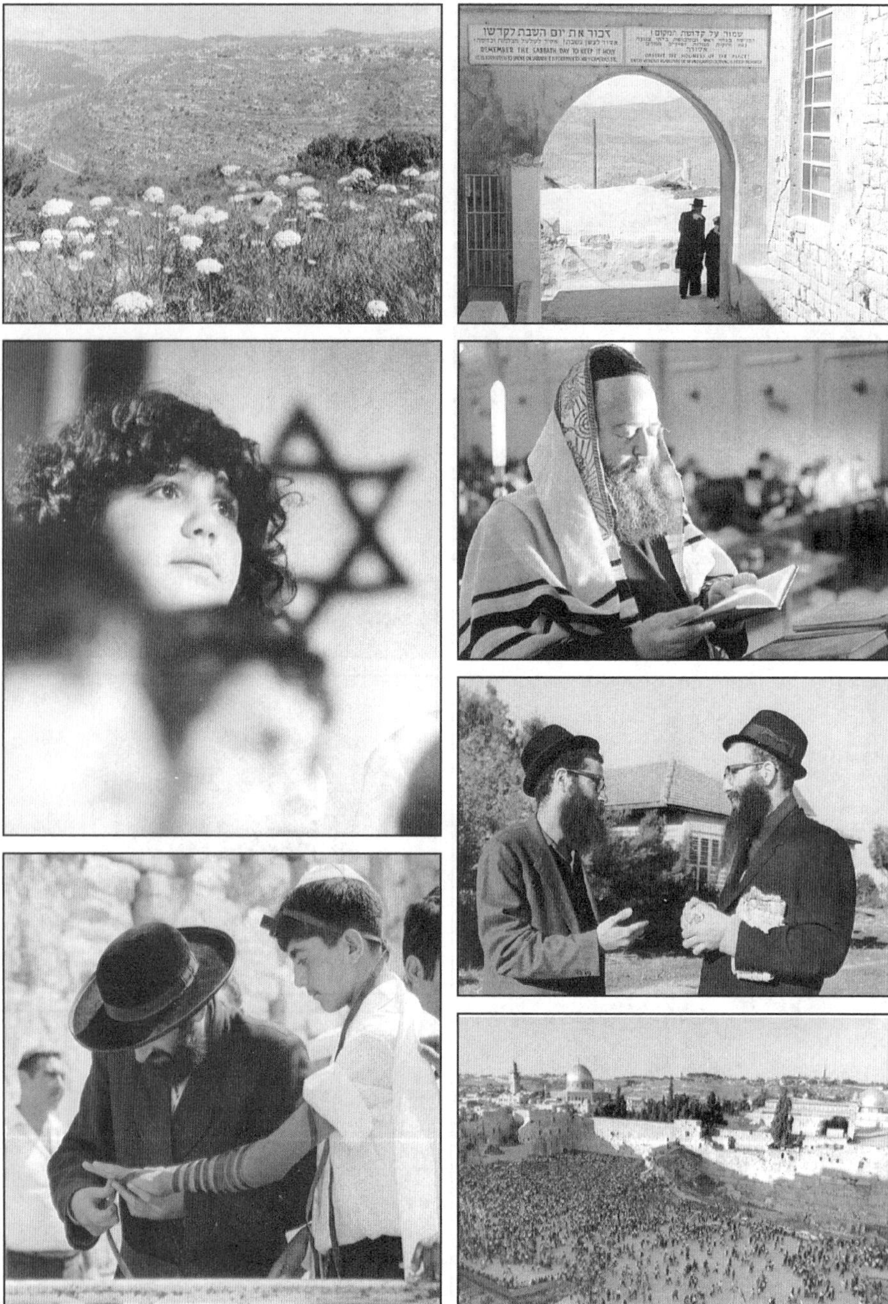

Landscape and religion in Israel.

Religion and the army in Israel, and a soldiers' memorial at Kyriat Anayim.

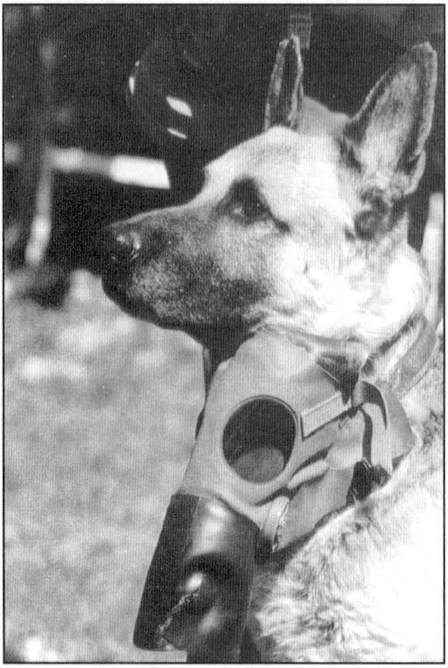

Names of fallen Israeli soldiers memorialized, and a German shepherd equipped with a gas mask in the service of the Israeli Army.

When the Messiah comes, He will arrive through the Golden Gate as the shofar sounds and the religious realize He is Yeshua—Jesus...

...then all will celebrate and rejoice.

" '...On that day when My people Israel are living securely, will you not know *it*? And you will come from your place out of the remote parts of the north, you and many peoples with you...a great assembly and a mighty army; and you will come up against My people Israel like a cloud to cover the land. It will come about in the last days...in order that the nations may know Me when I shall be sanctified through you before their eyes, O Gog.' " The biblical prophet, Ezekiel 38:14-16 NASB, 600 BC

"If you desire to know the manner...of the war of Gog and Magog you may see them both described by Ezekiel chap 38 and 39...where he represents how the Jews after their return from captivity dwell safely and quietly upon the mountains of Israel in unwalled towns without either gates or barrs to defend them untill they are grown very rich in Cattel and gold and silver and goods and Gog of the land of Magog stirrs up the nations round about. Persia and Arabia and Afric and the northern nations of Asia and Europe against them to take a spoile, and God destroys all that great army, that the nations may from thenceforth know that the...Jews went formerly into captivity for their sins but now since their return are become invincible...."[1] Isaac Newton, 1600's

"When the ships of the kingdom of Russia will cross the Dardannels you [Israel] should dress in Sabbath clothes because this means that the arrival of the Messiah is close."[2]
Rabbi Elija ben Solomon, the famed Vilna Gaon, 1700's

"When you see the Russian army begin to move southward and enter Turkey, put on your Sabbath garments and get ready to welcome the Messiah."[3] Rav Valoshiner,1800's

"Russia, then, according to the Scriptures, is the headship or leading power around which the multitudinous armies of allied monarchy shall be gathered together. 'Persia, Ethiopia, and Libya with them; all of them with shield and helmet' (Ezek. 38:5). Persia here represents the swarming hosts from the Asiatic possessions; Ethiopia, Libya, and the armies of Africa. 'Thou shalt ascend and come like a storm, thou shalt be like a cloud to cover the land, thou, and all thy bands, and many people with thee' (Ezek. 38:9). The invasion is here announced by an armament such as the world never saw. For the millions that are to assemble under Gog or Russia embrace nearly all of Europe, as well as a large portion of Asia and Africa."[4] Reverend Pitts, to Congress, 1857

"This king of the North I conceive to be the autocrat of Russia...that Russia occupies a place, and a very momentous place, in the prophetic word has been admitted by almost all expositors."[5] Dr. John Cumming, 1864

"We are not going to let them [Russia] issue an ultimatum to the world of surrender or die." Ronald Reagan, from the program, *Reagan on Reagan*, 1989. [ ] mine

19

RUSSIA IS CRUSHED IN GOG

These quotes, which span 2600 years, indicate that Russia will one day become the mortal enemy of Israel. In reference to our third

---

[1] *Yahuda Manuscript 6, fol. 17-18.*
[2] רפאל הלוי אייזנברג, חבלי משיח בזמננו, p. קלה. ירושלים, © 1970, used by permission.
[3] Hal Lindsey, *The 1980s: Countdown to Armageddon*, p. 65.
[4] F.E. Pitts, *The U.S.A. in Prophecy.* Baltimore: J.W. Bull, 1862. From his speech to the U.S. Congress. The theological library at Emory University, Atlanta, is named after Pitts!
[5] Hal Lindsey with C.C. Carlson, *The Late Great Planet Earth*, p. 63.

quote from the 1700's, we note that *Gaon*, in Hebrew, means "genius." Vilna is the town of Wilna, where he resided. These words of the rabbi are cited in the name of his students, which this author and Mike Bentley translated into English from the original Hebrew book *Chevlet Mashiach BIZemaneinu* ("Birth Pangs of the Messiah"), by Rabbi Raphael Eisenberg. We located this book in the Givat Ram branch of the Hebrew University Library in Jerusalem, Israel. The quote serves to illustrate that our biblical view of Armageddon, including the Russian attack from the north, as described in the Old Testament book of Ezekiel (chapter 38), has been interpreted by the rabbis of old as being Russia. This flies in the face of many liberal Christians who claim that some "wild-eyed fundamentalist evangelical groups" invented this idea.

Gary DeMar, author of *Last Days Madness,* infers that the prophecy of Russia is just that. He appears to infer that Dr. John Cumming (quoted earlier) was the first to identify Russia with Ezekiel's prophecy of Gog.[6] DeMar read this in Hal Lindsey's book, *The Late Great Planet Earth*, which DeMar's book attempts to disprove. He admits this in his footnote 15. However, Cumming is just the earliest source Hal mentions in this particular instance. We, along with Gaon, a genius rabbi who lived in the 1700's, do not attribute this interpretation to nineteenth century Christians. Vilna Gaon was, no doubt, unknown to most Christians, including DeMar, until now.

AN ORTHODOX JEWISH COMMENTARY LENDS CREDENCE TO OUR VIEW—WE DO NOT HAVE TO WAIT ANOTHER HALF-CENTURY, AS OTHERS HAVE SEEN TWENTY-SIX PASS!

The Gaon of Vilna's understanding of Ezekiel's prophecy will be realized before another half-century will pass. We believe it, even though today Russia is proclaiming "peace" (Ezek. 38:11).

If you are living a decade or so after the year 2000, look at the copyright date of this book. Are you impressed that the prophecies are being fulfilled? Even the modern Orthodox Jewish commentary on Ezekiel, the *Art Scrolls Series,* has commented on this: "In this light, one may understand an oral tradition passed down from the *Vilna Gaon*...that when the Russian navy passes through the Bosporus (that is, on the way to the Mediterranian through the Dardanelles) it will be time to put on Sabbath clothes [in anticipation of the coming of *Mashiach.*]"[7]

[6]Gary DeMar, *Last Days Madness*, p. 201.

[7]Rabbi Moshe Eisemann, *Yechezkel*. Jerusalem: Mesorah Publications, Ltd., © 1980, p. 581, used by permission. We, as well as Gaon, believe that Gog is Russia. The very word *Gog* in Hebrew means "roof" and Russia is above Israel, to the north!

A MODERN RINKY-DINK "CHRISTIAN" DENIAL THAT RUSSIA IS GOG, PROVEN FALSE

DeMar ridiculously criticizes the prophecy of a Russian attack against Israel in Armageddon, when he says: "Russia plays a significant role in today's last days madness because of its...geographic location, and a curious game of sound-alike. Modern Russia is supposedly found in Ezekiel 38-39. Here's how it works. In Ezekiel 38:2 and 39:1 the Hebrew word *rosh* is translated as if it were a nation. That nation is thought to be Russia because *rosh* sounds like Russia. In addition, *Meshech* (38:2) sounds like Moscow, and *Tubal* (38:2) is similar to the name of one of the prominent Asiatic provinces of Russia, the province of Tobolsk."[8]

This is an outright **lie**! I have never seen or read a prophetic scholar that used DeMar's "sound-alike" scenario. Hal Lindsey states that historians like Josephus, Pliny, Gesenius and Keil, actually pointed out that these ancient names were, in fact, the countries mentioned. For example, Lindsey's scholarly words are: "Gog is the symbolic name of the nation's leader and Magog is his land. He is also the prince of the ancient people who were called Rosh, Meshech, and Tubal.

In the Biblical chapter commonly called the 'Table of Nations' by scholars these names are mentioned. (See Genesis 10.) They are described as the grandsons of Noah through his son Japheth, with the exception of Rosh (Genesis 10:1, 2). Magog is the second son; Tubal is the fifth son; and Meshech is the sixth son."[9]

OUR WITNESSES AGAINST DEMAR'S ACCUSATIONS IN *LAST DAYS MADNESS* INCLUDE: JOSEPHUS, PLINY, GESENIUS AND DR. KIEL

"Josephus, a Jewish historian of the first century, says that the people of his day known as the Moschevi and Thobelites were founded by Meshech and Tubal respectively. He said, '...Magog is called the Scythians by the Greeks.' He continued by saying that these people lived in the northern regions above the Caucasus mountains.

Pliny, a noted Roman writer of early Christian times, said, 'Hierapolis, taken by the Scythians, was afterward called Magog.' In this he shows that the dreaded barbaric people called the Scythians were identified with their ancient tribal name. Any good history book of ancient times traces the Scythians to be a principal part of the people who make up modern Russia.

---

[8]Gary DeMar, *Last Days Madness*, p. 200.

[9]Hal Lindsey with C.C. Carlson, *The Late Great Planet Earth*, p. 52.

Wilhelm Gesenius, a great Hebrew scholar of the early nineteenth century, discusses these words in his unsurpassed Hebrew Lexicon. 'Meshech', he says, 'was founder of the Moschi, a barbarous people, who dwelt in the Moschian mountains'....the Greek name, 'Moschi,' derived from the Hebrew name Meshech is the source of the name for *the city of Moscow*. In discussing Tubal he said, 'Tubal is the son of Rapheth, founder of the Tibereni, a people dwelling on the Black Sea to the west of the Moschi.'

Gesenius concludes by saying that these people undoubtedly make up the modern Russian people.

There is one more name to consider in this line of evidence. It is the Hebrew word, 'Rosh,' translated 'chief' in Ezekiel 38:2, 3 of the King James and Revised Standard Versions. The word literally means in Hebrew the 'top' or 'head' of something. According to most scholars, this word is used in the sense of a proper name, not as a descriptive noun qualifying the word 'prince.'

The German scholar, Dr. Keil, says after a careful grammatical analysis that it should be translated as a proper name, i.e., Rosh. He says, 'The Byzantine and Arabic writers frequently mention a people called Ros and Rus, dwelling in the country of Taurus, and reckoned among the Scythian tribes.'

Dr. Gesenius in his Hebrew Lexicon says, '...Rosh was a designation for the tribes then north of the Taurus Mountains, dwelling in the neighborhood of the Volga.

He concluded that in this name and tribe we have the first historical trace of the Russ or Russian nation."[10]

PATTON'S PROVIDENTIAL DENIAL HAS CAST RUSSIA INTO HER MOLD OF PROPER PROPHETIC PERSPECTIVE

In this chapter, we will discuss the history and fate of communism as we see how it has propelled Russia into her proper prophetic perspective in the twenty-first century.

At the end of World War II, the great General George Patton, wanted to free the Russians from communist domination! We can all appreciate this gesture of freedom and democracy which could have been.[11] However, for some reason, this dream was not carried out. It is not a total loss, for the prophets of the Bible tell us that this victory, along with world peace, is being saved for the Savior Jesus!

---

[10]Ibid, pp. 52-54.

[11]This would have cut short communism by more than one-half of its seventy years of tyranny and saved millions of lives, not to mention the billions of dollars spent on the Cold War arms race!

Meanwhile, the current situation is fulfilling the end time prophecies of the Bible. Read on in this chapter and you will see what we mean.

THE ANCIENT RABBINICAL WRITINGS PROCLAIM ISRAEL'S REDEMPTION WHEN THE MESSIAH DESTROYS GOG IN THE END DAYS

The book of Revelation teaches that when Jesus returns He will save us from Armageddon! Zechariah, said that when the Israelis see Him coming, all of Israel shall weep, as if in mourning for their first-born (Zech. 12). Though many Jews believe in Jesus now, the New Testament says one day, they will all be saved (Rom. 11:26). Likewise, the rabbinical commentaries of ages past, pinpointed Israel's final redemption to the Messiah's victory over Gog in the end days! "NUMBERS. XI. 26. 'And they prophesied in the camp.' The *Jerusalem Targum*: And both of them prophesied together, and they said, In the end of the heel of days, Gog and Magog and their army shall ascend against Jerusalem, but by the hand of King Messiah they shall fall."[12]

"SONG OF SOLOMON....VIII. 4. 'I charge you, O daughter of Jerusalem.' *Targum*: King Messiah shall say, I adjure you, O my people of the house of Israel, wherefore do ye contend against the people of the land, (desiring) to go out of captivity? And wherefore do ye rise up against the army of Gog and Magog? Tarry ye a little, till the people be consumed who have gone up to wage war against Jerusalem, and afterwards the Lord of the world will remember unto you the mercies of the righteous, and it shall be pleasure before him to redeem you."[13] "In the End of Days, Gog and Magog and their armies will fall into the hands of King Messiah, and for seven years the Children of Israel will light fire from the shares of their weapons; they will not go out to the forest and will not cut down a [single] tree....(Targ. Yer. to Num. 11:26)."[14]

The Israelis were well prepared in the Gulf War, and we pray that they will also be on guard for the last war.

[12]Rev. B. Pick, Ph.D., *Old Testament Passages Messianically Applied by the Ancient Synagogue*, Vol. II, p. 28.
[13]Ibid, Vol. III, p. 34.
[14]Raphael Patai, *The Messiah Texts*, p. 146.

ORIGINAL HEBREW TEXT WRITTEN 587 BC

וְאָמַרְתָּ כֹּה אָמַר אֲדֹנָי יְהוִה הִנְנִי אֵלֶיךָ גּוֹג נְשִׂיא רֹאשׁ מֶשֶׁךְ וְתֻבָל׃ וְשֹׁבַבְתִּיךָ וְנָתַתִּי
חַחִים בִּלְחָיֶיךָ וְהוֹצֵאתִי אוֹתְךָ וְאֶת־כָּל־חֵילֶךָ סוּסִים וּפָרָשִׁים לְבֻשֵׁי מִכְלוֹל כֻּלָּם קָהָל
רָב צִנָּה וּמָגֵן תֹּפְשֵׂי חֲרָבוֹת כֻּלָּם׃ פָּרַס כּוּשׁ וּפוּט אִתָּם כֻּלָּם מָגֵן וְכוֹבָע׃ גֹּמֶר וְכָל־
אֲגַפֶּיהָ בֵּית תּוֹגַרְמָה יַרְכְּתֵי צָפוֹן וְאֶת־כָּל־אֲגַפָּיו עַמִּים רַבִּים אִתָּךְ׃ .... וּבָאתָ מִמְּקוֹמְךָ
מִיַּרְכְּתֵי צָפוֹן אַתָּה וְעַמִּים רַבִּים אִתָּךְ רֹכְבֵי סוּסִים כֻּלָּם קָהָל גָּדוֹל וְחַיִל רָב׃ וְעָלִיתָ
עַל־עַמִּי יִשְׂרָאֵל כֶּעָנָן לְכַסּוֹת הָאָרֶץ בְּאַחֲרִית הַיָּמִים תִּהְיֶה וַהֲבִאוֹתִיךָ עַל־אַרְצִי לְמַעַן
דַּעַת הַגּוֹיִם אֹתִי בְּהִקָּדְשִׁי בְךָ לְעֵינֵיהֶם גּוֹג׃ .... עַל־הָרֵי יִשְׂרָאֵל תִּפּוֹל אַתָּה וְכָל־אֲגַפֶּיךָ
וְעַמִּים אֲשֶׁר אִתָּךְ לְעֵיט צִפּוֹר כָּל־כָּנָף וְחַיַּת הַשָּׂדֶה נְתַתִּיךָ לְאָכְלָה׃ עַל־פְּנֵי הַשָּׂדֶה תִּפּוֹל
כִּי אֲנִי דִבַּרְתִּי נְאֻם אֲדֹנָי יְהוִה׃

יחזקאל לח:ג-ז; טו-טז; לט:ד-ה

OLD TESTAMENT SCRIPTURE TRANSLATION

"...Thus says the Lord GOD, 'Behold, I am against you, O Gog, prince of Rosh [Russia], Meshech [Moscow], and Tubal [Tubalsk]....Persia [modern Iraq and Iran], Ethiopia, and Put with them, all of them *with* shield and helmet; Gomer [Germany] with all its troops; Beth-togarmah [Turkey] *from* the remote parts of the north with all its troops—many peoples with you....And you will come from your place out of the remote parts of the north, you and many peoples with you...a great assembly and a mighty army; and you will come up against My people Israel like a cloud to cover the land. It will come about in the last days....You shall fall on the mountains of Israel, you and all your troops, and the peoples who are with you; I shall give you as food to every kind of predatory bird and beast of the field. You will fall on the open field; for it is I who have spoken,' declares the Lord GOD."

Ezekiel 38:3-6, 15-16; 39:4-5 NASB. [ ] mine

ANCIENT RABBINICAL COMMENTARY

"R. Levi said: 'In the Future to Come, Gog and Magog will say: 'The first ones were fools, for they occupied themselves with plans against Israel, and did not know that they have a Patron in Heaven. I shall not act like them, but first of all shall attack their Patron, and thereafter attack them....' But the Only One, blessed be He, says to him: 'You wicked one! Me you want to attack? By your life, I shall wage war against you....' "[15] **Leviticus Rabba 27:11**

SEMI-ANCIENT RABBINICAL COMMENTARY

"*When you see the Russian army begin to move southward and enter Turkey, put on your Sabbath garments and get ready to welcome the Messiah.*"[16]

Rabbi Chaim Valoshiner, mid-19th century

NEW TESTAMENT RECORDED 96 AD

"...for they are spirits of demons, performing signs, which go out to the kings of the whole world, to gather them together for the war of the great day of God, the Almighty. ('Behold, I [Messiah Jesus] am coming like a thief. Blessed is the one who stays awake and keeps his garments....') And they gathered them together to the place which in Hebrew is called HarMagedon."

Revelation 16:14-16 NASB. [ ] mine

---

[15] Raphael Patai, *The Messiah Texts*, p. 148.

[16] Hal Lindsey, *The 1980's: Countdown to Armageddon*, p. 65, italics Lindsey's..

MODERN RABBINIC COMMENT/REFUTATION

"Ezekiel's great prophecy about Gog of the Land of Magog...became the basis in Talmudic and Medieval times of the myth of the global Armageddon between the armies of Gog and Magog and the forces of the Messiah."

***The Messiah Texts*, by Raphael Patai, p. 145; © 1979**

MODERN DOCUMENTED POLITICAL RUSSIAN STATEMENTS

"We will grapple with the Lord God in due season. We shall vanquish Him in His highest heaven."

G. E. Zinoviver, former chairman of the Leningrad Soviet

"If the Israelis threaten us, we will wipe them out within two days. I can assure you our plans are made for this eventuality."

Soviet Ambassador Anatoly Dobrynin

AUTHOR'S COMMENT—EVANGELICAL CHRISTIAN POSITION

Presently, Russia appears to have given up its aspirations to communist world domination and has been split up, precisely as Ezekiel foresaw just prior to its attack on Israel. Ezekiel foresaw a great Russia splitting into several allied countries (Ezek. 38:7), only to then make a pretense of peace (Ezek. 38:11), later causing Israel to be without gates and bars (idiom for a time of peace when there is no fear of war) before they attack. These changes in Russia have brought us ever closer to the biblically predicted barrage on Israel.

Philip Moore

RECENT MODERN POLITICAL COMMENT—ISRAELI VIEW

"We will have a war with Russia because Ezekiel 38 and 39 predicts it."[17]

Former Israeli President Yitzhak Navon, 1993

WHAT BROKE THE SOVIETS SO BADLY THAT THEY HAD TO PRETEND FREE ENTERPRISE TO GET OUR SUPPLIES?

Are Russia's new attitudes toward democratic reform and the release of people who are an economic burden really the old ideas of 1921? Have the modern Soviets learned a lesson from old Lenin?

Ronald Reagan built one of the mightiest military forces[18] on the face of the earth, including the Strategic Defence Initiative which

---

[17]*Perhaps Today*, May/June 1993. Available through Jack Van Impe Ministries, POB 7004, Troy, MI, USA 48007.

[18]He went over the heads of the liberal, seemingly "pro-socialist," democratic Congress of his day, straight to the American people, by using television to show the dangers the Soviets possessed and how plans for a safer America (and world), through strength, would benefit all! Peace through strength is taught by Jesus in the Bible (Luke 14:31) and was once quoted by the President to the liberal media, angering them! Remember, the prophecy in Jeremiah regarding the release of the Jews from the North (Russia) of Israel says, "I will say to the North, give up." We believe the Lord spoke through Reagan and those who influenced him, to the Russian government. It was virtually a miracle that Ronald Reagan was able to bypass Congress and get his defense program approved, budgeted, built and deployed, all within eight years. This provided bargaining power, which resulted in pressure on the Soviets to *give up their Jews and their present offensive status or starve!* Hal Lindsey reported: "Former top Soviet officials have admitted it, but the American press seems loath to report that it was President Reagan's Strategic Defense

nearly caused the Soviet government to have a nervous breakdown. The President placed "Star Wars" satellites in orbit using the space shuttle Columbia, thereby strengthening the American armed forces. The Soviets went bankrupt trying to compete, and had to temporarily give up. This is why they tore down the Berlin Wall, allowed reform, stopped the war in Afghanistan and began to release Soviet Jews (as predicted in Jer. 23:7-8). None of these moves were gestures of good will, but rather measures of desperation, as by the winter of 1991, Russian citizens were starving. They could not afford to still enforce a strict communist system and had to relax the economy.

HOOVER DOCUMENTS THE FACT THAT CAPITALISM (NEP) WAS USED ONCE BEFORE TO SALVAGE COMMUNISM

Once before in Soviet history, they reverted to a temporary capitalistic economy rather than see communism dismantled (for those of you who keep up with your history, this should not be a surprise). Former FBI Director, J. Edgar Hoover, documents in his book, *Masters of Deceit*: "By 1921, when the last 'enemies' had been driven from Russia, the nation was a shambles. The Bolsheviks, trying to adapt Marxist theory to a nation predominantly rural, had compounded confusion. Industrial production was down, peasants were in open revolt. Private incentive had been ruined. By 1922 famine raged, with tens of millions of people starving or on a semistarvation diet. Some estimates place the loss of life at five million. This was Russia's introduction to communism.

Fanatical Lenin, after years of working for the revolution, would not let it slip away from him now. He struck back furiously. Slave labor camps were increased; dreaded secret police compelled conformity; churches were closed. 'Enemies of the people,' those who opposed the Bolsheviks, were ruthlessly executed. Uprisings were cruelly suppressed.

However, terror was not the answer. In March, 1921, sailors of the Red navy in Kronstadt, formerly strong Bolshevik supporters, rebelled. Lenin, with his keen sense of timing, realized that a change had to be made.

***

Initiative that led to a shift in Soviet policy and the end of the Cold War. At a conference in Princeton University earlier this year, the officials said the Soviet economy could not compete with Reagan's efforts to develop a space-based defense against nuclear missiles." Hal Lindsey, "The Most Censored Stories of 1993," *Countdown...*, Feb. 1994. Palos Verdes, CA: Hal Lindsey Ministries, used by permission.

The result was the NEP[19]—New Economic Policy. **Capitalist practices, so denounced by the Bolsheviks, were temporarily introduced to save the Russian government**. Peasants were now allowed to keep surpluses of grain after taxation, instead of having them confiscated. They could even dispose of their surplus products as they chose, and private trade was allowed to develop. In the industrial field many businesses were returned to private owners, although the government retained control over larger concerns.

To the surprise of Bolshevik leaders the NEP proved a relative success. **It gave them the breathing spell they so desperately needed to consolidate their gains.** Both agricultural and industrial production jumped. Lenin never lived to see the final results of the temporary NEP, but the revolution was no longer in immediate danger.

Lenin's scheming mind was laying the groundwork for extending the communist conspiracy throughout the world....The whole world, they said, must go communist. '...victory is ours,' Lenin proclaimed at the First Congress of the Comintern in 1919; 'the victory of the world Communist revolution is assured.' "[20]

***

[19]What happened to the NEP? Hoover tells us: "...in barely a generation Russia had moved swiftly forward in its campaign of world conquest. In the name of Karl Marx....Such a dictatorial empire grows out of the very nature of Marxist thought and is inevitable wherever it is applied. In the Kremlin the dream of world conquest still persists. It threatens free peoples everywhere. This Russian conquest was made possible, in large measure, by the tremendous strengthening of the Soviet state. In 1928 the first of a series of Five Year Plans, designed to strengthen heavy industry and collectivize agriculture, was launched. Step by step the New Economic Policy, adopted by Lenin in 1921, disappeared. The government now undertook to control everything. Production quotas, which had to be met, were set. Compulsory labor increased. Private trade disappeared. A system of rationing was introduced. Consumer goods virtually disappeared. In rural areas small farms were abolished. Peasants were compelled to live in giant cooperatives. Many of the more well-to-do farmers, called kulaks, were dispossessed and shipped to Siberia. Entire families were liquidated. The secret police became more active. As under Lenin's 'war communism,' the Five Year Plan brought untold human misery. The forced collectivization of agriculture caused a shortage of food. Transportation broke down in many areas. In the Ukraine, the food basket of Russia, famine reappeared. Millions of people died. Disease stalked the land." J. Edgar Hoover, *Masters of Deceit*. New York: Henry Holt and Company, © 1956, p. 44, used by permission. What happened to the NEP will also, no doubt, happen to the present Russian reforms, once the state is again financially secure!

[20]Ibid, pp. 33-34. Bold mine.

Israeli demonstration in Jerusalem, supporting
the immigration of Russian Jews to Israel.

GOD USED THE CHRISTIAN PRESIDENT, REAGAN, TO INITIATE THE PROPHESIED RELEASE OF THE JEW FROM COMMUNISM

We must remember one important point about the Soviet troubles. Ronald Reagan, on his own initiative and under the influence of Godly evangelical preachers[21] and leaders, bargained and made secret agreements with Russia to release the Jews during his presidential term. Our President stood up to the Soviets. They cracked, and since 1988 have released Jews by the hundreds of thousands, as predicted by the prophet Jeremiah in the Old Testament more than 2600 years ago. "Therefore, behold, the days come, saith

---

[21]In a 1983 television special, "Israel, America's Key to Survival," evangelist Mike Evans garnered hundreds of thousands of signatures for a petition in support of Israel, which was presented to President Reagan. Many ministers, including Evans, Jerry Falwell and Pat Robertson, met with the Chief Executive and shared with him the prophetic importance of working for the good of Israel.

the LORD, that they shall no more say, The LORD liveth, which brought up the children of Israel out of the land of Egypt; But, The LORD liveth, which brought up and which led the seed of the house of Israel out of the north country, and from all countries whither I had driven them; and they shall dwell in their own land" (Jer. 23:7-8 KJV).

THE SOVIETS WHO WERE HERE YESTERDAY WILL BE BACK TOMORROW—THEIR MOTIVE IS TOTAL OWNERSHIP OF ALL PROPERTY

The Bible says that the Russians, who are releasing Jews today, will attack Israel tomorrow. Hoover, a great expert on the dangers of communism, informs us: "The ex-communist is today one of our most potent weapons against communism."[22] An important example of this is documented in Dr. Arthur Kac's book, *The Messiahship of Jesus.* Dr. Kac is a Jewish believer in Jesus. He writes concerning communism: "Under Communism all political power and all economic power are vested in the hands of the government. When private enterprise is made illegal, every person is an employee of the government. His whole economic existence, his chance for advancement, his seniority—all depend on some government functionary. He cannot quit his job or look for another job without permission from the government. He is at the mercy of the government in a way that is unthinkable and intolerable in a true democracy.

What became of the Marxist doctrine of equality and the classless society is best told by one who knew the system from inside. One of the most important documents on the social system under Communism is a book written by Milovan Djilas, formerly vice president of communist Yugoslavia. For writing that book he was put in prison. The following excerpt from his work concerns the new ruling class in communist countries.

'Property is legally considered social and national property. But, in actuality, a single group manages it in its own interest....In communism, power and ownership are almost always in the same hands but this fact is concealed under a legal guise....The formal owner is the nation. In reality, because of monopolistic administration, only the narrowest stratum of administrators enjoys the rights of ownership....While promising to abolish social difference, [the new class] must always increase them by acquiring the products of the nation's workshops and granting privileges to its adherents....This is a class whose power over men is the most complete known to history....Having achieved industrialization, the new class can now do nothing more than strengthen its brute force and pillage the people.' "[23]

---

[22]J. Edgar Hoover, *Masters of Deceipt*, p. 117.
[23]Arthur W. Kac, *The Messiahship of Jesus*, pp. 283-284.

Even though we can appreciate that the Russians have been pressured into what appears to be a democracy (releasing Jews today), we must remember that tomorrow they will attack Israel. The same Bible that predicted the release of the Jews also foretold the attempted destruction of the Jewish state shortly thereafter (see our chapter 26, "We Win Armageddon—Our Final Battle" for a detailed examination of this).

WHEN THE BEAR SHOWS ITS TEETH AGAIN, OR SHORTLY THEREAFTER, IT WILL BE TO BITE ISRAEL[24]

You may ask why Russia has apparently relaxed their policy regarding Jewish emigration at the moment. Well, for one thing, we all know Russia has felt for some time that Israel is standing in the way of their expansion into the Middle East because of Israel's nuclear capabilities. But there is another reason hinted at in a speech President Reagan made about Russia's inability to feed themselves.[25] This speech ran as follows: "In the 1950's, Khrushchev predicted: 'We will bury you.' But in the West today, we see a free world that has achieved a level of prosperity and well-being unprecedented in all human history. In the communist world, we see failure, technological backwardness, declining standards of health, even want of the most basic kind, too little food. Even today, the Soviet Union still cannot feed itself....the Soviets themselves may, in a limited way, be coming to understand the importance of freedom. We hear much from Moscow about a new policy of reform....Are these the beginnings of profound changes in the Soviet state? Or are they token gestures, intended to raise false hopes in the West, or to strengthen the Soviet system without changing it....Mr. Gorbachev, tear down this [Berlin] wall!"[26]

---

[24]Before another fifty years pass, most probably.

[25]In 1991, Hal Lindsey pointed out that: "...the Soviet Union remains a giant Third World country with the mightiest military machine on earth. Here are some sobering statistics about the lumbering beast that still threatens the world with nuclear annihilation: * 40 million live in poverty—even by the Soviet Union's own conservative means of measuring such conditions. * Every sixth hospital bed is in an institution with no running water. One in three hospitals has no indoor toilets. A 950-bed hospital gets an average of one or two hypodermic needles a day. * Half the schools have no central heating, running water or indoor toilets. The average Soviet citizen has a worse diet than he did under the rule of Czar Nicholas II in 1913. Then, Russia was the world's largest food exporter. Now it is the largest importer. Meanwhile...Gorbachev has contradicted such hopeful thoughts in recent speeches. Late in the 1980s, for instance, in a speech to a national student conference he rejected claims that reform in Eastern Europe spells the demise of socialism and insisted that the communist revolution that brought such misery to the people 'was not a mistake.' " Hal Lindsey, *The 1990s: Prophecy on Fast Forward.* Palos Verdes, CA: Hal Lindsey Ministries, © 1990, chapter 13, p. 4, used by permission.

[26]Hal Lindsey, *Countdown...* [ ] mine.

DESPITE THE BOLD CLAIMS OF FINANCIAL CHANGE, RUSSIA WILL FOIL IT AND DESCEND ON ISRAEL TO TAKE THEIR SPOIL, SO SAYS EZEKIEL

We know from subtle hints in the prophecies of the Bible that the Russians will never allow the present promise of reform to continue. In all probability they will fall back into hard-line socialism the moment the government is financially stable, once they have strengthened the Soviet system without really changing it, as Ronald Reagan suspected. They will repeat the same pattern from 1921, when after the success of NEP,[27] they proceeded to "pillage their people." Thus they will become doubly poor[28] again, which will facilitate the fulfillment of Ezekiel's prophecy.

Ezekiel prophesied that one of the reasons "Gog, the land of Magog, the chief prince of Meshech and Tubal" (Ezek. 38:2 KJV) attacks Israel, is because Israel has "gotten goods" (Ezek. 38:12 KJV). Listen to the eloquent description of this prophetic scenario currently coming together in political events right before our eyes, as described by Ezekiel: "Thus saith the Lord GOD; It shall also come to pass, *that* at the same time shall things come into thy mind, and thou shalt think an evil thought: And thou shalt say, I will go up to the land of unwalled villages; I will go to them that are at rest, that dwell safely, all of them dwelling without walls, and having neither bars nor gates, To take a spoil, and to take a prey; to turn thine hand upon the desolate

---

[27]The 1921 NEP versus the 1991 NEP—If Russia was truly granting freedom to their citizens without some sort of secret plan to re-socialize them, they would have turned all the government-owned factories to private ownership and invited us in to supervise their "new capitalist system." Instead, they are raising prices in order to destroy the spirit of the people, so when they accomplish a "coup," the government can say that "capitalism" did not work. Meanwhile, in 1995...we are refinancing them. Where do you think all of our money is going? That's right, a good chunk of it is going into the "former" communist party members' hands within a subdued government. When the money slows, their hand will tighten its grip on the people once again. Watch and see what happens after 2003, or somewhere in-between, whenever the money begins to dry up. Pat Robertson mentioned that 400 million dollars was sent to Russia by the U.S. in 1994, for the sole purpose of dismantling nuclear weapons. In this interesting piece of literature, we quote this startling fact: "Some of the Russian scientists who worked on Novichok say U.S. money has been diverted to weapons development." "The 700 Club Fact Sheet," March 29, 1994, Christian Broadcasting Network, Inc., © used by permission. Available through CBN, 700 CBN Center, Virginia Beach, VA, USA 23463. It turns out that almost all of the weapons that will be dismantled are obsolete. On the same broadcast, Randall Brooks reported: "Just before he died last year, Andrei Zheleznyakov, a scientist who worked on Novichok, told the Russian newspaper, Novoye Vremya, 'The generals cannot be trusted with the destruction of chemical weapons. The money received from the Americans for this purpose will definitely be channeled into the development of new and more powerful toxic substances.' " Ibid.

[28]Wasting whatever aid the U.S. has provided for them to attempt a capitalist system.

places *that are now* inhabited, and upon the people that are gathered out of the nations, which have **gotten cattle and goods**, that dwell in the midst of the land....Art thou come to take a spoil? hast thou gathered thy company to take a prey? to carry away silver and gold, to take away cattle and goods, to take a great spoil? Therefore, son of man, prophesy and say unto Gog, Thus saith the Lord GOD; In that day when my people of Israel dwelleth safely, shalt thou not know *it?* And thou shalt come from thy place out of the north parts, thou, and many people with thee....it shall be in the latter days....Thus saith the Lord GOD; *Art* thou he of whom I have spoken in old time by my servants the prophets of Israel...." (Ezek. 38:10-17 KJV).

GOD TELLS US OF HIS IMPENDING JUDGMENT OF RUSSIA, IN THE FIRST PERSON, FOR THEIR ATTEMPT TO DESTROY ISRAEL

Ezekiel reports God's judgment on Russia: "And I will plead against him with pestilence and with blood; and I will rain upon him, and upon his bands, and upon the many people that *are* with him, an overflowing rain, and great hailstones, fire, and brimstone. Thus will I magnify myself, and sanctify myself; and I will be known in the eyes of many nations, and they shall know that I *am* the LORD....Thou shalt fall upon the mountains of Israel, thou, and all thy bands, and the people that *is* with thee: I will give thee unto the ravenous birds of every sort, and *to* the beasts of the field to be devoured. Thou shalt fall upon the open field: for I have spoken *it*, saith the Lord GOD. And I will send a fire on Magog, and among them that dwell carelessly in the isles: and they shall know that I *am* the LORD" (Ezek. 38:22-23; 39:4-6 KJV).

SIR ISAAC NEWTON CONFIRMS GOG'S ATTACK ON A RESTORED ISRAEL AFTER A FUTURE FALSE PEACE AGREEMENT IS THWARTED

Sir Isaac Newton commented on this prophecy in Ezekiel over three hundred years ago. Newton, our greatest scientist, wrote: "If you desire to know the manner...of the war of Gog and Magog you may see them both described by Ezekiel chap 38 and 39...represents how the Jews after their return from captivity dwell safely and quietly upon the

***

mountains of Israel in unwalled towns without either gates or barrs[29] to defend them untill they are grown very rich in Cattel and gold and silver and goods and Gog of the land of Magog stirrs up the nations round about, Persia and Arabia and Afric and the northern nations of Asia and Europe against them to take a spoile, and God destroys all that great army, that the nations may from thenceforth know that the...Jews went formerly into captivity for their sins but now since their return are become invincible."[30]

EVEN A MODERN ISRAELI RABBI, WHO TO MY KNOWLEDGE NEVER PROFESSED FAITH IN THE NEW TESTAMENT, UNDERSTANDS RUSSIA'S HIDDEN MOTIVES

From this prediction we can clearly see that the present apparent bloom of freedom and break-up of Russia will not continue, allowing the Soviet people to prosper. Rather, these reforms are a cruel hoax to give false hope and help the **government** consolidate its gains and prepare for a war of conquest of the free world, as Lenin promised and the Bible prophesied.

The late Rabbi Rafael Eisenberg was one of the few who observed Russia from a pure and biblical view. His comments reveal his biblical knowledge of chapters 38 and 39 of Ezekiel. They also serve to illustrate his frustration with the present political situation, which parallels the end time events culminating in the Coming of Messiah. He wrote in his book, *A Matter of Return*: "Russia is the obvious embodiment of the rule of evil and apostasy which will expand over the entire world...being the most tyrannical and despotic of all nations....The Russian descendants of Edom...have become one of Yisrael's deadliest enemies and will remain so until the days of the Messiah. It was the Russians...supplying the Arab governments with an abundance of modern weaponry with which to murder the People of Yisrael and expell their remnants from their land.

The Russians' ambition in so doing was to expand their own wicked government over Eretz Yisrael and the entire Middle East—which is the axis of the world, thus guaranteeing themselves unhampered, absolute control over the entire globe. Nevertheless, in spite of the superior and unlimited aid which Russia gave to the Arabs, God saved and rescued Yisrael, as we have clearly experienced in 1956, 1967 and in 1973.

---

[29] These words, "unwalled towns without either gates or barrs," are biblical idioms for peace. Even with all the current Russian and Arab peace proclamations, we do not have to guess how it will all end up, not if we are up on our Ezekiel, do we?

[30] *Yahuda Manuscript 6, fol.17-18.*

Even the irreligious Israel press reported the Divine aid given to Yisrael in June '67, when the Arab nations declared war against Yisrael."[31]

WHERE WILL RUSSIA FIND THESE SPOILS? ISRAEL IS NOT VERY WEALTHY NOW, BUT...

Ezekiel tells us in 38:12: "To take a spoil, and to take a prey; to turn thine hand upon the desolate places *that are now* inhabited, and upon the people *that are* gathered out of the nations, which have gotten cattle and goods, that dwell in the midst of the land" (KJV).

Where will the riches Ezekiel mentioned come from? Modern Israel is not yet full of the riches he described. We believe there are two possibilities. One is that Israel may discover oil herself. On my last trip to Israel I saw several oil rigs drilling off the coast near the city of Elat.[32] The second is that Israel may well expand its present boundaries before the Messiah returns.

According to Genesis 15, Israel will one day possess the land from the river of Egypt to the great river, the river Euphrates (Gen. 15:18). This will include Iraq, Egypt and a portion of Saudi Arabia. We all know Israel will possess this huge plot of land when Jesus returns, however, some feel it could happen before then.

Nathan, an Israeli friend of mine, once told me that Israeli General Ariel Sharon said: "If America ever cuts off aid to Israel, it won't be the end of the world. We can take Saudi Arabia, have all the oil and do the rest of the world a favor by selling it at a much more reasonable price."

Since Reagan left office, America's left-wing is less in favor of the great grants and sums of money his administration advanced to Israel. Should there be a shift in the American government to the far left some time in the future, Ariel Sharon's suggestion may just have to become reality! This is in addition to all of the wealth[33] brought back from the Diaspora communities, especially the United States, once the false Messiah has world Jewry convinced he is truly the Messiah. For a full explanation of this subject, see our chapter 26, "We Win Armageddon—Our Final Battle."

---

[31] Rafael Eisenberg, *A Matter of Return*. Jerusalem: Feldheim Publishers, © 1980, pp. 15, 39, used by permission.

[32] See our chapter 26, "We Win Armageddon—Our Final Battle," for a photograph of one of these oil wells.

[33] This would include, you name it: stocks; bonds; precious metals; precious stones; diamond mines in Africa; overseas real estate holdings; entertainment royalty rights; overseas banking and lending; worldwide business capital in general. We are not picking on the Jews. Any group of people, Italians, Greeks, etc., who would return from all over the world at once, to a small homeland, bringing their life savings, would of course make that country considerably richer.

Remember, if a large sector of the American Jewish population goes to Israel to live, the wealth Ezekiel predicted will have arrived. This is intended as a compliment to the Jewish people, and Ezekiel's prophecy agrees with our compliment. Don't we wish all peoples could amass wealth as successfully as the Jewish people have? Africa and India would not be starving today, would they?

THREE CHRISTIAN SCHOLARS OF THE 1800'S FORESAW THE PREDICTED INVASION LONG BEFORE MODERN ISRAEL AND RUSSIA EXISTED

Regarding Israel and her future invasion by Russia, Hal Lindsey illustrates in chapters 4 and 5 of his book, *The Late Great Planet Earth*, that several Bible believing Protestant Christian scholars of the past four centuries interpreted this very same scheme of events long before Israel or present day Russia were in existence. Hal notes: "The fact that the Jews had to be restored as a nation before Christ could return was seen by James Grant, an English Bible scholar writing in 1866.

'The personal coming of Christ, to establish His Millennial reign on earth, will not take place *until the Jews are restored to their own land*, and the enemies of Christ and the Jews have gathered together their armies from all parts of the world, and have commenced the siege of Jerusalem...now the return of the Jews to the Holy Land, and the mustering and marshalling of these mighty armies, with a view to capturing Jerusalem, must require a *considerable time yet.*'

(This was written eighty-two years before Israel was made a nation.) [Hal remarks]...the case is that this physical restoration to the land is directly associated with triggering the hostility which brings about a great judgment upon all nations and the Messiah's return to set up God's Kingdom. In other words, it is the presence of this reborn nation of Israel, flourishing in prosperity, that excites a great enemy from the uttermost north of Palestine to launch an attack upon them which sets off the last war of the world. This war is to be ended with such a display of divine intervention that a great many of the surviving Gentiles and Jews put their whole trust in the true Messiah, Jesus Christ....Since the restoration of Israel as a nation in 1948, we have lived in the most significant period of prophetic history. We are living in the times which Ezekiel predicted in chapters 38 and 39.

In 1854 a scholar named Chamberlain summed up the crux of what has just been said. In commenting on Ezekiel 38, he observed, 'From all which I should infer, the coming restoration of Israel will at first be gradual and pacific; a restoration permitted, if not assisted and encouraged or protected. They will return to occupy the whole land, both cities and villages; they will be settled there, become prosperous and increasing in wealth, before this great confederacy of northern people will be formed against them.'

Consider that Chamberlain wrote this over one hundred years ago—long before Israel was a nation 'assisted and encouraged' by other countries....For centuries, long before the current events could have influenced the interpreter's ideas, men have recognized that Ezekiel's prophecy about the northern commander referred to Russia.

Dr. John Cumming, writing in 1864, said, 'This king of the North I conceive to be the autocrat of Russia...that Russia occupies a place, and a very momentous place, in the prophetic word has been admitted by almost all expositors.' "[34]

SDI—STAR WARS—WHY A RESPONSIBLE PRESIDENT *WOULD* DEPLOY THE SHIELD

We should not forget about Gorbachev's secret meeting with top communist leaders, as reported by Sir William Stephenson, head of Combined Intelligence Operations. Stephenson revealed at an American Bar Association address that: "...in November, 1987 Gorbachev made a secret speech to the top leadership of Russia on the anniversary of the Communist coup of 1917. The thrust of Gorbachev's speech was that Russia must adopt policies 'that stops the U.S. Strategic Defense Initiative (SDI) and puts the Americans to sleep.' "[35]

IS THE 1991 NEP A PRELUDE TO RUSSIA'S PREDICTED INVASION OF ISRAEL?

We have good reason to believe that all of Russia's promises and "steps of freedom and democracy" are not permanent, but a rehash of the 1921 NEP. Until they are firmly back on their feet, keep your eyes on the bear and don't be fooled by his sleep—he has his eyes opened just a crack, and is waiting for you to doze off before his snack!

Stephenson, our military friend who revealed this secret Russian meeting to us, predicted: "...that the West would accept the proclamations of peace and democracy at their utmost peril. In the same way that Adolf Hitler promised Neville Chamberlain 'Peace in our Time', the Soviets are talking peace while rapidly continuing the most massive buildup of armaments in the history of the world."[36]

---

[34]Hal Lindsey, *The Late Great Planet Earth*, pp. 49-50, 52, 62-63 [ ] mine.
[35]Grant R. Jeffrey, *Armageddon, Appointment with Destiny*, p. 206.
[36]Ibid.

What better way to put the U.S. to sleep than to proclaim an end to the Cold War and appear to break into "republics of democracy," which will one day be resubverted. We doubt that the "democracy" portrayed in the Russian republics will be a permanent thing. Rather, we have good reason to think the communists are hoodwinking the West to draw as much aid as possible before they reinstate communism or some other similar form of totalitarianism, which involves governmental control of wealth and people. However, this should remind us that all of the prophecies in Ezekiel 38-39, which we read in our study of the Russian attack against Israel in the last days, **do not** necessitate that Russia be communist at the time they attack. The land in Russia now is the same land, the military is the same and their governments remain nuclear.

The fact that Russia is financially bankrupt and divided into republics, makes their biblically predicted invasion far more likely to be sooner than later; probably within the next twenty-five years rather than in the next fifty, because Ezekiel predicted that they would be divided when they attack. As he emphasized: "And thou shalt come from thy place out of the north parts, thou, and many people with thee, all of them riding upon horses, a great company, and a mighty army...." (Ezek. 38:15 KJV).

As you can see, this does not say a single army, but many. Also, their motive, as revealed by the Bible, is: "To take a spoil, and to take a prey; to turn thine hand upon the desolate places *that are now* inhabited, and upon the people that are gathered out of the nations, which have gotten cattle and goods, that dwell in the midst of the land" (Ezek. 38:12 KJV).

Obviously they are doing this because they need it. At present, these "former" communist countries are very poor, more than ever before. If they are not given goods, they will no doubt take them, using any means necessary to accomplish their goal. Remember the big question. If they really want peace why have they not surrendered their weapons to us?

IS RUSSIA SINCERE IN THEIR PEACE PROPOSALS?

Reverend Pat Robertson suggested that if Russia really wanted peace and was sincere about her new change to democracy being permanent, then she should sell her nuclear weapons to us.[37] Relating: Let us get them into a truly peaceful situation with us. Since we are giving them so much aid, why couldn't they give us some of these big bombs in exchange? If they are genuine.

---

[37] *The 700 Club,* Apr. 14, 1992, Christian Broadcasting Network.

I agree with Pat, because many keen and astute believers in Jesus do not believe the Russians are sincere, nor do we believe this is a permanent change. Rather, it is a ploy to procure the wealth of the West. In fact, the Russians now are more dangerous to Israel and the rest of the world than ever before because they are selling nuclear weapons, while posing as a benign group of independent republics. If an A-bomb were launched, Russia could easily say they did not know who did it, thus evading a retaliatory U.S. strike. This would afford Russia the opportunity to indirectly attack Israel or the West without assuming responsibility.

The nature of the deterrent in the 1962 Cuban Missile Crisis was that President Kennedy informed Russia that if they attacked the U.S. from Cuba, a full-scale counterattack would follow. Today, it is getting harder to tell exactly who "they" are and that is not by accident!

STAR WARS SAVED ME IN ISRAEL—WHY WOULD ANYONE DARE TO PROTEST THIS DEFENSIVE PEACE SHIELD? INSANITY!

Stanley and Ethel Marks, in their anti-Christian book, *Judaism Looks at Christianity, 7 B.C.E. - 1986 C.E.*, wrote in regard to our Star Wars national defense program: "Science, all fields of destruction, can never be held in secret. The Star War dream of Reagan is nothing more than a dream....The Nuclear Armageddon will arrive solely due to the obsession of the leaders of the Pauline christianity to 'hate your enemies.' The proof of that statement is found in the history of the Western World....The course of history flows inexorably and it flows toward the Nuclear Armageddon desired by Pauline christianity before the end of this decade."[38] Armageddon did not happen before 1990, as these authors so adamantly predicted!

To those of us who lived in Israel in 1990,[39] and the majority of Israelis, Star Wars was *not* a dream! The Patriot Missile, a product of the Star Wars program, was said to have saved the lives of thousands of Israelis and was our only defense against the incoming missiles. We are concerned that President Clinton has not deployed the nuclear shield which Reagan initiated. In the future, this may cause Americans to suffer a higher casualty rate in any upcoming confrontation, most notably the predicted war of Armageddon!

---

[38]Stanley J. and Ethel M. Marks, *Judaism Looks at Christianity, 7 B.C.E - 1986 C.E.* Newell, IA: Bureau of International Affairs, © 1986, p. 193, used by permission.

[39]I lived in Jerusalem from 1987 to mid-1991 and enjoyed watching the Patriot missiles chase Hussein's Scud missiles from the roof of an apartment building in French Hill. Israel is presently developing the arrow anti-ballistic missile system which works, meanwhile, our liberal congressmen place us in jeopardy by denying us the development of such a system in the United States.

Thus, if it had not been for the conservative revolution in the 1980's under President Ronald Reagan, there would have been no Patriot missiles. It was reported many times in the Israeli press that these missiles prevented a great number of casualties that would have ensued from Hussein's Russian-made Scud missiles hitting Israel.

It is predicted that the Arabs and Russians will attempt to launch devastating military actions against Israel, and possibly the West (Ezek. 38-39), in the future. Consequently, we should be militarily prepared, to the best of our ability. Jesus said: "...what king, going to make war against another king, sitteth not down first, and consulteth whether he be able with ten thousand to meet him that cometh against him with twenty thousand? Or else, while the other is yet a great way off, he sendeth an ambassage and desireth conditions of peace" (Luke 14:31-32 KJV).

This is certainly not the time to cut defense—not in the face of the worldwide communist arms race.[40] We should remember every time we go to the voting polls to cast our ballot in favor of those who have a documented history in support of the defense of our nation (women, children and little ones)! Your vote literally decides whether you live or die. To **not** continue with the most advanced Star Wars defense program would invite a more imminent and higher casualty rate, no matter how big the smile on the faces of Yeltsin or any future Russian leaders.

We know from the Bible that in the future the "Russians will indeed be coming." Thus we should be ready because the Bible does not show a clear-cut victory for the West. This may be deliberate. God is leaving our fate up to us, depending on how well we help His people, Israel (Gen. 12:3), and how much we are willing to care about ourselves by defending ourselves (Luke 14:31). This is all based on placing Godly conservative leaders within our government, who will make defense decisions based on the production and use of the latest equipment, and by our willingness to vote and vote right (I mean right as in correct and as far away from left as possible)! Woops, I hope I don't lose my tax exempt status to the IRS—just kidding, not really, I don't have any. But if I did, I would gladly sacrifice it for the betterment of my country. My right of free speech to advise my loved ones of the facts isn't for sale to the IRS!

The very idea that the IRS should be allowed to blackmail Christian ministers for endorsing candidates for office should be called into question and abolished. Where is it said in our free society, that a person's or religious organization's tax exempt status can be revoked if

---

[40]This arms race includes North Korean and Chinese nuclear proliferation on an ever-increasing scale. It is possible in the future that some communist countries will drop the name of communist and form totalitarian national governments (possibly after pretending to convert to Democracy), but I can assure you they will not drop their arms.

it chooses to voice its view on the candidates? Nowhere—this is unconstitutional. This was rigged after the television ministers helped elect Ronald Reagan to two terms and helped Bush, so that a liberal could have a chance. Next time you vote, pray to God to give you discernment before punching the ballot. He will answer your prayer!

CLINTON TRAITOROUSLY KILLS OUR STAR WARS-SDI NUCLEAR PROTECTION SHIELD

Ken Watts, of WAGA news in Atlanta, Georgia, reported: "Former President Ronald Reagan took a few shots at his successor, Bill Clinton, for killing his Star Wars Program, at the Citadel Military Academy in South Carolina today. Mr. Reagan said he's proud he launched the Strategic Defense Initiative. He said the space-based anti-missile system played a key role in ending the Cold War." The video-tape of Reagan speaking at the Citadel, filmed that mid-day in May of 1993, was then shown, as Reagan said: "I am not a Rhodes scholar, but I do know this; if we can protect Americans with a defensive shield from incoming missile attacks, we should by all means do so." A standing ovation followed. Reagan continued: "If a new administration in Washington thinks we are no longer at risk, they need to open their eyes and take a long hard look at the world...."

We, as Bible believing defense-minded Christians, also criticize Clinton[41] for violating Jesus' defense program in Luke 14:31[42] and placing us and our loved ones in jeopardy! May we all pray that Clinton and those like-minded and irresponsible come to swift judgment! May our Lord place a responsible godly man over our nation once again.

---

[41] You may be asking whose side he is on? Don't forget, during the Vietnam War, he was protesting that war against the communists on Russian soil. He is a very mixed-up and dangerous fellow, having never had a father's guidance at home during his early years. Not to mention his denial of guidance from his Heavenly Father. He is unstable, even in his adult life. No doubt, by the time you are reading this, he will be long gone. We emphasize that most political candidates from the left who attempt to disarm are not worthy of our vote. A believer's vote belongs to the godly patriot, in our opinion! Jerry Falwell produced a remarkable videotape entitled *Circle of Power, A Prescription for Disaster,* which documents not only laughed-upon Clinton adulteries, but the pleas of mothers who claim their sons and loved ones were murdered, on orders from Clinton, to protect his then-presidential political future.

[42] A modern English translation of Luke 14:31-32 records the words of Jesus as follows: "Or what king, when he sets out to meet another king in battle, will not first sit down and take counsel whether he is strong enough with ten thousand *men* to encounter the one coming against him with twenty thousand? Or else, while the other is still far away, he sends a delegation and asks terms of peace" (NASB). See Appendix 1, page 1127-9 and *Vol. II*, chapter 42, "Wealth and Pacifism Clarified with Scripture," to see where the Bible and Jesus draw the line between self-defense and turning the other cheek, based on the meaning of Hebrew words! Interestingly, Christians are not required to be sitting ducks, as some believe.

THE CREATURE WHO HAS SEIZED OUR PRESIDENCY IS KILLING SDI, DESPITE ITS SUCCESS IN TESTS

It was mentioned on Reverend Hal Lindsey's radio program *Weekend in Review*, May 15, 1993, that a very successful Star Wars test was recently performed. The gist of the program was that it was a shame for President Clinton[43] of "Aspen, Clinton and Company," to destroy what Ronald Reagan said was the key that brought the Cold War to an end. Are we going to let the Russian communists come back? Hopefully not, if we vote conservative Republican. No doubt, we may see several Democrat and Republican presidents before the showdown begins. Let's pray for godly conservative victories from now on, so that until the Lord comes, we will be as safe as possible!

RUSSIA TALKS PEACE BUT KEEPS BUILDING "RED OCTOBER" SUBMARINES

Hal Lindsey, in his 1992 publication, *The Magog Factor, A Special Report*, noted of Russia's recent defense build-up: "The provocative aspect of the Soviet building program is the cost: a Trident (and a Typhoon) costs in excess of $1 billion, fully equipped. In 1988 we had 34 ballistic missile submarines commissioned; the Soviets had 63. That gave them a capability to hold over 12,000 cities hostage. Not bad. But, apparently, that wasn't enough. In 1989 they built 9 more submarines. In 1990, they built 9 more. In 1991, they built 12 more. That's 30 more 'Red October'-type subs."[44]

THE MORE MONEY WE GIVE THEM, THE MORE WEAPONS THEY BUILD!

Hal Lindsey, who has access to U.S. intelligence, informed us in his June 1993 *Countdown...* article entitled, "Russians Modernize Strategic Arsenal," that: "As President Clinton and the European powers offer Russian President Boris Yeltsin a virtual blank check to help revitalize his suffering economy, Moscow continues to spend billions modernizing its strategic nuclear arsenal.

---

[43]Clinton walked in with forty-three percent because Perot split the conservative vote. In future elections we suggest conservative voters beware of Perot and similar candidates. We suspect that he is a vote-splitter for some secret special interest group. When Reagan won, in 1984, by the greatest landslide in history, it was Mondale who *lost* with forty-three percent of the vote. How did Clinton win with this small number? We have someone we never voted for, tearing down our national defenses.

[44]Hal Lindsey and Chuck Missler, *The Magog Factor, A Special Report*. Palos Verdes, CA: Hal Lindsey Ministries, pp. 50-51. This report is available through Hal Lindsey Ministries, POB 4000, Palos Verdes, CA, USA 90274.

Yes, I know. You've been told that the Russians are scrapping their nuclear weapons and that's why we need to encourage them with foreign aid. Well, let me tell you, Russia's nuclear weapons are as well-positioned to destroy the United States in a first strike as they have ever been. And it is the United States, not Russia, that is unilaterally disarming at a dangerous pace.

Let me be clear about something. I am not suggesting Yeltsin is anything but a true reformer who wants to move Russia toward market economics and democratic reforms. However, he is one man. He may not even have total control over the military in Russia. And he is literally surrounded by men who more closely resemble the hard-line, Communist totalitarian leaders of the old Soviet Union.

Take Vice President Alexander Rutskoi, for instance. He is calling for reinstating state control of the economy and disagrees with Yeltsin on moves toward widening freedoms for average Russians. This man is one bullet away from taking over the reins of power in a nation that still has a gun to our head—a nuclear gun.

The way the nuclear weapon modernization program continues at full speed in Russia should, therefore, give every American reason to be alarmed. With the MIRV (Multiple Independently-targeted Re-entry Vehicle) ICBMs due to be eliminated under the terms of START and START II, Russian modernization efforts are concentrated on single warhead missile systems like the SS-25. Intelligence reports suggest that by the end of this decade the Russians will deploy three new strategic systems, an SS-25 mobile, a silo-based version of the SS-25 and a new missile to replace the SSN-20 on the Typhoon class submarine.

Reports also indicate that the modernized versions of the SS-25 will have larger throw-weights and much greater accuracy.

'This is being done by the Russian republic at the very time that the U.S. has basically halted much of our own strategic modernization program and is proceeding unilaterally in many respects to dismantle the existing strategic systems in advance of entry into force of either START I or START II treaties,' Sen. John Warner said during confirmation hearings for Secretary of Defense Les Aspin.

The modernization effort is not a violation of any treaty with the United States. START restricts the size of the strategic forces but not their capabilities. So the Russians are accomplishing more with less.

'The continued deployment of Soviet mobile ICBMs (such as the SS-25) will give the (Russians) a monopoly on a survivable, land-based strategic reserve,' says Lawrence Fink, a Soviet and defense analyst writing in Defense News.

The modernization effort began long before the Soviet Union collapsed. U.S. intelligence experts have been predicting it would come to a halt for several years, but it continues unabated.

'The SS-25's modernization has been ignored by the media, while aid to Russia has dominated the headlines, as well as the administration's policy,' stated Defense Media Review.

The most disturbing part of this revelation, however, is the fact that the U.S. is leaving itself totally vulnerable to whatever fate dictates for Russia. After spending $32 billion developing a strategic defense, the U.S. program has been virtually abandoned by the Clinton administration.

No strategic defense. No modernization effort. Combine that with the massive military cutbacks and you have a prescription for disaster.

I was among those who warned about the dangers posed by the old Soviet Union for years. Were we right? According to newly discovered documents in East Germany, were we ever. The Washington Post reported earlier this year that the Soviet Union and East Germany were planning a full-scale invasion of West Germany 'so detailed and advanced that the Communists had already made street signs for western cities, printed cash for their occupation government and built equipment to run eastern trains on western tracks.'

When western officers took over eastern bases after the reunification of Germany in 1990, they found more ammunition for the 160,000-man East German army than the West Germans had for their 500,000-man force.

'The operational planning was far more advanced than anything our intelligence had envisioned,' said Vice Admiral Ulrich Weisser, chief of the planning staff for the German Bundeswehr, or armed forces.

Could it be that certain forces in Moscow are still preparing for the goals they had established for over 70 years? Wouldn't it be better to be safe than sorry?

The Bible tells us that Russia will play an important military role in the last days. Though all of the talk these days is about Russia disarming, it is clear she is still well-equipped to play out that final endtimes role scripted for her in prophecy."[45]

***

---

[45]Hal Lindsey, "Russians Modernize Strategic Arsenel," *Countdown...*, June 1993. Palos Verdes, CA: Hal Lindsey Ministries, pp. 1, 15, used by permission.

NEW STUDENTS CAN LEARN FROM OLD TEACHERS ABOUT THE GOALS AND AIMS OF SOCIALISM, ACCORDING TO ITS CREED

How do we know that the Russians do not really want a permanent peace with the West? Can we be sure that co-existence between the free and communist world is an illusion in their view? Is there anything in their ancient creed which points to their philosophy which states, "Be Red or be dead"? Hoover writes of Lenin: "Borrowing from the autocratic character of Marx himself, Lenin made Marxism a highly disciplined, organized, and ruthless creed. How can revolution be achieved? Not by democratic reforms, ballots, or good will but by naked, bloody violence. The sword is the weapon. Everything must be dedicated to this aim: one's time, talents, one's very life. Revolutions do not just happen. They are made."[46] Lenin himself wrote: "The dictatorship of the proletariat is necessary, and victory over the bourgeoisie is impossible without a long, stubborn and desperate war of life and death....As long as capitalism and socialism exist, we cannot live in peace: in the end, one or the other will triumph—a funeral dirge will be sung either over the Soviet Republic or over world capitalism."[47]

RUSSIAN THREATS FROM THE PAST WILL BECOME THE REALITIES OF THE FUTURE, AS THE ULTIMATE PEACE TREATY IS BROKEN

Have the Russians voiced their intent to attack Israel? In answer to this question, we will quote Russia's own ambassador: "...if the Israelis threaten us, we will wipe them out within two days. I can assure you our plans are made for this eventuality."[48]

By the time you read Dobrynin's quote in this book, don't be surprised if the Russians are talking "peace" with Israel. It was predicted the Antichrist will ultimately achieve this peace (see our chapter 23, "The False Messiah Armilus Equals Antichrist") for a short time. However, remember that Russia will never, according to the Bible, change her mind about Israel and will ultimately attempt to carry out the Soviet Ambassador's threat. We know this from Ezekiel 38:8-12 where it states: "After many days thou shalt be visited: in the latter

---

[46]J. Edgar Hoover, *Masters of Deceit*, pp. 28-29.

[47]Ibid, p. 35.

[48]William Goetz, *Apocalypse Next.* Sussex, England: Kingsway Publications Ltd., © 1980, p. 123. This was stated by Soviet Ambassador Anatoly Dobrynin to Henry Kissinger.

years thou shalt come into the land *that is* brought back from the sword, *and is* gathered out of many people, against the mountains of Israel, which have been always waste: but it is brought forth out of the nations, and they shall dwell safely all of them. Thou shalt ascend and come like a storm, thou shalt be like a cloud to cover the land, thou, and all thy bands, and many people with thee. Thus saith the Lord GOD; It shall also come to pass, *that* at the same time shall things come into thy mind, and thou shalt think an evil thought: And thou shalt say, I will go up to the land of unwalled villages; I will go to them that are at rest, that dwell safely, all of them dwelling without walls, and having neither bars nor gates, To take a spoil, and to take a prey; to turn thine hand upon the desolate places *that are now* inhabited, and upon the people *that are* gathered out of the nations, which have gotten cattle and goods, that dwell in the midst of the land" (KJV).

THOUGH ISRAEL WILL BE CAUGHT OFF GUARD, AS EZEKIEL PREDICTS, ZECHARIAH SAYS JESUS WILL NOT!

According to God's predictions, Israel will be caught off guard, as they were by Egypt in the 1973 Yom Kippur War. The phrases "unwalled villages" and "them that are at rest living without walls and without gates and bars," indicate that the false Messiah, who at that time will be thought to be truly the Jewish Messiah (see chap. 23), will have such a massive false peace treaty in force worldwide that Israel will appear to have little security and will look like "open game" to the Russians. However, the Russians have a surprise waiting for them, and that surprise is the true Jewish Messiah, Jesus Christ, and His return to defeat them and their allied Arab invading armies at the time the attack in question takes place. "And it shall come to pass in that day, *that* I will seek to destroy all the nations that come against Jerusalem. And I will pour upon the house of David, and upon the inhabitants of Jerusalem, the spirit of grace and of supplications: and they shall look upon me whom they have pierced, and they shall mourn for him, as one mourneth for *his* only *son*, and shall be in bitterness for him, as one that is in bitterness for *his* firstborn. In that day shall there be a great mourning in Jerusalem, as the mourning of Hadadrimmon in the valley of Megiddon. And the land shall mourn, every family apart; the family of the house of David apart, and their wives apart; the family of the house of Nathan apart, and their wives apart...." (Zech. 12:9-12 KJV).

***

THREE ESSENTIAL POINTS ON THE RELEASE OF SOVIET JEWS WHICH WILL BRING US CLOSER TO COMBAT!

The release of the Soviet Jews prophesied in Jeremiah 23:7-8, which seems to be surprising everyone now, is a definite necessity in the end time scheme of events and the final war the Russians will launch against Israel, as predicted in the Bible. For one thing, many have said the Russians will not start a war with Israel with so many Jews within their own country, because mutiny would almost instantly occur. Secondly, many believe the Russians want to kill two birds with one stone (their Jews and the Israeli Jews) because of their virulent anti-Semitism (which they are now keeping under wraps). In other words, they would like to release their Jews to Israel and then destroy Israel and the Russian Jews in one attack.

The emigration of Russian Jews would also make it easier for Israel to retaliate. With approximately three million Jews still in Russia, Israel would have to think twice about launching a counterattack; they would not want to kill so many fellow Jews inside Russian borders. However, once Russia releases most of her Jews to Israel, there will be nothing to stop Israel from a counterattack (Zech. 9)! What do the Soviets think of the God of Israel and the true Christians and why?

Israeli soldiers practice self-defense with Uzis.

" 'We will grapple with the Lord God in due season'....'We shall vanquish Him in His highest heaven.' "[49] Russian Ambassador Zinoviev, 1924

This quote brings to mind these questions. Why do the communists hate the idea of God and those who teach others about Him? Why are missionaries more feared than military forces in some instances? Why are Christians on the communist hit list (as Hal Lindsey documents)?[50] Hoover again answers these questions beautifully: "It cannot permit man to give his allegiance to a Supreme Authority higher than Party authority, for such allegiance to a higher authority carries with it a sense of freedom, of immunity to Party edict and discipline. Neither can it afford to have its members made hesitant in acts of cruelty and deception, which are ordained parts of its revolutionary program."[51] What did the contrivers of the communist theory and the soviet state say about Christians? "...Karl Marx... religion is 'the opium of the people'....Nikita Khrushchev....'...we are doing as much as we can to liberate those people who are still under the spell of this religious opiate'....Lenin...'...we must fight against...the 'Christians'....' "[52]

THE COMMUNISTS AND POLITICAL LIBERALS ARE NOT VERY FOND OF THE FUNDAMENTAL FAITH! ANY IDEA WHY?

We may ask ourselves why Marx calls religion "opium"? Could it be because, if we believe in the utopia Jesus will one day bring at His Second Coming (see our chapter 29 "After the Messiah Arrives and Ends the War—Paradise!") to Earth, it might make work, hard work, which leads to success and higher living standards (unattainable under communism), much easier, much more painless. Remember, opium is a pain killer—so if you kill the pain of toiling the ground (Gen. 3:17) with compensation for work[53] and Jesus' promise of Paradise upon His

---

[49]William Goetz, *Apocalypse Next*, p. 129.

[50]Hal documents: "The communists fear a powerful ideal or religion more than they fear military threats. Bible-believing Christians are viewed as one of the most powerful threats of all. They are among the few, for example, who did not break down under the brainwashing tactics used on POWs in the Korean War. Christianity...has been severely persecuted by the communists in the Soviet Union, Red China, Eastern Europe, North Korea, Cuba, Vietnam, Kampuchea, Laos, Nicaragua, Angola, Zimbabwe, and so on, where millions have been massacred." Hal Lindsey, *Combat Faith*, p. 18, © 1986 by the Aorist Corporation, used by permission of Bantam Books, A Division of Bantam Doubleday Dell Pub. Group, Inc.

[51]J. Edgar Hoover, *Masters of Deceipt*, p. 323.

[52]Ibid, p. 321.

[53]"...the workman is worthy of his meat [wages]" (Matt. 10:10 KJV; [ ] mine). Jesus also granted believers the right of ownership in the present and in the future when He said:

return (the ultimate Bible promise and Christian hope), you in essence, inoculate people against communism. That is why Marx hated the Christian faith. It was, and still is, the strongest victory over communism in the free world.

Lenin himself admitted to almost exactly what we have said, when he wrote: "...it is quite natural for the exploiters to sympathize with a religion that teaches us to bear 'uncomplainingly' the woes of hell on earth, in the hope of an alleged paradise in the skies."[54]

There is really no difference between liberals and communists in their desire to control the private citizen. The liberals make laws to help the communist, because the communist promises the liberal they will be the new communist "leaders" once the takeover is complete! Of course, the liberals are always the first shot, if you just take the time to check the record of history. It is too bad the liberals do not, for our and their sakes!

WHO'S PUTTING THE BAN ON SCHOOL PRAYER AND TRYING TO OUTLAW CHRISTIAN ACTIVITIES?

The liberals and communists want gun control for you, not for them. Why? President Clinton succeeded in getting his crime bill passed in late August of 1994. However, Charlton Heston said that what President Clinton was **not** telling us about the crime bill was, in fact, a crime. Heston stated in television advertisements aired a few days before the bill was passed, that it would put ten thousand felons on the street almost immediately, through early release programs.

This bill also puts a ban on what some feel are assault weapons, so in essence, it puts criminals on our streets and takes guns out of our hands. Sounds like it is going to create more crime against the working man—as it removes his ability to defend himself.

Anyone who saw the film *Red Dawn* (depicting a U.S. take-over by communists), knows that the first thing the communists try to accomplish is to take the guns out of the hands of the people. They do not want you to be able to defend yourself against them. They want guns, but they do not want you to have one.

Jesus taught peace through strength (Luke 14:31), which includes bearing arms. Our Constitution gives us the right to bear arms. Gun control would contradict this.

"And I appoint unto you a kingdom, as my Father hath appointed unto me; That ye may eat and drink at my table in my kingdom, and sit on thrones judging the twelve tribes of Israel" (Luke 22:29-30 KJV).

[54] J. Edgar Hoover, *Masters of Deceit*, p. 322.

The facts clearly show that more guns leads to less violence, while fewer guns in the hands of law abiding citizens leads to an unbelievable increase in armed crimes and murders. In one U.S. city (New York), guns were outlawed and the crime rate rose eight hundred percent. In another city (Kennesaw, GA), a law was passed that required home-owners to keep at least one gun in their home. The crime rate plummeted, amazing everyone.

J. Edgar Hoover speaks of Russia's past in his book, *Masters of Deceipt*. It sounds much like our present. Do the following lines sound familiar to you? "From the earliest days when communism came to power in the Soviet Union, communists have conducted a systematic campaign to cripple and destroy organized Judaism. On January 23, 1918, the Soviets issued a sweeping decree 'On the Separation of the Church from the State, and of the School from the Church.' All church property was nationalized; churches were denied rights of legal recourse; the teaching of religion was banned in public and private schools....This Marxian doctrine has been restated by William Z. Foster and applied to communist action in these words, '...God will be banished from the laboratories as well as from the schools.' "[55]

Communists and liberals—are they the same? Ask yourself this question as you compare the current activities of liberals against God, with those outlined and documented by J. Edgar Hoover regarding the communists.

In recent years in the U.S., all the talk about banning prayer in schools and passing laws prohibiting Christian activities was not sponsored by conservatives, but liberals. Read the angry statements made by left-wing liberal groups and individuals in the U.S. in response to the Supreme Court's June 1990 ruling that said we may have Bible clubs on campus again! Rev. Robert Maddox, Americans United for Separation of Church and State, said public school grounds could "become some kind of revival campground."[56] "Atheist activist Madalyn Murray O'Hair called the victory a 'major intrusion of religion into our secular public schools'....The School Board asserted that to allow Bible and Prayer Clubs would create a 'readymade audience for student evangelists'...."[57] "Anne Gaylor, president of the Freedom From Religion Foundation, was more vehement. 'It was a

---

[55]J. Edgar Hoover, *Masters of Deceit*, pp. 259, 321.

[56]Tony Mauro, "Court Opens Schools To Religious Clubs," *USA Today*, Tues., June 5, 1990.

[57]Jay Alan Sekulow, "Running the Race," *C.A.S.E.* (*Christian Advocates Serving Evangelism*), July 1990. Available through C.A.S.E., POB 450349, Atlanta, GA, USA 30345.

dumb decision,' she said. 'It's going to invite all sorts of cults and evangelists to establish beachheads in our public[58] schools.' "[59]

THE SOVIETS LIQUDATED JEWISH CULTURE AND EXECUTED JEWISH WRITERS

What is the recent Russian attitude toward Jewry? Even though they are releasing Jews to Israel—we believe because of prophecy and circumstances, not by coincidence—what is their true deep-seated attitude toward the Jew and Judaism? What is the record?

The Jews are the ones who gave us the Word, the entire Bible, both the Old and New Testaments. We must remember that Jesus and all of His disciples were practicing Jews all of their lives. Jesus merely claimed to be the Jewish Messiah as prophesied and His disciples believed Him.[60]

What have the Soviets done to the Jews? Hoover documents: "No mention was made by Khrushchev of any anti-Semitic crimes committed by Stalin. However, on April 4, 1956, an article entitled 'Our Pain and Our Solace' appeared in the Warsaw Yiddish-language newspaper *Folks-Shtimme*, which charged that Jewish culture had been largely liquidated under Stalin and many Jewish leaders executed. To date these allegations have never been denied by the Kremlin and American communists have reluctantly accepted them as true. On April 13, 1956, the East Coast communist paper, the *Daily Worker*, in an editorial entitled 'Grievous Deeds,' made mention of the earlier Polish 'disclosures...that a large number of Jewish writers and other Jewish leaders were framed up and executed and that Jewish culture was virtually wiped out' in the Soviet Union."[61]

***

---

[58]Reverend D. James Kennedy preached a wonderful sermon on education. Portions of this sermon are in our chapter 23. In this sermon, he pointed out that in the first one hundred years of our country, the Bible and religion were a major part of our educational system. At that time the literacy rate was much higher and there was much less crime. Members of cults may believe what they want to believe, at least I have my freedom to share my faith with them. Why is Gaylor so upset? If she wants to be free, she is free not to listen or talk to me—she is not free to mute me.

[59]William Robbins, "Joy and Foreboding Greet Bible Club Ruling," *New York Times*, Thurs., June 7, 1990.

[60]*Christ* is Greek for "Messiah" and Christian is anglicized Greek for "one who follows the Messiah."

[61]J. Edgar Hoover, *Masters of Deceit*, p. 50.

COMMUNISTS HATE THE FOLLOWERS OF MOSES AND CONSIDER JEWISH ZIONISTS THEIR ENEMY

Hoover documented the following atrocities committed by the Soviets against the Jews and Zionists. "The communist propagandist, Paul Novick, reflected the communist line both in the Soviet Union and the United States when he wrote: 'Ever since its inception Zionism has been an instrument of the Jewish bourgeoisie to hamper the struggle of the Jewish masses....a means of diverting the attention of the Jewish workers from the class struggle and of keeping them separated from the progressive forces of other nationalities....'

In the Soviet Union, Zionism is ruthlessly suppressed. In the United States communists have a more complex problem and avoid direct public attacks on the Zionist movement, so as not to alienate that large section of Jewish people who favor Zionism....Party leaders, however, in the face of the overwhelming evidence of communist hate for the followers of Moses, still are attempting to deceive unsuspecting persons of Jewish origin and, as this is being written, communist tacticians are at work on a program of infiltrating Jewish groups....The Party is today desperately working to mold atheistic materialism as a weapon of revolution, a revolution which, if it is to succeed, must first sap religion's spiritual strength and then destroy it....[their] *Final goal*: the utter elimination of all religion (called 'bourgeois remnants') from the heart, mind, and soul of man, and the total victory of atheistic communism."[62]

THEY WANT TO DESTROY JUDAIC-CHRISTIAN HERITAGE AND REPLACE IT WITH A WORLDWIDE COMMUNIST SOCIETY

Communist expert and FBI Director Hoover further notes: "The full implications of the Communist challenge are shocking. The ultimate Communist goal—as defined by Marx, Lenin, and other Communist leaders—is the ruthless overthrow of our Judaic-Christian heritage and the establishment of a worldwide communist society. By its very nature, communism is expansionist and universalist. In fact, the Communists feel that they can find their true fulfillment only by conquering non-Communist areas and bringing the whole planet under their dominion....Lenin proclaimed. 'We, of course, say that we do not believe in God, and that we know perfectly well that the clergy, the landlords, and the bourgeoisie spoke in the name of God in order to

---

[62]Ibid, pp. 266, 270, 328-329.

pursue their own exploiters' interests.' This rejection of God gives communism a demonic aspect—transforming it into a fanatical, Satanic, brutal phenomenon."[63]

RELIGION IS TEMPORARILY BEING PERMITTED TO INITIATE A FUTURE ONE-WORLD WORSHIP OF THE ANTICHRIST, AS FORETOLD!

Russia's new tolerance of religious activities and economic reform is because they are so poor, they cannot afford to fight. They must give the people back some temporary religious and economic hope to reinstate their status, power and purpose for a global takeover of our planet, just as they did in the 1921 NEP Freedom Reforms, before they took over so many of the countries which are now communist.

This includes one-third of the people living today. Hal Lindsey indicates correctly in his prophetic teachings that this unprecedented freedom concerning the present communist world, especially in the realm of religion, must occur to allow the Antichrist his opportunity to create a one-world religion in which, in the end, he will attempt to force mankind to worship him as predicted in the Bible. Hal notes: "A short while ago—even two years ago—it was very difficult to look at the world situation and see how the Antichrist could ever get the whole communist bloc to join some world federation. But, yet, the Bible says there is going to be a federation of the whole world. One man is actually going to be worshipped as the leader of the whole world....I think it's very significant that there is a new allowance for religious experience."[64]

UNBELIEVABLE ANTI-SEMITISM FROM THE SOVIET UNION, AS REPORTED BY DR. NUDELMAN

The following lengthy quotes are from a 1978 seminar conducted by Dr. Nudelman at the Hebrew University of Jerusalem Centre for Research and Documentation of East European Jewry. Dr. Nudelman comments: "In recent years Soviet anti-Semitism has increased dramatically. Its most important feature at the present is that it has

---

[63]J. Edgar Hoover, *J. Edgar Hoover Speaks Concerning Communism.* Nutley, NJ and Washington D.C.: The Capital Hill Press in cooperation with The Craig Press, © 1972, p. 2, used by permission.

[64]Hal Lindsey, *The 1990s: Prophecy on Fast Forward*, chapter 13, p. 2. Hal also notes in this work, that 100 million people have been murdered to keep communism in power as of the decade of the 1990's.

turned into a phenomenon of international dimensions, and has become a threat to the existence of the Jewish people. The other special feature is that internationally, Soviet imperialism, Arab and Afro-Asian nationalism, and left-wing anti-Zionism, combine with Soviet anti-Semitism to provide the ideological base for an all-out attack against Zionism, the State of Israel, and Jews in general....In 1971 a Soviet author, V. Bolishukhin, wrote in Pravda that every person who becomes a Zionist automatically becomes an enemy of the Soviet people. Enemy of the people is the same official term that was the watchword during all of Stalin's mass reprisals of the 1930s. Finally, soon afterwards, G. Artatov, an advisor of the Kremlin politburo, said that 90 percent of soviet Jews who remain in the USSR 'appear in an unfavourable light,' meaning they are suspicious elements....This new global doctrine of indiscriminate distrust toward Jews has become a theoretical basis for the systematic displacement of Soviet Jews from all spheres of social, industrial, and cultural life in the USSR—a process which has intensified and reached global proportions in recent years. The facts about this discrimination are widely known: numerus clausus for Jews who wish to enter institutions of higher learning or who seek employment, limitations in social activities, in the sciences....Other examples include the ruthless persecution of the Jewish religion and culture as well as suppression of every attempt at Jewish self-expression, such as the trial of Hebrew teachers I. Begun and P. Abramovich, the closing of the Moscow symposium on Jewish culture, and extra legal persecution of the Jewish Samizdat journal The Jews in the USSR....Mass circulation in the USSR of anti-Semitic books, articles, and brochures (by Kichko, Evseev, Ivanov and others) is now widely acknowledged. The use of mass media such as cinema and television for the same purposes is relatively new. On January 22, 1977 Soviet television showed a one-hour documentary, 'Traders in Souls.' The program featured caricatures of Jews and Israelis portrayed in the spirit of Nazi newspapers and journals....Another film, 'The Overt and the Covert'....begins with a revolver shot and the voice of the announcer saying: 'That was how the Jewess Kaplan attempted to murder Vladimir Il'ich Lenin'....When German tanks are shown entering a Soviet city, the announcer says, 'Hitler was brought to power by Jewish capital'....During last year alone Korne-yev published more than 10 articles under such characteristic titles as 'Nazism from Tel Aviv,' 'Zionism's Mercenaries,' 'Israel's Army—An Instrument of Aggression,' 'Raiders and Bandits,' 'Terror—the Weapon of Zionism,' 'The Espionage, Tentacles of Zionism,' 'Zionism's Secret War,' and 'The Poisonous Weapon of Zionism.' Korne-yev claims that Zionists are at the head of the American Mafia and that the Magic chief Meyer

Lansky received Golda Meir's personal invitation to settle in Israel. Quoting the Arab press, Korne-yev further claims that the Israeli army recruits disguised criminals after they have change their appearance, and that strikes in Israel are suppressed by some 'Civil Guard Corps' numbering 50,000 men. He also reports that Zionists are in control of 158 out of 163 of the world's largest arms factories....One such lecture delivered by Moscow party committee representative V. Eemel 'ianov, which arrived through Samizdat channels, may serve as an example of this propaganda. The lecture is entitled 'Judaism and Zionism:' 'Of all Semitic peoples the Jews are the youngest. The Bedouins, i.e., Arabs are the most ancient. The principle of Judaism has been formulated in the Torah. The Torah is the blackest book in mankind's entire history. Its main theses are that the Jews are a chosen people and should seize the territories of others. Joshua is like Genghis Khan. Jerusalem is translated as 'the city of peace,' but in reality it is a den of thieves and criminals. The Jews have contributed nothing original, they have proclaimed the racist principle: Jews must not work, work is for the Goyim. That was the origin of the division of humankind into humans proper—the Jews, and two-legged cattle—the Goyim. All nations must become the Jews' slaves. The Zionists have planned to achieve world domination by the year 2000. But....There will be a struggle, but we shall be victorious. But victory requires sacrifices. This does not mean that we must distrust all Jews, but we must take into account the fact that 40,000 leave annually for a state which is not just capitalist, but fascist.' "[65]

INDICATIONS THAT RUSSIAN ANTI-SEMITISM MAY RESURFACE IN THE LATE 1990'S

You may be familiar with Vladimir Zhirinovsky and his recent anti-Semitic slurs reported by the media. Many feel that he could revive the Cold War and stir up anti-Semitism if he comes to power in Russia. Hal Lindsey documents: "Who is Zhirinovsky....he is strongly anti-Semitic and fascistic, yet received the largest number of votes in Russia's December 1993 parliamentary elections. This man, sometimes called the 'Russian Hitler,' is poised for a presidential run in 1996. He enjoys good support among the Russian military. And his autobiography, apocalyptically titled *The Last Dash to the South*, promotes the idea of Russian expansion into the Middle East and

---

[65]Dr. R. Nudelman, "Anti-Semitism in the Soviet Union, Its Roots and Consequences," Vol. I-II, © 1979, pp. 25, 31, 35-38, used by permission. The publication of this book was supported by the Memorial Foundation for Jewish Culture, New York and the Society for Research on Jewish Communities, Jerusalem.

Persian Gulf....he [Zhirinovsky] says....'I will beat the Americans in space. I will surround the planet with our space stations, so that they'll be scared of our space weapons. I don't care if they call me a fascist or a Nazi. Workers in Leningrad told me, 'Even if you wear five swastikas, we'll vote for you all the same. You promise a clear plan.' There's nothing like fear to make people work better. The stick, not the carrot. I'll do it all without tanks in the streets. Those who have to be arrested will be arrested quietly at night. I may have to shoot 100,000 people, but the other 300 million will live peacefully. I have the right to shoot 100,000. I have this right as president.'

Listen to more Zhirinovsky: • 'I am the almighty! I am a tyrant! I will follow in Hitler's footsteps.' • 'From time to time, Russia is overwhelmed with anti-Semitism. This phenomenon is provoked only by the Jews themselves.' "[66]

Zhirinovsky may well come and go. We may never hear of him again following the 1996 Russian parliamentary elections. However, it is frightening to contemplate his popularity in light of his virulent anti-Semitism.

THE EARLY HISTORY AND TRAUMA OF KARL MARX! A KEY TO COMMUNISM'S ANTI-SEMITISM?

Even though Karl Marx himself was a Jew, he was an anti-Semite. Before we examine his anti-Jewish writings, let's read about his family life, when he was writing and formulating ideals that would later be adopted by Lenin and the Bolsheviks to forge a ruthless takeover of the Russian people. Former FBI Director, J. Edgar Hoover, documents: "Marx, in contrast, lived in squalor. He was often sick; he suffered from boils, headaches, and rheumatism. Jenny's health began to give way. Her seventh child was born dead. She became wretchedly nervous, irritable, and upset. 'Daily, my wife tells me she wishes she were lying in the grave with the children,' Marx wrote in 1862. 'And truly I cannot blame her....'

Marx did not have a regular job but depended on pittances, especially from Engels. He lived from pawnshop to pawnshop. It is a bitter irony of history, indeed, that the founder of communism should be literally kept alive by a wealthy industrialist, and that a 'capitalist's' son, turned communist, should become the second 'father' of this revolutionary movement."[67] Hoover further illustrates from Marx's

---

[66]Hal Lindsey, *The Final Battle*. Palos Verdes, CA: Western Front, Ltd., © 1995, pp. 130-133, used by permission. [ ] mine.

[67]J. Edgar Hoover, *Masters of Deceit*, p. 16.

own writings that his main problem with society was his lack of money. "Money was always short. Little Franziska died before her first birthday. There was no money for the funeral. A pittance was obtained from a neighbor which, as Jenny says, '...paid for the small coffin in which my poor child now sleeps in peace.' Marx sometimes couldn't go out of the house: his overcoats were pawned. His wife was sick, but he couldn't call a doctor. There was no money for medicine. [Marx complained] 'For a week or more I have kept my family alive feeding them bread and potatoes, and it is questionable whether or not I will be able to scare any up today'....Marx was stubborn. He kept plugging away, writing, reading, denouncing 'capitalist' poverty, and letting his family starve. No wonder a remark, attributed to his mother, was made that instead of writing about capital it would have been better if Karl had made some."[68]

WAS A JEWISH KARL MARX JEALOUS OF HIS BROTHERS BECAUSE MOST OF THEM DID BETTER THAN HE? MAYBE!

Many believe Marx was jealous of the Jews because somehow it always seemed to him that they had a bit more money than he. This is evident from his anti-Semitic remark: "Money is the jealous God of Israel, by the side of which no other god may exist....Exchange is the Jew's real God."[69]

Hoover tell us: "Karl Marx described Judaism as 'anti-social' and an expression of Jewish 'egoism.' Marx, better than any other communist leader, illustrates the gulf between Jewish tradition and communism."[70]

KARL MARX'S CONCEALED ANTI-SEMITIC WRITINGS HAVE RECENTLY BEEN REVEALED, ALTHOUGH NOT WIDELY PUBLISHED!

Karl Marx's little-known book, *A World Without Jews*, unveils his evil thoughts and intentions toward the Jew, which we believe have been intricately integrated into today's communist philosophy. A few of Marx's anti-Semitic slurs can be found in this rare book, which states: "The booklet presented here is the first unexpurgated English language publication of papers written by Karl Marx originally published in Germany as a review of the writings of Dr. Bruno Bauer,

---

[68]Ibid, p. 17. [ ] mine.
[69]Ibid, p. 259. Also see Karl Marx, *A World Without Jews*.
[70]Ibid.

a contemporary theologian and social philosopher, on 'the Jewish question.'

It is interesting to note that most of Marx's anti-Semitic references, in his correspondence, his journalistic writings and his books, were entirely eliminated by his various editors. Their full text, however, is now being published by the decidedly anti-Jewish-oriented State Publishing House in Moscow....Anti-Semitic expressions of his are to be found mainly in the present essay, in his *Class Struggles in France, In the Eighteenth Brumaire of Louis Bonaparte,* and in his *Letters to Engels,* censored by Bebel and Bernstein. Some of the editors of his writings attempted to modify the vindictiveness of Marx's aggression."[71] The book quotes the following Jew-baiting remarks of Marx: " 'It is the circumvention of law that makes the religious Jew a religious Jew.' (*Die Deutsche Ideologie,* MEGA V, 162) 'The Jews of Poland are the smeariest of all races.' (*Neue Rheinische Zeitung,* April 29, 1849) He called Ferdinand Lassalle, 'Judel Itzig—Jewish Nigger.' (*Der Jüdische Nigger,* MEKOR III, 82, July 30, 1862) 'Ramsgate is full of Jews and fleas.' (MEKOR IV, 490, August 25, 1879)"[72]

WHAT YOU DON'T KNOW *CAN* HURT YOU—RUSSIA IS DEVELOPING A NEW GENERATION OF ATOMIC WEAPONS AND GERM WARFARE MATERIAL!

We realize that we are quoting from a book over thirty years old. However, we believe that this information is relevant and should not be concealed. For now, as in the past, we have learned that *what you don't know* ***can*** *hurt you.*

Recently, on a *700 Club* interview, J. Michael Waller of the American Foreign Policy Council stated: "...the Cold War will...be back, and will probably much earlier than anybody expects."[73] We believe this is very probable and could occur before another decade has passed.

The same *700 Club* publication mentioned that "many of the key reformers in his [Yeltsin's] government are now gone."[74] They also quoted a Russian scientist who came forth and admitted Russia was still developing new generations of atomic weapons, working on a

---

[71]Karl Marx, *A World Without Jews.* New York: Philosophical Library Inc., © 1959, p. xii, vii, used by permission.
[72]Ibid, p. vii.
[73]"The 700 Club Fact Sheet," Mar. 29, 1994, © used by permission. Available through Christian Broadcasting Network, Inc., 700 CBN Center, Virginia Beach, VA, USA 23463.
[74]Ibid. [ ] mine.

new, more potent nerve gas and a "super plague" viral biological weapon.

RUSSIA HAS CHECKMATED ITS FREEDOM-LOVING REPUBLICS AND IS POISED TO RECONQUER

We should mention that on June 21, 1994, after several Russian republics joined NATO against the will of the present Russian establishment, Russia herself joined! The situation which was created, knowing NATO must be loyal to itself, was that if Russia attempts to recover other present Russian republic members of NATO, NATO cannot stop them because now Russia herself is a member of NATO.

On *The 700 Club*, Paul Strand of CBN News reported: "Today, Russia joined NATO's partnership for peace....Russia's signing means NATO stretches all the way around the world....All year, former Soviet Republics and satellites have been signing on the dotted line to get into the partnership for peace. But most of them wanted much more from NATO. They wanted full membership and its precious guarantee that if they were ever attacked by outside forces, all the NATO allies would rush to their rescue. Russia objected though, which made much of the world suspicious that some Russians still had their eye on reconquering what was the Soviet empire. NATO backed away from giving full membership to strategic countries, like Poland and the Czech Republic, leaving them worried that even if Russia is now an official NATO partner for peace, if it gets in the mood, it may still reconquer them someday without NATO putting up a fight."[75]

KARL MARX WAS THE FATHER OF POLITICAL ANTI-SEMITISM, WHICH HAS LED TO COMMUNIST ANTI-ZIONISM, THUS FEEDING ARAB TERRORISM

Having quoted the above, we would like to quote another passage from *A World Without Jews*, so as to inform and alert contemporary Jews and pro-Zionist Christians. In the near future, if Russia returns to her old ways, we had better be prepared to protect our loved ones.

Anti-Semitism has been deeply embedded in Russian politics since 1917. Truly, Karl Marx can be called "the father of modern political anti-Semitism." Prior to Marx, most anti-Semitism was based on religion, not official political policy. Dagobert D. Runes writes in the introduction to *A World Without Jews*: "The official Soviet Socialist attitude toward Israel and the Jewish people in general was unmistakably stated in their State publication of 1958, entitled *The State of Israel—Its Position and Policies*, by K. Ivanov and Z. Sheinis.

---

[75]Paul Strand, *The 700 Club*, June 21, 1994, Christian Broadcasting Network.

From this State document we translate '...The Zionist movement represents a form of the nationalistic ideology of the rich Jewish bourgeoisie, intimately tied to imperialism and to colonial oppression of the people of Asia. Zionism has tied itself to American and other Western capitalism and, with Jewish terrorist tactics, attacked its Arab neighbors. The national liberation movement of the people of the Middle East, spearheaded by its native leaders (such as President Nasser, King Ibn Saud of Saudi Arabia and King Iman Ahmad of Yemen) is constantly threatened by naked Jewish aggression...'

'The clear duty of all Marxists and Communists in this situation is to help the Asian and African people **crush the reactionary Jewish forces.**'

Such reads the widely-propagated platform of the Khrushchev-Mao Marxist axis. In fundamentals, it differs little from the Hitler-Stalin resolves of a generation ago, and it forebodes no less terror today than the previous anti-Jewish onslaught. Marxism may have failed in many of its postulates and prognostications, but its anti-Semitism lives on unabated.

It is indeed possible that these terrorist practices may succeed where the Roman *soldateska* of Titus and the pyres of Torquemada failed, namely, to bring to reality the sanguinary **dream of Karl Marx—a world without Jews.**"[76]

Though Runes quotes long dead Arab kings, there is no mistake that their anti-Semitism did not die with them. Current Moslem leaders, including Louis Farrakhan of the Nation of Islam, are even turning blacks against the Jews, calling them "blood suckers." This quote was recently documented in a 1994 broadcast of *20/20*, an ABC news magazine, with Barbara Walters and Hugh Downs.[77]

YELTSIN'S RUSSIA HAS MADE A PACT TO SIDE WITH THE ARABS AGAINST ISRAEL, WHILE STILL MODERNIZING HER WEAPONS!

Hal Lindsey documented in his 1994 book, *Planet Earth—2000 A.D.*: "As President Clinton and the European powers offer Russian President Boris Yeltsin a virtual blank check to help revitalize his suffering economy, Moscow continues to spend billions modernizing its strategic nuclear arsenal.

---

[76]Karl Marx, *A World Without Jews*, p. xi. Bold mine.

[77]Farakhan consistently denies the title of anti-Semite and has denied saying such things, thus, we cite a credible source.

Yes, I know. You've been told that the Russians are scrapping their nuclear weapons and that's why we need to encourage them with foreign aid. Well, let me tell you, Russia's nuclear weapons are as well-positioned to destroy the United States in a first strike as they have ever been. And it is the United States, not Russia, that is unilaterally disarming at a dangerous pace....Back in 1992, Yeltsin made it clear to all those who were listening just what his intentions were when he said: 'Now we will move in the East.' By this, Yeltsin explained that he meant closer ties with Islamic nations like Iran.

My intelligence sources, who have not been wrong so far about this area, tell me that Russia has already signed an accord with Iran that *will commit them to fight on the side of Islam in the next Islam-Israeli war.*"[78]

On the last day of 1993, the Associated Press reported a suspicious synagogue fire in Moscow.[79]

RUTSKOI ALMOST BROUGHT BACK THE COMMUNIST SOVIET UNION IN 1993, DIDN'T HE?

We cannot dismiss Boris Yeltsin's former vice-president, Alexander Rutskoi, and his attempt to force Yeltsin back into hard-line communism. Ted Koppel reported in an ABC News *Nightline* segment, "Moment of Crisis: Anatomy of a Revolution": "We Americans have always had a lot of misconceptions about this country, but rarely more so than now....Russia is no more a democracy in the sense that Americans understand the term than the Russian White House is where the President lives or works....Consider for only a moment the likelihood of an armed rebellion against President Clinton led by Al Gore and Tom Foley and you begin to appreciate how misleading terms like vice-president and speaker of the parliament can be, for all our frustration. With legislation gridlock back home, we don't count on the joint chiefs of staff to break that gridlock; here, they still do. Boris Yeltsin has won a battle, the war is an ongoing thing....behind the scenery, the military in Russia remains the decisive power. Had they chosen to throw their support behind Rutskoi, he would be president today and the Kremlin might once again be flying the Soviet flag."[80]

***

[78]Hal Lindsey, *Planet Earth—2000 A.D.*, pp. 197, 201.

[79]*Atlanta Journal and Constitution*, Fri., Dec. 31, 1993 p. A8. This fire completely destroyed the synagogue and had the earmarks of anti-Semitism.

[80]"Moment of Crisis: Anatomy of a Revolution," *Nightline*, ABC News, Oct. 22, 1993.

RUTSKOI'S REVOLT—A HINT OF WHAT MAY HAPPEN IN RUSSIA—IT IS TIME TO EMIGRATE, *NOW*!

The immigration of Russian Jews to Israel between 1988 and 1996, though it has been massive, is still far from complete. In other words, you ain't seen nothin' yet. Hal Lindsey confirms in his book, *Planet Earth—2000 A.D.*, that: "Natan Sharansky, head of the Zionist Forum and a former Russian refusenik, says he thinks a massive aliya from Russia is imminent.

'Masses of Jews could decide to come to Israel before the flames spread,' he said. 'The government must be ready to set aside resources to absorb a mass aliya.[81] This is the time to show the Jewish people and the world that Israel is the only safe and open home for the Jewish people'....Israeli sources estimate there may be as many as 1 million Russian Jews vacillating about moving to Israel. Though Yeltsin has improved the political climate for these people, they fear his grip on power is tenuous at best.

'Rutskoi [Yeltsin's chief rival] would not have encouraged attacks on Jews, but in the circumstances he could not control the forces of the city,' explained Anatoly Shabad. 'Pogroms would have begun immediately. I saw leaflets inciting people to kill Jews. I was shocked—we've had plenty of anti-Semitic material here, but I had never seen such direct incitement before. One leaflet showed a Russian child pleading, 'Daddy, kill a Jew for my future.' ' "[82]

BE ON GUARD TO HELP YOUR JEWISH FRIENDS—SOON THEY WILL NEED YOU MORE THAN EVER—RALLY TO THEIR SIDE—HELP AND SUPPORT THEM

Do we need any more proof to show we must be on the alert, now more than ever, to be ready to protect our Jewish friends, as did the righteous Gentiles during the Holocaust? Oh, it is true that when Jesus returns, there will be a kingdom and peace for all where anti-Semitism will have died forever. But until then, we as true believers have to rally to the side of the Jews and their true God-given right to return to their land. There they have an inalienable right to security, no matter how much the Arabs, ecumenicists and the communists, even those still hiding in Russia, dislike it!

***

[81] This is Hebrew for "coming up to immigrate" to Israel.

[82] Hal Lindsey, *Planet Earth—2000 A.D.*, pp. 135-136.

Books by Dagobert D. Runes

TREASURY OF PHILOSOPHY
TREASURY OF WORLD LITERATURE
DICTIONARY OF PHILOSOPHY
ON THE NATURE OF MAN
OF GOD, THE DEVIL AND THE JEWS
A BOOK OF CONTEMPLATION
LETTERS TO MY SON
LETTERS TO MY DAUGHTER
THE HEBREW IMPACT ON WESTERN CIVILIZATION
THE SOVIET IMPACT ON SOCIETY
SPINOZA DICTIONARY
LETTERS TO MY GOD
THE WISDOM OF THE TORAH
THE WISDOM OF THE KABBALAH
PICTORIAL HISTORY OF PHILOSOPHY
DICTIONARY OF JUDAISM

A WORLD WITHOUT JEWS

By KARL MARX

Translated from the Original German

With an introduction by Dagobert D. Runes

PHILOSOPHICAL LIBRARY
New York

COMMUNISM IS AGAINST BIBLICAL OWNERSHIP AND CAPITAL

John R. Rice, in his book, *False Doctrine*, sheds interesting light on Marx by taking actual quotes from his *Communist Manifesto,* scarcely read by most of us today! Do any of the following quotes from Marx sound familiar or in-line with a current particular political party? Rice points out: "You may begin to see some likeness to Roosevelt's New Deal."

Indeed, higher taxes created to discourage and cripple small and big business, have been, and still are, the practice of the U.S. liberals and Democrats. It was only Ronald Reagan who temporarily gave us a break. After he was elected, economic production jumped, to everyone's surprise.

Recently, President Clinton attempted to push through his health care plan, which would have closed down many "mom and pop" businesses, as it would make them unable to pay for their employees' benefits by striking a deathblow to private insurance.

One of my favorite fundamental Christian ministers, Jerry Falwell, described this plan as "a tax plan in disguise of health care," in his highly documented and excellent video, *Circle of Power, A Prescription for Disaster*.[83]

No doubt, many attempts will be made by future liberal leaders worldwide. We only pray they do not succeed. What is the desired

[83]Available through Liberty Alliance, Inc., POB 6000, Madison Heights, VA, USA 24572.

long-term goal of these liberals in undermining our economic status and the money and property we have managed to acquire? Would it be taking away our personal freedom, thus putting us in the position of having to work for them, "the government"? Rice answers this question as follows: "Along with the abolition of private property, communism plans the destruction of individual freedom. Karl Marx again speaks: *'The abolition of this state of things is called by the bourgeoisie, abolition of individuality and freedom! And rightly so'*....the plan is to put people in the greatest bondage possible.

Here is another word. Another quotation. Dr. Edman says: *'To that end the bases of society must be destroyed. First, the 'individual...the middle-class owner of property...must, indeed, be swept out of the way.'* "[84]

COMMUNISM IS AGAINST THE FAMILY

John Rice comments: "Next comes the family. The *Communist Manifesto* becomes savage in what it says about the family. Karl Marx, the founder of communism, the founder of socialism, says: *'Abolition of the family!....The bourgeois family will vanish as a matter of course when its complement vanishes, and both will vanish with the banishing of capital....The bourgeois claptrap about the family and education, about the hallowed co-relation of parent and child, becomes all the more disgusting...by the action of Modern Industry.'*

Then Marx goes on to say, *'the community of women,* [that is, making women property of everybody and passing the women around;] *it has existed almost from time immemorial'*....Now that is communism according to the author himself, Karl Marx, as quoted from the *Communist Manifesto*....Communists and socialists are not only not Christians, but they hate Christianity and deliberately fight and seek to destroy Bible Christianity....Let us turn to the Ten Commandments. It is a surprising thing, when you come to think of it, that two of the Ten Commandments deal directly with this matter of private ownership of property. Is it really a sin to own property? Should all property be owned by the state and so collectively owned by the people, as communism teaches and as socialism teaches? That is not what the Bible says.

For example, there is a command in Exodus 20:15, in the Ten Commandments—the eighth one which says, 'Thou shalt not steal.' Now stealing is taking property that belongs to someone else. Stealing is taking what is not your own. It necessarily involves private ownership.

***

---

[84]John R. Rice, D.D., Litt.D., *Communism and Socialism.* Murfreesboro, TN: Sword of the Lord Publishers, © 1970, p. 377, used by permission.

And in the same chapter, Exodus 20, verse 17, the tenth of the commandments says, 'Thou shalt not covet thy neighbour's house.' Then a neighbor has a right to own a house. 'Thou shalt not covet thy neighbour's house...."[85]

THE COMMUNISTS ARE STILL PROCLAIMING JESUS A MARXIST, DESPITE THE TRUTH THAT HE ESTABLISHED AND TAUGHT CAPITALIST PRINCIPLES

Even as late as 1992, **after** the Soviet leader Mikhail Gorbachev visited Israel, he made the age-old false statement which attempts to infer that Jesus was a Marxist. He said: "He declared himself a lifelong socialist, following in the footsteps of Jesus, the first socialist."[86]

Here, we will confront this devious acusation that Jesus somehow changed the Jewish laws of the Bible and became a socialist. Nothing could be further from the truth. Jesus kept and fulfilled the ancient Jewish oracles of God and gave proper examples of them as he taught our future responsibilities as believers. Two examples of this are mentioned by the evangelist John Rice. He noted: "...in Luke 19:11-27 Jesus clearly taught that the man who took one pound (a certain weight of money) and invested it in business and gained ten pounds, was to be commended, 'Well, thou good servant: because thou hast been faithful in a very little, have thou authority over ten cities.' The man who gained five pounds was praised, but not so much. And the man who did not have any profit on the investment is called 'Thou wicked servant.' Those who would try to limit legitimate profits are contrary to the Bible....in the parable of the sower Jesus plainly shows that men should expect profit from their labor. He tells about a farmer who sowed the ground and of the results of the seed sown. 'But other fell into good ground, and brought forth fruit, some an hundredfold, some sixtyfold, some thirtyfold.' In other words, it is not wrong, but proper and right, if a farmer can get his seed back a hundred times over. And the least figure given is an increase of thirtyfold, that is, three thousand per cent! This illustrates that people are to invest their time and their property and use it and expect profit from it. That is the Bible doctrine which socialists deny and which communists deny."[87]

---

[85]Ibid, pp. 377-380.

[86]Hal Lindsey, "Gorbachev Calls Jesus 'The First Socialist,' " *Countdown...*, Vol. 3, Sept. 1992. Palos Verdes, CA: Hal Lindsey Ministries, p.12, used by permission. Lindsey's source was *Jerusalem Post*, June 27, 1992.

[87]John R. Rice, *Communism and Socialism*, pp. 400-401.

"...the world had never before known a godlessness as organized, militarized, and tenaciously malevolent as that preached by Marxism. Within the philosophical system of Marx and Lenin and at the heart of their psychology, *hatred of God* is the principal driving force, more fundamental than all their political and economic pretensions."[88]

Alexander Solzhenitsyn, quoted from his
acceptance speech for the Templeton Prize, 1983

Hal Lindsey, in his book, *Combat Faith*, reminds us of relatively recent communist persecution of Christians. He gives us the true reason they fear the powerful message of Jesus' Gospel and its followers. Hal noted: "Faith is being tested by fire in those countries. According to a BBC special television report (April 1985), 33 percent of all prisoners in the vast Soviet prison system are 'born-again Christians,' mostly from the Pentecostal and Baptist underground churches....The communists fear a powerful ideal or religion more than they fear military threats. Bible-believing Christians are viewed as one of the most powerful threats of all. They are among the few, for example, who did not break down under the brainwashing tactics used on POWs in the Korean War.

Christianity...has been severely persecuted by the communists in the Soviet Union, Red China, Eastern Europe, North Korea, Cuba, Vietnam, Kampuchea, Laos, Nicaragua, Angola, Zimbabwe, and so on, where millions have been massacred."[89]

EVOLUTION: MARX'S TRICK KEY TO SUCCESS WITHIN A GENERATION, REACHING INTO OUR OWN TIME

We say with assurance, if there is ever to be a cessation of worldwide communism (China alone is one-fifth the population of the world and has recently outlawed Christian conversion), the death of socialism must be preceded by the death of the false concept of evolution!

Marx knew that Darwinism (the theory of human evolution), like terrorism, was a most potent propaganda tool which could be used to catapult communism into our age and break the spirit of the people. This would cause them to lose all hope and bring them to respect a "government" of a few elite men instead of God as their supreme hope and authority. This is why Marx personally asked if he could dedicate his book, *Das Kapital*, about the "collapse" of capitalism and free government, to Darwin.

***

---

[88]Hal Lindsey, *Combat Faith*, p. 18.
[89]Ibid, p. 16-18.

Darwin was the one who seemed to give the theory of evolution a reasonable cause.[90] Marx knew this would be both a catalyst and continuing oppressive force to bring in and sustain socialism in the modern world. Evidence that the communists know how to use the power of *the opiate of Darwin* can be seen further in the coins pictured below.

In 1959, Moscow struck these coins in commemoration of the one hundred-year anniversary of Darwin's book, *The Origin of Species.*

---

[90]See the section on Huxley and Columbus in our *Vol. II*, chapter 5, "Darwinian Evolution: Fact, Fraud or Fiction?" Huxley, Darwin's closest friend, exposed Darwin's theory of natural selection as a deceiption by comparing it to Columbus and his egg trick.

Das Kapital.

Kritik der politischen Oekonomie.

Von

Karl Marx.

Erster Band.

Buch I: Der Produktionsprocess des Kapitals.

Zweite verbesserte Auflage.

Das Recht der Uebersetzung wird vorbehalten.

Hamburg

Verlag von Otto Meissner.

1872.

The second edition of *Das Kapital*, personally inscribed by Marx to Darwin. Darwin turned down Marx's offer to dedicate the book to him due to his wife's objections; she was of Judeo-Christian background.

NATURAL SELECTION WAS USED TO DUPE THE PUBLIC, THUS PROVIDING A FOUNDATION FOR THE ANTI-CHRISTIAN SYSTEM OF COMMUNISM

Henry Morris, Ph.D, in his book, *The Troubled Waters of Evolution*, exposes the reason the communists have used the tool of evolution to destroy free enterprise and human freedom by replacing the biblical truths of creation with the false visions of evolution. He says: "...the industrial revolution had drastically increased public awareness and respect for science and technology, and the great scientists of the day were mostly Bible-believing Christians.... Sir Isaac Newton is generally acknowledged to have had the greatest scientific intellect of all time, and the weight of his great authority had long been cited in favor of belief in the full authority of the Bible. He, as did his successor at Cambridge, John Woodward, believed in the literal creation account of Genesis....In fact, the period from 1650 to 1850 was an era of scientific giants, and many of the greatest among them—men such as Pascal, Faraday, Maxwell, Kelvin, and others—were men who believed in the inspiration and authority of the Bible. The marvelous discoveries and achievements of science, revealing the complexities and orderly relationships in nature, seemed more and more to confirm the fact of design and therefore the existence of a Creator.

Therefore, if the great complex of anti-Christian movements and philosophies was to be successful in its struggle for control of the minds and hearts of men, something would have to be done first of all to undermine biblical creation and to establish evolution as the accepted cosmogony. The biblical doctrine of origins of course is foundational to all other doctrines, and if this could be refuted, or even diluted, then eventually the other doctrines of biblical theology would be undermined and destroyed.

The powerful argument from design in nature, as evidence for God and His creation, would need to be explained by some other means, some naturalistic means, before evolution could really become acceptable to most people. And such a new explanation would need to be a 'scientific' explanation, sufficiently so to convince the scientific community that it would really explain evolution. If the scientists could be converted to evolution, then the science-honoring public would soon go along....The idea of natural selection in the struggle for existence was the perfect solution. Everyone was familiar with the effectiveness of artificial selection in breeding, so why wouldn't the same process work in nature? Add the factor of the great spans of geologic time conveniently provided by Lyell's uniformitarianism, and everything was present to explain away the evidence of design and even the real necessity of a Creator. Or at least this was the way it would seem, and that was all that was necessary."[91]

T. H. HUXLEY'S GRANDSON, JULIAN, PERHAPS WITHOUT REALIZING IT, ADMITS THE DISASTERS CAUSED BY DARWINISM

Julian Huxley, grandson of T. H. Huxley, Darwin's strongest supporter, wrote in his book, *Charles Darwin and His World*: "Karl Marx venerated Darwin and wanted to dedicate the English translation of *Das Kapital* to him—a request which was courteously refused. Darwin has become an intellectual hero in the Soviet Union. There is a splendid Darwin Museum in Moscow, and the Soviet authorities struck a special Darwin medal in honour of the centenary of *The Origin*....In some quarters, especially in Germany, the attempt was made to apply Darwinian concepts, such as the struggle for existence and the survival of the fittest, directly to human affairs, under the guise of 'social Darwinism'. 'Social Darwinism' was of course only a pseudo-science, and its extrapolations from biology to social science and politics were quite unjustified. They led to...an unscientific eugenics and racism, and eventually to Hitler and Nazi ideology.

Within a dozen years from the publication of *The Origin*, biology had [falsely] become an evolutionary science, though by a strange irony most biologists concentrated merely on comparative anatomy and embryology....Only Darwin himself, together with a few others like Wallace, Bates, Fritz Müller, Cope, and Marsh, continued to pursue the study of scientific natural history."[92]

RUSSIAN RELIGION TODAY?

Lately, under Boris Yeltsin and his reforms, there is some degree of religious toleration; partly, of course, to receive good public opinion, and partly in order to revive the broken spirit of the people. However, as recently as 1993, we have seen the beginning of a reversal of this with the passing of a new law which prohibits evangelism (see our chapter 10, "Early Christian History Versus Catholicism," on church history).

***

---

91 Henry M. Morris, Ph.D., *The Troubled Waters of Evolution*, pp. 60-62. [ ] mine.

92 Julian Huxley and H.B.D. Kettlewell, *Charles Darwin and His World*. New York: The Viking Press, © 1965, pp. 80-81, used by permission. [ ] mine.

Portrait of Raoul Wallenberg.

WALLENBERG, IMPRISONED BY THE SOVIETS FOR SAVING JEWS—PERHAPS STILL ALIVE BUT SWORN BY RUSSIA TO BE DEAD

Raoul Wallenberg, a Christian Swedish diplomat, utilized the power and privilege of his position to save more Jews from the Holocaust than any other single person (100,000). He was captured by the KGB on January 17, 1945, and taken to Soviet-occupied Budapest and later imprisoned (apparently for his heroic rescue efforts).

For years, there were outcries for his release, while Russian agents only replied, "He is dead." Finally, in mid-October, 1989, the Russians invited his sister, Nina, and secretary, Sonia Sonnenfeld, to the Soviet Union to give them his diplomatic passport and a copy of a report by a deceased doctor which stated that Wallenberg had died in a Soviet jail in 1947. However, the October 17, 1989, edition of the Israeli newspaper, *The Jerusalem Post*, reported that while the Soviets claimed he died in 1947, after two years of imprisonment: "A criminal file on Wallenberg has never been found and a number of former camp inmates reported seeing him **alive** in the 1970s."[93]

Some believe he is still alive today in the 1990's and still in prison. For what? That's right, saving Jews—another example of Russian anti-Semitism being covered up by an outright lie. To release him would be the ultimate embarrassment and, of course, an admission of unforgettable guilt in the eyes of nearly all, thus negatively influencing world opinion—something they will not allow at any price.

SEALED FILES INDICATE RUSSIA WILL ONE DAY SOON REUNITE THE COMMUNIST SOVIET UNION OVERNIGHT

A *20/20* segment entitled, "The Men We Left Behind," featured American MIA's from World War II, the Korean War and Vietnam, who were secretly shipped to Russia! Certain numbered graves in Russia were proven to contain the bodies of American MIA's.[94]

The program made another interesting point. The Russians refused to open the GRU (Russian military intelligence) files,[95] which contain vital information on the MIA's. Tom Jarriel, reporting for *20/20* said: "Those reports would be invaluable in determining the fate of missing U.S. servicemen, but **Russian military intelligence refuses**

---

[93]Reuter, "Irrefutable Fact That Wallenberg Died In '47,' " *Jerusalem Post*, Oct. 17, 1989, p. 12. If you are interested in the evidence supporting the fact that Wallenberg may be alive, we suggest you read the interesting book by Efim Moshinsky entitled, *Raoul Wallenberg is Alive! The Amazing Autobiograhy of the KGB Officer Who Arrested Him In 1945*. Jerusalem: Rescue Publishing Company, © 1987. Available through Good Times Publishing Company, POB 3576, Jerusalem, Israel. Tel. 011-972-2-525353.

[94]Tom Jarriel of *20/20* reported the story of American soldiers in Vietnam who were secretly buried under Russian tombstones: "...American soldiers Richard Larson, Lyle Timmerman, Ted Yates and Alberto Cairo are found anonymously interred beneath Russian tombstones. And who is to explain why another American is resting beneath Marker 22 in a POW cemetery on Russian soil?" "The Men We Left Behind," *20/20*, ABC News, Sept. 11, 1992. Jarriel located Colonel Aleksei Kirichenko, a retired KGB and POW expert, who admitted: "I found some dates about the American prisoners of war...I saw the document recently." Ibid. Jarriel provides absolute proof in his report: "Major Robert Brown was a technical genius whose mind was crammed with classified data." Ibid. Brown was an experienced F-111 fighter pilot, he understood the U.S. anti-ballistic missile system and worked with NASA as a top engineer. Terry Minarcin, a National Security agent in Vietnam, tracked Brown and his co-pilot by intercepting radio transmissions. He still believes that the men were taken to the Soviet Union. Within the following year, the Soviet Union's technical advances in space and missile technologies—Major Brown's field of expertise—were monumental. For an in-depth understanding of this subject, a recent book, *Soldiers of Misfortune*, by J. Sanders, M. Sauter and R. Kirkwood (National Press Books, Washington, D.C.) would be an invaluable reference tool.

[95]These were agents who interrogated captured Americans in Vietnam. Their reports were returned to Moscow.

to open those files to anyone. So, U.S. POW search teams here in Moscow don't have access to a potential treasure chest of data."[96]

Can we put two and two together? If Russia was really free and intended to remain free, why would these MIA files never be opened? Obviously, the KGB is still powerful and waiting underground to reemerge in a future communist Soviet Union after the free world has bankrolled Russia back into financial stability.

At this point, to give anything other than the Gospel[97] to the Russians is nothing short of a "capital" crime against the people they will one day suppress with U.S. money! Meanwhile, many of the Soviet Jews continue to immigrate to Israel, fulfilling the prophecy of Jeremiah 16:15,[98] which had to take place before the Russians and Arabs launch their attack on Israel.

THE UNDERGROUND KGB EXISTS, ACCORDING TO A MAJOR RUSSIAN JOURNALIST

" 'I see Russian soldiers gathering for this last southern campaign. I see Russian commanders in the headquarters of Russian divisions and armies, tracing the route of movement of troop formations and the final destinations of the routes. I see planes at air bases in the southern military districts of Russia. I see submarines surfacing at the shores of the Indian Ocean and aircraft carriers approaching the shores, where the soldiers of the Russian army are already marching, where armed assault vehicles are moving, and enormous masses of tanks are converging. At last, Russia is completing its final military campaign'....'...The system of political police has been preserved, and could easily be resurrected,' stated the decree's preamble....the second part of the decree didn't merely contradict the preamble, but undoes it altogether, proposing that the very same Chekist bosses use the very same KGB officers to create a new secret service. And this transformation was to be accomplished by Nikolai Golushko, director of the new Federal Counterintelligence Service, who had made his career in ideological counterintelligence. Under the decree, Golushko was given two weeks to design a charter for the new intelligence agency and submit it to the President for approval.

---

[96]Ibid.

[97]We are not against private U.S. citizens helping Russian families with finances and physical help or the U.S. setting up businesses and commerce there, but giving billions of dollars, which fall into the hands of wealthy government officials, is not fair to us or the freedom-loving Russian citizens.

[98]"...As the LORD lives, who brought up the sons of Israel from the land of the north and from all the countries where He had banished them. For I will restore them to their own land which I gave to their fathers" (NASB).

Golushko, a career KGB officer who had reached the rank of colonel general after thirty-one years of service, had been security minister at the time of the decree. Prior to 1991, he had been chairman of the Ukrainian KGB, and before that, for many years, an officer of the KGB's Fifth Directorate.

The second presidential decree came only two weeks later, and contained none of the radical fervor that had characterized the first one. The charter of the Federal Counterintelligence Service was issued at the same time, and a commission was created to recertify 250 top KGB officials. Most passed the test: out of 250, 236 remained in place....The Committee for Border Troops, which had become an independent agency in the fall of 1991 and had returned to the KGB in May 1992, was again declared an independent organization. It was also announced that the Federal Counterintelligence Service would no longer act as a law enforcement body; its power to conduct investigations was revoked, and it's former Investigative Directorate was transferred to the curator General. (Actually, only the function was transferred; all five hundred KGB investigators remained just where they were in state security.)

Evidence for my assertions was given to me by Nikolai Golushko himself in a February 4, 1994, interview...."[99]

The Vilna Gaon (Rabbi Elijah ben Solomon; 1720-1797), one of the wisest men in Jewish history. He foresaw the future Russian invasion of Israel, which will probably occur sometime after 2020.

---

[99]Yevgenia Albats, *The State Within a State: The KGB and Its Hold on Russia—Past, Present and Future*. New York: Farrar, Straus and Giroux, © 1994, pp. 348-351, used by permission. First quote is Albats quoting Zhirinovsky, second quote is Albats quoting Yeltsin, third quote is Albats.

PAST AND PRESENT POLITICAL STATEMENTS WE SHOULD ALWAYS CONSIDER, REGARDING THE SUBJECTS OF PROPERTY OWNERSHIP AND COMMUNISM

"Property is the fruit of labor; property is desirable; it is a positive good in the world. That some should be rich shows that others may become rich and hence is just encouragement to industry and enterprise. Let not him who is homeless pull down the house of another, but let him work diligently and build one for himself, thus by example assuring that his own shall be safe from violence when built...."[100] "I know that I am right in loving liberty and justice, for Christ loved liberty and justice, and Christ is God."[101]

Abraham Lincoln, 16th President of the United States, 1857

"The democratic concept of man is false; because it is Christian. The democratic concept holds that each man has a value as a sovereign being. This is the illusion, dream and postulate of Christianity."[102] " 'The theory of the communists may be summed up in the single sentence: Abolition of private property'....'You are horrified at our intending to do away with...**your** property. Precisely so; that is just what we intend.' "[103] Leftist communist thug, Karl Marx, 1858

"To the Christian doctrine of the infinite significance of the individual human soul, I oppose with icy clarity the saving doctrine of the nothingness and insignificance of the individual human being."[104] Adolf Hitler, 1932

"Communism is the major menace of our time. Today, it threatens the very existence of our Western civilization. In November 1917, the Bolsheviks seized control in Russia, gaining state power for the first time. That breach has today widened into a vast communist empire. The attack is still being pressed. International communism will never rest until the whole world, including the United States, is under the hammer and sickle. This is what happened to the Russian people, now held in bondage, who would be free if they could....Communism is more than an economic, political, social, or philosophical doctrine. It is a way of life; a false, materialistic 'religion.' It would strip man of his belief in God, his heritage of freedom, his trust in love, justice, and mercy. Under communism, all would become, as so many already have, twentieth-century slaves."[105] J. Edgar Hoover, FBI Director, 1958

---

[100] *The Dawn*, Vol. XVII, No. 1, Jan.-Feb. 1946. An Anti-Defamation League publication recorded an interesting mention made by this President regarding the Jewish people. It reads: "Abraham Lincoln was revered by his Jewish compatriots. In 1862 General Grant issued a strange order that all Jews be expelled from the territories where his authority ran; Lincoln revoked the order after a plea from a Jewish delegation who said they came once again, as of old, seeking protection in 'Father Abraham's bosom.' His death was mourned deeply by Jews, and for the first time the prayer for the dead was recited in the synagoguge for someone not of the Jewish faith." Frederick M. Schweitzer, *A History of the Jews Since the First Century A.D.* New York: The Macmillan Company, © 1971, p. 272, used by permission. "Rabbi Isaac M. Wise, in an address following Lincoln's death, said that Lincoln had told him he believed himself to be of Hebrew parentage." *The Dawn*, Vol. IX, No. 1, Jan.-Feb. 1938, p. 3.

[101] "The Religion of Abraham Lincoln," *The Dawn*, Vol. XVIII, No. 1, Jan.-Feb., 1947.

[102] Samuel M. Shoemaker, "Christianity and Patriotism," *The Dawn*, Vol. XXXI, No. 3, May-June, 1960, p. 7.

[103] John R. Rice, *Communism and Socialism*, p. 375. Bold mine. Rice's source was *The Communist Manifesto.*

[104] Samuel M. Shoemaker, "Christianity and Patriotism," *The Dawn*, Vol. XXXI, No. 3, May-June, 1960, p. 7.

[105] J. Edgar Hoover, *Masters of Deceit*, p. vi.

"If we do not recognize the connection between freedom and faith, I can tell you that the dictators do. And this is why they seek to exterminate religion, root and branch....William Penn once said that men must be governed by God, or they will be ruled by tyrants. Nobody knows that so well as would-be-tyrants...."

Samuel M. Shoemaker, author of "Christianity and Patriotism," 1960

"He [JFK] leaves little doubt that his idea of the 'challenging new world' is one in which the Federal Govt. will grow bigger and do more and of course spend more. I know there must be some short sighted people in the Republican party who will advise that the Republicans should try to 'out liberal' him. In my opinion this would be fatal....Under the trusted boyish hair cut it is still old Karl Marx—first launched a century ago. There is nothing new in the idea of a Govt. being Big Brother to us all. Hitler called his 'State Socialism' and way before him it was 'benevolent monarchy."

Ronald Reagan's letter to Vice President Richard Nixon regarding JFK, 1960. [ ] mine

"We are not going to let them [Russia] issue an ultimatum to the world of surrender or die."

Ronald Reagan, from the television special, *Reagan on Reagan*, 1989. [ ] mine

ARE THE RUSSIANS COMING? ANSWERS FROM PROPHECY AND STUDENTS OF PROPHECY!

"What about the August 19th, 1991, coup against Gorbachev? The KGB deserve an Academy Award for the staging and plot development of this so-called 'coup.' Private polls in Russia reveal that some 62 percent of the citizens believe that the coup was staged....the August 1991 coup was the most inept military-political operation in the history of coups....Why did the coup leader call himself the 'acting president' if he truly intended overthrowing President Gorbachev? In every other coup in this century the rebels immediately attack the telephone system, water supplies, electricity, media access, airports and transportation. Not one of these targets was attacked. The telephones, radio and television stations, airports, and media broadcasting continued normally throughout the coup. The water, electricity, and phone lines to Yeltsin and the Russian Parliament also stayed open. Why did the plotters not attempt to kill Yeltsin, Gorbachev, and the other reformers since the Soviet Union had 250,000 superbly trained special forces Spetznaz troops available?....Why have the trials of the plotters been delayed, evidence 'lost' by the KGB, and a veil of secrecy been drawn over the proceedings? Two and a half years later not one of the coup plotters has gone to trial! Recently the Russian state judge fired all of prosecutors working on the case. The real reason Gorbachev and the KGB planned the 'coup' was to deceive the West about their true intentions. They knew some skeptics in western intelligence and military circles doubted the sincerity of their recent conversion to democracy. Some in the West warned of the dangers as Russia continued to massively arm its military while we disarmed believing the Cold War was over. The Soviets also knew that the New World Order planners in the Council on Foreign Relations and the Bilderbergers desperately wanted to believe that Russia was truly abandoning hard line communism. As Sun Tzu suggested: 'Offer your enemy a bait to lure him; pretend disorder. Then strike him.' The coup was planned to convince the West that Russia had truly reformed and communism was finished forever. When the reformers 'won,' as they naturally did, they would still need Gorbachev to deal with the West and the hard liners would go underground and out of sight. They hoped the failed coup would encourage the west to drop our reservations to the Soviet continued buildup of military power. Their goal was to encourage us to provide the high technology and western aid desperately needed by Russia. The western nations are providing billions in aid and investments. The 'failure' of the coup supposedly proved that the 'hard line communists had lost' and were now out of power. The West could safely disarm and ignore the largest military build-up in history because the new democratic leaders of the C.I.S. would never dream of using their superior weapons against the West."[106]

Grant R. Jeffrey, February 1994

" 'And you, son of man, prophesy against Gog, and say, 'Thus says the Lord GOD, 'Behold, I am against you, O Gog, prince of Rosh, Meshech, and Tubal; and I shall turn you around, drive you on, take you up from the remotest parts of the north, and bring you against the mountains of Israel. And I shall strike your bow from your left hand, and dash down your arrows from your right hand. You shall fall on the mountains of Israel, you and all your troops, and the peoples who are with you; I shall give you as food to every kind of predatory bird and beast of the field. You will fall on the open field; for it is I who have spoken,' declares the Lord GOD. 'And I shall send fire upon Magog and those who inhabit the coastlands in safety; and they will know that I am the LORD. And My holy name I shall make known in the midst of My people Israel; and I shall not let My holy name be profaned anymore. And the nations will know that I am the LORD, the Holy One in Israel.' "

Ezekiel 39:1-7 NASB

" 'Whether you like it or not, we are back again,' said Viktor Gogitiedse. The diplomat of Georgian origin is directing Moscow's return to the Middle East on the orders of the Russian president, Boris Yeltsin. Gogitiedse was able to set a first signal: Foreign Minister Andre Kozyrev traveled to Jerusalem to Israel's head of state, Yitzhak Rabin, and to Tunis to PLO chief, Yassir Arafat. (!!!) Is Gogitiedse thinking of creating new spheres of influence? The diplomat denies this, 'We only want to play a positive part.' Further facts which show that Russia is returning to the great Middle East playing field are: Moscow demanded a reduction of the sanctions against Iraq. A Russian friendship fleet appeared in the Iraqi port Um-Kassar. Russian 'technical experts' went to Damascus to discuss the sale of spare parts for the Soviet weapons supplied to Syria. The Soviet spy ship, 'Ariel,' now sailing under Russian flag, has returned to the Persian Gulf for the first time since 1989, supposedly for environmental research. Despite the difficult financial situation, the Russian government granted new scholarships to students from Arab lands. The renowned Soviet Institute for Oriental Languages has opened its doors again. Russia's diplomatic elite are to learn Arabic, Persian and Turkish."[107]

Arno Froese, October 1994

"The Russians have not forsaken intercontinental ballistic missiles. In fact, they are preparing three new models of ICBMs. The Russians have also built up their navy and plan to have a force of 24 (Red October style) Typhoon-class SSBNs equipped with upgraded SS-N-20 ballistic missiles by the year 2000."[108]

Hal Lindsey, March 1995

What a few have realized and revealed about Russia returning to its anti-Israel/pro-Islamic policies of destruction, may be only foreshadowed here by Froese. We believe Russia will hide this activity to the best of their ability, so long as our

---

[106]Grant R. Jeffrey, *Prince of Darkness.* Toronto: Frontier Research Publications, © 1994, pp. 164-165, used by permission.

[107]"Military Resistance Against Jesus," *Midnight Call,* © Oct., 1994, p. 9, used by permission.

[108]Hal Lindsey, *The Final Battle*, p. 178.

billions in aid continue to line their leaders' pockets. Soon, however, somewhere between the twenty to forty year range, this wise foresight will be proven accurate as the Russians openly defy us. However, at the very end, just prior to Ezekiel's predicted Russian attack, a pretense of peace will seem final as the prophet Ezekiel has foretold in Ezekiel 38:11: "And thou shalt say, I will go up to the land of unwalled villages; I will go to them that are at rest, that dwell safely, all of them dwelling without walls, and having neither bars nor gates" Philip Moore, 1996

"They [the communists within the Russian government] are an **evil** empire....they are the focus of **evil** in the modern world."

Astute, fearless, Bible-believing American President Ronald Reagan

"Thus saith the Lord God; It shall also come to pass, *that* at the same time shall things come into thy mind, and thou shalt think an **evil** thought....Therefore, son of man, prophesy and say unto Gog, Thus saith the Lord GOD; In that day when my people of Israel dwelleth safely, shalt thou not know *it*? And thou shalt come from thy place out of the north parts, thou, and many people with thee, all of them riding upon horses, a great company, and a mighty army: And thou shalt come up against my people of Israel....*Art* thou he of whom I have spoken in old time by my servants the prophets of Israel....when Gog shall come against the land of Israel, saith the Lord GOD, *that* my fury shall come up in my face....I will call for a sword against him [Russia]....great hailstones, fire, and brimstone."

Ezekiel 38:10, 14-18, 21-22 KJV. [ ] mine

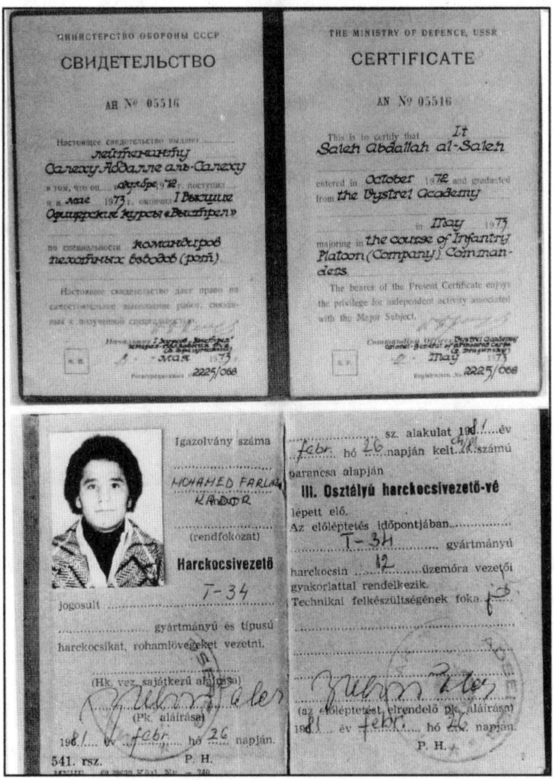

МИНИСТЕРСТВО ОБОРОНЫ СССР
СВИДЕТЕЛЬСТВО
АН № 05516
Лейтенанту Салеху Абдалле аль-Салеху
командиров пехотных взводов (рот)
2225/068

THE MINISTRY OF DEFENCE, USSR
CERTIFICATE
AN № 05516
This is to certify that Lt Saleh Abdallah al-Saleh
entered in October 1972 and graduated from the Vystrel Academy
in May 1973
majoring in the course of Infantry Platoon (Company) Commanders.
The bearer of the Present Certificate enjoys the privilege for independent activity associated with the Major Subject.
Commanding Officer
May 1973
Registration No. 2225/068

Igazolvány száma
MOHAMED FARLAH KADOR
(rendfokozat)
Harckocsivezető
jogosult T-34 gyártmányú és típusú harckocsikat, rohamlövegeket vezetni.
(Hk. vez. sajátkezű aláírása)
(Pk. aláírása)
1981. év febr. hó 26 napján.
541. rsz. P. H.

sz. alakulat 1981. év febr. hó 26 napján kelt ... számú parancsa alapján
III. Osztályú harckocsivezető-vé
lépett elő.
Az előléptetés időpontjában T-34 gyártmányú harckocsin 12 üzemóra vezetői gyakorlattal rendelkezik.
Technikai felkészültségének foka
(az előléptetést elrendelő pk. aláírása)
1981. év febr. hó 26 napján.
P. H.

МИНИСТЕРСТВО ОБОРОНЫ СССР

СВИДЕТЕЛЬСТВО

АН № 19441

Настоящее свидетельство выдано Тагер Хасан Хуссейн

в том, что он в мае 1976 г. поступил и в ноябре 1976 г. окончил офицерские курсы

по специальности командира артиллерийско-минометной батареи

Настоящее свидетельство дает право на самостоятельное выполнение работ, связанных с полученной специальностью.

Начальник

М. П. 11 ноября 1976 г.

Регистрационный № 394

THE MINISTRY OF DEFENCE, USSR

CERTIFICATE

AN № 19441

This is to certify that Taher Hassan Hussein

entered in May 1976 and graduated from the officers' course in November 1976

majoring in the speciality of the artillery and mortar battery commander

The bearer of the Present Certificate enjoys the privilege for independent activity associated with the Major Subject.

Commanding Officer

L. S. 11 November 1976

Registration No. 394

An Arab receives his graduation certificate after having been trained by Russia in the 1970's. Many Arab terrorists apprehended in Israel were trained in Russia or China.

"Make war upon those who believe not...even if they be people of the book [Jews or Christians]. Make war upon them until idolatry is no more and Allah's religion reigns supreme."[1] The Koran (Moslem Bible), circa 600 AD

"Mohammed was an impostor, since he completely rules out that freedom which was recognized by the universal religion revealed by the natural light and the light of the prophets...."[2] The famous Jewish philosopher, Baruch Spinoza, 1600's

"The greatest contemporary hero in the Arab world is Hitler."[3]
John Gunther, in his travelogue, *Inside* Asia, 1939

"There will be a war of extermination and massacre [against the Jews]...like the Mongolian massacres...."[4] Azzam Pasha, secretary general of the Arab League, 1948

"...It's time to pull out this cankerous tumor [Israel] from the body of the Muslim world. Every problem in our religion can be traced to this single dilemma—the everlasting struggle between Ishmael and Isaac."[5] President Rafsanjani of Iran, 1993

"The Jews are destined to be persecuted, humiliated and tortured forever, and it is a Muslim duty to see to it that they reap their due. No petty arguments must be allowed to divide us. Where Hitler failed, we must succeed."[6]
Sheikh Tamimi, Grand Mufti, the leader of Islam in Jerusalem, 1994

"...therefore, thus says the Lord GOD, 'Surely in the fire of my jealousy I have spoken against the rest of the nations, and against all Edom [Arab nations sprung from Esau; Gen. 25:30], who appropriated My land [Israel] for themselves as a possession with wholehearted joy *and* with scorn of soul, to drive it out for a prey.' Therefore, prophesy concerning the land of Israel, and say to the mountains and to the hills, to the ravines and to the valleys, 'Thus says the Lord GOD, 'Behold, I have spoken in My jealousy and in My wrath because you have endured the insults[7] of the nations'....I will multiply men on you, all the house of Israel, all of it; and the cities will be inhabited, and the waste places will be rebuilt."
The Bible, Ezekiel 36:5-6, 10 (NASB), prophesied 2600 years ago, as it applies today and in our future. [ ] mine

20

MOHAMMED IS MAD

The Arabs' ancient hatred of Israel may be the spark that lights the Armageddon fuse. Presently, many have been led to believe that the Arabs who are hostile to the Jews hold their position because of Israel's existence and control of Judea and Samaria, which the

---

[1]Mike Evans, *The Return*, p. 149.
[2]*The Books of Nature and Scripture*, p. 34.
[3]Aharon Lapid, "Terrible—The Terrorist," *Jerusalem Times/Jewish Press*, May 6, 1988, p. 63.
[4]Ibid. [ ] mine.
[5]*Perhaps Today*, May/June 1993, p. 7.
[6]Hal Lindsey, *Planet Earth—2000 A.D.*, p. 257.
[7]One of these insults is the Moslem doctrine, "Convert to Islam or die!" We note that scholar Joshua Bloch confirms Evans' interpretation of the "people of the book" in the

Moslems refer to as "occupied Arab territories." However, the root of this conflict is much deeper.

The Arab-Israeli question is among the most important in history, since the Bible foretells that it will be the cause of the world's last war, called Armageddon. Armageddon will be a war to end all wars because it will bring back the Messiah, who will herald the beginning of a **real** *new age* of peace! We want to give you the true story of the source of Arab/Israeli difficulties, which goes all the way back to the wombs which held Isaac and Ishmael, and nurtured the twins, Jacob and Esau.

MURDER, HORRENDOUS AND INHUMAN ACTS AGAINST THE JEWS, ARE THE RESULT OF ARAB RACISM

The ancient hatred of the Arab peoples against the Jews spans four millennia. It first manifested when Ishmael (the Arab son[8] of Abraham) discovered that he was not the chosen one after all, but that Isaac (the Jewish son) was. The result was that in order to keep Ishmael from killing Isaac out of jealousy, he and his mother Hagar were exiled from the city! Since then, all through history, Arabs have perpetrated terrible attacks of terror against innocent Jewish victims.

Tombstones from the Mount of Olives cemetery, used as part of a stairway in the Azaria Arab Legion camp on the Jerusalem-Jericho Road.

Koran to be the two groups shown in Evans' brackets. Bloch documents: " 'The Israelites were 'a people of the Book' (to use Mohammed's term); meaning, that their faith was based on divine revelation which was written down.' The Nazarenes wanted to enlarge upon this record of revelation by adding to it 'their 'Gospel' for which they evidently claimed the character of sacred Scripture.' " Joshua Bloch, "Outside Books," *Mordecai M. Kaplan, Jubilee Volume*, pp. 100-102.

8 *The Random House College Dictionary* says of Ishmael: "1....the son of Abraham and Hagar: he and Hagar were cast out of Abraham's family by Sarah. Gen. 16:11, 12. 2.an outcast. 3.an Arab." For Ishmaelite, the dictionary says: "...a descendant of Ishmael. 2. a wanderer or outcast. 3.an Arab." *The Random House College Dictionary*. New York: Random House, Inc., © 1975, p. 708, used by permission.

Professor Erhard, in 1967, visiting a former Arab Legion camp where Jewish tombstones from the Mount of Olives were used as building material.

Mohammed, who led the Arabs from multi-god religions into the Islam of the Koran in the seventh century, exterminated "the Jews of Arabia."[9] Did Zionism have anything to do with this? No, only racism! Racism against Jews. Many accuse Israel of racism when referring to Zionism (love of the Jewish nation). We assert that for the same reason that Jews were exiled from Yemen to Mauza by the Arabs in 1778, so also, the Algerian pogroms took place in 1801, and the infamous Damascus blood-libel in 1840. All of these tragic happenings are directly linked with Arab racial hatred of the Jew, which is traceable all the way back to his origin, as we will soon see!

A JEWISH BELIEVER IN JESUS TELLS OF AN ANTI-JEWISH PASSAGE IN THE MOSLEM KORAN

Meanwhile, we ask why the majority of Moslems are so particularly anti-Jew, anti-Israel, anti-Christian and anti-Bible. Could it be that their "Bible," the Koran, is filled with anti-Jewish and anti-Christian slurs? Liebes Feldman, a Jewish believer in Jesus, tells us in his article, "Islam, the Great Competitor": "Islam stepped into history tumultuously in the sixth century C.E. in the person of Muhammad, a descendant of Ishmael, Abraham's first son, born by the slave Hagar. Muhammad, although uneducated, was endowed with a mysterious ability....Islam attacked both Judaism and Christianity. It called them 'the people of the Book,' and accused them of altering and corrupting the 'book'....Concerning the Jews Muhammad says, 'They (the Jews) are those whom Allah has cursed and upon whom He brought His wrath and of whom He made apes and swine. and who serve the devil. These are in a worse plight and further astray from the straight path. (The Koran 5:60)' "[10]

MOHAMMED SETS US STRAIGHT ON THE CRUCIFIXION AND RESURRECTION OF JESUS—HE SAYS THEY NEVER OCCURRED

The central most important belief of our Messianic Christian faith is Jesus' death and resurrection. The Moslem arrogantly cuts this out of our historic faith, six hundred years after the fact, in the Koran! Liebes Feldman points out: "...the Koran, chapter 4, verse 157 [says]

---

[9]Aharon Lapid, "Terrible—The Terrorist," *Jerusalem Times/Jewish Press*, May 6, 1988, p. 63.

[10]Liebes Feldman, "Islam, the Great Competitor," *The Messianic Outreach*, Vol. 4:3, Mar.-May 1985, pp. 14-15, © used by permission. Available through Messianic Literature Outreach, POB 37062, Cincinnati, OH, USA 45222.

'...they killed him not, nor did they cause his death on the cross, but he was made to appear to them as such....' "[11] Feldman rightly notes: "Judaism and Christianity are but one tree, planted and planned by the eternal God of love and truth. But Islam pretends to be a tree by itself. The only link between the former religions and this 'new one' of Muhammad lies in the fact that Islam claims to correct the errors which crept into the holy books of Moses, and the Gospel of Jesus. This was wrought by the scribes of both Judaism and Christianity according to Islam. Therefore, Allah sent Muhammad to set aright the former books by sending down a new book void of any error. That book is the holy Koran. It was given to Muhammad, the prophet, in the Arabic language, with the express intention of proving the corruption of the Torah and the Gospel, perpetrated by Jews and Christians. Islam is not a God-planted tree, but a man-made construction, containing false accusations against the Bible whose author is the true and blessed God YHVH."[12]

IS "ALLAH'S" NAME A COUNTERFEIT COPY?

Regarding the identity of "Allah," Feldman enlightens us: "Allah was known in Arabia even before Muhammad. The Arabs being idolaters, worshipped Allah alongside with all the 360 idols. Allah was kept in greater honor than the other gods.

The word 'Allah' is doubtless of Hebrew origin: El...means God, in Hebrew. In Aramaic, Alh, Alaha, means God. The Jews which lived in Arabia spoke Aramaic. Muhammad heard God's Name Alh, Alaha, from them. But the Name of the God of Israel is YHVH. Exodus 3:14-15 tells us how God spoke to Moses and revealed to him his Name and memorial. The Name YHVH means Eternity in the past, present and future: 'I am that I am'....When we know the nature of God, as compared to the nature of Allah, we shall discover that Allah is God's adversary, who by a false prophet managed to make people believe that he and YHVH are the same God."[13]

DID MOHAMMED BELIEVE IN ONE GOD, AS MOST MOSLEMS BOASTFULLY CLAIM?

As far as Mohammed's creation of the idea of one god goes, this concept was only solidified within Islam after his death. Robert Morey

---

[11]Ibid, p. 14. [ ] mine.
[12]Ibid, p. 16.
[13]Ibid, p. 18.

informs us: "In order to appease his pagan family members and the members of the Quraysh tribe, he decided that the best thing he could do was to admit that it was perfectly proper to pray to and worship the three daughters of Allah: Al-Lat, Al-Uzza, and Manat.

This led to the famous 'satanic verses' in which Muhammad in a moment of weakness and supposedly under the inspiration of Satan (according to early Muslim authorities) succumbed to the temptation to appease the pagan mobs in Mecca (Sura 53:19).

The literature on the 'satanic verses' is so vast that an entire volume could be written just on this one issue. Every general and Islamic reference work, Muslim or Western, deals with it as well as all the biographies of Muhammad.

The story of Muhammad's temporary appeasement of the pagans by allowing them their polytheism cannot be ignored or denied. It is a fact of history that is supported by all Middle East scholars, Western and Muslim.

We are aware that there are a few modern Muslim apologists who reject the story of the 'satanic verses.' But we must point out that they do so not on the basis of any historical or textual evidence. Their objection is based solely on the grounds that Muhammad was sinless and therefore could not have done this!"[14]

ISLAM'S "BIBLE," THE SO-CALLED "HOLY" KORAN, IS ANTI-SEMITIC AND ANTI-CHRISTIAN

Most Jews and Christians have never bothered to pick up the Koran and see for themselves just what it has to say about us! We, in the course of writing this book, felt this was necessary to reveal the truth of what Islam really teaches regarding both the Jews and Christians. Once you realize what these teachings are, you will understand one reason why we have been so ruthlessly terrorized in the past.

Anti-Jewish and anti-Christian statements to the exalted followers of Allah in the Koran include: "Say: 'People of the Book! Come now to a word common between us and you, that we serve none but God, and that we associate not aught with Him, and do not some of us take others as Lords, apart from God.' And if they turn their backs, say: 'Bear witness that we are Muslims.'

People of the Book! Why do you dispute concerning Abraham? The Torah was not sent down, neither the Gospel, but after him. What, have you no reason?

---

[14]Robert Morey, *Islamic Invasion, Confronting the World's Fastest Growing Religion.* Eugene, OR: Harvest House Publishers, © 1992, pp. 78-79, used by permission.

Ha, you are the ones who dispute on what you know; why then dispute you touching a matter of which you know not anything? God knows, and you know not.

No; Abraham in truth was not a Jew, neither a Christian;[15] but he was a Muslim and one pure of faith; certainly he was never of the idolaters.

Surely the people standing closest to Abraham are those who followed him, and this Prophet, and those who believe; and God is the Protector of the believers.

There is a party of the People of the Book yearn to make you go astray; yet none they make to stray, except themselves, but they are not aware.

People of the Book! Why do you disbelieve in God's signs, which you yourselves witness? People of the Book! Why do you confound the truth with vanity, and conceal the truth and that wittingly?

Yet pardon them, and forgive....And with those who say 'We are Christians' We took compact; and they have forgotten a portion of that they were reminded of. So We have stirred up among them enmity and hatred....People of the Book, now there has come to you Our Messenger, making clear to you many things you have been concealing of the Book, and effacing many things. There has come to you from God a light, and a Book Manifest whereby God guides whosoever follows....They are unbelievers who say, 'God is the Messiah, Mary's son.' Say: 'Who then shall overrule God in any way if He desires to destroy the Messiah, Mary's son, and his mother, and all those who are on earth?'....Say the Jews and Christians, 'We are the sons of God, and His beloved ones.' Say: 'Why then does He chastise you for your sins?....O believers [Moslems], take not Jews and Christians as friends; they are friends of each other. Whoso of you makes them his friends is one of them. God guides not the people of the evildoers....The Jews have said, 'God's hand is fettered.' Fettered are their hands, and they

---

15We do not know of anyone who has ever said Abraham was a Christian. The New Testament, along with evangelicals, agrees that a Gentile can be adopted into God's covenant begun with Abraham, the father of the Jews, by accepting Jesus as the Messiah. Galatians 3:7-9 says: "Know ye therefore that they which are of faith, the same are the children of Abraham. And the scripture, foreseeing that God would justify the heathen through faith, preached before the gospel unto Abraham, *saying*, In thee shall all nations be blessed. So then they which be of faith are blessed with faithful Abraham" (KJV). By this we acknowledge Abraham, the faithful father of the Jew. The Moslem, on the other hand, is taught that Abraham was a Moslem, and he will swear to that. I have personally heard "them" say this in Israel. This is laughable, since there were no Moslems until Mohammed, in the seventh century AD. Abraham lived nearly 4000 years ago, long before Mohammed created the Moslem religion.

are cursed for what they have said....As often as they light a fire for war, God will extinguish it. They hasten about the earth, to do corruption there; and God loves not the workers of corruption.

But had the People of the Book [Jews and Christians] believed and been godfearing [converted to Islam], We would have acquitted them of their evil deeds [believing our Bible], and admitted them to Gardens of Bliss....And they supposed there should be no trial; but blind they were, and deaf. Then God turned towards them; then again blind they were, many of them, and deaf; and God sees the things they do.

They are unbelievers who say, 'God is the Messiah, Mary's son'....The Jews say, 'Ezra is the Son[16] of God'; the Christians say, 'The Messiah is the Son of God.' That is the utterance of their mouths, conforming with the unbelievers before them. God assail them! How they are perverted!....surely those who forge against God falsehood shall not prosper. A little enjoyment, then for them awaits a painful chastisement. And those of Jewry—We have forbidden them what We related to thee before, and We wronged them not, but they wronged themselves....Say: 'You of Jewry, if you assert that you are the friends of God, apart from other men, then do you long for death, if you speak truly.' But they will never long for it, because of that their hands have forwarded; God knows the evildoers. Say: 'Surely death, from which you flee, shall encounter you; then you shall be returned to the Knower of the Unseen....' "[17]

WHAT DOES *TIME* MAGAZINE SAY?

An older, more conservative *Time* magazine accurately described the real situation between the Arabs and Israel in June of 1967. They even used common biblical lingo—Isaac and Ishmael. "**The Promised Land**. To the Jews of the world, Israel is both a state and a state of mind. Named for Jacob, whose battle with the Angel of God (*Genesis 32:24-28)* led him to be called Israel ('He who struggles with God'), it is the fulfillment of a struggle that has pitted the Jew against the world for 2,000 years. It is the Land of Canaan to which Abraham was given a divine deed after he left Ur in the 18th Century B.C.....Isaac and Ishmael never really understood each other, but both were sons of Abraham—and both at least forgot their differences long enough to

---

[16]During our study, we have not found anywhere in Jewish belief the idea that Ezra was the son of God. Most rabbis deny the entire doctrine of God's son. The Arabs, it appears, are quite mixed up and misinformed concerning the Jewish faith.

[17]Arthur J. Arberry, *The Koran Interpreted*. London: Oxford University Press, © 1982, pp. 54-55, 102, 108, 110-111, 182, 272, 583-584, used by permission. [ ] mine.

bury their father. Their descendants in Israel and the Arab world today, even if they never embrace as brothers, need to come to terms with each other not only for the sake of world order but for selfish reasons. The Arabs need help—and the lessons—that Israel is willing to give. The Israelis need peace....Israel's hardest task is not just to survive the onslaught of Arab enmity, but to convince the Arabs that the Jewish state, here to stay, is worth having as a neighbor."[18]

Time went on to identify its biblical terminology in a footnote, which read: "Ishmael is traditionally considered the ancestor of the Arabs, Isaac of the Jews."

TIME TO STAY

The continued existence, or being "here to stay," as *Time* magazine puts it, is the essence of Zionism among modern Jews, particularly in regard to their permanent existence in Israel. Therefore, we ask "What do key Arab/Moslem leaders, past and present, say about the subject of Israel's Jewish existence and of her being 'here to stay'?" Their answers may startle you. Here are a few:

"It is extremely astonishing to see that the Jews of today are exactly a typical picture of those mentioned in the Holy Qur'an and they have the same bad manners and qualities of their forefathers."[19] Muhammad Azzah Darwaza, Moslem *'alim* (scholar/cleric)

"...the Jews as represented by their Holy Book are hostile to all human values...their evil nature is not to be easily cured through temporary or half measures....this book [the Bible] inculcated in their [the Jews] minds such rules of individual conduct and international policies as only the devil could approve of....the Jews' wicked nature never changes."[20] Kamal Ahmad Own, Egyptian religious educator

"...we as Arabs did not regard the Jews in a different light from that of other peoples, i.e., a pest which humanity had to tolerate and live with like other calamities of life and other diseases."[21] Professor Abdul Satta al-Sayed, of Tursos, Syria

"...all countries should wage war against the Zionists."[22]
King Faisal of Saudi Arabia, 1972

"...the Jews don't like Farrakhan, so they call me Hitler. Well, that's a good name. Hitler was a very great name....Jews know their wickedness, not just Zionism,

---

[18]"Israel: A Nation Under Seige," *Time*, June 9, 1967, pp. 39, 42, used by permission.
[19]Dr. M. S. Stern, "Islam and Jews, Moslem Hatred of The Jew Runs Deep," *The Jewish Press*, Fri., Dec. 7, 1990, p. 20. For more recent/current quotes, see p. 830-831.
[20]Ibid.
[21]Ibid.
[22]Michael L. Brown, *Our Hands are Stained with Blood, The Tragic Story of the "Church" and the Jewish People*, p. 54.

which is an outgrowth of Jewish transgression....sucking the blood of the black community...The Jews cannot defeat me. I will grind them and crush them into little bits'...."[23] "The present State called Israel is an outlaw act...she will never have any peace, because there can be no peace structured on injustice, thievery, lying, and deceit and using the name of God to shield your gutter religion under His holy and righteous name."[24]

Louis Farrakhan, founder and leader of the Nation of Islam[25]

"We shall never stop until...Israel is destroyed...the goal of our struggle is the end of Israel, and there can be no compromises...."[26] PLO Chairman Yassar Arafat

"We shall not rest until our usurped land is liberated and until the Palestinian people return with dignity and pride to their independent state, with Jerusalem its capital."[27] King Fahd of Saudi Arabia

"Our army will be satisfied with nothing less than the disappearance of Israel."[28]

Salah Jadid, Syrian Chief of Staff, October 30, 1964

"The Arab national aim is the elimination of Israel."[29]

President Nasser of Egypt to President Aref of Iraq, May 25, 1965

---

[23]Ibid, p. 51.

[24]National PAC (Political Action Committee) newsletter.

[25]In a recent *Atlanta Journal and Constitution* article entitled, "The Growing Rift Between Blacks and Jews, When Friends Feud," Rabbi Goodman made the true and accurate statement: "Farrakhan and Khalid Muhammad represent to us the voice of the Holocaust." Cynthia Tucker, the mediator of the discussion, posed the question, "Why is it important to so many in the Jewish community to have black leaders refute a Farrakhan or a Khalid Muhammad? What does that represent?" John Blake, "The Growing Rift Between Blacks and Jews, When Friends Feud," *Atlanta Journal and Constitution*, Sun. June 5, 1994, Section G3, reprinted by permission. Reproduction does not imply endorsement. Lawrence Jeffries, a black student, responded: "The fact of the matter is the Jewish community has no right to select black people's leaders. They have no right to tell black leaders how they should respond to other black leaders. Jews have never had this right, but in the past they had the *power* to. They had the power to pick and choose who black people were going to uphold as their leaders. Now the Jewish community does not have the power to do that." It seems ironic to us that such a sizable number within the black community are leaning toward anti-Semitism while simultaneously denying it, especially since the Jews were so helpful during the 1960's in support of the Civil Rights Movement! The article pictured Andrew Goodman and Michael Schwerner, who were killed in 1964 while organizing black voters in Mississippi. Truly, the evangelical born-again believer, both black and white, few that we may be, are the only true lasting loyal friends of the Jew. We can be counted upon to even give our lives, as many did in the Holocaust. We ask for nothing in return. We help only because of the love and word God gives us in the Bible. Even so, we are often referred to as "dangerous" by the rabbis because of our faith and because we share it with our Jewish friends! Have you ever seen a contrast so absurd? We pray that our Jewish friends realize we are their true friend, one who will never sell out—and we pray they not be afraid, because we teach that Jesus is the Messiah, even based on their Bible. We love you!

[26]Martin Gilbert, *The Arab-Israeli Conflict, Its History in Maps*, 4th Edition. Jerusalem: Steimatzky Ltd., © 1984, p. 103, used by permission.

[27]National PAC.

[28]Martin Gilbert, *The Arab-Israeli Conflict, Its History in Maps*, 4th Edition, p. 63.

[29]Ibid, p 52.

"This is a fight for the homeland—it is either us or the Israelis. There is no middle road. The Jews of Palestine will have to leave. We will facilitate their departure to their former homes. Any of the old Palestine Jewish population who survive may stay, but it is my impression that none of them will survive."[30]

Ahmed Shukairy, Chairman of the PLO, June 1, 1967

"Zionism...is a racist and a fanatical movement in its formation: aggressive, expansionist and colonialist in its aims: and Fascist and Nazi in its means. Israel is the tool of the Zionist movement and a human and geographical base for world imperialism."[31] Palestine National Covenant, July 17, 1968

WHAT DO THEY SAY ABOUT CHRISTIAN ZIONISM?

Large numbers of contemporary Arabs are not only incensed by Jewish Zionism but are becoming increasingly alarmed at Christian Zionism, which supports the Jews' right to return to their land, while helping to assist as many as possible in immigrating to Israel.

Few people realize it, but Christian Zionism has been with us since the first century. As already mentioned in a previous chapter, Regina Sharif, in her book, *Non-Jewish Zionism*, traces Christian Zionism for some four hundred years! In her thesis, she more or less tries to blame premillennial Evangelical Christians for the existence of modern Israel, rather than God and His prophecies. Still, believing Christians realize we have been given the honor by God to assist in pulling together the strings of the new State of Israel. We are all flattered by her thesis, to say the least!

REGINA SHARIF SAYS THAT CHRISTIAN ZIONISM (BASED ON BIBLICAL PROMISE AND PROPHECY) IS A "MYTH"

In our inquiry into Arab hostility toward the Jew, and particularly the new State of Israel of 1948, we ask, "What does the modern Arab have to say about Christian Zionists who love Israel and the Jewish people?" Sharif, a writer sympathetic to Arab fantasies, who is married to a Palestinian, remarks: "...Zionism as an idea pre-dates both the 19th Century and Jewish Zionism....Zionist pre-supposition, including their underlying mythology....can be traced back 300 years prior to the 1st Zionist Congress in Basle in 1897 when a select group of European Jews for the first time publicly rallied behind the Zionist banner....The non-Jewish Zionist tradition is thus based on a whole constellation of Zionist myths which managed to creep into Western history most noticeably via the Protestant Reformation of the 16th Century.

---

[30]Ibid.

[31]Ibid, p 103.

The Zionist myths which began to be cultivated at that early stage within the non-Jewish environment were...namely the myth of the Chosen People, the myth of the covenant and the myth of the Second Coming of the Messiah. The myth of the Chosen People set the Jews up as a nation and one favoured above all others. The myth of the covenant centred upon the continuous and indissoluble connection, as promised by God, between the Chosen People and the Holy Land, thus giving Palestine to the Jewish nation as its predestined territory. Finally the myth of messianic expectancy guaranteed that the Chosen People would in due time finally set an end to its exile and return to Palestine in order to establish there their national existence once and for all."[32]

SHARIF CORRECTLY CONCLUDES THAT INTEREST IN THE BIBLE AWAKENED PROTESTANT INTRIGUE WITH THE JEWS' PROPHETICAL RETURN TO ISRAEL

Sharif further reminds us: "Non-Jewish Zionism began to take on a recognizable form in the early 16th Century when Renaissance and Reformation combined to lay the foundation of modern European history. The revived interest in Biblical literature and its exegesis awakened public interest in the Jews and their return to Palestine. Thus what came to constitute the 'Jewish Question' in the 16th Century was not Jewish emancipation—the granting of citizens' rights—but the role assigned to the Jews in such new doctrinal questions as the fulfilment of Biblical prophecies, the Latter Times and the Second Coming of Christ the Messiah....Hence, by opening up the question of Jewish national revival and the Jews' collective return to Palestine, the Protestant Reformation initiated a continuous non-Jewish Zionist record as an important element in Protestant theology...."[33]

THOUGH SCORNFUL, SHARIF IS RIGHT AGAIN—WE RECOGNIZE JESUS AS A JEWISH PROPHET AND BEN-GURION'S REFERENCE TO THE CHRISTIAN BIBLE, AS THE JEWS' SACROSANCT TITLE-DEED TO ISRAEL

Sharif is correct in that she realizes: "The 'Judaizing' strain of the Protestant Reformation was further stimulated and enhanced by the rediscovery of the Old Testament so central to the Reformation, for: 'if it is doubtful whether Protestantism could have arisen without the knowledge of the Old Testament, it is certain that without it the Reformed Church could not have assumed the shape it took.' The so-called Old Testament not only constitutes the largest part of the

---

[32]Regina Sharif, *Non-Jewish Zionism*, p. 9.
[33]Ibid, p. 10.

Christian Bible, but is known as the Jewish or Hebrew Bible. As such, it is the only record of the history of the ancient Jewish state, made up of a collection of myths, legends, historical narratives, poems, prophetic and apocalyptic pronouncements. It is because of this common heritage that Ben-Gurion referred to the Christian Bible as the 'Jews' sacrosanct title-deed to Palestine...with a genealogy of 3,500 years....The Old Testament stories and characters became as familiar as bread and many Protestants could recite passages by heart. Jesus himself became known and thought of not so much as the son of Mary but as one of a long line of Hebrew prophets. Old Testament heroes like Abraham, Isaac, and Jacob came to replace the Catholic saints."[34]

SHE IS CORRECT ABOUT OUR INTEREST IN PROPHECIES RIGHT ON DOWN TO THE TWENTIETH CENTURY, BUT SHE IS WRONG ABOUT THE HISTORY OF THE OLD TESTAMENT BEING FANTASY

In truth, contrary to what many liberal theologians would have us believe, there were true Christian Zionists prior to the Reformation in the 1600's, dating all the way back to the time when Jesus walked the earth (Acts 1:16).[35] However, when Augustine abolished millennial Zionism in 380 (the biblical Christian teaching that Jesus would return to Israel in His Second Coming and reign 1000 years), the true Christians were underground in hiding to avoid persecution by the Catholic "Church."

You cannot go wrong in understanding the importance of the Jew, Israel, and the Messiah if you take the Bible at face value. Regina Sharif supports this conclusion, as she writes: "One of the most definite effects of the Protestant[36] Reformation was the emerging

[34]Ibid, p. 13.

[35]This author's opinion.

[36]Not all evangelicals realize the importance of Israel in prophecy and support her. There are a very minute number of evangelicals who claim to be born-again, yet do not recognize the prophetic importance of Israel. The majority of evangelicals have an answer for them. "There are a few rotten apples in every barrel!" or "There is always a fly in the ointment." Hal Lindsey identifies these people and shows how and why they are in error according to the New Testament. He mentions in his excellent treatise that anti-Semitism was caused, and can still be caused, by people who do not hold to the literal, premillennial/evangelical interpretation of the Bible. He notes: "The modern champions of this method of interpreting the Scriptures call themselves Christian Reconstructionists. They believe that they have a mandate from God to *reconstruct society* by strictly instituting the civil code of the Law of Moses over the governments of the world, beginning with the United States. They believe that this is the way the Church will establish the Kingdom of God on earth *before* the personal return of the Lord Jesus Christ....The arrogance manifested by the Dominion preachers against Israel as a distinct national people is awesome. A prime example of this is the book by Earl Paulk entitled *To Whom is God Betrothed*. One of the main issues he raises is that most teachers of prophecy today exhort us to bless a nation that is godless...." Hal Lindsey, *The Road To*

interest in the fulfilment of biblical prophecies concerning the End of Time. The core of millenarianism was the belief in the Second Coming of Christ whose return would establish God's kingdom on earth, which was to last for 1,000 years (that is, a millennium). Millenarians regarded the future of the Jewish people as an important element in the events to precede the End of Time. In fact, the literal interpretation of the apocalyptic writings in the Bible led them to conclude that the Millennium was to be heralded by the physical Restoration of the Jews as a nation (Israel) to Palestine....After Christianity [Catholicism] became the official religion of the Roman Empire in AD 380....Augustine in his [book] *City of God* seemed to have settled this problem [of millennial teachings], at least until the 16th Century. Using the allegorical methodology, Augustine interpreted the Millennium as a spiritual state into which the Church collectively had already entered at the time of Pentecost, i.e. just after the death and resurrection of Christ. Pre-Reformation semi-sectarian minority movements expressing millenarian yearnings had to remain underground. They were persecuted and suppressed by the Church in Rome....It [millenarianism] continued to find followers in every period of history after the Reformation and finally culminated in 20th Century American fundamentalism which insists that the state of Israel presents the literal fulfilment of prophecy in modern history."[37]

Sharif further writes: "The present-day Zionist falsification of history which claims 'historical right' to Palestine found its Christian precursor in Protestant Biblicism. The total history of Palestine was gradually reduced to those episodes concerning only the Jewish presence. People in Europe became conditioned to believing that nothing had happened in Palestine except the legends, historical narratives and myths recorded in the Old Testament. Only they were not regarded as such, but accepted as true history."[38]

CHRISTIAN ZIONISTS BRING BACK HEBREW AND STUDY RABBINICAL LITERATURE, DESPITE CATHOLIC PERSECUTION

Sharif has uncovered the little-known but very interesting fact that the true Christians' revival of Hebrew and study of rabbinical commentaries began, in some cases, *before* the Jews! She enlightens

---

Holocaust. New York: Bantam Books, Inc., © 1989, The Aorist Corporation, pp. 27, 194, used by permission. The official evangelical view can be summed up in the article entitled, "Whose Land: Can Christians be Neutral or Non-Aligned?", by Dr. Ulla Järvilehto, which we have reprinted in our *Vol. II*, chapter 39, "True Evangelical Christians Support Israel in the Ongoing Political Arena."

[37]Regina Sharif, *Non-Jewish Zionism*, pp. 16-17. [ ] mine.

[38]Ibid, p. 14.

many a scholar as she notes: "Of major importance for the post-Reformation development of Christian Zionism was the great weight the Reformation gave to the Hebrew language....In traditional Catholic circles the study of Hebrew, or even of Greek, was often regarded as the pastime of heretics and Hebrew learning was styled by many as a 'Jewish heresy.' Vigorous steps were often undertaken to uproot the study of Hebrew during the era of medieval scholasticism....knowledge of Hebrew soon became a recognized part of general European secular culture. The Reformation gave it a specifically religious sanction and made it a standard part of the theological curriculum.

The Reformation's interest in the Hebrew language was stimulated by its strict Biblicism. In order to understand correctly the infallible word of God....Already before the close of the 16th Century, Hebrew typefaces were employed in printing. This new knowledge of Hebrew was by no means confined to the books of the Biblical canon, i.e. the books of the Old Testament. Rabbinical literature was also studied deeply by others than rabbis, and by the Christian laity as well as the clergy....Among many Protestant groups and sects, this new appreciation for Hebrew as a language very often combined with an appreciation of Jewish traditions and values. The best example of this was Puritan England....General appreciation of the Jewish past led to respect for contemporary Jewry, often resulting in greater degrees of toleration in territories under the political influence of Protestantism. The Protestant Netherlands, under the ruling House of Nassau-Orange, was a case in point. During the 16th and 17th Centuries, Amsterdam was known among Europe's Jews as the new Jerusalem. Hugo Grotius, the well known Hebraist, philosopher, theologian and lawyer, and frequently cited today as the founder of public international law, established the common sources of Christianity and Judaism in his treatise *Ueber die Wahrheit der Christlichen Religion* (The Truth about the Christian Religion). He strongly objected to traditional Christendom's degradation of Judaism as an inferior religion....the influence of Judaism and Hebraism in those early days of the Reformation have deeply affected the mind of modern Europe....that was later to result in what we call the phenomenon of non-Jewish Zionism."[39]

***

[39]Ibid, pp. 14-16.

SHARIF FALSELY CLAIMS THAT CHRISTIAN ZIONISM IS A PRODUCT OF EUROPEAN RACIST PHILOSOPHY AS SHE COMPARES THIS BIBLICAL TRUTH TO NAZISM—ABHORRENT!

This author's biblical misunderstanding leads her to falsely conclude: "A clear understanding of the phenomenon of non-Jewish Zionism in its full historical perspective enables us to 'demythologize' Zionism and see it for what it originally was—a product of European racist and colonial philosophies. It was not even in its origins a distinctively Jewish movement, encountering opposition, on the one hand, from religious Jews....Non-Jewish Zionists held a specific racist outlook on the Jews which was deeply rooted in the 19th Century colonial racial myth. The Jews were glorified as a chosen race....With non-Jewish Zionism on the rise, a whole complex of prejudices against the Arabs was systematically fostered in the consciousness of the Western people....On the whole, the belief in the Jewish race and its racial distinctiveness had stronger protagonists among non-Jews than among Western Jews themselves....the ideological and political fathers of Nazism shared the premises with the Zionists. The concept of the 'chosen race' in Nazism differed from the concept of the 'chosen race' in Zionism only in the identity of this race; Aryan or Jewish."[40]

This perverted statement of Sharif's is quite inaccurate. The Bible says the Jew was chosen to bring the knowledge of God and Messiah to all peoples (Gen. 12:2-3),[41] while the racism of Hitler's Nazi party dictated that all non-Aryans were inferior and should be either enslaved or murdered. How can anyone compare the murderous deeds of Hitler to the Bible's promises to the world through God's chosen people? Regina Sharif has, no doubt, much hate and envy ingrained within her heart against the Jewish people and those who care for them!

***

[40]Ibid, pp. 120, 122-125.

[41]In the New Testament it is made clear that this promised blessing to *all* the families of the earth was, and is, to be fulfilled in Messiah Jesus Coming to redeem humanity.

SHARIF IS WRONG AGAIN—CHRISTIANS *DO*[42] CARE ABOUT JEWS BECAUSE THEY ARE PEOPLE, NOT BECAUSE THEY ARE FULFILLING PROPHECIES

Regina Sharif, while sympathetic to the Arabs, has correctly observed that true believers realized the Bible foretold the return of the Jewish people to Israel and that this event is concisely tied to the Second Coming of Jesus. However, she refers to these facts and the concept of the chosen people as "myths" and "historic falsifications." She also says that Christians were not concerned with Jewish emancipation but only the fulfillment of prophecies concerning the Jews and their future return to Israel. In her very words: "...what came to constitute the 'Jewish Question' in the 16th Century was not Jewish emancipation—the granting of citizens' rights—but the role assigned to the Jews in such new doctrinal questions as the fulfilment of Biblical prophecies, the Latter Times and the Second Coming of Christ the Messiah....Early Restorationists often expounded a love for God's Chosen People. But this was not out of concern for the Jews, but for their role in God's plan, as revealed by his promise to them."[43]

I believe most Arabs not only dislike and abhor the true Christian's love of Israel, but also are not able to bring themselves to accept the fact that true believers really do care for the freedom, rights and well-being of the Jews, simply because of Jesus' teaching. "This is my commandment, That ye love one another, as I have loved you. Greater love hath no man than this, that a man lay down his life for his friends" (John 15:12-13 KJV).

JEWISH SCHOLARS AND RABBIS ATTEST TO OUR LOVE IN THAT MANY CHRISTIANS HAVE PUT THEIR LIVES ON THE LINE TO SAVE JEWS

As you have read in this book, many Christians such as Corrie Ten Boom, risked their lives to save Jews in the Holocaust. Yad VaShem, the Holocaust museum in Israel, is filled with trees

---

[42]Sharif insists that in the sixteenth century Christians did not care for the rights of Jews. However, Rabbi Emden of the eighteenth century wrote that in *every generation* the true "Christian wise men" rise up and save us. Rabbi Emden differentiates between true and non-true believers. Author Pinchas Lapide says: "Rabbi Emden's remarks on Jew-baiters and anti-Jewish theologians have even today lost none of their relevance: 'These perverse scholars stir up great hatred against the children of Israel instead of inspiring the hearts of their people with love for the Jews, who are truly devoted to their God. Since their teacher [Jesus] bade them love their enemies, how much more should they not love us!' " Pinchas Lapide, *Israelis, Jews, and Jesus*, pp. 105-106.

[43]Regina Sharif, *Non-Jewish Zionism*, pp. 10, 19.

representing Christians who risked and lost their lives to save Jews. The Jewish writer, Sholem Asch,[44] writes: "...[concerning] *events associated with the Nazi period*....'Christianity also distinguished itself, in the particular of rescuing Jewish children, by the highest degree of self-sacrifice. It may be stated without exaggeration that almost the entire remnant of Israel which was found in the liberated countries—no matter how small its number—has the Christians to thank for its preservation. Christians who, by performing this action, placed their own lives in danger.'"[45]

Rabbi Emden of Hamburg uttered perhaps the most profound words ever spoken by a rabbi: " '...For if it had not been for the Christians, our remnant would surely have been destroyed, and Israel's hope would have been extinguished amidst the Gentiles, who hate us because of our faith....But God, our Lord, has caused the Christian wise men to arise, who protect us in every generation.' "[46]

ISAAC WAS CHOSEN, NOT ISHMAEL, AND JESUS IS THE GREATEST HEBREW PROPHET, DESPITE MOSLEM AND CATHOLIC OBJECTIONS

Some believe Arabs, and especially Moslem Arabs, are jealous of the fact that Isaac and not Ishmael (the Arab child of Abraham) was chosen to be the father of the people God would use to bring the Bible (God's revelation of redemption for man), the Messiah and salvation to the world. Their Koran, in fact, claims that Ishmael was the chosen one, in a direct denial of the Bible, which indicates Isaac. This also runs hand in hand with Sharif's insinuation that Protestants changed Jesus from "Mary's son" into "one of a long line of Hebrew prophets."[47]

The New Testament genealogy of Jesus has maintained this truth from the beginning, regardless of what Islam or Catholicism would like us to believe—Jesus is, in fact, the end of the line and the greatest of all Hebrew prophets, as foretold in Deuteronomy 18:15. The first sixteen verses of the New Testament read: "The book of the generation of

---

[44]Sholem Asch was born in Poland in 1880. He was one of the best known Jewish writers of his day. He wrote in Yiddish, the language used by the bulk of East European Jewry. In 1910, he settled in the United States, where he was catapulted into world prominence with his book, *Nazarene*, in 1939. His novel *Apostle* came out in 1943, and *Mary* in 1949. Asch died in England in 1957, with more than fifty novels, plays and short stories to his credit. For a more impressive and detailed story of his life, see Sholem Asch, *One Destiny*. New York: Putnam, 1945.

[45]Arthur W. Kac, *The Messiahship of Jesus*, p. 18. [ ] mine.

[46]Pinchas Lapide, *Israelis, Jews, and Jesus*, p. 103.

[47]Regina Sharif, *Non-Jewish Zionism*, p. 13.

Jesus Christ, the son of David, the son of Abraham. Abraham begat Isaac; and Isaac begat Jacob; and Jacob begat Judas and his brethren; And Judas begat Phares and Zara of Thamar; and Phares begat Esrom; and Esrom begat Aram; And Aram begat Aminadab; and Aminadab begat Naasson; and Naasson begat Salmon; And Salmon begat Booz of Rachab; and Booz begat Obed of Ruth; and Obed begat Jesse; And Jesse begat David the king; and David the king begat Solomon of her *that had been the wife* of Urias; And Solomon begat Roboam; and Roboam begat Abia; and Abia begat Asa; And Asa begat Josaphat; and Josaphat begat Joram; and Joram begat Ozias; And Ozias begat Joatham; and Joatham begat Achaz; and Achaz begat Ezekias; And Ezekias begat Manasses and Manasses begat Amon; and Amon begat Josias; And Josias begat Jechonias and his brethren, about the time they were carried away to Babylon: And after they were brought to Babylon, Jechonias begat Salathiel; and Salathiel begat Zorobabel; And Zorobabel begat Abiud; and Abiud begat Eliakim; and Eliakim begat Azor; And Azor begat Sadoc; and Sadoc begat Achim; and Achim begat Eliud; And Eliud begat Eleazar; and Eleazar begat Matthan; and Matthan begat Jacob; And Jacob begat Joseph the husband of Mary of whom was born Jesus, who is called Christ" (Matt. 1:1-16 KJV).

SHARIF CALLS OUR PRO-ISRAEL FAITH "PREJUDICE" AND WOULD HAVE US LEAVE IT, THUS THWARTING ISRAEL—DISGUSTING AND ARROGANT

Sharif then gives her definition of justice for the Palestinians—giving Israel to the Palestinians. This would be equivalent to giving America's thirteen colonies back to England. No one ever asked us to do this, did they? What's more, aside from the few territories we purchased, we conquered our land. Israel's land was given to the Jew by God (Gen. 17:8). The modern Israelis simply resettled it. When they were attacked, they rightfully repossessed their land by force, only after it became clear their enemies were unwilling to share and live in peace.

It is important to remember that Israel was never "Palestine" by national right. The Romans, when they exiled Israel, renamed the land after the Philistines to punish the Jews for the rebellion of Bar Kochba.

To get back to our point, Sharif feels that the cure for the Palestinian problem is to change, in essence, the religious heritage of the United States of America. She calls on the American evangelicals, in so many words, to stop supporting Israel, which is tantamount to asking them to become hypocrites. Her solution is, in her own words:

"It will also be obvious that current Western attempts to find a solution to the Palestine problem will remain futile as long as the West does not come to grips with its own inherent Zionist prejudices embedded in its past and present....It is highly unlikely that any proposed 'solution' to the problem of Palestine coming from the West will ever do justice to the Palestinian or Arab cause until the West faces up to the intrinsic nature of Zionism and frees itself from its deeply entrenched Zionist prejudices. Nothing less than a major re-orientation is required....Biblical fundamentalism, as an outgrowth of the Protestant tradition, further developed the myth of Israel's Restoration. What was posited was a supra-rational relationship between the land of Palestine and the Jewish people as the direct descendants of the ancient Biblical Hebrew tribes of Israel. It was Protestant Christian theology which established the unbroken continuity between the two, the land and the people....Viewing American support for Israel from the vantage point of the long history and tradition of non-Jewish Zionism, it is evident....that American attitudes towards the Middle East reflect not only a strong emotional pro-Israel bias, but that this bias is accompanied by an equally pervasive dislike and distrust of the Arabs....There exists a long historical tradition of anti-Arab prejudice going back to the early 19th Century, and a consistent disinclination on the part of Western scholars to acknowledge the contributions of Islamic civilization to the West."[48]

Oh, is there really? Israel has been abused and terrorized. U.S.-drilled and owned oil wells in Arab states were nationalized, petrol costs were raised and Israelis were (and continue to be) murdered. Can you blame us for our reservations?

CHRISTIAN ZIONISM HAS NOTHING TO DO WITH WESTERN DISLIKE OF THE ARAB RECORD OF TERRORISM—MOSLEM ACTS SPEAK FOR THEMSELVES

Sharif speaks for many a Moslem when she writes: "Today popular culture is used to portray the Arabs as the villains of the world and as the number one enemy of Western civilization and all its values. The growth of non-Jewish Zionism is inseparable from the mass inculcation of a whole complex of anti-Arab prejudices....if the West finally comes to grips with its own Zionist leanings. On the rudimentary level we have first to examine our own pro-Israeli attitudes and predispositions and to recognize them as the outcome of a centuries long process of socialization and spiritual innoculation. We

---

[48]Ibid, pp. 4, 7, 133, 138.

will then discover that as a result of non-Jewish Zionism a whole complex of prejudices[49] against the Arabs, their culture and their religion, have been systematically inculcated into our own consciousness and have thus directly or indirectly influenced our views on Palestine, the Palestine problem and the Palestinian people....We can no longer afford to look at Israel and its policies through the Zionist prism and the coloured spectacles of our own mythological history of fundamentalist theology."[50]

We maintain that our history and biblically based Zionism, including our fundamental faith in Jesus and the prophecies, are neither prejudice nor myth. It is our right, God's will and we are proud of it. I will tell Regina Sharif and any Arab face-to-face any day of the week, with love, "Isn't it about time to stop bashing the Christians and to start respecting the rights of Evangelical Zionists?" Yes!

***

[49]We assert that there are no Christian Zionist prejudices against the Arabs because of their culture. To the contrary. Movies like *Lawrence of Arabia* and other early twentieth century films portray Arabs in a positive light. Rather, we are becoming increasingly alarmed concerning the Arabs' terrorist attacks on the West and our *civilization*, and their anger due to our friendship with our ally, Israel. Maybe we should ask those 1000 people who were injured in the 1993 Arab bombing of the World Trade Center in New York, which took five American lives, if they felt the Arabs might be a "danger to civilization." They most certainly are, in our opinion, and our opinion is expected to be validated more and more as we enter the first half of the twenty-first century. The conservative Jewish columnist, Don Feder, wrote in 1993: "Islamic fundamentalism is rapidly replacing communism as the major threat to Western civilization." Hal Lindsey, "Countdown...", Apr. 1993, Vol. 4, No. 4. Hal Lindsey noted in this same newsletter: "...the most radical of the Islamic leaders seem to bask in the knowledge that they are finally being recognized as a real threat. 'The Americans keep saying Iran is a threat,' explains Ayatollah Ahmad Jannah, a powerful radical Islamic leader. 'We are glad to learn that we're a threat to our enemies.' Jannah not only predicts that Iran will draw America into another Persian Gulf War, he declares that Iran is activating agents around the globe for 'the Third World War—between Islam and the West.' " Ibid. In May of 1993, fourteen Arabs confessed to plotting the assassination of President Bush in Kuwait. I, myself, recently became a first-hand victim of Arab terrorism. As I was going to the money-changer in Jerusalem, a gang of Arabs stepped out from around a corner and proceeded to pelt my taxi with baseball-sized rocks, shattering the windshield. I nearly lost my life—all because I had a beard and looked Jewish. More recently, when Israel's Prime Minister, Yitzhak Rabin, was assassinated for giving such ridiculous land concessions to the Arabs, many Arabs themselves celebrated his death, honking horns and shooting guns in the air. Can we call this civilized? No! The word assassination comes from assassins, which means *hashshashin* (hemp-eaters). This was a band of Moslems in twelfth century Persia who killed their enemies while under the influence of hashish, which is made from the hemp plant.

[50]Regina Sharif, *Non-Jewish Zionism*, pp. 138-139.

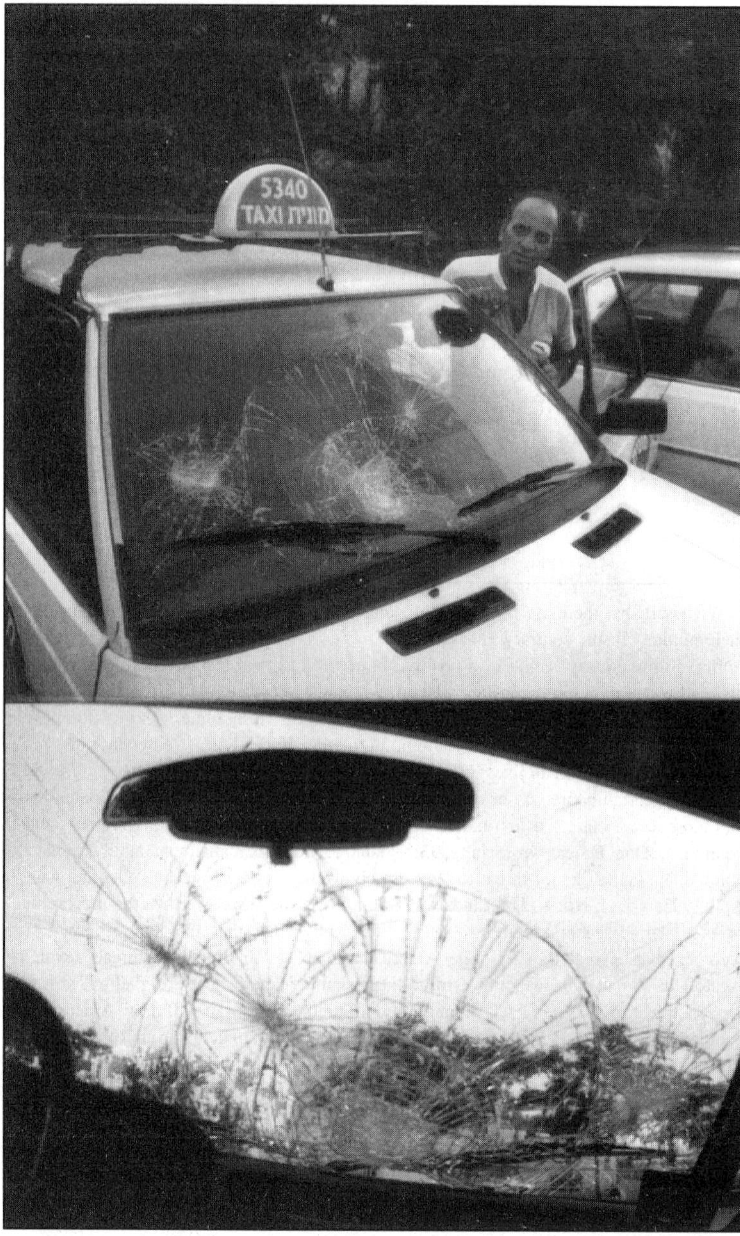

In 1989, while an Israeli cab driver took me through an Arab section in Jerusalem, we were attacked with stones. The reason for this, I was later told, was that my beard looked "too Jewish."

Children in one of the shelters at Kibbutz Gadot
during a barrage of Syrian shell-fire.

"People all over the world have come to realize that Hitler was right...the whole world...has...expelled them and despised them...and burnt them in Hitler's crematoria....Would that he had finished it!"[51] Anis Mansour, Egyptian writer, 1973

Mufti Haj Amin al-Husseini and Adolph Hitler in 1941.

Norma Archbold verifies the horrendous story of how the Mufti of Jerusalem, in cooperation with Hitler, succeeded in disallowing nearly 1000 Jews passage to Palestine, resulting in their murder by the Führer. She shares with us this little-known story: "During World War II, the Arab Moslem leader in Jerusalem was Mufti Haj Amin al-Husseini (*cousin of PLO Chairman, Yassar Arafat*). The Mufti supported the Nazis. He met with Hitler on November 21, 1941 as reported in his diary....In 1943 the Hungarian government planned to send Jewish children to the Holy Land to escape the Nazis. In a letter the Mufti demanded that Hungary reverse the plan. The 900 children were sent to extermination camps in Poland."[52]

***

[51]*Al-Akhbar*, Aug. 19, 1973.

[52]Norma Archbold, *The Mountains of Israel: The Bible & the West Bank*. Jerusalem: A Phoebe's Song Publication, © 1993, pp. 68-69, used by permission.

Hitler's book, *Mein Kampf*, in Arabic, issued to Arab military officers. These were recovered from the posts of Egyptian soldiers during the Sinai Campaign of 1956.

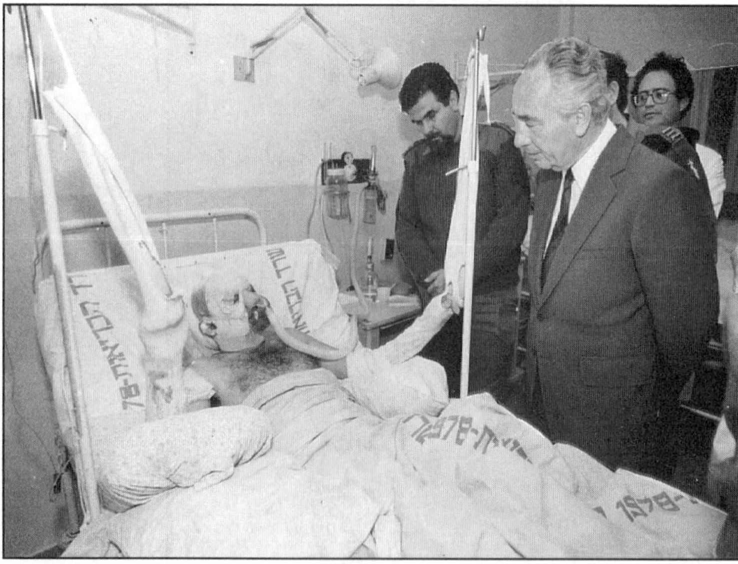

In March 1985, Israeli Prime Minister Shimon Peres visits a soldier wounded near the Good Fence, at the Lebanon-Israeli border.

An Israeli bus blown up by Arab terrorists.
This occurred several times between 1995 and 1996.

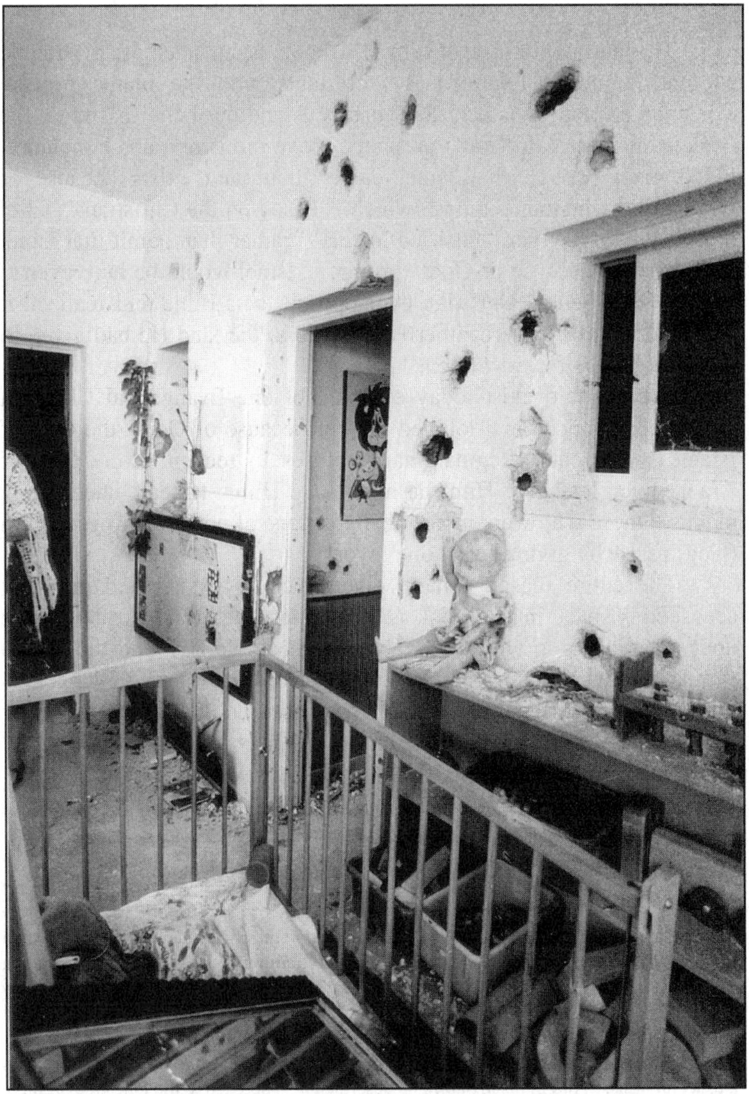

The children's dormitory of Kibbutz Misgav Am
after an Arab terrorist raid, March 1980.

SHARIF TRIES TO BLAME THE EXISTENCE OF ISRAEL ON EVANGELICAL CHRISTIANS AND THEIR POLITICAL LEADERS, INCLUDING PRESIDENT TRUMAN

The entire premise of Sharif's book is an attempt, a pathetic attempt, to credit Evangelical Protestants with the blame for the existence of modern Israel. She insults us and our belief based on the Bible, which foretold God's prophetic move in history, and concludes, in so many words, that Israel came about and exists because of Evangelical Christian support, which is based on the Christians' belief in biblical "myth" and "falsified history," rather than admit that Israel is really here because of God's promise. Israel would be here even if not one Evangelical Christian ever opened their Bible and realized it was God's purpose to regather His people to the land He had given to their forefathers forever! (Gen. 17:8)

Israel would exist today even if not one Evangelical Christian supported, financed and lobbied for her because of God—the God of Israel! Apparently Regina Sharif refuses to recognize the God of Israel, much less give Him the honor due Him. Instead, she bitterly mocks[53] those who were in political positions of power, who gave Him (God) praise by giving Israel due favor!

The entire reason I have given such a woman and her silly accusations space in this book is to attempt to give my readers some understanding as to why the Arabs of the Middle East and those who sympathize with them are so jealous and envious of true evangelical born-again supporters of Israel. This is based on the Bible's prophecy

---

[53]Sharif says of our beloved pro-Zionist Chief Executive Truman: "President Truman was the personification of American non-Jewish Zionism on the political level, as is universally agreed in Zionist histories. But there has always existed a controversy over the reasons for his Zionism, with one historian even portraying him as an indecisive opportunist oscillating under Zionist pressure and allowing the Jewish vote to dictate his Palestine policy....Without disputing the validity of any of these factors, we seek merely to point out the omission of perhaps the most important of all, namely Truman's own personal participation in the non-Jewish Zionist tradition. Shortly after succeeding President Roosevelt, Truman made the following press statement: 'The American view of Palestine is, we want to let as many of the Jews into Palestine as it is possible to let into that country. Then the matter will have to be worked out diplomatically with the British and the Arabs, so that if a state can be set up there they may be able to set it up on a peaceful basis.' And in his *Memoirs* he described his approach to the Palestine problem in the following way: 'My purpose was then and later to help bring about the redemption of the pledge of the Balfour Declaration and the rescue of at least some of the victims of Nazism....'...On the contrary, an American President forthrightly declared American policy on Palestine to be in line with the Zionist aims....Truman's Palestine policy was a presidential policy unilaterally carried out despite the opposition of various government advisers and the overwhelmingly negative view of the Department of State....Long before he had become President, Truman had shown a sympathetic

of a true chosen son, Isaac. His descendants will one day rule the world after the Second Coming of the Messiah. We can see that this is not far off, as we observe the present political climate in light of Bible prophecy.

ARAB JEALOUSY OVER ISRAEL WILL PRECIPITATE ARMAGEDDON

According to the Bible, this jealousy of the Arabs concerning the return of the Jews to Israel will lead to the greatest war history has ever known! This is the war of Gog and Magog, as predicted in the Old Testament book of Ezekiel, chapters 38-39, and the New Testament book of Revelation—as you will later see described in chapter 26, "We Win Armageddon—Our Final Battle." This war includes the Russians using Arabs in an attempt to destroy Israel, which they (Russia) feel is the reason for their retarded expansion[54] in the Middle East.

The Russians have in the past, and will in the future, arm the Arabs against Israel, and will then attack her directly, because the Arabs are not as capable as the Russians of using such sophisticated equipment. When Russia enters the war, nuclear weapons will be used (Zech. 14:12) and only the Second Coming of the Messiah Jesus will be able to stop this global holocaust. Jesus said: "And except those days should be shortened, there should no flesh be saved: but for the elect's sake those days shall be shortened" (Matt. 24:22 KJV).

ZECHARIAH SAYS ATOMIC WEAPONS WILL BE USED AGAINST ISRAEL

As Zechariah prophesied 2500 years ago: "And this shall be the plague wherewith the LORD will smite all the people that have fought against Jerusalem; Their flesh shall consume away while they stand upon their feet, and their eyes shall consume away in their holes, and their tongue shall consume away in their mouth" (14:12 KJV).

---

understanding of Zionism. His own Southern Baptist background and training stressed the theme of the Jews' Restoration to Zion. The members of the Southern Baptist convention were the most enthusiastic pro-Zionist congregations, championing both the religious and historical claims of the Jews to the land of Palestine. Most Baptists were theologically conservative or even fundamentalist and tended to regard the creation of the Jewish state as the evident fulfilment of Biblical prophecies....Truman's autobiography, full of Biblical quotations and allusions, also indicates his marked tendency to dwell upon the Judaeo-Christian tradition....Truman once confessed that he could never read the account of the giving of the Ten Commandments at Sinai without a tingle going down his spine." Regina Sharif, *Non-Jewish Zionism*, pp. 101-107.

[54]Though the Russians are presently claiming to be at peace, which is to be expected, we are confident that they will sadly return to their Cold War ideology of conquest within twenty to forty years, if not sooner.

We now know that a person can melt while on their feet from the intense heat radiated by atomic weapons. This was illustrated quite realistically in the movie, *The Day After*.

A SPEEDY END AND ARAB/RUSSIAN DEFEAT IS PROPHESIED IN THIS WAR

Zechariah predicted and Jesus prophesied a speedy Russian/Arab defeat in this future war! Zechariah 14:4 says: "And his feet shall stand in that day upon the mount of Olives, which *is* before Jerusalem on the east, and the mount of Olives shall cleave in the midst thereof toward the east and toward the west, *and there shall be* a very great valley; and half of the mountain shall remove toward the north, and half of it toward the south" (KJV).

We have hope and comfort for the future. However, all of the terrible things that are predicted would not have to occur if the Arabs and their sympathizers could work out their envy. Jesus is the only remedy for jealousy! Until people recognize the biblical (not Catholic or ecumenical) Jesus, there will be strife of heart. Jesus is the only one who can heal the human heart.

THE PEOPLE OF THE MIDDLE EAST KNOW NO PEACE BECAUSE THEY REFUSE TO HEED THE WORDS OF JESUS AND REJECT HIS COVENANT

There will be no hope for lessening the severity of Armageddon until people are ready to realize Jesus is truth and not myth. There will be wars and rumors of wars, and the ultimate war, Armageddon, because the communist and Middle Eastern nations will not, as predicted, heed the truths of the New Testament. They will plunge the world into a war of annihilation, which only Jesus will end. When He ends the slaughter at His return, then the entire world will know peace, because all will realize who He is.

The Old Testament speaks of the Egyptians, who are mostly Moslems today. "And it shall be for a sign and for a witness unto the LORD of hosts in the land of Egypt: for they shall cry unto the LORD because of the oppressors, and he shall send them a saviour, and a great one, and he shall deliver them" (Isa. 19:20 KJV).

When there is no longer any way to deny Jesus as the Messiah, there will be peace. Then Jesus will set up a new world order and establish the earth anew. It is either that or, if there really is no Jesus, nuclear annihilation with no flesh saved. Take your choice.

***

BELIEVING IN JESUS IS NOT FORSAKING ARAB CULTURE, AS MOSLEM LEADERS TEACH—RATHER THERE ARE ARABS WHO LOVE JESUS, ISRAEL AND THEIR ARAB HERITAGE!

We must add that becoming a believer in Jesus does not mean taking a stand against Arab culture, as some like to infer. Many Eastern Orthodox, Catholic and Moslem Arabs have invited Jesus into their hearts and still appreciate their Arab and national heritage! They also accept Israel as a nation, with love and trust that it is God's sign that Jesus will soon return to this planet to save it. This is attested to by the Arab Bible Baptist Church in Bethlehem today. Their pastor, Musa, once showed me the book he was using to teach the over three hundred-member congregation about prophecy. It was Larkin's *Dispensational Truth*. He also expressed his approval of Hal Lindsey's book, *The Late Great Planet Earth.*

You cannot become more pro-Israel than the authors of these two books, politically or biblically. Only Jesus can break down the four millenia-long animosity the Arabs have borne against the Jew and Israel. There has been strife, bombing of synagogues worldwide and terrorism against Israel. Jesus alone can remove this hatred. You must truly ask Him into your heart and be born-again, before love can triumph over hate and become reality.

ORIGINAL HEBREW TEXT WRITTEN 997 BC

אֱלֹהִים אַל־דֳּמִי־לָךְ אַל־תֶּחֱרַשׁ וְאַל־תִּשְׁקֹט אֵל: כִּי־הִנֵּה אוֹיְבֶיךָ יֶהֱמָיוּן וּמְשַׂנְאֶיךָ נָשְׂאוּ
רֹאשׁ: עַל־עַמְּךָ יַעֲרִימוּ סוֹד וְיִתְיָעֲצוּ עַל־צְפוּנֶיךָ: אָמְרוּ לְכוּ וְנַכְחִידֵם מִגּוֹי וְלֹא־יִזָּכֵר
שֵׁם־יִשְׂרָאֵל עוֹד: כִּי נוֹעֲצוּ לֵב יַחְדָּו עָלֶיךָ בְּרִית יִכְרֹתוּ: אָהֳלֵי אֱדוֹם וְיִשְׁמְעֵאלִים
מוֹאָב וְהַגְרִים: גְּבָל וְעַמּוֹן וַעֲמָלֵק פְּלֶשֶׁת עִם־יֹשְׁבֵי צוֹר: גַּם־אַשּׁוּר נִלְוָה עִמָּם הָיוּ
זְרוֹעַ לִבְנֵי־לוֹט סֶלָה: **תהלים פג:ב-ט**

OLD TESTAMENT SCRIPTURE TRANSLATION

"Keep not thou silence, O God: hold not thy peace, and be not still, O God. For, lo, thine enemies make a tumult: and they that hate thee have lifted up the head. They have taken crafty counsel against thy people, and consulted against thy hidden ones. They have said, Come, and let us cut them off from *being* a nation; that the name of Israel may be no more in remembrance. For they have consulted together with one consent: they are confederate against thee: The tabernacles of Edom, and the Ishmaelites; of Moab, and the Hagarenes; Gebal, and Ammon, and Amalek; the Philistines with the inhabitants of Tyre; Assur also is joined with them: they have holpen the children of Lot. Selah."

Psalms 83:1-8 KJV

ANCIENT RABBINICAL COMMENTARY

"What did they [the hosts of Gog] do? They stood on their feet and looked up toward the Holy One, blessed be He, and said: '*Come, let us cut them off from being a nation, that the name of Israel may be no more in remembrance* (Ps. 83:5)'....'Let us uproot Him who wrote, *Blessed be the Lord, the God of Israel* (Ps. 41:14)'....The Holy One, blessed be He, says to them: 'At first you [Arab nations] were not at peace with one another. And now you made peace with one another so as to come against Me....I, too, shall do likewise. I shall call the birds and the beasts who were not at peace with one another, and I shall cause them to be at peace with one another in order to go forth against you. And because you said, *That the name of Israel may be no more in remembrance* (Ps. 83:5), by your life, you will die and they [Israel] will bury you and will take a name [i.e., become famous] in the world.' "[55] **Midrash, Aggadat B'reshit, ed. Buber, pp. 5-7**

NEW TESTAMENT RECORDED 60 AD

"...neither are they all children because they are Abraham's descendants, but: 'THROUGH ISAAC YOUR DESCENDANTS WILL BE NAMED.' That is, it is not the children of the flesh who are children of God, but the children of the promise are regarded as descendants. For this is a word of promise: 'AT THIS TIME I WILL COME, AND SARAH SHALL HAVE A SON [Isaac].' And not only this, but there was Rebekah also, when she had conceived *twins* by one man, our father Isaac; for though *the twins* were not yet born, and had not done anything good or bad, in order that God's purpose according to *His* choice might stand, not because of works, but because of Him who calls, it was said to her, 'THE OLDER WILL SERVE THE YOUNGER.' Just as it is written, 'JACOB I LOVED, BUT ESAU I HATED[56] [Malachi 1:2-3]'....For the Scripture says to Pharaoh, 'FOR THIS VERY PURPOSE I RAISED YOU UP, TO DEMONSTRATE MY POWER IN YOU, AND THAT MY NAME MIGHT BE PROCLAIMED THROUGHOUT THE WHOLE EARTH'....*even* us, whom He also called,

---

[55]Raphael Patai, *The Messiah Texts*, pp. 149-150. Second and third [ ] mine.

[56]What God hated about Esau was the fact that he sold the precious God-given birthright given him by the Lord. This was a slap in the face to the giver. If you gave your entire inheritance, for which your parents worked all of their lives, to someone, in exchange for a meal of bean soup, you can imagine how your mother and father would feel.

not from among Jews only , but also from among Gentiles. As He says also in Hosea, 'I WILL CALL THOSE WHO WERE NOT MY PEOPLE, 'MY PEOPLE'....And you brethren, like Isaac, are children of promise. But as at that time he who was born according to the flesh [Ishmael, a principal father of the Arab peoples] persecuted him *who was born* according to the Spirit [Isaac, a principal father of the Jews], so it is now also."[57]

Romans 9:7-13, 17, 24-25; Galatians 4:28-29 NASB

MODERN RABBINIC COMMENT/REFUTATION

"Jews firmly believe that the Messiah will come. We believe that man will not self-destruct, that we will not disappear in a gigantic atomic blast. Man is basically good....However, it is not enough to believe in G-d. Faith alone is not adequate...."

***The Real Messiah*, by Aryeh Kaplan, *et al*, p. 50; 1976**

MODERN DOCUMENTED POLITICAL STATEMENTS MADE BY ARAB HEADS OF STATE

"...'Israel must be destroyed', 'We will swallow you up'; 'You invaders will be driven into the sea'...."[58] **President Nasser of Egypt**

"It's time to pull out this cankerous tumor [Israel] from the body of the Muslim world. Every problem in our religion can be traced to this single dilemma—the everlasting struggle between Ishmael and Isaac."[59]

President Rafsanjani of Iran, 1993

AUTHOR'S COMMENT—EVANGELICAL CHRISTIAN POSITION

Here, in the New Testament books of Galatians and Romans, Paul is making an analogy. He explains why the Arabs were always jealous of the Jews (Abraham, Isaac, Jacob and all their descendants). It was because Isaac was chosen over Ishmael and Jacob was chosen over Esau (Gen. 27:26-29). Ishmael and Esau have become principal fathers of the Arab peoples, thus we observed Arab hatred of the Jews from the beginning (Rom. 9:11), in the same way that true believers in Messiah have been subjected to rabbinical persecution. Those Jews and non-Jews who have believed in Messiah Jesus were persecuted by rabbinical Judaism. Today, the one who believes in the Jewish Messiah and invites Him into his heart becomes the chosen of God to receive all He has for us. The Arabs could have accepted the God of the Jews then, or now, and become chosen. Likewise, the Jews of Paul's era, and of today, can receive the Jewish Messiah and regain spiritually chosen status with us (they are already physically chosen). The reason we quoted these verses concerning the Middle East/Arab conflict with Israel is summed up in Paul's New Testament verses (Rom. 9:7-13; 17:24-25; Gal. 4:28-29). Just as the Arab (Ishmael) persecuted the Jew (Isaac) then, so it is today. The Arabs are still persecuting the Jews and will continue to do so until Jesus returns and they see and believe in Him as Messiah. This is predicted to occur at the end of the war. God mentions that His Grace will go to Egypt in Isaiah's Old Testament prophecy, after the Egyptians look to the Savior Jesus (Isa. 19:20).

Philip Moore

---

[57][ ] mine. Today, anyone can become a son of promise if he truly believes in Jesus, as Paul writes in Galatians: "And if ye *be* Christ's, then are ye Abraham's seed, and heirs according to the promise" (3:29 KJV). This includes Catholics, Arabs, pagans, anyone.

[58]Arthur W. Kac, *The Death and Resurrection of Israel.* Grand Rapids, MI: Baker Book House, © 1969, p. 253.

[59]*Perhaps Today*, May/June 1993, p. 7.

THOUGH THE ARABS WERE NOT PROMISED THE LAND OF ISRAEL, THEY WERE PROMISED THE OIL IN THE SURROUNDING LAND—WE SHOULD ALL BE CONTENT WITH OUR PROMISES

Many people today sympathize with the Arabs because they feel they have become outcasts in Israel. Genesis 17:8-9 of the Bible has given God's written promise of this land to Israel. Later on, Ezekiel 36-37 predicts God's planned return of the Jews to their land, yet most of the Arab nations feel that this promised land should be turned into a Palestinian Arab state.[60]

Many people sympathize with this Arab wish, thinking the Arabs should "have something." It would serve them well to know that the Arabs were given something! As a matter of fact, in the eyes of world materialism, much more than the Jews. Although Ishmael (Abraham's Arab child) was not promised the land as Isaac was, he was promised "the fat of the land." We ask, is it any coincidence that just a very short time ago, when the Arabs were on the verge of starvation, the gasoline engine was invented and oil became a necessity in the West? The Arabs were able to compound their wealth when they subsequently nationalized the oil wells and raised the prices. Thus, truly they have received the promise of the "fat" or "oil" of the land in the literal scientific sense of the twentieth century. In Hebrew, the word *shumon* means "fat," *shemin* means "oil," as in olive oil (see Gen. 27:39-40 KJV).[61]

GOD HAS KEPT HIS PROMISE TO THE ARABS BUT THE ARABS DO NOT WANT TO LET GOD KEEP HIS PROMISE TO GIVE THE LAND TO THE JEWS!

In Genesis 17:20, the sons of Ishmael were promised: "...I have blessed him, and will make him fruitful, and will multiply him exceedingly; twelve princes [nations] shall he beget, and I will make him a great nation" (KJV; [ ] mine).

The word nations here means a great Gentile people. Today, they possess lands so much more vast than Israel, it is

---

[60]The Bible predicts that in the general time of the Antichrist, a temporary peace will be made with Israel before the final liberation attempt. Thus, if you read this book in the early or near the mid-2000's, and peace between the sons of Isaac and Ishmael is beginning, expect action before the end of the century.

[61]This has a historical and prophetic significance. In ancient times, owning large herds and many fruit or olive trees was considered a sign of wealth. Animal fat and olive oil were burned in lamps as fuel. This parallels the Arabs' present prosperity due to oil, which is also burned for fuel.

incomprehensible. Just take out your map and you will see Israel, a tiny strip among the Arab countries!

The few Arabs who now live in Israel, called Palestinians,[62] have only wandered over this land for a few centuries and are from all of the surrounding Moslem nations. The majority came after Israel became a state where "good work" could be found in a productive Western-style capitalistic economy. The Arabs have full rights in Israel. There is no segregation as there was in the United States between blacks and whites a few decades ago. Why then are the Arabs so disturbed about living with a few Jews in a state called Israel, and why are all the mighty neighboring Arab countries, with their multi-billion dollar oil industries, so concerned about this? Remember, five Arab nations attacked Israel in 1948! If you really want to be let in on a biblical secret, it is a spiritual jealousy so deep only the Messiah Jesus can heal them.

GOD SAVED THE ARAB TWICE—ONCE WITH WATER AND ONCE WITH OIL—NEVERTHELESS HE IS STILL THE WILD MAN THE BIBLE PREDICTED

Genesis 21:8-14 reveals the origin of this jealousy in the account of Isaac and Ishmael's childhood relationship. Hagar and Ishmael were expelled to prevent Isaac's death (Gen. 21:8-14). They found themselves in a waterless desert (Gen. 21:17-18). Hagar prayed that she would not see the death of her child (Gen. 21:16) and God answered her, telling her she would not (Gen. 21:17-18). Her eyes were opened and water sprang from the ground just in time to save

---

[62]It is important to realize that Israel was never called Palestine by national right. The Romans gave the land this name out of contempt for the Jews two thousand years ago. This was admitted in early 1996 by the *Jerusalem Post*. An Israeli reporter, while exposing Arafat's false claim that "Jesus was a Palestinian," as Arafat proclaimed Bethlehem "liberated," noted that: "It should not be too painfully difficult for the Church to remind its Arab flocks that Jesus was a Jew who lived in Judea, as the New Testament testifies. Nor should its officials be diffident about mentioning that the name Palestine, which is never mentioned in the New Testament, is a distortion of 'Palestina,' a derisive appellation coined by the Romans to offend the Jews (including those who followed Jesus)." "Israeli Media Reminds Arafat: 'Jesus Belongs to Us,' " *Maoz "The Lord is My Strength,"* Feb. 1996, p. 1. Dallas, TX. *Maoz*'s source was the *Jerusalem Post*, Dec. 25, 1995. In another article entitled, "Mocking Jesus and the Jews," by Andrea Levin, the Israeli writer added: "No disclaimer, wry or otherwise, noted that Jesus was a Jew born in Judea, or that he died more than a hundred years before Rome imposed the name Syria-Palestina on the area in the aftermath of crushing a Jewish rebellion led by Bar Kochba. The name change was meant to add mockery to the Jews' defeat by recalling historic Jewish battles with the Philistines. All of these events preceded by many centuries the Arab invasion and conquest." Ibid, p. 2. *Maoz*'s source was the *Jerusalem Post*, Jan. 5, 1996.

Ishmael (Gen. 21:19). His descendants later made the surrounding lands very dangerous, as the Bible foretold: "And the angel of the LORD said unto her, Behold, thou *art* with child, and shalt bear a son, and shalt call his name Ishmael; because the LORD hath heard thy affliction. And he will be a wild man; his hand *will be* against every man, and every man's hand against him; and he shall dwell in the presence of all his brethren" (Gen. 16:11-12 KJV).

Today, on a larger scale, we see a replay of the same biblical story. The Arabs were on the edge of death and starvation and then oil sprang from the ground and not only saved them, but procured them billions of petrol dollars.

TODAY'S ARABS ARE AS DANGEROUS TO ISRAEL AS ISHMAEL WAS TO ISAAC!

These modern day descendants of Ishmael also make Israel dangerous for their half-brother, of whom they are jealous (they want Jerusalem). As you can observe in modern history, five Arab nations warred against Israel in only forty years. Saddam Hussein was on the verge of obtaining nuclear capability in 1991, before the U.S. removed this threat to the world. Hussein was also set on developing chemical and biological weapons, which he would have used against Israel had an opportunity presented itself.

THE ARAB'S MONETARY POWER THROUGH OIL

"The Achilles heel of the industrial nations is their need for oil. Entire economies stand or fall with the availability of petroleum. It influences every part of life in a modern industrial nation. From factories to transportation to farming to making synthetic fabrics to generating electricity, oil is the life-blood of the developed world.

The Organization of Petroleum Exporting Countries—OPEC—has had the potential to influence the world since the time it was formed, in 1960.

But it wasn't until 1973 that the Arab oil barons showed the world how easily they could cut off the supply of petroleum. When they flexed that muscle, the world panicked.

Then OPEC brought western Europe, the U.S. and Japan to their knees by increasing the price of crude oil fourfold. This move staggered the economies of the industrial nations. It helped cause a very serious recession-inflation syndrome in the U.S., a condition which still exists.

The 1970's were marked by one economic spasm after another ripping through the western nations—mostly due to oil price hikes.

As the Arabs see it, it's only a matter of time before Israel's one true ally, the U.S., will become so dependent on Middle East oil that we will have to either drop our support of Israel or be destroyed economically.

This tactic has already worked on other nations, especially in western Europe. No nation there will show support for Israel for fear of losing a favored bargaining position for Arab oil....Members of OPEC have already bought major shares of some of the largest companies in Europe. They also own banks, farmland, real estate and businesses in the U.S. as well.

The fact is that as more and more money goes to these foreign countries, and as the western nations' balance of payments become more lopsided, then the Arabs will become even more powerful in determining the foreign policies of the world's major powers....they now have two mighty tools—oil and money—to bring their grievances to the world's attention. And what grieves the Arabs? Israel, and particularly Jerusalem."[63]

STATEMENTS AGAINST ISRAEL, BY ARAB LEADERS AND HEADS OF STATE, INDICATE A PROJECTED HOLOCAUST

"The entire Jewish population in Palestine must be destroyed or be driven into the sea. Allah has bestowed on us the rare privilege of finishing what Hitler only began. Let the *Ji'had* begin. Murder the Jews. Murder them all!"[64]

Haj Amin Al-Husseini, Mufti of Jerusalem, 1948

"Kill the Jews wherever you find them. Kill them with your arms, with your hands, with your nails and teeth."[65] King Hussein,during the Six Day War, 1967

"Our forces continue to pressure the enemy and will continue to strike at him until we recover the occupied territory, and we will then continue until all the land is liberated."[66] President Hafez Assad of Syria, 1984

"The battle with Israel must be such that, after it, Israel will cease to exist."[67]

President Muammar Qaddafi of Libya

"We shall never call for nor accept peace. We shall only accept war. We have resolved to drench this land with your blood, to oust you aggressors, to throw you into the sea."[68] Hafiz Assad, Syrian Defence Minister, May 24, 1966

***

---

[63]Hal Lindsey, *The 1980's: Countdown to Armageddon*, pp. 54-56.

[64]Michael L. Brown, *Our Hands are Stained with Blood: The Tragic Story of the "Church" and the Jewish People*, p. 54.

[65]Ibid.

[66]National PAC.

[67]Ibid.

[68]Martin Gilbert, *The Arab-Israeli Conflict, Its History in Maps*, p. 63.

"The existence of Israel is an error which must be rectified. This is our opportunity to wipe out the ignominy which has been with us since 1948. Our goal is clear—to wipe Israel off the map."[69]
President Aref of Iraq, May 31, 1967

"We shall never stop until all Palestine is ours and Jerusalem is our capital!"[70]
Yassar Arafat, July 1994, *after* a treasonous Prime Minister Rabin handed Arafat a good chunk of Israel's God-given land[71]

"The former leaders of Israel met together, and they planned how they would control the world. And they added to those plans the color of religion, in order to gather support from all Jews from all over the world. In the Protocols of the Elders

---

[69]Ibid, p. 67.

[70]"Voice of Hope," Global Broadcasting Network, Issue No. 1, July 1994, p. 3. George Otis is Chairman/CEO. Available through GBN, POB 100, Simi Valley, CA, USA 93065. On July 25, a few days after this statement, a huge bomb exploded outside the Israeli Embassy in Britain. Need we ask "Do you, the Arabs, really want peace?" Rather, they want to disassemble Israel by any means possible: bombs, terror, false treaties, land exchanges "for peace," piece by piece.

[71]Religious Jews feel that key Scriptures indicate Rabin's assassination was foreseen in the Bible. In Genesis 15:17-18 we find God's covenant of the land of Israel to Abraham; it reads: "And it came about when the sun had set, that it was very dark, and behold, *there appeared* a smoking oven and a flaming torch which passed between these pieces. On that day the LORD made a covenant with Abram, saying, 'To your descendants I have given this land, From the river of Egypt as far as the great river, the river Euphrates....' " (NASB). The word "fire" in Hebrew is *esh* (אֵשׁ). *Lapide* means "fire torch" (לַפִּיד). *Avar* (עָבַר) means "passed," and *bean* (בֵּין) means "between." If you take the last letter of *avar* (ר), which is "r," and combine it with the word *bean*, you have the name Rabin (רבין), who was, in fact, killed by gun*fire* passing between his body, for attempting to give away large amounts of land God gave to Abraham and his people (עָבַר בֵּין). Once we combine the last letter "r" of עָבַר to spell Rabin with the next word, the remaining two letters spell "fire" (*esh*), so in two words where the last letter of one is joined to the first of the next word, you form two new words, which read, literally, "fire rabin." Genesis 15:9-10 mentioned animals that were sacrificed and set apart, then the fire passed between the pieces, sealing the covenant between God and Abraham, the father of the Jewish people. Some Orthodox Jews feel Rabin was sacrificed so that the covenant between the land and the people God made would not be broken. On a closer examination of this verse, we observed additional similarities. The Bible mentions that the fire passed between the sacrifices after the sun went down. It was also after the sun went down that Rabin was fired upon. What is even more interesting is that if you read this line of Genesis 15:17, אֵשׁ אֲשֶׁר עָבַר בֵּין, with the first "b" (ב) removed as אֵשׁ אֵשׁ רַע רַבִּין, it translates *esh esh ra rabin*, which means "fire, fire, bad rabin." The numerical equivalent of "b" in Hebrew is two; this was Rabin's second time in office. Prime Minister Rabin was hit with gun*fire twice* when he was assassinated, and was considered to be *bad* by his assassin and many religious Jews, who felt he was violating the biblical Scriptures by giving away important areas of the land of Israel in the name of peace. When Isaac Rabin's initials (Ude-e or i and Resh-r), the first and last letters are removed from the assassin's name, Egal Amir, reads Gal Ami, "Redeemer of My People," i.e., National Hero in Hebrew. In the Bible, forty represents judgment. The Israelites were forty years in the desert. For example, Noah was in the ark for forty days and forty nights while the world was underwater. Likewise, Rabin was buried on the fortieth day after he signed the Oslo Agreement in Washington DC, which handed key Israeli cities in the West Bank over to the Arabs, which violates God's covenant with Abraham. God's consequences???

of Zion, they claim that they are the masters of the world and the selected people of God, and they tried to implant those ideas and concepts into the minds of the Jews, as if it had been quoted directly by the Torah and the Talmud....we are calling on the world to helpus defeat the devil...It is clear from the Protocols of the Elders of Zion that the Jews want to conquer the world."[72] Dr. Ahmad Bahar, political spokesman for Hamas, 1995

THE EVANGELICAL COMMENT

"Since 1948, five brutal wars have been fought over the control of Jerusalem, over control of the Golan Heights and over the West Bank and now with one swing of the pen, what was purchased in a river of blood, has been given away in what President Clinton has called, 'a great gamble for peace.' "[73]

Reverend John Hagee, world renowned Zionist-Christian evangelist, 1993

One day soon, perhaps before twenty to thirty years pass, a conservative government will be elected in Israel, which will put a stop to the socialist/labor party giving away God's land to an avowed mortal and political enemy. At that time, or just prior to it, the Arabs will attempt to destroy Israel. The Antichrist will use this occasion to force a peace. Later, when his peace treaty folds, the Arabs will try again with Russia. This will initiate WW III. Philip Moore, 1996

The destructive attitude and threats of the Arab states seem more realistic when we take into account their arsenal of weapons.

ARAB ARSENALS OF THE 90'S

Recently, Arab League headquarters was moved back to Cairo, Egypt, and the PLO restored relations with Egyptian President Hosni Mubarak. An assassination attempt on Mubarak was foiled in June of 1995. If a future assassination[74] attempt were to succeed, it is almost

---

[72]"The Specter of the Holocaust," *Israel My Glory*, May 1995, p. 4.

[73]John Hagee, *Israel and the PLO Peace Pact: Hope or Hoax, Evidence of the Last Generation on Earth.* This video is available through John Hagee, POB 1400, San Antonio, TX, USA 78295-1400.

[74]As far as we know, we are the first to point out "fire fire bad Rabin" (in relation to Rabin's recent assassination), as an apparent encoded Hebrew text prophecy. We were absolutely amazed to discover that Hebrew text encoding has become an established field of study. In Hal Lindsey's February 1996 *Countdown...* newsletter, it was noted: "...a serious mathematical study of the Book of Genesis was conducted seven years ago by mathematicians at Hebrew University in Israel. The scientists discovered a mathematical code embedded in the Hebrew text of the Torah, the first five books of Moses. Of the study, the Bible Review concluded; *'The capacity to embed so many, meaningfully related, randomly selected word pairs in a body of text with a coherent surface meaning is so stupendously beyond the intellectual capacity of any human being or group of people, however brilliant and equally beyond the capacity of any conceivable computing device. Furthermore, that the word pairs were randomly selected strongly suggests that all possible word pairs are so embedded,'* (Bible Review, October, 1995). The study, first published by the prestigious Royal Statistical Society, was so staggering, that its editor, Robert Kass, prefaced the article with the following disclaimer. *'Our referees*

certain that a radical leader would replace him. Hal Lindsey, in his latest book, *The Final Battle*, consults Joseph de Courcy, one of the world's most respected intelligence analysts. Hal reminds us: " '...Egypt's stock of main battle tanks has gone up from 1,600 in 1979 to over 3,300 today....The dramatic increase in anti-tank guided weapons (from 1,000 in 1979 to 2,340 today) is particularly worrying for Israel as Israel's is the only armored force large enough to justify such an inventory of anti-tank weapons'....Since the Camp David peace agreement, American taxpayers have transferred about $30 billion to Egypt. About $17 billion of that aid was in direct military assistance....As of 1994, the total strength of the Syrian Armed forces was 808,000, including 408,000 on active duty. It has 4,500 main battle tanks and 591 combat aircraft, according to de Courcy....the desert kingdom [Saudi Arabia] has transformed its army, air force and navy, spending $250 billion in the last ten years alone....The Saudi air force has been reoriented, de Courcy says, from a predominately defensive force into a formidable offensive threat with the coming of the Tornado and F-15 strike aircraft. It now has a force of some 292 combat aircraft. The Saudis also can deploy 770 main battle tanks....The country [Iran] has 1,245 main battle tanks and 295 combat aircraft. Iran, however, is in the midst of a major rearmament program that will include a $15 billion deal for new MiGs and T-72 tanks from Russia....the combined troop strength of Syria, Lebanon, Egypt, Saudi Arabia, Jordan, Yemen, Libya, Iraq and Iran comes to *more than 5 million*.

---

were baffled: their prior beliefs made them think the Book of Genesis could not possibly contain meaningful references to ***modern day*** *individuals, yet when the authors carried out additional analyses and checks the effect persisted. The paper is thus offered to the Statistical Science readers as a challenging puzzle'*....The Bible Review article concluded: *'Mathematical statisticians have discovered words encoded into the Hebrew text of the Book of Genesis that could not have been accidental; nor placed there by human hand. After publication, the authors continued their work and found that same pairs of words were predictive—they could not possibly have been known to the supposedly human authors because they occurred long after the Bible was composed.'* In other words, no human being could have written the Book of Genesis. No conceivable computer could have embedded these mathematical codes. The codes themselves are predictive. The authors of the study were given the names of 34 prominent rabbis who lived between the 9th and 19th centuries AD. Each of the names, and the dates of death *were mathematically embedded in the original Textus Receptus Hebrew version of the Torah!* Each lived more than a thousand years after Christ! The authors examined another 32 prominent rabbis who lived during this same period. Each of them were also listed, including the dates of the deaths. Statistically speaking, the odds against these references occurring by chance were calculated as being 1 in 50 *quadrillion*....1 chance in 50,000,000,000,000,000." Hal Lindsey, *Countdown...*, Vol. 7, No. 1, Feb. 1996, pp. 6, 13, used by permission. Bold mine.

These armies could field *19,269 main battle tanks*, including T-72s, M1A1 Abrams and Britain's Chieftains. That is more than the United States can mobilize!

They could scramble *3,325 first-rate combat aircraft*, including F-16s, MIG 29s, MIG 31s and Mirage F-1s....If we add Turkey to the total, the troop level increases to *6.4 million men*, the tank total to more than *24,000* and the combat aircraft to *3,880*. When we factor Russia into the equation, we see that this coalition can march *10 million men* toward Jerusalem.

You don't hear much about some of the most awesome parts of the Russian arsenal anymore. But it hasn't been destroyed. It hasn't fallen off the face of the Earth. These weapons are still around, but where?....In 1970, a World Health Organization report said that if anthrax were to be sprayed over a city of 5 million in a developed country, it would kill 100,000 and incapacitate 150,000 more. The same report said that if botulism were introduced into the water supply of an average town of 50,000, nearly 30,000 would die....Israeli intelligence predicts that Iran will be able to manufacture its own nuclear weapons by the year 2002."[75]

ISRAELI INTELLIGENCE ON ARAB A-BOMB POTENTIAL

In Hal Lindsey's July 1992 issue of his Christian Intelligence Journal, *Countdown...*, he noted: "In a meeting last year presided over by Rafsanjani, the Iranian leader told Arab political and religious leaders that Islam has replaced Marxism as the No. 1 ideology and power in the world to overthrow the Judeo-Christian world order.

'Our plan is to overthrow all Western influence in the Middle East and then overthrow the Judeo-Christian world order,' he said.

Because of this radical agenda, my Israeli military source believes the Islamic threat is the most important security issue for Israel and the West.

'Stopping the Iranian-Syrian axis and their lead over the Islamic world is the most important issue of this decade,' he said. 'It is even more important than it was in 1939 to stop Adolph Hitler. And remember I'm a Jew saying this'....In the spring of 1991, a top Iranian official met with nuclear scientists of the former Soviet republics to negotiate for the sale of nuclear weapons. That summer, an Iranian intelligence agent educated at the University of California, Berkeley, went to Kazakhstan, now the fifth leading nuclear power in the world. In October 1991, the agreement for three bombs was signed for $150 million.

---

[75]Hal Lindsey, *The Final Battle*, pp. 180-184, 188-189. [ ] mine.

The same Iranian agent then went to Russia and hired 250 nuclear scientists for $5,000 a month plus bonuses. They are all currently in Iran developing a nuclear stockpile for the world's leading terrorist, renegade nation. Iran has also reportedly hired 21 specialists in multi-warhead weapons.

In November, Iran's Operation Grand Design went into full-scale military maneuvers that included an amphibious invasion in chemical environment. This tactic is clearly designed for the eventual overthrow of the House of Saud. By taking out Saudi Arabia, the Iran-Syria alliance would remove a vital Western military base, control the Islamic holy places and deprive the West of its supply of oil. According to intelligence sources, the plan then calls for an all-out airborne chemical and nuclear assault on the state of Israel."[76]

WILL THE ARABS UTILIZE THEIR ARSENALS?

The Arabs are clearly predicted to launch an attack on Israel in unison with Russia in the end days. Daniel, a prophet of the Old Testament, wrote centuries ago of this final conflict: "And at the time of the end shall the king of the south push at him: and the king of the north shall come against him like a whirlwind, with chariots, and with horsemen, and with many ships; and he shall enter into the countries, and shall overflow and pass over. He shall enter also into the glorious land, and many *countries* shall be overthrown: but these shall escape out of his hand, *even* Edom, and Moab, and the chief of the children of Ammon" (Dan. 11:40-41 KJV).

Daniel clearly shows that the king of the south (Egypt) shall push at him (Russia). This of course, causes Russia to move in, giving her an excuse to conquer the Middle East in a pretense of "sympathy" for the "Palestinian cause" of liberty. As soon as Russia enters the war before her (Russia's) destruction by the Messiah (Jesus) for attempting to destroy His people (Israel), she will, while in combat, betray the Arabs by attacking them, hoping to gain control of the oil fields of the Middle East. This is indicated by Daniel's words: "He [king of the north, i.e. Russia] shall stretch forth his hand also upon the countries [Arab]: and the land of **Egypt** shall not escape. But he shall have power over the treasures of gold and of silver, and over all the precious things [oil] of Egypt: and the Libyans and the Ethiopians *shall be* at his steps" (Dan. 11:42-43 KJV).[77]

***

[76]Hal Lindsey, "The Hook in the Jaw of Magog," *Countdown...*, Vol. 3, No. 7, July 1992, p. 12, used by permission. Available through 1-800-Titus-35.

[77][ ] and bold mine.

This sudden unsuspected attack of the Egyptian Arabs by Russia during their almost simultaneous attack on Israel, will also include several other Arab nations. It is clear that Russia wants "all"—not only the future riches of Israel (see our chapter 26, "We Win Armageddon—Our Final Battle"), but the oil of Egypt and the rest of the Arab world as well.

A couple of the other (yet-to-be conquered) Arab countries are mentioned in Ezekiel, chapter 30: "The word of the LORD came again unto me, saying, Son of man, prophesy and say, Thus saith the Lord GOD; Howl ye, Woe worth the day! For the day *is* near, even the day of the LORD *is* near, a cloudy day; it shall be the time of the heathen. And the sword shall come upon Egypt, and great pain shall be in Ethiopia, when the slain shall fall in Egypt, and they shall take away her multitude, and her foundations shall be broken down. Ethiopia, and Libya, and Lydia, and all the mingled people, and Chub, and the men of the land that is in league, shall fall with them by the sword. Thus saith the LORD; They also that uphold Egypt shall fall; and the pride of her power shall come down: from the tower of Syene shall they fall in it by the sword, saith the Lord GOD. And they shall be desolate in the midst of the countries *that are* desolate, and her cities shall be in the midst of the cities *that are* wasted. And they shall know that I *am* the LORD, when I have set a fire in Egypt, and *when* all her helpers shall be destroyed. In that day shall messengers go forth from me in ships to make the careless Ethiopians afraid, and great pain shall come upon them, as in the day of Egypt: for, lo, it cometh" (Ezek. 30:1-9 KJV).[78]

It very well may be between twenty and forty years before we see the Arabs lead their final attack on Israel. In other words, all of the present Arab heads of state will have died. We have no reason to imagine that their successors will be any more rational than their predecessors. With the A-bomb firmly at their disposal, their over-confidence of victory over Israel will probably be too much for their egos to resist, won't it? The Bible has told (in prophecies) and time will tell (in actions)!

GOD LOVES THE ARABS TOO, THOUGH THEY REJECTED HIM AND HIS PEOPLE, WHO GAVE US OUR SAVIOR—THUS, IN THE END, SOME WILL REALIZE REDEMPTION

At the end, when all seems lost, Jesus returns to save Israel from the invading Russian and Arab armies. Once the Egyptians witness

---

[78]The "day of the Lord" phrase in this passage from Ezekiel indicates that verses 1-9 of Ezekiel 30 are prophetic, applying to the time of the Messiah's Second Coming. Verses 10 and on are historical and past.

what the Russians have done to them, they will be utterly hopeless. As in ancient times, the Bible said that during the first Passover (of the Exodus from Egypt): "...a mixed multitude went up also with them; and flocks, and herds, *even* very much cattle" (Exo. 12:38 KJV).

Some of the Egyptians accepted the God of Israel, placed the blood of a Passover lamb on their door, and left Egypt for Israel with the Israelites. So it will be when Jesus returns. Some of the Egyptians will call on the Jewish Messiah and Savior Jesus. This is clearly indicated by the words of the prophet Isaiah. Isaiah predicts of this future spectacular event: "And it shall be for a sign and for a witness unto the LORD of hosts in the land of Egypt: for they shall cry unto the LORD because of the oppressors, and he shall send them a saviour, and a great one, and he shall deliver them. And the LORD shall be known to Egypt, and the Egyptians shall know the LORD in that day...." (Isa. 19:20-21 KJV). Where do the Chinese fit in? This is the subject of our next chapter.

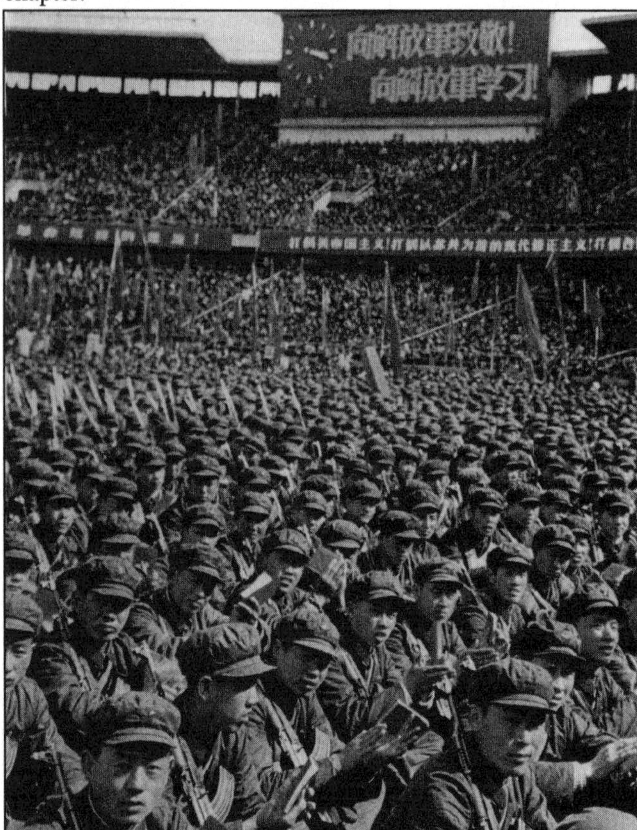

Chinese soldiers are armed and ready.

"...the great river, the Euphrates; and its water was dried up, that the way might be prepared for the kings from the east....for the war of the great day of God, the Almighty....they gathered them together to the place which in Hebrew is called Har Magedon....so that they might kill a third of mankind. And the number of the armies of the horsemen was two hundred million; I heard the number of them. And this is how I saw in the vision the horses and those who sat on them: *the riders* had breastplates *the color* of fire and hyacinth and of brimstone; and the heads of the horses are like the heads of lions; and out of their mouths proceed fire and smoke and brimstone. A third of mankind was killed by these three plagues, by the fire and the smoke and the brimstone, which proceeded....For the power of the horses is in their mouths and in their tails; for their tails are like serpents and have heads; and with them they do harm [could these be modern-day missiles and guns?]."[1]

John the apostle,
predicted in Revelation 16:12, 14, 16; 9:15-18, 19 NASB, AD 96

"Political power comes out of the barrel of a gun. The gun must never slip from the grasp of the Chinese communist party."[2] "Israel...[is] 'the Formosa [free China] of the Mediterranean' which should be swept into the sea."[3]

Mao Tse-tung, Communist China's first Premier, 1949

"China will always firmly support...the PLO as the sole legitimate representative of the Palestinian people and firmly support the revolutionary leadership of **Brother** Arafat."[4]

Premier Zhao Ziyang of China, 1984

"As China marches southwestward, China is grabbing all the deep water ports in the China Sea and expanding its exploration for oil. We believe that the 'Mid-East' is a prime target and oil is the magnet that is drawing China Southwestward. The sleeping giant is awakening and the Far/Mid-East will become more dangerous in the coming years!"[5]

"Taipan," 1995

21

THE CHINA CHAPTER

We have already examined the role of Russia and the Arab spheres of power predicted in Armageddon. The apostle John and prophet Isaiah also identify an Eastern power bloc, which will mortify the world. These "kings of the East" are the Orientals, chiefly

---

[1][ ] mine.

[2]Hal Lindsey, *The 1980's: Countdown to Armageddon*, p. 87.

[3]Karl Marx, *A World Without Jews*, p. viii. [ ] mine. In case you don't know, Formosa is the last vestige of freedom left in China. It is a small unconquered island located off the coast of China and is still a democracy as of 1996. Formosa is known to the world as Taiwan. Is there any hint at why China continues to openly and secretly train PLO terrorists?

[4]Michael Parks, "Arafat, on China Visit, Promised Support," *Los Angeles Times*, May 8, 1984, p. 17. Bold mine.

[5]"International Intelligence Briefing," Feb. 1995. Palos Verdes, CA: Hal Lindsey Ministries, p. 6. Available through HLM, 1-800-TITUS-35.

designated today as China. The word "east" in the original biblical language (Rev. 16) means "the rising of the sun," thus the unmistakable designation of the Orient, which includes China!

AMERICA GIVES BIRTH TO COMMUNIST CHINA BY WITHDRAWING LOGISTIC SUPPORT—FIFTY-FIVE MILLION CHINESE MURDERS FOLLOW

Communist China was born in October 1949, when the United States withdrew its logistic support under the ridiculous order of U. S. General George C. Marshall. This order was given because China's president, Chiang Kai-shek, refused to allow Communists Chou En-lai and Mao Tse-tung into his government. Senator and former U.S. presidential candidate, Barry Goldwater, documented this in his book, *With No Apologies.* " 'We were told that Chou En-Lai and Mao Tse-tung were amiable, benevolent reformers determined to free the Chinese people from the oppressive, corrupt government of Chiang Kai-shek. General George Marshall ordered Chiang to admit Chou and Mao into a coalition government. When Chiang refused, we withdrew American logistic support. Chiang was forced to flee to Formosa, and Mainland China came under communist rule.' "[6]

Once this occurred, Communist Premier Mao Tse-tung and his friend, Chou En-lai, murdered fifty-five million Chinese for their independent beliefs; in other words, because they did not accept communism. General MacArthur wanted to free the Chinese people from this tyranny and had mapped out a military rescue operation which would have accomplished this. His plan would have also ended China's ability to wage war into our era. At that time, we were the only ones who possessed the atomic bomb, thus, Russia could not have interfered. However, he was prevented from executing this by President Truman, and as the Bible foretold, China's part in the mold of the end time scenario was cast.

THE ONCE BENEVOLENT CHINESE PEOPLE ARE MILITARIZED, JUST AS THE BIBLE AND HER STUDENTS FORESAW

This new communist state of China, bent on expansion and conquest like all other totalitarian communists, began to spread throughout Asia! The once benevolent feudal landlords were forced into the die of militarized aggression common to all communists. Read the words of Dr. Robinson, a student of prophecy, uttered in the latter

---

[6]Hal Lindsey, *The 1980's: Countdown to Armageddon*, p. 91.

part of the nineteenth century: "Before another half century shall have rolled away in the providence of God there will be seen revolutions in the Oriental mind of which no one has even a foreboding."[7] This foreshadows their role in the war predicted to occur in the last days before the return of the Messiah to bring lasting peace!

On June 6, 1989, after the American news cameras were turned off during the coverage of the pro-democracy demonstration in Tiananmen Square near Beijing, the Chinese Communist government opened fire on the unarmed protesters, killing hundreds, if not thousands, of innocent Chinese students.[8]

[7]John Cumming D.D., *The Destiny of Nations*. London: Hurst & Blackette, 1864.

[8]While in Tiananmen Square, *CBS News* anchor Dan Rather gave some sort of excuse and then signaled to a technician behind him to cut the satellite transmission. The television picture became static, then the massacre began. What judgment lies ahead for those who could have helped but turned a deaf ear.

ORIGINAL HEBREW TEXT WRITTEN 712 BC

הַעִירֹ֤ותִי מִצָּפֹון֙ וַיַּ֔את מִמִּזְרַח־שֶׁ֖מֶשׁ יִקְרָ֣א בִשְׁמִ֑י וְיָבֹ֤א סְגָנִים֙ כְּמֹו־חֹ֔מֶר וּכְמֹ֥ו יֹוצֵ֖ר יִרְמָס
טִֽיט׃ .... הָאֹמֵ֥ר לַצּוּלָ֖ה חֳרָ֑בִי וְנַהֲרֹתַ֖יִךְ אֹובִֽישׁ׃

ישעיה מא:כה; מד:כז

OLD TESTAMENT SCRIPTURE TRANSLATION

"...he has come; From the rising of the sun....*It is I* who says to the depth of the sea, 'Be dried up!' And I will make your rivers dry."

Isaiah 41:25; 44:27 NASB

ANCIENT RABBINICAL COMMENTARY

"And again the spirit carried me and took me to the east of the world, and I saw there stars battling one another and resting not."[9]

Sefer Eliyahu, BhM 3:65-67

"...the kings of the East will congregate....They will offer sacrifices in Jerusalem....The kings of the East will say, 'He is giving the Israelites permission to build the house of the sanctuary,' and they will come to burn it. Then the holy One blessed be He will go out and fight with them, to fulfill that which is said, *The Lord will go out and fight with those Gentiles* (Zech 14:3)."[10]

Midrash Suta Hagadische Abhandlungen uber
Schir haSchirim, Ruth, Eikah, und Koheleth

"...Gog and Magog will come against Israel, he and all the kings of the East...."[11]

The Book of Zerubbabel, text of Pirke Hecalot Rabbati

NEW TESTAMENT RECORDED 96 AD

"And the number of the armies of the horsemen was two hundred million; I heard the number of them....And the sixth *angel* poured out his bowl upon the great river, the Euphrates; and its water was dried up, that the way might be prepared for the kings from the east...." **Revelation 9:16; 16:12 NASB**

MODERN RABBINIC COMMENT/REFUTATION

"Jews....believe that man will not self-destruct, that we will not disappear in a gigantic atomic blast. Man is basically good...."

***The Real Messiah*, by Aryeh Kaplan, *et al*, p. 50; 1976**

AUTHOR'S COMMENT—EVANGELICAL CHRISTIAN POSITION

It is quite clear that many modern rabbis' conception of a permanent peace, formulated and enforced with no nuclear confrontation, is in error, as far as the Bible verses and rabbinical writings we have quoted are concerned. There will be peace, but lasting peace will only come when Jesus is received by His people. Only the Messiah can bring peace upon His acceptance, and this, as the Bible teaches, will only occur when He saves the world from Armageddon!

Philip Moore

---

[9] Raphael Patai, *The Messiah Texts*, p. 150.

[10] George W. Buchanan, *Revelation and Redemption*, p. 449.

[11] Ibid, p. 345.

GENERAL MACARTHUR WARNS AGAINST APPEASING CHINA DUE TO THEIR MILITARIZATION—AGAIN, WE IGNORE THE LESSONS OF HISTORY

In 1951, General MacArthur alerted the United States Congress regarding the militarization of China and the potential consequences. In his Congressional speech, the General warned: "The Chinese people have become thus militarized in their concepts and their ideals....This has produced a new and dominant power in Asia....There are some who for various reasons would appease Red China. They are blind to history's clear lesson. For history teaches, with unmistakable emphasis, that appeasement but begats new and bloodier war. It (history) points to no single instance where the end has justified that means—where appeasement has led to more than a sham peace. Like blackmail, it lays the basis for new and successively greater demands until, as in blackmail, violence becomes the only alternative."[12]

THE CHINESE COMMUNISTS HAVE OBTAINED THE H-BOMB, FOMENTED SEVERAL REVOLUTIONS AND ARE PRESENTLY SIGNING TERRORIST AGREEMENTS WITH THE PLO ARABS

It was not long after MacArthur's speech that Red China shocked the world by detonating a hydrogen bomb.[13] Later, in the 1970's, these communists obtained intercontinental ballistic missiles and launchers, which can now carry nuclear warheads to Europe and Asia. Shortly after the fall of the Chinese people to the communists, their "government" started the Korean War, and since then has fomented Vietnam and is presently aggravating subversion in Africa and the Middle East.

In 1984, the *Los Angeles Times* documented that Premier Zhao Ziyang of China said: "China will always firmly support the Palestinian people in their just struggle, firmly support the PLO as the sole legitimate representative of the Palestinian people and firmly support the revolutionary leadership of **Brother** Arafat."[14]

***

[12]Hal Lindsey, *The 1980's: Countdown to Armageddon*, p. 92.

[13]*The World Book Encyclopedia* mentions: "China exploded its first atomic bomb in 1964, and successfully fired its first guided missile with a nuclear warhead in 1966. In 1967, China exploded its first hydrogen bomb." *The World Book Encyclopedia*, 1970 Edition, p. 390r.

[14]Michael Parks, "Arafat, on China Visit, Promised Support," *Los Angeles Times*, May 8, 1984, p. 17. Bold mine.

A 1988 issue of *Al Bayader Assiyasi (*a left-wing Arab publication printed in Jerusalem) stated: "Peking has told PLO Chairman Yasser Arafat that it supports any PNC decision including the establishment of a provisional government-in-exile. During Arafat's recent visit to China, he signed several accords including one for training Palestinian military [terrorist] personnel in China."[15]

CHINA'S COMPLETION OF A HIGHWAY IN 1979 PAVES THE WAY TO THE PROPHETIC FULFILLMENT OF "A DRIED UP EUPHRATES" FROM REVELATION

In the 1990's, China is selling nuclear military technology to Arab nations which are unstable and as dangerous to Israel as Iran.[16] We read in Revelation 9:14-16 that China's two hundred million-man army will cross the Euphrates River, which will have dried up!

Some have asked how the Orientals could move a mechanized force to the border of this river, considering the rough terrain. The answer is China's completion of Karakoram Highway in 1979, which runs: "...from Singkiang province through Pakistan to the Indian Ocean. A spur of this highway goes through Afghanistan and Iran to Iraq where the Euphrates River runs from Turkey to the Persian Gulf."[17]

CHINESE FAMINE

In the 1960's, just ten years after the communist takeover of China, twenty million Chinese starved to death as the result of famine. This famine was caused by the ineffeciency of communism. Free enterprise had been completely obliterated.

When Mao died in 1976, his successor, Deng Xiaoping, transformed China's half-empty and mismanaged factories into a semi-efficient economic industry by adopting capitalist principles. He allowed private ownership of land and profit after quotas were met. Thus the Chinese are no longer starving and the country has been

---

[15]*Al Bayader Assiyasi, Independent Weekly*. Jerusalem, Oct. 14, 1988, p. 7, used by permission. [ ] mine.

[16]In his 1994 book, Hal Lindsey documents: "According to some intelligence sources, Iran already has at least four nuclear warheads, from the former Soviet republic of Kazakhstan. Iran reportedly plans to fit the warheads to Chinese Silkworm missiles. And yes, China has admitted supplying missiles to several Islamic states....Iran has also purchased a 300-megawatt reactor from China despite U.S. efforts to block the deal, and may be negotiating to buy another....The Iranians have acquired military nuclear technology from China...." Hal Lindsey, *Planet Earth—2000 A.D.*, pp. 209 -211.

[17]William Goetz, *Apocalypse Next*, p. 114.

provided with a viable means of producing the weapons to be used in the final conflict of Armageddon.

Once China becomes fully industrialized with the help of Western technology,[18] she will no doubt, become vulnerable to pressure and control by the future world leader, known to us as the Antichrist. You will read about him in chapter 23, "The False Messiah Armilus Equals Antichrist."

SHE LEARNED HER LESSON FROM FAMINE, BUT HAS SHE FROM WAR?

Hal Lindsey brings us up-to-date on China's war goals using inside information he obtained in 1994. He notes: "Interestingly, my intelligence sources tell me that the Chinese leadership had to promise its military that a large sum of the revenue raised through China's prosperous transition into capitalism will go directly into the military[19] forces. That was one of the compromises that needed to be made to minimize opposition to departing from the Marxist-Leninist path. In fact, they promised that the military will be built up to the point where it is *second to none*....Today, of course, China is a major thermo-nuclear power with intercontinental missiles[20] capable of hitting anywhere in the West. China also has intermediate-range nuclear weapons and nuclear submarines. It is a real power with first-class bombers and fighter planes."[21]

***

---

[18]I remember when Deng Xiaoping visited the assembly line of General Motors in my home state of Georgia. He was very impressed. This incident, among other things, led him to approve the importation of vital U.S. technology into China.

[19]Recently, Clinton (the traitor) recklessly and treasonously gave our super computer to China. Also, we note that a recent ABC news magazine, *48 Hours*, documented that the Chinese military factories are making dolls, toys and stuffed animals at a labor cost of twenty cents per hour. These same products have been found on Wal-Mart and Kmart shelves in the U.S. The program emphasized that the capital from this huge operation is being used to massively upgrade China's military hardware, which may result in an unforeseen powerful Chinese military in the early to mid-twenty-first century.

[20]When John the apostle makes strange predictions, he is most likely describing, with his first-century understanding, what he saw in his glimpse into the twenty-first century. For instance, in Revelation 9:18-19, he says: "A third of mankind was killed by these three plagues, by the fire and the smoke and the brimstone, which proceeded out of their mouths. For the power of the horses is in their mouths and in their tails; for their tails are like serpents and have heads; and with them they do harm" (NASB). His descriptions sound like missiles and modern weaponry. Certainly nothing of his time could fit this description! And the text here is not symbolic in its context, as it sometimes is in other passages in the Scripture, such as parables.

[21]Hal Lindsey, *Planet Earth—2000 A.D.*, p. 208.

THE EXPERTS SAY CHINA HAS HER BIBLICALLY PREDICTED TWO HUNDRED MILLION SOLDIERS!

The mindset of China is forever changed. They, as prophecy has foretold (Rev. 9:16; 16:12), will launch a two hundred million-man army into the Middle East in the final war. Alexander Solzhenitsyn, the famous Russian novelist, remarked over a decade ago: "In expectation of World War III, the West again seeks cover, and finds Communist China an ally! This is another betrayal, not only of Taiwan, but of the entire oppressed Chinese people. Moreover, it is a mad, suicidal policy: Having supplied billion-strong China with American arms, the West will defeat the U.S.S.R., but thereafter no force on earth will restrain communist China from world conquest."[22]

The renowned prophecy teacher, Hal Lindsey, rightly remarks of our Russian friend: "Solzhenitsyn echoes the Biblical prophets, who said that the Oriental people, led by China, will battle the western nations in the planet's last great war. So it is plain to see that the arms we are now sending the Chinese will be turned against us after the Russians are destroyed in the Middle East."[23]

Hal notes: "The Bible foretold this development 20 centuries ago when there were not 200 million people on earth. This vast, turbulent sea of humanity is now being equipped with the latest military technology of the West—mainly by the USA. Several American administrations have fallen for the fatal lie—that friendship with China is somehow indispensable to our overall best interests. According to Bible prophecy, we are feeding the tiger that will one day eat us."[24]

Hal also says: "We believe that China is the beginning of the formation of this great power called 'the kings of the east' by the apostle John. We live at a time in history when it is no longer incredible to think of the Orient with an army of 200 million soldiers. In fact, a recent television documentary on Red China, called 'The Voice of the Dragon,' quoted the boast of the Chinese themselves that they could field a 'people's army' of 200 million militiamen. In their own boast they named the same number as the Biblical prediction. Coincidence?"[25]

***

[22]Hal Lindsey, *The 1980's: Countdown to Armageddon*, p. 95.
[23]Ibid.
[24]Hal Lindsey, *The 1990's: Prophecy on Fast Forward*, chapter 13, p. 7.
[25]Hal Lindsey with C.C. Carlson, *The Late Great Planet Earth*, p. 86.

"The Bible clearly tells us that God is in control. There is hope. The world is racing towards a climax. But instead of a disastrous catastrophe, it will be Christ's dynamic return to earth to set up a thousand year reign of peace....Daniel has become a focal point of critics' attacks upon the Old Testament prophecies because it contains detailed, accurately fulfilled predictions which demonstrate their divine inspiration. Because of Daniel's devotion to God and his great concern for the Jewish people...the Lord seems to have given him a special understanding of what the future held for his people. These prophetic insights extend even to the end time of Hebrew history and the destiny of other nations of the world."[1] Josh McDowell

"Jesus Christ regarded the book as a prophetic preview of future history, and, indeed, of the divine program for a future that still lies ahead (Matthew 24:4 ff., Mark 13:5 ff., Luke 21:8 ff.). If He is wrong in His interpretation of the book then He must be less than an omniscient, inerrant God incarnate. On the other hand, if His appraisal is right, then we cannot question His claim to deity in this regard."[2]

Bruce Waltke, professor of Semitics and Old Testament at
Dallas Theological Seminary, Ph.D. from Harvard University

"If the keys of the Bible, up to the book of Psalms, hang on Moses' books, those of the rest of the Bible, through Revelation, hang on Daniel; and indeed very many of the prophetic Psalms fail to open to us till we see their solution in the wonderful visions of the faithful seer of the captivity."[3] William R. Newell

22

ROME RESURRECTED

The book of Daniel is the most controversial book in the Old Testament. The rabbis have often warned their students not to read it because it "tells the time of Messiah." The Jews in Israel have difficulty with chapters 2:4-7:28, which describe the end time in detail, because they are written in Aramaic, the language of Babylon. The Babylonians captured the prophet Daniel as a boy, and held him and his people for seventy years, an occurrence predicted by the prophet Jeremiah.

***

---

[1] Josh McDowell, *Prophecy, Fact or Fiction?*, pp. 4-5. McDowell works for Campus Crusade for Christ and has lectured at over five hundred college campuses in fifty-three countries, speaking to over five million students as of 1981. In his book, McDowell does a very good job of exposing liberal Bible critics who have attempted to discredit Daniel as a sixth century BC prophet. If you have friends who have doubts about Daniel, have them read McDowell! Then they will have no more doubts.

[2] Ibid, p. 6.

[3] Ibid.

LIBERAL DISAPPROVAL OF DANIEL

Most contemporary liberal scholars avoid Daniel's book altogether due to the supernatural element of future-telling. Daniel foretold the future of the Gentile nations. His predictions about the rise and fall of world empires can only be explained by divine inspiration. However, for this explanation to be palatable, we of course would need to believe in the divine. Many who like to teach the Bible do not. This is where the conflict of Daniel's dream comes into play. Daniel provided the king with answers when no one else could, through God's power. As it has been said: "Daniel answered before the king and said, 'As for the mystery about which the king has inquired, neither wise men, conjurers, magicians, *nor* diviners are able to declare *it* to the king' " (Dan. 2:27 NASB).

Daniel lived well into his nineties and his writings span a period of seventy-three years. He wrote his book in the first part of the sixth century BC, when Babylon was still the ruling world empire. In chapters 2 and 7 he describes the four major empires which would rule the world until the Messiah ushers in the eternal kingdom. Daniel's prophecy is centered on the interpretation of a dream which God gave the Babylonian king. Significantly, none of the king's astrologers, soothsayers or fortune tellers were able to interpret the king's dream, which he had forgotten. Only Daniel was able to refresh the king's memory. This is why the king recognized Daniel's power.

NEBUCHADNEZZAR'S DREAMS FORETOLD HISTORY TO OUR DAY AND BEYOND

The dream, which revealed and outlined the rise and fall of the world's major empires, reads as follows: "Now in the second year of the reign of Nebuchadnezzar, Nebuchadnezzar had dreams; and his spirit was troubled and his sleep left him. Then the king gave orders to call in the magicians, the conjurers, the sorcerers and the Chaldeans, to tell the king his dreams. So they came in and stood before the king. And the king said to them, 'I had a dream, and my spirit is anxious to understand the dream.' Then the Chaldeans spoke to the king in Aramaic: 'O king, live forever! Tell the dream to your servants, and we will declare the interpretation.' The king answered and said to the Chaldeans, 'The command from me is firm: if you do not make known to me the dream and its interpretation, you will be torn limb from limb, and your houses will be made a rubbish heap. But if you declare the dream and its interpretation, you will receive from me gifts and a reward and great honor; therefore declare to me the dream and its interpretation.' They answered a second time and said, 'Let the king tell the dream to his servants, and we will declare the interpretation.' The king answered and said, 'I know for certain that you are bargaining for time, inasmuch as you have seen that the command from me is firm, that if you do not make the dream known to me, there is only one decree for you. For you have agreed together to speak lying and corrupt words before me until the situation is changed; therefore tell me the dream, that I may know that you can declare to me its interpretation.' The Chaldeans answered the king and said, 'There is not a man on earth who could declare the matter for the king, inasmuch as no great king or ruler has *ever* asked anything like this of any magician, conjurer or Chaldean. Moreover, the thing which the king demands is difficult, and there is no one else who could declare it to the king except gods, whose dwelling place is not with *mortal* flesh.' Because of this the king became indignant and very furious, and gave orders to destroy all the wise men of Babylon. So the decree went forth that the wise men should be slain; and they looked for Daniel and his friends to kill *them*. Then Daniel replied with discretion and discernment to Arioch, the captain of the king's bodyguard, who had gone forth to slay the wise men of Babylon; he answered and said to Arioch, the king's commander, 'For what reason is the decree from the king *so* urgent?' Then Arioch informed Daniel about the matter. So Daniel went in and requested of the king that he would give him time, in order that he might declare the interpretation to the king. Then Daniel went to his house and informed his friends, Hananiah, Mishael and Azariah, about the matter, in order that they might request compassion from the God of heaven concerning this mystery, so that Daniel and his friends might not be destroyed with the rest of the wise men of Babylon. Then the mystery was revealed to Daniel in a night vision. Then Daniel blessed the God of heaven; Daniel answered and said, 'Let the name of God be blessed forever and ever, for wisdom and power belong to Him. And it is He who changes the times and the epochs; He removes kings and establishes kings; He gives wisdom to wise men, And knowledge to men of understanding. It is He who reveals the profound and hidden things; He knows what is in the darkness, And the light dwells with him. To Thee, O God of my fathers, I give thanks and praise, For Thou hast given me wisdom and power; Even now Thou hast made known to me what we requested of Thee, For Thou hast made known to us the king's matter.' Therefore, Daniel went in to Arioch, whom the king had appointed to destroy the wise men of Babylon; he went and spoke to him as follows: 'Do not destroy the wise men of Babylon! Take me into the king's presence, and I will declare the interpretation to the king!' Then Arioch hurriedly brought Daniel into the king's presence and spoke to him as follows: 'I have found a man among the exiles from Judah who can make the interpretation known to the king!' The king answered and said to Daniel, whose name was Belteshazzar, 'Are you able to make known to me the dream which I have seen and its interpretation?' Daniel answered before the king and said, 'As for the mystery about which the king has inquired, neither wise men, conjurers, magicians, *nor* diviners are able to declare *it* to the king. However, there is a God in heaven who reveals mysteries, and He has made known to King Nebuchadnezzar what will take place in the latter days. This was your dream and the visions in your mind *while* on your bed. As for you, O king, *while* on your bed your thoughts turned to what would take place in the future; and He who reveals mysteries has made known to you what will take place. But as for me, this mystery has not been revealed to me for any wisdom residing in me more than *in* any *other* living man, but for the purpose of making the interpretation known to the king, and that you may understand the thoughts of your mind. You, O king, were looking and behold, there was a single great statue; that statue, which was large and of extraordinary splendor, was standing in front of you and its appearance was awesome. The head of that statue *was made* of fine gold, its breast and its arms of silver, its belly and its thighs of bronze, its legs of iron, its feet partly of iron and partly of clay. You continued looking until a stone was cut out without hands, and it struck the statue on its feet of iron and clay, and crushed them. Then the iron, the clay, the bronze, the silver and the gold were crushed all at the same time, and became like chaff from the summer threshing floors; and the wind carried them away so that not a trace of them was found. But the stone that struck the statue became a great mountain and filled the whole earth. This *was* the dream; now we shall tell its interpretation before the king. You, O king, are the king of kings, to whom the God of heaven has given the kingdom, the power, the strength, and the glory; and wherever the sons of men dwell, *or* the beasts of the field, or the birds of the sky, He has given *them* into your hand and has caused you to rule over them all. You are the head of gold. And after you there will arise another kingdom inferior to you, then another third kingdom of bronze, which will rule over all the earth. Then there will be a fourth kingdom as strong as iron; inasmuch as iron crushes and shatters all things, so, like iron that breaks in pieces, it will crush and break all these in pieces. And in that you saw the feet and toes, partly of potter's clay and partly of iron, it will be a divided kingdom; but it will have in it the toughness of iron, inasmuch as you saw the iron mixed with common clay. And *as* the toes of the feet *were* partly of iron and partly of pottery, *so* some of the kingdom will be strong and part of it will be brittle. And in that you saw the iron mixed with common clay, they will combine with one another in the seed of men; but they will not adhere to one another, even as iron does not combine with pottery. And in the days of those kings the God of heaven will set up a kingdom which will never be destroyed, and *that* kingdom will not be left for another people; it will crush and put an end to all these kingdoms, but it will itself endure forever. Inasmuch as you saw that a stone was cut out of the mountain without hands and that it crushed the iron, the bronze, the clay, the silver, and the gold, the great God has made known to the king what will take place in the future; so the dream is true, and its interpretation is trustworthy.' Then King Nebuchadnezzar fell on his face and did homage to Daniel, and gave orders to present to him an offering and fragrant incense. The king answered Daniel and said, 'Surely your God is a God of gods and a Lord of kings and a revealer of mysteries, since you have been able to reveal this mystery' " (Dan. 2:1-47 NASB).

THE SEVENTH CHAPTER OF DANIEL

Daniel 7 was written in the first year of Belteshazzar[4] (553 BC), an incredible five and one-half centuries before the birth of Jesus. In 33 AD, Jesus presented His case before the Sanhedrin. He quoted the thirteenth verse of this chapter in His claim of Messiahship. "Again the high priest asked him, and said unto him, 'Art thou the Christ, the Son of the Blessed?' And Jesus said, 'I am: and ye shall see the Son of man sitting on the right hand of power, and coming in the clouds of heaven' " (Mark 14:61-62 KJV).

As we mentioned, Daniel is a major source of Messianic prophecy, especially the time-frame of Jesus' First Coming and the destruction of Jerusalem (Dan. 9:24-27). However, in keeping with the subject of this chapter, we will investigate certain portions of Daniel, which have remained cryptic or hidden for centuries.

Daniel himself had a dream, which he described in the seventh chapter of his work. The dream pertained not only to the future empires and historical Rome but also to contemporary reality. The dream God allowed Daniel to have revealed major world empires prior to their actual appearance in history. The dream also exposed the current revival of the fourth empire, Rome. Daniel's dream reads as follows: "...I was looking in my vision by night, and behold, the four winds of heaven were stirring up the great sea. And four great beasts were coming up from the sea, different from one another. The first

[4]See Daniel 7:1 to authenticate this date.

was like a lion and had *the* wings of an eagle....a second one, resembling a bear....and behold, another one, like a leopard, which had on its back four wings of a bird; the beast also had four heads, and dominion was given to it. After this I kept looking in the night visions, and behold, a fourth beast, dreadful and terrifying and extremely strong; and it had large iron teeth. It devoured and crushed, and trampled down the remainder with its feet; and it was different from all the beasts that were before it, and it had ten horns. While I was contemplating the horns, behold, another horn, a little one, came up among them, and three of the first horns were pulled out by the roots before it; and behold, this horn possessed eyes like the eyes of a man, and a mouth uttering great *boasts*....I approached one of those who were standing by and began asking him the exact meaning of all this. So he told me and made known to me the interpretation of these things: 'These great beasts, which are four *in number*, are four kings *who* will arise from the earth'....Then I desired to know the exact meaning of the fourth beast, which was different from all the others, exceedingly...and *the meaning* of the ten horns that *were* on its head, and the other *horn* which came up...that horn which had eyes and a mouth uttering great *boasts*, and which was larger in appearance than its associates. I kept looking, and that horn was waging war with the saints and overpowering them until the Ancient of Days came, and judgment was passed in favor of the saints of the Highest One, and the time arrived when the saints took possession of the kingdom. Thus he said: 'The fourth beast will be a fourth kingdom on the earth, which will be different from all the *other* kingdoms, and it will devour the whole earth and tread it down and crush it. As for the ten horns, out of this kingdom ten kings [ten nations of the end times] will arise; and another [Antichrist—false Messiah] will arise after them, and he will be different from the previous ones....And he will speak out against the Most High and wear down the saints of the Highest One, and he will intend to make alterations in times and in law; and they will he given into his hand for a time, times, and half a time' " (Dan. 7:2-8, 16-17, 19-25 NASB; [ ] mine).

DOES YOUR MIND HAVE WISDOM?

Daniel wrote: "As for the ten horns, out of this kingdom ten kings will arise; and another will arise after them, and he will be different from the previous ones and will subdue three kings" (Dan. 7:24 NASB). The apostle Paul added: "Here is the mind which has wisdom. The seven heads are seven mountains on which the woman sits, and they are seven kings; five have fallen, one is, the other has not yet come; and when he comes, he must remain a little while. And the beast which was and is not, is himself also an eighth, and is *one* of the seven, and he goes to destruction. And the ten horns which you saw are ten kings, who have not yet received a kingdom, but they receive authority as kings with the beast for one hour" (Rev. 17:9-10 NASB).

You have just read prophetic verses which have baffled the most brilliant interpreters for centuries. However, we who live in the twentieth century can safely say we have the "wisdom" mentioned by the apostle John nearly 2000 years ago! We have the vantage point of hindsight to see John's foresight, as the prophet quoted these words from God: "But as for you, Daniel, conceal these words and seal up the book until the end of time; many will go back and forth, and knowledge will increase....none of the wicked will understand, but those who have insight will understand....as for you, go *your way* to the end; then you will enter into rest and rise *again* for your allotted portion at the end of the age" (Dan. 12:4; 10:13 NASB).

We can understand because some of the events mentioned have actually begun to occur. Daniel's words "the time of the end" apply to us! Because we live near the "time of the end," our knowledge of biblical prophecy is increased. The things you are reading in this book escaped the most brilliant scholars of the past because they were sealed!

The seven heads and ten horns may still sound strange to you—let's examine them. The seven heads are synonomous with six former kingdoms which ruled the world, with one yet to come. They also represent the trademark of the seventh coming kingdom, which is a revival of the sixth. Since a key part of the prophecy features seven hills, the seventh coming kingdom will be Rome, a city built on seven hills.

LET US DOCUMENT

The seven heads were ancient world kingdoms including Assyria, Egypt, Babylon, Media-Persia, Greece and Rome, which existed in John's day. One is revived Rome, made up of ten nations which have not yet received a kingdom. However, they will receive a kingdom with the beast (Antichrist; Rev. 17:13), when the seven heads culminate in a New Rome.

Daniel 7:24 explains that the ten kings arise out of the fourth world empire,[5] which he predicted while Babylon (the first) still

[5]Daniel does not count Assyria and Egypt because they were not in the king's dream. Therefore, Daniel's fourth kingdom is John's sixth. The first ruling kingdom mentioned in Daniel (Babylon) is documented as John's third because Daniel begins with the Europe of his day. In the book of Revelation, John gives us a complete view of the three kingdoms which existed before Babylon (Rev. 17:10).

existed. History documents this fourth power as Rome, which was the strongest world power to that date. Daniel predicted that out of that kingdom, ten horns (nations) would come. We see the EEC (European Economic Community) as the power predicted by Daniel and John now being reassembled in its final ten-horned form.

Ancient Rome, by no coincidence, was known as the city of seven hills, which is verified throughout Roman literature and on their coins. Notice above, the woman is sitting upon seven hills etched on the coin.

"HUMPTY DUMPTY" IS PUT BACK TOGETHER AGAIN! ROME IS RESURRECTED

The children's nursery rhyme containing the line, "They [all the king's men] couldn't put Humpty Dumpty back together again," was written, believe it or not, as a result of the many failed attempts to rebuild Rome. As one Bible teacher tells us: "By reconstructing a world government out of the ruins of the ancient Roman Empire, the Antichrist will have accomplished what no one else has been able to do since A.D. 476, the year the Roman Empire officially died. Charlemagne tried to put it together but failed. Napoleon did his best, but met his Waterloo! Bismarck dreamed of making Germany the capital of revived Rome, and did succeed in defeating France.

"Then Hitler came along. He envisioned the Mediterranean Sea as a German lake and the whole world as his empire. He saw himself as the caesar of the third Roman Empire—the 'Third Reich.' His efforts resulted in the downfall of his own nation.

"So fruitless were the efforts of men to reconstruct the Roman Empire that poets wrote sonnets about the futility of it…the children's nursery rhyme *Humpty Dumpty* was originally written about the fallen Roman Empire and all of the attempts to put it back together again."[6]

THE ANCIENT RABBINIC LITERATURE CONFIRMS OUR INTERPRETATION

We believe that New Rome, which will soon be consolidated by the Antichrist, has already seen its primary reassembly, as Daniel predicted 2600 years ago in his famous Old Testament prophecy (Dan. 7:24). In the book of Revelation in the New Testament, John adds even more vivid details: "And I stood upon the sand of the sea, and saw a beast rise up out of the sea, having seven heads and ten horns, and upon his horns ten crowns, and upon his heads the name of blasphemy" (Rev. 13:1 KJV).

The ancient rabbinical writers adhered to the same interpretation of a ten nation revived Rome headed by an evil king who would attempt to destroy Israel: "...Armilus...will rule over the entire world, and there will be nobody to stand up against him. And all those who do not believe in him will die by his cruel sword. And he will come to the land of Israel with ten kings, to Jerusalem....And then there will be trouble in Israel the like of which never was in the world. And they will flee in to crevices and caves in the deserts....And these are...ten kings who will arise over the nations in those seven years."[7]

We, as Bible believers and political spectators, see before our very eyes a group of countries known as the EEC (European Economic Community) or Common Market. We believe that they are soon to be consolidated into a final form,[8] which will be the fulfillment of the prophecies contained in the ancient text of the Bible! This will be

---

[6]Hal Lindsey, *There's A New World Coming*, p. 177.

[7]Raphael Patai, *The Messiah Texts*, pp. 126, 128. Patai's source was Sefer Zerubbabel, BhM 2:54-57.

[8]Interestingly, a Brussels, Belgium, Associated Press report on this issue surmises: "With more of a whimper than a bang, the European Community is ushering in a new era in its decades-old drive for a unified Europe. The dozen nations have put into place their Treaty of European Union, linking the political and economic fates of their 346 million people more closely than ever. Over time, EC citizens will be able to vote and run for office in other EC countries. Foreign ministers will speak with a single voice on world issues. Their currencies will one day fold into one." Hal Lindsey, *Countdown...*, Vol. 4, No. 12.

accomplished by the greatest evil leader who has ever lived. He will attempt to become a world caesar over a one-world government energized by Satan himself. This event, to take place shortly before the return of the Messiah, will be expanded upon in the next chapter.

HOW MANY KINGS?

The EEC's original goal when it was established by the Treaty of Rome in 1957, was a confederacy numbering ten nations. More than twenty-five years ago, when the association consisted of only six nations, a *Time* magazine article entitled, "Europe's Dreams of Unity Revived," said: "Should all go according to the most optimistic schedules, the Common Market could someday expand into a ten-nation economic entity whose industrial might would far surpass that of the Soviet Union."[9]

For many years, the nations in this group numbered fewer than ten: in 1958, they numbered six; in 1973, they numbered nine; and in 1981, they numbered ten—drawing Greece into the fold. In 1986, they included Spain and Portugal, bringing their total to twelve-fold, a number that could increase again. One day their numbers will decline again to precisely ten,[10] as predicted in the Scriptures. However, it may be possible that this may be more than twenty years away. It is also possible that one ancient nation may have covered the same area as several modern countries. If we look at it from this perspective, current numbers would be meaningless (see our footnote below for Rev. Chuck Smith's observations). At that time, they will be used by the Antichrist to accomplish a counterfeit one-world Messianic

---

[9]"Europe's Dreams of Unity Revived," *Time,* July 4, 1969, p. 23.

[10]The ten nations of the EEC match the ten toes mentioned in Daniel's prediction. Concerning this, the learned Reverend Chuck Smith of Calvary Chapel in Costa Mesa, CA, tells us: "The original idea for the formation of the EEC came from a group of intellectuals known as the Club of Rome. The confederacy of European nations is relevant to this discussion because each nation in the EEC was once a part of the old Roman Empire....However....The latest maps of Europe list the nation north of France as Benelux. This is a combination of the three small nations of Belgium, the Netherlands, and Luxembourg. All are listed separately as member-nations of the Community. If they were recognized as one, there would then be ten nations corresponding to the ten toes....Daniel 7:8 tells us that an eleventh horn shall arise which will destroy three of the horns. This eleventh horn is identified as the Antichrist who will rise to rule over the world. [If one more enters and he destroys Benelux, you will still end with ten]....the nations of the EEC have a greater potential gross national product than the United States, and could conceivably become the greatest economic power in the world...." Chuck Smith, *The Final Curtain.* Eugene, OR: Word for Today, © 1991, pp. 11-12, used by permission. Available through Word for Today, POB 8000, Costa Mesa, CA, USA 92628. Tel. (800) 272-WORD or (714) 979-0706.

Kingdom, which will be terminated by Armageddon. Only then will true peace be possible through the real Messiah.

ONE MIGHTY SUPERPOWER? WHERE IS THE CONTEMPORARY EVIDENCE?

Is there any proof that these nations in the modern EEC have the ambition to become one mighty power, consolidated in a ten-nation confederacy of Europe? Dr. Walter Hallstein, former president of the EEC, wrote: " 'Three phases of the European unification are to be noted. First, the customs union, second, the economic union, third, the political union...what we have created on the way to uniting Europe is a mighty economic-political union of which nothing may be sacrificed for any reason. Its value exists not only in what it is, but more in what it promises to become....we may fully expect the great fusion of all economic, military, and political communities together into the United States of Europe.' "[11]

BACK TO BABYLON AND ALEXANDER'S PREDICTED CONQUEST

Babylon became an empire in 606 BC and was still in power when God began to give Daniel his famous visions. The second kingdom, "like a bear," was Media-Persia (Dan. 8:20).

Around 530 BC, the Babylonians were conquered by the Medes and Persians, who replaced them as the world empire. Daniel predicted that the Greeks would rise and defeat Media-Persia. He recorded this in 530 BC. Did it occur? History records that in 331 BC, Alexander the Great conquered them! Interestingly enough, Dr. Louis Bauman noted: "It is said that Alexander the Great, when he marched his swift-moving columns into Palestine, entered the Temple in Jerusalem. While there, the high priest showed him the scroll of the prophet Daniel. Alexander was greatly interested in discovering that his own plans, as he thought they were, were the plans of the God of Israel, and were all written down by Daniel before he (Alexander) was born!"[12]

DANIEL'S PREDICTION OF GREEK DESTRUCTION

Daniel 8 predicted that the Greek Empire of Alexander would crumble into four separate parts when its king died abruptly. His

---

[11]Hal Lindsey with C.C. Carlson, *The Late Great Planet Earth*, p. 96.

[12]Louis S. Bauman, D.D., *Light from Bible Prophecy, As Related to the Present Crisis.* New York: Fleming H. Revell Company, © 1940, p. 66, used by permission.

prediction also said that four powers would divide his empire: "And I saw him come beside the ram, and he was enraged at him; and he struck the ram and shattered his two horns, and the ram had no strength to withstand him. So he hurled him to the ground and trampled on him, and there was none to rescue the ram from his power. Then the male goat magnified *himself* exceedingly. But as soon as he was mighty, the large horn was broken; and in its place there came up four conspicuous *horns* toward the four winds of heaven....And the shaggy goat *represents* the kingdom of Greece, and the large horn that is between his eyes is the first king. And the broken *horn* and the four *horns that* arose in its place *represent* four kingdoms *which* will arise from *his* nation, although not with his power" (Dan. 8:7-8, 21-22 NASB).

History also bears witness to the fact that Alexander died of alcoholism at the age of thirty-three. On his deathbed, he was asked who would take over the empire. Traditionally, it had gone to the son; however, Alexander said, "Give it to the strongest." The kingdom was then divided up amongst his four strongest generals: Lysymmacus, Casander, Selecus and Ptolemy. The divided Greek Empire was considerably weakened and in 68 BC, four hundred years after the rule of Alexander, it was overthrown by Rome, which became the greatest world power to date.

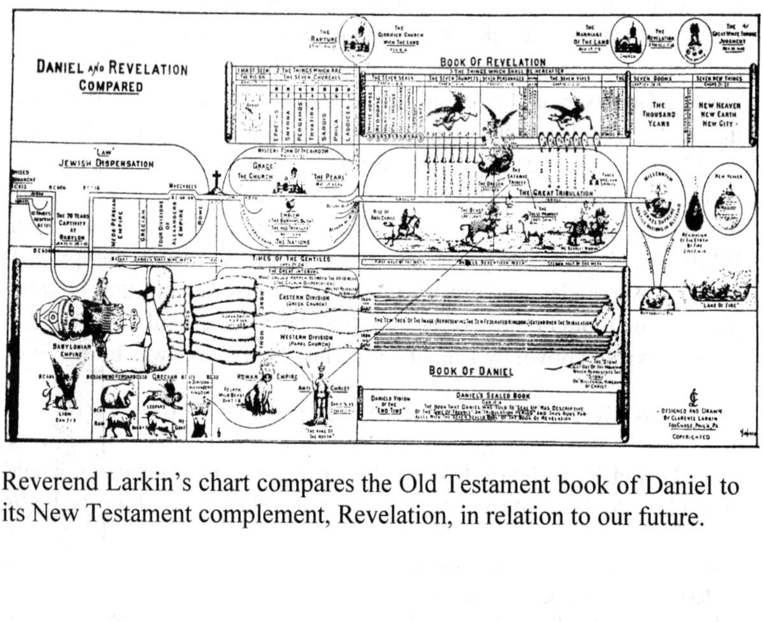

Reverend Larkin's chart compares the Old Testament book of Daniel to its New Testament complement, Revelation, in relation to our future.

ORIGINAL ARAMAIC TEXT WRITTEN 555 BC

כֵּן אֲמַר חֵיוְתָא רְבִיעָיְתָא מַלְכוּ רְבִיעָיָא תֶּהֱוֵא בְּאַרְעָא דִּי תִשְׁנֵא מִן־כָּל־מַלְכְוָתָא וְתֵאכֻל
כָּל־אַרְעָא וּתְדוּשִׁנַּהּ וְתַדְּקִנַּהּ׃ וְקַרְנַיָּא עֲשַׂר מִנַּהּ מַלְכוּתָה עַשְׂרָה מַלְכִין יְקֻמוּן וְאָחֳרָן יְקוּם
אַחֲרֵיהוֹן וְהוּא יִשְׁנֵא מִן־קַדְמָיֵא וּתְלָתָה מַלְכִין יְהַשְׁפִּל׃ וּמִלִּין לְצַד עִלָּיָא יְמַלִּל וּלְקַדִּישֵׁי
עֶלְיוֹנִין יְבַלֵּא וְיִסְבַּר לְהַשְׁנָיָה זִמְנִין וְדָת וְיִתְיַהֲבוּן בִּידֵהּ עַד־עִדָּן וְעִדָּנִין וּפְלַג עִדָּן׃

דניאל ז:כג-כה

OLD TESTAMENT SCRIPTURE TRANSLATION

"Thus he said: 'The fourth beast will be a fourth kingdom on the earth, which will be different from all the *other* kingdoms, and it will devour the whole earth and tread it down and crush it. As for the ten horns, out of this kingdom ten kings will arise; and another will arise after them, and he will be different from the previous ones and will subdue three kings. And he will speak out against the Most High and wear down the saints of the Highest One, and he will intend to make alterations in times and in law; and they will be given into his hand for a time, times, and half a time.' " **Daniel 7:23-25 NASB**

ANCIENT RABBINICAL COMMENTARY

"...Armilus...he will rule over the entire world, and there will be nobody to stand up against him. And all those who do not believe in him will die by his cruel sword. And he will come to the land of Israel with ten kings, to Jerusalem....And then there will be trouble in Israel the like of which never was in the world. And they will flee into crevices and caves in the deserts....And these are...ten kings who will arise over the nations in those seven years."[13]

Sefer Zerubbabel, BhM 2:54-57

NEW TESTAMENT PREDICTION 96 AD

"And the ten horns which you saw are ten kings, who have not yet received a kingdom, but they receive authority as kings with the beast for one hour. These have one purpose and they give their power and authority to the beast. These will wage war against the Lamb [Messiah], and the Lamb will overcome them, because He is Lord of lords and King of kings, and those who are with Him *are the* called and chosen and faithful."

Revelation 17:12-14 NASB. [ ] mine

MODERN POLITICAL SPECULATIONS

"Should all go according to the most optimistic schedules, the Common Market could someday expand into a ten-nation economic entity whose industrial might would far surpass that of the Soviet Union."

"Europe's Dreams of Unity Revived,"
***Time*, p. 23; July 4, 1969**

"Europe declared 1993 the year they would begin to unify! During 1992, they took the first steps towards a common currency and common defense policy. They began to mesh their varied economic policies into a free trade agreement, and join their individual armed forces under a common command presenting a unified military front....February of 1992, member nations signed the European Community Unity Treaty, commonly called the Maastricht Treaty, which set Europe on the course to union by 1999."[14]

"Europe: The Rocky Road to Unity,"
***Future Times*, pp. 2-3; 1993**

---

[13]Raphael Patai, *The Messiah Texts*, pp. 126-128.

[14]"Europe: The Rocky Road to Unity," *Future Times*, Spring 1993. World Prophetic Ministry, pp. 2-3, © used by permission. Available through World Prophetic Ministry, Colton, CA, USA 92324-0907.

DANIEL FORESEES ROME AND RESURRECTED ROME

Daniel's fourth kingdom was described as a beast more terrible than all the rest! Daniel wrote: "Then I desired to know the exact meaning of the fourth beast, which was different from all the others, exceedingly dreadful, with its teeth of iron and claws of bronze, *and which* devoured, crushed, and trampled down the remainder with its feet...." (Dan. 7:19 NASB).

Daniel described the Roman Empire in its initial stage. Daniel 7:20 begins to outline Rome's resurrection into ten separate kingdoms in our time: "...and *the meaning* of the ten horns that *were* on its head, and the other *horn* which came up, and before which three *of them* fell, namely, that horn which had eyes and a mouth uttering great *boasts*, and which was larger in appearance than its associates" (NASB).

TEN KINGS AND THEN ONE—NO FUN

This second phase of Rome, which is yet to be consolidated in the form of ten separate but unified kingdoms under "the king" Antichrist, is elaborated upon in verses 23-24. It is clear that the fourth kingdom was Rome. This passage adds: "Thus he said, 'The fourth beast will be a fourth kingdom on the earth, which will be different from all the *other* kingdoms, and it will devour the whole earth and tread it down and crush it. As for the ten horns, out of this kingdom ten kings will arise; and another will arise after them, and he will be different from the previous ones and will subdue three kings' " (Dan. 7:23-24 NASB).

Then the Antichrist, who took over the ten kings, will challenge the true Messiah. Daniel's startling words read: " 'And in the latter period of their rule, When the transgressors have run *their course*, A king will arise Insolent and skilled in intrigue. And his power will be mighty, but not by his *own* power, And he will destroy to an extraordinary degree And prosper and perform *his will*; He will destroy mighty men and the holy people. And through his shrewdness He will cause deceit to succeed by his influence; And he will magnify *himself* in his heart, And he will destroy many while *they are* at ease. He will even oppose the Prince of princes, But he will be broken without human agency. And the vision of the evenings and mornings Which has been told is true; But keep the vision secret, For *it* pertains to many days *in the future*' " (Dan. 8:23-26 NASB).

***

JOHN, PAUL AND DANIEL REVEAL AN ATTEMPT AT WORLD DOMINATION BY THE ANTICHRIST—JESUS OVERTHROWS NEW ROME AND THE FALSE MESSIAH

Daniel 7:21-22 shows resurrected Rome's plans for those who believe in the real Messiah (Jesus) after the Rapture (see our chapter 25, "The Rapture Factor"), with the power of the false Messiah, Antichrist (little horn): "I kept looking, and that horn was waging war with the saints and overpowering them until the Ancient of Days came, and judgment was passed in favor of the saints of the Highest One, and the time arrived when the saints took possession of the kingdom" (NASB).

Daniel 7:13 gives the only remedy for this evil leader the Bible calls the Antichrist: "I kept looking in the night visions, And behold, with the clouds of heaven One like a Son of Man was coming, And He came up to the Ancient of Days And was presented before Him" (NASB). This remedy is Jesus as He fulfills His promise of the Second Coming, as mentioned in Mark 14:61-62. "But He kept silent, and made no answer. Again the high priest was questioning Him, and saying to Him, 'Are you the Christ, the Son of the Blessed *One*?' And Jesus said, 'I am; and you shall see the THE SON OF MAN SITTING AT THE RIGHT HAND OF POWER, and COMING WITH THE CLOUDS OF HEAVEN' " (NASB).

Concerning the fact that Jesus will overthrow the revived Roman Empire and its leader (the false Messiah), Paul wrote: "And then that lawless one will be revealed whom the Lord will slay with the breath of His mouth and bring to an end by the appearance of His coming; *that is*, the one whose coming is in accord with the activity of Satan, with all power and signs and false wonders, and with all the deception of wickedness for those who perish, because they did not receive the love of the truth so as to be saved" (II Thes. 2:8-10 NASB).

This is confirmed by Daniel: " 'And in the days of those kings the God of heaven will set up a kingdom which will never be destroyed, and *that* kingdom will not be left for another people; it will crush and put an end to all these kingdoms, but it will itself endure forever. Inasmuch as you saw that a stone [Messiah] was cut out of the mountain without hands and that it crushed the iron, the bronze, the clay, the silver, and the gold, the great God has made known to the king what will take place in the future; so the dream is true, and its interpretation is trustworthy' " (Dan. 2:44-45 NASB; [ ] mine).

The apostle John revealed: " 'And the ten horns which you saw are ten kings, who have not yet received a kingdom, but they receive authority as kings with the beast for one hour. These have one purpose and they give their power and authority to the beast. These will wage war against the Lamb, and the Lamb will overcome them, because He is Lord of lords and King of kings, and those who are with Him *are the* called and chosen and faithful' " (Rev. 17:12-14 NASB).

ZECHARIAH'S INCREDIBLE REVELATION—THE JEWS ACCEPT THEIR MESSIAH, JESUS, AS HE RETURNS AT HIS PEAK OF VICTORY

The Jews will accept Messiah Jesus at the same moment that He destroys Gog and Magog. The Arab-Russian assault is mounted on Israel from the north (see our chapter 19, "Russia is Crushed in Gog"), which results in the Jews realizing that Jesus was their Messiah all along. " 'And I [God] will pour out on the house of David and on the inhabitants of Jerusalem, the Spirit of grace and of supplication, so that they will look on Me whom they have pierced; and they will mourn for Him, as one mourns for an only son, and they will weep bitterly over Him, like the bitter weeping over a first-born. In that day there will be great mourning in Jerusalem, like the mourning of Hadadrimmon in the plain of Megiddo. And the land will mourn, every family by itself; the family of the house of David by itself, and their wives by themselves; the family of the house of Nathan by itself, and their wives by themselves; the family of the house of Levi by itself, and their wives by themselves; the family of the Shimeites by itself; and their wives by themselves; all the families that remain, every family by itself, and their wives by themselves' " (Zech. 12:10-14 NASB; [ ] mine).

This will mark the moment when Jesus' condition for return will be uttered by the religious leaders of Israel, as He dictated in Matthew 23:39: "For I say to you, from now on you shall not see Me until you say, 'BLESSED IS HE WHO COMES IN THE NAME OF THE LORD!' " (NASB).

Once the Jews in Israel grasp what the Messiah has done by saving them from the destruction intended by the Russians and Antichrist, they will realize their mistake. As Zechariah predicted, they will look upon His pierced hands and receive Him as their Blessed Messiah, as He returns to the Mount of Olives (Zech. 12:10; 14:4, 15). "Then the LORD will go forth and fight against those nations, as when He fights on a day of battle. And in that day His feet will stand on the Mount of Olives, which is in front of Jerusalem on the east; and the Mount of Olives will be split in its middle from east to west by a very large valley, so that half of the mountain will move toward the north and the other half toward the south. And you will flee by the valley of

My mountains, for the valley of the mountains will reach to Azel; yes, you will flee just as you fled before the earthquake in the days of Uzziah king of Judah. Then the LORD, my God, will come, *and* all the holy ones with Him!" (Zech. 14:3-5 NASB).

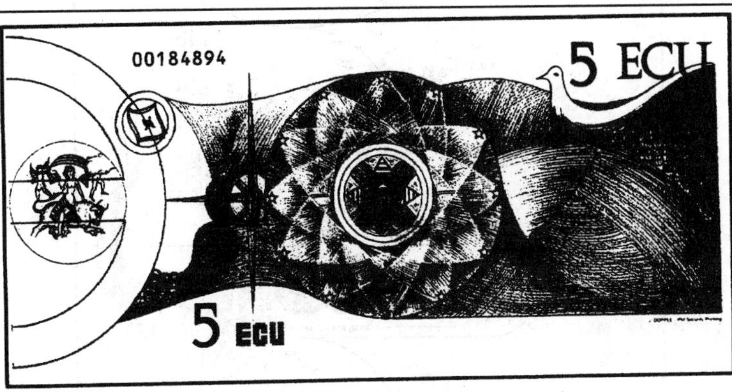

The New European Currency Unit

Enlargement of Symbol of Woman and Beast

The New European Currency Unit, issued on January 1, 1993, includes the symbol of a woman riding a two-horned beast. This is an ancient mythological symbol for the god, Europa. In his Apocalypse, John saw a two-horned beast, as well as a woman riding a scarlet-colored beast.[15]

[15]Photos courtesy of Grant R. Jeffrey, from his book, *Apocalypse, The Coming Judgement of the Nations.*

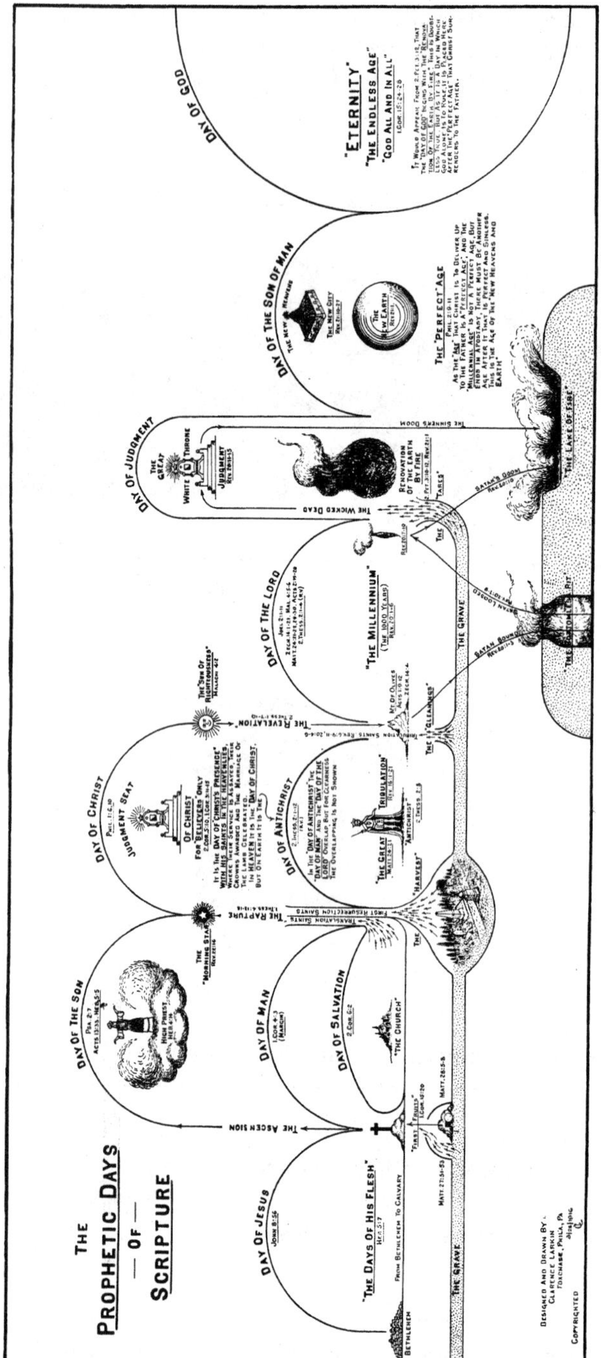
THE PROPHETIC DAYS OF SCRIPTURE
DAY OF JESUS
"THE DAYS OF HIS FLESH"
THE ASCENSION
DAY OF THE SON
DAY OF MAN
DAY OF SALVATION
"THE CHURCH"
THE RAPTURE
DAY OF CHRIST
JUDGMENT SEAT
DAY OF ANTICHRIST
"THE GREAT TRIBULATION"
THE REVELATION
DAY OF THE LORD
"THE MILLENNIUM"
DAY OF JUDGMENT
THE GREAT WHITE THRONE
THE WICKED DEAD
DAY OF THE SON OF MAN
THE NEW CITY
THE NEW EARTH
THE "PERFECT AGE"
DAY OF GOD
"ETERNITY"
"THE ENDLESS AGE"
"GOD ALL AND IN ALL"
THE GRAVE
"THE LAKE OF FIRE"
DESIGNED AND DRAWN BY CLARENCE LARKIN FOXCHASE, PHILA, PA
COPYRIGHTED

"This king will make a seven-year treaty with the people, but after half that time, he will break his pledge and stop the Jews from all their sacrifices and their offerings; then, as a climax to all his terrible deeds, the Enemy shall utterly defile the sanctuary of God. But in God's time and plan, his judgment will be poured out upon this Evil One."

Daniel the prophet, 9:27 *The Living Bible*, 538 BC

"...this gospel of the kingdom shall be preached in all the world for a witness unto all nations; and then shall the end come. When ye therefore shall see the abomination of desolation, spoken of by **Daniel the prophet,** stand in the holy place, (whoso readeth, let him understand:) Then let them which be in Judæa flee into the mountains...."

Jesus' warning of Antichrist in the New Testament, Matthew 24:14-16 KJV, 33 AD

"...it is also our duty to search with all diligence into these Prophesies. And if God was so angry with ye [the] Jews for not searching more diligently into the Prophesies wch [which] he had given them to know Christ by: why should we think he will excuse us for not searching into ye Prophesies wch he hath given us to know Antichrist by?....& therefore he may easily seduce thee if thou beest not well prepared to discern him. But if he should not be yet come into ye world yet amidst so many religions of wch there can be but one true [faith] & perhaps none of those [religions] that thou art acquainted with it is great odds but thou mayst be deceived & therefore it concerns thee to be very circumspect."[1]

Sir Isaac Newton,1642-1727

"...I believe the end of the age is very near. Why?....there is a growing tendency within Christendom to make room for the rise of the Antichrist."[2] Israeli Professor Flusser

"Into a world prepared to receive him, the Messiah will then be born. He will be a mortal human being, born normally of human parents....Now, imagine a charismatic leader greater than any other in man's history. Imagine a political genius surpassing all others. With the vast communication networks now at our disposal, he could spread his message to the entire world and change the very fabric of our society....One possible scenario could involve the Middle East situation. This is a problem that involves all the world powers. Now imagine a Jew, a Tzadik, solving this thorny problem....such a demonstration of statesmanship and political genius would place him in a position of world leadership. The major powers would listen to such an individual....Thus, the Rambam (Maimonides) writes, 'If he is further successful in rebuilding the Temple on its original site and gathering the dispersed of Israel, then his identity as the Messiah is a certainty'....these accomplishments are a minimum for our acceptance of an individual as the Messiah."[3]

Rabbi Kaplan, *The Real Messiah,* 1976,
his modern anti-Christian rabbinical opinion, if heeded, may set the stage for world Jewry to be deceived into believing that the Antichrist is the "real Messiah."

23

THE FALSE MESSIAH
ARMILUS EQUALS ANTICHRIST

For those of you who do not take the Antichrist seriously—for those of you who take the Bible lightly or with "a grain of salt"—for

---

[1] *Yahuda Manuscript 1.* [ ] mine.

[2] Arthur W. Kac, *The Messiahship of Jesus,* p. 41.

[3] This is a quote from a modern anti-missionary rabbinical polemic, designed to disprove

those of you who are "scientifically-minded"—let me present Sir Isaac Newton and what he had to say about the Antichrist. As you may remember from our chapter 18, "Israel—Is Real," Sir Isaac Newton predicted that the "Jews will return to Jerusalem in the twentieth century." Newton was right on the money with his law of gravitation, he was right on the return to Zion and he is right on the Antichrist.

ARMILUS IS ANTICHRIST—THREE QUESTIONS WHICH COULD COST YOU YOUR SANITY

1. Armi-what? 2. Who, what, where and when is Armilus? 3. Does anyone know? The Armilus is virtually unknown to the vast majority of people, even those who are Jewish and consider themselves religious! A handful of Bible scholars have looked up the word in various encyclopedias and then take the person for which it stands about as seriously as do the encyclopedias. If you do not believe this, just ask a rabbi, or any person who professes to have a knowledge or interest in the Jewish religion, about Armilus ("the Jewish Antichrist" or "the last evil king against Israel and the Messiah"). I am willing to bet that they either look completely bewildered, or look at you like you should be put in an asylum!

LET US ENLIGHTEN OURSELVES AND FIND OUT WHO "ARMILUS" REALLY IS, OR SHOULD WE SAY, "WILL BE"

Many believe the Antichrist is a Christian concept, having nothing to do with Judaism. This is not true! The ancient rabbis wrote about him under the name of Armilus. In this chapter we will quote rabbinical commentaries (such as certain Midrashim, Targums and selected writings of Bar Yohai) to illustrate this point.

In *The Jewish Encyclopedia*, it is admitted that a "Jewish Antichrist,"[4] called Armilus in ancient Jewish legend/tradition, will come to wreak havoc on the Jews of Jerusalem just prior to the Messiah coming to destroy him and save them. *The Jewish Encyclopedia* says: "ARMILUS: In later Jewish eschatology and legend, a king who will arise at the end of time against the Messiah,

---

the Messiahship of Jesus. Aryeh Kaplan, *et al*, *The Real Messiah*, pp. 69-71. Our annotation of their statement is our opinion. Rabbi Rafael Eisenberg, in his book, *A Matter of Return*, makes the same deadly conclusion as does the NCSY publication on how to establish a foolproof credential for the Jews to recognize an individual as Messiah or not, when he quotes Rambam: "If he will have succeeded in...building the Temple on its proper site, and gathering the exiled of Yisrael, then he will surely be the Messiah." Rafael Eisenberg, *A Matter of Return*, p. 149.

[4]The Jewish scholar, Pinchas Lapide, documents this in his book, *Israelis, Jews and Jesus*, as we will quote later in this chapter.

and will be conquered by him after having brought much distress upon Israel. The origin of this Jewish Antichrist (as he can well be styled in view of his relation to the Messiah) is as much involved in doubt as the different phases of his development, and his relation to the Christian legend....[Rabbi] Saadia (born 892; died 942)...speaks of Armilus. He mentions the following as a tradition of the ancients....If the Jews do not prove themselves worthy of Messianic salvation, God will force them to repentance by terrible persecutions. In consequence of these persecutions, a scion of the tribe of Joseph [known as Messiah ben Joseph] will arise and wrest Jerusalem from the hands of the Edomites....Thereupon the king, Armilus, will conquer and sack the Holy City....then begin a general campaign against the Jews, forcing them to flee into the desert [Petra],[5] where they will suffer untold misery. When they have been purified by sorrow and pain, the Messiah will appear, wrest Jerusalem from Armilus, slay him, and thereby bring the true salvation....This creature, Armilus by name—the Gentiles called him Antichrist, says the 'Otot'—will set himself up as Messiah, even as God Himself, being recognized as such by the sons of Esau....Armilus, inflamed against the Jews, will march against the Messiah. But now God Himself will war against Armilus and his army and destroy them; or the Messiah, as one version has it, will slay Armilus by the breath of his mouth (Jellinek, 'B.H.' ii. 51, line 3...[the encyclopedia goes on to instruct its readers] compare II Thess. ii. 8) [of the New Testament]."[6]

THE U.J.E.'S ANTI-MESSIAH SECTION REVEALS ADDITIONAL DETAILS

Incredibly enough, *The Universal Jewish Encyclopedia* admits, in so many words, that Armilus is the Antichrist. In this encyclopedia, under another heading near Antichrist and Armilus, there is a section called "Anti-Messiah." This encyclopedia reads: "ANTI-MESSIAH, legendary opponent of the Messiah and leader of the heathen forces in the battle against the latter which will take place at the end of time. Such a figure, under the name of Armilus, becomes a definite part of Jewish eschatology....[who] will overcome and destroy the Messiah of the house of Joseph and rule over the entire world, but will ultimately be defeated and slain by the Messiah of the line of David. In *Pesikta Rabbathi* (edit. Friedmann, p. 161b) the Anti-Messiah is apparently

[5]See our *Vol. II*, chapter 38, "They Escaped to Petra," which deals with Petra's role of protecting the Jews from the Antichrist just prior to the return of Jesus, illustrated with my own recent personal photos.

[6]Isidore Singer, Ph.D., *et al*, *The Jewish Encyclopedia,* Vol. II. [ ] mine.

identified with Satan and the Angel of Death....According to Bousset and Moritz Friedlaender, the idea of an Anti-Messiah goes back to...Ezekiel's prophecy of Gog, the prince of Magog, who was to attack Israel and to be miraculously overcome (*Ezek.* 38 and 39). The pseudepigraphic writings describe him as a powerful tyrant, with the characteristic traits of Antiochus Epiphanes, Herod the Great, Caligula or Nero, or else as a false prophet, who established his power by means of deceptive signs and miracles (*Ascension of Moses* 8; *IV Esdras* 13:33 et seq.; *Sibylline Oracles* 3:46-92)."[7]

THE U.J.E.'S ARMILUS SECTION INDICATES THAT ANCIENT RABBIS KNEW HIS (ARMILUS/ANTICHRIST FUTURE) WARS WOULD LEAD TO THE FINAL—"GOG"!

This encyclopedia continues along these lines in its section on Armilus, where it reads: "ARMILUS, representative of Roman power and arch-enemy of the Jews, who will rise at the end of time against the Messiah and will be vanquished by him only after he has brought much distress upon Israel....The name of this last king is debated by the rabbis. Saadia (882-942), in his *Emunoth Vedeoth* (8:6), speaks of an Armilus, king of Edom (Rome), who will arise and defeat the Messiah ben Joseph....but will in turn be defeated by the Messiah ben David. This is the opinion also of Hai Gaon (d. 1038), who states that the wars with Armilus will precede the final struggle with the hosts of Gog."[8]

THE *E.J.J.* SECTIONS ON "ANTICHRIST" AND "ARMILUS" REVEAL ANCIENT JEWISH ORIGINS AND WRITINGS ABOUT HOW THE WORLD WILL END—FIGHTING OVER JERUSALEM

The *Encyclopaedia Judaica Jerusalem* contains two headings, Antichrist and Armilus, both deserving of our interest. This encyclopedia reads: "ANTICHRIST, Gr. 'Αντιχριστος,' a term first occurring in the Johannine epistles in the New Testament (I John 2:18; 22:4:3; II John 7). It refers to an eschatological figure, the opponent of God, the pseudo-messiah who will be revealed at the end of days as the great enemy of Jesus. According to II Thessalonians 2:2-4 the second coming will be preceded by apostasy, and the 'man of lawlessness' will be revealed, the 'son of perdition' so evil that 'he

---

[7] *The Universal Jewish Encyclopedia*, Vol. I. New York: Universal Jewish Encyclopedia Co., © 1948, p. 337, used by permission. [ ] mine.
[8] Ibid, p. 483.

shall sit in the Temple of God, showing himself to be God.' Perhaps this figure too is to be identified with Antichrist, and he is destroyed by 'the breath of the Messiah's mouth' (cf. Isa. 11:4, Targ. *ibid.*, and many other places in Jewish writings).

The background to this figure lies in Jewish eschatology, where the ideas of the wicked king of the last generation and of the rise of evil to the highest point preceding salvation are found at an early period (cf. Ezek. 28:2; Dan. 7:24-25; 11:36; cf. 9:27). Another form of the same idea can be found in the eschatological battle in which the forces of evil and their leader are finally to be overcome (QM xviii:1; 1 QS iv:18-19, Test. Patr., Levi 3:3, et al.)....One particular form, basing itself on Jewish traditions (see Test. Patr., Dan. 5:6), makes the Antichrist a Jewish pseudo-messiah of the tribe of Dan....The idea of the rise of evil to its height before the coming of salvation, the embodiment of this evil in the eschatological king (cf. Test. Patr., Dan. 11:36, 37, Ass. Mos. 8), the overweening pride and blasphemy of the figure (Test. Patr., Dan. 7:11, 20, II Thess. 2:2-4, etc.), all these are old Jewish motifs."[9]

THE *E.J.J.* "ARMILUS" SECTION ADMITS THIS ONE, WHO WILL FIGHT OVER JERUSALEM, IS THE GENTILE ANTICHRIST

Concerning Armilus, the *Encyclopaedia Judaica Jerusalem* says of this wicked creature: "ARMILUS, legendary name of the Messiah's antagonist or anti-Messiah. Armilus appears frequently in the later Apocalyptic Midrashim, such as *Midrash Va-Yosha, Sefer Zerubbavel, and Nistarot shel R. Shimon b. Yohai.* He is also mentioned in the Targum pseudo-Jonathan, Isa. 11:4 and in the Targum Yerushalmi A (Deut. 34:3). Armilus is...mentioned otherwise in Saadiah Gaon's *Emunot ve-De'ot* (*Ma'amar* 8)....the talmudic legend of Messiah the son of Joseph, who would be slain in the war between the nations prior to the redemption that would come through Messiah the son of David (Suk. 52a). In *Otot ha-Mashi'ah* (*Midreshei Ge'ullah*, p. 320), there is reference to 'the Satan Armilus whom the Gentiles call Antichrist'....This Armilus will deceive the whole world into believing that he is God and will reign over the entire world. He will come with ten kings and together they will fight over Jerusalem."[10]

***

[9] *Encyclopaedia Judaica Jerusalem,* Vol. III.
[10] Ibid.

THE N.E.B. ADMITS THAT SOME JEWISH SOURCES SAY THAT ARMILUS IS THE SON OF SATAN

The New Encyclopædia Britannica tells us: "Armilus, in Jewish legends, an enemy who will conquer Jerusalem and persecute Jews until his final defeat at the hands of God or the true Messiah. His inevitable destruction symbolizes the ultimate victory of good over evil in the messianic era. Some sources depict Armilus as...the frightful offspring of Satan...."[11]

THE MODERN JEWISH SCHOLAR, PINCHAS LAPIDE, ENLIGHTENS US REGARDING THE SAGE SAADIA AND ARMILUS

The Jewish scholar, Pinchas Lapide, writes of the famed ancient Rabbi Saadia Gaon of the tenth century and his warning regarding Armilus! Lapide says: "Saadia describes—he is the first writer to do so—the Jewish eschatological legend of...Armilos, who has been called, not altogether inaccurately, 'the Jewish antichrist.' In the fourth chapter of his major work, *The Book of Beliefs and Opinions*, we read, '[Our fathers] have also handed down to us...that a man will appear in Galilee from among the sons of Joseph, and men of the Jewish nation will gather around him....This man will go up to Jerusalem....There he will be surprised by a man named Armilos, who will wage war on him and take the city, whereafter he will murder its inhabitants, dishonor them, and take them prisoners....' "[12]

Lapide goes on to reveal that fragments of the Midrash (ancient rabbinical commentary), which speaks of the Armilus, can be traced to the second century.[13] It is common knowledge that most Midrashim, before committed to writing, were oral traditions handed down for hundreds of years. This illustrates that ancient Judaism[14] expected the Antichrist before Jesus walked the earth. This is something liberal

---

[11]*The New Encyclopædia Britannica*. Chicago: Encyclopædia Britannica, Inc., © 1974.

[12]Pinchas Lapide, *Israelis, Jews, and Jesus*, p. 86. The spelling of "Armilos" is Lapide's English translators.

[13]Ibid, p. 86.

[14]The world-renowned Jewish scholar and professor, Dr. David Flusser, confirms: "The idea of Antichrist is surely Jewish and pre-Christian....the Antichrist is a human exponent of the Satanic forces of evil." Dr. David Flusser, *Judaism and the Origins of Christianity*, p. 210 (from his section "The Hubris of the Antichrist in a fragment from Qumran"). As further proof of his claim, he cites on pp. 621-622 of *Geschichte des jüdischen Volkes II*, by Emil Schürer and pp. 281-282 of *Die Eschatologie der jüdischen Gemeinde*, by Paul Volz. He also cites pp. 95-103 of "Taxo or the Apocalyptic Doctrine of Vengeance," *Journal of Jewish Studies* 12 (1961) as evidence.

Bible "scholars" do not want to face. That the Antichrist is prophesied in Daniel, chapter 8 (553 BC), as Jesus Himself pointed out (Matt. 24:15), is unthinkable! Most liberals like to imagine the Antichrist to be a late or comparatively modern superstitious fantasy.[15]

A MODERN LIBERAL TRIES TO DISPROVE OUR PROPHETICAL FUNDAMENTAL BIBLICAL VIEW OF THE ANTICHRIST, IN VAIN

One such modern liberal who attempts to refute the Bible's predicted Antichrist is Gary DeMar of the Christian Reform Movement. This arrogant individual, in his book *Last Days Madness,* attempts to discredit nearly all of the reputable dispensational authors on biblical prophecy. In respect, or I should say disrespect, to the Bible's teachings on the Antichrist, DeMar has said: "Modern advocates of the Armageddon doctrine have combined these and other Megiddo battles into one great future 'Great Tribulation' conflict where the 'Antichrist' will bring all the nations of the world into a final war against Israel....Revelation is describing a past battle between first-century Rome and Israel: 'The notion that Armageddon refers to some great cataclysm of the world's affairs in the future is hardly warranted.' "[16]

DeMar may truly believe that the idea of the Antichrist leading the last war on Israel is a modern concept, thus disproving the Antichrist's role in future events, as he also said: "...the modern doctrine of the Antichrist is an amalgamation of biblical concepts and events that are either unrelated or find their fulfillment in past events....Modern Antichrist hunters are pursuing a figure who does not exist."[17]

As you have just read, *The Jewish Encyclopedia* documents a very early belief in the Antichrist coming against Israel in the last days, except it calls him by the name Armilus. D. S. Russell tells us: "Although the expression 'Antichrist' first appears in Christian writings the idea is to be found in earlier Jewish apocalyptic works. M. R. James, basing his findings on Bousset's studies on the subject, states that in his opinion 'there was among the Jews a fully developed legend of Antichrist....' "[18]

---

[15]Legends and fairytales which grow up around every prominent person, per se, can also be found in some literature about the Armilus. However, this does not make the truth about him, which agrees with the Scriptures, any less valid.
[16]Gary DeMar, *Last Days Madness*, p. 167.
[17]Ibid, p. 145.
[18]D.S. Russell, *The Method and Message of Jewish Apocalyptic, 200 BC - AD 100*, p. 191.

Doesn't the old saying, "Don't knock it till you've tried it" have a familiar ring here? DeMar and liberal theologians the world over would do well to read all of the ancient Jewish and Christian literature before claiming ancient doctrines to be modern. Then he would know better.

GAON ON GAON, REGARDING THE *THEN* FUTURE JEWISH REGATHERING TO ISRAEL AND THE *REASON* FOR THEIR PERSECUTION THEREAFTER

The famous rabbi and scholar, Saadia Gaon, who died over 1000 years ago, spoke about the ancient traditional rabbinical warnings by the Jewish forefathers concerning Armilus. The Gaon (a Hebrew title meaning "genius") wrote: "Hence, if after our having lingered in exile for a long time without returning to God, God would bring us back to our land even though we should not have improved, [might one not ask whether] our exile has [not] been in vain?

However, it has been transmitted by the traditions of the prophets that God would cause misfortunes and disasters to befall us that would compel us to resolve upon repentance so that we would be deserving of redemption. That is the sense of the remark of our forebears: *If the Israelites will repent, they will be redeemed. If not, the Holy One, Blessed Be He, will raise up a king whose decrees will be even more severe than those of Haman, whereupon they will repent and thus be redeemed* (Sanh. 97b.)

<239> [Our forebears] also tell us that the cause of this [visitation]....they will be surprised by a man named Armilus, who will wage war against them and conquer the city and subject its inhabitants to massacre, captivity, and disgrace."[19]

DR. PATAI IS AMAZED THAT THE MIDRASH EQUATES THE ANTICHRIST WITH ARMILUS

The Jewish Bible scholar, Dr. Raphael Patai, notes regarding the Midrash Otot haMashiah (an ancient Jewish Bible commentary on the signs of the Messiah), which compares Armilus to Antichrist: "It is remarkable that, in speaking of Armilus, this Midrash identifies him with Satan on the one hand, and with the 'Antichrist' of the nations of the world, on the other....[The Midrash reads] and his name is Armilus the Satan. This is the one whom the nations of the world call Antichrist."[20]

---

[19]Samuel Rosenblatt, *Saadia Gaon, The Book of Beliefs and Opinions*. New Haven: Yale University Press, © 1948, p. 301, used by permission.
[20]Raphael Patai, *The Messiah Texts*, pp. 310-314. [ ] mine.

Patai also illustrates his amazement that these beliefs (now virtually unknown) were once common knowledge among Jews. He writes: "...Sa'adya Gaon (882-942), the great Jewish philosopher, scholar, and head of the academy of Sura in Babylonia. The fact that a scholar of his stature unquestioningly accepts all...about the Messiah indicates that these beliefs were a heritage common to the simple folk and the most learned in medieval Jewry."[21]

COLUMBUS' INTEREST IN THE ANTICHRIST ILLUSTRATED AS HE QUOTES D'AILLY

In *Christopher Columbus's Book of Prophecies,* it is noted: "The Calabrian abbot Joachim [of Fiore] said that the man who was to rebuild the Temple on Mount Zion would come out of Spain....Peter d'Ailly wrote a great deal about the end of the Mohammedan sect and the coming of the Antichrist in his treatise, *De concordia astronomie, veritatis & narrationis historice....*The philosopher Ethicus says in his cosmography that the people who were confined within the Caspian Gates will burst forth into the world and will go out to meet the Antichrist and will call him...the God of gods....I know that if the Church should wish to consult the sacred text and the sacred prophecies...greater certitude would be found concerning the time of the Antichrist."[22]

Columbus included excerpts from D'Ailly's book, *On Law and Sects,* in his *Book of Prophecies* (*Libro de las Profecias*), thus attesting to his interest in the Antichrist and the Messiah Jesus, who is to follow the Antichrist in His triumphant return. Amazing events, which are soon to occur, occupied Columbus over five hundred years ago. Interesting, wouldn't you say?

HITLER FORESAW AN ANTICHRIST LIKE HIMSELF APPEARING APPROXIMATELY ONE HUNDRED YEARS AFTER HIS DEATH

Hitler is reported by a reputable source to have said in his bunker: "In a hundred years time, perhaps a great man will appear who may offer them a chance of salvation. He will take me as his model, use my ideas and follow the course I have charted."[23]

---

[21]Ibid, p. 310.

[22]Kay Brigham, *Christopher Columbus's Book of Prophecies*, pp. 183-219.

[23]John Heyman, Ennio De Concini, Paramount Pictures, *Hitler: The Last Ten Days*. World Film Services, Ltd., © 1973, used by permission.

The movie *Hitler: The Last Ten Days*, from which these words are taken, was dictated from first-hand testimony. These words are certified as true by the eyewitness, Rittmeister Gerhard Boldt, who was in the bunker with Hitler. The Bible says that the Antichrist will persecute Jews and Christians to an extent never before witnessed.

If Hitler was truly demon-possessed, we speculate that he may have foreseen Satan's plans and their schedule in the future. We cannot help but notice that these words stand out in light of the prophecies of the Antichrist. Hitler's estimated one hundred years would end somewhere in the 2030's or 2040's, and would line up with the biblical calculation for the generation of the Messiah's arrival to stop the Antichrist and Armageddon, which we have detailed in chapter 27, "Speculating on Messiah's *Second* Coming—Whether They Know It or Not."

WILL JEWS AND OTHERS BE DECEIVED BY THE ARMILUS/ANTICHRIST BECAUSE THEY HAVE NOT READ THEIR ANCIENT WRITINGS AND THE NEW TESTAMENT?

In truth, all branches of modern Judaism: Orthodox, Conservative, Reformed, Lubavitch and Hasidic, do not take the Armilus seriously! In fact, most are not even aware that he exists[24] in the writings of the ancient Jewish sages, or that he is one and the same with the Antichrist of the New Testament, about whom Jesus warned. This ignorance is very dangerous because it leaves the Jewish person who is unfamiliar with the New Testament, and for that matter, the Old Testament predictions of the Antichrist, open to be deceived by Armilus into thinking that he is the Messiah. This, as predicted by Daniel,[25] would set up the Jewish people for political and spiritual sabotage in the mid-twenty-first century.

Shortly, we will present what the ancient rabbinical commentaries, and more importantly, what the Old and New Testaments have to say about Antichrist. But first, let us take a look at how history is setting the stage for his arrival and acceptance by millions of innocent, unsuspecting people.

***

[24]With the exception of Messianic Judaism, or Jews who accept Jesus as Messiah, who are acquainted with a knowledge of the Antichrist from the New Testament and teachings of Jesus.

[25]The future coming one, who will pretend to be Israel's Messiah, will be, as predicted by Daniel, a religious and political leader.

WHO CAN MAKE WAR WITH THE COMING CAESAR? ONLY JESUS

The Antichrist, or rather the false Messiah, will not be the first mere man in history to have terrifying control and be worshipped as God! William Barclay, in his book, *The Revelation of John*, documented: "The first temple to be erected to the godhead of the emperor was built in Pergamum in 29 B.C. Caesar worship had begun."[26]

The worship of Caesar began before the birth of Christ! The historian, Arnold Toynbee, commented during a radio broadcast: "...technology has brought mankind to such a degree of distress that we are ripe for the deifying of any new Caesar who might succeed in giving the world unity and peace."[27]

This coming false Messiah will be like the Caesars in many respects. The people who lived in the days of the Roman Caesars often said, "Who can make war with Caesar?" The New Testament says of the future Antichrist: "...they worshipped the beast,[28] saying, 'Who is like the beast, and who is able to wage war with him?' " (Rev. 13:4 NASB).

Near the end of the seven-year Tribulation period, when the beast and his helper, the false prophet, attempt to use nuclear force to exterminate man from the planet, the prophet Isaiah and apostle Paul foretell[29] that Jesus the Messiah returns to stop him! Only Jesus will be able to defeat this Satanic personality in his attempt at a future showdown with God Almighty!

***

---

[26]Hal Lindsey with C.C. Carlson, *The Late Great Planet Earth*, p. 100.

[27]Ibid, p. 103.

[28]John the apostle's synonym for the Antichrist.

[29]Isaiah prophesied: "But with righteousness He will judge the poor, And decide with fairness for the afflicted of the earth; And He will strike the earth with the rod of His mouth, And with the breath of His lips He will slay the wicked" (Isa. 11:4 NASB). Paul predicts: "And then that lawless one will be revealed whom the Lord will slay with the breath of His mouth and bring to an end by the appearance of His coming...." (II Thes. 2:8 NASB). The Jewish interpretative Targum Jonathan to Isaiah 11:4 also says: "But he shall judge the poor in truth, and shall reprove in faithfulness for the needy of the people. He shall smite the guilty of the land with the words of his mouth, and with the speech of his lips he shall slay Armilus the wicked." Samson H. Levey, *The Messiah: An Aramaic Interpretation, The Messianic Exegesis of the Targum*, p. 49. Levey's footnote to Armilus interestingly admits: "Armilus...is found in the late apocalypses and is a Messianic legend mentioned by Saadia Gaon, representing the anti-Messiah." Ibid, p. 154.

THE MODERN, SOON-TO-COME, CAESAR/BEAST WILL BE LIKE A LEOPARD, BEAR AND LION, ALL IN ONE

The New Testament (Rev. 13:2) describes the Antichrist as being like a "leopard," "bear" and "lion." The key to understanding this animal puzzle can be found in the Old Testament book of Daniel. Daniel describes these animals as the monstrous Gentile empires which will rule the world (see our chapter 22, "Rome Resurrected," for more details and information).

In Daniel 8 we see that the lion beast was Babylon. The second beast, "like a bear," was Media Persia. The third beast, the leopard, was Greece. Daniel predicted a fourth beast and its leader (Antichrist) in his seventh chapter, verses 23-24. He wrote that the fourth beast (Rome) would "devour the whole earth." This did occur, as we know from the history of the Roman Empire.

Verse 24 of Daniel identifies a new revived Rome consisting of ten nations, which we previously discussed in chapter 22. This new Roman-like one-world government is still in the future.

If we take a look at Revelation 13, it is not hard to guess who the ten horns of the Antichrist represent. Obviously, they are the ten kings of Daniel, which the Antichrist will use as a power base from which to rule the world for a short time.

SATAN OFFERS JESUS THE CROWN FIRST BEFORE GOD'S CROSS

In the Gospel of Luke, Satan offered Jesus the temptation of becoming *world ruler*: "And he [Satan] led Him up and showed Him all the kingdoms of the world in a moment of time. And the devil said to Him, 'I will give You all this domain and its glory; for it has been handed over to me, and I give it to whomever I wish. Therefore if You worship before me, **it** shall all be Yours' " (Luke 4:5-7 NASB; [ ] and bold mine).

Jesus, at that time, refused this offer. Why? Remember Satan's words: " '...it [the title deed to world dominion] has been handed over to me,[30] and I give it to whomever I wish.' "

Adam, the first man, was given world dominion (ownership of the earth) in Genesis, chapters 2 and 3. Adam forfeited this title deed when he gave in to Satan's deception in the third chapter of Genesis. The rulership of the earth can only be taken back from Satan by someone who will redeem the earth.

---

30 See the biblical verses Ephesians 2:2, John 12:31, and I John 5:19.

Redemption (*Ligol,* לגאל in Hebrew) means to "buy back." If someone gives you something, they can take it back; however, if you redeem it, they cannot. This was the crux of Satan's offer to Jesus. The New Testament tells us Jesus redeemed the world spiritually when He said "Paid in Full" (*Tetelastai*)[31] on the cross. However, the world will not be physically redeemed until Israel receives and honors Him as their Messiah (Zech. 12-14; Acts 3:21; Matt. 19:28). When Jesus returns in His Second Coming, He will *physically* take back world dominion, legally!

WHEN THE JEWS FINALLY BELIEVE IN THE REAL MESSIAH, IT WILL BE LIKE "DEAD PEOPLE COMING BACK TO LIFE"

The New Testament details this as follows: "For all creation is waiting patiently and hopefully for that future day when God will resurrect his children....For we know that even the things of nature, like animals and plants, suffer in sickness and death as they await this great event. And even we Christians, although we have the Holy Spirit within us as a foretaste of future glory, also groan to be released from pain and suffering. We, too, wait anxiously for that day when God will give us our full rights as his children, including the new bodies he has promised us—bodies that will never be sick again and will never die....Does this mean that God has rejected his Jewish people forever? Of course not! His purpose was to make his salvation available to the Gentiles, and then the Jews would be jealous and begin to want God's salvation for themselves. Now if the whole world became rich as a result of God's offer of salvation, when the Jews stumbled over it and turned it down, think how much greater a blessing the world will share in later on when the Jews, too, come to Christ....And how wonderful it will be when they become Christians [Messianic believers in their Messiah]![32] When God turned away from them it meant that he turned to the rest of the world to offer his salvation; and now it is even

---

[31]This Greek word from the Greek translation of the New Testament (the Gospels were originally written in Hebrew. See our appendix 1, "It's All *Hebrew* to Me") is translated literally in English as "paid in full." However, most English versions of the Bible render it as "it is finished."

[32]*The Living Bible* beautifully simplifies the more difficult renderings of certain English translations of the New Testament. However, when it says Christians, it may confuse some Jews who do not realize that the word Christian does not designate a religion foreign to Judaism. This word is derived from the Greek *Christos*, which means "Messiah" (*Meshiak* in Hebrew), which the Jewish Bible (our Old Testament) predicts of our true faith. *Ian* simply means "one who follows Christ," i.e., Messiah!

more wonderful when the Jews come to Christ. It will be like dead people coming back to life. And since Abraham and the prophets are God's people, their children will be too. For if the roots of the tree are holy, the branches will be too....I want you to know about this truth from God, dear brothers, so that you will not feel proud and start bragging. Yes, it is true that some of the Jews have set themselves against the Gospel now, but this will last only until all of you Gentiles have come to Christ—those of you who will. And then all Israel will be saved. Do you remember what the prophets said about this? 'There shall come out of Zion a Deliverer....' " (Rom. 8:19-23; 11:11-12, 15-16, 25-26 *The Living Bible*; [ ] mine).

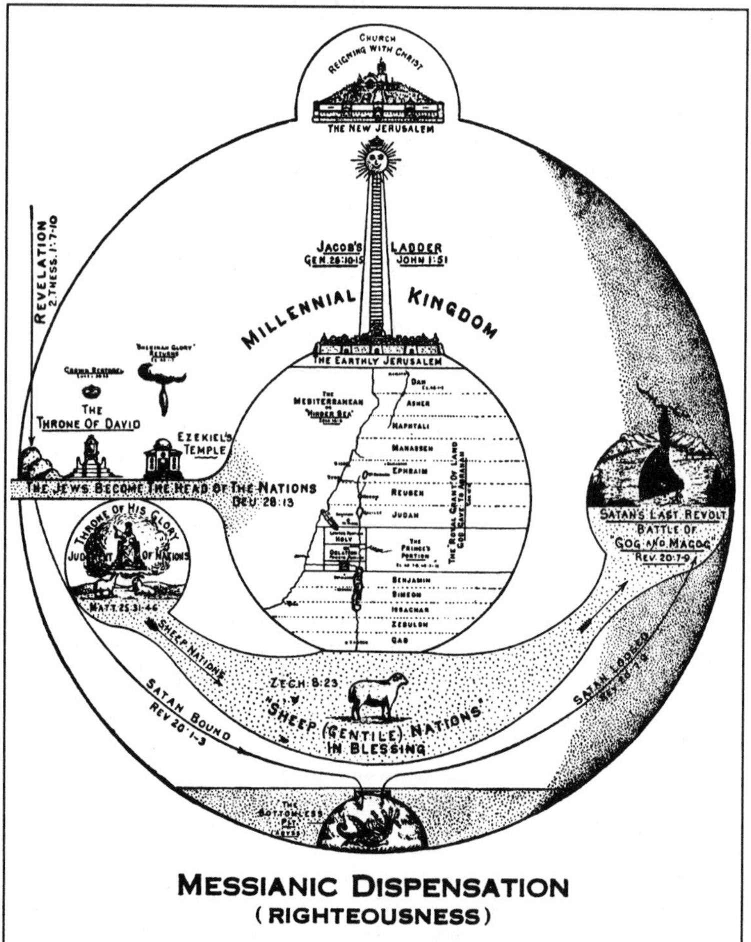

Reverend Larkin illustrates the Messianic dispensation which will take place during the millenial kingdom of Messiah after Jesus returns.

ORIGINAL HEBREW TEXT WRITTEN 553 BC

וּבְאַחֲרִית֙ מַלְכוּתָ֔ם כְּהָתֵ֖ם הַפֹּשְׁעִ֑ים יַעֲמֹ֞ד מֶ֤לֶךְ עַז־פָּנִ֖ים וּמֵבִ֥ין חִידֽוֹת: וְעָצַ֤ם כֹּחוֹ֙ וְלֹ֣א

בְכֹח֔וֹ וְנִפְלָא֤וֹת יַשְׁחִית֙ וְהִצְלִ֣יחַ וְעָשָׂ֔ה וְהִשְׁחִ֥ית עֲצוּמִ֖ים וְעַם־קְדֹשִֽׁים: וְעַל־שִׂכְל֗וֹ וְהִצְלִ֤יחַ

מִרְמָה֙ בְּיָד֔וֹ וּבִלְבָב֖וֹ יַגְדִּ֑יל וּבְשַׁלְוָ֖ה יַשְׁחִ֣ית רַבִּ֑ים וְעַל־שַׂר־שָׂרִים֙ יַעֲמֹ֔ד וּבְאֶ֥פֶס יָ֖ד יִשָּׁבֵֽר:

וּמַרְאֵ֨ה הָעֶ֧רֶב וְהַבֹּ֛קֶר אֲשֶׁ֥ר נֶאֱמַ֖ר אֱמֶ֣ת ה֑וּא וְאַתָּה֙ סְתֹ֣ם הֶֽחָז֔וֹן כִּ֖י לְיָמִ֥ים רַבִּֽים:

דניאל ח:כג-כו

OLD TESTAMENT SCRIPTURE TRANSLATION

"And in the latter period of their rule, When the transgressors have run *their course,*
A king will arise Insolent and skilled in intrigue. And his power will be mighty, but
not by his *own* power, And he will destroy to an extraordinary degree And prosper
and perform *his will*; He will destroy mighty men and the holy people. And
through his shrewdness He will cause deceit to succeed by his influence; And he
will magnify *himself* in his heart, And he will destroy many while *they are* at ease.
He will even oppose the Prince of princes, But he will be broken without human
agency. And the vision of the evenings and mornings Which has been told is true;
But keep the vision secret, For *it* pertains to many days *in the future.*"

Daniel 8:23-26 NASB

ANCIENT RABBINICAL COMMENTARY

"...he will break the languages of all religions and laws, for he will say that there
will be one law and one religion, that of the Lord of Hosts. And he will slay the
warriors of the Children of Ishmael and the Children of the East, and also the
inhabitants of Tyre. And he will gather the gold and the silver into the city of
Jerusalem. Then his name will become great, and his heart will be lifted up....And
in his days will rise up a false Messiah, a speaker of lies and emptiness and deceit.
And his name will grow great and his heart become haughty, and many people will
go astray after him and will die."[33]

**Manuscript from Yemen in the Cambridge
University Library, no. 890, Add. 3381**

"And he will [further] say to them: 'I am your god, I am your Messiah and your
god!' In that hour he will send [a messenger] to...all Israel, and say to them: 'Bring
me your Tora and testify that I am god.' Instantly all Israel becomes confused and
frightened."[34]   **T'fillat R. Shim'on ben Yohai, BhM 4:124-26**

"He will capture the West. And many wicked men, lovers of war, will be in those
days, and they will gather around him from the whole earth, and will tell him that he
is the Messiah, and this rumor will spread all over the world. And the whole earth
will submit to him, and he will slay those who do not submit. There will be
suffering in the whole world....And the people will have to bear and suffer distress
and much trouble, and the Children of Israel more than all the others....And he [the
evil king] will become angry and will command that they be killed...."[35]

Ma'ase Daniel, pp. 222-25

---

[33]Raphael Patai, *The Messiah Texts,* p. 162. This manuscript refers to the false Messiah
prophet who will work hand-in-hand with the false Roman Messiah world ruler. See our
paragraph "Two for the Price of One, Though Believe Me, We Could Do Without the
One, Who Is Not Going To Be Very Fun," coming up, which distinguishes between the
two future Antichrist figures.

[34]Ibid, p. 158.
[35]Ibid, p. 163.

NEW TESTAMENT RECORDED 54 AD

"Let no one in any way deceive you, for *it will not come* unless the apostasy comes first, and the man of lawlessness is revealed, the son of destruction, who opposes and exalts himself above every so-called god or object of worship, so that he takes his seat in the temple of God, displaying himself as being God....*that is*, the one whose coming is in accord with the activity of Satan, with all power and signs and false wonders, and with all the deception of wickedness for those who perish, because they did not receive the love of the truth so as to be saved. And for this reason God will send upon them a deluding influence so that they might believe what is false, in order that they all may be judged who did not believe the truth...."

The second epistle of Paul to the Thessalonians,
II Thessalonians 2:3-4, 9-12 NASB

MODERN RABBINIC COMMENT/REFUTATION

None of the modern Jewish writing I examined seemed to know anything of an Armilus in relation to taking him seriously or attempting to dispute the Antichrist of II Thessalonians and the Messianic Jewish and evangelical New Testament teachings which we have outlined in this chapter. In 1983, Rabbi Shalom Lewis in Atlanta, Georgia told me: "There is no belief in Judaism of an Antichrist at all. Obviously, there is no belief in Christ so there is no belief in an Antichrist." All of the polemical books were silent on the subject of Armilus. However, we do not doubt that once this is read, someone will attempt to write a refutation of our work, thereby addressing him. **Philip Moore**

HISTORICAL/POLITICAL COMMENT

"By forcing on mankind more and more lethal weapons, and at the same time making the world more and more interdependent economically, technology has brought mankind to such a degree of distress that we are ripe for the deifying of any new Caesar who might succeed in giving the world unity and peace."[36]

Eminent historian, Arnold Toynbee

AUTHOR'S COMMENT—EVANGELICAL CHRISTIAN POSITION

The fact that contemporary rabbis are not even aware that the Armilus/Antichrist will soon be masquerading as the Jewish Messiah, tells us that the biblical predictions of his acceptance are accurate. The silence of the anti-Christian writers on this subject is all the more proof that millions will be fooled. Furthermore, when modern historians, who are not even aware of biblical prophecy, begin to link political events with a one-world ruler, which would leave us "ripe for the deifying of any new Caesar," any fool should be able to read the handwriting on the wall. We, who are not foolish, do! **Philip Moore**

THE ENIGMA OF HOW THE ANTICHRIST FOOLS THE JEWS IS IN HIS TIMING

The Antichrist will come before Jesus, but after the Rapture. As established by the Scriptures, seven years prior to Armaggedon, Jesus will come in a veiled form to rescue His people. During this event known as the Rapture, believers will be caught up in the air and removed from Earth. Their absence will give the Antichrist the opportunity to present himself as the true Messiah, a lie that will be exposed at the Second Coming.

---

[36]Hal Lindsey with C.C. Carlson, *The Late Great Planet Earth*, p. 103.

The New Testament adds: "...Jesus said unto them, 'Verily I say unto you, That ye which have followed me, in the regeneration when the Son of man shall sit in the throne of his glory, ye also shall sit upon twelve thrones, judging the twelve tribes of Israel' " (Matt. 19:28 KJV).

Before this occurs, Satan will bring in his masterpiece (the Antichrist) and attempt to rule the world through the physical incarnation of this creature,[37] before the world's Jews realize who their true Messiah is, was, and will be—Jesus.

ANTICHRIST'S RESURRECTION WILL BE IMPRESSIVE TO THE WORLD AND ESPECIALLY TO THE JEWS

The Antichrist, since he is Satan in human flesh,[38] will deceive the world through incredible miracles. Paul tells us of this in one of his letters to the Thessalonians: "*Even him*, whose coming is after the working of Satan with all power and signs and lying wonders...." (II Thes. 2:9 KJV).

The greatest of Satan's deceptive miracles, which he will use to fool the world into receiving the Antichrist as the Messiah, will be a counterfeit of the resurrection of Jesus! Revelation 13:3 speaks of this world leader receiving a fatal wound to his head, which is supernaturally healed. This is the way Satan will catapult himself onto the world's stage as the Messiah and Savior, and as the answer to the world's quest for peace, including the solution to the Middle East Crisis. He will accomplish this through a false miracle that will appear to be so great, all the world's people will sit up and take notice—a man resurrected from the dead.

HOW DOES THIS FALSE MESSIAH/ANTICHRIST COME ONTO THE SCENE IN OUR PRESENT WORLD

In order to give you a modern, updated and educated idea about how the Antichrist comes to power, we will quote Hal Lindsey, who is more than qualified on this issue. "The way in which this dictator is

---

[37]"And I saw one of his heads as it were wounded to death; and his deadly wound was healed: and all the world wondered after the beast" (Rev. 13:3 KJV). Once he is healed, the spirit of Satan will take over his body, giving him even more incredible intelligence and deceptive talent than that with which he was born!

[38]What an ironic tragedy for Jews, religious Jews who occupy their lives in an attempt to worship a true God, to be fooled into accepting Satan. Offer a helping hand to your Jewish friends. Give them this book and tell them to read this chapter, so that they may be aware of the Antichrist's lies, soon to be told in the twenty-first century.

going to step onto the stage of history will be dramatic. Overnight he will become the byword of the world. He is going to be distinguished as supernatural; this will be done by an act which will be a Satanic counterfeit of the resurrection. This writer does not believe it will be an actual resurrection, but it will be a situation in which this person has a mortal wound. Before he has actually lost life, however, he will be brought back from this critical wounded state. This is something which will cause tremendous amazement throughout the world.

We could draw a comparison to the tragic death of John F. Kennedy. Imagine what would have happened if the President of the United States, after being shot and declared dead, had come to life again! The impact of an event like that would shake the world.

It is not difficult to imagine what will happen when this coming world leader makes his miraculous recovery. This man, the Antichrist, will probably not be known as a great leader until the time of his revival from the fatal wound. After that the whole world will follow him.

He will have a magnetic personality, be personally attractive, and a powerful speaker. He will be able to mesmerize an audience with his oratory.

'Who is like the beast, and who is able to wage war with him?' These are the expressions the people who live at the time of the appearance of the Antichrist will be saying. They will accept anyone who offers peace, since this is the great cry of the world.

What does this indicate? We recall that the *Pax Romana*, the Roman peace, was the reason the provincials willingly turned to Rome and eventually initiated Caesar worship. Law and order—peace and security—freedom from war. The same needs, the same desires were expressed in ancient times that the Bible says will be prevalent before the Antichrist begins his rule. He will be swept in at a time when people are so tired of war, so anxious for peace at any price, that they willingly give their allegiance to the world dictator who will promise them peace."[39]

YOU NEED NOT WORRY, IF YOU BELIEVE IN JESUS! IF YOU DON'T, OH BOY! WE HOPE YOU REMEMBER WHAT ISAAC NEWTON SAID—BE CIRCUMSPECT

You may have read, in one of this chapter's opening quotes, the recommendation of the famed scientist Sir Isaac Newton, concerning the Antichrist: "...it is also our duty to search with all diligence into

[39]Hal Lindsey with C.C. Carlson, *The Late Great Planet Earth*, pp. 108-109.

these Prophesies. And if God was so angry with the Jews for not searching more diligently into the Prophesies which he had given them to know Christ by: why should we think he will excuse us for not searching into the Prophesies which he hath given us to know Antichrist by?....Antichrist was to seduce the whole Christian world and therefore he may easily seduce thee if thou beest not well prepared to discern him. But if he should not be yet come into the world yet amidst so many religions of which there can be but one true and perhaps none of those that thou art acquainted with it is great odds but thou mayst be deceived and therefore it concerns thee to be very circumspect."[40]

WHERE WILL WE BE?

In the New Testament, II Thessalonians 2:6-12 makes it very clear that people who have believed in Jesus before the Rapture will not be here during the terrible reign of the Antichrist. "And now ye know what withholdeth that he might be revealed in his time. For the mystery of iniquity doth already work: only he who now letteth *will let*, until he be taken out of the way. And then shall that Wicked be revealed...." (II Thes. 2:6-8 KJV).

We believe the restrainer is the Holy Spirit,[41] who takes up residence in all who put their faith in Jesus as Messiah. The Holy Spirit can never[42] be separated from the receptacles in which He dwells. Since the New Testament promises that the Antichrist cannot be revealed until the Spirit is removed (see our chapter 25, "The Rapture Factor"), we believe God will remove the Spirit by removing all the receptacles in which He dwells. That's us folks—all who believe in Jesus. We believe that during this time, known to us as the seven-year Tribulation (a period of persecution following the Rapture; Matt. 24:21; Jer. 30:7), we will be with Jesus celebrating the marriage supper of the Lamb (Rev. 19:9; I Thes. 4:13-18; I Cor. 15:51-57).

***

[40] *Yahuda Manuscript 1*. As rendered by Frank Manuel.

[41] The Holy Spirit, in Hebrew, is called *Rauch Ha Kodesh*. He is not exclusive to the New Testament, as many have falsely taught. The Old Testament speaks of the Spirit of God in Isaiah: "Come ye near unto me, hear ye this; I have not spoken in secret from the beginning; from the time that it was, there *am* I: and now the Lord GOD, and his Spirit, hath sent me" (Isa. 48:16 KJV).

[42] See our *Vol. II*, chapter 11, "Eternal Security for True Believers."

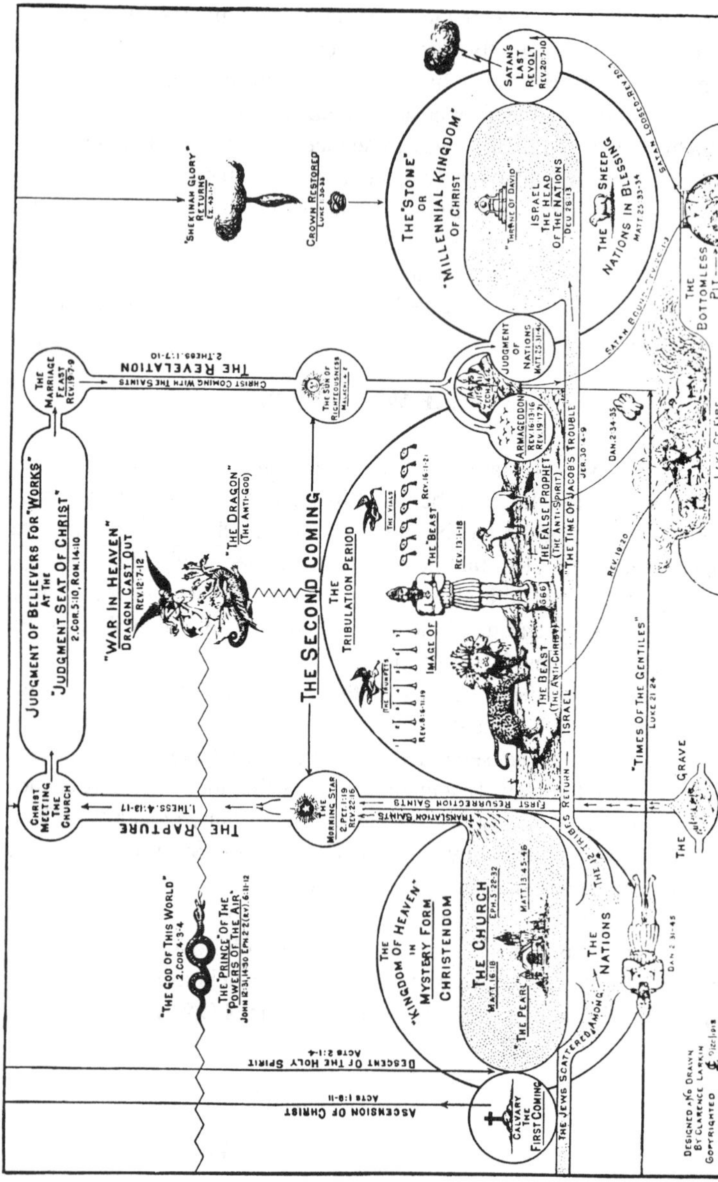

A chart drawn by Clarence Larkin illustrating the Tribulation period of the Antichrist reign, in relation to the Rapture of the church and the millenial kingdom of Jesus. At this time, Israel will be the head of the nations (Deut. 28:13), in their acceptance of Him as their Messiah. The following two charts are also courtesy of Clarence Larkin Estate.

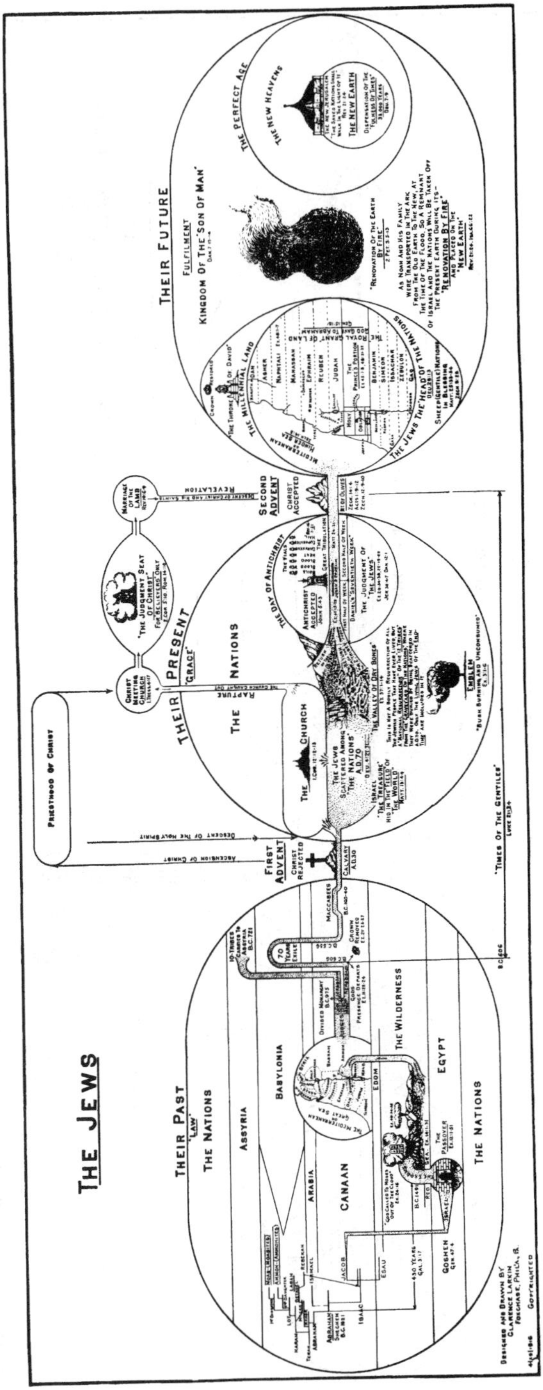
THE JEWS
THEIR PAST
"LAW"
THE NATIONS
ASSYRIA
BABYLONIA
ARABIA
CANAAN
EDOM
THE WILDERNESS
EGYPT
THE NATIONS
FIRST ADVENT
CHRIST REJECTED
CALVARY A.D.30
PRIESTHOOD OF CHRIST
ASCENSION OF CHRIST
DESCENT OF THE HOLY SPIRIT
THEIR PRESENT
"GRACE"
THE NATIONS
THE CHURCH
RAPTURE
"THE JUDGMENT SEAT OF CHRIST"
MARRIAGE OF THE LAMB
REVELATION
THE DAY OF ANTICHRIST
THE VALLEY OF DRY BONES
EMBLEM
SECOND ADVENT
CHRIST ACCEPTED
"TIMES OF THE GENTILES"
LUKE 21:24
THEIR FUTURE
FULFILMENT
KINGDOM OF THE "SON OF MAN"
THE MILLENNIAL LAND
THE JEWS THE "HEAD" OF THE NATIONS
THE PERFECT AGE
THE NEW HEAVENS
THE NEW EARTH
DESIGNED AND DRAWN BY CLARENCE LARKIN FOX CHASE, PHILA., PA.
COPYRIGHTED

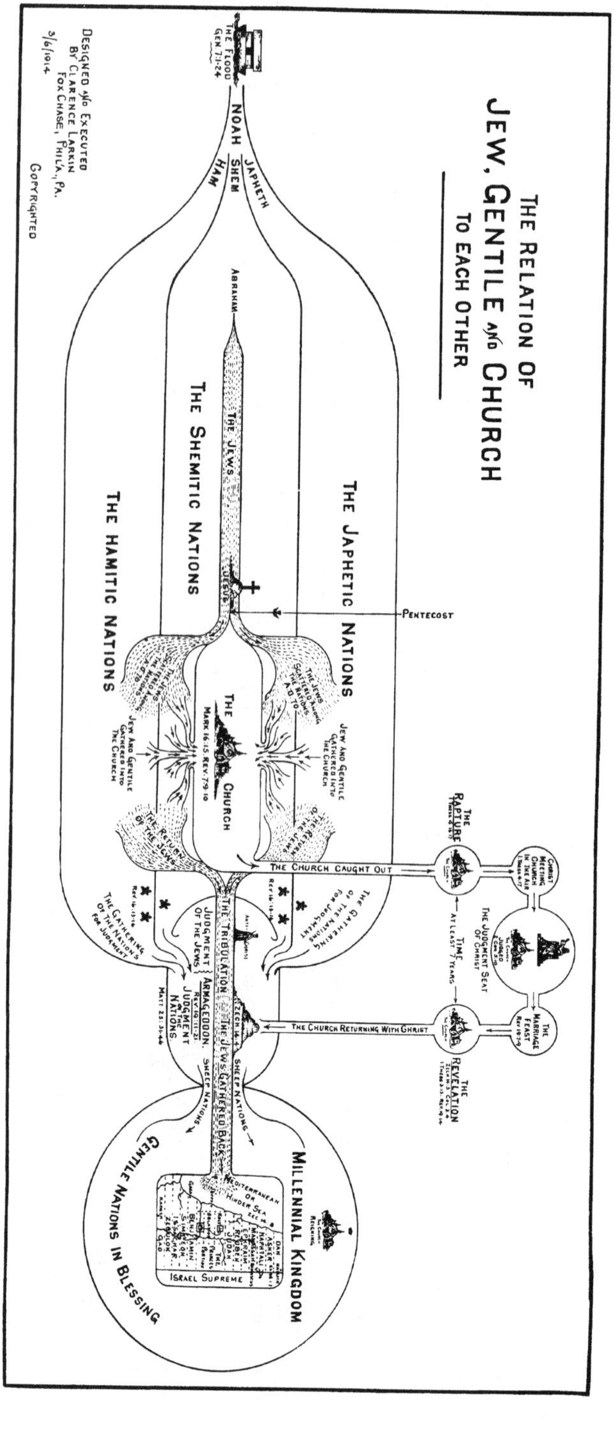

THE RELATION OF
JEW, GENTILE AND CHURCH
TO EACH OTHER
THE FLOOD
GEN. 7:1-24
NOAH
JAPHETH
SHEM
HAM
ABRAHAM
THE JEWS
JESUS
PENTECOST
THE JAPHETIC NATIONS
THE SHEMITIC NATIONS
THE HAMITIC NATIONS
THE CHURCH
MARK 16:15. REV. 7:9-10
JEW AND GENTILE GATHERED INTO THE CHURCH
THE RETURN OF THE JEWS
THE CHURCH CAUGHT OUT
THE RAPTURE
CHRIST MEETING CHURCH IN THE AIR
THE JUDGMENT SEAT OF CHRIST
TIME AT LEAST 7 YEARS
THE MARRIAGE FEAST
REV. 19:7-9
THE CHURCH RETURNING WITH CHRIST
THE REVELATION
THE GATHERING OF THE NATIONS FOR JUDGMENT
THE TRIBULATION
JUDGMENT OF THE JEWS
ARMAGEDDON
JUDGMENT OF THE NATIONS
MATT. 25:31-46
ZECH. 14:4
THE JEWS GATHERED BACK
SHEEP NATIONS
MEDITERRANEAN OR HINDER SEA
ISRAEL SUPREME
MILLENNIAL KINGDOM
GENTILE NATIONS IN BLESSING
DESIGNED AND EXECUTED
BY CLARENCE LARKIN
FOX CHASE, PHILA., PA.
3/6/1914.
COPYRIGHTED

AN ANGRY ANTICHRIST MUST EXPLAIN

Once believers have been removed from the earth, the Antichrist, of course, will be angry. The ones he hates the most are out of his reach, rescued to safety. But most of all, in order to divert the world from Jesus, he will try to explain away the Rapture by denying its miraculous nature. He will insist that the disappearance of believers was not a rescue by Jesus as was predicted by many evangelical Christians who are mysteriously missing! Armilus will give the world a blasphemous explanation that seems logical.

HOW WILL HE DO IT?

Does the Bible mention anything about what the Antichrist will say regarding believers who were removed to Heaven because of his reign? The apostle John informs us in the book of Revelation: "Then the Dragon encouraged the Creature to speak great blasphemies against the Lord; and gave him authority to control the earth for forty-two months. All that time he **blasphemed** God's Name and his temple and **all those living in heaven**. The Dragon gave him power to fight against God's people and to overcome them, and to rule over all nations and language groups throughout the world. And all mankind—whose names were not written down before the founding of the world in the slain Lamb's Book of Life—worshiped the evil Creature" (Rev. 13:5-8 *The Living Bible*; bold mine).

The Antichrist blasphemes the saints by saying they are not in Heaven. How? Maybe he borrows a line or two from the film, *Close Encounters of the Third Kind*, which dramatized a cosmic kidnapping, or some of the other films[43] which have depicted a portion of the world's people being abducted by aliens and taken aboard ships from

---

[43]Films such as *This Island Earth*, and the 1993 Paramount release, *Fire in the Sky*, both of which portray a cosmic *kidnapping* of earthlings by aliens. The movie, *Fire in the Sky*, has some of the same special effects and similar scenes (such as a breathable compartment, tunnels, cocoon-like hibernation and the appearance of an alien studying humans) as does the old, nearly forgotten 1964 film, *First Men in the Moon*. This film depicts two Englishmen and a woman who went to the moon in 1899 using a make-shift space sphere. There, they found a subterranean atmosphere and moon creatures, etc. This movie is available on videotape and is based on H.G. Wells' 1901 novel, *The First Man in the Moon*. We do not believe there are any UFO's or aliens, rather these ships being sighted are demons. Zola Levitt comments on this truth with interesting proof in some of his works. We suggest you read the book *Encounters with UFO's*, available through Zola Levitt, POB 12268, Dallas, TX, USA 75225. Also, *This Week in Bible Prophecy* produced an excellent video entitled, *UFO's—The Hidden Truth*, available through This Week in Bible Prophecy, POB 1440, Niagara Falls, NY, USA 14302-1440. We believe the Antichrist will use this UFO kidnapping explanation in the future sudden disappearance of Christians in the Rapture, in an attempt to logically explain it all away.

outer space. I wonder who is inspiring the plots of these films, at a time when the Rapture is so close at hand. Could it be Satan himself? They certainly provide an explanation for millions of missing persons—something the Antichrist will grasp as an answer for those who may have heard about the Rapture.[44] According to Revelation 13:6, the Antichrist will blaspheme "all those living in heaven" (*The Living Bible*).

WHAT HAPPENS TO THE 144,000 JEWS WHO WERE TOLD THAT JESUS IS MESSIAH *BEFORE* THE RAPTURE? WHAT HAPPENS AFTER THEIR CHRISTIAN FRIENDS ARE GONE?

Many Jews who do not presently believe in Jesus, have been told by their Christian friends, and perhaps even other Jewish believers, known to us as "Messianic Jews" or "Jews for Jesus," that Jesus is the Messiah. They have been shown countless Old Testament prophecies which prove Jesus conclusively to be the Jewish Messiah. Only the pressure of religious identity and peer acceptance seems to hold many back from believing.

When these 144,000 (12,000 from each of the twelve tribes) see the Rapture take place, they will begin to tell the world, including their fellow Jews, that Jesus really is the Messiah. They will suddenly realize that their Gentile Christian and Jews for Jesus friends were right. They will see through the sham of the Antichrist's lies and become, as Revelation 7:4 says, 144,000 sealed witnesses.

Revelation, chapter 7, speaks of them bringing a multitude to believe in Jesus—so great they cannot even be numbered! Of course, the Antichrist will try to persecute them (Rev. 13:7), but God's seal will protect them. In the end, those who live in Jerusalem with all of those who believe because of them (multitudes), will escape into the mountains of Petra, where God has promised protection (Rev. 12:6). We will discuss this further in our chapter 26, "We Win Armageddon—Our Final Battle," and our *Vol. II*, chapter 38, "They Escaped to Petra").

---

[44]In the Rapture, we will be "beamed up," so to speak, but not by Scotty! Recent books relating this theme of cosmic kidnapping include: *Communion*, and *Breakthrough the Next Step* by Whitley Strieber; *Close Encounters of the Fourth Kind* by C.D.B. Bryan; *Abduction, Human Encounters with Aliens* by John Mack, M.D.; *UFO Abductions in the Gulf Breeze* by Ed and Frances Walters; *The Alien Abduction Survival Guide* by Michelle LaVigne; *Secret Life*, by David M. Jacobs, Ph.D.; *Intruders*, by Budd Hopkins; *Alien Contact: Top-Secret UFO Files Revealed*, by Timothy Good; *Watchers*, by Raymond E. Fowler; *The Tujunga Canyon Contacts*, by Ann Druffel and D. Scott Rogo; and *Into the Fringe*, by Karla Turner, Ph.D.

ORIGINAL HEBREW TEXT WRITTEN 760 BC

וּבָאוּ בִּמְעָרוֹת צֻרִים וּבִמְחִלּוֹת עָפָר מִפְּנֵי פַּחַד יְהוָה וּמֵהֲדַר גְּאוֹנוֹ בְּקוּמוֹ לַעֲרֹץ הָאָרֶץ׃
....לֵךְ עַמִּי בֹּא בַחֲדָרֶיךָ וּסְגֹר דְּלָתֶיךָ בַּעֲדֶךָ חֲבִי כִמְעַט־רֶגַע עַד־יַעֲבוֹר זָעַם׃ כִּי־הִנֵּה
יְהוָה יֹצֵא מִמְּקוֹמוֹ לִפְקֹד עֲוֹן יֹשֵׁב־הָאָרֶץ עָלָיו וְגִלְּתָה הָאָרֶץ אֶת־דָּמֶיהָ וְלֹא־תְכַסֶּה
עוֹד עַל־הֲרוּגֶיהָ׃ **ישעיה ב:יט; כו:כ-כב**

OLD TESTAMENT SCRIPTURE TRANSLATION

"And *men* will go into caves of the rocks, And into holes of the ground....Come, my people, enter into your rooms, And close your doors behind you; Hide for a little while, Until indignation runs *its* course. For behold, the LORD is about to come out from His place To punish the inhabitants of the earth for their iniquity; And the earth will reveal her bloodshed, And will no longer cover her slain."

Isaiah 2:19; 26:20-21 NASB

ANCIENT RABBINICAL COMMENTARY

"At that time the Israelites will be in great trouble. Some of them will hide themselves in caves and pits, and those who remain of them will flee to the wilderness of Ammon and Moab. *The outcasts of Moab will dwell in you* (Isa. 16:4)....Then Armilos, the son of Satan, will go to the wilderness of Moab (...*He will bring forth the top stone* [Zech. 4:7]). The Israelites will cry out bitterly to Heaven, and *Michael the prince* of the throne of glory, will provide mercy for them. He will *stand* in prayer before the holy One blessed be He, as it is written, *In that time Michael, the great prince who stands for the sons of your people, will arise* (Dan 12:1)."[45] **Midrash fragment, Marmorstein, REJ 52, p. 183; 1906**

NEW TESTAMENT PROPHECY RECORDED 37 AD

"Therefore when you see the ABOMINATION OF DESOLATION which was spoken of through Daniel the prophet, standing in the holy place (let the reader understand), then let those who are in Judea flee to the mountains [of Ammon]; let him who is on the housetop not go down to get the things out that are in his house; and let him who is in the field not turn back to get his cloak. But woe to those who are with child and to those who nurse babes in those days! But pray that your flight may not be in the winter, or on a Sabbath...."

Matthew 24:15-20 NASB. [ ] mine

AUTHOR'S COMMENT—EVANGELICAL CHRISTIAN POSITION

There is no rabbinical refutation of this Petra prophecy to date, since very little is known of the obscure predictions about Israel's flight to Petra in the Bible. The material you are reading here and in our *Vol. II*, chapter 38, "They Escaped to Petra," involved hundreds of hours of research and study; thus, you have the opportunity to read our original discoveries involving Old Testament and rabbinical literature, never before thought to refer to Petra. In these findings, we strongly felt the hand of the Lord and His wonderful guidance. We illustrate throughout our *Vol. II*, that from the context of said biblical prophecies and ancient writings, it is quite obvious that Petra is indicated, even though the name "Petra" is not always spelled out. **Philip Moore**

---

[45]George W. Buchanan, *Revelation and Redemption*, pp. 500-501. Regarding this manuscript, Buchanan says: "This is a text from Cairo Geniza which is damaged at the beginning and in some places throughout the ms. It originally had ten signs, and parts of the second sign survive, but the clear text begins with the sign three." Ibid, p. 490.

The author examines the three hundred and fifty-foot-high entrance to Petra known as the *Siq*, which is one mile in length. These stone structures are capable of protecting people from radiation, nuclear bomb blasts and the Antichrist!

At the end of the *Siq*, at the opening to the city of Petra, lies the magnificent building known as the Treasury, hewn from the solid rose-red rock of Petra.

As we travel further into the city of Petra, we see the ancient homes of the Nabateans, carved from the rock. Many Bible teachers believe that the Jews will take refuge here during the Tribulation.

Bait Jubrine Cave, near Kibbutz Bait Jubrine in Kiryat Gat, Israel. These Bell Caves are so named because they were carved from a hole which was bored in the top of the mountain, and then extended hundreds of feet into the rock in the shape of a bell. These caves could also provide shelter for Israelis during the time of the Antichrist.

ANTICHRIST HIGH-TECH MARK—ECONOMIC COMPUTER BLACKMAIL

The Antichrist will offer solutions to the world's problems that will seem incredible. The Bible foretells that the masses of the world will be saying: "...who is able to make war with him?" (Rev. 13:4 KJV).

Toward the middle of his seven-year rule, his solutions will begin to fail. Ultimately, they will crumble. He will use economics to blackmail all who will not worship him or swear allegiance to him as God. The book of Revelation predicts this: "And he causeth all, both small and great, rich and poor, free and bond, to receive a mark in their right hand, or in their foreheads: And that no man might buy or sell, save he that had the mark, or the name of the beast, or the number of his name. Here is wisdom. Let him that hath understanding count the number of the beast: for it is the number of a man; and his number *is* Six hundred three score *and* six" (Rev. 13:16-18 KJV).

THE TECHNOLOGY THAT WILL ULTIMATELY FULFILL JOHN'S PROPHECY IS PRESENTLY BEING DEVELOPED AND TESTED

Through our new and ever advancing computer technology, it is now possible to number everyone. They have even experimented with electronic money in our own country. Hal Lindsey, in his updated book, *There's A New World Coming*, notes: "Along with the governments of France, Holland, and Norway, the U.S. is testing what is known as the 'Smart Card.' This plastic credit card contains a microchip feature which allows the card to retain and sort information. The cardholder, of course, has a secret code number to activate the card, which carries a 'memory' of past financial transactions and the sum of the person's account. Amazingly, France, according to *U.S. News and World Report*, is testing the cards 'for use as children's portable school records and for storage of vaccination and other personal health information'...Germany may be the next nation to try out the Smart Card.

In an article on the Smart Card entitled 'Your Life May Be Sandwiched in a Card,' the Commercial Appeal of Memphis, Tennessee, stated, 'It may well be the ultimate transaction vehicle of our consuming world. It could bring about the much-discussed cashless, paperless society....And it may also end up as a national identification card—a prospect that chills many....' The article pointed out the various functions the card could be used for, including: crediting and debiting, all other banking functions, computer data access, medical information, telephone access, passport use, Social Security information, identification purposes, security access....the Defense Department is eyeing the card for its security value. In seeking to think through all the possible problems that could arise from this, one of the first considerations has been the problem of theft of your card or loss of it in some other manner. Since your whole financial and personal history might be wrapped up in your card, a thief or spy could wipe you out overnight. The apostle John says that the Antichrist will require everyone to have an identifying mark on either his forehead or right hand. Strangely enough, that is the same solution that's being talked about by some who have been wrestling with this problem for a decade. There's no way to lose your number or have your identification subverted if it's tattooed on you!"[46]

IT WILL PROBABLY BE READY SOMETIME *AFTER* 2020, AS TECHNOLOGY ADVANCES

Sometime in the near future, not too many decades into the twenty-first century, we will see fingerprints,[47] blood vessel prints,[48] handprints (bio-metrics) and possibly microchip Smart Cards used in conjunction with bio-metrics and even microchip implantation[49] to keep track of us in a global government system. No doubt, this system will be appropriated by the Antichrist and used against those left behind after the Rapture; they will have to receive his terrible mark and worship him or starve. Modern technology is setting the stage for this very scenario!

---

[46]Hal Lindsey, *There's A New World Coming*. Eugene, OR: Harvest House Publishers, © 1973, pp. 182-183, used by permission.

[47]A humorous but somewhat sobering real example of this is incorporated in Steven Spielberg's 1987 movie, *Back to the Future Part II*. Jennifer (Lea Thompson) is helped into her home in the year 2015 by a policewoman who puts her thumb print on the door plate in order to unlock the entrance. Also, Biff follows Dr. Brown to Marty's future home (so he can steal the time machine in order to make himself a millionaire in his youth). Biff pays the cab driver by pressing his thumb on the driver's portable computer account register, which records his thumbprint. Presently, this idea is just science fiction in the movies, but remember that going to the moon was fiction a few years before we did it. Yesterday's fictional movies have a habit of becoming tomorrow's science fact, don't they?

[48]In the *Star Trek* film, *The Wrath of Khan*, Captain Kirk's retinal blood vessels are scanned by a computer before he is given security clearance to open the file of "Project Genesis." Sounds like we are being conditioned for such futuristic implementations.

[49]This is also portayed in the 1993 futuristic film *Demolition Man*, which starred Sylvester Stallone. The reason the two twentieth century men were so hard for the authorities in the 2030's to locate, was because they lacked the chip implanted in everyone of that era.

Peter Lalonde, in his videotape, *Mark of the Beast II*, recalled a conversation with his Israeli friend, Daniel Man. Lalonde said: "...he was saying, I would like to propose to the Israeli government that we implant a chip under the skin of all of our diplomats and leading political figures. And then if they get kidnapped, we won't have to search around in Lebanon for two years, like the Americans had to do, or five years or longer trying to search someone out, because you now have tracking satellites...that can pinpoint the location of a microchip, even if you had it implanted under the skin, within three feet of where it's located on the earth....One of the big developments they're talking about now are the no-contact Smart Cards. And what that means is, leave your card in your wallet and when you walk through the machine, it will just read the card, right on the seat of your pants and you just keep walking without even knowing it's there and it's all done. They're doing it with toll highways and so on....but these kind of ideas of the ability to track people sound like very good ideas. It doesn't sound fearful anymore. It sounds like it's being done for your own good, to help find missing children, to help people with Alzheimer's, to help people in a medical emergency. Suddenly, the aura of Big Brother is gone and it just sounds like such a very good idea."[50]

WHAT THEY ARE DOING TO DOGS TODAY, THEY WILL BE DOING TO YOU TOMORROW!

Paul Lalonde (Peter's brother) added: "A general rule of thumb in scientific research is that if you want to see what will be a part of everyday life in the future, go see what's in the labs today. Nowhere is that truer than in the study of implantable microchips. However, the 'lab' may be a little different than you'd expect. That's right, it's your black lab or golden lab that we're talking about here. You see, a program is now being carried out all over North America in which cats, dogs, horses, cattle and every type of animal that you can imagine are being implanted with computer readable microchips. As part of an effort to keep track of lost pets and as a way to identify livestock, InfoPet Systems of California and several other microchip developers have created a unique system that has effectively replaced the old system of dog tags and branding. The animals are implanted with a microchip that contains an electronically encoded number.

---

[50]Peter and Paul Lalonde, *Mark of the Beast II*, 1993. This video is available through This Week in Bible Prophecy, POB 1440, Niagara Falls, NY, USA 14302-4429. Tel. (800) 776-7432.

That number is matched to a file and entered into a computer database. Then, if the animal runs away and is found by someone, they can simply bring it in to the local Humane Society. All the Humane Society has to do is run a scanner, no more technologically advanced than the bar code readers in your supermarket, over the skin of the animal and a nation-wide database can identify your lost pet. At last count, the system had the capability to track over 34 billion animals' identification devices. The Colorado based manufacturer of the chip, however, leaves the door open to future uses. According to their promotional materials: '...consider how these innovations might be employed to solve the age-old problem of providing positive identification **of people**, animals and equipment.' So once again, it's not only the Bible prophecy teacher who sees where all of this may be leading us."[51]

BOTH COMPUTER AND FINANCIAL EXPERTS ALIKE TESTIFY THAT THE CURRENT TECHNOLOGICAL GROUNDWORK IS LAYING THE FOUNDATION FOR REVELATION'S FULFILLMENT

At the beginning of the same program, Paul Shantz[52] said: "It will be done so that you can extract information off people's bodies and it'll be done for very good...very practical reasons; for security, for protection of an individual's identity and so on." Paul Lalonde asked Shantz what he thought of all of this, in light of Revelation, and he answered: "So, I would say, yes. I think the prophecies in Revelation are quickly, quickly becoming reality, as we look at the developments in the marketplace today." Lalonde further noted: "When we spoke to computer systems expert Randy Sistelli, on our video, *The Mark of the Beast* [*I*], we asked him the same question. [He answered:] 'Do I think that the prophecies in Revelation are coming true? I think the technology is there...that's a serious concern. Yeah, I can see it happening.' "[53]

Peter Lalonde mentioned that the EEC is contemplating a law which would require all of their cattle to be implanted with microchips. He observed: "The groundwork for this whole thing is being tested right now. You have the work on the Smart Card technology, you have the work on the electronic banking systems. You have the need to make sure that the card is attached to the person and at the same time you are implanting microchips under the skin of

---

[51]Ibid. Bold mine.

[52]Paul Shantz is the senior manager of a major Canadian bank.

[53]Ibid. [ ] mine.

animals and then, on top of that, you're building a database that can keep track of thirty-four billion different cats and dogs. You're building a system that **could be utilized in Revelation 13**. A system that did not exist in any other generation before this one....This is the kind of technology that exists today and it's a great concern to us because the Scripture says, speaking of the false prophet working under the Antichrist: 'And he causeth **all**, both small and great, rich and poor, free and bond, to receive a mark....' [Rev. 13:16 KJV]. He causeth all. This system eventually is going to be developed in such a way that you have to be within the system to conduct any business. If you're outside of that electronic system, you are locked out of everything and that's exactly what the Scriptures say."[54]

When you couple this economic mark with the one-world religion and global government predicted in the book of Revelation, you have a prescription for disaster—a disaster that will befall you if you become a believer *after* the Rapture.

TWO FOR THE PRICE OF ONE, THOUGH BELIEVE ME, WE COULD DO WITHOUT THE ONE, WHO IS NOT GOING TO BE VERY FUN

We know from the New Testament and rabbinical writings that there will be two people involved in this world leadership of Antichrist (Rev. 16:13-14). One is referred to as the false prophet (Rev. 16:13; 19:20; 20:10), the other, the beast (Rev. 13:11). One will wield ruthless control over Israel and is a Jew, the other will have dominion over the entire world (Rev. 13:2). The rabbinical commentary, Otot haMashiah, points this out as it parallels the two, agreeing with the books of Revelation and Thessalonians regarding the claim of the Antichrist that he "is God," along with the words of Jesus: "For then shall be great tribulation, such as was not since the beginning of the world to this time, no, nor ever shall be" (Matt. 24:21 KJV). The commentary reads as follows: "...And another king[55] will arise in Rome and will rule over the whole world...and will destroy many countries. And his wrath will be kindled against Israel,

---

[54]Ibid. [ ] and bold mine.

[55]This indicates the rabbinical writers interpreted the Bible with the understanding of two anti-Messiah kings. Rome indicates the world and *Harutz* is Hebrew for "the land" of Israel! We have confirmation of one of the Antichrists specifically coming out of, and controlling Israel, from the early Christian writer, Jerome, of the fourth century. In his commentary, on Daniel xi. 21, he tells us: " 'But our [expositors] interpret both better and more correctly that at the end of the world these things shall be done by the Antichrist, who is to rise up from a small nation—that is, the nation of the Jews." Wilhelm Bousset, *The Antichrist Legend.* London: Hutchinson and Co., 1896, p. 135.

and he will impose upon them heavy taxes. And Israel will be in greatest distress in that hour because of the many decrees and disturbances which will become renewed over them every day. And Israel will diminish and perish in that time, and will have no helper....a man emerges...his name is Armilus the Satan. This is the one whom the nations of the world call Antichrist....he will go to Edom the wicked and say to them: 'I am Messiah, I am your god!' Instantly they believe in him, and make him king over them, and all the Children of Esau [Arab Moslems] join themselves to him and come to him. And he goes forth and conquers all the countries, and says to the Children of Esau: 'Bring me my Tora [Koran] which I gave you!' And they bring him their obscenity, and he says to them: 'Is it true what I gave you?' And he tells the nations of the world: 'Believe in me, for I am your Messiah.' And instantly they believe in him....he sends to...Israel and says to them: 'Bring me your Tora and testify to me that I am god.' Instantly they are afraid and confused....and they take the Tora scroll and read before him: *I am the Lord thy God, thou shalt have no other gods before Me* (Exod. 20:2-3). And he says to them: 'There is nothing in this Tora of yours; come and testify to me that I am god, as did all the nations'....Instantly the wicked Armilus becomes wroth, and gathers all the armies of the nations of the world to the Valley of Harutz, and fights Israel, and heaps and heaps are killed of them, and Israel will be smitten a little....And it will be a suffering for Israel the like of which has not been ever since the world exists and to that time."[56]

A MODERN POPULAR CHRISTIAN AUTHOR CONFIRMS OUR STUDY OF TWO ANTICHRISTS, ONE FOR THE WORLD AND THE OTHER FOR ISRAEL

Hal Lindsey commented on Revelation 13:11-18 in his book *There's A New World Coming*, regarding these evil twins: "Despite the merciless, sweeping tyranny of the first beast (the Roman Antichrist), Satan will not be content to stop there. He'll raise up a conspirator who is an even more ruthless tyrant because he will enslave the *minds* and *souls* of men.

Basically the second Beast will be similar to the first one. The Greek word translated 'another' in verse 11 specifically means *another of the same kind*. He will have the same scintillating

[56]Raphael Patai, *The Messiah Texts*, pp. 313-315. [ ] mine. Patai's source was the *Otot haMashiah*, BhM 2:58-63.

personality, the same tireless dynamism, the same oratorical finesse as the first Beast. He will also have the same Satanic powers.

But there will be some differences too. While the first Beast emerged from the sea (the unrest of troubled nations), the second beast emerges from the *land*. ('Earth' in verse 11 could just as well be translated 'land.') When the Bible uses the word 'land' symbolically, it usually refers to the land that belongs to Israel. So the second beast will come from the region of the Middle East, and I believe he will be a Jew."[57]

SATAN IN THE SANCTUARY BRINGS ON THE WAR MANY HAVE FEARED FROM TIME IMMEMORIAL

There is a chamber in the Jewish Temple known as the Holy of Holies, where God Himself has resided in past Temples. The Antichrist will enter this chamber and try to cause all to worship his statue, proclaiming himself God (II Thes. 2:4), which will cause his delicately balanced peace to collapse. Regarding this event, the Bible says: "For when they shall say, Peace and safety; then sudden destruction cometh upon them, as travail upon a woman with child...." (I Thes. 5:3 KJV). This will herald the arrival of Armageddon/Gog and Magog, the war everyone has feared from time immemorial.

Jesus warned that this individual would come to deceive His people shortly before His return to save them. Jesus said: "I am come in my Father's name, and ye receive me not: if another shall come in his own name, him ye will receive" (John 5:43 KJV). Jesus also gives special instructions for safety to those living in Jerusalem at this time. He said: "When you therefore shall see the abomination of desolation, spoken of by Daniel[58] the prophet, stand in the holy place, (whoso readeth, let him understand:) Then let them which be in Judæa flee into the mountains....But pray ye that your flight be not in the winter, neither on the sabbath day: For then shall be great tribulation, such as was not since the beginning of the world to this time, no, nor ever shall be. And except those days should be

---

[57]Hal Lindsey, *There's A New World Coming*, pp. 179-180.

[58]What Jesus was warning us of in Daniel's writings approximately six hundred years earlier (almost 2600 years ago, from our time), was the yet-to-come Antichrist. Daniel's words were: "And his power shall be mighty, but not by his own power: and he shall destroy wonderfully, and shall prosper, and practise, and shall destroy the mighty and the holy people. And through his policy also he shall cause craft to prosper in his hand; and he shall magnify *himself* in his heart, and by peace shall destroy many: he shall also stand up against the Prince of princes; but he shall be broken without hand....And he shall confirm the covenant with many for one week: and in the midst of the week he shall cause the sacrifice and the oblation to cease, and for the overspreading of abominations he shall make *it* desolate, even until the consummation, and that determined shall be poured upon the desolate" (Dan. 8:24-25; 9:27 KJV).

shortened, there should no flesh be saved: but for the elect's[59] sake those days shall be shortened. Then if any man shall say unto you, Lo, here *is* Christ, or there; believe *it* not" (Matt. 24:15-16, 20-23 KJV).

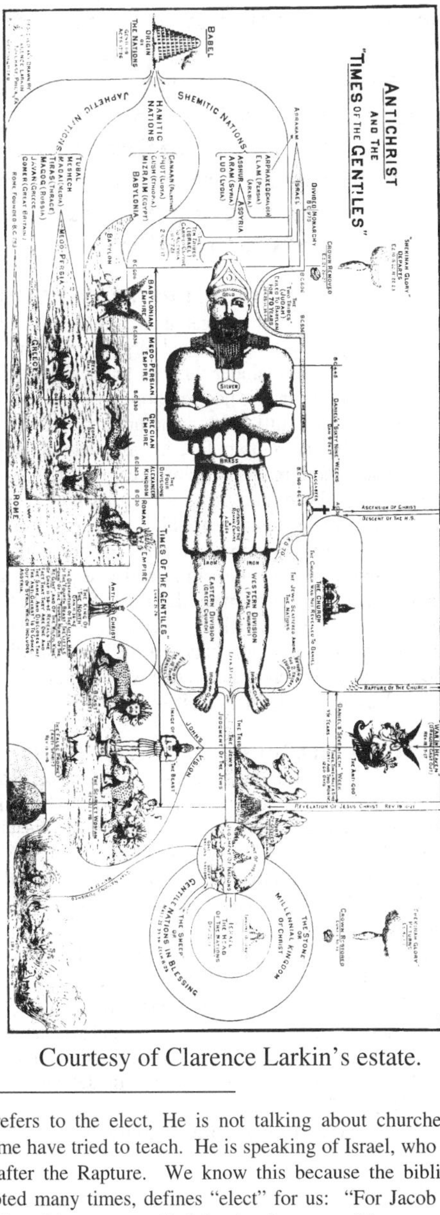

Courtesy of Clarence Larkin's estate.

59When Jesus refers to the elect, He is not talking about churches or contemporary Christians, as some have tried to teach. He is speaking of Israel, who is yet to believe, in the Tribulation after the Rapture. We know this because the biblical prophet Isaiah, whom Jesus quoted many times, defines "elect" for us: "For Jacob my servant's sake, and Israel mine **elect**, I have even called thee by thy name: I have surnamed thee, though thou hast not known me" (Isa. 45:4 KJV).

ORIGINAL HEBREW TEXT WRITTEN 555 BC

בָּאתַר דְּנָה חָזֵה הֲוֵית בְּחֶזְוֵי לֵילְיָא וַאֲרוּ חֵיוָה רְבִיעָיָה דְּחִילָה וְאֵימְתָנִי וְתַקִּיפָא יַתִּירָא
וְשִׁנַּיִן דִּי־פַרְזֶל לַהּ רַבְרְבָן אָכְלָה וּמַדֱּקָה וּשְׁאָרָא בְּרַגְלַיהּ רָפְסָה וְהִיא מְשַׁנְּיָה
מִן־כָּל־חֵיוָתָא דִּי קָדָמַיהּ וְקַרְנַיִן עֲשַׂר לַהּ׃ מִשְׂתַּכַּל הֲוֵית בְּקַרְנַיָּא וַאֲלוּ קֶרֶן אָחֳרִי
זְעֵירָה סִלְקָת בֵּינֵיהֵון וּתְלָת מִן־קַרְנַיָּא קַדְמָיָתָא אֶתְעֲקַרוּ מִן־קֳדָמַיהּ וַאֲלוּ עַיְנִין
כְּעַיְנֵי אֲנָשָׁא בְּקַרְנָא־דָא וּפֻם מְמַלִּל רַבְרְבָן׃ ....וְעַל־קַרְנַיָּא עֲשַׂר דִּי בְרֵאשַׁהּ וְאָחֳרִי
דִּי סִלְקַת וּנְפַלוּ מִן־קֳדָמַיהּ תְּלָת וְקַרְנָא דִכֵּן וְעַיְנִין לַהּ וּפֻם מְמַלִּל רַבְרְבָן וְחֶזְוַהּ
רַב מִן־חַבְרָתַהּ׃ חָזֵה הֲוֵית וְקַרְנָא דִכֵּן עָבְדָה קְרָב עִם־ קַדִּישִׁין וְיָכְלָה לְהוֹן׃ עַד
ים: וּלְהַחֲרִיםדִּי אֲתָה עַתִּיק יוֹמַיָּא וְדִינָא יְהִב לְקַדִּישֵׁי עֶלְיוֹנִין וְזִמְנָא מְטָה וּמַלְכוּתָא הֶחֱסִנוּ
קַדִּישִׁין׃ .... וּשְׁמֻעוֹת יְבַהֲלֻהוּ מִמִּזְרָח וּמִצָּפוֹן וְיָצָא בְּחֵמָא גְדֹלָה לְהַשְׁמִיד רַבִּ
וְיִטַּע אָהֳלֵי אַפַּדְנוֹ בֵּין יַמִּיםלְהַר־צְבִי־ קֹדֶשׁ וּבָא עַד־ קִצּוֹ וְאֵין עוֹזֵר לוֹ׃

דניאל ז:ז-ח; כ-כב; יא:מד-מה

OLD TESTAMENT SCRIPTURE TRANSLATION

"After this I kept looking in the night visions, and behold, a fourth beast, dreadful and terrifying and extremely strong; and it had large iron teeth. It devoured and crushed, and trampled down the remainder with its feet; and it was different from all the beasts that were before it, and it had ten horns. While I was contemplating the horns, behold, another horn, a little one, came up among them, and three of the first horns were pulled out by the roots before it; and behold, this horn possessed eyes like the eyes of a man, and a mouth uttering great *boasts*....and *the meaning* of the ten horns that *were* on its head, and the other *horn* which came up, and before which three *of them* fell, namely, that horn which had eyes and a mouth uttering great *boasts*, and which was larger in appearance than its associates. I kept looking, and that horn was waging war with the saints and overpowering them until the Ancient of Days came....But rumors from the East and from the North will disturb him, and he will go forth with great wrath to destroy and annihilate many. And he will pitch the tents of his royal pavilion between the seas and the beautiful Holy Mountain; yet he will come to his end, and no one will help him."

Daniel 7:7-8, 20-22; 11:44-45 NASB

ANCIENT RABBINICAL COMMENTARY

"...at the end of four kingdoms [Babylon, Medo-Persia, Greece, Rome], in the days of the fourth king [newly revived Rome in ten nation form] who will be in the....end of the future will be at the end of days, in the days of the king who will be in the future....And these will be the signs which Daniel foresaw in him...between his eyes is haughtiness....he will stretch forth his hand on that day against the faithful nation [Israel], and he will shake it....They [the Antichrist's armies]...will oppress houses and rob fields, and slay the orphan and the widow in the marketplace....a king will rise from the sea and destroy and shake the world, and he will come to the holy mountain of the gazelle [i.e., the Temple Mount in Jerusalem] and will burn it. Accursed be among the Women she who will bear him! [This is] that horn which Daniel saw. And on that day there will be suffering and war against Israel....'Woe to you, you evil ones, for at the end of the four kingdoms all of you will be ejected from the world!'....And each tree will be loaded with delicacies and fruits....And Israel will eat and rejoice...."[60]

Sefer Eliyahu, BhM 3:65-67

[60] Raphael Patai, *The Messiah Texts*, pp. 150-152. First, second and fourth [ ] mine.

NEW TESTAMENT RECORDED 96 AD
"...And I saw a beast coming up out of the sea, having ten horns and seven heads, and on his horns *were* ten diadems, and on his heads *were* blasphemous names....And there was given to him a mouth speaking arrogant words and blasphemies; and authority to act for forty-two months was given to him....the ten horns which you saw are ten kings, who have not yet received a kingdom, but they receive authority as kings with the beast for one hour. These have one purpose and they give their power and authority to the beast. These will wage war against the Lamb, and the Lamb will overcome them, because He is Lord of lords and King of kings, and those who are with Him *are the* called and chosen and faithful. And he said to me, 'The waters which you saw where the harlot sits, are peoples and multitudes and nations and tongues....' "

Revelation 13:1, 5; 17:12-15 NASB

MODERN RABBINIC COMMENT/REFUTATION
None of the modern Jewish writing I examined seemed to know anything about Armilus. All of the polemical books were silent on the subject of Armilus.

Philip Moore

WHEN THE FALSE MESSIAH'S PEACE FAILS, JESUS WILL PREVAIL

The false Messiah deceitfully establishes peace and leads mankind into a third world war, which, according to Zechariah 14:12,[61] Revelation and Ezekiel, will apparently involve nuclear weapons. This heralds the return of Jesus, who will end the war, kill the false Messiah[62] (II Thes. 2:8), arrange for the burial of Arab and Russian troops and finally, at long last, bring peace.

The physical redemption of the earth will be accomplished only by the one who spiritually redeemed it nearly 2000 years ago, and only after His covenant people recognize and accept Him as the Messiah. This occurs when Jesus comes to stop the war and all Israel looks into the sky and recognizes Him. Zechariah predicted: "And it shall come to pass in that day, *that* I will seek to destroy all the nations that come against Jerusalem. And I will pour upon the house of David, and upon the inhabitants of Jerusalem, the spirit of grace and of supplications: and they shall look upon me whom they have pierced, and they shall mourn for him, as one mourneth for *his* only *son*, and shall be in

---

[61]"And this shall be the plague wherewith the LORD will smite all the people that have fought against Jerusalem; Their flesh shall consume away while they stand upon their feet, and their eyes shall consume away in their holes, and their tongue shall consume away in their mouth" (Zech. 14:12 KJV). Only thermo-nuclear heat can cause the body to melt (consume away) before it has the opportunity to fall from its feet to the ground.

[62]"Who opposeth and exalteth himself above all that is called God, or that is worshipped; so that he as God sitteth in the temple of God, shewing himself that he is God" (II Thes. 2:4 KJV).

bitterness for him, as one that is in bitterness for *his* firstborn. In that day shall there be a great mourning in Jerusalem, as the mourning of Hadadrimmon in the valley of Megiddon" (Zech. 12:9-11 KJV).

MODERN RABBINICAL COMMENTS ON MISTAKEN MESSIANIC CREDENTIALS ARE SETTING THE JEWS UP TO BE DECEIVED! HELP[63]

Not only is the lost Armilus legend opening the door for millions of Jews to be deceived into thinking the Antichrist is the Messiah, there are modern orthodox religious publications which use what the Bible predicted about the Antichrist to set up minimal criteria for accepting an individual as Messiah! In a recently published book ironically entitled *The Real Messiah*, Rabbi Aryeh Kaplan writes: "Into a world prepared to receive him, the Messiah will then be born.

He will be a mortal human being, born normally of human parents[64]....Now, imagine a charismatic leader greater than any other in man's history. Imagine a political genius surpassing all others. With the vast communication networks now at our disposal, he could spread his message to the entire world[65] and change the very fabric of our society.[66]

Now imagine that he is a religious Jew, a Tzadik. It may have once seemed far-fetched for a Tzadik to assume a role in world leadership, but the world is becoming increasingly more accustomed to accepting leaders of all races, religions, and ethnic groups. We may soon have reached the stage where it is not far-fetched to picture a Tzadik in such a role.

One possible scenario could involve the Middle East situation. This is a problem that involves all the world powers. Now imagine a Jew, a Tzadik, solving this thorny problem. It would not be

---

63Give this book, or a similar one, to your Jewish loved ones. This may help them avoid the deception we are documenting, hopefully providing a beacon to the Bible's truth, which the Lord so adamantly and lovingly wishes them to have!

64This will be true of the Antichrist, not the true Messiah, who was predicted: 1. to be God Incarnate (Isa. 9:6); 2. to be born of a virgin (Isa. 7:14); 3. to die at the time Jesus died (Dan. 9:26; see our chapter 5, "Which Prophecies Did Jesus Fulfill?"); 4. to come into a world **not yet** ready to receive Him (Hos.5:15; see New Testament evidence in Matt. 23:39; John. 5:43); 5. to arrive in Jerusalem on a donkey (Zech. 9:9, as Jesus did); 6. and return miraculously on the clouds of heaven (Dan. 7:13), as Jesus promised to do (Mark 14:62, at His trial before the Sanhedrin).

65The New Testament book of Revelation foretells: "And he causeth all, both small and great, rich and poor, free and bond, to receive a mark in their right hand, or in their foreheads...." (13:16 KJV).

66Six hundred years before the birth of Jesus, the Old Testament prediction of Daniel foretold: "He [the Antichrist]....shall...think to change times and laws...." (Dan. 7:25 KJV; [ ] mine).

inconceivable that such a demonstration of statesmanship and political genius would place him in a position of world leadership.[67] The major powers would listen to such an individual[68]....If this Tzadik was so ordained by the entire community, he could then re-establish the Sanhedrin. This is a necessary condition for the rebuilding of the Temple....In his position of leadership, through direct negotiation and perhaps with the concurrence of the world powers, this Tzadik might just be able to regain the Temple Mount for the Jewish people....the Rambam (Maimonides) writes, '...If he is further successful in rebuilding the Temple on its original site and gathering the dispersed of Israel, then his identity as the Messiah is a certainty.'

It is very important to note that these accomplishments are a minimum[69] for our acceptance of an individual as the Messiah."[70]

AN ADDITIONAL MISTAKE IN TRIBAL GENEALOGY IS SETTING OUR JEWISH LOVED ONES UP FOR GREATER MESSIANIC DECEPTION

In the Midrash Rabbah, a rabbi claims the Messiah will come from the tribe of Dan, but the Bible clearly prophesied the tribe of Judah, on both sides! The Bible even hints, in Genesis 49:17, that the Antichrist will come from Dan, as many commentators have recognized.[71] Therefore, if today's rabbinical community follows the

---

[67] The Bible predicts the Antichrist will temporarily solve the Middle East Crisis, which will boil over into war. Jesus, the true Messiah, will end Armageddon, the last war (Matt. 24:22), which will occur when the false Messiah's peace collapses. Daniel 8:25 predicts: "...and by peace [the Antichrist] shall destroy many...." (KJV; [ ] mine).

[68] Revelation, the last book in the New Testament, says: "...who is able to make war with him?" (13:4 KJV). The Old Testament Book of Psalms relates: "...let all the inhabitants of the world stand in awe of him" (33:8 KJV).

[69] When Jesus returns as Messiah, He will rebuild the Temple, the fourth Temple predicted in Ezekiel 48 and Revelation 11, after the destruction of the third Temple of the Antichrist. The third Temple is spoken of in II Thessalonians 2:3-4, as Paul warns us about the Antichrist: "Let no man deceive you by any means: for *that day shall not come*, except there come a falling away first, and that man of sin be revealed, the son of perdition; Who opposeth and exalteth himself above all that is called God, or that is worshipped; so that he as God sitteth in the temple of God, shewing himself that he is God" (KJV). Daniel alludes to it being desecrated by the Antichrist/false Messiah in its Holy of Holies, and Jesus, in the New Testament, confirms this (Matt. 24:15) in a warning before He comes to establish the fourth Temple. The Antichrist, king of false Messiahs, will negotiate to build and afterward desecrate the third Temple of Israel—a future Temple **yet to be built!** This is before the real, or rather, true Messiah, Jesus, builds the final millennial Temple in the land of Israel to reign in peace forever.

[70] Rabbi Aryeh Kaplan, *et al*, *The Real Messiah*, pp. 69-71.

[71] Hal Lindsey points out: "Many scholars believe that the tribe of Dan is missing [from being mentioned in the New Testament book of Revelations] because the Jewish Antichrist (the False Prophet), will come from it. This certainly seems to be the meaning of an ancient prophecy that Jacob gave about the tribes of Israel in the last days: 'Dan

belief that the Messiah will come from Dan, according to a commentary which is in error, they are further deceiving themselves, and are once again setting their people up to be taken into the hands of the Antichrist when he steps onto the stage of history.

The Midrash Genesis Rabbah (p. 906) says that the Messiah will be from the tribe of Dan on one side of his lineage. This is the tribe from which the Antichrist will come. The New Testament firmly shows that Jesus came from the tribe of Judah on both sides of His lineage (Matt. 1; Luke 3), as the Hebrew Bible foresaw of the Messiah (Gen. 49:10). Thus, there still exists the false idea within Judaism that if someone claiming to be Messiah can be traced to Dan (the tribe the Antichrist will come from), he's eligible to be Messiah, an exceedingly dangerous concept which will one day aid in the deceiption of millions of Jews!

May we always tell our Jewish friends that, according to their Bible, the Messiah came from Judah, and Judah only (Gen. 49:10). The portion of the Midrash we mentioned that is in error, reads: "JUDAH IS A LION'S WHELP (XLIX, 9). R. Hama b. R. Hanina said: 'This alludes to Messiah the son of David who was descended from two tribes, his father being from Judah and his mother from Dan....' "[72] Remember, the *Encyclopaedia Judaica Jerusalem*, quoted earlier, mentioned: "One particular form, basing itself on Jewish traditions (see Test. Patr., Dan. 5:6), makes the Antichrist a Jewish pseudo-messiah of the tribe of Dan."[73]

AN ANTICHRIST COMIC BOOK INFORMS US OF THE FUTURE OUTLOOK (NOT SO GOOD) FOR THE UNBELIEVER

Jack Chick, though not infallible, produced a small biblical cartoon explaining the Antichrist. Though its overtones are comical, it conveys the essence of the personality of the Antichrist, as predicted by the Bible.

***

---

will be a serpent in the way, a venomous viper by the path, that bites the horse's heels so that his rider falls backward' (Genesis 49:17). Ephraim is left out because it led the way in causing the civil war which divided the ten tribes of the North from the two in the South. The tribes of Dan and Ephraim were the first to lead Israel into idolatry. Individual members of these tribes can certainly be brought into God's kingdom by faith, but no representatives of these tribes are given the honor of being the great evangelists of God in the Tribulation. The priestly tribe of Levi is substituted for Dan, and Joseph (Ephraim's father) is substituted for Ephraim." Hal Lindsey, *There's A New World Coming*, pp. 109-110. [ ] mine.

[72] *Midrash Rabbah, Genesis*, Vol. II, p. 906, Rabbi Dr. H. Freedman, B.A., Ph.D., editor.

[73] *Encyclopaedia Judaica Jerusalem,* Vol. 3.

THE BEAST

I'LL KILL YOU FOR THAT!
YOU REMIND ME OF MY 4th WIFE!
STOP IT! MY HUSBAND IS WATCHING US!
YOU KNOW HE DOESN'T CARE!
I'LL BET ON THE LITTLE MAN!

YOU KNOW YOU'RE THE ONLY MAN FOR ME!
HAW HAW
THAT WAS A FILTHY STORY! THAT WAS GREAT!
HEY EVERYBODY! ---LET'S HAVE SOME FUN— LET'S GO SEE CRAZY OLD NOAH, AND GIVE HIM A BAD TIME!
NOTHING IS REALLY FILTHY! FILTH IS ONLY IN YOUR MIND!—IF YOU THINK IT'S FILTHY— THEN IT'S FILTHY!
AND GOD SAW THAT THE WICKEDNESS OF MAN WAS GREAT IN THE EARTH, AND THAT EVERY IMAGINATION OF THE THOUGHTS OF HIS HEART WAS ONLY EVIL CONTINUALLY. Gen. 6-5

HE'S OUT OF HIS MIND!
THE OLD FOOL IS PREACHING ABOUT GOD'S COMING JUDGMENT AGAIN.. WHAT A LAUGH!
IF THERE WAS A GOD—HE WOULDN'T DESTROY US---WE'RE NOT THAT BAD!

GOD'S JUDGMENT FINALLY STRIKES AFTER YEARS OF WARNING!
IN THE SIX HUNDREDTH YEAR OF NOAH'S LIFE, IN THE SECOND MONTH, THE SEVENTEENTH DAY OF THE MONTH, THE SAME DAY WERE ALL THE FOUNTAINS OF THE GREAT DEEP BROKEN UP, AND THE WINDOWS OF HEAVEN WERE OPENED. AND THE RAIN WAS UPON THE EARTH FORTY DAYS AND FORTY NIGHTS. Gen. 7:11-12

ALL IN WHOSE NOSTRILS WAS THE BREATH OF LIFE, OF ALL THAT WAS IN THE DRY LAND, DIED. Gen. 7:22
AND EVERY LIVING SUBSTANCE WAS DESTROYED WHICH WAS UPON THE FACE OF THE GROUND, BOTH MAN, AND CATTLE, AND THE CREEPING THINGS, AND THE FOWL OF THE HEAVEN; AND THEY WERE DESTROYED FROM THE EARTH: AND NOAH ONLY REMAINED ALIVE, AND THEY THAT WERE WITH HIM IN THE ARK. Gen. 7:23

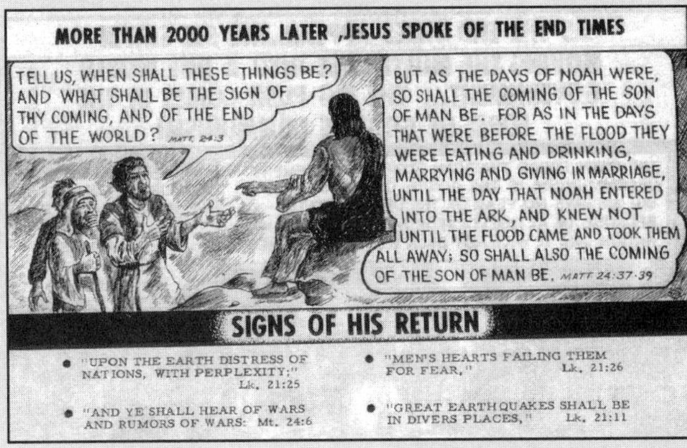
MORE THAN 2000 YEARS LATER ,JESUS SPOKE OF THE END TIMES
TELL US, WHEN SHALL THESE THINGS BE? AND WHAT SHALL BE THE SIGN OF THY COMING, AND OF THE END OF THE WORLD? MATT 24:3
BUT AS THE DAYS OF NOAH WERE, SO SHALL THE COMING OF THE SON OF MAN BE. FOR AS IN THE DAYS THAT WERE BEFORE THE FLOOD THEY WERE EATING AND DRINKING, MARRYING AND GIVING IN MARRIAGE, UNTIL THE DAY THAT NOAH ENTERED INTO THE ARK, AND KNEW NOT UNTIL THE FLOOD CAME AND TOOK THEM ALL AWAY; SO SHALL ALSO THE COMING OF THE SON OF MAN BE. MATT 24:37-39
SIGNS OF HIS RETURN
"UPON THE EARTH DISTRESS OF NATIONS, WITH PERPLEXITY;" Lk. 21:25
"AND YE SHALL HEAR OF WARS AND RUMORS OF WARS: Mt. 24:6
"MEN'S HEARTS FAILING THEM FOR FEAR," Lk. 21:26
"GREAT EARTHQUAKES SHALL BE IN DIVERS PLACES," Lk. 21:11

AS THE END TIMES APPEAR...WE SEE SATAN MOVING THE MULTITUDES INTO A ONE WORLD GOVERNMENT... THE BIG PUSH COMES IN THE FORM OF GODLESS COMMUNISM!
THE ONLY FORCE THAT CAN STOP THE MOVEMENT OF COMMUNISM IS THE GOSPEL OF JESUS CHRIST— BUT WE HAVE NO FEAR OF THE UNITED STATES --- BECAUSE IN ACTUALITY IT IS NOT A CHRISTIAN NATION AND IT WILL NOT BACK ITS MISSIONARIES!
REGARDLESS COMRADES, WE WILL INFILTRATE THEIR SEMINARIES AND NEUTRALIZE THE EFFECTS OF THE GOSPEL!

THE MODERN COUNCILS OF CHURCHES THAT CLAIM TO SPEAK FOR MILLIONS OF PROTESTANTS
DISCREDIT THE BIBLE
VIRGIN BIRTH IS A FABLE
GOD IS DEAD!
WE DO NOT ACCEPT THE DEITY OF CHRIST!
WE SUPPORT CIVIL DISOBEDIENCE
ONE WORLD GOVERNMENT
CO-EXIST WITH THE REDS
ONE SUPER CHURCH THROUGH THE ECUMENICAL MOVEMENT!
THE WAY THINGS ARE GOING,—WE WILL SOON BE ABLE TO FORCE EVERY GOSPEL PROGRAM OFF RADIO AND TELEVISION!
HEAR HEAR!
THAT'S WONDERFUL NEWS!
FOR THE TIME WILL COME WHEN THEY WILL NOT ENDURE SOUND DOCTRINE; BUT AFTER THEIR OWN LUSTS SHALL THEY HEAP TO THEMSELVES TEACHERS, HAVING ITCHING EARS; AND THEY SHALL TURN AWAY THEIR EARS FROM THE TRUTH, AND

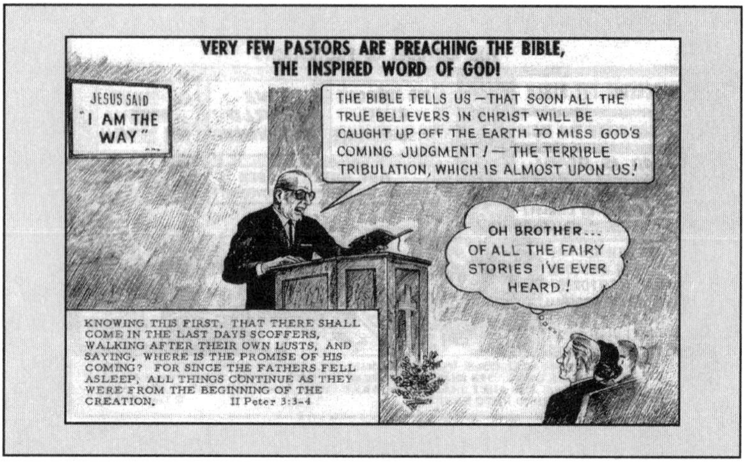
VERY FEW PASTORS ARE PREACHING THE BIBLE, THE INSPIRED WORD OF GOD!
JESUS SAID "I AM THE WAY"
THE BIBLE TELLS US—THAT SOON ALL THE TRUE BELIEVERS IN CHRIST WILL BE CAUGHT UP OFF THE EARTH TO MISS GOD'S COMING JUDGMENT!—THE TERRIBLE TRIBULATION, WHICH IS ALMOST UPON US!
OH BROTHER... OF ALL THE FAIRY STORIES I'VE EVER HEARD!
KNOWING THIS FIRST, THAT THERE SHALL COME IN THE LAST DAYS SCOFFERS, WALKING AFTER THEIR OWN LUSTS, AND SAYING, WHERE IS THE PROMISE OF HIS COMING? FOR SINCE THE FATHERS FELL ASLEEP, ALL THINGS CONTINUE AS THEY WERE FROM THE BEGINNING OF THE CREATION. II Peter 3:3-4

C'MON NOW, DO YOU ACTUALLY BELIEVE THAT YARN ABOUT JESUS RAISING THE DEAD BELIEVERS AND THE REAL CHRISTIANS OFF THE EARTH?
YOU MEAN THE RAPTURE? OH YES, IT'S THE NEXT EVENT ON THE PROPHETIC CALENDAR—IT COULD HAPPEN TONIGHT AND I'D BE GONE! I WISH YOU'D SURRENDER YOUR LIFE TO CHRIST—BEFORE IT'S TOO LATE!
HAW HAW.. THAT'LL BE THE DAY!
MORE RACE RIOTS
MAJOR WAR LOOMS

I'LL KILL YOU FOR THAT!
YOU REMIND ME OF MY 4th WIFE!
STOP IT! MY HUSBAND IS WATCHING US!
I'LL BET ON THE LITTLE MAN!
YOU KNOW HE DOESN'T CARE!

YOU KNOW YOU'RE THE ONLY MAN FOR ME!
HAW HAW @@!!!★ THAT WAS A FILTHY STORY! THAT WAS GREAT!
HEY! THERE'S AN OLD NUT OUTSIDE—PREACHING THE GOSPEL!— LET'S GO GIVE HIM THE BUSINESS! HAW HAW HAW
THIS KNOW ALSO, THAT IN THE LAST DAYS PERILOUS TIMES SHALL COME. FOR MEN SHALL BE LOVERS OF THEIR OWN SELVES, COVETOUS, BOASTERS, PROUD, BLASPHEMERS, DISOBEDIENT TO PARENTS, UNTHANKFUL, UNHOLY, WITHOUT NATURAL AFFECTION, TRUCE BREAKERS, FALSE ACCUSERS, INCONTINENT, FIERCE, DESPISERS OF THOSE THAT ARE GOOD, TRAITORS, HEADY, HIGH-MINDED, LOVERS OF PLEASURES MORE THAN LOVERS OF GOD; HAVING A FORM OF GODLINESS, BUT DENYING THE POWER THEREOF. II Tim. 3:1-5
NOTHING IS REALLY FILTHY! FILTH IS ONLY IN YOUR MIND!—IF YOU THINK IT'S FILTHY— THEN IT'S FILTHY!
AS IT WAS IN THE DAYS OF NOAH . .

THE NEXT EVENT ON GOD'S PROPHETIC CALENDAR
"FOR THE LORD HIMSELF SHALL DESCEND FROM HEAVEN WITH A SHOUT, WITH THE VOICE OF THE ARCHANGEL, AND WITH THE TRUMP OF GOD: AND THE DEAD IN CHRIST SHALL RISE FIRST: THEN WE WHICH ARE ALIVE AND REMAIN SHALL BE CAUGHT UP TOGETHER WITH THEM IN THE CLOUDS, TO MEET THE LORD IN THE AIR: AND SO SHALL WE EVER BE WITH THE LORD. WHEREFORE COMFORT ONE ANOTHER WITH THESE WORDS."
I Thess. 4:16-18

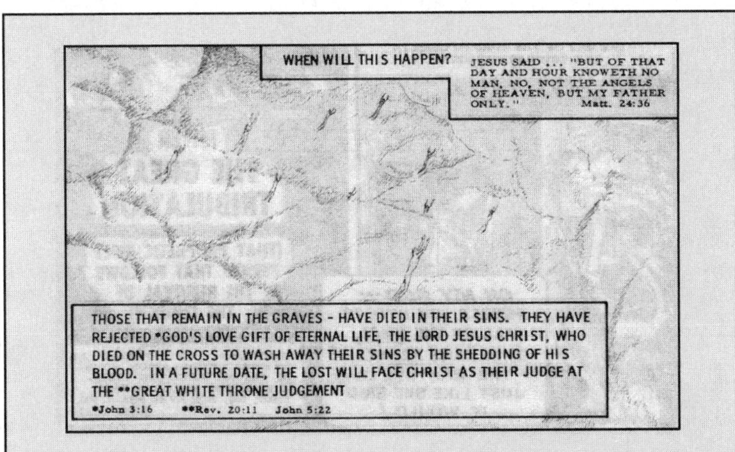
WHEN WILL THIS HAPPEN?
JESUS SAID ... "BUT OF THAT DAY AND HOUR KNOWETH NO MAN, NO, NOT THE ANGELS OF HEAVEN, BUT MY FATHER ONLY." Matt. 24:36
THOSE THAT REMAIN IN THE GRAVES - HAVE DIED IN THEIR SINS. THEY HAVE REJECTED *GOD'S LOVE GIFT OF ETERNAL LIFE, THE LORD JESUS CHRIST, WHO DIED ON THE CROSS TO WASH AWAY THEIR SINS BY THE SHEDDING OF HIS BLOOD. IN A FUTURE DATE, THE LOST WILL FACE CHRIST AS THEIR JUDGE AT THE **GREAT WHITE THRONE JUDGEMENT
*John 3:16 **Rev. 20:11 John 5:22

I Thess. 5:2
OH MY GOD---
WHERE'S MY WIFE??
ALL OF THE REAL
CHRISTIANS ARE GONE!
--- THE RAPTURE CAME,
JUST LIKE SHE SAID
IT WOULD!
THE CONQUEROR
DESTROYER OF PEACE
FAMINE
DEATH
ENTER
THE GREAT
TRIBULATION
(THAT PROPHETIC BIBLE
PERIOD THAT FOLLOWS
THE REMOVAL OF
THE CHURCH)
JESUS SAID ... "FOR THEN SHALL
BE GREAT TRIBULATION, SUCH
AS WAS NOT SINCE THE BEGIN-
NING OF THE WORLD TO THIS
TIME, NO, NOR EVER SHALL BE.
Matt. 24:21

RUSSIA (MAGOG)
MOVES ON ISRAEL
"THOU SHALT FALL UPON THE MOUNTAINS OF ISRAEL, THOU, AND ALL THY
BANDS, AND THE PEOPLE THAT IS WITH THEE: I WILL GIVE THEE UNTO
THE RAVENOUS BIRDS OF EVERY SORT, AND TO THE BEASTS OF THE FIELD
TO BE DEVOURED.
Ezekiel 39:4
RUSSIA IS DEFEATED - A MIRACLE OF GOD'S INTERVENTION

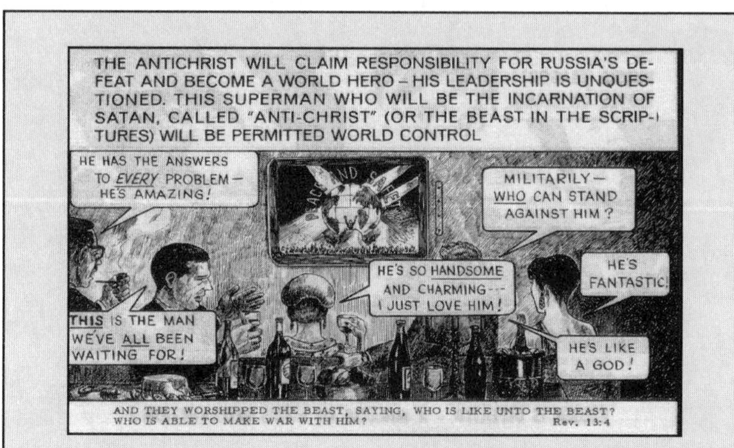
THE ANTICHRIST WILL CLAIM RESPONSIBILITY FOR RUSSIA'S DE-
FEAT AND BECOME A WORLD HERO – HIS LEADERSHIP IS UNQUES-
TIONED. THIS SUPERMAN WHO WILL BE THE INCARNATION OF
SATAN, CALLED "ANTI-CHRIST" (OR THE BEAST IN THE SCRIP-
TURES) WILL BE PERMITTED WORLD CONTROL
HE HAS THE ANSWERS
TO EVERY PROBLEM –
HE'S AMAZING!
MILITARILY –
WHO CAN STAND
AGAINST HIM?
HE'S SO HANDSOME
AND CHARMING---
I JUST LOVE HIM!
HE'S
FANTASTIC!
THIS IS THE MAN
WE'VE ALL BEEN
WAITING FOR!
HE'S LIKE
A GOD!
AND THEY WORSHIPPED THE BEAST, SAYING, WHO IS LIKE UNTO THE BEAST?
WHO IS ABLE TO MAKE WAR WITH HIM?
Rev. 13:4

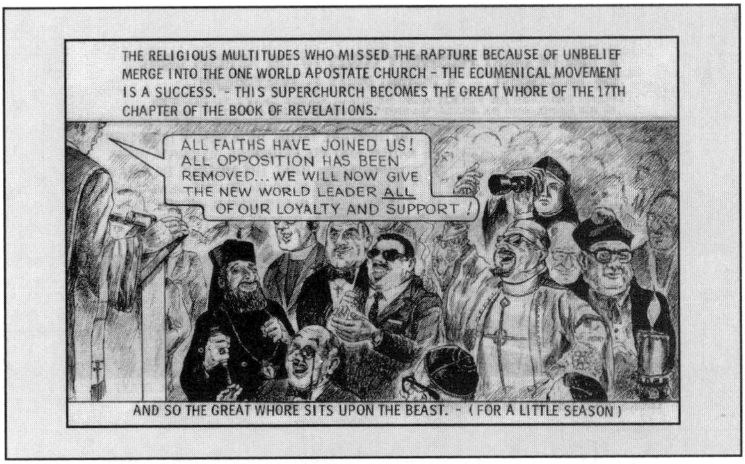
THE RELIGIOUS MULTITUDES WHO MISSED THE RAPTURE BECAUSE OF UNBELIEF MERGE INTO THE ONE WORLD APOSTATE CHURCH - THE ECUMENICAL MOVEMENT IS A SUCCESS. - THIS SUPERCHURCH BECOMES THE GREAT WHORE OF THE 17TH CHAPTER OF THE BOOK OF REVELATIONS.
ALL FAITHS HAVE JOINED US! ALL OPPOSITION HAS BEEN REMOVED... WE WILL NOW GIVE THE NEW WORLD LEADER ALL OF OUR LOYALTY AND SUPPORT!
AND SO THE GREAT WHORE SITS UPON THE BEAST. - (FOR A LITTLE SEASON)

A TIME OF GREAT PROSPERITY COMES TO THE NATIONS UNDER THE ANTI-CHRIST. A PSEUDO PEACE IS EVERYWHERE! -
("AND THROUGH HIS POLICY ALSO HE SHALL CAUSE CRAFT TO PROSPER IN HIS HAND; AND HE SHALL MAGNIFY HIMSELF IN HIS HEART" -) Daniel 8:25
MOSQUE OF OMAR
THE JEWS ARE TAKING THEIR WEALTH FROM EVERY NATION AND ARE RETURNING TO ISRAEL—SEE THAT THE MOSQUE OF OMAR IS GIVEN TO THE JEWS AS A PEACE TOKEN.—THEY CAN RECONSTRUCT SOLOMON'S TEMPLE ON THAT SITE!
YES, MASTER!
KNOWING FULL WELL THAT HIS FALSE PROSPERITY WILL COME TO AN END - THE BEAST LOOKS UPON THE WEALTH OF ISRAEL. - HE NOW PLANS FOR THEIR DESTRUCTION

ISRAEL BELIEVES THAT PEACE HAS COME AT LONG LAST - SOLOMON'S TEMPLE IS RECONSTRUCTED ON IT'S ORIGINAL SITE. - THE MOSQUE OF OMAR IS GONE
FINALLY WE HAVE PEACE AND SAFETY!
YES!
"FOR WHEN THEY SHALL SAY, PEACE AND SAFETY; THEN SUDDEN DESTRUCTION COMETH UPON THEM," I Thess. 5:3

WITH THE USE OF COMPUTERS, THE BEAST WILL BE ABLE TO CONTROL EVERY PERSON ON THE GLOBE.
EVERYONE SHALL RECEIVE MY MARK ON THEIR FOREHEADS OR ON THEIR RIGHT HAND, WITHOUT THIS MARK-YOU WILL BE UNABLE TO BUY OR SELL! REV 13:16-17
" IF ANY MAN WORSHIP THE BEAST AND HIS IMAGE, AND RECEIVE HIS MARK IN HIS FOREHEAD, OR IN HIS HAND"-------" HE SHALL BE TORMENTED WITH FIRE AND BRIMSTONE IN THE PRESENCE OF THE HOLY ANGELS,"......... Rev. 14:9-10

THERE ARISES A FALSE PROPHET WHO CAUSES THE MULTITUDES TO WORSHIP THE BEAST.
I COMMAND FIRE TO COME OUT OF THE HEAVENS (REV 13:13)
HE'S NOT A MAN...HE'S A GOD!
AND DECEIVETH THEM THAT DWELL ON THE EARTH, BY THE MEANS OF THOSE MIRACLES WHICH HE HAD POWER TO DO IN THE SIGHT OF THE BEAST; ... SAYING TO THEM THAT DWELL ON THE EARTH, THAT THEY SHOULD MAKE AN IMAGE TO THE BEAST, Rev. 13:14

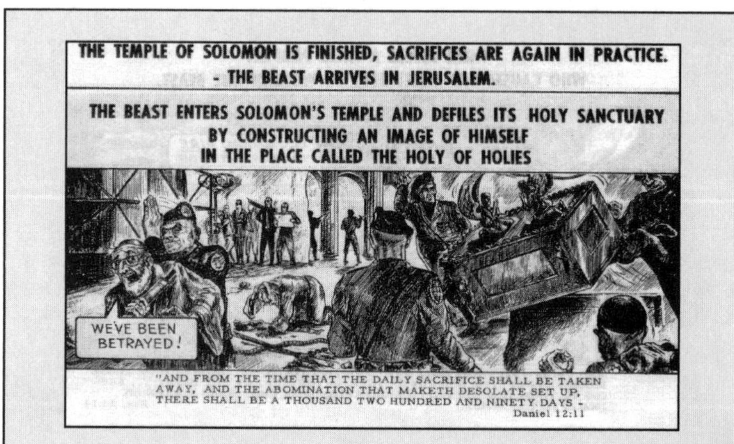
THE TEMPLE OF SOLOMON IS FINISHED, SACRIFICES ARE AGAIN IN PRACTICE. - THE BEAST ARRIVES IN JERUSALEM.
THE BEAST ENTERS SOLOMON'S TEMPLE AND DEFILES ITS HOLY SANCTUARY BY CONSTRUCTING AN IMAGE OF HIMSELF IN THE PLACE CALLED THE HOLY OF HOLIES
WE'VE BEEN BETRAYED!
"AND FROM THE TIME THAT THE DAILY SACRIFICE SHALL BE TAKEN AWAY, AND THE ABOMINATION THAT MAKETH DESOLATE SET UP, THERE SHALL BE A THOUSAND TWO HUNDRED AND NINETY DAYS - Daniel 12:11

AND HE (THE FALSE PROPHET) HAD POWER TO GIVE LIFE UNTO THE IMAGE OF THE BEAST, THAT THE IMAGE OF THE BEAST SHOULD BOTH SPEAK, AND CAUSE THAT AS MANY AS WOULD NOT WORSHIP THE IMAGE OF THE BEAST SHOULD BE KILLED. Rev. 13:15
I COMMAND YOU TO BECOME A LIVING THING!
IT'S A MIRACLE!
IT'S ALIVE!
THIS IS THE DEATH SENTENCE FOR EVERY JEW!

JESUS SAID ... WHEN YE THEREFORE SEE THE ABOMINATION OF DESOLATION, SPOKEN OF BY DANIEL THE PROPHET, STAND IN THE HOLY PLACE, (WHOSO READETH, LET HIM UNDERSTAND:)
THEN LET THEM WHICH BE IN JUDAEA FLEE INTO THE MOUNTAINS: LET HIM WHICH IS ON THE HOUSE-TOP NOT COME DOWN TO TAKE ANYTHING OUT OF HIS HOUSE: NEITHER LET HIM WHICH IS IN THE FIELD RETURN BACK TO TAKE HIS CLOTHES. AND WOE UNTO THEM THAT ARE WITH CHILD, AND TO THEM THAT GIVE SUCK IN THOSE DAYS. Matt. 24:15-19
MEDITERRANEAN SEA
SEA OF GALILEE
JERUSALEM
DEAD SEA
PETRA
MANY BIBLE SCHOLARS BELIEVE THEY WILL FIND REFUGE IN PETRA, THE INCREDIBLE RUINS OF AN EMPTY CITY, MYSTERIOUSLY CONCEALED FROM THIS MODERN WORLD IN A REMOTE BASIN OF TRANS-JORDANIA

144,000 JEWISH SERVANTS ARE SEALED BY GOD TO GO FORTH AND PREACH THE GOSPEL OF THE KINGDOM. Rev. 7
THE MESSIAH WILL COME SHORTLY!
DON'T YOU THINK HE SHOULD BE REPORTED?
YES, I'LL CALL IN AT ONCE!
AND THIS GOSPEL OF THE KINGDOM SHALL BE PREACHED IN ALL THE WORLD FOR A WITNESS UNTO ALL NATIONS; AND THEN SHALL THE END COME. Matt. 24:14

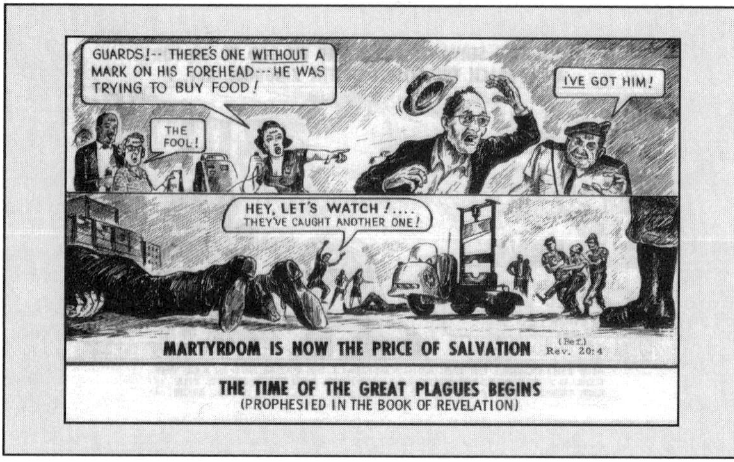
GUARDS!-- THERE'S ONE WITHOUT A MARK ON HIS FOREHEAD--- HE WAS TRYING TO BUY FOOD!
THE FOOL!
I'VE GOT HIM!
HEY, LET'S WATCH!.... THEY'VE CAUGHT ANOTHER ONE!
MARTYRDOM IS NOW THE PRICE OF SALVATION (Ref.) Rev. 20:4
THE TIME OF THE GREAT PLAGUES BEGINS
(PROPHESIED IN THE BOOK OF REVELATION)

AND THE THIRD PART OF THE WATERS BECAME WORMWOOD; AND MANY MEN DIED OF THE WATERS, BECAUSE THEY WERE MADE BITTER Rev. 8:11
AND THE THIRD PART OF THE SEA BECAME BLOOD AND THE THIRD PART OF THE CREATURES WHICH WERE IN THE SEA AND HAD LIFE, DIED, AND A THIRD PART OF THE SHIPS WERE DESTORY-ED Rev. 8: 8-9
AND THERE CAME OUT OF THE SMOKE LOCUSTS UPON THE EARTH: AND UNTO THEM WAS GIVEN POWER AS THE SCORPIONS OF THE EARTH HAVE POWER. Rev. 9:3
AND THEIR POWER WAS TO HURT MEN FIVE MONTHS. Rev. 9:10
AND MEN WERE SCORCHED WITH GREAT HEAT, AND BLASPHEMED THE NAME OF GOD, WHICH HATH POWER OVER THESE PLAGUES: Rev 16:9
PLAGUE AFTER PLAGUE STRIKES REBELLIOUS MAN...
AND STILL HE WILL NOT REPENT

THE SUPER APOSTATE CHURCH IS NO LONGER OF ANY USE TO THE BEAST. THE GREAT WHORE (REPRESENTING THE SUPER CHURCH) IS DESTROYED.
THE FINAL SHOWDOWN BEGINS
EVERY LAST JEW MUST DIE! ALERT MY ARMIES!
666
THIS IS IT!
SO ECCLESIASTICAL BABYLON IS NO MORE...ALAS BABYLON! Rev. 18:10

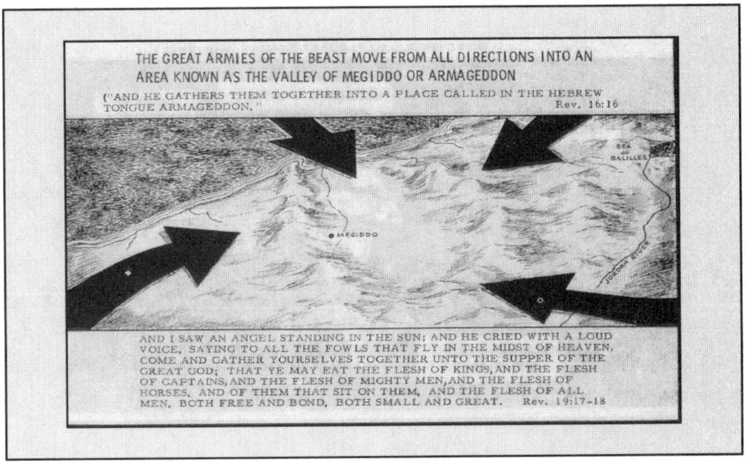
THE GREAT ARMIES OF THE BEAST MOVE FROM ALL DIRECTIONS INTO AN AREA KNOWN AS THE VALLEY OF MEGIDDO OR ARMAGEDDON
("AND HE GATHERS THEM TOGETHER INTO A PLACE CALLED IN THE HEBREW TONGUE ARMAGEDDON." Rev. 16:16
SEA OF GALILEE
MEGIDDO
JORDAN RIVER
AND I SAW AN ANGEL STANDING IN THE SUN; AND HE CRIED WITH A LOUD VOICE, SAYING TO ALL THE FOWLS THAT FLY IN THE MIDST OF HEAVEN, COME AND GATHER YOURSELVES TOGETHER UNTO THE SUPPER OF THE GREAT GOD; THAT YE MAY EAT THE FLESH OF KINGS, AND THE FLESH OF CAPTAINS, AND THE FLESH OF MIGHTY MEN, AND THE FLESH OF HORSES, AND OF THEM THAT SIT ON THEM, AND THE FLESH OF ALL MEN, BOTH FREE AND BOND, BOTH SMALL AND GREAT. Rev. 19:17-18

JESUS SAID: "AND EXCEPT THOSE DAYS SHOULD BE SHORTENED, THERE SHOULD NO FLESH BE SAVED:" Matt. 24:22
ISRAEL IS FINISHED!
ALL HOPE IS GONE!
THERE IS NO ESCAPE!
OUR GOD HAS FORSAKEN US!
WHERE IS OUR MESSIAH?

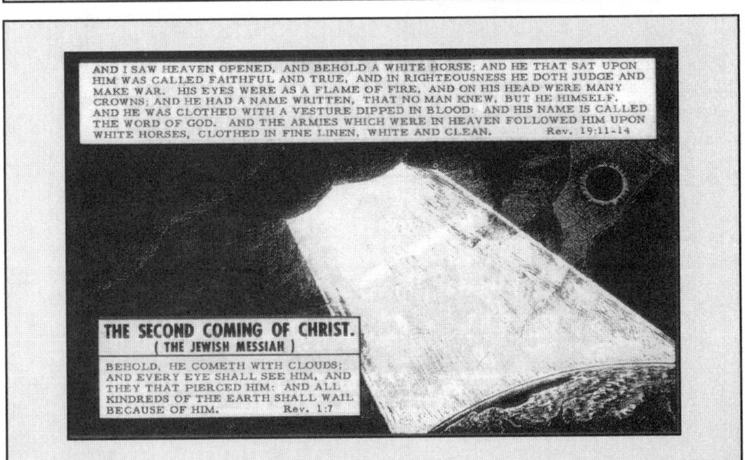
AND I SAW HEAVEN OPENED, AND BEHOLD A WHITE HORSE; AND HE THAT SAT UPON HIM WAS CALLED FAITHFUL AND TRUE, AND IN RIGHTEOUSNESS HE DOTH JUDGE AND MAKE WAR. HIS EYES WERE AS A FLAME OF FIRE, AND ON HIS HEAD WERE MANY CROWNS; AND HE HAD A NAME WRITTEN, THAT NO MAN KNEW, BUT HE HIMSELF. AND HE WAS CLOTHED WITH A VESTURE DIPPED IN BLOOD: AND HIS NAME IS CALLED THE WORD OF GOD. AND THE ARMIES WHICH WERE IN HEAVEN FOLLOWED HIM UPON WHITE HORSES, CLOTHED IN FINE LINEN, WHITE AND CLEAN. Rev. 19:11-14
THE SECOND COMING OF CHRIST.
(THE JEWISH MESSIAH)
BEHOLD, HE COMETH WITH CLOUDS; AND EVERY EYE SHALL SEE HIM, AND THEY THAT PIERCED HIM: AND ALL KINDREDS OF THE EARTH SHALL WAIL BECAUSE OF HIM. Rev. 1:7

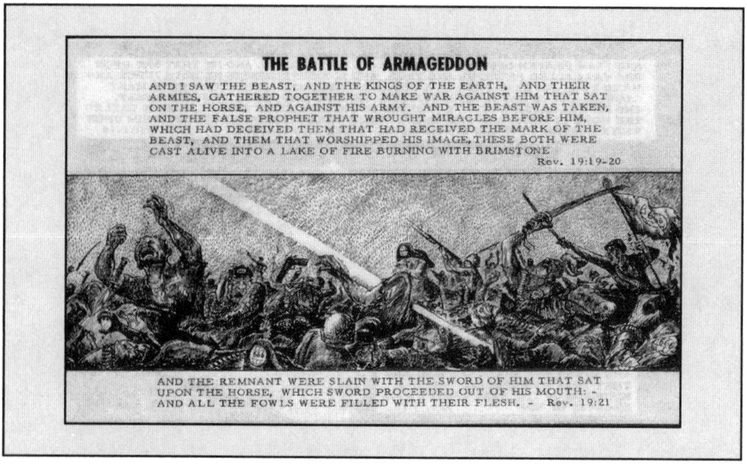
THE BATTLE OF ARMAGEDDON
AND I SAW THE BEAST, AND THE KINGS OF THE EARTH, AND THEIR ARMIES, GATHERED TOGETHER TO MAKE WAR AGAINST HIM THAT SAT ON THE HORSE, AND AGAINST HIS ARMY. AND THE BEAST WAS TAKEN, AND THE FALSE PROPHET THAT WROUGHT MIRACLES BEFORE HIM, WHICH HAD DECEIVED THEM THAT HAD RECEIVED THE MARK OF THE BEAST, AND THEM THAT WORSHIPPED HIS IMAGE. THESE BOTH WERE CAST ALIVE INTO A LAKE OF FIRE BURNING WITH BRIMSTONE
Rev. 19:19-20
AND THE REMNANT WERE SLAIN WITH THE SWORD OF HIM THAT SAT UPON THE HORSE, WHICH SWORD PROCEEDED OUT OF HIS MOUTH: - AND ALL THE FOWLS WERE FILLED WITH THEIR FLESH. - Rev. 19:21

JESUS CHRIST, "THE PRINCE OF PEACE", NOW RULES OVER THE EARTH - "SWORDS ARE BEATEN INTO PLOWSHEARS" AND THERE SHALL BE WAR NO MORE. THE GREAT MILLENNIUM HAS COME.
I LOOKED AND I ACTUALLY SAW THE NAIL PRINTS IN OUR MESSIAH'S HANDS!
THY KINGDOM COME. THY WILL BE DONE IN EARTH, AS IT IS IN HEAVEN. Matt. 6:10

1000 YEARS LATER
THAT GREAT AND TERRIBLE DAY FINALLY COMES - THE DAY, WHEN ALL WHO DIED IN THEIR SINS WILL BE JUDGED BY THEIR CREATOR,* THE LORD JESUS.
DO THEIR NAMES APPEAR IN THE BOOK OF LIFE ?
NO LORD, THEIR NAMES DO NOT APPEAR !
"AND I SAW THE DEAD, SMALL AND GREAT, STAND BEFORE GOD; AND THE BOOKS WERE OPENED: AND ANOTHER BOOK WAS OPENED, WHICH IS THE BOOK OF LIFE: AND THE DEAD WERE JUDGED OUT OF THOSE THINGS WHICH WERE WRITTEN IN THE BOOKS, ACCORDING TO THEIR WORKS." Rev. 20:12
* Ref. John 1:10 and 5:22

"AND WHOSOEVER WAS NOT FOUND WRITTEN IN THE BOOK OF LIFE WAS CAST INTO THE LAKE OF FIRE." Rev. 20:15
GOD'S LOVE GIFT - WHICH IS ETERNAL LIFE IS STILL EXTENDED TO YOU IN THESE CLOSING HOURS.
"FOR GOD SO LOVED THE WORLD, THAT HE GAVE HIS ONLY BEGOTTEN SON, THAT WHOSOEVER*BELIEVETH IN HIM SHOULD NOT PERISH BUT HAVE EVERLASTING LIFE!" John 3:16
(* trusts, clings to, relies on)

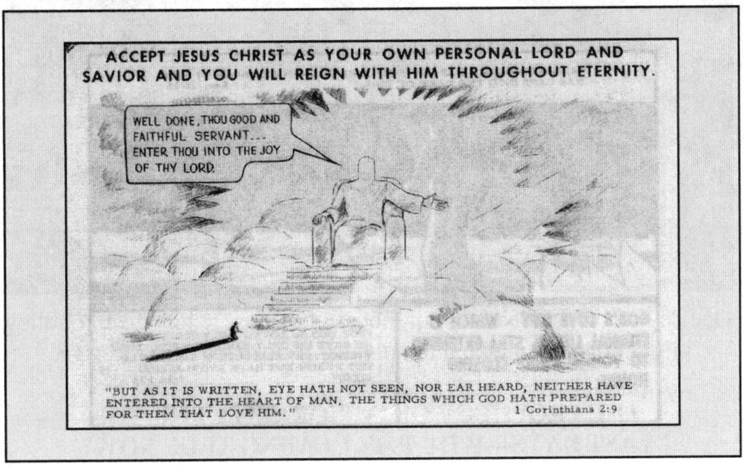
ACCEPT JESUS CHRIST AS YOUR OWN PERSONAL LORD AND SAVIOR AND YOU WILL REIGN WITH HIM THROUGHOUT ETERNITY.
WELL DONE, THOU GOOD AND FAITHFUL SERVANT... ENTER THOU INTO THE JOY OF THY LORD.
"BUT AS IT IS WRITTEN, EYE HATH NOT SEEN, NOR EAR HEARD, NEITHER HAVE ENTERED INTO THE HEART OF MAN, THE THINGS WHICH GOD HATH PREPARED FOR THEM THAT LOVE HIM." 1 Corinthians 2:9

One day rabbis will lead tens of thousands astray, telling them to follow the Antichrist, thinking blindly that he is in fact, the Messiah.

THE PROPHECY OF IMMORALITY FOR THE LAST DAYS—WHY IS IT COMING TRUE NOW?

Why does the mass media, including soap operas, talk shows and other Hollywood productions, endorse homosexuality, living together, public distribution of condoms, and other behavior which contributes to the destruction of the traditional family unit? Good question—we are glad you asked. We believe many members of the media, along with other influential people and groups on the financial level of the Rockefellers and Turner, are members of the Trilateral Commission for world government.[74] We believe that they feel they have much to gain in a global government economy.

---

[74]Hal Lindsey interestingly notes of the Trilateral Commission for world government: "*Newsweek* described the commission's inception: '...The Trilateral Commission, a brainchild of David Rockefeller, was transformed into reality by Zbigniew Brzezinski'....new provisions to the system are the need for relationships with communist, Third World and OPEC groups. This system indeed intends to unite the

There are those who feel that they (certain ultra-wealthy individuals and government security divisions) want to depopulate the middle and lower classes to *manageable levels, possibly through genetically engineered germ warfare* (see our *Vol. II*, chapter 41, "Was AIDS Made?"), and to levy high taxes on all the products the *selected to live* population can produce. They can then sit back and enjoy the rewards and fruits with little work. The way to create a global government and one which suppresses the masses, so the governement elite can gather their taxes, is to destroy the sovereignty of all nations. The children are the future of any nation. Hitler once said, "Let me control the textbooks, and I will control Germany."[75]

---

whole world economically....Carter became a charter member of the commission in 1973. He received a thorough indoctrination in trilateralist views, particularly on foreign policy, from Brzezinski himself. There is no question that the commission groomed Carter to be President. He was virtually a political unknown. Yet because of the enormous behind-the-scenes power of the Trilateralists in the news media, he came from nowhere to capture the White House....It's been interesting to me to watch various news media heavyweights rush to defend the commission against charges that it has gained undue power in the world's governments. Publications such as the *Wall Street Journal*, *Time*, *Newsweek* and *U.S. News and World Report* have all said pretty much the same things. In general, they publish articles which minimize the commission's influence....simply a floating study group with no essential power, and...or Marxist-leaning leftists. I wonder if the fact that so many news media executives are also commission members has anything to do with these published defenses. The Trilateral Commission's members include men like the editor-in-chief of *Time* magazine, directors of the *New York Times*, the *Wall Street Journal,* the *Los Angeles Times* and the *Washington Post*, and the editorial director of the *Chicago Sun-Times*....For the media to say that the Trilateral Commission has no essential political power, however, is an insult to the intelligence of the American public. It also assumes that most Americans didn't read or don't remember the many articles which detailed the commission's growing power and were published in those same newspapers and magazines in the 1977 era." Hal Lindsey, *The 1980's: Countdown to Armageddon*, pp. 122-126. I believe that it will be this organization, or one similar to it, that within approximately fifty years or less will set up a global economy, which the Antichrist of the end times will take over and use as his machinery to rule the world and attempt to force human worship of himself. This will occur shortly before Jesus returns, just after the Rapture of true believers, but before His triumphant return seven years after that Rapture with us (Rev. 19), to rule the world during the Kingdom Age (Rev. 20; Isa. 11; 65).

[75]D. James Kennedy, Ph.D., "A Godly Education." Kennedy went on to note: "Dr. John Goodland of the National Education Association (the teachers union) wrote a report for the NEA entitled 'Schooling For the Future' in which he stated: 'Our goal is...' What is their goal? Is it educating the children? 'Our goal is *behavioral change* [emphasis added]. The majority of our youth still hold to the values of their parents and if we do not recognize this pattern, if we do not resocialize them to accept change, our society may decay.' Did you realize that teachers were in the classroom to disengage children from the values of their parents?....there is the censoring of anything Christian out of textbooks....it is the opinion of a study funded by a grant from the National Institute of Education....The study was directed by Dr. Paul C. Vitz, a professor of psychology at New York University. He says the textbooks in our schools are biased....May I say that the greatest amount of censorship going on anywhere, is the censorship taking place in

If you plan to destroy a nation and its sovereignty and replace it with some type of global-socialist philosophy, you have to destroy the building blocks of that nation. The family is the building block of a nation. Once this institution falls, chaos follows: illegitimate children, drugs, disease, homosexuality, improper education and character, will contribute to the fall of civilization as we have known it. If present trends continue to escalate, within twenty to thirty years we are going to fall. The super rich will have their way and a liberally oriented world government, which is antithetical to traditional morality, will then thrive. This will create an atmosphere for the Antichrist to take over! Thus, your question has been answered.

The immorality the Bible predicted on a large scale (II Tim. 3:1-5)[76] for the last days, has an un-Christian and selfish motive, fueled by secular economic profit, and is well on its way! George Orwell might have miscalculated the date in his *1984* "Big Brother" speculation, but those wise ideas will hit all of us in some terrible way, someday, probably between 2020 and 2040!

***

American schools, censoring Christianity into non-existence. Here is what the National Institute of Education says is the nature of the bias: 'Religion, traditional family values, and conservative political and economic positions have been reliably excluded from children's textbooks. This exclusion is particularly disturbing because it is found in a system paid for by taxpayers, and one that claims, moreover, to be committed to impartial knowledge and accuracy....'....The report goes on to say: 'The fifth-grade U.S. history texts included modest coverage of religion in Colonial America and at the early Southwest missions; however, the treatment of the past 100 years was so devoid of reference to religion as to give the impression that it has ceased to exist in America.' The sixth-grade textbooks dealing with religion and culture in world history, displayed a consistent bias against Christianity. The report states that 'In several books Mohammed's life gets much more coverage than that of Jesus.' " Ibid, pp. 6-8. Available in its entirety through Coral Ridge Ministries, POB 40, Fort Lauderdale, FL, USA 33302.

[76]"This know also, that in the last days perilous times shall come. For men shall be lovers of their own selves, covetous, boasters, proud, blasphemers, disobedient to parents, unthankful, unholy, Without natural affection, trucebreakers, false accusers, incontinent, fierce, despisers of those that are good, Traitors, heady, highminded, lovers of pleasures more than lovers of God; Having a form of godliness, but denying the power thereof: from such turn away" (II Tim 3:1-5 KJV).

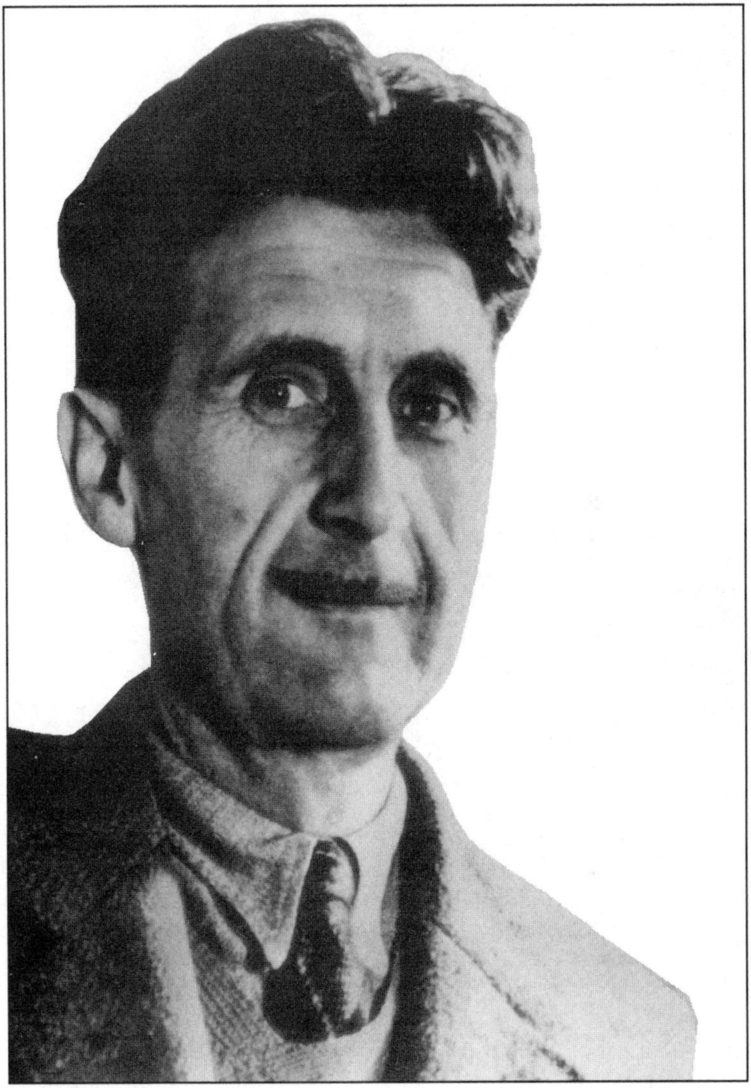

George Orwell (Eric Arthur Blair), 1903-1950, author of *1984*.

Orwell's novel, *1984*, written in 1948, dealt with a future of Totalitarian rule, where little privacy exists. It would seem that we are presently witnessing the birth of his fears, in that almost everywhere we go, we are "on camera": in the Post Office, the bank, the department store, etc. We are deterring crime at the expense of our privacy. Another twenty to thirty years may indeed bring his novel into the realm of reality.

An aerial view of Jerusalem.[77] Numbered sites include: 1. The Garden Tomb of Jesus; 2. Mount Calvary (location of the Crucifixion); 3. Arab bus station landmark; 4. The Bible Society; where the New Testament is available in many different languages, including Hebrew; 5. Bank Lumi; 6. Main Post Office; 7. The King David Hotel; 8. The YMCA; 9. Intercontinental Hotel, near the summit of the Mount of Olives.

[77]Courtesy of State of Israel Government Press Office, photography department.

"The LORD thy God will raise up unto thee a Prophet from the midst of thee, of thy brethren, like unto me; unto him ye shall hearken...." Moses, the chief prophet of Judaism, Deuteronomy 18:15 KJV[1]

"...This is of a truth that prophet that should come into the world."
The words of those who witnessed Jesus' miracles, John 6:14 KJV

"...I am the way, the truth, and the life: no man cometh unto the father, but by me."
Jesus, John 14:6 KJV

"When ye therefore shall see the abomination of desolation, spoken of by Daniel the prophet, stand in the holy place, (whoso readeth, let him understand:) Then let them which be in Judæa flee into the mountains...." Jesus' instruction to the Jews of Israel at the time of the end, Matthew 24:15-16 KJV

"Hold fast to the Bible as the sheet anchor of our liberties. To the influence of this book we are indebted for all the progress made in true civilization and to this we must look as our guide in the future."[2] U.S. Grant,
18th President of the United States

" 'Can you give me one single irrefutable proof of God?' 'Yes, your Majesty, the Jews.' " Marquis D'Argens to Frederick the Great

"About the time of the End, a body of men will be raised up who will turn their attention to the prophecies, and insist on their literal interpretation in the midst of such clamor and opposition." Sir Isaac Newton

24

TRUTH OR CONSEQUENCES—WILL THE REAL FAITH PLEASE STAND?

How can we know the many counterfeits from the real thing? The apostle John warned us 2000 years ago: "BELOVED, believe not every spirit, but try the spirits whether they are of God: because many false prophets are gone out into the world" (I John 4:1 KJV).

Jesus Himself also mentions that there will be wolves in sheep's clothing posing as prophets, who would be false. In His exact words, He warns us: "...narrow *is* the way, which leadeth unto life, and few there be that find it. Beware of false prophets, which come to you in sheep's clothing, but inwardly they are ravening wolves....For there shall arise false Christs, and false prophets, and shall shew great signs and wonders; insomuch that, if *it were* possible, they shall deceive the very elect. Behold, I have told you before. Wherefore if they shall say

---

[1] *The New Scofield Reference Bible.*

[2] "The Interpreter," Vol. XXXVII, No. 2, Spring 1995. Lutherville: MD, © 1995, p. 21. Available through The Interpreter, POB 110, Lutherville, MD, USA 21093-0110.

unto you, Behold, he is in the desert; go not forth: behold, *he is* in the secret chambers; believe *it* not" (Matt. 7:14-15; 24:24-26 KJV). Thus, if we seek the truth for ourselves, we should remember Jesus' answer when Pilate asked Him who He was: "...Thou sayest that I am a king. To this end was I born, and for this cause came I into the world, that I should bear witness unto the truth. Every one that is of the truth heareth my voice" (John 18:37 KJV). Earlier He said: "...I am the way, the truth, and the life: no man cometh unto the Father, but by me" (John 14:6 KJV).

We should, of course, very carefully avoid that which is untrue! For instance, bank tellers can tell the difference between a real dollar bill and a counterfeit one, due to the fact that they are very well acquainted with the real one.

I expect this to be the most criticized chapter of this book. That is because anyone who is not spiritually close to Jesus, who is perhaps only a curious spectator to the promises of the New Testament, may, upon reading this chapter, find these concepts to be offensive. However, it is our conviction that the darkness will never comprehend the light (John 1:1-5). We are gambling that most of our readers have a spark of light within their spirit placed there by God, due to their openness, which has brought them this far through reading the various Old Testament prophecies and New Testament fulfillments concerning the prophesied Messiah! We hope to fan this spark of Messianic curiosity and hope into heartfelt fires of salvation!

WITH NO APOLOGIES

With no apologies, we proceed with this chapter, which we are aware that not all will be able to accept. We believe the Antichrist will coerce the worship of himself through ecumenical and economic pressure, as he forcefully creates a one-world religion. This one-world union will contain elements of every religion except the true one!

To understand the significance of what the book of Revelation calls "mystery Babylon" (Rev. 17:5), we should be aware of these "false spirits" to which John alluded (I John 4:1). Hopefully, we will then be equipped to steer our loved ones away from the deceptions which are presently plaguing our society,[3] as predicted.

***

[3]The spirits of New Age and witchcraft are exploding like wildfire. See our *Vol. II*, chapter 4, "Cults, the Occult and the New Age."

RELIGIOUS DECEPTION AND THOSE OTHER GODS

From the time of Adam, there has been religious deception, alternatives, if you please, to the true God who loves us. In Adam's time, Satan used the serpent to deceive. We will investigate in this chapter and our *Vol. II*, chapter 4, "Cults, the Occult and the New Age," the many current deceptions, in order that Christians may be better equipped to avoid the many techniques being used by the master of darkness in his ongoing work to exterminate the souls of men, which are so very precious to God.

Dagon, the fish-god of the Philistines.

A pagan priest offers a new-born baby as
a sacrifice to Molech, god of the Canaanites.

LOOKING BACK ON THE WORSHIP OF LIES

In past ages, Baal, Molech and Ashtoreth were worshipped (II Kings 23:10, 13). Dagon was the fish-god of the Philistines whose temple was destroyed by Samson (Jer. 7:31; 32:35). Molech,[4] to whom even Israelites sacrificed their children, was the god of the Canaanites (Lev. 20:2-5; Ezek. 16:20-22; Jer. 32:35; Amos 5:26). The Egyptian sun-god, Ra, and the many Hindu dieties, have deceived millions.

In the holy book of Islam, the Koran, Mohammed instructs in the name of Allah: "Make war upon those who believe not...even if they be people of the Book [Jews or Christians]. Make war upon them until idolatry is no more and Allah's religion reigns supreme."[5] In the past, Islam contributed to the murder of Jews and Christians and presently continues to perpetrated acts of terrorism!

Moslems claim that they are monotheistic and threaten those who realize otherwise! We recall that Salman Rushdie, author of *The Satanic Verses*, was placed under a death sentence in 1989 because he implied that Islam is polytheistic. This Islamic contract on Rushdie's life was instituted by the Ayatollah Khomeini, and is still enforced by Iran today. God forbid if they should ever find him. They have already murdered some of the foreign translators of his book.

FALSE PROPHETS AND RELIGIONS —WHAT DID MOSES SAY?

What does the Bible, which contains the record of God's creation of the universe and man's very beginnings,[6] have to say about this? "There shall not be found among you *any one* that maketh his son or his daughter to pass through the fire, *or* that useth divination, *or* an observer of times, or an enchanter, or a witch, Or a charmer, or a consulter with familiar spirits, or a wizard, or a necromancer. For all that do these things *are* an abomination unto the LORD: and because of these abominations the LORD thy God doth drive them out from before thee....But the prophet, which shall presume to speak a word in my name, which I have not commanded him to speak, or that shall speak in

---

[4]Leviticus 18:21-22 expressly forbade the Israelis to allow their children to pass through the fires of Molech and warned against the wickedness of homosexuality. The New Testament describes a horrifying consequence of homosexual activity, which sounds very much like AIDS (see Rom. 1:24-27). It goes without saying that we should heed this ancient Hebrew injunction, so that we may live today and inherit life in the world to come. The spelling of Molech is from the King James Version of the Bible.

[5]Mike Evans, *The Return*. New York: Thomas Nelson Publishers, © 1986, p. 149, used by permission.

[6]See Genesis 1-3.

the name of other gods, even that prophet shall die" (Deut. 18:10-12, 20 KJV).

Moses certainly illustrated God's opinion of false religions. It was not very flattering, was it? If Mohammed had chanced to meet some of the righteous of Israel, he might well have become a rock pile (stoning was the required method of execution for false prophets). As a result, the killings done in the name of Islam, which we have witnessed from the seventh century until now, might never have happened.[7]

ASTROLOGY IS A RELIGION!

Few realize that astrology is really the religion of the ancient Babylonians. The seers of Babylon, known as Chaldeans, assigned perverted meanings[8] to the stars and began to teach that a person's life was governed by them. Hal Lindsey tells us: "...the Chaldeans studied a person's birthday, asking the very hour a person was born, and then they would cast a horoscope of his destiny....The ancient astrologers believed that your fate was written in the stars before you were born and you can't alter the course of your destiny."[9]

The beginnings of the religion of astrology are recorded in Genesis 11:4: "And they said, Go to, let us build us a city and a tower, whose top *may reach* unto heaven; and let us make us a name, lest we be scattered abroad upon the face of the whole earth" (KJV). Notice the words "may reach" in italics. They were not in the original Hebrew. The "Tower of Babel" we read about as children was not built by stupid people trying to physically reach God; it was the first ziggurat used by the astrological priests to chart and study the stars in their false attempt to foretell the destiny of men.[10]

GOD JUDGES THE IDOLATRY OF ASTROLOGY

Astrology was exported from the plains of Shinar, in ancient Babylon, to Egypt (Exo. 7:11). The chief reason God allowed Israel to be destroyed in 606 BC, and kept in Babylonian captivity for seventy years, was because of the sin of idolatry, which at that time, was

---

[7]However, the Middle East Crisis, between Israel and the Arabs along with the Russians, is clearly forecast in the Bible. We must be prepared for it (Ezek. 38, 39).

[8]See our *Vol. II*, chapter 30, "The Gospel in the Stars." A sermon by Dr. D. James Kennedy documents this while explaining the true Christian Bible meaning in the constellations of the stars—the true meaning which God intended!

[9]Hal Lindsey with C.C. Carlson, *The Late Great Planet Earth*, p. 109.

[10]Bible scholar Henry H. Halley explains: "Genesis 11:4, 'a tower with its top in heaven' is an expression of the vast pride of the first builders of 'ziggurats,' the artificial temple hills of Sumeria and Babylonia." Henry H. Halley, *Halley's Bible Handbook*, p. 84.

associated with astrology. This can be seen in the biblical book of II Kings, which records many of the deeds performed by the righteous Israeli King Josiah, with God's favor.

The Bible tells us: "...he put down the idolatrous priests, whom the kings of Judah had ordained to burn incense in the high places in the cities of Judah, and in the places round about Jerusalem; them also that burned incense unto Baal, to the sun, and to the moon, and to the planets, and to all the host of heaven....Moreover the *workers with* familiar spirits, and the wizards, and the images, and the idols, and all the abominations that were spied in the land of Judah and in Jerusalem, did Josiah put away, that he might perform the words of the law....And like unto him was there no king before him, that turned to the LORD with all his heart, and with all his soul, and with all his might, according to all the law of Moses; neither after him arose there *any* like him" (II Kings 23:5, 24-25 KJV). When the Scripture speaks of "them also that burned incense unto....the planets and to all the host of heaven," it is clearly identifying ancient astrology.

A display of occult artifacts and astrological items at a local New Age store in Atlanta, GA.

"Thou art wearied in the multitude of thy counsels. Let now the astrologers, the stargazers, the monthly prognosticators, stand up, and save thee from *these things* that shall come upon thee. Behold, they shall be as stubble; the fire shall burn them; they shall not deliver themselves from the power of the flame: *there shall* not *be* a coal to warm at, *nor* fire to sit before it."

Isaiah 47:13-14 KJV

ASTROLOGY WAS ALMOST STRANGLED IN ITS BABYLONIAN CRIB

Daniel's power of prophecy from God so amazed the king, that he made Daniel a ruler, recognized his God, and at Daniel's urging spared the lives of his astrologers and wise men. Moreover, Daniel the prophet had a curious run-in with the astrologers of his day.

The king of Babylon was very upset with the astrologers. They were not able to fill him in on his forgotten dream. He was ready to execute them when, through the power of God, Daniel told the king not only of his dream, but of its true prophetic interpretation. "Then the king commanded to call the magicians, and the astrologers, and the sorcerers, and the Chaldeans, for to shew the king his dreams. So they came and stood before the king" (Dan. 2:2 KJV). The king told the astrologers: "...if ye will not make known unto me the dream, *there is but* one decree for you: for ye have prepared lying and corrupt words to speak before me, till the time be changed: therefore tell me the dream, and I shall know that ye can shew me the interpretation thereof. The Chaldeans answered before the king, and said, There is not a man upon the earth that can shew the king's matter: therefore *there is* no king, lord, nor ruler, *that* asked such things at any magician, or astrologer, or Chaldean....Then Arioch brought in Daniel before the king in haste, and said thus unto him, I have found a man of the captives of Judah, that will make known unto the king the interpretation. The king answered and said to Daniel, whose name *was* Belteshazzar, Art thou able to make known unto me the dream which I have seen, and the interpretation thereof? Daniel answered in the presence of the king, and said, The secret which the king hath demanded cannot the wise *men*, the astrologers, the magicians, the soothsayers, shew unto the king; But there is a God in heaven that revealeth secrets, and maketh known to the king Nebuchadnezzar what shall be in the latter days. Thy dream, and the visions of thy head upon thy bed, are these...." (Dan. 2:9-10, 25-28 KJV).

Daniel then revealed the king's dream. As previously mentioned, the dream was about a statue, which represented the rise and fall of the mightiest Gentile powers from that time until the Second Advent of the

Messiah. From our vantage point, the final portion of this prophecy, concerning revived Rome, is yet to culminate in the EEC.

After the king heard Daniel's recounting and interpretation, he was so awed that he: "...fell upon his face, and worshipped Daniel, and commanded that they should offer an oblation and sweet odours unto him. The king answered unto Daniel, and said, Of a truth *it is*, that your God *is* a God of gods, and a Lord of kings, and a revealer of secrets, seeing thou couldest reveal this secret. Then the king made Daniel a great man, and gave him many great gifts, and made him ruler over the whole province of Babylon, and chief of the governors over all the wise *men* of Babylon" (Dan. 2:46-48 KJV).

THE FAMILY TREE OF ASTROLOGY

The Medes conquered the Babylonians, and in turn, were conquered by the Persians, who inherited the craft. When the Greeks took over Media-Persia, they continued this fortune-telling. Finally, when the Romans overran the Greek kingdom, astrology became a worldwide practice. The astrological augurs of Rome were even consulted by the caesars.

ASTROLOGY—A MULTI-BILLION DOLLAR-A-YEAR INDUSTRY, PAVING THE WAY TO ANTICHRIST

We now see astrology as a multi-billion dollar-a-year industry—almost every newspaper has an astrology column. There are "do it yourself" witchcraft courses and an increasing number of outlets which carry books on the subject. Advertisments for 900 telephone numbers and call-in fortune-telling shows direct a steady stream of this brand of witchcraft at the layman. Even President Reagan's wife, Nancy, our former First Lady, was caught in its web, driven by the fear of another assassination attempt on her husband.

No one seems to be immune to this deceptive religion of Nimrod (the world's first dictator mentioned in Gen. 10), who wanted to use this religion to rule the world. God destroyed the Tower of Babel and introduced many different languages (Gen. 11). Thus, if there are many separate nations, it is almost impossible to have a one-world dictator until the false Messiah takes over at the end of history. Therefore, we know that the Antichrist must, and will, unify the world in economics and religion, to gain a unified control of the earth's people.

As already mentioned, the EEC, computer technology and a cashless society, which is now in the planning stages, are bringing us closer to the new world order. Astrology will be a key ingredient. The

Antichrist knows, in order to assume control, he must create a religious world in which all people have some common religious "values." Remember the two things you are not supposed to discuss if you want to remain friends—religion and politics. The Scriptures say these are the very two things he will reorganize—no doubt in an attempt to get all of us to worship him.

Mount Sinai in Egypt, where Moses
spoke to God and God spoke to Moses.

"Come down, and sit in the dust, O virgin daughter of Babylon, sit on the ground: *there is* no throne, O daughter of the Chaldeans: for thou shalt no more be called tender and delicate. Take the millstones, and grind meal: uncover thy locks, make bare the leg, uncover the thigh, pass over the rivers. Thy nakedness shall be uncovered, yea, thy shame shall be seen: I will take vengeance, and I will not meet *thee* as a man."
Isaiah 47:1-3 KJV

DAUGHTER OF BABYLON

Not only will astrology be a key piece in this religion of the end times, but we can also see from subtle hints in the Scripture that the Roman Catholic Church seems to be indicated. Isaiah 47 makes mention of "the daughter of Babylon."

As we look into the chief tenets of the Babylonian religions, we find the origin of mother and child worship. Once Nimrod died, his wife Semiramis proclaimed him the sun-god.[11] She claimed that when her son, Tammuz, was born he was, in fact, Nimrod reincarnated. She also claimed that he was supernaturally conceived and the promised seed of Genesis 3:15, which predicted God would send just such a one, coming from a woman to save mankind. As this religion developed, Semiramis and her son were both worshipped.

In Genesis 11:9, we see that the men of Babel were scattered "unto all the earth," having been confounded by God through the creation of many different languages. Thus, this pagan mother/child tenet of worship was also spread throughout the world. As the people scattered into many different nations, regrouping according to language, the mother goddess and child assumed a different name in each new nation. Here is the evidence:

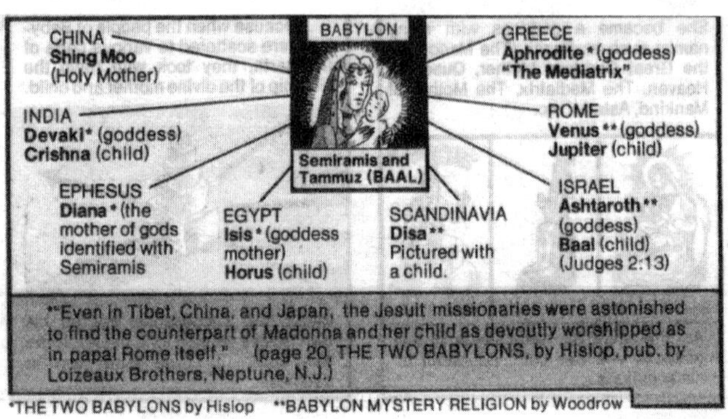

---

[11]"The mother of Tammuz had probably heard the prophecy of the coming Messiah to be born of a woman for this truth was known from the earliest times (Gen. 3:15). She claimed her son was supernaturally conceived and that he was the promised seed, the 'savior.' In the religion that developed, however, not only was the child worshipped, but the *mother* was worshipped also!" Ralph Woodrow, *Babylon Mystery Religion*, p. 9.

Much later, when Jesus was born, He was indeed born of a virgin—having been conceived of the Holy Spirit, with God as His Father. The Jewish Scriptures foretold that the Messiah would be the Son of God in reference to His flesh (see our chapter 5, "Which Prophesies Did Jesus Fulfill"). However, nowhere in the New Testament does it say that Mary is to be worshipped, and nowhere does she remain[12] a virgin after the birth of Jesus, as the Roman Catholic Church claims! In fact, it was documented that after Constantine, the Roman Catholic Church took the statues of Isis and Horus (one such goddess/child pair) and renamed them Mary and Jesus.[13]

A holy effigy of the Virgin Mary being carried on Mount Carmel by Greek and Catholic residents of Israel.

[12]Mark 6:3 mentions: "Is not this the carpenter, the son of Mary, the brother of James, and Joses, and of Juda, and Simon? and are not his sisters here with us? And they were offended at him" (KJV). Matthew clearly tells us: "...and kept her a virgin **until** she gave birth to a Son; and he called His name Jesus" (Matt. 1:25 NASB). A psalm predicting the alienation of the Messiah from His family reads: "I am become a stranger unto my brethren, and an alien unto my mother's children" (Ps. 69:8 KJV).

[13]Ralph Woodrow tells us: "...'the ancient portrait of Isis and the child Horus was ultimately accepted not only in popular opinion, but by formal episcopal sanction, as the portrait of the Virgin and her child'....In numerous ways, leaders of the falling away attempted to make Mary appear similar to the goddess of paganism and exalt her to a divine plane. Even as the pagans had statues of the goddess, so statues were made of 'Mary'....in some cases, the *very same* statues that had been worshipped as Isis (with her child) were simply renamed as Mary and the Christ child." Ralph Woodrow, *Babylon Mystery Religion*, p. 19.

" ' I know that I am right in loving liberty and justice,' he says, 'for Christ loved liberty and justice, and Christ is God.' "[14]
Abraham Lincoln,
16th President of the United States

"For unto us a child is born, unto us a son is given: and the government shall be on his shoulder: and his name shall be called Wonderful, Counsellor, The **mighty God,** The everlasting Father, The Prince of Peace. Of the increase of *his* government and peace *there shall be* no end, upon the throne of David, and upon his kingdom, to order it...."
Isaiah 9:6-7 KJV

"But unto the Son *he saith*, Thy throne, O God, *is* for ever and ever: a sceptre of righteousness *is* the sceptre of thy kingdom."
Hebrews 1:8-9 KJV

"For many deceivers are entered into the world, who confess not that Jesus Christ is come in the flesh. This is a deceiver and an antichrist."
II John 1:7 KJV

"What is the name of the King Messiah? Rabbi Abba, son of Kahana, said: Jehovah; for it is written, 'This is his name whereby he shall be called, the Lord our Righteousness.' "
Midrash on Lamentations I.16

AN ONSLAUGHT OF CULTS DENY JESUS' DIETY, ETERNAL SECURITY AND THAT HE WAS SUFFICIENT TO SAVE WITHIN HIMSELF

In the past few centuries, there has been an explosion of cults proclaiming to be a way, or even "the only way," to the truth of God. The Scriptures—Isaiah 9:6-7, Hebrews 1:8, II John 1:7, and John 9:9—teach how to discern a cult from the truth. Cults deny the two most important truths: 1. Jesus is God, and; 2. He is solely sufficient to save us without external work on our part.

---

[14] "The Religion of Abraham Lincoln," *The Dawn*, Vol. XVIII, Jan.-Feb., 1947. D. James Kennedy mentions in one of his lectures, that Lincoln once said to Mr. Bateman in 1860, during his early presidency: " 'I am not a Christian. God knows I would be one. I have carefully read the Bible.' And he pulled a New Testament out of his pocket where it always was kept. 'But I do not understand this book.' " He later quotes Lincoln's letter to a friend: " 'When I came to Springfield, I was not a Christian. When I left Springfield for Washington and asked you to pray for me, I was not a Christian. When I received the bitterest blow of my life—the death of my son—I was not a Christian. When I went to Gettysburg, I was not a Christian; but there at Gettysburg, I consecrated my heart to Christ.' " Kennedy also quotes from a letter written by Mary Todd Lincoln after her husband was shot, relating her last conversation with him: "These were his last words. He was not interested in the play, but he was leaning forward talking to her. He said, 'Mary, you know what I would like most of all to do now? I would like to take you with me on a trip to the Near East.' John Wilkes Booth silently opened the door to the presidential box. He [Lincoln] said, 'We could go to Palestine, where He lived. We could visit Bethlehem, where He was born.' You could see about whom he was thinking. A pistol was lifted behind him. 'We could go up to Bethany. We could go up to Jeru...' BOOM! Lincoln's last words. 'We could go up to Jeru...' " D. James Kennedy, *Was Abraham Lincoln a Christian?* Tape 20D. Fort Lauderdale: Coral Ridge Ministries, © used by permission. This tape is available through CRM, POB 40, Fort Lauderdale, FL, USA 33302. This tape also includes books and references to document what we have written.

There was an excellent article in the *Moody Monthly* magazine of July/August 1979, listing what particular groups or cults had to say about Jesus' deity. We have reproduced it in our *Vol. II*, chapter 4, "Cults, the Occult and the New Age."[15]

An A to Z list of these cults includes: Ahmadiyya Movement, American Atheist Center, Ananda Marga Yoga, Anthroposophical Society, Arica, Assemblies of Yahweh, Baha'i, Bawa Muhaiyaddeen Fellowship, Black Muslim, Buddhism, Cabala, Center for Spiritual Awareness, Children of God, Christian Scientists, Church of the Living Word, Church Universal and Triumphant, Dhyana-Mandiram, Divine Light Mission, ECKANKAR, Findhorn Foundation University of Light, Freemasonry, Hare Krishna, "I Am" Movement, Iglesia Ni Cristo, Inner Peace Movement, Integral Yoga Institute, Islam, Jainism, Jehovah's Witnesses, Laymen's Home Missionary Movement, Liberal Catholic Church, Megiddo Mission, Mormons, Nichiren Shoshu Soka Gakkai, Peace Mission Movement, Psychiana, Radha Soami Society, Rajneesh Meditation Centers, Rosicrucianism, Ruhani Satsang, Sacred Mushroom of the Cross, Sanatana Dharma Foundation, Satanism, Scientology, Self Realization Fellowship, Shintoism, Shree Guru Dev Siddha Yoga Ashram, Sikhism, Sivananda Yoga Vedenta Centers, Spiritual Advancement of the Individual Foundation, Spiritual Frontiers Fellowship, Spiritualists, Sri Chinmoy Centers, Still Point Institute, Subud, Sufism, Swedenborgism, Taoism, Tarotology, The Farm, The Foundation Church of the Millennium, The Holy Order of MANS, The Himalayan International Institute of Yoga Science and Philosophy, The Local Church, The Process Church of the Final Judgment, The 3 HO Foundation, The Unification Church, The Way, Theosophists, Transcendental Meditation, Unitarians, Unity School of Christianity, Vedanta Society, Witchcraft, Worldwide Church of God, Zen Buddhism, and Zoroastrianism.

SIR ISAAC NEWTON TRACES THE TRUE BIBLICAL FAITH FROM NOAH TO US

Assuming that you just finished glancing over the nearly one hundred cults and where they stand regarding the diety of Jesus in our *Vol. II*, chapter 4, "Cults, the Occult and the New Age," you may be asking, "What is true faith?" The Bible, through its hundreds of

---

[15] If you have a chance, stop and read through this chapter in our *Volume II*. It contains a thorough list of cults, proof from the Jewish standpoint of the deity of Jesus and enlightening information on the occult. These are all facts that true believers should know so that they will not be deceived. The New Age is also covered from the vantage point of Satan's plan to take over the earth in the person of the Antichrist.

prophecies, guides us to the born-again (John 3) Messianic truth that Jesus is the Messiah.

Sir Isaac Newton, using the Scripture, traces the true faith throughout history, beginning as early as Noah. Newton wrote: "The true religion was propagated by Noah to his posterity, & when they revolted to the worship of their dead Kings & Heroes & thereby denied their God & ceased to be his people, it continued in Abraham & his posterity who revolted not. And when they began to worship the Gods of Egypt & Syria, Moses & the Prophets reclaimed them from time to time till they rejected the Messiah from being their Lord, & he rejected them from being his people & called the Gentiles, & henceforward the believers both Jews & Gentiles became his people....The God of the Jews & Gentiles was one & the same God the creator of heaven & earth, & the Christian religion was one & the same with the Jewish till the calling of the Gentiles, with this only addition that Jesus who was crucified under Pontius Pilate was the Prince of the host or head of the Church the seed of the Woman which was to bruise the serpent's head, the Shiloh who was to come before the scepter departed from Israel, the Prophet promised by Moses & prefigured by the Paschal lamb, the holy David who was not to be left in the grave nor to see corruption, the servant of God who was wounded for our transgressions & bruised for our iniquities & brought as a lamb to the slaughter & made an offering for sin, & the Messiah or Christ the Prince predicted by Daniel (whence came the name of the Christian religion;) & that he rose from the dead & shall judge the quick & the dead; & that we are to give him honour & glory on account of his death & to commemorate it often & to direct our prayers to God in his name as our great high Priest the mediator between God & man. But when this doctrine had been preached to the nation of the Jews about seven years, & they received it not, God began to call the Gentiles without obliging them to observe the law of Moses, & soon after caused the Jewish [Temple] worship to cease & the Jews to be dispersed into all nations."[16]

NEWTON'S VIEWS ON THE DIETY OF JESUS

In his work, David Castillejo comments on Newton's conviction of the diety of Jesus as follows: "Newton believed that Christ dominates both the Old and the New Testament. All appearances of Jehova in the Bible are in fact appearances of Christ: it was Christ who

---

[16]David Castillejo, *The Expanding Force in Newton's Cosmos*. Madrid: Ediciones de Arte y Bibliofilia, © 1981, pp. 58-60, used by permission. [ ] mine. Castillejo's source was *Yahuda Manuscript 15*.

walked in the Garden of Eden, who gave Moses the ten Commandments, who appeared to Abraham as an Angel, who fought with Jacob, who gave the prophecies to the prophets. He is the Prince Michael mentioned by Daniel, and he will come to judge the quick and the dead. The Jews are ruled by Christ in an absolute monarchy, and he is their lord."[17]

RELIGIOUS DECEPTION AND THE PROPHETICAL ACCURACY OF OUR BIBLE VERSUS THE MODERN BIBLICAL CRITICAL FRAUD

Today, many claim that we cannot rely on the Scriptures because they have been repeatedly copied, translated and mistranslated. Nothing could be further from the truth. We will show that the ancient Dead Sea copies of the original Hebrew manuscript of our Bible disprove much modern liberal "scholarship," which purports to show that the Bible, through the process of translation, underwent changes. This "scholarship" claims that we cannot take the Scriptures seriously because we "supposedly" do not know what earlier copies might have said. However, to the dismay of critics, scrolls of Bible copies were discovered in the caves of Qumran near the Dead Sea, which are 1100 years older than any previously known copies. The scrolls show us that no considerable changes were made in that span of time.

The Bible we have today, in all legitimate translations, and certainly the original Hebrew, is the Bible written by God, through His prophets, in its original authorized version. Ezekiel wrote, "Thus saith the Lord" (5:5 KJV). Many, however, say **man** wrote the Bible. Ezekiel, one of the major writers of the Bible, said the Lord told him what to write. There are no neutrals. Either Ezekiel is a liar or the Bible is God's message to mankind. Prophecy has shown the latter to be true, disproving the self-appointed liberal Bible "scholars." Or perhaps we should say Bible haters; people who, for moral reasons, hope and try to prove to themselves that the Bible is not true. Deep inside their innermost being they are afraid of God, because they are unwilling to come to Him. They are: "Ever learning, and never able to come to the knowledge of the truth" (II Tim. 3:7 KJV). On the other hand, there are many sincere laymen who want to believe but have been led by the liberals to think that the Scriptures have been discredited. Many have not been enlightened by the many archaeological discoveries and fulfilled prophecies which authenticate

---

[17] Ibid, p. 60.

the truth of the Bible. Our solution to this dilemma is to **tell them** so they will be with us in God's beautiful coming kingdom.

We point out here that, of the many cults and religions proliferating in the world, whose followers claim they are "the way," not one has had the accuracy of the Hebrew prophets! Prophecy, apart from everything else, should be sufficient to set the Bible apart from all of the other religions which purport to be an alternative to Jesus. However, if foretelling the future with immutable manuscripts is not enough in the eyes of those who try to find something lacking, we have reproduced actual press photos of classified displays in the Israel Museum in Jerusalem (not usually permitted to be photographed), of the ancient Dead Sea Scrolls found at Qumran. Many of these scrolls are the earliest Hebrew copies we now possess of the Bible.

מתחת לרצפת חדר זה
נמצאו קטעי מגילות אשר נגנזו כאן
בין הקטעים נכלל ,חזון העצמות
היבשות"- יחזקאל פרק ל"ז
UNDER THE FLOOR OF THIS ROOM WERE
FOUND FRAGMENTS OF SCROLLS A PART
OF A "GENIZA" INCLUDING THE "VISION OF
THE DRY BONES" EZEKIEL CHAP. 37

This is the oldest synagogue in the world, located atop Masada, where many brave Jews once committed suicide rather than be enslaved by the Romans. Here, in 1947, the first of the Dead Sea Scrolls were discovered, including Ezekiel 37, which speaks of "Israel standing on her feet from dry bones." Interestingly enough, Israel became a nation in 1948. A very timely find, wouldn't you say?

These are the most ancient copies we have of the Bible, eleven centuries older than those we possessed prior to 1947.

The Dead Sea Scrolls, here on display, are carefully preserved between panes of glass.

Individuals are in awe as they view the entire book of Isaiah.

The earliest copies of Isaiah's prophecies, displayed in a scroll-shaped encasement, under the dome of the Shrine of the Book, in the Israel Museum.

Government officials carefully scrutinize Isaiah's handwritten words.

A meticulous manuscript from the Dead Sea.

Workers take a rest during excavations at the Bar Kochba cave near the Dead Sea caves of Qumran, where the scrolls were found. Perhaps more are still to come.

A rabbi recopies a Torah. This is reminiscent of the method in which the Dead Sea Scrolls of the Bible were copied—very meticulously.

GAON AND JESUS ON THE DIVINE INSPIRATION OF THE BIBLE'S HEBREW TEXT

Recently, in an October 1995 *Bible Review* article entitled, "Divine Authorship?" (concerning inspired mathematical Bible codes, as mentioned earlier in our chapter 20), it was noted that: "In 1988 an obscure paper was published—in a prominent, rigorous, indeed premier, scientific journal—with results that may demolish the claims of the 'higher' critics, and support, rather, the Orthodox Jewish contention as to the nature of the Torah. The paper, by Doron Witzturn, Eliyahu Rips and Yoav Rosenberg of the Jerusalem College of Technology and the Hebrew University, is innocuously entitled 'Equidistant Letter Sequences in the Book of Genesis' and was published in the eminent *Journal of the Royal Statistical Society*....They were rather words composed of letters selected at various equal skip distances....It was as though 'behind' the surface meaning of the Hebrew there was a second, hidden level of embedded meaning....Following publication of this paper, a public statement was issued, signed by five mathematical scholars—two from Harvard, two from Hebrew University and one from Yale. ‘The present work,’ they said, ‘represents serious research carried out by serious investigators....results obtained are sufficiently striking to deserve a wider audience and to encourage further study.’ The work was also critiqued and endorsed by Dr. Andrew Goldfinger, a senior research physicist at Johns Hopkins University in Baltimore, and by Harold Gans, an analyst with the U.S. Department of Defense.

According to Jewish tradition, the Torah contains all knowledge; therefore the codes embedded in the Torah also encompass information that transcends the limitation of time. The Vilna Gaon, the great 18th century Rabbi of Vilna, Lithuania, a child prodigy and one of the most brilliant men in Jewish history, wrote that ‘all that was, is, and will be unto the end of time is included in the Torah...and not merely in a general sense, but including the details of every species and of each person individually, and the most minute details of everything that happened to him from the day of his birth until his death.’

Some may be reminded of the words of the Rabbi from Nazareth [Jesus], seen in a different light: ‘I tell you the truth, until heaven and earth disappear, not the smallest letter [literally *iota*, equivalent to the Hebrew *yod*, the smallest letter in the Hebrew alphabet], not the least stroke of a pen [literally *tittle*, a reference to the small decoration or ‘crown’ on some Hebrew letters in handwritten scrolls of the Torah], will by any means disappear from the Torah [Law] until everything is accomplished’ (Matthew 5:18)....The phenomenon cannot be attributed to anything within the known physical universe, human beings included. Moreover, rigorous proof of the existence and validity of the phenomenon requires both high-speed computation and only recently developed techniques of statistical analysis....What then was the purpose of encoding this information into the text? Some would say it is the Author’s signature. Is it His way of assuring us that at this particular, late moment—when our scientific, materialistic doubt has reached its apotheosis, when we have been driven to the brink of radical skepticism—that He is *precisely* who He had said He is in that astonishing, radical core document of the Judeo-Christian tradition?”[18]

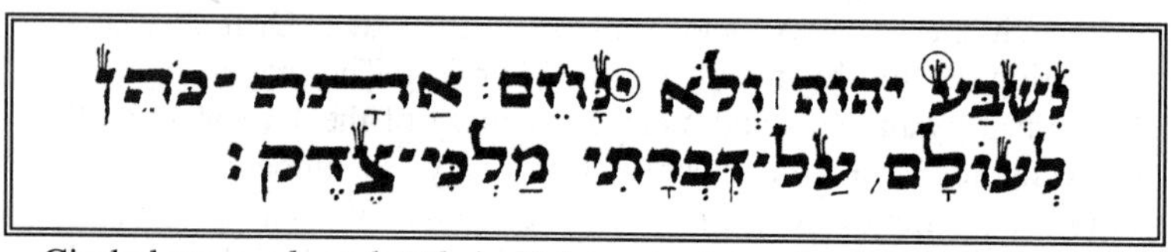

Circled are a *ude* and *tittle* in Hebrew text, to which Jesus referred.

[18]Jeffrey B. Satinover, “Divine Authorship?”, *Bible Review*, © Oct. 1995, pp. 28-29, 44-45, used by permission. First [ ] mine. Second and third [ ] are my insertion of the article’s footnotes to Jesus’ words, *letter*, and *pen*.

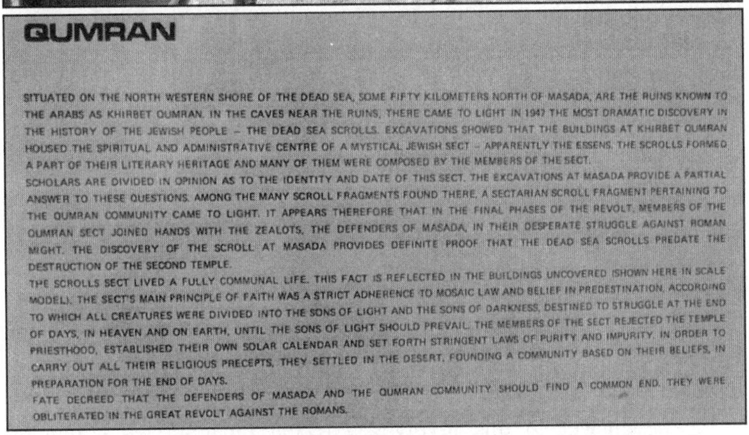

QUMRAN
SITUATED ON THE NORTH WESTERN SHORE OF THE DEAD SEA, SOME FIFTY KILOMETERS NORTH OF MASADA, ARE THE RUINS KNOWN TO THE ARABS AS KHIRBET QUMRAN. IN THE CAVES NEAR THE RUINS, THERE CAME TO LIGHT IN 1947 THE MOST DRAMATIC DISCOVERY IN THE HISTORY OF THE JEWISH PEOPLE – THE DEAD SEA SCROLLS. EXCAVATIONS SHOWED THAT THE BUILDINGS AT KHIRBET QUMRAN HOUSED THE SPIRITUAL AND ADMINISTRATIVE CENTRE OF A MYSTICAL JEWISH SECT – APPARENTLY THE ESSENS. THE SCROLLS FORMED A PART OF THEIR LITERARY HERITAGE AND MANY OF THEM WERE COMPOSED BY THE MEMBERS OF THE SECT.
SCHOLARS ARE DIVIDED IN OPINION AS TO THE IDENTITY AND DATE OF THIS SECT. THE EXCAVATIONS AT MASADA PROVIDE A PARTIAL ANSWER TO THESE QUESTIONS. AMONG THE MANY SCROLL FRAGMENTS FOUND THERE, A SECTARIAN SCROLL FRAGMENT PERTAINING TO THE QUMRAN COMMUNITY CAME TO LIGHT. IT APPEARS THEREFORE THAT IN THE FINAL PHASES OF THE REVOLT, MEMBERS OF THE QUMRAN SECT JOINED HANDS WITH THE ZEALOTS, THE DEFENDERS OF MASADA, IN THEIR DESPERATE STRUGGLE AGAINST ROMAN MIGHT. THE DISCOVERY OF THE SCROLL AT MASADA PROVIDES DEFINITE PROOF THAT THE DEAD SEA SCROLLS PREDATE THE DESTRUCTION OF THE SECOND TEMPLE.
THE SCROLLS SECT LIVED A FULLY COMMUNAL LIFE. THIS FACT IS REFLECTED IN THE BUILDINGS UNCOVERED (SHOWN HERE IN SCALE MODEL). THE SECT'S MAIN PRINCIPLE OF FAITH WAS A STRICT ADHERENCE TO MOSAIC LAW AND BELIEF IN PREDESTINATION, ACCORDING TO WHICH ALL CREATURES WERE DIVIDED INTO THE SONS OF LIGHT AND THE SONS OF DARKNESS, DESTINED TO STRUGGLE AT THE END OF DAYS, IN HEAVEN AND ON EARTH, UNTIL THE SONS OF LIGHT SHOULD PREVAIL. THE MEMBERS OF THE SECT REJECTED THE TEMPLE PRIESTHOOD, ESTABLISHED THEIR OWN SOLAR CALENDAR AND SET FORTH STRINGENT LAWS OF PURITY AND IMPURITY. IN ORDER TO CARRY OUT ALL THEIR RELIGIOUS PRECEPTS, THEY SETTLED IN THE DESERT, FOUNDING A COMMUNITY BASED ON THEIR BELIEFS, IN PREPARATION FOR THE END OF DAYS.
FATE DECREED THAT THE DEFENDERS OF MASADA AND THE QUMRAN COMMUNITY SHOULD FIND A COMMON END. THEY WERE OBLITERATED IN THE GREAT REVOLT AGAINST THE ROMANS.

The Dead Sea Scrolls are priceless. Two signs at the discovery site.

Publications, such as the *Los Angeles Times, Atlanta Journal and Constitution* and *Time,* featured headlines regarding newly discovered, yet repressed, Dead Sea Scroll evidence. This evidence supports the suffering role of the Messiah, and hints at the fact that these very same things happened to Jesus during this time period.

BACK TO THE TRUE GOD AND HIS AUTHENTIC RELIGION

In the first chapters of this book, we have covered the original meanings of Hebrew words and resolved apparent contradictions regarding creation as opposed to evolution, and seeming "contradictions" pertaining to the two Comings of the redeeming Messiah to buy us back from the Fall that occurred in Genesis 3. Since that time, Satan has introduced many counterfeit religions in an attempt to deceive man by steering him away from the truth!

We mentioned earlier that the main way to determine a counterfeit from the real thing, is to be well acquainted with the feel of the real thing, as a bank teller distinguishes a phony bill from a real one! In our century, and especially this decade, one of the most intriguing discoveries authenticating the Bible's genuineness and its claim of two Comings of the Messiah, often denied by "scholars," are the Dead Sea Scrolls! There has been an effort to keep certain portions of the scrolls concealed and away from the public. Why? Read on and see if you can guess.

WHAT'S ALL THE FUSS ABOUT THE MYSTERY REGARDING THE CONCEALMENT OF THE DEAD SEA SCROLLS?

The answer to this involves a recent unauthorized computer reconstruction, which apparently precipitated the unexpected release of secret copies kept in a Huntington Library vault! The *Atlanta Journal and Constitution* brought this to light when they revealed several facts on the subject in two articles, "Dead Sea Scrolls" and "Dead Sea Scrolls Refer to Messiah's Execution." A portion of the first article reads: "...a Palestinian shepherd boy chasing a stray goat tossed a stone into a narrow cave near the Dead Sea. The stone hit a clay jar, causing a tinkling noise that is still echoing in the halls of academia. When he and his cousin crawled into the hole, they found eight stone jars containing foul-smelling manuscripts, each wrapped in linen, coated with black pitch and hidden for 1,900 years: the first of the Dead Sea Scrolls....'...the scrolls originated in Jerusalem and were taken to hiding places in the Judaean wilderness for safekeeping either before or during the Roman siege of Jerusalem in 70 A.D.'....The scrolls contain every book of the Hebrew Bible except Esther [and]....*ancient Hebrew commentaries* on the Bible....The first two-thirds of the Dead Sea Scrolls appeared in scholarly journals a generation ago. Then, for no apparent reason, the flow of information *stopped*....Two professors of Hebrew Union College in Cincinnati revealed that they had used a computer to reconstruct a secret text that the authorized scholars had not gotten around to publishing.

The Cincinnati scholars had started with a bootlegged copy of an index to the scrolls showing each word and its context....Soon after publication of the computer-generated texts began, the director of the private Huntington Library in California announced that he was going to break the academic monopoly once and for all by releasing 3,000 photographic negatives showing the original scrolls in their complete form.

The library had obtained its set of photos in a roundabout way....after the 1967 Arab-Israeli war, a California philanthropist, Elizabeth Hay Bechtel, persuaded the Israeli antiquities authorities to let her personal photographer make a photographic record of the original scrolls so that a future war couldn't rob the world of the Dead Sea treasure.

Before her death in 1987, Mrs. Bechtel endowed a vault in the Huntington Library and secretly deposited a master set of negatives **without** the knowledge of the scholarly establishment."[19]

Within days of the release, William A. Moffett, the library director, said "he would allow anyone with an established interest to see a microfilm of the original Dead Sea Scrolls in Hebrew",[20] adding it was "like bringing down the Berlin Wall."[21]

One aspect which may have had some bearing on whether or not to release the scrolls is revealed in an Associated Press article entitled "Dead Sea Scrolls Refer to Messiah's Execution," which appeared in the November 8, 1991, *Atlanta Journal and Constitution.* In a previous article on October 12, Dr. Newsom of Emory University was quoted as saying the unreleased portions of the scrolls would not be embarrassing to Judaism. She also said that "bomb shell" rumors that Jews "were sitting on the scrolls," fearing publication could in some way undermine Judaism,[22] would now be dispelled. The November 8, 1991 article

---

[19]Joseph Albright and Gayle White, "Dead Sea Scrolls," *Atlanta Journal and Constitution*, Sat., Oct. 12, 1991, p. E6, reprinted by permission. Reproduction does not imply endorsement. [ ], bold and italics mine.

[20]Apparently to prevent further computerized reconstructions of the Dead Sea Scrolls using the concordance!

[21] Ibid.

[22]In our opinion, the scrolls, in a very real sense, undermine "*Rabbinical* Judaism" in its exclusion of the execution of the suffering Messiah, since these Dead Sea Scrolls were written before the foundation of Rabbinic Judaism. If we were allowed to peer into true Judaism in its pure form, we would be flabbergasted at the openness toward the concept of a suffering Messiah. Devora Demad, an Israeli scholar, appeared on a *Nova* program entitled, "Secrets of the Dead Sea Scrolls," produced by Nancy Porter. On the subject of Rabbinic Judaism in relation to the scrolls, Demad said: "This is a crucial moment in the Jewish history because after the destruction of the temple, all Judaism was codified and

reveals that: "The execution of a Messiah-like leader is mentioned in newly released text from the Dead Sea Scrolls, indicating the Christian concept was shared by ancient Jews who wrote the documents, scholars say."[23]

THE REAL CRUX—A SUFFERING MESSIAH IS REVEALED WITHIN JUDAISM, WHICH AUTHENTICATES CHRISTIAN CLAIMS

The article continues: "The fragmentary, five-line text has 'far-reaching significance' because it shows the scrolls' authors 'had the same Messianic ideas that are familiar in early Christian teachings,' said Robert Eisenman, chairman of religious studies at California State University, Long Beach. Mr. Eisenman said he found the text among 3,000 photographs of the scrolls opened to scholarly study last month by the Huntington Library in San Marino. The text describes...being 'put to death' and mentions 'piercings' or 'wounds.' It also uses Messiah-related terms such as 'the staff,' 'the Branch of David,' and the 'Root of Jesse,' Mr. Eisenman said....'the idea of **a dying Messiah—is new and explosive**,' said Michael Wise of the University of Chicago."[24]

THE REAL REASON THESE SCROLLS ARE SO EXPLOSIVE IS BECAUSE THEY PROVE JESUS IS THE JEWISH MESSIAH

It is quite obvious that the reason these scrolls are "explosive," and have such "far reaching significance," is that they bring us all one step closer to proving that ancient Judaism anticipated the death of the Messiah, and consequently, that Jesus is the Jewish Messiah; a thought scorned by many modern scholars. Thus, the supporting evidence of

---

fixed into the form we now know and currently called 'Rabbinic Judaism.' This means that the scrolls reflect the variety, the openness that existed before this date." Nancy Porter, "Secrets of the Dead Sea Scrolls," *Nova*. The narrator of this television special made an incredible, but true statement which backs up everything we have said. His exact words were: "The scrolls do offer new insights. We now know that ideas later identified with Christianity existed much earlier within a **Judaism** which was far richer and more varied than scholars had ever realized." Ibid. We might ask opponents of Messianic Judaism, who claim it is a contradiction to be a Jew and a believer in Jesus, to consider these words. Incidentally, this was an unbiased, scholarly research program which did not favor or foster the viewpoints held by evangelicals or *Jews for Jesus*. This *Nova* special was advertised in the *Atlanta Journal and Constitution*, Sat., Oct. 12, 1991.

[23]"Dead Sea Scrolls Refer to Messiah's Execution," *Atlanta Journal and Constitution*, Nov. 8, 1991, p. A7, reprinted by permission of the Associated Press. Reproduction does not imply endorsement. [ ] and bold mine.

[24]Ibid. Bold mine.

the scrolls is not easily accepted by those who do not believe Jesus to be the Jewish Messiah, which includes a majority of the rabbinical community.

PROFESSOR GOLB UPSETS THE SCHOLARS AND THE STATUS QUO IN HIS NEW BOOK

We discovered additional evidence regarding the Dead Sea Scrolls and their relation to ancient Judaism, Christian origins and who we are in relation to both of these subjects, in the *Jerusalem Post* article, "Who Wrote the Dead Sea Scrolls?" In this article, reporter Gail Lichtman quotes Professor Norman Golb[25] of the University of Chicago, who is a manuscript scholar and has studied with paleographer S. Goitein. Lichtman, quoting Golb in connection with his book which was released in 1995, writes: "The Scrolls do contain many new works in Hebrew which strongly resemble Jewish intertestamental writings—writings which eventually lost their popularity among Jews and have survived as translations appended to the Christian Bible. 'These and other texts from Qumran have made possible a much fuller reconstruction of Judaism of that period, which in many ways was radically different from...the rabbinic Judaism that followed. The ideas of this intermediate Judaism are not always familiar or comforting, and sometimes even inspire repugnance. But they are there nevertheless'....'Whether scholars will continue to indefinitely...make these texts the corpus of belief of a minority sect is a question whose answer it is still too early to venture. It is, however, becoming obvious that traditional Qumranologists have yet to offer a cogent refutation of the Jerusalem-origin theory. Much depends on the outcome—mainly, our understanding of Christian origins and of ancient Judaism and its evolution, and the manner in which the Bible came to be what it is today. For those of us concerned with the question of who we are, this understanding matters profoundly.' "[26] Under the professor's picture were his words: "I feel it is my responsibility to write the truth as I see it and it doesn't matter if scholars get angry."[27]

***

[25]Professor Golb is the first holder of the Rosenberger Chair in Jewish History and Civilization at the University of Chicago.

[26]Gail Lichtman, "Who Wrote the Dead Sea Scrolls?" *The Jerusalem Post International Edition*, Oct. 30, 1993, © used by permission.

[27]Ibid.

GOLB PROVES THE SCROLLS WERE THE PRODUCT OF ANCIENT JUDAISM AND THE SON OF GOD MESSIAH IS JEWISH, NOT PAGAN!

The cover flap of Golb's book quite eloquently states: "The Scrolls have been the subject of unending fascination and controversy ever since their discovery in the Qumran caves beginning in 1947. Intensifying the debate, Professor Norman Golb now fundamentally challenges those who argue that the writings belonged to a small, desert-dwelling fringe sect. Instead, he shows why the scrolls must have been the work of many groups in ancient Judaism, kept in libraries in Jerusalem and smuggled out of the capital just before the Romans attacked in A.D. 70."[28]

Using the Dead Sea discovery of a certain text, Golb exposes the lie that the Son of God Messiah concept was pagan[29] (Greco-Roman). Many critics of the past have laid this accusation at the feet of Christian missionaries. This is one of the major claims of Samuel Golding's anti-missionary book, *A Guide to the Misled.* In our opinion, Dr. Golb proves the Son of God Messiah idea is not pagan, but thoroughly Jewish, and from God. He states: "In one important text (4Q246) written in Aramaic, a figure called 'the Son of God, Son of the Most High' appears....it has been plausibly suggested that this figure is none other than the Messiah.[30] This apocalyptic fragment may thus provide

---

[28]Norman Golb, *Who Wrote the Dead Sea Scrolls? The Search for the Secret of Qumran*, p. cover flap.

[29]An example of this misconception that the Son of God is a pagan idea, is expressed by Rabbi Kaplan in *The Real Messiah.* This anti-missionary book was published in 1976, long before the release of the Dead Sea Scrolls. Kaplan, unaware of what the scrolls said about the Son of God, wrote: "The Greeks already had legends about men who had been fathered by gods who had visited mortal human women. Legends like these had even sprung up about such eminent men as Plato, Pythagoras, and Alexander the Great. Why should Jesus be any less? They therefore interpreted his poetic expression quite literally, to mean that he had an actual genetic relationship with G-d. Jesus therefore became the 'son of G-d,'...." Rabbi Aryeh Kaplan, *et al*, *The Real Messiah*, p. 31. Though Kaplan did not have the Dead Sea Scroll fragment in 1976, he could have opened his Bible to the Jewish prophet Isaiah, who wrote about the Messiah over seven hundred years before Jesus was born. "For unto us a child is born, unto us a son is given: and the government shall be upon his shoulder: and his name shall be called Wonderful, Counsellor, The mighty God, The everlasting Father, The Prince of Peace" (Isa. 9:6 KJV). Kaplan could also have read Proverbs 30:4: "Who hath ascended up into heaven, or descended? who hath gathered the wind in his fists? who hath bound the waters in a garment? who hath established all the ends of the earth? what *is* his name, and what *is* his son's name, if thou canst tell?" (KJV)

[30]Golb's footnote to Messiah states: "See Eisenman and Wise, *The Dead Sea Scrolls Uncovered*, pp. 68-69. See also John Collins, 'A Pre-Christian 'Son of God' Among the Dead Sea Scrolls," *Bible Review* (June 1993), pp. 34-39; and Emile Puech, 'Fragment d'une apocalypse en Araméen (4Q246 = pseudo-Dan[b]) et le 'Royaume de Dieu,' ' *Revue Biblique 99* (1992), pp. 98-131." Norman Golb, *Who Wrote the Dead Sea Scrolls? The Search for the Secret of Qumran*, p. 421.

an important precursor to the New Testament's designation of Jesus as the 'Son of God.' Prior to its publication, the idea of the Messiah as God's son had not been attested in pre-Christian Jewish texts. It was often suggested that the idea derived not from Judaism, but from the Greco-Roman royal ideology, where kings were believed to have been adopted by the gods. (We may observe the appearance of similar themes also in ancient Near Eastern texts.) This scroll may thus provide a Jewish antecedent to an idea once thought to be a Hellenistic-Christian innovation."[31]

Golb's findings are particularly valuable to us because he is a Jewish scholar and does not profess Jesus as Messiah. His illumination of these facts is truly fair and not in any way biased, which no doubt, will capture the favor of many evangelical leaders!

THE *TIME* MAGAZINE ARTICLE "IS JESUS IN THE DEAD SEA SCROLLS?" SUPPORTS OUR CONCLUSION

Further evidence supporting our conclusions was reported in an astounding *Time* magazine article in September of 1992, entitled, "Is Jesus in the Dead Sea Scrolls?" The well-known, worldwide, news magazine reported: "...the latest discoveries on actual details in the scrolls are startling enough to generate legitimate headlines. Texts that are only now becoming widely available establish the first connection between the scrolls and Jesus' New Testament words about his role as the Messiah. The debate over all the possible interpretations is bound to be **fierce**....the scrolls do speak of the coming Jewish Messiah...Two of the fragments made newly available in the *Review's* photo books are especially striking....the most important phrases are clear. Apparently referring to the coming Messiah, the text declares that he will 'heal the wounded, resurrect the dead [and] preach glad tidings to the poor.' The passage closely resembles the words of Jesus in the Nazareth synagogue (*Luke 4*)....The text, which echoes *Isaiah 11*, also anticipates another primary New Testament teaching, that the Messiah must die as Jesus did....Wise, Eisenman's sometime ally, says the evidence could equally back the conservatives who believe God prepared the way for the true Messiah: 'Many of Christianity's ideas were there at the time of Jesus. I believe the things that happened wouldn't have happened if the ground were not already fertile.' The scrolls have another important effect, underscoring anew the Jewishness of Jesus. In any event, those angry, locked-out Dead Sea scholars turn out to have been correct in their assertions that highly important material remained tucked away for decades."[32]

---

[31]Ibid, p. 379.

[32]Richard N. Ostling, contributor, "Is Jesus in the Dead Sea Scrolls?", *Time*, Sept. 21, 1992.

THE SON OF GOD SUFFERING MESSIAH IS SOMETHING ANCIENT JEWS WANTED US TO KNOW ABOUT

Professor Golb beautifully illustrates that the ancient Jews wanted the world to know about these ancient beliefs. This is why they hid them at Qumran prior to the Roman destruction of Jerusalem. He tells us: "The parallels between the scrolls and the New Testament do serve to make an important point, however: They unequivocally testify to the fact that various Christian traditions recorded in the New Testament were at home in the world of ancient Judaism....Taken from Jerusalem libraries and personal collections at a crucial hour and hidden away in many places in the wilderness, the Dead Sea Scrolls are the remnants, miraculously recovered, of a hoard of spiritual treasures of the Jewish people....The Jews, for their part, deeply feared that the Romans intended to destroy the Temple, the physical embodiment of the Jewish ideals. They hoped that by saving their collections of scrolls and thereby the words that expressed their beliefs and aspirations of centuries—by literally hiding those words, that is, until the terror had passed—the time would yet come when the message of the Jews and of Judaism to the nations of the world might be heard again."[33]

THE QUESTION OF THE CENTURY!

Shouldn't we all, Jew and non-Jew, lovingly invite Jesus into our hearts—especially now, as more conclusive evidence surfaces proving that He is the only one[34] who can guarantee us life in the eternal world to come?! In light of what these Hebrew scrolls have revealed, we challenge every Jew who has not yet done so, to read the New Testament and visit a Messianic congregation![35]

***

[33]Norman Golb, *Who Wrote the Dead Sea Scrolls? The Search for the Secret of Qumran*, pp. 382-384.

[34]When brought before the Sanhedrin (Jewish Supreme Court of Israel), Jesus was asked by the high priest: "Art thou the Christ, the Son of the Blessed?" Jesus replied: "I am..." (Mark 14:61-62 KJV). He told the religious Pharisees: "I said therefore to you, that you shall die in your sins; for unless you believe that I am *He* [Messiah], you shall die in your sins" (John 8:24 NASB; [ ] mine). He also told the Samaritan woman at the well: "...I that speak unto thee am *he*" (John 4:26 KJV). This was in reply to her statement: "I know that Messias cometh, which is called Christ: when he is come, he will tell us all things" (John 4:25 KJV).

[35]For more information, see our *Vol. II*, chapter 19, "Messianic Synagogues—How to Get There."

A special vault protects the Dead Sea Scrolls
in a controlled environment.[36]

[36]Photo courtesy of the State of Israel Government Press Office, photography department.

Religious Jews in Israel pray at the Wailing Wall
and study at a *yeshiva*.

" 'May it be Thy will, O Jehovah our God and the God of our fathers, that as we have been granted the dawn of redemption, so may we be granted to hear the **trumpet** of the Messiah.' "[1] A Jewish prayer recited on Israel's Independence Day following one blast of the trumpet

"Behold, I tell you a mystery; we shall not all sleep, but we shall all be changed, in a moment, in the twinkling of an eye, at the last trumpet; for the **trumpet** will sound, and the dead will be raised imperishable, and we shall be changed."
The apostle Paul, I Corinthians 15:51-52 NASB. Bold mine

" 'He who has an ear, let him hear what the Spirit says to the churches.' After these things I looked, and behold, a door *standing* open in heaven, and the first voice which I had heard, like *the sound* of a **trumpet** speaking with me, said, 'Come up here, and I will show you what must take place after these things.' "
John the apostle, of the first century, speaking of his own time-warp Rapture, Revelation 3:22-4:1 NASB. Bold mine

"For the grace of God has appeared, bringing salvation to all men, instructing us to deny ungodliness and worldly desires and to live sensibly, righteously and godly in the present age, looking for **the blessed hope** and **the appearing** of the glory of our great God and Savior, Christ **Jesus;** who gave Himself for us, that He might redeem us from every lawless deed and purify for Himself a people for His own possession, zealous for good deeds. These things speak and exhort and reprove with all authority. Let no one disregard you." The apostolic teacher, Titus, reaffirms our future hope of the Rapture in the New Testament, Titus 2:11-15 NASB. Bold mine

" '...the feasts of the *Jews* were typical of things to come. The Passover related to the first coming of *Christ*, and the feasts of the seventh month to his **second coming**....' "[2] Sir Isaac Newton

25

THE RAPTURE FACTOR

Where did they all go? They didn't disappear into thin air, did they? This will be the question many non-believers will ask in the future, once we are gone. Don't worry, we will explain everything before the end of this chapter.

The word "Rapture"[3] is not in the Bible, it is a modern term describing the "catching away" of believers, as promised in the New

---

[1] Arthur W. Kac, *The Rebirth of the State of Israel: Is It of God or of Men?*, p. 88. Bold mine. A Jewish prayer: "...found in the Order of Prayer compiled with the approval of the Chief Rabbinate of the State of Israel...recited...on [Israel's] Independence Day....following one blast of the trumpet...." Ibid, p. 88. [ ] mine.

[2] Leroy Edwin Froom, *The Prophetic Faith of our Fathers*, p. 668. Bold mine.

[3] The word "Rapture" is a cognate of the Latin for "caught up." Zola Levitt, *The Signs of the End*, p. 19.

Testament. All of a sudden, Jews and Gentiles, many of whom have accepted the Messiahship of Jesus, will disappear from the face of the earth, and a great world dictator will start raving about alien abductions. You may recall, in the movies *Close Encounters of the Third Kind*, and *Fire in the Sky*, that humans were stolen or kidnapped[4] by extra-terrestrial beings and no one knew what had happened to them. Revelation 13:6 states: "And he opened his mouth in blasphemy against God, to blaspheme his name, and his tabernacle, and them that dwell in heaven" (KJV).

This certainly sounds familiar. This beast (Antichrist) is really angry at those "in heaven." The very suggestion that those who are in Heaven, who have been rescued by God, are not with God but in a UFO, constitutes blasphemy. The book of Revelation predicts that the excuse of extra-terrestrial kidnapping will be used by the Antichrist and those who assist him. It would certainly explain and coordinate the Bible's statement with the modern UFO theories recently portrayed on the cinema screen, wouldn't it?

SEPARATING THE WHEAT FROM THE CHAFF

True believers (in Jesus; Jew and Gentile) are separated from unbelievers at the Rapture, seven years prior to Jesus' physical return to the earth, by being taken into the heavens. We know the period is seven years because God's stopwatch, which counted out seventy sevens of years in Daniel 9, stopped at Jesus' First Coming at the end of sixty-nine sevens of years, leaving one remaining seven to be fulfilled. In the New Testament, the book of Revelation speaks of a period made up of forty-two months and twelve hundred and sixty days. Of course, these two figures add up to seven years!

WHY SEVEN YEARS?

In the time of the Old Testament, prior to the First Coming of Jesus, God was, of course, using the Israelites to introduce Himself to the world (Gen. 12:1-3; Jonah 3:10; Ps. 22:28; 72:17). However, when Jesus came and was rejected, God decided to use those who believed in Him in the dispensation of grace. Thus we have Israel as the tool of God until Jesus, then an approximate 2000-year parenthesis of true

---

[4]The number of books claiming to give the testimonies of people kidnapped by UFO's is rising rapidly. They include: *Communion*, by Whitley Strieber; *Secret Life*, by David M. Jacobs, Ph.D.; *Intruders*, by Budd Hopkins; *Alien Contact: Top-Secret UFO Files Revealed*, by Timothy Good; *Watchers*, by Raymond E. Fowler; *Into the Fringe*, by Karla Turner, Ph.D., and some of the additional books we mentioned on page 886.

believers (born-again Christians and Messianic Jews) being used as His chosen instruments of evangelism until now.

One day soon, the Bible tells us that He will remove the believers in the twinkling of an eye (I Thes. 4:13-17; I Cor. 15:50-55). Starting at that moment and running through the final seven years, God has promised to use Israel, primarily through the 144,000 Jews mentioned in Revelation 7:4. They will evangelize the world throughout the seven-year Tribulation period on Earth. God will give them the chance to fulfill their previously allotted time grant, while the true believers, who were removed, are consecrated to the Messiah Jesus in the heavens. These 144,000 evangelists are Jews whom you may have told about Jesus. They will keep the knowledge in their hearts, hesitating—but once the Rapture occurs, they will say, "Oh, my Christian friend was right. He just disappeared. Jesus must be the Messiah. I now accept Him. What's next, Lord?" Tell the world for seven years!

Our point is that God uses only one program at a time. First the Jews of Israel, who were still proselytizing, though perhaps wrongly, in Jesus' day (Matt. 23:15).[5] Then, once Israel officially sealed the rejection of the Messiah, a new program, the Church—or rather, the true believers—became the new evangelists.

God's Church program has been used for two millenia. However, once again, when the Church is removed in the Rapture, God will use Israel. This can clearly be seen in certain cryptic verses in the New Testament book of Revelation. In chapters 1-3, the Church is mentioned thirty times, but in chapter 4, John is called up[6] into that open door in Heaven (a symbol of the Rapture). Afterwards, in chapters 6-18, we read nothing of the Church, for this is the Tribulation period. Only in chapter 19 do we again see the Church, as it returns to Earth after the Tribulation is ended by Jesus and His believers.

After the seven years are completed, Jesus' Second Coming to Earth will reunite the Tribulation believers who came to faith under the ministry of the 144,000 Jews, with those of us who were previously caught up in the Rapture. He will defeat the Antichrist and hostile

---

[5]"Woe unto you, scribes and Pharisees, hypocrites! for ye compass sea and land to make one proselyte, and when he is made, ye make him twofold more the child of hell than yourselves" (KJV).

[6]We believe John the Revelator, who apart from other prophets, received God's prophecies in visions, was actually catapulted by God into a time-warp. He was there in the future witnessing the Rapture in real time. Perhaps he actually saw us. The door was a time portal, through which he was physically transported. Remember, there was a rumor of him: "Peter seeing him saith to Jesus, Lord, and what *shall* this man [John] do? Jesus saith unto him, 'If I will that he tarry till I come, what *is that* to thee? follow thou me.' Then went this saying abroad among the brethren, that this disciple should not die...." (John 21:21-23 KJV; [ ] mine).

armies of the world, proceed to judge the goats from the sheep and begin the 1000-year Messianic Kingdom. Those of us who were raptured will enter the millenial kingdom as immortals; those who survived the Tribulation and were on the side of the sheep in the judgment mentioned in Matthew 25, enter as mortals. These people will have greatly increased longevity, and will receive their new bodies at the end of the millennium, when the New Heaven and Earth are begun! Oh, what fun!

In the Middle East, farmers separate the wheat from the chaff by throwing both into the air. The wind blows away the lighter chaff and the heavier wheat remains.

ORIGINAL HEBREW TEXT WRITTEN 712, 725 BC

בִּלַּע הַמָּוֶת לָנֶצַח וּמָחָה אֲדֹנָי יְהוִה דִּמְעָה מֵעַל כָּל־פָּנִים וְחֶרְפַּת עַמּוֹ יָסִיר מֵעַל
כָּל־הָאָרֶץ כִּי יְהוָה דִּבֵּר׃ **ישעיה כה:ח**
מִיַּד שְׁאוֹל אֶפְדֵּם מִמָּוֶת אֶגְאָלֵם אֱהִי דְבָרֶיךָ מָוֶת אֱהִי קָטָבְךָ שְׁאוֹל נֹחַם יִסָּתֵר
מֵעֵינָי׃ **הושע יג:יד**

OLD TESTAMENT SCRIPTURE TRANSLATION

"He will swallow up death for all time, And the Lord GOD will wipe tears away from all faces, And He will remove the reproach of His people from all the earth; For the LORD has spoken." **Isaiah 25:8 NASB**

"I will ransom them from the power of Sheol; I will redeem them from death. O Death, where are your thorns? O Sheol, where is your sting? Compassion will be hidden from My sight." **Hosea 13:14**

ANCIENT RABBINICAL COMMENTARY

"In the future the Holy One, blessed be He, will resurrect the dead. How will He do it? He takes the Great Shofar and blows it seven times. At the first blast, the whole world shakes and suffers pangs like a woman in childbirth. At the second, the dust is scattered and the graves open. At the third, the bones gather together. At the fourth, the limbs are stretched out. At the fifth, skin comes into being. At the sixth, spirits and souls enter the bodies. At the seventh, they live...."[7]

Pesiqta Hadta, BhM 6:58

NEW TESTAMENT RECORDED 54, 59, 90 AD

"...we do not want you to be uninformed, brethren, about those who are asleep, that you may not grieve, as do the rest who have no hope. For if we believe that Jesus died and rose again, even so God will bring with Him those who have fallen asleep in Jesus. For this we say to you by the word of the Lord, that we who are alive, and remain until the coming of the Lord, shall not precede those who have fallen asleep. For the Lord Himself will descend from heaven with a shout, with the voice of *the* archangel, and with the trumpet of God; and the dead in Christ shall rise first. Then we who are alive and remain shall be caught up together with them in the clouds to meet the Lord in the air, and thus we shall always be with the Lord."

I Thessalonians 4:13-17 NASB

"Now I say this, brethren, that flesh and blood cannot inherit the kingdom of God; nor does the perishable inherit the imperishable. Behold, I tell you a mystery; we shall not all sleep, but we shall all be changed, in a moment, in the twinkling of an eye, at the last trumpet; for the trumpet will sound, and the dead will be raised imperishable, and we shall be changed. For this perishable must put on the imperishable, and this mortal must put on immortality. But when this perishable will have put on the imperishable, and this mortal will have put on immortality, then will come about the saying that is written, 'DEATH IS SWALLOWED UP in victory. O DEATH, WHERE IS YOUR VICTORY? O DEATH, WHERE IS YOUR STING?' "

I Corinthians 15:50-55 NASB

"...I go to prepare a place for you. And if I go and prepare a place for you, I will come again, and receive you to Myself; that where I am, *there* you may be also."

John 14:2-3 NASB

[7] Raphael Patai, *The Messiah Texts*, p. 203.

AUTHOR'S COMMENT—EVANGELICAL CHRISTIAN POSITION

Modern rabbis are not aware of the event known to us believers as the Rapture. This first century Jewish teaching[8] was lost early in the Christian era as a result of the activity of Roman Catholic subversive forces against the early believers. Thus, the early Jewish Christian teaching known as the Rapture was rediscovered and widely taught among Dispensational Evangelicals recently, for the past few hundred years or so. Grant Jeffrey sheds light on this on page 93 of his 1992 book *Apocalypse: The Coming Judgment of the Nations*, when he tells us: "Many writers ignorantly assert that the pretribulation Rapture theory was invented in 1820. While the clearest statement of the pretribulation position was articulated by N. Darby at that time, they ignore these writings of the early Christians that anticipate Christ's coming to deliver His saints before the Tribulation period. Furthermore, many of these writers are ignorant of the other men who developed a clearer understanding of the Rapture in the centuries before 1820....Peter Jurieu was a French Calvinist preacher and was considered 'the Goliath of the French Protestants.' He wrote in A.D. 1687 about the Rapture and the premillennial return of Christ. Jurieu discussed the coming of Jesus to translate the saints prior to the time He returns in judgment. He preached in Rotterdam as one of the greatest of the Reformers in his day. I found his rare and fascinating book, *Approaching Deliverance of the Church*, in a small bookstore in Wales. In his book, Jurieu refuted the amillennial teaching of his day and clearly argued for the premillennial position regarding Christ's return. He also believed that Christ would come in the air to Rapture the saints and return to heaven before the Battle of Armageddon....his book disproves the theory of the posttribulation teachers that assert that the pretribulation Rapture was first invented by Darby and the Plymouth Brethren. As my research indicates, the pretribulation Rapture was articulated in both the New Testament, the writings of some of the Ante-Nicene Fathers and Peter Jurieu, long before 1820. Over one hundred and thirty years before Darby, Jurieu spoke of a secret Rapture, 'a kind of a

---

[8]A modern Christian teacher, Ms. Relfe, said: " 'The recent pre-trib doctrine teaches that this 'he' is the Holy Spirit. There are many blatant inconsistencies which render this untrue.' " Hal Lindsey, *The Rapture: Truth or Consequences*. New York: Bantam Books, Inc., © 1983, p.133. However, the learned and copious prophecy author, Hal Lindsey, quotes Gundry, an opponent of our pre-Trib Rapture faith, as noting: "...'Far from being novel, the view just might reflect apostolic teaching...the charge of novelty against this view, as we have seen, does not survive investigation....' " Ibid, pp. 133-134. Thus this view supports our belief in the pre-Trib Rapture, which stretches back to the New Testament time of Jesus, Himself. The point about the Spirit being the restrainer of the Antichrist (II Thes. 2:7-9) is very important. There are many believers in Jesus today, all of whom receive the Holy Spirit from the moment of salvation (Rom. 8:9). Our point is, if God's Spirit in us is restraining the evil of the coming of the Antichrist as the Bible teaches (II Thes. 2:7), the Spirit would have to be momentarily absent for him (the Anti-Messiah) to step upon his seven-year Tribulation stage. Thus the only way to remove the Spirit is to remove the receptacles in which the Holy Spirit dwells, and that is the believers. Once we are gone, just prior to the 144,000 Jewish believers being sealed with the Spirit, the Antichrist (in the absence of the Spirit on Earth) will quickly make his entry! Soon after, as the Spirit of God is reinstated through the 144,000 Jews (Rev. 7:4) and their converts, the Antichrist will persecute the Tribulation saints as Christians have never been persecuted before (Dan. 7:25), until the Raptured believers are reunited with the Tribulation saints at the end of the seven years. Thus it goes without saying that we should share with as many of our friends as possible that Jesus is the only one who can rescue us, before the Rapture, so that they can believe and come with us, too!

clandestine coming of Christ' prior to His coming in glory and judgment at Armageddon.' "[9] In Grant's 1995 book *FINAL* WARNING (p. 306), he quotes the Christian writer Ephram of AD 373, who wrote of the pre-trib. rapture! Death brings the soul face-to-face with Jesus (I Cor. 13:12).[10] The resurrection reunites the body, once again, with the soul and Spirit in order that it may experience eternal blissful existence. The Rapture of the living occurs a split second after the resurrection and Rapture of the dead believers in Messiah (I Cor. 15:51-52). It serves the purpose of a "resurrection" for the living believers who have not had their spirit separated from them by death. Their bodies are changed from mortal to immortal. Thus, we who are alive, receive our new eternal resurrected bodies (I Thes. 4:17), just as the dead bodies are transformed from "corruption to incorruption." Corruption means dead, as mortal refers to a body "subject to death." Jesus was referring to this event when He said: "I am the resurrection and the life: he that believeth in me, though he were dead, yet shall he live: And whosoever liveth and believeth in me shall never die...." (John 11:25-26 KJV). Those who will never die are those of us alive at the moment of His Coming for us, and those who are dead at the Rapture (the first part of the Second Advent of Messiah) will be raised to spend that seven-year period with Him, before His return to the earth with us, to destroy Antichrist and institute the 1000-year kingdom (Zech. 14:4, 5; Rev. 19-20). **Philip Moore**

SOME DENY AND RIDICULE THE RAPTURE—THEY SHOULD STUDY!

There are those who claim to be Christian and who, I guess because they have a spiritual chip on their shoulder, like to ridicule the Rapture. By this I mean they outright deny it. Gary DeMar, who is called "one of the [Christian Reconstructionist] movement's most popular and prolific apologists,"[11] wrote a book, *Last Days Madness*, about which the *Atlanta Journal and Constitution* article entitled, "A 'World View' Based on the Bible," says: "...describes as 'folly' the fear of the imminent end of the world." The article mentions that this view of end time events "has pitted him against such popular writers as Hal Lindsey, Dave Hunt and John Walvoord." I might add that these three authors' books far surpass the writings of Mr. DeMar in the depth of their understanding of eschatology (study of the end times).

---

[9]Grant R. Jeffrey, *Apocalypse: The Coming Judgment of the Nations.* Toronto: Frontier Research Publications, © 1992, p. 93, used by permission.

[10]I Corinthians 13:12 reads: "For now we see through a glass, darkly; but then face to face: now I know in part; but then shall I know even as also I am known" (KJV). A precious hope for all who now draw breath!

[11]Gayle White, "A 'World View' Based on the Bible," *Atlanta Journal and Constituton*, Sat. Sept. 26, 1992, p. E6, © 1992, reprinted by permission, [ ] mine. Reproduction does not imply endorsement. Hal Lindsey exposes this movement and its leaders' deceptions and false doctrine, with emphasis on their anti-Israel stance in relation to our biblical prophetic beliefs. If you are interested in researching this subject, Hal Lindsey has a great book entitled, *The Road To Holocaust.*

The article went on to say that DeMar "credits the belief in Armageddon, soon with what he calls a 'general malaise' in the Christian church."[12] These words bring to mind the apostle Peter's warning to us regarding liberal preachers who deny truth: "This is now, beloved, the second letter I am writing to you in which I am stirring up your sincere mind by way of reminder, that you should remember the words spoken beforehand by the holy prophets and the commandment of the Lord and Savior *spoken* by your apostles. Know this first of all, that in the last days mockers will come with *their* mocking, following after their own lusts, and saying, 'Where is the promise of His coming? For *ever* since the fathers fell asleep, all continues just as it was from the beginning of creation' " (II Pet. 3:1-4 NASB). Where is the promise of His Coming? DeMar says: " 'They think they're going to be raptured out of here and there's nothing they can do....' "[13]

THE CRM'S MISDIAGNOSIS—JESUS CLEANS UP THE HEART, NOT CRM

Here we should mention that many within the Christian Reform Movement (CRM) feels it is their duty to clean up the world by enforcing biblical justice on all who live. We, as true believers, know it is impossible to legislate morality and "perfect human behavior." Only Jesus can change the heart. That is why true Christians are interested in introducing their friends to Jesus, who, once received, transforms the human heart! True believers in Jesus do not "think they can do nothing" because they are going to "be raptured," rather they follow Jesus' biblical command: "...**Occupy till I come**" (Luke 19:13 KJV). They are instrumental in placing responsible people in office who will enact laws protecting the right of the unborn to be born.

Jay Sekulow and Pat Robertson have been most active and successful in securing our right to continue evangelism in certain public areas, an activity for which the ACLU and similar organizations have taken us to court![14]

While we share the Gospel without trying to clean up the fish pond, we fish like Peter. Jesus told Peter and Andrew: "...I will make you fishers of men" (Matt. 4:19 KJV).

---

[12]Ibid.

[13]Ibid.

[14]The Supreme Court ruled that *Jews for Jesus* had the legal right to distribute literature in airports and other public places. The ACLU had challenged the right of believers to this form of free speech! It seems to me that they should call themselves anti-ACLU instead of the American Civil Liberties Union, if they want to remove the Christians' civil liberty of free speech.

Many people will believe in Jesus if told the truth about Him, but the pond of the world cannot be cleansed, because there will always be unbelievers. Until Jesus returns, we share the Gospel, catch a few fish out of the corrupt pond and await the Messiah, who is coming soon, as the end times indicate.

DeMar, by calling the true believers "Eschatalogical couch potatoes," is of course, irresponsible and slanderous. I, for one, have spent twelve years in libraries and universities, working long hours researching and writing this book, to help educate both the Christian and non-Christian about biblical history and prophecies. Who can call me a couch potato? No one. Not DeMar and not the CRM, which borders on being a "cult" in the minds of many evangelical authorities!

The Rapture will come soon, we believe hopefully, while we are being examples to our, as of yet, unwon loved ones! We do not legislate morality, we live it, though we may sometimes fail. We are in the world but not of the world (John 15:19). Substitute "pond" for "world" and you see where the true believer parts from the CRM activist and his theological error.

BACK TO OUR POINT ABOUT THE RAPTURE—WHAT DOES HAL SAY?

Hal Lindsey commented on this momentous event we know as the Rapture: "We have been examining the push of world events which the prophets foretold would lead the way to the seven-year countdown before the return of Jesus Christ to earth. The big question is, will you be here during this seven-year countdown? Will you be here during the time of the Tribulation when the Antichrist and the False Prophet are in charge for a time? Will you be here when the world is plagued by mankind's darkest days?

It may come as a surprise to you, but the decision concerning your presence during this last seven-year period in history is entirely up to you.

God's Word tells us that there will be one generation of believers who will never know death. These believers will be removed from the earth before the Great Tribulation—before that period of the most ghastly pestilence, bloodshed, and starvation the world has ever known.

Examine the prophecies of this mysterious happening—of the 'Rapture.' Here is the real hope for the Christian, the 'blessed hope' for true believers (Titus 2:13-15).

As we see the circumstances which are coming on the world, this hope gets more blessed all the time. This is the reason we are optimistic about the future. This is the reason that in spite of the headlines, in spite of crisis after crisis in America and throughout the world, in spite of the dark days which will strike terror into the hearts of many, every Christian has the right to be optimistic!

You may be thinking now, 'Count me out. I like it right here and I have a lot of plans for my future.'

Exactly. This is what we are talking about—your plans for the future....According to all the Scriptures we are told that the place He is preparing for us will be utterly fantastic. Eternal life will surpass the greatest pleasures we have known on earth."[15]

Paul tells us in the New Testament: "...We shall not all sleep...." (I Cor. 15:51 KJV). "Sleep" here indicates a Christian's death. While his spirit becomes instantly united with the Lord (II Cor. 5:1-10; Phil. 1:21-23), his body sleeps until resurrection.

Hal answers the question this way: "So what does sleep? Your body. The body that disintegrates, Christ will raise into a body which can never see corruption again. 'For our citizenship is in heaven, from which also we eagerly wait for a Savior, the Lord Jesus Christ; who will transform the body of our humble state into conformity with the body of His glory, by the exertion of the power that He has even to subject all things to Himself' (Philippians 3:20, 21 NASB).

What about the mystery? The mystery has to do with the believers who will be *alive* when Christ comes for them. 'In a moment, in the twinkling of an eye, at the last trumpet; for the trumpet will sound, and the dead will be raised imperishable, and we shall be changed' (I Corinthians 15:52 NASB)."[16]

THE RAPTURE, ACCORDING TO THE JEWISH CHRISTIAN ZOLA LEVITT

Zola Levitt, the author of a number of famous books[17] on prophecy, has commented on the pre-Tribulation Rapture and the wonderful things in store for believers. Levitt, who shows that the ancient Jewish wedding feast is a prophetic preview of this wonderful event, tells us: "We have been invited, every one of us believers, to the most thrilling and mystical seven-year sojourn this side of eternity. We are to be the house guests of Almighty God!....Jesus' overwhelming promise of John 14:1-3 separates the true Biblical faith from all

---

[15]Hal Lindsey with C.C. Carlson, *The Late Great Planet Earth*, pp. 137-138.
[16]Ibid, p. 140.
[17]His books are available through Zola Levitt, POB 12268, Dallas, TX, USA 75225. His book, *The Rapture,* can be obtained through Harvest House Publishers, Eugene, OR, USA 97402. John F. Walvoord, president of Dallas Theologian Seminary, wrote *The Rapture Question*, which is clear and to the point on our pre-Trib view of the Rapture.

religions man has concocted. It is not some wishful thinking on our part that provides us a visit to heaven but God's own pronouncement.

On that particularly tense Passover night when our Lord was to face arrest, trial and conviction, and finally crucifixion, he uttered the promise that makes Christianity what it is: Let not your heart be troubled: ye believe in God, believe also in me. In my Father's house are many mansions: if it were not so, I would have told you. I go to prepare a place for you. And if I go and prepare a place for you, I will come again, and receive you unto myself; that where I am, there ye may be also (John 14:1-3)....There are plenty of churches that are teaching that Jesus is not going to return and that what we see is what we get. The liberal Protestant churches—if they really believe that Jesus existed as characterized in the gospels at all—are really not expecting His return or preaching it....The Roman Catholics have a vague idea of some Kingdom to come or some general trip to heaven, but no appreciation of the details of the Rapture, the Second Coming, etc....He told them [his disciples] plainly: 'I go to prepare a place for you.'

Every religious leader has died and left a group of devout followers on earth, but one has announced that He died for a purpose; one has promised that He was merely departing to do work on behalf of His disciples. The leaders of the various cults will not be making return trips and are not able to promise that reassurance to their followers, but Jesus asserted just that. He went further: He said, 'I will come again and receive you unto myself that where I am ye may be also.' He has not only gone to prepare us a place in His Father's house but He will come personally to escort us there. This is very much in keeping with what the bridegroom did on behalf of his bride. After he proposed he left to prepare the bridal chamber, or mansion, and then later returned to take her there personally. We are so very literally the Bride of Christ, as Paul described us. We are being treated as the best of all brides by that one-of-a-kind Bridegroom, who came to us from an unearthly place and who will one day come to take us there....The verses about the Rapture of the Church are most clear in the New Testament. They are objective and decisive—not given in the language of poetry or parables so they may be 'spiritualized' away by those who have difficulty believing in the Lord's return. If a person does not believe that Jesus Christ will come back from heaven to take His church to His Father's house, that person does not believe in Christianity. He may believe in the moral messages of Jesus and in the principles of Christian behavior and the like, but he is not believing in the principle that makes the biblical faith what it is. We count on—we live for—the Lord's return. That visit to His Father's house, and the

Kingdom and eternity beyond, are our very basis for being believers in Him.

But we are concerned in this book with the details of what will happen in Jesus' Father's house when we go there. We are not going to heaven merely to luxuriate in that mystical place but to accomplish two things necessary to our own perfection as the Bride of Christ. In His Father's house we will each enter the Judgment Seat of Christ, and then we will celebrate our wedding to the Lord at the Marriage Supper of the Lamb."[18]

THE ANCIENT JEWISH WEDDING FEAST FITS THE PRE-TRIBULATION RAPTURE

Levitt continues his analogy of the wedding feast by telling us: "...to understand this magnificent idea more completely we need to review the custom...basically the wedding breaks down into seven parts: The contract; The cup; The price; The departure of the bridegroom; The stealing of the bride; The bridal chamber; The marriage supper." The first part is the contract which Levitt[19] describes as follows: "Israeli marriages were by contract....The bridegroom would see the girl he wanted (she could be a perfect stranger) and simply go to her house with a contract of marriage. It would have in it the rules of the waiting period before the bridegroom would come back for his bride....typically the marriages were arranged and the contracts drawn by the parents long before the youngsters got the news. As Tevye sings to his wife in *Fiddler on the Roof*, 'The first time I saw you was on our wedding day...' Rebecca married a man she never met."[20]

LET'S TALK PRICE

We emphasize that there was a price a man had to pay in dollars, or rather shekels (ancient Israeli money), for his wife. The bridal price varied. Sometimes the bridegroom-to-be would ask his father, "Is she worth it?" If the price was a high one, Levitt says: "Many a bridegroom probably returned to his father after learning the price for a particular bride and asked his advice on whether he should pay it. 'Do you realize how much they want for her?' must have been a question

---

[18]Zola Levitt, *In My Father's House*. Dallas: Zola Levitt, © 1981, pp. 1, 4, 8, used by permission. [ ] mine.

[19]See our *Vol. II*, chapter 35, "The Secrets of Jesus in Passover Versus the Errors of Easter," for lengthy quotes from Levitt illustrating how the development of a baby prophetically parallels the Jewish feasts, advocating the pre-Trib Rapture—obstetrically!

[20]Zola Levitt, *In My Father's House*, p. 12.

repeated often in the old tradition. The Jewish bridegroom was wise enough to know that his father's judgments in these matters were trustworthy...."[21] However, once the price was decided, it was final.

Jesus, in the Garden of Gethsemane, asked that judgment (this cup) be lifted if it were possible, but then said, "nevertheless not my will, but thine, be done" (Luke 22:42 KJV), thus deciding to pay the price of His life for the sins of all mankind.

THE CUP OF THE NEW COVENANT ANSWERS THE PROPOSAL

With regard to the cup, Zola Levitt notes: "The cup was a formality establishing the bride's answer to the proposal. When the contract and the price had both been presented, the bridegroom would pour a cup of wine for his intended and propose a toast to her. She could pick up the cup or she could withdraw, and this was her way of saying yes or no to the proposal."[22]

Levitt continues: "We see Him [Jesus] drinking the cup with His bride in Matthew 26:27. It was at the Passover table that the Lord did this so appropriately. He was to die that day (the next morning actually, but the Jewish day begins at sundown). He took this last opportunity to drink the cup with His bride and seal the New Covenant: And He took the cup, and gave thanks, and gave it to them, saying, Drink ye all of it; For this is my blood of the New Testament, which is shed for many for the remission of sins (Matt. 26:27-28).

Looking at verse 27, we might ask, 'What did the Lord say when He gave thanks?' Any Jew can tell you—there is just one Jewish blessing over the wine and it has been said for all time: Blessed art Thou, O Lord our God, King of the universe, Creator of the fruit of the vine.

The fruit of the vine, ultimately, is the Church. Jesus said that He was the true vine, and the disciples were the branches. Finally, we become the fruit in this figure, and this brings out the toast aspect of this cup. Jesus praised the Creator for bringing forth this bride and He toasted the bride for becoming the true fruit. Then He told all the believers to drink this cup so that they would answer His proposal affirmatively and become His promised bride.

In verse 28, He announced that the cup was His blood of the New Covenant ('testament' and 'covenant' are the same word), and that it is

---

[21]Zola Levitt, *A Christian Love Story*. Dallas: Zola Levitt, © 1978, p. 15, used by permission.

[22]Zola Levitt, *In My Father's House*, pp. 12-13.

shed for the remission of sins. Obviously, this fulfilled Jeremiah's announcement of the New Covenant—the covenant which would forgive sins. It's interesting to consider that the New Testament itself is our copy of the contract. Should anyone accuse you of sin, you need only show him your copy of the contract to prove that your sins are forgiven....Jesus made it very clear that this one sacrifice—this one cup—would be sufficient to forgive everyone's sins, all the way up to the Kingdom of God: But I say unto you, I will not drink henceforth of this fruit of the vine, until that day when I drink it new with you in my Father's Kingdom (v. 29).' "[23]

JESUS FULFILLED THE JEWISH FEAST OF PASSOVER AND UNLEAVENED BREAD BY COMING DOWN FROM THE CROSS AT THE RIGHT TIME

When Jesus went to the cross and paid for all of our shortcomings, it was on Passover. Levitt elaborates: "The symbol of Passover is the sacrifice of the lamb, and Jesus fulfilled it on the cross. The symbol of Unleavened Bread is the body of the Lord buried in the earth ('if a kernel of wheat fall into the ground...', 'This bread is My body'). Thus, to fulfill the second feast, the Lord had to be buried at the beginning of Unleavened Bread, or at sundown on the day of Passover. He was placed on the cross at 9:00 in the morning and taken down at 3:00. Sundown in April in Israel is about 4:30 or 5:00, and thus the Lord was buried exactly in time to commemorate the Feast of Unleavened Bread.

And so the fulfillments progress through the rest of the feasts. First Fruits, which we now call ('Easter'), came on the following Sunday (Lev. 23:10-12), and indeed the Lord rose as the first fruits of those to be resurrected (I Cor. 15:22-23). The fourth feast is Pentecost, 50 days later (Lev. 23:15-16), and the Lord sent the Holy Spirit in a great harvest. Three thousand people were saved that day, just as 3,000 people were killed on the day the Law came. They had made a golden calf and the Lord was infuriated: And the children of Levi did according to the word of Moses: and there fell of the people that day about three thousand men (Exodus 32:28).

But when the Lord sent the Holy Spirit, He returned to Israel exactly 3,000 souls. The Lord is a good bookkeeper, and indeed, the letter kills, the Spirit gives life (II Cor. 3:6).

Thus the Lord performed exactly in accordance with the first four feasts of Israel. He will do the same in the future, it is clear. We expect

---

[23]Zola Levitt, *A Christian Love Story*, pp. 12-13.

the Rapture of the church on the fifth feast, the Feast of Trumpets (I Thess. 4:16-17). We expect the return of the Lord to the earth for the start of the Kingdom on the Day of Atonement, when 'all Israel will be saved' (Zech. 12:10; 13:1; Rom. 11:26). And finally, the Lord will set up His Tabernacle in Jerusalem appropriately enough on the final feast, the Feast of Tabernacles. The tabernacles hark back to the shelters the Lord gave the children of Israel in the wilderness, and indeed the Lord's Tabernacle will shelter us on this earth for the duration of the Kingdom. These final three feasts are explained in Leviticus 23:24, 27 and 34, respectively.

We say all of that above to show that the Lord, who never omitted a Jewish feast, fulfilled each one even in His crucifixion and burial, as well as in His resurrection, His sending of the Holy Spirit, His return at the sound of the trumpet, His second coming on the day when Israel atones, and His establishment of His Kingdom on Tabernacles. Thus, it is valid that the Lord had to come off the cross in six hours for the simple reason that He was a law abiding Jew and He had a feast to keep."[24]

THEN, MANSIONS WERE PREPARED FOR THE BRIDE, AND NOW THEY ARE PREPARED FOR BELIEVERS

Regarding the departure, Levitt notes: "As soon as the bride drank the cup the bridegroom would make a little speech on the order of, 'I go to prepare a place for you.' He then returned to his father's house to build her a bridal chamber—a little mansion—for their honeymoon. The bride would spend her time (up to two years!) gathering her trousseau, getting her oil lamp ready to travel at night (Matt. 25:1-13) and keeping her veil on whenever she went out (in effect, keeping her faith in good order and not mixing with the world). She waited at home every night for her bridegroom as the contract normally specified. 'Ye are not your own for ye are bought with a price,' Paul admonishes us (I Corinthians 6:19-20). She did not know her wedding day. At the bridegroom's father's house the young man would build a beautiful bridal chamber as fast as he could. His father would be the judge of when it was properly finished (to prevent the excited youngster from throwing up some sort of lean-to and going to get the girl)! So the bridegroom did not know the wedding day either. If one came along and asked him he would say, 'I don't know, only my father knows' (Acts 1:7)."[25]

---

[24]Ibid, pp. 16-18.
[25]Zola Levitt, *In My Father's House*, p. 13.

Levitt continues: "[Jesus says of His Second Coming] We saw in the Jewish wedding custom that the bridegroom would depart to his father's house after he made the covenant, drank the cup and paid the price. Likewise, our Lord went on to His Father's house with an announcement to His disciples virtually in the same words as the Israeli bridegroom must have used: Let not your heart be troubled: ye believe in God, believe also in Me. In My Father's house are many mansions: if it were not so, I would have told you. I go to prepare a place for you. And if I go and prepare a place for you, I will come again, and receive you unto Myself; that where I am, there ye may be also (John 14:1-3)....In our case, we have been waiting a long time. But we must continue to wait in a manner that would gratify our Bridegroom. The veil worn by the bride is simply our good testimony before the world. Our consecrated, set-apart ways speak to the unbelievers around of our loyalty to God and our agreement to marry His Son. Paul put it very strongly when he said simply, 'You are not your own.'

We must all fully realize, as we wait, that the Lord *is coming*. The bridegroom always returned. We hear many a sermon on the Lord's return but we falter in our walk, reasoning that if He didn't come last year or last week, He probably won't come tonight. But there *will* be a night when the Lord will come, and He requires that we be ready and waiting. We can believe that that Jewish bride waited at home every night and trusted constantly in that marvelous night when she would at last hear the shout."[26]

THE SECRET, SWIFT STEALING OF THE ANCIENT JEWISH BRIDE WAS A PROPHECY OF OUR RAPTURE!

With regard to the stealing of the bride, Levitt tell us: "The bride was 'stolen' in the sense that the groom would come completely unannounced in the middle of the night and seize her out of her bed. She did not know where she was going, and with lamp in hand could only be led along over hill and dale to her bridal chamber. Now it's getting romantic! All the Jewish brides were stolen out of their beds in the middle of the night by young strangers they may have seen once, two years before, and that is the way they did things back then! Their divorce rate was nil, by the way. The bridegroom comes therefore 'like a thief in the night.' "[27]

Zola also says: "The return of the Lord for His bride, the church, is most clear in the Scriptures: For the Lord Himself shall descend

---

[26]Zola Levitt, *A Christian Love Story*, pp. 18-20. [ ] mine.

[27]Zola Levitt, *In My Father's House*, pp. 13-14.

from heaven with a shout, with the voice of the archangel, and with the trump of God: and the dead in Christ shall rise first: Then we which are alive and remain shall be caught up together with them in the clouds, to meet the Lord in the air: and so shall we ever be with the Lord (I Thess. 4:16-17)....Now when the Lord comes for us, we are to have oil lamps ready and waiting. Oil in the Bible is the Holy Spirit, and we are to have the oil and be ready to travel even in the dark of night. The parable of the ten virgins (Matt. 25:1-13) is correctly applied to the Kingdom, but has marvelous application to this wedding story. In that parable, there were ten virgins 'which took their lamps and went forth to meet the bridegroom': And five of them were wise, and five were foolish. They that were foolish took their lamps, and took no oil with them: But the wise took oil in their vessels with their lamps (Matt. 25:2-4).

The bridegroom in this parable acted in accordance with the Jewish tradition of totally surprising the bride and catching her asleep: While the bridegroom tarried, they all slumbered and slept (v. 5).

But then he comes with a shout: And at midnight there was a cry made, Behold, the bridegroom cometh; go ye out to meet him (v. 6)....only those virgins with their lamps trimmed with oil were able to go with the bridegroom. The others, suddenly realizing that they were not properly prepared, went out to purchase oil, but they were too late: And while they went to buy, the bridegroom came; and they that were ready went in with him to the marriage: and the door was shut. Afterward came also the other virgins, saying, Lord, Lord, open to us. But he answered and said, Verily I say unto you, I know you not (vs. 10-12).

The message is very clear: We must have the Holy Spirit—we must be true believers in the Lord Jesus—to go with Him when He comes.

The oil was established as a very essential ingredient as far back as the building of the Tabernacle in the wilderness: And thou shalt command the children of Israel, that they bring thee pure olive oil beaten for the light, to cause the lamp to burn always (Exodus 27:20).

We can learn a great deal from the above Scripture. We are just like the lampstand in the Tabernacle. We are set aflame once when we believe in the Messiah, but as we walk, we must constantly take in the oil—the Holy Spirit—in order to keep our flame burning brightly. The flame is a beautiful symbol of the Christian faith. With one flame I can light all the candles in the world and mine will not be diminished.

Understanding the symbol of the oil and the symbol of the trumpet as well, we are in a position to see how powerful we really are in this world. Gideon went forward with only 300 men and attacked a force of Midianites totaling over 100,000! Gideon, like the U.S. Marines, came forward with 'a few good men', but the Lord had armed these soldiers in a special way. They carried trumpets in their right hands and oil lamps in their left hands. Remarkably, they won that battle with their peculiar attack: And the three companies blew the trumpets, and brake the pitchers, and held the lamps in their left hands, and the trumpets in their right hands to blow withal: and they cried, The sword of the Lord, and of Gideon (Judges 7:20).

Armed with God's symbol of deliverance, the trumpet, and the symbol of the Holy Spirit, the oil in the lamps, Gideon's army prevailed over the pagans. God had chosen to have Gideon attack with such a small force so that the glory would certainly go to Him. And likewise, we carry the Holy Spirit in the same sort of pottery jars used by Gideon's men: But we have this treasure in earthen vessels, that the excellency of the power may be of God, and not of us (II Cor. 4:7).

When we break the earthen vessels that are our earthly bodies, the light pours out of us and the oil within convicts the unbeliever. We are a small army, like Gideon's, but outfitted with God's special weaponry, we are invincible in this spiritual battle."[28]

IN THE BRIDAL CHAMBER, WE GAIN OR LOSE REWARDS OF PRECIOUS STONES AND MORE, IN OUR SEVEN YEARS OF FUN

Regarding the bridal chamber, Zola emphasizes that we will be going to the "judgment seat of Christ" (I Cor. 3:11-15; II Cor. 5:10), which is a judgment for believers only. There we receive or lose rewards for serving the Lord based on our motives. If the motive was genuine and carried out by relying on the power of the Holy Spirit, we get rewards for our works of "precious metals and stones." If it was not,[29] they (the works) are burned up, being made of wood, hay and stubble.

The parallel with the Jewish wedding is informative here. While the bridegroom learned physical secrets in this chamber, where he stayed with his bride for seven days, Jesus reviews our spiritual strengths and weaknesses in an intimate manner. That is, we remain with the Lord seven years, having been caught up seven years before

---

[28]Zola Levitt, *A Christian Love Story*, pp. 20, 22-24.

[29]An example of this would be sharing the Gospel with someone to impress them, with no thought for that person's needs or feelings regarding an understanding of Jesus; telling someone about Jesus without relying on God's Holy Spirit. Impious pride is an example. Piety and pride were also the worst among the Pharisees, as you can see from Jesus' rebuke of them for it in the Gospels (Matt. 23:15).

He returns to Earth. Zola mentions this detail of the feast: "The bride and groom would remain in the chamber for seven days, at last emerging for the marriage supper."[30]

THE ROYAL RECEPTION, WITH ALL OF OUR BROTHERS AND THE PROPHETS

Levitt says with respect to the marriage supper: "This is what we would call the reception, in effect, a banquet for the new couple. In heaven presumably all the Old Testament saints will be at that magnificent celebration and we as the wife of Christ will be the guests of honor: Let us be glad and rejoice, and give honour to him: for the marriage of the Lamb is come, and his wife hath made herself ready. And to her was granted that she should be arrayed in fine linen, clean and white: for the fine linen is the righteousness of saints (Rev. 19:7-8).

After the meal the bride and groom would typically leave his father's house and go to the housing that the groom had arranged for them. And thus it will be that after seven years (the seven days of the wedding) we will return to earth with our Bridegroom. We will not stay in heaven, as some preach, but instead return to the Kingdom that has been prepared for us on earth. And so at last 'the meek shall inherit the earth,' and 'God's will shall be done on earth as it is in heaven'....we are now in that lengthy waiting period while He prepares our bridal chamber. We can see clearly that the stealing away of the bride is the Rapture of the Church. As a matter of fact, in order to prevent the young man from literally snatching the girl out of her bed and to give her just a moment or two to prepare herself, the rules were that when he got close enough to her house to be heard, someone in the wedding party had to shout. And it is clear from Scripture that the Lord will play the part of the bridegroom, even at the time of the Rapture; 'For the Lord himself shall descend from heaven with a shout, (I Thess. 4:16)...."[31]

Zola beautifully concludes the pre-Trib wedding feast analogy by enlightening us: "The real purpose, as we said above, is to take care of our last vestiges of imperfection, our bad works. Our sins were forgiven long ago at the cross but we carry the memory of our bad works with us to heaven. Those will be taken care of in the Judgment Seat so that at the point when we marry the Lord at that marriage supper we will be simply perfect; as perfect as He is.

---

[30]Zola Levitt, *In My Father's House*, p. 14.
[31]Ibid, pp. 14-15.

He would marry nothing less....the marriage supper of the Lamb is the very last activity of the Church in heaven because it is immediately followed by the Second Coming of Christ (Rev. 19:11). We go with our Husband when He returns to the earth (vs. 14). We put a stop to Armageddon before it puts a stop to the entire human race and we begin at long last the Kingdom of God. We will happily undertake our best 1,000 years to that point. Clearly the Scriptures indicate nothing further for the Church but only chronicle the battle of Armageddon, the doom of the Antichrist, Satan bound and the final judgment. We then go on to eternity. The final judgment, the 'Great White Throne' judgment, does not concern the Church at all but those who were unbelievers in their earthly lives. It will follow the Kingdom Age and it is the judgment we are exempted from when we receive Christ.

But to go back to our subject of what will happen to us in Jesus' Father's house, we will be married and that will end our visit. Therefore the events in heaven, climactic as they are, are only two in number—the Judgment Seat of Christ and the Marriage Supper of the Lamb. Both will be enormous in size since both will concern every believer of the Church Age, every soul who ever believed in Jesus from the cross to the Rapture, will have to be dealt with individually, at least in the Judgment Seat. Can God do this in seven years and still save time for a wedding? Can He create the universe in six days and save the seventh for a rest?"[32] Yes!

LEVITT'S TIME IS ON THE DIME

As mentioned, Zola's analogy based on the Jewish tradition, settles conclusively the question of when the Rapture will occur. He reminds us: "A knowledge of the Jewish wedding as outlined above contributes a great deal to the understanding of prophecy. Currently, for example, there is quite a discussion about whether the Rapture will come before or after the Tribulation Period. Instantly, however, we can see by consulting the wedding that it must be before. To have it afterward would put the stealing of the bride after the honeymoon and ruin the entire analogy....The seven years in heaven so neatly fit the events on earth below and, after all, the Church has to be somewhere. If it were on earth then where would the Judgment Seat and the wedding happen? Those who place the Rapture after the Tribulation Period or the midpoint seldom go into such fine detail but these particular events seem heavenly in nature, supernatural as they are, and

---

[32]Ibid, pp. 16-17.

have no place in the earthly Biblical reportage....Paul made it so clear that we are to have individual interviews with our King. Again, that vital admonition: 'For we must all appear before the judgment seat of Christ: that every one may receive the things done in his body, according to that he hath done, whether it be good or bad (II Cor. 5:10).

Another important prophetic conclusion that is borne out by this splendid analogy is that of the Rapture itself. Some believers question whether it will really happen just the way it is spelled out in the Scriptures, but after all it wouldn't be much of a wedding if the groom did not come back to take the bride away. Again we are urged by the accuracy of the thing toward the inevitable conclusion that it will all happen in orderly fashion with the Rapture first, then the Judgment Seat, then the marriage supper, then the return to earth and the Kingdom. Any change, even in the order of these events, would ruin the whole picture."[33]

REVEREND CHARLES RYRIE'S DIARY

Reverend Charles Ryrie, who compiled the *Ryrie Study Bible*, also uses the Jewish wedding model to make the same point in his book, *What You Should Know About the Rapture*.[34] Hal Lindsey makes an interesting comment on Ryrie's work in his book, *The Rapture: Truth or Consequences*. Hal states: "All of the symbols and imagery used in the New Testament were based upon the common Hebrew culture of the day. Otherwise there would be no hope of understanding the rich use of parable, allegory and illustrations. Therefore, the standard Hebrew marriage tradition of that time gives insight into the Church as the bride of Christ, particularly in Revelation chapters 19 and 21.

I believe that these passages we have examined contribute significantly toward the case for a pre-Tribulation Rapture. The promise of being kept from the hour; the identity of those who dwell in heaven; the Church's absence from earth in chapters 4 through 19; the bride's presence in heaven before the second coming, all fit into the pattern of a pre-Tribulation Rapture scenario."[35]

***

[33]Ibid, pp. 17-18.

[34]Rev. Charles Ryrie, *What You Should Know About the Rapture*. Chicago: Moody Press, © 1981, pp. 60-61.

[35]Hal Lindsey, *The Rapture: Truth or Consequences*, p. 111.

ON A POSITIVE CLOSING RAPTURE NOTE

If you want to have some small inkling of what is in store for you during those great seven years of Rapture before the Second Coming, read Revelation, chapters 4 and 5! Remember, according to God's prophets, there is nothing more to be fulfilled before Jesus comes to catch us up. It could happen tomorrow.

Israelis prepare for a poison gas attack,
and an Israeli soldier guards the border of Israel.

"...all the armies of the world could maneuver for battle here [the valley of Armageddon]."[1] Napoleon Bonaparte breathed these words as he looked out over the valley of Armageddon in Israel, 1798

"We have had our last chance. If we will not devise some greater and more equitable system, ARMAGEDDON will be at the door. The problem basically is theological and involves a spiritual recrudescence and improvement of human character that will synchronize with our almost matchless advances in science, art, literature, and all material and cultural developments of the past 2000 years. It must be the spirit if we are to save the flesh."

General Douglas MacArthur, at Japanese surrender, 1945

"You know, I turn back to your ancient prophets in the Old Testament and the signs foretelling Armageddon, and I find myself wondering if — if we're the generation that is going to see that come about. I don't know if you've noted any of those prophecies lately, but, believe me, they certainly describe the times."[2] "We see around us today the marks of a terrible dilemma, predictions of doomsday. Those predictions carry weight because of the existence of nuclear weapons, and the constant threat of global war...so much so that no president, no congress, no parliament can spend a day entirely free of this threat."[3]

President Ronald Reagan, 1983

"...the danger of a nuclear war is greater now than during the Cold War."[4]

Former President Richard M. Nixon, 1994

"The End Times are now, we're living in them. The enemies of Israel will attack Israel during the night with a major chemical and biological attack and the numbers of casualties will be tremendous, and it is said that Israel will respond strategically with nuclear weapons, beginning a WWIII....here in the U.S. you will see horrible things. Our prophecies do teach us that there will be a nuclear strike against an American city. Our prophecies teach us that America...will fall from racial rioting from within."[5] Rabbi Ariel R. Tzadok, 1994

"A nuclear confrontation in the Middle East is not just likely, it is certain. It is just a matter of timing." Robert Hunter, U.S. Ambassador to NATO, 1996

26

WE WIN ARMAGEDDON— OUR FINAL BATTLE

The word Armageddon is known to most people from one verse in the New Testament portion of the Bible, namely Revelation 16:16.

---

[1]Hal Lindsey with C.C. Carlson, *The Late Great Planet Earth*, p. 164. [ ] mine.
[2]"Reagan: Is Apocalypse Now?" *Atlanta Journal and Constitution*, Sat., Oct. 29, 1983, reprinted by permission of Associated Press. Reproduction does not imply endorsement.
[3]Mike Evans, *The Return*, p. 94.
[4]Richard Nixon, *Beyond Peace*, p. 36. Nixon's reference was to North Korea and the Arab nations, who were trying to join the nuclear club, but did not have the same restraint as the super-powers.
[5]*Ancient Prophecies II*, NBC News, Nov. 18, 1994.

The meaning of the English word, Armageddon, is a complete mystery to most who read or hear about it. Armageddon is an anglicized version of two Hebrew words: *Har* meaning "mountain" and *Magedon*, meaning "slaughter." "And they gathered them together to the place which in Hebrew is called HarMagedon" (Rev. 16:16 NASB). So reads verse 16, of chapter 16, of the last book of the New Testament.

HarMagedon is located in northern Israel near Galilee. It is one of the bloodiest historical sites known on Earth. Twenty-eight different battles were waged in this immediate area. It is the key to strategic military needs, to any and every army which desires to gain a foothold in the surrounding territory. Today, it is a peaceful mountain overlooking a pleasant valley, and at the moment, one of Israel's national parks. Peaceful, perhaps, for only a few moments more, for one day soon, it will become the scene of the last and worst battle ever fought!

You will recall the battles of Gog and Magog mentioned earlier in our chapter 19, "Russia is Crushed in Gog." Well, the army that originates with Russia and the Arabs, terminates here at Armageddon in Israel, together with a 200 million-strong horde from Red China and the rest of the world's armies, concentrating their forces in and around the valley.

A view of the Valley of Megiddo, from the summit of Mount Megiddo.

Mount Megiddo (Armageddon) from street level.

A road sign points the way to Mount Megiddo.

The actual landscape where the battle of Armageddon will occur. Today, the hill of Megiddo is a national park in Israel.

ORIGINAL HEBREW TEXT WRITTEN 587 BC

ויהי דבר־יהוה אלי לאמר: בן־אדם שים פניך אל־גוג ארץ המגוג נשיא ראש משך ותבל
והנבא עליו: ואמרת כה אמר אדני יהוה הנני אליך גוג נשיא ראש משך ותבל: ....
פרס כוש ופוט אתם כלם מגן וכובע: גמר וכל־אגפיה בית תוגרמה ירכתי צפון
ואת־כל־אגפיו עמים רבים אתך: .... מימים רבים תפקד באחרית השנים תבוא ׀
אל־ארץ ׀ משובבת מחרב מקבצת מעמים רבים על הרי ישראל אשר־היו לחרבה תמיד
והיא מעמים הוצאה וישבו לבטח כלם: ועלית כשאה תבוא כענן לכסות הארץ תהיה
אתה וכל־אגפיך ועמים רבים אותך: כה אמר אדני יהוה והיה ׀ ביום ההוא יעלו דברים
על־לבבך וחשבת מחשבת רעה: .... והיה ׀ ביום ההוא ביום בוא גוג על־אדמת ישראל
נאם אדני יהוה תעלה חמתי באפי: ובקנאתי באש־עברתי דברתי אם־לא ׀ ביום ההוא
יהיה רעש גדול על אדמת ישראל: ורעשו מפני דגי הים ועוף השמים וחית השדה
וכל־הרמש הרמש על־האדמה וכל האדם אשר על־פני האדמה ונהרסו ההרים ונפלו
המדרגות וכל־ חומה לארץ תפול: וקראתי עליו לכל־הרי חרב נאם אדני יהוה חרב
איש באחיו תהיה: ונשפטתי אתו בדבר ובדם וגשם שוטף ואבני אלגביש אש וגפרית
אמטיר עליו ועל־אגפיו ועל־עמים רבים אשר אתו: .... על־הרי ישראל תפול
אתה וכל־אגפיך ועמים אשר אתך לעיט צפור כל־כנף וחית השדה נתתיך לאכלה:
על־פני השדה תפול כי אני דברתי נאם אדני יהוה:....ואתה בן־אדם כה־אמר אדני יהוה
אמר לצפור כל־כנף ולכל ׀ חית השדה הקבצו ובאו האספו מסביב על־זבחי אשר אני
זבח לכם זבח גדול על הרי ישראל ואכלתם בשר ושתיתם דם: בשר גבורים תאכלו
ודם־נשיאי הארץ תשתו אילים כרים ועתודים פרים מריאי בשן כלם: ואכלתם־חלב
לשבעה ושתיתם דם לשכרון מזבחי אשר־זבחתי לכם: ושבעתם על־שלחני סוס
ורכב גבור וכל־איש מלחמה נאם אדני יהוה: ונתתי את־כבודי בגוים וראו כל־הגוים
את־משפטי אשר עשיתי ואת־ידי אשר־שמתי בהם: וידעו בית ישראל כי אני יהוה
אלהיהם מן־היום ההוא והלאה:

יחזקאל לח:א-ג ,ה-ו ,ח-י ,יח-כב ;לט:ד-ה ,יז-כב

OLD TESTAMENT SCRIPTURE TRANSLATION

"And the word of the LORD came to me saying, 'Son of man, set your face toward Gog of the land of Magog, the prince of Rosh, Meshech, and Tubal, and prophesy against him, and say, 'Thus says the Lord GOD, 'Behold, I am against you, O Gog, prince of Rosh, Meshech, and Tubal....Persia, Ethiopia, and Put with them, all of them *with* shield and helmet; Gomer with all its troops; Beth-togarmah [Turkey] *from* the remote parts of the north with all its troops—many peoples with you....After many days you will be summoned; in the latter years you will come into the land that is restored from the sword, *whose inhabitants* have been gathered from many nations to the mountains of Israel which had been a continual waste; but its people were brought out from the nations, and they are living securely, all of them. And you will go up, you will come like a storm; you will be like a cloud covering the land, you and all your troops, and many peoples with you.' Thus says the Lord GOD, 'It will come about on that day, that thoughts will come into your mind, and you will devise an evil plan....And it will come about on that day, when Gog comes against the land of Israel,' declares the Lord GOD, 'that My fury will mount up in My anger. And in My zeal and in My blazing wrath I declare *that* on that day there will surely be a great earthquake in the land of Israel. And the fish of the sea, the birds of the heavens, the beasts of the field, all the creeping things that creep on the earth, and all the men who are on the face of the earth will shake at My presence; the mountains also will be thrown down, the steep pathways will collapse, and every wall will fall to the ground. And I shall call for a sword against him on all My mountains,' declares the Lord GOD. 'Every man's sword will be against his brother. And with pestilence and with blood I shall enter into judgment with him; and I shall rain on him, and on his troops, and on the many peoples who are with him, a torrential rain, with hailstones, fire, and brimstone'....'You shall fall on the mountains of Israel, you and all your troops, and the peoples who are with you; I shall give you as food to every kind of predatory bird and beast of the field. You will fall on the open field; for it is I who have spoken,' declares the Lord GOD....'And as for you, son of man, thus says the Lord GOD, 'Speak to every kind of bird and to every beast of the field, Assemble and come, gather from every side to My sacrifice which I am going to sacrifice for you, as a great sacrifice on the mountains of Israel, that you may eat flesh and drink blood. You shall eat the flesh of mighty men, and drink the blood of the princes of the earth, as *though they were* rams, lambs, goats, and bulls, all of them fatlings of Bashan. So you will eat fat until you are glutted, and drink blood until you are drunk, from My sacrifice which I have sacrificed for you. And you will be glutted at My table with horses and charioteers, with mighty men and all the men of war,' declares the Lord GOD. 'And I shall set My glory among the nations; and all the nations will see My judgment which I have executed, and My hand which I have laid on them. And the house of Israel will know that I am the LORD their God from that day onward.' "

Ezekiel 38:1-3, 5-6, 8-10, 18-22; 39:4-5, 17-22 NASB. [ ] mine

ANCIENT RABBINICAL COMMENTARY

"...for seven years there will gather great hosts and many peoples [Arabs], officers and charioteers....And at the end of seven years up will go a great company and a huge army....Gog and Magog will come upon the Land of Israel and will launch three wars against the Messiah and the People of Israel....And in one hour the earth will jump [an earthquake is indicated as Ezekiel predicted] [and they will advance] five hundred parasangs...And when they [Russia] reach the Land of Israel, the nations of the world will hear it, and many peoples [Arabs] will come up with them....they will come and sit in the gates of Jerusalem and drive half of the city into exile....In that hour the Messiah will come forth from Jerusalem to make war with them, and all the pious will be with him, a great multitude....In that hour the Holy One, blessed be He, will descend from the highest heaven above, and the ministering angels with Him....And they will make war against Gog and Magog....And how will be the wars of Gog and Magog? The Holy One, blessed be He, will wage war against them with...pestilence, blood, pouring rain, hailstones, fire, and brimstone....And the Holy One, blessed be He, fights for them, and He caused fire and brimstone to rain upon them...."[6]

Midrashim Alpha Betot, 2:438-42

"And thereafter will come Messiah ben David....And he will kill the wicked Armilus [Antichrist]....And thereafter the Holy One, blessed be He, will gather all Israel who are dispersed here and there."[7]

Midrashim waYosha', BhM 1:56

"Thereafter the inhabitants of Jerusalem, by permission of the Messiah, go out, company by company....And for three months they will gather all their belongings and all the weapons they had...and bring all of it into Jerusalem, and they will fill Jerusalem like a pomegranate with the riches of Gog and Magog....And for seven months all the winged birds and all the fowl of heaven and all the beasts of the field will eat their flesh and drink their blood, and lick their fat, until they sate and fatten

---

[6]Raphael Patai, *The Messiah Texts*, pp. 153-154. All [ ] mine except third [ ].

[7]Ibid, p. 160. [ ] mine.

their bones to such an extent that they will be unable to flee and to run because of the abundance of their fat...."[8]

Midrashim Alpha Betot, 2:438-42

NEW TESTAMENT RECORDED 96 AD

"And they gathered them together to the place which in Hebrew is called Har-Magedon....And there were flashes of lightning and sounds and peals of thunder; and there was a great earthquake, such as there had not been since man came to be upon the earth, so great an earthquake *was it, and* so mighty....And huge hailstones, about one hundred pounds each, came down from heaven upon men; and men blasphemed God because of the plague of the hail, because its plague was extremely severe....And I saw heaven opened; and behold, a white horse, and He who sat upon it *is* called Faithful and True; and in righteousness He judges and wages war....And the armies which are in heaven, clothed in fine linen, white *and* clean, were following Him on white horses....And on His robe and on His thigh He has a name written, 'KING OF KINGS, AND LORD OF LORDS'....he cried out with a loud voice, saying to all the birds which fly in midheaven, 'Come, assemble for the great supper of God; in order that you may eat the flesh of kings and the flesh of commanders and the flesh of mighty men and the flesh of horses and of those who sit on them and the flesh of all men, both free men and slaves, and small and great.' "

Revelation 16:16, 18, 21; 19:11, 14, 16-18 NASB

An aerial view of Armageddon.[9]

---

[8]Ibid, p. 155.

[9]Courtesy of the State of Israel Government Press Office, photography department.

ORIGINAL HEBREW TEXT WRITTEN 487 BC

וְזֹאת ׀ תִּהְיֶה הַמַּגֵּפָה אֲשֶׁר יִגֹּף יְהוָה אֶת־כָּל־הָעַמִּים אֲשֶׁר צָבְאוּ עַל־יְרוּשָׁלִָם הָמֵק ׀ בְּשָׂרוֹ
וְהוּא עֹמֵד עַל־רַגְלָיו וְעֵינָיו תִּמַּקְנָה בְחֹרֵיהֶן וּלְשׁוֹנוֹ תִּמַּק בְּפִיהֶם׃ וְהָיָה בַּיּוֹם הַהוּא תִּהְיֶה
אֹד׃ מְהוּמַת־יְהוָה רַבָּה בָּהֶם וְהֶחֱזִיקוּ אִישׁ יַד רֵעֵהוּ וְעָלְתָה יָדוֹ עַל־יַד רֵעֵהוּ׃ וְגַם־יְהוּדָה
תִּלָּחֵם בִּירוּשָׁלִָם וְאֻסַּף חֵיל כָּל־הַגּוֹיִם סָבִיב זָהָב וָכֶסֶף וּבְגָדִים לָרֹב מְ

זכריה יד:יב-יד

OLD TESTAMENT SCRIPTURE TRANSLATION

"Now this will be the plague with which the LORD will strike all the peoples who have gone to war against Jerusalem; their **flesh** will rot while they stand on their feet, and their eyes will rot in their sockets, and their tongue will rot in their mouth. And it will come about in that day that a great panic from the LORD will fall on them; and they will seize one another's hand, and the hand of one will be lifted against the hand of another. And Judah also will fight at Jerusalem...."

Zechariah 14:12-14 NASB

ANCIENT RABBINICAL COMMENTARY

"And what did Gog think? He said: 'Pharaoh who went forth against Israel was a fool, for he let their Patron [i.e., God] be and went against them, and likewise Amalek and Sisera, and all those who arose against them. They let the Holy One, blessed be He, be; they were fools. But I, what will I do? I shall go forth first against the Patron of Israel, [since] if I first slay the Messiah, he will cause other Messiahs to arise. Therefore I shall go against the Holy One, blessed be He....' What did they [the hosts of Gog] do? They stood on their feet and looked up toward the Holy One, blessed be He, and said: '*Come, let us cut them off from being a nation, that the name of Israel may be no more in remembrance* (Ps. 83:5).' What does 'the Name of Israel' mean? They said: 'Let us uproot Him who wrote, *Blessed be the Lord, the God of Israel* (Ps. 41:14).' And what does the Holy One, blessed be He, do to them from Above? They stand on their feet, and He punishes them....[He says:] 'Those feet which wanted to stand up against Me, *Their **flesh** shall consume away while they stand upon their feet* (Zech. 14:12). And those eyes which looked up, *And their eyes shall consume away in their sockets* (ibid.). And that tongue which spoke against the Lord, *And their tongue shall consume away in their mouth* (ibid.).' The Holy One, blessed be He, says to them: 'At first you were not at peace with one another....And now you made peace with one another so as to come against Me....I, too, shall do likewise. I shall call the birds and the beasts who were not at peace with one another, and I shall cause them to be at peace with one another in order to go forth against you. And because you said, *That the name of Israel may be no more in remembrance* (Ps. 83:5), by your life, you will die and they will bury you and will take a name [i.e., become famous] in the world.' "[10]

Aggadat B'reshit, ed. Buber, pp. 5-7

"The tradition may have even anticipated the tremendous destructive powers of our modern technology. Thus, we have the teaching of Rabbi Elazar that the Messianic Age will begin in a generation with the power to destroy itself."[11]

Rabbi Elazar of the first century

NEW TESTAMENT RECORDED 37AD

"...'Take heed that no man deceive you....And ye shall hear of wars and rumours of wars: see that ye be not troubled: for all *these things* must come to pass, but the

---

[10]Ibid, pp. 149-150. Bold mine.

[11]Rabbi Aryeh Kaplan, *et al*, *The Real Messiah*, p. 67.

end is not yet. For nation shall rise against nation, and kingdom against kingdom: and there shall be famines, and pestilences, and earthquakes, in divers places....ye shall be hated of all nations for my name's sake....many false prophets shall rise, and shall deceive many....When ye therefore shall see the abomination of desolation, spoken of by Daniel the prophet, stand in the holy place, (whoso readeth, let him understand:) Then let them which be in Judæa flee into the mountains....then shall be great tribulation, such as was not since the beginning of the world to this time, no, nor ever shall be. And except those days should be shortened, there should no **flesh** be saved: but for the elect's sake those days shall be shortened....Behold, I have told you before.' "

Matthew 24:4, 6-7, 9, 11, 15-16, 21-22, 25 KJV

MODERN RABBINIC COMMENT/REFUTATION

"There are some pessimists who say that mankind is approaching its end. They predict that we will either pollute ourselves off the face of this planet or overpopulate to the barest marginal existence. Others see man doing the job more quickly, bringing his civilization crashing down on his head in a nuclear war."

***The Real Messiah*, by Rabbi Aryeh Kaplan, *et al*, p. 63; 1976**

MODERN POLITICAL SCIENTIFIC FACT

"There is no defense[12] in science against the weapons which can now destroy civilization." [13] **Albert Einstein**

"If the Israelis threaten us, we will wipe them out within two days. I can assure you our plans are made for this eventuality."[14]

Soviet Ambassador Anatoly Dobrynin

AUTHOR'S COMMENT—EVANGELICAL CHRISTIAN POSITION

In light of the Old Testament biblical prophet Zechariah's awesome description of end time war, which could only be nuclear, coupled with Rabbi Elazar's point that the Messianic age would only begin in a generation with the power to destroy itself, we see interesting illumination in Albert Einstein's comment, as stated above, and in those who politically threaten the security of Israel and the West today. Thus Jesus' words of warning about the war in the last days and His advice to the Jews to flee to the mountains until His return, take on an immense importance. All of this undermines Rabbi Kaplan's irresponsible statement in *The Real Messiah*, to the effect that we will graduate into a Messianic peace without the war predicted by Jesus. Had Rabbi Kaplan read the commentaries of his own Jewish predecessors, he would have been more informed in this matter. If Mr. Kaplan were alive today, I would love to discuss these commentaries with him. Shouldn't we all heed the words of the Bible and New Testament as they become more evident in the end time scenario presently developing? Yes!

Philip Moore

---

12 It is interesting that just as we were developing a defense (President Reagan's Star Wars nuclear defense shield), in late 1993, President Clinton cancelled this would-be life-saving project, further validating Einstein's statement. We pray that we get a responsible President who will invest in the protection of this nation's families, hopefully redeploying this scientific, space-age Strategic Defense Initiative before it is too late. For the Bible does not state whether anyone will or will not escape annihilation; apparently God is leaving this up to us. Though we know some areas of the world will suffer, the Bible does not mention the U. S. or its number of casualties!

13 Hal Lindsey with C.C. Carlson, *The Late Great Planet Earth*, p. 146.

14 Mike Evans, *The Return*, p. 184.

THE PRECIPITATION OF THE BATTLE AT THE BIBLICALLY PREDICTED ARMAGEDDON

The land bridge of HarMagedon connects Africa, Asia and Europe. Thus anyone trying to gain control of the Middle East and its precious oil reserves, makes Har Megiddo (in Israel) their first and foremost target. No wonder the apostle John foretold such a war for the future hill of Megiddo!

We should note that World War III, or Armageddon,[15] and Gog,[16] as the Bible also calls this war, will be a war of wars, the fiercest and most horrible ever fought (Dan. 12; Matt. 24:5), with only the personal intervention of the Messiah able to bring it to an end (Matt. 24:22). All of the United Nation's peace treaties will not be able to stop this war! It will certainly be the worst, due to the most sophisticated nuclear arsenal ever designed, which presently includes weaponry[17] you could not imagine in your wildest nightmares. The prophets and Jesus, repeating the very words of God, emphasize the certainty of this war. Thus we dare not ignore it or try to lull ourselves into a world of dreams by pretending it does not have to happen!

The components of this war include: 1. the most evil personality ever to live, known to us as the Antichrist; 2. Russia, a nation filled with more nuclear weapons than the world has yet seen, and; 3. China, where 55 million innocent people[18] were murdered during the communist takeover.

When oil, money, an unregenerate human nature and a global economy are all combined, we can only wonder at the horrors man and the most inhuman man (the Antichrist/False Messiah) will perpetrate upon the world!

WHY ARE WE UNABLE TO AVOID THIS WAR, APART FROM THE BIBLE'S PREDICTION?

The heart of man, without the God-given nature which we lost in the Fall (Gen. 3), is deceitfully wicked. The prophet Jeremiah says in the Old Testament: "The heart *is* deceitful above all *things*, and desperately wicked: who can know it?" (Jer. 17:9 KJV).

---

[15]Revelation 16:16.
[16]Ezekiel 38-39.
[17]These weapons include: 1. the H-bomb, much more powerful than the A-bomb; 2. the cobalt bomb; 3. the neutron bomb, which, when exploded above a city, preserves the buildings, but kills all of the people within days, and; 4. genetically engineered germ warfare, capable of wiping out entire cities. You name it, they have it, and more!
[18]These were their **own** people, Chinese who did not agree with communism.

Only Jesus, once invited into our hearts, can give us the power in our lives needed to avoid war. However, most of the people alive today, violently reject Jesus and His love. The Bible tells us the Antichrist will order the mass murder of those who believe in Jesus, just prior to this last war.

Hal Lindsey, in his book, *The Late Great Planet Earth*, writes: "After three and a half years of remarkable progress, the Antichrist will become worshiped for his brilliant statesmanship and the wonderful progress in the world. The believers in Christ will oppose his rule and be ruthlessly exposed. Publicly, they will not be able to buy, sell, or hold a job. They will be executed en masse as examples to those who would hinder the 'brotherhood of man,' because they will insist that Christ is the only lasting hope for man.

Riding upon the crest of public worship the Roman Dictator will go to Jerusalem and in the Temple proclaim himself to be God incarnate (II Thessalonians 2:4; Matthew 24:15). As mentioned, this will be the great warning sign to the believers of that day that Armageddon is about to begin. The residents of Israel who believe in Jesus will flee to the mountains and canyons of Petra for divine protection, as promised (Matthew 24:16; Revelation 12:6, 14)."[19]

In the New Testament, God diagnoses the cause of war among men. He says: "From whence *come* wars and fightings among you? *come they* not hence, *even* of your lusts that war in your members? Ye lust, and have not: ye kill, and desire to have, and cannot obtain: ye fight and war, yet ye have not...." (James 4:1-2 KJV).

Only through a change in heart, possible only through Jesus, can lust and evil be eliminated. Satan, who is mentioned in both the Old and New Testament,[20] does all he can to divert our eyes from seeing the truth in the Messiah Jesus. He wishes us to be destroyed, hopelessly bound and alienated from our loving Father, God. Satan wants us to take part in his final destiny in the lake of fire prepared for him and his angels (Rev. 20:14).

THE ANTICHRIST'S TRICK OF FALSE PEACE LEADS TO DESTRUCTION!

When Satan personally indwells his masterpiece—the Antichrist—he will deceive the world (everyone except the believers in Messiah Jesus) into falsely believing that he has finally established a working solution for peace in the Middle East and throughout the

---

[19]Hal Lindsey with C.C. Carlson, *The Late Great Planet Earth*, pp. 152-153.

[20]See I Chronicles 21:1, Job 1-2, Psalms 109, Zechariah 3, The Acts 5:3; 26:18, and I Corinthians 7:5.

globe. Some Orthodox Jews believe their Messiah, yet to come, will do this (remember Rabbi Aryeh Kaplan's statement in *The Real Messiah*, in connection with the Antichrist?).[21]

In the New Testament, Paul writes regarding the false hopes of peace the Antichrist will give people: "For when they shall say, Peace and safety; then sudden destruction cometh upon them, as travail upon a woman with child; and they shall not escape" (I Thes. 5:3 KJV).

Today, since the re-establishment of the biblically predicted State of Israel in 1948, we see an angry[22] Arab world bent on "liberating Palestine," which in their minds means the total annihilation of the State of Israel! The Israelis know that to surrender the land God gave them would be risking another Holocaust, since it would leave them defenseless and without a country.

While pretending to be the Jewish Messiah and a friend of the Arabs, the Antichrist will contrive a covenant between the two parties, and overnight, the Middle East Crisis will appear to be resolved. The Antichrist will appease the Arabs while allowing the Israelis to fulfill the prophecy of rebuilding the Temple (see our *Vol. II*, chapter 17, "Jewish Plans for Rebuilding the Temple").

There is an ancient church writing about the Antichrist rebuilding the Temple called Hippolytus, c. 6, 5, 11. It reads: "The Saviour raised up and manifested His holy body as a temple; in the same way he also [the Antichrist] shall raise up the temple of stone in Jerusalem."[23]

ISRAEL'S FUTURE PEACE PACT WITH HELL RESULTS IN A GREAT JEWISH PERSECUTION

Soon after the Rapture, the Scriptures predict that the Antichrist will sign an agreement[24] with Israel to rebuild the Temple, seven years before the return of Jesus and those believers previously raptured. Once this agreement is signed, actual Temple construction will begin.

---

[21]See this false expectation regarding the Jewish Messiah quoted on the opening page of chapter 23, "The False Messiah Armilus Equals Antichrist."

[22]We do not doubt that the welcomed false Messiah will make "peace," a false peace, with most Arab countries, just prior to the great war of Armageddon and Gog. Remember Paul's words in I Thessalonians 5:3.

[23]Wilhelm Bousset, *The Antichrist Legend*, p. 162.

[24]Some believe the actual construction may begin several years before the Rapture, with the belligerent objection of the Arabs, and that the Antichrist comes in and signs an agreement, whereby the Arabs officially recognize the right of the Israelis to finish their Temple in exchange for land concessions or whatever—this is also a possibility! It is quite possible that we may, within twenty to thirty years, see Temple construction begin, if not before.

The Fourth Temple, for worship in Messianic Kingdom, is constructed upon the return of Jesus (Ezek. 40-48; Zech. 6:12-13). However, the third Temple, built under the supervision of the Antichrist as he impersonates the Messiah, is an absolute disappointment and a no-no, as far as God is concerned.

Regarding this covenant, Isaiah predicted: "Because ye have said, We have made a covenant with death, and with hell are we at agreement; when the overflowing scourge shall pass through, it shall not come unto us: for we have made lies our refuge, and under falsehood have we hid ourselves....Judgment also will I lay to the line, and righteousness to the plummet: and the hail shall sweep away the refuge of lies, and the waters shall overflow the hiding place. And your covenant with death shall be disannulled, and your agreement with hell shall not stand; when the overflowing scourge shall pass through, then ye shall be trodden down by it" (Isa. 28:15, 17-18 KJV).[25]

Daniel says of this agreement: "And he shall confirm the covenant with many for one week: and in the midst of the week he shall cause the sacrifice and the oblation to cease, and for the overspreading of abominations he shall make *it* desolate, even until the consummation, and that determined shall be poured upon the desolate" (Dan. 9:27 KJV).

Even though the Third Temple will not be God's Temple, it's prospected rebuilding is of interest to Evangelical believers because this prophesied event indicates the Rapture is imminent!

After the Antichrist seemingly settles the Middle East Crisis, all nations will cooperate with him, saying, "Who can make war with him?" He will create a false, but seemingly real, worldwide peace treaty for a short while. That is, until he enters the Holy of Holies in the Temple in Jerusalem, three and one-half years after the signing of the Temple peace pact.

Once this happens (as foretold in Matt. 24:15; II Thes. 2-4), his peace agreement will crumble, the Jews will not worship him as he had hoped and he will become very angry. At this point, his vicious but hidden anti-Semitism will be revealed, as he attempts the greatest

---

[25]Isaiah 28:16 indicates that the hope of Jesus is available all through this time of desperation during the reign of the Antichrist. This cornerstone is Jesus (Dan. 2:34-5; Exo. 17:6; I Pet. 2:8). "Therefore, thus saith the Lord GOD, Behold, I lay in Zion for a foundation a stone, a tried stone, a precious corner *stone*, a sure foundation: he that believeth shall not make haste" (Isa. 28:16 KJV). In the New Testament, Jesus claims to be this cornerstone to the Pharisees who were rejecting Him: "...'What is this then that is written, The stone, which the builders rejected, the same is become the head of the corner? Whosoever shall fall upon that stone shall be broken; but on whomsoever it shall fall, it will grind him to powder' " (Luke 20:17-18 KJV).

Jewish persecution of all time. God will then break out *Operation Petra* (see our *Vol. II*, chapter 38, "They Escaped to Petra," where it is shown that God supernaturally hides and protects the Jews from Antichrist there).

THE PERSECUTION IS CUT SHORT BECAUSE OF PETRA, GOD'S FORTRESS

Once the Jews—women, men and children, many of them believing at that time—have safely established themselves in God's fortress of Petra, the battle between the earth's powers begins. The prophet Daniel outlines the movement of troops very clearly in the eleventh chapter of his book.

THE STRATEGIC BATTLE PLAN OF THE LAST WAR IS ALMOST BEFORE US, AS LAID OUT BY THE BIBLE!

Daniel 11:41 says that at the end, the kingdom of the South (Egypt, leading Arab forces) will collide with "him" (the Jewish Antichrist), and the king of the North (Russia, see Ezek. 38-39) will storm against him with chariot, horsemen and many ships. He will enter in the countries and overflow them and press through. Verse 41 says: "He [the king of the North] shall enter also into the glorious land [Israel], and many *countries* shall be overthrown: but these shall escape out of his hand, *even* Edom, and Moab, and the chief of the children of Ammon" (KJV; [ ] mine).

The three areas mentioned refer to Petra in modern Jordan, where Jesus warned *end time Israel* to flee, to escape from the Antichrist's abomination of desolation (claiming he is God) in the New Testament book of Matthew.[26]

Verse 42 continues: "Then he will stretch out his hand against *other* countries, and the land of Egypt will not escape" (NASB). Thus the future Russian forces will wipe out everything in their path, not stopping at Egypt, but moving on into her, double-crossing the Egyptians and other surrounding Arab nations.

Verse 43 precisely predicts that: "...he [the king of the North or future Russia] will gain control over the hidden treasures of gold and silver, and over all the precious things of Egypt; and Libyans and

---

[26]For some very exciting and fascinating details, don't miss our *Vol. II*, chapter 38, "They Escaped to Petra."

Ethiopians[27] *will follow* at his heels" (NASB) In the original language this infers complete cooperation with this Russian commander.

After this, in verse 44, the prophet explains that while this leader is still standing in Egypt: "...rumors from the East and from the North will disturb him, and he will go forth with great wrath to destroy and annihilate many [referring to the Jewish people in Israel]" (NASB; [ ] mine).

The Bible continues with verse 45: "And he will pitch the tents of his royal pavilion between the seas [the Dead and Mediterranean Seas] and the beautiful Holy Mountain [Mount Moria, with its temple, in Jerusalem]; yet he will come to his end, and no one will help him" (NASB; [ ] mine).

Remember that the Russian commander in Egypt heard troubling news as he looked northward toward Western Europe. The Antichrist's armies are apparently mobilizing to counter-attack Russia. When Daniel mentions his eastward look toward the Euphrates, this no doubt, refers to Red China's approaching armies. This is why the Russian commander moves his army out of Egypt and into Israel, only to meet his fate of total destruction: "...no one will help him" (Dan. 11:45 NASB).

ISRAEL WINS, AS RUSSIA IS TOTALLY ANNIHILATED BY THE HOUSE OF DAVID AND THE LORD (MESSIAH)

Ezekiel 38 and 39 describe future Russia's total annihilation, along with their allies, on the very mountains of Israel. Zechariah 12-14 identifies those in Israel who have apparently become believers by this time, as *the mightiest army of all time*, defeating their Arab/Russian enemies. "In that day shall the LORD defend the inhabitants of Jerusalem; and he that is feeble among them at that day shall be as David; and the house of David *shall be* as God, as the angel of the LORD before them" (Zech. 12:8 KJV).

RUSSIAN MOTIVES FOR ATTACKING THE MIDDLE EAST

The key culprits in the aforementioned attack plan were Russia and Turkey of the North. Why? God revealed to Ezekiel the reason the Russians want the Middle East. Ezekiel made predictions 2600 years ago that in our future will become all too obvious. Ezekiel predicted that they would: "...capture spoil and...sieze plunder...." (Ezek. 38:12 NASB).

27"Put" and "Cush" indicates North and Black Africa in the biblical Hebrew, not the present Libyans and Ethiopians, as translated.

It is clear that Israel is to have tremendous wealth. As Ezekiel predicted: "...the people [Jews] who are gathered from the nations [non-Jewish countries], who have acquired **cattle** and **goods**...." (Ezek. 38:12 NASB; [ ] mine).

WHERE WILL ISRAEL GET HER WEALTH?

We all know Israel is not presently considered one of the world's wealthiest countries, so something has to change. We believe Israel is destined to find oil, for in Deuteronomy it is predicted: "...may he [Asher] dip his foot in oil" (Deut. 33:24 NASB; [ ] mine).

One of the oil wells presently drilling in search of oil in Israel.

Salt crystal formations in the Dead Sea. The Dead Sea is thirty percent salt, the highest natural concentration on Earth. Because of the high concentration of salt, a person cannot sink in the Dead Sea. It is three hundred and ninety-seven meters below sea level; the lowest point in the world.

ISRAELIS CONFISCATE ARAB OIL, WHILE AMERICAN JEWS IMPORT THEIR JEWELS

We also know that any future wars between the Arabs and Israel could lead to Israel having to confiscate Arab oil, in order to arrest the Arabs' power to make war. This would produce untold wealth for the Israelis. We also speculate that unbelievable amounts of personal wealth will be imported by people emigrating to Israel. Ezekiel said, if you will read again closely, that the northern enemy would come: "To take a **spoil**, and to take a prey; to turn thine hand upon the desolate places *that are now* inhabited, and upon the **people** *that are* **gathered** out of the nations, which have **gotten** cattle and **goods**, that dwell in the midst of the land" (Ezek. 38:12 KJV; bold mine).

HOW AND WHEN DO THE AMERICAN JEWS GET TO ISRAEL?

1. If anti-Semitism[28] ever gets a foothold in the U.S. (we pray not, but if so), this would provide a reason for American Jews to visit Israel and consider a prolonged stay with their "goods." 2. A seeming peace in Israel and a Middle East free of war, due to the Antichrist peace treaty, would reduce fear of coming to Israel among those who otherwise have never been there or planned to come. 3. Tremendous improvement in the Israeli economy, due to capitalistic economic plans presently[29] being implemented and any newly discovered or captured oil (Deut. 33:24), would relieve fears of monetary difficulties, as previously discussed. 4. A man claiming to be the Messiah, awaited for

---

[28]I, along with the vast majority of Evangelical Christians, pray that anti-Semitism be abolished! However, as previously mentioned in our chapter 23, the age-old famous Rabbi Saadia Gaon wrote: "Hence, if after our having lingered in exile for a long time without returning to God, God would bring us back to our land....it has been transmitted by the traditions of the prophets that God would cause misfortunes and disasters to befall us that would compel us to resolve upon repentance...." Samuel Rosenblatt, *Saadia Gaon, The Book of Beliefs and Opinions*, p. 301. We fearfully wonder if all of the modern hate groups like the KKK, neo-Nazis, and certain radical militia, may end up playing a role in persecuting American Jews, causing a mass emigration to Israel. (What we witnessed in Oklahoma City alerts us to such dangers.) We hope not, but if they do, we cannot help but ask the same question as did Gaon, "Did the prophets see it?"

[29]Some consider Israel to be a socialistic country because of its socialized medicine, *kupot holim*, which operates concurrently with private medical practice. Its government bounces back and forth between the socialist Labor party and the capitalist Likud, but all the time, it is undergoing reform to U.S. capitalist standards. Many government companies such as the telephone company, are being handed from the government to the people. It no longer takes a year to get a phone in Israel, as it did a few years ago, when the government ran the telephone company! Just wait, Israel will soon be capitalistic and wealthy.

4000 years by religious Jews, would no doubt, draw untold numbers of secular[30] and religious Jews.

With war and poverty out of the way, the discomfort of anti-Semitism held at bay outside of Israel, and a man in Israel who appears to be the long awaited Messiah, you better believe this will draw most of the world's Jews to this nation! This is not only my assumption based on the Bible, it is also the reasoning of an Orthodox Jewish publication.

This recent orthodox work, using speculation of current events regarding this very same situation, reached the same biblically based conclusion as their own expected hope and aspiration toward their goal of migration to Israel, which has truly amazed all of us in the prophetically-minded evangelical community!

CONTEMPORARY ORTHODOX HOPES VERIFY THE BIBLE'S PREDICTIONS OF A FUTURE WORLDWIDE RETURN TO ISRAEL!

A book from which we have already quoted entitled, *The Real Messiah*, says: "There is even evidence that the majority of the Jews will have to return to their homeland before the Messiah comes in a non-miraculous manner. One of our important traditions regarding the advent of the Messiah is that it will mark the return of prophecy....there is a basic teaching that prophecy can only exist in the Land of Israel, and then, only when the majority of Jews live there. Thus, unless we assume that this rule is to be broken, the majority of Jews will have to live in the Land of Israel before the Messianic Age commences....Into a world prepared to receive him, the Messiah will then be born.

He will be a mortal human being, born normally of human parents....Now, imagine a charismatic leader greater than any other in man's history. Imagine a political genius surpassing all others. With the vast communication networks now at our disposal, he could spread his message to the entire world and change the very fabric of our society....Let us go a step further. With peace established in the Land of Israel, he could induce many more Jews to emmigrate to Israel. Perhaps he would negotiate with the Russian government to allow all of their Jews to leave. Things might by then have become *uncomfortable* enough for *American Jews to induce them to emmigrate* as well....In such an unassuming manner, the ingathering of the exiles could take place....If he is further successful in rebuilding the Temple

[30]The worldly Jews would find their curiosity aroused, while the religious Jews would find their dedication challenged. If they are truly dedicated to God's principles, they had better come to Israel to honor the one they think is God's Messiah.

on its original site and gathering the dispersed of Israel, then his identity as the Messiah is a certainty.

It is very important to note that these accomplishments are a minimum for our acceptance of an individual as the Messiah....As the Messiah's powers develop, so will his fame. The world will begin to recognize his profound wisdom and come to seek his advice. As a Tzadik, he will teach all mankind to live in peace...."[31] Thus we do not have to guess how Israel becomes wealthy. If the majority of world Jewry returns, bringing with them their wealth, you can be certain that Israel, even without oil, will be one of the wealthiest countries on Earth.

Ezekiel's **goods** take on new meaning, don't they? Thus if the world's Jews have returned under this false idea that the Antichrist is the Messiah who has brought peace to the Middle East, and bring untold quantities of the world's wealth to Israel, this will make Israel seem, to the Russians, to be a land well worth robbing. By that time, Russia will probably have starved most of their country's people because of their communist "economic system," to which we believe they may shortly relapse, using what little money they have obtained to secretly build weapons in their underground arms race! Let us not forget the CIA/Russian Ames case, which made national headlines on February 23, 1994.[32] It is also possible that they may become a nationalistic empire, which would have the same goal of obtaining cold cash through robbing Israel because of their geographical location.[33]

***

[31]Rabbi Aryeh Kaplan, *et al*, *The Real Messiah*, pp. 69-71. Italics mine.

[32]We wonder if the current talk of Russia coming clean, being on the up and up, and truly wanting peace, is true, because they were caught spying by our own CIA as late as February of 1994. Agent Ames, of the CIA, was paid over one million dollars for top-secret information, which reportedly resulted in over ten American deaths. While we pray for, and take every opportunity to preach the Gospel to, and help the common, innocent Russian citizen who is eager to hear, we maintain a skeptical watch on the Russian government, its nuclear arsenal and its military intelligence officials.

[33]Keep in mind that these events will most probably be more than thirty and possibly less than forty years away! Why do we dare say such a thing? Well, if: 1. a generation is approximately one hundred years, as Moses specifies in Genesis 15:13-16; 2. the fig tree parable of Jesus is Israel (Matt. 24:32-34), as the document of the apocalypse of Peter verifies, and; 3. since Jesus said that it would be *less* than one generation before all would be fulfilled concerning the Second Coming (Matt. or Luke), since Israel was born in 1948; then most probably twenty to thirty years short of 2048, will be the Bible's target date! Seventy years seems to be a Bible number. It was the length of the Babylonian captivity of the Jews! Israel is presently forty-eight years old. We definitely do not have long to wait! Twenty years may sound like an eternity, when you are looking forward. I am thirty-eight, but when I think back to when I was eighteen, it seems as if it were only yesterday. It is nothing, and remember, the older you get, the faster time seems to pass—you have time to wait.

A TEMPLE FOR *A*-BOMB

What will give the Russians the courage and confidence to attack Israel? Apparently the Antichrist, in his deceitful negotiations between the Arabs and Israelis, will have to negotiate on the Arab side. He will cause them to give in and allow the Temple to be built. On the Israeli side, he may ask that she give in and give up her nuclear capability; something the Arabs and Russians will drool over. This author does not think Israel would be so stupid, but she may play along with the game. Thus the politicians may promise there will be no more bombs, but the military will secretly keep a number of them hidden, leading the Arab/Russian forces to think Israel has become defenseless. This will provide the Russians with the opportunity to attack without fear of being annihilated. This situation would then provide Israel (still having her bomb) with the strength to fight back with sure might, though the real strength of the defense of Israel will come from the supernatural strength of the Messiah (Zech. 12:9-10). As Zechariah 12:8 predicts: "In that day shall the LORD defend the inhabitants of Jerusalem; and he that is feeble among them at that day shall be as David; and the house of David *shall be* as God, as the angel of the LORD before them" (KJV).

The northern border of Israel.

THE TRIBULATION

ORIGINAL HEBREW TEXT WRITTEN 534 BC

וּבָעֵת הַהִיא יַעֲמֹד מִיכָאֵל הַשַּׂר הַגָּדוֹל הָעֹמֵד עַל־בְּנֵי עַמֶּךָ וְהָיְתָה עֵת צָרָה אֲשֶׁר
לֹא־נִהְיְתָה מִהְיוֹת גּוֹי עַד הָעֵת הַהִיא וּבָעֵת הַהִיא יִמָּלֵט עַמְּךָ כָּל־הַנִּמְצָא כָּתוּב
בַּסֵּפֶר׃ .... לֵךְ דָּנִיֵּאל כִּי־סְתֻמִים וַחֲתֻמִים הַדְּבָרִים עַד־עֵת קֵץ׃ יִתְבָּרֲרוּ וְיִתְלַבְּנוּ
וְיִצָּרְפוּ רַבִּים וְהִרְשִׁיעוּ רְשָׁעִים וְלֹא יָבִינוּ כָּל־רְשָׁעִים וְהַמַּשְׂכִּלִים יָבִינוּ׃ וּמֵעֵת הוּסַר
הַתָּמִיד וְלָתֵת שִׁקּוּץ שֹׁמֵם יָמִים אֶלֶף מָאתַיִם וְתִשְׁעִים׃

דניאל יב:א; ט-יא

OLD TESTAMENT SCRIPTURE TRANSLATION

"Now at that time Michael, the great prince who stands *guard* over the sons of your people, will arise. And there will be a time of distress such as never occurred since there was a nation until that time; and at that time your people, everyone who is found written in the book, will be rescued....Many will be purged, purified and refined; but the wicked will act wickedly, and none of the wicked will understand, but those who have insight will understand. And from the time that the regular sacrifice is abolished, and the abomination of desolation is set up, *there will be* 1,290 days." **Daniel 12:1, 10-11 NASB**

ANCIENT RABBINICAL COMMENTARY

"In that hour all the nations of the world will expel Israel from their countries and will not allow them to dwell with them in their countries, and will say: 'Have you seen this despised and lowly people who rebelled against us and chose a king [Antichrist]?' And it will be a suffering for Israel the like of which has not been ever since the world exists and to that time. And in that hour Michael will rise to sort out the wicked from Israel....Instantly all Israel will flee to the deserts...."[34]

Otot haMashiah, BhM 2:58-63

NEW TESTAMENT RECORDED 37AD

"...the disciples came to Him privately, saying, 'Tell us, when will these things be, and what *will be* the sign of Your coming, and of the end of the age?' And Jesus answered and said to them, 'See to it that no one misleads you. For many will come in My name, saying, 'I am the Christ,' and will mislead many. And you will be hearing of wars and rumors of wars....For nation will rise against nation, and kingdom against kingdom, and in various places there will be famines and earthquakes....Therefore when you see the ABOMINATION OF DESOLATION which was spoken of through Daniel the prophet, standing in the holy place (let the reader understand), then let those who are in Judea flee to the mountains....for then there will be a great tribulation, such as has not occurred since the beginning of the world until now, nor ever shall. And unless those days had been cut short, no life would have been saved; but for the sake of the elect those days shall be cut short.' "

Matthew 24:3-7, 15-16, 21-22 NASB

MODERN RABBINIC COMMENT/REFUTATION

"Jews firmly believe that the Messiah will come. We believe that man will not self-destruct, that we will not disappear in a gigantic atomic blast. Man is basically good...." **Rabbi Pinchas Stolper; *The Real Messiah*, by Rabbi Aryeh Kaplan, *et al*, p. 50; 1976**

---

[34]Raphael Patai, *The Messiah Texts*, pp. 314-315. [ ] mine.

AUTHOR'S COMMENT—EVANGELICAL CHRISTIAN POSITION

In Jeremiah 17:9, the Old Testament clearly teaches that man is not basically good, as Rabbi Stolper states, but that humanity is evil (in its fallen state). Jeremiah 17:14 clearly says that *we need a savior*. Modern Rabbinical Judaism fosters this anti-biblical idea that man is basically good, in order to discredit the need for the savior Messiah, the Messiah ben Joseph, as the ancient rabbis called him. Need we remind Rabbi Stolper that he should review the *Midrash Otot haMashiah* we quoted, for though we will not disappear in a gigantic nuclear blast, this rabbinic commentary, along with the New Testament and the Old, all indicate that there will be some blasts in the last war before the Messiah comes. Rabbi Stolper and others should not propagate the idea that we can comfortably glide into a Messianic age of peace. The Bible teaches that there will be war *before* peace. These rabbis are seemingly setting a trap into which many Jews will fall by accepting the Antichrist's promises of peace. We pray that all be on their guard, for deception is evil!

Philip Moore

TRIBULATION PAST AND FUTURE, INVOLVING FALSE JEWISH MESSIAHS, RESULTING IN PERSECUTIONS AND DISAPPOINTMENTS

The Tribulation period spoken of in the Old Testament will indeed be an actual period of time just prior to the return of Jesus. The prophet Jeremiah spoke of it in these words: "Alas! for that day is great, There is none like it; And it is the time of Jacob's distress, But he will be saved from it" (Jer. 30:7 NASB).

Though there have been many mini-tribulations in the past involving the false Messiahs, nothing will measure up to this terrible day of great Tribulation, of which Daniel, Jeremiah and the New Testament warn us. The tribulations of the past involved Jewish persecution in different areas of the world, whereby different individuals claimed to be the Messiah. These "Messiahs" and dates run as follows: Bar Kochba—second century; Moses of Crete—fifth century; Abu Isa—eighth century; David Alroy—twelfth century; Abraham Abulafia—1240-1291; Abraham ben Samuel—circa 1300; Hayyim Vital—1574; David Reuveni—sixteenth century; Solomon Molko—1700s; Sabbatai Zevi and Jacob Frank—eighteenth century. Some of these Messianic claims resulted in persecution of the Jews who followed these self-styled Messiahs, persecutions they obviously could have done without!

Prior to his death in June of 1994, hundreds of thousands of Jews believed that Menachem Schneerson, the Lubavitcher rabbi in New York, was their Messiah. Granted, their numbers out of the total Jewish population were small, but this contemporary example illustrates how someone can be hailed as the Messiah without biblical credentials. It goes without saying that many were greatly and grievously disappointed!

THE FALSE MESSIAHS OF THE PAST WILL PALE IN COMPARISON TO *THE FALSE MESSIAH* (ANTICHRIST) OF THE FUTURE—YOU AIN'T SEEN NOTHIN' YET

Little do the great majority of rabbis realize that a giant false Messiah is presently waiting in the wings to deceive most of world Jewry. Though he may now be only a teenager, we all pray that you will give them this work and emphasize that they should read chapter 23, "The False Messiah Armilus Equals Antichrist," so that possibly, *only* the most minimal number will be deceived.

Jesus' words of the past have proved to be all too true in regard to the false Messiahs we mentioned! "For many shall come in my name, saying, I am Christ [Messiah]; and shall deceive many" (Matt. 24:5 KJV; [ ] mine).

All[35] of the Jews we listed led many Jews astray by claiming to be Messiah. Even today, people think of Bar Kochba as a hero, though he led nearly one million Jews to their death in a futile, suicidal battle with the Romans, under the leadership of Rabbi Akiva, who proclaimed him to be the Messiah.

We as believers, pray for the rabbis to open the Bible with an open mind, and investigate all of their many Messianic prophecies, which God has given for all of us! We petition the Lord to evoke in them a new and clean spirit of investigative honesty, so that the truth of this "controversy" will be realized—too many Jews were led astray at the whim of dangerous men claiming to be the Messiah!

All throughout history, from the first century to the twentieth, rabbis have set dates for the Messiah's Coming, which have been incorrect. We are entering the Apocalypse spoken of by the Bible and Jesus, in which the true Messiah will arrive. It is of paramount importance for us to know the biblical signs of the Messiah, and how they differ from the tall tales handed down concerning Him. This is the subject of our next chapter.

***

[35]As far as we know, Schneerson never claimed outright to be the Messiah. His followers more or less bestowed this title upon him.

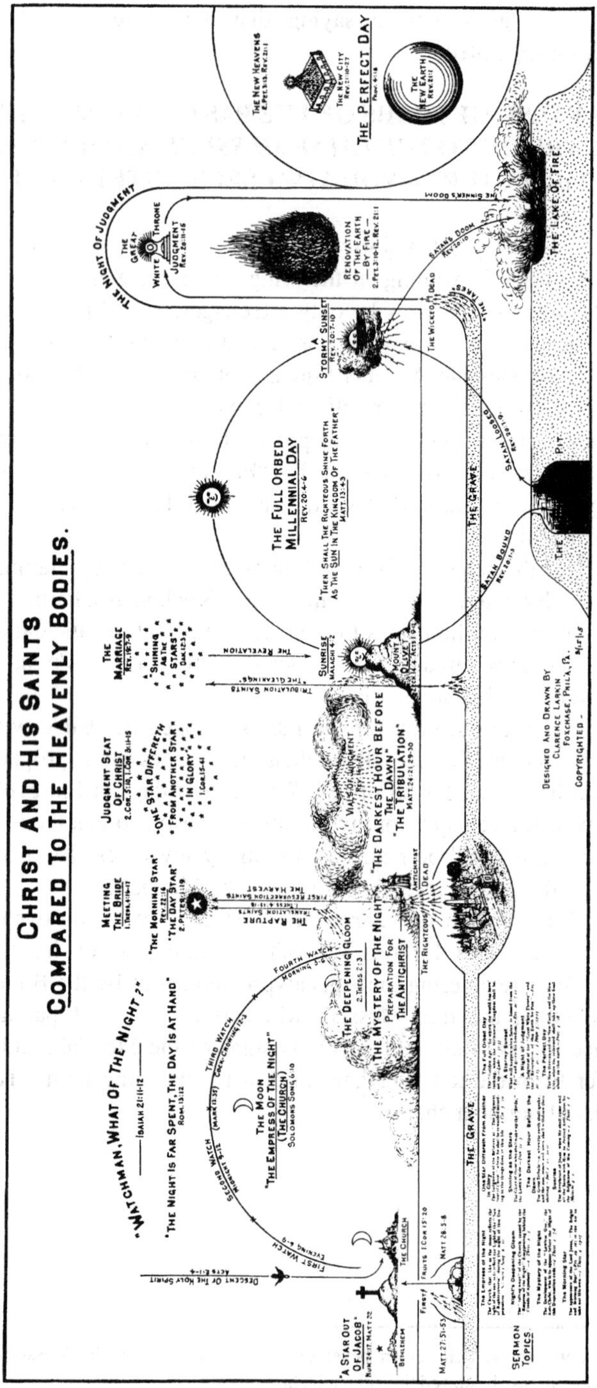

CHRIST AND HIS SAINTS
COMPARED TO THE HEAVENLY BODIES.
"WATCHMAN, WHAT OF THE NIGHT?" ISAIAH 21:11-12
"THE NIGHT IS FAR SPENT, THE DAY IS AT HAND" ROM. 13:12
"A STAR OUT OF JACOB" NUM. 24:17. MATT. 2:2
BETHLEHEM
DESCENT OF THE HOLY SPIRIT ACTS 2:1-4
THE CHURCH
FIRST WATCH EVENING 6-9
SECOND WATCH MIDNIGHT 9-12
THIRD WATCH COCK-CROWING 12-3
FOURTH WATCH MORNING 3-6
THE MOON "THE EMPRESS OF THE NIGHT" (THE CHURCH) SOLOMONS SONG 6:10
THE DEEPENING GLOOM 2. THESS 2:3
THE MYSTERY OF THE NIGHT PREPARATION FOR THE ANTICHRIST
THE RAPTURE
THE HARVEST
MEETING THE BRIDE 1. THESS. 4:16-17
"THE MORNING STAR" REV. 22:16
"THE DAY STAR" 2. PETER 1:19
JUDGMENT SEAT OF CHRIST 2. COR. 5:10, 1. COR. 3:11-15
"ONE STAR DIFFERETH FROM ANOTHER STAR IN GLORY" 1. COR. 15:41
THE MARRIAGE REV. 19:7-9
"SHINING AS THE STARS" DAN. 12:3
TRIBULATION SAINTS
"THE GLEANINGS"
THE REVELATION
THE DARKEST HOUR BEFORE THE DAWN
"THE TRIBULATION" MATT. 24:21, 29-30
VIALS OF JUDGMENT
ANTICHRIST
SUNRISE MALACHI 4:2
MOUNT OLIVET
THE FULL ORBED MILLENNIAL DAY REV. 20:4-6
"THEN SHALL THE RIGHTEOUS SHINE FORTH AS THE SUN IN THE KINGDOM OF THEIR FATHER" MATT. 13:43
STORMY SUNSET REV. 20:7-10
SATAN BOUND REV. 20:1-3
SATAN LOOSED REV. 20:7-9
THE PIT
SATAN'S DOOM REV. 20:10
THE TARES
THE WICKED DEAD
THE RIGHTEOUS DEAD
THE NIGHT OF JUDGMENT
THE GREAT WHITE THRONE JUDGMENT REV. 20:11-15
RENOVATION OF THE EARTH BY FIRE 2. PET. 3:10-12. REV. 21:1
THE SINNER'S DOOM
THE LAKE OF FIRE
THE NEW HEAVENS
THE NEW CITY
THE NEW EARTH
THE PERFECT DAY
THE GRAVE
FIRST FRUITS 1 COR 15:20
MATT. 27:51-53
MATT. 28:5-8
SERMON TOPICS
DESIGNED AND DRAWN BY CLARENCE LARKIN FOXCHASE, PHILA., PA.
COPYRIGHTED

"R. Shim'on said to them: 'It is not the will of the Holy One, blessed be He, that too much be revealed to the world. But when the days of the Messiah approach, even the children of the world will be able to discover secrets of wisdom, and to know through them the Ends and the Calculations....'"[1] Zohar 1:117b-118a

"For thus saith the LORD of hosts; Yet once, it *is* a little while, and I will shake the heavens, and the earth, and the sea, and the dry *land*; And I will shake all nations, and the **desire**[2] of all nations shall come...." Haggai 2:6-7 KJV

"And there shall be signs in the sun, and in the moon, and in the stars; and upon the earth distress of nations, with perplexity; the sea and the waves roaring; Men's hearts failing them for fear, and for looking after those things which are coming on the earth: for the powers of heaven shall be shaken....And when these things begin to come to pass, then look up, and lift up your heads; for your redemption draweth nigh." Jesus — Luke 21:25-26, 28 KJV

"...our Forefathers wrongfully put [him] [Jesus] to death and that Sin lies upon us unto this day."[3] Rabbi Nathan Shapira of Jerusalem, 1657

"...radioactive poisoning of the atmosphere, and hence, annihilation of any life on earth, has been brought within the range of technical possibility."[4] Albert Einstein, warning of the results of the imminent development of the hydrogen bomb

"In my opinion....We must aim at a stable state society and the destruction of nuclear stockpiles. Otherwise, I don't see how we can survive much later than 2050."[5] Dr. Jacques Monod, French molecular biologist

27

SPECULATING ON MESSIAH'S *SECOND* COMING—WHETHER THEY KNOW IT OR NOT

In connection with our quotation of Luke, we believe an indication that we are nearing the very end of the apocalyptic era may be found in the fact that, since 1944, we have possessed atomic energy. As it turns out, the word "Heaven" in Greek (οὐρανῶν), is pronounced *ouranós*, from which we derive the words Uranus and uranium. Could this be a two-fold Bible meaning?

---

[1]Raphael Patai, *The Messiah Texts*, p. 63.
[2]Desire, in this passage, refers to the Messiah Jesus Christ.
[3]*Jewish Christians and Christian Jews*, p. 65. Second [ ] mine.
[4]"Einstein," *Nova*, 1976. The hydrogen bomb was developed shortly after Einstein made this comment, though as of this date, it has never been used in warfare.
[5]Josh McDowell, *Prophecy, Fact or Fiction*, p. 3, © 1981, San Bernadino, Here's Life Publishers.

Jesus knew that the powers of uranium would be unleashed. Uranium's power is released when two portions are fired together to achieve critical mass, bringing about nuclear fission, which creates the explosion.

In an atomic hydrogen explosion, hydrogen and oxygen are the key components for ignition; an A-bomb is used to detonate an H-bomb, creating fusion. Interestingly, in the Hebrew from which the Greek was translated, Heaven is *shamaim* meaning "water there" (above in Heaven). *Sham* means "there" and *maim* means "water." The symbol for water is H_2O. Two hydrogen atoms and one oxygen atom combine to make one water molecule! When the heavens are disturbed by the same atomic components from which they are derived, it will be time for Jesus to stop the warfare! Interesting, don't you think?

The Hebrew word for Heaven was used in Genesis. It was used to describe the original water vapor canopy[6] which enveloped the earth before it was precipitated in Noah's flood. Truly, the heavens will be shaken after Armageddon has progressed to the point of multi-megaton nuclear delivery, requiring the return of Jesus to rescue the planet.

DR. MONOD'S YEAR IS ACCURATE BUT HIS METHODS ARE INCONSISTENT WITH TODAY'S INSANITY

This author believes that we must maintain the maximum amount of technical, nuclear/Star Wars defenses possible, in order to deter our enemies. It is also a possibility that an enemy could accidentally launch a missile. Would it not be better for us to neutralize this accident harmlessly in space rather than retaliate?

We cannot responsibly destroy our weapons because we are in an arms race in which it is impossible to completely monitor the opponents! Most scientists, including Dr. Monod, do not understand that to attain the goal of maximum survival, we must do just the opposite of what they suspect. Science is not politics and cannot anticipate the Qaddafis and Saddam Husseins of our future world! Ironically, Dr. Monod's date closely matches our biblically projected maximum era for the return of the Messiah!

***

[6]This water vapor canopy is described in the following books and is very interesting reading: Dave Balsiger and Charles E. Sellier, Jr., *In Search of Noah's Ark*. Los Angeles: Sun Classic Pictures, Inc., © 1976, chapter 4, and; John C. Whitcomb, Jr., and Henry M. Morris, *The Genesis Flood*. Nutley, NJ: Presbyterian and Reformed Publishing Co., © 1961, p. 121.

SOME RABBIS CLAIM CHRISTIANS ARE MISTAKEN, AND THAT THEY CANNOT BE WRONG *JUST BECAUSE* THEY ARE RABBIS

When will the Second Coming of the Messiah occur? Does anyone know? Did the rabbis miss the First Coming and make a laughable guessing game out of *when* the Promised One *will* come? Let's see. Are the rabbis right in agreeing that Jesus is not the Messiah simply because they are rabbis?

In an anti-missionary tape I purchased some years ago in Jerusalem, the argument was put forth that rabbis have an edge over Christians on knowing how to interpret the Messianic prophecies, because they have a direct lineage of interpretation leading back to the prophets themselves.

The rabbi then introduced the argument that said, more or less, we know our own prophets and we are not wrong in our understanding of the Messianic prophecies, while you Christians have picked up a Jewish work, "our writings," and made off-the-wall assertions that Jesus is the Messiah. We know He is not and we cannot be wrong, because we understand how to decipher our own prophets on Messianic ideals and expectations.

Rabbi Shalom Lewis advanced this false train of thought in a 1994 class I attended called, "The Jewish View of Jesus." Lewis used what he called the "Abner Doubleday argument," in an inapplicable way, attempting to disprove the Christian interpretation of the Messiah. However, we invalidate his entire thesis as we quote from both sides of two debates with him, separated by eleven years, in our *Vol. II*, chapter 23, "Rabbi Lewis Says Christians Reinterpreted the Messiah—But Really He Has!"

MESSIANIC DATES AND FAKES—THE RABBIS MAKE MORE MISTAKES THAN FABLES AND IT ACHES

We would like to point out that the rabbis do not have a monopoloy on interpreting the Bible, and that this argument, while it may sound plausible to some, is in fact, off the wall! This leads us to ask, "Can the rabbis make mistakes about the Messiah?" Could they mistake His identity or the time of His Coming? Have they, throughout history, made mistakes regarding the identity[7] of the Messiah, and given incorrect dates for His arrival? Many of the most famous rabbis did just that!

---

[7]Concerning the Messiah's identity, see our section on false Messiahs near the end of our chapter 5, "Which Prophecies Did Jesus Fulfill?"

Since it is documented that they did make mistakes, could it be possible that they misunderstood their own prophets regarding the identity and time clock of the Messiah, while others, who are not Jewish, realize who He is? It was a Jewish biblical prophet himself who told us and the world's Jews that God said: "I permitted Myself to be sought by those [non-Jews] who did not ask *for Me;* I permitted Myself to be found by those who did not seek Me....I have spread out My hands all day long to a rebellious people, Who walk *in* the way which is not good, following their own thoughts....I called, but you [Jews] did not answer; I spoke, but you did not hear" (Isa. 65:1-2, 12 NASB). Need we ask if there could really be truth to the New Testament claim: "He came to His own [the Jewish people], and those who were His own did not receive Him" (John 1:11 NASB; [ ] mine).

The great scientist and Bible scholar, Sir Isaac Newton, commented: "For they [the Jews] had some regard to these prophesies insomuch as to be in generall expectation of our Savior about that time when he came, onely they were not aware of the manner of his two comings; (and were mistake) they understood the description of his second coming, and onely were mistaken in applying that to the time of his first coming....Consider therefore, if the description of his second coming was so much more plain and perspicuous then that of the first, that the Jews who could not so much as perceive any thing of the first could yet understand the second."[8]

A WORLD OF MESSIANIC MISTAKES AND ERRORS

There are many examples which illustrate just how often Jewish leaders and rabbis have been mistaken in dating the Coming of the Messiah! Nearly 2000 years ago, Rabbi Yohanan Ben Zakkai felt the Messiah would be coming in his time.[9] Rabbi Jose, the Galilean, said the Messiah would come in 130 AD.[10] Rabbi Eleazar ben Azariah predicted He would come in 140 AD.[11] Rabbi Judah ha-Nasi (circa 135-220), redactor of the Mishnah, said 435 AD[12] would be the date of His Coming. Rabbi Hanina of the third century said He would be here by 470 AD.[13]

***

[8]Frank E. Manuel, *The Religion of Isaac Newton*, p. 110. [ ] mine. Manuel's source was *Yahuda Manuscript 1*.

[9]Raphael Patai, *The Messiah Texts*, p. 54.

[10]Abba Hillel Silver, D.D., *A History of Messianic Speculation in Israel*, p. 20.

[11]Ibid.

[12]Ibid, pp. 25-26.

[13]Ibid, p. 26.

Rabbi Elazar ben Arak maintained Messiah would come in 620 AD.[14] Salmon ben Yeroham, a Karaite, thought He would be here in 968 AD.[15] Judah Halevi, poet and author of *Kuzari* (1080-1141), said 1130 AD[16] would be the date for the Messiah. Rabbi Moshe ben Maimon, the great Rambam (1135-1204), set the date for the Coming of the Messiah at 1210 AD.[17] Rabbi Abraham bar Hiyya (d. 1136) said 1230 AD.[18] Abraham ben Alexander of Cologne, author of *Keter Shem Tov*, and the mid-thirteenth century student of Eliazar of Worms, "gives the year 1329 as the Messianic year."[19]

The French Rabbi Levi ben Abraham (circa 1240-1315) gave 1345 AD as the Messianic year in his manuscript, *Liwyat Hen*.[20] Levi ben Gershon, known to us as Gersonides (1288-1344), maintained 1358 AD was the date.[21] Benjamin Ben Moses Nahawendi, the great Karaite of the eighth and ninth centuries, insisted 1358 AD would be the time.[22] Rabbi Sh'lomo ben Yitzhay, the great and famed Rashi, (1040-1105), set the Messiah's date of arrival at 1352 AD.[23] Rabbi Moshe ben Nahman, the well-known Nahmanides (1194-1268), predicted a date of 1403 AD.[24] Joseph ben Isaac Bekor Shor, a French Tosafist/exegete, and Bahya ben Asher of Saragossa both said 1403.[25]

Abraham Halevi, a Cabbalist who was exiled from Spain in the sixteenth century, wrote in his 1508 commentary on Daniel, *Mashre Kitrin* (The Loosener of Knots), that the Messiah would come in 1530.[26] Italian Rabbi Mordecai ben Judah Dato (1527-1585), who wrote *Migdal David,* was of the conviction that the Messiah would come in 1575.[27] Eliezer Ashkenazi ben Eli Rofe (d. 1586), who wrote *Ma'ase Adonai,* a commentary on the Pentateuch, offered 1594 as "the Messianic year."[28] Gedalia ibn Yahya, in his book *Sefer Shalshelet ha-Kabbala*, suggested 1598.[29] Even one hundred and ten-year-old David ben Solomon ibn Abi Zimra (1479-1589), who wrote *Magen*

---

[14]Ibid, p. 40.
[15]Ibid, p. 52.
[16]Ibid, p. 68.
[17]Raphael Patai, *The Messiah Texts*, p. 55. There are many who deny that Rambam set a date. You are free to consider Patai's evidence and decide for yourself.
[18]Abba Hillel Silver, D.D., *A History of Messianic Speculation in Israel*, pp. 69-71.
[19]Ibid, p. 99.
[20]Ibid, pp. 99-100.
[21]Ibid, p. 94.
[22]Ibid, p. 55.
[23]Raphael Patai, *The Messiah Texts*, p. 55.
[24]Abba Hillel Silver, D.D., *A History of Messianic Speculation in Israel*, pp. 83-84.
[25]Ibid, pp. 66, 94, 96-97.
[26]Ibid, p. 130.
[27]Ibid, p. 135.
[28]Ibid, p. 139.
[29]Ibid, p. 140.

David, a mystical interpretation of the Hebrew alphabet, said He would come in 1640.[30] Rabbi Moses de Leon (1240-1305), Isaiah Horowitz (1555-1630), and Yom-Tov Lippmann Heller, all three, said 1648 was the date.[31]

Isaac Cohen, who published *Pa'aneah Raza* in 1607, said 1713-14 was pristine, the perfect date.[32] Rabbi Nathan Nata Spira (circa 1584-1633) of Cracow said 1725.[33] Rabbi Simeon ben Zemah Duran (1361-1444), who wrote *Oheb Mishpat*, a commentary on Job, gave the year of 1850.[34]

Rabbi Samuel ben Judah Velerio, physician and biblical commentator, who died in the second half of the sixteenth century, after writing *Hazon la-Mo'ed*, said 1868 was the Messiah's date.[35] Rabbi Meir Loeb ben Y'hiel Mikhael Malbim (1809-1879), who was the chief rabbi of Rumania, said 1913.[36] Joseph ben David ibn Yahya (the fourth, 1494-1539) said the Messiah would come in the year 1931.[37]

In the early 1980's, we spoke to more than one rabbi in Israel who felt that because the Hebrew spelling of the Jewish year which would occur in 1984, was Tishmad, meaning "destruction," that would be the year. Needless to say, we were unable to convince them until 1985, but this date, too, was in error.

THE *SAN FRANCISCO CHRONICLE* REVEALED THE MESSIANIC MISTAKE OF THE 1990'S IN ITS INTERVIEW WITH RABBI LANGER

The *San Francisco Chronicle* ran an article entitled "Jewish Sect is Expecting Its Messiah by Sept. 9," stipulating His possible Coming three years ago, as expected by Lubavitcher Jews. Their Rabbi Schneerson was also thought by some of them to be the Messiah, until he died in mid-1994 at the age of ninety-two, God bless his soul. The article went on to report: "...last fall...Schneerson accurately predicted that the gulf war would take few Jewish lives and be over by Purim, the Jewish holiday of February 28.

Schneerson hit the prophetic jackpot when, at midnight on February 26th, President Bush ended Operation Desert Storm, a war

---

[30] Ibid, pp. 141-142.

[31] Raphael Patai, *The Messiah Texts*, pp. 55-56.

[32] Abba Hillel Silver, D.D., *A History of Messianic Speculation in Israel*, pp. 186-187.

[33] Ibid, p. 187.

[34] Ibid, p. 107.

[35] Ibid, p. 143.

[36] Raphael Patai, *The Messiah Texts*, p. 56.

[37] Abba Hillel Silver, D.D., *A History of Messianic Speculation in Israel*, p. 142.

that went much more quickly and had far fewer allied and Israeli casualties than most observers—except Schneerson—expected.

His prophecies did not end with the war. Schneerson has also predicted that the Hebrew Messiah will be revealed by Rosh Hashana, the Jewish New Year that begins September 9.

Schneerson based his prediction on an 1800-year-old Jewish prophecy that in the year the Jewish Messiah appears, 'the nations will challenge one another. The King of Paras (Persia) will challenge an Arab king...and the entire world will panic and be stricken with consternation....Israel will also panic and be confounded....' "[38]

THE PROPHECY OF THE MESSIAH WILL COME TRUE IN ITS TIME, AND WE HAVE *TIME* TO WAIT!

No doubt this Jewish prophecy will come true. Schneerson, in his zealous interpretation, hurried it up too much for its own good—for the time being, that is. Toward the end of the article, the prospect was raised to Rabbi Langer of Chabad, in the Richmond district, "What if the Messiah does not appear by September 91?" His answer was, "We will deal with that, God forbid, at the time!"[39]

No doubt this will not be the last *mistaken Messianic date* given by well-meaning, but misinformed rabbis![40] This apocalyptic guesswork is slated for increase as we approach the first quarter of the twenty-first century—toward the middle, someone may just get incredibly close to it! Time will tell—we will see.

SETTING A SPECIFIC YEAR FOR THE MESSIAH'S COMING, BEFORE THE REBIRTH OF ISRAEL, WAS WITCHCRAFT

We want to emphasize that we are not alone in criticizing these rabbis for their mistakes. Rabbi Y'huda heHasid, author of *Sefer*

---

[38]Don Lattin, "Jewish Sect Is Expecting Its Messiah by Sept. 9," *San Francisco Chronicle*, Apr. 15, 1991, p. A5, © used by permission. Sadly, Rabbi Schneerson passed away in June of 1994. Our condolences to his family.

[39]Ibid.

[40]We hope that other rabbis will realize, as did Rabbi Nathan Shapira: "...our Forefathers wrongfully put [him] to death and that Sin lies upon us unto this day." *Jewish Christians and Christian Jews*, p. 65. Professor Popkin noted of this incredible rabbi of the seventeenth century: "...the Millenarians so loved rabbi Shapira that they took on his fund-raising, and in the first known case, Christians were raising substantial sums for the Jews in Jerusalem....The Millenarians found in rabbi Shapira a striking case of a Christian Jew. He avowed Christian sentiments....and held Jesus's views in the highest regard....The Millenarians...got him to take a copy of the New Testament back to Palestine to have it properly rendered into Hebrew." He further notes of the famed Jewish philosopher, Baruch Spinoza: "...he spent the rest of his life with Christians, mainly Millenarian ones." Ibid, pp. 65-66. This is a fact not generally known by most laymen.

Hasidim (the book of the Pious), a renowned Hasidic Jewish work, said: "When you see a person prophesying about the Messiah, you should know that he is either engaged in witchcraft, or has dealings with demons, or has adjured them with the Ineffable Name. Because such a sorcerer importunes the angels or the spirits, they say to him: 'Speak not in this manner, [rather] reveal [the coming of the Messiah] to the whole world.' But at the end he will be put to shame before the whole world, because he importuned the angels or the demons. And in its place misfortunes come because of him who adjured. And demons come and teach him calculations and secrets, to his shame and the shame of those who believe his words...for no man knows about the coming of the Messiah."[41]

THE RABBIS' MISTAKEN SPECULATION ABOUT THE MESSIAH'S "ONLY" COMING COULD ONLY TRULY APPLY TO HIS SECOND, ACCORDING TO THE PROPHECY OF MOSES IN GENESIS 49!

We maintain that the rabbis have speculated about the Messiah's **Second Coming** with good reason. Risto Santala documented: "Rabbi Rahmon says: 'When the members of the Sanhedrin discovered that the rights of life and death had been torn from their hands a general consternation seized hold of them. They covered their heads with ashes and their bodies with sackcloth, shouting, 'Woe to us! The sceptre of Judah has been taken away and the Messiah has not yet come.' ' In the light of all this the Rabbis' speculation about the possible **first advent** of the Messiah is **completely illogical**—he must already have come. R. Rahmon saw the Bible's own time limits."[42]

In other words, in the first century, before Rome sacked Jerusalem in 70 AD and abolished capital punishment (John 18:31), twenty-two years before Jesus was crucified, when Judea had already become a Roman province, the Messianic prophecy of Genesis 49:10 had already been fulfilled:[43] "The sceptre shall not depart from Judah, nor a lawgiver from between his feet, until Shiloh come; and unto Him shall the obedience of the people be."[44]

This showed that the time limit for the Messiah's Coming had expired, except the rabbis did not realize this (the significance of Gen. 49:10 in relation to Rome taking over the law and Jesus' subsequent

---

[41]Raphael Patai, *The Messiah Texts*, p. 57. Patai's source was *Sefer Hasidim*, pp. 76-77.

[42]Risto Santala, *The Messiah in the Old Testament in the Light of Rabbinical Writings*, pp. 103-104. Santala's source was Fred John Meldau, *The Messiah in Both Testaments*.

[43]See Fred John Meldau, *The Messiah in Both Testaments*, p. 30.

[44]Ibid, p. 29. Genesis 49:10.

appearance). Many had rejected Jesus, who was the Messiah and had just come—right on time.[45]

To put it more simply, a set of conditions which had been prophesized were fulfilled by Jesus: 1. The Messiah had to come before the Temple was destroyed (Hag. 2:7-9); 2. That He had to come after the Jews lost their political power.

The second condition was in fulfillment of Genesis 49:10. The appearance of the Messiah in this narrow window of opportunity fits the bill perfectly. Twelve years after the birth of Jesus, Judah became a full-fledged Roman province and the Jews lost their right to mete out capital punishment, their last vestige of sovereign power. Yet the Messiah could still preach in the Temple, which was not destroyed until 70 AD. The Messiah had come right on schedule. Now we wait for His Second Advent (Matt. 24)!

THE MESSIAH'S SECOND COMING! COULD IT BE IN OUR GENERATION?

Our answer concerning a date for the Second Coming of the Messiah is the same as Jesus': "...of that day and hour knoweth no *man*...." (Matt. 24:36 KJV). Our rabbi friends we have quoted, who speculated and made such trivial predictions involving the exact time, should have realized that it was impossible to know even the year. Suffice it to say that it would have done them good to take Jesus' statement seriously—had they read it, of course.

In our search for the generation of His Advent, we will also examine the words of Jesus which, unlike the rabbis', have yet to be proven in error! Jesus tells us in the first book of the New Testament: "Now learn a parable of the fig tree [Israel's rebirth].[46] When his branch is yet tender, and putteth forth leaves, ye know that summer *is* nigh: So likewise ye, when ye shall see all these things, know that it [the Second Advent of Messiah] is near, *even* at the doors. Verily I say unto you, This generation [the generation which sees Israel become a nation, us!] shall not pass, till all these things [the Second Advent and

---

[45]Even the twentieth century Jewish author, Abba Hillel Silver, whom we have quoted, admitted: "Jesus appeared in the procuratorship of Pontius Pilate (26-36 C.E.). The first mention of the appearance of a Messiah in Josephus is in connection with the disturbances during the term of office of the procurator....The Messiah was expected around the second quarter of the first century C.E., because the Millennium was at hand. Prior to that time he was not expected, because according to the chronology of the day the Millennium was still considerably removed." Abba Hillel Silver, D.D., *A History of Messianic Speculation in Israel*, pp. 6-7.

[46]For conclusive proof that the fig tree is Israel, see our *Vol. II*, chapter 1, "A Liberal Interpretation on the Prophecy of Israel—Disproved."

its accompanying end time events] be fulfilled" (Matt. 24:32-34 KJV; [ ] mine).

We know from Genesis 15:13-16 that a generation can be as long as one hundred years.[47] Since Israel was born in 1948, then according to Jesus who spoke of Israel's beginning generation, and Moses who wrote of the maximum length of a generation in Genesis (two prophets who have never been wrong), we should see something by 2048, shouldn't we?

We also have Hosea's calendar in the Old Testament, which speaks of one who had returned to His place after 2000 years, to begin a third 1000-year kingdom (see our chapter 6, "The Handwriting on the Wall Spelled 'The Temple Falls' ").

Don't get me wrong, we do not believe in setting dates, we are just relying on the limits Jesus set on time parameters drawn on certain events, some of which have already occurred, thus giving us numerical boundaries. Therefore, we suspect that sometime between the year you read this and the year 2048, or shortly thereafter, the ultimate redemption of the planet you and I inhabit, will be brought in by our Messiah, Jesus.

COULD HE RETURN SOONER?

On the other hand, we might see the Messiah return a few years sooner! Nate Krupp, in his book, *The Omega Generation*, points out: "The maximum number of eclipses of the sun and the moon combined that can possibly occur in any single year is seven. Many believe that the year the Balfour Declaration was signed (1917) giving the Jews the right to return to Palestine, ushered in the time of the last generation mentioned by Jesus in Matthew 24:34, also called the time of the 'beginning of sorrows.' In the year 1917 there were seven eclipses of the sun and the moon. As the seventh eclipse appeared, General Allenby marched into Jerusalem, thereby putting into effect the agreements contained within the Balfour Declaration."[48]

---

[47]To be even more precise, the children of Israel were in Egypt four hundred and thirty years, which the Bible equates to be four generations in Genesis 15. Thus if we divided four into four hundred and thirty, we come up with four generations of one hundred seven and one-half years. So a maximum generation of one hundred seven and one-half years, from May 1948, would end in November of 2055, and even sooner if these were three hundred and sixty-day biblical years instead of our three hundred and sixty-five-day solar year. Will we see Jesus before then? This prophetic writer bets his life on it!

[48]Nate Krupp, *The Omega Generation*. Harrison, AR: New Leaf Press, Inc., © 1977, p. 137, used by permission.

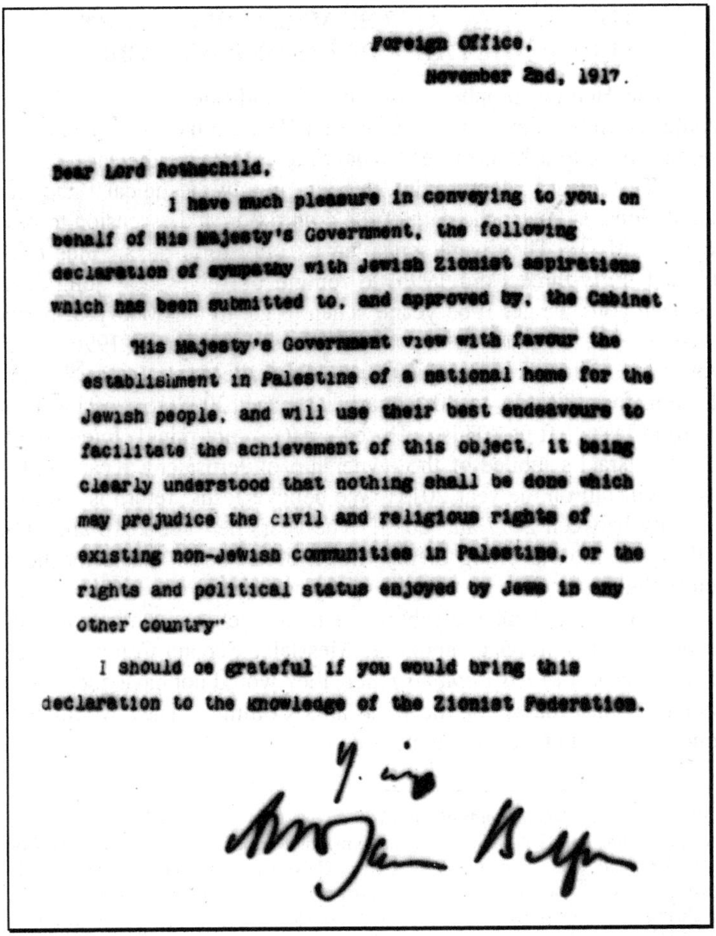

Foreign Office,
November 2nd, 1917.

Dear Lord Rothschild,

I have much pleasure in conveying to you, on behalf of His Majesty's Government, the following declaration of sympathy with Jewish Zionist aspirations which has been submitted to, and approved by, the Cabinet.

"His Majesty's Government view with favour the establishment in Palestine of a national home for the Jewish people, and will use their best endeavours to facilitate the achievement of this object, it being clearly understood that nothing shall be done which may prejudice the civil and religious rights of existing non-Jewish communities in Palestine, or the rights and political status enjoyed by Jews in any other country"

I should be grateful if you would bring this declaration to the knowledge of the Zionist Federation.

We could deductively reason, if this is true and a generation is one hundred years, according to Genesis 15:13-16, that the earliest date for the Coming of Jesus could be 2017 (causing the Rapture to occur in 2010). So we will wait and see with excitement, as Jesus tells us in the New Testament to: "...look up, and lift up your heads; for your redemption draweth nigh" (Luke 21:28 KJV).

The greatest scientist of all time, Isaac Newton, believed the Jews would return to Jerusalem in the twentieth century and that Jesus would return in the twenty-first century, so we believe Christ's most probable appearance will be between 2017 and 2048. Not long to wait, is it? When you consider that nearly forty half-century increments of time have passed, another fifty years, or less, leaves about one-and-a-half minutes before twelve o'clock midnight, if we are right.

THE REAL ERA OF THE MESSIAH'S RETURN VERSUS THE FALSE DATES OF PAST RABBIS

The Hebrew prophet Hosea clearly indicated that the Messiah would return two days (2000 years) after He went back to His place, so we only have to ask ourselves "When did Jesus leave the earth?" The New Testament, along with recent highly technical scientific calculations, indicates the date of the crucifixion and ascension to have been 33 AD.[49] They were separated by only forty days; thus if we subtract thirty-three from 1996, to remind ourselves how long Jesus has been gone we get 1963 years. Then to get to the 2000-year period since He left, we must add another thirty-seven years to 1996, which would put us into the era of 2033, give or take a few years.[50] Time elapsing from 33 AD. to 2033 marks an exact 2000-year period from the time Jesus left us. This is Hosea's date,[51] not mine! Interestingly enough, Israel's jubilee of the ownership of Jerusalem, recaptured in 1967, will fall on the year 2017! We believe Jesus' return is almost a certainty between 2017 and 2033! The years between 2010 and 2033 will be the most exciting of my life, if Jesus doesn't take me home before then.

Just think, if all the rabbis we mentioned had understood and heeded Hosea's prophecy about the Messiah's Second Coming in light of Jesus' *return to His Father's place*, they would not have guessed the numerous false dates for the Messiah's Coming. They would have done a service to God and themselves.

---

[49]We note that an *Atlanta Journal and Constitution* article mentioned several intriguing points regarding our 33 AD date. The article mentioned that two British scientists, Colin Humphreys and W.G. Waddington, of Oxford University, concluded that Jesus died in April of 33 AD. The British science magazine, *Nature*, reported that they based their conclusions on astronomical, biblical and historical references. The article reported: "The scientists said they were able to reconstruct the Jewish calendar at the time and to date a lunar eclipse which the Bible and other historical sources suggest followed the crucifixion....By a process of elimination they went on to conclude that within the decade from A.D. 26 to A.D. 36, the only possible year for the crucifixion to have occurred was A.D. 33. In the second half of their article, the scientists turn to references in the Bible and in the Apocrypha to the moon's being 'turned to blood,' saying that 'in our view the phrase...probably refers to a lunar eclipse, in which case the crucifixion can be dated unambiguously.' 'The reason an eclipsed moon is blood red is well known,' they wrote. 'Even though the moon is geometrically in the earth's shadow, sunlight still reaches it by refraction in the earth's atmosphere and is reddened by having traversed a long path through the atmosphere where scattering (of light) preferentially removes the blue end of the spectrum....' " "2 Scientists Determine Exact Crucifixion Date," *Atlanta Journal and Constitution*, Dec. 22, 1983, © reprinted by permission of the Associated Press. Reproduction does not imply endorsement.

[50]This would be even sooner if three hundred and sixty-day biblical years are considered.

[51]Hosea, as he was a prophet of God, speaking and writing the Lord's very own inspired words, cannot be wrong. The many critics of the Second Coming who admit biblical inspiration and inerrancy, few as they may be, may disagree with me, but can they argue with God about His word written through His prophet Hosea? No!

It is because so many have set dates which came and passed, that presently, many doubt the Coming of the Messiah. So much so among many Jewish theologians, that the famous Jewish philosopher, Martin Buber, in his book, *Hasidic Stories Retold,* relates a question put to the Rabbi of Sadagora: "How can this be? A number of holy men who lived before our time alluded to a date on which redemption was to come. The era they indicated has come and gone, but redemption has not come to pass."[52] In answer to this, the *Tzaddiq* replies: "The light of redemption is spread about us at the level of our heads. We do not notice it because our heads are bowed beneath the burden of exile. Oh, that God might lift up our heads!"[53]

We hope to see the words of Jesus and Hosea fulfilled as prophecies in our day. No doubt, many are, as we see the rapid growth of Jews for Jesus around the globe. An April 14, 1989, Glasgow newspaper article entitled, "The Numbers of 'Messianic' Jews is Said To Be Growing," by Susan Birnbaum, predicted that by the year 2000, the number of Messianic Jews would probably be one-half million. This will be a historic record!

SIR ISAAC NEWTON WARNS OF THE FOLLY OF DATES AND FALSE PROPHECY VERSUS GOD'S PROVIDENCE

Sir Isaac Newton, who knew the Bible inside and out, in both Greek and Hebrew, was an ardent student of the rabbis[54] and the ancient rabbinical literature, as well! No doubt he had some of these "brilliant" rabbis in mind when he wrote: "The folly of interpreters has been to foretel[55] times and things by this Prophecy, as if God designed to make them Prophets. By this rashness they have not only exposed themselves, but brought Prophecy also into contempt. The design of God was much otherwise. He gave this and the Prophecies of the Old Testament, not to gratify men's curiosities by enabling them to foreknow things, but that after they were fulfilled they might be interpreted by the event, and his own Providence, not the Interpreters, be then manifested thereby to the world. For the event of things predicted many ages before, will then be a convincing argument that the world is governed by Providence."[56]

---

[52]Raphael Patai, *The Messiah Texts*, p. 64.

[53]Ibid. Patai's source was *Tales of the Hasidim II: The Later Masters*. New York: A Schocken Book with Farrar, Straus & Young, © 1948. Hasidic stories retold in Buber's style.

[54]For documentation, see *The Books of Nature and Scripture*, James E. Force and Richard H. Popkin, ed.

[55]This spelling is Newton's of three hundred years ago.

[56]Frank E. Manuel, *A Portrait of Isaac Newton*, p. 361. Manuel's source was Isaac Newton's *Observations Upon the Prophecies of Daniel, and the Apocalypse of St. John.* See also the *Yahuda Manuscript*, where Newton says: "I mention this period not to assert

IF THE RABBIS WERE MISTAKEN BEFORE, MIGHT THEY ALSO BE WRONG NOW ABOUT JESUS BEING AN IMPOSTER?

Finally, we conclude that since so many rabbis have shamefully been mistaken so many times in the past about the Messiah, could it be that they also erred in failing to recognize who the Messiah was and His generation? We believe the Messiah is Jesus and His generation is now.

Jesus gave certain eminent signs, which He said would clearly indicate the nearness of His Coming. He said: "...brother will deliver up brother to death, and a father *his* child; and children will rise up against parents, and cause them to be put to death. And you will be hated by all on account of My name....and A MAN'S ENEMIES WILL BE THE MEMBERS OF HIS HOUSEHOLD....And you will be hearing of wars and rumors of wars; see that you are not frightened, for *those things* must take place, but *that* is not yet the end. For nation will rise against nation, and kingdom against kingdom, and in various places there will be famines [and pestilences][57] and earthquakes[58]....And because

---

it, but only to show that their is little reason to expect it earlier and therby to put a stop to the rash conjectures of interpreters." *Yahuda Manuscript, Var. 1.7:3, fol. 13.* Spelling is Newton's.

57"Pestilences" is from Matthew 24:7 of the King James Version of the Bible. See our *Vol. II*, chapter 41, "Was AIDS Made?" for the statistics of its predicted potential to infect one-quarter of the globe, as foretold in Revelation 6:8.

58Concerning Jesus' end time sign of earthquakes, Zionist evangelist television preacher, John Hagee, documented at the end of 1993: "In the 15th century there were 115 earthquakes; in the 16th there were 253; in the 17th there were 378; in the 18th century there were 640; in the 19th century there were 2119; in the 20th century we've had so many earthquakes so fast we can hardly keep records of them. We have a department now trying to predict where the next big one is going to take place...." John Hagee, *Israel and the PLO Peace Pact: Hope or Hoax, Evidence of the Last Generation on Earth.* Fairly recently, earthquakes have increased exponentially. Over a decade ago, Hal Lindsey noted: "...the number of earthquakes per decade has roughly doubled in each of the 10-year periods since 1950....In fact, the dramatic increase in quakes in 1976 led many scientists to say we are entering a period of great seismic disturbances....The new wave of quakes indicates that we are well on the way to the final stages of the prophetic timetable." Hal Lindsey, *The 1980's: Countdown to Armageddon*, p. 30. Gary DeMar attempts to refute Jesus' earthquake prophecy, in his book, *Last Day's Madness.* He asserts: "Jesus had a different era in mind when He uttered words describing... earthquakes, and wars on the Mount called Olivet." Gary DeMar, *Last Day's Madness*, p. 187. This was in spite of the brilliant Zionist television evangelist John Hagee's statistical list of earthquakes from the past six centuries. "There is nothing unique about the number of earthquakes that the world is now experiencing." Ibid. DeMar arrogantly states: "The way some prophecy analysts talk, only a dozen or so major earthquakes have been recorded over the centuries. This is far from the truth." Ibid. I have never heard an evangelist make such a statement! Have you? In the book, *Sign of the Last Days* (1987, p. 52), by Carl Olof Jonsson and Wolfgang Herbst, there is an attempt to lawlessness is increased, most people's love will grow cold....Therefore when you see the ABOMINATION OF DESOLATION which was spoken of through Daniel the prophet, standing in the holy place (let the reader understand), then let those who are in Judea flee to the mountains....there will be a great tribulation...." (Matt. 10:21-22, 36; 24:6-12, 15-16, 21 NASB; [ ] mine).

During this time, the book of Revelation says the average wage paid will be a *denarius*, a coin the King James Version translates as "penny." It was a day's wages for a laborer. The whole point is that a day's wage only buys a small amount of wheat or bread. The New Testament says inflation and starvation will be the norm before the return of Jesus. "And I heard as it were a voice...saying, 'A quart of wheat for a denarius...and do not harm the oil and the wine" (Rev. 6:6 NASB).

This all takes place during the era when the Antichrist attempts to force Jewish worship of himself in place of God. The New Testament says: "Now we request you, brethren, with regard to the coming of our Lord Jesus Christ, and our gathering together to Him, that you may not be quickly shaken from your composure or be disturbed either by a spirit or a message or a letter as if from us, to the effect that the day of the Lord has come. Let no one in any way deceive you, for *it will not come* unless the apostasy comes first, and the man of lawlessness is revealed, the son of destruction, who opposes and exalts himself above every so-called god or object of worship, so that he takes his seat in the temple of God, displaying himself as being God" (II Thes. 2:1-4 NASB).

SOMETIMES THE RABBIS ARE RIGHT, ESPECIALLY WHEN THEIR END TIME SIGNS ARE IN LINE WITH THOSE OF JESUS!

Even though we do not believe in the inspiration of the rabbinical writings, due to their documented mistakes, it is interesting to see that a number of them do correctly identify some of these same signs noted by Jesus. These rabbis also comment on a seven-year Tribulation

---

poke fun at Lindsey's statement, which is true. They attempt to refute the fact that earthquakes are getting worse and more frequent. We suppose this is because they want to prove Jesus wrong. However, modern scientific evidence can be assembled to disprove false claims and reveal the truth. Bruce Bolt, professor of seismology and director of seismographic stations at UC-Berkeley, in his book, *Earthquakes Newly Revised and Expanded*, displays a remarkable appendix entitled, "World Earthquakes and Seismicity Rates." His irrefutable sources are the U.S. National Oceanic and Atmospheric Administration and the U.S. Geological Survey. His appendix, listing average to large quakes and deaths, has been reprinted in our *Vol. II*, chapter 10, "Earthquakes."

period, of which the last three-and-a-half years will be the worst and most horrible—just as foreseen in Daniel and Revelation! Here are a few general, but correct lines from our ancient rabbinical friends on the Coming of Messiah! "In the footsteps of the Messiah [when the Messiah is about to come], insolence will multiply and honor will disappear, the vine will give its fruit but wine will be expensive....Youths will shame the faces of the old, old men will stand up before children. *The son dishonoreth the father, the daughter riseth up against her mother, the daughter-in-law against her mother-in-law, a man's enemies are the people of his own house* (Mic. 7:6)....(M. Sota 9:15)[59] R. Yitzhaq said....'The generation in which the Son of David comes, the scholars will diminish in it, and as for the rest, their eyes will be consumed because of sorrow and sighs....'The rabbis taught: The septenary in which the Son of David comes, in its first year the verse will be fulfilled, *I shall cause it to rain upon one city and shall cause it not to rain upon another city* (Amos 4:7). In the second year arrows of famine will be sent out; in the third, there will be great famine, and men, women, and children, the pious and the men of [good] deeds, will die, and the Tora will be forgotten by its students. In the fourth, there will be plenty and yet no plenty. In the fifth, there will be great plenty, they will eat and drink and rejoice, and the Tora will return to her students. In the sixth, there will be sounds [of trumpets]. In the seventh there will be wars, and at the end of the seventh the Son of David will come....The rabbis taught: The Son of David will not come until....the penny disappears from the pocket...Until they despair of the Redemption....When, as it were, Israel will have neither supporter nor helper....(B. Sanh. 97a)[60]....[In the days of the Messianic sufferings] *All faces will be turned into paleness* (Jer. 30:6)....(B. Sanh. 98b)[61]....R. Berekhia in the name of R. Levi: 'The Last Redeemer [the Messiah] will be like the First Redeemer [Moses]. Just as the First Redeemer was revealed and then again was hidden from the Children of Israel...so the Last Redeemer will be revealed to them and then will be hidden from them....'R. Yitzhaq ben Marion said: 'In the end the Holy One, blessed be He, will reveal Himself to them and will cause manna to descend for them, [for] *There is nothing new under the sun* (Eccles. 1:9).' (Ruth Rabba 5:6)[62]....In the third year of the pestilence, the exiles will make atonement, and at the end of the year the king will be killed, and the

---

59Raphael Patai, *The Messiah Texts*, p. 97. M. Sota 9:15 is a rabbinical commentary.

60Ibid, p. 98. Sanhedrin 97a is a rabbinical commentary found in the Talmud.

61Ibid, p. 99. This is also a rabbinical commentary.

62Ibid. Ruth Rabba is a rabbinical Midrash.

people will flee into the deserts....a great evil will be in the world, and he will rebel and rule for three and a half years. And the princes of Edom will fall....for seven years Israel will burn the wood of their bows and their shields and their lances. (Pirqe Mashiah, BhM 3:70-73)[63]....It was taught in the name of the rabbis: In the septenary in which the Son of David comes, in the first year there will be insufficient food; in the second, arrows of famine are sent out; in the third, great famine; in the fourth, neither famine nor abundance; in the fifth, great abundance....in the sixth, sounds and rumors; in the seventh, wars. And at the end of the seventh the Messiah will be expected, and the Children of the West will become overbearing and will come and will maintain a reign with insolence, and they will come unto Egypt and capture all the captivity. And in those days will arise an insolent king over a poor and destitute people....And Israel will be exiled to the desert of marshes to graze in the salt plants and roots of broom bushes....(Aggadat Mashiah, BhM 3:141-43)"[64]

THE SIGNS ARE BEGINNING TO MANIFEST THEMSELVES

We are now seeing great famine in many parts of the world. In this century we have witnessed two world wars, with more casualties than in all the wars throughout human history. We have witnessed inflation on an unforeseen scale, due in large part, to tremendous amounts of Western currency sent to the Arab nations for oil.

The Antichrist will come and bring in peace *for a limited time*. His coming as a fake Messiah will succeed in deceiving most of the world's Jewry into believing he is the "real Messiah" for only a short while. However, once his true identity is discovered, just before Jesus returns, toward the end of the seven-year Tribulation period,[65] great war and famine, which this self-styled Messiah seemed to eliminate, will return on an unbelievable scale.

Presently, millions starve in Africa, despite many Christian organizations' importation of food rations, but at the time of the Antichrist, there will be worldwide famine and accompanying war, leading toward the predicted Magog-Armageddon war, which will become reality after the false peace of the Antichrist falls. The New Testament foresees his persecution of Jews and true Christians who

---

[63]Ibid, pp. 174-176. Pirqe Mashiah, BhM, is a rabbinical Midrash from the collection *Bait ha Midrash.*

[64]Ibid, pp. 97-99, 174-177. *Aggadat Mashiah* is also a Midrash from the collection *Bait ha Midrash.*

[65]This period is known as "Jacob's trouble" in the Old Testament passage of Jeremiah 30:6.

recognize Jesus, instead of him, as Messiah. Thus, Micah's prophecy of family member turning against family member, spoken of by Jesus, becomes reality, as unbelievers turn in secret believers for their faith. War, famine, inflation and persecution (death sentences) are rendered to the faithful of Jesus, before He defeats the Antichrist, saving Israel and the rest of mankind from a thermal nuclear annihilation.

THE ANTICHRIST OF THE NEW TESTAMENT IS THE ARMILUS OF THE RABBIS, NOT CHRISTIAN LEGEND AS MANY HAVE ALLEGED!

The ancient Jewish commentary, *Midrash Otot HaMashiah*, gives us an incredible picture of an end time prophetic scenario, in which the Antichrist (the rabbis refer to him as Armilus) favors the Jews, only to finally turn on them, while the true Messiah, ben David, rescues them by defeating the false Messiah-Antichrist, just as the New Testament says will occur with Jesus. *Otot* is an incredible piece of scholarship, worth quoting at length: "...his name is Armilus the Satan. This is the one whom the nations of the world call Antichrist....he will go to Edom the wicked and say to them: 'I am Messiah, I am your god!' Instantly they believe in him, and make him king over them, and all the Children of Esau join themselves to him and come to him. And he goes forth and conquers all the countries....In that hour he sends to...all Israel and says to them: 'Bring me your Tora and testify to me that I am god.' Instantly they are afraid and confused. In that hour Nehamiah son of Hushiel arises, and thirty thousand warriors from among the Children of Ephraim, and they take the Tora scroll and read before him: *I am the Lord thy God, thou shalt have no other gods before Me* (Exod. 20:2-3). And he says to them: 'There is nothing in this Tora of yours; come and testify to me that I am god....'...Instantly the wicked Armilus becomes wroth, and gathers all the armies of the nations of the world to the Valley of Harutz, and fights Israel, and heaps and heaps are killed of them, and Israel will be smitten a little....And it will be a suffering for Israel the like of which has not been ever since the world exists and to that time....In that hour the Holy One, blessed be He, will examine Israel and purify them like silver and like gold....And all the rest of Israel, the saintly ones and the pure ones, will be in the desert of Judah....fear and trembling will fall upon the nations of the world, and evil illnesses[66] will seize them. And Israel will gird to march out, and Messiah ben David will come, and the

---

66 Some believe this phrase (evil illnesses) denotes genetically (deliberate evil) engineered sickness. See our *Vol. II*, chapter 41, "Was AIDS Made?"

prophet Elijah, with the pious who have returned from the desert of Judah and with all Israel who have gathered, and he will come to Jerusalem....Armilus will hear that a king arose in Israel and will say: 'How far will this despised and lowly nation do this?' Instantly he will gather all the armies of the nations of the world, and will come to fight the Messiah of the Lord....Instantly the Holy One, blessed be He, fights them, as it is written, *Then shall the Lord go forth, and fight against those nations, as when He fighteth in the day of battle* (Zech. 14:3). And the Holy One, blessed be He, will cause fire and brimstone to descend from heaven....Instantly the wicked Armilus will die, he and all his army, and the wicked Edom which destroyed the house of our God and exiled us from our land. In that hour Israel will wreak great vengeance upon them....And He will open for them the sources of the Tree of Life, and will give them to drink....(Otot haMashiah, BhM 2:58-63)"[67]

[67]Ibid, pp. 314-316.

An illustration of the elders before the throne in the book of Revelation by William Blake (1757-1827).

"I saw in the night visions, and, behold, *one* like the Son of man came with the clouds of heaven, and came to the Ancient of days, and they brought him near before him." The prophet Daniel of the Old Testament, 537 BC

"Again the high priest asked him, and said unto him, Art thou the Christ, [Messiah] the Son of the Blessed? And Jesus said, 'I am: and ye shall see the Son of man sitting on the right hand of power, and coming in the clouds of heaven.' "

Jesus of the New Testament, 33 AD

"Behold, he cometh with clouds; and every eye shall see him, and they *also* which pierced him: and all kindreds of the earth shall wail because of him."[1]

The apostle John of the New Testament, 96 AD

"...I say that not only does the Holy Spirit reveal the future to rational creatures, but he shows us what is yet to come by summoning signs in the heavens (Rev. 6:12-14)....The Holy Scriptures testify in the Old Testament, by the mouth of the prophets, and in the New [Testament], by our Savior Jesus Christ, that this world will come to an end: Matthew, Mark, and Luke have recorded the signs of the end of the age; the prophets had also abundantly foretold it....Our Savior said that before the consummation of this world, all that was written by the Prophets must be fulfilled. The Prophets, in their writings, spoke, more or less clearly and in various manners, of things belonging to the future as if past [to their view] and of things past as future, and in the same way [they spoke] of things present. Many prophecies have a double meaning and refer to different events of similar character [the one near, the other remote; the one temporal, the other spiritual]; some prophecies are [interpreted] figuratively and others literally. **Prophecy may be fulfilled partially in the near future or more completely at a much later date**....I will speak of one [scriptural truth] because it is relevant to me, and every time I meditate on it, I feel rest and contentment. I am the worst of sinners. (1 Tim. 1:15) The pity and mercy of our Lord have completely covered me whenever I have called [on him] for them. I have found the sweetest consolation in casting away all my anxiety...."[2]

Admiral Christopher Columbus, the discoverer of America, 1400's

28

THE SECOND COMING EVENT—WILL HE YET BE SENT?

"Then shall the LORD go forth, and **fight against those nations**, as when he fought in the day of battle. And his feet shall stand in that day upon the mount of Olives, which *is* before Jerusalem on the east, and the mount of Olives shall cleave in the midst thereof toward the east and toward the west, *and there shall be* a very great valley; and half of the mountain shall remove toward the north, and half of it

[1]First three quotes, KJV, *The New Scofield Reference Bible*. [ ] mine.

[2]Kay Brigham, *Christopher Columbus's Book of Prophecies*, pp. 180-182. Bold mine. Kay Brigham's scriptural footnotes inserted with ( ).

toward the south. And ye shall flee *to* the valley of the mountains; for the valley of the mountains shall reach unto Azal: yea, ye shall flee, like as ye fled from before the earthquake in the days of Uzziah king of Judah: and **the LORD my God shall come,** *and* all the saints with thee" (Zech. 14:3-5 KJV; bold mine).

This is a prediction of the final battle of Armageddon (known as the battle of Gog and Magog in Ezek. 38-39), which will take place at the end of the seven-year Tribulation period (Matt. 24:21; Dan. 12:1; Rev. 4; 19). Notice it is mentioned that the Mount of Olives will *split.*[3] Zechariah 14:4, written 500 BC, foretold: "...the mount of Olives shall **cleave** in the midst thereof toward the east and toward the west, *and there shall be* a very great valley; and half of the mountain shall remove toward the north, and half of it toward the south" (KJV).

This face of the Mount of Olives reveals thousands of Jewish gravesites, placed there in anticipation of the Coming of the Messiah.

[3]When the Mount of Olives is cloven at the moment of the Messiah Jesus' arrival, there will be a resurrection of the dead (John 5; Rev. 20; Dan. 12). Religious Jews have been buried on the Mount of Olives for centuries, due to the belief that the Messiah would first come to this mountain and raise the dead. This belief comes from Zechariah 14:5, where it says, "the LORD my God shall come." Thus it is shown that in their ancient Jewish belief, the Messiah was to be God. As you can see in this picture of the Mount, there are literally thousands of Jewish graves covering its face, awaiting Messiah, because of these words of Zechariah, written 2500 years ago!

THE MESSIAH'S BOMB SHELTER AND GATE—MOST LIKELY NOT A LONG WAIT

The Messiah's foot is scheduled to touch the Mount of Olives just before it breaks apart. Why? Is God planning to let the mountain split just as Jesus returns? The answer is found in Zechariah 14:5, which says: "And ye shall flee *to* the valley of the mountains...." (KJV). This is the *valley* which will soon be opened by the splitting of the Mount of Olives.

Before long, there will be warfare in this area like never before. The Messiah will return to destroy Israel's enemy invaders, the Arabs and the Russians of Ezekiel 38, in order to protect the Jews in the immediate area. When He returns to drive off their enemies, He provides a place of shelter—a natural bomb shelter, if you will.

Many geologists surveyed for oil in various locations in Israel. When they examined this area on the Mount of Olives, they found a deep fault running lengthwise from the top of the mountain right through the Golden Gate. This is the location where Ezekiel 44:3 predicts the Messiah will enter a second time when He returns to Earth. The first entrance was made when He rode into Jerusalem in 33 AD, as He was proclaimed Messiah, the son of David (Luke 19:37).

Ezekiel 44:2-3 explicitly says: "...the LORD God of Israel has entered by it; therefore it shall be shut" (NASB). And: "*It is* for the prince...." (KJV).

This refers to the Messiah, the Prince, at His Second Advent. Truly, none have entered this gate because it has been walled up with huge Jerusalem stones. Only the splitting of the Mount of Olives will open this gate, and this will occur only when Messiah returns to save His people, Israel. By then, they will have realized that the Antichrist is the false Messiah and will be anxiously awaiting the Messiah Jesus.

TWO STRIKES, THREE AND YOU'RE OUT!

In modern history, the Arabs attempted to open this gate twice. Both attempts failed, we believe not coincidentally! Providentially, God has kept this gate shut.

Because the Arabs are aware of the Hebrew belief that the Jewish Messiah will enter this gate, they purposely laid their graves there to prevent Him. Grant Jeffrey, in his book *Heaven, the Last Frontier*, details: "The prophet Ezekiel declared that the promised Messiah would enter the sealed Eastern Gate of the Temple Mount into the rebuilt sanctuary. 'And, behold, the glory of the God of Israel came from the way of the east: and His voice was like a noise of many waters: and the earth shined with His glory...And the glory of the Lord came into the house by the way of the gate whose prospect is toward the east. So the spirit took me up, and brought me into the inner court and behold, the glory of the Lord filled the house' (Ezekiel 43:1,2,4,5)....Amazingly, this gate has been shut now for many centuries. The original Eastern gate is also sealed under the accumulated rubble directly in front of the present sealed Eastern Gate which you can see today. The Moslems under Suleiman the Magnificent were aware of the ancient prophecy of the coming Jewish Messiah and they sealed this gate when they rebuilt the city walls four hundred years ago. To prevent the coming of the Messiah through the gate they built a large graveyard in front of it....a priest...will be defiled by walking through a graveyard so they felt that a grave site would prevent the Messiah fulfilling Ezekiel's prophecy.

"Several months ago I approached and touched these ancient stones of the Eastern Gate. On the ground directly in front of the sealed gate the Arabs had placed the gravestones of several children only two inches from the bottom of the huge foundation blocks of the gate. Poignantly, a shell casing from an ejected bullet had fallen onto the child's small grave from the soldier's guard post above the gate. I discovered an amazing inscription which was written on the stones which had sealed the gate for so many centuries. 'Ba Ha Moshiach'—'Come Messiah.' Some orthodox Jewish believer, who understood the ancient prophecy of Ezekiel, had secretly approached the Eastern Gate recently and written this welcoming message to the Messiah upon these stones.

"Twice in this century an attempt to open the sealed Eastern Gate failed. First, on December 9th, 1917 the Grand Muffti, the Arab leader of Jerusalem, tried to open this gate. He had ordered the other gates to Jerusalem sealed to deter the approaching Allied Expeditionary Army led by the British General Lord Allenby. Since he needed one gate open, he ordered his workmen to open the mysterious sealed gate. As the workmen picked up their sledgehammers, Lord Allenby's biplane flew over the city telling the Arabs to 'Flee Jerusalem.' Miraculously, without a shot being fired the soldiers fled the city. It was delivered into the hands of Britain which had one month earlier promised the Jews 'a national homeland' with the famous Balfour Declaration. The workmen fearfully put down their sledgehammers and the gate remained sealed as God had prophecied.

"Again in 1967, the ancient prophecy was fulfilled. Tensions were rising in the Middle East as the Arabs commanded the United Nations peacekeeping forces out of the Sinai. Egypt stopped Israeli shipping and moved its forces into attack formations. King Hussein of

Jordan had conquered the old city of Jerusalem in 1948, including the Temple Mount. For the first time in centuries the Jews were forbidden to worship at their sacred Western Wall. The Moslem King Hussein decided to build a hotel for Arab pilgrims on this section of the Western Wall closing off this area of Jewish worship forever. However, the planned hotel would be built over the Magreb Gate which all pilgrims presently use to enter the Temple Mount. The King needed to open another gate to allow Moslem worshippers entrance to the El Aksa Mosque on the Temple Mount. In violation of the prophecy he ordered his workmen to open the sealed Eastern Gate. On June 5, 1967 as the workmen prepared their air hammers to shatter the huge stones, Israeli aircraft preemptively responded to the Arab war preparations. The warplanes flew out of their underground air bases to devastate their enemies' air forces and armored formations. As the stunningly successful Six Day War began, the workmen put down their tools. The Eastern Gate is still sealed. The gate will remain sealed until the day when the promised Messiah will enter into His Kingdom."[4]

The Golden Gate.

[4]Grant R. Jeffrey, *Heaven, The Last Frontier*, pp. 128-131.

ORIGINAL HEBREW TEXT WRITTEN 487 BC

וְזֹאת ׀ תִּהְיֶה הַמַּגֵּפָה אֲשֶׁר יִגֹּף יְהוָה֙ אֶת־כָּל־הָעַמִּים אֲשֶׁר צָבְאוּ עַל־יְרוּשָׁלִָם הָמֵק ׀
בְּשָׂרוֹ וְהוּא֙ עֹמֵד עַל־רַגְלָיו וְעֵינָיו֙ תִּמַּקְנָה בְחֹרֵיהֶן וּלְשׁוֹנוֹ תִּמַּק בְּפִיהֶם׃

זכריה יד:יב

OLD TESTAMENT SCRIPTURE TRANSLATION

"And this shall be the plague with which the LORD will smite all the peoples that have fought against Jerusalem: their flesh shall consume away while they stand upon their feet, and their eyes shall consume away in their holes, and their tongue shall consume away in their mouth."

Zechariah 14:12 KJV[5]

ANCIENT RABBINICAL COMMENTARY

"...what did Gog think? He said: '...I shall go forth first against the Patron of Israel'....What did they [the hosts of Gog] do? They stood on their feet and looked up toward the Holy One, blessed be He, and said: '*Come, let us cut them off from being a nation, that the name of Israel may be no more in remembrance* (Ps. 83:5)'....And what does the Holy One, blessed be He, do to them from Above? They stand on their feet, and He punishes them....[He says:] 'Those feet which wanted to stand up against Me, *Their flesh shall consume away while they stand upon their feet* (Zech. 14:12). And those eyes which looked up, *And their eyes shall consume away in their sockets* (ibid.). And that tongue which spoke against the Lord, *And their tongue shall consume away in their mouth* (ibid.).' The Holy One, blessed be He, says to them: 'At first you were not at peace with one another....And now you made peace with one another so as to come against Me....I, too, shall do likewise. I shall call the birds and the beasts who were not at peace with one another, and I shall cause them to be at peace with one another in order to go forth against you. And because you said, *That the name of Israel may be no more in remembrance* (Ps. 83:5), by your life, you will die and they will bury you and will take a name [i.e., become famous] in the world.' "[6]

Aggadat B'reshit, ed. Buber, pp. 5-7

NEW TESTAMENT RECORDED 37 AD

"And ye shall hear of wars and rumours of wars: see that ye be not troubled: for all *these things* must come to pass, but the end is not yet. For nation shall rise against nation, and kingdom against kingdom: and there shall be famines, and pestilences, and earthquakes, in divers places. All these *are* the beginning of sorrows....For then shall be great tribulation, such as was not since the beginning of the world to this time, no, nor ever shall be. And except those days should be shortened,[7] there should no flesh be saved: but for the elect's sake those days shall be shortened."

Matthew 24:6-8, 21-22 KJV

MODERN RABBINIC COMMENT/REFUTATION

"Jews firmly believe that the Messiah will come. We believe that man will not self-destruct, that we will not disappear in a gigantic atomic blast. Man is basically good, and G-d's Kingdom will be established. However, it is not enough to believe in G-d. Faith alone is not adequate,—G-d demands deeds and actions....What is the future bringing? There are some pessimists who say that mankind is approaching its end. They predict that we will either pollute ourselves off the face of this planet

---

5 *The New Scofield Reference Bible.*

6 Raphael Patai, *The Messiah Texts*, pp. 149-150.

7 By Jesus the Messiah, who is speaking these words.

or overpopulate to the barest marginal existence. Others see man doing the job more quickly, bringing his civilization crashing down on his head in a nuclear war. On the other hand, there are optimists who predict a utopian future...."

***The Real Messiah*, by Rabbi Aryeh Kaplan, *et al*, pp. 50, 63; 1976**

AUTHOR'S COMMENT—EVANGELICAL CHRISTIAN POSITION

It seems clear to us that any honest observer would notice that the New Testament "War of End Times" agrees with the Old Testament prophet Zechariah, and the ancient rabbinical commentary, Aggadat B'reshit. Rabbi Kaplan's modern disagreement in *The Real Messiah* not only goes against the grain of the New Testament, but against Jewish tradition, as expressed in the previous commentary. Rabbi Kaplan is not being honest when he says faith is not enough. Faith was enough for the thief on the cross, who had not done one good work, and for Abraham. Moses recorded of Abraham: "And he believed in the LORD; and he counted it to him for righteousness" (Gen. 15:6 KJV). Finally, Christians do not believe there will be a nuclear Armageddon and—puff—we are all gone, as our friendly rabbi seems to imply. The Messiah Jesus will bring a halt to the war, and thereafter initiate world peace! **Philip Moore**

WORLDWIDE DEVASTATION OCCURS, AS THE MESSIAH ARRIVES TO BRING PEACE

The Old Testament prophet Zechariah said, 2500 years ago: "And this shall be the plague wherewith the LORD will smite all the people that have fought against Jerusalem; Their flesh shall consume away while they stand upon their feet, and their eyes shall consume away in their holes, And their tongue shall consume away in their mouth" (Zech. 14:12 KJV).

Again, nearly 2000 years ago, in the New Testament book of Matthew, Jesus says: "...for then there will be a great tribulation....And unless those days had been cut short, no life would have been saved; but for the sake of the elect those days shall be cut short" (Matt. 24:21-22 NASB).

The apostle Luke's book of Acts, in the New Testament, affirms that Jesus will return to Earth in the same way He left, so that He may put an end to the Tribulation war. "And after He had said these things, He was lifted up while they were looking on, and a cloud received Him out of their sight. And as they were gazing intently into the sky while He was departing, behold, two men in white clothing stood beside them; and they also said, 'Men of Galilee, why do you stand looking into the sky? **This Jesus**, who has been taken up from you into heaven, **will come in just the same way as you have watched Him go** into heaven.' Then they returned to Jerusalem from the mount called Olivet, which is near Jerusalem, a Sabbath day's journey away" (Acts 1:9-12 NASB).

Tradition has it that Jesus ascended into Heaven from this highest point on the Mount of Olives, in fulfillment of David's prophetic

Psalm: "The LORD said unto my Lord, Sit thou at my right hand, until I make thine enemies thy footstool....The LORD hath sworn, and will not repent, Thou *art* a priest for ever after the order of Melchizedek" (Ps. 110:1, 4 KJV).

According to prophecy, He will only return from His place at God's right hand, to Earth, at the peak of the most terrible global war against Israel (Rev. 16:16; Ezek. 38-39). The prophet Hosea, even in the Old Testament, confirms of the Rejected One: "I will go away *and* return to My place Until they acknowledge their guilt and seek My face; In **their affliction** [world war] **they** [the Jews] will earnestly **seek Me** [Messiah]" (Hos. 5:15 NASB; [ ] and bold mine).

Once Messiah has come to the Mount of Olives, the people in Jerusalem will see His pierced hands and recognize Jesus for who He has always been—Messiah!

ORIGINAL HEBREW TEXT WRITTEN 487 BC

וְיָצָא יְהוָה וְנִלְחַם בַּגּוֹיִם הָהֵם כְּיוֹם הִלָּחֲמוֹ בְּיוֹם קְרָב׃ וְעָמְדוּ רַגְלָיו בַּיּוֹם־הַהוּא עַל־הַר
הַזֵּתִים אֲשֶׁר עַל־פְּנֵי יְרוּשָׁלִַם מִקֶּדֶם וְנִבְקַע הַר הַזֵּיתִים מֵחֶצְיוֹ מִזְרָחָה וָיָמָּה גֵּיא גְּדוֹלָה
מְאֹד וּמָשׁ חֲצִי הָהָר צָפוֹנָה וְחֶצְיוֹ־נֶגְבָּה׃ וְנַסְתֶּם גֵּיא־הָרַי כִּי־יַגִּיעַ גֵּי־הָרִים אֶל־אָצַל
וְנַסְתֶּם כַּאֲשֶׁר נַסְתֶּם מִפְּנֵי הָרַעַשׁ בִּימֵי עֻזִּיָּה מֶלֶךְ־יְהוּדָה וּבָא יְהוָה אֱלֹהַי כָּל־קְדֹשִׁים
עִמָּךְ׃ **זכריה יד:ג-ה**

OLD TESTAMENT SCRIPTURE TRANSLATION

"Then the LORD will go forth and fight against those nations, as when He fights on a day of battle. And in that day His feet will stand on the Mount of Olives, which is in front of Jerusalem on the east; and the Mount of Olives will be split in its middle from east to west by a very large valley, so that half of the mountain will move toward the north and the other half toward the south. And you will flee by the valley of My mountains, for the valley of the mountains will reach to Azel; yes, you will flee just as you fled before the earthquake in the days of Uzziah king of Judah. Then the LORD, my God, will come, *and* all the holy ones with Him!"

Zechariah 14:3-5 NASB

ANCIENT RABBINICAL COMMENTARY

"...And the Holy One, blessed be He, will go forth and fight them [Gog and Magog]...and the mountains will move and the hills will shake, and the Mount of Olives split asunder....And the Holy One, blessed be He, will descend upon it, and Israel will flee and escape...."[8]

Midrash Leqah Tov, pp. 258-59

NEW TESTAMENT RECORDED 33 AD

"He said to them, '...you shall receive power when the Holy Spirit has come upon you; and you shall be My witnesses both in Jerusalem, and in all Judea and Samaria, and even to the remotest part of the earth.' And after He had said these things, He was lifted up while they were looking on, and a cloud received Him out of their sight. And as they were gazing intently into the sky while He was departing, behold, two men in white clothing stood beside them; and they also said, 'Men of Galilee, why do you stand looking into the sky? This Jesus, who has been taken up from you into heaven, will come in just the same way as you have watched Him go into heaven.' " **Acts 1:7-11 NASB**

MODERN RABBINIC COMMENT/REFUTATION

"...the Messiah comes in a non-miraculous manner....Into a world prepared to receive him, the Messiah will then be born....He will be a mortal human being, born normally of human parents."

***The Real Messiah*, by Rabbi Aryeh Kaplan, *et al*, p. 69; 1976**

AUTHOR'S COMMENT—EVANGELICAL CHRISTIAN POSITION

While the Messiah Jesus was born in a miraculous manner, He will return with might, power and eternal dominion. However, the Antichrist (coming false Messiah), who will come before Jesus returns to save our planet, will in fact, be born of natural parents, as Rabbi Kaplan mentions regarding his expectation of the Messiah yet to arrive! The Jewish people are being set up to be deceived, along with many others, by modern rabbinical teachings. As Isaac Newton wrote: "...it is also our duty to search with all diligence into these Prophesies. And if God was so angry with the Jews for not searching more diligently into the Prophesies which he had given them to know Christ by: why should we think he will excuse us for not searching into the Prophesies which he hath given us to know Antichrist by? For

---

[8]Raphael Patai, *The Messiah Texts*, p. 170.

certainly it must be as dangerous and as easy an error for Christians to adhere to Antichrist as it was for the Jews to reject Christ. And therefore it is as much our duty to indeavor to... be able to know him that we may avoyd him....he may easily seduce thee if thou beest not well prepared to discern him."[9] We should all heed these biblical verses and share them with our Jewish friends, if we are truly going to be witnesses of Jesus. **Philip Moore**

Upon the arrival of Jesus to the Mount of Olives, the Jews in that future time will, in the words of Zechariah: "...look on Me [Jesus] whom they have pierced; and they will mourn for him...." (Zech. 12:10 NASB; [ ] mine).

This fantastic biblical prophecy was written five centuries before the birth of Jesus. It is incredible that its fulfillment, as the political climate seems to indicate, is just around the corner. We await it with anticipation and hope as we share our faith with not only the Jews, but all who yearn and desire to know!

The Mount of Olives, where Jesus stood before ascending into the heavens, and to which He will soon return!

[9] *Yahuda Manuscript 1.*

Back view of the Mount of Olives with its many Jewish tombstones.

An illustration of the Second Coming, as predicted in the Scriptures.

The third face of the Mount of Olives,
as viewed from an Arab neighborhood.

The Mount of Olives, with its chambers,
and the Intercontinental Hotel, fully visible.

Presently, the general area near the summit of the Mount of Olives contains a Moslem graveyard. Arab leaders are aware of the ancient Jewish tradition that Jewish priests could not defile themselves by touching the dead or even passing through a graveyard.[10] As a result, the Arabs felt that since the Messiah is also a priest, He could be prevented from returning to the Mount of Olives by placing a cemetery there. The Moslems are not happy about the predicted return of the Jewish Messiah Jesus, so they took this "precaution." Their superstition is just that. Even though the Messiah is a priest, He has the power to **raise** all believers to life—and He will!

---

[10]*The Babylonian Talmud*, Baba Mezi'a 30a, p. 186.

The steeple in the center of the graveyard is surrounded by a playground. It marks the exact place from which Jesus left and to which He will return (Acts 1:11). Quite a fitting setting, for Jesus once said: "...'Suffer little children, and forbid them not, to come unto me: for of such is the kingdom of heaven' " (Matt. 19:14 KJV).

ORIGINAL HEBREW TEXT WRITTEN 487 BC

בַּיּוֹם הַהוּא יָגֵן יְהוָה בְּעַד יוֹשֵׁב יְרוּשָׁלִַם וְהָיָה הַנִּכְשָׁל בָּהֶם בַּיּוֹם הַהוּא כְּדָוִיד וּבֵית
דָּוִיד כֵּאלֹהִים כְּמַלְאַךְ יְהוָה לִפְנֵיהֶם׃ וְהָיָה בַּיּוֹם הַהוּא אֲבַקֵּשׁ לְהַשְׁמִיד אֶת־כָּל־הַגּוֹיִם
הַבָּאִים עַל־ יְרוּשָׁלִָם׃ וְשָׁפַכְתִּי עַל־בֵּית דָּוִיד וְעַל יוֹשֵׁב יְרוּשָׁלִַם רוּחַ חֵן | וְתַחֲנוּנִים
וְהִבִּיטוּ אֵלַי אֵת אֲשֶׁר־דָּקָרוּ וְסָפְדוּ עָלָיו כְּמִסְפֵּד עַל־ הַיָּחִיד וְהָמֵר עָלָיו כְּהָמֵר
עַל־הַבְּכוֹר׃ בַּיּוֹם הַהוּא יִגְדַּל הַמִּסְפֵּד בִּירוּשָׁלִַם כְּמִסְפַּד הֲדַד־רִמּוֹן בְּבִקְעַת מְגִדּוֹן׃

זכריה יב:ח-יא

OLD TESTAMENT SCRIPTURE TRANSLATION

"In that day the LORD will defend the inhabitants of Jerusalem, and the one who is feeble among them in that day will be like David, and the house of David *will be* like God, like the angel of the LORD before them. And it will come about in that day that I will set about to destroy all the nations that come against Jerusalem. And I will pour out on the house of David and on the inhabitants of Jerusalem, the Spirit of grace and of supplication, so that they will look on Me whom they have pierced; and they will mourn for Him, as one mourns for an only son, and they will weep bitterly over Him, like the bitter weeping over a first-born. In that day there will be great mourning in Jerusalem...."

Zechariah 12:8-11 NASB

ANCIENT RABBINICAL COMMENTARY

"What is the cause of his mourning? In this Rabbi Dosa....said it was for Messiah, the son of Joseph, who is to be slain....If the cause will be the violent death of Messiah, the son of Joseph, one can understand that which is written, 'And they shall look to him whom they have pierced.' "[11]

Talmud Succah, fol. 52, col. 1

NEW TESTAMENT RECORDED 96 AD

"BEHOLD, HE IS COMING WITH THE CLOUDS, and every eye will see Him, even those who pierced Him; and all the tribes of the earth will mourn over Him. Even so. Amen." **Revelation 1:7 NASB**

MODERN RABBINICAL COMMENT/REFUTATION

" '...they shall look upon me whom they have pierced,' etc. The prophet having, in this manner, alluded to the great superiority of the Jews in the latter days, says now, that they will look to him in humility and contrition, on account of those who have been pierced and killed in war. The Jews will be so assured of the Divine assistance in their restoration, that they will feel afflicted on account of those who shall become the first victims of their warfare with the Gentiles."

***Faith Strengthened*, by Isaac ben Abraham, p. 183; 1850**

"But I will pour upon the house of David, and upon the inhabitants of Jerusalem, the spirit of grace and of supplications: and they whom the *nations* were piercing shall look upon me, and shall mourn over it, as one mourneth for *his* only *son*, and shall be in bitterness over it, as one that is in bitterness for *his* firstborn."[12]

***The Holy Scriptures: A Jewish Bible According to the Masoretic Text*, pp. 1331-1332; © 1977**

---

[11] Rev. B. Pick, Ph.D., *Old Testament Passages Messianically Applied by the Ancient Synagogue*, published in the compilation *Hebraica, A Quarterly Journal in the Interests of Semitic Study*, Vol. IV, p. 248.

[12] *The Holy Scriptures: A Jewish Bible According to the Masoretic Text.* Tel Aviv, Israel: "Sinai" Publishing, © 1977, pp. 1331-1332.

AUTHOR'S COMMENT—EVANGELICAL CHRISTIAN POSITION

As Jesus returns, the Jews will realize that their leaders, along with Rome, pierced the one who was their Messiah. We also ask, "Are the rabbis desperate about Zechariah 12:10?" For nearly 2500 years, the Hebrew words of Zechariah's prophetic jewel have been preserved in their purity. However, as we examined various newer English translations, we found that an increasing number of them had begun to mutilate these ancient words of the Jewish prophet. For example, though it says in the original Hebrew (וְהִבִּיטוּ אֵלַי אֵת אֲשֶׁר־דָּקָרוּ): "...they [the people of Jerusalem] will look upon him, whom they have pierced," one modern translation (*The Holy Scriptures: A Jewish Bible According to the Masoretic Text*, by Sinai Publishing) now reads: "...they whom the *nations* were piercing shall look upon me, and shall mourn over it, as one mourneth for *his* only <u>son</u>, and shall be in bitterness over it, as one that is in bitterness for *his* firstborn."[13] In recent times, the rabbis have found it expedient to take it upon themselves to change and alter the words of Zechariah, apparently to ward off missionaries. To change Scripture is strictly forbidden by the Bible, Jewish culture and tradition. In ancient times, when Hebrew scribes hand-copying a manuscript of a book of the Bible made a one-letter mistake, they would discard the entire manuscript and begin again. These ancient rabbis would have the heads of those responsible for changing entire words and sentences in Zechariah's ancient prophecy, breathed by God, if they knew about it today—no matter what the reason. Why has it become common practice in the twentieth century to arbitrarily change portions of Zechariah's prophecy, especially after they have been maintained in their purity for over 2500 years? We believe this has happened as the result of the latter day continuation of the Messiah Conspiracy, orchestrated by the rabbis to prevent Jews from finding biblical reasons to believe in Messiah Jesus. Clearly, the comments in *Faith Strengthened* and *The Holy Scriptures: A Jewish Bible According to the Masoretic Text* (which in our opinion, is more of a commentary, since it is such a dishonest translation),[14] are both deceptive and untrue. We can see this when we look at Rabbi Dosa's unbiased ancient interpretation recorded in the Talmud. We support the original Hebrew of Zechariah, the New Testament and Rabbi Dosa's rabbinic comment, over modern frauds perpetrated to deceive the innocent! Don't you?

Philip Moore

AFTER HE RETURNS, FIRST THINGS FIRST

After the Messiah returns and destroys the invading enemies of Israel, He will enter the eastern Golden Gate (Ezek. 44:3), which will be opened when His foot touches down on the Mount of Olives. According to Zechariah, the mount will cleave, providing shelter for those fleeing from the ongoing war. Once He enters this gate, He will inaugurate the kingdom, set up David's throne, on which He will reign, and rebuild the Temple so precisely described in Ezekiel 40-48. The New Temple will be the center of God's new capital on Earth in the new millennium.

***

---

[13]Ibid, pp. 1331-1332.

[14]In our *opinion,* the translation is dishonest for the reasons we have stated.

The Golden Gate, a spectacular piece of architecture. This is where Jesus will enter after returning to the Mount of Olives, a few hundred yards away. Directly under this gate lies the original gate of Jesus' day, which is also walled up, as predicted by Ezekiel. We await the Prince Messiah. "*It is* for the prince...he shall enter by the way of the porch of *that* gate, and shall go out by the way of the same" (Ezek. 44:3 KJV).

Back view of the majestic Golden Gate, still awaiting the Messiah.

This author stood in front of the Golden Gate, just to the left of a Moslem tombstone, to give a perspective of its size.

RADIATION CLEAN-UP—THE CONTAMINATED BONES OF GOG ARE PROPERLY BURIED

Jesus will also clean up all the radiation brought on by the war, and order a seven-month clean-up of Russian and Arab bones (Ezek. 39:11-16). Ezekiel says there will be professional buriers to bury Gog in their graveyard called "the valley of Hamon-gog," which means "the valley of the multitudes of Gog." " 'And it will come about on that day that I shall give Gog a burial ground there in Israel, the valley of those who pass by east of the sea, and it will block off the passers-by. So they will bury Gog there with all his multitude, and they will call *it* the valley of Hamon-gog. For seven months the house of Israel will be burying them in order to cleanse the land. Even all the people of the land will bury *them*; and it will be to their renown *on* the day that I glorify Myself,' declares the Lord GOD. 'And they will set apart men who will constantly pass through the land, burying those who were passing through, even those left on the surface of the ground, in order to cleanse it. At the end of seven months they will make a search. And as those who pass through the land pass through and anyone sees a man's bone, then he will set up a marker by it until the buriers have buried it in the valley of Hamon-gog. And even *the* name of *the* city will be Hamonah. So they will cleanse the land' " (Ezek. 39:11-16 NASB).

When Jesus returns He puts an end to war. One of the first things He does is neutralize the one who has become the king of war, the Antichrist! The prophet Isaiah called the Antichrist "the wicked," the rabbinical Targum Jonathan refers to him as "Armilus" and the New Testament, the "lawless one," as you see in our comparison layout.

The Golden Gate as seen through the olive trees from the Garden of Gethsemane in Jerusalem.

ORIGINAL HEBREW TEXT WRITTEN 713 BC

וְשָׁפַט בְּצֶדֶק דַּלִּים וְהוֹכִיחַ בְּמִישׁוֹר לְעַנְוֵי־אָרֶץ וְהִכָּה־אֶרֶץ בְּשֵׁבֶט פִּיו וּבְרוּחַ שְׂפָתָיו יָמִית רָשָׁע

ישעיה יא:ד

OLD TESTAMENT SCRIPTURE TRANSLATION

"But with righteousness He will judge the poor, And decide with fairness for the afflicted of the earth; And He will strike the earth with the rod of His mouth, And with the breath of His lips He will slay the wicked."

Isaiah 11:4 NASB

ANCIENT RABBINICAL COMMENTARY

"But he shall judge the poor in truth, and shall reprove in faithfulness for the needy of the people. He shall smite the guilty of the land with the word of his mouth, and with the speech of his lips he shall slay Armilus the wicked."[15]

Targum Jonathan

NEW TESTAMENT RECORDED 54 AD

"And then that lawless one will be revealed whom the Lord will slay with the breath of His mouth and bring to an end by the appearance of His coming...."

II Thessalonians 2:8 NASB

MODERN RABBINIC COMMENT/REFUTATION

None was found, since this doctrine of a false Messiah deceiving the Jewish people, only to turn on them, has been lost to mainstream Judaism. This will contribute to the success of Satan's deception!

AUTHOR'S COMMENT—EVANGELICAL CHRISTIAN POSITION

Within Judaism, the ancients realized that a terrible creature, the Antichrist they called the "Armilus," would wreak havoc on Jerusalem. *The Jewish Encyclopedia* says: "Thereupon the king Armilus, will conquer and sack the Holy City....then begin a general campaign against the Jews, forcing them to flee into the dessert, where they will suffer untold misery."[16] Modern Jews are relatively unaware of this ancient but true doctrine. At any rate, the Old Testament, rabbinic commentaries and the New Testament, all indicate that he will be terminated in the war by "the lips" of the Messiah. Since modern Judaism apparently lost the original knowledge of Armilus, all the anti-Christian polemics we reviewed do not comment on this aspect of the Gog/Magog war.

Philip Moore

ONCE THE ANTICHRIST IS PUT AWAY, JESUS STRAIGHTENS OUT THE EARTH RIGHT AWAY

Once Jesus destroys the Antichrist, He will take over the proper and rightful administration of the earth as He inaugurates the kingdom. The first thing He will do is establish the throne predicted in Isaiah. The Old Testament rabbinical writings and New Testament agree on Isaiah's prophecy and the deity of the Messiah.

---

[15]Samson H. Levey, *The Messiah: An Aramaic Interpretation, The Messianic Exegesis of the Targum*, p. 49.

[16]Isidore Singer, Ph.D., *et al*, *The Jewish Encyclopedia*, Vol. II.

ORIGINAL HEBREW TEXT WRITTEN 740 BC

כִּי־יֶלֶד יֻלַּד־לָנוּ בֵּן נִתַּן־לָנוּ וַתְּהִי הַמִּשְׂרָה עַל־שִׁכְמוֹ וַיִּקְרָא שְׁמוֹ פֶּלֶא יוֹעֵץ אֵל גִּבּוֹר
אֲבִיעַד שַׂר־שָׁלוֹם׃ לְםַרְבֵּה הַמִּשְׂרָה וּלְשָׁלוֹם אֵין־קֵץ עַל־כִּסֵּא דָוִד וְעַל־מַמְלַכְתּוֹ
לְהָכִין אֹתָהּ וּלְסַעֲדָהּ בְּמִשְׁפָּט וּבִצְדָקָה מֵעַתָּה וְעַד־עוֹלָם קִנְאַת יְהוָה צְבָאוֹת תַּעֲשֶׂה־זֹּאת׃

ישעיה ט:ה-ו

OLD TESTAMENT SCRIPTURE TRANSLATION

"For a child will be born to us, a son will be given to us; And the government will rest on His shoulders; And His name will be called Wonderful Counselor, Mighty God, Eternal Father, Prince of Peace. There will be no end to the increase of *His* government or of peace, On the throne of David and over his kingdom, To establish it and to uphold it with justice and righteousness From then on and forevermore. The zeal of the LORD of hosts will accomplish this."

Isaiah 9:6-7 NASB

ANCIENT RABBINICAL COMMENTARY

"The prophet said to the house of David, For unto us a child is born, to us a son is given, and he shall receive the law upon him to keep it, and his name is called from eternity, Wonderful, Counsellor, Mighty God, Continuing for ever, the Messiah; for peace shall be multiplied upon us in his days."[17]

Targum

NEW TESTAMENT RECORDED 63 AD

"And behold, you will conceive in your womb, and bear a son, and you shall name Him Jesus. He will be great, and will be called the Son of the Most High; and the Lord God will give Him the throne of His father David; and He will reign over the house of Jacob forever; and His kingdom will have no end."

Luke 1:31-33 NASB

MODERN RABBINIC COMMENT/REFUTATION

"Jesus was *never called these names*; i.e., Wonderful, Prince of Peace, etc., even in the New Testament, and yet the verse says explicitly that the person referred to will be *called* those names. Furthermore, in desperation, the Christians say that Isaiah 9:6 refers to Isaiah 7:14. The absurdity of 7:14 referring to Jesus has been discussed before....How can this refer to Jesus—his government never began, let alone had any peace! If someone tells you that it refers to the second coming—well, by now, I think that you should be able to seek the weakness of that. Thus, this verse refers to someone, but surely not to Jesus [in his footnote 18 to names, he says]....many Jewish commentaries translate the verse like this: 'And the Wonderful Counseler, the Mighty God, the Everlasting Father will call him (the boy that is born) the Prince of Peace.' Thus, the verse does not say that the Prince of Peace will be another name for God."

***You Take Jesus, I'll Take God*, by Samuel Levine, p. 54; © 1980. [ ] mine**

AUTHOR'S COMMENT—EVANGELICAL CHRISTIAN POSITION

With all due respect to Mr. Levine, if he is going to criticize Isaiah's Messianic prophecy using the New Testament, he should take the time to fully inform himself. Though Jesus may not have been called all these titles in His day, He is projected to be just who Isaiah proclaims in the future, as the Angel Gabriel affirmed to Jesus'

---

[17]Rev. B. Pick, Ph.D., *Old Testament Passages Messianically Applied by the Ancient Synagogue*, published in the compilation *Hebraica, A Quarterly Journal in the Interests of Semitic Study*, Vol. III, p. 35.

mother Mary, as recorded in Luke 1 in the New Testament. Revelation 22:6 assures us that the Messianic Kingdom of Jesus will soon take place. Apparently Levine knows this prophecy in question is about the Second Coming, otherwise why would he have mentioned it?! I assure you there is not any "weakness" in that (see our chapters 26-30 for details on the Second Coming). Jesus pointed out that His Messianic Kingdom was postponed because He was rejected (see Matthew 23:37-39). It will only begin when He is accepted by the Jews. Lastly, Levine mentions that Jewish commentaries retranslate this passage. We have not seen them and he does not go to the trouble to name them, if they exist. Even if they did, that would only prove our point regarding the rabbis' cover-up of the Messianic prophecies. The Jewish Targum clearly refers to the Messiah in this passage, a claim that Jesus fulfilled (Luke 24:42; John 4:26).

Philip Moore

SEAPORT—AND VISITORS OF PEACE

After Jesus executes His judgment on the Antichrist and the false prophet, and makes preliminary plans to establish the kingdom, the Mount of Olives, which sheltered the Jews, will continue to split. Since the Mount of Olives is part of the Great Rift which runs from Syria to Lake Tanganyika in Africa, Hal Lindsey points out that a shift accompanying the Coming of the Messiah could connect the Mediterranean Sea and the Dead Sea, thus creating a seaport in Jerusalem.[18]

For the first time in history, Jerusalem will have a seaport. The purpose of this seaport will be to accommodate ships arriving from the nations of the world. According to Zechariah 14:16, all nations during the 1000-year reign of Messiah Jesus, will visit annually and pay homage to Him. They will be very thankful that He finally returned and brought peace to this old Earth, which previously had known so much war and so little peace.

EARLIER CURSES REMOVED—NO ONE WHO BELIEVES WILL EVER GO HUNGRY AGAIN

During this 1000-year reign, the Messiah will remove the curse which was placed on the ground after Adam chose to rebel against God (Gen. 3:23). Genesis 3:17-19 tells us that the ground was cursed as punishment for man, so that hard work would be required to wrest a living from it. He was to sweat, and today, is still toiling the ground by the sweat of his brow to provide what he needs to live; food, shelter and security.

Currently, all men[19] must "toil" as doctors, lawyers, fire fighters, carpenters, farmers, and so on, to provide what he calls his "bread

---

[18]Noted by Hal Lindsey during a 1984 tour of the Holy Land.

[19]All except those who inherit their parents' hard-earned properties, or those who are on welfare. In this awkward arrangement, the government confiscates the liquid work assets

money," which is necessary to purchase the essentials for life. During the time of the millennium, we will once again receive these essentials of life, as we did in the Garden of Eden before the fall of Adam, as a gift.

Ancient rabbis agree with what the Bible has to say about this: "R. Y'huda said: 'In This World the crops ripen in six months, and a tree yields fruit in twelve months, but in the Future to Come the crops will ripen every month....' R. Yose said: '...In the Future to Come the crops will ripen in fifteen days, and the trees yield fruit every month.' "[20]

The New Testament says: "And he showed me a pure river of water of life, clear as crystal, proceeding out of the throne of God and of the Lamb. In the midst of the street of it, and on either side of the river, *was there* the tree of life, which bore twelve *kinds of* fruits, *and* yielded her fruit every month; and the leaves of the tree *were* for the healing of the nations" (Rev. 22:1-2 KJV).[21]

To be able to harvest fruit from trees every month without fertilizing or "toiling" with them, as the Bible puts it, will be a real change for man; an alternative that he has not known for the past 6000 years. We will devote our time to enjoying the kingdom the Lord will bring, instead of toiling the earth. There will be peace and equality for all.[22]

WHICH BELIEVERS RULE WHICH CITIES? POSITIONS OF POWER

Those who presently do not believe in Jesus, but survive the Tribulation and become[23] believers after the Rapture, through the ministry of the 144,000 Jewish evangelists, will enter the kingdom of mortals. They will become subjects and at the end of the 1000 years, will receive their new and glorified bodies (Rev. 20:22). Those who

---

(money) of others in the form of "taxes," by force, allocating it to those who are too lazy or unable to work (while we believe in voluntary charity and donations to the disabled, we are sceptical of forced government programs). The only other way is stealing, which of course, profits from the work of others. Work is the bottom line until....

[20]Raphael Patai, *The Messiah Texts*, pp. 231-232. Patai's source was *Y. Sheqalim 50a Midrash.*

[21]*The New Scofield Reference Bible.*

[22]See our comparison pages in chapters 29-30 for details of these biblical promises and Jewish interpretive confirmation of them through recently published ancient rabbinical text.

[23]If prophecy proves satisfactory to you that Jesus is the Messiah, it would be wise to accept Him into your heart now, because not all of us can count on the future. To put it off is almost like playing Russian roulette. We say this because the New Testament predicts many will be blinded at the Rapture. Those who have not believed will be allowed to believe a lie, as Thessalonians predicts: "And for this cause God shall send them strong delusion, that they should believe a lie...." (II Thes. 2:11 KJV).

presently believe, or come to believe prior to the Rapture, will enter this kingdom as administrators, having already received new eternal bodies (I Cor. 15:50; II Thes. 4:16-17; Rev. 19; Matt. 19:28).

During the millennium, Jesus said certain of us would be "rulers over cities" (Luke 19:17). We shall be appointed into these administrative positions as immortals, after we return with Jesus to Earth.

In our last chapters, 29-30, we will cover in detail, different interesting and pleasant aspects of the millennial and eternal kingdoms yet to come—after we backtrack and review a bit!

When Jesus returns we will finally have peace.

"For I know *that* my redeemer liveth, and *that* he shall stand at the latter *day* upon the earth: And *though* after my skin *worms* destroy this *body*, yet in my flesh shall I see God...."
The book of Job 19:25-27 KJV, 1520 BC

"Thy dead *men* shall live, *together with* my dead body shall they arise. Awake and sing, ye that dwell in dust: for thy dew is as the dew of herbs, and the earth shall cast out the dead."
The prophet Isaiah 26:19 KJV, 712 BC

"And many of them that sleep in the dust of the earth shall awake, some to everlasting life, and some to shame *and* everlasting contempt. And they that be wise shall shine as the brightness of the firmament; and they that turn many to righteousness as the stars for ever and ever."
The Hebrew captive, Daniel, 12:2-3 KJV, 534 BC

"And the LORD shall be king over all the earth: in that day shall there be one LORD, and his name one."
The prophet Zechariah, 14:9 KJV, 487 BC

"And shall come forth; they that have done good, unto the resurrection of life; and they that have done evil, unto the resurrection of damnation....And this is the Father's will which hath sent me, that of all which he hath given me I should lose nothing, but should raise it up again at the last day. And this is the will of him that sent me, that every one which seeth the Son, and believeth on him, may have everlasting life: and I will raise him up at the last day."
Messiah Jesus, John 5:29; 6:39-40 KJV, spoken 31 AD

29

AFTER THE MESSIAH ARRIVES AND ENDS THE WAR—PARADISE!

Many philosophies and religions alike teach that there is no bodily resurrection, only a lonesome wandering spirit which floats around after a person dies. We of course, as true believers in the Bible and its unique proofs of prophecy, know better! Both our Old and New Testaments lavishly illustrate a beautiful kingdom which God and His Messiah Jesus will create. This kingdom will be created for our bodies (John 14:1-3),[1] which will be resurrected and transformed into an eternal state of permanence, in which to live forever.

The resurrection and eternal existence in this new kingdom is the central point of all that God promises in the Bible.[2] Jesus will

---

[1]Jesus comforted His disciples: "Let not your heart be troubled; believe in God, believe also in Me. In My Father's house are many dwelling places; if it were not so, I would have told you; for I go to prepare a place for you. And if I go and prepare a place for you, I will come again, and receive you to Myself; that where I am, *there* you may be also" (John 14:1-3 NASB).

[2]While there are liberal theologians who deny this, we need only to direct them to Paul's New Testament words: "Now if Christ be preached that he rose from the dead, how say some among you that there is no resurrection of the dead? But if there be no resurrection

inaugurate redemption in this soon coming Messianic Kingdom, thus restoring us and the earth to a state **even better** than the Garden of Eden. We will regain the rights to all that we lost[3] in Genesis 3, when our first parents fell in Eden, and more.

THOUGH SOME DOUBT THE RESURRECTION, ATTEMPTING TO BASE THEIR BELIEF ON "SCIENCE," SIR ISAAC NEWTON, THE GREATEST OF SCIENTISTS, BELIEVED IN IT!

The central feature of this redemption is the resurrection of the dead! Some may snicker, however they should bear in mind that all the prophecies regarding the First Coming of Jesus and the troublesome Middle East Crisis have occurred literally, not figuratively.

Sir Isaac Newton, the greatest scientist of all time, who lived in the seventeenth century, was eternally right when he instructed us: "Let me therefore beg of thee not to trust to the opinion of any man concerning these things....search the scriptures thy self....if thou desirest to find the truth. Which if thou shalt at length attain thou wilt value above all other treasures....search into the scriptures which God hath given to be a guide...and be not discouraged by the gainsaying which these things will meet with in the world....the world loves to be deceived, they will not understand, they never consider equally, but are wholly led by prejudice, interest, the praise of men....Wherefore when thou art convinced be not ashamed of the truth but profess it openly

---

of the dead, then is Christ not risen: And if Christ be not risen, then *is* our preaching vain, and your faith *is* also vain. Yea, and we are found false witnesses of God; because we have testified of God that he raised up Christ: whom he raised not up, if so be that the dead rise not. For if the dead rise not, then is not Christ raised: And if Christ be not raised your faith *is* **vain**....Then they also who are fallen asleep in Christ are **perished**. If in this life only we have hope in Christ, we are of all men **most miserable**" (I Cor. 15:12-19 KJV). Thus we all long in our hearts, those of us who believe, for our new resurrection bodies promised to us in the New Testament book of Romans: "For we know that even the things of nature, like animals and plants, suffer in sickness and death as they await this great event. And even we Christians, although we have the Holy Spirit within us as a foretaste of future glory, also groan to be released from pain and suffering. We, too, wait anxiously for that day when God will give us our full rights as his children, including the new bodies he has promised us—bodies that will never be sick again and will never die. We are saved by trusting. And trusting means looking forward to getting something we do not yet have—for a man who already has something doesn't need to hope and trust that he will get it. But if we must keep trusting God for something that hasn't happened yet, it teaches us to wait patiently and confidently" (Rom. 8:22-24 *The Living Bible*).

[3]See our comparison list of prophecies and rabbinical commentary in chapter 1, which proves that in the "original sin," we **lost** much that we will regain. Some rabbis state that this teaching is unique to the New Testament, but it is not, as we proved in our chapter 1.

and indeavour to convince thy Brother also that thou mayst inherit at the resurrection the promis made in Daniel 12.3, that they who turn many to righteousness shall shine as the starrs for ever and ever. And rejoyce if thou art counted worthy to suffer in thy reputation or any other way for the sake of the Gospel, for then great is thy reward."[4]

Let's not let anyone try to cheat us out of our resurrection promise, which Jesus maintained would be a physical resurrection when He said: "Do not marvel at this; for an hour is coming, in which all who are in the tombs shall hear His voice, and shall come forth; those who did the good *deeds*, to a resurrection of life...." (John 5:28-29 NASB).

JOB AND JESUS TELL IT (THE RESURRECTION) LIKE IT IS (LITERAL), NO MATTER HOW MUCH LIBERALS DISLIKE IT

In the Bible's Old Testament, Job proclaimed 4000 years ago: "For I know *that* my redeemer liveth, and *that* he shall stand at the latter *day* upon the earth: And *though* after my skin *worms* destroy this *body*, yet in my flesh shall I see God" (Job 19:25-26 KJV).

It should be noted that some liberal "scholars" try to say resurrection is a recent idea. However, they either choke or change the subject when you quote this verse to them, and remind them that Job is among the oldest books of the Bible; perhaps the oldest!

Job, under the prophetic inspiration of God, could not have made himself more clear in these verses, could he? Jesus, the very Messiah Himself—God in the flesh—made the strongest statement about bodily resurrection in the New Testament: "For as the Father hath life in himself; so hath he given to the Son to have life in himself; And hath given him authority to execute judgment also, because he is the Son of man. Marvel not at this: for the hour is coming, in the which all that are in the graves shall hear his voice, And shall come forth; they that have done good, unto the resurrection of life; and they that have done evil, unto the resurrection of damnation" (John 5:26-29 KJV).

***

---

[4]*Yahuda Manuscript 1.*

ORIGINAL HEBREW TEXT WRITTEN 534 BC

וְרַבִּים מִיְּשֵׁנֵי אַדְמַת־עָפָר יָקִיצוּ אֵלֶּה לְחַיֵּי עוֹלָם וְאֵלֶּה לַחֲרָפוֹת לְדִרְאוֹן עוֹלָם׃
וְהַמַּשְׂכִּלִים יַזְהִרוּ כְּזֹהַר הָרָקִיעַ וּמַצְדִּיקֵי הָרַבִּים כַּכּוֹכָבִים לְעוֹלָם וָעֶד׃

דניאל יב:ב-ג

OLD TESTAMENT SCRIPTURE TRANSLATION

"And many of those who sleep in the dust of the ground will awake, these to everlasting life, but the others to disgrace *and* everlasting contempt. And those who have insight will shine brightly like the brightness of the expanse of heaven, and those who lead the many to righteousness, like the stars forever and ever."

Daniel 12:2-3 NASB

ANCIENT RABBINICAL COMMENTARY

"R. 'Azaria said: 'The Holy One, blessed be He, opens the graves and opens the storehouses of the souls and puts back each soul into its own body....' "[5]

Pirqe R. Eliezer, ch. 34

"Rabbi [Y'huda haNasi] said....the Holy One, blessed be He, too, will bring the soul, cast it into the body, and judge them as one."[6]

B. Sanhedrin 91a-b

NEW TESTAMENT RECORDED 31 AD

"Do not marvel at this; for an hour is coming, in which all who are in the tombs shall hear His voice, and shall come forth; those who did the good *deeds* to a resurrection of life, those who committed the evil *deeds* to a resurrection of judgment." **John 5:28-29 NASB**

MODERN RABBINIC COMMENT/REFUTATION

"However, the life after which there is no death is the life of the World to Come, in which there is no body. For we believe it, and it is the truth [held] by all those who have a mind, that the World to Come is souls without bodies, like the angels."[7]

***Treatise on Resurrection*, by Maimonides, p. 17**

AUTHOR'S COMMENT—EVANGELICAL CHRISTIAN POSITION

Again, we have Maimonides (Rambam—Rabbi Moshe ben Maimon), who presently has many admirers and followers, advocating an off-the-wall, controversial, contrived position, contrary to the Bible's promise of resurrection. The Scriptures promise that we will receive bodies at the resurrection in which our souls will reside during the eternal world to come.

Philip Moore

WILL WE RECOGNIZE EACH OTHER BEFORE THE RESURRECTION?

Some ask, "Do we have *recognizable* bodies after we die and during eternity, or are we just lonesome spirits?" While many cults teach soul sleep and that we will become just a spirit of some sort, we

---

[5]Raphael Patai, *The Messiah Texts*, p. 202.

[6]Ibid, p. 219.

[7]Ibid, p. 206. While Maimonides lived in the thirteenth century, he originated this modern rabbinical view.

as Bible believers know, even before we are resurrected, that we retain a recognizable spiritual body. We know this from Matthew 17:1-3, where 1700 years after Moses physically died, he and Elijah were seen in beautiful radiating **recognizable** bodies, with Jesus on the Mount of Transfiguration. A comforting thought, isn't it?!

UNDERSTANDING WHAT HAPPENS BETWEEN DEATH AND THE RESURRECTION

Here, we should take some space to clarify some misunderstood details about soul sleep, resurrection, Heaven and Hell, which vary in their dispensations.

Once death occurs, the soul of the person leaves the body through the mouth. The body begins to deteriorate and rigor mortis sets in. Thereafter, the body decomposes into the dust from which it was taken, as God promised would happen as a consequence of the Fall: "In the sweat of thy face shalt thou eat bread, till thou return unto the ground; for out of it wast thou taken: for dust *thou* art, and unto dust shalt thou return" (Gen. 3:19 KJV). That is, until the resurrection predicted by Daniel and Jesus occurs (Dan. 12:2; John 5:28-29).[8]

The soul, upon its departure, continues its eternal existence which began at conception in the womb (Ps. 139:14-15, 24). It continues in a constant state of consciousness, either with the Lord or in a state of agony separated from Him. Whether the soul ends up in Paradise or Hell depends on a person's decision to accept God's sacrificial provisions for redemption.

God always provided a sacrifice for those who would receive it. Prior to the Messiah, there was a long line of sacrifices, from the Garden of Eden, to Passover, to the Temple, to Yom Kippur. All of these foreshadowed the Messiah's fulfilled work, until Jesus, Himself, came and died for us in our place, providing our forgiveness. God clearly said there is no remission of sins (redemption) without the shedding of blood, in the Jewish Old Testament book of Leviticus: "... for it is the blood by reason of the life that makes atonement" (Lev. 17:11 NASB).

***

[8]Except for some very rare cases in which doctors have been able to revive dead people through cardiac resuscitation. Some of these people, who were clearly dead and had no heartbeat or brain activity for a number of minutes, reported startling stories of seeing Jesus or experiencing unbelievable Hell. For a fuller explanation on the subject of near death experiences, correctly called temporary death experiences, see our appendix 2, "Life After Death Experiences That People Have Lived to Tell About." In this appendix, we quote doctors who published interviews with their patients who experienced this. One doctor even retrieved first-hand testimony from a patient on the operating table.

Concerning where those who died went before Jesus' Coming to be and seal all sacrifices of past and future, the Old Testament spoke of Sheol, and the New Testament, of Hades. Some have mistakenly thought that these were Hell and were for eternal punishment only. This is not true. Both Sheol and Hades were the same place, where all people went—both the redeemed and the unredeemed (by their own choice)—before Jesus rose from the dead.

Hades had two chambers. One chamber contained Paradise, also called "Abraham's bosom," where the people who believed in God's blood sacrifice went; and another compartment called "Torments" where those who rejected God's blood provision were, and still are, deposited.

The New Testament tells us that there was a great gulf between these two areas, which allowed none to move across, only to see across. "And in hell he lift up his eyes, being in torments, and seeth Abraham afar off, and Lazarus in his bosom. And he cried and said, Father Abraham, have mercy on me, and send Lazarus, that he may dip the tip of his finger in water, and cool my tongue; for I am tormented in this flame. But Abraham said, Son....between us and you there is a great gulf fixed: so that they which would pass from hence to you cannot; neither can they pass to us, that *would come* from thence" (Luke 16:23-26 KJV).

WHAT HAPPENED WHEN JESUS VISITED HADES?

It is written that when Jesus died at the crucifixion He went down into Hell (Hades) and into the Paradise portion of Hades. He then stated that the promised redemption, which all of these people anticipated with their blood sacrifices and faith, was now an accomplished reality through His death. He also endured Torments, the place where He preached to those spirits who had rejected God's loving plan for an innocent to take our punishment by shedding His blood as an atonement (I Pet. 3:19).

It should be noted that the word Peter uses, "preached," in the original Bible language, means to "announce" and not to attempt to "convert," as Mormons believe. The Scriptures clearly teach that a man dies once, and is then judged (Heb. 9:27). No reincarnation or second chance is even hinted at in our Judeo/Christian Bible. Jesus announced to the individuals within this second chamber of Hades that they had made the wrong decision in not accepting God's loving gifts of sacrifice through faith. As a result, there was no doubt about the fact that they had lost their chance for redemption and condemned themselves to eternal punishment.

Jesus, Himself, told the thief on the cross beside Him, who changed his mind and believed[9] in Him, that he would be in Paradise! As the apostle Luke related: "And he [the thief] said unto Jesus, **Lord**, remember me when thou comest into thy kingdom. And Jesus said unto him, Verily I say unto thee, To day shalt thou be with me in paradise" (Luke 23:42-43 KJV; [ ] and bold mine).

When the thief called Jesus *Lord,* it was clear that he had changed his mind about Jesus. He had accepted Him as Messiah and redeemer!

JESUS LIBERATES THE CAPTIVES IN HADES' PARADISE COMPARTMENT

This travel to Hell occurred while the body of Jesus still lay in the tomb. When His resurrection and ascension into Heaven took place, He took all the souls in the Paradise chamber of Hades into Heaven above with Him. "But unto every one of us is given grace according to the measure of the gift of Christ. Wherefore he saith, When he ascended up on high, he led captivity captive, and gave gifts unto men. (Now that he ascended, what is it but that he also descended first into the lower parts of the earth? He that descended is the same also that ascended up far above all heavens, that he might fill all things)" (Eph. 4:7-10 KJV).

These events were also foreseen 1000 years earlier in King David's biblical book of Psalms. He prophesied: "Thou hast ascended on high, thou hast led captivity captive, thou hast received gifts for men...." (Ps. 68:18 KJV).

Now, since the First Coming of Jesus and His resurrection, all those who believe are taken to be face-to-face with Jesus in the heavens above: "For now we see | in a mirror |, darkly; but then, face to face; now I know in part, but then shall I know [Him] even as also I am known" (I Cor. 13:12 KJV; [ ] mine).[10]

We are told in the Scriptures that to be absent from our bodies is to be instantly present with the Lord, which is far better (II Cor. 5:8; Phil. 1:21-23)!

OUR MORTAL BODIES ARE REFORMED INTO IMMORTAL HAPPINESS AT THE RAPTURE

The body of a person may be buried, cremated, mutilated by a catastrophe or even disintegrated in a ship like the famed Titanic in the

---

[9]That he believed in Jesus is indicated clearly by verse 42. The designation of Jesus as "Lord" is evidence of this.

[10]*The New Scofield Reference Bible.*

depths of the ocean; however, when the Rapture occurs (as you read about earlier in our chapter 25, "The Rapture Factor"), a person's body is reunited with their soul, never again to be separated. This new reunion of body and soul is unique in that our new bodies (spoken of in Romans) will have four "no-mores." The New Testament book of Revelation tells us: "He will wipe every tear from their eyes. There will be no more death or mourning or crying or pain, for the old order of things has passed away" (Rev. 21:4 NIV).

THOSE OF YOU WHO DO NOT BELIEVE, STILL HAVE A CHANCE TO GET IN ON THE *ETERNAL* ASPECT OF THE REST OF YOUR LIFE

The soul of every person in every period of history, who dies rejecting God's love gift of sacrifice, will go to Torments. This includes Cain, those who reverted to paganism between Adam and Abraham, those who rejected the Jewish Temple sacrifice, those in Egypt who did not put the lamb's blood on the door, and those who now say, "The death of Jesus is meaningless and I do not want forgiveness or redemption from any part of it."

There they will all remain until the end of the 1000-year Messianic Kingdom, when they will be reunited with their suffering bodies of shame. Daniel spoke of the resurrection of everlasting contempt: "...there shall be a time of trouble, such as never was since there was a nation *even* to that same time: and at that time thy people shall be delivered, every one that shall be found written in the book. And many of them that sleep in the dust of the earth shall awake, some to everlasting life, and some to shame *and* everlasting contempt" (Dan. 12:1-2 KJV).

Jesus spoke of the resurrection of life and damnation: "...the hour is coming, in the which all that are in the graves shall hear his voice, And shall come forth; they that have done good, unto the resurrection of life; and they that have done evil, unto the resurrection of damnation" (John 5:28-29 KJV).

The two modes of resurrection are made very clear by both Hebrew sages, Daniel and Jesus, who have never been wrong in their prophecies. Do we dare take them lightly or neglect God's precious love gift of Jesus' death for us, while we still draw breath and have the opportunity to receive it?[11]

---

[11]If you want to receive Jesus' eternal gift of forgiveness, say a simple prayer to Him. Admit your wrongs and accept His death in your place for all the wrongs you have and will perpetrate, inviting Him into your heart (Rev. 3:20; Rom. 10:9). You will then be removed from eternal judgment and be given eternal life. Paul tells us in the New

Testament that by believing He arose from the dead and confessing Him, we will be saved. In his very words: "That if thou shalt confess with thy mouth the Lord Jesus, and shalt believe in thine heart that God hath raised him from the dead, thou shalt be saved" (Rom. 10:9 KJV). See Philip Moore, *Eternal Security for True Believers.* This mention of good and evil (in John 5:28-29) is, in the original language, preceeded by **the**—*the* good, *the* evil; singular. The only truly evil thing a person can do is to reject the Messiah who died for *all* their evil. The only truly good thing a person can do is to *receive* the Messiah's death in their place as payment for all of their evils.

A memorial for the victims of the Holocaust, at Yad VaShem, in Jerusalem, Israel.

An Israeli mother weeps over the grave of her eighteen-year-old son, killed in battle. This picture clearly illustrates that if there is no resurrection, as liberals teach, then we live in utter hopelessness. This picture helps us appreciate the promises the Bible gives us concerning resurrection.

RESURRECTION AND RAMBAM—THE WHO, WHAT AND WHY OF THE ATTEMPTED RESURRECTION COVER-UP

Rabbi Moshe ben Maimon (Rambam) changed the already reconstructed rabbinical view of the Jewish Messiah, even more radically, ten centuries after the changes made at Yavne. He did this to build a wall around "Judaism" and keep Jews who believed in Jesus as Messiah outside that wall. What Rambam did was make a radical change in the traditional biblical view of resurrection! The Bible always taught that the Messiah would be the one who would raise the dead; the ancient rabbis agreed on this point in many important commentaries and writings.[12] Rambam changed this view, and attempted to universalize his own "new" ideas within "Judaism." Why would he do a thing like that? What possible motive could he have had?

It is interesting to see that after Jesus met the conditions elaborated upon by the Bible and ancient rabbinical authorities, Rambam and other rabbis simply attempted to change the tasks which the Messiah had always been understood to fulfill. Jesus fulfilled over three hundred prophecies in His First Coming and promised to fulfill the remaining prophecies upon His return, when Israel, as a nation, accepts Him as Messiah. This will occur when Jesus wins Israel's great future battle, known as Gog and Magog (Armageddon—Ezek. 38; Rev. 16:16; Matt. 24:22).

Jesus made very specific solemn promises about resurrecting the dead. One of the promises was: "...this is the Father's will which hath

---

[12]A *Time* magazine article entitled "Is Jesus in the Dead Sea Scrolls?" illustrates certain tasks the Messiah was to accomplish and compares them with the text of the Dead Sea Scrolls and portions of Jesus' New Testament record. The article portrays Luke 7:20-23 beside the recently released Dead Sea Scroll text 4Q521, which reads: "Surely the Lord shall visit the pious and shall call the righteous by name. His spirit shall hover over the poor; by his strength he shall renew the faithful. He shall glorify the pious upon the throne of the eternal kingdom. He shall release the captives, restore sight to the blind, make straight those who are bent double...He shall heal the wounded, **resurrect** the dead, preach glad tidings to the poor." An interesting portion of the article, connecting Jesus to the Jewish Messiah's resurrecting role, mentions: "...the scrolls do speak of the coming Jewish Messiah....Two of the fragments made newly available in the *Review's* photo books are especially striking....the most important phrases are clear. Apparently referring to the coming Messiah, the text declares that he will 'heal the wounded, resurrect the dead [and] preach glad tidings to the poor.' The passage closely resembles the words of Jesus in the Nazareth synagogue (Luke 4)....[James] Tabor [of the University of North Carolina at Charlotte] notes that Jesus spoke virtually the same words about resurrection in *Luke 7* when John the Baptist asked for proof that he was the Messiah. This, Tabor says, is the closest parallel yet found between the Dead Sea Scrolls and the recorded words of Jesus." Richard N. Ostling, contributor, "Is Jesus in the Dead Sea Scrolls?" *Time*, © Sept. 21, 1992, reprinted by permission. [ ] mine.

sent me, that of all which he hath given me I should lose nothing, but should raise it up again at the last day. And this is the will of him that sent me, that every one which seeth the Son, and believeth on him, may have everlasting life: and I will raise him up at the last day" (John 6:39-40 KJV).

Jesus' promise firmly supports Job's Old Testament words: "For I know *that* my redeemer liveth, and *that* he shall stand at the latter *day* upon the earth: And *though* after my skin *worms* destroy this *body*, yet in my flesh shall I see God...." (Job 19:25-26 KJV).

I believe Rabbi Maimon had Jesus' words in mind when he attempted to lead the Jewish population away from the bodily resurrection which was to be accomplished by the Messiah. Rabbi Maimon says: "...think not that the Messiah must perform signs and portents and bring about new things in the world, or that he will resuscitate the dead, or the like. Not so" (Hilkhot M'lakhim 11-12).[13]

IF YOU CAN'T TAKE JESUS OUT OF THE OLD TESTAMENT, YOU HAD BETTER TAKE THE OLD TESTAMENT OUT OF JESUS

It is rather convenient, isn't it? If you cannot change Jesus' fulfillment of past prophecies and future promises, you can just say the Messiah was never meant to suffer and fulfill Isaiah 53, nor was He ever to return and raise the dead. Thus, as people no longer have these specific expectations of Messiah, He is not as easily recognized.

This ingenious technique of blinding the Jew was applied in an attempt to curb assimilation. However, we must remember, when Jews accept their Messiah (Jesus) today, they are much more proud of being a Jew, a Messianic Jew, who threw off those old rusty chains of modern rabbinical Judaism for the fresh vitality of biblical Judaism. After all, the Bible is the document which originally recorded the life of the first Jew, Abraham, and his history, as a standard for what Judaism is. If at any time, the rabbis begin to deviate from the Bible, they are teaching a false religion under the name of Judaism, which absolutely, in our opinion, should not be accepted as Judaism.

***

[13]Raphael Patai, *The Messiah Texts*, p. 324. Though other texts purported to be his seem to look forward to the resurrection, this one is for sure and clearly against a Messianic resurrection. It denies the Messiah would bring about this resurrection supernaturally, as Judaism historically taught and maintained!

"I beheld till the thrones were cast down, and the Ancient of days did sit, whose garment *was* white as snow, and the hair of his head like the pure wool: his throne *was like* the fiery flame, *and* his wheels *as* burning fire. A fiery stream issued and came forth from before him: thousand thousands ministered unto him, and ten thousand times ten thousand stood before him: the judgment was set, and **the books were opened**. I beheld then because of the voice of the great words which the horn spake: I beheld *even* till the beast was slain, and his body destroyed, and given to the burning flame." Daniel 7:9-11 KJV. Bold mine

"And I saw a great white throne, and him that sat on it, from whose face the earth and the heaven fled away; and there was found no place for them. And I saw the dead, small and great, stand before God; and **the books were opened**: and another book was opened, which is *the book* of life: and the dead were judged out of those things which were written in the books, according to their works. And the sea gave up the dead which were in it; and death and hell delivered up the dead which were in them: and they were judged every man according to their works. And death and hell were cast into the lake of fire. This is the second death. And whosoever was not found written in the book of life was cast into the lake of fire."

Revelation 20:11-15 KJV. Bold mine

The apostle John and prophet Daniel give very vivid and, for the unbeliever, frightening accounts of future prophetic occurrences, resurrections and judgments. At this point, we as believers, can certainly say, "It pays!" As we read Daniel and John's ancient parchments above, we probably wondered about the details, and especially about the books mentioned therein! That is, if we are believers; if not, maybe it is better not to read on.

THE BOOK OF LAW

Which books are the apostle John and the Hebrew prophet Daniel talking about? The books of law, works and life. At the great white throne of judgment, we believe that the first of the books to be opened will be the book of the law.[14] In several biblical verses, the written word of God is called "the book of the law." This book will be used to illustrate to millions that anyone who has heard or read God's law must keep it perfectly, or accept the consequences of judgment, unless they received God's mercy through the sacrifices before Jesus came or Jesus' *perfect salvation* (Isa. 53) itself once He did come. Of course, once Jesus paid the penalty for all who have broken the law, He fulfilled the final sacrifice! The New Testament book of Galatians makes this clear: "CURSED IS EVERYONE WHO DOES NOT ABIDE BY ALL THINGS WRITTEN IN THE BOOK OF THE LAW....Christ redeemed us from

---

[14]Deuteronomy 28:58, 61; 29:20-21, 27; 30:10; 31:24, 26; Joshua 1:8; 8:31, 34; 23:6; II Kings 14:6; 22:8, 11; II Chronicles 17:9; 34:15; Nehemiah 8:1, 3, 8, 18; 9:3 and; Galatians 3:10.

the curse of the Law, having become a curse for us...." (Gal. 3:10, 13 NASB).

To those who will claim a lack of knowledge of God's law, it will be shown that God placed the knowledge of good and evil within their conscience (Rom. 2:11-16). By not always following their "good" conscience, without the Messiah's blood atonement, they will find themselves in a position of perilous judgment.

WHAT ABOUT THE PAGAN IN AFRICA?

At this point, we should say that there have been many instances throughout history whereby anyone desiring to receive God's salvation has been shown many times, through miraculous circumstances, who and what Jesus was, in order that they may receive Him.

A friend[15] of mine once told me of an African chief who had realized that his idols were not really God. He was on his knees daily asking to be shown the truth of the true God. Then this chief had a series of dreams of a man with nail-scarred hands who told him, "I am the atonement for your evils." A few days later a group of missionaries passed through his village. When he told them of his dream through their interpreter, they told him of Jesus and gave him a New Testament in his own language. Once he read the life story of Jesus, he was so impressed that he, and the majority of this group of African natives, became devout followers of the Jewish Messiah. This shows one thing; if anyone wants to know God's truth, He will move Heaven and Earth to get the correct information to them! This means there is no one who has wanted to hear that has not heard. They do not exist except in the minds of critics of the faith.

THE BOOK OF WORKS

The second book to be opened is called "the book of works." Today, some well-meaning ministers teach that if you are sincere and

[15]Reverend Jeff Williams, former pastor of Northside Park Baptist Church in Atlanta, is truly an incredible Christian. He was the one who prayed with me that the man who killed my father would be apprehended. After a year of no clues, within a week of our prayer together, the murderer, through a set of miraculous circumstances, was caught, and is still behind bars today—nineteen years later. This episode with Jeff helped me to answer the many people who asked me, "Have you ever seen God do a miracle in your life? Has God ever answered a prayer?" Jeff presently ministers at Lebanon Community Fellowship in Lebanon, VA, USA. Also, I will never forget my school teacher, Mrs. Parko, who once wrote me when I was only fifteen, saying, "I pray to God every night that things will work out for you." Shortly thereafter, I became a Christian, and so far, everything has worked out (Rom. 8:28). By praying for others you edify yourself and bless those for whom you pray.

do many good deeds, this is enough to salvage you into forgiveness and eternal bliss.

Clearly, Jesus taught that works don't cut it. He said there would be only two catergories of people standing before His judgement throne: those that have done *the evil*[16] (there is only one evil that is unforgivable and that is rejecting the one who has paid the price for all evil deeds), and those who have done the good[17] (the only truly good thing a person can do is to accept the penalty Jesus paid in your place, which forgives all sin past and future). Thus, those who will boast of their works will be shown that, no matter how many good deeds they performed, they cannot erase those evil things which only the atoning death of Jesus can erase. Thus judgment falls and they are not allowed into a kingdom which they have no key to enter—Jesus.

Jesus is the key to the kingdom. The Jewish Bible and Jesus both taught that, aside from those who are forgiven, all deeds will be exposed and judged in the end (Ecc. 12:14; Matt. 12:36).

THE BOOK OF LIFE

The book of life[18] contains the names[19] of every human being who was ever conceived,[20] including all those who have not reached the age of accountability[21] and died without receiving the forgiveness of Jesus, and those who received the mark of the beast (Antichrist) in the Tribulation. However, their names will be removed immediately upon their acceptance of this false Messiah's economic/spiritual

---

[16]This is the literal translation, singular, of Jesus' words recorded in the Gospel of John (I John 5:29).

[17]Ibid.

[18]The book of life is mentioned in Philippians 4:3, and Revelation 3:5; 20:12, 15; 21:27; 22:19, as the book containing the names of all who are redeemed. The book of life is also mentioned in Jewish holidays, ceremonies and throughout the ancient rabbinical writings. In Hebrew, it is known as *Sefer Hayyim.* We documented earlier that it was mentioned in the Birkat ha Minim, a curse used to excommunicate Jewish Christians of the first and second centuries from their synagogues. The BHM was a curse primarily due to the phrase, "May they (Jewish-Christians) be erased from the *book of life.*" G. Alon, *The Jews in Their Land in the Talmudic Age*, p. 289.

[19]Those who were miscarriages or purposely killed by abortion and never given a name by their parents, have a name given by God.

[20]See our *Vol. II*, chapter 13, "Heaven and Abortion," on the eternal future existence of aborted children.

[21]This age varies with the intelligence of the person and their ability to distinguish good from evil. We should all ask and pray with our children to receive Jesus as soon as our children are able to understand! A man named Bill Gothard told me, "Draw a picture of a heart and a door within it, and tell the child, open the door and invite Jesus in to forgive." This is known as a childhood salvation and is, no doubt, wise. For in the course of time, existential philosophy, socialism, evolution, atheism and all the "isms" can blind people.

computer chip sell-out.[22] Thus, when God opens this book, as He sits upon His great white throne, the only names left are those who accepted the atonement of Jesus (He died for their wrongs and one cannot be tried twice for the same crime).

The story is told about the judge whose daughter committed the crime of murder. He stood up and asked to be executed in her place. He was executed and she was set free, because the crime required a "human life for a human life." "Eye for eye, tooth for tooth...." (Exo. 21:23-24 NASB).

No one who witnessed this was able to fathom such mercy. This is the case of Jesus, who is sitting on the judgment seat. He already paid for us, but we can only claim that redemptive sacrificial death if we receive it. If someone holds out ten dollars to you, it is not yours until you take it into your hand! Thus, at the judgment, this book only contains the names of those who have believed in Jesus. This is why its name was changed from the book of life to the *lamb's* book of life (Rev. 21:27). Jesus is our lamb (John 1:29, 36).

THE ORDER AND LOGIC OF THE BOOK OF JUDGMENTS

As we have seen, God first opens "the book of the law" and illustrates to all those who claim they kept the law, that this law was to be perfectly kept, and nothing short of perfection could merit forgiveness. He will explain that this is why the Messiah Himself came to keep the law perfectly and then die as an eternal atoning sacrifice for all those from Adam until **the end of history**. Thus, the law, without sacrificial payment, does not win Heaven (*olam haba* in Hebrew) and forgiveness. Secondly, God opens "the book of works" and shows the person all of their good deeds. He emphasizes that all of these deeds and works were not enough, especially when they fall short of what was demanded in the book of the law, since there was no blood sacrifice to intercede for and cover these offenses.

Finally, God opens "the book of life," which contains the names of all who inherit eternal life. He then shows the person (while wishing all the time that their name were there), that only the acceptance of the Messiah's righteous blood sacrifice for all their shortcomings prior to their death would have assured that their name remain inscribed. He will then remind the person of all those times

[22]To get this mark enabling you to buy and sell or even hold a job, you will have to worship or swear allegiance to the Antichrist, who is Satan in the flesh. It is also highly probable that this mark may be accompanied by a computer chip similar to those that are in today's Smart Cards, placed under the skin of your hand, or your forehead (if you are an amputee), as a means of credit, banking and general indentification.

true believers presented this beautiful opportunity of Messiah to them, then He will say with sadness, "Your name was removed when you died, rejecting My provision for you; thus, your name does not remain as it would have otherwise." Then his nail-scarred hands close the book and the Lord says with tears in His eyes: "...I never knew you; depart from me...ye cursed into everlasting fire" (Matt. 7:23; 25:41 KJV).[23]

The tomb of Rambam.

---

[23]See the evidence of the reality of Hell, as taught within ancient Judaism, which is shunned by most modern rabbis! Ancient Jews believed and wrote about Hell as Gehenna, though there are many within the modern rabbinical community who deny there ever was a theology of Hell within Judaism. See Philip Moore, *Nightmare of the Apocalypse*, Appendix 2, "The Reality of the Ancient Jewish Acknowledgment of Hell, Covered Up Until Now." This section also gives critical information on Rambam discouraging the reading of the end time Midrashim (Jewish commentaries) and his "proofs" that Jesus is not the Messiah. He once wrote: "You know that the Christians falsely ascribe marvelous powers to Jesus the Messiah, may his bones be ground to dust. We should not be convinced by their reality that Jesus is the Messiah for we can bring a 1,000 proofs from scripture that he is not." This rabbi's statement is, of course, untrue, as we have shown in the scriptural comparison charts on the Jewish view of the Messiah in Chapter 5. Rambam also attempted to apply the prophecies of the Antichrist (the yet to come false Messiah) in Daniel, to Jesus (see Abraham Halkin, trans., Crisis and Leadership: Epistles of Maimonides, New York: The Jewish Publication Society of America, 1985), which is the epitome of absurdity.

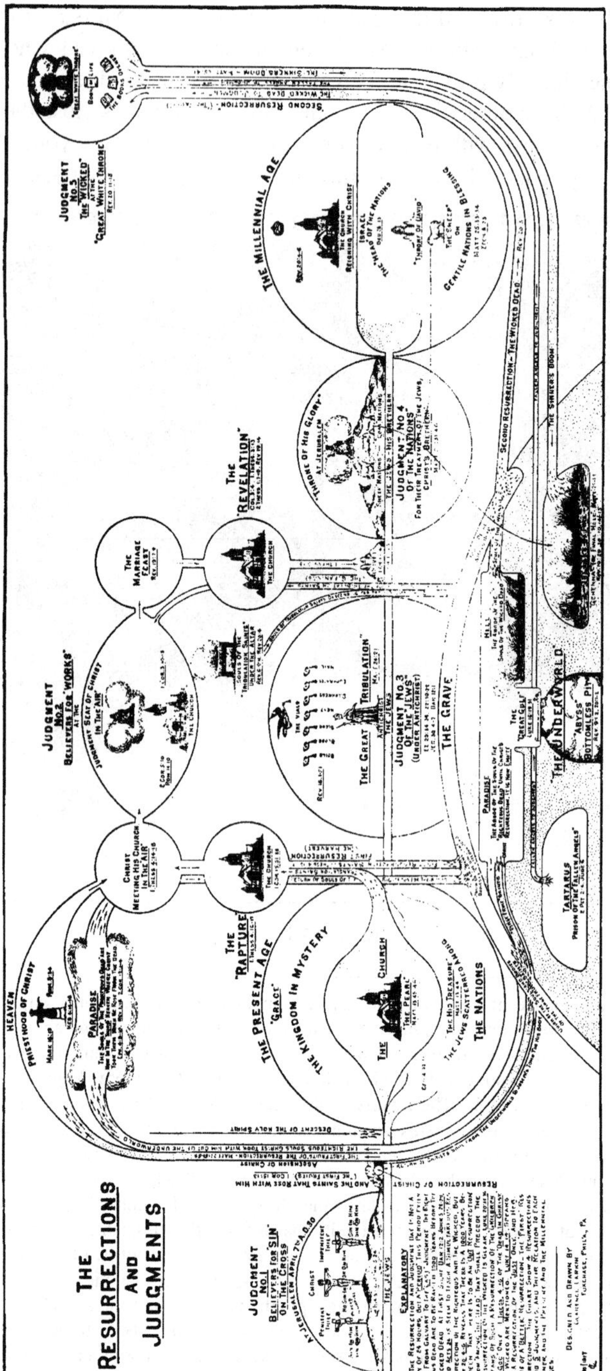
THE RESURRECTIONS AND JUDGMENTS
JUDGMENT No.1 BELIEVERS FOR SIN ON THE CROSS
THE PRESENT AGE
"GRACE"
THE KINGDOM IN MYSTERY
THE CHURCH
THE NATIONS
THE "RAPTURE"
CHRIST MEETING HIS CHURCH IN THE AIR
JUDGMENT No.2 BELIEVERS FOR "WORKS"
"JUDGMENT SEAT OF CHRIST" IN THE AIR
THE MARRIAGE FEAST
THE GREAT TRIBULATION
JUDGMENT No.3 OF THE JEWS
THE "REVELATION"
JUDGMENT No.4 OF THE NATIONS
THE MILLENNIAL AGE
JUDGMENT No.5 THE WICKED AT THE "GREAT WHITE THRONE"
THE GRAVE
PARADISE
THE "GREAT GULF"
THE UNDERWORLD
"ABYSS" BOTTOMLESS PIT
TARTARUS PRISON OF THE FALLEN ANGELS
SECOND RESURRECTION - THE WICKED DEAD
THE SINNER'S DOOM
HEAVEN
PRIESTHOOD OF CHRIST
EXPLANATORY
DESIGNED AND DRAWN BY CLARENCE LARKIN

ORIGINAL HEBREW TEXT WRITTEN 997, 713, 698 BC

טָבְעוּ גוֹיִם בְּשַׁחַת עָשׂוּ בְּרֶשֶׁת־זוּ טָמָנוּ נִלְכְּדָה רַגְלָם׃ נוֹדַע ׀ יְהוָה מִשְׁפָּט עָשָׂה בְּפֹעַל
כַּפָּיו נוֹקֵשׁ רָשָׁע הִגָּיוֹן סֶלָה׃ **תהלים ט:טו-טז**

וְנָמַקּוּ כָּל־צְבָא הַשָּׁמַיִם וְנָגֹלּוּ כַסֵּפֶר הַשָּׁמָיִם וְכָל־צְבָאָם יִבּוֹל כִּנְבֹל עָלֶה מִגֶּפֶן וּכְנֹבֶלֶת
מִתְּאֵנָה׃ .... וְיָצְאוּ וְרָאוּ בְּפִגְרֵי הָאֲנָשִׁים הַפֹּשְׁעִים בִּי כִּי תוֹלַעְתָּם לֹא תָמוּת לֹא תִכְבֶּה
וְהָיוּ דֵרָאוֹן לְכָל־בָּשָׂר׃ **ישעיה לד:ד; סו:כד**

OLD TESTAMENT SCRIPTURE TRANSLATION

"The LORD is known *by* the judgment, *which* he executeth....The wicked shall be turned into hell [sheol], *and* all the nations that forget God."
Psalms 9:16-17 KJV. [ ] mine

"...the host of heaven shall be dissolved, and the heavens shall be rolled together as a scroll: and all their host shall fall down, as the leaf falleth off from the vine, and as a falling *fig* from the fig tree....of the men that have transgressed against me: for their worm shall not die, neither shall their fire be quenched; and they shall be an abhorring...." **Isaiah 34:4; 66:24 KJV**

ANCIENT RABBINICAL COMMENTARY

"...The Holy one, Blessed be He, will sit on the Throne of Judgment in the Valley of Yehoshaphat. And instantly the heaven and the earth will decay, and the sun will become ashamed, and the moon and the mountains will shake, and the hills tremble so as not to remind Israel of its sins. And the gates of Gehenna will open in the Valley of Yehoshaphat, and the gates of the Garden of Eden in the east."[24]
Nistarot R. Shim'on ben Yohai, BhM 3:80-81

NEW TESTAMENT RECORDED 37 and 96 AD

"Immediately after the tribulation of those days shall the sun be darkened, and the moon shall not give her light, and the stars shall fall from heaven,[25] and the powers of the heavens shall be shaken....Then shall he say also unto them on the left hand, Depart from me, ye cursed, into everlasting fire, prepared for the devil and his angels...." **Matthew 24:29; 25:41 KJV**

---

24 Raphael Patai, *The Messiah Texts*, p. 217.

25 These words have puzzled many people. Hal Lindsey speculates on the meaning of this verse when he comments on a similar passage written by John in the book of Revelation. Hal says: "I believe this passage describes the initial stages of an all-out nuclear war. '*Seismos*' (σε ισμοσ) in the Greek does not necessarily mean an earthquake, as it is usually translated. It can also mean a terrible shaking of the earth by forces not known to the 1st century writer who witnessed it. As a result of this violent shaking on the earth, the **sun** becomes black like sack cloth and the **moon** becomes red like blood. This sounds remarkably like the 'nuclear winter' scenarios that scientists predict will follow a thermo-nuclear war. The debris that is blasted into the atmosphere will blot out a great deal of light and heat from the sun and moon. Note that John predicts that multiple **stars** fall out of the sky to earth. To a 1st century man, this would appear like falling stars. But he could have well been describing multiple independently targeted warheads blazing through the atmosphere as they streak toward their targets. The clincher is '**the sky was rolled up like a scroll.**' In a thermonuclear blast, the atmosphere is violently pushed back upon itself as a great vacuum is created. Then it rushes back into the vacuum with almost equal force. The double violent movement of the atmosphere is one of the great destructive parts of the bomb's explosion." Hal Lindsey, *The Final Battle*, pp. 248-249. This prophecy could also be literally interpreted as a divine judgment.

"And I saw a great white throne, and him that sat on it, from whose face the earth and the heaven fled away; and there was found no place for them. And I saw the dead, small and great, stand before God; and the books were opened; and another book was opened, which is *the book* of life: and the dead were judged out of those things which were written in the books, according to their works. And the sea gave up the dead which were in it; and death and hell delivered up the dead which were in them: and they were judged every man according to their works. And death and hell were cast into the lake of fire. This is the second death. And whosoever was not found written in the book of life was cast into the lake of fire."

Revelation 20:11-15 KJV

MODERN RABBINIC COMMENT/REFUTATION

"...eternal punishment for the wicked finds no official acceptance in Judaism."[26]

Rabbi Abba Hillel Silver

"...even the tarnished souls will not be forever denied spiritual bliss. Judaism rejects the doctrine of eternal damnation."[27]

Chief Rabbi Dr. J. H. Hertz

AUTHOR'S COMMENT—EVANGELICAL CHRISTIAN POSITION

These statements by our rabbi friends, which are shared by the vast majority of contemporary rabbis, are not really accurate when you glance up at the Old Testament and ancient rabbinical commentary, are they? For detailed documentation, using many verses from the ancient rabbinical commentary, proving Rabbis Hertz and Silver are absolutely misrepresenting Jewish belief on the subject of eternal judgment, see our *Vol. II*, chapter 33, "The Reality of the Ancient Jewish Acknowledgment of Hell, Covered Up Until Now."

Philip Moore

THE ORDER OF RESURRECTION

There are many ecumenical and liberal theologians who are very confused as to the order of God's Messianic resurrection of humanity. In the past, some believed that the teachings of Augustine[28] were valid.

---

[26]Dan Cohn-Sherbok, *Rabbinic Perspectives on the New Testament*. Lampeter, Dyfed, Wales, UK: The Edwin Mellen Press, Ltd., © 1990, p. 2, used by permission.

[27]Ibid, p. 1.

[28]Augustine, of the fourth century, purposely altered the early New Testament and biblical teachings, which were so precious to believers. Incredibly, many of them were only rediscovered recently, thanks to modern reasonable sound Bible scholarship in an absence of ecumenical persecution! *Israel My Glory* quotes Augustine on this issue, which threw prophetic teachings into the Dark Ages for centuries. We have every right to ask, "Why did Augustine alter the early true New Testament interpretation of resurrection, and the 1000-year promise of a literal kingdom?" Hal Lindsey comments on this question in his 1983 publication, *The Rapture: Truth or Consequences*. Hal correctly notes: "...Augustine (A.D. 354-430) dealt the doctrine of prophecy the most damaging blow of anyone in history. He plunged the study of prophecy into darkness for almost 1,400 years by systematically teaching that prophecy could not be interpreted literally. Augustine held to a literal, grammatical and historical interpretation of every other field of Bible doctrine, but taught that prophecy must be interpreted allegorically. He did this in order to be able to sustain his views....He taught that Jews had no more purpose in God's plan; that they would never be reborn as a nation." Hal Lindsey, *The Rapture: Truth or Consequences*, p. 167. I, along with millions of other true Christians, support

His pretense indicated that there would occur just a general resurrection of all the dead at once and that would be all. However, the Bible definitely teaches us of "dispensational resurrections" that occur at different times and to different divisions of people! "The apostle Paul uses an extremely important term in relation to the stages of resurrection. He says again, 'But each in his ***order***...' (1 Corinthians 15:23a). 'Order' is the translation of the Greek word *tagma* which was primarily a military term. It was most frequently used to designate a division or battalion of soldiers. The best available Greek New Testament lexicon says about this term, 'Of a number of persons who belong together and are therefore arranged together; *division; group*. A military term for bodies of troops in various numbers such as divisions or battalions of soldiers...in 1 Corinthians 15:23f the gift of life is given to various ones in turn, and at various times. [F. W. Gingrich and Frederick Danker, *A Greek-English Lexicon of the New Testament*, p. 802]....Paul paints a word picture which descibes army divisions on parade passing by a reviewing stand at different intervals in time....the believers are to be resurrected...each one in **his own division**. The very term, *tagma*, implies a number of phases."[29]

The order of resurrection, according to the specifications in our Judeo/Christian Bibles, occurs as follows:

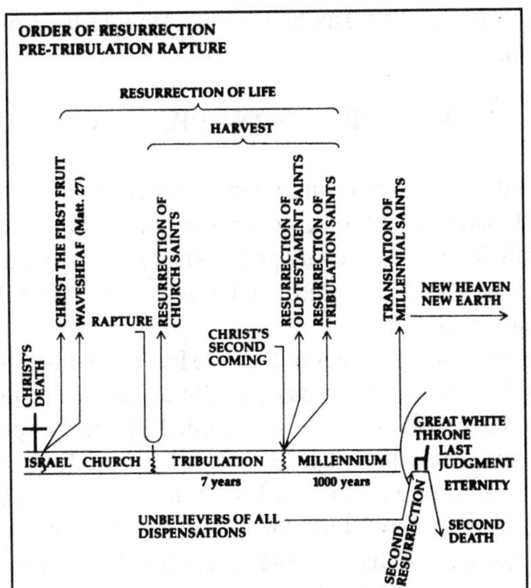

Israel, as God would have it. So much for Augustine's false teachings. Israel has become a nation and we are very happy about it! See our chapter 18, "Israel—Is Real."

[29] Hal Lindsey, *The Rapture: Truth or Consequences*, pp. 159-160. The diagram is Hal Lindsey's. Ibid, p. 161, courtesy of Bantam Books.

RESURRECTION—PHASE I

In the first resurrection, there are four phases (the second resurrection occurs at the end of the millennium and is for unbelievers only; John 5:29; Rev. 20:6). The first resurrection, which is composed of believers only, has four stages. The first stage of phase one was the resurrection of Jesus nearly 2000 years ago. We are told that Jesus was the "first fruits" of the resurrection (I Cor. 15:20-25).

Jesus as Messiah, was the first man in the long history of men to receive a permanent resurrection body which can never be destroyed. Lazarus and the boy in the Old Testament were only raised back into their mortal bodies and died again shortly thereafter. There is a clear difference between raising the dead and resurrection. Resurrection is permanent and encompasses a resurrection body. This resurrection of first fruits, which corresponds to the Jewish feast of "first fruits" in the Bible (Lev. 23:16), contained a token of believers (Matt. 27:52-53) in ancient Israel.

The first fruits of the harvest were waved before God in the tabernacle by the high priest. This was an offering of thanks, which also assured a bountiful harvest (the second stage). It was only offered with a lamb sacrifice, therefore Jesus, our high priest (Heb. 5-7; 13:11-12), offered these believers His first fruits. Thus Jesus is our Passover lamb for all time.

RESURRECTION—PHASE II

The second phase of resurrection is hinted at in Revelation 4:1: "After this I looked, and behold, a door *was* opened in heaven: and the first voice which I had heard *was* as it were of a trumpet talking with me; which said, Come up hither, and I will shew thee things which must be hereafter" (KJV).

John, who is writing, sees a door in Heaven and is told to "come up hither" in his vision. This may provide an answer to the puzzling conversation Jesus had with Peter, recorded in the Gospel of John: "Peter therefore seeing him said to Jesus, 'Lord, and what about this man [John]?' Jesus said to him, 'If I want him to remain until I come, what *is that* to you? You follow Me!' This saying therefore went out among the brethren that that disciple would not die; yet Jesus did not say to him that he would not die, but *only*, 'If I want him to remain until I come, what *is that* to you?' " (John 21:21-23 NASB; [ ] mine).

The apostle John was told to "**come** up hither" so he could see and record the vision of the end days and Second **Coming** of the Messiah. This second phase will occur in our future and is known as the Rapture. All that John wrote, until he was told to "come up," was history.

After he was taken, he was given visions which are predicted to occur **after** the Rapture portion of the resurrection, lasting seven years, before the Lord returns to stop Gog and Magog in Revelation 19. This resurrection contains all of those who were born-again at Jesus' Pentecost (the beginning of His true church, fifty days after the Passover from which He rose until the day of the event known as the Rapture occurs—still future). As we know, in the Rapture we will all be taken up (see our chapter 25, "The Rapture Factor"). You will get a taste of being a benefactor, which you will be, if you are a believer!

RESURRECTION—PHASE III

In the third phase of the resurrection, the Old Testament believers, from Adam until John the Baptist's ministry, prior to the dispensation of the church age (Acts 1:22), are resurrected. This resurrection also contains the Tribulation believers in Jesus, both Jew and Gentile, who were martyred (not the 144,000 specially appointed Jewish witnesses; see our chapter 25, "The Rapture Factor"). This resurrection occurs after the seven-year Tribulation—after the previous "Rapture resurrection"—at Jesus' judgment of the nations (Matt. 25:32-46; Dan. 12:2).

RESURRECTION—PHASE IV

The fourth phase of the resurrection occurs when the mortal kingdom believers receive their new immortal resurrected bodies. It consists of those who survived the seven-year Tribulation, the last war of Gog and Magog, and lived through the 1000-year Messianic Kingdom (Matt. 25), due to the biblically predicted alteration of nature, which resulted in greatly increased longevity. This happens at the end of the kingdom, just prior to Jesus' creation of the New Heaven and Earth, which is the beginning of eternity future, the subject of our forthcoming chapter 30, "New Heavens and a New Earth."

AFTER PHASE III, THERE ARE MESSIANIC JUDGMENTS OF JEWS AND GENTILES HERE ON EARTH

After the resurrection (third phase), the Hebrew prophet Daniel elaborates on the beginnings of the millennial kingdom: "I saw in the night visions, and, behold, *one* like the Son of man came with the clouds of heaven, and came to the Ancient of days, and they brought him near before him. And there was given him dominion, and glory, and a kingdom, that all people, nations, and languages, should serve him: his dominion *is* an everlasting dominion, which shall not pass away, and his kingdom *that* which shall not be destroyed....And the kingdom and dominion, and the greatness of the kingdom under the whole heaven, shall be given to the people of the saints of the most High, whose kingdom *is* an everlasting kingdom, and all dominions shall serve and obey him" (Dan. 7:13-14, 27 KJV).

Two major judgments occur before the joys of this kingdom are realized. Hal Lindsey, in his book, *The Rapture: Truth or Consequences*, precisely covers the major events of these judgments. Therefore, we will quote him at length: "The *second prophetic theme* that relates to this question of who populates the Kingdom concerns *two* great judgments of the Tribulation survivors which takes place on earth immediately after Christ's return. These judgments are the Lord's first major act after returning to the earth.

There is an extremely important condition on earth which is demonstrated by the Lord's judgment of the survivors. These survivors are segregated into two judgments: one of Jews and one of Gentiles....

THE JUDGMENT OF SURVIVING ISRAELITES

Throughout the Old Testament, prophecies were made about the coming of the promised Messianic Kingdom. Many of these spoke of a judgment of the physical descendants of Abraham, Isaac and Jacob to determine who would enter. Paul warned that not all who are called Israel are Israel (Romans 9:6).

Ezekiel clearly forewarned what would immediately precede the Messiah's founding of the Kingdom. In Chapter 20 he said that the Messiah would become king over them with great judgment upon the earth (Verse 33); that He would bring them out of the lands where He had scattered them (Verse 34); that He would bring all living survivors of Israel into the wilderness (probably the Sinai Desert) and judge them face-to-face (Verses 35 and 36); that the judgment would be made according to the covenant He made with them (which demanded faith in His provision for sin) (Verse 37); that He would purge from them all rebels who had transgressed against Him (Verse 38); and that those who remained would be established in the Kingdom (Verses 40-44).

The prophet Zephaniah predicts the same sequence of events. First, he predicts the terrible judgment of the Tribulation (1:14-18); then, the coming of the Lord to earth with great worldwide destruction and judgment (3:8). Next, he predicts a judgment of survivors in which all proud and exulting ones, and all deceitful and lying people, will be removed from their midst (3:11). He also said that only a humble and lowly people who take refuge in the name of the Lord will remain to enter the Kingdom and land of Israel (3:12-13). Finally, the Lord will become the king of Israel and remain in their midst (3:15-17).

These two passages make it very clear that all Jewish survivors will be gathered for judgment 'face-to-face' with the Messiah Jesus, and that the believers alone will enter the Messiah's Kingdom.

THE JUDGMENT OF THE GENTILE SURVIVORS

After the Lord Jesus judges the Israelites (illustrated by the parables of Matthew 25:1-30), He will then gather all Gentiles to Jerusalem (the place of His glorious throne of Matthew 25:31) and conduct a very personal judgment of all those who survive the Tribulation (Matthew 25:31-46).

This passage very clearly indicates when and upon whom this judgment takes place, 'But when the Son of Man comes in His glory, and all the angels with Him, then He will sit on His glorious throne. And all the nations [Gentiles] will be gathered before Him; and He will separate them from one another, as the shepherd separates the sheep [believers] from the goats [unbelievers]; and he will put the sheep on His right, and the goats on the left.' (Matthew 25:31-33)

At the end of the judgment and separation the Lord Jesus says, 'And these [that is, the goats on the left] will go away into eternal punishment, but the righteous [that is, the sheep on His right] shall go into eternal life'....The Lord uses a unique test to determine whether these Tribulation survivors are true believers in Him. This is evaluated on the basis of how they treated a very special group that the Lord Jesus calls 'these brothers of mine' (Matthew 25:40, 45). Judging by the unusual survival of this group in spite of hunger, thirst, estrangement, lack of adequate clothing, sickness and imprisonment, it seems certain that they are the 144,000 Jewish witnesses....At the end of the Tribulation, the same 144,000 are pictured standing with Jesus the Messiah on Mount Zion in Jerusalem (Revelation 14:1-5). The indication is that they all survived the Tribulation and are in *unresurrected* bodies."[30]

***

[30]Hal Lindsey, *The Rapture: Truth or Consequences*, pp. 144-146.

"And I saw thrones, and they sat upon them, and judgment was given unto them: and I *saw* the souls of them that were beheaded for the witness of Jesus, and for the word of God... they lived and reigned with Christ a thousand years."

Revelation 20:4 KJV

"...The Jews kept ye Passover partly in memory of their coming out of Egypt, partly as an anniversary type of the passion of the Messiah to come: & we now keep it in memory of his passion past: And so ye feast of the seventh month kept by ye Jews as a type Christ second coming of ye kingdom of God. Then to be founded may be hereafter kept in memory of ye coming & as ye anniversary or birthday of the kingdom of God which from thence shal stand forever."[31]

Sir Isaac Newton, 1600's

"...the Holy Communion is to be understood as a Messianic meal which hints at an eternal perspective."[32]

Risto Santala, 1992

WHAT WILL BELIEVERS DO? PLENTY!

The Scriptures teach that we will rule over angels: "Do ye not know that the saints [believers] shall judge the world? and if the world shall be judged by you....Know ye not that we shall judge angels?" (I Cor. 6:2-3 KJV; [ ] mine).

We believe we will assist Jesus in the governing of the universe. This will be a rule which is shrouded in love. The mortals who survive the Tribulation and live through the 1000-year kingdom, will definitely rely on our direction before they are given their new eternal resurrection bodies. They will receive these bodies at the end of the kingdom, pending our entry into the New Jerusalem, New Heaven and Earth, so beautifully described in Revelation 21:1-4.

THE NEWTONIAN VIEW OF THE MILLENNIUM IS A COMFORTING AND CORRECT CONFIRMATION

Sir Isaac Newton, our scientific friend, wrote in great anticipation of enjoying this future world of the millennium: "But you will say how then comes it to pass that in the thousand years there are Mortals on earth?....Doth the earth last after the day of judgment, and do mortals live on it, and do the Sons of the resurrection live among them like other men and reign over them in the beloved city? I answer that its true the beloved city is a city of mortals, and I say further that the glorious description of the new Jerusalem under the types of pretious stones and pearles is a commentary upon this city....Christ at his second coming must...rule....when the Martyrs and Prophets live again they may reign here with Christ, a thousand years till...the dominion of the new Jerusalem be established and death be vanquished by raising the

[31] *Yahuda Manuscript 9.2 151.* Read "ye" as "the."

[32] Risto Santala, *The Messiah in the New Testament in the Light of Rabbinical Writings*, p. cover flap.

rest of the dead...and all this time they may be in the same state of happiness...."[33]

HEY FOLKS, WE WILL GET TO MEET ISAAC NEWTON, IN SPITE OF MANUEL'S SARCASM

I, myself, look forward to seeing Isaac Newton there, the man who opened the way to so much understanding of our scientific universe in the fields of calculus, optics, mathematics, physics and gravity. Newton anticipated his place with us, resurrected in the millennial kingdom. We are informed of this by a sarcastic comment in the writings of Frank Manuel: " 'Such as is his body [Jesus], such shall ours be', wrote Newton, with more than a touch of self-assurance that he would be among those 'children of the resurrection.' "[34]

It goes without saying, if you are a scientific fan of Newton's and would like to meet him and ask a few questions, it would no doubt pay to become a believer. Wouldn't it? Yes!

THE MILLENNIAL PARADISE OF THE AGES FINALLY REALIZED—WE COULD ALL USE THE REST, COULDN'T WE? YES!

In our forthcoming and final chapter, we will take up the crowning subject of the New Heavens and New Earth. I cannot wait! But before we get into those jewels, we will examine the beautiful conditions which will prevail once Jesus returns, executes the Antichrist (Isa. 11:4; II Thes.2:8) and convenes the resurrections and judgments that we have read so much about.

The millennium, once put into operation, will be one of the most beautiful states the world has ever known. It will be very similar to the condition our father, Adam, was accustomed to in Eden[35] (see Gen. 1). The curse placed on the ground will be removed so that we will no longer have to "work by the sweat of our face" (Gen. 3:19). Food will again become the gift of God, as it was in the Garden.

The fact that men have had to strive for their upkeep has been the result of God's original judgment, for the original sin[36] of distrusting

---

[33]*Yahuda Manuscript 9.2, fol. 138r, 6 fol. 12.*

[34]Frank E. Manuel, *The Religion of Isaac Newton*, p. 100. Manuel's source was *Yahuda Manuscript 9.2, fol. 138r, 6 fol. 12.* [ ] mine.

[35]See our *Vol. II*, chapter 29, "The Garden of Eden, Immortality and Today—Will We Stop Aging?"

[36]Those of you reading this, who are Jews, and have been taught that original sin is not originally Jewish, see our comparision page in our chapter 1, where we show the parallels between the ancient rabbinical view and that of the New Testament. You will see that

Him and disobeying Him. Few take Genesis 3:17 seriously, which describes the curse placed on the ground so that man would have to work vigorously to extract a living from the earth.[37] There is no such thing as free money. All of us must work for "money," the liquid result of labor. The only other methods are stealing or taxing, both of which take from someone else's hard work! Thus in Revelation 22:3, God says clearly that He removes this curse.

Once this obstacle is removed, the world, under the personal rulership of Jesus, undergoes a transformation in which our present earth of war, famine and death, will be changed into a world of peace, plenty and fairness.

HOW DO THE TESTAMENTS DESCRIBE THIS 1000-YEAR MILLENNIAL KINGDOM? BEAUTIFULLY!

The rulership of this Messianic Kingdom, which Jesus will inaugurate as the Jewish Messiah, is beautifully foretold in Jeremiah and I Chronicles of the Old Testament: "Behold, the days come, saith the LORD, that I will raise unto David a righteous Branch, and a King shall reign and prosper, and shall execute judgment and justice in the earth. In his days Judah shall be saved, and Israel shall dwell safely: and this *is* his name whereby he shall be called, THE LORD OUR RIGHTEOUSNESS" (Jer. 23:5-6 KJV).

I Chronicles also predicted: "And it shall come about when your days are fulfilled that you must go *to be* with your fathers, that I will set up *one* of your descendants after you, who shall be of your sons; and I will establish his kingdom. He shall build for Me a house, and I will establish his throne forever. I will be His father, and He shall be My son; and I will not take My loving kindness away from him, as I took it from him who was before you. But I will settle him in My house and in My kingdom forever, and his throne shall be established forever. According to all these words and according to all this vision, so Nathan spoke to David" (I Chr. 17:11-15 NASB).

---

ancient Judaism agrees with the New Testament regarding original sin. Modernists deny Judaism ever taught such a doctrine! There is really no difference, though some would like you to think there is, and will tell you so in order to keep you away from a Messiah who redeems from sin—Jesus!

[37]The very words God spoke to Adam, recorded by Moses in Genesis, were: "And unto Adam he said, Because thou hast hearkened unto the voice of thy wife, and hast eaten of the tree, of which I commanded thee, saying, 'Thou shalt not eat of it: **cursed** *is* the ground for thy sake; in sorrow shalt thou eat *of* it all the days of thy life; Thorns also and thistles shall it bring forth to thee; and thou shalt eat the herb of the field; In the sweat of thy face shalt thou eat bread, till thou return unto the ground; for out of it wast thou taken: for dust thou *art*, and unto dust shalt thou return" (Gen. 3:17-19 KJV).

Isaiah wrote the prophetic words: "For unto us a child is born, unto us a son is given: and the government shall be upon His shoulder: and His name shall be called Wonderful, Counsellor, The mighty God, The everlasting Father, The Prince of Peace. Of the increase of *his* government and peace *there shall be* no end, upon the throne of David, and upon his kingdom, to order it, and to establish it with judgment and with justice from henceforth even for ever. The zeal of the LORD of hosts will perform this" (Isa. 9:6-7 KJV).

Luke writes in the New Testament: "And the angel said unto her, Fear not, Mary: for thou hast found favour with God. And, behold, thou shall conceive in thy womb, and bring forth a son, and shalt call his name JESUS. He shall be great, and shall be called the Son of the Highest: and the Lord God shall give unto him the throne of his father David: And he shall reign over the house of Jacob for ever; and of his kingdom there shall be no end" (Luke 1:30-33 KJV).

THOUGH THE WORLD IS PRESENTLY ONE-QUARTER COMMUNIST AND OPPRESSED, THAT IS GOING TO CHANGE SOON WHEN THE MESSIAH TAKES THE REINS

At present, the world is one-fourth communist. The communists (dishonest people artificially placed in ruling leadership positions) force their citizens (slaves) to work, but not for themselves. They then confiscate their money or goods and sell them to others.[38] This now goes on, on a large scale, throughout the world. However, the Bible foretells this will not be the case when Jesus returns and sets up the Messianic Kingdom. Isaiah, the Old Testament prophet, clearly tells of the equality and plenty once the kingdom begins: "And they shall build houses, and inhabit *them*; and they shall plant vineyards, and eat the fruit of them. They shall not build, and another inhabit; they shall not plant and another eat: for as the days of a tree *are* the days of my people,[39] and mine elect shall long enjoy the work of their hands.

---

[38]For example, the finest candies, jams and novelties, which are forbidden for the worker to eat and are not available in these countries, are sold to the West. It was recently documented on a national news show that the workers in China's military factories only receive twenty cents an hour. The seemingly harmless products, such as stuffed toys and dolls, end up on the shelves of stores like Kmart, here in the West, at a high profit margin. China, in turn, uses the funds to enhance their military for an aspired battle that will be to all of our detriment!

[39]This was especially true of the Jewish people in Russia, who until recently, were forced to produce food in factories so the state could sell it to the West. It would seem, in this case, that God's people (the Russian Jews) were exploited by the capitalistic principle of the communist elite. This will totally halt in the millennium when Jesus returns, though the tide seems to be beginning to turn at the moment. My favorite President, Ronald Reagan, might have spoken a bit prematurely (as far as the freedom we

They shall not labour in vain, nor bring forth for trouble; for they *are* the seed of the blessed of the LORD, and their offspring with them" (Isa. 65:21-23 KJV).

"Peace," by William Strutt. During the millennial reign of the Messiah, all of God's creatures will love one another, as was intended in the beginning.

---

will have in the millennium) when he said: "I've always maintained that the struggle now going on for the world will never be decided by bombs or rockets; by armies or military might. The real crisis we face today is a spiritual one. At root, it is a test of moral will and faith. I believe that communism is another sad, bizarre chapter in human history whose last...pages, even now, are being written. I believe this because the source of our strength and the quest for human freedom is not material, but spiritual, and because it knows no limitation. It must testify and ultimately triumph over those who would enslave their fellow man. For in the words of Isaiah: 'He giveth power to the faint and to them that have no might; he increases strength that they that wait upon the Lord shall renew their strength. They shall mount up with wings as eagles. They shall run and not be weary.' " These words were spoken to the National Association of Evangelicals in Orlando, FL, March 8, 1983, by President Reagan. In the early 1990's, this biblical dream was partially realized in the present demise of communism in Russia. For the moment, the people are free, though we do not know how long this will last. However, as we know, in the millennium, the Bible has promised all people will be free for all time in dignity and freedom to serve God.

THE CONDITIONS OF THE MILLENNIUM INCLUDE A WORLD FREE OF GERMS, DEFORMITIES AND DISEASE

Isaiah also foretells of a world free of disease, deformities, handicaps and illnesses, which are presently incurable. All of these sicknesses will be cured, and in fact, made extinct by the Messiah when He comes to establish His kingdom. The prophet states: "Say to them *that are* of a fearful heart, Be strong, fear not: behold, your God will come *with* vengeance, even God *with* a recompence; he will come and save you. Then the eyes of the blind shall be opened, and the ears of the deaf shall be unstopped. Then shall the lame *man* leap as an hart, and the tongue of the dumb sing: for in the wilderness shall waters break out and streams in the desert....And the ransomed of the LORD shall return, and come to Zion with songs and everlasting joy upon their heads: they shall obtain joy and gladness, and sorrow and sighing shall flee away" (Isa. 35:4-6, 10 KJV).

ONCE FEROCIOUS ANIMALS WILL AGAIN BE TAME, AS THEY WERE IN THE GARDEN!

Other beautiful passages show that even the animals and beasts, some of which are presently hostile toward each other and man himself, will once again become friendly. Even a child will be able to put his hand in a snake's den without the fear of being bitten. Isaiah predicts: "And the wolf will dwell with the lamb, And the leopard will lie down with the kid, And the calf and the young lion and the fatling together; And a little boy will lead them. Also the cow and the bear will graze; Their young will lie down together; And the lion will eat straw like the ox. And the nursing child will play by the hole of the cobra, And the weaned child will put his hand on the viper's den....'The wolf and the lamb shall graze together, and the lion shall eat straw like the ox; and dust shall be the serpent's food. They shall do no evil or harm in all My holy mountain,' says the LORD" (Isa. 11:6-8; 65:25 NASB).

***

ORIGINAL HEBREW TEXT WRITTEN 713, 574, 487 BC

וְגָר זְאֵב עִם־כֶּבֶשׂ וְנָמֵר עִם־גְּדִי יִרְבָּץ וְעֵגֶל וּכְפִיר וּמְרִיא יַחְדָּו וְנַעַר קָטֹן נֹהֵג בָּם׃
וּפָרָה וָדֹב תִּרְעֶינָה יַחְדָּו יִרְבְּצוּ יַלְדֵיהֶן וְאַרְיֵה כַּבָּקָר יֹאכַל־תֶּבֶן׃ וְשִׁעֲשַׁע יוֹנֵק עַל־חֻר
פָּתֶן וְעַל מְאוּרַת צִפְעוֹנִי גָּמוּל יָדוֹ הָדָה׃ לֹא־יָרֵעוּ וְלֹא־יַשְׁחִיתוּ בְּכָל־הַר קָדְשִׁי כִּי־מָלְאָה
הָאָרֶץ דֵּעָה אֶת־יְהוָה כַּמַּיִם לַיָּם מְכַסִּים׃ .... וַיְשִׁבֵנִי אֶל־פֶּתַח הַבַּיִת וְהִנֵּה־מַיִם יֹצְאִים
מִתַּחַת מִפְתַּן הַבַּיִת קָדִימָה כִּי־פְנֵי הַבַּיִת קָדִים וְהַמַּיִם יֹרְדִים מִתַּחַת מִכֶּתֶף הַבַּיִת הַיְמָנִית
מִנֶּגֶב לַמִּזְבֵּחַ׃ .... וְעַל־הַנַּחַל יַעֲלֶה עַל־שְׂפָתוֹ מִזֶּה ׀ וּמִזֶּה ׀ כָּל־עֵץ־מַאֲכָל לֹא־יִבּוֹל עָלֵהוּ
וְלֹא־יִתֹּם פִּרְיוֹ לָחֳדָשָׁיו יְבַכֵּר כִּי מֵימָיו מִן־הַמִּקְדָּשׁ הֵמָּה יוֹצְאִים וְהָיוּ פִרְיוֹ לְמַאֲכָל וְעָלֵהוּ
לִתְרוּפָה׃ .... וְהָיָה ׀ בַּיּוֹם הַהוּא יֵצְאוּ מַיִם־חַיִּים מִירוּשָׁלַםִ חֶצְיָם אֶל־הַיָּם הַקַּדְמוֹנִי וְחֶצְיָם
אֶל־הַיָּם הָאַחֲרוֹן בַּקַּיִץ וּבָחֹרֶף יִהְיֶה׃ וְהָיָה יְהוָה לְמֶלֶךְ עַל־כָּל־הָאָרֶץ בַּיּוֹם הַהוּא יִהְיֶה
יְהוָה אֶחָד וּשְׁמוֹ אֶחָד׃

ישעיה יא:ו-ט ; יחזקאל מז:א-יב; זכריה יד:ח-ט

OLD TESTAMENT SCRIPTURE TRANSLATION

"The wolf also shall dwell with the lamb, and the leopard shall lie down with the kid; and the calf and the young lion and the fatling together; and a little child shall lead them. And the cow and the bear shall feed; their young ones shall lie down together: and the lion shall eat straw like the ox. And the sucking child shall play on the hole of the asp, and the weaned child shall put his hand on the cockatrice' den. They shall not hurt nor destroy in all my holy mountain: for the earth shall be full of the knowledge of the LORD as the waters cover the sea....Afterward, he brought me again unto the door of the house, and behold, waters issued out from under the threshold of the house eastward: for the forefront of the house *stood toward* the east, and the waters came down from under from the right side of the house, at the south *side* of the altar....And by the river upon the bank thereof, on this side and on that side, shall grow all trees for |meat|, whose leaf shall not fade, neither shall the fruit thereof be consumed; it shall bring forth new fruit according to his months, because their waters issued out of the sanctuary: and the fruit thereof shall be for |meat|, and the leaf thereof for medicine....And it shall be in that day, *that* living waters shall go out from Jerusalem; half of them toward the former sea, and half of them toward the hinder sea: in summer and in winter shall it be. And the LORD shall be king over all the earth...."

Isaiah 11:6-9 KJV; Ezekiel 47:1, 12 KJV;[40] Zechariah 14:8-9 KJV

ANCIENT RABBINICAL COMMENTARY

"Why was it [one of the Temple gates] called Water Gate? R. Eliezer ben Ya'aqov said: 'Because in it water bubbled forth.' This teaches us that the waters were bubbling forth and rising as if coming out of a flask. In the future they will come forth from under the threshold of the Temple....All the waters of Creation will in the future come forth as if coming from the mouth of a flask."[41]

M. Middot 2:6; T. Suk, 3:3, 10; B. Yoma 77b-78a

"And He will open for them the sources of the Tree of Life, and will give them to drink on the way...."[42] **Otot haMashiah, BhM 2:58-63**

"R. Y'huda said: 'In This World the crops ripen in six months, and a tree yields fruit in twelve months, but in the Future to Come the crops will ripen every month'....R. Yose said: '...In the Future to Come the crops will ripen in fifteen days, and the trees yield fruit every month.' "[43]

Y. Sheqalim 50a mid.

---

[40] *The New Scofield Reference Bible.*
[41] Raphael Patai, *The Messiah Texts*, p. 231.
[42] Ibid, p. 316.
[43] Ibid, pp. 231-232. Patai's source was the Jerusalem Talmud.

"[In the days of the Messiah] *I will cause evil beasts to cease out of the land* (Lev. 26:6). R. Y'huda said: 'He [God] will calm them so that they should do no damage.' R. Shim'on said...'God will calm those who cause injury in the world, so that they will cause no injury. To this refers the verse, *And the wolf shall dwell with the lamb, and the leopard shall lie down with the kid...and the cow and the bear...and the suckling child shall play on the hole of the asp* (Isa. 11:6-8).' "[44]

Sifra b'Huqotai 2:1, Yalqut haMakhiri, p. 86

NEW TESTAMENT RECORDED 60; 96 AD

"...the creature itself also shall be delivered from the bondage of corruption into the glorious liberty of the children of God. For we know that the whole creation groaneth and travaileth in pain together until now. And not only *they*, but ourselves also, which have the first fruits of the Spirit, even we ourselves groan within ourselves, waiting for the adoption, *to wit*, the redemption of our body....And he shewed me a pure river of water of life, clear as crystal, proceeding out of the throne of God and of the Lamb. In the midst of the street of it, and on either side of the river, *was there* the tree of life, which bare twelve *manner* of fruits, *and* yielded her fruit every month: and the leaves of the tree *were* for the healing of the nations."

Romans 8:21-23; Revelation 22:1-2 KJV

MODERN RABBINIC COMMENT/REFUTATION

"It should not come to one's mind that in the days of the Messiah anything in the customary order of the world will be annulled, or that there will be something new in the order of Creation. For the world will continue in its path. And that which Isaiah said, *The wolf shall dwell with the lamb, and the leopard shall lie down with the kid* (Isa. 11:6), is but an allegory and a riddle....*The lion shall eat straw like the ox* (Isa. 11:7). And likewise, all the similar things said about the Messiah are but allegories."[45] **Maimonides (Rambam),[46] Yad haHazaqa, Shoftim, Hilkhot M'lakhim 11-12**

AUTHOR'S COMMENT—EVANGELICAL CHRISTIAN POSITION

The name Rambam stands for Rabbi Mosha ben Maimon (Rabbi Mosha "son of" Maimon). It is clear to us that Rambam and the many modern rabbis who agree with his allegorical interpretation/opinion, not only contradict the New Testament Scriptures, but also those cherished literal hopes which lie within the core of ancient (true) Judaism, as noted in the above commentaries. We who believe, look forward to the new world and its new order, which Jesus the Messiah foretold! He Himself promised: "...Verily I say unto you, That ye which have followed me, in the

---

[44]Ibid, pp. 231-232, 259.

[45]Raphael Patai, *The Messiah Texts*, p. 325.

[46]Rambam was a rabbi who died in 1204, and is still considered a giant within rabbinic circles. Why? I do not know! His opinions seem blasphemous when compared to the earlier literal rabbinic commentaries. Concerning Rambam and certain modern rabbis who deny these wonderful promises, claiming they are "allegory," this author believes the words of Newton, the world's most famous scientist, are appropriate. He wrote: "He that without better grounds then his private opinion or the opinion of any human authority whatsoever shall turn scripture from the plain meaning to an Allegory or to any other less naturall sense declares thereby that he reposes more trust in his own imaginations or in that human authority then in the Scripture (and by consequence that he is no true beleever). And therefore the opinion of such men how numerous soever they be, is not to be regarded." Frank E. Manuel, *The Religion of Isaac Newton*, p. 118. Manuel's source was *Yahuda Manuscript 1*. Spelling per original text quoted.

regeneration when the Son of man shall sit in the throne of his glory, ye also shall sit upon twelve thrones, judging the twelve tribes of Israel" (Matt. 19:28 KJV).
Philip Moore

WE HAVE A LOT TO LOOK FORWARD TO AT JESUS' SECOND COMING—PERFECT PEACE IN PARADISE—TAILOR-MADE FOR ALL WHO LOVE HIM!

The Scripture foretells: "And he shall judge among many people, and rebuke strong nations afar off; and they shall beat their swords into plowshares, and their spears into pruninghooks: nation shall not lift up a sword against nation, neither shall they learn war any more. But they shall sit every man under his vine and under his fig tree; and none shall make *them* afraid: for the mouth of the LORD of hosts hath spoken *it*" (Micah 4:3-4 KJV).

It is also foretold that there will be a perfect one-world government, that the Messiah will be king over the whole world and that far-off nations will come once a year to pay homage to Him: "And the LORD will be king over all the earth; in that day the LORD will be *the only* one, and His name *the only* one....Then it will come about that any who are left of all the nations that went against Jerusalem will go up from year to year to worship the King, the LORD of hosts, and to celebrate the Feast of Booths. And it will be that whichever of the families of the earth does not go up to Jerusalem to worship the King, the LORD of hosts, there will be no rain on them. And if the family of Egypt does not go up or enter, then no *rain will fall* on them; it will be the plague with which the LORD smites the nations who do not go up to celebrate the Feast of Booths. This will be the punishment of Egypt, and the punishment of all the nations who do not go up to celebrate the Feast of Booths. In that day there will *be inscribed* on the bells of the horses, 'HOLY TO THE LORD.' And the cooking pots in the Lord's house will be like the bowls before the altar. And every cooking pot in Jerusalem and in Judah will be holy to the LORD of hosts; and all who sacrifice will come and take of them and boil in them" (Zech. 14:9, 16-20 NASB).

We can say with confidence that we have a lot to look forward to, to say the least. All of us who are believers, will soon be in a Shangri-La of perfect peace. A paradise so unimaginable, with a harmony of man and nature so fantastic that we may only dream and read about it. That is, until it actually arrives, which will not be long!

The time key is that there is a biblical history of 7000 years marked off—the kingdom lasts 1000 years and we are nearing the end of 6000 years; thus soon (no one knows the day or hour), things will start happening! This author believes most probably *before* another forty years have passed!

Though the Scriptures teach that no one may know the exact time, they do not negate our hope and Scriptural speculation. Jesus taught: "And when these things begin to come to pass [end time signs], then look up, and lift up your heads; for your redemption draweth nigh" (Luke 21:28 KJV; [ ] mine).

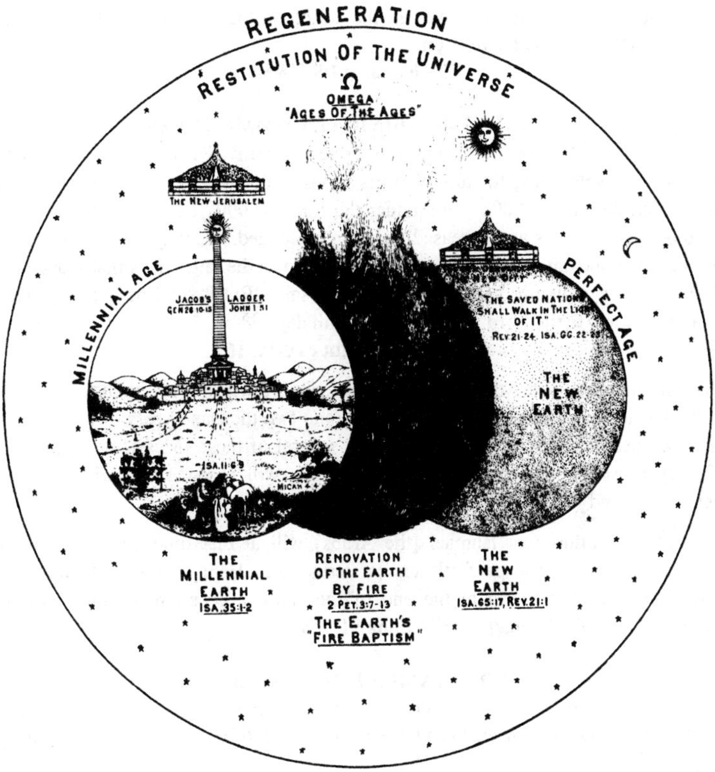

Reverend Clarence Larkin beautifully
illustrates the regeneration of the universe.[47]

[47]Courtesy of Rev. Clarence Larkin Estate, from the book *Dispensational Truth*. Available through Rev. Clarence Larkin, Est., POB 334 Glenside, PA, USA 19038.

ORIGINAL HEBREW TEXT WRITTEN 997; 487 BC

כִּי אֶלֶף שָׁנִים בְּעֵינֶיךָ כְּיוֹם אֶתְמוֹל כִּי יַעֲבֹר וְאַשְׁמוּרָה בַלָּיְלָה׃

תהלים צ:ד

וְהָיָה יְהוָה לְמֶלֶךְ עַל־כָּל־הָאָרֶץ בַּיּוֹם הַהוּא יִהְיֶה יְהוָה אֶחָד וּשְׁמוֹ אֶחָד׃

זכריה יד:ט

OLD TESTAMENT SCRIPTURE TRANSLATION

"For a thousand years in Thy sight Are like yesterday when it passes by, Or *as* a watch in the night." **Psalms 90:4 NASB**

"And the LORD will be king over all the earth; in that day the LORD will be *the only* one and his name *the only* one."

Zechariah 14:9 NASB

ANCIENT RABBINICAL COMMENTARY

"Another interpretation of 'There was none of them' (Ps. cxxxix. 16) is that it means the seventh day, for this world is to last 6,000 years; 2,000 years....It was waste and desolate; 2,000 years under the Law; 2,000 years under the Messiah. And because our sins are increased, they are prolonged. As they are prolonged, and as we make one day a Sabbatic year, so will God in the latter days make one day a Sabbatic year, which is 1,000 years, and it is said, 'But it shall be one day, which shall be known to the Lord,' this is the seventh day."[48]

Yalkut on Psalm cxxxix. 16

"For six thousand years the world will exist: [there will be] two thousand years of *Tohu* ['void'], two thousand years of Tora, and two thousand years of the Messiah. But because of our sins, which are many, several of these [Messianic years] have already passed....the Holy One, blessed be He, will renew His world only after seven thousand years."[49] **B. Sanhedrin 97a-b**

"...And the Children of Ishmael [the Arabs] will at that time arise with all the nations of the world to go forth against Jerusalem....Happy will be all those who will remain on the world at the end of the sixth millennium to enter into [the millennium of] the Sabbath...."[50] **Zohar 1:119a**

NEW TESTAMENT RECORDED 96 AD

"Blessed and holy is the one who has a part in the first resurrection; over these the second death has no power, but they will be priests of God and of Christ and will reign with Him for a thousand years."

Revelation 20:6 NASB

---

[48]Rev. B. Pick, Ph.D., *Old Testament Passages Messianically Applied by the Ancient Synagogue*, published in the compilation *Hebraica, A Quarterly Journal in the Interests of Semitic Study*, Vol. IV, pp. 248-249.

[49]Raphael Patai, *The Messiah Texts*, p. 60.

[50]Ibid, p. 64.

AT THE END OF THE MILLENNIUM, THERE IS A SMALL REBELLION AGAINST THE MESSIAH WHICH IS QUICKLY QUASHED

Near the end of paradise, which lasts 1000 years (Rev. 20:4-6), at the end of the last year, there will be one final attempt at battle. Apparently it will be instigated by the descendants of Gog (Rev. 20:8); those who were born into the kingdom through mortals who had survived the Tribulation, but who secretly, within their hearts, rejected the Messiah. The Messiah will quickly halt this attempted rebellion, as He allows these people to make themselves known for the first time, as they chose to reject the truth. Even in a perfect environment, they will finally illustrate that positive surroundings do not heal man's fallen heart of sin—only Jesus does, and He only does it when invited personally to do so. He loves us beyond all, but will never violate our free will.

ANTI-PREMILLENNIAL (MESSIANIC KINGDOM) TEACHERS WOULD RATHER YOU NOT KNOW ABOUT THE PARADISE OF JESUS, BECAUSE THEY ARE JEALOUS, OR UNBELIEVERS THEMSELVES!

Now you have been enlightened in the revelation of this beautiful kingdom. If it was the first time you heard this, you should know why you did not hear about it before from your church or minister!

There are many "ministers" today, and untold numbers of religious leaders of centuries past, who taught violently against God's 1000-year kingdom of peace, promised to you in the many prophecies of the Old Testament and the last book of the New Testament (Rev. 20:4). We ask ourselves, "Why?" Some, of course, do not feel worthy themselves of going there, and thus, they very definitely do not want you to have the hope which they do not! They simply cannot stand the thought of Abraham, Isaac and Jacob, and all of the believing[51] Jews, together with the Evangelical Christians, enjoying eternity in a physical, literal kingdom in which they have no part.

Others, of course, do not believe in the Bible, but are only "frocked" because their profession requires it. Thus they adhere to the most liberal and unorthodox position, allowing them the maximum comfort in their hopeless unbelief! There are even liberal rabbis who neither believe in a Messiah nor a Messianic Kingdom.

---

[51]Believers in Jesus as Messiah.

JESUS TAUGHT THE APOSTLES AS WELL AS US, THROUGH PRAYERS AND PROMISES, THAT THERE WILL BE AN EARTHLY MESSIANIC KINGDOM

Jesus taught us in the Lord's prayer to pray for this kingdom. He said: "After this manner therefore pray ye: Our Father which art in heaven, Hallowed be thy name. Thy **kingdom** come. Thy will be done in earth, as *it is* in heaven" (Matt. 6:9-10 KJV).

We can know with certainty that this is a literal kingdom for the future of believers and believing Israel, because Jesus' very own apostles later asked: "...Lord, wilt thou at this time restore again the **kingdom** to Israel?" (Acts 1:6 KJV). Jesus' reply was: "...It is not for you to know the times or the seasons, which the Father hath put in his own power" (Acts 1:7 KJV).

An answer like this gives us hope for the future, even though we don't know exactly when this kingdom begins. We were told previously by Jesus there would be a regeneration upon the earth in which the apostles and believers would rule (Matt. 19:28).

DESPITE JESUS AND JOHN'S REVELATORY PROMISE OF A KINGDOM, LIBERALS AND ECUMENICALS SELDOM TAKE A "POSITION"—THUS, CONVENIENTLY AVOIDING THE QUESTION

I once asked a Greek "priest"[52] what the Greek Orthodox Church believed regarding the 1000-year reign of Jesus over all the world as Messiah, while pointing to verse 4 in Revelation 20: "...they lived and reigned with Christ, one thousand years." He raised his eyebrows and snapped defensively, "I know it says 1000 years, but we do not take a position on that!"[53]

---

[52]One named Homer p. Goumenis in Atlanta, GA.

[53]*Israel My Glory*, a Jewish-Christian magazine, notes that the Christian writer, Harnack: "...claimed that in their eschatology the early Christians preserved the Jewish hopes for the future presented in ancient Jewish literature." Dr. Renald E. Showers, "A Description and Early History of Millennial Views," *Israel My Glory*, June-Oct. 1986, used by permission. The same magazine reminds us, using Harnack as its authority, that: "As early as 170 A.D. a church group (known as the Alogi) in Asia Minor rejected the prophetic writings from which the premillennial view was derived. This group 'denounced the Apocalypse of John as a book of fables'....Because of the great influence of the Alexandrian scholars, most of the Greek Church followed their lead in rejecting Premillennialism. Concerning this rejection of the premillennial views in the East, Harnack wrote: 'It was the Alexandrian theology that superseded them; that is to say, Neo-Platonic mysticism triumphed over the early Christian hope of the future'....Harnack related the following information concerning the controversy between Dionysius and Nepos: 'During this controversy Dionysius became convinced that the victory of mystical theology over 'Jewish' Chiliasm would never be secure so long as the

If you ask around, you will see that nearly all the ecumenical, Catholic and liberal Protestant "Churches" deny this great promise of the New Testament to Israel and the believing world.

TRUE BIBLE BELIEVING CHRISTIANS HOLD FIRM TO GOD'S PRECIOUS PROMISE OF THE MILLENNIAL KINGDOM, FOR OURSELVES AND THE BELIEVING JEW

We, as true Bible believing pro-Israel believers in Jesus, accept the literal promises of the Bible. Hal Lindsey, one of the more well-known premillennialists, who has sold millions of **popular** books supporting our true, literal viewpoint, reminds us: "This view holds that Christ will literally and bodily return to earth *before* the thousand-year Kingdom begins. He will set up this Kingdom and reign from the throne of David out of a rebuilt city of Jerusalem....Pre-millennialists also believe that God made many unconditional promises and covenants with Israel, and that...God will *literally fulfill* all His promises during this thousand-year Kingdom period. Church-age believers and Tribulation believers will also be the recipients of these promises as the adopted sons of Abraham."[54]

LINDSEY REMINDS US THAT MOST MINISTERS DENY THE LITERAL TRUTH OF THE KINGDOM, EVEN THOUGH THE PROPHECIES OF JESUS' FIRST COMING WERE LITERAL

Hal Lindsey elaborates in his book, *The Late Great Planet Earth*: "Most ministers and religious leaders today reject even the possibility that Christ will establish an actual physical kingdom of God upon the earth. Many who believe in a personal return of Christ reject that He

---

Apocalypse of John passed for an apostolic writing and kept its place among the homologoumena of the canon. He accordingly raised the question of the apostolic origin of the Apocalypses and by reviving old difficulties, with ingenious arguments of his own, he carried his point.' Dionysius so prejudiced the Greek Church against the Book of Revelation and its canonicity that during the fourth century that church removed it from its canon of Scripture, 'and thus the troublesome foundation on which Chiliasm might have continued to build was got rid of.' The Greek Church kept the Book of Revelation out of its canon for several centuries, 'and consequently Chiliasm remained in its grave.' The Greek Church restored the book to its canon late in the Middle Ages, but by that time the damage to the premillennial view could not be remedied." Ibid. It goes without saying that even though these ecumenical churches have greatly persecuted us in the past, we are proud to be free premillennial evangelical believers today, just as our forefathers were, who lived in the generation of Jesus' life on Earth. We are proud of our biblical faith in which we love the Jew. This faith has proven superior and true to Jesus' teachings over all other "Christian" faiths that have gone against the wishes of Jesus—even to the point of attempting to relegate portions of the Scripture to fables!

[54]Hal Lindsey, *There's A New World Coming*, p. 267.

will establish a thousand year kingdom of God and rule mortals from the throne of David out of Jerusalem after His return. The Latin word for '1000' is 'millennium' and down through history the teaching concerning this earthly kingdom came to be known as the 'millennial kingdom.' Those who reject that Christ will establish a 1000 year kingdom after His return, are known theologically as 'amillennialists,' meaning 'no millennium.' Those who believe that Christ will return and set up a 1000 year kingdom are called 'premillennialists,' meaning Christ returns first, then establishes the kingdom on earth....We are 'premillennialists' in viewpoint. The real issue between the amillennial and the premillennial viewpoints is whether prophecy should be interpreted literally or allegorically. As it has been demonstrated many times in this book, all prophecy about past events has been fulfilled literally, particularly the predictions regarding the first coming of Christ. The words of prophecy were demonstrated as being literal, that is, having the normal meaning understood by the people of the time in which it was written. The words were not intended to be explained away by men who cannot believe what is clearly predicted.

The opponents[55] of the premillennial view all agree grudgingly that if you interpret prophecy literally it does teach that Christ will set

---

55On the subject of the 1000-year kingdom, many modern critics of the literal interpretation of the Bible, shout, "Premillennialism is a new fundamentalist view, a modern Christian invention of this century!" They should do their homework. Justin's biblical view that Jesus would return and inaugurate a 1000-year earthly kingdom was believed by the apostles. The first century Christian apologist, Justin Martyr, who was killed as a result of his faith, wrote: " '... But I and others, who are right-minded Christians on all points, are assured that there will be a resurrection of the dead, and a thousand years in Jerusalem, which will then be built, adorned, and enlarged, [as] the prophets Ezekiel and Isaiah and others declare'....there was a certain man with us, whose name was John, one of the apostles of Christ, who prophesied, by a revelation that was made to him, that those who believed in our Christ would dwell a thousand years in Jerusalem; and that thereafter....the eternal resurrection and judgment of all men would likewise take place." Dr. Renald E. Showers, "A Description and Early History of Millennial Views," *Israel My Glory*, June-Oct. 1986. Tertullian wrote: "...we do confess that a kingdom is promised to us upon the earth, although before heaven, only in another state of existence; inasmuch as it will be after the resurrection for a thousand years....After its thousand years are over...there will ensue the destruction of the world and the conflagration of all things at the judgments...." Ibid. *Israel My Glory*'s source was *Tertullian Against Marcion*, Book III, Anti-Nicene Fathers, p. 342. Irenaeus, second century Bishop of Lyons/church father and student of Polycarp, was a disciple of John the apostle. John was Jesus' closest buddy and the author of Revelation, the last book of the New Testament. Irenaeus wrote of the miraculous paradise of the millennium. "The predicted blessing, therefore, belongs unquestionably to the times of the kingdom, when the righteous shall bear rule upon their rising from the dead; when also the creation, having been renovated and set free, shall fructify with an abundance of all kinds of food, from the dew of heaven, and from the fertility of the earth: as the elders who saw John, the disciples of the Lord, related that they had heard from him how the Lord used to teach in regard to these times...." Ibid. *Israel My Glory*'s source was *Irenaeus Against* up a literal kingdom in time which will last in history a thousand years and then go into an eternal form which will never be destroyed.

To us the biggest issue is the question, 'Does God keep His promises?' For God unconditionally promised Abraham's descendants a literal world-wide kingdom over which they would rule through their Messiah who would reign upon King David's throne. The Jews who believe in the Messiah will also possess the land which is bordered on the east by the Euphrates River, and on the west by the Nile (Genesis 15:18-21).

It is promised that Jerusalem will be the spiritual center of the entire world and that all people of the earth will come annually to worship Jesus who will rule there (Zechariah 14:16-21; Isaiah 2:3; Micah 4:1-3). The Jewish believing remnant will be the spiritual leaders of the world and teach all nations the ways of the Lord (Zechariah 8:20-23; Isaiah 66:23)."[56]

LINDSEY EXPOSES THE FALSE TEACHING ABOUT THE MILLENNIUM, BY THE DOMINIONISTS, AS ANTI-SEMITIC

Hal Lindsey exposes some of the teachers of the Christian Reform Movement, Dominionists and others, showing Scriptural proof of their false teachings against the Messianic Kingdom, in his book, *The Road to Holocaust.* The cover flap of this work reads: "Now, from bestselling author Hal Lindsey, here is the shocking revelation of a spiritual movement that would take over our churches and government and lead us to disaster. At just the time current events are

---

Heresies, Book V, pp. 562-563. Lactantius wrote of this future kingdom: "Then, those who will be living in bodies will not die, but will generate an infinite multitude during those same thousand years....Those who will be raised from the dead will be in charge of the living as judges." Ibid, p. 25. The church father, Lactantius (240-320 AD), was known as the Christian Cicero because of his famous writings defending the Christian faith. Jerome referred to him as "the most learned man of his time." Ibid. The word *Chiliasm* is Greek for belief in a 1000-year literal Messianic Kingdom. Thus, this view is not a new view, as the liberals would have us believe. So much for their "scholarship." Rather, this is the original Christian view revived! Even the Jewish Talmud teaches that the Messiah will rule over the 1000-year Messianic Kingdom. Today's liberal "Christians," who are not really Christian at all, will be told one day by Jesus, "I never knew you" (Matt. 7:23), because they mock being born-again, which is the only way to know Jesus personally. They late date prophecy and claim the promises of the Bible, like the millennial kingdom mentioned in Revelation 20:4, nearly 2000 years ago, are recent ideas which were invented in an effort to discredit them. They do this in order to make us lose hope and the spirit of sharing Jesus with others, because they do not want us to be given what they have rejected out of bitterness. We define the word "Christian" as the New Testament does. Remember, Newton said that such liberal allegorizing individuals are "no true beleever and are not to be regarded as such" (see our chapter 11, "Newton's Forbidden Works Rescued").

[56]Hal Lindsey with C.C. Carlson, *The Late Great Planet Earth*, pp. 164-165.

converging into the precise pattern the biblical Prophets predicted would occur before the return of Jesus Christ, a new movement has sprung up within the Evangelical Church that denies it all. With subtle appeal to the politically conservative Christian, the movement allegorizes away the clear meaning of prophecy....Hal Lindsey sounds a warning about Dominion Theology and explains why, in his estimation, it poses such a great danger to the Church and to the Jew."[57] For a fuller understanding of the millennium, we recommend all believers and interested people read these quality books!

ISAAC NEWTON AFFIRMS ONE OF GOD'S PREDICTED PURPOSES FOR THE MILLENNIUM—TO KEEP THE PROMISE TO HIS ANCIENT PEOPLE, THE JEWS

The scientist, Isaac Newton, in affirming that the millennial kingdom and the city of the New Jerusalem were promised by God to the Jews, quotes Isaiah 65, and comments: "These mortal inhabitants of this city the Prophet afterwards...describes to be the nation of the **Jews** returned from captivity...."[58]

Newton then quotes Isaiah 54: "*...thy seed shall inherit the Gentiles, and make the desolate cities to be inhabited....*For a small moment have I forsaken thee [during thy captivity] but with great mercy will I gather thee [from among the nations.] In a little wrath I hid my face from thee for a moment but with everlasting kindness will I have mercy on thee saith the Lord thy redeemer."[59]

After this, Isaac Newton emphatically states: "This [kingdom] was God's covenant with Abraham when he promised that his seed should inherit the land of Canaan for ever, and on this ⟨promise⟩ covenant was founded the Jewish religion as on that is founded the Christian; and therefore this point is of so great moment that it ought to be considered and understood by all men who pretend to the name of Christians."[60]

THE BORDERS OF THE FUTURE MILLENNIAL KINGDOM—TERRIFIC!

One may ask, "How will Israel become the center of the world, at its present size? How could every nation on Earth come once a year to

---

[57]Hal Lindsey, *The Road To Holocaust*, p. cover flap.

[58]Frank E. Manuel, *The Religion of Isaac Newton*, p. 128. Bold mine. Manuel's source was *Yahuda Manuscript 1*.

[59]Ibid, p. 128.

[60]Ibid, p. 130. [ ] mine.

pay homage to Jesus in His 1000-year kingdom on Earth?" The answer to this is recorded in Genesis, where it says: "In the same day the LORD made a covenant with Abram, saying, Unto thy seed have I given this land, from the river of Egypt unto the great river, the river Euphrates: The Kenites, and the Kenizzites, and the Kadmonites, And the Hittites, and the Perizzites, and the Rephaims, And the Amorites, and the Canaanites, and the Girgashites, and the Jebusites" (Gen. 15:18-21 KJV).

This is known, in biblical terms, as the royal grant to Abraham. This land, as of yet, has never been possessed by Israel in ancient or modern times. Only when Jesus returns will this glorious grant be honored! In order to give you an idea of the increased ratio of land area which will be given to Israel in this kingdom, we have illustrated two charts drawn by Rev. Clarence Larkin in the early 1900's. The present Israel is only a fraction of these areas which are shaded by Larkin,[61] which were promised along with much more lands, as outlined to become part of Israel during the kingdom, according to Genesis 15:18-21.

Sir Isaac Newton.

[61]Should we call them territories, like our leftist news media? No! By the way, I do not believe we will have news networks in this kingdom. If we do, they will probably be the Crouch/Robertson-type, rather than Dan Rather!

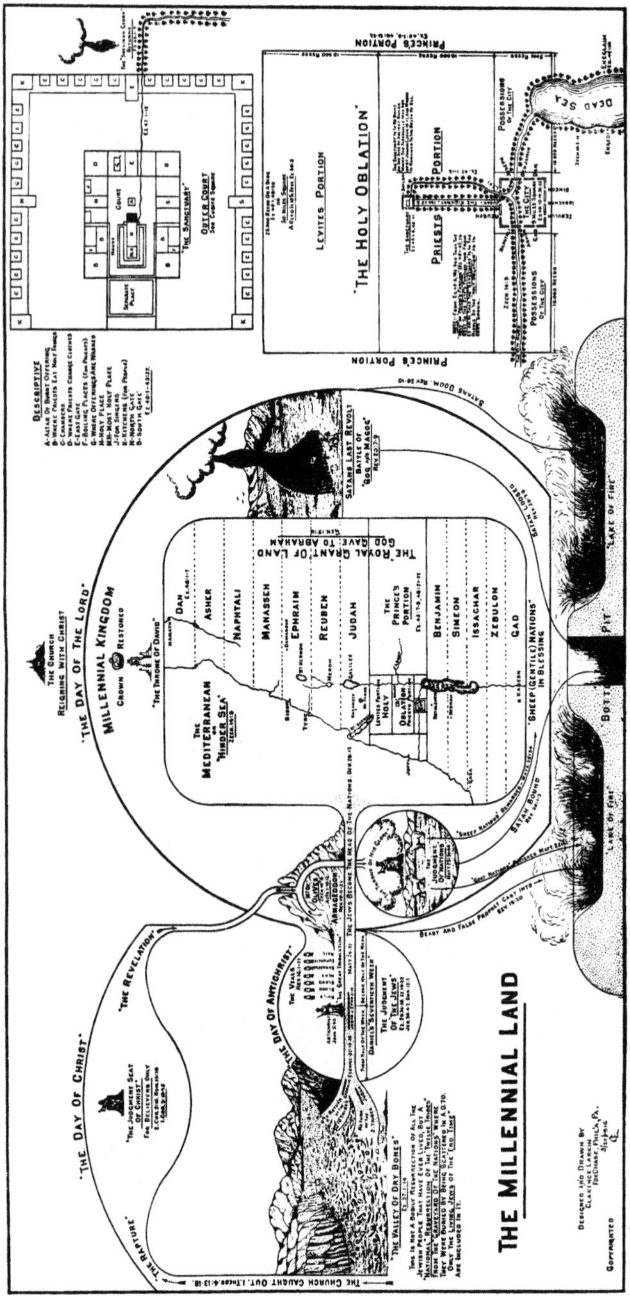

The New World, New Jerusalem and Israel's promised land, are shown here in their prophetical entirety.

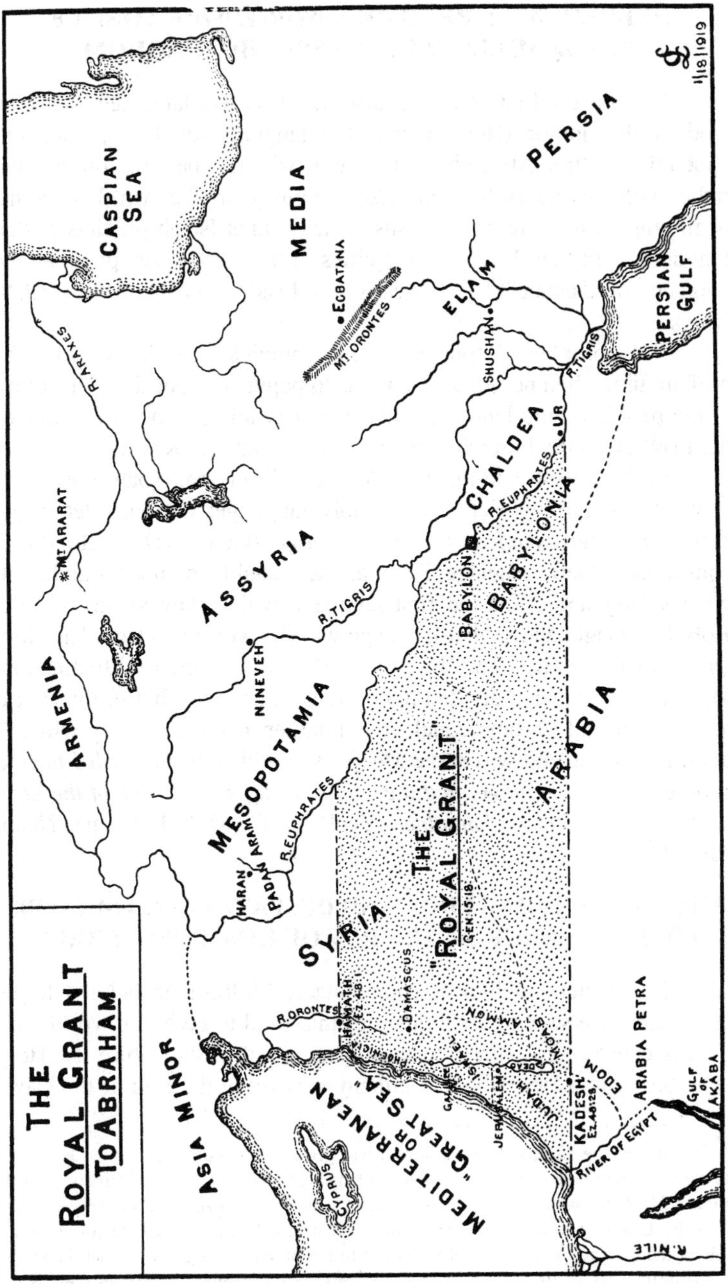

The royal grant of the land of Israel, promised to Abraham for the age of the millennial kingdom, soon to be realized.

HEBREW WILL BECOME A *WORLDWIDE* TONGUE IN THE MILLENNIAL MESSIANIC KINGDOM

Perhaps the first and, of course, most perfect language, of which God is the author (Hebrew was the language of Jesus; see our appendix 1, "It's All *Hebrew* to Me"), will not be lost forever, but rather will be the earth's universal language in the world to come, beginning with the return of Jesus. The prophet Isaiah predicts of that kingdom: "In that day shall five cities in the land of Egypt speak the language of Canaan,[62] and swear to the LORD of hosts...." (Isa. 19:18 KJV).

The prophet Zephaniah also predicted Hebrew for the millennium, when he set God's words to papyrus: "For then will I turn to the people a pure language, that they may all call upon the name of the LORD, to serve him with one consent" (Zeph. 3:9 KJV).

In the Jewish commentary, Midrash Tanhuma, Noah, Par. 19, it is written regarding Zephaniah's holy language: "*Come, let us go down and there confound their language* (Gen. 11:7). He [God] confounded their languages so that they could not understand each other's language. For the first language which they spoke was the Holy Language, and in that language was the world created. The Holy One, blessed be He, said: 'In This World, through the Evil Inclination, My creatures became divided into seventy languages, but in the World to come all will become equal, and shoulder to shoulder they will call upon My Name and will serve Me, as it is said, *For then will I turn to peoples a pure language, that they may call upon the name of the Lord to serve him with one shoulder* (Zeph. 3:9)" (Mid. Tanhuma, Noah, par., 19).[63]

THE MIDRASH HAGADOL AND DR. PATAI LEND SUPPORT TO OUR EVANGELICAL VIEW OF KINGDOM HEBREW

The ancient rabbinical commentary, Midrash haGadol, tells us that there were several good qualities that used to be in the world, but: "...sins caused all of them to disappear. And in the future the Holy One, blessed be He, will restore them to Israel at the End of the Days.

---

[62]Canaan was the name of Israel before it was given to and colonized by the Jews, and its name became Israel. Thus, we know the language spoken of here is Hebrew. Verses 20 and 21 of the same passage in Isaiah state concerning Egypt: "...for they shall cry unto the LORD because of the oppressors, and he shall send them a savior...he shall deliver them. And the LORD shall be known to Egypt, and the Egyptians shall know the LORD in that day...." (Isa. 19:20-21 KJV). Thus we see here that the time-frame is the kingdom once Jesus returns. Only then will the Egyptians, who are now Moslems, recognize the true God of Israel, and of course, the Savior, who saves those who believe, will be the Jewish Messiah Jesus.

[63]Raphael Patai, *The Messiah Texts*, p. 260.

And they are: The image and the stature and the Garden of Eden and the Tree of Life and the heroism and the years and many children and the peace and the **Holy Language**...."[64]

Raphael Patai's footnote to "image" indicates Genesis 1:26, whereby we were originally created in God's image. Patai's footnote to years is: "I.e. the long life, such as the 930 years of Adam, cf. Gen. 5:5." His footnote to peace is: "I.e., safety from harmful demons, and the absence of suffering, p. 137." And to add our point, his footnote to "Holy Language" states: "The Aggadic view is that until the Generation of the Dispersion (the tower of Babel), the whole world spoke Hebrew." Patai references Genesis 11:1 and Midrash haGadol (p. 137) to support his point!

THE EVANGELICAL WRITER, GRANT JEFFREY, NOTES THAT THE PRESENT RETURN OF HEBREW IS "A PHENOMENON WITHOUT PRECEDENT"

The popular Evangelical Christian writer, Grant Jeffrey, beautifully pointed out: "The revival of the ancient language of Hebrew in modern Israel, is another miraculous fulfillment of prophecy in our day. This recovery of a 'dead' language and its revival after some two thousand years is a phenomenon without precedent in human history. It is interesting that God calls Hebrew a 'pure' language. Several Israelis have stated that an unusual characteristic of Hebrew, is that one cannot use it to swear[65] or take the name of the Lord in vain."[66] What better reason for the world to speak such a language during the millennium?

WHAT IS BETTER THAN THE MILLENNIUM? ETERNITY!

We have now covered everything unbelievers were not aware they would be missing in the kingdom. We realize, with sympathy, the tragedy of their absence from us. However, God will wipe away our tears and the memory of this sadness (Rev. 21:4). Our next question may well be, "What could be better than the 1000-year Messianic Kingdom?" This is the subject of our next chapter.

---

[64]Ibid, p. 263. Bold mine.

[65]You may be saying to yourself that nearly everyone swears now and then. How could an entire nation never swear? Messianic rabbi and teacher, Manny Brotman, in his tapes, "How to Share the Messiah With Your Jewish Friends," mentions that the Hebrew language prophecy is coming true and that Hebrew will be spoken in the kingdom. He points out that Israelis have told him that, in order to curse, slang words have been invented and borrowed from the Arabic. Biblical Hebrew is truly a pure language. These tapes are available through The Messianic Jewish Movement International, POB 30313 Bethesda, MD, USA 20824. Tel. 301-656-7875

[66]Grant R. Jeffrey, *Armageddon, Appointment with Destiny*, p. 120.

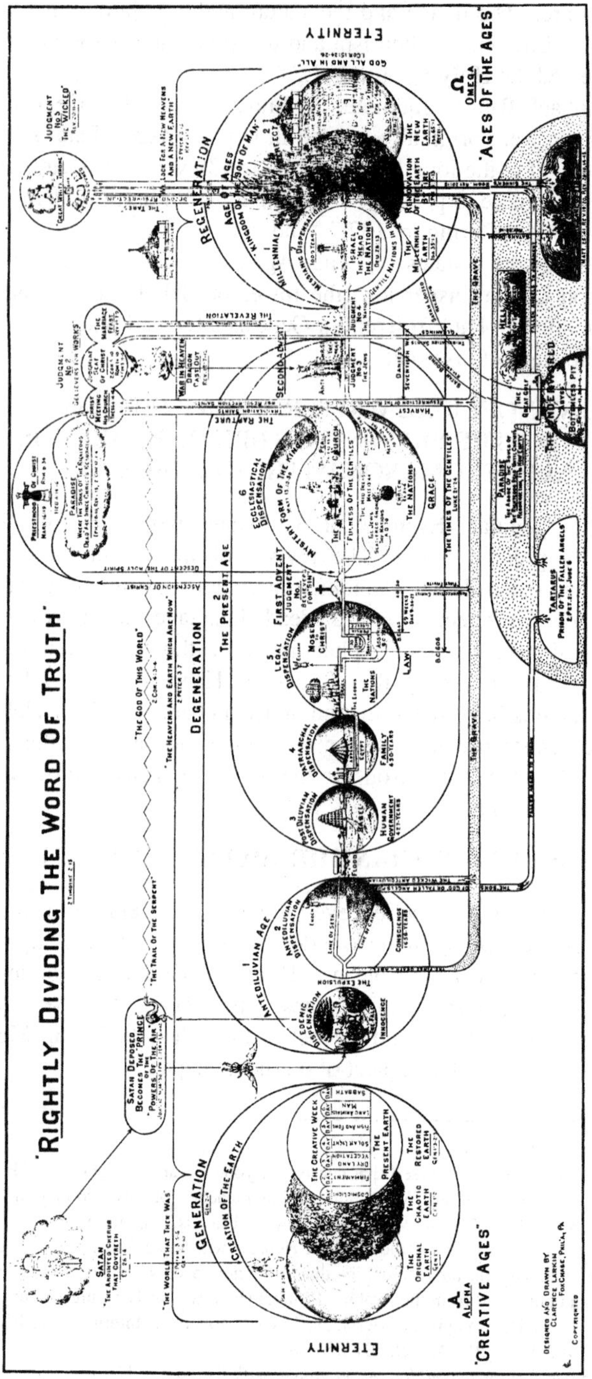
'RIGHTLY DIVIDING THE WORD OF TRUTH'
2 TIMOTHY 2:15
ETERNITY
ALPHA
'CREATIVE AGES'
GENERATION
CREATION OF THE EARTH
THE ORIGINAL EARTH
THE CHAOTIC EARTH
THE PRESENT EARTH
THE RESTORED EARTH
THE CREATIVE WEEK
SATAN DEPOSED BECOMES THE 'PRINCE OF THE POWERS OF THE AIR'
'THE TRAIL OF THE SERPENT'
'THE GOD OF THIS WORLD'
'THE HEAVENS AND EARTH WHICH ARE NOW'
DEGENERATION
ANTEDILUVIAN AGE
EDENIC DISPENSATION
INNOCENCE
ANTEDILUVIAN DISPENSATION
CONSCIENCE
POST DILUVIAN DISPENSATION
HUMAN GOVERNMENT
PATRIARCHAL DISPENSATION
FAMILY
LEGAL DISPENSATION
LAW
THE PRESENT AGE
FIRST ADVENT
ECCLESIASTICAL DISPENSATION
GRACE
'THE TIMES OF THE GENTILES'
THE RAPTURE
SECOND ADVENT
REGENERATION
AGE OF AGES
MILLENNIAL
THE NEW EARTH
THE GRAVE
TARTARUS
PARADISE
HELL
OMEGA
'AGES OF THE AGES'
ETERNITY
DESIGNED AND DRAWN BY CLARENCE LARKIN FOX CHASE, PHILA, PA
COPYRIGHTED

"For, behold, I create new heavens and a new earth: and the former shall not be remembered, nor come into mind. But be ye glad and rejoice for ever *in that* which I create: for, behold, I create Jerusalem a rejoicing, and her people a joy. And I will rejoice in Jerusalem, and joy in my people: and the voice of weeping shall be no more heard in her, nor the voice of crying." Isaiah 65:17-19 KJV

"...we, according to his promise, look for new heavens and a new earth....Wherefore, beloved, seeing that ye look for such things, be diligent that ye may be found of him in peace...." II Peter 3:13-14 KJV

"And I saw a new heaven and a new earth: for the first heaven and the first earth were passed away; and there was no more sea. And I John saw the holy city, new Jerusalem, coming down from God out of heaven, prepared as a bride adorned for her husband. And I heard a great voice out of heaven saying, Behold, the tabernacle of God *is* with men, and he will dwell with them, and they shall be his people, and God himself shall be with them, *and be* their God. And God shall wipe away all tears from their eyes; and there shall be no more death, neither sorrow, nor crying, neither shall there be any more pain: for the former things are passed away. And he that sat upon the throne said, Behold, I make all things new. And he said unto me, Write: for these words are true and faithful. And he said unto me, It is done. I am Alpha and Omega, the beginning and the end. I will give unto him that is athirst of the fountain of the water of life freely." Revelation 21:1-6 KJV

30

NEW HEAVENS AND A NEW EARTH

When the end of the 1000-year kingdom is reached, there will be a judgment of the unbelievers from every era, known as the Great White Throne, on which Daniel and Jesus elaborate considerably.[1] After this judgment is conducted, the present Heaven and Earth are transformed by fire into a new eternal form.

In his inspired writings, the apostle Peter graphically describes the way God terminates the millennium in order to make room for the eternal kingdom, known to us as the New Heavens (universe) and Earth. "But the heavens and the earth, which are now, by the same word are kept in store, reserved unto fire against the day of judgment and perdition of ungodly men. But, beloved, be not ignorant of this one thing, that one day *is* with the Lord as a thousand years, and a thousand years as one day. The Lord is not slack concerning his promise, as some men count slackness; but is longsuffering to us-ward, not willing that any should perish, but that all should come to repentance" (II Pet. 3:7-9 KJV).

[1]See Daniel 12 and John 5 in the Bible.

PETER PROPHESIED THE POWER OF ATOMS

The phrase "stored with fire" illustrates that Peter, although not knowledgeable himself about the atom, accurately described the immense power stored within it, which when split, emits much heat and fire, thus causing the disintegration of matter. Peter continues: "But the day of the Lord will come as a thief in the night; in the which the heavens shall pass away with a great noise, and the elements shall melt with fervent heat, the earth also and the works that are therein shall be burned up. *Seeing* then *that* all these things shall be dissolved, what manner *of persons* ought ye to be in *all* holy conversation and godliness. Looking for and hasting unto the coming of the day of God, wherein the heavens being on fire shall be dissolved, and the elements shall melt with fervent heat? Nevertheless we, according to his promise, look for new heavens and a new earth, wherein dwelleth righteousness" (II Pet. 3:10-13 KJV).

Here, in what God inspired Peter to reveal to us, we have the explanation of how God creates room for us to live in His New Earth! It is interesting to note that we could not have clearly understood these verses until the age of Einstein, nearly 2000 years after they were inscribed on papyrus. Through our modern understanding of nuclear physics, we can grasp something of God's description to Peter of the immense heat and fire released when He explodes every atom.[2]

[2]Hal Lindsey enlightens us: "The word translated 'elements' is *stoicheiov*, which means the most basic element of nature. Today we know the atom is the smallest building block of nature. Now Peter says that these elements will be 'destroyed.' The literal meaning of the word 'destroyed' is 'to loose something.' It was frequently used for untying a rope, or a bandage as in John 11:44. In other words, Christ is going 'to loose' the atoms of the

Furthermore, we now know Einstein was not the first to realize the power of the atom. We see it was also encoded by God in the Holy Scriptures long ago.

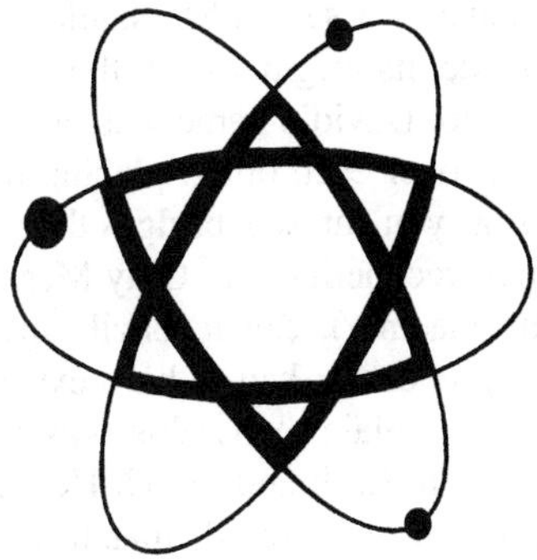

Since the Godhead is three in one, we present a diagram of an atom with three electrons in orbit around its nucleus, which contains protons and neutrons. Notice that the inner design forms the six-pointed Star of David. Notice also that the Star of David is composed of a triangle pointing up toward God, and another pointing down toward man. A triangle has three sides, illustrating man's complete essence of: 1. mind; 2. body; 3. spirit; which were made in God's image. God is also one, yet three at the same time (Gen. 1:26).[3] In the Old Testament, Isaiah 48:16 relates, in God's own words: "Come ye near unto me, hear ye this; I have not spoken in secret from the beginning; from the time that it was, there *am* I: and now the Lord GOD [Father], and his Spirit ["Holy Spirit," in Hebrew, *Rauch ha Kodesh*], hath sent me [Messiah]" (KJV; [ ] mine).

Remember, the Messiah, who is said to be both man and God, would comprise both of these triangles which are interlocked in the Star of David ("shield of David" in Hebrew). Megan David ✡, David's true shield, was Messiah. The very phrase, "Son of David," is in itself, a Messianic idiom. The Messiah created every atom. "He was in the world, and the **world** was made **by him**, and the world knew him not" (John 1:10 KJV). Therefore, as you can see, His emblem is inscribed[4] in this molecular diagram designed by twentieth century science! We also believe He will recreate all matter in the new universe (Rev. 21)!

---

galaxy in which we live. No wonder there will be a great roar and intense heat and fire. Then Christ will put the atoms back together to form a new heaven and earth...." Hal Lindsey with C.C. Carlson, *The Late Great Planet Earth*, p. 179.

[3]Genesis 1:26 reads: "And God said, Let **us** make man in **our** image, after **our** likeness: and let them have dominion...." (KJV; bold mine).

[4]It is inscribed on the basic atom, which contains protons, neutrons and electrons. The electrons circle the nucleus of the atom at incredible speed, completing billions of revolutions in only one-millionth of a second.

In modern Israel, some religious Jews believe that the ancient Jewish King, David, signed his name with this star. The ancient Hebrew *daled* is shaped like a triangle, and the Hebrew name David has two D's! If you have ever seen a Messianic Jew wearing a Star of David with a cross inside, its origin was in the ancient name of David itself; for, 3000 years ago, David's name was not spelled דוד but ΔTΔ. If you invert the *daleds* over each other, placing the *vav* in the center, you get ✡. The cross, as you can see, bridges the gap between the God ∇ and man Δ triangles—reconciliation. Only Messiah, being both man and God (a kinsman redeemer), can reconcile man to God! As Hal Lindsey puts it: "...the redeemer had to be 'next of kin' to the human race. Hebrews 2:14,15 explains why this was so: 'Since then the children [mankind] share in flesh and blood, He Himself likewise also partook of the same [flesh and blood], that through death He might render powerless him who had the power of death, that is, the devil; and might deliver those who through fear of death were subject to slavery all their lives.'

You see, the price of redemption for man has always been the shed blood of an innocent substitute. Moses taught in the Law, 'Without the shedding of blood, there is no remission of sin' (Hebrews 9:22). However, the blood of animals could never take the sin away; it only atoned for, or covered it, temporarily until God provided a complete remission of sins through His ultimate sacrifice of Jesus (Hebrews 10:11-14).

But, since the redemption price had to be the shed *blood* of an *innocent* sacrifice, the redeemer had to be someone with blood in his veins who could actually experience death. In other words, a man, but one who was completely innocent of any sins."[5]

[5]Hal Lindsey, *The Liberation of Planet Earth*, pp. 106-107.

THE MOLECULAR TRANSFORMATION

The entire planet will undergo a molecular transformation of temporal material and natural substances into eternal, non-perishable elements! The grass, trees, animals, and of course, people, will not die or age, nor will it be possible to damage them. The entire planet will be breathtaking, refreshing, lush and green, full of beautiful plants, minerals and stones of perfection (no flawed diamonds), which will serve as the building materials in this new world! No more ugly cement, but diamonds, emeralds, rubies, sapphires, topaz, gold and many other precious materials will be used in building and construction. God will be our source of light (Isa. 60:19; Rev. 21:23) and the immortality of the Garden of Eden from before the Fall, will be restored and last forever! This might be the new physics Isaac Newton spoke of for the New Jerusalem.[6] Gravity, and other physical laws in force today, that many believe were the result of the Fall and which cause many undesirable effects on human life, will no longer be in effect! You will not walk off a building, fall and be crushed by gravity, as you would now.

The astrophysicist Hugh Ross noted on his April 29, 1995, broadcast, *Reasons to Believe*: "The law of decay will be taken away; the law of gravity will be taken away....it's easy to see in picking our way through that twenty-first chapter [of Revelation] that the law of gravity has been replaced. The laws of thermodynamics have been replaced, and it's the law of gravity and the laws of thermodynamics that cause things to wear down, cause order to evolve into disorder that results in the increase of chaos. That will be taken care of. There will be no decay, no wearing down from the laws of gravity and thermodynamics."[7]

The Bible, both Old and New Testaments, and even the ancient rabbinical writings, describe the glories of the New Heavens, Earth and Jerusalem, which we believe will become a reality within the next thirty years!

***

---

[6]The article in the Hebrew newspaper, *Al Hamishmar*, July 26, 1985, speaks of Newton's conviction of a new physics in the New Jerusalem. The long-term time spent in space on our space shuttle flights justified this assumption. There are many health benefits which are gained in a weightless environment. Some believe that our present gravity, which kills if you fall more than a few feet, was part of the curse put on the ground in the Garden (Gen. 3). Jim Irwin, the Apollo 15 astronaut who walked on the moon, told me of the incredible mental clarity he experienced in weightlessness.

[7]*Reasons to Believe*, TBN, Apr. 29, 1995. [ ] mine. *Reasons to Believe* has many teaching materials with a biblical/astrophysical point of view, available through *Reasons to Believe*, POB 5978, Pasadena, CA, USA 91117.

ORIGINAL HEBREW TEXT WRITTEN 698 BC

כִּי־הִנְנִי בוֹרֵא שָׁמַיִם חֲדָשִׁים וָאָרֶץ חֲדָשָׁה וְלֹא תִזָּכַרְנָה הָרִאשֹׁנוֹת וְלֹא תַעֲלֶינָה עַל־לֵב׃
כִּי־אִם־שִׂישׂוּ וְגִילוּ עֲדֵי־עַד אֲשֶׁר אֲנִי בוֹרֵא כִּי הִנְנִי בוֹרֵא אֶת־יְרוּשָׁלִַם גִּילָה וְעַמָּהּ מָשׂוֹשׂ׃
וְגַלְתִּי בִירוּשָׁלִַם וְשַׂשְׂתִּי בְעַמִּי וְלֹא־יִשָּׁמַע בָּהּ עוֹד קוֹל בְּכִי וְקוֹל זְעָקָה׃ .... כִּי כַאֲשֶׁר
הַשָּׁמַיִם הַחֲדָשִׁים וְהָאָרֶץ הַחֲדָשָׁה אֲשֶׁר אֲנִי עֹשֶׂה עֹמְדִים לְפָנַי נְאֻם־יְהוָה כֵּן יַעֲמֹד זַרְעֲכֶם
וְשִׁמְכֶם׃ וְהָיָה מִדֵּי־חֹדֶשׁ בְּחָדְשׁוֹ וּמִדֵּי שַׁבָּת בְּשַׁבַּתּוֹ יָבוֹא כָל־בָּשָׂר לְהִשְׁתַּחֲוֹת לְפָנַי אָמַר
יְהוָה׃ **ישעיה סה:יז-יט; סו:כב-כג**

OLD TESTAMENT SCRIPTURE TRANSLATION

"For, behold, I create new heavens and a new earth: and the former shall not be remembered, nor come into mind. But be ye glad and rejoice for ever *in that* which I create: for, behold, I create Jerusalem a rejoicing, and her people a joy. And I will rejoice in Jerusalem, and joy in my people: and the voice of weeping shall be no more heard in her, nor the voice of crying....For as the new heavens and the new earth, which I will make, shall remain before me, saith the LORD, so shall your seed and your name remain. And it shall come to pass, *that* from one new moon to another, and from one sabbath to another, shall all flesh come to worship before me, saith the LORD." **Isaiah 65:17-19; 66:22-23 KJV**

ANCIENT RABBINICAL COMMENTARY

"...in the future the Holy One, blessed be He, will cause built-up Jerusalem to descend from heaven, and will set her upon the tops of four mountains: Upon Sinai, and upon Tabor, and upon Hermon, and upon Carmel. And she will stand on the tops of mountains and give good tidings to Israel about the End, the Redemption."[8]

Pesiqta diRabbi Kahana, ed. Mandelbaum, p. 466

"...There will be no more weeping and wailing in the world....There will be no more death in the world....There will be no more sigh, no more groan, no more sorrow, but all will rejoice...."[9] **Exodus Rabba 15:21**

NEW TESTAMENT RECORDED 96 AD

"And I saw a new heaven and a new earth: for the first heaven and the first earth were passed away; and there was no more sea. And I John saw the holy city, new Jerusalem, coming down from God out of heaven, prepared as a bride adorned for her husband. And I heard a great voice out of heaven saying, Behold, the tabernacle of God *is* with men, and he will dwell with them, and they shall be his people, and God himself shall be with them, *and be* their God. And God shall wipe away all tears from their eyes; and there shall be no more death, neither sorrow, nor crying, neither shall there be any more pain: for the former things are passed away. And he that sat upon the throne said, Behold, I make all things new. And he said unto me, Write: for these words are true and faithful....And the nations of them which are saved shall walk in the light of it: and the kings of the earth do bring their glory and honour into it. And the gates of it shall not be shut at all by day: for there shall be no night there. And they shall bring the glory and honour of the nations into it."

Revelation 21:1-5; 24-26 KJV

---

[8]Raphael Patai, *The Messiah Texts*, pp. 224-225.

[9]Ibid, p. 261.

If you are a gemologist, then the eternal
New Jerusalem will be your dream come true!

ORIGINAL HEBREW TEXT WRITTEN 712, 997 BC

עֲנִיָּה סֹעֲרָה לֹא נֻחָמָה הִנֵּה אָנֹכִי מַרְבִּיץ בַּפּוּךְ אֲבָנַיִךְ וִיסַדְתִּיךְ בַּסַּפִּירִים׃ וְשַׂמְתִּי כַּדְכֹד
שִׁמְשֹׁתַיִךְ וּשְׁעָרַיִךְ לְאַבְנֵי אֶקְדָּח וְכָל־גְּבוּלֵךְ לְאַבְנֵי־חֵפֶץ׃ וְכָל־בָּנַיִךְ לִמּוּדֵי יְהוָה וְרַב .
שְׁלוֹם בָּנָיִךְ׃ .... עֹמְדוֹת הָיוּ רַגְלֵינוּ בִּשְׁעָרַיִךְ יְרוּשָׁלִָם׃ יְרוּשָׁלִַם הַבְּנוּיָה כְּעִיר
שֶׁחֻבְּרָה־לָּהּ יַחְדָּו׃ **ישעיה נד:יא-יג; תהלים קכב:ב-ג**

OLD TESTAMENT SCRIPTURE TRANSLATION

"O thou afflicted, tossed with tempest, *and* not comforted, behold, I will lay thy stones with fair colours, and lay thy foundations with sapphires. And I will make thy windows of agates, and thy gates of carbuncles, and all thy borders of pleasant stones. And all thy children *shall be* taught of the LORD; and great *shall be* the peace of thy children....Our feet shall stand within thy gates, O Jerusalem. Jerusalem is builded as a city that is compact together...."

Isaiah 54:11-13; Psalms 122:2-3 KJV

ANCIENT RABBINICAL COMMENTARY

"Elijah said: 'I see a beautiful and great city descend from heaven, built up, as it is written, *Jerusalem that art builded as a city that is compact together* (Ps. 122:3). Built up and embellished, and her people dwell in her midst...and every *ris* comprises twenty-five thousand cubits of smaragds and precious stones and pearls....I see the houses and gates of the pious. Their lintels and sideposts are of precious stones, and the treasuries of the Sanctuary open right unto their doors. And Tora and peace are among them....' "[10]

Sefer Eliahu, BhM 3:67-68

"In the future there will be found in Jerusalem ten kinds of precious stones, and they are: ruby, topaz, emerald, beryl, onyx, jasper, carbuncle, sapphire, diamond, and gold—these are ten. And the Holy One, blessed be He, will add to them two...and they are: *kodkod* and *eqdah* [different varieties of rubies and carbuncles]."[11]

Milhamot Melekh haMashiah, BhM 6:118

"In Jerusalem there will be in the future, three thousand towers....And seven walls will surround Jerusalem, of silver, of gold, of precious stones, of stibium, of sapphire, of chalcedony, and of fire. And its glow will light up the world from one end to the other. And the Temple will be built on four mountains, of purified gold, of clear gold, of drawn gold, and of Parwayim gold....And it will be set in sapphires and capped in greatness."[12] **Pirqe Mashiah, BhM 3:74-75**

NEW TESTAMENT TRANSLATED 96 AD

"And he carried me away in the spirit to a great and high mountain, and shewed me that great city, the holy Jerusalem, descending out of heaven from God, Having the glory of God: and her light *was* like unto a stone most precious, even like a jasper stone, clear as crystal; And had a wall great and high, *and* had twelve gates, and at the gates twelve angels, and names written thereon, which are *the names* of the twelve tribes of the children of Israel: On the east three gates; on the north three gates; on the south three gates; and on the west three gates. And the wall of the city had twelve foundations, and in them the names of the twelve apostles of the Lamb....And the building of the wall of it was *of* jasper: and the city *was* pure gold, like unto clear glass. And the foundations of the wall of the city *were* garnished

---

[10] Ibid, p 225.
[11] Ibid, p. 226.
[12] Ibid, pp. 226-227.

with all manner of precious stones. The first foundation *was* jasper; the second, sapphire; the third, a chalcedony; the fourth, an emerald; The fifth, sardonyx; the sixth, sardius; the seventh, chrysolyte; the eighth, beryl; the ninth, a topaz; the tenth, a chrysoprasus; the eleventh, a jacinth; the twelfth, an amethyst. And the twelve gates *were* twelve pearls; every several gate was of one pearl: and the street of the city *was* pure gold, as it were transparent glass."

Revelation 21:10-14, 18-21 KJV

AUTHOR'S COMMENT—EVANGELICAL CHRISTIAN POSITION

We ask ourselves, "Can there be justice through stones, but not the ones you throw?" In the future, Rabbi Levi expounds on how the gems of Jerusalem will be used to perpetuate peace. "R. Levi said: 'In the future, the area of Jerusalem, measuring twelve by eighteen miles, will be full of precious stones and pearls. For in this world, if a man owes his neighbor something and he says to him, 'Let us go and be judged by the judge,' at times the judge makes peace between them and at times he does not make peace between them, and the two do not come out satisfied. But in the future to come, if a man owes his neighbor something, and he says to him, 'Let us go and be judged by King Messiah in Jerusalem,' as soon as they reach the outskirts of Jerusalem they will find them full of precious stones and pearls, and he will take two of them and say to him, 'Do I owe you more than these?' And the other will answer him, 'Not even this much! Let it be forgiven to you, let it be left to you!' "[13] (Pes. diR. Kahana, ed. Mandelbaum, pp. 299-300). Today's precious stones were formed from the immense build-up of pressure and heat in volcanoes and underground chambers and chasms. Thus, they are small in size and few in quantity. The Bible describes a time when tremendous heat and pressure will be released (II Pet. 3:10-13), as God transforms the earth from its millennial condition into its new eternal state. Thus we believe that this immense heat will naturally produce these precious stones in great abundance and size. If you enjoy precious jewels, you will be in Heaven! Won't you? The earth will radiate with an unfathomable beauty! **Philip Moore**

THE NEW JERUSALEM

John the revelator tells us of his eyewitness of the New Jerusalem: "And I John saw the holy city, New Jerusalem, coming down from God out of heaven, prepared as a bride adorned for her husband. And I heard a great voice out of heaven saying, Behold, the tabernacle of God *is* with men, and he will dwell with them, and they shall be his people, and God himself shall be with them, *and be* their God" (Rev. 21:2-3 KJV).

The New Jerusalem has been in existence since Jesus began to build mansions there for the believers after He left the earth in 33 AD. He once told the apostles, as it is written to us: "Let not your heart be troubled: ye believe in God, believe also in me. In my Father's house are many mansions: if *it were* not *so*, I would have told you. I go to prepare a place for you. And if I go and prepare a place for you, I will

[13]Ibid, p. 224.

come again, and receive you unto myself; that where I am, *there* ye may be also" (John 14:1-3 KJV).

At the Rapture, seven years before the millennium starts, believers will get their first chance to enjoy this completed city, soon to be on Earth! Once the New Heavens (cosmos) and Earth are created, then the city will be brought down to be the center of the world, for us to enjoy forevermore, as John saw: "...the holy city, New Jerusalem, coming down from God out of heaven...." (Rev. 21:2 KJV).

During the millennial kingdom, this city was suspended above the Earth. Those who received resurrection bodies at the Rapture will enjoy free access to it. This includes both Old Testament believers like Abraham, Isaac and Jacob, and us New Testament folks, who are alive when Jesus removes us before the Antichrist's reign. We shall travel back and forth between the city and the Earth below, administrating the Earth and angels (I Cor. 6:2-3). As Jesus promised, He would make us rulers over cities (Luke 19:16).

THE MILLENNIAL PEOPLE GET THEIR NEW BODIES AND WE WILL LIVE WITH THEM FOREVER!

Of course, during the time of the millennium, mortals with extended life spans would have lived on an Earth greatly transformed, but short of the perfection of the Garden of Eden. Now, in the New Heaven, Earth and Jerusalem, these people and their children have also received their resurrection bodies. This occurred after the Great White Throne judgment, when God transformed the old Earth, by fire, in order to create the new one. Thus everyone is in a permanent state and all who are redeemed are permitted, in the eternal kingdom, to go in and out of the twelve gates of pure pearl created for the nations. The New Jerusalem is going to be the center of our universe. Eventually, everything will revolve around the beautiful city God will give to us to live in forever!

ABRAHAM GETS HIS CITY, NEW JERUSALEM, PROMISED TO THE BELIEVING JEWS IN THE BOOK OF HEBREWS

Just think, Abraham will finally get the city for which he was looking! In the New Testament book of Hebrews, it is told that Abraham was promised this city: "By faith Abraham....looked for a city which hath foundations, whose builder and maker *is* God....all died in faith, not having received the promises, but having seen them afar off, and were persuaded of *them*, and embraced *them*....But now they desire a better *country*, that is, an heavenly: wherefore God is not ashamed to be called their God: for he hath prepared for them a city" (Heb. 11:8, 10, 13, 16 KJV). This city of foundations, spoken of in

Hebrews, is New Jerusalem. This city is for the saved of Israel, as well as for the bride of Jesus, mentioned in the New Testament; that is, all those who have believed in Him, from the time He came, until He returns (from Pentecost until the Rapture). This is made clear by the twelve foundation stones, which bear the apostles' names, and the twelve gates,[14] which are embossed with the names of the twelve tribes of Israel (Rev. 21:12)![15] Thus we can be sure that we will be in the presence of our creator, in a state of constant and perfect acceptance of love. Our old sin nature, which sometimes controls us and causes us to stumble now, will be gone. We will be made into perfection. The Scripture teaches: "Beloved, now we are children of God, and it has not appeared as yet what we shall be. We know that, when He appears, we shall be like Him, because we shall see Him just as He is" (I John 3:2 NASB).

The Holy City, New Jerusalem as illustrated by Reverend Clarence Larkin.

---

[14]Ezekiel 38:31-35, in the Old Testament, details these gates.

[15]"...Behold, the tabernacle of God *is* with men, and he will dwell with them, and they shall be his people, and God himself shall be with them, *and be* their God. And God shall wipe away all tears from their eyes; and there shall be no more death, neither sorrow, nor crying, neither shall there be any more pain: for the former things are passed away" (Rev. 21:3-4 KJV).

"And when thou art convinced be not ashamed to profess the truth. For otherwise thou mayst become a stumbling block to others, and inherit the lot of those **Rulers** of the Jews who beleived in Christ but yet were afraid to confess him least they should be put out of the Synagogue. Wherefore when thou art convinced be not ashamed of the truth but profess it openly and indeavour to convince thy Brother also that thou mayst inherit at the resurrection the promis made in Daniel 12.3, that they who turn many to righteousness shall shine as the starrs for ever and ever. And rejoyce if thou art counted worthy to suffer in thy reputation or any other way for the sake of the Gospel, for then great is thy reward."[16]

Sir Isaac Newton (1642-1727)

If we are as He is, there will be no worries or sorrows, no more tears—for Jesus wipes them away—no more death. Just think of it, in the New Jerusalem, there will be no graveyards or monuments of marble to painfully cry over, as we have and do now. We will, as Jesus shone forth at His transfiguration (Matt. 17:1-5), shine. As Daniel promised to those who win many to righteousness (believing in the forgiveness of Messiah), we will "shine...like the stars **forever and ever**" (Dan. 12:3 NASB), in our new and beautifully indestructible eternal bodies.

WHAT IS THE EVIDENCE OF THE NEW JERUSALEM? HAS ANYONE LIVED TO TELL ABOUT IT?

Jesus began to build this city and its mansions, for all of us, immediately upon His ascension to Heaven. This is where believers go "to Heaven" to be "face-to-face" with the Lord until His Second Coming and the subsequent resurrection of the physical body! There are some who would deny us the possibility of Paradise! Many liberal ministers and atheists alike may scoff at God's promises and say, "There's no proof—no one ever lived to tell us!" To such an accusation, we as believers, have a question and an answer: 1. "Has anybody ever disproved Heaven's New Jerusalem?" The answer (if honest) will be no; 2. Many have indeed survived death and, after an extended temporary death experience and medical resuscitation, describe just such a city.

A DOCTOR'S ENCOUNTER WITH HIS PATIENTS' CONFESSIONS

Dr. Raymond Moody, author of *Life After Life* and *Reflections on Life After Life,* interviewed over 1000 people who experienced clinical death and were successfully resuscitated. These people gave similar vivid descriptions of their experiences! In his second book, *Reflections on Life After Life*, Moody dealt with advanced cases of people

---

[16]Frank E. Manuel, *The Religion of Isaac Newton*, pp. 112-113. Manuel's source was *Yahuda Manuscript 1*. The spellings are Newton's from over three hundred years ago.

surviving bodily death of extreme duration, up to twenty minutes,[17] who then reported unusual events which occurred once death had advanced considerably. These individuals are seldom successfully revived. However, in some cases, they saw this city just prior to resuscitation. Excerpts from two of Dr. Moody's interviews reveal: "I had heart failure and clinically died....I remember everything perfectly vividly....Suddenly I felt numb. Sounds began sounding a little distant....All this time I was perfectly conscious of everything that was going on. I heard the heart monitor go off. I saw the nurse come into the room and dial the telephone, and the doctors, nurses, and attendants came in....I rose up and I was a few feet up looking down on my body. There I was, with people working on me. I had no fear. No pain. Just peace. After just probably a second or two, I seemed to turn over and go up. It was dark—you could call it a hole or a tunnel—and there was this bright light....I seemed to be in a countryside with streams, grass, and trees, mountains....there were people there....There was a sense of perfect peace and contentment; love. It was like I was part of it."[18] And: "...when it vibrated, I became separated. I could then see my body....I stayed around for a while and watched the doctor and nurses working on my body, wondering what would happen....And after I floated up, I went through this dark tunnel...I went into the black tunnel and came out into brilliant light....A little bit later on I was there with my grandparents and my father and my brother, who had died....There was the most beautiful, brilliant light all around. And this was a beautiful place. There were colors—bright colors—not like here on earth, but just indescribable. There were people there, happy people....People were around, some of them gathered in groups....Off in the distance...I could see a city. There were buildings—separate buildings. They were gleaming, bright. People were happy in there. There was sparkling water, fountains...a city of light I guess would be the way to say it....It was wonderful....Everything was just glowing, wonderful....But if I had entered into this, I think I would never have returned....I was told that if I went there I couldn't go back...that the decision was mine."[19] After an elderly man experienced a cardiac

---

[17]In extreme cases, when the body temperature plummets drastically, it is possible to survive without oxygen for a considerable period of time. This sometimes occurs when a person dies on a cold winter day, when the temperature is near freezing. Once resuscitated, the person may not suffer brain damage.

[18]Raymond A. Moody, Jr., M.D., *Reflections on Life After Life*. New York: Bantam Books, © 1977, pp. 15-16, used by permission.

[19]Ibid, pp. 16-17. While some may assert that these people had unfortunate dreams, Dr. Moody reminds doubters of unusual corroborations: "Numerous persons have told me that while they were out of their bodies during apparent 'death,' they witnessed events at a distance—even outside the hospital—which were later confirmed by the reports of independent observers." Ibid, p. 110.

arrest, he was asked what he remembered from before he was brought back. Dr. Moody recalls the man's answer: "Well, it's a place...It's really beautiful, but you just can't describe it. But it's really there. You just can't imagine it. When you get on the other side, there's a river. Just like in *The Bible*, 'There is a river....' It had a smooth surface, just like glass....There's no way to describe it. We have beauty here, there's no question, with all these flowers and everything. But there is no comparison....There was no darkness."[20]

THE FOREVER FAMILY REUNION WITH OUR FRIENDS—IT NEVER ENDS!

Just think what it will be like to walk up to your beloved friends to whom you have told the story of the wonderful redemption of Jesus! They will thank you for telling them and you will probably say, "No, thank you for listening and believing, for we are both here together **forever**. Here!" Oh, how wonderful it will be. I am wondering how many beautiful people I never knew in this life may walk up and say, "I read your book that God finally prompted you to finish, and that is one reason I am here. Thanks!" I will thank them for reading it, and rejoice over the fact that we[21] will have eternity to make some new friends and get to know everyone we helped to be with Jesus, the Messiah.

And why shouldn't all of us who are believers tell all our friends, while there is still time, as Jesus commissioned: "...'Go into all the world and preach the Gospel to all creation' " (Mark 16:15 NASB). "...and that repentance for forgiveness of sins should be proclaimed in His name to all the nations, beginning from Jerusalem" (Luke 24:47 NASB). As He emphasized through Paul (Rabbi Saul), who wrote more than half of the New Testament: "...for it is the power of God unto salvation to every one that believeth; to the Jew first, and also to the Greek [Gentile/non-Jew]" (Rom. 1:16 KJV; [ ] mine).

Regarding Jesus' unconditional free forgiveness, if only they will say, "I accept your death for my shortcomings. I believe you are Lord and that God has raised you from the dead. Come into my heart. Amen." Jesus said clearly that this is all that is needed (Rom. 10:8; Rev. 3:20).

***

---

[20]Ibid, pp. 17-18.

[21]Every one of us who has received the Messiah into our hearts is permanently joined with God's Holy Spirit. That is why believers can say *we* will see you, referring to no one else excepting God's Spirit. The Holy Spirit gets the real credit! We are just privileged to serve and rejoice in that.

Once we have accepted this gift, we will not lose it![22] Although we may fail Him from time to time, we will find ourselves filled with a new power so electrifying, that we will even be able to act and respond with love toward those who hate us. People will look at us in a way that shows they know there is something different, better and powerful in us, and they will secretly want this power. Paul, quoting Moses' words from God, wrote: "...I will provoke you to jealousy by *them that are* no people, *and* by a foolish nation I will anger you" (Rom. 10:19 KJV). Thus, even though our friends, and especially our Jewish friends, know we are different, we are adjured by Jesus to tell them, when they are ready to hear us in the power of the spirit, that **He is** the reason.

Israeli Prime Minster Gola Meir, the unknown believer, returns to Israel from a visit to the United States. If, by chance, you are Jewish, and have some reservations about receiving Jesus because you may have heard it is not "kosher," you can rest at ease—it is the most Jewish thing in the world to believe in the Jewish Messiah. Through prophecy, Jesus claimed and proved Himself as such. Remember, if Golda Meir, Israel's Prime Minister, could do so and remain Jewish, so can you! Don't forget, Jesus is Jewish, too!

---

[22]God does not take back His gifts once they are given. See Philip Moore, *Eternal Security for True Believers*.

EPILOGUE

Imagine yourself as a new-born baby. You are on the way home from the hospital. You see buildings and telephone poles out the window of the car, yet you know nothing of this new world you have entered. You grow a little older and learn to speak a few words. Just when you begin to feel secure, you hurt yourself by skinning your knee or burning your finger on your mother's stove.

Later, you learn about death. Just when you thought you were going to learn that all the world was safe, you found out that there is something terribly wrong. Nothing seems to be for sure anymore. Is there any way to fix it? No. The more you learn about the intricate complexities of life, the more impossible it is to understand how to revive it once it is truly gone. Everything is winding down! Thermodynamics—Maxwell's demon—yes!

This was your life, until one day you discover the one true God, whose Messiah has promised to put this troubled world back together again. We can trust God's Messiah because He was foretold, in every detail, hundreds of years prior to His birth!

He did what He said He would do during His First Advent 2000 years ago. So we know one day soon He will remove the curse of death and bring us into a world of everlasting harmony; the world we thought we had been born into the first time around, when He returns in glory. He has promised to do this for us at His Second Coming, which cannot be more than sixty years away and may be as close as thirty! Incredible!

For 6000 years we have wondered and tinkered in the stone age of knowledge. Now, before the Messiah returns at the end of time, we witness God's words spoken by the great prince, Michael, recorded by Daniel becoming reality: "But as for you, Daniel, conceal these words and seal up the book until the end of time; many will go back and forth, and **knowledge will increase**" (Dan. 12:4 NASB). We see this increase of knowledge occurring now, before our eyes!

View of the planet Mars from the U.S. Viking mission.

We started making cars, antibiotics, trains, computers and telephones, reaching anywhere there was a wire (today, we have even gone wireless). We built planes and space ships which could land on the moon and planets. We built bombs that could destroy all life on Earth if our time were not cut short (Matt. 24:22). As the Messiah foretold in that incredible book we have come to know as the New Testament, our time (of war) will definitely be cut short thanks to Messianic intervention.

Without the New Testament's predictions and its pleasant prophecies of assurance, I would still be waking up in the middle of the night asking myself, "Why am I here? How did humanity get here? What if I die in my sleep? Where will I go? Will I just cease to exist? I do not want to. What happens to people after they close the lid on that long box and start shoveling dirt on top while they are still inside?" What a nightmare!

Now I know about **the prophecies,** since quite a few have come true. Now I know about the promised resurrection and the new body (Rom. 8:23); a body that will never die once I have been resurrected into it (John 5:28-29). We did not get it right the first time, but the Lord is going to do it right for us the second time, if we receive Him and allow Him to forgive us by receiving Jesus! Though there seems to be nothing for sure in this world, everything will be assured in the next.

So now that you have read all of this, don't blow it. Believe in it and receive it before it is too late. Once you have done that, be sure to share with a Jewish friend, as the apostle Paul asked (Rom. 1:16), for God chose a Jew to write the New Testament. Paul wrote over one-half of the New Testament. He was a Jew and he gave his life for you. The Romans executed him for his faith, but not before he wrote those precious promises. Read his message of grace, read his **prophecies**—if for no other reason, read them because he was killed for writing them—so **you** could read them.

If you take that step and buy a New Testament, I suggest both *The Living Bible* and the King James Version (KJV). *The Living Bible* is extremely easy to read and fun while the KJV is very accurate and a must for study!

I have also risked my life, in more ways than one, especially in my forthright statements against Arab terror, to bring these treasures to you. While I appreciate your value of my research, I know that I may one day pay for it with my very life. However, it was worth it to bring this to you so that **your** eternal future will be all the better; because you are worth it! I believe it and I am willing to die for what I believe regarding Messiah Jesus. It would prove wise that we all receive

Messiah Jesus while we still can. When we die, He is the journey's end and we may never pass His way again. Philip Moore

ספרי

הברית החדשה

הַבְּשׂוֹרָה הַקְּדוֹשָׁה עַל־פִּי מַתָּי

סֵפֶר תּוֹלְדֹת יֵשׁוּעַ הַמָּשִׁיחַ בֶּן־דָּוִד בֶּן־אַבְרָהָם:
אַבְרָהָם הוֹלִיד אֶת־יִצְחָק וְיִצְחָק הוֹלִיד אֶת־יַעֲקֹב
וְיַעֲקֹב הוֹלִיד אֶת־יְהוּדָה וְאֶת־אֶחָיו: וִיהוּדָה הוֹלִיד
אֶת־פֶּרֶץ וְאֶת זֶרַח מִתָּמָר וּפֶרֶץ הוֹלִיד אֶת־חֶצְרֹן
וְחֶצְרוֹן הוֹלִיד אֶת־רָם: וְרָם הוֹלִיד אֶת־עַמִּינָדָב
וְעַמִּינָדָב הוֹלִיד אֶת־נַחְשׁוֹן וְנַחְשׁוֹן הוֹלִיד אֶת־
שַׂלְמוֹן: וְשַׂלְמוֹן הוֹלִיד אֶת־בֹּעַז מֵרָחָב וּבֹעַז הוֹלִיד
אֶת־עוֹבֵד מֵרוּת וְעוֹבֵד הוֹלִיד אֶת־יִשָׁי: וְיִשַׁי הוֹלִיד
אֶת־דָּוִד הַמֶּלֶךְ וְדָוִד הַמֶּלֶךְ הוֹלִיד אֶת־שְׁלֹמֹה
מֵאֵשֶׁת אוּרִיָּה: וּשְׁלֹמֹה הוֹלִיד אֶת־רְחַבְעָם וּרְחַבְעָם
הוֹלִיד אֶת־אֲבִיָּה וַאֲבִיָּה הוֹלִיד אֶת־אָסָא: וְאָסָא
הוֹלִיד אֶת־יְהוֹשָׁפָט וִיהוֹשָׁפָט הוֹלִיד אֶת־יוֹרָם וְיוֹרָם
הוֹלִיד אֶת־עֻזִּיָּהוּ: וְעֻזִּיָּהוּ הוֹלִיד אֶת־יוֹתָם וְיוֹתָם
הוֹלִיד אֶת־אָחָז וְאָחָז הוֹלִיד אֶת־חִזְקִיָּהוּ: וְחִזְקִיָּהוּ
הוֹלִיד אֶת־מְנַשֶּׁה וּמְנַשֶּׁה הוֹלִיד אֶת־אָמוֹן וְאָמוֹן
הוֹלִיד אֶת־יֹאשִׁיָּהוּ: וְיֹאשִׁיָּהוּ הוֹלִיד אֶת־יְכָנְיָהוּ וְאֶת־
אֶחָיו לְעֵת גָּלוּת בָּבֶל: וְאַחֲרֵי גְּלוֹתָם בָּבֶלָה הוֹלִיד
יְכָנְיָהוּ אֶת שְׁאַלְתִּיאֵל וּשְׁאַלְתִּיאֵל הוֹלִיד אֶת־
זְרֻבָּבֶל: וּזְרֻבָּבֶל הוֹלִיד אֶת־אֲבִיהוּד וַאֲבִיהוּד הוֹלִיד
אֶת־אֶלְיָקִים וְאֶלְיָקִים הוֹלִיד אֶת עַזּוּר: וְעַזּוּר הוֹלִיד
אֶת־צָדוֹק וְצָדוֹק הוֹלִיד אֶת־יָכִין וְיָכִין הוֹלִיד אֶת־
אֱלִיהוּד: וֶאֱלִיהוּד הוֹלִיד אֶת־אֶלְעָזָר וְאֶלְעָזָר הוֹלִיד
אֶת־מַתָּן וּמַתָּן הוֹלִיד אֶת־יַעֲקֹב: וְיַעֲקֹב הוֹלִיד אֶת־
יוֹסֵף בַּעַל מִרְיָם אֲשֶׁר מִמֶּנָּה נוֹלַד יֵשׁוּעַ הַנִּקְרָא
מָשִׁיחַ: וְהִנֵּה כָּל־הַדֹּרוֹת מִן־אַבְרָהָם עַד־דָּוִד
אַרְבָּעָה עָשָׂר דֹּרוֹת וּמִן־דָּוִד עַד־גָּלוּת בָּבֶל אַרְבָּעָה
עָשָׂר דֹּרוֹת וּמֵעֵת גָּלוּת בָּבֶל עַד־הַמָּשִׁיחַ אַרְבָּעָה
עָשָׂר דֹּרוֹת:

The first page of the Hebrew New Testament traces Jesus' genealogy through forty-two generations of the ancient Hebrews.

"The spoken languages among the Jews of that period were Hebrew, Aramaic, and to an extent Greek. Until recently, it was believed by numerous scholars that the language spoken by Jesus' disciples was Aramaic...Jesus did, from time to time, make use of the Aramaic language. But during that period Hebrew was both the daily language and the language of study. The Gospel of Mark contains a few Aramaic words, and this was what misled scholars. Today, after the discovery of the Hebrew Ben Sira (Ecclesiasticus), of the Dead Sea Scrolls and of the Bar Kokhba Letters, and in the light of more profound studies of the language of the Jewish Sages, it is accepted that most people were fluent in Hebrew. The Pentateuch was translated into Aramaic for the benefit of the lower strata of the population. The parables in the Rabbinic literature, on the other hand, were delivered in Hebrew in all periods. There is thus no ground for assuming that Jesus did not speak Hebrew; and when we are told (Acts 21:40) that Paul spoke Hebrew, we should take this piece of information at face value. This question of the spoken language is especially important for understanding the doctrines of Jesus. There are sayings of Jesus which can be rendered both into Hebrew and Aramaic; but there are some which can only be rendered into Hebrew, and none of them can be rendered only in Aramaic. One can thus demonstrate the Hebrew origins of the Gospels by retranslating them into Hebrew."[1]

Israeli Jewish professor David Flusser, 1989

APPENDIX 1
IT'S ALL *HEBREW* TO ME

You have probably heard the old expression that is often uttered when you are having a hard time understanding something in *your tongue,* "It's all Greek to me." Our real question in understanding the origins of the New Testament as a God-inspired piece of Jewish literature is, "Was it Greek or was it Hebrew?"

In recent years, many Israelis have pointed out to me that they cannot accept the New Testament as a Holy Book from God if its original rendering was in a heathen tongue—Greek! The first time I heard this, I did not know what to say. However, since that time, I have devoted myself to extensive study on this subject. I reached the conclusion that if this issue was a stumbling stone, preventing some Jews from realizing the truth of Jesus, I should undertake an effort to discover the entire truth, and to remove the stumbling stone, which has caused Jews to ask, "Is Jesus our Messiah or Not?"

I searched and discovered some rather interesting literary treasures supporting the Hebrew origin of the Gospels of Jesus! I am only giving my answer here for the purpose of helping the Jews of the world out of a difficult situation, which has caused many problems and questions for quite some time. We suspect not only "Christian" liberal theologians but many Diaspora rabbis as well, will probably be upset to see the proofs of the Hebrew origin, since the theory that the Gospels

---

[1]David Flusser, Ph.D., *Jewish Sources in Early Christianity*. p. 11.

were originally Greek has caused many Jews, the world over, to dismiss the New Testament on that basis alone.

SCHONFIELD HELPS ELIMINATE THE "GREEK" STUMBLING STONE WHICH LEVINE PRAISED

An example of this stumbling stone used by rabbis past and present, can be seen in the book, *You Take Jesus, I'll Take God*, by Samuel Levine. As far as our studies are concerned, Levine untruthfully and vainly claims: "...the New Testament was written originally in Greek, even though Jesus was a Jew who probably spoke Hebrew as his native language, and all of the apostles were Hebrew speaking Jews. This shows the strong antipathy which the Jewish people felt towards the whole idea. As Gibbon, in his famous history of the Roman Empire, points out, the Jews in Israel found it unnecessary to publish or at least preserve any Hebrew text of the New Testament. So why accept Jesus if the vast majority of his own people rejected him?"[2]

However, Hugh Schonfield, a Jewish scholar who did not profess Jesus' Messiahship at the time, pointed out: "The famous Cæsarean MS. may have been the very one brought back by Pantænus from India, having descended through Clement of Alexandria to Origen, who may have brought it to Cæsarea, where, with the rest of Origen's collection of MSS, it may finally have passed into the hands of Pamphilus who deposited it in his library. The library is believed to have been burnt by the Arabs at the capture of Cæsarea in A.D. 653. The last we hear of a Hebrew Gospel is in the ninth century. Cod. Tisch. 3 (Λ), a Greek MS. of the Gospels, dating from this period, having in Matthew four marginal quotations from 'the Jewish,' one of which is identical with one of Jerome's quotations from the *Gospel of the Hebrews*."[3]

BIVIN AND BLIZZARD BLOW AWAY THE GREEK THEORY AND EXPOSE THE HEBREW FACTS

For some reason, God chose to write the Old Testament in Hebrew. He also used a Hebrew dialect called Aramaic in certain places, such as Daniel 2:4-7:28, Ezra 4:8-6:18; 7:12-26, Jeremiah 10:11 and Genesis 31:47. Likewise, many would expect that if the

---

[2]Samuel Levine, *You Take Jesus, I'll Take God*, pp. 69-70.

[3]Hugh J. Schonfield, *An Old Hebrew Text of St. Matthew's Gospel*. Edinburgh: T. & T. Clark, 1927, pp. 194-195.

New Testament was also God's message to mankind, it would use the same *language*. So what are the facts?

Here are a few which I uncovered in a very interesting book entitled, *Understanding the Difficult Words of Jesus: New Insights from a Hebraic Perspective,* by scholars David Bivin and Roy Blizzard, Jr.: "...Papias, Bishop[4] of Hierapolis, in Asia Minor (mid-second century A.D.). Concerning the Hebrew origin of the Gospels, he states: Matthew put down the words of the Lord in the Hebrew language, and others have translated them, each as best he could (Eusebius, *Ecclesiastical History* III 39, 16).

Irenaeus (120-202 A.D.) was Bishop of Lyons in France. Most of his literary endeavors were undertaken in the last quarter of the second century A.D. Irenaeus states: Matthew, indeed, produced his Gospel written among the Hebrews in their own dialect (Eusebius, *Ecclesiastical History* V8, 2).

Origen (first quarter of the third century), in his commentary on Matthew, states: The first [Gospel], composed in the Hebrew language, was written by Matthew...for those who came to faith from Judaism (Eusebius, *Ecclesiastical History* V1 25, 4).

Eusebius, Bishop of Caesarea (circa 325 A.D.), writes: Matthew had first preached to the Hebrews, and when he was about to go to others also, he transmitted his Gospel in writing in his native language (*Ecclesiastical History* III 24, 6).

These are but a few of the references in the writings of the early church fathers that indicate a Hebrew origin for the Gospels. In addition to these, there are many references in the later church fathers (the Post-Nicean Fathers, from approximately 325 A.D.). Epiphanius [died 403 A.D.] for instance, writes at length about the Jewish-Christian sect of the Nazarenes: They have the entire Gospel of Matthew in Hebrew. It is carefully preserved by them as it was originally written, in Hebrew script (*Refutation of All Heresies* 29, 9, 4)....Jerome (died 420 A.D.), was by far the most knowledgeable in

[4]The word "bishop," as used in the New Testament, describes a local autonomous simple personage, who had a place in caring for the membership of his congregation. It was different from what we see today in the Roman Catholic and Greek Orthodox "Churches." The meaning was altered and falsely expanded upon many centuries after Jesus when these two "churches" were used as political entities. From within, the architects attempted to overturn the true church's belief in an individual relationship with Messiah. This forced the true believers' church underground for over 1000 years until after the Reformation in the sixteenth century, when they were able to reemerge without fear of papal and Byzantine persecution for their pure faith. The bishops we see today in the Roman Catholic and Greek Orthodox Churches act as heads of diocese and still dress as if they possessed some special political authority—their costume, of course, being only symbolic.

Hebrew of all the church fathers....Concerning Matthew's Gospel, Jerome writes: Matthew was the first in Judea to compose the gospel of Christ in Hebrew letters and words...Who it was that later translated it into Greek is no longer known with certainty. Furthermore, the Hebrew text itself is still preserved in the library at Caesarea which the martyr Pamphilus assembled with great care (*De Viris Inlustribus* 3)....A revolution is taking place in our understanding of the New Testament. With the rebirth of Israel in 1947-1948 came the dramatic discovery of the Dead Sea Scrolls. These priceless, ancient manuscripts, followed a few years later by the discovery of the Bar-Cochba letters, became vital contributions to a fuller understanding of the New Testament writings.

Many scholars in Israel are now convinced that the spoken and written language of the Jews in the Land of Israel at the time of Jesus was indeed Hebrew; and that the Synoptic Gospels were derived from original Hebrew sources.

These scholars, fluent in both Greek and Hebrew, have proposed impressive solutions to major problems of New Testament interpretation. Important discoveries which they have made serve to illuminate the very Hebraic style of speech used by Jesus and his first followers, and to make possible a more accurate translation of the Gospels....Professor David Flusser[5] of the Hebrew University of Jerusalem, and the world's leading Jewish authority on the New Testament and early Christianity, holds strongly to the view that the *Life of Jesus* was originally composed in Hebrew. He claims there are hundreds of Semitisms (Semitic idioms) in the Synoptic Gospels which could only be Hebrew....Dr. Moshe Bar-Asher, who has inherited the

---

[5]In his review of the book, *Understanding the Difficult Words of Jesus*, Jeffrey Magnuson addressed the subject of the New Testament Gospels having been originally written in Hebrew. "...Professor David Flusser and Dr. Robert Lindsey have been working together in a unique and fruitful collaboration. They have gathered around them a group of other scholars, Jewish and Christian, and formed the Jerusalem School for the Study of the Synoptic Gospels, whose research is challenging some of the most basic traditional assumptions of New Testament scholarship....Anyone who speaks Hebrew and lives in modern Israel will be familiar with the meaning of idioms that apparently were unknown to the Greek translators of the original Hebrew 'Life of Jesus,' such as *asoor* and *mootar* which are translated literally in Matthew 16:19 as 'bound' and 'loosed,' but in context mean 'forbidden' and 'permitted'....For those trained in the field of biblical studies, the new approach to the New Testament advocated in this book will either offer a key to unlocking **long-hidden mysteries**, or signal a challenge to interpretations which many consider sacrosanct. However the book is received, it certainly marks the first time in history that Christian scholars, fluent in the Hebrew language and living and working in Israel, have collaborated with Jewish scholars on New Testament studies." Jeffrey Magnuson, "The Original Text," *Jerusalem Post*, July 12, 1985, © used by permission. Bold mine.

late Professor Yehezkiel Kutscher's reputation as the foremost Aramaic scholar at the Hebrew University, says that he believes the Synoptic Gospels go back to a Greek translation of an original Hebrew....Dr. Pinchas Lapide, Director of the School for Translators and Interpreters at Bar-Ilan University in Tel Aviv, has written an article entitled "The Missing Hebrew Gospel" (Lapide 1974). In this article he discusses the Hebrew origins of the Gospels. Dr. Lapide, a scholar fluent in more than a dozen languages, states: No less significant is the fact, borne out by subsequent documentary finds at Murabba'at, Nahal Heber, and on Masada, that throughout the first Christian century (and later), religious topics were mainly recorded in Hebrew (Lapide 1974:169).

Dr. Lapide concludes: The past century has witnessed the unexpected discovery of such literary treasure-troves as in the Cairo Geniza and the Qumran and Murabba'at caves. It is not impossible than an excavator may yet unearth a fragment of that earliest Hebrew Gospel 'according to the Jews' (Lapide 1974:170)."[6]

The greatest Jewish scholars of our generation, David Flusser, Moshe Bar-Asher and Pinchas Lapide, all agree that the first book of the New Testament was originally written in Hebrew. Lapide is even optimistic about a soon-to-come archaeological unearthment of the original Hebrew Gospel. It is interesting that most rabbis, when technically referring to the New Testament, call it the "Greek Testament." They refer to it this way to distance it from the Hebrew Scriptures, known as the Jewish Bible, which is the Christian Old Testament. I have yet to hear of a rabbi, contemporary or medieval, who ever commented on whether the New Testament was in Hebrew or not. Why? Because a Hebrew New Testament could provoke further Jewish interest in Jesus!

THE ATTEMPTED DECEPTION OF AN ISRAELI FRIEND

Rachel, an Israeli friend of mine, told me that the rabbis tried to challenge her Jewish faith in the New Testament by telling her, "The New Testament couldn't possibly be a holy book because it was written in Greek, not Hebrew."

These were the rabbis of Safed, Israel, known as *Sphat* in Hebrew. They are famous for a Jewish mysticism called "cabbala," which has caused insanity in some of their students. I know of a man who had to be hospitalized in a mental institution after studying "cabbala." His only desire was to sit in a room, day and night, with the

---

[6]David Bivin and Roy Blizzard, Jr., *Understanding the Difficult Words of Jesus: New Insights from a Hebraic Perspective*, pp. 46-48, 39-42.

lights off. Many of those rabbis will not accept a student for cabbalistic study unless they are over the age of forty, because they say "insanity could more easily occur."

These same rabbis are also famous for their deceptive attempts to convince Messianic Jews/Jews for Jesus, that Jesus is not their Messiah. After I showed Rachel some of the evidence supporting the Hebrew Gospel, it put her mind at ease.

RABBIS ARE SILENT ON THE HEBREW GOSPELS—HOPING TO HINDER JEWISH INTEREST?

If the greatest Jewish scholars of our generation concede that the original language of the New Testament was Hebrew, why do rabbis the world over remain silent regarding this exciting new knowledge? My belief is that they fear it may nurture a Jewish interest in Jesus at the layman's level. Because of their perpetual fear of assimilation, this is something they want to avoid at any cost, even at the cost of knowledge!

Non-Jewish scholars outside of Israel are also reaching the same conclusion, based on the new finds at Qumran.

There are many who now say that Hebrew was not in common use in Jesus' day. However, modern research proves otherwise. These liberal scholars assert, for reasons that do not make sense, that the language of Jesus' day was Aramaic.

TWO PROFESSORS DISPROVE THE ARAMAIC THEORY

In response to the assertions of these "scholars," David Bivin and Ray Blizzard, Jr. quote two outstanding scholars who cannot be refuted: "William Sanford LaSor, professor emeritus at Fuller Theological Seminary in Pasadena, California, is an outstanding Semitic scholar. In a lecture delivered in Jerusalem on April 24, 1982, he stated: With the discovery of the Dead Sea Scrolls, it now seems highly probable that the language Jesus spoke was Hebrew and not Aramaic. The sectarians at Qumran not only wrote their commentaries on books of the Bible in Hebrew, but their manual for new members (the *Manual of Discipline)* and books regulating the life of the community, such as the *Damascus Covenant*, were also written in Hebrew.

Professor Frank Cross, of Harvard University, is probably the leading living authority on the handwriting of the Dead Sea Scrolls. Professor Cross has stated that by observing the handwriting of the various scribes who copied the scrolls over the centuries at Qumran, it can be seen that the dominant language of Palestine, beginning about 130 B.C., was Hebrew. Since, after 130 B.C., the scribes of Qumran no longer made mistakes when copying Hebrew texts, Cross determined that their principal language was Hebrew, and that they had an inferior knowledge of Aramaic grammar and syntax."[7]

JESUS' ARAMAIC PHRASES EXPLAINED

There still remains the question, "Why do some of Jesus' phrases use Aramaic words which transliterate to English as Aramaic?" As we have noted, there are sections of Aramaic in the Old Testament, so likewise, there are some in the New Testament. For example: "And he took the damsel by the hand, and said unto her, Talitha cumi; which is, being interpreted, Damsel, I say unto thee, arise" (Mark 5:41 KJV).[8]

Our answer is that a few families in Israel at that time were from Babylon, and knew Aramaic better than Hebrew. Thus, Jesus spoke Aramaic to these people, because they understood it.

Proof of this is recorded in a story in the Talmud. David Bivin and Roy Blizzard, Jr. quote an article by the Jewish scholar Jehushua Grintz. They write: "The late Johoshua M. Grintz wrote an article entitled 'Hebrew as the Spoken and Written Language in the Last Days of the Second Temple' (Grintz 1960)....Grintz further emphasizes: 'Moreover, Hebrew was then the main vehicle of *speech* [emphasis, the authors'] in Jewish Palestine, or at least in Jerusalem and Judea.' He provides evidence for this statement with a relevant story, narrated in the Talmud (Nedarim 66b) about the difficulties an Aramaic-speaking Jew from Babylon had in communicating with his Jerusalemite wife (Grintz 1960: 46-47)."[9]

***

---

[7]Ibid, pp. 42-43.

[8]W.E. Vine says that Talitha is: "...an Aramaic feminine meaning 'maiden,' [that has been]...transliterated in the N.T. Greek mss. *Koumi* or *Koum* (Heb. and Aram., *qûm* arise), which follows, is interpreted by 'I say unto thee, arise.' " W.E. Vine, *An Expository Dictionary of New Testament Words, With Their Precise Meanings for English Readers*, Vol. IV, Reference Library Edition. Old Tappan, NJ: Fleming H. Revell Company, © 1940, p. 109. Vine notes that this word appears in the Talmud seven times on one page. During my eight visits and over eight years of work in Israel, I have had many friends named either Tal or Tali, which in Hebrew means "dew" and "my dew," respectively. Jesus may well have said, "My Tal, arise to me," in Hebrew, "Tali ta cumi."

[9]David Bivin and Roy Blizzard, Jr., *Understanding the Difficult Words of Jesus, New Insights from a Hebraic Perspective*, p. 40.

A HEBREW-SPEAKING BAPTIST PASTOR CORROBORATES THE HEBREW WORD ORDER OF THE NEW TESTAMENT

The late Dr. Robert Lindsey,[10] a Baptist pastor who grew up and lived in Israel most of his life, made a monumental contribution to this issue from an evangelical perspective. Dr. Lindsey set out to translate the present Greek New Testament into Hebrew. He wrote the following in the foreword for the book, *Understanding The Difficult Words of Jesus, New Insights from a Hebraic Perspective*: "It gives me pleasure to commend this book to those who desire a closer acquaintance with what Jesus said and did in Galilee and Judea at the beginning of the Christian era. Scholars David Bivin and Roy Blizzard have here provided an introduction to the basic question of how best to approach and understand the words of Jesus—whether by limiting ourselves to the translation of the Greek texts, preserved so faithfully by the Church, or by exploring more deeply into the Hebrew texts lying behind our Greek ones.

My own encounter with the strong Hebraism of the Gospels of Matthew, Mark, and Luke came several years ago when I had occasion to attempt the translation of the Gospel of Mark to Hebrew. What first caught my attention was the very Hebraic word order of the Greek text of Mark. Usually I only needed to find the correct Hebrew equivalents to the Greek words in order to give good sense and understanding to the text. In other words, the syntax or word relationships were just such as one would expect in Hebrew.

All this was particularly surprising to me, for I remembered the problems I had as a student studying classical Greek in trying to juggle the words of Xenophon, Homer, Aeschylus, and Plato into the patterns of word order that English demands. What difficulty I had making those ancient Greeks speak English! And now, translating New Testament Greek into Hebrew, I was finding Greek[11] written as if it were Hebrew."[12]

---

[10]Bob went on to be with the Lord in 1995, while at his home in Tulsa, Oklahoma. Notices of his passing were published in Israeli papers. He lost the lower portion of one of his legs while rescuing an Israeli child from a mine field. He was the pastor of the Narkiss Street Baptist Congregation in Jerusalem from 1945-1987, and the author of *Jesus Rabbi & Lord: The Hebrew Story of Jesus Behind our Gospels* (1990). I knew him personally and attended his congregation many times. His warmth and kindness is already missed.

[11]What Pastor Robert Lindsey did that was new and monumental was retranslate the Greek Gospel back into Hebrew. While some may deny the validity of what this brilliant man has done, I know enough Hebrew and Greek to see that his proof is irrefutable. Aside from that, an interesting commentary that the Gospels were later translated into Greek is found in C.C. Torrey's book, *Documents of the Primitive Church,* where he tells us: "Out of this condition of things, it may be remarked here, came the designation of the

AN ORTHODOX ISRAELI TYPESETTER BECOMES A BELIEVER

Thanks to Dr. Lindsey, and many other scholars, both Jewish and non-Jewish alike, the United Bible Society has produced one of the finest Hebrew translations of the New Testament to date, which is easily available in Israeli bookstores today.

An Israeli Yemenite Jew, Batya, a personal friend, typeset the New Testament to be printed by the Israeli publishing firm, Yanetz. She was an Orthodox Jew prior to doing the work. Originally, she was reluctant to do[13] the project, yet after completing it, she became a staunch follower of Jesus as Messiah. Presently, she works with her husband, Barry, who is head of one of Israel's Messianic publishers

---

Christian gospel as *gilyon*. The origin of the word in the Greek εὐαγγέλιον has already been mentioned and taken for granted. But why a *Greek* name? The Semitic gospels mentioned in the Talmud in connection with canonicity certainly were not issued under a foreign title! Those who wished to gain acceptance for them as a new chapter in the revelation to Israel could never have made this grotesque blunder. The obvious fact is, that εὐαγγέλιον is the title originally appearing *in the Greek translation*, and that is was adopted by the Jews, in disparagement, after the gospels had been definitely rejected. The...gospel had been entitled בְּשׂוֹרְא,'good tidings,' a word (either Hebrew or Aramaic) which is regularly rendered by εὐαγγέλια or εὐαγγέλιον.See, for example, LXX 2 Sam. 18:19-7; 2 Kings 7:9. The first of the Gospels, Mark, was introduced with the words: רֵישׁ בורתא די ישׁוע משׁיחא, 'The Beginning of the Good Tidings of Jesus the Messiah,' and in the Greek translation which soon followed (*Our Translated Gospels,* p. li) this was rendered: 'Αρχὴ τόυ εὐαγγελίου 'Ιησοῦ Χριστου. Henceforth, the story of the Nazarene Messiah...in Greek, *evangelion*. But the orthodox Jews would never have applied to an arch-heretical writing the term בשׂורא (!); so when the Nazarenes were definitely classed with the Gentiles, the Greek name, or rather, a convenient and perfectly harmless disguising of it, *gilyon*, was made to serve." Torrey's footnote to *gilyon* states: "...the Talmud itself by the mildly malicious puns on εὐαγγέλιου, אָוֶן גִּלְיוֹן and עָוֺנְגִּלְיוֹן, the two former members of the compound meaning respectively 'falsity' and 'wickedness.' See the *Aruch* under the former compound, and the Munich manuscript of the Talmud in Shabbath 116a." Torrey also tells us of rabbis who hate the New Testament, as told in the Talmud: "Rabbi Tarphon would not only burn the books, but would also keep far away from any Christian place of assembling: If I were fleeing for my life, I would take refuge in a heathen temple rather than in one of their houses. Rabbi Ishmael, after agreeing as to the desirability of destroying the Gospels, expresses his horror of the heretics, quoting from Psalm 139: 'I hate them with perfect hatred.' " Charles Cutler Torrey, *Documents of the Primitive Church*, pp. 100-101, 103.

12David Bivin and Roy Blizzard, Jr., *Understanding the Difficult Words of Jesus: New Insights from a Hebraic Perspective*, p. foreword.

13After much thought and hesitation, she accepted the job of typesetting the New Testament because she needed the money. She said to herself, "I'll just type and ignore the subject matter." However, that proved to be impossible and her rich knowledge of the Old Testament gave way to her realization that Jesus is the Messiah in the revelations of the New Testament.

and ministries, which produces many books about Jesus' Jewish Messiahship.[14]

WHY WAS THE NEW TESTAMENT TRANSLATED FROM HEBREW TO GREEK?

The reason the New Testament was translated into Greek in the first place was the same reason the Old Testament was translated into Greek centuries before the birth of Jesus. The Old Testament translation to which I am referring, the famous Septuagint, is so named because seventy rabbinical scholars worked on its translation. There was a simple reason for this translation. Although many Jews spoke fluent Hebrew in Israel during that era, the Jews who lived in the Greek-speaking countries, after the Babylonian captivity, needed to have a translation made available to them.

Greek was the universal language of that time (as English is in our time). In the book of Acts, Jesus told the Christians, of that time and onward, concerning the New Testament: "...you shall be My witnesses...to the remotest part of the earth" (Acts 1:8 NASB).

You cannot very well take a Hebrew Gospel produced in Israel to a Greek-speaking pagan (Gentile) world. Therefore, a Greek translation of the New Testament was necessary to take the message of the Messiah to the millions of Greek-speaking people, Jew and non-Jew, throughout the world! However, today, because Hebrew is a revived language in the new State of Israel (which was the predicted pure language; Zeph. 3:9),[15] the Hebrew New Testament has been reassembled in its original form, through the art of Hebraic translation by brilliant translators!

THE JEWISH PROFESSOR PINCHAS LAPIDE CORROBORATES THE HEBREW NEW TESTAMENT

In conclusion, we quote Professor Pinchas Lapide, a Jew with unsurpassed qualifications, and who, to our knowledge, has not professed Jesus as his Messiah. Supporting his conviction that the New Testament was originally Hebrew, Lapide says: "It is certain,

---

[14]If you are interested in obtaining information on other Messianic Hebrew publications, fax us at: (404) 816-9994.

[15]Hebrew will be the language of the millennial kingdom. Isaiah predicts for our future: "In that day shall five cities in the land of Egypt speak the language of Canaan, and swear to the Lord of hosts...." (Isa. 19:18 KJV). Remember, Canaan was the land of Israel before the Israelites took residence there under God's divine providence. The language of Canaan is Hebrew. For additional evidence, see our chapter 29, "After the Messiah Arrives and Ends the War—Paradise!"

however, that all four Greek Gospels display distinct traces of an original Hebrew text in their vocabulary, grammar, syntax, and semantic patterns. Hence we cannot seriously question the existence of a 'Hebrew gospel'—no fewer than ten Fathers of the Church testify to it." Lapide's footnote reads: "1. Papias (Eusebius, *Hist. Eccl.* III, 39, 1); Irenaeus (*ibid.*, V, 8, 2); Hegesippus (*ibid.*, IV, 22, 4); Jerome (*Contra Rufinum* VII, 77; *De vir. ill.* II; *In Matt.* 6, 11; *In Ezech.* 18, 7; *Adv. Pel.* III, 2 et al.); Origen (*In Matt.* XV, 14); Epiphanius (*Panarion* I, 29, 7 and 9); Theodoret of Cyprus (*Haer. Fab.* II, 1); Nicephorus Callistus (*Eccl. Hist.* III, 13); Clement of Alexandria (*Strom.* II, IX, 45, 5); Pantaneus (Eusebius, *ibid.*, V, 10, 3).[16]

WHY IS IT WORTHWHILE TO STUDY THE NEW TESTAMENT IN HEBREW?

We believe, by studying the New Testament in Hebrew, we can better understand exactly what Jesus said and in greater detail than we can from any other language. For example, there is a misconception that Jesus taught pacifism and that He was against capital punishment. However, when we study the Hebrew, this is not the case! The very important teachings of Jesus regarding our behavior toward one another is illustrated by David Bivin and Roy Blizzard. "It is widely accepted that Jesus taught a higher ethic epitomized in his statement, 'Turn the other cheek.' This has led to the belief that when attacked, one should not injure or kill in order to defend self, family, or country.

The idea that pacifism was a part of the teaching of Jesus was popularized in the writings of Tolstoy. Pacifism, however, is not today, nor was it ever, a part of Jewish belief. The Jewish position is summed up in the Talmudic dictum, 'If someone comes to kill you, anticipate him and kill him first' (Sanhedrin 72[a]). In other words, it is permissible to kill in order to defend oneself.

Can it be, then, that Jesus was the first and only Jew to teach pacifism? It is very unlikely. We know that at least some of Jesus' disciples were armed (Luke 22:38; 22:50). Add to this the fact that, at one point, Jesus even suggested to his disciples that they purchase swords (Luke 22:35-37), and we begin to ask ourselves, Did Jesus really believe or teach pacifism? In reality, pacifism is a theological misunderstanding based on several mistranslations of the sayings of Jesus.

The first of these mistranslations is Matthew 5:21, where most English versions of the Bible read, 'You shall not kill.' This is a

---

[16]Pinchas Lapide, *Israelis, Jews, and Jesus*, p. 3.

quotation of Exodus 20:13. The Hebrew word used there is 'murder' (*ratzach*), and not kill (*harag*). In Hebrew there is a clear distinction between these two words. The first (*ratzach*) means premeditated murder, while the second (*harag*) encompasses everything from justifiable homicide, manslaughter and accidental killing, to taking the life of an enemy soldier in war. The commandment very precisely prohibits murder, but not the taking of a life in defense of oneself or others.

It is difficult to explain how English translators made this mistake since the Greek language also has separate words for 'murder' and 'kill,' and it is the Greek word for 'murder' (not 'kill') which is used in Matthew 5:21. Even with no knowledge of Hebrew, the English translators of the New Testament should here have correctly translated 'murder,' and not 'kill.'

A second saying of Jesus on which pacifism is based is Matthew 5:39[a], usually translated, 'Do not resist evil,' or 'Do not resist one who is evil.' Could Jesus possibly have said this to his disciples? If he did, his statement contradicts other scriptures such as, 'Hate what is evil' (Romans 12:9), and 'Resist the devil' (James 4:7).

Again, Hebrew provides the answer. When we translate this verse back into Hebrew, we see that Jesus was not creating a new saying, but quoting a well-known Old Testament proverb. This proverb appears, with slight variations, in Psalm 37:1, 8, and Proverbs 24:19. In modern English we would translate this maxim: 'Don't compete with evildoers.' In other words, do not try to rival or vie with a neighbor who has wronged you.

Jesus is not teaching that one should lie down in the face of evil or submit to evil; rather, he is teaching that we should forego trying to 'get back at,' or take revenge on a quarrelsome neighbor. As Proverbs 24:29 says: 'Do not say, 'I will do to him as he has done to me. I will pay the man back for what he has done.' '

Jesus is expressing an important principle which applies to our relationships with friends and neighbors. It does not apply when we are confronted with a murderer, rapist, or like person of violence; nor when we are facing the enemy on the field of battle. Jesus is not talking about how to deal with violence. He is talking about the fundamentals of brotherly relationships, about how to relate to our neighbor. If, for instance, a neighbor dumps a pail of garbage on our lawn, we are not to retaliate by dumping two pails on his lawn. If someone cuts in front of us in traffic, we are not to catch up and try to run him off the road. Wanting to 'get even' is, of course, a natural response; however, it is not *our* responsibility to punish our neighbor for his action. That responsibility is God's. We are to respond to our neighbor in a way that will disarm and shame him for his actions. Proverbs 25:21 says: 'If your enemy is hungry, give him bread to eat, and if he is thirsty, give him water to drink. In so doing, you heap red-hot coals on his head, and the Lord will reward you.'

Once we discover how to correctly translate Matthew 5:39[a], we can then correctly understand the verses which follow. Each verse is an illustration of how we should react to a hostile neighbor. If, for example (Matthew 5:39[b]), a friend insults and embarrasses us by slapping us on the cheek, we are not to slap him back, but instead offer our other cheek. This, by the way, is probably the best-known of all the sayings of Jesus. It also is another of the sayings on which pacifism is based. Properly understood, however, it has nothing to do with battlefield situations, defending oneself against a murderer, or resisting evil. It is an illustration of how to deal with an angry neighbor, a personal 'enemy.'

Mistranslation of Matthew 5:39[a] has created a theological contradiction. But, when this saying is understood Hebraically, rather than contradict, it harmonizes beautifully with the rest of Scripture. Our response to evil *does* have to be resistance! It is morally wrong to tolerate evil. Our response to a 'hot-headed' neighbor, on the other hand, must be entirely different. His anger will only be temporary if we respond in a biblical manner....The responsibility of the godly person is to defuse a potentially divisive situation by 'turning away wrath.' We are not to seek revenge. If a neighbor or friend has wronged us and is in need of punishment, God is the only one who can administer it properly: 'Do not say, 'I will repay the evil deed in kind.' Trust in the LORD. He will save you' [i.e., 'He will take care of it'] (Proverbs 20:22). Our responsibility is not to react, not to respond in kind, to a belligerent neighbor. We are not to 'be overcome by evil,' but to 'overcome evil with good' (Romans 12:21)."[17]

***

[17]David Bivin and Roy Blizzard, Jr., *Understanding the Difficult Words of Jesus*, pp. 106-110.

וַיִּדַּמֶּה לֵאלֹהִים׃ וַיַּעַן יֵשׁוּעַ וַיֹּאמֶר אֲלֵיהֶם אָמֵן
אָמֵן אֲנִי אֹמֵר לָכֶם לֹא־יוּכַל הַבֵּן לַעֲשׂוֹת דָּבָר
מִנַּפְשׁוֹ בִּלְתִּי אֵת אֲשֶׁר־יִרְאֶה אֶת־אָבִיו עֹשֶׂה כִּי
אֶת־אֲשֶׁר עֹשֶׂה הוּא גַּם־הַבֵּן יַעֲשֶׂה כָּמֹהוּ׃ כִּי הָאָב
אֹהֵב אֶת־הַבֵּן וּמַרְאֶה אֹתוֹ כֹּל אֲשֶׁר יַעֲשֶׂה וְעוֹד
מַעֲשִׂים גְּדוֹלִים מֵאֵלֶּה יַרְאֵהוּ לְמַעַן תִּתַּמָּהוּ׃ כִּי
כַּאֲשֶׁר הָאָב יָעִיר וִיחַיֶּה אֶת־הַמֵּתִים כֵּן גַּם־הַבֵּן
יְחַיֶּה אֶת־אֲשֶׁר יֶחְפָּץ׃ כִּי הָאָב לֹא־יָדִין אִישׁ כִּי
אִם־כָּל־הַמִּשְׁפָּט נָתַן לַבֵּן לְמַעַן יְכַבְּדוּ כֻלָּם אֶת־
הַבֵּן כַּאֲשֶׁר יְכַבְּדוּ אֶת־הָאָב׃ מִי אֲשֶׁר לֹא־יְכַבֵּד
אֶת־הַבֵּן גַּם אֶת־הָאָב אֲשֶׁר שְׁלָחוֹ אֵינֶנּוּ מְכַבֵּד׃ אָמֵן
אָמֵן אֲנִי אֹמֵר לָכֶם הַשֹּׁמֵעַ דְּבָרַי וּמַאֲמִין לְשֹׁלְחִי
יֶשׁ־לוֹ חַיֵּי עוֹלָמִים וְלֹא יָבֹא בַּמִּשְׁפָּט כִּי־עָבַר מִמָּוֶת
לַחַיִּים׃ אָמֵן אָמֵן אֲנִי אֹמֵר לָכֶם כִּי־תָבוֹא שָׁעָה
וְעַתָּה הִיא אֲשֶׁר יִשְׁמְעוּ הַמֵּתִים אֶת־קוֹל בֶּן־הָאֱלֹהִים
וְהַשֹּׁמְעִים חָיֹה יִחְיוּ׃ כִּי כַּאֲשֶׁר לָאָב יֵשׁ חַיִּים בְּעַצְמוֹ
כֵּן נָתַן גַּם־לַבֵּן לִהְיוֹת־לוֹ חַיִּים בְּעַצְמוֹ׃ וְאַף־שָׁלְטָן
נָתַן לוֹ לַעֲשׂוֹת מִשְׁפָּט כִּי בֶן־אָדָם הוּא׃ אַל־תִּתְמְהוּ
עַל־זֹאת כִּי הִנֵּה שָׁעָה בָאָה אֲשֶׁר כָּל־שֹׁכְנֵי קֶבֶר
אֶת־קוֹלוֹ יִשְׁמָעוּן׃ וְיָצְאוּ עֹשֵׂי הַטּוֹב לִתְקוּמַת הַחַיִּים
וְעֹשֵׂי הָרַע לִתְקוּמַת הַמִּשְׁפָּט׃ לֹא אוּכַל לַעֲשׂוֹת דָּבָר

A passage from the Gospel of John in Hebrew on the life to come.

"I knew a man in Christ above fourteen years ago, (whether in the body, I cannot tell; or whether out of the body, I cannot tell: God knoweth;) such an one caught up to the third heaven. And I knew such a man, (whether in the body, or out of the body, I cannot tell: God knoweth;) How that he was caught up into paradise, and heard unspeakable words, which it is not lawful for a man to utter"

The apostle Paul, describing his NDE in 60 AD, II Cor. 12:2-4 KJV

APPENDIX 2
LIFE AFTER DEATH EXPERIENCES THAT PEOPLE HAVE LIVED TO TELL ABOUT

Many people, who were clearly dead, with no heartbeat or brain activity for a number of minutes, have reported startling accounts of seeing Jesus or experiencing unbelievable Hell.[1]

We suggest that for a fuller explanation of this subject, near death experiences (NDE), which should be more correctly called temporary death experiences, you read the book, *Beyond Death's Door*, by Maurice S. Rawlings, M.D. This book is based on his research of several cases, drawn from the first hand testimonies of people who died, were revived and who later recalled very remarkable and similar experiences.

In a 1991 *Reader's Digest* article entitled "Children of the Light," by Melvin Morse, M.D., the author noted: "A 1982 Gallup Poll found that an estimated eight million people have had an NDE."[2]

THREE DEAD GIVE THEIR TESTIMONY

Some quotes from Dr. Raymond A. Moody's book, *Life After Life*, include: "I was in a very dark, very deep valley. Later I thought,

---

[1]Concerning an experience which sounds like Hell to us, Dr. Moody documents an interview with a man who said: " '...I seen a lot of people down there, screaming, howling....almost a million....They were miserable and hateful. They were asking me for water.' " Moody further reports that a young man who attempted to commit suicide and had a cardiac arrest, experienced: "...images of some horrific beings clutching and clawing at him. It was something like descending into Dante's inferno. He had a claustrophobic, hostile, nightmarish NDE, without the slightest positive experience....no being of light, nothing beautiful, nothing pleasant." Raymond A. Moody, Jr., M.D., *The Light Beyond*. New York: Bantam Books, © 1988, pp. 26-27, 151, used by permission.

[2]Melvin Morse, M.D., "Children of the Light," *Reader's Digest*, Mar., 1991, p. 84. Condensed version of the book *Closer to the Light*, by Melvin Morse, M.D.

'Well, now I know what the Bible means by *the valley of the shadow of death* because I've been there.' '

'After I came back, I cried off and on for about a week because I had to live in this world after seeing that one.'

'I heard a voice telling me what I had to do—go back—and I felt no fear.' "[3]

DR. ROSS CORROBORATES THE RESEARCH

Elisabeth Kübler-Ross, M.D., wrote, in the foreword to Moody's book: "...it is evident from his findings that the dying patient continues to have a conscious awareness of his environment after being pronounced clinically dead. This very much coincides with my own research, which has used the accounts of patients who have died and made a comeback, totally against our expectations and often to the surprise of some highly sophisticated, well-known and certainly accomplished physicians. All of these patients have experienced a floating out of their physical bodies....It is also corroborated by my own research and by the findings of other very serious-minded scientists...who have had the courage to investigate in this new field of research in the hope of helping those who need to know, rather than to believe."[4]

DR. MOODY'S "BEING OF LIGHT"

Dr. Moody said that many of the people he interviewed claimed to have seen a "being of light," which they felt was Jesus. This "being" radiated love and warmth. In Dr. Moody's words: "What is perhaps the most incredible common element in the accounts I have studied, and is certainly the element which has the most profound effect upon the individual, is the encounter with a very bright light. Typically, at its first appearance this light is dim, but it rapidly gets brighter until it reaches an unearthly brilliance. Yet, even though this light (usually said to be white or 'clear') is of an indescribable brilliance, many make the specific point that it does not in any way hurt their eyes, or dazzle them, or keep them from seeing other things around them (perhaps because at this point they don't have physical 'eyes' to be dazzled).

***

[3]Raymond A. Moody, Jr., M.D., *Life After Life*. New York: Bantam Books, © 1975, p. cover flap, used by permission
[4]Ibid, p. foreword.

Despite the light's unusual manifestation, however, not one person has expressed any doubt whatsoever that it was a being,[5] a being of light. Not only that, it is a personal being. It has a very definite personality. The love and the warmth which emanate from this being to the dying person are utterly beyond words, and he feels completely surrounded by it and taken up in it, completely at ease and accepted in the presence of this being. He senses an irresistible magnetic attraction to this light. He is ineluctably drawn to it."[6]

Dr. Moody, at the time of his third book, *The Light Beyond*, has interviewed over one thousand people who claim to have survived bodily death. This refers to medically proven cases in which there was no heartbeat for a number of minutes prior to resuscitation.

THREE, HAVING DIED, DESCRIBED THE LIGHT—ONE SAID IT WAS JESUS

The following are three personal testimonies regarding this "being of light," recorded by Dr. Moody: "I heard the doctors say that I was dead, and that's when I began to feel as though I were tumbling, actually kind of floating, through this blackness....I could see this light. It was a very, very, brilliant light, but not too large at first. It grew larger as I came nearer and nearer to it. I was trying to get to that light at the end, because I felt that it was Christ....being a Christian....I said to myself, 'If this is it, if I am to die, then I know who waits for me at the end, there in that light.' "[7]

Another person who witnessed this light, described it as a: "...pure crystal clear light, an illuminating white light. It was beautiful and so bright, so radiant, but it didn't hurt my eyes. It's not any kind of light you can describe on earth. I didn't actually see a person in this light, and yet it has a special identity, it definitely does. It is a light of perfect understanding and perfect love. The thought came to my mind, 'Lovest thou me?' This was not exactly in the form of a question, but I guess the connotation of what the light said was, 'If you do love me, go back and complete what you began in your life.' And all during this time, I felt as though I were surrounded by an overwhelming love and compassion."[8]

---

[5]Some have correctly pointed out that Satan can masquerade as an angel of light; thus, this author would have no doubt that this manifestation was not Jesus, if the person who saw him had not received Jesus as their Messiah-atonement. However, a Christian's testimony of this beauty leaves little doubt in our minds that, at least in these cases, this may very well be Jesus. Remember what Paul wrote: "We are confident, *I say*, and willing rather to be absent from the body, and to be present with the Lord" (II Cor. 5:8 KJV).

[6]Raymond A. Moody, Jr., M.D., *Life After Life*, p. 58.

[7]Ibid, p. 62.

[8]Ibid, p. 63.

Still another person testified: "I knew I was dying and that there was nothing I could do about it, because no one could hear me....I was out of my body, there's no doubt about it, because I could see my own body there on the operating room table. My soul was out! All this made me feel very bad at first, but then, this really bright light came. It did seem that it was a little dim at first, but then it was this huge beam....And it gave off heat to me; I felt a warm sensation.

It was a bright yellowish white—more white. It was tremendously bright; I just can't describe it. It seemed that it covered everything, yet it didn't prevent me from seeing everything around me—the operating room, the doctors and nurses, everything. I could see clearly, and it wasn't blinding....it asked, it kind of asked me if I was ready to die. It was like talking to a person....the voice that was talking to me actually realized that I wasn't ready to die. You know, it was just kind of testing me more than anything else. Yet, from the moment the light spoke to me, I felt really good—secure and loved. The love which came from it is just unimaginable, indescribable. It was a fun person to be with! And it had a sense of humor, too—definitely!"[9]

THE IDENTITY OF THE LIGHT, AS DEFINED BY THE APOSTLE PAUL'S EXPERIENCE

A New Testament clue to the identity of this light may be in the book of Acts 9:1-9 and 26:13-32, where Paul gives a testimony of his conversion. Before Paul accepted Jesus as Messiah, he was a renegade rabbi responsible for the deaths of many of the early Jewish believers in Jesus (Acts 26:9-10). In his description of seeing Jesus after His resurrection and ascension to the heavens, Paul said: "At midday, O king, I saw in the way a light from heaven, above the brightness of the sun, shining around about me and them which journeyed with me. And when we were all fallen to the earth, I heard a voice speaking unto me, and saying in the Hebrew tongue, Saul, Saul, why persecutest thou me? *it is* hard for thee to kick against the pricks. And I said, Who art thou, Lord? And he said, I am Jesus whom thou persecutest. But rise and stand upon thy feet: for I have appeared unto thee for this purpose....Delivering thee from the people, and *from* the Gentiles, unto whom now I send thee, To open their eyes, *and* to turn *them* from darkness to light, and *from* the power of Satan unto God, that they may receive forgiveness of sins, and inheritance among them which are sanctified by faith that is in me. Whereupon, O king Agrippa, I was not disobedient unto the heavenly vision....I continue unto this day, witnessing both to small and great, saying none other things than those

---

[9]Ibid, pp. 63-64.

which the prophets and Moses did say should come: That Christ should suffer, *and* that he should be the first that should rise from the dead, and should shew light unto the people, and to the Gentiles....King Agrippa, believest thou the prophets? I know that thou believest. Then Agrippa said unto Paul, Almost thou persuadest me to be a Christian" (Acts 26:13-19, 22-23, 27-28 KJV).[10]

The only difference in Paul's encounter was that his human, mortal eyes (he was still alive) were burdened by the light (Acts 9:9). This light identified Himself as **Jesus**, whom Paul had been persecuting.

The passage mentions that Jesus spoke in the Hebrew tongue. It is interesting to note that Jesus' Hebrew name, *Yeshua* (ישוע, in Hebrew), lights the Jewish candelabra called the menorah (lamp) described in Exodus 25:31-35, which has seven lamp stands. For interesting details about Jesus' name in Hebrew, see our section in chapter 9, "The Messiah Conpriracy Concludes," entitled "The Equation of the Ages." No doubt, these facts take on new meaning.

A woodcut, made in 1515, of Rabbi Sauls conversion to faith in Messiah as he is knocked from his horse while witnessing a light from Heaven brighter than the sun.

[10]These events were recorded by the apostle Luke.

In Hebrew, the shape of the four Hebrew letters spelling Jesus (*Yeshua,* ישוע) light God's candelabra, the Jewish menorah!

REXELLA VAN IMPE'S NDE

Rexella Van Impe, the wife of Dr. Jack Van Impe, the famous Bible scholar and television evangelist, was injured in a car accident in Brussels in 1982. She found herself outside of her body watching her husband crying as he held her in his arms. This was reported in their video, *Heaven, an Out-of-Body Adventure, Who, Why, When?* [11]

THE APOSTLE PAUL'S NEAR DEATH EXPERIENCE WITH JESUS IN THIRD HEAVEN

The apostle Paul describes his Heaven experience, when he was stoned to death at Lystra, in the year 46 AD. This is recorded in the book of Acts: "And there came thither *certain* Jews from Antioch and Iconium, who persuaded the people, and, having stoned Paul, drew *him* out of the city, supposing he had been dead' " (Acts 14:19 KJV).

After Paul was dragged to a garbage heap outside the city, he was resurrected: "Howbeit, as the disciples stood round about him, he rose up" (Acts 14:20 KJV).

Fourteen years later, in 60 AD, when Paul penned II Corinthians, he tells us: "I knew a man in Christ above fourteen years ago, (whether in the body, I cannot tell; or whether out of the body, I cannot tell: God knoweth;) such an one caught up to the third heaven. And I knew such a man, (whether in the body, or out of the body, I cannot tell: God knoweth;) How that he was caught up into paradise, and heard unspeakable words, which it is not lawful for a man to utter" (II Cor. 12:2-4 KJV).

Paul reminds us of our home in Heaven when he relates: "...Eye hath not seen, nor ear heard, neither have entered into the heart of man, the things which God hath prepared for them that love him" (I Cor. 2:9 KJV).

JESUS AND HIS APOSTLE JOHN DESCRIBE THE BEAUTY THAT IS IN STORE FOR US

Jesus said: "In my father's house are many mansions: if *it were* not so, I would have told you. I go to prepare a place for you" (John 14:2 KJV).

***

---

[11] This videotape, produced in 1992, is available through JVI Ministries, POB 7004, Troy, MI, USA 48007.

In the last book of the New Testament, the apostle John, through a prophetic vision of the future shown to him by God, tells us, where we, as believers, will all end up: "And I John saw the holy city, new Jerusalem, coming down from God out of heaven, prepared as a bride adorned for her husband" (Rev. 21:2 KJV).

We can all imagine how wonderful it will be when Jesus returns to stop Armageddon, resurrecting all the dead bodies of the Tribulation believers. What a beautiful sight we will see in our new eternal bodies—His divinity—which peered out only a little at His transfiguration, which was, in itself, a preview of His Second Coming.

Jesus' disciple, Matthew, recorded this dazzling event, which startled all who saw it nearly 2000 years ago: "And after six days Jesus taketh Peter, James, and John his brother, and bringeth them up into an high mountain apart, And was transfigured before them: and his face did shine as the sun, and his raiment was white as the **light**. And, behold, there appeared unto them Moses and Elias[12] talking with him: While he yet spake, behold, a bright cloud overshadowed them: and behold a voice out of the cloud, which said, This is my beloved Son, in whom I am well pleased; hear ye him. And when the disciples heard *it*, they fell on their face, and were sore afraid" (Matt. 17:1-3, 5-6 KJV; bold mine).

FOR THE UNBELIEVER, THERE IS NO BEAUTY, ONLY MISERY

Regarding some of the unpleasant experiences, Moody documents: "A man who was despondent about the death of his wife shot himself, 'died' as a result, and was resuscitated. He states: 'I didn't go where [my wife] was. I went to an awful place....I immediately saw the mistake I had made....I thought, 'I wish I hadn't done it.' ' "[13]

Dr. Moody emphasizes that many: "...say that although they had read religious writings, such as *The Bible*, they had never really understood certain things they had read there until their near-death experiences."[14]

***

[12]This is Elijah of the Old Testament.

[13]Raymond A. Moody, Jr., M.D., *Life After Life*, p. 143.

[14]Ibid, p. 141.

WHY ARE THERE SO MANY NEAR DEATH EXPERIENCES TODAY?

As to why there has been such an explosion of near-death experiences in our time, the doctor explains: "...it has only been in fairly recent times that advanced resuscitation technology has been available. Many of the people who have been brought back in our era would not have survived in earlier years. Injections of adrenaline into the heart, a machine which delivers a shock to the heart, and artificial heart and lung machines are examples of such medical advances."[15]

HAVE THESE EXPERIENCES BEEN CORROBORATED?

Dr. Moody addressed the issue of NDE corroboration and the bewilderment of the doctor in one of these cases. The patient told Moody: "After it was all over the doctor told me that I had a really bad time, and I said, 'Yeah, I know.' He said, 'Well, how do you know?' and I said, 'I can tell you everything that happened.' He didn't believe me, so I told him the whole story, from the time I stopped breathing until the time I was kind of coming around. He was really shocked to know that I knew everything that had happened. He didn't know quite what to say, but he came in several times to ask me different things about it."[16]

Moody also mentioned an old woman who had been blind since she was a young girl, long before the advent of the modern shock paddle defibrillator used for cardiac resuscitation. After her successful resuscitation, she described, in detail, the exact configuration of the equipment used to save her life.

Other patients reported seeing accidents and unusual events which took place outside the hospital just prior to their resuscitation—while they were dead!

MORE CORROBORATION—CASES OF THE BLIND LEADING THE SIGHTED—HEARING IS BELIEVING!

Cardiac surgeon Maurice Rawlings reminds us regarding this unexplainable evidence of: "...how blind individuals with NDEs report visual reconstructions of clothing colors, types of jewelry, and other visual details occurring in the room; how victims visualize events and people located in other rooms and how they see loved ones in another

---

[15]Ibid, p. 145.
[16]Ibid, p. 99.

world, with no prior knowledge of their deaths."[17] If an NDE were nearly a dream, as some claim, the above would not be possible.

THE CORROBORATION OF CHILDREN, DESCRIBING DETAILS WHILE OUTSIDE OF THEIR BODIES

Gary R. Habermas and J. P. Moreland, in their work, *Immortality, The Other Side of Death,* document two cases. The first case, a young girl named Katie, nearly drowned in a pool. After being resuscitated in the emergency room, a CAT scan showed she had massive brain swelling. She was attached to an artificial lung to keep her breathing. She had a ten percent chance of survival. Three days later, she completely recovered and told a remarkable story. Though she had been "profoundly comatose," with her eyes closed throughout her entire treatment, she gave exact details regarding the physical features of her doctors, the hospital rooms in which she had been treated, and the medical procedures her doctors employed to save her. Amazingly, she was also able to describe, in minute detail, what her family was doing at home, awaiting news of her status, while she lie in the hospital! Then, Katie said she met "Jesus and the heavenly Father."[18]

Another case from Habermas and Moreland involves five-year-old Rick, who suffered from meningitis. As Rick was rushed to the hospital in an ambulance, he decided to "stay behind." He later reported seeing his father crying in the car while he drove the family to the hospital. Rick then rushed to the hospital, "arriving" before the ambulance. He saw hospital orderlies move a young girl out of the room he would occupy. Rick's memories were corroborated by his family, and were particularly amazing due to the fact that he was

---

[17]Maurice S. Rawlings, M.D., *To Hell and Back.* Nashville: Thomas Nelson Publishers, © 1993, p. 94, used by permission.

[18]Gary R. Habermas and J.P. Moreland, *Immortality, The Other Side of Death.* Nashville: Thomas Nelson Publishers, © 1992, pp. 74-75. This book is very accurate and written by two highly qualified Christians. We highly recommend it. The authors' impressive credentials read as follows: "*Gary R. Habermas* is the Chairman of the Department of Philosophy and Theology and professor of apologetics and philosophy at Liberty University, Lynchburg, Virginia. He has written numerous books on life-after-death issues....published numerous scholarly and popular articles....He received a B.R.E. from William Tyndale College, a M.A. in religious studies from the University of Detroit, and a Ph.D. in history and philosophy of religion from Michigan State University....*J. P. Moreland* is professor of philosophy of religion at Talbot School of Theology, Biola University, La Mirada, California, and serves as director of Talbot's M.A. program in philosophy and ethics....He has earned four academic degrees: a B.S. in chemistry from the University of Missouri, a Th.M. in theology from Dallas Theological Seminary, a M.A. in philosophy from the University of California at Riverside, and a Ph.D. in philosophy from the University of Southern California." Ibid, p. "About the Authors."

comatose before he was taken in the ambulance and for several days afterward.

HOW REAL IS HELL? AS REAL AS DEATH!

Appearing on *The 700 Club* at the end of 1993, Dr. Rawlings related that while resuscitating some patients with shock paddles, they would say to him, "Don't stop Doctor, you're getting me out of Hell!" Dr. Rawlings has written two excellent books on the subject of near death experiences from a Christian perspective. They are *Beyond Death's Door* and *To Hell and Back.*

In our opinion, Dr. Rawlings is more qualified[19] to write on this subject because, unlike Dr. Moody (a psychiatrist), he is a surgeon who has had first hand experience with patients on the operating table.[20]

Dr. Rawlings' books are highly recommended, considered much more accurate, and also provide us with a more biblical perspective on the experience of the patients. These patients remember their Hell experiences more vividly than those interviewed by other doctors, days or weeks after the event.

Dr. Rawlings reports that the Hell experience is more easily and quickly forgotten than seeing Jesus, which accounts for the low percentage of hellish NDE's in the other research. The subconscious, in time, is much more apt to suppress a negative experience than a positive one. Rawlings testifies: " 'I was resuscitating a terrified patient who told me he was actually in hell. He begged me to get him

---

[19]Dr. Rawlings' credentials and unique qualifications read as follows: "Dr. Maurice Rawlings, specialist in cardiovascular diseases at the Diagnostic Center and the area hospitals of Chattanooga, graduated with honors from the George Washington University Medical School. He served in both the Army and the Navy and became chief of cardiology at the 97th General Hospital in Frankfurt, Germany. He then was promoted to personal physician at the Pentagon for the Joint Chiefs of Staff, which included Generals Marshall, Bradley, Patton, and Dwight Eisenhower before he became president of the United States. In civilian life Dr. Rawlings was appointed to the National Teaching Faculty of the American Heart Association, specializing in teaching methods for the retrieval of patients from sudden death. He taught at various medical schools and hospitals and conducted courses for doctors and nurses in many countries. Dr. Rawlings is clinical assistant professor of medicine for the University of Tennessee at Chattanooga, a member of the International Committee on Cardiovascular Diseases, a past governor for the American College of Cardiology for the state of Tennessee, founder of the area's Regional Emergency Medical Services Council, faculty instructor for the Advanced Cardiac Life Support programs, and Fellow of the American College of Physicians, the College of Cardiology, and the College of Chest Physicians. In addition, he has authored three previous books and written several articles on heart disease for national medical journals." Maurice S. Rawlings, M.D., *To Hell and Back*, p. "About the Author."

[20]Dr. Rawlings and I do not endorse any claims by Dr. Moody, which venture outside the Christian perspective.

out of hell and not to let him die. When I fully realized how genuinely and extremely frightened he was, I too became frightened....Now I feel assured that there is life after death, and not all of it good'....Public interest in these questions continues to grow as more people survive the death experience through modern restorative techniques called *resuscitation*....As a cardiologist exposed to critically ill patients in the coronary care units of several hospitals, I have had many opportunities to resuscitate people who have clinically died. I have found that an interview immediately after patients are revived reveals as many bad experiences as good ones."[21]

AN ISRAELI'S TESTIMONY REGARDING SURVIVAL AFTER BODILY DEATH

I would like to include the testimony of my close friend, Esther, an Israeli Jew who told me first hand of her experience during an operation: "Someone said to me, 'Where do you want to go? *Gan Eden*[22] or *Gehenom*?" In Hebrew these words mean "Heaven" and "Hell."

Esther continued: "...and I felt terrible in this time. I said, 'Take me where you want.' After I said that, he gave me my life back and I wondered, 'Why?' I was very happy. It was like waking up in the movie *Flat Liners*." *Flat Liners* is a movie on this subject, now available on video.

Esther continues: "After the operation, something inside me said, 'You have to believe in God, but also someone else.' " She told me that she felt this someone else was Jesus. Later, after reading many of the Messianic prophecies in the Old Testament, she received Jesus as her personal Messiah.

THE MEDIA IS DETERMINED TO DESTROY THE NDE

In a June, 1994, episode of *Turning Point*, entitled "Life After Death: Personal Experiences," host Diane Sawyer asked: "Is it possible that nature evolved a near death experience, an NDE, because the calmer you are in stress, the better chance you'll survive it?" She then introduced the audience to Madelaine Lawrence, a registered

---

[21]Maurice S. Rawlings, M.D., *Beyond Death's Door*. New York: Bantam Books, © 1978, pp. foreword and introduction, used by permission.
[22]This is Hebrew for "Paradise"—the Garden of Eden.

nurse whom she referred to as "one of the new breed of scientifically trained near-death detectives."[23]

Lawrence showed Sawyer a sign at the top of the room facing toward the ceiling, impossible to read from eye level. Sawyer explained that the nurse hopes someone will be revived and tell her what the sign says, which would "challenge all of established science."[24]

We ask honestly, "What evidence in all of established science proves that there is not life after death or out of body experiences?" Science cannot prove this. Furthermore, Dr. Moody documented several cases of patients describing, in accurate detail, events which occurred while their hearts were stopped. Thus, Sawyer's nonchalant reference to science is absurd, seeing that it also conflicts with Dr. Moody's work, which documents patients accurately describing events which occurred around them while their hearts were stopped.

THE DREAMS OF SAWYER ARE WISHFUL THINKING—HOPES THAT WILL NEVER BE REALIZED!

Diane Sawyer interviewed Susan Blackmore, a professor of psychology in England, who "doesn't buy it." Blackmore said: "They are valid experiences in themselves, only they're happening in the brain and not in the world out there."[25] As Blackmore was talking, a section by section CAT scan of a brain was shown to the television audience, as it seemed that the old announcer from *The Outer Limits* informed us: "We will control all that you see."

Then Sawyer clarified: "In other words, a kind of movie our brains run at times of extreme traumatic stress, like this movie...." She then gave an awkward interpretation of the film, *The Wizard of Oz*, as excerpts were aired. She said that scientists "theorize that under extreme stress, say the end of life, large amounts of endorphins[26] will produce a dream-like state, a natural drug trip, if you will...."[27]

They then replay the beautiful testimonies of those who had previously described their experiences—something here smells of brainwashing! This is not honest journalism but a cleverly devised

---

[23]"Life After Death: Personal Experiences," *Turning Point*, ABC News. Transcript #116, June 8, 1994, © American Broadcasting Companies, Inc.
[24]Ibid.
[25]Ibid.
[26]Endorphins are morphine-like pain reducing substances, which can induce euphoria naturally, produced by the body during exercise or stress.
[27]"Life After Death: Personal Experiences," *Turning Point*, ABC News. Transcript #116, June 8, 1994.

slant against the facts toward the dreams of Diane Sawyer, her writers and producers. We believe they simply hope there is no life after death, because if there is, then that proves there is a God; a God other than the media elite! Though they try to make some pretense of being fair to both sides, a careful examination of their phrasing and stress on certain words clearly indicates disgust and abhorrence toward the Christian perspective (in our opinion).

SAWYER'S DRUG TRIP MISFIRES IN SHOCKING UN-COLLABORATION

Sawyer then introduced Ronald Siegel, M.D., who said these experiences can be reproduced with LSD. Dr. Moody, in his book, *Life After Life*, devotes a chapter to proving that this is not true! However, Sawyer never addressed Moody's explanation; instead she had Blackmore explain the experience as the "misfiring of a million neurons."

Another experiment was introduced in which electrodes were used to shock a man's brain. After the episode, the patient said: "I definitely felt it. It was like an out-of-body experience....it was like I was looking from behind me, or something [not above]."[28] However, he appeared to be drugged, and furthermore, how could he have had an out-of-body experience while completely conscious? Perhaps he was paid by the producers to say what they wanted.

Can his statement explain how others have seen details which relatives and doctors have corroborated?[29] No, there can be no corroboration from this drugged-looking man, who had just had his brain "shocked"! However, Sawyer reacted as if she were immensely impressed, as if this man had done the world some great favor. I would bet many who have experienced genuine NDE's, would love to have a

---

[28] "Life After Death: Personal Experiences," *Turning Point*, ABC News. Transcript #116, June 8, 1994. [ ] mine. The name of the patient was Jerrod Jimanez.

[29] On the program Sawyer said: "And we heard of people who had seen objects physically impossible to see unless they were out-of-body. But in every case, we couldn't find the person or the proof of what happened." Ibid. However, a few moments before, she made mention of a lady who described the exact clothing her sisters were wearing one hundred miles away on the day she died and came back! Apparently, Sawyer has a short memory. It was also interesting that while she interviewed authors of some of the top-selling NDE books—Melvin Morse, Kenneth Ring, Dr. Moody and Dr. Willem Van Lomo—she mysteriously failed to mention the famous cardiac surgeon, Maurice Rawlings, whose books document that one-half of his NDE patients report going to a very unpleasant place (Hell). This, of course, would have exploded her endorphin/euphoria alternative explanation as given by Blackmore and others—and this she couldn't have, could she? Obviously not!

chance to shock Sawyer's brain and hear what kind of NDE she would claim to have.

SAWYER AND HER COHORTS ARE HARD TO STOMACH, ESPECIALLY WHEN THEY GET THE FACTS WRONG

I hope you will excuse me for being upset with Diane Sawyer, but putting up with the biased left-wing, anti-God/family slant of today's news media, especially when they purposely distort the facts and ignore the scholarship, evidence and the documentation of leading medical doctors, gets to be unbearable. By the way, Diane Sawyer mentioned on her show that seven million people claim to have had an NDE. In reality, as we mentioned earlier, *Reader's Digest*'s documented Gallup Poll said eight million, as of 1982. The numbers are now much higher. We do wish that before Sawyer broadcasts statistics on such an important topic all over the United States, she would first get her facts straight!

This irresponsible error-laden journalism comes as no surprise when you consider the source! Later, in 1994, reporter Sam Donaldson narrated a segment about Pat Robertson on the ABC News magazine, *Prime Time*. It contained many inaccuracies. Robertson later made a special tape that was aired on his television show, *The 700 Club*. Robertson pointed out the dishonest reporting, and mentioned that, though he had good cause for a defamation suit according to his attorneys, he would pray for his enemies instead.

In many cases, the media, instead of honestly reporting, have in fact, become our enemies. This is sad! We pray it does not persist, especially in the area of the NDE's, because people are interested in knowing the truth, not a dishonest slant.

***

A painting of Charles Darwin, by John Collier, 1883. Darwin is credited as the founder of the *Theory* of Evolution. Darwin once said: "Real good [in attacking Christianity] seems only to follow the slow and silent side attacks"([ ] mine), and, "I have...done good service in aiding to overthrow...creation." The following appendix will see him concede to creation.

"...keep that which is committed to thy trust, avoiding profane *and* vain babblings, and oppositions of science falsely so called...." I Timothy 6:20 KJV

"The fact that the synthetic (evolutionary) theory is now so universally accepted is not in itself proof of its correctness.... The basic theory is in many instances hardly more than a postulate".[1] Professor Ernst Mayr of Harvard, heavyweight among evolutionists

"The more one studies paleontology, the more certain one becomes that evolution is based on faith alone, exactly the same sort of faith which it is necessary to have when one encounters the great mysteries of religion."[2]

Staunch evolutionist, Dr. Louis T. More,
Dean of the Graduate School, University of Cincinnati

"The idea that mankind is descended from any simian species whatever, is certainly the most foolish ever put forth by a man writing on the history of man."

Dr. Trass, famous paleontologist

"The record of the rocks is decidedly against evolutionists, especially in the abrupt appearance of new forms under specific types, and without apparent predecessors... Paleontology furnishes no evidence as the actual transformation of one species into another. No such case is certainly known. Nothing is known about the origin of man except what is told in Scripture." Sir William Dawson, eminent Canadian geologist

"The attempt to find the transition from the animal to man has ended in total failure. The middle link has not been found and never will be. Evolution is all nonsense. It can not be proved by science that man descended from the ape or from any other animal."[3] Professor Virchow of Berlin, world famous naturalist

APPENDIX 3
APES, FAKES AND MISTAKES

In this appendix, I attempt to step aside and let the experts talk. Thus, with your benefit in mind, I shall quote from the works of scholars who have dealt with the various aspects of evolution.

---

[1]*Prophecy in the News*, April 1990, p. 11, © used by permission. "...(a postulate, by the way, is defined by Webster as 'a position or supposition assumed without proof.')...." Ibid.

[2]Ibid. What the wise Dr. More failed to realize about our "religion" is that we have the sure word of prophecy (II Pet. 1:19) in hundreds of predictions, many of which have been fulfilled to the letter and many more which are on the verge of being fulfilled in the Messiah's Second Coming, whereby we may **know** that we are saved (I John 2:3, 3:14). All other religions are truly shrouded in mystery and uncertainty, apart from the God of Israel, who has told us all worth knowing beforehand. For God, speaking through the Hebrew prophet Isaiah, tells us: "...for **I** *am* God, and *there is* none else; **I** *am* God, and *there is* none like me, Declaring the end from the beginning, and from ancient times *the things* that are not *yet* done...." (Isa. 46:9-10 KJV).

[3]Previous three quotes, Gordon Lindsay, *Evolution—The Incredible Hoax*. Dallas, TX: Christ for the Nations, © 1977, p. 16, used by permission.

COMMON ANCESTOR

At the apex of Charles Darwin's theory of evolution stands the idea that apes and men share a common ancestor. Yet, after reading a large number of books on the subject, I realized that this is just a theory—not one shred of evidence, not even a tooth was found to support it. Incidentally, when you leaf through the volumes on "human evolution," you will see how many drawings of these alleged ancient predecessors of man sprang from the imagination of evolutionary artists—creatures who have yet to be found, and never will be, because they simply did not exist.

RAMAPITHECUS

"Ramapithecus" is said to be second in line to the common ancestor. It is an extinct ape which is now considered by the majority of anthropologists to be in no way related to humanity. The renowned Dr. Henry M. Morris reveals to us the truth regarding this ape: "*Ramapithecus.* The suffix 'pithecus' means 'ape,' and a considerable number of fossils have been publicized of extinct 'pithecine' animals....*Dryopithecus, Oreopithecus, Limnopithecus, Kenyapithecus* and others, all dated roughly 14 million years ago.

Most evolutionary anthropologists consider *Ramapithecus* to be the most important of this group. This fossil was found in India in 1932 and consisted of several teeth and jaw fragments....Dr. Robert Eckhardt of Pennsylvania State University, in a thorough study of this entire group of fossils, said: '....They themselves nevertheless seem to have been apes—morphologically, ecologically and behaviourally.' "[4]

A HARVARD MAN REPENTS

Professor Marvin Lubenow, in his unsurpassed work, *Bones of Contention: A Creationist Assessment of the Human Fossils*, points out that David Pilbeam, the famous Harvard paleoanthropologist, had convinced many of his colleagues that "Ram" was our ancestor, only to later realize he was wrong. Lubenow notes: "For many years David Pilbeam (Harvard University) had convinced his fellow paleoanthropologists that a fossil form known as *Ramapithecus* was a hominid. This assessment was almost universally accepted even though it was based on the flimsiest of fossil evidence. Later, when

---

[4]Henry M. Morris, Ph.D, *Scientific Creationism.* San Diego, CA: Creation-Life Publishers, © 1974, p. 172, used by permission.

Pilbeam found more abundant fossil evidence, it became obvious that *Ramapithecus* had nothing to do with human origins. In explaining where he and the paleoanthropological world had gone astray, Pilbeam's confession reads almost like a Shakespearean soliloquy:

Theory shapes the way we think about, even perceive, data....We are unaware of many of our assumptions.

Conflicting visions of these [evolutionary] human ancestors probably says more about our conflicting views of ourselves than about the actual fossil data.

In the course of rethinking my ideas about human evolution, I have changed somewhat as a scientist. I am aware of the prevalence of implicit assumptions and try harder to dig them out of my own thinking."[5]

AUSTRALOPITHECUS

Australopithecus means "Southern Ape." This name has been assigned to Zinjanthropus, Paranthropus Plesithropus, Telanthropus and Homo habilis—fancy names for unfancy claims. Australopithecus dated at 1 million BC. Some of the classifications mentioned are set by some authorities at between 2 and 3 million years of age.

Australopithecus is now conceded by many scientists to be an extinct ape, who walked with his knuckles on the ground, as apes still walk today.[6] This ape had a brain the size of approximately five hundred cc's, which is smaller than that of a gorilla. Marvin Lubenow informs us: " '....Australopithecine authority Charles Oxnard (University of Western Australia) concludes: 'The genus *Homo* may, in fact, be so ancient as to parallel entirely the genus *Australopithecus*, thus denying the latter a direct place in the human lineage.' "[7]

Australopithecus were found in groups with the back of their skulls bashed in. Tools nearby obviously belonged to true man, who used them to slaughter these monkeys and extract their brains for food. Evolutionists would have us believe that the tools[8] belonged to the

---

[5]Marvin L. Lubenow, *Bones of Contention: A Creationist Assessment of the Human Fossils*. Grand Rapids, MI: Baker Book House, © 1992, p. 24, used by permission.

[6]"Australopithecus, a Long-Armed, Short-Legged Knuckle-Walker," *Science News*, Vol. 100, Nov. 27, 1971, p. 357.

[7]Marvin L. Lubenow, *Bones of Contention: A Creationist Assessment of the Human Fossils*, p. 166. Lubenow's source was Charles E. Oxnard, "The Place of the Australopithecines in Human Evolution: Grounds for Doubt?" *Nature*, Dec. 4, 1975.

[8]In Josh McDowell and Don Stewart's book, *The Creation*, they rightly note: "The tools found in the proximity of the *Australopithecus* fossils could have been used by some other human rather than by *Australopithecus*, who even could have been an ancient human prey....If we classify those as extinct apes instead of primitive humans, Johanson's

monkeys. This is absurd, since human skulls were found in the same area.

One reason that Ramapithicus and Australopithecus were thought by evolutionists to be our "ancestors" was because their teeth were more "human-like" and smaller in relation to modern apes and monkeys. However, today in Ethiopia, there is a species of high altitude baboon called "theropithecus galada,"[9] which has teeth and a jaw structure almost identical to the extinct Ramapithecus and Australopithecus.

Concerning Ramapithecus, Dr. Duane Gish notes in his pamphlet, *Have You Been...Brainwashed?*: "Dr. Jolley has recently reported that a species of baboon in Ethiopia has the same dental and jaw characteristics as Ramapithecus. These characteristics are therefore not those of man! Other anthropologists have agreed that Ramapithecus was simply an ape."[10]

Today, most paleoanthropologists and anthropologists have removed these two apes from their hominid class status. Ramapithecus is no longer considered to have been a creature in the line leading to man.[11] So much for that theory!

EAST AFRICAN ZINJANTHROPUS—NUTCRACKER "MAN"?

Zinjanthropus is said to be 1.8 million years old! Professor Lubenow goes behind the scenes to reveal little-known information about this creature, which he rightly calls "*Homo habilis*: The Little Man Who Isn't There." Lubenow informs us: "Louis and Mary Leakey had worked at Olduvai Gorge, Tanzania, for many years. The gorge, part of the East African Rift System, had produced many stone tools and animal fossils, but no hominids. Yet, Louis felt that hominid fossils had to be there. One day in 1959, because Louis was ill, Mary went out alone. At a certain spot she saw teeth sticking out of the

---

finds present no problem to creationists. The only real connection between *Australopithecus* and man is the tools found in the vicinity of the fossils. The evolutionists assume, without evidence, that *Australopithecus* used the tools. Creationists are just as reasonable in assuming that the tools belonged to true humans who hunted *Australopithecus*." Josh McDowell and Don Stewart, *Family Handbook of Christian Knowledge: The Creation*. San Bernardino, CA: Here's Life Publishers, Inc., © 1984, p. 122.

[9]Henry M. Morris, Ph.D, *Scientific Creationism*, p. 173.

[10]Duane T. Gish, Ph.D., "Have you Been...Brainwashed?" South Holland, IL: The Bible League, © 1986, used by permission. Dr. Gish has a Ph.D. in biochemistry from the University of California, Berkeley.

[11]Duane T. Gish, Ph.D., *Evolution: The Challenge of the Fossil Record*. El Cajon, CA: Creation-Life Publishers, © 1985, pp. 140-145, used by permission.

ground. Excavation revealed....*Zinjanthropus*, 'East Africa Man.' The ridiculously large molars indicated that the individual probably lived on nuts and berries, and so it became affectionately known as 'Nutcracker Man.'

Some of us suspect that Louis knew all along that 'Zinj' was just a variant of a robust australopithecine. But the financial support Louis desperately needed to continue his work does not come from the discovery of fossil primates. It comes from finding human ancestors. The long financial association the Leakeys had with the National Geographic Society began at this time. Telling of the discovery of 'Zinj' in *National Geographic*, Louis began his report: 'The teeth were projecting from the rock face, smooth and shining, and quite *obviously human*'....[later] Louis began to realize that 'Zinj' really was just a super-robust australopithecine, and it is now known as *Australopithecus boisei*. What Louis claimed was 'obviously human' turned out to be obviously nonhuman."[12]

NEBRASKA MAN

Nebraska Man, who was supposed to have been 1 million years old, was admitted as evidence in the trial of a teacher accused of teaching evolution. The Scopes Trial became a celebrated liberal cause in the 1920's and is featured in many textbooks. However, the same textbooks do not always mention that the Nebraska Man used in the trial was in fact, later discovered to be a mistake.

Nebraska Man was reconstructed from a single tooth that actually came from an extinct pig! Gordon Lindsay notes: "One of these [fraudulent fossils] is the so-called 'Nebraska Man'. At the Scopes evolution trial in Dayton, Tennessee, William Jennings Bryan was confronted by evolutionists who declared that the 'Nebraska Man' was one of a sub-human evolutionary race that lived some million years ago. Therefore he, William Jennings Bryan, should discard the Bible record of creation as an exploded myth. When Mr. Bryan rejected their 'evidence', he was mocked and jeered at as a fool.

But of what did the 'findings' of the Nebraska Man consist....Only one tooth! Years after the Scopes trial, the whole of the skeleton was discovered. Then it was learned that the tooth had come from an extinct pig!"[13]

***

---

[12]Marvin L. Lubenow, *Bones of Contention*, pp. 157-158. [ ] mine.

[13]Gordon Lindsay, *Evolution—The Incredible Hoax*, p. 17. [ ] mine.

Josh McDowell and Don Stewart comment on the Nebraska find in their book, *The Creation*: "...a molar found in Nebraska in 1922....was identified as coming from an important transition form between man and his primate ancestors by at least four well-known scientists: H. Cook, H.F. Osborn, H.H. Wilder, and G. E. Smith. Osborn declared, on the day he first saw the tooth:

'The instant your package arrived I sat down with the tooth, in my window, and said to myself: 'It looks one hundred percent anthropoid'...it looks to me as if the first anthropoid ape of America has been found.'

However, in 1927 the molar was correctly identified as that of a pig: 'The men from the museum also found more of the fossil material for which they were looking, and it turned out that the tooth which had caused such a sensation was the tooth of an animal which had previously been named *Prosthennops*. This was very embarrassing, because *Prosthennops* was a peccary, which is a type of pig!' "[14]

Dr. Gish exposes that this fake "ape-man" received a scientific name, a model drawing made of himself, and even news coverage, before anyone realized the fossil was a pig! Gish wrote in his book, *Evolution*: *The Challenge of the Fossil Record:* "Osborn and his colleagues could not quite decide whether the original owner of this tooth should be designated as an ape-like man or a man-like ape. He was given the designation *Hesperopithecus haroldcookii* and became known popularly as Nebraska Man. An illustration of what this creature and his contemporaries supposedly looked like was published in the *Illustrated London News*. In this illustration, *Hesperopithecus* looks remarkably similar to modern man, although brutish in appearance."[15]

JAVA MAN?

Java Man, named after the island in Indonesia where he was found, is dated at 700,000 BC. The Java Man—in actuality, a femur and skull fragment—was found along the bank of the Solo River by a Dutchman, Eugene Dubois.

Dubois went to Indonesia specifically in search of the missing link and once he found the bones—a fulfillment of his life's ambition—he wasted no time naming them. He called the find

---

[14]Josh McDowell and Don Stewart, *Family Handbook of Christian Knowledge: The Creation*, p. 116.

[15]Duane T. Gish, Ph.D., *Evolution: The Challenge of the Fossil Record*, p. 187. The illustration mentioned by Dr. Gish can still be found. It was originally published in the *Illustrated London News*, June 24, 1922.

Pithecanthropus Erectus. *Pithecos* is Greek for "ape," *anthropus* is Greek for "man" and of course, *erectus* means "erect." Thus, we are dealing with an impressive-sounding Greek name, which literally means "the ape-man who walks upright."

Gordon Lindsay, in his book, *Evolution—The Incredible Hoax*, notes that it was heralded as the "missing link" until Dr. Eugene Dubois, who discovered this "man," reversed his opinion. The doctor concluded "the bones he had found were the remains of a gibbon."[16]

Professor Lubenow tells us: "The work by Bert Theunissen, *Eugene Dubois and the Ape-Man from Java*, published in the Netherlands, brings to light information that has hitherto been unavailable to most researchers....[He notes] Dubois seriously misinterpreted the Java Man fossils, and there was abundant evidence available to him at that time that he had misinterpreted them...the evolutionists' dating of Java Man at half a million years is highly suspect....Java Man was eventually accepted as our evolutionary ancestor in spite of the evidence because he could be interpreted to promote evolution....Accurate dating is essential to the proper interpretation of a fossil. Since Dubois claimed that Java Man was *the* missing link between apes and humans, he had to show that it dated at the appropriate time when a certain ape stock was allegedly evolving into humans. If Java Man were rather recent in date, as may well be the case, he could not serve as an evolutionary transitional form because modern humans were already on the scene at that time.

Dubois claimed that the skullcap and the femur came from a rock stratum known as the Trinil layer, named after a nearby village in central Java. He believed that these rocks were below what is known as the Pleistocene-Pliocene (Tertiary) boundary. Dubois was convinced that 'real' humans evolved later in the Middle Pleistocene. Hence, his dating of Java Man was quite appropriate for a missing link. However, his interpretation was not exactly straightforward, as...G. H. R. von Koenigswald, tells us:

When Dubois issued his first description of the fossil Javanese fauna he designated it Pleistocene. But no sooner had he discovered his *Pithecanthropus* than the fauna had suddenly to become Tertiary. He did everything in his power to diminish the Pleistocene character of the fauna,....

The criterion was no longer to be the fauna as a whole, but only his *Pithecanthropus*. Such a primitive form belonged to the Tertiary!

---

[16]Gordon Lindsay, *Evolution—The Incredible Hoax*, p. 18. A modern gibbon is a slender, long-armed ape of the East Indies and southern Asia.

Dubois' view...did not go uncontested. But there was no getting at him until he had described his whole collection and laid all his cards on the table. That was why we all had to wait for a study of his finds, and to wait in vain....Weidenreich concluded that the Java Man femur was not a true *Homo erectus* femur but was instead a modern one....Here, then, is the problem faced by evolutionist paleoanthropology. If the Java skullcap and femur actually belong together, then it is difficult to maintain a species difference between *Homo erectus* and *Homo sapiens.* The distinction would be an artificial one, and it would compromise these fossils as evidence for human evolution. If, on the other hand, the skullcap belongs to *Homo erectus*, and the femur belongs to *Homo sapiens*, it shows that these two forms likely lived together as contemporaries. It likewise removes these fossils as evidence for human evolution, because fluorine analysis indicates that the fossils are both the same age."[17]

Regarding the Java Man, Dr. Gish informs us of a few little-known facts, such as: "...Marcellin Boule (then Director of the French Institute of Human Paleontology and one of the world's foremost experts on human fossils) and H. V. Vallois (Boule's successor) stated:

Following Dubois, several naturalists have laid stress on the resemblance between the *Pithecanthropus* remains and the corresponding portions of a Gibbon's skeleton....

'Taken as a whole, these structures are very similar to those of chimpanzees and gibbons.' They report that von Koenigswald, a German paleontologist who also spent time in Java and discovered some additional material, attributed the two molar teeth that Dubois had discovered to an orangutan and premolar tooth to a true Man....Boule and Vallois thus assert that if one looked only at the skull one would say, 'Ape,' while if one looked only at the femur one would say, 'Man.' Perhaps this is the true assessment of these specimens—the femur was that of a true Man and the skull, as Dubois himself finally concluded...was that of an exceptionally large ape....As noted earlier, the three teeth that Dubois also associated with the skull cap did not belong to the owner of the skull cap and there appears little justification in attributing the femur to the owner of that skull cap."[18]

---

[17]Marvin L. Lubenow, *Bones of Contention: A Creationist Assessment of the Human Fossils*, pp. 87-89, 98. [ ] mine. Lubenow's sources were Bert Theunissen, *Eugene Dubois and the Ape-Man from Java* (Dordrecht: Kluwer Academic Publishers, 1989), p.158; and G.H.R. von Koenigswald, *Meeting Prehistoric Man* (New York: Harper and Brothers, 1956), pp. 34, 38-39.

[18]Duane T. Gish, Ph.D., *Evolution: The Challenge of the Fossil Record*, pp. 181-182, 184.

To put icing on this fraudulent cake, we note that thirty years after the find, Dr. Dubois produced two human skulls, which he had originally hidden. He concealed them because they were found at the same level as his "missing link," proving that ape and man co-existed. This, of course, destroyed any possibility of the bones being those of an ape-man! It seems that when we try to get down to the facts regarding evolution, we find that they are just not there!

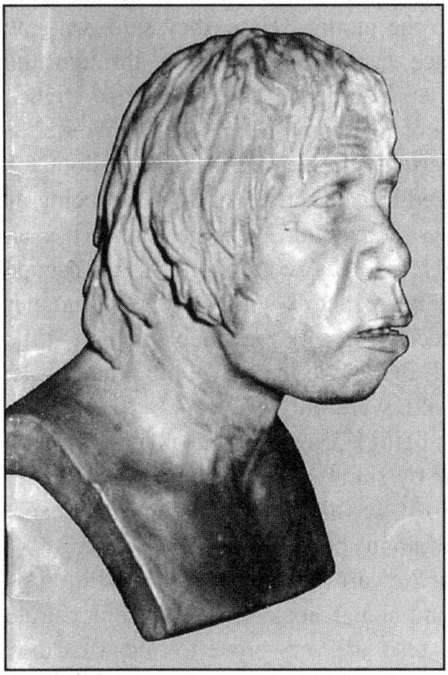

Left: A bust at the American Museum of Natural History in New York City, which was made to show what "Piltdown Man" was supposed to look like. Right: A stone marker commemorating the site where "Piltdown Man" was found.

PILTDOWN "MAN"

Piltdown Man, discovered in Piltdown, England, was believed to be the missing link for nearly fifty years. Sometimes called the "fraud of the century," this "man" was created from a modern jaw bone, a portion of a skull, and filed down teeth, all stained with iron salts to produce an aged color and fossilized appearance. Gordon Lindsay tells us: "The 'Piltdown Man' was 'discovered' by one Charles Dawson, an amateur fossilologist. He declared that he had found the remains of a 'man' in a gravel pit near Piltdown, in Sussex, England. Brought to the

British Museum, the fossils were acclaimed by paleontologists, as about half a million years old. The prized 'find' was called 'The Dawn Man.' The Piltdown Man received unusual publicity. From these worthless relics of a contrived fraud was reconstructed a monstrous, gibbering sub-human man. His likeness adorned schoolbooks of children in grade and high school, as well as college textbooks. The Piltdown 'fossil' was accepted as authentic by evolutionists and flaunted before those who revered the Bible. Once more the 'missing link,' was proudly hailed before the public. Here, they said, was the final proof that the human race came into existence through the processes of evolution....In the October 1956, Reader's Digest, appeared the full story of 'The Great Piltdown Hoax.' A Dr. Weiner of Oxford, revolved in his mind certain strange circumstances about the Piltdown man. The teeth appeared to be the teeth of a human being as they were worn down flat, which could not be done by an ape....Somebody had deliberately filed the teeth flat!....A microscope showed that the teeth had indeed been filed down! They used a geiger counter with modern dating techniques, not available at the time Charles Dawson had 'discovered' the jaw in the gravel pit....the fossils, instead of being 500,000 years old, were only 50 years old, and came from an ape, instead of a human being! Dawson, the faker, now dead, had cunningly fossilized the jaw by staining it a mahogany color with an iron salt and bichromate! So it was that the evolutionists became the victim of the world's most infamous hoax."[19]

Josh McDowell and Don Stewart correctly noted of Piltdown Man: "The success of this monumental hoax served to demonstrate that scientists, just like everyone else, are very prone to find what they are looking for whether it is there or not. The success of the Piltdown hoax for nearly 50 years in spite of the scrutiny of the world's greatest authorities, along with other stories nearly as dubious, led Lord Zuckerman to declare that it is doubtful if there is any science at all in the search for man's fossil ancestry."[20]

THE HYPOCRISY OF LEAKEY

Dr. Bolton Davidheiser also notes regarding the famous Piltdown hoax: "In 1960 L. S. B. Leakey, famous for his anthropological discoveries in Africa, published the fourth edition of his book *Adam's Ancestors.* The book was originally written before the Piltdown

---

[19]Gordon Lindsay, *Evolution—The Incredible Hoax*, pp. 18-19.
[20]Josh McDowell and Don Stewart, *Family Handbook of Christian Knowledge: The Creation*, p. 118.

material was exposed as a fraud, but this edition was published seven years after the hoax was disclosed. Dr. Leakey added more material to bring the book up-to-date, but left the original text unchanged. Thus we find in the same volume two different versions of the Piltdown affair. At one place he says, '...the jaw was that of a modern ape, while the skull was that of a modern type man....' At another place he says, 'The famous Piltdown skull agrees with *Homo sapiens* [modern man] in this one respect [that the brow ridges are similar to ours], but differs markedly in others, and so is ruled out from the species.' Thus at one place he says that the skull is the type of modern man, and at another place in the same book he says that it differs so much from that of modern man that it cannot be considered to belong to the same species!"[21]

FOUR DOWN, HOW MANY MORE TO SCORE?

Since we found four out of four "men" to be apes, fakes or mistakes, perhaps we should also ask, "If we have been deceived in the past, could present 'evolutionary evidence' also be deceptive?"

You have the right to demand tests, tests and more tests. As the science of testing becomes more advanced, we believe new revelations will appear—evidence that we must hear—evidence that will show that the missing link is missing because it truly never existed! As Dr. Davidheiser has wondered: "In the Piltdown case the truth has been revealed; one cannot help wondering how much fantasy may be involved in the interpretations of other cases which cannot be checked."[22]

1470 "MAN"

The 1470 Man is said to be over 2 million years old (the date keeps changing, as you will see). Found by Richard Leakey in Kenya in 1972, this australopithecine-type animal was reconstructed in a deceptive manner!

Regarding the 1470 skull, Professor Lubenow points out: "...the face had a bit of an australopithecine slant to it. Pictures taken before plaster was used to fill in the missing pieces reveal that the face of the fossil is rather free floating. It is attached to the skull only at the top,

---

[21]Bolton Davidheiser, Ph.D., *Evolution and Christian Faith*. Phillipsburg, NJ: The Presbyterian and Reformed Publishing Company, © 1969, p. 344, used by permission. Available through POB 817, Philipsburg, NJ, USA 08865. Davidheiser's source was L.S.B. Leakey, *Adam's Ancestors*, Harper and Brothers, 1960.

[22]Ibid, p. 340.

with nothing to stabilize the slant of the face. Further, the maxilla (upper jaw) is not attached to the rest of the face.

Others have also questioned the reconstruction of skull 1470. On several occasions, Richard Leakey protested that the skull was reconstructed in the only way possible. There were no other options. However, it seems that Leakey was not being straightforward. Roger Lewin, associated with Leakey on several projects, tells a different story regarding skull 1470.

One point of uncertainty was the angle at which the face attached to the cranium. Alan Walker remembers an occasion when he, Michael Day, and Richard Leakey were studying the two sections of the skull. 'You could hold the maxilla [upper jaw] forward, and give it a long face, or you could tuck it in, making the face short,' he recalls. '*How you held it really depended on your preconceptions.* It was interesting watching what people did with it.' Leakey remembers the incident too: 'Yes, if you held it one way, it looked like one thing; if you held it another, it looked like something else.'[23]

There is no question that bias intervened in the reconstruction of skull 1470. The face was given the larger slant off of the perpendicular to make it look more like a transitional form between primates and humans, especially when at the time of its reconstruction it was thought to be 2.9 million years old.

Bias is also obvious in the way famed artist Jay Matternes put 'flesh' on the bones of skull 1470, as seen in the June 1973 issue of *National Geographic*. Matternes shows the possessor of skull 1470 to be a young black woman who looks very human except that she has an apelike nose. Human noses are composed of cartilage which normally does not fossilize, and the nose is missing on 1470. It is obvious that the purpose in giving the reconstructed skull 1470 woman an apelike nose was to make her look as 'primitive' as possible. The decision of what kind of nose to give her was an entirely subjective one made by Matternes or his advisers. With a human nose, none would question the full humanity of that woman in *National Geographic*.

The very modern morphology and the very old date (2.9 m.y.a.) of skull 1470 presented an intolerable situation for human evolution. The ten-year controversy concerning the date of this fossil was finally 'settled' in 1981, when the accepted date became 1.9 m.y.a. The account of this controversy, showing that the dating methods are not independent of evolution or independent of each other, is found in the

---

[23]Lubenow's footnote states: "Roger Lewin, *Bones of Contention: Controversies in the Search for Human Origins*, (New York: Simon and Schuster, 1987), 160. Emphasis mine. Bracketed material added for clarity." Marvin L. Lubenow, *Bones of Contention: A Creationist Assessment of the Human Fossils*, p. 280.

appendix of this book. That case study of the dating of the KBS Tuff and of skull 1470 offers clear evidence that when the chips are down, factual evidence is prostituted to evolutionary theory."[24]

Dr. Gish rightly noted concerning the 1470 Man: "In Leakey's *National Geographic* article he is quoted as saying 'Either we toss out this skull or we toss out our theories of early man....It simply fits no previous models of human beginnings'....In his *National Geographic* article, Leakey (p. 820) refers to Skull 1470 as 'this surprisingly advanced early man.' In press conferences and public lectures Leakey emphasized that his Skull 1470 had many advanced human-like features, in some respects....even more advanced than *Homo erectus.* Yet, he declared, this creature was nearly three million years old....The estimated cranial capacity of 800 cc (other estimates have been somewhat lower), and the morphology of the calvaria (skull cap), Leakey believed, warranted inclusion of the fossil in the genus *Homo....*" Interestingly enough for us, the experts on evolution seldom agree. Gish continues: "Leakey declares that his Skull 1470 should be attributed to *Homo habilis*, although his co-author of the paper, Alan Walker, an anthropologist now at Johns Hopkins University, believes that it should be placed in the genus *Australopithecus* [an extinct ape]."[25]

THE 1470 CONTROVERSY

With regard to the 1470 controversy, Josh McDowell and Don Stewart point out that Dr. Gish said: "Early in 1973, Richard Leakey gave a lecture in San Diego describing his latest results. He stated his convictions that these findings simply eliminate everything we have been taught about human origins and, he went on to say, he had nothing to offer in its place! Creationists *do* have something to offer in its place, of course. We believe that these results support man's special creation rather than his origin from an animal ancestry. These results also strongly support our belief that man and the ape have always coexisted."[26]

---

[24]Ibid, pp. 163-164.

[25]Duane T. Gish, Ph.D, *Evolution: The Challenge of the Fossil Record*, pp. 165-166. [ ] mine.

[26]Josh McDowell and Don Stewart, *Family Handbook of Christian Knowledge: The Creation*, p. 122. McDowell and Stewart's source was Duane T. Gish, Ph.D., *Evolution: The Fossils Say No*. San Diego, CA: Creation-Life Publishers, 1978, p. 59. In 1974, Donald Johnson found some fragments which were thought to be missing links because tools were found nearby. As it turned out, these "links" were merely a sub-class of Australopithecus, an extinct ape which coexisted with humans—the tools belonged to the

PEKING "MAN"

Peking Man, discovered in China, is said to be one-half million years old and, like Australopithecus, has been considered by many to be an extinct ape. Dr. Davidson Black found a tooth in 1927, and in 1929, a fragment of skull was located. It is most interesting to us that "in 1941, the bones disappeared while being shipped out of China for safekeeping."[27]

We wonder who's keeping the bones safe from future tests for the sake of evolution? We may never know! We wonder—do we have another hoax on our hands? Dennis Petersen informs us: "French scientist, Marcellin Boule, examined the actual fragments of skull, and in 1937 published his opinion that the find was decidedly monkey-like. Boule and others report that **the model did not correspond objectively to the fossils.** It was clear that the fragments of skull found belonged to creatures hunted by true humans....**Human fossils have been excavated from the same site!**"[28]

---

humans. When we talk about extinction, we may think of the dinosaurs who lived millions of years ago, before the recreation of Earth, which excludes man's original creation just 6000 years ago. Modern animals become extinct every day. Thus, we have the environmental agencies of the twentieth century trying to prevent such extinction. My brother Paul, a bird expert, pointed out one example: the ivory-billed woodpecker, last seen in the 1940's. Our point is that modern man has coexisted with apes who are now extinct. If you combine this with inaccurate dating, there is no evidence to create an evolutionary hypothesis, much less a law. The theory of evolution contradicts the second law of thermodynamics, which is a proven fact. Thus, to an honest scientist who has knowledge of both evolution and thermodynamics, evolution is clearly impossible! To document an example of the errors and inaccuracies involved in some of the most advanced dating techniques being used today, we quote Richard Bliss, from his book, *Origins: Creation or Evolution*. He tells us of Leakey's 1470 Man: "This fossil was touted by the popular media as the 'Oldest Man.' It was dated using the potassium-argon method. John Reader in his book *Missing Links* (1981) gives us a glimpse of the method in use. 'The Worldwide admiration and congratulations that greeted the twenty-eight-year-old Richard Leakey and his two-and-a-half million-year-old 1470 (number given to the fossil skull) were subsequently marred by just one thing—an authoritative suggestion that the skull was not as old as Leakey claimed... Fitch and Miller's tests on the first samples...that Leakey sent to Cambridge actually gave an average age of 221 million years. Such an age was impossible—so Leakey sent more samples. From these the scientists selected crystals that seemed fresher than others and produced an age of 2.4 million years...They subsequently tested many more samples (including some they had collected themselves) and their results range from a minimum of 290,000 years to a maximum of 19.5 million.' (pages 205-206)." Richard Bliss, Ed.D., *Origins: Creation or Evolution*. Santee, CA: Creation-Life Publishers, Inc., © 1988, p. 68, used by permission.

[27]*The World Book Encyclopedia*, Vol. 15, 1970 edition, p. 204.

[28]Dennis R. Petersen, B.S., M.A., *Unlocking the Mysteries of Creation*, Vol. I. South Lake Tahoe, CA: Creation Resource Foundation, © 1986, p. 118, used by permission.

Regarding Peking Man, Dr. Gish notes: "A close examination of the reports related to Peking Man...reveal a tangled web of contradictions, highly subjective treatment of the data, a peculiar and unnatural state of the fossil bones, and the loss of essentially all of the fossil material.

At Choukoutien, about twenty-five miles from Peking, China, in the 1920s and 1930s, were found fragments of about thirty skulls, eleven mandibles (lower jaws), and about 147 teeth. Except for a very few and highly fragmentary remains of limb bones, nothing else from these creatures was found. One of the initial finds was a single tooth, and without waiting for further evidence, Dr. Davidson Black...declared that this tooth established evidence for the existence of an ancient hominid, or man-like creature, in China. He designated this creature *Sinanthropus pekinensis*, which soon came to be known as Peking Man."[29]

NEANDERTHAL "MAN"

Neanderthal Man, whose name is derived from the valley where it was discovered in Germany, is not the Neanderthal Man you have seen portrayed in movies. They are "us." So, our "evolutionary" list of men thus far consists of a fictional character called a "common ancestor," several early "ape-men," which were found to be ordinary apes that are now extinct, and several missing link "ape-men" who were supposedly half-human, but turned out to be fakes or mistakes.

Now we have a man whose severely deformed skeleton was used to prove "evolution." Is there anything further from the truth??? " '...Hooten says that you can model on a Neanderthal skull either the features of a chimpanzee or those of a philosopher. He concludes by saying that the alleged restorations of ancient types of man have very little, if any scientific value and are likely only to mislead the public.' "[30]

Dennis Peterson notes: "The very name, Neanderthal, seems to automatically arouse thoughts of a hunch-backed primitive brute with a heavily over-hanging forehead and a gorilla-like face. But what is the real story on Neanderthal Man?

***

Available through CRF, POB 16100, South Lake Tahoe, CA, USA 95706. Tel. (916) 542-1509.

[29]Duane T. Gish, Ph.D., *Evolution: The Challenge of the Fossil Record*, p. 185.

[30]Josh McDowell and Don Stewart, *Family Handbook of Christian Knowledge: The Creation*, p. 113.

The name comes from the Neander Valley near Dusseldorf, Germany. It was here in 1856 that the first skeleton of Neanderthal Man was discovered. Since then there have been many Neanderthal graves found in Europe and the Middle East.

At the time of the initial discovery and for many years after, it was publicly implied that Neanderthal Man was the missing link in man's heritage, connecting him to apes. During the late nineteenth century, with Darwin's theory shaking the scientific world, these early 'ape-men' were 'proof' that human evolution was a fact.

Models of Neanderthal Man were once exhibited as bent over, club-swinging cave men. But eventually it was discovered that Neanderthal man walked upright after all. In a news article of the Sacramento Union (California) dated September 16, 1981, the sub-headline reads: '**He may not have been the hairy ape we thought he was.**'

But why were Neanderthals depicted as hunchbacked and rather retarded looking? It turns out the reason is that ***'one skeletal find'*** proved to ***'have been severely deformed by age and arthritis.'***

Now the truth is known. If you were to give Mr. Neanderthal a shave and haircut, put him in a business suit, and send him downtown to pay the bills, he wouldn't stand out from the crowd at all. In fact you've likely seen individuals on the street that looked a whole lot more primitive than Mr. N."[31]

JOACHEM NEANDER'S VALLEY OF PRAISE

Professor Marvin Lubenow documents unusual, little-known and very interesting facts regarding Neanderthal Man. "In the late 1600s, an evangelical (Lutheran) theologian and school rector, gifted in poetry and hymn writing, took long walks in the country near Hochdal, Germany. As he strolled, he composed hymns and sang them in praise to God. One of his favorite spots was a beautiful gorge through which the Dussel River flowed, about ten miles east of Dusseldorf. He strolled in this one valley so often that it became identified with him and was eventually named after him. His name was Joachem Neander, and the valley became known as the Neanderthal—the Neander Valley (*tal,* or *thal* in Old German, means 'valley,' with the *h* being silent).

Almost two hundred years later, this valley was owned by Herr von Beckersdorf. As the owner quarried limestone in the valley for the manufacture of cement, his workmen came across some caves in the side wall of the gorge. One cave, known as the Feldhofer Grotto, had

[31]Dennis R. Petersen, B.S., M.A., *Unlocking the Mysteries of Creation*, Vol. I, p. 121.

human bones in the soil of its floor. Because the prime interest of the workmen was to quarry the limestone, what probably had been a complete skeleton was largely destroyed. Only the skullcap, some ribs, part of the pelvis, and some limb bones were saved. The year was 1856. The first Neandertal had been discovered....Eventually, the bones came to the attention of Rudolf Virchow, a professor at the University of Berlin. A brilliant man and a true scientist, Virchow is recognized as the father of pathology. Virchow questioned the antiquity of the bones. He felt that they belonged to a modern *Homo sapiens* who had suffered from rickets in childhood, arthritis in old age, and had received several severe blows to the head. As we shall see, Virchow's diagnosis is as valid today as when he first made it.

William King, professor of anatomy at Queen's College, Galway, Ireland, however, read an evolutionary history into the bones, and it was he who eventually gave them their first scientific name: *Homo neanderthalensis*....'Darwin's bulldog,' Thomas Huxley, recognized that Neandertal was fully human and not an evolutionary ancestor. Donald Johanson, in his book *Lucy's*[32] *Child*, writes:

From a collection of modern human skulls Huxley was able to select a series with features leading 'by insensible gradations' from an average modern specimen to the Neandertal skull. In other words, it wasn't qualitatively different from present-day *Homo sapiens*."[33]

NEANDERTHAL WAS HERE LESS THAN 6000 YEARS AGO

Regarding the dating[34] of so-called Neanderthal Man, Professor Lubenow informs us: "...there is evidence that the Neandertals persisted long after their alleged demise. The Neandertal skull known as Amud I from Upper Galilee, Israel, was found as a burial just below the top of layer BI. If Amud I was buried into layer BI, it follows that he cannot be older than Layer BI but could be younger. The radiocarbon date for Upper BI is 5,710 y.a. Michael Day (British Museum—Natural History) states: 'These dates are believed to be too 'young' as the result of contamination by younger carbon'....this is also the standard excuse given whenever a radiocarbon date is too young to

[32] In case you have ever wondered where they came up with the name "Lucy," we are informed that when the bones in question were found, The Beatles' song, "Lucy in the Sky with Diamonds," was playing on the radio.

[33] Marvin L. Lubenow, *Bones of Contention: A Creationist Assessment of the Human Fossils*, pp. 59-61.

[34] Professor Lubenow documents that evolutionists *say* that Neanderthals extend back as far as 200,000 y.a., while they disappeared rapidly 34,000 years ago. See Marvin L. Lubenow, *Bones of Contention: A Creationist Assessment of the Human Fossils*, p. 65.

fit the system. Day gives no evidence that young carbon was present. It is understood by evolutionists that if a radiocarbon date is too young to fit the evolutionary scenario, that is proof enough that the sample was contaminated, since a 'good' date would unquestionably fit the scheme."[35]

Professor Lubenow rightly points out that if there is any legitimacy to the recent date: "...for Neandertal, it could mean that Neandertal, like his smaller edition known as *Homo erectus*, persisted until quite recently. That would be additional evidence that the differences between Neandertal and anatomically modern humans had nothing to do with the [alleged] evolutionary process. For evolutionists, the Neandertal problem remains unsolved."[36]

However, we believe Rudolf Virchow has solved the Neanderthal problem! Lubenow notes: "Health factors can be reflected in the skeleton, especially a vitamin D deficiency resulting in rickets. J. Lawrence Angel (Smithsonian Institution) writes: 'Pelvis and skull base tend to flatten if protein or vitamin D in diet is inadequate.' This was the diagnosis of Rudolf Virchow, 'the father of pathology,' when he examined the flattened skullcap of the first Neandertal discovery. He was overruled by those who favored an evolutionary interpretation. In 1970, Francis Ivanhoe published in *Nature* an article entitled, 'Was Virchow Right about Neandertal?' He presented a strong case based on diagnostic evidence that the Neandertals were really modern humans who suffered from rickets."[37]

SMITH'S PILTDOWN ENDOCRANIAL CAST—A BLAST

Dr. Bolton Davidheiser, a professor of biology, tells us that G. Elliot Smith claimed in his 1924 book that Neanderthal was less intelligent than us. He based his findings on an endocranial cast, which he claimed showed that the brain of the Neanderthal, although larger than human, was less developed. However, Straus and Cave point out that Smith made a cast of Piltdown, which was a hoax—a modern skull. Smith said the same thing about Piltdown as he did about Neanderthal!

Dr. Davidheiser also points out that Neanderthals are not ancestral to humans because modern-shaped human skulls[38] older than

---

[35]Ibid, pp. 73-74.

[36]Ibid, p. 74. [ ] mine.

[37]Ibid, pp. 76-77.

[38]Keep in mind what Hooten said: "...you can model on a Neanderthal skull either the features of a chimpanzee or those of a philosopher." Dennis R. Petersen, B.S., M.A., *Unlocking the Mysteries of Creation*, Vol. I, p. 121. Remember, if Neanderthal was

Neanderthal have been found.[39] We believe, of course, that they are a little older than the date recorded in the Israeli find mentioned earlier, which gives us an interpretation consistent with biblical claims!

As we can see from this evidence, the fact that Neanderthal was malformed by rickets and thus, mistakenly claimed by many to be a very old "missing link," is preposterous! Professor Lubenow comments: "When Joachem Neander walked in his beautiful valley so many years ago, he could not know that hundreds of years later his name would become world famous, not for his hymns celebrating creation but for a concept that he would have totally rejected: human evolution."[40]

found in an Israeli grave, dating back less than 6000 years, he is obviously not anything less than human, though some of the skulls were malformed from rickets, due to a deficient diet. This is the difference between modern human skulls and those "ancient ones" deformed by rickets.

[39]See Bolton Davidheiser, Ph.D., *Evolution and Christian Faith*, p. 333.

[40]Marvin L. Lubenow, *Bones of Contention: A Creationist Assessment of the Human Fossils*, p. 77.

In the January 1996 issue of *National Geographic*, in an article entitled, "Neandertals," by Rick Gore, this photo was shown. A portion of the caption read: "All dressed up...and no place to evolve. A display at the Neanderthal Museum in Erkrath, Germany, near the original fossil discovery site, pays homage to the caveman of modern imagination. From his bestial 19th-century persona to just another guy in a suit."[41]

---

[41]Rick Gore, "Neandertals," *National Geographic*. Jan. 1996, © National Geographic. Photo by Kenneth Garrett/National Geographic Society, Image Collection ©.

A DECEPTIVE DISPLAY DESPITE THE THEORY

Dr. Lubenow reminds us that evolutionists like to link head shape (morphology) to missing links! A segment in his book, *Bones of Contention*, entitled "The Skull Size Argument" points out: "In seeking to establish the concept of human evolution, the evolutionist leans heavily on skull morphology and, to a lesser degree in recent years, on skull size. Both are spurious arguments and prove nothing. Typical of the charts and illustrations used by evolutionists is a display at the American Museum of Natural History in New York City. It is titled 'Increasing Brain Size' and shows an increase in brain sizes as follows:

Increasing Brain Size	
Homo Sapiens	1450 cc [cubic centimeters]
Neanderthal	1625 cc
Pithecanthropus [*Homo erectus*]	914 cc
Australopithecinae	650 cc
Gorilla	543 cc
Chimpanzee	400 cc
Gibbon	97 cc

(Bracketed material added for clarity.)

The obvious question is, What is the purpose of this display? or, What does this display say? The obvious answer, since it is a part of the museum's display on 'The Evolution of Man,' is to show that the hominid brain has enlarged by evolution over time. However, no evolutionist in the world—past or present—believes that it [evolution] happened in the way the chart implies it did. No evolutionist believes that evolution went from gibbon to chimpanzee to gorilla to the australopithecines to *Homo erectus* to Neandertal and then to modern humans....They assure us that we came from some transitional form that was the ancestor of both humans and living primates. (The fact that that transitional form—if ever existed—would readily be called an ape by anyone who saw it was admitted by the famous evolutionist George Gaylord Simpson.) The museum display is an absurd mixing of past and present forms having no relationship to what evolutionists themselves teach. It is a cheap form of propaganda, Madison Avenue style, to convince the uninformed public of the 'truth' of evolution.

Although that chart was still in the American Museum as of 1991, that type of illustration is not seen as much in recent years. We now know that relative brain size means very little. The relationship between brain size and body size must be factored in, and the crucial element is not brain size but brain organization. A large gorilla brain is no closer to the human condition than is a small gorilla brain. The human brain varies in size from about 700 cc to about 2200 cc with no differences in ability or intelligence. That variation, more than a factor of three, is an incredible difference in size variation but indicates no difference in quality. Those brain-size charts are meaningless. Yet, the idea of increasing brain size has been injected into the human thought stream so effectively by evolutionists that most nonspecialists still think of it as significant evidence for evolution."[42]

PROFESSOR LUBENOW'S EVALUATION OF RHODESIAN/BROKEN HILL/KABWE MAN—BRILLIANT AND INSIGHTFUL

Rhodesian Man is claimed to be between forty and 400,000 years old. Here we have a man with a brain size within human range (1280 cc), who apparently died with three other humans in a mine shaft while mining lead. Professor Lubenow writes: "Nothing illustrates the futility of basing an evolutionary sequence on skull morphology more than does the skull of Rhodesian Man..."[43]

Professor Lubenow has researched the subject of Mr. R. so well that we will quote him at length. "Rhodesian Man was so named because he was found in 1921 in what was then known as Northern Rhodesia, now Zambia. The fossil is also called Broken Hill Man (after the mine in which he was found), or Kabwe Man (after the city near which he was found). Because the browridges on this fossil skull are more pronounced than those found on any other human fossil, no human fossil appears to be more 'primitive'...than does Rhodesian Man. Yet, his brain size of 1280 cc is so large that the fossil demands to be classified as *Homo sapiens*. We need to be constantly reminded that there is nothing in the contours of the skull of an individual that gives clues as to his degree of civilization, culture, or morality....Rhodesian Man had been dated at about 40,000 y.a. Richard Klein gives the newer date as between 200,000 and 400,000 y.a. Yet, there is reason to believe that the fossil is actually quite recent in age. The original 1921 report in *Nature*, telling of its discovery, says: 'The skull is in a remarkably fresh state of preservation, the bone having merely lost its animal matter and not having been in the least mineralised.'

[42]Ibid, pp. 82-83. Last [ ] mine.
[43]Ibid, p. 83.

It is difficult to understand why a fossil buried for 200,000 to 400,000 years (or even 40,000 years) would have no mineralization whatsoever. That fact suggests that the fossil could be quite recent in age....the most remarkable feature of this fossil is that it was found about sixty feet underground at the far end of a shaft in a lead and zinc mine. The skull was found with the remains of two or possibly three other individuals. The maxilla (upper jaw) of one of those individuals is considerably more modern in morphology than is Rhodesian Man....The associated postcranial bones are all very modern in appearance.

Found under other circumstances, Rhodesian Man... could serve as an excellent illustration of an evolutionary transitional form between apes and humans."[44]

Professor Lubenow further points out: "...this individual was either mining lead and zinc himself or was in the mine shaft at a time when lead and zinc were being mined by other humans. This smacks of a rather high degree of civilization and technology.

It is amusing that many evolutionists, when reporting on the details of Rhodesian Man, say that he was found in a cave. Technically, I suppose, they are right. A mine shaft is just a cave, of sorts, in the same way that diamonds and emeralds are just pebbles....In spite of the obvious lesson to be learned from the Rhodesian and Saldanha skulls, evolutionists continue to base much of their evidence for human evolution on the alleged primitive-to-advanced contours of fossil skulls. Creationists maintain that in light of the evidence of the wide genetic diversity in the human family, skull contour is an inadequate basis for determining relationships. Evolution's illegitimate children, the archaic *Homo sapiens* fossils, give eloquent testimony to that fact."[45]

DOUBTS, ANYONE?

Anyone questioning our quotation of Professor Lubenow may find it interesting to read the foreword on the back cover of his book. Written by Michael Charney, emeritus professor of anthropology and affiliate professor of zoology at Colorado State University, the foreword reads: "On the question of biological, especially human, origins, Lubenow is not content to merely quote biblical theory (if I may use that word). Like a true scholar he researches in depth the literature in the scientific journals, sifting the evidence, searching out the areas open to interpretation....He does his homework so thoroughly

---

[44]Ibid, p. 84.
[45]Ibid, p. 85.

that he makes someone like me who would carry on a dialogue with him (as we did on creationism vs. Darwinism) also do his homework....He is a pleasure to fence with intellectually."[46]

CRO-MAGNON "MAN"

In 1992, a frozen man was discovered in Europe buried in the snow and ice. News magazines and television networks, which dubbed him "The Ice Man," reported that he was 5000 years old. He was a man just as we are—we could see his flesh. He was as modern as men have always been, from the beginning of Adam.

"In 1940 some boys were out running with their dog in the countryside near Lascaux, France. The dog fell into a crack in the ground. When the boys rescued their pet they prodded their way into an ancient cavern. It was several hundred feet long and the walls were covered with colorful paintings of horses, deer, and bison.

These paintings are now famous as the skilled artwork of people we call Cro-Magnon (KRO-MAN-YO). Some of their skeletons were found buried in another cave at Les Eyzies, France in 1868. **The name Cro-Magnon simply refers to the local name of the stone cave** in which they were found. It literally means 'great big.' There are more than 70 sites of Cro-Magnon art in France alone.

Based on evolutionary assumptions, the Cro-Magnon people are supposed to date back 12,000 to 30,000 years. The fact they lived in caves does not mean they were less human. Do some humans live in caves today? They do, but does that make them any less human? Realizing that, you can understand how easily tribal groups can become isolated over time and actually 'de-volve' to social and technological degenerates. Is it any wonder why *Smithsonian magazine* (October 1986) carried an article titled: '**Cro-Magnon hunters were really us, working out strategies for survival**'."[47]

In a *Time* magazine article entitled "How Man Began" by Michael D. Lemonick (March 14, 1994) the opening paragraph made the accusation "No single, essential difference separates human beings from other animals—but that hasn't stopped the phrasemakers from trying to find one." He then lists several things we and God's other creatures obviously have in common, reason, laughter, etc. But tell me, do you know of any other of God's creatures who can write language (such as the Bible) and pass it down from one generation to another? Perhaps this "phrasemaker" has resolved Lemonick's (and evolutionists who believe likewise) dilemma? Perhaps!

---

[46]Ibid, p. back cover.

[47]Dennis R. Petersen, B.S., M.A., *Unlocking the Mysteries of Creation*, p. 120.

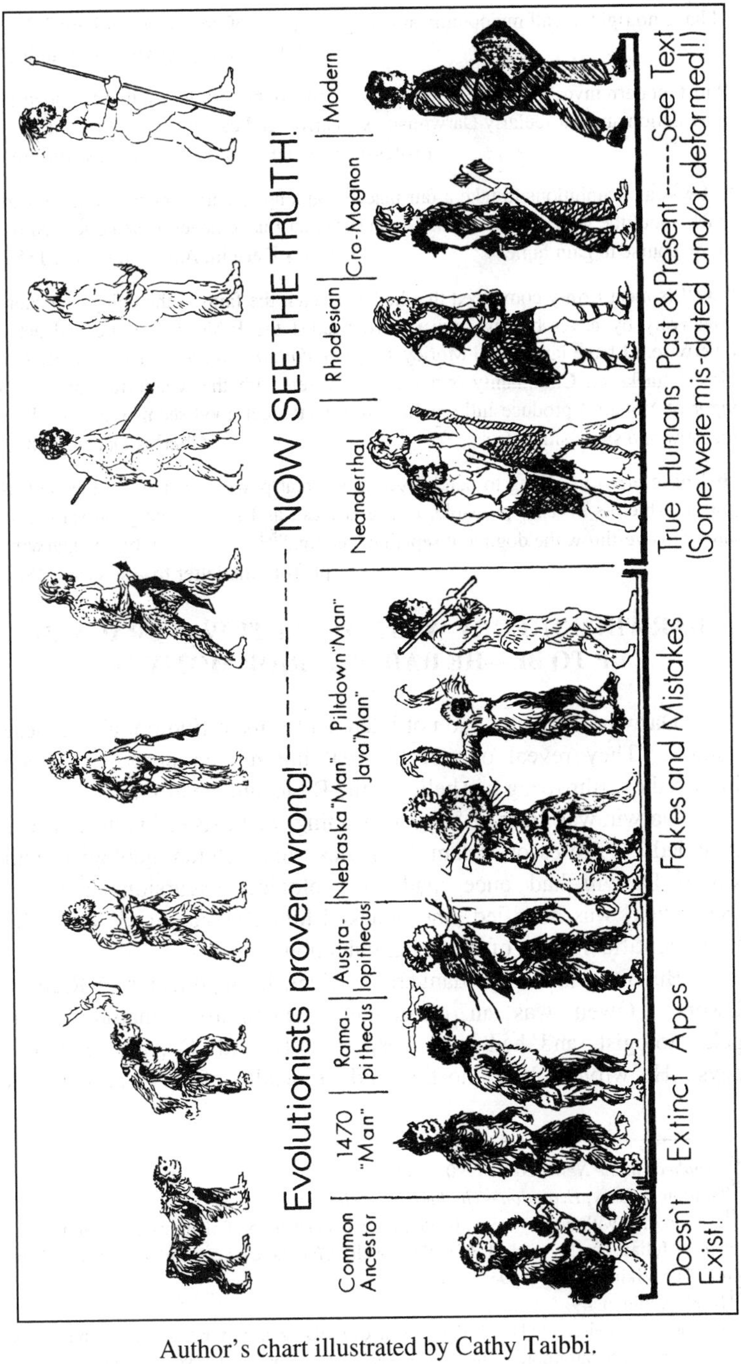

Author's chart illustrated by Cathy Taibbi.

"I have no right to call my opinion anything but an act of philosophical faith."[48]
T.H. Huxley, Darwin's "bulldog"

"Most modern investigators of science have come to the conclusion that the doctrine of evolution and particularly Darwinism is an error, and can not be maintained."[49]
Professor Haeckel, a most extreme evolutionist

"...I was also ambitious to take a fair place[50] among scientific men. I did not care much about the general public....and I am sure that I have never turned one inch out of my course to gain fame."[51] Charles Darwin, *Autobiography*, 1887

"Lyell is most firmly convinced that he has shaken the faith in the deluge far more effectively by never having said a word against the Bible than if he had acted otherwise....I have lately read Morley's *Life of Voltaire* and he insists strongly that direct attacks on Christianity (even when written with the wonderful forces and vigor of Voltaire) produce little permanent effect: real good seems only to follow the slow and silent side attacks."[52] Charles Darwin, 1873

"If I have erred in giving to natural selection great power...having exaggerated its power, which is in itself probable, I have at least, as I hope, done good service in aiding to overthrow the dogma of separate creation."[53] Charles Darwin,
excerpt from his letter to Asa Gray, 1861

DARWIN'S THEORY WAS NOT ALL IT WAS CRACKED UP TO BE—HE HAD ULTERIOR MOTIVES

Darwin, no doubt, had not intended for us to find out about these quotes. They reveal one of his real but hidden purposes, which involved overthrowing our belief in the Bible and creation!

Darwin was criticized by two leading scientists of his day. These included: "Professor Adam Sedgwick, the veteran geologist with whom Darwin had once made a geological excursion in Wales [Sedgwick] was horrified, and attacked him...for having deserted the true scientific method of Baconian induction.

But Darwin's most dangerous scientific opponent was Richard Owen. Owen was an outstanding comparative anatomist and paleontologist, and had been very friendly with Darwin in earlier days....He wrote a long, hostile, and—typically of him—anonymous

---

48 *Prophecy in the News,* April 1990, p. 11.
49 Gordon Lindsay, *Evolution—The Incredible Hoax*, p. 16.
50 Darwin died without any scientific degrees whatsoever and failed miserably in medical school. Julian Huxley and H.B.D. Kettlewell, *Charles Darwin and His World.* New York: The Viking Press, © 1965, p. 12.
51 Huxley, Ibid, p. 49.
52 Bolton Davidheiser, Ph.D., *Evolution and Christian Faith*, p. 67. Bolton Davidheiser is a graduate of Swarthmore College (A.B.) and Johns Hopkins University (Ph.D.).
53 Ibid, p. 67.

review of *The Origin*, which Darwin himself described as 'extremely malignant'....[to his theory]."[54]

Dr. Davidheiser reveals Darwin's ambivalence and admitted self-doubt from sources few have ever laid eyes on. "In 1844, seven years after Darwin had begun his work on evolution, he broached the subject to a friend in the following words, 'I am almost convinced (quite contrary to the position I started with) that species are not (it is like confessing a murder) immutable.'

When he finally published his book, he sent out presentation copies to various scientists with such notes as the following. '...how savage you will be, if you read it, and how you will try to crucify me alive.' 'There are so many valid and weighty arguments against my notions, that you, or anyone, if you wish [to be] on the other side, will easily persuade yourself that I am wholly in error, and no doubt I am in part in error, perhaps wholly so, though I can not see the blindness of my ways.' "[55]

WHEN WE CONSIDER THE LAWS OF THERMODYNAMICS, "EVOLUTION" IS VIRTUALLY IMPOSSIBLE

Scott Huse, author of *The Collapse of Evolution,* is more than qualified to present his evidence on the complex subject of thermodynamics. Huse tells us: "The first law of thermodynamics is known as the *Law of Energy Conservation.* It states that energy can be converted from one form into another, but it can neither be created nor destroyed. This law teaches conclusively that the universe did not create itself! There is absolutely nothing in the present economy of natural law that could possibly account for its own origin. This scientific fact is in direct contradiction with the basic concept of naturalistic, innovative evolution. The present structure of the universe is one of conservation, not innovation as required by the theory of evolution....the theory of evolution is to receive its fatal blow from the second law of thermodynamics. The second law of thermodynamics is known as the *Law of Energy Decay.* It states that every system left to its own devices tends to move from order to disorder....evolution requires billions of years of constant violations of the second law of thermodynamics to be considered even remotely feasible! Thus, we find that the **second law of thermodynamics renders the theory of**

---

[54]Julian Huxley and H.B.D. Kettlewell, *Charles Darwin and His World*, p. 76. [ ] mine.

[55]Bolton Davidheiser, Ph.D., *Evolution and Christian Faith*, p. 62. Davidheiser's sources were Francis Darwin, ed., *More Letters, loc. cit.*, Vol. I, p. 40; and Francis Darwin, ed., *Life and Letters, loc. cit.*, Vol. II, pp. 12, 14.

evolution not only statistically highly improbable, but virtually impossible. In the words of British astronomer, Arthur Eddington: '...if your theory is found to be against the second law of thermodynamics I can give you no hope; there is nothing for it but to collapse in deepest humiliation.'

The principle of increasing entropy (increasing disorder and randomness) from the second law of thermodynamics is interpreted by many creationists to be a direct result of the curse placed on creation due to the Fall of man (Genesis 3:17-19). Creationists also believe that the creation will ultimately be released from this bondage of decay and corruption (Romans 8:18-23).

The second law of thermodynamics constitutes a grave problem for evolutionists, and it is not surprising to find that they usually choose to ignore it. When pressed for an explanation....a pile of lumber, bricks, nails and tools will not automatically evolve into a building apart from a directing code, despite the fact that it is an open system receiving more than enough energy from the sun to carry out the job. And remember, a complex building is impossibly primitive compared with even the simplest living cell. Second, there is no such thing as a closed system. Therefore, to argue that the second law is inapplicable to open systems such as the earth is meaningless since all other systems are also open....life really is not increasing in complexity contrary to the second law of thermodynamics. Rather adult organisms are simply the unfolding, outward expression of the pre-existing order in the genes....It should also be noted that apparent *decreases* of entropy can only be produced at the expense of a still greater *increase* of entropy in the external environment. Thus, the entire system as a whole continues to run down as required by the second law of thermodynamics....Life forms attempt to postpone the second law of thermodynamics, but entropy eventually wins out. After all, biological systems and processes are merely complex chemical and physical processes, and to these the laws of thermodynamics do certainly apply. Dr. Harold Blum, an evolutionary biochemist, has recognized this fact and writes: 'No matter how carefully we examine the energetics of living systems we find no evidence of defeat of thermodynamic principles'....Thus, we find the second law of thermodynamics completely negates the concept of organic evolution. The creation model, however, predicts that the second law of thermodynamics will be operative and is thus, once again, substantiated by the facts of science.

The two most reliable scientific laws, the first and second laws of thermodynamics, prove that conservation and deterioration are the processes that characterize and direct the physical universe. These facts are in direct contradiction with the expectations and requirements of the evolutionary framework which hopes for a universe which is getting better and better, progressing ever-upward. Thus, the evolutionary model of origins is scientifically indefensible."[56]

THE *THEORY* OF EVOLUTION CONTRADICTS THE *LAW* OF BIOGENESIS!

Evolution states that, in the beginning, life came from non-life; once upon a time chemicals somehow made a transformation into living matter. Over one century ago, the eminent French scientist, Louis Pasteur, disproved[57] the superstition that said, "if you left meat out, flies, roaches and other living creatures would develop out of the dead non-living matter." This theory was known as "Spontaneous Generation," and was accepted by many scientists in the past.

Pasteur demonstrated this through his sterilization technique. Once a broth was heated hot enough to kill micro-organisms, and kept sealed from the environment, it did not become clouded.[58] In other words, bacteria did not spontaneously evolve out of soup! This soup stayed sterile because there was no life in or coming from it.

Evolution suggests that, from its origin, life develops from non-living chemicals, such as amino acids. This was disproved years ago by Pasteur in the law of biogenesis, which proves life comes from life and that life cannot come from non-living material—including amino acids.

IF EVOLUTION IS IMPOSSIBLE, A NEW ANTI-CREATION THEORY IS NEEDED

Today, as Darwin's ideas about our origins are becoming increasingly difficult to believe, the notion that we were planted by UFO's is being popularized. This author would not be surprised if within another twenty to thirty years, the Antichrist or a major government stages a fake UFO landing with phony "aliens" claiming they planted us here, in an attempt to discredit the Scriptures before millions. An act like this could precipitate an avalanche of Christian persecution—these beings will proclaim they have the answer to peace and Christians will disagree! This hypothesis, by no coincidence,

---

[56]Scott M. Huse, *The Collapse of Evolution*. Grand Rapids, MI: Baker Book House, © 1983, pp. 59-64, used by permission.

[57]Francesco Redi also conducted experiments to disprove spontaneous generation.

[58]This technique became known as pasteurization, and saved the French wine industry. Pasteur also developed the technique of artificially weakening germs and then injecting them into a host to prevent the disease. He also developed the first rabies vaccine and saved a young boy who had been bitten by a rabid dog.

conveniently avoids the creator God, which the Scriptures prove through biblical prophecy! When we challenge this theory by asking, "Who created the extraterrestrials that manned the UFOs which were supposed to have visited?", no one seems to know the answer!

God is the "extraterrestrial"[59] who created *us*—who will one day resurrect all who have believed, so we can take part in His kingdom, forever.

OUR CONCLUSION OF HUMAN EVOLUTION

Our conclusion is that contemporary anthropology, which attempts to trace man's ancestry through lower primates (monkeys or apes), is, and should be, dubbed a pseudo-science[60]—a theory (idea) with no foundation in true science or fact!

We recommend that you show this chapter to all of those who claim that evolution is an established fact. Parents, show your children who have forcibly been "taught" evolution over creation in "science class." Show this chapter to your school board. Stop your children from being deceived!

We pray that authors and journalists alike will take advantage of this chapter and help to expose the hoax that man came from monkey.

Evolution is the central thesis which today's liberal elitests use to undermine our biblical beliefs. They do this in order to bring us under their control, as the communists have done in our recent past. This is well illustrated in the film, *The Evolution Conspiracy*, which dismantles the so-called facts of the theory, piece by piece, using scientific and historical evidence.[61]

---

[59]The definition of "extraterrestrial" is: "...outside or originating outside, the limits of the earth." *The Random House College Dictionary*, 1975 edition, p. 469.

[60]*Pseudo* is Greek for "false." D. James Kennedy notes: "...a recent newspaper article indicated that one group of over five hundred scientists disbelieved it completely, in every single facet. One of the world's leading scientists, Sir Cecil Wakeley, whose credentials are rather impressive—K.B.E., C.B., LL.D., M.CH., Doctor of Science, F.R.C.S., past president of Royal College of Surgeons of Great Britain—aid, 'Scripture is quite definite that God created the world, and I for one believe that to be a fact, not fiction. There is no evidence, scientific or otherwise, to support the theory of evolution.' As famous a scientist as Sir Ambrose Fleming completely rejects it, as does the Harvard scientist, Louis Agassiz, probably one of the greatest scientists America has produced." Kennedy further notes of scientists who do believe in evolution, "Robert T. Clark and James D. Bales wrote an interesting and heavily documented book entitled *Why Scientists Accept Evolution*. It contains numerous letters written by Darwin, Huxley, Spencer, and other early evolutionists. It points out that these men indicated in their letters, by their own admission, that because of their hostility toward God and their bias against the supernatural, they jumped at the doctrine of evolution." D. James Kennedy, *Why I Believe*, pp. 52, 51-52.

[61]This film is available through Jeremiah Films. Tel. (800) 828-2290. The film documents the first things the communists did, immediately after their successful

In an article entitled "Dumping on Darwin," featured in an issue of *Time* Magazine, by Michael LeMonick, it was pointed out that "...polls consistently show that nearly half of all Americans reject Darwin's theory of evolution. They prefer to believe, against all scientific evidence, the Old Testament account of how God created the world...The Constitution protects their right to express that view, of course. But in decisions dating back at least 30 years, courts have ruled that the separation of church and state forbids religious groups to make the Bible part of the public-school curriculum."

LeMonick seems upset as he notes that: "the school board of Hall County, Georgia, just outside Atlanta, ruled last month that teachers must put forward a variety of theories on the origin of life, not just evolution. Beginning next fall, all biology textbooks in Alabama must have a disclaimer inserted stating that evolution is a 'controversial theory' accepted by 'some scientists.' And school boards in Washington State and Ohio are considering adopting a textbook titled *Of Pandas and People*, which contains something that would make an evolutionist squirm on virtually every page."

LeMonick then asked the question: "Why shouldn't anti-evolutionists [i.e., procreationist] be able to present their side of the controversy in the classroom?"[62] He then answers his own question with an intolerant fictitious answer.* "The reason, scientists say, is that there is no controversy, except among Bible literalists. It's true that evolution is 'just a theory.' So is Einstein's theory of relativity...."[63]

Notice LeMonick qualifies his statement with the endorsement "scientists say". In reality, I believe LeMonick should crawl out of his shell and graduate past his severely limited view, which implies (to me and some) God could have had nothing to do with our creation and that the theory of evolution is on a par with relativity. Truly the theory of relativity can be shown to be legitimate through all kinds of postulates and mathematical formulas[64] ($E = MC^2$), speeds add and subtract against

---

revolution. They hauled people off to reeducation camps to be taught, not about Marx or Lenin, but about evolution. Only when evolution is accepted, can someone be indoctrinated with Marxist ideals, which allow the population to be controlled by other mere humans in the hierarchy. Another interesting video entitled, *Ancient Man, Created or Evolved*, by Roger Oakland, is available through Oakland Communications, Inc. and distributed by Bridgestone Group.

62 Michael D. LeMonick, contributor "Dumping on Darwin", *Time,* March 18, 1996, Quebecor Printing Book Group, © 1996 Time Inc. [ ] mine. Reprinted by permission.

63 Ibid.

* In my opinion

64 When Einstein applied mass & energy to his theory of special relativity, he rendered the provable equation $E = MC^2$, (*energy* in ergs = *mass* moved at the speed of light in *centimeters squared*) illustrating that the energy contained in an object is equal to its mass times the speed of light squared. This equation indirectly proved the possible release of atomic energy directly from matter possible long before it was accomplished in the A-bomb.

each other, the faster you travel, the slower time passes, etc. Einstein's general theory of relativity, the theory of gravity of 1916, is defined by $G_{\mu\nu} = 8\pi T_{\mu\nu}$ (Space & Time = Matter & Energy) However, "evolution" is not a "theory" in this sense of the word, there is no postulate, no math, no proof at all. The *theory* of evolution is in and of itself an untrue title in that evolution is only a hypothesis, an idea, a conception, with no supporting evidence!

Time should find a more informed individual to write their *anti*-creation articles if they would like to appear more reasonable, credible, and believable, because as it appears to me here, LeMonick has not shown that the Christians[65] have "dumped on Darwin", but rather that LeMonick himself, in his leftist anti-Christian bias, has "dumped on *Time*" in his own intellectual insufficiency.

Dr. Wernher von Braun, the scientist who helped put men on the moon, endorsed teaching creation science in our classrooms. In May, 1974, he wrote: "One cannot be exposed to the law and order of the universe without concluding that there must be design and purpose behind it all...The better we understand the intricacies of the universe and all it harbors, the more reason we have found to marvel at the inherent design upon which it is based...To be forced to believe only one conclusion—that everything in the universe happened by chance—would violate the very objectivity of science itself...What random process could produce the brains of a man or the system of the human eye?...They (evolutionists) challenge science to prove the existence of God. But must we really light a candle to see the sun?...They say they cannot visualize a Designer. Well, can a physicist visualize an electron?....It is in scientific honesty that I endorse the presentation of alternative theories for the origin of the universe, life and man in the science classroom. It would be an error to overlook the possibility that the universe was planned rather than happening by chance."[66]

---

[65] Christians have not "dumped on Darwin" as Bible literalist as inferred above, rather, Christians and many scientists have discounted the "theory" of evolution because, in reality, it is not a theory as the phrase has been coined, over the years – evolution by the scientific standard is only a hypothesis with no solid evidence to back it up. The dictionary defines hypothesis as "a mere assumption or guess." (Random House Dictionary, 1975 edition, page 654). Understanding how the hypothesis of evolution came to be known as the *theory of evolution* can be seen in the Random House Dictionary's definition of theory, it notes that: "THEORY, HYPOTHESIS are both often used colloquially to mean an untested idea or opinion. A THEORY properly is a more or less verified or established explanation accounting for known facts or phenomena: *the theory of relativity.* A HYPOTHESIS is a conjecture put forth as a possible explanation of certain phenomena or relations, and serves as a basis of argument or experimentation by which to reach the truth: *This idea is offered only as a hypothesis* ..." (Ibid, p. 1362).

[66] Dennis R. Petersen, B.S., M.A., *Unlocking The Mysteries of Creation*, Vol. I, p. 63. Petersen's source was "The Bible Science Newsletter," May 1974, p. 8. *The World Book*

EVOLUTION—THE REASON WHY

It is our belief that the political movements of liberalism,[67] socialism, communism and humanism—where large numbers of people are easily controlled by a central elite[68]—are greatly fueled by a belief in "human evolution."

Scott Huse states: "The fruit of evolution has been all sorts of anti-Christian systems of beliefs and practice. It has served as an intellectual basis for Hitler's nazism and Marx's communism. It has prompted apostasy, atheism, secular humanism, and libertinism....The mind and general welfare of mankind has suffered greatly as a result of this naturalistic philosophy."[69]

We expect that the secular media and left-wing politicians, who seek to gain political control over us through restrictive laws,[70] may want to use the misconceptions of evolution over creation[71] to break the spirit of our youth. If evolution is presently being forced on your children in the public school system, we recommend that you transfer

---

Encyclopedia documents that Wernher von Braun was: "...considered the foremost rocket engineer in the world....When Hitler took personal control of rocket work, Von Braun resigned and was put in jail." *The World Book Encyclopedia*, Vol. 19, 1970 edition, p. 365. In 1955, Von Braun became a U.S. citizen and, later, the director of the George C. Marshall Space Flight Center in Huntsville, Alabama.

[67]Kennedy notes: "It is well known that Karl Marx asked Darwin to write the introduction to *Das Kapital* since he felt that Darwin had provided a scientific foundation for Communism. All over the world, those who are pushing the Communist conspiracy are also pushing an evolutionary, imperialistic, naturalistic view of life, endeavoring to crowd the Creator right out of the cosmos." D. James Kennedy, *Why I Believe*, p. 53.

[68]The elite are people who think they are better than you, which entitles them to rule over you.

[69]Scott M. Huse, *The Collapse of Evolution*, p. 124.

[70]Under the guise of "Separation of Church and State." On February 25, 1996, Reverend D. James Kennedy delivered a sermon documenting that the founding fathers intended no such separation, using extensive quotation from early documents and letters of the founding fathers. He pointed out that such separation is a hoax, from beginning to end, to rob us of our free exercise of religious freedom.

[71]Reverend Kennedy informs us: "Professor Enoch, zoologist at the University of Madras, said: 'The facts of Paleontology seem to support creation and the flood rather than evolution. For instance, *all the major groups of invertebrates appear 'suddenly'* in the first fossiliferous strata (Cambrian) of the earth with their distinct specializations indicating that they were all created almost at the same time.' The vocal evolutionist T. H. Morgan said in his book *Evolution and Adaptation*: 'Within the period of human history we do not know of a single instance of the transformation of one species into another one....It may be claimed that the theory of descent is lacking, therefore, in the most essential feature that it needs to place the theory on a scientific basis. This must be admitted.' Not a single instance, and yet Huxley claims that if the evidence isn't there, it is nowhere to be found." D. James Kennedy, *Why I Believe*, pp. 58-59.

them to a private school. If this is beyond your means, we advise you to pressure the teachers and principals, in the interest of protecting your children, as the Bible teaches (Ps. 1:1-6). If we do not fight to eliminate the misconceptions about evolution now, our children will suffer later! Let's win this fight, in the name of Jesus!

IF YOU CAN'T BEAT THEM, LEAVE THEM

We are familiar with the old saying, "If you can't beat them, join them." However, this is not what our American forefathers did. They left England to form a new country where they would be afforded the freedom of religion and lower taxes.

It appears that we are on the verge of losing many of our religious rights. We already surrender a good portion of our income—paying huge amounts of taxes bestowed upon us by liberals. This author wants to suggest to you that we are not helpless before the liberals. In the final analysis, we can do what our forefathers did—leave and form a new nation. Though it may sound radical, it would definitely make a statement: "We do not have to put up with you!"

We could call our new nation "Christian U.S.A.", or "God's New U.S.A." Though it sounds out of this world, if Christians were to organize, purchase land, move a few hundred thousand people there, a few from all the industries, we would have a working model.

How would we persuade people to move there? How about a one percent tax bracket rather than the current thirty percent—freedom to pray and teach the Bible rather than evolution—a vow to eliminate the teachings of homosexuality,[72] socialism and humanism? Wouldn't it be nice if Christians could organize and try this today?

On the other hand, as our only other alternative, we can stay in our land and fight. Our fight will be at the voting booth, to elect those who pledge to uphold our traditional family values. This is one of the main reasons why our forefathers founded the U.S.A. Freedom of religion—not freedom from religion, as today's radical left would have you believe. Since prayer was removed and evolution was added to the public school system, kids have stopped throwing spitballs and paper planes and started raping and shooting each other. Something is wrong and something must be done to vanquish the liberal who has robbed us of our dignities as human beings!

We can think of no better tools to use than prayer and the ballot box, provided "third party candidates" spare us! Remember if we are true believers—until the rapture—we are to be the light and salt of the earth. (Matt. 5:13-16; 7:24-27). And salt preserves!

---

[72]As a legitimate alternative lifestyle, as has been done in our recent past.

BIBLIOGRAPHY

BOOKS BY AUTHOR

דון יצחק אברבנאל, מעיני הישועה, 1948. (Abarbanel, Don Itzhak. *Matters of Salvation*, 1948, originally published in the sixteenth century).

Abrahams, Israel. *Studies in Pharisaism and the Gospels*, published in the compilation by Harry M. Orlinsky, ed., *Library of Biblical Studies*. New York: KTAV Publishing House, Inc., 1917, 1967.

Abrahams, M. *Aquila's Greek Version of the Hebrew Bible*. London: Spottiswoode, Ballantyne & Co. Ltd., 1919.

Albats, Yevgenia, Catherine A. Fitzpatrick, trans. *The State Within a State: The KGB and Its Hold on Russia—Past, Present and Future*. New York: Farrar, Straus and Giroux, Inc., 1994.

Alon, G. *The Jews in Their Land in the Talmudic Age*, Vol. I. Jerusalem: EJ Brill, The Magnes Press, The Hebrew University, 1980.

Anderson, Robert. *The Coming Prince*. Grand Rapids, MI: Kregel Publications, 1984.

Ankerberg, John, and John Weldon. *The Facts on Creation vs. Evolution*. Eugene, OR: Harvest House Publishers, 1993.

Arberry, Arthur J. *The Koran Interpreted*. London: HarperCollins Publishers, 1982.

Archbold, Norma. *The Mountains of Israel The Bible & The West Bank*. Jerusalem: A Phoebe's Song Publication, 1993.

Baker, Robert A. *A Summary of Christian History*, Nashville: Broadman Press, 1959, 1987.

Barnes, Albert. *Notes on the Old Testament*, Psalms Vol. I. Grand Rapids, MI: Baker Book House, 1985.

Baron, David. *Rays of Messiah's Glory, Christ in the New Testament*. Grand Rapids, MI: Zondervan Publishing House, 1886.

Bauman, Louis S. *Light from Bible Prophecy, As Related to the Present Crisis*. New York: Fleming H. Revell Company, 1940.

Bauminger, Arieh L. *The Righteous*, Third Edition. Jerusalem: Yad VaShem Martyrs and Heroes Remembrance Authority, 1983.

Ben-Sasson, H.H., and Shmuel Safrai. *Part IV A History of the Jewish People*. Tel Aviv: Dvir Publishing House, 1969, 1976.

Beresford, Gary, and Shirley. *The Unpromised Land: The Struggle of Messianic Jews*. Baltimore, MD: Lederer Messianic Publications, 1994.

Berger, David, and Michael Wyschogrod. *Jews and "Jewish Christianity."* New York: KTAV Publishing House, Inc., 1978.

Beshore, F. Kenton. *"The Messiah" of the Targums, Talmuds, and Rabbinical Writers*. Los Angeles, CA: World Bible Society, 1971.

Bivin, David, and Roy Blizzard, Jr. *Understanding the Difficult Words of Jesus: New Insights from a Hebraic Perspective*. Austin, TX: Center for Judaic-Christian Studies, 1983, 1984.

Bliss, Richard. *Origins: Creation or Evolution*. El Cajon, CA: Master Books, 1988. Available through Master Books, POB 1606, El Cajon, CA, USA 92022.

Bloch, Joshua. *Mordecai M. Kaplan, Jubilee Volume*. New York: The Jewish Theological Seminary of America, 1953.

Booker, Richard. *Jesus in the Feasts of Israel*. Shippensburg, PA: Destiny Image Publishers, 1987.

Bousset, Wilhelm. *The Antichrist Legend.* London: Hutchinson and Co., 1896.

Branley, Franklyn M., and Stephen Foster. *The Christmas Sky*. New York: HarperCollins Publishers, 1966, 1990.

Braude, William G. *Pesikta Rabbati*, from *Pesikta Rabbati: Discourses for Feasts, Fasts, and Special Sabbaths*. New Haven, CT: Judaica Research at Yale University, 1968.

Brennan, J.H. *Nostradamus, Visions of the Future*. London: The Aquarian Press, 1992.

Brigham, Kay. *Christopher Columbus's Book of Prophecies: Reproduction of the Original Manuscript with English Translation*. Barcelona: Clie, 1991. Clie books may be ordered from TSELF, POB 8337, Fort Lauderdale, FL, USA 33310. Tel. (800) 327-7933.

Brigham, Kay. *Christopher Columbus: His Life and Discovery in the Light of His Prophecies*. Barcelona: Clie, 1990. Clie books may be ordered from TSELF, POB 8337, Fort Lauderdale, FL, USA 33310. Tel. (800) 327-7933.

Brown, Michael L. *Our Hands are Stained with Blood: The Tragic Story of the "Church" and the Jewish People*. Shippensburg, PA: Destiny Image Publishers, 1992.

Bruce, F.F. *Jesus and Christian Origins Outside the New Testament*. Grand Rapids, MI: William B. Eerdmans Publishing Company, 1984.

Bruce, F.F. *New Testament History*. New York: Doubleday & Company, Inc., a division of Doubleday, Dell Publishing Group, Inc., 1971.

Bruce, F.F. *The Spreading Flame*. Grand Rapids, MI: William B. Eerdmans Publishing Company, 1958.

Buchanan, George W. *Revelation and Redemption*. Dillsboro, NC: Western North Carolina Press, 1978.

Carr, Joseph. *The Twisted Cross*. Shreveport, LA: Huntington House, Inc., 1985.

Carrington, Philip. *The Early Christian Church*, Vol. I, *The First Christian Century*. London: The Syndics of The Cambridge University Press, 1957.

Castillejo, David. *The Expanding Force in Newton's Cosmos*. Madrid: Ediciones de Arte y Bibliofilia, 1981.

Chandler, Walter M. *The Trial of Jesus, From a Lawyer's Standpoint*, Illustrated Edition, Vol. I-II. Norcross, GA: The Harrison Company Publishers, 1976.

Cheetham, Erika. *The Prophecies of Nostradamus*. New York: Berkley Books, 1973.

Chernoff, David. *7 Steps to Knowing the God of Abraham, Isaac & Jacob*. Havertown, PA: MMI Publishing Co., 1984.

Christian, John T. *A History of the Baptists: Together With Some Account of Their Principles and Practices*, Vol. I-II. Nashville, TN: Sunday School Board of the Southern Baptist Convention, 1922, 1926.

Cohn-Sherbok, Daniel. *Rabbinic Perspectives on the New Testament*. Lampeter, Dyfed, Wales: The Edwin Mellen Press, Ltd., 1990, 1991.

Constantelos, Demetrios J. *Understanding the Greek Orthodox Church: Its Faith, History and Practice*. New York: The Seabury Press, 1982.

Crenshaw, Charles A. *JFK: Conspiracy of Silence*. New York: Signet, 1992.

Cumming, John. *The Destiny of Nations*. London: Hurst & Blackette, 1864.

Curtis, William Eleroy. *The Authentic Letters of Columbus*, Vol. 1, No. 2. Chicago: Field Columbian Museum, 1895.

Darby, J.N. *'The Holy Scriptures,' A New Translation from the Original Languages*. Addison, IL: Bible Truth Publishers, 1976.

David, Maurice. *Who Was "Columbus"?* New York: The Research Publishing Co., 1933.

Davidheiser, Bolton. *Evolution and Christian Faith.* Phillipsburg, NJ: The Presbyterian and Reformed Publishing Company, 1969.

Deal, Colin. *The Day and Hour Jesus Will Return.* NC: Rutherford College, 1981.

DeMar, Gary. *Last Days Madness*. Brentwood, TN: Wolgemuth & Hyatt Publishers, Inc., 1991.

Dimont, Max I. *Jews, God and History*. New York: Dutton Signet, a division of Penguin Books USA, Inc., 1962, 1990.

Dixon, Jeane. *The Call to Glory*. New York: William Morrow & Company, 1972

Drazin, Michoel. *Their Hollow Inheritance: A Comprehensive Refutation of Christian Missionaries*. Safred, Israel: G.M. Publications, 1990.

Durant, Will. *Caesar and Christ: A History of Roman Civilization and of Christianity from Their Beginnings to A.D. 325*. New York: Simon and Schuster, 1944.

Duvernoy, Claude. *The Prince and the Prophet*. Jerusalem: Claude Duvernoy, 1979.

Eastman, Mark, and Chuck Smith. *The Search for Messiah.* Costa Mesa, CA: The Word for Today, 1993.

Eckstein, Yechiel. *What Christians Should Know About Jews and Judaism.* Dallas, TX: Word, Inc., 1984.

Edersheim, Alfred. *The Life and Times of Jesus the Messiah.* Grand Rapids, MI: William B. Eerdmans Publishing Co., 1971.

Einstein, Albert. *Cosmic Religion with Other Opinions and Aphorisms*. New York: Covici Friede, 1931.

Eisemann, Moshe. *Yechezkel*. Jerusalem: Mesorah Publications, Ltd., 1980.

Eisenberg, Rafael. *A Matter of Return*. Jerusalem: Feldheim Publishers, 1980.

חבלי משיח בזמננו, רפאל הלוי אייזנברג, 1970. (Eisenberg, Rafael. *Hevly Meshak Bizmanu, Birth Pains of the Messiah*, 1970).

Evans, Mike. *The Return*. New York: Thomas Nelson Publishers, Inc., 1986.

Falls, Thomas B. *Saint Justin Martyr*. Washington: Catholic University Press, 1948.

Flusser, David. *Jewish Sources in Early Christianity*. Tel Aviv: The Israel MOD Publishing House, 1989.

Force, James E., and Richard H. Popkin, eds. *Essays on the Context, Nature, and Influence of Isaac Newton's Theology*. Boston: Kluwer Academic Publishers, 1990.

Force, James E., and Richard H. Popkin, eds. *The Books of Nature and Scripture: Recent Essays on Natural Philosophy, Theology, and Biblical*

Criticism in the Netherlands of Spinoza's Time and the British Isles of Newton's Time. Boston: Kluwer Academic Publishers, 1994.

Forkman, Göran, Pearl Sjölander, B.A., trans. *The Limits of the Religious Community, Expulsion from the Religious Community Within the Qumran Sect, Within Rabbinic Judaism, and Within Primitive Christianity*. Sweden: Studentlitteratur Lund, 1972.

Froom, Leroy Edwin. *The Prophetic Faith of Our Fathers,* Vol. I. Washington, DC: Review and Herald, 1948.

Fruchtenbaum, Arnold G. *Israelology: The Missing Link in Systematic Theology*. Tustin, CA: Ariel Ministries Press, 1993.

Frydland, Rachmiel. *When Being Jewish Was a Crime*. Nashville: Thomas Nelson Publishers, Inc., The Messianic Outreach, 1978.

Gaebelein, A.C. *The Prophet Daniel*. New York: Our Hope Press, 1911.

Galimir, Mosco. *Christobal Colón, The Discoverer of America*. New York: Galimir, 1950.

Geisler, Norman. *Is Man the Measure? An Evaluation of Contemporary Humanism*. Grand Rapids, MI: Baker Book House, 1983.

Gilbert, Martin. *The Arab-Israeli Conflict, Its History in Maps*, Fourth Edition. Jerusalem: Steimatzky Ltd., 1984.

Gish, Duane T. *Evolution: The Challenge of the Fossil Record*. El Cajon, CA: Master Books, 1985. Available through Master Books, POB 1606, El Cajon, CA, USA 92022.

Goble Phillip E. *Everything you Need to Grow a Messianic Synagogue*. S. Pasadena, CA: William Carey Library, 1974.

Goetz, William. *Apocalypse Next*. Sussex, England: Kingsway Publications Ltd., 1980.

Goguel, Maurice. *The Birth of Christianity*. London: George Allen & Unwin Ltd., 1953.

Golb, Norman. *Who Wrote the Dead Sea Scrolls? The Search for the Secret of Qumran*. New York: Scribner, 1995.

Goldwurm, Hersh. *History of the Jewish People, The Second Temple Era*, adapted from Dr. Eliezer Ebner's translations of Yekutiel Friedner's *Divrei Y'mei HaBayit HaSheini*. Brooklyn, NY: Mesorah Publications, Ltd., 1982.

Good, Joseph. *Rosh HaShanah and the Messianic Kingdom to Come, A Messianic Jewish Interpretation of the Feast of Trumpets*. Port Arthur, TX: Hatikva Ministries, 1989.

Graetz, H. *History of the Jews,* Vol. II. Philadelphia: The Jewish Publication Society of America, 1893.

Grayzel, Solomon. *A History of the Jews*. Philadelphia: The Jewish Publication Society of America, 1970.

Habermas, Gary R., and J.P. Moreland. *Immortality, The Other Side of Death*. Nashville: Thomas Nelson Publishers, Inc., 1992.

Hagner, Donald. *The Jewish Reclamation of Jesus*. Grand Rapids, MI: Academie Books, Zondervan Publishing House, 1984.

Halkin, Abraham. *Crisis and Leadership: Epistles of Maimonides*. Philadelphia: The Jewish Publication Society of America, 1985.

Halley, Henry H. *Halley's Bible Handbook*. Grand Rapids, MI: Zondervan Publishing House, 1965.

Hare, Douglas. *The Theme of Jewish Persecution of Christians in the Gospel According to St Matthew*. London: Cambridge University Press, 1967.

Harnack, Adolf. *The Mission and Expansion of Christianity in the First Three Centuries*. New York: G.P. Putnam's Sons, 1908.

Herford, R. Travers. *Christianity in Talmud & Midrash*. New York: KTAV Publishing House, Inc., 1903.

Hewitt, V.J., and Peter Lorie. *Nostradamus, The End of the Millennium, Prophecies to 2001*. New York: Simon and Schuster, 1991.

Higgins, A.J.B. *Jewish Messianic Belief in Justin Martyr's Dialogue with Trypho*, published in the compilation by Leo Landman, *Messianism in the Talmudic Era*. New York: KTAV Publishing House, Inc., 1979.

Highfield, Roger, and Paul Carter. *The Private Lives of Albert Einstein*. New York: St. Martin's Press, Inc.,1994.

Hislop, Alexander. *The Two Babylons*. England: A&C Black, Ltd., 1916.

Hoover, J. Edgar. *J. Edgar Hoover Speaks Concerning Communism*. Nutley, NJ and Washington DC: The Capital Hill Press in cooperation with The Craig Press, 1972.

Hoover, J. Edgar. *Masters of Deceipt*. New York: Henry Holt and Company, Inc., 1958.

Hunt, Dave. *Global Peace and the Rise of Antichrist*. Grand Rapids, MI: Harvest House Publishers, 1990.

Huse, Scott M. *The Collapse of Evolution*. Grand Rapids, MI: Baker Book House, 1983.

Huxley, Julian, and H.B.D. Kettlewell. *Charles Darwin and His World*. New York: The Viking Press, 1965.

Huxley, Thomas Henry. *Agnosticism and Christianity and Other Essays*. Buffalo, NY: Prometheus Books, 1992.

Hymers, R.L. *Holocaust II*. Van Nuys, CA: Bible Voice, Inc., 1978.

Irwin, James B., with William A. Emerson, Jr. *To Rule the Night, The Discovery Voyage of Astronaut Jim Irwin*. Nashville, TN: Broadman Press, 1973, 1982.

Jeffrey, Grant R. *Apocalypse: The Coming Judgment of the Nations*. Toronto: Frontier Research Publications, Inc., 1992.

Jeffrey, Grant R. *Armageddon, Appointment with Destiny*. New York: Bantam Books, 1988.

Jeffrey, Grant R. *Heaven...The Last Frontier*. New York: Bantam Books, 1990.

Jeffrey, Grant R. *Messiah, War in the Middle East & The Road to Armageddon*. Toronto: Frontier Research Publications, Inc., 1991.

Jeffrey, Grant R. *Prince of Darkness, Antichrist and the New World Order*. Toronto: Frontier Research Publications, Inc., 1994.

Jocz, Jakob. *The Jewish People and Jesus Christ*. London: SPCK Holy Trinity Church, 1949.

Josephus. *Wars of the Jews*, published in the compilation *Josephus: Complete Works*. Grand Rapids, MI: Kregel Publications, 1981.

Kac, Arthur W. *The Death and Resurrection of Israel*. Grand Rapids, MI: Baker Book House, 1969.

Kac, Arthur W. *The Messiahship of Jesus*. Grand Rapids, MI: Baker Book House, 1980.

Kac, Arthur W. *The Messianic Hope*. Grand Rapids, MI: Baker Book House, 1975.

Kac, Arthur W. *The Rebirth of the State of Israel: Is It of God or of Men?* Grand Rapids, MI: Baker Book House, 1976.

Kahle, Paul E. *The Cairo Geniza*. Oxford: Basil Blackwell, 1959.

Kaplan, Rabbi Aryeh, *et al*. *The Real Messiah*. New York: National Conference of Synagogue Youth, 1976.

Kayserling, Meir. *Christopher Columbus and The Participation of the Jews in the Spanish and Portugese Discoveries*. New York: Hermon Press, 1968.

Kennedy, D. James. *Why I Believe*. Dallas, TX: Word, Inc., 1980.

Koch, Kurt E. *The Coming One*. Grand Rapids, MI: Kregal Publishing, 1972. First published in German under the title *Der Kommende*, 1971.

Koenig, John. *Jews and Christians in Dialogue*. Pennsylvania: Westminster Press, 1979.

Krupp, Nate. *The Omega Generation*. Harrison, AR: New Leaf Press, Inc., 1977.

Lambert, Lance. *Israel: A Secret Documentary*. Wheaton, IL: Tyndale House Publishers, Inc., 1975.

Lapide, Pinchas. *Israelis, Jews, and Jesus*. New York: Doubleday & Company, Inc., a division of Doubleday, Dell Publishing Group, Inc., 1979.

Lapide, Pinchas. *The Resurrection of Jesus, A Jewish Perspective*. Minneapolis, MN: Augsburg Publishing House, 1983.

Larkin, Clarence. *Dispensational Truth or God's Plan and Purpose in The Ages*. Glenside, PA: Rev. Clarence Larkin Est., 1918.

Larson, Bob. *Larson's Book of Cults*. Wheaton, IL: Tyndale House Publishers, 1982.

Lee, Richard, and Ed Hindson. *Angels of Deceipt: The Masterminds Behind Religious Deceptions*. Eugene, OR: Harvest House Publishers, 1993.

Levey, Samson H. *The Messiah: An Aramaic Interpretation, The Messianic Exegesis of the Targum*. Jerusalem: Hebrew Union College/Jewish Institute of Religion, 1974.

Levine, Samuel. *You Take Jesus, I'll Take God*. Los Angeles: Hamoroh Press, 1980.

Levitt, Zola. *A Christian Love Story*. Dallas: Zola Levitt Ministries, 1978. Available through Zola Levitt Ministries, Inc., POB 12268, Dallas, TX, USA 75225.

Levitt, Zola. *In My Father's House*. Dallas: Zola Levitt Ministries, 1981.

Levitt, Zola. *The Seven Feasts of Israel*. Dallas: Zola Levitt Ministries, 1979.

Levitt, Zola. *The Signs of the End*. Dallas: Zola Levitt Ministries, 1978.

Liberman, Paul. *The Fig Tree Blossoms: Messianic Judaism Emerges*. Indianola, IA: Fountain Press, 1976.

Lindsay, Gordon. *Evolution—The Incredible Hoax*. Dallas, TX: Christ for the Nations, 1977.

Lindsey, Hal. *A Prophetical Walk Through the Holy Land*. Eugene, OR: Harvest House Publishers, 1983.

Lindsey, Hal. *Combat Faith*. © The Aorist Corporation. New York: Bantam Books, a division of Bantam Doubleday Dell Publishing Group, Inc., 1986.

Lindsey, Hal. *Planet Earth—2000 A.D.* Palos Verdes, CA: Western Front, Ltd., 1994.

Lindsey, Hal. *The 1980's: Countdown to Armageddon.* © The Aorist Corporation. New York: Bantam Books, Inc., a division of Bantam Doubleday Dell Publishing Group, Inc., 1980.

Lindsey, Hal. *The 1990s: Prophecy on Fast Forward.* Palos Verdes, CA: Hal Lindsey Ministries, 1990.

Lindsey, Hal. *The Final Battle*. Palos Verdes, CA: Western Front, Ltd., 1995.

Lindsey, Hal. *The Liberation of Planet Earth.* Palos Verdes, CA: Western Front, Ltd., 1974.

Lindsey, Hal. *The Promise*. Palos Verdes, CA: Western Front, Ltd., 1984.

Lindsey, Hal. *The Rapture: Truth or Consequences.* © The Aorist Corporation. New York: Bantam Books, Inc., a division of Bantam Doubleday Dell Publishing Group, Inc., 1983.

Lindsey, Hal. *There's A New World Coming.* Trade Paper Edition. Eugene, OR: Harvest House Publishers, 1973.

Lindsey, Hal. *The Road To Holocaust.* © The Aorist Corporation. New York: Bantam Books, Inc., a division of Bantam Doubleday Dell Publishing Group, Inc., 1989.

Lindsey, Hal, with C.C. Carlson. *Satan is Alive and Well on Planet Earth.* Grand Rapids, MI: Zondervan Books, 1972.

Lindsey, Hal, with C.C. Carlson. *The Late Great Planet Earth.* Grand Rapids, MI: Zondervan Publishing House, 1970, 1977.

Lowenthal, Marvin. *The Diaries of Theodor Herzl.* New York: Dial Press, 1956. From Esther Yolles Feldblum, *The Introduction of The American Catholic Press and The Jewish State 1917-1959.* New York: KTAV Publishing House, Inc., 1977.

Lubenow, Marvin L. *Bones of Contention: A Creationist Assessment of the Human Fossils*. Grand Rapids, MI: Baker Book House, 1992.

Mantel, Hugo. *Studies in the History of the Sanhedrin.* Cambridge, MA: Harvard University Press, 1961.

Manuel, Frank E. *A Portrait of Isaac Newton.* London: Frederick Muller Limited, 1980.

Manuel, Frank E. *The Changing of the Gods.* Hanover: University Press of New England, 1983.

Manuel, Frank E. *The Religion of Isaac Newton.* London: Oxford University Press, 1974.

Marks, Stanley J., and Ethel M. *Judaism Looks at Christianity, 7 B.C.E. - 1986 C.E.* Newell, IA: Bureau of International Affairs, 1986.

Marx, Karl. *A World Without Jews.* New York: Philosophical Library Inc., 1959.

McCall, Thomas S., and Zola Levitt. *Satan in the Sanctuary.* Dallas, TX: Zola Levitt Ministries, 1983.

McDowell, Josh. *Evidence that Demands a Verdict, Historical Evidences for the Christian Faith.* San Bernardino, CA: Campus Crusade for Christ International, 1972.

McDowell, Josh and Don Stewart. *Family Handbook of Christian Knowledge: The Creation.* San Bernardino, CA: Here's Life Publishers, Inc., 1984.

McDowell, Josh, *Prophecy, Fact or Fiction*, San Bernadino, Here's Life Publishers.

McEntire, Walter F. *Was Christopher Columbus a Jew*. Boston: The Stratford Company, 1925.

Meldau, Fred John. *Messiah in Both Testaments.* Denver, CO: The Christian Victory Publishing Company, 1956.

Michaelsen, Johanna. *Like Lambs to the Slaughter.* Eugene, OR: Harvest House Publishers, 1989.

Montefiore, C.G., and H. Loewe. *A Rabbinic Anthology.* New York: Schocken Books, Inc. Published by Pantheon Books, a division of Random House, Inc., 1974.

Moody, Raymond A., Jr. *Life After Life.* St. Simons Island, GA: Life After Life, Inc., 1975.

Moody, Raymond A., Jr. *Reflections on Life After Life.* St. Simons Island, GA: Mockingbird Books, Inc., 1977.

Moody, Raymond A. Jr. *The Light Beyond.* New York: Bantam Books, a division of Bantam Doubleday Dell Publishing Group, Inc., 1988.

Moore, George Foot. *Judaism In The First Centuries Of the Christian Era, The Age of The Tannaim,* Vol. I. London: Humphrey Milford Oxford University Press, 1927.

Morey, Robert. *Islamic Invasion, Confronting the World's Fastest Growing Religion.* Eugene, OR: Harvest House Publishers, 1992.

Morison, Samuel Eliot. *Christopher Columbus, Admiral of the Ocean Sea.* London: Oxford University Press, 1939.

Morris, Henry, M., ed. *Scientific Creationism.* El Cajon, CA: Master Books, 1974. Available through Master Books, POB 1606, El Cajon, CA, USA 92022.

Morris, Henry M. *The Troubled Waters of Evolution.* El Cajon, CA: Master Books, 1974. Available through Master Books, POB 1606, El Cajon, CA, USA 92022.

Mosley, John. *The Christmas Star.* Los Angeles: Griffith Observatory, 1987.

Munk, Michael L. *The Wisdom in the Hebrew Alphabet.* Brooklyn, NY: Mesorah Publications, 1983.

Neusner, Jacob. *First-Century Judaism in Crisis, Yohanan Ben Zakkai and the Renaissance of Torah.* New York: Abingdon Press, 1975.

Newton, Isaac. *Mathematical Principles of Natural Philosophy*, published in the compilation *Great Books of the Western World*, Vol. 34. Chicago: William Benton for Encyclopedia Brittanica, Inc., in cooperation with the University of Chicago, 1952.

Nixon, Richard M. *Beyond Peace.* New York: Random House, Inc., 1994.

Oesterley, W.O.E., and G.H. Box. *The Religion and Worship of the Synagogue.* London: Sir Isaac Pitman and Sons, 1911.

O'Neill, Dan, and Don Wagner. *Peace or Armageddon.* Grand Rapids, MI: Zondervan Publishing House, 1993.

Otis, George. *The Ghost of Hagar.* Van Nuys, CA: Time-Light Books, 1974.

Parkes, James. *Judaism and Christianity.* Chicago: The University of Chicago Press, 1948.

Parkes, James. *The Conflict of the Church and the Synagogue.* Philadelphia: Jewish Publication Society of America, 1981.

Parkes, James. *The Foundations of Judaism and Christianity.* London: Vallentine, Mitchell & Co. Ltd., 1960.

Patai, Raphael. *The Messiah Texts.* Detroit: Wayne State University Press, 1979.

Pember, G.H. *Earth's Earliest Ages*. Grand Rapids, MI: Kregel Publications, 1979.

Petersen, Dennis R. *Unlocking the Mysteries of Creation*, Vol. I. South Lake Tahoe, CA: Creation Resource Foundation, 1986.

Pfeiffer, Robert. *History of New Testament Times*. New York: Harper & Brothers Publishers, 1949.

Pick, B. *Old Testament Passages Messianically Applied by the Ancient Synagogue*, published in the compilation *Hebraica, A Quarterly Journal in the Interests of Semitic Study*, Vol. I-IV. New York: Charles Scribner's Sons, 1886-1888.

Pitts, F.E. *The U.S.A. in Prophecy*. Baltimore: J.W. Bull, 1862.

Popkin, Richard H., and Gordon M. Weiner, eds. *Jewish Christians and Christian Jews*. Boston: Kluwer Academic Publishers, 1994.

Popkin, Richard, H. *Predicting, Prophecying, Divining and Foretelling from Nostradamus to Hume*. Published in the compilation *History of European Ideas,* Vol. 5, No. 2. London: Pergamon Press, 1984.

Pritz, Ray. *Nazarene Jewish Christianity*. Jerusalem: Magnes Press, 1988.

Randi, James. *The Mask of Nostradamus, The Prophecies of the World's Most Famous Seer*. Buffalo, NY: Prometheus Books, 1993.

Rausch, David A. *Messianic Judaism: Its History, Theology, and Polity*. New York: The Edwin Mellen Press, 1982.

Rawlings, Maurice S. *Beyond Death's Door*. New York: Bantam Books, 1978.

Rawlings, Maurice S. *To Hell and Back*. Nashville: Thomas Nelson Publishers, Inc., 1993.

Reider, Joseph. *Prolegomena to a Greek-Hebrew & Hebrew-Greek Index to Aquila*. Philadelphia: College of Hebrew and Cognate Learning, 1916.

Rice, John R. *Communism and Socialism*. Murfreesboro, TN: Sword of the Lord Publishers, 1970.

Ridpath, John Clark. *Cyclopædia of Universal History*, Vol. II - Part II/The Modern World. Cincinnati: The Jones Brothers Publishing Company, 1885.

Roper, Albert. *Did Jesus Rise from the Dead?* Grand Rapids, MI: Zondervan Publishing House, Inc., 1965.

Rosenblatt, Samuel. *Saadia Gaon, The Book of Beliefs and Opinions*. New Haven: Yale University Press, 1948.

Rosen, Moishe. *Y'shua, The Jewish Way to Say Jesus*. Chicago: Moody Bible Institute, Jews for Jesus, 1982.

Russell, D.S. *The Method & Message of Jewish Apocalyptic, 200 BC - AD 100*. Philadelphia: The Westminster Press, 1964.

Ryrie, Charles. *What You Should Know About the Rapture*. Chicago: Moody Press, 1981.

Santala, Risto. *Paul: The Man and the Teacher, In the Light of Jewish Sources*. Jerusalem: Keren Ahvah Meshihit, 1995.

Santala, Risto. *The Messiah in the New Testament in the Light of Rabbinical Writings*. Jerusalem: Keren Ahvah Meshihit, 1992.

Santala, Risto. *The Messiah in the Old Testament in the Light of Rabbinical Writings*. Jerusalem: Keren Ahvah Meshihit, 1992.

Schiffman, Lawrence. *Who Was a Jew? Rabbinic and Halakhic Perspectives on the Jewish-Christian Schism.* New York: KTAV Publishing House, Inc., 1985.

Schonfield, Hugh, J. *An Old Hebrew Text of St. Matthew's Gospel.* Edinburgh: T&T Clark, 1927.

Schonfield, Hugh J. *Saints Against Caesar, The Rise and Reactions of the First Christian Community.* London: Macdonald & Co., Ltd., 1948.

Schonfield, Hugh J. *The History of Jewish Christianity, from the First to the Twentieth Century.* London: Duckworth, 1936.

Schonfield, Hugh J. *The Passover Plot: New Light on the History of Jesus.* Rockport, MA: Element Books, Inc., 1971.

Schweitzer, Frederick M. *A History of the Jews Since the First Century A.D.* New York: The Macmillan Company, Anti-Defamation League of B'nai B'rith, 1971.

Sharif, Regina. *Non-Jewish Zionism.* London: Zed Press, 1983.

Sigal, Gerald. *The Jew and the Christian Missionary: A Jewish Response to Missionary Christianity.* New York: KTAV Publishing House, Inc., 1981.

Sigal, Phillip. *Judaism, The Evolution of a Faith.* Grand Rapids, MI: William B. Eerdmans Publishing Co., 1988.

Sigal, Phillip. *The Emergence of Contemporary Judaism.* Pittsburgh: The Pickwick Press, 1980.

Singer, Isidore, *et al. The Jewish Encyclopedia, A Descriptive Record of the History, Religion, Literature, and Customs of the Jewish People, from the Earliest Times to the Present Day*, Vol. II. New York: Funk and Wagnalls Company, 1902.

Smith, Chuck. *The Final Curtain.* Eugene, OR: Harvest House Publishers, The Word for Today, 1991.

Spong, John Shelby. *Resurrection, Myth or Reality?* San Francisco, CA: HarperCollins Publishers, 1994.

Stoddard, John L. *John L. Stoddard's Lectures,* Vol. II. Boston: Balch Brothers Co., 1897.

Tenney, Merrill C. *The Reality of the Resurrection.* New York: Harper & Row, 1963.

Thayer, H.S. *Newton's Philosophy of Nature,* Third Edition. New York: Hafner Publishing Company, 1953.

Thompson, Frank Charles. "Condensed Cyclopedia of Topics and Texts," *Thompson Chain Reference Bible.* Indianapolis, IN: B.B. Kirkbride Bible Co., Inc., 1964.

Torrey, Charles Cutler. *Documents of the Primitive Church.* New York: HarperCollins Publishers, 1941.

Troki, Isaac. *Faith Strenghthened.* New York: Hermon Press, 1850.

Vine, W.E. *An Expository Dictionary of New Testament Words, With Their Precise Meanings for English Readers*, Vol. IV, Reference Library Edition. Old Tappan, NJ: Fleming H. Revell Company, 1940.

Weiss, Johannes. *Earliest Christianity: A History of the Period A.D. 30-150,* Vol. II. New York: Harper & Row Publishers, 1959.

Williams, A. Lukyn. *Justin Martyr, The Dialogue With Trypho.* India: Diocesan Press, 1930.

Woodrow, Ralph. *Babylon Mystery Religion.* Riverside, CA: Ralph Woodrow Evangelistic Association, Inc., 1966. Available through RWEA, POB 124, Riverside, CA, USA 92502.

Wurmbrand, Richard. *Christ on the Jewish Road.* Bartlesville, OK: Living Sacrifice Book Company, The Voice of the Martyrs, Inc., 1970.

Yaseen, Leonard C. *The Jesus Connection: To Triumph Over Anti-Semitism.* New York: The Crossroad Publishing Company, 1985.

Yavari, Birgitta. *Min Messias.* Jerusalem: Rahm & Stenström Interpublishing, 1979.

Yonah, M. Avi. *The Jews of Palestine*, 1976.

BOOKS BY TITLE

'Atiqot, Vol. XXI. Jerusalem: Israel Antiquities Authority, 1992.

Barnhart Dictionary of Etymology. Bronx, NY: The H.W. Wilson Company, 1988.

Commemoration of the Fourth Centenary of the Discovery of America. From the Report of the Madrid Commission, 1892. Washington: Government Printing Office, 1895.

Jerusalem to Jabneh: The Period of the Mishnah and its Literature—Units 11, 12. Tel Aviv: The Open University of Israel, 1981.

Midrash Rabbah, Vol. II. New York: The Soncino Press, Ltd., 1983.

Mishkan, Winter 1985, No. 2. Jerusalem: Arnold Fruchtenbaum, 1985.

New Dictionary. Jerusalem: Kiryat Sephen, 1973.

Pesikta Rabbati, Yale Judaica Series, Vol. XVIII. New Haven, CT: Yale University Press, 1968.

Septuaginta. Stuttgart: Deutsche Bibelgesellschaft, 1935.

The Holy Scriptures: A Jewish Bible According to the Masoretic Text. Tel Aviv, Israel: "Sinai" Publishing, 1977.

The Babylonian Talmud. London: The Soncino Press, Ltd., 1938.

The Encyclopaedia Judaica Jerusalem. Jerusalem: Keter Publishing House, Ltd., 1971.

The Fifty-Third Chapter of Isaiah, According to the Jewish Interpreters, published in the compilation *The Library of Biblical Studies.* New York: KTAV Publishing House, Inc., 1969.

The Holy Scriptures. New York: Hebrew Publishing Company, 1930.

The Jesus Connection: To Triumph Over Anti-Semitism. New York: The Crossroad Publishing Company, 1985.

The New Encyclopædia Britannica, 15th Edition, Chicago: Encyclopædia Britannica, Inc., 1974.

The Oxford English Dictionary, Vol. III. Oxford: Clarendon Press, 1989.

The Random House College Dictionary. New York: Random House, Inc., 1975.

The Universal Jewish Encyclopedia, Vol. I. New York: Universal Jewish Encyclopedia Co., 1948.

The World Book Encyclopedia. Chicago: Field Enterprises Educational Corporation, 1970 Edition, 1957.

The Zohar, Vol. II. New York: The Soncino Press, Ltd., 1984.

ARTICLES BY TITLE

"2 Scientists Determine Exact Crucifixion Date." *Atlanta Journal and Constitution*, Dec. 22, 1983.

"A Description and Early History of Millennial Views," by Dr. Renald E. Showers. *Israel My Glory*, The Friends of Israel Gospel Ministry, Inc., June-Oct. 1986.

"Ads For Jesus Who's Right the Bishop of Oxford or the American Based Organisation Jews for Jesus? Asks Steve Parish," by Steve Parish. *CWN Series*, Jan. 30, 1989.

"A 'World View' Based on the Bible." *Atlanta Journal and Constitution*, Sept. 26, 1992.

Al Bayader Assiyasi, Independent Weekly. Jerusalem, Oct. 14, 1988.

"An Interview with Pope John Paul II," by Tad Szulc. *Atlanta Journal and Constitution*, Apr. 3, 1994.

"A Leap in the Dark." *Jerusalem Post* magazine, Mar. 10, 1989.

"An Oliphant Not Forgotten," by Beth Uval. *The Jerusalem Post*, Mar. 3, 1989.

"A Pierced or Piercing Messiah?—The Verdict is Still Out," by James Tabor. *Biblical Archaology Review*. Washington, DC: Biblical Archaeology Society, Nov./Dec. 1992.

"Beware of Missionary Forge S'Dorim," by Aryeh Julius. *Jerusalem Times/Jewish Press*, Apr. 10-16, 1987.

"Christianity and Patriotism," by Samuel M. Shoemaker. *The Dawn*, Vol. XXXI, No. 3, May-June 1960.

"Christian Zionism," by Malcolm Hedding. *Jerusalem Courier*, Vol. 7, No. 2, 1988.

"Children of the Light," by Melvin Morse. Condensed version of the book *Closer to the Light*, by Melvin Morse. *Reader's Digest*, Mar., 1991.

"Court Opens Schools to Religious Clubs," by Tony Mauro. *USA Today*, Tues., June 5, 1990.

"Dead Sea Scrolls," by Joseph Albright and Gayle White. *Atlanta Journal and Constitution*, Sat., Oct. 12, 1991.

"Dead Sea Scrolls Refer to Messiah's Execution." *Atlanta Journal and Constitution*, Nov. 8, 1991.

"Dialogue with Evangelicals," by Charles Hoffman. *The Jerusalem Post*, Aug. 8, 1987.

"Doubting the Blessings of Christian Zionism," by Pnina Peli. *The Jerusalem Post*, Sept. 20, 1985.

"Europe: The Rocky Road to Unity." *Future Times*, Spring 1993.

"Europe's Dreams of Unity Revived." *Time*, July 4, 1969.

"Evangelical Challenge," by Geoffrey Wigoder. *The Jerusalem Post*, Oct. 14, 1984.

"Filling in the Blanks," by Abraham Rabinovich. *ERETZ, The Geographic Magazine from Israel*, May-June 1994.

"Gentiles Who Dared to Save Jews," by Peter Colón. *Israel My Glory*, Apr./May 1995.

"Gorbachev Calls Jesus 'The First Socialist,' " by Hal Lindsey. *Countdown...*, Vol. 3, Sept. 1992. Palos Verdes, CA: Hal Lindsey Ministries.

"Have you Been...Brainwashed?", by Duane T. Gish. South Holland, IL: The Bible League, 1986.

"Hebrew Christians," by Menahem Benhayim. *The Jerusalem Post*, Fri., July 3, 1987.

"Hebrew Christians," letter to the editor, by Julius Berman. *The Jerusalem Post*, Mar. 2, 1988.

"High Court Asked: Is a Jew Who Believes in Jesus Still a Jew?" *The Jerusalem Post*, Feb. 5, 1988.

"Holocaust: A Christian Atrocity?", by Elwood McQuaid. *Israel My Glory*, Apr./May 1995.

"Irrefutable Fact that Wallenberg Died in '47.' " *The Jerusalem Post*, Oct. 17, 1989.

"Is Jesus in the Dead Sea Scrolls?", by Richard N. Ostling, contributor. *Time*, Sept. 21, 1992.

"Islam, the Great Competitor," by Liebes Feldman. *The Messianic Outreach*, Vol. 4:3, Mar.-May 1985.

"Israel: A Nation Under Seige," *Time*, June 9, 1967.

"Israel's New Closer Links to Europe," by Hal Lindsey. *Countdown...*, Feb. 1994. Palos Verdes, CA: Hal Lindsey Ministries.

"Israel, Vatican Begin Diplomatic Ties: But Animosities Aren't All Buried," by Clyde Haberman. *Atlanta Journal and Constitution*, Dec. 31, 1993.

"Issues in the Separation of Judaism and Christianity after 70 C.E.: A Reconsideration," by Steven T. Katz. *Journal of Biblical Literature*, Mar. 1984.

"Jamnia During the Presidency of Gamaliel II, C. A.D. 80-117," by Archdeacon Dowling. *Palestine Exploration Fund*. London: Palestine Exploration Fund, 1914.

"Jerusalem Temple, Preparing for the Messiah," by Gareth G. Cook and David Makovshy. *U.S. News & World Report*, Dec. 19, 1994.

"Jewish Fear of Fundamentalist Activism Exaggerated," by Jerry Falwell. *The Fundamentalist Journal*, Oct. 1986.

"Jewish Sect is Expecting Its Messiah by Sept. 9," by Don Lattin. *San Francisco Chronicle*, Apr. 15, 1991.

"Jewish Thought and Spirituality, Christian Influences in the Zohar," by Yehudah Liebes. *Immanuel*, No. 17, Winter 1983-84.

"Joy and Foreboding Greet Bible Club Ruling," by William Robbins. *New York Times*, Thurs., June 7, 1990.

Love Song to the Messiah, by Neil and Jaime Lash. Ft. Lauderdale, FL, Jan. 1993.

"Market-place of Ideas," by David Krivine. *The Jerusalem Post*, Oct. 1, 1985.

"Messianic Judaism, Topic of Discussion," by James D. Davis. *The Ft. Lauderdale Sun-Sentinel*, Dec. 4, 1992.

"Messianics Welcomed at Temple," by James D. Davis. *The Ft. Lauderdale Sun-Sentinel*, Dec. 4, 1992.

"Military Resistance Against Jesus." *Midnight Call*, Oct., 1994.

"Neandertals," by Rick Gore. *National Geographic*, Jan. 1996, Vol. 189, No. 1.

"Newton on the Restoration of the Jews," by Franz Kobler. *The Jewish Frontier*, Mar. 1943.

"Newton's Theological Manuscripts," by Richard S. Westfall. *Contemporary Newtonian Research*. Boston: D. Reidel Publishing Company, 1982.

"New Wave of Missionaries Includes Many Americans: Are Americans Too Pushy About Their Beliefs?", by Elizabeth Kurylo. *Atlanta Journal and Constitution*, July 25, 1993.

"Notes for Bibliophiles." *New York Herald Tribune Books*, July 12, 1936.

"Pope Urges Mexicans to Keep Faith," by Jim Jones. *Fort Worth Star-Telegram*, Mon., A.M., May 14, 1990.

Prophecy in the News, Apr. 1990.

"Qumran Corner: The Oxford Forum for Qumran Research Seminar on the Rule of War from Cave 4 (4Q285)," by Geza Vermes. *Journal of Jewish Studies*,Vol. 43, No. 1. Oxford Centre for Hebrew and Jewish Studies: Oxford, England, 1992.

"Rallies Tout Opposing Views on Uprisings," by Julius Liebb. *Jewish Press*, May 6, 1988.

"Reader Criticizes Liberals," by Lee Halpern. *Jewish Tribune*, Miami, Mar. 10, 1989.

"Reagan: Is Apocalypse Now?" *Atlanta Journal and Constitution*, Sat., Oct. 29, 1983.

"Resurrection? A Jew Looks at Jesus." *Time*, Vol. 113, No. 19, May 7, 1979.

"Running the Race," by Jay Alan Sekulow. *C.A.S.E. (Christian Advocates Serving Evangelism)*, July 1990.

"Russians Modernize Strategic Arsenel," by Hal Lindsey. *Countdown...*, June 1993. Palos Verdes, CA: Hal Lindsey Ministries.

"Sholem Asch in the Eye of the Storm," by Nahaman Tamid. *Maariv*, Apr. 21, 1989.

"Some Observations on the Attitude of the Synagogue Towards the Apocalyptic-Eschatological Writings," by Louis Ginzberg. *Journal of Biblical Literature*, Vol. XLI, 1922.

"Sparks Fly Over 'Messianic' Congregation," by Rick Hellman. *The Kansas City Jewish Chronicle*, Apr. 16, 1993.

"Terrible—The Terrorist," by Aharon Lapid. *Jerusalem Times/Jewish Press*, May 6, 1988.

"The Biblical Injunction," by Elwood McQuaid. *Israel My Glory*, Apr.-May 1993.

"The Christian Messiah in Light of Judaism 327-328," by Henry Frowde. *Journal of Theological Studies*, Vol. XIII. London: Oxford University Press, 1912.

"The Christmas Covenant," by Jeffrey L. Sheler. *U.S. News & World Report*, Dec. 19, 1994.

"The Crucified Man from Giv^{c}at ha-Mivtar-A Reappraisal," by Joseph Zias and Eliezer Sekele. *Biblical Archaologist*, Sept. 1985.

"The Growing Rift Between Blacks and Jews, When Friends Feud," by John Blake. *Atlanta Journal and Constitution*, June 5, 1994.

"The Hook in the Jaw of Magog," by Hal Lindsey. *Countdown...*, July 1985. Palos Verdes, CA: Hal Lindsey Ministries.

"The Mask is Off," by Yaakov Spivak. *Jerusalem Times/Jewish Press*, Fri., July 3, 1987.

"The Most Censored Stories of 1993," by Hal Lindsey. *Countdown...*, Feb. 1994. Palos Verdes, CA: Hal Lindsey Ministries.

"The New Testament's Unsolved Mysteries, by John Elson. *Time*, Dec. 18, 1995, Vol. 146, No. 25.

"The Numbers of 'Messianic' Jews is Said to be Growing," by Susan Birnbaum. *Jewish Echo*, Glasgow, Scotland, Apr. 14, 1989.

"The Original Text," by Jeffrey Magnuson. *The Jerusalem Post*, July 12, 1985.

"The Ostracized Newton," by Ruvic Rosenthal. *Al Hamishmar*, July 26, 1985.

"The Prophecies of Nostradamus," by John Kinsella. *This Week in Bible Prophecy*, Vol. 2, Issue 3, Mar. 1994.

"The Religion of Abraham Lincoln." *The Dawn*, Vol. XVIII, Jan.-Feb. 1947.

"The Two Zadokite Messiahs," by G. Margoliouth. *The Journal of Theological Studies*, Vol. XII, 1911.

"1999? Global March to Israel," by Jack and Rexella Van Impe. *Perhaps Today*, May/June 1993. Troy, MI: Jack Van Impe Ministries.

"Thoughts on the Star of Bethlehem," by Roger W. Sinnott. *Sky & Telescope*, Dec. 1968.

"Time for a New Temple," by Richard K. Ostling. *Time*, Oct. 25, 1989.

"Tomb in Jerusalem May Be That of Priest Who Doomed Jesus," *New York Times*, Aug. 14, 1992.

"Vying for the Soul of Russia, Some Sects Fear Persecution," by Marcia Kunstel and Joseph Albright. *Atlanta Journal and Constitution*, July 25, 1993.

"Was Hitler a Christian?", by David Allen Lewis. *Jerusalem Courier*, Vol. 7, No. 2, 1988.

"Was the Discoverer of America Jewish?", by Newton Frohlich. Washington, DC: *Moment*, Dec. 1991.

"West Bank Uprising, Christian Zionists Have No Doubts Over the Outcome," by Herb Keinon. *Jerusalem* magazine, of *The Jerusalem Post*, Apr. 15, 1988.

"Who Makes the Horn of Jesus to Flourish," by Yehudah Liebes. *Immanuel*, No. 21, Summer 1987. Israel: The Ecumenical Theological Research Fraternity in Israel and The Anti-Defamation League of B'nai B'rith.

"Who Wrote the Dead Sea Scrolls?", by Gail Lichtman. *The Jerusalem Post International Edition*, Oct. 30, 1993.

"Why Should Catholic Church Honor Queen Isabella?", by Arnold Fine. *Jerusalem Times/Jewish Press*, Fri., Jan. 18, 1991.

"Yavneh's Liturgy and Early Christianity," by Asher Finkel. *The Journal of Ecumenical Studies*, Spring 1981.

UNPUBLISHED MATERIAL BY TITLE

"Anti-Semitism in the Soviet Union, Its Roots and Consequences," by R. Nudelman. 1979. Jerusalem: Center for Research and Documentation of East European Jewry, Givat Ram.

"A Study of the Alleged 'Two Messiah' Expectation of the Dead Sea Scrolls Against the Background of Developing Eschatology," by Jay Junior Smith. May 1970. Produced on microfilm-xerography in 1971 by University Microfilms, A Xerox Company, Ann Arbor, MI, USA.

"Catalogue of The Newton Papers." Compiled for the auction of Newton's papers by Sotheby & Co. on May 13, 1936.

"Testimony Pamphlet of Carlo Fumagalli." Dayton, VA: Sunrise, Inc.

"The Magog Factor, A Special Report," by Hal Lindsey and Chuck Missler. Palos Verdes, CA: Hal Lindsey Ministries.

Raymon Hanson, "The Schism Between the Judeo-Christians and Mainstream Judaism," Hebrew University, May 24, 1984.

"Yahuda Manuscript." Jerusalem: Hebrew University Manuscript Department, Jewish National and University Library.

"Yavney: Achievements and Significance," by Julie Baker. The Moody Bible Institute of Chicago, Apr. 16, 1986.

NEWSLETTERS AND PAMPHLETS BY TITLE

"A Godly Education," by D. James Kennedy. Fort Lauderdale, FL: Coral Ridge Ministries.

"Backgrounder," June 1980. Jewish Community Relations Council of Greater Philadelphia, a constituent of the Federation of Jewish Agencies.

"Evangelical Newsletter," by Morris Cerillo, 1987.

"Footprints on the Moon," by James B. Irwin. Colorado Springs, CO: High Flight Ministries.

"Golda Meir and the Christian Professor from America," by Larry Samuels. *The Interpreter*, Vol. 37, No. 1, Winter 1995. Lutherville, MD.

"International Intelligence Briefing," by Hal Lindsey. Feb. 1995. Palos Verdes, CA: Hal Lindsey Ministries.

"Israeli Media Reminds Arafat: 'Jesus Belongs to Us,' " *Maoz "The Lord is My Strength,"* Feb. 1996. Available through Maoz, POB 763100, Dallas, TX, USA 75376-3100.

"Jerusalem Garden Tomb" Booklet, Fifth Edition. Jerusalem: The Garden Tomb.

"Jewishness and Hebrew Christianity," by Arnold G. Fruchtenbaum. Englewood Cliffs, NJ: Sar Shalom Publications.

"Jewishness and the Trinity," by Arnold Fruchtenbaum. San Francisco, CA: Jews for Jesus, 1987.

National PAC (Political Action Committee) Newsletter.

"The 700 Club Fact Sheet," Mar. 29, 1994. Virginia Beach, VA: Christian Broadcasting Network, Inc.

"The Fourth Gospel and the Exclusion of Christians from the Synagogues," by Kenneth L. Carroll. *Bulletin of the John Rylands University Library of Manchester*, 40, 1957-58. Manchester, England.

"The God of Marxism," by Richard Wurmbrand. Oct. 1967. *Jesus to the Communist World, Inc., "The Voice of the Martyrs," 1967-1977.* Glendale, CA: Jesus to the Communist World, Inc.

"The Interpreter," Vol. 37, No. 2, Spring 1995, by Arthur W. Kac., ed. Lutherville, MD.

"Voice of Hope," Issue 1, July 1994. Simi Valley, CA: Global Broadcasting Network.

VIDEO CASSETTE TAPES BY TITLE

Charlton Heston Presents the Bible. Irving, TX: TTV Educational Media Company, 1993.

Führer, Rise of a Madman. Videotape MP 1203, Matjack Productions, Inc.

Heaven, an Out-of-Body Adventure, Who, Why, When?, by Jack and Rexella Van Impe. Troy, MI: Jack Van Impe Ministries, 1992.

Hitler: The Last Ten Days, by John Heyman, Ennio De Concini, and Paramount Pictures. World Film Services, Ltd., 1973.

Israel and the PLO Peace Pact: Hope or Hoax, Evidence of the Last Generation on Earth, by John Hagee. San Antonio, TX: John Hagee.

Mark of the Beast II, by Paul and Peter Lalonde. This Week in Bible Prophecy. Niagara Falls, NY: This Week in Bible Prophecy, 1993.

The Rise and Fall of Adolf Hitler: Black Fox, by Louis Clyde Stoumen. W. Long Beach, NJ: White Star, 1962.

AUDIO CASSETTE TAPES BY TITLE

From Abraham to the Middle East Crisis, by Hal Lindsey. Palos Verdes, CA: Hal Lindsey Ministries.

Selections from Ask the Rabbi, by Yechiel Eckstein. Chicago, IL: Holyland Fellowship of Christians and Jews, 1988.

The Reemergence of Messianic Judaism, by Ruth Fleischer. Tape 30 CF179. Grantham, PA: 1993 Messiah Conference at Messiah College. Albuquerque, NM: Manna Conference Taping, Inc., 1993.

Was Abraham Lincoln a Christian?, by D. James Kennedy. Tape 20D. Fort Lauderdale, FL: Coral Ridge Ministries.

Why We Honor the Jews, by John Hagee. San Antonio, TX: John Hagee.

TELEVISION BROADCASTS BY TITLE

Ancient Prophecies II, NBC News, Nov. 18, 1994.

"Life After Death: Personal Experiences," *Turning Point*, ABC News, Transcript #116, June 8, 1994.

"Moment of Crisis: Anatomy of a Revolution," *Nightline*, ABC News, Oct. 22, 1993.

Reasons to Believe, Trinity Broadcasting Network, Apr. 29, 1995.

"Secrets of the Dead Sea Scrolls," *Nova*, Oct. 19, 1991.

The 700 Club, Christian Broadcasting Network, Dec. 8, 1994.

"The Fire Unleashed," *Close Up*, ABC News, 1986.

"The Men We Left Behind," *20/20*, ABC News, Sept. 11, 1992.

***

PHOTO AND ILLUSTRATION CREDITS

P. numbers following names represent the P. numbers in this book.

American Museum of Natural History, New York: P. 1155.

Bartour, Ron: P. 526.

Bauminger, Rabbi Arieh L. *The Righteous*, Third Edition: P. 587 (bottom).

Ben-Gurion, David: P. 618.

Bentley, Michael David: Pp. 26-36, 1042, 1065.

Biblioteca Colombina, Seville: P. 666.

Breu, Jorg the Elder: P. 469 (top).

Chaplin, Carl: P. i.

Chick, Jack: Pp. 905-917, 932.

Collier, John: P. 1146.

El Hamishmar: P. 519.

Från, Judiskt Bokmärke: P. 15.

Frankenberger, James: P. 1200 (top).

Friends of Israel: P. 166.

Froom, Leroy Edwin. *The Prophetic Faith of Our Fathers*: P. 852.

Garden Tomb Association: Pp. 255, 257, 265, 268, 270, 272 (top).

Gilbert, Martin: P. 278.

Hyer: P. 508 (right).

Hargrave, Alice Q. *Time* magazine: P. 945 (bottom; far right photo).

International Christian Embassy, Jerusalem: Pp. Vi, 532, 574-575, 593-597, 605 (bottom), 1112.

Israel Antiquities Authority: Pp. 79, 201 (bottom).

Jeffrey, Grant R. *Apocalypse, The Coming Judgement of the Nations*: P. 861.

Jerusalem Post: Pp. 334 (article), 540, 567, 606, 633, 635, 638-639, 645.

Jerusalem Post Supplement: P. 588.

Jewish Echo: P. 623.

Jewish National and University Library: Pp. 491, 498-503, 520.

Kedler, Sir Godfrey: P. 680 (top portion of photo).

Kneller, G., and William Sharp: P. 1091.

Kormosh Shosh: P. 1205 (bottom).

Larkin, Clarence (The Clarence Larkin Estate): Pp. 2-3, 14, 18, 54, 68, 74, 154, 687, 856, 862, 876, 882-884, 899, 1002, 1066, 1083, 1092-1093, 1096, 1107.

Lauderdale, George S.: Pp. 610, 619.

Levitt, Zola: P. 288.

Lindsey, Hal. *The Rapture: Truth or Consequences*: P. 1069.

Livingston, Grant: P. 622.

Maariv: P. 611.

Miller, Vernon D.: P. 248.

Moore, Paul: p. Acknowledgments.

Moore, Philip N. Pp. Xvii, 75, 81, 105, 118, 128, 171, 173-174, 192-193, 195, 206, 221, 241, 249 (bottom), 253, 256, 258-260, 266, 272 (bottom), 273, 306, 315, 318, 388-389, 497, 512-516 (top; bottom arrangement), 527, 577, 579, 581-583, 586-587 (top; arrangement), 589, 592, 595 (bottom left), 597 (bottom right 3), 598, 602, 607 (top), 609 (bottom), 611 (inset)-614, 616, 622 (inset), 624-625 (arrangement)-626 (arrangement), 632, 647, 650-655 (arrangement), 657, 662 (arrangements), 674 (arrangement), 691, 703-704, 712 (bottom right), 719 (bottom left)-720 (excluding bottom right), 742 (inset), 814, 888-890, 928, 931, 938, 945 (bottom; arrangement), 978-981, 1024, 1027, 1032, 1033, 1035-1037, 1040-1041, 1099-1100, 1103, 1136.

Moss, Gary, for *Time* magazine: P. 945 (bottom; second photo from right).

National Aeronautical Space Administration (NASA): Pp. Front Cover, 671, 673, 676-678, 695, 1113.

National Geographic Society: P. 1166.

Newton, Sir Isaac: P. 281.

New York Herald Tribune Books: P. 488.

New York Times: P. 80.

Organ of the Jewish Messianic Movement: P. 648.

Ori, Shimon: Pp. 504-505.

P-Haeton (פ האתון): P. 644.

Picart: P. 469 (bottom).

Ridpath, John Clark, *Cyclopædia of Universal History*: Pp. 470, 473.

Rubens, Peter Paul: P. 145.

Santala, Risto: P. 201 (top).

Septuaginta: P. 394.

Suran, Shmuel: Pp. 627-629.

State of Israel Government Press Office, photography department: Pp. Xxiv, xxvi, 10, 40, 52, 114, 151, 157 (bottom), 183 (top), 186, 264, 390, 403, 422, 564, 576, 591, 603, 605 (top), 607 (bottom)-609 (top), 615, 617, 621, 649, 672, 680 (bottom portion of photo), 683 (top), 689-690, 709-710 (excluding top right)-712 (excluding bottom right)-719 (excluding bottom left)-720 (bottom right)-732, 737, 742, 760, 791-792, 794-795, 815-819, 823, 891, 918, 922, 933, 939, 940-943, 953-954, 958, 976, 984, 993-994, 998, 1013, 1021, 1030, 1057, 1058, 1098, 1111, 1115, 1205 (top).

Strutt, William, "Peace": P. 1078.

Sussman, Eddie: P. 280.

Syndics of Cambridge University Library: Pp. 334 (photo), 338, 351, 396.

Taibbi, Cathy: Pp. 104, 177, 249, 416, 419, 1034, 1171.

Van Eyck, Jan: P. 133.

Van Rijn, Rembrandt: Pp. 107, 179, 199, 247, 282.

Weiser, Rafael: Pp. 507, 525.

Winkler, Ilan: P. 506.

Woodrow, Ralph, *Babylon Mystery Religion*: Pp. 453, 474, 925.

Wide World Photo: P. 660.

Yerushlime: P. 508 (left).

Zurbaran, Francisco de: P. 126.

Author with a few of the books he used in his research.

Author with Lt. Col. Oliver North who, as head of President Reagan's National Security Council, foiled many Arab terrorist attempts.

ABOUT THE AUTHOR

Dr. Philip Moore was born in Atlanta, Georgia, in 1957. He attended Georgia State University and received his doctorate of divinity degree in Jewish-Messianic research from Immanuel Bible College and Baptist Seminary in Sharpsburg, Georgia. He studied Greek, and ancient Jewish biblical beliefs for many years in the U.S. and Israel. In the 1980s, Moore assisted in research for the well-known author Hal Lindsey. He dedicated much time and effort into the research of Sir Isaac Newton's theological writings at the Hebrew University in Jerusalem and has worked with Campus Crusade for Christ (CCC) in the voluntary preparation and coordination of the Hebrew edition of the film *Jesus*. Some of his responsibilities were to oversee, choose and approve the dubbed voices; answer news reporters' questions regarding the astonishment of the Israelis over such a production; and to be the go-between for the arrangement of public showings of *Jesus* in a Jerusalem cinema. This film premiered in Jerusalem in the spring of 1990. He wishes to thank Dr. Bill Bright, President of CCC, for his sensitivity and kindness in helping with and approving the Jerusalem Hebrew premiere.

In *The Hebrew Christian*, an article entitled "News from the Homeland, 'Yeshua' speaking Hebrew," writer Menahem Benhayim commented: "Philip Moore is an enthusiastic 32 year old Georgian U.S. Evangelical, a familiar face among U.S. and Israeli Messianic Jews. He decided one day that the Genesis Project production of Luke's Gospel, featuring 16 Israeli actors, must be completely restored to its natural setting. The scenery, the costumes, the story, were all Israeli enough, but the languages were '*goyish.*' Although screened originally in English, the sound had been dubbed into over 100 tongues. Hebrew was not one of them.

Moore invested some $30,000[1] of his own funds....He employed major Israeli announcers and actors....It was Moore's desire to have the film screened in public commercial cinemas for the wider Israeli public....Advertisements were placed in Jerusalem Hebrew weeklies, posters were spread around the city, local believers were alerted, and a P.R. firm was employed....The film was advertised on posters and in the media in Hebrew letters 'YESHUA' beside bold Latin letters 'JESUS' and snapshots of 16 of the Israeli actors....the film is an attempt to visualize the Gospel of Luke, almost exclusively relating to the original texts. The Jewishness of the original story is brought out more effectively in the Hebrew dubbing amid familiar Israeli and Jewish settings (synagogue scrolls, the *talit*, traditional Hebrew blessings)....It can still be shown on video privately."[2]

---

[1]Dr. Moore wishes to thank Sid Roth, President of the Messianic Vision national radio program, for his contribution of $3000 to the project and Campus Crusade for Christ (CCC), who spent many thousands of dollars on the 35mm print and its Hebrew soundtrack transfer, made available for them from Moore's Jerusalem costs and work.

[2]*The Hebrew Christian,* The Quarterly Organ of the International Hebrew Christian Alliance, No. 2 Vol. LXIII, July, 1990-Sept., 1990, pp. 46-47. Available through POB 7329, Jerusalem, Israel 91072. Tel. (02) 814228 or 249480. In the US: POB 438,

Ronan Tal, writing for the Tel Aviv newspaper *Hyer*, in Israel, reported that the original Genesis Project[3] production included "John Heyman and Hyam Topol." The latter was famous for his role in *Fiddler on the Roof.* An impressed Tal wrote regarding the Hebrew translation: "Moore presents the dubbing project as a gift to Israel and the Jews. 'Even as a child I had within me a love for the Jews. I knew that there was something special about them, that God loved them—I knew that I wanted to help them whenever I would be able.' When he was eighteen, his father was robbed and murdered....Moore said, 'I decided that I had to give the Israelis an opportunity to see the movie in their language. I contacted the organization, who purchased the rights of distribution concerning the movie and suggested that it be translated to Hebrew. Just then the funds from my father's will were released and I used them'....He chose in certain places in the movie to place subtitles quoting the Hebrew Bible. The quotes prove, according to him, the connection between Jesus and the prophets, which he felt would cause the Israelis to see Jesus in a new light. 'Even though Jesus is the most famous Jew in history, he's the least understood,' says Moore. 'Now this injustice will be resolved'....On the advertisement he wanted to add the following quote: 'Even though, today, Jesus has over a billion followers, his people (Israel) have not as of yet seen his true story, as it is told in this movie. And why shouldn't they? After all Yeshua was an Israeli.' The advertising agency objected, the quotation was removed, but Moore didn't despair. From his wallet he retrieved a wrapper of a bazooka gum, which he gave me, on which it was written: [in its "Believe it or Not" Hebrew fact/cartoon insert] 'Did you know that the first Christians were Jews in every way—only they believed the Messiah had already come?' Moore concluded with the following story: 'As I stood at the bus stop with the posters of the movie, there were there a number of children, and they thought that it was referring to *The Last Temptation of Christ*[4]—until they saw the Israeli actors. One of the girls asked: Does this movie have a good ending? I said that this is the only true movie of Jesus, which shows what others did not show. It shows that Jesus resurrected from the dead, ascended to

---

Hinghamn, MA 02043. Tel. (617) 826-7119 or (617) 826-7973. The video tape, *Jesus: According to the Gospel of Luke* is available in more than three hundred languages from: Campus Crusade for Christ Keynote Communications, 23181 Verdugo Drive, Suite 106, Laguna Hills, CA, USA 92653-1313. Tel. (800) 266-7741 or the *Jesus* film project, POB 7690, Laguna Niger, CA, USA 92607. Tel. (714) 495-7383. Selections and languages available at www.internetsermons.com/Jesus-movie.htm

[3]It was the Genesis Project who produced a movie of Genesis, word for word with a soundtrack, loyal to the text of the first book of the Bible. They also produced a four-hour movie from the Gospel of Luke in the New Testament in their new Media Bible Series. CCC, recognizing the authenticity of Luke, bought the rights to distribute the film in a more condensed form. In our opinion, this is the greatest and most touching film ever made about the Savior.

[4]A film considered by evangelical Christians to be fictional and derogatory, with regard to the life of Jesus, which was playing in the cinemas at that time.

heaven and secured redemption for the entire world for those who would believe, including Israel. Then she had a very big smile on her face. That really touched me. I simply can't forget it.' "[5]

Moore has spent more than twelve years researching this work. While doing so he has taken time to volunteer much effort in his support of Israel, which he feels, along with other pre-millennial Christians, is a biblical command and duty (Genesis 12:3; Romans 10:14), for the last days, in fervent expectation of the imminent return of the Messiah Jesus. His tasks included volunteer work in several kibbutzim in 1980 and work for the temple archaeological dig, under archaeologist Eilat and Professor Binyamin Mazar, which yielded the discovery of the "first temple gateway" in 1986.[6] Moore also committed himself to volunteer work in the Israel Defense Force at the army base near Bersheva, in 1985.[7]

He is included in *Marquis Who's Who in America* biography and the *Dictionary of International Biography* at the International Biographical Center at Cambridge, for his literary work.

Dr. Moore is the grandson of George Moore, Sr., who was founder and president of the George Moore Ice Cream Company in Atlanta, Georgia, and the son of Nick G. Moore, the president of Moore Foods until his untimely death in 1976. Moore's present occupation is real estate. He has spent over eight years in Israel studying Hebrew and giving out thousands of Hebrew New Testaments to friends and acquaintances. He thanks you for any prayers[8] you may offer up on his behalf now or in the future!

George Moore, Sr., and his trademark from over a generation ago.

[5]Ronan Tal, "After 12 Years the Hebrew Dubbed Film 'Jesus' Comes to Israel," *Hyer* newspaper, April 6, 1990, © 1990, pp. 78-79, used by permission.
[6]For details of this dig, see the *Jerusalem Post* article entitled, "First Temple Gateway," by Abraham Rabinovich (April 22, 1986).
[7]Mr. Moore thanks Major Smulic, his base commander, from Makhena Natan, for his kind letter of thanks for his work.
[8] Pray that this book makes its way onto film/video, so that those who are more acclimated to this medium have an opportunity to hear this message on the messiah conspiracy and biblical prophecy.

Philip Moore (left) with Israeli military personnel, Tamar Borria, and Shosh Abraham, at Base Machena Natan, in Beersheba.

Philip Moore (left) with archaeologists Eilat and Binyamin Mazar.

Philip Moore. Photo courtesy of Shosh Kormosh
from the Israeli Press.

"...I say that not only does the Holy Spirit reveal the future to rational creatures, but he shows us what is yet to come by summoning signs in the heavens...."[1]
Christopher Columbus

"...the conjunction of Jupiter and Saturn in the constellation Pisces....[will] precede the birth of the Messiah...."[2]
Rabbi Abarbanel

COVER ART AND ILLUSTRATIONS

The snake poised to strike the heels of Jesus represents the first Messianic prophecy in the Bible, as you may have read in the body of the King Cobra. "And the LORD God said to the serpent, 'Because you have done this, Cursed are you more than all cattle, And more than every beast of the field; On your belly shall you go, And dust shall you eat All the days of your life; And I will put enmity Between you and the woman, And between your seed and her seed; He shall bruise you on the head, And you shall bruise him on the heel' " (Gen. 3:14-15 NASB).

For truly the Messiah's heel would be bruised in a life and death struggle as He redeemed the earth! At His Second Coming, He will destroy the serpent (evil). Did these things occur and are they happening? Jesus was crucified by the Romans, thus His heels were bruised as the nails were driven into His feet. Because He died for our sins, this will give Him the right, at the advent of His Second Coming, to physically redeem Earth and crush Satan's head in the process. However, until He does this, the earth is under the dominion of the prince of the power of the air (Eph. 2:2). We will continue to struggle with sickness, disease, hunger and crime until He initiates His kingdom, *physically* redeeming Earth!

As you see, the cover art depicts Earth in the constricted tail of the serpent! Notice the "Y" of the word conspiracy in the serpent's head as he strikes at the Messiah's heels. This illustrates that Jesus has been, and is still under attack by the rabbinic conspiracy, which denies Him His true title—MESSIAH!

The three planets are the conjunction of Mars, Saturn and Jupiter in the constellation Pisces. According to the tradition of the ancient rabbis, this was to signal the birth of the Messiah at Bethlehem. This occurrence, known as the Star of Bethlehem, is recorded in the New Testament (Matt. 2) and confirmed by the astronomer Kepler as occuring during the nativity of Jesus. The famous Rabbi Abarbanel

---

[1]Kay Brigham, *Christopher Columbus's Book of Prophecies*, p. 180

[2]Alfred Edersheim, *The Life and Times of Jesus the Messiah*, p. 211. [ ] mine.

said that just such a planetary conjunction in Pisces, which occurred at the birth of Moses, "must renew" at the Coming of the Messiah. The astronauts on the moon is a tribute to Jim Irwin, a very special person and precious believer. Jim was the first and only of the moonwalkers to have died.

Both covers were designed by Philip Moore and beautifully illustrated by Cathy Taibbi. The front cover was edited by the author with NASA photos of the earth, Saturn, moon and sun. Cathy also illustrated several other designs of ours throughout this book, including: "The Star of Bethlehem" p. 104, "The Undisturbed Graveclothes of Jesus" p. 249, "Jesus in the Garden of Gethsemane" p. 177, "The Changing of Jesus' Hebrew Name by the Removal of the Last Letter" p. 416, "Jesus' Hebrew Name Lighting the Menorah" p. 419 (modeled after a photo from the State of Israel Government Press Office, photography department), "The Second Coming of Jesus to the Mount of Olives" p. 1034, and our chart illustrating the deception of human evolution, p. 1171. We thank Cathy Taibbi for her work and contribution.

We would like to hear your questions and comments on our work. We would also appreciate any news articles or documentation supporting our theses. Please feel free to contact us at: Rams Head Press International, Inc., POB 12-227, Atlanta, GA, USA 30355; 1-800-726-7432 (1-800-RAMSHEAD) or 1-404-233-8023. Fax: 404-816-9994. This work can also be ordered through your local bookstore by request of author/title through the books in print database. This work is also available through www.bookwire.com, Borders, Barnes & Noble, Brodart Co. 1-800-233-8467 and amazon.com.

***

Philip Moore may be contacted for interviews and speaking engagements through RamsHead Press International, (404) 233-8023.

Attention Valued Reader:

We at RamsHead Press thank you in advance for showing and requesting acquisition of this book at your local public, university, high school and church libraries so that others may benefit.

To read selected sections of this text and others by the same author, visit the web site www.ramsheadpress.com or http://members.aol.com/theconinc/publish.htm on the internet.

Order other titles by Philip Moore.

ORDER FORM

Please Print

Name ______________________________

Address ______________________________

City ____________ State ________ Zip ________ Phone ____________

Quantity	Code	Description	Price	Total
	Book 1	The End of History—Messiah Conspiracy, Volume I (1200 pgs.)	$29.00	
	Book 2	Israel and the Apocalypse Prophecies of Newton	$17.00	
	Book 3	Nightmare of the Apocalypse—The Rabbi Conspiracy	$15.00	
	Book 4	Eternal Security for True Believers	$ 5.00	
	Book 5	A Liberal Interpretation of the Prophecy of Israel—Disproved	$ 5.00	
	Book 6	What If Hitler Won The War?	$19.95	
	Book 7	The End of Earth as We Know It (Available 1999)	$15.00	
	Tapes	Testimony Tapes of Israeli Messianic Believers	$ 3.00	
	Video	Garden Tomb Tour Video	$17.00	
		One low shipping and handling fee (per order)	$ 4.95	$ 4.95
			Total	

Mail along with your check or money order to:
Ramshead Press International, Inc., P.O. Box 12-227, Atlanta, Georgia, USA, 30355-2227
Toll Free 1-800-RAMSHEAD (1-800-726-7432) or FAX (404) 816-9994 - Main (404) 233-8023

Please do not remove this page from book.
Photocopy this form and order your new book today!

ISBN 1-57915-998-2

ISBN 1-57915-996-6

ISBN 1-57915-999-0

Eternal Security
For True Believers
The Rabin Assassination—Predicted
An Excerpt from The End of History—
Messiah Conspiracy Volume II—Essays
Included is an appendix on Hebrew Bible word codes which have foretold the future. One made nearly four thousand years ago seems to have predicted the fate and
assassination of the Israeli Prime Minister Isaac Rabin in 1995! We present new insights into the second coming of the Messiah, which may take us to the 2020s-2030s.
PHILIP N. M
Researcher for Hal
"Now if any man build upon this fo
cious stones ... If any man's work
upon it, he shall receive a reward.
burned, he shall suffer loss; but he hi
by fire." (I Corinthians 3:12,

Is Israel's Rebirth Represented by Jesus ( ) in the New Testament Fig Tree Parable? Yes!
A LIBERAL INTERPRETATION ON THE PROPHECY OF ISRAEL—DISPROVED
NOSTRADAMUS: BIBLICAL SAGE OR SORCERER?
An exerpt from
THE END OF HISTORY—MESSIAH CONSPIRACY
VOLUME II—ESSAYS
Israel Is
The Fig Tree
PHILIP N. MOORE
Researcher for Hal Lindsey
Featured is an astonishing Hebrew word equidistant Bible code associating Israel with the Fig Tree and an Appendix on the false prophecies of Edgar Cayce, Jeane Dixon and Nostradamus (versus the truth of the Bible), revealing novel information on the 'inerrant prophecy' of the Kennedy assassination.

ISBN 1-57915-997-4

Order other titles by Philip Moore.

ORDER FORM

Please Print

Name ______________________________

Address ______________________________

City ______________ State ________ Zip __________ Phone ______________

Quantity	Code	Description	Price	Total
	Book 1	The End of History—Messiah Conspiracy, Volume I (1200 pgs.)	$29.00	
	Book 2	Israel and the Apocalypse Prophecies of Newton	$17.00	
	Book 3	Nightmare of the Apocalypse—The Rabbi Conspiracy	$15.00	
	Book 4	Eternal Security for True Believers	$ 5.00	
	Book 5	A Liberal Interpretation of the Prophecy of Israel—Disproved	$ 5.00	
	Book 6	What If Hitler Won The War?	$19.95	
	Book 7	The End of Earth as We Know It (Available 1999)	$15.00	
	Tapes	Testimony Tapes of Israeli Messianic Believers	$ 3.00	
	Video	Garden Tomb Tour Video	$17.00	
		One low shipping and handling fee (per order)	$ 4.95	$ 4.95
			Total	

Mail along with your check or money order to:
Ramshead Press International, Inc., P.O. Box 12-227, Atlanta, Georgia, USA, 30355-2227
Toll Free 1-800-RAMSHEAD (1-800-726-7432) or FAX (404) 816-9994 - Main (404) 233-8023

Please do not remove this page from book.
Photocopy this form and order your new book today

ISBN 1-57915-994-X

ISBN 1-57915-995-8